WILEY
Publishers Since 1807

FROM THE PUBLISHER

We are pleased to present this new Active Learning Edition of **PSYCHOLOGY IN ACTION.**

In working with you and your students, we have consistently found that two of the most important things that students want from a textbook are lower price and greater value for their money.

This new Active Learning Edition offers all the features and content of **PSYCHOLOGY IN ACTION, 7/E** in a new modular format with integrated study material—all at a new low price.

• The new modular format presents material in smaller, more manageable chunks, making the content easier to absorb. This flexible format also enables instructors to cover the text's material in any order they wish.

• The Active Learning Edition costs less than other introductory psychology texts.

• In addition to the modular format and new low price, students get integrated self-study material and practice tests that reinforce key concepts and provide them with instant assessment feedback. The study material appears on special perforated pages, which allows instructors to assign and grade material directly from the text. And the durable spiral binding enables students to work right in the book.

Lower price, a new modular format, free integrated study resources—all this means greater value for your students!

Dear Reader and Student of Psychology:

Welcome to the Active Learning Edition of *Psychology in Action* (7e). I believe that studying psychology can change your life. I think I've always loved psychology—long before I knew there was an entire science devoted to its study. But once I took my first college course in psychology, I was really "hooked." I discovered a scientific way of looking at behavior that I never fully understood in the past. I found psychology so uniquely intriguing and exciting because it studies you and me, and because it holds the key to so much understanding of our personal and social life.

My goals as a college instructor and author of this text are to introduce you to the incredible wealth of information in our field, and to show you how this information can be usefully applied to your own life and the world around you. Please consider this book as a long letter from me to you. I will guide you through a fascinating world that can transform your relationships with others and with yourself.

But I cannot do this alone. I've done all that I could imagine to make this text as engaging and worthwhile as possible. In order to truly understand and appreciate psychology (or any other discipline), however, you must become an active participant. As a lifelong advocate of active learning, I am firmly convinced that this is the very best method for mastering any important task—or for maintaining any important relationship. To encourage you to read and study actively, I've included a wide variety of active learning tools, including: **Tools for Student Success** and **Integrated Study Tips, Visual Summaries** and **Chapter Summary Tables, Visual Quizzes, Check and Review** sections, **Try This Yourself** activities, **Critical Thinking/Active Learning Exercises, Applying Psychology to Work, Relationships, and Everyday Life,** and other additional techniques.

As you can see, this book can be part of an exciting intellectual adventure. If you use these tools to become an active participant, the study of psychology can lead you to an entirely new way of looking at the social world around you. I wish you the very best in college and in your life afterward. It is my fondest hope that *Psychology in Action* will contribute to your lifelong success.

Warmest regards,

Karen Huffman

Karen Huffman

ACTIVE LEARNING EDITION

PSYCHOLOGY IN ACTION

(SEVENTH EDITION)

KAREN HUFFMAN

PALOMAR COLLEGE

WILEY

John Wiley & Sons, Inc.

Executive Editor	Ryan Flahive
Associate Editor	Lili DeGrasse
Editorial Assistant	Aliyah Vinikour
Media Editor	Tom Kulesa
Associate Director of Development	Johnna Barto
Production Editor	Sandra Dumas
Senior Marketing Manager	Kate Stewart
Senior Designer	Kevin Murphy
Illustration Editor	Sandra Rigby
Photo Editor	Sara Wight
Photo Researcher	Elyse Rieder
Production Management Services	Hermitage Publishing Services
Cover Photo	Scott Morgan/Taxi/Getty Images

This book was typeset in 10/12 Janson by Hermitage Publishing Services and printed and bound by Von Hoffmann Corporation. The cover was printed by Von Hoffmann Corporation.

The paper in this book was manufactured by a mill whose forest management programs include sustained yield harvesting of its timberlands. Sustained yield harvesting principles ensure that the number of trees cut each year does not exceed the amount of new growth.

This book is printed on acid-free paper. ∞

To order books or for customer service please, call 1(800)-CALL-WILEY (225-5945).

Huffman, Karen.
Psychology In Action, seventh edition

ISBN 0-471-47957-8

Printed in the United States of America.

10 9 8 7 6 5 4 3 2 1

CONTENTS IN BRIEF

CONTENTS

MEMORY

THINKING, LANGUAGE, AND INTELLIGENCE

PREFACE TO THE ACTIVE LEARNING EDITION

While reading a traditional college text with 40 or 50 page chapters, do you find it difficult to concentrate? Do you frequently count ahead to find out how many pages are left in the chapter until you reach the end? As an instructor, have you asked yourself how other teachers "cover" a full-length introduction to psychology text? Do you want to assign parts of chapters and not others? These and related questions led to the creation of this Active Learning Edition of Psychology in Action.

How does the modular version differ from Psychology in Action, Seventh Edition? Rather than presenting material in a traditional 16 chapter format, the information is organized into 48 separate, independent modules. This allows increased flexibility for teachers and smaller study units for students.

Although the material and information in this modular version is exactly the same as the Sixth Edition, there are two major changes: *Reorganization* and *Increased Pedagogy*.

Reorganization

Each of the previous 16 chapters in the Seventh Edition has been broken into 2 to 5 modules. This format allows instructors to pick and choose specific topics they wish to assign their students. For example, instructors who wish to talk about intelligence, but not thinking or language, could assign Module 24 and skip Modules 22 and 23. Because each Module is truly *independent* from the others, the instructor can safely skip from topic to topic.

In addition to the benefit of "customization" for the professor, the modular approach also allows students the benefit of distributed versus massed practice. As research has shown, we all learn and retain information better when it is divided into smaller chunks (see Modules 4, 20 and 21).

Increased Pedagogy

Beginning with the first edition, *Psychology in Action* has been known for its extensive pedagogy, including Critical Thinking/Active Learning Exercises, the SQ4R method, Try This Yourself exercises, Check and Review sections (with brief summaries and practice test questions), Tools for Student Success, built in short Study Tips, Visual Summaries, and so on. All of our previous "tools" and student aids are retained in this *Active Learning Edition*.

To further increase student mastery, this Modular version of Psychology in Action also includes a new, ACTIVE LEARNING WORKSHEET at the end of each module. Some worksheets allow the reader to test his or her comprehension with fun and quick crossword puzzles based on key terms within the module. Other worksheets involve personal applications, matching exercises, fill-in the blanks, and other engaging forms of self-testing. Immediate feedback is provided with sample answers found in Appendix B.

"WHAT'S NEW? ACTIVE LEARNING WITH RESULTS

The Seventh Edition of *Psychology in Action* takes active learning to an even higher level. I have added new pedagogical features and organized all the active learning elements into three distinct, but overlapping, "As"— *Application*, *Achievement*, and *Assessment* (Figure 1).

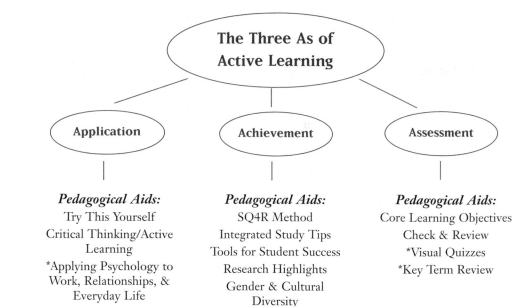

Figure 1 *The Three As of Active Learning*
(*New to the Seventh Edition)

▣ Application

The first "A," **Application**, is essential to active learning. As most instructors (and students) know, true understanding is much more than a simple memorization of terms and concepts to be retrieved during exams — and then quickly forgotten. To truly master psychology, you must question, debate, experiment, and apply psychological principles to your everyday life.

As you can see in Figure 1, the Seventh Edition includes numerous pedagogical aids dedicated to helping you apply psychology, including a new element called **"Applying Psychology to Work, Relationships, and Everyday Life."** This feature was added in response to reviewer requests and the changing demographics of today's "typical" college student. Modern college campuses include a wide assortment of people: full and part-time students, unemployed, part-time, and fully employed workers, non-native speakers and visiting students from around the globe, returning older students, and general interest students searching for new hobbies, interests, and first or second careers. The Seventh Edition's expanded focus on application serves these diverse needs by showing the reader how psychology can be usefully applied at home, work, and around the globe. For example, Module 1 includes a special section, **"Applying Psychology to Work: Careers in the Field,"** that provides job descriptions and opportunities within the field of psychology, whereas Module 15, **"Applying Psychology to Everyday Life: Club Drug Alert,"** provides the latest information and guidance regarding club drugs such as Ecstasy, Rohypnol, and GHB.

In addition to the new feature of applying psychology to work, I continue two previous forms of application: **"Try This Yourself"** and **"Critical Thinking/Active Learning"** exercises. The widely copied **"Try This Yourself"** activities are high-interest and simple-to-do experiments, demonstrations, and self-tests, which give you, the reader, an opportunity to personally test and apply basic psychological principles and concepts. Further application is provided with each section's in-depth **"Critical Thinking/Active Learning Exercise,"** which is based on that unit's content and devoted to developing specific critical thinking skills. For example, the Active Learning Exercise in Module 48 asks readers, "Would you have obeyed Milgram's directions?" and helps develop independent thinking as a critical thinking skill.

Achievement

The second "A" is for Achievement. To fully master and understand information, you must employ a form of *metacognition*, which requires watching and evaluating your own thought processes. In other words, you must "think about your thinking and learning."

To help insure metacognition, and this type of achievement, the Seventh Edition helps you examine and refine your personal studying and learning style. For example, in an upcoming section of this preface, you will learn to use one of the most respected study techniques, the **"SQ4R method."** In addition to the SQ4R method, this text also includes "Integrated Study Tips" (which appear throughout the text offering specific techniques to improve learning and retention), and **"Tools for Student Success"** (an expanded discussion in Module 4 featuring numerous "tools" for improved learning).

To further increase metacognition and achievement, the Seventh Edition also offers the following special features:

- *Research Highlights* — Aids understanding of the intricacies of scientific research.

- *Gender and Cultural Diversity* — Encourages appreciation of similarities and differences between men and women and various cultures.

- *Web Resources* — Suggested Web sites that further Internet exploration of important psychological topics.

- *Summary Tables and End-of-Section Visual Summaries* — Synthesize numerous concepts and graphically demonstrate their interrelationships.

Assessment

The third A, **Assessment**, requires you to demonstrate your learning — to yourself and others. To do this, each section opens with 4 to 6 **"Core Learning Objectives"** that model the type of questions you should ask and answer as you read the modules. These objectives are repeated as a reminder and guidepost in the margin next to the section where the topic is discussed.

In addition to the core learning objectives, numerous **"Check and Review"** sections are sprinkled throughout the text. This pedagogical aid provides a brief review of the preceding material, followed by a self-scoring quiz with 4 to 5 multiple-choice, fill-in, or short-answer questions.

New to the seventh edition are two unique assessment features: **"Visual Quizzes"** and **"Key Term Reviews."** After many years of watching students open their books and turn immediately to the photos and cartoons, I wondered how I could use this innate interest to foster greater mastery and appreciation of important psychological concepts and terms. My answer? Turn these photos and cartoons into a form of assessment. Like the "Try This Yourself" exercises, which require active learning, the new "Visual Quizzes" require active participation and provide a form of self-testing and assessment for the reader. As a reader, you are asked to answer a specific question about a photo, cartoon, or figure, which requires a mastery of key terms or concepts. To assess your understanding, the correct answer is printed upside down directly below the photo or cartoon (Figure 2).

Students and professors who have seen these Visual Quizzes are excited by this new feature — and wondering why other texts do not include such a valuable pedagogical aid.

In addition to the Visual Quizzes, another new feature for the Seventh Edition is the end-of-section **"Key Term Review."** Rather than just listing the terms and providing the page references, you are reminded: "To assess your understanding of the

Assessment

VISUAL QUIZ

THE FAMILY CIRCUS.   By Bil Keane

"Look what I can do, Grandma!"

Reprinted with special permission of King Features Syndicate.

Can you identify this child's Piagetian stage of cognitive development? Why does he think his Grandma can see him?

Answer: The child is in the preoperational stage, and his egocentism prevents him from recognizing that Grandma does not see everything he sees.

Figure 2

Key Terms in Modules ___, write a definition for each term (in your own words), and then compare your definitions with those in the text." This is an important assessment tool and a great way to review before quizzes or exams.

NEW BIOPSYCHOSOCIAL MODEL

There are seven major perspectives in modern psychology: *biopsychology/neuroscience, cognitive, behavioral, sociocultural, evolutionary, humanistic,* and *psychoanalytic/psychodynamic.* As you will discover in the upcoming modules, these seven perspectives are widely overlapping and somewhat inseparable. In response to this overlap, many psychologists (and this seventh edition of *Psychology in Action*) have adopted a **biopsychosocial model**, which incorporates all seven perspectives. This model proposes that three major forces — biological (e.g., genetics, brain functions, neurotransmitters, and evolution), psychological (e.g., learning, thinking, emotion, personality, and motivation), and social (e.g., family, school, culture, ethnicity, social class, and politics) affect and are affected by one another. For example, feelings of depression are often influenced by genetics and neurotransmitters (biology), our learned responses and patterns of thinking (psychology), and our socioeconomic status and cultural views of emotion (social).

TWO OPTIONAL, APPLIED CHAPTERS

In response to increasing demand for more coverage of how psychology applies to business and work in the 21st century, I have completely revised the previous Chapter 17, "Industrial/Organizational Psychology," and added an entirely new chapter, "Human Performance in a Global Economy." These two chapters are available as a shrink-wrapped option to interested professors and their students. Both chapters were co-written with Gary Piggrem, a professor of psychology at DeVry University, and they provide a general overview of industrial/organizational psychology, along with an extended discussion of communication, conflict management, leadership, and persuasion techniques.

ADDITIONAL CHANGES

In addition to the increased focus on the 3 A's (application, achievement, and assessment), incorporation of the biopsychosocial model, and two new or revised optional chapters, the new edition of *Psychology in Action* includes changes in organization and includes the most recent research findings.

Please note that the following list includes only some of the most important new changes and additions. A full, detailed list, including material that was deleted, is available on our Web site (http:www.wiley.com/college/huffman) for instructors who used the sixth edition and will be using the seventh. I also invite all instructors and their students to contact me directly if you have questions about these changes. I sincerely appreciate your choice of *Psychology in Action* (7th ed.) as your text, and I want to make your teaching and learning experience as easy as possible. ,

Organizational changes from 6/e to 7/e

* *Movement of biological research methods from Neuroscience and Biological Foundations to Introduction and Research Methods.* Introductory psychology texts have traditionally presented biological research methods (e.g., anatomical dissection and PET scans)

in the biology unit. In recent years, however, neuroscience and its research methods are being used in almost every field of psychology, including developmental, abnormal, therapy, and social psychology. I believe it no longer makes sense to separate biological research from the other mainstream psychological research methods. Combining the research methods into one streamlined section (in Module 2) also improves the flow of Modules 5, 6 and 7, the biology unit, which is often one of the most lengthy and difficult of all sections.

- *The discussion of health psychology has been moved from the beginning to the end of the unit called Stress and Health Psychology.* This movement improves the flow and allows a greater focus on stress.

- *Movement of language development from Life Span Development I to Module 23 Thinking, Language, and Intelligence.* Given that many instructors follow the text in a sequential pattern, combining all coverage of language into this earlier module allows for less duplication of topics and streamlining of coverage.

- *The Research Highlight of "The Art and Science of Flirting" was moved from Gender and Human Sexuality to Social Psychology.* Reviewers enjoyed this topic and requested that it be placed near the section on interpersonal attraction in Module 47.

Research updates

To keep pace with the rapid progress in neuroscience, behavioral genetics, evolutionary psychology, cognitive psychology, sociocultural research, and positive psychology, I have added more than 800 new references from 2000 to 2003. I also have included new "Research Highlight" sections, such as "Does Stress Cause Cancer?" (Module 9), "Discovering a Delicious New Taste — Umami" (Module 12), and "Is Cybersex Harmful?" (Module 30).

New Critical Thinking/Active Learning Exercises

For example, "Using Reflective Thinking to Improve Your Memory" (Module 21), "Are Your Marital Expectations Unrealistic?" (Module 28), and "What's Wrong With Movie Portrayals of Therapy?" (Module 42).

Expanded and Innovative Technology

Exciting new online resources can be used by the student who wants to improve skills or enrich his or her study of psychology, or by instructors who teach online courses or as a resource for their traditional lecture courses. These resources include practice quizzes, graded quizzes, demonstrations, simulations, Critical Thinking/Active Learning exercises, and additional features. Each section of the text also contains specific Web site icons ⬤ located near topics that have important Web site resources.

As a user of *Psychology in Action*, you have guaranteed access to John Wiley & Sons student resource Web site http://www.wiley.com/college/huffman. The site includes special online student tutorial quizzes and practice tests, active learning exercises, links to psychology related topics, Internet activities, as well as other valuable features and activities. Check us out!

TABLE 1 SAMPLE HIGHLIGHTS FROM THE SEVENTH EDITION

Application of Psychology
(in addition to the shorter discussions and examples throughout the text):

- Applying Psychology to Work: Careers in the Field (p. 7)
- Applying Psychology to Everyday Life: Overcoming Genetic Misconceptions (p. 87)
- Applying Psychology to Student Life: Why You Shouldn't Procrastinate (p. 105)
- Applying Psychology to Everyday Life: Taking Action Against Stress (p. 117)

- Applying Psychology to Work: Would You Like to Be a Health Psychologist? (p. 120)
- Applying Psychology to Everyday Life: Self-Help for Insomnia (p. 190)
- Applying Psychology to Everyday Life: Club Drug Alert! (p. 201)
- Applying Classical Conditioning to Everyday Life (p. 224)
- Applying Operant Conditioning to Everyday Life (p. 238)
- Applying Cognitive-Social Learning to Everyday Life (p. 246)
- Applying Psychology to Student Life: Using Retrieval Strategies on Exams (p. 270)
- Applying Psychology to Student Life: Overcoming Problems with Forgetting (p. 278)
- Applying Psychology to Student Life: Improving Memory and Exam Scores (p. 289)
- Applying Psychology to Everyday Life: Recognizing Barriers to Problem Solving (p. 306)
- Applying Psychology to Everyday Life: Dealing with Your Own Death Anxiety (p. 398)
- Applying Psychology to Relationships: Protecting Yourself and Others Against STIs (p. 431)
- Applying Psychology to Student Life: Overcoming Test Anxiety (p. 443)
- Applying Psychology to Everyday Life: Birth Order and Personality (p. 493)
- Applying Psychology to Everyday Life: Suicide and Its Prevention (p. 531)
- Applying Psychology at Work: Careers in Mental Health (p. 557)
- Applying Psychology to Relationships: The Art and Science of Flirting (p. 609)
- Applying Psychology to Everyday Life: Improving Communication (Optional Chapter 18)
- Applying Psychology to Everyday Life: Improving Your Powers of Persuasion (Optional Chapter 18)
- Applying Psychology to Everyday Life: Five Approaches to Conflict Resolution (Optional Chapter 18)

Neuroscience
(in addition to the expanded and general updating in Modules 5, 6, and 7):

- Rewiring, repairing, and transplanting brains and spinal cords (p. 82)
- Neuroplasticity and neurogenesis (p. 82)
- The importance of stem cell research (p. 82)
- Why mapping the human genome is important (p. 89)
- Phantom pain and phantom limbs (p. 136)
- Addictive drugs as the brain's "evil tutor" (p. 205)
- Neuroscience and learning (pp. 249–252)
- Brain scans of learning (p. 250)
- Neuronal and synaptic changes in memory (pp. 272–273)
- Where is memory stored? (p. 274)
- Traumatic brain injury and Alzheimer's disease (pp. 282–284)
- Biological influences on intelligence, including brain size, speed, and efficiency (pp. 330–332)
- Brain changes during development (pp. 349–351, 354–355)
- Brain's role in gender differences and sexual behavior (pp. 411, 423–424)
- Brain and emotion (p. 456)
- Biological aspects of personality (pp. 502–504)
- Biological contributors to mental disorders (pp. 525–526, 529, 538–540, 546)
- Biomedical psychotherapy (pp. 560–563)
- Biology of aggression (pp. 626–628)

Behavioral Genetics
(in addition to the expanded and general updating in Modules 5, 6, and 7):

- Genetics and evolution (pp. 86–89)
- Methods for studying (pp. 86–87)
- Genetic mutant "smart mice" (pp. 272–273)
- Genetic influences on intelligence (pp. 330–332)
- The Bell Curve debate (pp. 332–334)
- Nature versus nurture controversy (pp. 343–343)
- Genetics and aging (p. 354)
- Attachment and imprinting (p. 358)

- Nature versus nurture sex and gender differences (pp. 410–413)
- Genetic influences on eating disorders (pp. 441–442)
- Genetic contributions to personality (pp. 503–504)
- The role of genetics in mental disorders, such as schizophrenia (p. 538)
- Genetic contributors to aggression (p. 626)

Evolutionary Psychology
(in addition to the expanded and general updating in Modules 5, 6, and 7):

- Basic principles such as natural selection (pp. 90–91)
- The evolution of sex differences (pp. 91–92)
- Evolutionary advantages of sensory adaptation (pp. 134–135)
- Evolutionary/circadian theory of sleep (p. 185)
- Classical conditioning and biological preparedness (pp. 250–251)
- Operant conditioning and instinctive drift (pp. 251–252)
- Theories of language development (pp. 316–317)
- Are there evolutionary advantages to female nonmonogamy? (pp. 420–421)
- Evolution and emotions (pp. 458–460)
- Animal personalities (pp. 483–484)
- Evolution and aggression (p. 626)
- Evolution and altruism (p. 628)

Cognitive Psychology
(in addition to the expanded and general updating in Modules 20–24):

- Bottom-up and top-down processing (pp. 131, 154)
- Cognitive view of dreams (p. 187)
- Memory problems (pp. 282–288)
- Stereotype threat and intelligence tests (pp. 332–333)
- Intellectual processes of resilient children (p. 392)
- Cognitions and sexual dysfunctions (pp. 425–427)
- Cognitive theories of motivation and emotion (pp. 452, 455, 465–466)
- Social/cognitive approaches to personality (pp. 500–502)
- Cognitive processes in mental disorders (pp. 525, 529–530, 544–545)
- Cognitive therapy (pp. 570–573)
- Attitude change and cognitive processing (pp. 601–602)
- Cognitive processes in prejudice (pp. 604–605)

Positive Psychology

- Ethical research (pp. 27–30)
- Wellness (pp. 96–126, 142–143, 195–201)
- Hardiness (pp. 110–111)
- Coping with stress (pp. 114–117)
- Overcoming sleep disorders (pp. 189–190)
- Alternative routes to alternate states (pp. 206–209)
- Alternatives to punishment (pp. 234–235, 239)
- Improving memory (pp. 271, 277, 289–292)
- Creativity (pp. 310–311)
- Multiple intelligences (pp. 322–324)
- Positive aspects of aging (pp. 352–355, 371)
- Promoting secure attachment and positive parenting (pp. 356–361)
- Moral behavior (pp. 378–380)
- Resilient children (pp. 392)
- Benefits of androgyny (pp. 413–414)
- High achievers (pp. 445–446)
- Emotional intelligence (pp. 461–462)
- Overcoming prejudice and discrimination (pp. 600–607)
- Love and interpersonal attraction (pp. 607–613)
- Reducing aggression (pp. 628–629)
- Altruism and helping behaviors (pp. 629–630)

A COMPLETE LEARNING SYSTEM

Beginning with the first edition, *Psychology in Action*, has won acclaim for its extensive pedagogy. The Seventh Edition includes even more tools and aids to increase student learning.

■ Tools for Student Success

To help students become more efficient and successful, this Seventh Edition includes a special feature called, "Tools for Student Success." Beginning in Module 4, there is a special end-of-section segment that includes tips for active reading, time management, and improving course grades, as well as important resources for college success.

In addition, several student success sections (identified with a light bulb icon ♀) are sprinkled throughout the text. For example, Modules 16–24 and 38 all include strategies for improving learning strategies, memory, test performance, and overall achievement.

■ Visual Summaries

In addition to the Tools for Student Success, each section of the text ends with a unique study tool that visually summarizes and organizes the main concepts. This Visual Summary is a two-page spread that can be used both as an overview "to get the big picture" before reading the modules in that section, and as a quick review after completing the reading. Our students, readers, reviewers, and adopters are all very excited by this feature. They report finding it "extremely helpful" and "the best study tool ever invented!"

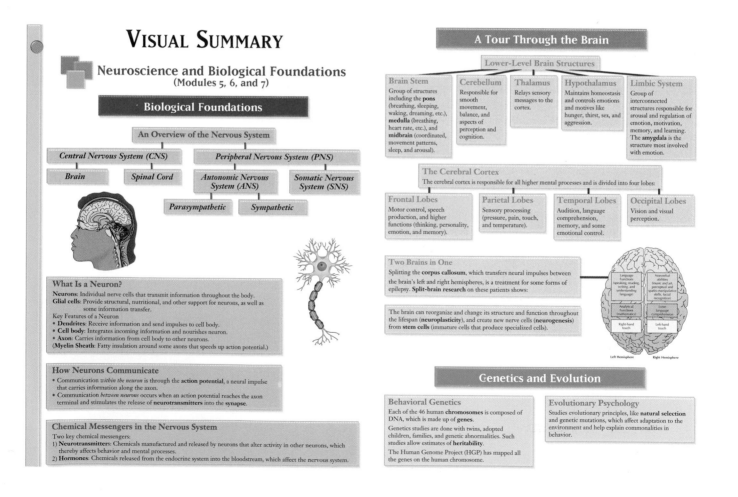

■ Research Highlights

These recent, high interest topics are explored in enough detail to fully explain the topic, yet remain brief enough to maintain full reader attention. These sections show the achievement of scientific research.

■ Focus on Critical Thinking and Active Learning

To promote both critical thinking and active learning, I include "Try This Yourself" activities in every module. These high-interest and simple-to-do experiments, demonstrations, and self-tests give students an opportunity to apply basic principles and concepts. In Module 37, for example, one "Try This Yourself" activity debunks myths about mental illness and another presents a checklist for recognizing serious depression.

In addition to "Try This Yourself" activities, each section also presents an in-depth "Critical Thinking/Active Learning Exercise" based on text content and devoted to developing specific critical thinking skills. For example, the Active Learning Exercise in Module 33 asks readers, "Why are pseudo personality tests so popular?" and aims to expose persuasive appeals as a critical thinking skill.

Student and reader comments indicate that both the "Try This Yourself" and "Critical Thinking/Active Learning Exercises" are enjoyable and educational. One student wrote, "I looked forward to the 'Try This Yourself' sections because they were a fun, quick, and easy way to try out the ideas in the text." Another student wrote: "The 'Try This Yourself' feature was always interesting to do. I especially liked the one about culture and the 'proper' ways to ride an elevator. My friends and I still have fun going into an elevator and facing toward the people instead of away from them." As for the "Critical Thinking/Active Learning Exercises," one student wrote that they "made me really think about what I was studying and how it pertained to my life," and another said they were "not only useful in this course, but could be applied to other courses and daily life as well."

■ SQ4R Learning Activities

To further encourage active learning, the text is designed to include the SQ4R (Survey, Question, Read, Recite, Review, and "wRite") method of learning:

Survey and Question

Each section begins with four survey and question techniques: core learning objectives, a section outline, a vignette that introduces essential concepts, and an introductory paragraph that previews content and organization.

Read

Each module has been carefully evaluated for clarity, conciseness, and student reading level.

Recite and Review

To encourage recitation and review, the text offers a short "Check & Review" section that summarizes the previous material and offers four or five multiple-choice, fill-in, and short answer questions. An additional aid to review is the previously mentioned "Visual Summaries" at the end of each section that visually organizes and connects essential concepts. Each section also concludes with a review activity for the key terms, which is topically organized with page references.

wRite

As part of the fourth R in the SQ4R method, this book is designed to incorporate writing as a way of improving student retention. In addition to the writing students do in the survey, question, and review sections, note taking is encouraged in the margin of each page, which have been kept as clear as possible. The Instructor's Manual, which accompanies this text, also describes a special "marginal marking" technique that can be easily taught to students. The accompanying Student Study Guide discusses the SQ4R method in more detail.

◼ Additional Learning Aids

In addition to the previously mentioned pedagogical aids, *Psychology in Action* incorporates other learning aids known to increase comprehension and retention and contribute to active learning with results:

Key terms

Important terms are put in **boldface type** and immediately defined in the text.

Running glossary

Key terms also appear with their definitions and a phonetic pronunciation in the margin of each page near where they are first introduced. Calling out and defining key terms in the margin not only increases overall comprehension; it also provides a useful review tool.

End-of-text glossary

All key terms are also gathered in a complete, cumulative glossary at the end of the text.

Summary tables

To increase student insight and "aha" experiences, I include numerous summary tables, some containing important illustrations, such as the table on drug actions and neurotransmitters in Module 15. The tables that compare classical and operant conditioning in Module 17 and contrasting theories of memory in Module 20 also serve as important educational tools.

Study tips

In addition to the Tools for Student Success discussed earlier, I also include specific short study tips that students have found very useful. For example, the study tip in Module 23

(p. 316) helps clarify overgeneralization and overextension. The study tip on positive and negative symptoms of schizophrenia in Module 40 (p. 537) incorporates earlier concepts of positive and negative reinforcement found in Module 17 (p. 231).

Historical timeline
The grouping of famous contributors to psychology on the text's front endpapers provides a visual organizer and overview of the history of psychology.

Emphasis on the Science of Psychology

> The pursuit of scientific understanding is among the noblest of all human goals. Like the pursuit of great art or the preservation of a beautiful wilderness, it is good in and of itself.
>
> RANDY GALLISTEL [cited in Loftus, E. (1999, January), Higher intolerance. *APS Observer*, 12(1), 3, 20.]

It is important to recognize that a century of psychological research has greatly increased our understanding of human behavior. Therefore, in preparing this Seventh Edition, I have sought to enhance students' appreciation of psychology as an empirical study of human experience and to demonstrate the advantages of the scientific method over speculation and "common" sense.

Modules 1 and 2 set the stage with a thorough discussion of the scientific method, bias in research, and types of correlation, but every section also includes extended research examples that demonstrate the scientific nature of psychology. In addition, all biological figures have been reviewed and when necessary redrawn to clarify difficult concepts, such as neurotransmitter reuptake at the synapse.

SUPPLEMENTS

Psychology in Action (Seventh Edition) is accompanied by a host of ancillary materials designed to facilitate the mastery of psychology. Ordering information and policies may be obtained by contacting your local Wiley sales representative.

Instructor's Supplements

Computerized Test Bank
Wendy J. Hunter, Ph.D., Palomar College, prepared the Computerized Test Bank, a multiplatform CD-ROM, that fully supports graphics, prints tests, student answer sheets and answer keys. The software's advanced features allow you to create an exam to your exact specifications, within an easy-to-use interface. The test generation program has nearly 2,000 test items that include approximately 10 essay questions for each chapter (with suggested answers) and a variety of multiple-choice questions. Each multiple-choice question has been linked to the student learning objective it pertains to, coded "Factual" or "Applied," the correct answer indicated, and page referenced to its source in the text. Also included are several "humorous questions" that can be inserted in tests to reduce test anxiety. In addition, the Computerized Test Bank includes questions from the Student Study Guide and the main text's "review questions." These can be easily added to the test to reinforce student efforts or simply for the professor's reference.

Instructor's Resource Guide (available in hard copy and electronic format — Microsoft Word files)
Prepared by Kathleen Weatherford, Trident Technical College, this comprehensive resource includes for each text chapter: an outline, student learning objectives, out-

line/lecture organizer (page referenced to text), lecture lead-ins, supplemental lectures ("hot" topics), key terms (page referenced to text), chapter summary/lecture organizer, discussion questions, suggested films and videos, activities section, three active learning/critical thinking exercises, and a writing project. This edition also includes a Cross-Cultural Focus (either an activity or a brief lecture) and numerous Active Learning Exercises specifically created for use with any size class.

Transparency Acetates
One hundred full-color overhead transparencies are created from text illustrations, resized with bold type for use in large lecture halls.

Videos
Please contact your Wiley sales representative for information on videos that are available to adopters of the text, such as Roger Bingham's series on the brain, and many other titles.

Faculty Resource Network
The Faculty Resource Network is a group of psychology instructors ready to support the use of online course management tools and discipline specific software/learning systems in the classroom. They will help you apply innovative classroom techniques, implement specific software packages and tailor the technology experience to the needs of each individual class. Get connected with the Faculty Resource Network at www.FacultyResourceNetwork.com.

WebCT
In addition to the Web site, we also offer a WebCT course management system in the highly customizable WebCT format. The course includes: chapter overviews, chapter reviews for each section, assignments, Web links, discussion questions, self-tests, quiz questions and test questions, as well as all standard features of WebCT, such as bulletin board, calendar, e-mail and chat. A brief Instructor's Manual will be available (in electronic format only) to assist you in your use of this course.

Blackboard
Due to its popularity, we also offer a Web course management system in the popular Blackboard format. The course includes: chapter overviews, chapter reviews for each section, homework assignments, Web links, discussion questions, self-tests, quiz questions and test questions, as well as all standard features of Blackboard.

■ Student's Supplements

Student Study and Review Guide (Seventh Edition)
Prepared by Karen Huffman and Richard Hosey, this valuable resource offers students an easy way to review the textbook material and ensures that they know it. For each textbook chapter students have numerous tools that help them master the material, including: chapter outline, learning objectives, key terms, key term crossword puzzles, matching exercises, fill-in exercises, an additional Active Learning Exercise, and two Sample Tests (20 items each) with answers. New to this edition, each chapter of the student study and review guide also includes a copy of the visual summaries that appear at the end of each chapter in the text. Students in the past have xeroxed these summaries to use during class lecture or text reading, so we've made their studying easier by including them in this supplement.

Media Package: Web Site

An exciting new Web site has been created expressly for the Seventh Edition that will include both student and instructor materials. All of the assets can be accessed directly from the Web site.

The media package includes the following supplementary material: multimedia mini-modules to enhance teaching of complex topics such as conditioning; HTML-based exercises, homework assignments, and more; self-tests and Web Links. The package also includes additional free downloads, such as the following:

- *PowerPoint Files.* Two sets of files will be available for both student and instructor use: art slides and lecture note slides. Students will be able to access the Power Point files on the Web, and instructors will have the files on the Instructor's Resource CD-ROM, as well as, on the Web.

- *Vocabulary Flash Cards.* The vocabulary flash cards comprise an interactive module that allows students to test their knowledge of vocabulary terms. Students will also be able to take self-tests on these vocabulary terms and monitor their progress.

- *Simulations.* These exciting and new interactive modules will help students understand introductory and complex concepts that are featured in the text. Each interactive simulation will include summaries and thought-provoking questions to help support the student's understanding of the module.

- *Online Guide.* This guide offers information about how to use the Web for research, and how to best find the information you are seeking.

ACKNOWLEDGMENTS

The writing of this text has been a group effort involving the input and support of my families, friends, and colleagues. To each person I offer my sincere thanks. A special note of appreciation goes to Jay Alperson, Bill Barnard, Haydn Davis, Tom Frangicetto, Ann Haney, Herb Harari, Sandy Harvey, Richard Hosey, Terry Humphrey, Teresa Jacob, Kandis Mutter, Bob Miller, Roger Morrissette, Harriett Prentiss, Jeanne Riddell, Sabine Schoen, and Katie Townsend-Merino.

To the reviewers, focus group, and telesession participants who gave their time and constructive criticism, we offer our sincere appreciation. We are deeply indebted to the following individuals and trust that they will recognize their contributions throughout the text.

Student Reviewers

To help us verify that our book successfully shaped active learning, we asked introductory psychology students about their experience studying from *Psychology in Action*. Their reactions confirmed our belief that the book is an effective learning tool. We are grateful to the following students who took the time to share their honest opinions with us:

Erin Decker, *San Diego State University*, Laura Decker, *University of California at Davis*, Amanda Nichols, *Palomar College*, Idalia S. Carrillo, *University of Texas at San Antonio*, Sarah Dedford, *Delta College (Michigan)*, Laural Didham, *Cleveland State University*, Danyce French, *Northampton Community College (Pennsylvania)*, Stephanie Renae Reid, *Purdue University–Calumet*, Betsy Schoenbeck, *University of Missouri at Columbia*, Sabrina Walkup, *Trident Technical College (South Carolina)*

■ Reviewers for *Psychology in Action* (Seventh Edition)

The following professionals evaluated the previous edition and offered suggestions for revision, reviewed manuscript, or responded to surveys.

Thomas Alley, *Clemson University*
David R. Barkmeier, *Northeastern University*
Steven Barnhart, *Rutgers University*
Dan Bellack, *Trident Technical College*
JoAnn Brannock, *Fullerton College*
Michael Caruso, *University of Toledo*
Nicole Judice Campbell, *University of Oklahoma*
Sandy Deabler, *North Harris College*
Diane K. Feibel, *Raymond Walters College*
Richard Griggs, *University of Florida*
Richard Harris, *Kansas State University*
John Haworth, *Florida Community College at Jacksonville*
Guadalupe King, *Milwaukee Area Technical College*
Roger Morrissette, *Palomar College*
Barbara Nash, *Bentley College*
Maureen O'Brien, *Bentley College*
Jan Pascal, *DeVry University*
John Pennachio, *Adirondack Community College*
Gary E. Rolikowki, *SUNY, Geneseo*
Ronnie Rothschild, *Broward Community College*
Ludo Scheffer, *Drexel University*
Kathy Sexton-Radek, *Elmhurst College*
Matthew Sharps, *California State University–Fresno*
Richard Topolski, *Augusta State University*
Katie Townsend-Merino, *Palomar College*
Elizabeth Young, *Bentley College*

■ Focus Group and Telesession Participants

Brian Bate, Cuyahoga Community College; Hugh Bateman, Jones Junior College; Ronald Boykin, Salisbury State University; Jack Brennecke, Mount San Antonio College; Ethel Canty, University of Texas–Brownsville; Joseph Ferrari, Cazenovia College; Allan Fingaret, Rhode Island College; Richard Fry, Youngstown State University; Roger Harnish, Rochester Institute of Technology; Richard Harris, Kansas State University; Tracy B. Henley, Mississippi State University; Roger Hock, New England College; Melvyn King, State University of New York at Cortland; Jack Kirschenbaum, Fullerton College; Cynthia McDaniel, Northern Kentucky University; Deborah McDonald, New Mexico State University; Henry Morlock, State University of New York at Plattsburgh; Kenneth Murdoff, Lane Community College; William Overman, University of North Carolina at Wilmington; Steve Platt, Northern Michigan University; Janet Proctor, Purdue University; Dean Schroeder, Laramie Community College; Michael Schuller, Fresno City College; Alan Schultz, Prince George Community College; Peggy Skinner, South Plains College; Charles Slem, California Polytechnic State University–San Luis Obispo; Eugene Smith, Western Illinois University; David Thomas, Oklahoma State University; Cynthia Viera, Phoenix College; Matthew Westra, Longview Community College

■ Reviewers of Previous Editions

L. Joseph Achor, Baylor University; M. June Allard, Worcester State College; Joyce Allen, Lakeland College; Worthon Allen, Utah State University; Jeffrey S. Anastasi, Francis Marion University; Susan Anderson, University of South Alabama; Emir Andrews, Memorial University of Newfoundland; Marilyn Andrews, Hartnell College; Richard Anglin, Oklahoma City Community College; Susan Anzivino, University of Maine at Farmington; Peter Bankart, Wabash College; Susan Barnett, Northwestern State University (Louisiana); Patricia Barker, Schenectady County Community College; Daniel Bellack, College of Charleston; Daniel Bitran, College of Holy Cross; Terry Blumenthal, Wake Forest University; Theodore N.

Bosack, Providence College; Linda Bosmajian, Hood College; John Bouseman, Hillsborough Community College; John P. Broida, University of Southern Maine; Lawrence Burns, Grand Valley State University; Bernado J. Carducci, Indiana University Southeast; Charles S. Carver, University of Miami; Marion Cheney, Brevard Community College; Meg Clark, California State Polytechnic University–Pomona; Dennis Cogan, Texas Tech University; David Cohen, California State University, Bakersfield; Anne E. Cook, University of Massachessetts; Kathryn Jennings Cooper, Salt Lake Community College; Steve S. Cooper, Glendale Community College; Amy Cota-McKinley, The University of Tennessee, Knoxville; Mark Covey, University of Idaho; Robert E. DeLong, Liberty University; Linda Scott DeRosier, Rocky Mountain College; Grace Dyrud, Augsburg College; Thomas Eckle, Modesto Junior College; Tami Eggleston, McKendree College; James A. Eison, Southeast Missouri State University; A. Jeanette Engles, Southeastern Oklahoma State University; Eric Fiazi, Los Angeles City College; Sandra Fiske, Onondaga Community College; Kathleen A. Flannery, Saint Anselm College; Pamela Flynn, Community College of Philadelphia; William F. Ford, Bucks City Community College; Harris Friedman, Edison Community College; Paul Fuller, Muskegon Community College; Frederick Gault, Western Michigan University; Russell G. Geen, University of Missouri, Columbia; Joseph Giacobbe, Adirondack Community College; Robert Glassman, Lake Forest College; Patricia Marks Greenfield, University of California — Los Angeles; David A. Griese, SUNY Farmingdale; Sam Hagan, Edison County Community College; Sylvia Haith, Forsyth Technical College; Frederick Halper, Essex County Community College; George Hampton, University of Houston — Downtown; Joseph Hardy, Harrisburg Area Community College; Algea Harrison, Oakland University; Mike Hawkins, Louisiana State University; Linda Heath, Loyola University of Chicago; Sidney Hochman, Nassau Community College; Richard D. Honey, Transylvania University; John J. Hummel, Valdosta State University; Nancy Jackson, Johnson & Wales University; Kathryn Jennings, College of the Redwoods; Charles Johnston, William Rainey Harper College; Dennis Jowaisis, Oklahoma City Community College; Seth Kalichman, University of South Carolina; Paul Kaplan, Suffolk County Community College; Bruno Kappes, University of Alaska; Kevin Keating, Broward Community College; Guadalupe Vasquez King, Milwaukee Area Technical College; Norman E. Kinney, Southeast Missouri State University; Richard A. Lambe, Providence College; Sherri B. Lantinga, Dordt College; Marsha Laswell, California State Polytechnic University — Pomona; Elise Lindenmuth, York College; Allan A. Lippert, Manatee Community College; Thomas Linton, Coppin State College; Virginia Otis Locke, University of Idaho; Maria Lopez-Trevino, Mount San Jacinto College; Tom Marsh, Pitt Community College; Edward McCrary III, El Camino Community College; David G. McDonald, University of Missouri, Columbia; Yancy McDougal, University of South Carolina — Spartanburg; Nancy Meck, University of Kansas Medical Center; Juan S. Mercado, McLennan Community College; Michelle Merwin, University of Tennessee, Martin; Mitchell Metzger, Penn State University; David Miller, Daytona Beach Community College; Michael Millcr, College of St. Scholastica; Phil Mohan, University of Idaho; Ron Mossler, LA Valley College; Kathleen Navarre, Delta College; John Near, Elgin Community College; Steve Neighbors, Santa Barbara City College; Leslie Neumann, Forsyth Technical Community College; Susan Nolan, Seton Hall University; Sarah O'Dowd, Community College of Rhode Island; Joseph J. Palladino, University of Southern Indiana; Linda Palm, Edison Community College; Richard S. Perroto, Queensborough Community College; Larry Pervin, Rutgers University, New Brunswick; Valerie Pinhas, Nassau Community College; Leslee Pollina, Southeast Missouri State University; Howard R. Pollio, University of Tennessee — Knoxville; Christopher Potter, Harrisburg Community College; Derrick Proctor, Andrews University; Antonio Puete, University of North Carolina — Wilmington; Joan S. Rabin, Towson State University; Lillian Range, University of Southern Mississippi; George A. Raymond, Providence College; Celia Reaves, Monroe Community College; Michael J. Reich, University of Wisconsin — River Falls; Edward Rinalducci, University of Central Florida; Kathleen R. Rogers, Purdue University North Central; Leonard S. Romney, Rockland Community College; Thomas E. Rudy, University of Pittsburgh; Carol D. Ryff, University of Wisconsin — Madison; Neil Salkind, University of Kansas — Lawrence; Richard J. Sanders, University of North Carolina — Wilmington; Harvey Richard Schiffman, Rutgers University; Steve Schneider, Pima College; Michael Scozzaro, State University of New York at Buffalo; Tizrah Schutzengel, Bergen Community College; Lawrence Scott, Bunker Hill Community College; Michael B. Sewall, Mohawk Valley Community College; Fred Shima, California State University — Dominquez Hills; Royce Simpson, Campbellsville University; Art Skibbe, Appalachian State University; Larry Smith, Daytona Beach Junior College; Emily G. Soltano, Worcester State College;

Debra Steckler, Mary Washington College; Michael J. Strube, Washington University; Kevin Sumrall, Montgomery College; Ronald Testa, Plymouth State College; Cynthia Viera, Phoenix College; John T. Vogel, Baldwin Wallace College; Benjamin Wallace, Cleveland State University; Mary Wellman, Rhode Island College; Paul J. Wellman, Texas A & M University; I. Eugene White, Salisbury State College; Delos D. Wickens, Colorado State University — Fort Collins; Fred Whitford, Montana State University; Charles Wiechert, San Antonio College; Jeff Walper, Delaware Technical and Community College; Bonnie S. Wright, St. Olaf College; Brian T. Yates, American University; Todd Zakrajsek, Southern Oregon University; Mary Lou Zanich, Indiana University of Pennsylvania

■ Special Thanks

Special thanks also go to the superb editorial and production teams at John Wiley and Sons. This project benefited from the wisdom and insight of Sandra Dumas, Sandra Rigby, Sara Wight, Elyse Rieder, Karyn Drews, Kevin Murphy, and many others. Like any cooperative effort, writing a book requires an immense support team, and I am deeply grateful to this remarkable group of people.

In particular, I would like to thank my developmental editor, Johnna Barto, for her outstanding help in keeping the project on track and pulling all the loose ends together. Textbook production is a complex process that only works when everything comes together at the right time and in the right place. Johnna handled this with great patience and good humor. (Please, Johnna, don't ever leave Wiley and Sons!)

It's also a pleasure to thank my psychology editor, Tim Vertovec, who supervised the revision from start to finish with enthusiasm, skill, and lots of good ideas, while soothing his author's frazzled nerves. Thanks, Tim!

Next, I'd like to thank Leslie Carr, my developmental editor, for her careful, intelligent and constructive comments. Her guidance greatly improved the project. I also am deeply indebted to Anne Smith, Publisher, Kevin Molloy, Marketing Manager, Lisa Schnettler, media editor, and a host of others — all of whom helped enormously in the initial launch and ongoing work of this revision.

I also wish to thank Hermitage Publishing Services and Radiant Illustration and Design. Their careful and professional approach were critical to the successful production of this book.

Finally, I would like to express our continuing appreciation to my students. They taught me what students want to know and inspired me to revise the book. In addition, two individuals deserve special recognition for their research assistance, Chris Wagner and Sandy Harvey. My warm appreciation is also extended to Kandis Mutter and Richard Hosey. They provided careful editing of this text, library research, and a unique sense of what should and should not go into an introduction to psychology text. I sincerely appreciate their contributions. If you have suggestions or comments, please feel free to contact me at my email address: Karen Huffman (khuffman@palomar.edu).

PROLOGUE
CRITICAL THINKING/ACTIVE LEARNING

(With contributions from Thomas Frangicetto and his students at Northampton Community College)

This text's focus on active learning naturally contributes to the development of critical thinking. I believe that an active learner is by definition also a critical thinker. Critical thinking has many meanings and some books dedicate entire chapters to defining the term. The word critical comes from the Greek word *kritikos*, which means to question, makes sense of, be able to analyze. Thinking is the cognitive activity involved in making sense of the world around us. Critical thinking, therefore, is defined as thinking about and evaluating our thoughts, feelings, and behavior so that we can clarify and improve them (adapted from Chaffee, 1988, p. 29).

Critical thinking is a process. As a process — something you do — you can do it better. You can develop your critical thinking skills. Each unit of *Psychology in Action* (and corresponding section in the Student Study and Review Guide and Instructor's Resource Guide) includes a specific Critical Thinking/Active Learning Exercise devoted to improving one or more of the components of critical thinking. To learn more about each of these components, study the following three lists. They present the affective (emotional), cognitive (thinking), and behavioral (action) components of critical thinking. You will no doubt find that you already employ some of these skills. You also will no doubt recognize areas you could strengthen through practice.

AFFECTIVE COMPONENTS

The emotional foundation that either enables or limits critical thinking.

1. ***Valuing truth above self-interest.*** Critical thinkers hold themselves and those they agree with to the same intellectual standards to which they hold their opponents. This is one of the most difficult components to employ on a regular basis. We all have a tendency to cater to our own needs (see "self-serving bias"), and to ignore information that conflicts with our desires. Critical thinkers recognize that, even when it appears otherwise, the "truth" is always in our self-interst.

2. ***Accepting change.*** Critical thinkers remain open to the need for adjustment and adaptation throughout the life cycle. Because critical thinkers fully trust the processes of reasoned inquiry, they are willing to use these skills to examine even their most deeply held values and beliefs, and to modify these beliefs when evidence and experience contradict them.

   "As one becomes a parent for the first time, that individual must face the fact that accepting change plays a very big role. A new parent can no longer drop everything and do whatever they please, such as going to a club or bar to socialize or even just going out to dinner. They now have more responsibilities and different priorities." — James Cavanaugh

3. ***Empathizing.*** Critical thinkers appreciate and try to understand others' thoughts, feelings, and behaviors. Noncritical thinkers view everything and everyone in relation to the self.

   "Same sex marriage is a controversial subject in America today. I always thought that marriage between two men or two women was a mortal sin and I couldn't accept it. There are people who discriminate and protest against this and many violent crimes, even murder, are

committed because of one person's hatred for another's lifestyle. I now empathize with same sex couples because they are just trying to live their lives and be happy and they have a tough time being accepted. Who should determine what makes another person happy? Just because I didn't agree with their choice, it doesn't make it wrong." — *Troy Margeson*

4. ***Welcoming divergent views.*** Critical thinkers value examining issues from every angle and know that it is especially important to explore and understand positions with which they disagree.

5. ***Tolerating ambiguity.*** Although formal education often trains us to look for a single "right" answer, critical thinkers recognize that many issues are complex and subtle, and that complex issues may not have a ""right" answer. They recognize and value qualifiers such as ""probably," ""highly likely," and ""not very likely."

6. ***Recognizing personal biases.*** Critical thinkers use their highest intellectual skills to detect personal biases and self-deceptive reasoning so they can design realistic plans for self-correction.

"When I came to the United States I had my own views and understanding of the American way of life and of the American people. But I quickly learned that in order to really understand American values and the American people I must be open-minded and not be prejudiced in dealing with Americans—I had to recognize my personal biases." — *Banchalem Tesfaye*

COGNITIVE COMPONENTS

The thought processes actually involved in critical thinking.

7. ***Thinking independently.*** Critical thinking is independent thinking. Critical thinkers do not passively accept the beliefs of others and are not easily manipulated.

8. ***Defining problems accurately.*** A critical thinker identifies the issues in clear and concrete terms, to prevent confusion and lay the foundation for gathering relevant information.

"Sometimes I focus on things that are not important and blow them out of proportion; I do not define problems accurately. I don't know if this a defense mechanism or just a lack of sleep. I need to slow down, organize, prioritize, and do more critical thinking." — *Danielle LaBarre*

9. ***Analyzing data for value and content.*** By carefully evaluating the nature of evidence and the credibility of the source, critical thinkers recognize illegitimate appeals to emotion, unsupported assumptions, and faulty logic. This enables them to discount sources of information that lack a record of honesty, contradict themselves on key questions, or have a vested interest in selling a product or idea.

10. ***Employing a variety of thinking processes in problem solving.*** Among these thinking processes are inductive logic — reasoning that moves from the specific to the general; *deductive logic* — reasoning that moves from the general to the specific; *dialogical thinking* — thinking that involves an extended verbal exchange between differing points of view or frames of reference; and *dialectical thinking* — thinking that tests the strengths and weaknesses of opposing points of view.

11. ***Synthesizing.*** Critical thinkers recognize that comprehension and understanding result from combining various elements into meaningful patterns.

12. ***Resisting overgeneralization.*** Overgeneralization is the temptation to apply a fact or experience to situations that are only superficially similar.

13. ***Employing metacognition.*** Metacognition, also known as reflective or recursive thinking, involves reviewing and analyzing your own mental processes — thinking about your own thinking.

"I believe that I benefit from being able to employ metacognition. I am able to use this component extensively in my writings. I can be brutally honest about myself and really dig deeply into my own thoughts to find out how I truly feel about any given situation." — *Tara Torcivia*

BEHAVIORAL COMPONENTS

The actions necessary for critical thinking.

14. ***Delaying judgment until adequate data is available.*** A critical thinker does not make snap judgments.

15. ***Employing precise terms.*** Precise terms help critical thinkers identify issues clearly and concretely so they can be objectively defined and empirically tested.

16. ***Gathering data.*** Collecting up-to-date, relevant information on all sides of an issue is a priority before making decisions.

17. ***Distinguishing fact from opinion.*** Facts are statements that can be proven true. Opinions are statements that express how a person feels about an issue or what someone thinks is true.

"I like that this text teaches us to distinguish fact from opinion, for example, to 'recognize statements that can be proven true' versus statements that merely reveal the way we feel about something. We must learn to tell the difference between the 'truth' and popular opinions we have learned from our parents and society." — *Wendy Moren*

18. ***Encouraging critical dialogue.*** Critical thinkers are active questioners who challenge existing facts and opinions and welcome questions in return. Socratic questioning is an important type of critical dialogue in which the questioner deeply probes the meaning, justification, or logical strength of a claim, position, or line of reasoning.

"September 11th, 2001, is a time that Americans will always remember. The impact of massive death rocked our nation in a huge way. Our children were not spared this act of terror...there was no way to hide this event or to sugarcoat it. We needed to allow our children to express what they were feeling and to talk about what they were seeing on television and hearing from others by encouraging critical dialogue." — *Debbie Fegley*

19. ***Listening actively.*** Critical thinkers fully engage their thinking skills when listening to another.

20. ***Modifying judgments in light of new information.*** Critical thinkers are willing to abandon or modify their judgments if later evidence or experience contradicts them.

21. ***Applying knowledge to new situations.*** When critical thinkers master a new skill or experience an insight, they transfer this information to new contexts. Non-critical thinkers can often provide correct answers, repeat definitions, and carry out calculations, yet be unable to transfer their knowledge to new situations because of a basic lack of understanding.

A great many people think they are thinking when they are merely rearranging their prejudices.

WILLIAM JAMES

INTRODUCTION AND RESEARCH METHODS

Assessment
Core Learning Objectives

As you read Modules 1, 2, 3, and 4, keep the following questions in mind and answer them in your own words:

▶ What is psychology? What are its goals and main career specialties?

▶ What is the scientific method?

▶ What are the four major methods of psychological research?

▶ What are the key research and ethical issues?

▶ Who are the important contributors to psychology's past, and what are the primary perspectives that guide modern psychology?

Study Tip 💡

Learning Objectives
These objectives are general questions you should attempt to answer as you read the modules. For reinforcement, they are repeated in the margins at the place where they are discussed. These questions are an important part of the SQ4R method described in the Preface, and the Student Study and Review Guide, which accompanies this text. They foster **assessment.**

Study Tip 💡

Section Outline
Each section begins with an outline of major topics and subtopics that will be discussed in the following modules. The major topics are boldfaced. Under each are approximately three to five subtopics. This pattern of headings is repeated within each module. The section outline and the corresponding headings provide a mental scaffold to organize the new information you are learning.

Imagine yourself as Emily Rosa, a 9-year-old looking for a topic for your school's annual science fair. Like most fourth-graders, you turn to your parents for ideas. It so happens that your mom and stepfather have frequently discussed the controversial practice of therapeutic touch (TT) — an alternative nursing technique designed to treat many medical conditions by manipulating "human energy fields." Although acknowledging that massage or actual touch can help patients, your parents are highly skeptical that TT practitioners can cure illness by simply waving their hands above the patient's body. You've heard your parents complain that TT practitioners charge up to $70 an hour for their treatment, despite the lack of corroborating scientific evidence. Suddenly, it hits you! Why not design a science fair project that tests TT?

As it turns out, your simple but elegant scientific study so completely debunks TT that you're invited to publish your findings in the highly respected Journal of the American Med-

Study Tip 💡

Opening Vignette
Every section begins with a short opening story that sets the stage for the following modules. These vignettes introduce interesting real-world examples and applications of the theories covered.

■ Achievement
■ Assessment
■ Application

ical Association (JAMA). *As the youngest researcher to ever publish in a major medical journal, you are recognized by the Guinness Book of World Records, receive a $1,000 check from the Skeptics Society, and are invited to appear on several nationally televised news broadcasts.*

Although this sounds like a fourth-grader's fantasy, the story is true. Nine-year-old Emily Rosa (almost) single-handedly debunked an entire medical treatment employed by over 100,000 trained practitioners. As JAMA editor George Lundberg stated in a television interview, "Age doesn't matter. It's good science that matters, and this is good science" (Lemonick, 1998).

Now, think of yourself as Dr. Antonio Damasio, distinguished professor and head of the Department of Neurology at the University of Iowa College of Medicine in Iowa City. You are introduced to a tall, slender, and extremely pleasant young female patient, referred to as "S." Tests show that she has normal healthy sensory perceptions, language abilities, and intelligence. Shortly after being introduced, S hugs and touches you repeatedly. You discover that this same cheerful, touching behavior pervades all areas of her life. She makes friends and romantic attachments easily and is eager to interact with almost anyone. By all reports, S lives in an extremely pleasant world dominated by positive emotions.

So what's "wrong" with S? Can you diagnose her? Dr. Damasio discovered that a very small part of S's brain, the amygdala, is damaged, which makes her unable to recognize or respond to fear in a person's face. As a result, "she has not learned the telltale signs that announce possible danger and possible unpleasantness, especially as they show up in the face of another person" (Damasio, 1999, p. 66).

As a third challenge, imagine yourself as a highly respected research psychologist. The U.S. government asks you and your colleagues to develop better techniques for predicting violent behavior in convicted criminals. They also seek your help in two other areas. Do herbal products such as Ginkgo Biloba improve memory? Do smaller classes result in greater student achievement, and, if so, for what type of student? The government offers lucrative contracts, but do you have the psychological training to answer these questions?

The stories of Emily Rosa and S are true. And the research questions in the third case are similarly real. They are taken from a recent national research initiative, known as Psychological Science in the Public Interest (PSPI). Recognizing that psychological research is a critical resource in our society, the PSPI commissions panels of psychologists to study issues of national concern and strong public interest (Gold, Cahill, & Wenk, 2002; Swets, Dawes, & Monahan, 2000).

Welcome to the fascinating world of psychology. When I was a student and opened my first psychology text, I expected to read mostly about abnormal behavior. I thought many (or all) psychologists worked as therapists. Today, most of my college students seem to share these same expectations—and *misconceptions.*

This is why I chose to open this first section with the stories of Emily, Dr. Damasio, and the work of the PSPI. I wanted to demonstrate the diverse interests and concerns of psychology and psychologists. Although some psychologists do treat and study abnormal behavior, others study how the brain and nervous system affect and control our behavior, how we sense and perceive the world around us, what motivates us, what happens when we sleep and dream, how a child's mind grows and changes over time, and much more.

To help you understand and appreciate the enormous range of psychology, this opening section provides a brief introduction to the entire field. We begin with a formal definition of psychology and an exploration of its goals. The sec-

ond module discusses the various scientific methods used to collect the data that makes up the foundation of psychology. The third module, on psychology's past and present perspectives, helps you understand how the field developed and where it is today. The fourth module concludes with a special feature, *Tools for Student Success,* which will help you do well in this course. Be sure to read this section carefully.

(Nervous students take note: Before you begin your study of psychology, I would like to offer a little reassurance. Students sometimes are overwhelmed with the amount of material in a broad survey course like general psychology. Most instructors, however, do not expect you to master every term and concept in every module. If you pay close attention during class lectures and discussions, you can discover what areas your professor will emphasize on exams and quizzes. More important than test success, however, is the positive value of psychological knowledge. The wealth of information you will gain from this course in psychology will greatly increase your understanding of yourself and the world around you. It has direct (and useful) applications to your everyday life. Keep these benefits and the big picture in mind. Look at the forest—not just the trees.)

MODULE 1
UNDERSTANDING PSYCHOLOGY

Assessment

What is psychology? What are its goals and main career specialties?

Psychology *The scientific study of behavior and mental processes*

Critical Thinking *The process of objectively evaluating, comparing, analyzing, and synthesizing information*

Study**T**ip

Running Glossary

Another feature designed to promote achievement, the key terms and concepts are **boldfaced** *in the text the first time they appear. They also are printed again in the margin and defined in a "running glossary." The running glossary provides a helpful way of reviewing key ideas before tests. If you want to check the meaning of a term from another module, use the end-of-book glossary.*

What Is Psychology?

The term *psychology* derives from the roots, *psyche*, meaning *mind*, and *logos*, meaning *word*. Early psychologists focused primarily on the study of mind and mental life. By the 1920s, however, many psychologists believed the mind was not a suitable subject for scientific study, and they initiated a movement to restrict psychology to observable behavior alone. Today we recognize the importance of both areas. Modern day **psychology** is commonly defined as the *scientific study of behavior and mental processes. Behavior* is anything we do—talking, sleeping, blinking, or reading. And *mental processes* are our private, internal experiences—dreams, thoughts, perceptions, feelings, or remembrances.

For many psychologists, the most important part of this definition of psychology is its emphasis on the word *scientific*. Psychology places high value on *empirical evidence*, information acquired by direct observation and measurement using systematic scientific methods. Emily's skepticism and empirical approach, Dr. Damasio's careful observation and treatment of his patient, and the research-based goals of PSPI all exemplify that, at its core, psychology is a *science*.

Emily, Dr. Damasio, and the PSPI also demonstrate an essential part of the scientific method, that of **critical thinking,** the process of objectively evaluating, comparing, analyzing, and synthesizing information. Learning to think critically also is one of the most important and lasting benefits of a college education. The study of psychology will greatly improve your critical thinking abilities, and this text includes several unique features designed to build and expand these skills. For example, each section contains a "Critical Thinking/Active Learning" Exercise and numerous "Try This Yourself" activities.

If you would like to exercise your critical thinking skills, and test how much you already know about psychology, try the following "Try This Yourself" exercise.

Study**T**ip

Try This Yourself

In each module you will find several opportunities to **apply** *what you are learning. These "Try This Yourself" sections are clearly identified with a special heading shown above. These activities are brief and fun to do. Research shows that actively involving yourself in learning increases comprehension and retention.*

TRY THIS YOURSELF **A**pplication

____ 1. Most people only use about 10 percent of their brain.

____ 2. Most brain activity stops during sleep.

____ 3. Police departments often use psychics to help solve crimes.

____ 4. Punishment is the most effective way to permanently change behavior.

____ 5. Eyewitness testimony is often unreliable.

____ 6. Most adults go through a stormy midlife crisis in middle age.

____ 7. Polygraph ("lie detector") tests can accurately reveal if a person is lying.

____ 8. People who threaten suicide seldom follow through with it.

____ 9. People with schizophrenia have two or more distinct personalities.

____ 10. Males are naturally more aggressive than females.

Answers: 1. False (Module 6). 2. False (Module 14). 3. False (Module 13). 4. False (Module 17). 5. True (Module 21). 6. False (Module 27). 7. It depends on several factors (Module 32). 8. False (Module 39). 9. False (Module 41). 10. It depends on how you define *aggression*. (Module 48).

Beware of the pseudopsychologist.
Only scientific research enables us to reliably understand and predict behavior. Supposed psychics who claim to read palms and foretell the future make a lot of money, but their demonstrations do not meet scientific or critical thinking standards.

How did you do? Students in my classes often miss several questions because they've just begun their first psychology course and lack the information, or because they've mistakenly accepted common myths (e.g., questions 4 and 6). Errors also happen when we fail to critically examine widely accepted, but untrue, "pop psychology" beliefs like the one about only using 10 percent of our brains. Does anyone really believe they could lose 90 percent of their brain and it wouldn't matter?

In response to the question about psychics, college students are often surprised to learn that psychology professors are among the *least* likely to believe in psychics, palmistry, astrology, and other paranormal phenomena. This may be because students (and the public) often confuse *scientific* psychology with *pseudopsychologies*, which give the appearance of science but are actually false. (*Pseudo* means "false.") Pseudopsychologies include claims made by psychics (who supposedly help police locate missing children and foretell the future), palmistry (reading people's character from the markings on the palms of their hands), psychometry (the ability to determine facts about an object by handling it), psychokinesis (the movement of objects by purely mental means), and astrology (the study of how the positions of the stars and planets influence people's personalities and affairs).

For some, pseudopsychologies are mere entertainment, but about half of all Americans say they believe in them and some report spending thousands of dollars and many hours on calls to psychic hotlines and horoscope readings. James Randi ("The Amazing Randi") is a famous magician who has dedicated his life to educating the public about fraudulent pseudopsychologists. And for many years, he has offered $1 million to "anyone who proves a genuine psychic power under proper observing conditions" (About James Randi, 2002; Randi, 1997). Although some have tried, the money has never been collected. If you would like more information about James Randi (and his million-dollar offer), visit his website at http://www.randi.org.

■ Psychology's Goals: Describe, Explain, Predict, and Change

In contrast to pseudopsychologies, which rely on self-report, anecdotal evidence, and opinions, true psychology bases its findings on scientific research and critical thinking. Psychology has four basic goals: to describe, explain, predict, and change behavior and mental processes through the use of scientific methods.

Do you know why this magician is so widely respected?

Answer: It is because this particular magician, James Randi, helps educate and protect the public against fraudulent claims made by psychics and other pseudopsychologists. Along with the prestigious MacArthur Foundation, Randi has offered $1 million for scientific proof of any ESP or paranormal phenomena. After many years, the offer still stands.

Nature—Nurture Controversy
Ongoing dispute over the relative contributions of nature (heredity) and nurture (environment) to the development of behavior and mental processes

Interaction *A process in which multiple factors mutually influence one another and the outcome—as in the interaction between heredity and environment*

1. ***Description.*** Description tells "what" occurred. In some studies, psychologists attempt to *describe*, or name and classify, particular behaviors by making careful scientific observations. Description is usually the first step in understanding behavior. For example, if someone says, "Boys are more aggressive than girls," what does that mean? The speaker's definition of *aggression* may differ from yours. Science requires specificity.

2. ***Explanation.*** An explanation tells "why" a behavior occurred. In other words, *explaining* a behavior or mental process depends on discovering and understanding its causes. One of the most enduring debates in science has been the **nature–nurture controversy** (Pinker, 2002; McCrae et al., 2000). To what extent are we controlled by biological and genetic factors (the nature side) or by environment and learning (the nurture side)? As you will see throughout the text, however, psychology (like all sciences) generally avoids "either-or" positions and focuses instead on **interactions.** Today, almost all scientists agree that nature and nurture *interact* to produce most psychological traits and even most physical traits. For example, research on aggression reports numerous interacting causes or explanations, including culture and learning, as well as genes, brain damage, and higher levels of testosterone (Best, Williams, & Coccaro, 2002; Pahlavan, Bonnet, & Duda, 2000; Pinker, 2002; Zillman & Weaver, 1999).

3. ***Prediction.*** Once psychologists meet the goals of description and explanation (answering the "whats" and "whys"), they move on to the higher-level goal of *prediction*, specifying the conditions under which a behavior or event is likely to occur. For instance, knowing that alcohol leads to increased aggression (Goodwin, 2000), we can predict that more fights will erupt at sports matches where alcohol is sold than at those where alcohol isn't sold.

4. ***Change.*** For some people, having "change" as a goal of psychology brings to mind evil politicians or cult leaders "brainwashing" unknowing victims. However, to psychologists, *change* means applying psychological knowledge to prevent unwanted outcomes or bring about desired goals. In almost all cases, change as a goal of psychology is positive. Psychologists help people improve their work environment, stop addictive behaviors, become less depressed, improve their family relationships, and so on. Furthermore, as you know from personal experience, it is very difficult (if not impossible) to change someone against her or his will. (*Question:* Do you know how many psychologists it takes to change a lightbulb? *Answer:* None. The lightbulb has to want to change itself.)

Application
APPLYING PSYCHOLOGY TO WORK

Careers in the Field

Knowing what psychology is and understanding its four major goals, would you consider a career in the field? Many students think of psychologists only as therapists, but there are numerous career paths in psychology. Although many psychologists are employed as full-time therapists, a large percentage also work in academic, business, industrial, and government settings (Table 1.1).

Note that Table 1.1 is divided into several career specialties and that psychologists typically wear more than one hat. For example, your instructor may be an experimental psychologist by training, but devote his or her entire professional life to teaching. Another experimental psychologist might teach, conduct research, and serve as an industrial consultant all at the same time. Similarly, a clinical psychologist might teach college courses while also being a full-time therapist.

What is the difference between a psychiatrist and a clinical or counseling psychologist? The joke answer would be "about $100 an hour." The serious answer is that psychiatrists are medical doctors. They have M.D. degrees with a specialization in psychiatry and are licensed to prescribe medications and drugs. In contrast, most counseling and clinical psychologists have received M.A., M.S., Ph.D., Psy.D., or Ed.D. degrees after intense study of human behavior and methods of therapy. Many clinical and counseling psychologists work with psychiatrists in a team approach to therapy.

Because of its diversity, psychology is currently one of the most popular career choices, and the U.S. Department of Labor expects that increasing employment opportunities for psychologists will continue at least through the year 2005. To get an idea of the relative number of psychologists working in different fields of psychology, see Figure 1.1.

In this text, we will introduce many psychological fields of study and career options that may interest you. For example, Modules 5, 6, and 7 explores the world of neuroscience, and you may decide you would like the work of a neuroscientist/biopsychologist. Similarly, Module 11 discusses health psychology and the work of health psychologists, whereas Modules 37–47 examine problems in mental health and how therapists treat them. If you find a particular area of interest, ask your instructor and campus career counselors for further career guidance. We also encourage you to explore the American Psychological Association's (APA) home page (http://www.apa.org), and the American Psychological Society's (APS) website (http://www.psychologicalscience.org). Psychology is always looking "for a few good men"—and women.

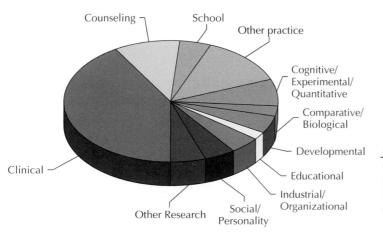

Figure 1.1 *Percentage of psychology degrees awarded by subfield.* Note that this is a small sampling of the numerous specialty areas in psychology. The percentages shown here are based on data from the *American Psychological Association* (APA), the largest professional psychological organization. The other major organization is the *American Psychological Society* (APS). *Source: Graduate Studies in Psychology, 2000.*

TABLE 1.1 SAMPLE SPECIALTIES IN PSYCHOLOGY

Neuroscientist Candace Pert (and others) discovered the body's natural painkillers called endorphins (Chapter 2).

Psychologists often wear many hats. Dan Bellack teaches full-time at Trident Technical College, serves as Department Chair, and also works with faculty on teaching improvement.

For most people, this is the role they commonly associate with psychology — that of clinical or counseling psychologist.

Dr. Louis Herman's research with dolphins has provided important insight into both human and nonhuman behavior.

Biopsychology neuroscience *[handwritten: L)research lab]*	Investigates the relationship between biology, behavior, and mental processes, including how physical and chemical processes affect the structure and function of the brain and nervous system
Clinical psychology	Specializes in the evaluation, diagnosis, and treatment of mental and behavioral disorders
Cognitive psychology	Examines "higher" mental processes, including thought, memory, intelligence, creativity, and language
Counseling psychology	Overlaps with clinical psychology but generally works with adjustment problems that are less severe, including marital, behavioral, or academic
Developmental psychology	Studies the course of human growth and development from conception until death
Educational and school psychology	Studies the process of education and works to promote the intellectual, social, and emotional development of children in the school environment
Experimental psychology	Examines processes such as learning, conditioning, motivation, emotion, sensation, and perception in humans and other animals (The term *experimental psychologist* is somewhat misleading because psychologists working in almost all areas of specialization also conduct experiments.)
Gender and/or cultural psychology	Investigates how men and women and different cultures differ from one another and how they are similar
Industrial/ organizational psychology	Applies the principles of psychology to the workplace, including personnel selection and evaluation, leadership, job satisfaction, employee motivation, and group processes within the organization
Social psychology	Investigates the role of social forces and interpersonal behavior, including aggression, prejudice, love, helping, conformity, and attitudes

Study **T**ip 💡

Illustrations

Don't skip over the photos, figures, and tables. They visually reinforce important concepts and often contain material that may appear on exams.

Assessment

CHECK & REVIEW

Understanding Psychology

Psychology is the scientific study of behavior and mental processes. It emphasizes the empirical approach and the value of **critical thinking.** Psychology is not the same as common sense, "pop psychology," or pseudopsychology. The goals of psychology are to *describe, explain, predict,* and *change* behavior and mental processes.

There are many opportunities for a career in psychology. Some examples are experimental, biopsychology or neuroscience, cognitive, developmental, clinical, counseling, industrial/organizational, educational, and school psychology.

Questions

1. Psychology is the _____ study of _____ and _____.
2. What is the definition of *critical thinking*?
3. List and describe the four goals of psychology.
4. Name the subfield of psychology that studies each of the following topics:
_____a. The brain and nervous system
_____b. Growth and development from conception to death
_____c. Thinking, memory, and intelligence
_____d. Evaluation, diagnosis, and treatment of mental and behavioral disorders
_____e. Application of psychological principles to the workplace

Answers to Questions can be found in Appendix B.

Study Tip

Check & Review
As a form of assessment, each module concludes with an interim summary and four to six self-test questions that allow you to stop and check your understanding of the important concepts just discussed. Use these questions to review for exams, too. Answers for all questions are in Appendix B in the back of the text.

ACTIVE LEARNING WORKSHEET   MODULE 1

Enter the correct letter from Column A in the blank space in Column B, and then double-check your answers with those in Appendix B.

Column A	Column B
a. Critical Thinking	1.____ Multiple factors influence the outcome.
b. Clinical Psychology	2.____ Describe, explain, predict, and change.
c. Interaction	3.____ Objectively evaluating information.
d. Nature-Nurture Controversy	4.____ Applies psychology to the workplace.
e. Psychology	5.____ Studies the biology of behavior.
f. Goals of Psychology	6.____ Studies growth and development.
g. Developmental Psychology	7.____ Concerned with "higher" mental processes.
h. Biopsychology	8.____ Diagnoses and treats psychological disorders.
i. Cognitive Psychology	9.____ Scientific study of behavior and mental processes.
j. Industrial/Organizational Psychology	10.____ Asks "Is it learned or innate?"

MODULE 2
DOING RESEARCH IN PSYCHOLOGY

Throughout this book you will read about numerous research studies (and see them cited parenthetically to support statements in the text). You will find this evidence easier to evaluate if you have a general understanding of research methods—or how psychologists collect, interpret, and evaluate data. First, you should know that research strategies are generally referred to as *basic* or *applied*. **Basic research** is usually conducted in universities or in research laboratories to explore new theories and advance general scientific understanding. Discoveries linking aggression to testosterone, instincts, genes, learning, and other factors came primarily from basic research. Because the application of findings usually occurs in the future, basic research may not have any immediate real-world uses. It is primarily seeking knowledge for its own sake.

Basic research meets the first three goals of psychology (description, explanation, and prediction). When we want to apply the fourth goal of psychology, to change existing real-world problems, scientists conduct **applied research.** As you can see in Figure 2.1, applied research has generated important safety and design improvements in automobiles, airplanes, and even stovetop burner arrangements.

Keep in mind that basic and applied research often interact, with one leading to the other. Once basic research identifies specific factors that contribute to aggression, for example, psychologists may conduct applied research to address problems related

Basic Research *Research conducted to advance scientific knowledge rather than practical application*

Applied Research *Research designed to solve practical problems*

(a) Spatial Correspondence

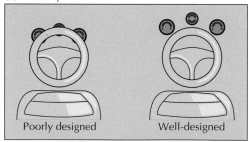

(b) Visibility

(c) Shape Indicates Function

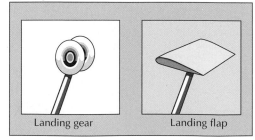

Figure 2.1 *Human factors design and the real world.* In the following examples, note how the well-designed appliances and machinery are easily understood and operated compared to the poorly designed ones. (a) The controls for stovetops should be arranged in a pattern that corresponds to the placement of the burners. (b) In an automobile, gauges for fuel, oil, and speed should be easily visible to the driver. (c) Controls and knobs are easier and safer to use if their shape corresponds to their function.

to aggressive behavior. And finding that alcohol is linked to aggression, some sports stadiums now limit the sale of alcohol during the final quarter of football and the last two innings of baseball.

Knowing the distinction between basic and applied research, we can now discuss the scientific method, general categories of research design, and important research and ethical dilemmas.

■ The Scientific Method: A Way of Discovering

Because psychology involves studying behavior and mental processes scientifically, psychologists approach research in the same way as scientists in biology, chemistry, or any other scientific field. First, they conduct an investigation and methodically collect data. They then piece together their findings, bit by bit, until they come to an objective conclusion. Throughout the entire process, psychologists follow standardized scientific procedures so that others—laypeople as well as scientists—can understand, interpret, and repeat their research. Most scientific investigations generally involve six basic steps, as summarized in Figure 2.2. Let's examine the key concepts associated with each step of this *scientific method.*

Step 1: Literature Review

Most research actually begins with informal questions: Emily Rosa asked about therapeutic touch. Students often ask about study methods for tests. And young parents want to know what to do about their small child who begs to sleep with them in their bed. If you asked 20 people these questions, you might get 20 different answers. For example, one of the most popular beliefs about sleeping arrangements in our Western culture is that, "Children should sleep alone. Otherwise, they will become overly attached and never leave their parents bed."

Let's look at this "theory" more closely. How would you scientifically investigate it? The first official step in the scientific method would be to *review the literature.* That is, as a scientific researcher, you would carefully check this popular belief against what has been published in major professional, scientific journals (such as *Psychological Science,*

Assessment

What is the scientific method?

www.wiley.com/college/huffman

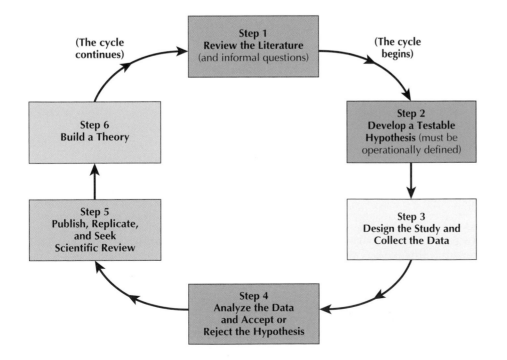

Figure 2.2 *The six steps of the scientific method.* Science is a dynamic field where new ideas are continually being tested and revised. Most investigations involve six carefully planned steps, beginning with a review of the existing theories and ending with a return to theory building. Note that the steps are arranged in a circle, which symbolizes the circular, cumulative nature of science. One scientific study generally leads to additional and refined hypotheses, further studies and clarification of the results, and improvement in the overall scientific knowledge base, known as *theories.*

Journal of Cross Cultural Psychology, and others). Scientific researchers do *not* rely on reports in the popular media (such as local newspapers or unofficial Internet reports).

If you did this type of literature review, you would find several studies about children's sleeping arrangements. For example, cross-cultural studies generally report that the "family bed," where the entire family sleeps in one bed, is a common arrangement in many parts of the world. In these cultures, shared sleeping arrangements are considered important to a child's social and emotional development (see Morelli, Rogoff, Oppenheim, & Goldsmith, 1999). You might also find *scientific* theories explaining why sleeping with parents may or may not be a good idea. (See Module 25 for a further discussion of theories of attachment.) Unlike casual, informal theories, scientific theories represent accumulated scientific knowledge developed from previous research and empirical observation. Contrary to common belief, theories are *not* just guesses or hunches or beliefs. A *scientific* **theory** is an interrelated set of concepts that explains a body of data.

Theory *An interrelated set of concepts, which explains a body of data*

Step 2: Develop a Testable Hypothesis

As you just saw with the sleeping arrangement example, theories can come from many sources, including an investigator's personal observations, empirical findings from previous studies, or extensions from previous studies. Once the review of literature is completed, the researcher is in a position to begin testing the original theory or a revised theory based on findings from the literature. A cardinal rule of a scientific theory is that it must make *testable predictions* about *observable* behavior. That is, the researcher must make predictions that can be objectively tested. The results then will support or not support the theory.

Step 2 begins with a *testable hypothesis.* A **hypothesis** is a specific prediction about how one variable is related to another. The *variables* in any given hypothesis are simply the factors that can vary or change. To explore the question about sleeping arrangements, a researcher might formulate this hypothesis: "Family bed sleeping arrangements lead to overly attached children" A hypothesis may or may not be correct; it is merely a possible explanation for a behavior that can be verified through scientific testing.

Hypothesis *A specific prediction about how one variable is related to another*

To be fully *testable,* a hypothesis must be formulated precisely (as opposed to vaguely or loosely), and the variables under study must be **operationally defined,** or stated in observable, measurable terms. With our previous hypothesis, how would you operationally define *sleeping arrangements?* What could you measure? One way might be to define *sleeping arrangements* as "one or more children sharing one bed for the majority of nights with one or both parents." This could be observed and measured as "the number of hours a week that a child sleeps alone or with one or both parents or caregivers." You then would operationally define "overly attached."

Operational Definition *A precise description of how the variables in a study will be observed and measured (For example, drug abuse might be operationally defined as "the number of missed work days due to excessive use of an addictive substance.")*

Step 3: Design the Study and Collect the Data

The third step in the scientific method is to design a way to test your hypothesis. As you will learn in the next section, there are various research methods to choose from, including naturalistic observation, case studies, surveys, experiments, and so on. The researcher considers the relative advantages and disadvantages of each method, and then selects the one deemed most appropriate and practical.

Once the method is chosen, the researcher decides how to collect *data,* or the measurements of behaviors. For example, if you were testing sleeping arrangements and attachment, you might choose to use the survey method. To begin, you would first decide when to conduct your survey, how many people you needed to question, and where you would get your subjects or *participants* (the people or nonhuman animals that are systematically observed and tested in a study.) In your sleeping and attachment survey, you might decide to mail 500 questionnaires to parents asking about their child's sleeping habits and attachment behaviors. Questions might include the following: "How many hours a day does your child sleep alone or with one or both parents?" "Does the child cry when you leave him or her in the care of another trusted adult?" "How does your child respond when you return after a brief (30-minute) separation?"

Step 4: Analyze the Data and Accept or Reject the Hypothesis

After the observations and measurements have been collected, the "raw data" must be analyzed so that you can decide whether they support or reject your initial hypothesis. To do such an analysis, researchers rely on *statistics*, mathematical methods used to organize, summarize, and interpret numerical data. Statistics play a vital role in the scientific method. If you are interested in learning more about statistical analysis, see Appendix A at the back of this book.

Step 5: Publish, Replicate, and Seek Scientific Review

To advance in any scientific discipline, researchers must share their work with one another and with the general public. Thus, the fifth step in the scientific method begins when the researcher writes up the study and its results and submits it to *peer reviewed* scientific journals for *publication*. (Peer reviewed journals ask other psychologists to critically evaluate material that is submitted for publication.) On the basis of these peer reviews, the study may then be accepted for publication.

Throughout this text, you'll see *citations*, authors' names and publication dates, at the end of many sentences, like this: (Kempermann, 2002). This tells you that the material comes from reputable sources and is as up-to-date as possible. Complete publication information (title of article or chapter, author, journal name or book title, date, and page numbers) is provided in the References section at the back of this book. You can use these references as a starting point for research projects, for additional information on a topic of interest, and to double-check any research cited in this text. As a critical thinker, never take the word of any one author or authors. Check their sources.

Once a study is published, other scientists interested in that topic attempt to replicate, or repeat, the study. *Replication* increases scientific confidence if the findings are the same. If not, researchers look for explanations and conduct further studies. As responsible scientists, psychologists almost never accept a theory on the basis of a single study; they wait for replication. The more times a study is replicated by other researchers using different participants in varied settings, the greater confidence psychologists have in the findings.

What if some replications find contradictory results? If the study can't be replicated or the findings are questionable, it is publicly questioned and criticized in follow-up journal articles. When different studies report contradictory findings, researchers can average or combine the results of all such studies and reach conclusions about the overall weight of the evidence, a popular statistical technique called **meta-analysis.** For example, researchers Daniel Voyer, Susan Voyer, and M. P. Bryden (1995) used meta-analysis of almost 50 years of research on gender differences in spatial abilities. They found that males do better than females on some, but not all, tests of spatial ability. This meta-analysis also found that the differences have decreased in recent years, possibly owing to changes in educational practices. As you can see, with time, the process of *scientific review* gradually discloses flaws, fine tunes the research, and helps eliminate erroneous findings.

Meta-analysis *Statistical procedure for combining and analyzing data from many studies*

Step 6: Build a Theory—And Then the Cycle Continues

In steps 1 through 5, the researcher reviews the literature, formulates a hypothesis, conducts the research, analyzes the data, and publishes the findings so they can be replicated and reviewed. Now, the fun begins. In addition to explaining existing research findings, a good theory also generates *new* hypotheses and suggests new

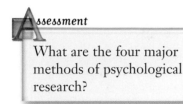

*A*ssessment

What are the four major methods of psychological research?

Experiment *Carefully controlled scientific procedure that determines whether variables manipulated by the experimenter have a causal effect on other variables*

methods of inquiry. Thus, the research cycle continues. As Figure 2.2 shows, the scientific method is *circular* and *cumulative*, and scientific progress is made by repeatedly challenging and revising existing theories.

Now that you have a good basic understanding of the scientific method, we can examine four major types of psychological research—experimental, descriptive, correlational, and biological. As Figure 2.3 shows, all four types of research have advantages and disadvantages. We will discuss each approach separately, but keep in mind that most psychologists use several methods to study a single problem. In fact, when multiple methods are used and the findings are mutually supportive, scientists have an especially strong foundation for concluding that one variable does affect another in a particular way.

■ Experimental Research: Looking for the Causes

We begin our discussion with the single most powerful research method, the **experiment,** where an experimenter manipulates and controls the variables to determine cause and effect. Only through an experiment can researchers isolate a single factor and examine the effect of that factor alone on a particular behavior (Ray, 2003). For example, in studying for an upcoming test, you probably use several methods—reading lecture notes, rereading highlighted sections of your textbook, and repeating key terms with their definitions over and over. Using multiple methods, however, makes it impossible to determine which study methods are effective or ineffective. The only way to discover which method is most effective is to isolate each one in an experiment. In fact, several experiments have been conducted to determine effective learning and study techniques (Son & Metcalfe, 2000). If you're interested in the results of this research or want to develop better study habits, refer to "Tools for Student Success" (Module 4) and in other special sections throughout the text identified with this lightbulb icon 💡 .

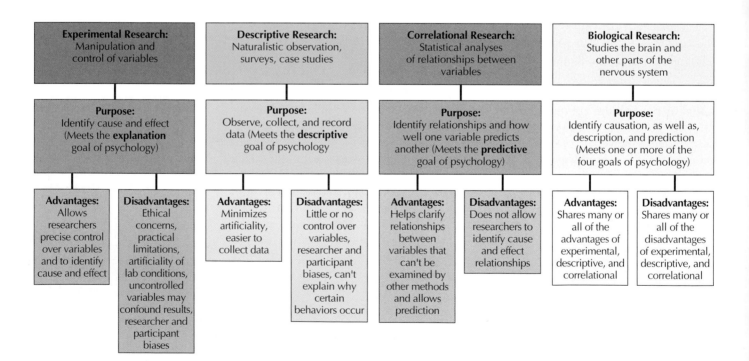

Figure 2.3 *The four major methods of psychological research.*

Key Features of an Experiment

An experiment has two critical components: independent and dependent variables, and experimental versus control groups.

Independent and Dependent Variables

If researchers choose to use an experiment to test a hypothesis, they must then decide which variables to manipulate and which to examine for possible changes. (A variable is simply anything that can *vary*.) The variables in an experiment are either independent or dependent. An **independent variable** (IV) is a factor that is selected and *manipulated* by the experimenter. In contrast, a **dependent variable** (DV) is a *measurable* behavior exhibited by the participant in the experiment. Because the IV is free to be selected and varied by the experimenter, it is called *independent*. The DV is called *dependent* because it is assumed to *depend* (at least is part) on manipulations of the IV. Keep in mind that the goal of any experiment is to learn how the dependent variable is affected by (*depends* on) the independent variable.

If you were designing an experiment to discover whether watching violence on television causes aggressiveness in viewers, you might randomly assign groups of children to watch three violent or nonviolent television programs (the IV). Afterward, you could put a large plastic doll in front of each child and record for one hour the number of times the child hits, kicks, or punches the plastic doll (the DV).

Experimental Versus Control Groups

In addition to IVs and DVs, each experiment must have one control group and one or more *experimental conditions*, or ways of treating the subject/participants. Having at least two groups allows the performance of one group to be compared with that of another.

In the simplest experimental design, the researcher *randomly assigns* one group of participants to the *experimental group* and the other participants to the *control group* (Dehue, 2000). In the violence on TV and aggression example, one group, the **experimental group,** is exposed to the IV—in this case violent TV programs. The **control group** members would be treated exactly the same way as those in the experimental group, except that they would be assigned to a zero, or *control condition*, which means they are not exposed to any amount of the IV. They would watch a nonviolent TV program for the same amount of time (see Figure 2.4).

We also could design the experiment with more than two *comparison groups* by using different levels of the independent variable. If one group watches 6 hours of violent TV, the comparison group watches 2 hours of violent TV, and the control group

Independent Variable *(IV) Variable that is manipulated to determine its causal effect on the dependent variable*

Dependent Variable *(DV) Variable that is measured; it is affected by (or dependent on) the independent variable*

Study$T$ip

Note that the IV (violent or nonviolent TV) was manipulated *by the experimenter, whereas the DV (aggression) was* measured. *Remember that IVs are* manipulated *and DVs are* measured.

Experimental Group *Group that receives a treatment in an experiment*

Control Group *Group that receives no treatment in an experiment*

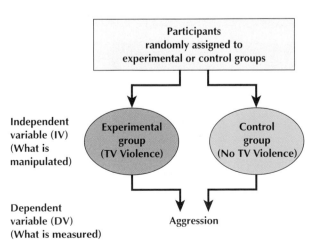

Figure 2.4 *Does TV increase aggression?* If experimenters wanted to test the hypothesis that watching violent TV increases aggression, they might begin by randomly assigning participants into one of two groups: the experimental group who watches a prearranged number of violent TV programs, or a control group who watches the same number of nonviolent TV programs. Then, they would observe and measure the subsequent level of aggression. Note that the violent TV or nonviolent TV was the *manipulated* variable (the IV), whereas the *measured* variable (the DV) was the amount of aggression.

CONTROL GROUP   OUT OF CONTROL GROUP

© Peter S. Mueller

watches no violent TV, then we could relate differences in aggressive behavior (DV) to the amount of violent TV viewing (IV).

While creating both control and comparison groups, experimenters also take care that all *extraneous variables* (those that are not being directly manipulated or measured) are held constant (the same). For example, time of day, heating, and lighting would need to be kept constant for all participants so that they do not affect participants' responses.

Experimental Safeguards

Every experiment is designed to answer essentially the same question: Does the IV *cause* the predicted change in the DV? To answer this question, the experimenter must establish several safeguards. In addition to the previously mentioned controls within the experiment itself (e.g., operational definitions, having a control group, and holding extraneous variables constant), a good scientific experiment also protects against potential sources of error from both the researcher and the participant. As we discuss these potential problems (and their possible solutions), you may want to refer several times to the summary in Figure 2.5.

Researcher Problems

Researchers must guard against two particular problems—*experimenter bias* and *ethnocentrism*.

Experimenter Bias *Occurs when researcher influences research results in the expected direction*

1. ***Experimenter bias.*** Experimenters, like everyone else, have their own personal beliefs and expectations. The danger in research, however, is that these personal matters may produce a *self-fulfilling prophecy:* The researchers find what they expect to find. In collecting data, they may *inadvertently* give subtle cues or treat participants differently in accordance with their expectations. For example, an experimenter may breathe a sigh of relief when a participant gives a response supporting the researcher's hypothesis. This tendency of experimenters to influence the results in the expected direction is called **experimenter bias.**

   Researchers can prevent this bias in several ways. One technique is to set up objective methods for recording data and enlist "blind observers" (neutral people

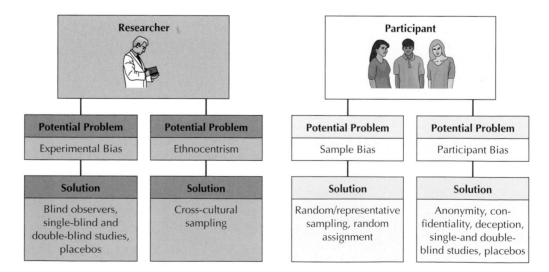

Figure 2.5 *Potential research problems and solutions.*

other than the researcher) to collect the data without knowing what the researcher has predicted. In addition, researchers can arrange the experiment so that *either* the observer or the participant is unaware of which group received the experimental treatment. This is called a *single-blind study.* When *both* the experimenter and the participants are unaware, it is known as a **double-blind study.**

In a typical double-blind experiment testing a new drug, both the experimenter administering the drug and the participants taking the drug are unaware (or "blind") as to who is receiving a **placebo,** a fake pill or injection, and who is receiving the drug itself. Researchers use placebos because they have found that the mere act of taking a pill or receiving an injection can change the condition of a participant. (The term *placebo* comes from the Latin verb *placere,* "to please.") Thus, to ensure that a particular effect is indeed due to the drug being tested and not to the *placebo effect,* control participants must be treated exactly as the experimental participants, even if this means faking the motions of giving them drugs or medications.

2. ***Ethnocentrism.*** When we assume behaviors typical in our culture are typical in all cultures, we are committing a bias known as **ethnocentrism.** ("Ethno" refers to *ethnicity* and "centrism" comes from *the center of.* Thus ethnocentrism refers to seeing your ethnic group as primary.) One way to avoid this problem is to have two researchers, one from one culture and one from another, conduct the same research study two times, once with their own culture and once with at least one other culture. When using this kind of *cross-cultural sampling,* differences due to researcher ethnocentrism can be isolated from actual differences in behavior between the two cultures.

Participant Problems

In addition to potential problems from the researcher, there also are several possibilities for error associated with participants, which can be grouped under the larger categories of *sample bias* and *participant bias.*

1. ***Sample bias.*** A *sample* is a group of research participants selected to represent a larger group, or *population.* When we do research, we obviously cannot measure the entire population, so we select and test a limited sample. However, using such a small group requires that the sample be reasonably similar to the composition of the population at large. If systematic differences exist among the groups being studied, **sample bias,** experimental results may not truly reflect the influence of the independent variable.

For example, much research has been done on the increased safety of having air bags in automobiles. Unfortunately, the research has been conducted almost exclusively with men. When car manufacturers apply findings from this research, with no regard for the sample bias, they create airbags sized for men, which may seriously damage (or even decapitate) small adults (mostly women) and kids. Because the purpose of conducting experiments is to apply, or *generalize,* the results to a wide population, it is extremely important that the sample represents the general population.

To safeguard against sample bias, research psychologists use random/representative sampling and random assignment:

- ***Random/representative sampling.*** Obviously, psychologists want their research findings to be applicable to more people than just those who took part in the study. For instance, critics have suggested that much psychological literature is biased because it is based primarily on white participants (see Robert Guthrie's 1998 book, *Even the Rat Was White*). One way to ensure less bias and more rel-

Double-Blind Study *A procedure in which both the researcher and the participants are unaware (blind) of who is in the experimental or control group*

Placebo [pluh-SEE-bo] *An inactive substance or fake treatment used as a control technique, usually in drug research, or given by a medical practitioner to a patient*

Ethnocentrism *Believing that one's culture is typical of all cultures; also, viewing one's own ethnic group (or culture) as central and "correct" and then judging the rest of the world according to this standard*

Sample Bias *Occurs when research participants are not representative of the larger population*

Would you like to volunteer as a participant in psychological research? The American Psychological Society (APS) has a website with links to ongoing studies that need participants. On a recent visit to this site, I found several exciting studies, including:

- *What Should be Done with Child Abusers?*
- *Reactions to September 11 Terrorist Attacks*
- *Leadership Styles and Emotional Intelligence*
- *Bem Sex Role Inventory*
- *Internet Usage, Personality, and Behavior*

- *Adult Attention Deficit Hyperactivity Disorder (ADHD/ADD)*
- *Sensation and Perception Laboratory*
- *Web of Loneliness*
- *Sexual Behavior and Alcohol Consumption*
- *Marriage Inventory*
- *Are You a Logical Thinker?*
- *Web Experimental Psychology Lab*

If you'd like to participate, go to http://www.psych.hanover.edu/research/exponnet.html

evance is to select participants who constitute a representative sample of the entire population of interest. Proper *random sampling* will likely produce a *representative*, unbiased sample.

- *Random assignment.* To ensure the validity of the results, participants must also be assigned to experimental groups using a chance, or *random*, system, such as a coin toss or drawing numbers out of a hat. This procedure of **random assignment** ensures that each participant is equally likely to be assigned to any particular group and that differences among the participants will be spread out across all experimental conditions.

Random Assignment *Participants are assigned to experimental conditions on the basis of chance, thus minimizing the possibility of biases or preexisting differences in the groups*

2. *Participant bias.* In addition to problems with initial sampling of participants, bias also can occur when participants try to present themselves in a good light (the *social desirability response*) or deliberately attempt to mislead the researcher. They also may be less than truthful when asked embarrassing questions or placed in awkward experimental conditions.

Researchers attempt to control for this type of participant bias by offering anonymous participation and other guarantees for privacy and confidentiality. Also, as mentioned earlier, single- and double-blind studies and placebos offer additional safeguards. If participants don't know which group they're in, or whether they're receiving the real drug or the "fake one," they won't try to overly please or deliberately mislead the experimenter.

Finally, one of the most effective, but controversial, ways to prevent participant bias is *deception*. Just like the unsuspecting subjects on popular TV programs, like "Jamie Kennedy's Experiment" or "Spy TV," research participants will behave more naturally when they don't know they are part of a research project. However, many researchers consider the use of deception unethical—a topic we discuss in a later section.

*A*ssessment

CHECK & REVIEW

Scientific Method and Experimental Research

The scientific method consists of six carefully planned steps: (1) reviewing the literature for existing **theories,** (2) formulating a testable hypothesis, (3) designing the study and collecting the data, (4) analyzing the data and accepting or rejecting the **hypothesis,** (5) publishing followed by replication and scientific review, and (6) building further theory. The steps are arranged in a circle to show the circular, cumulative nature of science.

The experimental method is the only research method that can be used to identify cause-and-effect relationships. **Independent variables** (IVs) are the factors the experimenter manipulates, and **dependent variables** (DVs) are measurable behaviors

of the participants. Experimental controls include having one control group and one or more experimental groups, and holding extraneous variables constant.

To safeguard against the researcher problem of **experimenter bias,** researchers employ blind observers, single-blind and **double-blind studies,** and **placebos.** To control for **ethnocentrism,** they use cross-cultural sampling. In addition, to offset participant problems with **sample bias,** researchers use random/representative sampling and **random assignment.** To control for participant bias, they rely on many of the same controls in place to prevent experimenter bias, such as double-blind studies. They also attempt to ensure anonymity and confidentiality and sometimes use deception.

Questions

1. What are the six steps of the scientific method?

2. Why is an experiment the only way we can determine the cause of behavior?

3. If researchers gave participants varying amounts of a new "memory" drug and then gave them a story to read and measured their scores on a quiz, the _____ would be the IV, and the _____ would be the DV. (a) response to the drug, amount of the drug; (b) experimental group, control group; (c) exposure to the drug, quiz scores; (d) researcher variables, extraneous variables.

4. What are the two primary sources of problems for both researchers and participants? What are the solutions?

Answers to Questions can be found in Appendix B.

■ Descriptive Research: Naturalistic Observation, Surveys, and Case Studies

The second major type of research, **descriptive research,** observes and describes behavior without manipulating variables. Almost everyone observes and describes one another in an attempt to understand them, but psychologists do it systematically and scientifically. In this section, we will examine three key types of descriptive research: naturalistic observation, surveys, and case studies. As you explore each of these methods, keep in mind that most of the problems and safeguards discussed with the experimental method also apply to the nonexperimental methods.

Descriptive Research *Research methods that observe and record behavior without producing causal explanations*

Naturalistic Observation

When using **naturalistic observation,** researchers systematically measure and record observable behavior of participants as it occurs in the real world, without interfering in any way. The purpose of most naturalistic observation is to gather descriptive information. Because of the popularity of researchers like Jane Goodall, who studied chimpanzees in the jungle, most people picture naturalistic observation occurring in wild, remote areas. But supermarkets, libraries, subways, airports, museums, classrooms, assembly lines, and other settings also lend themselves to naturalistic observation.

Recall from the introductory vignette that the Psychology in the Public Interest (PSPI) initiative is commissioning a review of studies asking, "Do smaller classes result in greater student achievement? If so, for what type of student?" A researcher who wanted to study these questions might not want to begin the investigation by bringing students and teachers into a controlled experimental laboratory setting. She or he might first go to several classrooms and observe how children and teachers behave in their natural setting.

Naturalistic Observation *Observing and recording behavior in the participant's natural state or habitat*

Naturalistic observation. *Studying behavior in its natural environment allows behavior to unfold naturally (without interference).*

In naturalistic observation, the researcher does not manipulate or control anything in the situation. The observer tries to be as unobtrusive as possible, to become, as they say, "like a fly on the wall." The researcher might conceal him- or herself in the background, stand behind a one-way mirror, or observe from a distance while the participants are (hopefully) unaware that they are being observed. If participants know someone is watching, their behavior becomes unnatural. For example, have you ever been driving down the street, singing along with the radio, and quickly stopped when you noticed the person in the next car was watching you? The same type of thing normally happens when participants in scientific studies realize they are being observed.

The chief advantage of naturalistic observation is that researchers can obtain data about a truly natural behavior rather than about a behavior that is a reaction to an artificial experimental situation. If Jane Goodall had observed chimpanzees in a lab (or zoo), their behavior would probably have been quite different than in their natural habitat. On the down side, naturalistic observation can be difficult and time-consuming, and the lack of control by the researcher makes it difficult to conduct observations for behavior that occurs infrequently.

Surveys

Survey *Research technique that assesses behaviors and attitudes of a sample or population*

Surveys, tests, questionnaires, and interviews (we will refer to them all as "surveys") are all techniques for sampling a wide variety of behaviors and attitudes. They range from personality inventories that probe the makeup of individuals to public opinion surveys such as the popular Gallup and Harris Polls, most known for their surveys of voting preferences prior to important state or national elections.

Surveys are typically used to determine general opinions, attitudes, feelings, or behaviors related to a specific issue. Have you ever wondered about the attitudes and beliefs of people who travel long distances to attend rallies against animal research? This was the question that intrigued Scott Plous and his fellow researchers. In 1990, they approached hundreds of people who were attending an animal rights rally in Washington, D.C., and asked them to complete a detailed questionnaire regarding their attitudes toward animal rights and animal research (Plous, 1991). He then conducted a follow-up survey of activists attending a similar event in 1996.

When he compared the two surveys, he found several interesting attitudinal changes, particularly in what participants believed should be the highest priorities of the animal rights movement. As you can see in Table 2.1, in 1990 a majority of activists saw animal research as the most important issue, whereas activists in 1996 considered animals used for food as the most important. The 1996 survey also found a modest decline among activists in their support for laboratory break-ins. A majority also supported a proposal designed to reduce tensions between activists and researchers. Plous suggests that these responses might help encourage dialogue and a possible "cease fire" in the ongoing animal rights debate (Plous, 1998). What do you think?

One key advantage to surveys is that they can gather data from a much larger sample of people than is possible with other research methods. Unfortunately, most surveys rely on self-reported data, and not all participants are completely honest. In

TRY THIS

YOURSELF

Application

Why not conduct your own informal survey? Station yourself at a conspicuous spot on campus, in your dorm, or some other place. Ask random passersby whether they consider themselves animal rights activists or nonac-tivists. If they are activists, read them the question in Table 2.1 and record their responses next to the appropriate item. How do your survey results compare with those of Plous?

TABLE 2.1 WHAT SHOULD THE ANIMAL RIGHTS MOVEMENT FOCUS ON MOST?

Issue	Year of survey	
	1990 (N = 346)	1996 (N = 327)
Animals used in research	54	38
Animals used for food	24	48
Animals used for clothing or fashion	12	5
Animals in the wild	5	3
Animals used in sports or entertainment	4	5
Animals used in education	1	2

Note. Figures indicate the percentage of respondents giving each answer.

addition, survey techniques cannot, of course, be used to explain *causes* of behavior. But they can be helpful in predicting behavior. Plous, for example, could not pinpoint the causes of the activists' beliefs, but the results of his survey might be used to predict the attitudes and goals of some animal rights activists in the United States. (As a critical thinker, can you see why his results are limited? Because he administered his survey only to participants at an animal rights rally, he lacked a *random/representative sample*).

Case Studies

What if a researcher wants to investigate *photophobia*, fear of light? Most people are not afraid of light, so it would be difficult to find enough participants to conduct an experiment or to use surveys or naturalistic observation. In the case of such rare disorders, researchers try to find someone who has the problem and study him or her intensively. Such an in-depth study of a single research participant is called a **case study.**

In a case study, many aspects of a person's life are examined in detail to allow full description of the person's problem behavior and evaluation of any treatment. Dr. Damasio's (1999) study of patient "S," mentioned in this section's opening vignette, provides an excellent example of a case study. Damasio and his colleagues began with comprehensive evaluations of the patient's physical and mental health, intelligence, and personality. Results showed that S was in good health with normal sensory perception, language ability, and intelligence. She also had remarkable artistic and drafting skills. Her one problem was that she could not identify facial expressions of fear. She easily recognized other emotions and could mimic them with her own facial muscles. And, interestingly, she could draw finely detailed faces showing all emotions—except fear.

After extensive neurological tests and extensive interviews, Damasio and his staff discovered that S's inability to recognize fear in someone's face resulted from damage to her amygdala. They also found that S does not experience fear in the same way as others. She intellectually knows "what fear is supposed to be, what should cause it, and even what one may do in situations of fear, but little or none of that intellectual baggage, so to speak, is of any use to her in the real world" (Damasio, 1999, p. 66). Her inability to recognize fear in herself and others causes her to be overly trusting of strangers and romantic partners, which creates serious problems in social interactions.

At this time, there is no "happy ending" for S and others with similar damage, but case studies like this may eventually provide valuable clues that will lead to successful treatment. Keep in mind, however, that case studies have their research lim-

Case Study *An in-depth study of a single research participant*

Correlational Research *Any scientific study in which the researcher observes or measures (without directly manipulating) two or more variables to find relationships between them*

Correlation Coefficient *A number that indicates the degree and direction of the relationship between the two variables*

its, including their lack of generalizability to others, and inaccurate or biased recall among participants.

Correlational Research: Looking for Relationships

Nonexperimental researchers sometimes want to determine the degree of relationship, or *correlation*, between two variables, so they turn to **correlational research.** As the name implies, when any two variables are *correlated*, they are "co-related," and a change in one variable is accompanied by a concurrent change in the other.

Using the correlational method, researchers begin with their topic of interest such as alcohol consumption during pregnancy. Then they select a group for study—in this case, pregnant women. After selecting the group, the variables of interest are measured for each participant in the study. In the alcohol study, the researchers might survey or interview the selected group of women about the amount and timing of any alcohol use during their pregnancies.

After the data are collected, the researchers analyze their results using a statistical formula that results in a *correlation coefficient*, a numerical value that indicates the degree and direction of the relationship between the two variables. (Note that there is an important distinction between correlational studies and correlation as a mathematical procedure. *Correlational studies* are a type of research methodology in which researchers set out to identify relationships between variables, whereas **correlation coefficients** are statistical procedures used in correlational studies, as well as with surveys and other research designs.)

Correlation coefficients are calculated by a formula (described in Appendix A) that produces a number ranging from +1.00 to –1.00. The sign (+ or –) indicates the *direction* of the correlation, positive (+) or negative (–), whereas the number (+1.00 to –1.00) indicates the *strength* of the relationship.

A *positive correlation* is one in which the two variables move (or *vary*) in the *same direction*—the two factors increase or decrease together. As you know, for most students there is a positive correlation between hours of study and scores on exams—when studying increases, exam scores increase. Or I could state it the other way—when studying decreases, exam scores also decrease. Can you see why both examples are positive correlations? The factors vary in the same direction—upward or downward.

In contrast, a *negative correlation* is one in which the two factors vary in *opposite directions*—as one factor increases, the other factor decreases. Have you noticed that the more hours you work (or party) outside of college, the lower your exam scores? This is an example of a negative correlation—working or partying both vary in opposite directions to exam scores.

On some occasions, researchers will discover there is no relationship between two variables—a *zero correlation*. Obviously, there is no relation (zero correlation) between your birthday and exam scores. And, despite popular belief, repeated scientific investigations of astrology have found no relationship between personality and the position of the stars (a zero correlation). Figure 2.6 provides a visual depiction and additional examples of positive, negative, and zero correlations.

Now that you understand the *direction* of correlations, let's go back to the number itself (+1.0 to –1.0), which represents the *strength* of the relationship. The closer the number is to 1.00, either positive or negative, the stronger the correlation between the variables. Thus, if you had a correlation of +.92 or –.92, you would have a high (or strong) correlation. On the other hand, a correlation of +.15 or –.15 would represent a low (or weak) correlation.

The Value of Correlations

Understanding correlational studies and correlational coefficients may be difficult, but it's worth the effort. As you will see in upcoming chapters, there are numerous

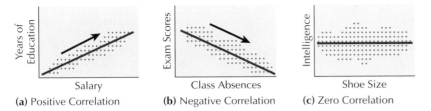

Figure 2.6 *Three types of correlation*. Each dot represents an individual participant's score on the two variables. For example, in the positive correlation (a), each dot corresponds to one person's salary and years of education.

questions about how two things relate: How is stress related to susceptibility to colds? Does smoking marijuana decrease motivation? How is intelligence related to achievement? When we report the data, "there is a strong correlation between ... and...," you will understand the significance. This also is true when you read news reports of the latest findings showing a strong (or weak) relationship between oatmeal and heart disease, or cellular phones and brain cancer.

In addition to greater understanding of psychological data and news reports, understanding correlations also may help you live a safer and more productive life. For example, correlational studies have repeatedly found high correlation coefficients between birth defects and a pregnant mother's use of alcohol, and between car accidents and the driver's use of cellular phones. This information enables us to reliably predict our relative risks and make informed decisions about our lives and behavior. If you would like additional information about correlations, see Appendix A at the back of the book.

Before we leave this topic, it's important to caution you that *correlation does not imply causation*. This is a logic error commonly associated with correlational studies. Although a high correlation allows us to predict one variable from another, it does not tell us whether a cause–effect relationship exists between the two variables. For example, what if we said there was a substantial positive correlation between the size of young children's feet and how fast they read? Would this mean that having small feet *causes* a child to be a slow reader? Obviously not! Nor do increases in reading speed *cause* increases in foot size. Instead, both are caused by a third variable — an increase in children's age. Although we can safely *predict* that as a child's foot size increases, his or her reading speed will also increase, this *correlation does not imply causation*.

We use this extreme example to make an important point about an all too common public reaction to research findings. People read media reports about *relationships* between stress and cancer or between family dynamics and homosexuality and then jump to the conclusion that "stress causes cancer" or that "withdrawn fathers and overly protective mothers cause their son's homosexuality." But they fail to realize that a third factor, perhaps genetics, may cause greater susceptibility to both cancer and increased rates of homosexuality.

Once again, as Figure 2.7 shows, a correlation between two variables does not mean that one variable *causes* another. Correlational studies do sometimes point to *possible* causes, like the correlation between alcohol and birth defects. However, only the experi-

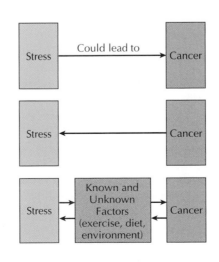

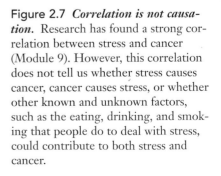

Figure 2.7 *Correlation is not causation*. Research has found a strong correlation between stress and cancer (Module 9). However, this correlation does not tell us whether stress causes cancer, cancer causes stress, or whether other known and unknown factors, such as the eating, drinking, and smoking that people do to deal with stress, could contribute to both stress and cancer.

Application

CRITICAL THINKING   ACTIVE LEARNING

Becoming a Better Consumer of Scientific Research

The news media, advertisers, politicians, teachers, close friends, and other individuals frequently use research findings in their attempts to change your attitudes and behavior. How can you tell whether their information is accurate and worthwhile?

    The following exercise will improve your ability to critically evaluate sources of information. It is based on the concepts you learned in the previous discussion of psychological research techniques. Read each "research" report and identify the primary problem or research limitation. In the space provided, make one of the following marks:

CC = The report is misleading because correlation data are used to suggest causation.

CG = The report is inconclusive because there was no control group.

EB = The results of the research were unfairly influenced by experimenter bias.

SB = The results of the research are questionable because of sample bias.

_____1. A clinical psychologist strongly believes that touching is an important adjunct to successful therapy. For two months, he touches half his patients (Group A) and refrains from touching the other half (Group B). He then reports a noticeable improvement in Group A.

_____2. A newspaper reports that violent crime corresponds to phases of the moon. The reporter concludes that the gravitational pull of the moon controls human behavior.

_____3. A researcher interested in women's attitudes toward premarital sex sends out a lengthy survey to subscribers of *Vogue* and *Cosmopolitan* magazines.

_____4. An experimenter is interested in studying the effects of alcohol on driving ability. Prior to testing on

an experimental driving course, Group A consumes 2 ounces of alcohol, Group B consumes 4 ounces of alcohol, and Group C consumes 6 ounces of alcohol. After the test drive, the researcher reports that alcohol consumption adversely affects driving ability.

_____5. After reading a scientific journal that reports higher divorce rates among couples living together before marriage, a college student decides to move out of the apartment she shares with her boyfriend.

_____6. A theater owner reports increased beverage sales following the brief flashing of a subliminal message to "Drink Coca-Cola" during the film showing.

Answers: 1. EB; 2. CC; 3. SB; 4. CG; 5. CC; 6. CG

Study Tip 💡

Critical Thinking/Active Learning Exercises
Special critical thinking/active learning exercises provide important insight into specific terms and concepts, while improving your basic critical thinking skills.

Biological Research *Scientific studies of the brain and other parts of the nervous system*

www.wiley.com/college/huffman

mental method manipulates the IV under controlled conditions and therefore can draw conclusions about cause and effect.

■ Biological Research: Tools for Exploring the Brain and Nervous System

In the previous section we discussed traditional research methods in psychology—experimental, descriptive, and correlational. Each of these methods explores the behavioral and mental processes of humans and nonhuman animals. But what about our internal, biological processes? This is the province of **biological research,** which scientifically studies the brain and other parts of the nervous system (Table 2.2).

    For most of history, examination of the brain was possible only after an individual died. The earliest explorers of the brain dissected the brains of deceased humans and conducted experiments on other animals using *lesioning techniques* (systematically destroying brain tissue to study the effects on behavior and mental processes) (Table 2.2). By the mid-1800s, this early research had produced a basic map of the peripheral nervous system and some areas of the brain. Early researchers also relied on clinical observations and case studies of living people. Tragic accidents and diseases or other brain disorders also offered valuable insights into brain functioning.

    Modern researchers still use dissection, lesioning, clinical observation, and case studies, but they also employ other techniques such as electrical recording and electrical brain stimulation. *Electrodes* (tiny electrified disks or wires) pasted to the skin or skull translate brain waves (electrical energy from the brain) to produce wavy lines on

TABLE 2.2 TOOLS FOR STUDYING THE BRAIN

Method	Description	Sample Results
Brain dissection *Brain dissection. Structures of the brain can be examined by dissecting the brains of deceased people who donated their bodies for scientific study.*	Careful cutting and study of a cadaver brain to reveal structural details.	Brain dissections of Alzheimer's disease victims often show identifiable changes in various parts of the brain (Chapter 7).
Ablation/lesions	Surgically removing parts of the brain (ablation), or destroying specific areas of the brain (lesioning), is followed by observation for changes in behavior or mental processes.	Lesioning specific parts of the rat's hypothalamus greatly affects its eating behavior (Chapter 12).
Clinical observations/ case studies	Observing and recording changes in personality, behavior, or sensory capacity associated with brain disease or injuries.	Damage to one side of the brain often causes numbness or paralysis on the body's opposite side; also Phineas Gage's injury and subsequent changes (Chapter 2).
Electrical recordings *Electroencephalogram (EEG). Electrodes are attached to the patient's scalp, and the brain's electrical activity is displayed on a computer monitor or recorded on a paper chart.*	Using electrodes attached to a person or animal's skin or scalp, brain activity is recorded to produce an electroencephalogram.	Reveals areas of the brain most active during a particular task or changes in mental states, like sleeping, and hypnosis; also traces abnormal brain waves caused by brain malfunctions, like epilepsy or tumors.
Electrical stimulation of the brain (ESB)	Using an electrode, a weak electric current stimulates specific areas or structures of the brain.	Penfield (1958) mapped the surface of the brain and found that different areas have different functions.

(Table continues)

TABLE 2.2 (CONTINUED)

Method	Description	Sample Results
CT (computed tomography) scan *This false color CT scan used X-rays to locate a brain tumor. The tumor is the deep purple mass at the top left.*	A computer that creates cross-sectional pictures of the brain reads X-rays directed through the brain at different angles; least expensive type of imaging and widely used in research.	Reveals the effects of strokes, injuries, tumors, and other brain disorders.
PET (positron emission tomography) scan *PET scans and brain functions. In these two scans, the top one shows brain activity when the eyes are open, whereas the one at the bottom is with the eyes closed. Note the increased activity, red and yellow, in the occipital lobe (the top of the photo) when the eyes are open.*	Radioactive form of glucose is injected into the bloodstream; scanner records amount of glucose used in particularly active areas of the brain and produces computer-constructed picture of the brain.	Originally designed to detect abnormalities, also used to identify brain areas active during ordinary activities (reading, singing, etc.).
MRI (magnetic resonance imaging) scan *Magnetic resonance imaging (MRI). Note the fissures and internal structures of the cerebral cortex, as well as the cerebellum and the brain stem. The throat, nasal airways, and cerebrospinal fluid surrounding the brain are dark.*	A high-frequency magnetic field is passed through the brain by means of electromagnets.	Produces high-resolution three-dimensional pictures of the brain useful for identifying abnormalities and mapping brain structures and function.
fMRI (functional magnetic resonance imaging) scan	A newer, faster version of the MRI that detects blood flow by picking up magnetic signals from blood that has given up its oxygen to activate brain cells.	Indicates which areas of the brain are active or inactive during ordinary activities or responses (like reading or talking); also, shows changes associated with disorders.

a moving piece of paper. This report is called an *electroencephalogram* (*electro-* means "electrical," *encephalon* means "brain," and *gram* means "record"). The instrument itself, called an *electroencephalograph* (EEG), is a major research tool for studying changes in brain waves during sleep and dreaming. For even more precise information, researchers can use *electrical stimulation of the brain* (ESB). Electrodes are inserted into the brain to record the naturally occurring electrical activity of neurons or to stimulate certain areas with weak electrical currents.

In recent years, advances in brain science have led to exciting, new techniques, including various types of brain-imaging scans (see again Table 2.2). Most of these methods are relatively *noninvasive*. That is, they are performed without breaking the skin or entering the body. They can be used in both clinical settings to examine suspected brain damage and disease, and in laboratory settings to study brain function during ordinary activities like sleeping, eating, reading, speaking, and so on (Dade, Zatorre, & Jones-Gottman, 2002; Senior, Ward, & David, 2002). For example, computed tomography (CT) scans (a computer-enhanced series of X-rays of the brain) have been used to look for abnormalities in brain structures among people suffering from mental illness, whereas positron emission tomography (PET) scans map actual *activity* in the brain. PET scans can be used to pinpoint brain areas that handle various activities, such as singing or fist clenching, and even areas responsible for different emotions (Craik et al., 1999; Mayberg et al., 1999).

It is important to note that each biological method has its particular strengths and weaknesses, but all provide invaluable insights and information. We'll discuss findings from these research tools in upcoming chapters on sleep and dreaming (Modules 14), memory (Modules 20 and 21), thinking and intelligence (Modules 22–24), and abnormal behavior and its treatment (Modules 37–45).

◼ Ethical Problems: Protecting the Rights of Others

The two largest professional organizations of psychologists, the *American Psychological Society* (APS) and the *American Psychological Association* (APA), both recognize the importance of maintaining high ethical standards in research, therapy, and all other areas of professional psychology. The preamble to the APA's publication *Ethical Principles of Psychologists and Code of Conduct* (1992) admonishes psychologists to maintain their competence, to retain objectivity in applying their skills, and to preserve the dignity and best interests of their clients, colleagues, students, research participants, and society. In this section, we will discuss three important areas of ethical concern: human participants, animal rights, and clients in therapy.

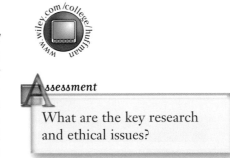

Assessment

What are the key research and ethical issues?

Respecting the Rights of Human Participants

The APA has developed guidelines regulating research with human participants. These are the key issues:

- **Informed consent and voluntary participation.** One of the chief principles set forth in the APA document is that an investigator should obtain the participant's **informed consent** before initiating an experiment. The researcher should fully inform the participant as to the nature of the study, including significant factors that might influence a person's willingness to participate, such as physical risks, discomfort, or unpleasant emotional experiences. The researcher also must explain that participants are free to decline to participate or to withdraw from the research at any time.

- **The use of deception.** Participation in research should be voluntary and informed, but what if you're studying topics like persuasion techniques or attitude change? If participants know the true purpose behind some studies, they will almost certainly not respond naturally. Therefore, APA acknowledges the need for some

Informed Consent *Participant's agreement to take part in a study after being told what to expect*

Debriefing *Informing participants after the research about the purpose of the study, the nature of the anticipated results, and any deceptions used*

deception research. When using deception, researchers are expected to follow strict guidelines, including **debriefing** participants at the end of the experiment. Debriefing involves explaining the reasons for conducting the research and clearing up any misconceptions or concerns on the part of the participant.

- **Confidentiality.** All information acquired about people during a study must be held confidential and not published in such a way that individual rights to privacy are compromised.

- **Students as research participants.** If research participation is a course requirement or an opportunity for extra credit, the student must be given the choice of an alternative activity of equal value.

Achievement

RESEARCH HIGHLIGHT

Study Tip

Research Highlights
In this section, recent, relevant, high interest topics are explored and summarized to help you understand and appreciate the latest developments in psychology.

An Elegant Study of Therapeutic Touch

Nine-year-old Emily Rosa, the child in our opening story, is a wonderful model of critical thinking and the scientific approach to everyday life. Therapeutic touch (TT) practitioners claim to heal or alleviate medical problems by passing their hands over the patient's body, supposedly realigning energy fields until they're "in balance" (Scheiber & Selby, 2000). This realignment reportedly stems disease and allows the patient's body to heal itself (Quinn & Strelkauskas, 1993). But rather than asking TT practitioners or their patients if their energy manipulations actually heal or relieve pain, Emily asked a more important question. She wanted to know whether *human energy fields* (HEF) even exist.

As you can see in Figure 2.8, Emily set up a small screen and then asked 21 TT practitioners to stick their hands, palms up, through the screen. The researcher (Emily) then held her hand over either the left or right hand of the practitioner — decided by a flip of coin. In 10 to 20 separate trials, the TT practitioners had to say which of his or her hands was nearer to the researcher's hand. Each participant was allowed to make any desired "mental preparations" ahead of time and to take as much time as necessary to make each determination. When the results were analyzed, the TT practitioners performed no better than chance (Rosa, Rosa, Sarner, & Barrett, 1998)!

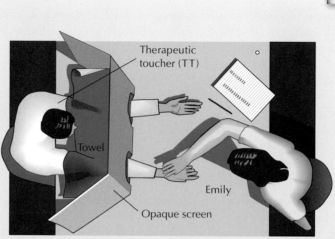

Figure 2.8 *Emily's clever design.* In Emily Rosa's simple (but scientifically sound) experiment, therapeutic touch practitioners placed their hands through the holes in a screen. Then Emily tossed a coin and held one of her hands over the practitioner's left or right hand to see if they could detect her "energy field." They couldn't.

Not only did Emily's research bring her personal recognition and science fair honors but it also demonstrated the importance of scientifically analyzing therapeutic claims. This fourth-grader's "simple" study demonstrated that 21 practitioners failed to even *detect* her energy field—much less modify it. As our earlier discussion of the goals of psychology and the scientific method explained, therapeutic techniques must meet basic scientific standards. Given the lack of scientific support for TT's most fundamental claim, members of the medical and scientific community now question its continued use.

Needless to say, TT practitioners and supporters dispute the findings of Emily's study and cite several studies of documented success (e.g., Engle & Graney, 2000; Kiernan, 2002). They say the research arrangement was unnatural, that "our hands are moving, not stationary. You don't just walk into a room and perform — it's a whole process" (Lemonick, 1998, p. 67). TT practitioners who fully believe in their work can contact the James Randi Educational Foundation. As mentioned earlier, Randi offers $1 million to anyone who can demonstrate proof of any HEF or other pseudopsychology under scientifically controlled conditions. Despite extensive recruiting efforts, only one TT practitioner has attempted the test. She failed (Rosa, Rosa, Sarner, & Barrett, 1998).

Respecting the Rights of Nonhuman Animal Participants

Research in psychology almost always involves human participants. Only about 7 to 8 percent of research is done on nonhuman animals, and 90 percent of that is done with rats and mice (American Psychological Association, 1984). There are important reasons for using nonhuman animals in psychological research. For example, the field of *comparative psychology* is dedicated to the study of behavior of different species. In other cases, nonhuman animals are used because researchers need to study participants continuously over months or years (longer than people are willing to participate), and occasionally they want to control aspects of life that people will not let them control and that would be unethical to control (such as who mates with whom or serious food restrictions). The relative simplicity of some nonhuman animals' nervous systems also provides important advantages for research.

Is nonhuman animal research ethical?
Opinions are sharply divided on this question.

Most psychologists recognize the tremendous contributions that laboratory animals have made—and continue to make—to science. Without nonhuman animals in *medical research*, how would we test new drugs, surgical procedures, and methods for relieving pain? *Psychological research* with nonhuman animals has led to significant advances in virtually every area of psychology, including the brain and nervous system, health and stress, sensation and perception, sleep, learning, memory, stress, emotion, and so on. Nonhuman animal research also has produced significant gains for animals themselves. More natural environments have been created for zoo animals, successful breeding techniques have been developed for endangered species, and more effective training techniques have been developed for pets and wild animals in captivity.

Despite the advantages, using nonhuman animals in psychological research continues to be a controversial and ethical problem. Opponents argue that, unlike humans, nonhuman animals cannot give *informed consent*. They also question the so-called benefits of animal research, especially considering the suffering and loss of freedom for the animals. Proponents counter some of this by saying that most nonhuman animal research involves naturalistic observation or learning experiments using rewards rather than punishments, and most research does *not* involve pain, suffering, or deprivation (Burgdorf, Knutson, & Panksepp, 2000; Neuringer, Deiss, & Olson, 2000; Shapiro, 1997). Like in most controversies, there are numerous unresolved questions—with no easy answers: How do we balance costs and benefits? To what extent do the costs to nonhuman animals justify the benefits? Is human life intrinsically more valuable than other animal life?

While the debate continues, psychologists take great care in the handling of research animals and actively search for new and better ways to protect them (Guidelines for the Treatment, 2000, 2002; Petrinovich, 1999). In all institutions where nonhuman animal research is conducted, animal care committees are established to ensure proper treatment of research animals, to review projects, and to set guidelines that are in accordance with the APA standards for the care and treatment of nonhuman (and human) research animals.

Respecting the Rights of Psychotherapy Clients

Ethics are important in therapy, as well as in research. Successful psychotherapy requires that clients reveal their innermost thoughts and feelings during the course of treatment. It follows, then, that clients must trust their therapists. This places a burden of responsibility on therapists to maintain the highest of ethical standards and uphold this trust.

Therapists are expected to conduct themselves in a moral and professional manner. They should remain objective while becoming sufficiently involved with the clients' problems to know how to best help them. They should encourage their clients to become involved not only in deciding the type of treatment but also in the treatment process itself. Therapists also are expected to evaluate their clients' progress and report that progress to them.

All personal information and therapy records must be kept confidential, with records available only to authorized persons and with the client's permission. Such confidentiality can become an ethical issue when a client reveals something that might affect or possibly injure another person. For example, if you were a therapist, what would you do if a client revealed plans to commit murder? Should you alert the police or uphold your client's trust?

In cases of serious threat to others, the public's right to safety ethically outweighs the client's right to privacy. In fact, a therapist is legally required to break confidentiality if a client threatens violence to self or others, in cases involving suspected or actual child or elderly abuse, and in some other limited situations. In general, however, a counselor's primary obligation is to protect client disclosures (Corey, 2001).

A Final Note on Ethical Issues

After discussing ways research can be flawed and ethics can be violated, you may be unnecessarily concerned. Remember that guidelines exist to protect the rights of humans, nonhuman animals, and therapy clients. Most importantly, a *human subjects committee* or *institutional review board* must first approve all research using human participants conducted at a college, university, or any reputable institution. This group ensures that every proposed study provides for informed consent, participants' confidentiality, and safe procedures. Similar committees also exist to oversee and protect the rights of animal participants.

Any member of APA who disregards these principles may be censured or expelled from the organization. Clinicians who violate ethical guidelines for working with clients risk severe sanctions and can permanently lose their license to practice. In addition, both researchers and clinicians are held professionally and legally responsible by their institutions, as well as by local and state agencies.

Assessment

CHECK & REVIEW

Descriptive, Correlational, and Biological Research and Ethical Problems

Unlike experiments, descriptive methods cannot determine the causes of behavior, but they can describe specifics. **Naturalistic observation** is used to study and describe behavior in its natural habitat. **Surveys** use interviews or questionnaires to obtain information on a sample of participants. Individual **case studies** are in-depth studies of a participant.

Correlational research examines how strongly two variables are related (0 to ±1.00) and whether the relationship is positively, negatively, or not at all (zero) correlated. Correlational studies and the correlation coefficient provide important research findings and valuable predictions. However, it is important to remember that *correlation does not imply causation.*

Biological research studies the brain and other parts of the nervous system through dissection of brains of cadavers, lesion techniques, and direct observation or case studies. Electrical recording techniques involve implanting electrodes into the brain or on its surface to study the brain's electrical activity. Computed tomography (CT), positron emission tomography (PET), magnetic resonance imaging (MRI), and functional magnetic resonance imaging (fMRI) scans are sophisticated techniques for studying intact, living brains.

Psychologists are expected to maintain high ethical standards in their relations with human and nonhuman animal research participants, as well as with clients in therapy. The APA has published guidelines detailing these ethical standards.

Questions

1. Maria is thinking of running for student body president, but she wonders whether her campaign should emphasize campus security, improved parking facilities, or increased health services. Which scientific method of research would you recommend she use to determine the focus of her campaign? (a) case study; (b) naturalistic observation; (c) an experiment; (d) a survey.
2. Which of the following correlation coefficients indicates the strongest relationship? (a) +.78; (b) −.84; (c) +.35; (d) 00.
3. The four major techniques used for scanning the brain are _____, _____, _____, and _____.
4. A participant's agreement to take part in a study after being told what to expect is known as _____. (a) participant bias; (b) placebo effect; (c) informed consent; (d) debriefing.

Answers to Questions can be found in Appendix B.

ACTIVE LEARNING WORKSHEET   MODULE 2

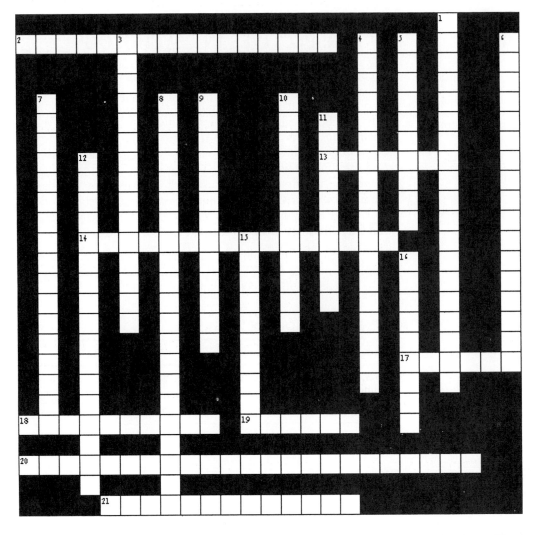

ACROSS

2 Experimenter influences the results of a research study in the expected direction.

13 An inactive substance or fake treatment used as a control technique in research.

14 Participant's chances of being assigned to each group in an experiment are equal.

17 Interrelated set of concepts, which explains a body of data.

18 Informing research participants about the purpose of the study, the nature of the anticipated results, and any deceptions used.

19 Nonexperimental research technique that assesses behaviors and attitudes of a sample or population.

20 Systematic recording of observable behavior in the participant's natural state or habitat with little or no experimenter intervention.

21 Believing behavior in your culture is typical of all cultures.

DOWN

1 Variables not directly related to the hypothesis under study and that the experimenter does not actively attempt to control.

3 Participant's agreement to take part in a study after being told what to expect.

4 Form of research that studies relationships between variables without the ability to infer causal relationships.

5 Statement of a predicted relationship between two or more variables.

6 Study in which neither the participant nor the experimenter knows which treatment is being given to the participant or to which group the participant has been assigned.

7 Variable that is observed and measured for change in an experiment.

8 Precise description of how the variables in a study will be observed and measured.

9 Statistical procedure for combining and analyzing data from many studies.

10 Research participants receiving a zero level of the independent variable.

11 Carefully controlled scientific procedure that determines whether certain variables manipulated by the experimenter have a causal effect on other variables.

12 Research participants receiving the independent variable.

15 Participants in a research study judged to be atypical of a larger population.

16 In-depth study of a single research participant.

MODULE 3
PERSPECTIVES IN PSYCHOLOGY

www.wiley.com/college/huffman

Assessment

Who are the important contributors to psychology's past, and what are the primary perspectives that guide modern psychology?

People have always been interested in human nature. Before psychology became a separate scientific discipline, the study of why people act as they do and how one person is different from another fell within the realm of philosophy. It was not until the first psychological laboratory was founded in 1879 that psychology as a science officially began. As interest in the new field grew, psychologists adopted various approaches to their research. Eventually, the different approaches and beliefs regarding the study of behavior came to be grouped into *schools of psychology*. In the next few pages, we will first explore those early schools in psychology's past and then briefly summarize the seven major approaches or *perspectives* in modern psychology.

▪ Psychology's Past: Important Pioneers

As you can see in Table 3.1, the early pioneers and approaches to psychology are grouped into six major schools: experimental psychology, structuralism, functionalism, psychoanalytic, behaviorism, and Gestalt.

TABLE 3.1 PSYCHOLOGY'S PAST — MAJOR SCHOOLS OF PSYCHOLOGY

School	Prominent Figures	Major Emphases	Study Techniques
Experimental psychology (1870s–1880s)	Wilhelm Wundt	Thought processes	Trained introspection
Structuralism (1890s)	Edward Titchener	Thought processes, structure of the mind, and identification of the elements of thought	Trained introspection
Functionalism (1890s)	William James John Dewey	Applying psychological findings to practical situations and the function of mental processes in adapting to the environment	Introspection Experimental method Comparative method (humans and animals)
Psychoanalytic/ psychodynamic (1895–present)	Sigmund Freud Carl Jung Alfred Adler Karen Horney	Unconscious determinants of behavior, effect of early life experiences on later personality development	Individual case studies of patients
Behaviorism (1906–present)	Ivan Pavlov Edward Thorndike John B. Watson B. F. Skinner	Objective, observable behavior, stimulus–response, and effect of the environment on overt behavior	Experiments, primarily on learning and often done with animals
Gestalt psychology (1910s)	Max Wertheimer Wolfgang Kohler Kurt Koffka	Organization and context in the perception of meaningful wholes	Sensation and perception experiments

Experimental Psychology

Wilhelm Wundt is generally known as the founder of experimental psychology. He established the first psychological laboratory at the University of Leipzig, Germany, in 1879 and wrote what is often considered the most important book in the history of psychology, *Principles of Physiological Psychology*.

In this laboratory, Wundt and his followers undertook the study of psychology, which to them consisted of the study of experience. They went about this study by trying to break down conscious experiences into basic elements. Their chief method was termed *introspection*, monitoring and reporting on the contents of consciousness. If you were one of Wundt's participants trained in introspection, you might be presented with the sound of a clicking metronome. You would focus solely on the clicks and report only your immediate reactions to them — your basic sensations and feelings.

Structuralism

Edward Titchener, one of Wundt's followers, brought Wundt's ideas to the United States. Titchener established a psychological laboratory and coined the term *structuralism* to embody Wundt's ideas. Like Wundt, structuralists believed that, just as the elements hydrogen and oxygen combine to form the compound water, the "elements" of conscious experience combined to form the "compounds" of the mind. They sought to identify the elements of thought through introspection and then determine how these elements combined to form the whole of experience. Thus, their study focused on the investigation of thought processes and the structure of the mind.

Functionalism

Structuralists inaugurated psychology as a science and established the importance of studying mental processes. However, psychologists, especially those in the United States, became impatient with structuralism. They felt it was limited to only one area of behavior (e.g., introspection) and had few practical applications. These American psychologists, feeling the need for application of psychological findings to practical situations, began a new school of psychology known as *functionalism*, which stressed the *functions* of behavior in enabling people and animals to adapt to their environment.

By the end of the nineteenth century, Charles Darwin's theory of evolution was beginning to have a significant impact on psychology (Segerstrale, 2000). Of particu-

"Well, you don't look like an experimental psychologist to me."

William James (1842–1910). James was a leading force in the functionalist school of psychology, which stressed the adaptive and practical functions of human behavior.

lar interest was his idea of *natural selection*, which stresses the function of superior biological structures in adapting organisms to their environment. It was this idea that led several American psychologists to investigate the function of mental processes in adapting the individual to the environment — thus the name *functionalism*. Darwin's theory of evolution also suggested the possibility that mental processes of animals and people might be part of a continuum. Therefore, *functionalists* studied mental processes of both animals and humans to test their theories. Many then applied their research findings to practical situations.

William James was the leading force in the functionalist school. In keeping with structuralism, he viewed psychology as the study of consciousness, but James did not believe consciousness could be separated into distinct elements. He felt that mental activities form a unit of experience — that they are continually changing, while remaining interrelated, one thought flowing into another in a continuous "stream of consciousness."

Functionalism had a great impact on the development of psychology. It expanded the scope of psychology to include research on emotions and observable behaviors, initiated the psychological testing movement, changed the course of modern education, and extended psychology's influence to diverse areas in industry.

Psychoanalytic

Sigmund Freud (1856–1939). Freud founded the psychoanalytic perspective, an influential theory of personality, and a type of therapy known as psychoanalysis.

During the late 1800s and early 1900s, while functionalism was prominent in the United States, the *psychoanalytic* school was forming in Europe (Gay, 2000). Its founder, Sigmund Freud, was an Austrian physician who was fascinated by the way the mind influences behavior. After encountering several patients with ongoing physical complaints that seemed to have no physiological basis, Freud assumed that their complaints must be psychological. Further studies of these patients convinced Freud that such problems are caused by conflicts between what people believe to be acceptable behavior and their unacceptable motives, which are primarily of a sexual or aggressive nature. Freud believed these motives, the driving forces behind behavior, were hidden in the *unconscious*, the part of the mind that is outside of our awareness. Freud developed psychoanalytic theory to explain these conflicts and to provide a basis for a system of therapy known as *psychoanalysis*.

Isn't there a lot of criticism of Freud? Freud's nonscientific approach and emphasis on sexual and aggressive impulses have caused a great deal of controversy over the years. Even some of Freud's most ardent followers, Carl Jung, Alfred Adler, Karen Horney, and Erik Erikson, later broke away from their mentor — in large part because they wanted less emphasis on sex and aggression and more on social motives and relationships. Some also objected to possible sexist bias in his writings and theories. These early followers and their theories are now referred to as *neo-Freudians* (*neo* means "new" or "recent").

Today, there are few strictly Freudian psychoanalysts left. But the broad features of his theory remain in the modern approach known as *psychodynamic*. Although psychodynamic psychologists are making increasing use of experimental methods, their primary method is the analysis of case studies, because their primary goal is to interpret complex meanings hypothesized to underlie people's actions.

In sum, the original psychoanalytic approach has had a profound impact on psychotherapy, psychiatry, and modern psychodynamic psychologists. Freud is generally credited with expanding the impact of psychology throughout the world.

Behaviorism

In the early 1900s, another major school of thought appeared that dramatically shaped the course of psychology. Whereas structuralism, functionalism, and the psychoanalytic school looked at nonobservable mental forces, *behaviorism* emphasized objective, observable behaviors. John B. Watson (1913), the acknowledged founder of behaviorism, strongly objected to the method of "introspection," the study of mental processes, and the influence of unconscious forces because he believed they were too obscure to be studied scientifically. Watson adopted Russian physiologist Ivan Pavlov's concept of conditioning to explain behavior as a result of observable *stimuli* (in the environment) and observable *responses* (behavioral actions). In Pavlov's famous experiment teaching a dog to salivate in anticipation of food to the sound of a bell, the bell is the stimulus and the salivation is the response.

Because nonhuman animals are ideal subjects for studying objective, overt behaviors, the majority of early behaviorist research was done with them or with techniques developed through nonhuman research. Using dogs, rats, pigeons, and other animals, behaviorists such as John Watson in the early 1900s and, more recently, B. F. Skinner focused primarily on learning and how behaviors are acquired. They formulated a number of basic principles about learning that are explained in Module 17.

It sounds like behaviorists are interested only in nonhuman animals. Aren't any of them interested in humans? Yes, behaviorists *are* interested in people. One of the most well-known behaviorists, B. F. Skinner, was convinced that we could use behaviorist approaches to actually "shape" human behavior and thereby change the present negative course (as he perceived it) of humankind. He did considerable writing and lecturing to convince others of this position. Behaviorists have been most successful in treating people with overt (observable, behavioral) problems, such as phobias (irrational fears) and alcoholism (Modules 38 & 45).

Ivan Pavlov (1849–1936). Pavlov earned Russia's first Nobel Prize in 1904 for his study of digestion, but his lasting contribution to psychology was his accidental discovery of classical conditioning

B. F. Skinner (1904–1990). Skinner was a prominent figure in behaviorism and one of the most influential psychologists of the twentieth century.

Gestalt Psychology

Another early influence on psychology was the school of *Gestalt psychology*, founded by a group of German psychologists headed by Max Wertheimer in the early 1900s. Unlike behaviorism, Gestalt psychology assigned an important role to mental activities, which they believed organized sensations into meaningful perceptions.

Although Wundt and the structuralists were also interested in perception, the underlying philosophy of the Gestaltists was quite different. Gestaltists rejected the notion that experiences can be broken down into elements, such as stimulus and response. Rather, they insisted that experience could be studied only as a whole — that the whole experience is qualitatively different from the sum of the distinct elements of that experience (*Gestalt* means roughly "organized whole" or "pattern" in German). As you will note in upcoming modules, Gestalt psychology remains an important contributor to modern studies of sensation, perception, personality, and a type of psychotherapy (e.g., Humphreys & Muller, 2000).

Women and Minorities

Before leaving the topic of "psychology's past," we need to explore the contributions of women and minorities. During the late 1800s and early 1900s, most colleges and universities provided little opportunity for women and minorities, either as students or faculty. Despite these early limitations, both women and minorities have made important contributions to psychology.

One of the first women to be recognized in the field was Mary Calkins. Calkins performed valuable research on memory and in 1905 served as the first female president of the APA. Her achievements are particularly noteworthy, considering the significant discrimination against women in those times. Even after completing all the requirements for a Ph.D. at Harvard and being described by William James as his brightest student, the university refused to grant the degree to a woman. The first woman to receive a Ph.D. in psychology was Margaret Floy Washburn (in 1894), who wrote several influential books and served as the second female president of APA.

Mary Calkins (1863–1930). Calkins was the first woman president of the American Psychological Association, established a psychology laboratory at Wellesley College, and conducted important research on memory.

Kenneth Clark 1914–). Clark was the first African-American president of the American Psychological Association, He and his wife, Mamie, also conducted research on prejudice that was cited in 1964 by the U.S. Supreme Court.

Francis Cecil Sumner, without benefit of a formal high school education, became the first African American to earn a Ph.D. in psychology from Clark University in 1920. He translated over 3,000 articles from German, French, and Spanish and founded one of the country's leading psychology departments. One of Sumner's students at Clark University, Kenneth B. Clark, later (in 1971) became the first African American to be elected APA president. Along with his wife, Mamie, Kenneth Clark also documented the harmful effects of prejudice. Their research had a direct effect on the Supreme Court's ultimate ruling against racial segregation in schools.

Sumner and Clark, Calkins and Washburn, along with other important minorities and women, made important and lasting contributions to the developing science of psychology. In recent years, several programs have been developed to encourage people of color and women to pursue graduate degrees in psychology.

■ Psychology's Present: Seven Perspectives and One Unifying Theme

In modern psychology, early schools like structuralism have almost entirely disappeared; whereas viewpoints like functionalism, psychoanalytic, and Gestalt have blended into newer, broader perspectives. In addition, rather than "schools of psychology," most psychologists today talk about different "perspectives." (A perspective is the psychologists's points of view or scientific assumptions, which influence the topics they choose to study, how they conduct their research, and what evidence they consider important.)

Today, there are seven major perspectives in psychology: *biopsychology* or *neuroscience, cognitive, behavioral, sociocultural, evolutionary, humanistic,* and *psychodynamic.* Many modern psychologists also recognize the value of using several perspectives and that no one view has all the answers. This *eclectic approach* is fast becoming the mainstream belief in modern psychology. It is becoming increasingly clear that psychology can no longer be divided into nature or nurture, biological versus psychological factors, evolutionary versus social factors, and so on.

One of the most widely accepted, and unifying, themes of modern psychology is that of a **biopsychosocial model,** which views *biological processes* (e.g., genetics, brain functions, neurotransmitters, and evolution), *psychological factors* (e.g., learning, thinking, emotion, personality, and motivation), and *social forces* (e.g., family, school, culture, ethnicity, social class, and politics) as interrelated influences. This new, integrative model proposes that all three forces *affect* and are *affected* by one another—they are inseparable. For example, feelings of depression are often influ-

Biopsychosocial Model *A unifying theme of modern psychology, which considers biological, psychological, and social processes*

ssessment

VISUAL QUIZ

Can you apply your psychology?

Research has shown that some animals, such as newly hatched ducks or geese, follow and become attached to (or imprinted on) the first large moving object they see or hear. The geese in this photo, which were hatched in an incubator by Konrad Lorenz, are following him in the water as if he were their mother. Which school or perspective of psychology would study and explain this behavior?

Answer: Evolutionary

TABLE 3.2 PSYCHOLOGY'S PRESENT — SEVEN MAJOR PERSPECTIVES AND ONE UNIFYING THEME

Perspectives	Prominent Figures	Major Emphases	Biopsychosocial Model
Psychoanalytic/ psychodynamic (1895–present)	Sigmund Freud Carl Jung Alfred Adler Karen Horney	Unconscious determinants of behavior, effect of early life experiences on later personality development	Takes into account all seven major perspectives
Behaviorism (1906–present)	Ivan Pavlov Edward Thorndike John B. Watson B. F. Skinner	Objective, observable behavior; stimulus–response; and effect of the environment on overt behavior	
Humanistic psychology (1950s–present)	Carl Rogers Abraham Maslow	Self-concept, free will, and human nature as naturally positive and growth-seeking	
Cognitive psychology (1950s–present)	Jean Piaget Albert Ellis Albert Bandura Robert Sternberg Howard Gardner	Mental processes, language, and perception	
Neuroscience/biopsychology (1950s–present)	Johannes Müller Karl Lashley David Hubel James Olds Roger Sperry Candace Pert	Genetics and physiological processes occurring in the brain and nervous system	
Evolutionary psychology (1980s–present)	Charles Darwin Konrad Lorenz E. O. Wilson David Buss	Natural selection, adaptation, and evolution of behavior patterns	
Sociocultural psychology (1980s–present)	John Berry Patricia Greenfield Richard Brislin	Social interaction and the cultural determinants of behavior	

enced by genetics and neurotransmitters (biology), our learned responses and patterns of thinking (psychology), and our socioeconomic status and cultural views of emotion (social). Table 3.2 summarizes the seven major modern perspectives and how they relate to the biopsychosocial model. In the coming modules, we frequently refer to one or more of these seven major perspectives, but the common theme of modern psychology, and this text, is an integrative, *biopsychosocial approach*.

A Final Note

One final note as you begin your study of psychology: You will learn a great deal about psychological functioning, but take care that you don't overestimate your expertise. Once friends and acquaintances know that you're taking a course in psychology, they may ask you to interpret their dreams, help them to discipline their children, or even offer your opinion on whether they should end their relationships. It is a good idea, therefore, to remember that the ideas, philosophies, and even experimental findings of the science of psychology are continually being revised. As David L. Cole, a recipient of the APA Distinguished Teaching in Psychology Award, stated, "Undergraduate psychology can, and I believe should, seek to liberate the student from ignorance, but also the arrogance of believing we know more about ourselves and others than we really do" (1982).

At the same time, psychological findings and ideas developed through careful research and study can make important contributions to our lives. As Albert Einstein once said, "One thing I have learned in a long life: that all our science, measured against reality, is primitive and childlike — and yet, it is the most precious thing we have."

Assessment

CHECK & REVIEW

Schools of Psychology

Among the early schools of psychology, the experimentalists focused on the study of experience and the use of introspection, whereas the structuralists sought to identify elements of consciousness and how those elements formed the structure of the mind. Functionalists studied how mental processes help the individual adapt to the environment. A later pioneer in psychology, Sigmund Freud developed psychoanalytic theory to explain psychological problems developed from unconscious conflicts. Behaviorism emphasizes observable behaviors and stimulus–response relationships. The Gestalt

school studied organizing principles of perceptual processes.

Seven major perspectives guide modern psychology: biopsychology or neuroscience, cognitive, behavioral, sociocultural, evolutionary, humanistic, and psychodynamic. These seven perspectives permeate the field of psychology and will be discussed in great detail in later modules. Today, the **biopsychosocial model** draws from all seven major perspectives.

Questions

1. The _____ school of psychology originated the method of introspection to examine thoughts and feelings.

2. _____ investigated the function of mental processes in adapting to the environment, and many applied their findings to real-world situations.

3. Why is Freud's theory so controversial?

4. Which of the following pairs of terms do not belong together? (a) structuralism, observable behavior; (b) behaviorism, stimulus–response; (c) psychoanalytic, unconscious conflict; (d) Gestalt; whole.

Answers to Questions can be found in Appendix B.

Achievement

GENDER & CULTURAL DIVERSITY

Are There Cultural Universals?

Psychology is a broad field with numerous subdisciplines and professions. Until recently, most psychologists worked and conducted research primarily in Europe and North America. Given this "one-sided" research, psychology's findings may not apply equally to people in other countries, or to minorities and women in Europe and North America, for that matter (Matsumoto, 2000; Shiraev & Levy, 2000). However, modern psychology, in particular *cultural psychology*, is working to correct this imbalance. Key research from cross-cultural and multiethnic studies is integrated throughout the text. Each section also includes an expanded "Gender and Cultural Diversity" discussion with a special icon in the margin that looks like this:

In this first gender and cultural diversity discussion, we explore a central question in cultural psychology: Are there *cultural universals?* That is, are there aspects of human behavior and mental processes that are true and *pancultural* or *universal* for all people of all cultures?

For many "universalists," emotions and facial recognition of emotions provide the clearest example of a possible cultural universal. Numerous studies conducted

Figure 3.1 *Do you recognize these emotions?* The recognition and display of facial expressions of emotion may be true "cultural universals."

over many years with people from very different cultures suggest that everyone can easily identify facial expressions for at least six basic emotions: happiness, surprise, anger, sadness, fear, and disgust. All humans supposedly have this capacity whether they are shown the face of a child or an adult, a Western or non-Western person (Ekman, 1993; Ekman & Friesen, 1971; Hejmadi, Davidson, & Rozin, 2000; Matsumoto, 1992, 2000). Moreover, nonhuman primates and congenitally blind infants also display similarly recognizable facial signals. In other words, across cultures (and some species), a frown is recognized as a sign of displeasure, and a smile, as a sign of pleasure (Figure 3.1).

Critics of the universalist position emphasize problems with these studies. For example, how do you label and study the emotion described by Japanese as *hagaii* (feeling helpless anguish mixed with frustration). How can Western psychologists study *hagaii* if they have no experience with these emotions and no English equivalent words? Other critics argue that *if* cultural universals exist, it is because they are biological and innate — and they should be labeled as such. However, equating biology with universality has its own problem. Behaviors or mental processes that are universal may be so because of culture-constant learning rather than biological destiny (Matsumoto, 2000). For example, *if* we found that certain gender roles were expressed the same in all cultures, it might reflect shared cultural training beginning at birth and not an "anatomy is destiny" position.

As we discussed earlier, scientists avoid the tendency to compartmentalize behaviors into "either–or" categories. Like the nature–nurture controversy, the answer once again is an *interaction*. Emotions and their recognition may be both biological and culturally universal. As a beginning student in psychology, you will encounter numerous areas of conflict, with well-respected arguments and opponents on each side. Your job is to adopt an open-minded, critical-thinking approach to each of these debates.

In addition to building your critical thinking skills, hearing arguments from both sides also will develop your understanding and appreciation for diversity, both intellectual and cultural. It might even improve your personal and business interactions. Richard Brislin (1993) told the story of a Japanese businessman who was asked to give a speech to a Fortune 500 company in New York. He was aware that Americans typically begin speeches by telling an amusing story or a couple of jokes. In contrast, Japanese typically begin speeches by apologizing for the "inadequate" talk they are about to give. This savvy businessman began his speech: "I realize that Americans often begin by making a joke. In Japan, we frequently begin with an apology. I'll compromise by apologizing for not having a joke" (p. 9). By appreciating cultural diversity, we can, like the Japanese businessman, learn to interact successfully in other cultures.

MODULE 3   ACTIVE LEARNING WORKSHEET

"What's My Line?"

Complete each statement with the correct psychological perspective (Experimental, Structuralism, Functionalism, Psychoanalytic/Psychodynamic, Behaviorism, Gestalt, Humanism, Cognitive, Neuroscience/biopsychology, Evolutionary, Sociocultural, Eclectic).

1. "As a(n) _____ psychologist, I believe that the whole experience is qualitatively different from the sum of the distinct elements."

2. "I believe that all behavior can be viewed as a response to a stimulus. My perspective is called _____."

3. "As a(n) _____ psychologist, I emphasize hidden forces within one's personality."

4. "I am concerned with conscious thought, perception, and information processing. My perspective is known as _____."

5. "As a(n) _____ psychologist, I emphasize natural selection, adaptation, and evolution of behavior patterns."

6. "I attempt to explain behavior and mental processes in terms of biological or physical mechanisms. My perspective is called _____."

7. "As a(n) _____ psychologist, I emphasize self-actualization, free will, and personal growth."

8. "I emphasize the application of psychological findings to practical situations. My perspective is known as _____."

9. "As a(n) _____ psychologist, I focus on social interaction and cultural determinants of behavior."

10. "I see value in using multiple perspectives because no one view has all the answers. My approach is known as _____."

MODULE 4
TOOLS FOR STUDENT SUCCESS

Congratulations! At this very moment, you are demonstrating one of the most important traits of a critical thinker and successful college student—your *willingness to accept suggestions for improvement.* Many students think they already know how to be a student, and that student success skills are only for "nerds" or "problem students." But would these same individuals assume they could become top-notch musicians, athletes, or plumbers without mastering the tools of those trades? Trying to compete in a college environment with minimal, or even average, study skills is like trying to ride a bicycle on a high-speed freeway. *All students* (even those who seem to get A's without much effort) can improve their "student tools."

In this section, you'll find several important *tools* (specific, well-documented study tips and techniques) guaranteed to make you a more efficient and successful college student. Mastering these tools will take a modest amount of time initially, but you'll save thousands of hours later on—I promise! Research clearly shows that good students tend to work smarter, not just longer or harder (Dickinson, O'Connell, & Dunn, 1996).

Do you want to learn how to "work smart?" The best place to start is with *active reading* and *time management.* I will then discuss several tips for *improving your grades*, and point you toward *additional resources for college success.* (*Study Tip:* One of the best resources for overall learning, memory, and motivation is psychology itself. Throughout this text you will find numerous topics and study tips that will help improve your study skills. Look for this icon 💡 in the margin. It identifies these special sections.)

Study Tip 💡

Tools for Student Success
This special feature in Module 4 includes tips for overall college success, as well as success in this course. In addition, the "lightbulb" icon identifies additional sections throughout the text that address other strategies for dealing with test anxiety, improving memory, performance, and overall **achievement.**

ACTIVE READING: How to Study (and Master) This Text

Have you ever read several pages of a text and then found you couldn't recall a single detail? Or have you read the assigned pages (possibly many times) and still did poorly on an exam? Do you want to know why? Try the Visual Quiz on this page.

Assessment

VISUAL QUIZ

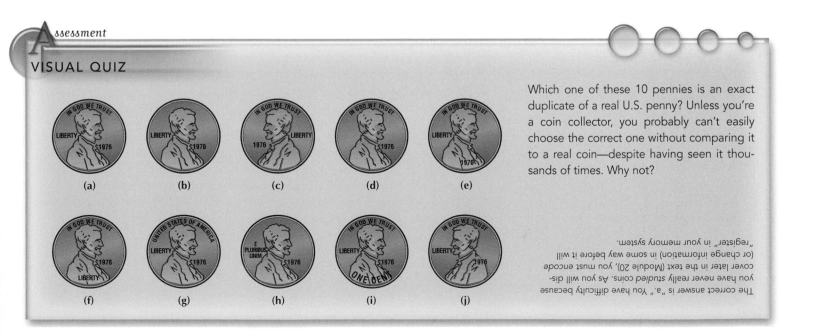

(a)   (b)   (c)   (d)   (e)

(f)   (g)   (h)   (i)   (j)

Which one of these 10 pennies is an exact duplicate of a real U.S. penny? Unless you're a coin collector, you probably can't easily choose the correct one without comparing it to a real coin—despite having seen it thousands of times. Why not?

The correct answer is "a." You have difficulty because you have never really *studied* coins. As you will discover later in the text (Module 20), you must encode (or change information) in some way before it will "register" in your memory system.

Can you see why I added this visual quiz to begin this section? I wanted to demonstrate how even a simple task of coin recognition requires *active* study. Just as you can't recognize a penny after years of looking at one, you can read modules many times and still remember nothing—unless you make a conscious effort. You must "intend to learn." Admittedly, some learning does occur effortlessly (as is the case when you learn the lyrics to your favorite song or find your way around your new home), but other information (like textbook reading) requires effort and deliberate attention. There are a number of ways to *actively read* (and remember) information in a text. Let's begin with Step One.

STEP ONE Familiarizing Yourself with the General Text

Your textbook is the major tool for success in any course. Most instructors rely on it to present basic course material, reserving class time for clarifying and elaborating on important topics. You can be a more successful student (and test taker) if you take full advantage of all the special features offered in *Psychology in Action*. Here's how to use these features:

- *Preface.* If you have not already read the preface, do it now. It is a road map for the rest of the text.

- *Table of Contents.* Scan the table of contents for a bird's-eye view of what you will study in this course. Get the big picture from the module titles and the major topics within each section.

- *Individual Modules.* Each module of *Psychology in Action* contains numerous learning aids to help you master the material. There are section outlines, learning objectives, introductory vignettes, running glossaries, Check and Review (summaries and self-test questions), visual summaries, and more. These learning aids are highlighted and explained in the margin of Modules 1–4.

- *Appendixes.* Two appendixes, A, *Statistics*, and B, *Answers to Review Questions and Activities*, present important information. The statistics appendix further discusses some of the concepts introduced in Module 2. It also explains how to read and interpret the graphs and tables found throughout the text. Appendix B contains answers to the Check and Review questions, Try This Yourself features, and various other activities found in the modules.

- *Glossary.* There are two glossaries in this text. A running glossary appears in the margins of each module to define key terms and concepts when they are first introduced. There is also an end-of-book glossary that gathers all the terms from the running marginal glossaries in one place. Use the end-of-book glossary to review terms from other modules.

- *References.* As you read each module, you will see references cited in parentheses, not in footnotes, as is common in other disciplines. For example, *(Ventner et al., 2001)* refers to an article written by Craig Ventner and his colleagues announcing the first successful mapping of the full human genome, which was published in 2001. All the references cited in the text are listed in alphabetical order (by the author's last name) in the References section at the back of the book.

- *Name index and subject index.* If you are interested in learning more about a particular individual, look for his or her name in the name index. The page numbers refer you to every place in the text where the individual is mentioned. If you are interested in a specific subject (e.g., anorexia nervosa or stress), check the subject index for page references.

Study **T**ip

Most instructors rarely (if ever) expect you to memorize these parenthetical citations. They are provided so you can look up the source of a study if you would like more information. At the same time, keep in mind that authors of certain key studies and famous psychologists are important to remember. Therefore, their names are emphasized in the text's discussion.

STEP TWO How to Read a Textbook

Once you have a sense of the book as a whole, your next step to success is improving your general reading skills. The most important tool for college success is the ability to read and master the assigned class text. Many colleges offer instruction in reading efficiency, and I highly recommend that you take the course. All students can become faster and more efficient readers, and this section can offer only the highlights of a full-length course.

One of the best ways to read *actively* is to use the SQ4R method, developed by Francis Robinson (1970). The initials stand for six steps in effective reading: Survey, Question, Read, Recite, Review, and wRite. Robinson's technique helps you better understand and remember what you read. As you might have guessed, *Psychology in Action* was designed to incorporate each of these six steps.

- *Survey.* Each section of the text opens with an outline, Learning Objectives in question format, an introductory vignette, and a short commentary on the vignette. Together, they provide an overview, or *survey*, of the following modules. Imagine trying to assemble a jigsaw puzzle without looking at the puzzle box cover to see what the overall picture should be. Similarly, knowing what to expect from a module can help you focus on the main points when you read.

- *Question.* To maintain your attention and increase comprehension as you read, turn the heading of each unit into a *question*. The Learning Objectives listed at the beginning of each section and repeated in the margins already do this for the main sections. Use them as models for turning the second- and third-level headings into questions. Also try to anticipate the questions your instructor might ask on an exam.

- *Read.* The first *R* in *SQ4R* refers to reading. Try to answer the questions you formed in the previous step as you read the module. Read carefully—in short, concentrated time periods.

- *Recite.* After you have read one small section, stop and *recite*. Try to summarize what you've just read—either silently to yourself or as written notes. Also, think of personal examples of major concepts and how you might apply a certain concept to real-life situations. This will greatly increase your retention of the material.

- *Review.* Read the Interim Reviews that conclude each major section and then answer the Review Questions. Write down your responses, before checking your answers in Appendix B. When you finish the entire module, look back over your answers, the module headings, and Interim Reviews. Before each class quiz or exam, repeat this review process.

- *wRite.* In addition to the writing you do in the above steps, take brief notes in the text margins or on a separate sheet. This helps keep you focused during your reading. (The Student Study Guide that accompanies this text teaches a special "marginal marking" technique that my students find extremely helpful.)

The SQ4R method may sound time consuming and difficult. However, once you've mastered the technique, it actually saves time. More important, it also greatly improves your reading comprehension—and exam grades!

TIME MANAGEMENT: How to Succeed in College and Still Have a Life

Time management is not only desirable; it is also essential to college success. If you answer *yes* to each of the following, congratulate yourself and move on to the next section.

1. **I** have a good balance among work, college, and social activities.

2. **I** set specific, written goals and deadlines for achieving them.

3. I complete my assignments and papers on time and seldom stay up late to cram the night before an exam.

4. I am generally on time for classes, appointments, and work.

5. I am good at estimating how much time it will take to complete a task.

6. I recognize that I am less productive at certain times of the day (e.g., right after lunch), and I plan activities accordingly.

7. I am good at identifying and eliminating nonessential tasks from my schedule and delegate work whenever possible.

8. I prioritize my responsibilities and assign time accordingly.

9. I arrange my life to avoid unnecessary interruptions (visitors, meetings, telephone calls during study hours).

10. I am able to say no to unnecessary or unreasonable requests for my time.

If you cannot answer yes to each of these statements and need help with time management, here are four basic strategies:

1. *Establish a baseline.* To break any bad habit (poor time management, excessive TV watching, overeating), you must first establish a *baseline*, a characteristic level of performance for assessing changes in behavior. The first step in a successful weight loss program, for example, is to establish a caloric baseline. Before beginning a diet, dieters are asked to continue their normal eating patterns for 1 to 2 weeks while meticulously recording every meal, snack, and caloric drink. The total number of calories consumed each day, as well as trouble spots—times when the dieter is likely to overeat—constitute a baseline against which to judge future behavior.

    A similar strategy also works for time management. Before attempting any changes, simply record your day-to-day activities for 1 to 2 weeks (see the sample in Figure 4.1). Like most dieters who are shocked at their daily eating habits, most students are unpleasantly surprised when they recognize how poorly they manage their time.

Figure 4.1 *Sample record of daily activities.* To help manage your time, draw a grid similar to this and record your daily activities in appropriate boxes. Then use it to fill in other necessities, such as extra study time and "down time."

	Sunday	Monday	Tuesday	Wednesday	Thursday	Friday	Saturday
7:00		Breakfast		Breakfast		Breakfast	
8:00		History	Breakfast	History	Breakfast	History	
9:00		Psychology	Statistics	Psychology	Statistics	Psychology	
10:00		Review History & Psychology	Campus Job	Review History & Psychology	Statistics Lab	Review History & Psychology	
11:00		Biology		Biology		Biology	
12:00		Lunch / Study		Exercise	Lunch	Exercise	
1:00		Bio Lab	Lunch	Lunch	Study	Lunch	
2:00			Study	Study			

2. *Set up a realistic activity schedule.* Once you realize how you normally spend your time each day, you can begin to manage it. Start by making a daily and weekly "to do" list. Be sure to include all required activities (class attendance, study time, work, etc.), as well as basic maintenance tasks like laundry, cooking, cleaning, and eating. Using this list, create a daily schedule of activities that includes time for each of these required activities and maintenance tasks. Also be sure to schedule a reasonable amount of "down time" for sports, movies, TV watching, and social activities with friends and family.

Try to be realistic. Some students try to replace all the hours they previously "wasted" watching TV or visiting friends with studying. Obviously, this approach inevitably fails. To make permanent time management changes, you must *shape* your behavior. That is, start small and build skills. For example, schedule 15 minutes increased study time for the first few days, then move to 30 minutes, 60 minutes, and so on.

3. *Reward yourself for good behavior.* The most efficient way to maintain good behavior is to reward it—the sooner, the better. But the rewards of college (a degree and/or job advancement) are generally years away. To get around this problem and improve your time management skills, give yourself immediate, tangible rewards for sticking with your daily schedule. Allow yourself a guilt-free call to a friend, for example, or time for a favorite TV program after studying for your set period of time.

4. *Maximize your time.* Time management experts, such as Alan Lakein (1998), suggest you should "work harder, not longer." Many students report that they're studying all the time, but they may be confusing "fret time" (worrying and complaining) and useless prep time (fiddling around getting ready to study) with real, *concentrated* study time.

Time experts also point out that people generally overlook important "time opportunities." For example, if you ride the bus to class, you can use this time to review notes or read a textbook. If you drive yourself and waste time looking for parking spaces, go earlier and spend the extra time studying in your car or classroom. While waiting for doctor or dental appointments or to pick up your kids after school, take out your text and study for 10 to 20 minutes. These hidden moments count!

IMPROVING YOUR GRADES: Note Taking, Study Habits, and General Test-Taking Strategies

- *Note taking.* Effective note taking depends on *active listening.* Find a seat in the front of the class and look directly at the instructor while he or she is talking. Focus your attention on what is being said by asking yourself, "What is the main idea?" Write down key ideas and supporting details and examples, including important names, dates, and new terms. Don't try to write down everything the instructor says, word for word. This is passive, rote copying– not active listening. Also, be sure to take extra notes if your professor says, "This is an important concept," or if he or she writes notes on the board. Finally, arrive in class on time and don't leave early—you may miss important notes and assignments.

- *Distributed study time.* The single most important key to improved grades may be *distributed* study time. Although it *does* help to intensively review before a quiz or exam, if this is your major method of studying, you are not likely to do well in any college course. One of the clearest findings in psychology is that spaced practice is a much more efficient way to study and learn than massed practice (Module 20).

Just as you wouldn't wait until the night before a big basketball game to begin practicing your free throws, you shouldn't wait until the night before an exam to begin studying.

- *Overlearning.* Many students study just to the point where they can recite the immediate information. For best results, you should know how key terms and concepts are related to examples other than the ones in the text. You also should repeatedly review the material (using visualization and rehearsal) until it is firmly locked in place. This is particularly important if you suffer from test anxiety. For additional help on test anxiety and improving memory in general, see Modules 20, 21, and 44.

- *Psyche out your instructor.* Pay close attention to the lecture time spent on various topics. This is generally a good indication of what the instructor considers important (and what may appear on exams).

    Try, too, to understand the perspective (and personality) of your instructor. Recognize that most instructors went into education because they *love* the academic life. They were probably model students who attended class regularly, submitted work on time, and seldom missed an exam. Try your hardest to be in class for every exam. Remember that instructors have many students and hear many excuses for missing class and exams. Also bear in mind that most instructors actually enjoyed lectures during college and were trained under this system. *Never* say, "I missed last week's classes. Did I miss anything important?" This is guaranteed to upset the most even-tempered instructor.

- *General test taking.* Here are several strategies to improve your performance on multiple-choice exams:

    1. *Take your time.* Carefully read each question and each of the alternative answers. Do not choose the first answer that looks correct. There may be a better alternative farther down the list.

    2. *Be test smart.* If you're unsure of an answer, make a logical guess. Begin by eliminating any answer that you know is incorrect. If two answers both seem reasonable, try to recall specific information from the text or professor's lecture. Be sure to choose "all of the above" if you know that at least two of the options are correct. Similarly, if you are confident that one of the options is incorrect, *never* choose "all of the above."

    3. *Review your answers.* After you finish a test, go back and check your answers. Make sure you have responded to all the questions and recorded your answers correctly. Also, bear in mind that information relevant to one question is often found in another test question. Don't hesitate to change an answer if you get more information — or even if you simply have a hunch about another answer. Although many students (and faculty) believe "your first hunch is your best guess," research suggests this may be bad advice (Johnston, 1978). Changing answers often pays off! The popular myth of *not* changing answers probably persists because we tend to pay more attention to losses than successes. Think about what happens when you get a test back. Most students pay attention to only the items they got wrong and fail to note the number of times they changed from an incorrect to a correct answer.

    4. *Practice your test taking.* Complete the *Check and Review* sections found throughout each module and check your answers in Appendix B. Make up questions from your lectures and text notes. Also, try the interactive quizzes on our website http://www.wiley.com/college/huffman. Each module of the text has its own sample quiz with individualized feedback. If you answer a question incorrectly, you get immediate feedback and further explanations that help you master the material.

RESOURCES FOR SUCCESS: Where Can I Get Additional Help?

In addition to college counselors and financial aid officers, there are several resources that students often overlook in their search for success:

1. ***Instructors.*** Get to know your instructors. They can provide useful tips for succeeding in their course. But it's up to you to discover their office hours and office location. If their office hours conflict with your schedule, ask for an alternative appointment, try to stop by right before or after class, or email them.

2. ***College Courses.*** College instructors often assign 2 or 3 books per course and numerous papers that must be typed. *All* students can improve their reading speed and comprehension, and their word processing/typing skills, by taking additional college courses designed to develop these specific abilities.

3. ***Friends and Family.*** Ask friends or family members to serve as your *conscience/coach* for improved time management and study skills. After completing your daily activity schedule (see page 44), set up weekly (or biweekly) appointments with a friend or family member to check your progress and act as your "conscience." You may think it would be easy to lie to your conscience/coach, but most people find it much harder to lie to another person than to lie to themselves (about calories, study time, TV watching, etc.). Encourage your conscience/coach to ask pointed questions about your *actual* study time versus your *fretting* and *prepping* time.

4. **Roommates, Classmates, and Study Groups.** Although college roommates and friendly classmates can sometimes be a distraction, you also can enlist their help as your conscience/coach or study partner. Also, ask your classmates and roommates what tricks/techniques they use to maintain their attention and interest during lectures or while reading texts.

If you would like more information on student success skills, consult the *Psychology in Action* website http://www.wiley.com/college/huffman. In addition to the interactive tutorials and quizzes mentioned earlier, we also offer specific Internet links for student success and recommend books and articles on time management and the other topics discussed here.

A FINAL WORD: Your Attitude

Imagine for a moment that the toilet in your bathroom is overflowing and creating a horrible, smelly mess. Whom should you reward? The plumber who quickly and efficiently solves the problem? Or someone who "tries very hard"?

Some students may believe they can pass college courses by simply attending class and doing the homework — that this shows their great interest and effort. This might have worked for *some* students in *some* classes in high school, but it probably won't work in college. Most college professors seldom assign homework and may not notice if you skip class. They assume students are independent, self-motivated adult learners.

Professors also generally consider college a last stop on the way to the real world and believe grades should reflect knowledge and performance — not effort. Although points may be given in some classes for attendance, participation, and effort, the heaviest weight will almost always come from exams, papers, and projects. Did you fix the toilet or not?

MODULE 4   ACTIVE LEARNING WORKSHEET

You have just discovered 15 Tools for Student Success. To help you apply this material to your own study skills, place a "+" mark by those activities or skills you currently use, and a "–" by those you don't. Then review the items with a "–" mark, and decide how you can incorporate them into your study skills "toolbag."

_____ Familiarizing Yourself with the General Text.

_____ Using the SQ4R Method to Read the Chapter

_____ Establishing a Baseline for Time Management

_____ Setting up a Realistic Activity Schedule

_____ Rewarding Myself for Good Behavior

_____ Maximizing My Time

_____ Effective Note Taking Through Active Listening

_____ Distributed Study Time versus Cramming

_____ Overlearning

_____ Psyching out my Instructor

_____ Taking My Time on Tests

_____ Being Test Smart

_____ Reviewing My Test Answers

_____ Practicing my Test Taking Skills

_____ Seeking Help from Instructors, College Courses, Family, and others

KEY TERMS

To assess your understanding of the **Key Terms** in this section, write a definition for each (in your own words), and then compare your definitions with those in the text.

Understanding Psychology
critical thinking (p. 4)
interaction (p. 6)
nature–nurture controversy (p. 6)
psychology (p. 4)

Doing Research in Psychology
applied research (p. 10)
basic research (p. 10)
biological research (p. 24)
case study (p. 21)
control group (p. 15)
correlational research (p. 22)
correlation coefficient (p. 22)

debriefing (p. 28)
descriptive research (p. 19)
dependent variable (DV) (p. 15)
double-blind study (p. 17)
ethnocentrism (p. 17)
experiment (p. 14)
experimental group (p. 15)
experimenter bias (p. 16)
hypothesis (p. 12)
independent variable (IV) (p. 15)
informed consent (p. 27)
meta-analysis (p. 13)
naturalistic observation (p. 19)
operational definition (p. 12)

Key Terms
The list of key terms at the end of each section is helpful to your mastery of the most important concepts. Try to recite aloud, or write a brief definition for each term. Then, turn to the relevant pages in the modules and check your understanding.

placebo [pluh-SEE-bo] (p. 17)
random assignment (p. 18)
sample bias (p. 17)
survey (p. 20)
theory (p. 12)

Perspectives in Psychology
biopsychosocial model (p. 36)

WEB RESOURCES

Huffman Book Companion Site
http://www.wiley.com/college/huffman
   This site is loaded with free Interactive Self-Tests, Internet Exercises, Glossary and Flashcards for key terms, Web links, Handbook for Non-Native Speakers, and other activities designed to improve your mastery of the material in this section.

American Psychological Association (APA)
http://www/apa.org/
   Richly layered home page of the APA with links to Internet resources, services, careers in psychology, member information, and more.

American Psychological Society (APS)
http://www.psychologicalscience.org
   Official web site of the American Psychological Society and a great place to start your search of psychology related web sites.

Cyberpsychlink
http://cctr.umkc.edu/~dmartin/psych2.html
   Provides an index of psychology sites, including list servers, electronic journals, self-help, newsgroups, and software for psychologists.

Today in the History of Psychology
http://www.cwu.edu/~warren/today.html
   Pick a date (any date) from the history of psychology calendar and see what happened.

Web Resources
Each section ends with a short list of suggested web links to further your achievement in psychology-both your grade in the course and your personal interest in the field.

Want to be a Research Participant?
http://www.psych.hanover.edu/research/exponent.html and
http://www.oklahoma.net/~jnichols/research.html
   Both sites offer great opportunities to participate in psychological research online.

Want to be an Experimenter?
http://www.uwm.edu/~johnchay/index.htm
   Provides two sets of programs that allow you to explore classic experiments in psychology.

Psychweb
http://www.psychwww.com
   Provides links to classic works in psychology, scholarly resources, psychology journals, and career information for psychology majors.

Ethical Principles of Psychologists
http://www.apa.org/ethics/code.html
   Offers the full text of the ethical guidelines for professional psychologists.

VISUAL SUMMARY

Introduction and Research Methods
(Modules 1, 2, 3, and 4)

Understanding Psychology

Psychology

The *scientific* study of behavior and mental processes. It values empirical evidence and **critical thinking,** unlike pseudopsychologies, which use nonscientific and nonverifiable methods.

Psychology's Goals

Describe, explain, predict, and change behavior and mental processes.

Careers or Specialties

Various areas, including biopsychology, clinical, cognitive, and so on.

Types of Research

Basic research studies theoretical questions.
Applied research attempts to answer real-world problems.

Doing Research in Psychology

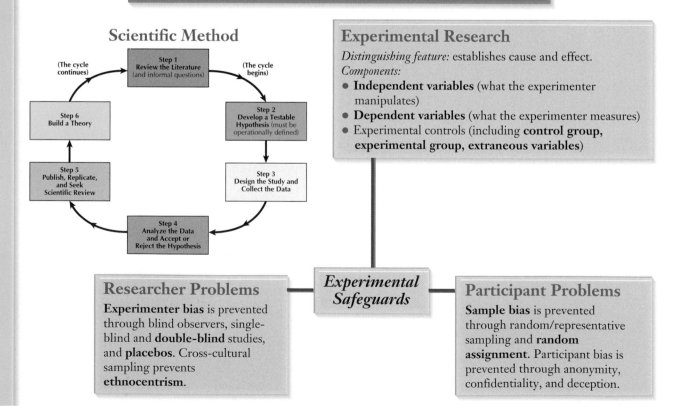

Scientific Method

(The cycle continues)

(The cycle begins)

Step 1
Review the Literature
(and informal questions)

Step 2
Develop a Testable Hypothesis (must be operationally defined)

Step 3
Design the Study and Collect the Data

Step 4
Analyze the Data and Accept or Reject the Hypothesis

Step 5
Publish, Replicate, and Seek Scientific Review

Step 6
Build a Theory

Experimental Research

Distinguishing feature: establishes cause and effect.
Components:
- **Independent variables** (what the experimenter manipulates)
- **Dependent variables** (what the experimenter measures)
- Experimental controls (including **control group, experimental group, extraneous variables**)

Experimental Safeguards

Researcher Problems

Experimenter bias is prevented through blind observers, single-blind and **double-blind** studies, and **placebos**. Cross-cultural sampling prevents **ethnocentrism**.

Participant Problems

Sample bias is prevented through random/representative sampling and **random assignment**. Participant bias is prevented through anonymity, confidentiality, and deception.

StudyTip

At the end of each section, all modules are summarized in a visual format. This unique study tool visually organizes the main concepts of each section in a clear, two-page layout. Use the summary as a quick review after completing your reading.

Doing Research in Psychology (cont.)

Descriptive Research

Distinguishing feature: Describes specifics about behavior, determines relationships between variables, and helps with prediction.

Naturalistic Observation

Systematic recording of observable behavior in the participant's natural habitat with little or no experimenter intervention.

Surveys

Assesses behaviors and attitudes of a sample or population.

Case studies

In-depth study of a single research participant.

Correlational Research

Statistical analyses of relationships between variables.

Biological Research

Methods include brain dissection, ablation, lesioning, clinical observation, case studies, electrical recordings, electrical stimulation of the brain (ESB), brain imaging (such as CT, PET, MRI, fMRI).

Ethical Problems

Human research participants have rights, including **informed consent** and voluntary participation, limited use of deception, **debriefing**, and confidentiality. Rights of animal participants and clients in therapy are protected through careful adherence to APA standards.

Perspectives in Psychology

Psychology's Past

- *Experimental psychology*: Studied experience through introspection.
- *Structuralism*: Focused on thought processes and the structure of the mind through introspection.
- *Functionalism*: Emphasized the function of mental processes in adapting to the environment and application of psychology to practical situations.
- *Psychoanalytic/Psychodynamic*: Emphasized unconscious processes and early life experiences.
- *Behaviorism*: Studied objective, observable behavior, and the effect of the environment.
- *Gestalt psychology*: Emphasized organization, context, and meaningful wholes.

Psychology's Present

- *Psychoanalytic/Psychodynamic*: Emphasizes unconscious processes and early life experiences.
- *Behaviorism*: Studies objective, observable, environmental influences.
- *Humanistic*: Focuses on self-concept, free will, and human nature as positive and growth-seeking.
- *Cognitive*: Emphasizes conscious thought, perception, and information processing.
- *Neuroscience/Biopsychology*: Studies genetics and physiological processes.
- *Evolutionary psychology*: Emphasizes natural selection and adaptation.
- *Sociocultural*: Focuses on social interaction and cultural determinants of behavior.
- *Unifying Theme*: Biopsychosocial model, which considers biological, psychological and social forces.

NEUROSCIENCE AND BIOLOGICAL FOUNDATIONS

Assessment

Core Learning Objectives

As you read Modules 5, 6, and 7, keep the following questions in mind and answer them in your own words:

▶ How is the nervous system organized?

▶ What are neurons, and how do they communicate information throughout the body?

▶ What are the lower-level structures of the brain, and what are their roles in behavior and mental processes?

▶ How does the cortex control behavior and mental processes?

▶ How are heredity and evolution linked to human behavior?

In 1848, when the Rutland and Burlington Railroad was laying new track through Vermont, 25-year-old Phineas P. Gage was a foreman in charge of blasting through the rocky terrain. Blasting a boulder into smaller, more easily removed rocks was a dangerous job, but not very complicated. First, a hole was drilled into the boulder and partially filled with blasting powder. Then a fuse was run into the blasting powder that was carefully tamped down, and the hole was filled with sand. The sand was tamped again with a metal rod to remove any air pockets that might diminish the blast, the fuse was lit, and everyone ran for cover.

Gage had done this hundreds of times, but on September 13, 1848, he failed to notice that his assistant had not yet put sand into the hole. So when Gage put down the tamping rod, it scraped against the rock and created sparks that ignited the blasting powder. But instead of shattering the boulder, the blast turned the iron rod into a missile. The 13-pound metal rod, $1\frac{1}{4}$ inches in diameter and $3\frac{1}{2}$ feet long, rocketed out of the hole and shot through Gage's head. Entering under his left cheekbone, the rod slammed

Achievement

Assessment

Application

through his brain, exiting out the top of his skull into the air, and eventually landing 60 to 80 feet away. Portions of his brain's frontal lobes littered the ground and smeared the tamping iron. This should have been the end of the story, but it wasn't.

Gage was stunned and his extremities shook convulsively. But in just a few minutes, he was able to talk to his men, and he even walked with little or no assistance up a flight of stairs before receiving medical treatment 1$^1/_2$ hours later. Although his mind was "clear" and Gage insisted he would be back at work in a day or two, the attending physician, John Harlow, doubted that he would recover and the town cabinetmaker even measured Gage so there would be a coffin "in readiness to use" (Harlow, 1848, 1868; Macmillan, 1986, 2000).

Gage did survive physically, but not psychologically. A serious personality transformation had occurred. Before the accident, Gage was "the most efficient and capable foreman," "a shrewd, smart business man," and very energetic and persistent in executing all his plans. After the accident, Gage "frequently changed what he proposed doing, and was, among other things, fitful, capricious, impatient of advice, obstinate, and lacking in deference to his fellows" (Macmillan, 2000, p. 13). In the words of his friends and acquaintances, "Gage was no longer Gage" (Harlow, 1868). Following months of recuperation, Gage attempted to return to work but was refused his old job. The damage to his brain had changed him too profoundly.

According to historical records by his physician, Gage never again held a job equal to that of foreman. He supported himself with odd jobs and traveled around New England, exhibiting himself and the tamping iron, and for a time he did the same at Barnum Museum. He even lived in Chile for 7 years before ill health forced a return to the United States. Near the end of his life, Gage experienced numerous epileptic seizures of increasing severity and frequency. Despite the massive damage to his frontal lobes caused by the tamping iron, Phineas Gage lived on for another 11$^1/_2$ years, eventually dying from the epileptic seizures.

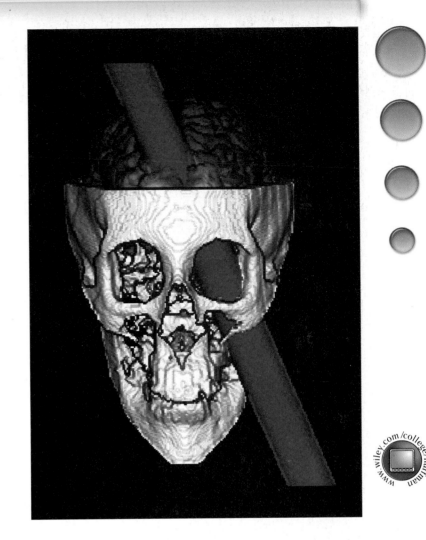

How did Gage physically survive? What accounts for his radical change in personality? If the tamping iron had traveled through the brain at a slightly different angle, Gage would have immediately died. But as you can see in the photo above, the rod entered and exited the front part of the brain, a section unnecessary for physical survival but intimately involved in motivation, emotion, and a host of other cognitive activities.

Phineas Gage's injury and "recovery" is a classic example from the field of **neuroscience** and *biopsychology*, the scientific study of the *biology* of behavior and mental processes. Most beginning psychology students expect to study only abnormal behavior and are surprised by the amount of biology. Obviously, the brain is critical to survival, but have you thought about how it is also the site of all your thoughts, fears, loves, and other behavior and mental processes? Your brain and nervous system control everything you do, feel, see, or think. *You are your brain.*

To help you fully understand and appreciate the wonders of your brain and the rest of your nervous system, Modules 5, 6, and 7 provide a basic overview and lays the foundation for the biological processes discussed throughout the text. Module 5 presents a brief overview of the nervous system. Then we examine the *neuron*, or nerve cell, and the way neurons communicate with one another. Module 6 explores the brain itself. Module 7 concludes with a look at heredity and evolutionary processes.

Neuroscience *An interdisciplinary field studying how biological processes relate to behavioral and mental processes*

MODULE 5
BIOLOGICAL FOUNDATIONS

One of the many advantages of studying psychology is learning about yourself and how you learn. As you'll discover in Module 20, when you are introduced to a large set of new terms and concepts, the best way to master this material (and get it "permanently" stored in long-term memory) is through *organization*. A broad overview showing the "big picture" helps you organize and file specific details. Just as you would use a large globe of the world that shows all the continents to learn about individual countries, you need a "map" of the entire nervous system before studying the individual parts. Thus, we begin with a broad overview of the nervous system, followed by a close examination of the neuron itself, communication between neurons, and chemical messengers in the nervous system.

Assessment

How is the nervous system organized?

■ An Overview of the Nervous System: The Central Nervous System and Peripheral Nervous System

Have you heard the expression "Information is power?" Nowhere is this truer than in the human body. Without information we could not survive. Our nervous system must take in sensory information from the outside world through our eyes, ears, and other sensory receptors, and then decide what to do with the information and follow through. Just as the circulatory system handles blood, our nervous system handles information.

To fully comprehend the intricacies of the nervous system, it helps to know the names of its major parts and how they are interrelated. Take a look at Figure 5.1. The

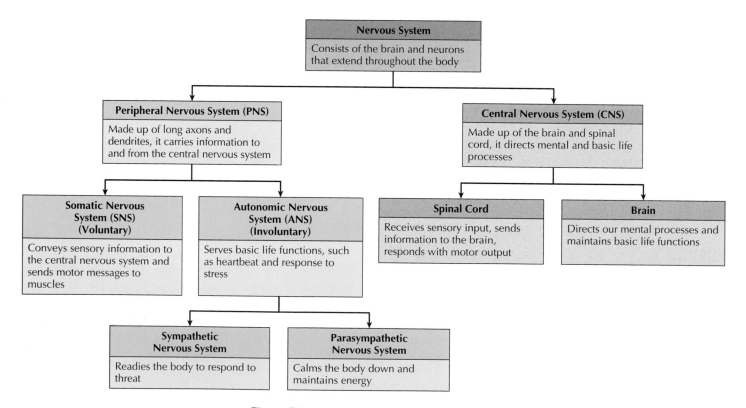

Figure 5.1 *The nervous system.* Note how the nervous system is divided and subdivided into various subsystems according to their differing functions. Review this diagram often as you study upcoming sections.

nervous system has two major divisions, the *Central Nervous System* (CNS), which processes and organizes information, and the *Peripheral Nervous System* (PNS), which serves primarily as a relay system getting information to and from the CNS.

Central Nervous System (CNS)

The **central nervous system (CNS)** consists of the *brain* and the *spinal cord.* Located *centrally* in the body, the brain and spinal cord both are surrounded by protective bony structures—the skull and spinal column. Unlike neurons in the PNS that can regenerate and require less protection, serious damage to cells in the CNS is usually permanent. However, the brain may not be as "hard wired" as we once believed. As you will discover throughout this text, the brain changes with learning and experience. In response to environmental demands (and some injuries), the brain can reorganize its functions, rewire itself with new connections, possibly reroute neurons around damaged areas, and even generate new brain cells (Gage, 2000; Kempermann, 2002; Song, Stevens, & Gage, 2002; Taub, Gitendra, & Thomas., 2002).

Because of its central importance for psychology and behavior, the brain is the major subject of this unit, but the spinal cord is also important. It is a great highway of information in and out of the brain. Beginning at the base of the brain and continuing down the back, the spinal cord contains nerve fibers that link the brain to other parts of the body. These fibers relay incoming sensory information to the brain and send messages from the brain to muscles and glands.

The spinal cord also is responsible for one of our simplest behavior patterns-the *reflex arc,* which occurs when a stimulus provokes an automatic response. Have you ever noticed that you automatically jerk your hand away from a hot pan *before* your brain has a chance to respond? Reflexes occur within the spinal cord, without any help from the brain (Figure 5.2). It is only later, when the spinal cord transfers the sensory information to the brain, that you actually experience the sensation called *pain.* If the top of your spinal cord were severed, you would not feel pain—or pleasure. As you will discover in Module 12, the brain receives and interprets sensory messages, while the independently operating spinal cord allows us to react automatically and protect ourselves.

Peripheral Nervous System (PNS)

The **peripheral nervous system (PNS)** is just what it sounds like — the part that involves nerves *peripheral* to (or outside of) the brain and spinal cord. The chief function of the PNS is to carry information to and from the CNS. It links the brain and spinal cord to the body's sense receptors, muscles, and glands.

The PNS is subdivided into the somatic nervous system and the autonomic nervous system. The **somatic nervous system (SNS)** (also called the skeletal nervous system) consists of all the nerves that connect to sensory receptors and control skeletal muscles. The name comes from the term soma, which means "body," and the somatic nervous system plays a key role in communication throughout the entire *body.* In a kind of "two-way street," the somatic nervous system first carries sensory information to the CNS, and then carries messages from the CNS to skeletal muscles. When you hear a question from your instructor and you want to raise your hand, your *somatic nervous system* will report to your brain the current state of your skeletal muscles and then carry instructions back, allowing you to lift your arm and hand.

Although the somatic system can help you respond to your college instructor's questions, it cannot make your pupils dilate or your heartbeat respond if a dangerous snake came sliding into the classroom. For this, you need the other subdivision of the PNS—the **autonomic nervous system (ANS).** The ANS is responsible for *involuntary* tasks, such as heart rate, digestion, pupil dilation, and breathing. Like an automatic pilot, the ANS can sometimes be consciously overridden. But as its name implies, the autonomic system normally operates on its own (autonomously).

Central Nervous System (CNS) *System located centrally in the body that includes the brain and spinal cord*

Peripheral Nervous System (PNS) *All nerves and neurons outside the brain and spinal cord. Its major function is to connect the CNS to the rest of the body*

Somatic Nervous System (SNS) *A subdivision of the peripheral nervous system (PNS) that connects to sensory receptors and controls skeletal muscles*

Autonomic Nervous System (ANS) *Subdivision of the peripheral nervous system (PNS) that controls involuntary functions, such as heart rate and digestion. It is further subdivided into the sympathetic nervous system, which arouses, and the parasympathetic nervous system, which calms*

Assessment

VISUAL QUIZ

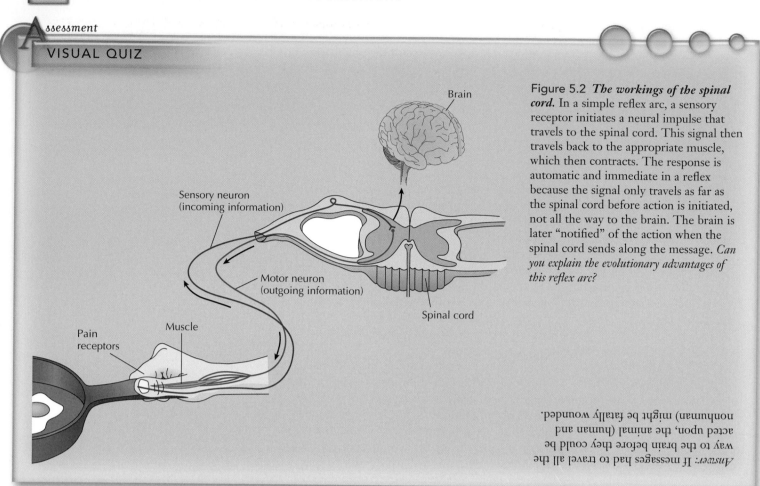

Brain

Sensory neuron
(incoming information)

Motor neuron
(outgoing information)

Spinal cord

Pain
receptors

Muscle

Figure 5.2 *The workings of the spinal cord.* In a simple reflex arc, a sensory receptor initiates a neural impulse that travels to the spinal cord. This signal then travels back to the appropriate muscle, which then contracts. The response is automatic and immediate in a reflex because the signal only travels as far as the spinal cord before action is initiated, not all the way to the brain. The brain is later "notified" of the action when the spinal cord sends along the message. *Can you explain the evolutionary advantages of this reflex arc?*

Answer: If messages had to travel all the way to the brain before they could be acted upon, the animal (human and nonhuman) might be fatally wounded.

Sympathetic Nervous System *Subdivision of the autonomic nervous system (ANS) responsible for arousing the body and mobilizing its energy during times of stress; also called the "fight or flight" system*

Parasympathetic Nervous System *Subdivision of the autonomic nervous system (ANS) responsible for calming the body and conserving energy*

The fight-or-flight response of the sympathetic nervous system is activated in both of these individuals

The autonomic nervous system is itself further divided into two branches, the **sympathetic** and **parasympathetic,** which tend to work in opposition to each other to regulate the functioning of such target organs as the heart, the intestines, and the lungs (Figure 5.3). A convenient, if somewhat oversimplified, distinction is that the sympathetic branch arouses the body for action (often called the "fight or flight" response), whereas the parasympathetic branch relaxes it—bringing it back to normal after stress. It's important to note, however, that these two systems are not an either/or arrangement. Like two children on a teeter-totter, one will be up while the other is down, but they essentially balance each other out.

During stressful times, either mental or physical, the *sympathetic nervous system* mobilizes bodily resources to respond to the stressor. If you noticed a dangerous snake coiled and ready to strike, your sympathetic nervous system would increase your heart rate, respiration, and blood pressure, stop your digestive and eliminative processes, and cause hormones, such as cortisol, to be released into the bloodstream. The net result of sympathetic activation is to get more oxygenated blood and energy to the skeletal muscles, thus allowing you to cope with the stress—to "fight or flee."

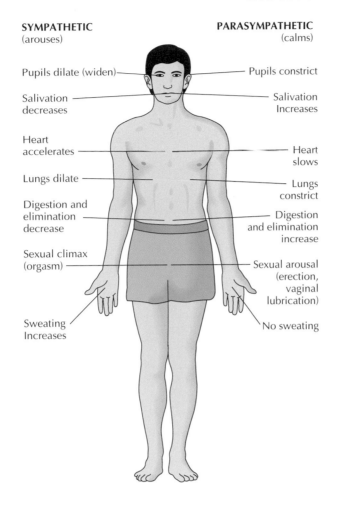

SYMPATHETIC
(arouses)

PARASYMPATHETIC
(calms)

Pupils dilate (widen) — — Pupils constrict

Salivation decreases — — Salivation Increases

Heart accelerates — — Heart slows

Lungs dilate — — Lungs constrict

Digestion and elimination decrease — — Digestion and elimination increase

Sexual climax (orgasm) — — Sexual arousal (erection, vaginal lubrication)

Sweating Increases — — No sweating

Figure 5.3 *Actions of the autonomic nervous system (ANS).* This figure illustrates the chief functions of the parasympathetic and sympathetic branches of the ANS.

In contrast to the sympathetic nervous system, which controls the emergency, fight or flight mode, the *parasympathetic nervous system* is responsible for returning your body to its normal functioning by slowing your heart rate, lowering your blood pressure, and increasing your digestive and eliminative processes.

Can you see why it's generally healthier to have the parasympathetic system predominate over your sympathetic? It activates processes that relax your body and allow it to save and store energy. On the other hand, the sympathetic system's fight or flight mode also provides an adaptive, evolutionary advantage.

At the beginning of human evolution, when we faced a dangerous bear or aggressive human intruder, there were only two reasonable responses—fight or flight! Today, this automatic mobilization of bodily resources and increased energy gained through activation of the sympathetic nervous system still has significant survival value. But as we all know, today our sympathetic nervous system may be activated by less life-threatening events, such as full-time college classes mixed with part or full-time jobs, multitasking jobs, dual career marriages, daily traffic jams and rude drivers on high-speed freeways—not to mention terrorist attacks and global pollution. Our bodies still respond to these sources of stress with sympathetic arousal. And, as you will see in the next section *(Stress and Health Psychology)*, ongoing sympathetic system response to such chronic, daily stress can become detrimental to our health.

Stud**y T**ip

One way to differentiate the two subdivisions of the ANS is to imagine yourself jumping out of an airplane. When you initially jump, your sympathetic nervous system has "sympathy" for your crisis situation. It responds by bringing your brain and body to full alert status. Once your "para" chute opens, your "para" sympathetic nervous system also can open, and you can relax as you float safely to earth.

Assessment

CHECK & REVIEW

An Overview of the Nervous System

Neuroscience is an interdisciplinary field that studies how biological processes relate to behavior and mental processes. The **central nervous system** is composed of the brain and the spinal cord. The spinal cord is the communications link between the brain and the rest of the body below the neck. It is involved in all voluntary and reflex responses of the body below the neck.

The **peripheral nervous system** includes all nerves going to and from the brain and spinal cord. Its two major subdivisions are the **somatic nervous system** and the **autonomic nervous system.**

The somatic nervous system includes all nerves carrying incoming sensory information and outgoing motor information to and from the sense organs and skeletal muscles.

The autonomic nervous system includes the nerves outside the brain and spinal cord that maintain normal functioning of glands, heart muscle, and the smooth muscle of blood vessels and internal organs.

The autonomic nervous system is further divided into two branches, the **parasympathetic** and the **sympathetic,** which tend to work in opposition to one another. The parasympathetic nervous system normally dominates when a person is relaxed. The sympathetic nervous system dominates when a person is under physical or mental stress. It mobilizes the body for fight or flight by increasing heart rate and blood pressure and slowing digestive processes.

Questions

1. The nervous system is separated into two major divisions: the _____ nervous system, which consists of the brain and spinal cord, and the _____ nervous system, which consists of all the nerves going to and from the brain and spinal cord.

2. The autonomic nervous system is subdivided into two branches called the _____ and _____ systems. (a) automatic, semiautomatic; (b) somatic, peripheral; (c) afferent, efferent; (d) sympathetic, parasympathetic

3. If you are startled by the sound of a loud explosion, the _____ nervous system will become dominant. (a) peripheral; (b) somatic; (c) parasympathetic; (d) sympathetic

4. What is the major difference between the sympathetic and parasympathetic nervous systems?

Answers to Questions can be found in Appendix B.

Assessment

What are neurons, and how do they convey information throughout the body?

Neuron *Individual nerve cell responsible for processing, storing, and transmitting information throughout the body*

Glial Cells *Cells that provide structural, nutritional, and other support for the neuron, as well as communication within the nervous system; also called glia or neuroglia*

Dendrites *Branching neuron structures that receive neural impulses from other neurons and convey impulses toward the cell body*

Cell Body *The part of the neuron that contains the cell nucleus, as well as other structures that help the neuron carry out its functions*

Axon *A long, tubelike structure that conveys impulses away from the neuron's cell body toward other neurons or to muscles or glands*

■ What Is a Neuron? Psychology at the Micro Level

Our brains and the rest of our nervous system essentially consist of **neurons,** individual cells that communicate information throughout the body, as well as within the brain. Each neuron is a tiny information processing system with thousands of connections for receiving and sending signals to other neurons. Although no one knows for sure, one well-educated guess is that each human body has as many as one *trillion* neurons.

These neurons are held in place and supported by **glial cells** (from the Greek word for "glue"). Glial cells surround neurons, perform cleanup tasks, and insulate one neuron from another so their neural messages do not get scrambled. Although recent research has found that glial cells also play a direct role in nervous system communication (Rose & Konnerth, 2002; Song, Stevens, & Gage, 2002), the "star" of the communication show is still the neuron.

Basic Parts of a Neuron

Just as no two people are alike, no two neurons are exactly the same, although most do share three basic features: dendrites, the cell body, and an axon (Figure 5.4). **Dendrites** look like leafless branches of a tree; in fact, the word "dendrite" means "little tree" in Greek. Dendrites act like antennas, receiving electrochemical information from other neurons and transmitting it to the cell body. Each neuron may have hundreds or thousands of dendrites and their branches. From the many dendrites, information flows into the **cell body,** or *soma*, which accepts the incoming messages. If the cell body receives enough stimulation from its dendrites, it will pass the message on to the **axon** (from the Greek word for "axle"). Like a miniature cable, this long, tubelike structure then carries information away from the cell body.

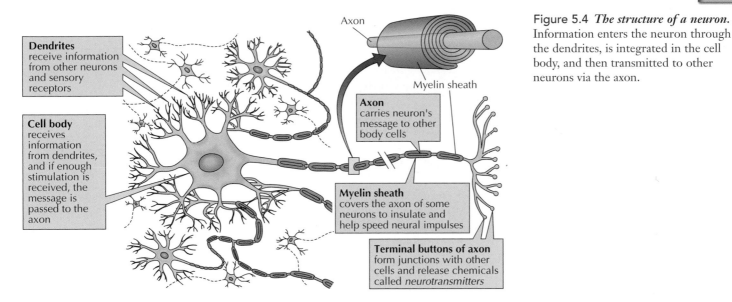

Figure 5.4 *The structure of a neuron.* Information enters the neuron through the dendrites, is integrated in the cell body, and then transmitted to other neurons via the axon.

The **myelin sheath,** a white, fatty coating around the axons of some neurons, is not considered one of the three key features of a neuron, but it is important because it helps insulate and speed neural impulses (Figure 5.4). Its importance becomes readily apparent in certain diseases, such as multiple sclerosis, where the myelin progressively deteriorates. This loss of insulation around the axons leads to disruptions in the flow of information between the brain and muscles, and the person gradually loses muscular coordination. For reasons not well understood, the disease often goes into remission, but it can be fatal if it strikes the neurons that control basic life-support processes, such as breathing or the beating of the heart.

Near each axon's end, the axon branches out, and at the tip of each branch are *terminal buttons,* which release chemicals (called *neurotransmitters*). These chemicals move the message from the end of the axon to the dendrites or cell body of the next neuron, and the message continues. Neurotransmitters will be studied in depth in the upcoming sections.

Myelin [MY-uh-lin] Sheath *A layer of fatty insulation wrapped around the axon of some neurons, which increases the rate at which nerve impulses travel along the axon*

Study Tip

To remember how information travels through the neuron, think of the three key parts in reverse alphabetical order: Dendrite → Cell Body → Axon.

How Neurons Communicate: An Electrical and Chemical Language

The basic function of neurons is to transmit information throughout the nervous system. Neurons "speak" to each other or, in some cases, to muscles or glands, in a type of electrical and chemical language. We begin our discussion by looking at communication *within* the neuron itself. Then we explore how communication occurs *between* neurons.

Communication Within the Neuron—the Action Potential
The process of neural communication begins within the neuron itself, when electrical "messages" are received by the dendrites and cell body. These messages are passed along the axon in the form of a neural impulse or **action potential** (Figure 5.5).

Because the neural impulse that travels down the axon is chemical, the axon does not transmit it in the same way a wire conducts an electrical current. The movement down the axon actually results from a change in the permeability of the cell membrane. Picture the axon as a tube filled with chemicals. This tube is floating in a sea of still more chemicals. The chemicals both inside and outside the tube are *ions,* molecules that carry an electrical charge, either positive or negative.

When the neuron is inactive, or *resting,* the fluid outside the axon has more positively charged ions than the fluid inside, leaving the axon *polarized.* This is similar

Action Potential *Neural impulse that carries information along the axon of a neuron. The action potential is generated when positively charged ions move in and out through channels in the axon's membrane*

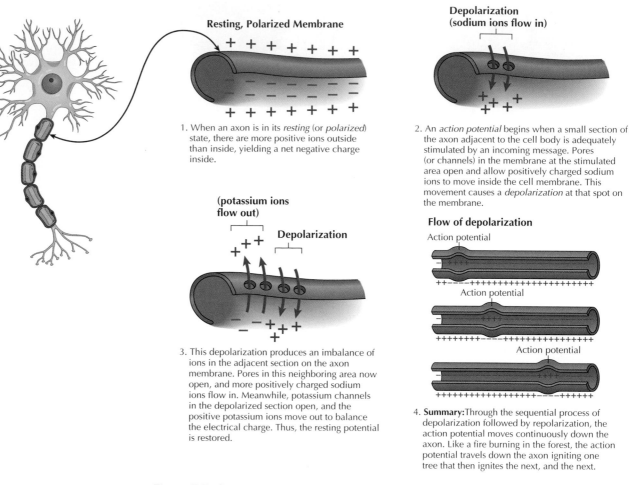

Resting, Polarized Membrane

1. When an axon is in its *resting* (or *polarized*) state, there are more positive ions outside than inside, yielding a net negative charge inside.

Depolarization (sodium ions flow in)

2. An *action potential* begins when a small section of the axon adjacent to the cell body is adequately stimulated by an incoming message. Pores (or channels) in the membrane at the stimulated area open and allow positively charged sodium ions to move inside the cell membrane. This movement causes a *depolarization* at that spot on the membrane.

(potassium ions flow out)

Depolarization

3. This depolarization produces an imbalance of ions in the adjacent section on the axon membrane. Pores in this neighboring area now open, and more positively charged sodium ions flow in. Meanwhile, potassium channels in the depolarized section open, and the positive potassium ions move out to balance the electrical charge. Thus, the resting potential is restored.

Flow of depolarization

Action potential

Action potential

Action potential

4. **Summary:** Through the sequential process of depolarization followed by repolarization, the action potential moves continuously down the axon. Like a fire burning in the forest, the action potential travels down the axon igniting one tree that then ignites the next, and the next.

Figure 5.5 *Communication within the neuron – the action potential.*

to a car or flashlight battery, which has positive and negative poles, which also are said to be "polarized." Just as a battery has an electrical potential difference between the poles (1.5 volts for a flashlight battery), the axon membrane has a potential difference of about –70 mVolts across it—the inside is more negative by 70 / 1000 of a volt.

When the neuron is activated by sufficient stimulation from other adjacent neurons, the electrical potential of the axon membrane near the cell body changes. When this potential change reaches a specific level, special voltage-controlled channels open, allowing a rapid inflow of positive sodium (NA) ions. This changes the previously negative charge inside the axon to positive—*depolarizing* the membrane. This change also causes nearby ion channels to open and the next section of the axon depolarizes, and the next, and the next, in a chain reaction. By this mechanism, the changed electrical potential is passed along the length of the axon—like a line of dominoes falling, each one toppling the next. This is called the *action potential*.

It is important to remember that once the action potential is started, it continues. There's no such thing as a "partial" action potential. Similar to the firing of a bullet from a gun, the action potential either fires completely or not at all. This is referred to as the *all-or-none law*. Immediately after a neuron fires, it enters a brief *refractory period* where it cannot fire again. During the refractory period, the neuron *repolarizes:* the resting balance is restored with negative ions inside and positive ions outside. Now the neuron is free to fire again.

How fast does a neural impulse travel? Actually, a nerve impulse moves slowly, much more slowly than electricity through a wire. Because electricity travels by a purely physical process, it can move through a wire at 97 percent of the speed of light, approximately 300 million meters per second. A neural impulse, on the other hand, travels along a bare axon at only about 10 meters per second.

Some axons, however, are enveloped in fatty insulation, the myelin sheath, which greatly increases the speed of an action potential. The myelin blankets the axon, with the exception of periodic *nodes*, points at which the myelin is very thin or absent (see again Figure 5.4). In a myelinated axon, the speed of the nerve impulse increases because the action potential jumps from node to node rather than traveling point by point along the entire axon. An action potential in a myelinated axon moves about 10 times faster than in a bare axon, at over 100 meters per second. The importance of the myelin sheath becomes apparent when it is destroyed in certain diseases such as multiple sclerosis. The greatly slowed rate of action potential conduction affects the person's movement and coordination.

Communication Between Neurons—Neurotransmitter Action at the Synapse

Communication *between* neurons is *not* the same as communication *within* the neuron itself. As we've just seen, messages travel *electrically* from one point to another within the neuron. Now let's watch and follow as the same message is transmitted *chemically* from one neuron to the next.

Once the action potential reaches the end of the axon, it continues traveling down the branching axon terminals until it reaches the axon terminal buttons. The transfer of information from one neuron to the next occurs at the junction between them, known as the **synapse.** This synaptic juncture includes the tips of the terminal branches of the axon (the terminal buttons), the tiny space between neurons (the synaptic gap), and the ends of the dendritic branches or the cell body of the receiving neuron (Figure 5.6). The electrical energy delivered by the action potential causes the knoblike terminal buttons at the axon's end to open and release a few thousand molecules of a chemical substance, known as a **neurotransmitter.** These molecules then move across the synaptic gap carrying the message from the sending neuron to the receiving neuron.

Once a neurotransmitter molecule travels across the tiny space of the synapse, and attaches to the membrane of the receiving neuron, it delivers either an *excitatory* or *inhibitory* message. Because the receiving neuron receives multiple, competing messages from other nearby neurons (Figure 5.7), the receiving neuron will only produce an action potential if the total amount of excitatory messages received from various neurons outweighs the total number of inhibitory messages. This process is somewhat analogous to everyday decisions in which we weigh the relative costs and benefits, and then decide to act if the benefits outnumber the costs.

Keep in mind that both *excitatory* and *inhibitory* messages are critical to your survival. Just as driving a car requires using both an accelerator and brake, your body needs both "on" and "off" neural switches. Your nervous system manages an amazing balancing act between *overexcitation*, leading to seizures, and *underexcitation*, leading to coma and death. Interestingly, poisons, such as strychnine, work by disabling many inhibitory messages, which may result in overexcitation and uncontrollable, possibly fatal convulsions.

Synapse [SIN-aps] *Junction between the axon tip of the sending neuron and the dendrite or cell body of the receiving neuron; during an action potential, chemicals called neurotransmitters are released and flow across the synaptic gap*

Neurotransmitter *Chemicals manufactured and released by neurons that alter activity in other neurons*

■ Chemical Messengers in the Nervous System: Neurotransmitters and Hormones

We have seen how communication within a neuron is the result of changes in the electrical charges along its membrane. And we have seen how communication between neurons occurs at the synapse and can excite or inhibit the receiving neuron's action

Figure 5.6 *Neurotransmitters – How neurons "talk" to one another.* In this schematic view of a synapse, neurotransmitter chemicals are stored in small terminal buttons at the end of the axon. When action potentials reach the axon terminal, they stimulate the release of neurotransmitter molecules into the synaptic gap. The neurotransmitter chemicals then travel across the synaptic gap, and bind to receptor sites on the dendrites or cell body of the receiving neurons.

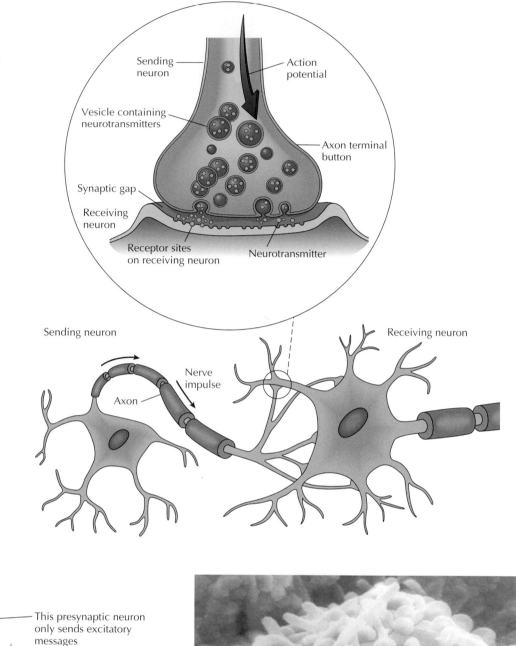

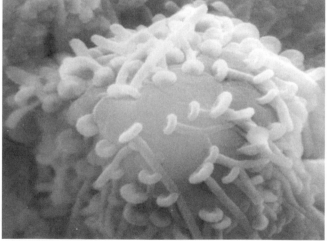

Figure 5.7 *Multiple messages.* (a) In the central nervous system, the cell bodies and dendrites receive input from many synapses, some excitatory and some inhibitory. (b) Note in this closeup photo how the axon terminals from thousands of other neurons almost completely cover the cell body of the receiving neuron.

potential. Now we look more closely at the major chemical messengers responsible for communication: *neurotransmitters* and *hormones*.

Neurotransmitters

Researchers have discovered hundreds of substances known or suspected to be neurotransmitters. Some neurotransmitters regulate the actions of glands and muscles; others promote sleep or stimulate mental and physical alertness; others affect learning and memory; and still others affect motivation, emotions, and psychological disorders, including schizophrenia and depression. Table 5.1 lists a few of the better-understood neurotransmitters and their known or suspected effects.

Endorphins   Perhaps the best known neurotransmitters are the *endogenous opioid peptides*, more commonly known as **endorphins.** These chemicals produce effects similar to those of opium-based drugs such as morphine — they reduce pain and promote pleasure.

Endorphins were discovered in the early 1970s, when Candace Pert and Soloman Snyder (1973) were doing research on morphine, a pain-relieving and mood-elevating opiate derived from opium, which is made from poppies. They found that the

Endorphins [en-DOR-fins] *Chemical substances in the nervous system that are similar in structure and action to opiates and are involved in pain control, pleasure, and memory*

SUMMARY TABLE 5.1 HOW NEUROTRANSMITTERS AFFECT US

Neurotransmitter	Known or Suspected Effects
Serotonin	Affects mood, sleep, appetite, sensory perception, temperature regulation, pain suppression, impulsivity, and aggression. May play a role in some psychological disorders, such as depression.
Acetylcholine (ACh)	Affects muscle action, cognitive functioning, memory, REM (rapid-eye-movement) sleep, emotion. Suspected role in Alzheimer's disease.
Dopamine (DA)	Affects movement, attention, memory, learning, and emotion. Too much DA is associated with schizophrenia, too little with Parkinson's disease. Also plays a role in addiction and the reward system.
Norepinephrine (NE) (or noradrenaline)	Affects learning, memory, dreaming, emotion, waking from sleep, eating, alertness, wakefulness, reactions to stress. Low levels of NE associated with depression, high levels with agitated, manic states.
Epinephrine (or adrenaline)	Affects emotional arousal, memory storage, and metabolism of glucose necessary for energy release.
GABA (gamma aminobutyric acid)	Neural inhibition in the central nervous system. Tranquilizing drugs, like Valium, increase GABA's inhibitory effects and thereby decrease anxiety.
Endorphins	Elevate mood, reduce pain, and affect memory, learning, etc.

morphine was taken up by specialized receptors in areas of the brain linked with mood and pain sensations.

But why would the brain have special receptors for morphine — a powerfully addicting drug? Pert and Snyder reasoned that the brain must have its own internally produced, or *endogenous*, morphine-like chemicals. They later confirmed that such chemicals do exist and named them *endorphins* (a contraction of *endogenous* [self-produced] and *morphine*). The brain evidently produces its own naturally occurring chemical messengers that elevate mood and reduce pain, as well as affect memory, learning, blood pressure, appetite, and sexual activity. Endorphins also help explain why soldiers and athletes continue to fight or play the game despite horrific injuries.

Neurotransmitters and Disease   One of the many advantages of studying your brain and its neurotransmitters is an increased understanding of your own or others' medical problems and their treatment. For example, do you remember why actor Michael J. Fox retired from his popular TV sitcom, *Spin City?* It was because of muscle tremors and movement problems related to a poorly understood condition called *Parkinson's disease* (PD). As Table 5.1 shows, the neurotransmitter *dopamine* is a suspected factor in PD, and its symptoms are reduced with L-dopa (levodopa), a drug that increases dopamine levels in the brain (Brundin et al., 2000; Diederich & Goetz, 2000).

Interestingly, when some Parkinson's patients are adjusting to L-dopa and higher levels of dopamine, they may experience symptoms that mimic schizophrenia, a serious psychological disorder that disrupts thought processes and produces delusions and hallucinations. As you will see in Module 40, excessively high levels of *dopamine* are a suspected contributor to some forms of *schizophrenia*, and when patients take antipsychotic drugs that suppress dopamine, their symptoms are sometimes reduced or even eliminated. However, some patients may develop some symptoms of PD. Can you explain why? (Laruelle, Abi-Dargham, Gil, Kegeles, & Innis, 1999; Reynolds, 1999). In sum, *decreased* levels of dopamine are associated with Parkinson's disease, whereas *increased* levels are related to some forms of schizophrenia.

Another neurotransmitter, *serotonin* (Table 5.1), may also be involved in the depression that often accompanies Parkinson's disease. Although some researchers believe Parkinson's patients become depressed in reaction to the motor disabilities of the disorder, others think the depression is directly related to lower levels of serotonin (Schapira, 1999). As Module 39 discusses, certain forms of depression are indeed related to lowered levels of serotonin. And popular antidepressant drugs, like *Prozac* and *Zoloft*, work by boosting levels of available serotonin (Margolis & Swartz, 2001; Tauscher et al., 1999; Wegerer et al., 1999). Even without medication, serotonin levels increase after successful psychotherapy for depression (Bransfod, 2000). (Recall from Module 2 that scientific research is "circular and cumulative" and that basic and applied research often overlap. Research with Parkinson's disease demonstrates these principles.)

Neurotransmitters, Poisons, and Mind-Altering Drugs   An understanding of neurotransmitters explains not only the origin of certain diseases and their pharmaceutical drug treatments but also how poisons, such as snake venom, and mind-altering drugs, such as nicotine, alcohol, caffeine, and cocaine, affect the brain (see also Module 15).

Most poisons and drugs act at the synapse by replacing, decreasing, or enhancing the amount of neurotransmitter. Given that transmission of messages *between* neurons is chemical, it's not surprising that many chemicals we ingest can significantly affect neurotransmission. They can do this because their molecules have shapes similar to various neurotransmitters.

Why study neurotransmitters? Actor Michael J. Fox suffers from Parkinson's disease, which involves a decrease in cells that produce dopamine. In this photo, he is testifying before a U.S. congressional subcommittee to urge increased funding for research on Parkinson's and other medical conditions.

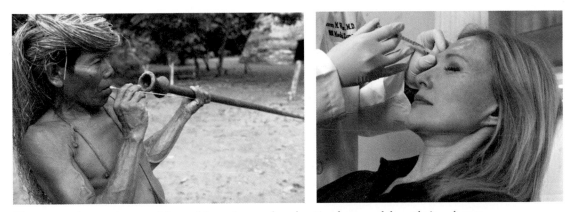

Neurotransmitters, poisons, and drugs. Most poisons and psychoactive drugs work by replacing, decreasing, or increasing the amount of certain neurotransmitters. The neurotransmitter acetylcholine (ACh) is responsible for muscular contractions, including the muscles responsible for breathing. The poison curare blocks the action of ACh and South American hunters sometimes apply it to the tips of their blowgun darts or arrows to paralyze their prey. Similarly, the botox poison also blocks ACh and it is used cosmetically to paralyze facial muscles. In contrast, nicotine in cigarettes increases the effects of ACh and smokers experience increased heart and respiration rates.

Neurotransmitters communicate with other neurons by binding to receptor sites in much the same way that a key fits into a lock. Just as different keys have distinct three-dimensional shapes, various chemical molecules, including neurotransmitters, have distinguishing three-dimensional characteristics. If a neurotransmitter has the proper shape, it will bind to the receptor site (Figure 5.8a and 5.8b) and thereby influence the firing of the receiving cell.

Some drugs, called *agonists* (from the Greek *agon*, meaning "contest, struggle"), mimic or enhance the action of neurotransmitters (Figure 5.8c). For example, both the poison in the black widow spider and the nicotine in cigarettes have a molecular shape similar enough to the neurotransmitter *acetylcholine (ACh)* that they can mimic its effect, including increasing the heart rate. Amphetamines have a similar excitatory effect by mimicking the neurotransmitter *norepinephrine.*

In contrast, *antagonist* drugs (from the Greek word meaning "a member of the opposing team"), work by opposing or blocking neurotransmitters (Figure 5.8d). Most snake venom and some poisons, like the *curare* that South American hunters use, act as antagonists to ACh. Because ACh is vital in muscle action, blocking it paralyzes muscles, including those involved in breathing, which can be fatal.

Hormones

Did you know that the human body actually has two communication systems? We've just seen how the nervous system uses *neurotransmitters* and *neurons* to carry messages throughout the body. But there is a second system, a network of glands that

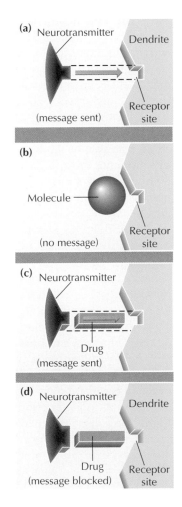

Figure 5.8 *Receptor sites.* (a) Receptor sites on dendrites recognize neurotransmitters because of their three-dimensional shape. (b) Molecules without the correct shape will not fit the receptors and therefore will not stimulate the dendrite. (c) Some *agonist* drugs, like nicotine, are similar enough in structure to a certain neurotransmitter (in this case, acetylcholine) that they mimic its effects on the receiving neuron. (d) Some *antagonist* drugs, like curare, block the action of neurotransmitters (again, acetylcholine) by filling a receptor site and thus not allowing the neurotransmitter to stimulate the receptor.

Figure 5.9 *The endocrine system.* The major endocrine glands are shown along with some internal organs to help you locate the glands.

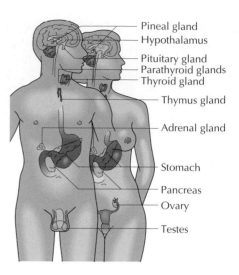

- Pineal gland
- Hypothalamus
- Pituitary gland
- Parathyroid glands
- Thyroid gland
- Thymus gland
- Adrenal gland
- Stomach
- Pancreas
- Ovary
- Testes

Hormones *Chemicals manufactured by endocrine glands and circulated in the bloodstream to produce bodily changes or maintain normal bodily functions*

Endocrine [EN-doh-krin] System *A collection of glands located throughout the body that manufacture and secrete hormones into the bloodstream*

uses a different set of chemicals, called **hormones,** to carry messages that stimulate and regulate important bodily functions. This network of glands, the **endocrine system,** is located throughout the body (Figure 5.9), and it manufactures and secretes hormones directly into the bloodstream. The endocrine system tends to be involved in long-term regulation of bodily processes because its action can't match the speed of neural transmission.

The chemical messengers of the neural and endocrine system, the neurotransmitters and hormones, are closely related. In fact, some neurotransmitters (e.g., norepinephrine) function as both a hormone and neurotransmitter—depending on whether they are released from the neural system or endocrine system. Also like neurotransmitters, hormones activate cells in the body, and the cells must have receptor sites for the particular hormone. But unlike neurotransmitters that are released immediately adjacent to the cells they are to excite or inhibit, hormones are released into the blood and travel throughout the entire circulatory system.

A further example of the close connection between the nervous system and the endocrine system can be seen in the way structures in the brain (especially the hypothalamus) stimulate or inhibit the release of most hormones. This is primarily because the hypothalamus controls the *pituitary gland*, which is considered the "master gland" of the body. This tiny structure, about the size of a pea, is responsible for releasing the hormones that flow throughout the body and stimulate actions in the other endocrine glands.

What does this have to do with you and your everyday life? Without the pituitary, the testes in men would not produce *testosterone* and the ovaries in women would not produce *estrogen*. As you may know, these hormones are of critical importance to sexual behavior and reproduction (see Module 29). In addition, the pituitary produces its own hormone that controls body growth. Too much of this hormone results in *gigantism;* too little will make a person far smaller than average, a *hypopituitary dwarf.*

Other hormones released by the endocrine system play important roles in maintaining your body's normal functioning. For example, hormones released by the kidneys help regulate blood pressure. The pancreatic hormone (insulin) allows cells to use sugar from the blood. And stomach and intestinal hormones help control digestion and elimination.

An additional function of the endocrine system is in its control of the "fight or flight" response described earlier. In times of crisis, the hypothalamus sends messages through two pathways—the neural system (sympathethic and parasympathetic nervous system) and endocrine system (primarily the pituitary). The pituitary sends hormonal messages to the adrenal glands (located right above the kidneys). The adrenal glands then release cortisol, a "stress hormone" that boosts energy and blood sugar levels, epinephrine (commonly called adrenaline), and norepinephrine. (Remember that these same chemicals also serve as neurotransmitters when released by the nervous system.)

In sum, the major functions of the endocrine system, including the pituitary, thyroid, adrenals, and pancreas, are to help with regulation of long-term bodily processes (such as growth and sex characteristics), maintain ongoing bodily processes, and assist in regulating the "fight or flight" response discussed earlier in relation to the sympathetic nervous system. This brief discussion has covered only a few of the endocrine glands' most important functions. Nevertheless, even this limited coverage provides a foundation for understanding the brain, genetics, and evolution—topics in the upcoming sections.

Assessment

CHECK & REVIEW

Neurons, Neural Communication, and Chemical Messengers

Neurons are cells that transmit information throughout the body. They have three main parts: **dendrites,** which receive information from other neurons; the **cell body,** which provides nourishment and "decides" whether the axon should fire; and the **axon,** which sends along the neural information. **Glial cells** support and provide nutrients for neurons in the central nervous system (CNS).

The axon is specialized for transmitting neural impulses, or **action potentials.** During times when no action potential is moving down the axon, the axon is at rest. The neuron is activated, and an action potential occurs, when the charge within the neuron becomes more positive than the charge outside the cell's membrane. Action potentials travel more quickly down myelinated axons because the **myelin sheath** serves as insulation.

Information is transferred from one neuron to another at synapses by chemicals called **neurotransmitters.** Neurotransmitters bind to receptor sites much as a key fits into a lock, and their effects can be *excitatory* or *inhibitory.* Most psychoactive drugs affect the nervous system by acting directly on receptor sites for specific neurotransmitters or by increasing or decreasing the amount of neurotransmitter that crosses the **synapse.**

Hormones are released from glands in the **endocrine system** directly into the bloodstream. They act at a distance on other glands and in the brain.

Questions

1. Draw and label the three major parts of a neuron and the myelin sheath.
2. An impulse travels through the structures of the neuron in the following order: (a) cell body, axon, dendrites; (b) cell body, dendrites, axon; (c) dendrites, cell body, axon; (d) axon, cell body, dendrites
3. Chemical messengers that are released by axons and stimulate dendrites are called _____. (a) chemical messengers; (b) neurotransmitters; (c) synaptic transmitters; (d) neuromessengers
4. Explain how neurotransmitters and hormones carry messages throughout the body.

Answers to Questions can be found in Appendix B.

MODULE 5   ACTIVE LEARNING WORKSHEET

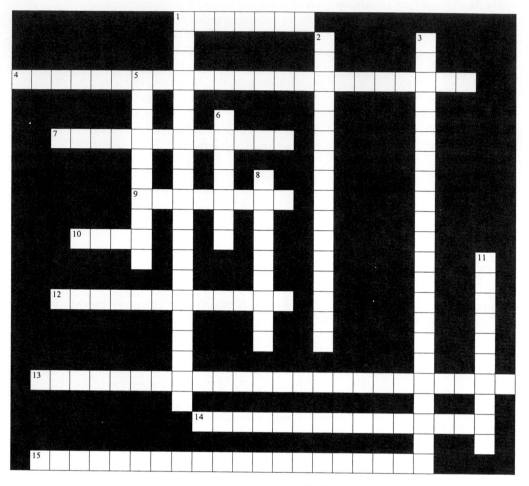

ACROSS

1 The junction between the axon tip of the sending neuron and the dendrite or cell body of the receiving neuron.

4 All nerves and neurons outside the brain and spinal cord. Its major function is to connect the CNS to the rest of the body.

7 An interdisciplinary field studying how biological processes relate to behavioral and mental processes.

9 Chemicals manufactured by endocrine glands and circulated in the bloodstream to produce bodily changes or maintain normal bodily functions.

10 A long, tube-like structure that conveys impulses away from the neuron's cell body toward other neurons or to muscles or glands.

12 A layer of fatty insulation wrapped around the axon of some neurons, which increases the rate at which nerve impulses travel along the axon.

13 Subdivision of the autonomic nervous system (ANS) responsible for arousing the body and mobilizing its energy during stress; also called the "fight or flight" system.

14 A neural impulse that carries information along the axon of a neuron. The action potential is generated when positively charged ions move in and out of channels in the axon's membrane.

15 The brain and spinal cord.

DOWN

1 A subdivision of the peripheral nervous system (PNS) that connects to sensory receptors and controls skeletal muscles.

2 Chemicals manufactured and released by neurons that alter activity in other neurons.

3 Subdivision of the peripheral nervous system (PNS) that controls involuntary functions, such as heart rate and digestion. It is further subdivided into the sympathetic nervous system, which arouses, and the parasympathetic nervous system, which calms.

5 Chemical substances in the nervous system that are similar in structure and action to opiates; involved in pain control, pleasure, and memory.

6 Individual nerve cells responsible for processing, storing, and transmitting information throughout the body.

8 Branching neuron structures that receive neural impulses from other neurons and convey impulses toward the cell body.

11 Nervous system cells that provide structural, nutritional, and other support for the neuron, as well as communication within the nervous system; also called glia or neuroglia.

MODULE 6
A TOUR THROUGH THE BRAIN

Having covered basic, biological foundations (neurons, neurotransmitters, divisions of the neural system, and hormones), we come now to the "main event" of neuroscience — the brain itself. We began this unit with the tale of Phineas Gage and his horrible brain injury because it emphasized the vital importance of this relatively tiny three-pound organ that sits atop your shoulders. Who would you be without your brain? Without its lower-level structures, you would not be alive. Without your cortex, you would not be capable of thinking, speaking, or perceiving. And as we saw with Phineas Gage, when the cortex is damaged, we lose much of what we define as "self."

We begin our exploration of the brain at the lower end, where the spinal cord joins the brainstem, and move upward toward the cerebral cortex. Note as we move from the brainstem to the cortex that the functions of brain structures change from regulating "lower," basic functions like breathing to "higher," more complex mental processes such as thinking.

◼ Lower-Level Brain Structures: The Oldest Parts of the Brain

Brain size and complexity vary significantly from species to species. Lower species such as fish and reptiles have smaller, less complex brains than do higher species such as cats and dogs. The most complex brains belong to whales, dolphins, and higher primates such as chimps, gorillas, and humans. The billions of neurons that make up the human brain control much of what we think, feel, and do.

As we begin our tour of the brain, keep in mind that certain brain structures are specialized to perform certain tasks, a process known as **localization of function.** However, don't make too much of the distinctions and differences. Most parts of the brain perform integrating, overlapping functions. Figure 6.1 shows the major structures of the brain. You should refer to it as you read.

The Brainstem

You are sleeping. Your eyes dart back and forth as you begin your last dream of the night. Your heart rate, blood pressure, and respiration increase, as the dream gets more exciting. But then your dream is shattered by a buzzing alarm clock. All your automatic behaviors and survival responses in this scenario have been either controlled by or influenced by parts of the brainstem. The **brainstem** looks like its name. The lower-end "stem" is a continuation of the spinal cord, and the higher end lies deep within the brain. Three structures generally are associated with the brainstem — the mid brain, pons, and medulla.

Messages to and from upper-level brain structures pass through all three of these structures. The **midbrain** contains neural centers that help us orient our eye and body movements to visual and auditory stimuli. It also works with the pons to help control sleep and level of arousal. The **pons,** located below the midbrain, is involved in respiration, movement, sleeping, waking, and dreaming (among other things). The **medulla** is below the pons, at the bottom of the brainstem and just above the spinal cord. Its functions are similar to those of the pons. Because the medulla is essentially an extension of the spinal cord, many nerve fibers pass through it carrying information to and from the brain. The medulla also contains many nerve fibers that control automatic bodily functions such as respiration and heart rate. Damage to the medulla can lead to failure of essential bodily functions and death. This is the area of the brain that was damaged when Senator Robert Kennedy was assassinated in 1968.

Running through the core of the brainstem and extending upward is the **reticular** (netlike) **formation** (RF). This diffuse, finger-shaped network of neurons filters

Assessment

What are the lower-level structures of the brain, and what are their roles in behavior and mental processes?

www.wiley.com/college/huffman

Localization of Function *Specialization of various parts of the brain for particular functions*

Brainstem *Area at the base of the brain in front of the cerebellum responsible for automatic, survival functions*

Midbrain *Neural centers located near the top of the brainstem involved in coordinating movement patterns, sleep, and arousal*

Pons *Structure at the top of the brainstem involved in respiration, movement, waking, sleep, and dreaming*

Medulla [muh-DUL-uh] *Structure at the base of the brainstem responsible for automatic body functions such as breathing and heart rate*

Reticular Formation (RF) *Diffuse set of neurons in the core of the brainstem that screens incoming information and arouses the cortex*

Corpus callosum
Thick band of axons connecting the two hemispheres of the cerebral cortex

Cerebral cortex
Divided into two hemispheres and responsible for higher mental functions

Amygdala
Part of the limbic system (see Fig.2.11). Involved in aggression, fear, and learning

Hypothalamus
Responsible for regulating emotions and drives like hunger, thirst, sex, and aggression

Midbrain
Helps control basic movement patterns, sleep, and level of arousal

Cerebellum
Coordinates smooth movement, balance, and some perception and cognition

Spinal cord
Responsible for transmitting information between brain and body; handles simple reflexes

Thalamus
Relays sensory messages to cortex

Pons
Involved with respiration, movement, waking, REM sleep, and dreaming

Reticular formation
Helps screen incoming sensory information and arouses the cortex

Medulla
Responsible for breathing, heartbeat, and other vital life functions

Brain stem
(Pons, Medulla, and Midbrain)

Summary Figure 6.1 *The human brain.* Although you wouldn't be alive to read this, if your brain were sliced down the center, lengthwise, it would look like the top right photo. The drawing highlights key structures of the right half of your brain and some of their principal functions. As you read about each of these structures, keep this drawing in mind and refer back to it as necessary.

incoming sensory information and arouses the higher centers of the brain when something happens that demands their attention. Basically, without your RF, you would not be alert or perhaps even conscious. Damage to this area can cause a coma.

Cerebellum [sehr-uh-BELL-um]

Structure at the base of the brain, behind the brainstem, responsible for maintaining smooth movement, balance, and some aspects of perception and cognition

The Cerebellum

The **cerebellum** ("little brain") is located at the base of the brain behind the brainstem. (Some say it looks like a cauliflower.) In evolutionary terms, it is a very old structure responsible for maintaining smooth movement and coordinating motor activity. Although the actual commands for movement come from higher brain centers in the cortex, the cerebellum coordinates the muscles so that movement is smooth and precise. The cerebellum is also involved with the sense of balance. In fact, roadside tests for drunk driving are essentially testing the cerebellum, because it is one of the first structures depressed by alcohol.

Research suggests that the cerebellum does much more than just coordinate movement and maintain physical balance. It may also have a role in perception and cognition. Using magnetic resonance imaging (MRI), researchers have documented that parts of the cerebellum are very active during perceptual and cognitive activities that require the processing of sensory data (Luft, Skalej, Stefanou, Klose, & Voight, 1998).

The Thalamus

The **thalamus** lies at the top of the brainstem. Resembling two little footballs, one on each side of the brain, connected by a thin group of nerve fibers, it serves as the major sensory relay center for the brain. Like an air traffic control center that receives information from all aircraft, and then directs them to the appropriate landing or take-off areas, the thalamus receives input from nearly all the sensory systems and then directs this information to the appropriate cortical areas. For example, while you're reading this page, your thalamus sends incoming visual signals to the visual area of your cortex. When your ears receive sound, the information is transferred to the auditory (or hearing) area of your cortex.

The thalamus plays an active role in integrating information from various senses and may be involved in learning and memory (Crosson, 1999). Injury to the thalamus can cause deafness, blindness, or loss of any other sense (except smell). This suggests that some analysis of sensory messages may occur here. Because the thalamus is the major sensory relay area to the cerebral cortex, damage or abnormalities also might cause the cortex to misinterpret or not receive vital sensory information. For example, research using brain-imaging techniques links abnormalities in the thalamus to schizophrenia (Andreasen, 1999, 2000; Hazlett et al., 2000; Omori et al., 2000). Schizophrenia is a serious psychological disorder characterized by problems with sensory filtering and perception. Can you see how a defective thalamus might produce characteristics of schizophrenia, such as hallucinations and delusion?

The Hypothalamus

Beneath the thalamus lies the **hypothalamus** (*hypo-* means "under"). Although no larger than a kidney bean, it has been called the "master control center" for emotions and many basic motives such as hunger, thirst, sex, and aggression (Fulton, Woodside, & Shizgal, 2000; Meston & Frohlich, 2000). Its general function is regulation of the body's internal environment, including temperature control, which it accomplishes by regulating the endocrine system. Hanging down from the hypothalamus, the *pituitary gland* is usually considered the master endocrine gland because it releases hormones that activate the other endocrine glands. The hypothalamus influences the pituitary through direct neural connections and by releasing its own hormones into the blood supply of the pituitary.

Despite its relatively small size, the hypothalamus influences important aspects of behavior either *directly*, by generating some behaviors itself, or *indirectly* by controlling parts of the autonomic nervous system (ANS) and endocrine system. An example of its direct effects are found when animals exhibit increased or decreased eating and drinking patterns depending on what area of the hypothalamus is affected. The indirect effects of the hypothalamus are seen in the interaction of stress and the ANS.

The Limbic System

The **limbic system** is an interconnected group of structures located roughly along the border between the cerebral cortex and the lower-level brain structures (hence the term *limbic*, which means "edge" or "border"). The limbic system includes the *fornix,*

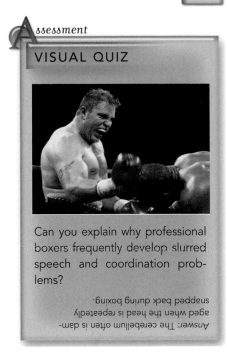

Thalamus [THAL-uh-muss] *A brain structure at the top of the brainstem that relays sensory messages to the cerebral cortex*

Hypothalamus [hi-poh-THAL-uh-muss] *A small brain structure beneath the thalamus that maintains the body's internal environment and regulates emotions and drives, such as hunger, thirst, sex, and aggression*

Limbic System *An interconnected group of lower-level brain structures involved with the arousal and regulation of emotion, motivation, memory, and many other aspects of behavior and mental processes*

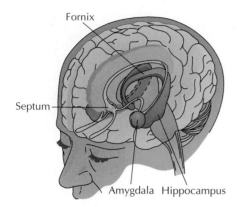

Fornix

Septum

Amygdala   Hippocampus

Figure 6.2 *The major brain structures associated with the limbic system.*

Amygdala [uh-MIG-dull-uh] *An almond-shaped lower-level brain structure that is part of the limbic system and is involved in emotion*

the *hippocampus*, the *amygdala*, and the *septum* (Figure 6.2). Scientists disagree about which structures should be included in the limbic system, and many also include the hypothalamus, parts of the thalamus, and parts of the cerebral cortex.

Recent research studying the fornix and hippocampus suggests that they, along with the amygdala, are involved in the formation of new and short-term memories (Chin, 2000; Giovagnoli, 2001; McGaugh, 2000). However, the major focus of interest in the limbic system, and particularly the **amygdala,** has been its production and regulation of emotional behavior, particularly aggression and fear. Research on cats and rats shows that stimulating the amygdala increases aggressive behavior, and research on the human amygdala demonstrates its role in aggression and violence, as well as the learning and expression of fear and the ability to recognize fear in the faces of others (Adolphs, Tranel, & Damasio, 1998; Cahill, Vazdarjanova, & Setlow, 2000; Davidson, Putnam, & Larson, 2000; Schmolck & Squire, 2001).

Perhaps one of the best-known functions of the limbic system is its role in pleasure or reward. James Olds and Peter Milner (1954) were the first to note that electrically stimulating certain areas of the limbic system caused a "pleasure" response in rats. The feeling was apparently so rewarding that the rats would cross electrified grids, swim through water (which they normally avoid), and press a lever thousands of times until they collapsed from exhaustion — just to have this area of their brains stimulated. Follow-up studies found somewhat similar responses in other animals and even among human volunteers (e.g., Dackis & O'Brien, 2001). Modern research suggests that brain stimulation may activate neurotransmitters rather than discrete "pleasure centers."

Keep in mind that even though limbic system structures and neurotransmitters are instrumental in emotional behavior, emotion in humans is also tempered by the cerebral cortex, especially the frontal lobes. As the case of Phineas Gage shows, damage to the frontal lobes, which have neural connections to the amygdala and other parts of the limbic system, can permanently impair social and emotional behavior. This is yet another example of the inseparable interconnectivity of the entire brain.

Assessment

VISUAL QUIZ

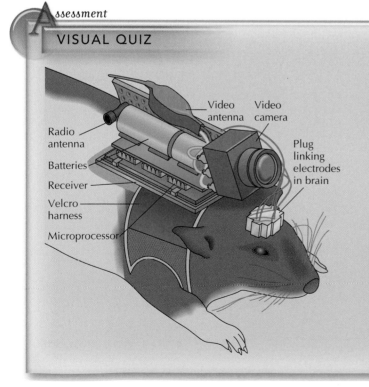

Radio antenna

Batteries

Receiver

Velcro harness

Microprocessor

Video antenna   Video camera

Plug linking electrodes in brain

In May 2002, a Brooklyn-based research team (Talwar et al., 2002) announced an ingenious technical breakthrough — "roborats." These live animals navigate complex terrain at the will of controllers at laptop computers more than 500 yards away (Dorfman, 2002). These "roborats" are important because researchers believe they may someday be sent into collapsed buildings to find survivors or for land-mine detection. The research itself also might lead to methods for artificial stimulation of brain regions that could bypass damaged nerves in paralyzed people.

Why do these rats respond to remote control? As you can see in the diagram, researchers implanted electrodes in the rat's brain that were connected to radio transmitters and miniature TV cameras. The researchers then sent electrical signals to the rat's brain to encourage them to turn right, left, or go straight ahead. When the rats responded correctly, they were rewarded with stimulation of their pleasure centers. Can you identify what area of the brain contains these pleasure centers?

Answer: The limbic center (or more specifically, the medial forebrain bundle).

CHECK & REVIEW

Lower-Level Brain Structures

The most important lower-level brain structures are the brainstem, cerebellum, thalamus, hypothalamus, and limbic system. The **brainstem** controls automatic functions such as heartbeat and breathing; the cerebellum contributes to balance, muscle coordination, and some higher mental operations. Parts of the brain stem (the **pons, medulla,** and **midbrain**) are involved in sleeping, waking, dreaming, and control of automatic bodily functions. The **reticular formation** screens incoming information and arouses the cortex. The **cerebellum** maintains smooth movement, balance, and some aspects of perception and cognition. The **thalamus** is the major incoming sensory relay area of the brain. The **hypothalamus** is involved in emotion and in drives associated with survival, such as regulation of body temperature, thirst, hunger, sex, and aggression. The **limbic system** is a group of brain structures (including the **amygdala**) involved with emotional behavior and memory.

Questions

1. What are the three major structures within the brainstem?
2. Roadside test for drunk driving primarily test responses of the _____.
3. What is the major sensory relay area for the brain? (a) hypothalamus; (b) thalamus; (c) cortex; (d) hindbrain?
4. Why is the amygdala a major focus of interest for researchers?

Answers to Questions can be found in Appendix B.

■ The Cerebral Cortex: The Center of "Higher" Processing

Above the lower-level brain structures, such as the brainstem, thalamus, and limbic system, lie the two *cerebral hemispheres*, the outer surface of which is called the **cerebral cortex.** (The word *cortex* means "bark," and the cerebral cortex surrounds most of the brain like the bark on a tree.) In general, the right hemisphere is in charge of the left side of the body, whereas the left hemisphere controls the right side of the body (Figure 6.3). We will later discuss how the two hemispheres have somewhat different tasks and special functions.

If you were able to open your skull and look inside at your own brain, you would note that the two hemispheres, each slightly larger than a clenched fist, take up most of the space. They balloon out and cover most of the lower-level structures from view. The thin surface layer of the cerebral hemispheres (the cortex) contains approximately 30 billion neurons and nine times as many glial cells. If the cortex of both hemispheres were spread out, it would cover an area almost the size of a standard newspaper page. How does all this material fit inside our skull? Imagine crumpling the newspaper sheet into a loose ball. You would retain the same surface area but in a much smaller space. The cortex contains numerous "wrinkles" (called *convolutions*), which allow it to hold billions of neurons in the restricted space of the skull.

Each of the two cerebral hemispheres is divided into four areas, or *lobes:* frontal (behind your forehead), parietal (at the top and to the rear of your skull), temporal (in the "temple" region above your ears), and occipital (at the back of your head). Divisions of these lobes are marked by prominent folds, which provide convenient geographic landmarks (Figure 6.4). Like the lower-level brain parts discussed earlier, each lobe specializes in somewhat different tasks — another example of *localization of function.* At the same time, some functions overlap between lobes. As we describe each lobe and its functions, you may want to refer frequently to Figure 6.4.

The Frontal Lobes

By far the largest of the cortical lobes, the **frontal lobes** are located at the top front portion of the two brain hemispheres — right behind your forehead. The frontal lobes receive and coordinate messages from the other three lobes of the cortex and are responsible for at least three additional major functions:

How does the cortex control behavior and mental processes?

Cerebral Cortex *The bumpy, convoluted area on the outside surface of the two cerebral hemispheres that regulates most complex behavior, including receiving sensations, motor control, and higher mental processes*

Frontal Lobes *Cortical lobes at the front of the brain, which govern motor control, speech production, and higher functions, such as thinking, personality, emotion, and memory*

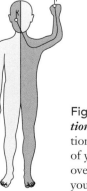

Figure 6.3 *Information crossover.* Information from the left side of your body crosses over to the right half of your brain.

Figure 6.4 *The cerebral cortex*. This is a view of the brain's left hemisphere with its four lobes, the frontal, parietal, temporal, and occipital, along with their major functions.

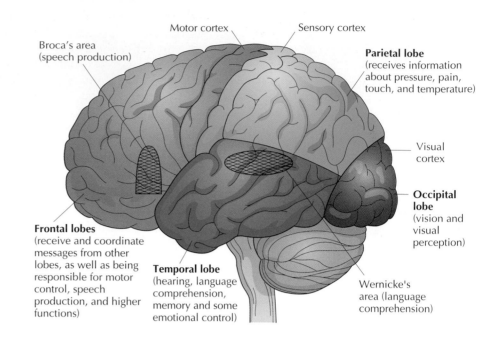

Motor cortex

Sensory cortex

Broca's area (speech production)

Parietal lobe (receives information about pressure, pain, touch, and temperature)

Visual cortex

Occipital lobe (vision and visual perception)

Frontal lobes (receive and coordinate messages from other lobes, as well as being responsible for motor control, speech production, and higher functions)

Temporal lobe (hearing, language comprehension, memory and some emotional control)

Wernicke's area (language comprehension)

1. ***Motor control.*** At the very back of the frontal lobes lies the *motor cortex*, which sends messages to the various muscles and glands in the body. All neural signals that instigate voluntary movement originate here. For instance, when you reach out to choose a candy bar from a vending machine, it is the motor control area of the frontal lobes that guides your hand in pulling the proper lever.

2. ***Speech production.*** In the *left* frontal lobe, on the surface of the brain near the bottom of the motor control area, lies *Broca's area*, which is known to play a crucial role in speech production. In 1865, French physician Paul Broca was the first to discover that patients with damage to this area had great difficulty speaking but could comprehend written or spoken language. This type of aphasia (or impaired language ability) has come to be known as *Broca's aphasia*.

3. ***Higher functions.*** Most functions that distinguish humans from other animals, such as thinking, personality, emotion, and memory, are controlled primarily by the frontal lobes. Abnormalities in the frontal lobes are often observed in patients with schizophrenia. And as the story of Phineas Gage shows, damage to the frontal lobe affects motivation, drives, creativity, self-awareness, initiative, and reasoning. Damage in this area also affects emotional behavior.

A modern day Phineas Gage? Construction worker Travis Bogumill was accidentally shot in the head with a nail gun. Like Phineas Gage, he was able to walk and talk immediately after the accident but also suffered some damage to his frontal lobes. The X-ray at the right shows the 3¹/₄-inch nail that was removed from his brain.

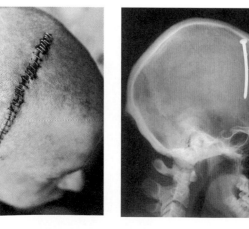

Using advanced research techniques, Hanna Damasio and her colleagues (1994) constructed computer images of Gage's brain, which showed the tamping iron most likely destroyed frontal lobe areas governing emotional control, social behavior, and decision-making. As Gage's case and other research indicates, what makes us uniquely human and what makes up our individual personalities is regulated by our frontal lobes.

A recent case reminiscent of Phineas Gage's experience also suggests that a person's short-term or "working memory" is located in the frontal lobes. In 1998, a construction worker named Travis Bogumill was accidentally shot in the head with a nail gun. The nail entered the right side of his brain near the rear of the frontal lobe. Like Gage, Bogumill was able to walk and talk after the accident. The nail was removed and, so far, Bogumill seems to be doing well. The only damage seems to be an impaired ability to perform complex mathematical problems in his head. Before the accident, Bogumill was able to easily multiply two-digit numbers in his head. After the accident, he was barely able to multiply two-digit numbers with a paper and pencil. This case supports other experimental research that shows that the frontal lobes and the working memory are responsible for reasoning, problem solving, mathematical calculation, and thinking about future rewards or actions (Giovagnoli, 2001; Hazlett, 2000; Koechlin, Basso, Pietrini, Panzer, & Grafman, 1999; O'Doherty, Kringelbach, Rolls, Hornak, & Andrews, 2001).

Parietal Lobes

At the top of the brain just behind the frontal lobes are the **parietal lobes,** the seat of body sensations and much of our memory about our environment. At the front of the parietal lobes is the *somatosensory cortex*, which receives information about pressure, pain, touch, and temperature. When you step on a sharp nail, you quickly (and reflexively) withdraw your foot because the messages travel directly to and from your spinal cord. However, you don't experience "pain" until the neural messages reach the parietal lobes of the brain.

As you can see in Figure 6.6, the more sensitive a body part is, the greater the area of sensory cortex devoted to it. Note how the face and hands receive the largest share of cortical tissue. These areas are much more sensitive than the rest of the body and require more precise control. Note also that the greater the area of motor cortex, the finer the motor control.

The Temporal Lobes

The **temporal lobes** (Latin for "pertaining to the temples") are found on the sides of the brain right above your ears. Their major functions are auditory perception (hearing), language comprehension, memory, and some emotional control. An area called the *auditory cortex* (which processes sound) is located at the top front of each temporal lobe. Incoming sensory information from the ears is processed in this area and then sent to the parietal lobes, where it is combined with visual and other body sensation information.

Parietal [puh-RYE-uh-tuhl] Lobes *Cortical lobes at the top of the brain where bodily sensations are interpreted*

Temporal Lobes *Cortical lobes above the ears involved in audition (hearing), language comprehension, memory, and some emotional control*

The motor and somatosensory cortex. The exaggerated size of the hands and mouth reflects the amount of cortex that is dedicated to them.

TRY THIS

YOURSELF

*A*pplication

Would you like a quick way to understand both your motor cortex and your sensory cortex?

1. *Motor cortex.* Try wiggling each of your fingers one at a time. Now try wiggling each of your toes. Note on Figure 6.6 how the area of your motor cortex is much larger for your fingers than for your toes, which correlates with your greater sensitivity and precise control in your fingers.
2. *Somatosensory cortex.* Ask a friend to close his or her eyes. Using a random number of fingers (one to four), press down on the skin of your friend's back for 1 or 2 seconds and ask your friend to report how many fingers you are using. Now repeat the same procedure on the palm or back of your friend's hand. Your friend should do much better with guessing when you're pressing on his or her hand than on his or her back. Again as in Figure 6.6, the area of the somatosensory cortex is much larger for the hands than for the back, which reflects more sensitivity and higher accuracy in detecting the finger pressure on the hand.

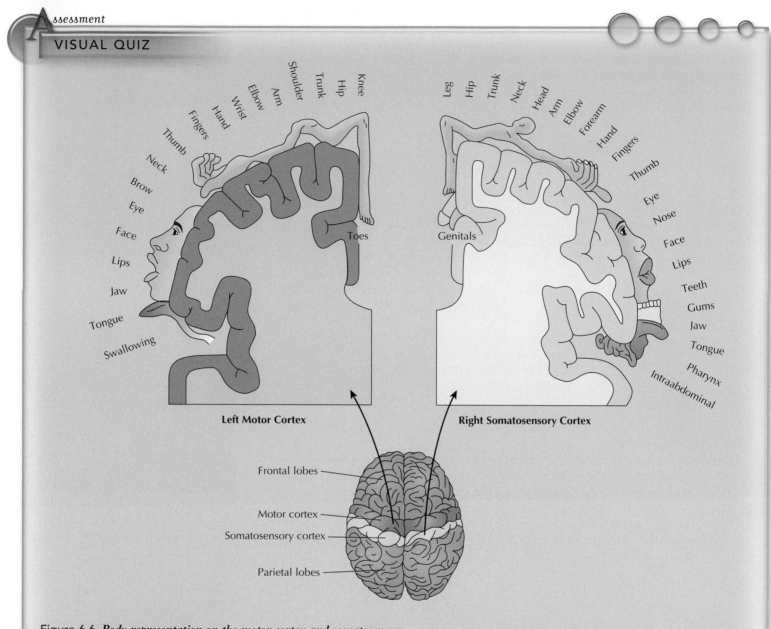

Figure 6.6 *Body representation on the motor cortex and somatosensory cortex.* This drawing represents a vertical cross-section taken from the left hemisphere's motor cortex and right hemisphere's somatosensory cortex. The amount of cortex devoted to a specific body part is depicted by the oddly shaped human figures draped around the outside edge of the cortex. Can you explain why the hands and the face on this drawing are so large, and why the proportions might be different in different animals?

Answer: The larger size of the hands and face reflects the larger cortical area necessary for the precise motor control and greater sensitivity humans need in our hands and faces. In other animals, the proportions are different. Spider monkeys, for example, have large areas of their motor and somatosensory cortices devoted to their tails, which they use like another arm and hand.

An area of the *left* temporal lobe, *Wernicke's area*, is involved in language comprehension. About a decade after Broca's discovery, German neurologist Carl Wernicke noted that patients with damage in this area could not understand what they read or heard, but they could speak quickly and easily. However, their speech was often unintelligible because it contained made-up words, like *chipecke*, sound substitutions (*girl* became *curl*), and word substitutions (*bread* became *cake*). This syndrome is now referred to as *Wernicke's aphasia*. (Study tip: Remember that *Broca's area* in the left frontal lobes is responsible for *speech* production, whereas *Wernicke's area* in the left temporal lobe is involved in *language* comprehension.)

Occipital Lobes

As the name implies, the **occipital lobes** (Latin for *ob*, "in back of," and *caput*, "head") are located at the lower back of the brain. Among other things, the occipital lobes are responsible for vision and visual perception. Damage to the occipital lobe can produce blindness, even though the eyes and their neural connection to the brain are perfectly healthy. The occipital lobes are also involved in shape, color, and motion perception.

Occipital [ahk-SIP-uh-tuhl] Lobes *Cortical lobes at the back of the brain responsible for vision and visual perception*

Association Areas

Thus far, we have focused on relatively small areas of the four lobes of the cortex that have specific functions. If a surgeon electrically stimulated the parietal lobe area of your brain, you would most likely report physical sensations, such as feeling touch, pressure, and so on. On the other hand, if the surgeon stimulated your occipital lobe, you would see flashes of light or color.

Surprisingly, most areas of your cortex, if stimulated, produce nothing at all. These so-called quiet sections are not dormant, however. They are clearly involved in interpreting, integrating, and acting on information processed by other parts of the brain. Thus, these collective "quiet areas" are aptly called **association areas** because they *associate* various areas and functions of the brain. The association areas in the frontal lobe, for example, help in decision making and planning. Similarly, the association area right in front of the motor cortex is involved in the planning of voluntary movement.

Association Areas *So-called quiet areas in the cerebral cortex involved in interpreting, integrating, and acting on information processed by other parts of the brain*

As you recall from Module 1, one of the most popular myths in psychology is that we use only 10 percent of our brain. This myth might have begun with early research on association areas of the brain. Given that approximately three-fourths of the cortex is "uncommitted" (with no precise, specific function responsive to electrical brain stimulation), researchers might have mistakenly assumed that these areas were nonfunctional.

■ Two Brains in One? A House Divided

As mentioned earlier, the two cerebral hemispheres control opposite sides of the body. Each hemisphere also has separate areas of specialization. (This is another example of *localization of function*, yet it is technically referred to as **lateralization.**)

By the mid-1800s, early researchers had discovered that the left and right hemispheres carry out different tasks. In addition to mapping the brain and nervous system, they also noted that injury to one side of the brain produced paralysis or loss of sensation on the opposite side of the body. Also around this same time, case studies like Phineas Gage's documented that accidents, strokes, and tumors in the left hemisphere generally led to problems with language, reading, writing, speaking, arithmetic reasoning, and other higher mental processes. The "silent" right hemisphere came to be viewed as the "subordinate" or "nondominant" half, lacking special functions or abilities.

Lateralization *Specialization of the left and right hemispheres of the brain for particular operations*

Split-Brain Research

In the 1960s, this portrayal of the left and right hemispheres as dominant and subordinate players began to change as a result of landmark research with **split-brain** patients.

The two cerebral hemispheres are normally connected at several places, but the primary connection between the left and right halves is a thick, ribbon-like band of nerve fibers under the cortex called the **corpus callosum.** (See Figure 6.7.)

Split-Brain *A surgical separation of the brain's two hemispheres used medically to treat severe epilepsy; split-brain patients provide data on the functions of the two hemispheres*

Corpus Callosum [CORE-puss] [cah-LOH-suhm] *Bundle of nerve fibers connecting the brain's left and right hemispheres*

Figure 6.7 *Crisscrossing of visual information.* (a) Imagine this as a drawing of your brain, and that you are being asked to stare straight ahead. Note how visual images from the left half of each of your two eyes connect only to the right half of your brain; whereas images from the right half of each eye connect to the left half. The information received by either hemisphere is transmitted across your corpus callosum to the other side. (b) When the corpus callosum is cut, however, the "split-brain" patient does not receive the normally shared information.

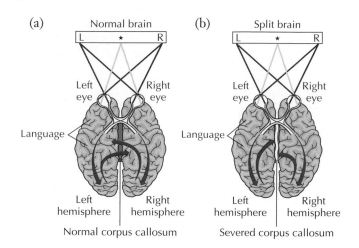

In some cases of *severe* epilepsy, surgeons cut the corpus callosum to stop the spread of epileptic seizures from one hemisphere to the other. Given that brain surgery is a radical and permanent procedure, such an operation is always a last resort and is performed only when patients' conditions have not responded to other forms of treatment. However, the results are generally successful — epileptic seizures are reduced and sometimes disappear entirely.

Split-brain patients also provide an unintended, dramatic side benefit to scientific research. Because this operation cuts the only direct communication link between the two hemispheres, it reveals what each half of the brain can do when it is quite literally cut off from the other. Although relatively few split-brain operations have been conducted since 1961, the resulting research has profoundly improved our understanding of how the two halves of the brain function. In fact, in 1981 Roger Sperry received a Nobel Prize in physiology/medicine for his split-brain research.

How do these patients function after the split-brain surgery? The surgery does create a few unusual responses. For example, one split-brain patient reported that when he dressed himself, he sometimes pulled his pants down with his left hand and up with his right (Gazzaniga, 2000). However, patients generally show very few outward changes in their behavior, other than fewer epileptic seizures. If you met and talked with a split-brain patient, you probably wouldn't even know he or she had had the operation. In fact, one famous psychologist, Karl Lashley, joked that the corpus callosum's only function is to keep the two hemispheres from sagging (Gazzaniga, 1995).

The subtle changes in split-brain patients normally appear only with specialized testing. For example, when a split-brain patient is asked to stare straight ahead while a photo of a fork is flashed to his left visual field, he cannot name it, although he can point to a similar photo with his left hand. Can you explain why?

To answer this question, you need to understand two major points about your brain. First, as you know, the left hemisphere receives and sends messages from and to the right side of the body, and vice versa. However, vision is different. Your eyes connect to your brain in such a way that, when you look straight ahead, the left half of your field of vision sends an image through both eyes to your right hemisphere (Figure 6.8). Likewise, the right side of your visual field is transmitted only to your left hemisphere.

Assuming you don't have a split-brain, if information were presented only to your right hemisphere, it would be quickly sent to your left hemisphere — where the speech center could name it. However, when the corpus callosum is split and experimenters present an image to only the left visual field, information cannot be transferred from the right hemisphere to the left. Thus, the patient cannot say what he saw, but he can point to a photo of the same object with his left hand. (Figure 6.9 offers a further example of split-brain testing.)

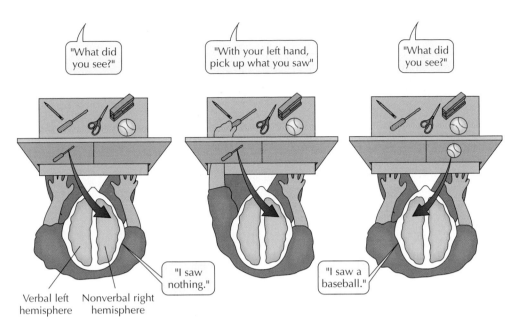

Verbal left hemisphere Nonverbal right hemisphere

Figure 6.8 Split-brain research. When a split-brain patient stares straight ahead and a picture of a screw driver is flashed only to the left visual field, the information goes only to the nonverbal right hemisphere, and he cannot name what he saw. However, when asked to "pick up what you saw," his left hand can touch the items hidden behind the screen and easily identify the screwdriver. This shows that the right hemisphere received the photo image of the screwdriver, but the patient could not name it because the information did not travel across the severed corpus callosum to the left hemisphere where language is normally processed. Note when the image of a baseball is presented to the left hemisphere, the patient easily names it. Can you see why split-brain research is so important to brain researchers interested in studying the various functions of the two hemispheres?

Keep in mind that split-brain surgery is a last resort medical treatment, which reduces the severity of epileptic seizures and generally has few effects on everyday functioning. An unexpected benefit of this surgery is that it has allowed researchers to demonstrate the functional specialization of each hemisphere (Schiffer, Zaidel, Bogen, & Chasan-Taber, 1998).

Hemispheric Specialization

Dozens of studies on split-brain patients, and newer research on people whose brains are intact, have documented several differences between the two brain hemispheres (summarized in Figure 6.9). In general, for roughly 95 percent of all adults, the left hemisphere is specialized not only for language functions (speaking, reading, writing, and understanding language) but also for analytical functions, such as mathematics. In contrast, the right hemisphere is specialized primarily for nonverbal abilities, including art and musical abilities and perceptual and spatiomanipulative skills, such as maneuvering through space, drawing or building geometric designs, working jigsaw puzzles, building model cars, painting pictures, and recognizing faces (Franz, Waldie, & Smith, 2000; Gazzaniga, 1970, 1995, 2000; Keenan, Nelson, O'Connor, & Pascual-Leone, 2001; Zaidel, 1985, 1998). Research with fMRI imaging suggests that the right hemisphere also may contribute to complex language comprehension (Knecht et al., 2002; Robertson et al., 2000).

In another study, a team of researchers led by Fredric Schiffer (1998) at McLean Hospital in Massachusetts reported that different aspects of personality appear in the different hemispheres. In one patient, the right hemisphere seemed more disturbed by childhood memories of being bullied than did the left. In another patient, the right

Figure 6.9 *Functions of the left and right hemispheres.* The left hemisphere specializes in verbal and analytical functions, whereas the right hemisphere focuses on nonverbal abilities, such as spatiomanipulative skills, art and musical abilities, and visual recognition tasks.

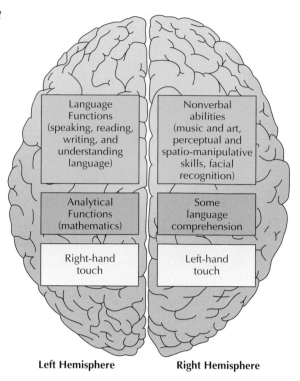

Left Hemisphere   **Right Hemisphere**

hemisphere seemed to regard the patient more positively, while also feeling more negative emotions such as loneliness and sadness (Schiffer, Zaidel, Bogen, & Chasan-Taber, 1998).

Is this left and right brain specialization reversed in left-handed people? Not necessarily. About 68 percent of left-handers (people who use their left hands to write, hammer a nail, and throw a ball) and 97 percent of right-handers have their major language areas on the left hemisphere. This suggests that even though the right side of the brain is dominant for movement in left-handers, other types of skills are often localized in the same brain areas as for right-handers.

TRY THIS

YOURSELF

Application

Would you like a demonstration of the specialized functions of your own two hemispheres? Some research suggests that the eyes tend to move to the right when a mental task involves the left hemisphere and to the left when the task involves the right hemisphere (see Kinsbourne, 1972). Read the following questions to a friend and record whether his or her eyes move to the right or to the left as he or she ponders the answers. Try to keep the monitoring of your friend's eye movements as natural as possible.

1. Define the word *neuroscience*.
2. What is a function of the corpus callosum?
3. What structure of the brain is located right above the pituitary gland?

4. If you are on top of the brain and traveling straight down, what is directly below the parietal lobes?

The first two questions involve language skills and the left hemisphere, which should produce more eye movement to the right. Questions 3 and 4 require spatial reasoning and the right hemisphere, which should elicit more eye movement to the left.

Try the same test on at least four other friends or family members. You'll note two major points: (1) cerebral lateralization is a matter of degree — not all or nothing, and (2) individual differences do exist, especially among left-handers.

Although left-handers are generally penalized for living in a right-handed world, there may be some benefits to being left-handed. For example, history shows that a disproportionate number of lefties have achieved greatness in art, music, sports, and architecture, including Leonardo da Vinci, Michelangelo, Picasso, and M. C. Escher. Because the right hemisphere is superior at imagery and visualizing three-dimensional objects, it may help to use the left hand for drawing, painting, or drafting (Springer & Deutsch, 1998). Moreover, left-handers tend to recover better from strokes that damage the language areas in the brain, which may be because the nonspeech hemisphere in left-handers is better able to compensate (Geschwind, 1979).

The Myth of the "Neglected Right Brain"

Courses and books directed at "right-brain thinking" and "drawing on the right side of the brain" often promise to increase your intuition, creativity, and artistic abilities by waking up your neglected and underused right brain (e.g., Bragdon & Gamon, 1999; Edwards, 1999). This myth of the neglected right brain arose from popularized accounts of split-brain patients and exaggerated claims and unwarranted conclusions about differences between the left and right hemispheres.

The fact is that the two hemispheres work together in a coordinated, integrated way, with each making important contributions. If you are a married student with small children, you can easily understand this principle. Just as you and your partner often "specialize" in different jobs (one giving the kids their baths, the other washing the dinner dishes), the hemispheres also divide their workload. However, both parents and both hemispheres are generally aware of what the other "half" is doing.

In our tour of the nervous system, the principles of *localization of function* and *specialization* are common — dendrites receive information, the occipital lobe specializes in vision, and so on. However, it's important to remember that all parts of the brain and nervous system play overlapping and synchronized roles.

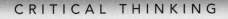

Application

CRITICAL THINKING

Understanding Central Nervous System Anatomy and Function

Being able to define a term or concept doesn't necessarily mean you fully comprehend it. The following exercise will help clarify your understanding of brain terminology and function. It also provides a model for the types of questions that lead to critical thinking.

Situation #1

A neurosurgeon is about to perform brain surgery. The surgeon stimulates (touches with an electrode) a tiny portion of the patient's brain, and the patient's right finger moves. After noting the reaction, the surgeon stimulates a portion of the brain a short distance away and the patient's right thumb moves.

Questions to Answer

1. What section of the brain has been stimulated? In which lobe of the brain is this section found?

2. Which hemisphere of the brain is being stimulated?

3. During this stimulation, would the patient experience pain? Why or why not?

Situation #2

The scene: An emergency room in a hospital. Two doctors are talking about a car crash victim who has just been wheeled in.

First Doctor: "Good grief! The whole cerebral cortex is severely damaged; we'll have to remove the entire area."

Second Doctor: "We can't do that. If we remove all that tissue, the patient will die in a matter of minutes."

First Doctor: "Where did you get your medical training — watching *General Hospital*? The patient won't die if we remove his whole cerebral cortex."

Second Doctor: "I resent your tone and insinuation. I went to one of the finest medical schools, and I'm telling you the

ACTIVE LEARNING

patient will die if we remove his whole cerebral cortex."

Questions to Answer

1. If the whole cerebral cortex is removed, will the patient die? Explain your answer.

2. If the patient were kept alive without a cerebral cortex, what kinds of behaviors or responses would be possible? What changes would you expect in personality, memories, and emotions?

3. What behaviors could be expected with only the subcortex, medulla, and spinal cord intact? What if only the medulla and spinal cord were functioning? Only the spinal cord?

4. If a patient could be kept alive without a cerebral cortex, would life be worth living? How much of your brain would have to be removed before you would rather die?

Achievement

R E S E A R C H   H I G H L I G H T

Rewiring, Repairing, and Transplanting Brains and Spinal Cords

Imagine being completely paralyzed and unable to speak. Each year, thousands of people suffer serious brain and spinal cord injuries, and until recently, these injuries were considered permanent and beyond medical help. Scientists have long believed that after the first 2 or 3 years of life humans and most animals lack the capacity to repair or replace damaged neurons in the brain or spinal cord. Though nerves in the *peripheral* nervous system sometimes repair and regenerate themselves, it was accepted doctrine that this could not occur in the *central* nervous system.

Thanks in part to recent research, this dogma has been overturned. We now know the human brain is capable of lifelong *neuroplasticity* and *neurogenesis*. Let's begin with **neuroplasticity.** Rather than being a solid

Can adult brains grow new neurons? Neuroscientists once believed that each of us was born with all the brain cells we would ever have, but Fred Gage and others have shown that neurons are renewed throughout our life span.

fixed organ, your brain is capable of changing its structure and function in response to changing environmental conditions (Cotman & Bechtold, 2002; D'sa & Duman, 2002; Reid & Stewart, 2001). Although the basic brain organization (cerebellum, cortex, and so on) is irreversibly established well before birth, the details are subject to revision. As you're learning a new sport or foreign language, for example, your brain changes and "rewires" itself. New synapses form and others disappear. Some dendrites grow longer and sprout new branches, whereas others are "pruned" away. This is what makes our brains so wonderfully adaptive.

Remarkably, this rewiring has even helped "remodel" the brain following strokes. For example, psychologist Edward Taub and his colleagues (2002) have had success with constraint-induced (CI) movement therapy in stroke patients. Immobilizing the unaffected ("good") arm (or leg) of the patient has restored function in some patients as long as 21 years after their strokes. Rather than coddling the affected arm, Taub requires rigorous and repetitive exercise, which he believes causes intact parts of the brain to take over for the stroke-damaged areas. In effect, Taub "recruits" intact brain cells.

Other scientists researching Alzheimer's disease suggest "rerouting" neurons around damaged areas of the brain (Begley, 2000). This treatment would be analogous to an electrician's wiring a shunt around the damaged part of an electrical circuit.

Obviously, there are limits to neuroplasticity. Even with the best "rewiring," most of us will never become another Tiger Woods or Albert Einstein. However, the fact that our brains continually reorganize themselves throughout our lives has enormous implications.

Perhaps the most dazzling recent finding is **neurogenesis** — the production of nerve cells. Until very recently, it was believed that we are born with all the neurons we'll ever have. Life was a slow process of dying neurons and increasing loss of brain tissue.

Today, however, we know that 80-year-olds have just as many neurons as 20-year-olds. Although we do lose hundreds of cells each day, our brains also replenish themselves with *new* cells that originate deep within the brain and migrate to become part of the brain's circuitry.

The source of these newly created cells is neural **stem cells** — rare, precursor

Stem cell research and Parkinson's disease. A fetal graft implanted in the brain of a Parkinson's patient 10 years ago still produces significant levels of dopamine (the brain scan on the left). Note, however, that the activity of this area of the brain is still below that of the normal brain on the right.

Neuroplasticity *The brain's ability to reorganize and change its structure and function throughout the life span*

Neurogenesis [nue-roh-JEN-uh-sis] *The division and differentiation of nonneuronal cells to produce neurons*

Stem Cell *Precursor (immature) cells that give birth to new specialized cells; a stem cell holds all the information it needs to make bone, blood, brain — any part of a human body — and can also copy itself to maintain a stock of stem cells*

("immature") cells that can grow and develop into any type of cell depending on the chemical signals they receive as they grow (Gage, 2000; Kempermann, 2002; Reh, 2002; Song, Stevens, & Gage, 2002; Svendsen, 2002).

Until now, physicians have used stem cells for bone marrow transplants, but many more clinical applications have already begun. For example, clinical trials using stem cells to repopulate or replace cells devastated by injury or disease have helped patients suffering from strokes, Alzheimer's, Parkinson's, epilepsy, stress, and depression (Jones, 2002; Kim et al., 2002; McKay et al., 2002; Qu, Brannen, Kim, & Sugaya, 2001; Wickelgren, 2002).

Does this mean that people paralyzed from spinal cord injuries might be able to walk again? At this point, neurogenesis in the brain and spinal cord is minimal, but one possible bridge might be transplanting embryonic stem cells in the damaged area of the spinal cord. In research with rats, researchers have transplanted mouse embryonic stem cells into a damaged rat spinal cord (McDonald et al., 1999). When the damaged spinal cord was viewed several weeks later, the implanted cells had survived and spread throughout the injured spinal cord area. More important, the transplant rats also showed some movement in previously paralyzed parts of their bodies. Medical researchers have also begun human trials using nerve grafts to repair damaged spinal cords (Lopez, 2002; Saltus, 2000).

Although it is unwise to raise unrealistic hopes, we are making remarkable breakthroughs in neuroscience. The rewiring, repairing, and transplanting we discussed in this section are just a small part of what was discovered in the last 10 years. Can you imagine what the next step (or the next decade) might bring?

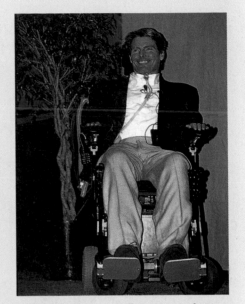

Is paralysis permanent? Recent research on neurogenesis and neuroplasticity may provide hope for actor Christopher Reeve who was paralyzed in a horse riding accident and for other people with serious medical conditions.

Assessment

CHECK & REVIEW

The Cerebral Cortex and Hemispheric Specialization

The left and right cerebral hemispheres of the brain take up most of the room inside the skull. The outer covering of the hemispheres, the **cerebral cortex,** is divided into four lobes. The **frontal lobes** control movement and speech and are involved with self-awareness and planning ahead. The **parietal lobes** are the receiving area for sensory information. The **temporal lobes** are concerned with hearing and language. The **occipital lobes** are dedicated to vision and visual information processing.

The two hemispheres of the brain are linked by the **corpus callosum,** through which they communicate and coordinate. However, **split-brain** research shows that each hemisphere does perform somewhat separate functions. In most people, the left hemisphere is dominant in verbal skills, such as speaking and writing, and also for analytical tasks. The right hemisphere appears to excel at nonverbal tasks, such as spatio-manipulative skills, art and music, and visual recognition.

Recent research shows the brain can reorganize and change its structure and function throughout the lifespan (**neuroplasticity),** and create new nerve cells (**neurogenesis**) from **stem cells.**

Questions

1. The bumpy, convoluted area making up the outside surface of the brain is the

   _____.

2. You are giving a speech. Name the cortical lobes involved in the following behaviors:
   a. Identifying faces in the audience
   b. Hearing questions from the audience
   c. Remembering where your car is parked when you're ready to go home
   d. Noticing that your new shoes are too tight and hurting your feet

3. The case of Phineas Gage suggests that the _____ lobes regulate our personality and are largely responsible for much of what makes us uniquely human. (a) frontal; (b) temporal; (c) parietal; (d) occipital

4. Although the left and right hemispheres of the brain are specialized, they are normally in close communication through the _____. (a) reciprocating circuits; (b) thalamus; (c) corpus callosum; (d) cerebellum

Answers to Questions can be found in Appendix B.

MODULE 6 ACTIVE LEARNING WORKSHEET

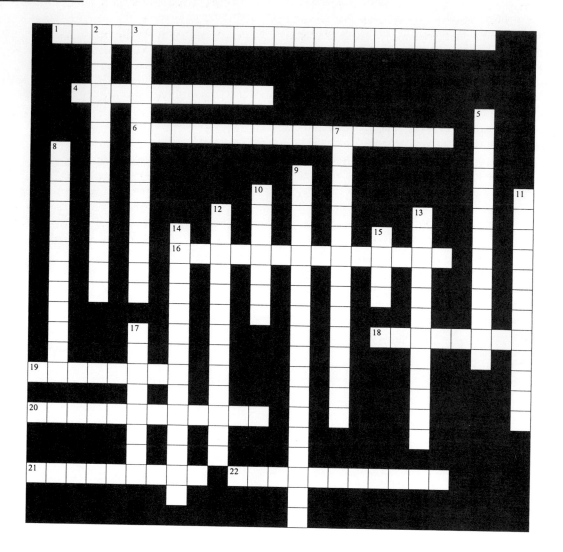

ACROSS

1 Specialization of various parts of the brain for particular functions.

4 The brain area responsible for maintaining smooth movement, balance, and some aspects of perception and cognition.

6 So-called "quiet areas" in the cerebral cortex involved in interpreting, integrating and acting on information processed by other parts of the brain.

16 Bundle of nerve fibers connecting the brain's left and right hemispheres.

18 Precursor (immature) cells that give birth to new specialized cells. A stem cell holds all the information it needs to make bone, blood, brain—any part of a human body-and can also copy itself to maintain a stock of stem cells.

19 An almond-shaped lower-level brain structure that is part of the limbic system and involved in emotion.

20 Cortical lobes in the front of the brain, which govern motor control, speech production, and higher functions, such as thinking, personality, emotion, and memory.

21 The part of the brain that begins as a continuation of the spinal cord and ends deep within the cortex; it is responsible for automatic, survival functions.

22 A surgical separation of the brain's two hemispheres used medically to treat severe epilepsy. Split-brain patients provide data on the functions of the two hemispheres.

DOWN

2 The bumpy, convoluted area on the outside surface of the two cerebral hemispheres that regulates most complex behavior, including receiving sensations, motor control, and higher mental processes.

3 Specialization of the left and right hemispheres of the brain for particular operations.

5 Cortical lobes above the ears involved in auditory (hearing), language comprehension, memory, and some emotional control.

7 The brain's ability to reorganize and change its structure and function throughout the life span.

8 An interconnected group of lower-level brain structures involved with the arousal and regulation of emotion, motivation, memory, and many other aspects of behavior and mental processes.

9 A diffuse set of neurons found in the core of the brain stem that are responsible for screening incoming information and arousing the cortex.

10 A structure in the brain stem responsible for automatic body functions such as breathing and heart rate.

11 A tiny structure in the brain that lies under the thalamus and regulates emotions and drives, such as hunger, thirst, sex, and aggression.

12 Cortical lobes at the top of the brain where bodily sensations are interpreted.

13 The division of nonneuronal cells to produce neurons.

14 Cortical lobes at the back of the brain responsible for vision and visual perception.

15 A structure located at the top of the brain stem that is involved with functions such as respiration, movement, waking, sleep, and dreaming.

17 A brain structure located on top of the brain stem that relays sensory messages to the cerebral cortex.

MODULE 7
GENETICS AND EVOLUTION

Assessment

How are heredity and evolution linked to human behavior?

Behavioral Genetics *The study of the effects of heredity on biological, behavioral, and mental processes*

Chromosome *Threadlike strands of DNA (deoxyribonucleic acid) molecules that carry genetic information*

Gene *A segment of DNA (deoxyribonucleic acid) that occupies a specific place on a particular chromosome and carries the code for hereditary transmission*

We began this unit with a look at the smallest part of the nervous system — the neuron — and then toured the structures of the brain. Now, we go backward in time to the moment of your own conception to see how *behavioral genetics* helps to explain your present adult being. Then we close this section by going even further back in history to look at the role of *evolution*.

Behavioral Genetics: How Much Can We Blame Our Parents?

A relatively new field called **behavioral genetics** has greatly increased our understanding of the relative contributions of genetic and environmental influences on behavior. Throughout this text, you will find numerous examples of how heredity contributes to various behaviors and mental processes, such as intelligence (Module 24), prenatal development (Module 25), and mental disorders (Modules 37–41). To provide a foundation for these upcoming discussions, we will explore a few basic principles of genetics and the methods used to study behavioral genetics.

Basic Principles of Genetics

Every cell in your body contains lifelong *messages* from your parents — and you thought it was just their phone calls that bothered you! At the moment of your conception, your mother contributed one set of 23 **chromosomes** and another set of 23 came from your father. Each of these 46 chromosomes is composed of a double-stranded molecule of *DNA (deoxyribonucleic acid)*, which, in turn, is made up of thousands of **genes** (Figure 7.1). Genes, the basic units of heredity, are themselves small segments of DNA. We share many of the same genes with other animals and even insects and plants. But it's the genes we share with other humans that set us apart from gorillas, spiders, and tomatoes.

Have you ever wondered why some children have blond hair if both parents have brown hair? It depends on the particular combinations of gene types inherited by the child. For most characteristics, the child inherits two genes, one from each parent. If the inherited gene is *dominant*, the trait encoded in the gene will always be expressed. If the gene is *recessive*, the trait for that gene will be expressed only if the other gene in the pair also carries the same trait. Because many people have single recessive genes that are not expressed, two brown-haired parents, who both have recessive genes for blond hair, could produce a blond-haired child.

Methods for Studying Behavioral Genetics

Beyond hair and eye color or vision, how much are you shaped by your genetic inheritance? Or by your environment? To answer these questions, researchers generally rely on four methods:

1. **Twin Studies** The study of identical (*monzygotic*) and fraternal (*dizygotic*) twins takes advantage of their increased proportion of shared genes—identical twins share 100 percent of the same genes, whereas fraternal twins (like all siblings) share, on average, 50 percent.

    Recall that each of us receives a unique combination of genes from our mothers and fathers. The only exception to this genetic uniqueness is *identical twins*— who are created when a fertilized mother's egg divides into two separate (but identical) cells. These cells then go on to produce two complete individuals with identical genetic information. *Fraternal twins*, on the other hand, occur when the mother's two separate eggs are fertilized by different sperm from the father. Although these twins share approximately the same moment of fertilization, womb

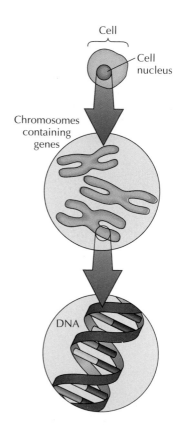

Figure 7.1 *DNA, genes, chromosomes, cell.* The nucleus of every cell in our bodies contain *genes*, which carry the code for hereditary transmission. Our genes are arranged along *chromosomes*, which are strands of paired DNA (deoxyribonucleic acid) that spiral around each other.

environment, and time of birth, they are genetically no more alike than brothers and sisters born at different times. They are simply nine-month "womb mates." However, because fraternal twins share the same developmental time period, from conception throughout most of their childhood, their study provides additional insight into the relative contributions of nature and nurture.

In contrast to identical and fraternal twin studies, which look at genetic similarity, psychologist Nancy Segal has studied "virtual twins" (pairs of unrelated siblings of the same age, one or both adopted, who have been raised together since infancy). Can you see why the study of virtual twins might be important? Because they share a common family environment but no common genes, their information can provide a valuable comparison to traditional studies of twins, which emphasize genetics and the prenatal environment (see Figure 7.2).

2. **Adoption Studies** In addition to studies of identical and fraternal twins who are occasionally adopted and reared apart, *adoption studies* also compare two other groups of relatives—biological parents and siblings ("blood relatives") and adoptive parents and siblings. Can you imagine why adoption studies are important? If adopted children more closely resemble their biological parents (and biological siblings) in personality, mental disorders, and so on, even though they were not raised in that family, then genetic factors probably had the greatest influence. On the other hand, if adopted children resemble their adopted family, even though they do not share similar genes, then environmental factors may predominate.

3. **Family Studies** If a specific trait is inherited, it should run in families—there should be increased trait similarity among biological/blood relatives. And those relatives who share more genes, like siblings or twins, should exhibit more similarity than cousins. This is why *family studies* conduct research on the genetic history of all blood relatives (siblings, parents, aunts, uncles, cousins, etc.) in great detail. For example, some research indicates mental disorders, such as schizophrenia and depression (Modules 38 and 39), run in families.

4. **Genetic Abnormalities** Research in behavioral genetics also explores disorders and diseases that result when genes malfunction. For example, an extra 21st chromosome fragment almost always causes a condition called *Down syndrome*. People with Down syndrome often have distinctive round faces, with small folds of skin across the inner edge of the eyes, and impaired psychomotor and physical development, as well as mental retardation. Abnormalities in several genes or chromosomes also are suspected factors in *Alzheimer's disease*, which involves serious brain deterioration and memory loss, and *schizophrenia*, a severe mental disorder characterized by loss of contact with reality. We will discuss these disorders in detail in upcoming modules.

Findings from these four methods have allowed behavioral geneticists to estimate the **heritability** of various traits. That is, the extent to which differences among individuals in biological, behavioral, or mental processes are determined by genetic factors, as opposed to differences in environment. If genetics contributed *nothing* to the trait, it would have a heritability estimate of 0 percent. If a trait were *completely* due to genetics, we would say it had a heritability estimate of 100 percent.

Figure 7.2 *"Virtual Twins" Julie (top) and Sara (bottom).* Traditionally, biological twins have been "the gold standard" for genetic studies, but psychologist Nancy Segal has recently studied "virtual twins" (pairs of unrelated siblings of the same age, one or both adopted, who have been raised together since infancy). Segal suggests these twins provide unique information because they share common family environment, but no common genes.

Heritability *A measure of the degree to which a characteristic is related to genetic, inherited factors*

Application
APPLYING PSYCHOLOGY TO EVERYDAY LIFE

Overcoming Genetic Misconceptions

Behavioral genetics and heritability are hot topics in modern psychology—and the general press. Each day we're bombarded with new discoveries regarding genes, and

TRY THIS

YOURSELF

Application

Can you curl your tongue lengthwise? This "ability" is one of the few traits that depends on only one dominant gene. You can increase your understanding of dominant versus recessive genes by doing a simple observation. If you can curl your tongue, one or both of your biological parents will probably also be able to curl his or her tongue — because this is a dominant trait. However, if both of your parents are "noncurlers," they both must have recessive genes for curling.

I've included this because it will help you appreciate material in upcoming sections and the world around you. When this text (or the media) talks about the heritability of intelligence, sexual orientation, or athletic abilities, you will have a deeper appreciation for, and be better able to evaluate, what is being asserted. But as you read this text and media reports, there are a few cautions to keep in mind:

1. *Genetic traits are not fixed or inflexible!* My students sometimes become unreasonably discouraged when they discover they are at increased risk for heart disease, depression, alcoholism, or other traits because of their particular biological inheritance. I reassure them (and you, Dear Reader) that even though genes may have a strong influence, your genetic inheritance says nothing about how an environmental intervention might change your individual outcome. If you inherited a possible genetic predisposition for some undesirable trait, learn all you can about this trait and investigate ways to prevent its development or minimize its effect on your life. The conclusion from behavioral genetics and all of psychology: If you don't like the outcome, change the environment. (Joke: Remember that nothing in life is 100 percent inherited—except *sex*. If your parents didn't have it, it's 100 percent sure you won't either.)

2. *Heritability estimates do not apply to individuals.* When you hear media reports that intelligence or athletic talents are 30 to 50 percent inherited, do you assume this applies to you as an individual? Do you believe that if intelligence is 50 percent inherited, then 50 percent is due to your parents and 50 percent to your environment? This is a common misconception. But these heritability statistics *describe groups, not individuals.* They are mathematical computations of the proportion of total variance in a trait that is explained by genetic variation within a *group*.

Height, for example, has one of the highest heritability estimates—around 90 percent (Plomin, 1990). However, your own personal height may be very different from your parents' or other blood relatives'. We each inherit a unique combination of genes (unless we are identical twins). Therefore, it is impossible to predict your individual height from a heritability estimate. You can only estimate for the group as a whole.

3. *Genes, individuals, and the environment are inseparable.* As first discussed in Module 1 (and throughout upcoming Modules), biological, psychological, and social forces all influence one another and are inseparable—the *biopsychosocial model*. Imagine your inherited genes as analogous to water, sugar, salt, flour, eggs, baking powder, and oil. When you mix these ingredients and pour them on a hot griddle (one environment), you get pancakes. Add more oil (a different combination of genes) and a waffle iron (a different environment), and you get waffles. With another set of ingredients and environments (different pans and an oven), you can have crepes, muffins, or cakes. How can you separate the effects of ingredients and cooking methods? You can't. Biological, psychological, and social forces all interact.

With a good heredity, nature deals you a fine hand at cards; and with a good environment, you learn to play the hand well.

WALTER C. ALVAREZ

Achievement

RESEARCH HIGHLIGHT

Why Mapping the Human Genome Is Important

Since the 1980s, an exciting, ambitious, multibillion dollar international scientific effort called the *Human Genome Project (HGP)*, led by Francis Collins, and the *International Human Genome Sequencing Consortium (IHGSC)*, led by Craig Venter, have been creating "the human book of life." Working with new, high-tech methods, these two research teams set out to map all of the estimated 100,000 genes on the human chromosome. (The full set of genes for any organism is known as the *genome*—the total DNA blueprint of heritable traits contained in every cell of the body.)

On February 12, 2001, the journals *Science* and *Nature* published the breakthrough news that the initial draft of the human genome was complete, and that humans have only about 30,000 to 40,000 genes, which compares to around 19,000 for the roundworm and 13,000 for the fruit fly (International Human Genome, 2001; Venter et al., 2001).

Although the mapping still has some holes, and sections that need redoing, researchers believe this initial draft sequence was one of the most significant landmarks of all time, comparable to landing a man on the moon or splitting the atom. Francis Collins, leader of the HGP, described the genome as a "book of life" with three volumes:

"It's a history book—a narrative of the journey of our species through time. It's a shop manual, with an incredibly detailed blueprint for building every human cell. And it's a transformational textbook of medicine, with insights that will give healthcare providers immense new powers to treat, prevent, and cure disease" (cited in Sherrid, p. 48).

Although the human genome mapping project has sparked concerns over how its information will be applied, this project is

Cracking the genetic code. J. Graig Venter and Francis Collins, lead researchers for the Human Genome Project, received joint credit for mapping the human genome. Their work is considered a monumental milestone in genetic research. Can you explain why?

making invaluable contributions to our knowledge of the hereditary basis of human biology, behavior, and disease—information that offers great promise for improving both our mental and physical health (Jegalian & Lahn, 2001; Rae-Dupree, 2002).

■ Evolutionary Psychology: Darwin Explains Behavior and Mental Processes

If you've traveled in many countries or taken courses in anthropology, your initial focus may have been on all the strange and unusual practices of other cultures. But over time, you also undoubtedly noted that people the world over seem to eat, work, play with their friends, care for their children, and fight with their enemies in remarkably similar ways. How do we explain this?

Evolutionary psychology suggests that many behavioral commonalities, from eating to fighting with our enemies, emerged and remain in human populations because they helped our ancestors (and ourselves) survive. This perspective is based on the writings of Charles Darwin (1859) who suggested that natural forces select traits that are adaptive to the organism's survival. This process of **natural selection** occurs when one particular genetic trait gives a person a reproductive advantage over others. Although some people mistakenly believe that natural selection means "survival of the fittest," what really matters is *reproduction* — the survival of the genome. Because of natural selection, the fastest or otherwise most fit organisms will be more likely than the less fit to live long enough to mate and thus pass on their genes to the next generation.

Imagine that you are camping alone in a remote area and see a large grizzly bear approaching. According to the principles of *natural selection*, your chances for survival depend on how quickly and intelligently you respond to the threat. But what if your child and a group of strangers and their children are also camping in the same spot? Whom do you protect? Most parents would "naturally" choose to help their own child. Why? Why does this feel so "natural" and automatic? According to evolutionary psychologists, natural selection favors animals whose concern for kin is proportional to their degree of biological relatedness. Thus, most people will devote more resources, protection, love, and concern to close relatives. This helps ensure their "genetic survival."

In addition to natural selection, *genetic mutations* also help explain behavior. Given that each of us inherits approximately 30,000 genes, the probability is quite high that everyone carries at least one gene that has *mutated*, or changed from the original. The vast majority of mutated genes have no effect on behavior whatsoever. But, on occasion, a mutated gene will change an individual's behavior. It might cause someone to be more social, more risk taking, more shy, more careful. If the gene gives the person reproductive advantage, he or she will be more likely to pass on the gene to future generations. Another common misunderstanding is that evolution translates into continuing, long-term improvement. A genetic mutation can produce a population that is perfectly adapted to a current environment, but which may later perish if the environment changes.

Evolutionary Psychology *A branch of psychology that studies evolutionary principles, like natural selection and genetic mutations, which affect adaptation to the environment and help explain commonalities in behavior*

Natural Selection *The driving mechanism behind evolution that allows individuals with genetically influenced traits that are adaptive in a particular environment to stay alive and produce offspring*

FEEDING TIME AT THE NATURAL SELECTION ZOO

WILEY@NON-SEQUITUR.NET   DIST. BY UNIVERSAL PRESS SYND.   WWW. NON-SEQUITUR.NET

As discussed in Module 3, biological, psychological, and social forces are overlapping and inseparable influences—the *biopsychosocial model*. In this case, psychological and social forces also affect evolution, as evidenced by the mating behavior of people (Segerstrale, 2000). For example, because the concept of beauty is culturally influenced those who best fit their culture's concept of beauty may find it easier to acquire mates and have more offspring, to whom they pass on their physical and behavioral traits. Similarly, in cultures that arrange marriages according to social class or religious factors, different traits may be selected and passed along to succeeding generations.

Evolutionary psychology is one of the seven major perspectives in modern psychology, and we will revisit this field many times throughout this text. For example, in Modules 8, 9, and 10, we examine the role of stress over the course of evolution, and Modules 23 and 25 explore the role of evolution in infant reflexes, language development, and attachment. In Modules 29 and 30, we look at modern controversies surrounding evolution and gender role development and supposed differences in sexual behavior. Modules 31 and 32 discuss the role of evolution in drives toward novelty and exploration and the universal recognition of facial expressions of emotion. Evidence of evolution in our helping and aggressive behaviors is discussed in Module 48.

In the following section, we explore biological differences between women and men that may have evolved from different gender-related adaptations.

Achievement
GENDER & CULTURAL DIVERSITY

The Evolution of Sex Differences

Because of the way our species evolved, modern men and women have many abilities that helped our ancestors adapt to their environment and hence to survive and reproduce. For example, Figures 7.3 and 7.4 show that men tend to score higher on tests of mathematical reasoning and spatial relationships, whereas women score higher on tests involving mathematical calculation and tasks requiring perceptual speed. Men also tend to be more accurate in target-directed motor skills, whereas women tend to be more efficient in skills requiring fine motor coordination. What accounts for these differences?

One possible answer from evolutionary psychologists is that ancient societies typically assigned men the task of "hunters" and women as "gatherers." The man's superiority on many spatial tasks and target-directed motor skills, for example, may have evolved from the adaptive demands of hunting. Similarly, activities such as gathering, child-rearing, and domestic tool construction and manipulation may have contributed to the woman's language superiority (Farber, 2000; Joseph, 2000; Silverman & Phillips, 1998). Some critics, however, suggest that evolution progresses much too

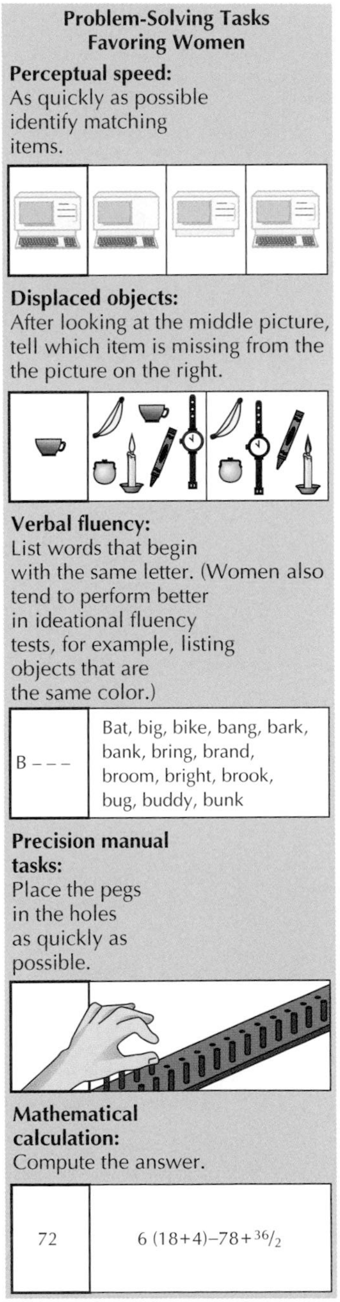

Problem-Solving Tasks Favoring Women

Perceptual speed: As quickly as possible identify matching items.

Displaced objects: After looking at the middle picture, tell which item is missing from the the picture on the right.

Verbal fluency: List words that begin with the same letter. (Women also tend to perform better in ideational fluency tests, for example, listing objects that are the same color.)

B - - - | Bat, big, bike, bang, bark, bank, bring, brand, broom, bright, brook, bug, buddy, bunk

Precision manual tasks: Place the pegs in the holes as quickly as possible.

Mathematical calculation: Compute the answer.

72 | 6 (18+4)−78+$^{36}/_2$

Figure 7.3 *Problem solving tasks favoring women.*

Problem-Solving Tasks Favoring Men

Spatial tasks: Mentally rotate the 3-d object to identify its match.

Spatial tasks: Mentally manipulate the folded paper to tell where the holes will fall when it is unfolded.

Target-directed motor skills: Hit the bull's eye.

Disembedding tests: Find the simple shape on the left in the more complex figures.

Mathematical reasoning: What is the answer?

5 1/2 | If you bicycle 24 miles a day, how many days will it take to travel 132 miles?

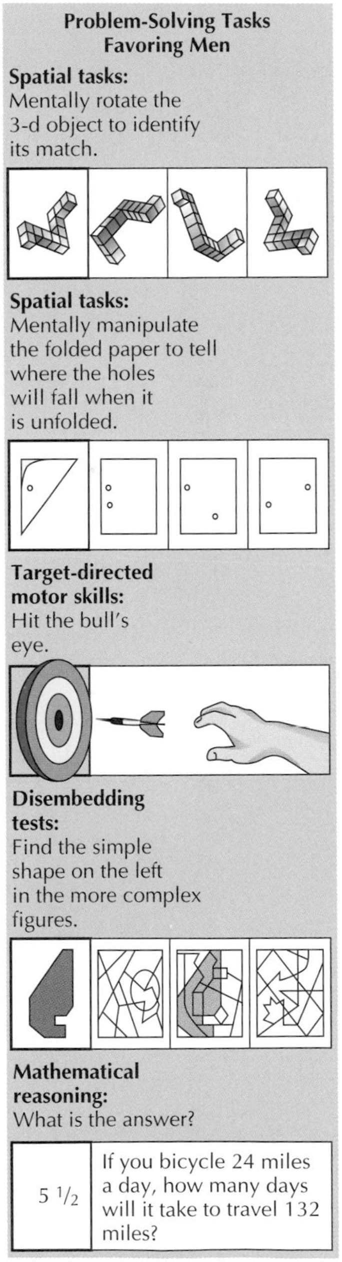

Figure 7.4 *Problem solving tasks favoring men.*

slowly to account for this type of behavioral adaptation. Furthermore, evolutionary explanations of sex differences are highly speculative and obviously difficult to test scientifically (Eagly & Wood, 1999).

Evolutionary psychology research emphasizes heredity and early biological processes in determining gender differences in cognitive behavior, but keep in mind that almost all sex differences are *correlational*. The mechanisms involved in the actual *cause* of certain human behaviors have yet to be determined. Furthermore, it is important to remember that all known variations *between* the two sexes are much smaller than differences *within* each sex. Finally, to repeat a theme discussed throughout this text, it is extremely difficult to separate the effects of biological, psychological, and social forces — the biopsychosocial model.

Assessment

CHECK & REVIEW

Genetics and Evolutionary Psychology

Genes are strings of chemicals that hold the code for certain traits that are passed on from parent to child, and they can be dominant or recessive. Genes are found on long strands of DNA molecules called **chromosomes**. **Behavioral geneticists** use twin studies, adoption studies, family studies, and genetic abnormalities to explore genetic contributions to behavior and make estimates of **heritability**.

Evolutionary psychology is the branch of psychology that looks at evolutionary changes related to behavior. Several different processes, including **natural selection,** mutations, and social and cultural factors can affect evolution.

Questions

1. Evolutionary psychology is the branch of psychology that looks at
   a. How fossil discoveries affect behavior
   b. The relationship between genes and the environment
   c. The relationship between evolutionary changes and behavior
   d. The effect of culture change on behavior

2. What are the four chief methods used to study behavioral genetics?

3. According to evolutionary theorists, why are people more likely to help their family members than strangers?

4. How would evolutionary psychology explain why men tend to score higher on mathematical reasoning, spatial relationships, and target directed motor skills, whereas women score higher on mathematical calculation, tasks requiring perceptual speed, and fine motor coordination?

Answers to Questions can be found in Appendix B.

MODULE 7   ACTIVE LEARNING WORKSHEET

Respond to the following questions, and then compare your answers with those of your classmates or friends.

1. Imagine you are the parent of 3-year-old identical twins. Your friends and relatives frequently comment on how much the twins are alike in their size and temperament. Can you conclude that these similarities are primarily genetic? Can you think of other explanations?

2. Which of the following methods for studying behavioral genetics is most likely to provide definitive evidence? a) twin studies, b) adoption studies, c) family studies, d) genetic abnormalities

3. An evolutionary psychologist has just reported a study showing males are more talkative than females. What questions would you ask before trusting the research findings?

Assessment
KEY TERMS

*To assess your understanding of the **Key Terms** in this section, write a definition for each (in your own words), and then compare your definitions with those in the text.*

neuroscience (p. 53)

Biological Foundations
action potential (p. 59)
autonomic nervous system (ANS)
   (p. 55)
axon (p. 58)
cell body (p. 58)
central nervous system (CNS) (p. 55)
dendrites (p. 58)
endocrine [EN-dohe-krin] system
   (p. 66)
endorphins [en-DOR-fins] (p. 63)
glial cells (p. 58)
hormones (p. 66)
myelin [MY-uh-lin] sheath (p. 59)
neuron (p. 58)
neurotransmitter (p. 61)
parasympathetic nervous system
   (p. 56)
peripheral nervous system (PNS)
   (p. 55)

somatic nervous system (SNS)
   (p. 55)
sympathetic nervous system (p. 56)
synapse [SIN-aps] (p. 61)

A Tour Through the Brain
amygdala [uh-MIG-dull-uh] (p. 72)
association areas (p. 77)
brainstem (p. 69)
cerebellum [sehr-uh-BELL-um]
   (p. 70)
cerebral cortex (p. 73)
corpus callosum [CORE-puss] [cah-
   LOH-suhm] (p. 77)
frontal lobes (p. 73)
hypothalamus [hi-poh-THAL-uh-
   muss] (p. 71)
lateralization (p. 77)
limbic system (p. 71)
localization of function (p. 69)
medulla [muh-DUL-uh] (p. 69)
midbrain (p. 69)

neurogenesis [nue-roe-JEN-uh sis]
   (p. 82)
neuroplasticity (p. 82)
occipital [ahk-SIP-uh-tuhl] lobes
   (p. 77)
parietal [puh-RYE-uh-tuhl] lobes
   (p. 75)
pons (p. 69)
reticular formation (RF) (p. 69)
split brain (p. 77)
stem cell (p. 82)
temporal lobes (p. 75)
thalamus [THAL-uh-muss] (p. 71)

Genetics and Evolution
behavioral genetics (p. 86)
chromosome (p. 86)
evolutionary psychology (p. 90)
gene (p. 86)
heritability (p. 87)
natural selection (p. 90)

Achievement

WEB RESOURCES

Huffman Book Companion Site
http://www.wiley.com/college/huffman
   This site is loaded with free Interactive Self-Tests, Internet
   Exercises, Glossary and Flashcards for key terms, Web links,
   Handbook for Non-Native Speakers, and other activities
   designed to improve your mastery of the material in this section.

Dissections of a Real Human Brain and Spinal Cord
http://www.vh.org/Providers/Textbooks/BrainAnatomy/
BrainAnatomy.html
   This site provides detailed photographs and drawings allowing
   an inside look at the Internal structures, appearance, and
   organization of the brain and spinal cord.

Brain Diseases
http://www.mic.ki.se/Diseases/c10.228.html
   The site contains a wealth of information related to brain diseases, including Alzheimer's, Parkinson's, stroke, and even
   migraine headaches.

Neuroscience for Kids
http://faculty.washington.edu/chudler/neurok.html
   A dynamic site designed for all ages to facilitate exploration of
   the human brain and nervous system.

VISUAL SUMMARY

Neuroscience and Biological Foundations
(Modules 5, 6, and 7)

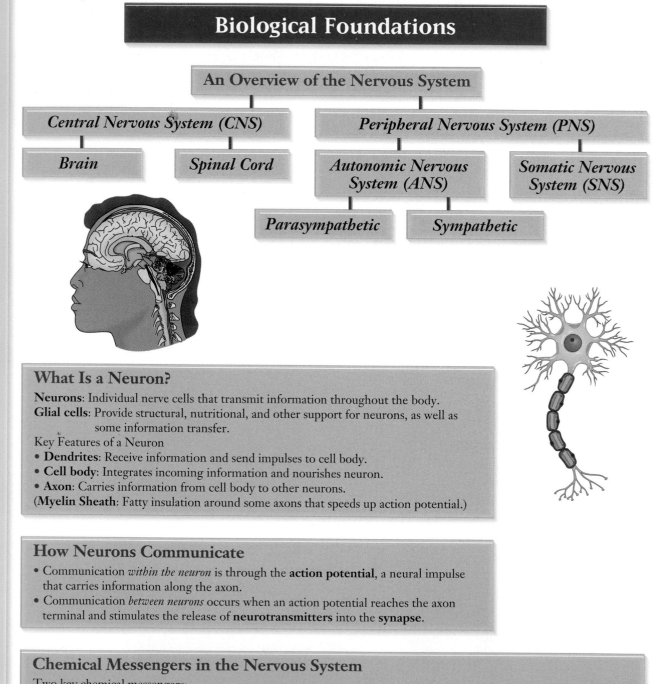

Biological Foundations

An Overview of the Nervous System

Central Nervous System (CNS)

Peripheral Nervous System (PNS)

Brain

Spinal Cord

Autonomic Nervous System (ANS)

Somatic Nervous System (SNS)

Parasympathetic

Sympathetic

What Is a Neuron?

Neurons: Individual nerve cells that transmit information throughout the body.
Glial cells: Provide structural, nutritional, and other support for neurons, as well as some information transfer.
Key Features of a Neuron
- **Dendrites**: Receive information and send impulses to cell body.
- **Cell body**: Integrates incoming information and nourishes neuron.
- **Axon**: Carries information from cell body to other neurons.
(**Myelin Sheath**: Fatty insulation around some axons that speeds up action potential.)

How Neurons Communicate

- Communication *within the neuron* is through the **action potential**, a neural impulse that carries information along the axon.
- Communication *between neurons* occurs when an action potential reaches the axon terminal and stimulates the release of **neurotransmitters** into the **synapse**.

Chemical Messengers in the Nervous System

Two key chemical messengers:
1) **Neurotransmitters**: Chemicals manufactured and released by neurons that alter activity in other neurons, which thereby affects behavior and mental processes.
2) **Hormones**: Chemicals released from the endocrine system into the bloodstream, which affect the nervous system.

A Tour Through the Brain

Lower-Level Brain Structures

Brain Stem
Group of structures including the **pons** (breathing, sleeping, waking, dreaming, etc.), **medulla** (breathing, heart rate, etc.), and **midbrain** (coordinating, movement patterns, sleep, and arousal).

Cerebellum
Responsible for smooth movement, balance, and aspects of perception and cognition.

Thalamus
Relays sensory messages to the cortex.

Hypothalamus
Maintains homeostasis and controls emotions and motives like hunger, thirst, sex, and aggression.

Limbic System
Group of interconnected structures responsible for arousal and regulation of emotion, motivation, memory, and learning. The **amygdala** is the structure most involved with emotion.

The Cerebral Cortex
The cerebral cortex is responsible for all higher mental processes and is divided into four lobes:

Frontal Lobes
Motor control, speech production, and higher functions (thinking, personality, emotion, and memory).

Parietal Lobes
Sensory processing (pressure, pain, touch, and temperature).

Temporal Lobes
Audition, language comprehension, memory, and some emotional control.

Occipital Lobes
Vision and visual perception.

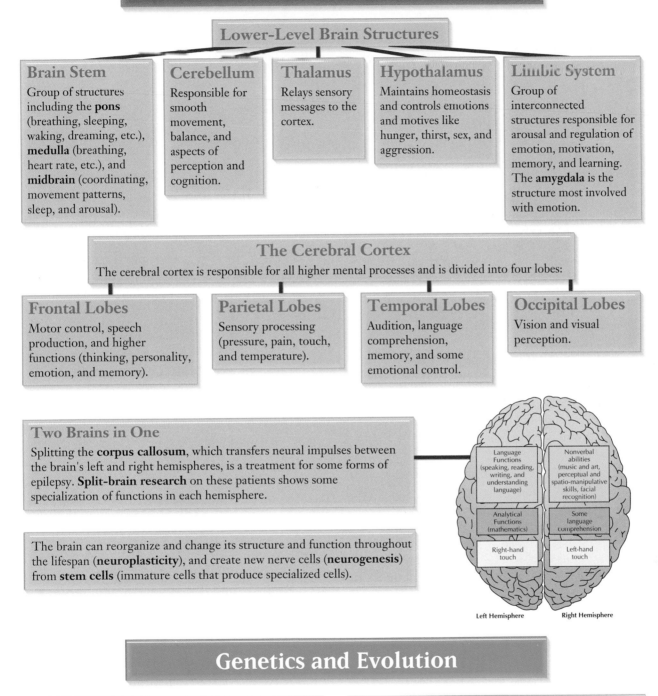

Two Brains in One
Splitting the **corpus callosum**, which transfers neural impulses between the brain's left and right hemispheres, is a treatment for some forms of epilepsy. **Split-brain research** on these patients shows some specialization of functions in each hemisphere.

The brain can reorganize and change its structure and function throughout the lifespan (**neuroplasticity**), and create new nerve cells (**neurogenesis**) from **stem cells** (immature cells that produce specialized cells).

Language Functions (speaking, reading, writing, and understanding language)

Nonverbal abilities (music and art, perceptual and spatio-manipulative skills, facial recognition)

Analytical Functions (mathematics)

Some language comprehension

Right-hand touch

Left-hand touch

Left Hemisphere   **Right Hemisphere**

Genetics and Evolution

Behavioral Genetics
Each of the 46 human **chromosomes** is composed of DNA, which is made up of **genes**.

Genetics studies are done with twins, adopted children, families, and genetic abnormalities. Such studies allow estimates of **heritability**.

The Human Genome Project (HGP) has mapped all the genes on the human chromosome.

Evolutionary Psychology
Studies evolutionary principles, like **natural selection** and genetic mutations, which affect adaptation to the environment and help explain commonalities in behavior.

STRESS AND HEALTH PSYCHOLOGY

Assessment

Core Learning Objectives

As you read Modules 8, 9, 10, and 11, keep the following questions in mind and answer them in your own words:

▶ What is stress and what are its major sources and effects?

▶ How is stress related to serious illness?

▶ What techniques and resources are available to help people cope with stress?

▶ How can health psychologists help with smoking, binge drinking, and chronic pain?

O n the morning of September 11, 2001, the woman in this photograph, Marcy Borders, was standing at a copying machine on the 81st floor of Tower One at the World Trade Center. She was busily daydreaming about her new job and thinking, "Here I am, in New York, doing something with my life." In the next moment, everything changed. The terrorists' plane hit and the building started "swaying like it was going to break off." Marcy frantically ran down the 81 flights of stairs and escaped to a world of panic and chaos.

Outside rescue workers screamed to her, "Run! Don't look back! Run!" But Marcy couldn't move. She was paralyzed by the horror that surrounded her—huge walls of smoke barreling down the street, people hanging out of windows, and then jumping to their

Achievement
Assessment
Application

death—and the smoke soon became so thick she could no longer see. Marcy stood alone in the dark screaming, "Help me, I don't want to die!"

Four months after the terrorist attack, Marcy is still having trouble adjusting. She is so depressed and terrified that she seldom leaves her apartment. Haunted by fears and memories of the attack, she cannot work and lives "off Lipton's chicken noodle soup." Officials from the Red Cross and other organizations have tried to help, but find that she seems reluctant to reach out. "I don't want to seem like I am taking away from the people who lost loved ones."

Alone at night, Marcy drinks alcohol to try to fall asleep. Unfortunately, when she succeeds she has nightmares of missiles flying overhead, or visions of her mother making her funeral arrangements. "Everything I've built up seems gone. ... My mother is so disappointed in me. She thinks I should bounce back. But she wasn't there on the 81st floor."

ADAPTED FROM CANNON, 2002.

Where were you on September 11, 2001? I hope your experience was not as traumatizing as Marcy's, but, like most Americans, you know that this day will never be forgotten. Whether in Kosovo, Jerusalem, Tokyo, Oklahoma City, or New York City, people know what's its like to be a victim of terrorism (Pomponio, 2002). We also now know what it's like to be a victim of ongoing stress. In the months and years following the attack, we've struggled with continuing threats of repeated terrorism, fears of Anthrax-laced mail and biological warfare, and the lingering sadness and grief for the loss of so many lives.

Marcy's story and our collective memories of the horrors of September 11 may be depressing, but stress, and ways of coping with it, have long been a core part of psychology. Throughout most of history, people have understood that emotions and thoughts affect physical health. However, in the late 1800s, the discovery of physiological causes for infectious diseases such as typhoid and syphilis led scientists to focus primarily on physiological causes of disease. As a result, medicine and public health made marked advances. Over the last century, life expectancy for Americans of all races and genders has steadily increased, and for those born in 1997 it is an all time high of 76.5 years (National Center for Health Statistics, 2001).

Interestingly, the major causes of death have shifted from contagious diseases (pneumonia, influenza, tuberculosis, measles, and typhoid fever) to noncontagious diseases (cancer, heart and cardiovascular disease, chronic lung disease) (National Center for Health Statistics, 2001). Can you see how today's key health problems are strongly related to behavior and lifestyle? Scientists and medical experts are now reemphasizing the close relationship between psychological behavior and physical health and illness, with an emphasis on wellness and the prevention of illness. This is the heart (and definition) of **health psychology** (Baum & Posluszny, 2001).

In this section, we will explore how biological, psychological, and social factors (the *biopsychosocial model*) all affect our health and well-being. We begin with the causes and effects of stress, along with the role stress plays in serious illnesses, such as cancer and heart disease. Then we explore various ways of coping with stress. The section concludes with a discussion of how the field of health psychology can help with problems related to smoking, binge drinking, and chronic pain.

Health Psychology *Studies the relationship between psychological behavior and physical health and illness*

MODULE 8
STRESS AND ITS ROLE IN HEALTH

Assessment

What is stress, and what are its major sources and effects?

Stress *A nonspecific response of the body to any demand made on it; the arousal, both physical and mental, to situations or events that we perceive as threatening or challenging*

Eustress *Pleasant, desirable stress*

Distress *Unpleasant, objectionable stress*

Hans Selye (Sell-yay), a physiologist renowned for his research and writing in the area of stress since the 1930s, defines **stress** as the nonspecific response of the body to any demand made on it. The trigger that prompts the stressful reaction is called a *stressor*. When you play two nonstop tennis matches in the middle of a heat wave, your body responds with a fast heartbeat, rapid breathing, and an outpouring of perspiration. When you find out 10 minutes before class starts that the term paper you just started is due today rather than next Friday, your body has the same physiological stress response to a very different stressor. Stress reactions can occur to either internal, cognitive stimuli or external, environmental stimuli (Sarafino, 2002).

The body is nearly always in some state of stress, whether pleasant or unpleasant, mild or severe. *Anything* placing a demand on the body can cause stress. When stress is beneficial, such as moderate exercise, it is called **eustress** and when it is objectionable, as from chronic illness, it is called **distress** (Selye, 1974). The total absence of stress would mean the total absence of stimulation, which would eventually lead to death. Because health psychology has been chiefly concerned with the negative effects of stress, we will adhere to convention and use the word "stress" to refer primarily to harmful or unpleasant stress (Selye's *distress*), even though there are some forms of beneficial *eustress*.

■ Sources of Stress: From Major Life Changes to Minor Hassles

Although stress is pervasive in our lives, some things cause more stress than others. The major sources of stress are life changes, chronic stressors, hassles, burnout, frustration, and conflict.

Life Changes

As we discovered earlier, the terrorist attack on September 11 caused such severe change in Marcy Border's life that she continued to suffer long after the attack. Early stress researchers Thomas Holmes and Richard Rahe (1967) believed that change, of any kind, that required some adjustment in behavior or lifestyle could cause stress. Moreover, they believed that exposure to numerous stressful events within a short period of time could have a direct, detrimental effect on health.

To investigate the relationship between change and stress, Holmes and Rahe created a Social Readjustment Rating Scale (SRRS) that asked people to check off all the life events they've experienced in the last year (Table 8.1). Each event is assigned a numerical rating expressed in *life change units* (LCUs). To score yourself on this scale, add up the LCUs for all life events you have experienced during the last year and compare your score with the following standards: 0–150 = No significant problems, 150–199 = Mild life crisis (33 percent chance of illness), 200–299 = Moderate life crisis (50 percent chance of illness), 300 and above Major life crisis (80 percent chance of illness).

The SRRS scale is an easy and popular way to measure stress, and cross-cultural studies have shown that most people rank the magnitude of stressful events in similar ways (McAndrew, Akande, Turner, & Sharma, 1998; Scully, Tosi, & Banning, 2000). However, the SRRS is not foolproof. First, it only shows a *correlation* between stress and illness, and as you recall from Module 2, *correlation does not prove causation*. Illnesses could be caused by stress or they also could be caused by other (yet unknown) factors.

In addition, as noted earlier, stress varies according to the individual. Any one event may be perceived as a stressful ordeal, a neutral occurrence, or even an exciting

TABLE 8.1 MEASURING LIFE CHANGES

Social Readjustment Rating Scale			
Life Events	Life Change Units	Life Events	Life Change Units
Death of spouse	100	Son or daughter leaving home	29
Divorce	73	Trouble with in-laws	29
Marital separation	65	Outstanding personal achievement	28
Jail term	63	Spouse begins or stops work	26
Death of a close family member	63	Begin or end school	26
Personal injury or illness	53	Change in living conditions	25
Marriage	50	Revision of personal habits	24
Fired at work	47	Trouble with boss	23
Marital reconciliation	45	Change in work hours or conditions	20
Retirement	45	Change in residence	20
Change in health of family member	44	Change in schools	20
Pregnancy	40	Change in recreation	19
Sex difficulties	39	Change in church activities	19
Gain of a new family member	39	Change in social activities	18
Business readjustment	39	Mortgage or loan for lesser purchase (car, major appliance)	17
Change in financial state	38	Change in sleeping habits	16
Death of a close friend	37	Change in number of family get-togethers	15
Change to different line of work	36	Change in eating habits	15
Change in number of arguments with spouse	35	Vacation	13
Mortgage or loan for major purchase	31	Christmas	12
Foreclosure on mortgage or loan	30	Minor violations of the law	11
Change in responsibilities at work	29		

Source: Holmes & Rahe (1967).

opportunity. It depends on your personal interpretation and appraisal (Whelan & Kirkby, 2000). You might find moving to another state a terrible sacrifice and a tremendous stressor, whereas your friend might see the move as a wonderful opportunity and experience little or no stress. Furthermore, different people have differing abilities to deal with change, perhaps because of good coping skills, general physical health, healthier lifestyles, or even genetic predisposition.

Chronic Stressors

Not all stressful situations are single, short-term events such as a terrorist attack, death, or a birth. A bad marriage, poor working conditions, or an intolerable political climate can be *chronic stressors*. Even the stress of low frequency noise is associated with measurable hormonal and cardiac changes (Waye et al., 2002). Our social lives also can be chronically stressful, because making and maintaining friendships involves considerable thought and energy (Griffith, Dubow, & Ippolito, 2000).

Perhaps the largest source of chronic stress is work. People often experience stress associated with keeping or changing jobs or with job performance (Grossi, Perski, Lundberg, & Soares, 2001). However, the most stressful jobs are those that make great demands on performance and concentration but allow little creativity or opportunity for advancement (Parasuraman & Purohit, 2000). Assembly-line work ranks very high in this category.

Is nursing a stressful career? People who think of their profession as a "calling" may lose their idealism when faced with the ongoing stresses and emotional turmoil. Over time they may suffer a type of mental and physical exhaustion known as "burnout."

Hassles *Small problems of daily living that accumulate and sometimes become a major stress*

Burnout *Physical, emotional, and mental exhaustion attributable to long-term involvement in emotionally demanding situations*

Researchers have documented that stress at work can also cause serious stress at home not only for workers but for other family members as well. And, of course, in our private lives, divorce, child and spouse abuse, alcoholism, and money problems can place severe stress on all members of a family (Pajer, Gardner, Kirillova, & Vanyukov, 2001; Thompson & Kaslow, 2000; Tien, Sandler, & Zautra, 2000).

Hassles and Burnout

In addition to chronic stressors, we also experience a great deal of daily stress from **hassles,** little problems of daily living that are not significant in themselves but that pile up to become a major source of stress. Some hassles tend to be shared by all: time pressures (getting to work or school on time, finding a parking place, fighting traffic jams), problems with family and coworkers (equitable sharing of work, scheduling conflicts, gossip), and financial concerns (competing demands for available funds, increasing prices). But our reactions to hassles may vary. For example, compared to women, men tend to have more impairment of their immune system and an increased heart rate in response to hassles (Delahanty et al., 2000).

Some authorities believe hassles can be more significant than major life events in creating stress (Kraaij, Arensman, & Spinhoven, 2002; Lazarus, 1999). For example, divorce is extremely stressful, but it may be so because of the increased number of hassles — change in finances, child-care arrangements, longer working hours, and so on. Similarly, a move is a stressful life change, but preparing to move or having your house up for sale for an extended period of time can be more stressful than the actual move itself.

Persistent hassles in your work situation can lead to a form of physical, mental, and emotional exhaustion known as **burnout.** Although the term has become an overused buzzword, health psychologists use it to describe a specific syndrome that develops most commonly in idealistic people who are exposed to chronically stressful and emotionally draining professions (Alexander & Hegarty, 2000; Linzer et al., 2002). People who think of their job as a "calling" enter their careers with a high sense of motivation and commitment. But over time, some become emotionally drained and disillusioned and feel a loss of personal accomplishment — they "burn out." The result may be increased absences from work, a sharp downturn in productivity, and an increased risk of physical problems. Police officers, nurses, doctors, social workers, and teachers are particularly vulnerable.

TRY THIS

YOURSELF

Application

Kanner and others developed a *Hassles Scale* to assess those everyday events on the job, at school, and in interpersonal relations that annoy, frustrate, and anger us (Kanner, Coyne, Schaefer, & Lazarus, 1981). Write down the top 10 hassles you most commonly experience and then compare your answers to the following list:

The 10 Most Common Hassles for College Students

Percentage of Times Checked

1. Troubling thoughts about the future	76.6
2. Not getting enough sleep	72.5
3. Wasting time	71.1
4. Inconsiderate smokers	70.7
5. Physical appearance	69.9
6. Too many things to do	69.2
7. Misplacing or losing things	67.0
8. Not enough time to do the things you need to do	66.3
9. Concerns about meeting high standards	64.0
10. Being lonely	60.8

Source: Kanner, A. D., Coyne, J. C., Schaefer, C., & Lazarus, R. S. (1981). Comparison of two modes of stress measurement: Daily hassles and uplifts versus major life events. *Journal of Behavioral Medicine, 4,* 1–39.

Frustration

Frustration is a negative emotional state generally associated with a blocked goal such as not being accepted for admission to your first-choice college. The more motivated we are, the more frustration we experience when our goals are blocked. After getting stuck in traffic and missing an important appointment, we may become very frustrated. On the other hand, if the same traffic jam causes us to be five minutes late to a painful medical appointment, we may experience little or no frustration.

Frustration *Unpleasant tension, anxiety, and heightened sympathetic activity resulting from a blocked goal*

Conflicts

Another source of stress is **conflict,** which arises when one is forced to make a choice between at least two incompatible alternatives. The amount of stress produced by a conflict depends on the complexity of the conflict itself, and the difficulty involved in resolving it. There are three basic types of conflict: *approach–approach, avoidance–avoidance*, and *approach–avoidance.*

In an **approach–approach conflict,** a person must choose between two or more *favorable* alternatives. Thus, no matter what choice is made, the result will be desirable. At first it might seem that this type of conflict shouldn't create any stress, but consider this example. Suppose you have to choose between two summer jobs. One job is at a resort where you will meet interesting people and have a good time; the other will provide you with valuable experience and look impressive on your résumé. No matter which job you choose, you will benefit in some way. In fact, you would like to take both jobs, but you can't. The requirement to choose is the source of stress.

An **avoidance–avoidance conflict** involves making a choice between two or more unpleasant alternatives that will lead to negative results, no matter which choice is made. In the book (and film) *Sophie's Choice*, Sophie and her two children are sent to a German concentration camp. A soldier demands that she give up (apparently to be killed) either her daughter or her son, or they both will be killed. Obviously, neither alternative is acceptable; both will have tragic results. Although this is an extreme example, avoidance–avoidance conflicts can lead to intense stress.

An **approach–avoidance conflict** occurs when a person must choose between alternatives that will have both desirable and undesirable results. We have all been faced with such decisions as "I want to spend more time in a close relationship, but that means I won't be able to see as much of my old friends." This conflict thus leads to a great deal of ambivalence. In an approach–avoidance conflict, we experience both good and bad results from any alternative we choose.

The longer any conflict exists or the more important the decision, the more stress a person will experience. Generally, the approach–approach conflict is the easiest to resolve and produces the least stress. The avoidance–avoidance conflict, on the other hand, is usually the most difficult because all choices lead to unpleasant results. Approach–avoidance conflicts are somewhat less stressful than avoidance–avoidance conflicts and are usually moderately difficult to resolve.

Conflict *Having to choose between two or more incompatible goals or impulses*

Approach—Approach Conflict *Having to choose between two or more desirable alternatives*

Avoidance—Avoidance Conflict *Forced choice between two or more undesirable alternatives*

Approach—Avoidance Conflict *Forced choice between two or more alternatives, which have both desirable and undesirable results*

Assessment

CHECK & REVIEW

Sources of Stress

Stress is the body's arousal, both physical and mental, to situations or events that we perceive as threatening or challenging. A situation or event, either pleasant or unpleasant, that triggers arousal and causes stress is known as a stressor.

The major sources of stress are life changes, chronic stressors, hassles, burnout, frustration, and conflicts. Chronic stressors are ongoing events such as poor working conditions. **Hassles** are little everyday life problems that pile up to cause major stress. Persistent hassles and a loss of initial idealism in your work situation can lead to a form of physical, mental, and emotional exhaustion known as **burnout.** **Frustration** has to do with blocked goals, whereas **conflict** involves two or more competing goals. Conflicts can be classified as **approach–approach, avoidance– avoidance,** or **approach–avoidance.**

Effects of Stress: How the Body Responds

HPA Axis *The hypothalamus, pituitary gland, and adrenal cortex, which are activated by stress*

When stressed either mentally or physically, your body undergoes several major and minor physiological changes, some of which we have already mentioned. The most significant changes are controlled by the *sympathetic nervous system* and the *HPA Axis* (see Figure 3.1). We will explore (and explain) both of these systems in this section.

Stress and the Sympathetic Nervous System

Stress has a domino effect on the neural system—as one domino falls, it topples the next. As you can see in the left side of Figure 8.1, stress activates the hypothalamus and the hypothalamus signals the sympathetic nervous system, which then activates the central part of the adrenal glands (the adrenal medulla) to release large amounts of norepinephrine and epinephrine. The net result is increased energy to help us "fight or flee" from a threat.

As you recall from Module 5, under low-stress conditions, the parasympathetic part of the autonomic nervous system tends to reduce heart rate and blood pressure, while increasing muscle movement in the stomach and intestines. This allows the body to conserve energy, absorb nutrients, and maintain normal functioning. Under stressful conditions, the sympathetic part of the autonomic nervous system is dominant. It increases heart rate, blood pressure, respiration, and muscle tension; decreases the movement of stomach muscles; constricts blood vessels; and so on.

Stress and the HPA Axis

The sympathetic nervous system obviously prepares us for immediate action. We see a shark and we quickly swim to shore, where our parasympathetic nervous system calms us and restores normal functioning. But what happens to our bodies when we face chronic stressors, like bad jobs or marriages?

We also have another stress response team that reacts a little more slowly and stays on the job. It is called the **HPA Axis**—the *H*ypothalamus, *P*ituitary gland, and *A*drenal cortex system. Look again at Figure 8.1. Note that stress creates a domino effect on the HPA Axis (the right side of the figure). Stimulation of the hypothalamus activates the pituitary gland, which in turn activates the core of the adrenal glands (the adrenal cortex), which then releases the hormone known as *cortisol*. Once again, the net effect is increased energy.

It is important for you to understand this arrangement because cortisol plays a critical role in the long-term effects of stress.

Figure 8.1 *How our bodies respond to stress — a dual system.* (a) The sympathetic nervous system helps us respond immediately to stress (such as seeing a snake). (b) The pituitary allows us to maintain this vigilant response and deal with chronic stressors (like a bad job).

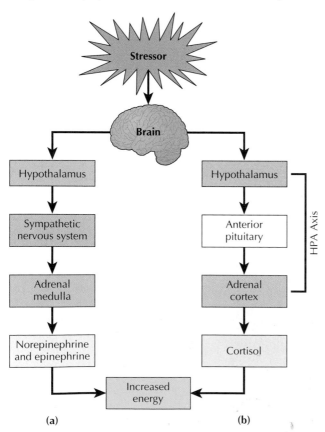

(a)   (b)

Would you like to be president of the United States? Note how the stress of this office has aged George W. Bush, as it has previous presidents.

Researchers call it a "stress hormone," and the level of circulating cortisol is the most commonly employed physiological measure of stress. During the initial crisis, cortisol increases blood sugar and metabolism, which helps us cope. However, with long-term stressors the HPA axis remains in service and cortisol remains in the bloodstream. Prolonged elevation of cortisol has been linked to increased levels of depression, post-traumatic stress disorder (PTSD), memory problems, unemployment, and even drug and alcohol abuse (Al'absi, Hugdahl, & Lovallo, 2002; Cowen, 2002; Grossi, Perski, Lundberg, & Soares, 2001; Gunnar & Donzella, 2002; Yehuda, Halligan, & Bierer, 2002). Perhaps most important, increased cortisol is directly related to impairment of immune system functioning.

Stress and the Immune System

The discovery of the relationship between stress and the immune system is very important. This system is our major defense against disease. When it is impaired, we

Stress in ancient times. *As shown in these early cave drawings, the automatic "fight or flight" response was adaptive and necessary for early human survival. However, in modern society it occurs as a response to ongoing situations where we often cannot fight or flee. This repeated arousal can be detrimental to our health.*

are at greatly increased risk of suffering from a number of diseases, including bursitis, ulcers, colitis, Alzheimer's disease, rheumatoid arthritis, periodontal disease, and even the common cold (Bowler, 2001; Cohen et al., 1999, 2002; Kiecolt-Glaser, McGuire, Robles, & Glaser, 2002; Rabin, 2002).

The connection between stress and the immune system also has had a great impact on the field of psychology. Knowledge that psychological factors have considerable control over infectious diseases has upset long held assumptions in biology and medicine that these diseases are "strictly physical." The clinical and theoretical implications are so important that a new field of biopsychology has emerged. That field is **psychoneuroimmunology,** and it studies the interactions of psychological factors (psycho-), the nervous and endocrine systems (neuro-), and the immune system (immunology).

Psychoneuroimmunology [sye-koh-NEW-roh-IM-you-NOLL-oh-gee] *Interdisciplinary field that studies the effects of psychological factors on the immune system*

Selye's General Adaptation Syndrome (GAS)

Stress clearly causes physiological changes that can be detrimental to health. Hans Selye, who was mentioned earlier in our definition of stress, described a generalized physiological reaction to severe stressors that he called the **general adaptation syndrome** (GAS) (1936). Figure 8.2 shows the three phases of this reaction. In the initial phase, called the *alarm reaction*, the body reacts to the stressor by activating the sympathetic nervous system (with increases in heart rate, blood pressure, secretion of hormones, and so on). The body has abundant energy and is alert and ready to deal with the stressor.

If the stressor remains, the body enters the *resistance phase*. Physiological arousal declines somewhat, but remains higher than normal as the body tries to adapt to the stressor. According to Selye, one outcome of this stage is that some people develop what he called *diseases of adaptation*, including asthma, ulcers, and high blood pressure. This adaptation and resistance phase is very taxing, and long-term exposure to the stressor may eventually lead to the *exhaustion phase* if the resistance is not successful. During this final stage, all adaptation energy becomes depleted, and our susceptibility to illness increases. In severe cases, long-term exposure to stressors can be life threatening because we become vulnerable to serious illness such as heart attack, stroke, and cancer.

General Adaptation Syndrome (GAS) *Selye's three-phase (alarm, resistance, and exhaustion) reaction to severe stress*

Figure 8.2 *The general adaptation syndrome (GAS).* According to Hans Seyle, when the body is exposed to severe, prolonged stress, it goes from an initial alarm reaction to an increased level of resistance. If the stress is prolonged, as it is for workers in some high risk occupations, it may lead to exhaustion and even death.

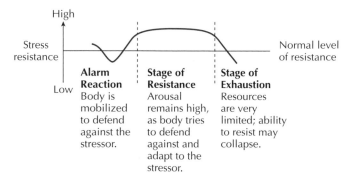

Application

APPLYING PSYCHOLOGY TO STUDENT LIFE

Why You Shouldn't Procrastinate

If your professor assigned a term paper for this class, have you already started working on it? Or are you putting it off until the last minute? Have you ever wondered if working continuously on a term paper from the first day of class until the paper is due might ultimately be more stressful than putting off the paper until the last minute?

To answer this question, Dianne Tice and Roy Baumeister (1997) at Case Western Reserve University assigned a term paper in their health psychology class at the beginning of the semester. Throughout the semester, they carefully monitored the stress, health, and procrastination levels of 44 student volunteers from the class. After the term papers were submitted at the end of the course, Tice and Baumeister found that procrastinators suffered significantly more stress and developed more health problems than nonprocrastinators. They were also more likely to turn in their papers late and earn lower grades on those papers.

In the Tools for Student Success section in Module 4, you learned that research shows that spacing out your studying rather than cramming the night before produces higher scores on exams. Now you have additional research showing that distributed work also produces better grades on term papers — as well as less stress. The bottom line is this: *Don't procrastinate.* It can be hazardous to your health, as well as your grades.

Assessment

CHECK & REVIEW

Effects of Stress

When stressed, the body undergoes physiological changes. The sympathetic branch of the autonomic nervous system is activated, increasing heart rate and blood pressure. Stressors also activate the **HPA axis** (hypothalamus, pituitary gland, and adrenal cortex), which increases the stress hormone cortisol. Increased cortisol decreases immune system functioning, which can render the body susceptible to a number of diseases.

Hans Selye described a generalized physiological reaction to severe stressors, which he called the **general adaptation syndrome** (GAS). It has three phases: the alarm reaction, the resistance phase, and the exhaustion phase.

Questions

1. How does the sympathetic nervous system respond to stress?
2. How does the HPA Axis respond to stress?
3. The GAS consists of three phases: the _____ reaction, the _____ phase, and the _____ phase.
4. As Michael watches his instructor pass out papers, he suddenly realizes this is the first major exam and he is totally unprepared. Which phase of the GAS is he most likely experiencing? (a) resistance; (b) alarm; (c) exhaustion; (d) phase-out.

MODULE 8   ACTIVE LEARNING WORKSHEET

Respond to the following questions, and then compare your answers with those in Appendix B.

1. The text defines stress as "a _____ response of the body to any _____ made on it."
   a. nonspecific; demand
   b. nonspecific; psychological demand
   c. specific; demand
   d. psychological; demand

2. Hans Selye called beneficial stress _____.
   a. unstress
   b. pseudo-stress
   c. positive stress
   d. eustress

3. You wake up late for your college classes. In your rush to get out of the house, you forget your books and homework assignment. When you arrive on campus, you find that you must park several blocks away from your class and your professor refuses to accept late homework. Each of these "small" problems may be considered _____.
   a. chronic stressors
   b. acute stressors
   c. hassles
   d. approach-approach conflicts

4. You work at a convalescent hospital for elderly people who are seriously ill or dying. The facility is severely underfunded and everyone is asked to work long hours for little pay. You are upset and continually frustrated by the inferior care given to the patients. If you work at this facility for many years, you are likely to develop _____.
   a. an avoidance-avoidance conflict
   b. the general-aversion-syndrome
   c. burnout
   d. chronic stress

5. Isabel needs to wash the dishes, but the dishwasher is broken and she can't find dishwashing soap. She may experience a negative emotion called _____.
   a. eustress
   b. distraction
   c. conflict
   d. frustration

6. A negative emotional state caused by an inability to choose between two or more incompatible goals or impulses is known as _____.
   a. frustration
   b. conflict
   c. hassles
   d. distress

7. When forced to make a choice leading to both desirable and undesirable results, you're likely to experience _____.
   a. double frustration
   b. an approach-approach conflict
   c. an approach-avoidance conflict
   d. an avoidance-avoidance conflict

8. Under everyday low-stress conditions, the _____ part of the nervous system tends to lower heart rate and blood pressure, while increasing muscle movement in the stomach and intestines.
   a. parasympathetic
   b. reflexive
   c. ventromedial
   d. cortical

9. The level of circulating _____ is the most commonly employed physiological measure of stress.
   a. endorphins
   b. enkephalins
   c. adrenaline
   d. cortisol

10. In Selye's general adaptation syndrome (GAS), the initial response of the autonomic nervous system to a stressor occurs in the _____ phase.
   a. resistance
   b. primary response
   c. sympathetic
   d. alarm reaction

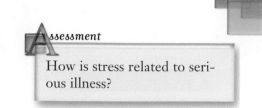

MODULE 9
STRESS AND SERIOUS ILLNESS

As we've just seen, stress has dramatic effects on our bodies. In this section, we will explore how stress is related to four serious illnesses — *cancer*, *coronary heart disease*, posttraumatic stress disorder, and gastric ulcers.

■ Cancer: A Variety of Causes — Even Stress

The word *cancer* is frightening to nearly everyone, and for good reason: Cancer is among the leading causes of death for adults in the U.S. It occurs when a particular type of primitive body cell begins rapidly dividing, and then forms a tumor that invades healthy tissue. Unless destroyed or removed, the tumor eventually damages organs and causes death. To date, over 100 types of cancer have been identified. They appear to be caused by an interaction between environmental factors and inherited predispositions.

To understand how the environment contributes to cancer, it helps to know what normally happens to cancerous cells. Whenever cancer cells start to multiply, the immune system checks the uncontrolled growth by attacking the abnormal cells (see the accompanying photograph). This goes on constantly, with abnormal cells arising, and, in a healthy person, the immune system keeping cancer cells in check.

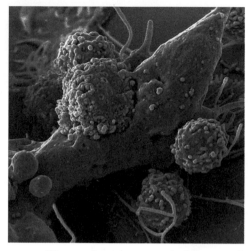

The round structure near the left center of this photomicrograph is a T-lymphocyte, a type of white blood cell produced by the immune system. It has just killed a cancer cell, the sweet potato-shaped structure.

Something different happens when the body is stressed. As you read earlier, the stress response involves the release of adrenal hormones that suppress immune system functioning. The compromised immune system is less able to resist infection and cancer development. An experimental animal study found that stress inhibited immune system defenses against cancer and promoted tumor growth (Wu et al., 2000). Other research with humans suggests that stress can also suppress lymphocytes, the main immune system cells that control cancer (Goebel & Mills, 2000).

The good news is that we can substantially reduce our risk of cancer by making changes that reduce our stress level and enhance our immune system. For example, when researchers interrupted the sleep of 23 men and then measured their *natural killer cells* (a type of immune system cell), they found the number of killer cells was 28 percent below average (Irwin et al., 1994). Can you see how staying up late studying for an exam (or partying) can decrease the effectiveness of your immune system? Fortunately, these researchers also found that a normal night's sleep after the deprivation returned the killer cells to their normal levels.

■ Cardiovascular Disorders: The Leading Cause of Death in the United States

Cardiovascular disorders are the cause of over half of all deaths in the United States (Centers for Disease Control, 2002). Understandably, health psychologists are concerned because stress is a major contributor to these deaths. *Heart disease* is a general term for all disorders that eventually affect the heart muscle and lead to heart failure. *Coronary heart disease* results from *arteriosclerosis*, a thickening of the walls of the coronary arteries that reduces or blocks the blood supply to the heart. Arteriosclerosis causes *angina* (chest pain due to insufficient blood supply to the heart) or *heart attack* (death of heart muscle tissue). Controllable factors that contribute to heart disease include stress, smoking, certain personality characteristics, obesity, a high-fat diet, and lack of exercise (American Heart Association, 2000; King et al., 2002; Krantz & McCeney, 2002).

How does stress contribute to heart disease? Recall that one of the major autonomic nervous system fight–flight reactions is the release of epinephrine and cortisol into the bloodstream. These hormones increase heart rate and release fat and glucose from the body's stores to give muscles a quickly available source of energy.

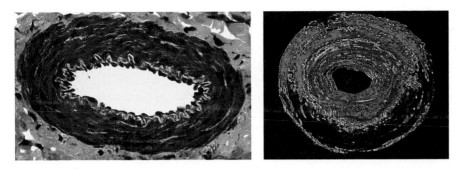

Figure 9.1 *Fatty deposits in arteries.* One major cause of heart disease is the blockage of arteries that supply blood to the heart. The artery at the left is normal; the one on the right is almost completely blocked. Reducing stress, exercising, and eating a low-fat diet can help prevent the buildup of fatty deposits in the arteries.

If no physical action is taken (and this is most likely the case in our modern lives), the fat released into the bloodstream is not burned as fuel and may become fatty deposits on the walls of blood vessels (Figure 9.1). These deposits are a major cause of blood supply blockage that causes heart attacks.

Personality Types

The effects of stress on heart disease may be amplified if an individual tends to be hard driving, competitive, ambitious, impatient, and hostile. People with such **Type A personalities** are chronically on edge, feel intense time urgency, and are preoccupied with responsibilities. The antithesis of the Type A personality is a **Type B personality,** having a laid-back, calm, relaxed attitude toward life.

Two cardiologists, Meyer Friedman and Ray Rosenman (1959), were the first to identify and describe the Type A personality. The story goes that in the mid-1950s, an upholsterer who was recovering the waiting room chairs in Friedman's office noticed an odd wear pattern. He mentioned to Friedman that the chairs looked like new except for the front edges, which were badly worn, as if all the patients sat only on the edges of the chairs. Initially, this didn't seem too important to Friedman. However, he later came to believe that this chronic sense of time urgency, being literally "on the edge of your seat," was a possible contributing factor to heart disease and the hallmark of the Type A personality.

Initial research into Type A behavior suggested Friedman and Rosenman were right, but more recent research has been less supportive. When researchers examined the relationship between characteristics of the Type A behavior pattern and heart disease, they found that the critical component and strongest predictor of heart disease was *hostility* (Fredrikson, Wik, & Fischer, 1999; Miller, Smith, Turner, Guijarro, & Hallet, 1996).

Actually, *cynical* hostility appears to be the most important factor in the Type A relationship to heart disease. Cynical people always expect problems and are constantly alert and "on watch," trying to foresee problems and possibly avert them. This attitude produces a nearly constant state of stress, which translates physiologically into higher blood pressure and heart rate, and production of stress-related hormones. In addition, because of their hostile, suspicious, argumentative, and competitive style, these people tend to have more interpersonal conflicts (Friedman, Hawley, & Tucker, 1994). Constant interpersonal conflicts can lead to a loss of social support and heightened autonomic activation, which can then lead to increased risk of cardiovascular disease (Sher, 2000; Tennant, 1999).

Can people with a Type A personality change their behavior? Health psychologists have developed two types of behavior modification to help people with

Type A Personality *Behavior characteristics including intense ambition, competition, exaggerated time urgency, and a cynical, hostile outlook*

Type B Personality *Behavior characteristics consistent with a calm, patient, relaxed attitude toward life*

Copyright 1997 by Randy Glasbergen.
www.glasbergen.com

"I'm learning how to relax, doctor—but I want to relax *better* and *faster!* I want to be on the *cutting edge of relaxation!*"

Type A personality — the *shotgun approach* and the *target behavior approach*. The *shotgun approach* aims to change all the behaviors that relate to the Type A personality. Friedman and his colleagues (1986) use the shotgun approach in their Recurrent Coronary Prevention Program. The program provides individual counseling, dietary advice, exercise, drugs, and group therapy to eliminate or modify Type A behaviors. Type A's are specifically encouraged to slow down and perform tasks incompatible with their personalities. For example, they might try to listen to other people without interrupting or stand in the longest supermarket line on purpose. The major criticism of the shotgun approach is that it eliminates desirable Type A traits, such as ambition, as well as undesirable Type A traits, like cynicism and hostility.

The alternative therapy, the *target behavior approach*, focuses on only those Type A behaviors that are likely to cause heart disease — namely, cynical hostility. By modifying specific behaviors, the person will likely reduce his or her risk of heart disease.

Hardiness

In addition to Type A and Type B personalities, there may be other personality patterns that affect the way we respond to stress. Have you ever wondered how some people survive in the face of great stress (repeated personal tragedies, demanding jobs, and even a poor home life) but others do not? Suzanne Kobasa was among the first to study this question (Kobasa, 1979; Maddi et al., 2002; Pengilly & Dowd, 2000).

*A*chievement

RESEARCH HIGHLIGHT

Does Stress Cause Ulcers?

Do you have gastric ulcers or know someone who does? If so, you know that these lesions to the lining of the stomach (and duodenum—the upper section of the small intestine) can be quite painful. In extreme cases, they may even be life threatening. Have you been told ulcers are caused by bacteria and not by stress, as previously thought? Would you like to know what psychologists believe?

Beginning in the 1950s, psychologists reported strong evidence that stress can lead to ulcers. Correlational studies have found that people who live in stressful situations develop a higher incidence of ulcers, and numerous experiments with laboratory animals have shown that stressors, such as shock or confinement to a very small space for a few hours, can produce ulcers in some laboratory animals (Andrade & Graeff, 2001; Desiderato, Mackinnon, & Hissom, 1974; Woods & Ramsay, 2000).

The relationship between stress and ulcers seemed well established, until researchers reported a bacterium (*Helicobac-ter pylori* or *H. pylori*), which appears to be associated with ulcers. Because many people prefer medical explanations, like bacteria or viruses, to psychological ones, the idea of stress as a cause of ulcers has been largely abandoned.

Is this warranted? Let's take a closer look at the research. First, most ulcer patients do have the *H. pylori* bacterium in their stomachs, and it clearly damages the stomach wall. In addition, antibiotic treatment does help many patients. However, approximately 75 percent of *normal control* subjects' stomachs also have the bacterium. This suggests that the bacterium may cause the ulcer, but only in people whose systems are compromised by stress. Furthermore, behavior modification and other psychological treatments, working alongside antibiotics, can help ease ulcers. Finally, studies of the amygdala (a part of the brain involved in emotional response) show that it plays an important role in gastric ulcer formation (Henke, 1992; Tanaka, Yoshida, Yokoo, Tomita, & Tanaka, 1998). Apparently, stressful situations, and direct stimulation of the amygdala, cause an increase in stress hormones and hydrochloric acid, and a decrease in blood flow in the stomach walls. This combination leaves the stomach more vulnerable to attack by the *H. pylori* bacteria.

In sum, it appears that *H. pylori*, increased hydrochloric acid and stress hormones, and decreased blood flow lead to the formation of gastric ulcers. Once again, we see how biological, psychological, and social forces influence one another (the biopsychosocial model), and for now the psychosomatic explanation for ulcers is back in business (Overmier & Murison, 2000).

*S*tudy *T*ip

Psychosomatic illness is not the same as an imagined, hypochondriacal illness. Psychosomatic [psyche = mind, soma = body] refers to symptoms or illnesses that are caused or aggravated by psychological factors, especially stress (Lipowski, 1986). Most researchers and health practitioners believe that almost all illnesses are partly psychosomatic in this sense.

Examining male executives with high levels of stress, she found that some people are more resistant to stress than others because of a personality factor called **hardiness,** a resilient type of optimism that comes from three distinctive attitudes:

1. *Commitment.* Hardy people feel a strong sense of commitment to both their work and their personal life. They also make intentional commitments to purposeful activity and problem solving.

2. *Control.* These people also see themselves as being in control of their lives, rather than as victims of their circumstances.

3. *Challenge.* Finally, hardy people look at change as an opportunity for growth and improvement — not as a threat. Hardy people welcome challenges.

The important lesson from this research is that hardiness is a *learned behavior* — not something based on luck or genetics. If you're not one of the *hardy* souls, you can develop the trait. The next time you face a bad stressor, such as four exams in one week, try using the 3 C's: "I am fully *committed* to my college education." "I can *control* the number of tests by taking one or two of them earlier than scheduled, or I can rearrange my work schedule." "I welcome this *challenge* as a final motivation to enroll in those reading improvement and college success courses I've always planned to take."

Before we go on, it's also important to note that Type A personality and lack of hardiness are not the only controllable risk factors associated with heart disease. Smoking, obesity, and lack of exercise are very important factors. Smoking restricts blood circulation, and obesity stresses the heart by causing it to pump more blood to the excess body tissue. A high-fat diet, especially one high in cholesterol, contributes to the fatty deposits that clog blood vessels. Lack of exercise contributes to weight gain and prevents the body from obtaining important exercise benefits, including strengthened heart muscle, increased heart efficiency, and the release of neurotransmitters such as serotonin that alleviate stress and promote well-being.

■ Posttraumatic Stress Disorder (PTSD): A Disease of Modern Times?

Perhaps the most powerful example of the effects of severe stress is **posttraumatic stress disorder (PTSD).** Children as well as adults can experience the symptoms of PTSD, which include feelings of terror and helplessness during the trauma and recurrent flashbacks, nightmares, impaired concentration, and/or emotional numbing afterward. As we discovered in the opening story of Marcy Borders, these symptoms may continue for months or years after the event itself, and some victims of PTSD turn to alcohol and other drugs, which often compound the problem.

We have an interesting history with the diagnosis of PTSD. During the Industrial Revolution, workers who survived horrific railroad accidents sometimes developed a condition very similar to PTSD that was called "railway spine" because it was thought the worker's problems resulted from a twisting or concussion of the spine. In later times, PTSD was primarily associated with military combat. Doctors called it "shell shock" because they believed it was a response to the physical concussion caused by exploding artillery. Today, we know that PTSD is caused by any exposure to extraordinary stress.

The essential feature of PTSD is *severe anxiety* (a state of constant or recurring alarm and fearfulness) that develops after experiencing a traumatic event (such as rape, natural disaster, war), learning about a violent or unexpected death of a family member, or even being a witness or bystander to violence (American Psychiatric Association, 2002).

According to the Facts for Health website http://www.factsforhealth.org, approximately 10 percent of Americans have had or will have PTSD at some point in their lives. The primary symptoms of PTSD are summarized in Table 9.1. The table also includes five important tips for coping with traumatic events.

Hardiness *Resilient personality that includes a strong commitment to personal goals, control over life, and viewing change as a challenge rather than a threat*

Posttraumatic Stress Disorder (PTSD) *Anxiety disorder following exposure to a life-threatening or other extreme event that evoked great horror or helplessness; characterized by flashbacks, nightmares, and impaired functioning*

TABLE 9.1 IDENTIFYING PTSD AND COPING WITH CRISIS

Primary Symptoms of Posttraumatic Stress Syndrome (PTSD)

- Re-experiencing the event through vivid memories or flashbacks
- Feeling "emotionally numb"
- Feeling overwhelmed by what would normally be considered everyday situations
- Diminished interest in performing normal tasks or pursuing usual interests
- Crying uncontrollably
- Isolating oneself from family and friends and avoiding social situations
- Relying increasingly on alcohol or drugs to get through the day
- Feeling extremely moody, irritable, angry, suspicious, or frightened
- Having difficulty falling or staying asleep, sleeping too much and experiencing nightmares
- Feeling guilty about surviving the event or being unable to solve the problem, change the event, or prevent the disaster
- Feeling fear and sense of doom about the future

Five Important Tips for Coping with Crisis

1. Recognize your feelings about the situation and talk to others about your fears. Know that these feelings are a normal response to an abnormal situation.
2. Be willing to listen to family and friends who have been affected and encourage them to seek counseling if necessary.
3. Be patient with people; fuses are short in times of crisis and others may be feeling as much stress as you.
4. Recognize normal crisis reactions, such as sleep disturbances and nightmares, withdrawal, reverting to childhood behaviors, and trouble focusing on work or school.
5. Take time with your children, spouse, life partner, friends, and co-workers to do something you enjoy.

Source: American Counseling Association and adapted from Pomponio, 2002.

Assessment

CHECK & REVIEW

Stress and Serious Illness

Cancer appears to result from an interaction of heredity, environmental insults (such as smoking), and immune system deficiency. Stress may be an important cause of decreased immunity. During times of stress, the body may be less able to check cancer cell multiplication because the immune system is suppressed.

The leading cause of death in the United States is heart disease. Risk factors include smoking, stress, obesity, a high-fat diet, lack of exercise, and **Type A personal**-ity (if it includes cynical hostility). The two main approaches to modifying Type A behavior are the shotgun approach and the target behavior approach. People with psychological **hardiness** are less vulnerable to stress because of three distinctive personality characteristics — commitment, control, and challenge.

Exposure to extraordinary stress (like war or rape) may lead to posttraumatic stress disorder (PTSD). Contrary to current opinion that gastric ulcers are caused only by the *H. pylori* bacterium, psychological research shows that stress also plays a major role.

Questions

1. Stress can contribute to heart disease by releasing the hormones _____ and _____, which increase the level of fat in the blood.
2. Which of the following is *not* among the characteristics associated with Type A personality? (a) time urgency; (b) patience; (c) competition; (d) hostility.
3. Explain how the three characteristics of the hardy personality help reduce stress.
4. What is the essential feature of PTSD?

Answers to Questions can be found in Appendix B.

ACTIVE LEARNING WORKSHEET   MODULE 9

Respond to the following questions, and then compare your answers with those in Appendix B.

1. Which of the following is a factor in the development of cancer?
   a. hereditary predispositions
   b. environmental substances
   c. changes in the immune system
   d. all of the above

2. A person with a _____ personality tends to be chronically on edge, feels a sense of intense time urgency, and is preoccupied with responsibilities, whereas a person with a _____ personality tends to have a laid-back, calm, relaxed attitude toward life.
   a. conflict ridden; conflict free
   b. distress type; eustress type
   c. Type-A; Type B
   d. internal locus of control; external locus of control

3. Why did cardiologists Meyer Friedman and Ray Rosenhan first become interested in the relationship between personality characteristics and heart disease?
   a. They noted that heart patients tend to sit on the front edge of chairs.
   b. There were frequent arguments among patients in their waiting rooms.
   c. The divorce rate of their patients was much higher than that of the general population.
   d. Their patients frequently brought work to do while waiting to see the cardiologists.

4. What is the most important factor in the Type A personality and the increased risk in heart disease?
   a. The sense of time urgency.
   b. Chronic feelings of irritability.
   c. Perception of chronic and increasing responsibilities.
   d. Feelings of cynical hostility.

5. Individuals with a hardy personality type tend to share a form of optimism that comes from three attitudes—commitment, control, and _____.
   a. conscientiousness
   b. compassion
   c. challenge
   d. conservatism

6. Juan was brutally beaten and robbed. For years after the attack, he experienced nightmares, times of impaired concentration, and occasional flashbacks of the attack. Juan probably suffers from _____.
   a. schizophrenia
   b. burnout
   c. posttraumatic stress disorder
   d. somatoform disorder

7. According to recent research, gastric ulcers are caused by:
   a. a bacterium called H. pylori
   b. increased hydrochloric acid and stress hormones
   c. decreased blood flow
   d. all of the above

MODULE 10
COPING WITH STRESS

Assessment

What techniques and resources are available to help people cope with stress?

Emotion-Focused Forms of Coping *Coping strategies based on changing one's perceptions of stressful situations*

Defense Mechanisms *Unconscious strategies used to distort reality and relieve anxiety and guilt*

Problem-Focused Forms of Coping *Coping strategies that use problem-solving strategies to decrease or eliminate the source of stress*

Figure 10.1 *Is stress in the eye of the beholder?* Lazarus (1999) suggests that our emotional reaction to stress is largely a result of how we interpret it. Therefore, we can learn to cope with stress with cognitive, emotional, and behavioral strategies — instead of feeling threatened.

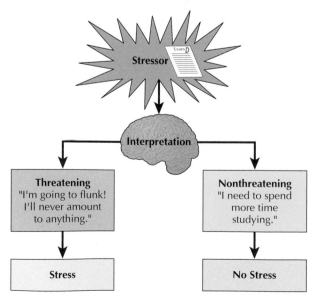

It would be helpful if we could avoid all negative stressful situations, but this is impossible. Everyone encounters pressure at work and school, long lines at the bank, and relationship problems. Because we can't escape stress, we need to learn how to effectively cope with it. Lazarus and Folkman (1984) defined *coping* as "constantly changing cognitive and behavioral efforts to manage specific external and/or internal demands that are appraised as taxing or exceeding the resources of the person." In simpler terms, coping is an attempt to manage stress in some effective way. It is not one single act but a process that allows us to deal with various stressors. As you can see in Figure 10.1, our level of stress depends on our interpretation and reaction. In this section, we first look at *emotion-focused* forms of coping that deal with our interpretation, and then we discuss *problem-focused* strategies that deal directly with our reactions.

■ Emotion-Focused Forms of Coping: Reappraising the Situation

Emotion-focused forms of coping are emotional or cognitive strategies that change how we view a stressful situation. Suppose you are refused a highly desirable job or rejected by a desired lover. You might reappraise the situation and decide that the job or lover might not have been the right match for you or that you weren't really qualified or ready for that specific job or relationship.

One of the most common forms of emotion-focused coping is the use of **defense mechanisms,** unconscious strategies that protect the ego and avoid anxiety by distorting reality (Module 35). The use of defense mechanisms reduces anxiety and often helps us cope with unavoidable stress. For instance, *fantasizing* about what you will do once you graduate from college or during the summer break can relax you when you're feeling stressed over final exams.

On the other hand, defense mechanisms can sometimes be destructive. You might decide you didn't get the job or the lover because you didn't have the right "connections" or "the perfect body." This is known as *rationalization*, fabricating excuses when frustrated in attaining particular goals. Not seeing the situation more clearly and realistically might prevent you from developing skills or qualities that could get you a desirable job or lover in the future.

In sum, emotion-focused forms of coping that are accurate reappraisals of stressful situations, and do not distort reality, may alleviate stress in some situations (Burke & Greenglass, 2000; Gold & Friedman, 2000). Many times, however, it is necessary and more effective to confront the stressor directly.

■ Problem-Focused Forms of Coping: Putting Problem-Solving Skills to Work

Problem-focused forms of coping deal directly with the situation or the stressor to eventually decrease or eliminate it (Bond & Bunce, 2000). Generally, these approaches are the same as the problem-solving strategies discussed in Module 22. Thus, the better a person is at solving problems, the more likely he or she will develop effective strategies. These strategies include identifying the stressful problem, generating possible solutions, selecting the appropriate solution, and applying the solution to the problem — thus eliminating the stress.

To illustrate the difference between the two forms of coping, let's suppose that you are flying to Denver to be in your best friend's wedding. You have an exam that lets out at 10:00 and your plane leaves at noon; the wedding is at 4:00. It will be tight, but you can

*A*pplication

CRITICAL THINKING · ACTIVE LEARNING

Is Your Job Stressful?

An important component of critical thinking is the ability to *define problems accurately.* By carefully identifying the problem in clear and concrete terms, critical thinkers prevent confusion and lay the foundation for gathering relevant information. Health psychologists (and industrial/organizational psychologists) have studied numerous factors in job-related stress. Their findings suggest that one way to prevent these stresses is to gather lots of information before making a career decision.

If you would like to apply this to your own career plans, start by identifying what you like and do not like about your current (and past) jobs. With this information in hand, you are then prepared to research jobs that will better suit your interests, needs, and abilities and avoid the stress caused by jobs failing to meet this criteria. To help your analysis, answer yes or no to these questions:

1. Is there a sufficient amount of laughter and sociability in your workplace?
2. Does your boss notice and appreciate your work?
3. Is your boss understanding and friendly?

4. Are you embarrassed by the physical conditions of your workplace?
5. Do you feel safe and comfortable in your place of work?
6. Do you like the location of your job?
7. If you won the lottery and were guaranteed a lifetime income, would you feel truly sad if you also had to quit your job?
8. Do you watch the clock, daydream, take long lunches, and leave work as soon as possible?
9. Do you frequently feel stressed and overwhelmed by the demands of your job?
10. Compared to others with your qualifications, are you being paid what you are worth?
11. Are promotions made in a fair and just manner?
12. Given the demands of your job, are you fairly compensated for your work?

Now score your answers. Give yourself one point for each answer that matches the following: 1. No; 2. No; 3. No; 4. Yes; 5. No; 6. No; 7. No; 8. Yes; 9. Yes; 10. No; 11. No; 12. No.

The questions you just answered are based on four factors that research shows are conducive to increased job satisfaction and

reduced stress: supportive colleagues, supportive working conditions, mentally challenging work, and equitable rewards (Robbins, 1996). Your total score reveals your overall level of dissatisfaction, whereas a look at specific questions can help identify which of these four factors is most important to your job satisfaction — and most lacking in your current job.

Supportive colleagues (items 1, 2, 3): For most employees, work fills important social needs. Therefore, having friendly and supportive colleagues and superiors leads to increased satisfaction.

Supportive working conditions (items 4, 5, 6): Not surprisingly, studies find most employees prefer working in safe, clean, and relatively modern facilities. They also prefer jobs close to home.

Mentally challenging work (items 7, 8, 9): Jobs with too little challenge create boredom and apathy, whereas too much challenge creates frustration and feelings of failure.

Equitable rewards (items 10, 11, 12): Employees want pay and promotions based on job demands, individual skill levels, and community pay standards.

---

make it. Unfortunately, on the way to the airport, the taxi has a flat tire. You can cognitively evaluate the situation and tell yourself that because this is your best friend, he'll understand that you did everything you could to be there; it wasn't your fault that the taxi had a flat (emotion-focused approach). Or, you could ask the driver to immediately call for another taxi to come and take you to the airport (problem-centered approach).

In general, the better a person is at solving problems, the more likely he or she will develop effective problem-focused coping strategies, including identifying the stressful problem, generating possible solutions, selecting the appropriate solution, and applying the solution to the problem.

Can people use both forms of coping strategies at once? Yes, most stressful situations are complex, and people often combine problem-focused and emotion-focused coping strategies. Furthermore, as you know from your own life, stressful situations change and the type of strategy we use depends not only on the stressor but also the changing nature of the stressor. In some situations, we may first need to use an emotion-focused strategy, which allows a step back from an especially overwhelming problem. Then, later on, when we have our emotional strength and our feet on the ground, we can reappraise the situation and use the problem-solving approach to look for solutions.

We also may use one coping strategy to prepare us to use the other. For example, humor is an emotion-focused coping strategy that is highly effective in altering negative moods. Also, in many situations, dealing with emotions helps us problem-solve (Keltner & Bonanno, 1997; Moran & Massam, 1999). Imagine that you are about to take your first exam in a difficult course. You are naturally very anxious: To calm yourself, you can first take an emotion-focused approach. You might say to yourself, "Relax and take a deep breath; it can't be as bad as you imagine." With reduced anxiety, you can then use problem-focused coping techniques and concentrate on the best strategy for taking the test.

■ Resources for Effective Coping: From Good Health to Money

A person's ability to cope effectively depends on the stressor itself — its complexity, intensity, and duration — and on the type of coping strategy used. It also depends on available resources. Researchers have identified several important coping resources:

1. *Health and energy.* All stressors cause physiological changes. Therefore, an individual's health significantly affects his or her ability to cope. Look again at Figure 8.2 on the GAS: The resistance stage is the coping stage. The stronger and healthier people are, the better they cope and the longer they stay in the resistance stage without entering the exhaustion stage.

2. *Positive beliefs.* A positive self-image and a positive attitude can be especially significant coping resources. Research shows that even temporarily raising self-esteem reduces the amount of anxiety caused by stressful events (Greenberg et al., 1993). Also, hope can sustain a person in the face of severe odds, as is often documented in news reports of people who have triumphed over seemingly unbeatable circumstances. According to Lazarus and Folkman, hope can come from a belief in oneself, which can enable us to devise our own coping strategies; a belief in others, such as medical doctors who we feel can effect positive outcomes; or a belief in a just and helpful God.

3. *Social skills.* Social situations — meetings, discussion groups, dates, parties, and so on — are often a source of pleasure, but they can also be a source of stress. Merely meeting someone new and trying to find something to talk about can be very stressful for some people. Therefore, people who acquire social skills (know appropriate behaviors for certain situations, have conversation-starters "up their sleeves," and express themselves well) suffer less anxiety than people who do not. In fact, people lacking social skills are more at risk for developing illness (Cohen & Williamson, 1991).

   Social skills not only help us interact with others, but also communicate our needs and desires, enlist help when we need it, and decrease hostility in tense situations. If you have weak social skills, you may find it worth the effort to learn how to act in a variety of social situations. Observe others and ask people with good social skills for advice. You can also practice your new skills by role-playing before applying them in real life.

4. *Social support.* Having the support of others helps offset the stressful effects of divorce, loss of a loved one, chronic illness, pregnancy, physical abuse, job loss, and work overload (Edwards, Hershberger, Russell, & Markert, 2001; Gold & Friedman, 2000; Yoshihama & Horrocks, 2002). When we are faced with stressful circumstances, our friends and family often help us take care of our health, listen and "hold our hand," make us feel important, and provide stability to offset the changes in our lives.

   For people with specific problems, support and self-help groups can be very helpful. There are groups for alcoholics and families of alcoholics, for former drug addicts, for divorced people, for single parents, for cancer patients, for parents who have had a young child die, and so on. Support groups help people

People need people. An important resource for coping with stress is social support from friends, families, and support groups.

cope not only because they provide other people to lean on but also because people can learn techniques for coping from others with similar problems (see Module 44).

5. *Material resources.* We've all heard the saying "Money isn't everything," but when it comes to coping with stress, money and the things that money can buy can be very real resources. Money increases the number of options available to eliminate sources of stress or reduce the effects of stress. When they are faced with the minor hassles of everyday living, with chronic stressors, or with major catastrophes, people with money and have the skills to effectively use that money generally fare better and experience less stress than people without money (Chi & Chou, 1999; Ennis, Hobfoll, & Schroeder, 2000).

6. *Personal control.* Do you believe that what happens to you is primarily the result of your own actions? That success is mostly a matter of hard work versus luck? Our sense of controlling our environment, rather than feeling helpless, is an important resource in effective coping. This perception of personal *locus of control* over the events in one's life tends to make people more sensitive to health messages and more likely to take actions to improve their health. It also buffers the negative effects of stress. In fact, one of the greatest threats to well-being occurs when people feel caught in a situation and unable to control their circumstances.

People with an **external locus of control** are more likely to believe in bad luck or fate. They feel powerless to change their circumstances and are less likely to make healthy changes, follow treatment programs, or positively cope with a situation. Conversely, people with an **internal locus of control** believe they are in charge of their own destiny and tend to adopt more positive coping strategies. For example, internals who believe their heart attacks happened because of their unhealthy choices, such as smoking or having a stressful job, are more likely to change their unhealthy behaviors and recover more quickly (Ewart & Fitzgerald, 1994). Studies in China (Hamid & Chan, 1998), Taiwan, and the UK (Lu, Kao, Cooper, & Spector, 2000) found that those who had a higher internal locus of control experienced less psychological stress than did those with a higher external locus of control.

External Locus of Control *Believing that chance or outside forces beyond one's control determine one's fate*

Internal Locus of Control *Believing that one controls one's own fate*

Application
APPLYING PSYCHOLOGY TO EVERYDAY LIFE

Taking Action Against Stress

In addition to coping styles and resources that rely primarily on cognitive and emotional strategies, there are other more direct, action-oriented approaches. Active coping methods "provide more direct and deliberate means of controlling and reducing the impact of stress ... [and] prepare us to deal with unexpected stress and keep us in stress-ready condition" (Gill, 1983, p. 84). The two major active methods are exercise and relaxation.

Exercise
If you exercise and keep yourself physically fit, you will probably experience less anxiety, depression, and tension than do people who do not exercise or who are less fit. Moreover, researchers have found that people engaging in strenuous exercise experienced greater reductions in anxiety than did those in moderate programs (Hong, 2000; Katula, Blissmer, & McAuley, 1999; McEntee & Halgin, 1999).

Exercise reduces the negative effects of stress in several ways. First, it uses up the hormones secreted into the bloodstream during stress, thereby helping the immune system return to normal functioning sooner. Second, exercise can help work out ten-

Coping with stress. Exercise and friends are important resources for effective stress reduction. As the song says, "I get by with a little help from my friends." John Lennon and Paul McCartney, Sgt. Pepper's Lonely Hearts Club Band, 1967.

You can use the following progressive relax-ation technique anytime and anywhere you feel stressed, such as while waiting for an exam to begin. Here's how:

1. Sit in a comfortable position, with your head supported.
2. Start breathing slowly and deeply.
3. Let your entire body go limp — let go of all tension. Try to visualize your body get-ting more and more relaxed.
4. Systematically tense and release each part of your body, beginning with your toes. Focus your attention on your toes and try to visualize what they are doing. Curl

them tightly, while counting to 10, then release them and feel the difference between the tense state and the relaxed state. Next, tense your feet to the count of 10, then relax them and feel the differ-ence between the two states. Continue with your calves, thighs, buttocks, abdomen, back muscles, shoulders, upper arms, forearms, hands and fingers, neck, jaws, facial muscles, and forehead.

Try practicing progressive relaxation twice a day for about 15 minutes. You will be sur-prised at how quickly you can learn to relax — even in the most stressful situations.

sion that has built up in muscles. Third, exercise increases strength, flexibility, and stamina for encountering future stressors and increases the efficiency of the cardio-vascular system. The best exercise for all these purposes is aerobic exercise — regular strenuous activity that heightens cardiovascular functioning, such as brisk walking, jogging, bicycling, swimming, dancing, and so on.

Relaxation

One of the most effective means of dealing with physical stress reactions is to make a conscious decision to relax during the stressful situation (Matuszek, 2000; Robert-McComb, 2001). There are a variety of relaxation techniques. As we will see in the next section, biofeedback is often used in the treatment of chronic pain, but it also is useful in teaching people to relax and manage their stress. Progressive relaxation is also very helpful in reducing or relieving the muscular tension commonly associated with stress. Using this technique, patients first tense and then relax specific muscles, such as in the neck, shoulders, and arms. This technique teaches people to recognize the difference between tense and relaxed muscles.

Assessment

CHECK & REVIEW

Coping With Stress

The two major forms of coping with stress are **emotion-focused** and **problem-focused.** Emotion-focused coping changes how we view stressful situations. Problem-focused coping deals directly with the situ-ation or the factor causing the stress so as to decrease or eliminate it. The ability to cope with a stressor also depends on the resources available to a person, including health and energy, positive beliefs, social

skills, social support, material resources, and personal control. Exercise and relax-ation are active methods people can use to cope with stress.

Questions

1. Which form of coping is being used in the following reactions to forgetting your best friend's birthday? (a) "I can't be expected to remember everyone's birthday"; (b) "I'd better put Cindy's birthday on my calen-dar so this won't happen again."

2. What are two common defense mecha-nisms, and why should people avoid using them?
3. People with a(n) _____ locus of control are better able to cope with stress.
4. What are the six major resources for cop-ing with stress? Which resource is most helpful for you? Least helpful?

Answers to Questions can be found in Appendix B.

ACTIVE LEARNING WORKSHEET   MODULE 10

This activity will help you review important concepts, as well as, helping you improve your coping responses to stress.

Briefly describe a recent time when you experienced significant stress. _____

_____

_____

Did you use an emotion-focused form of coping? If so, briefly describe it.

_____

_____

_____

Did you use a problem-focused form of coping? If so, briefly describe it.

_____

_____

_____

Your book describes several resources for coping with stress. Place a "+" mark by those activities or skills you currently use and a "–" by those you don't. Then review the items with a "–" mark, and decide how you can incorporate them into your daily life.

_____ health and energy
_____ positive beliefs
_____ social skills
_____ social support
_____ material resources
_____ personal control
_____ exercise
_____ relaxation

MODULE II
HEALTH PSYCHOLOGY IN ACTION

Assessment

How can health psychologists help with smoking, binge drinking, and chronic pain?

Psychological factors play a strong role in health problems. People use substances that are clearly unsafe and damaging to their health. Why? In this section, we'll consider the psychological components of two major health risks—*smoking* and *binge drinking*. We also will explore the psychological factors that increase and decrease *chronic pain*. But first, we must learn a little about the field of health psychology, and what health psychologists have learned about promoting healthy behaviors.

Application
APPLYING PSYCHOLOGY TO WORK

Would You Like To Be A Health Psychologist?

Health psychologists study how people's lifestyles and activities, emotional reactions, ways of interpreting events, and personality characteristics influence their physical health and well-being. Some health psychologists are involved primarily in research, whereas others work directly with physicians and other health professionals to implement research findings.

As researchers, they have been particularly interested in the relationship between stress and the immune system. As we discovered earlier, a normally functioning immune system helps detect and defend against disease, and a suppressed immune system leaves the body susceptible to a number of diseases.

As practitioners, health psychologists can work as independent clinicians or as consultants alongside physicians, physical and occupational therapists, and other health care workers. Their goal is to reduce psychological distress or unhealthy behaviors. They also help patients and families make critical decisions and prepare psychologically for surgery or other treatment.

In addition to their work as researchers and practitioners, health psychologists also educate the general public about health *maintenance*. They provide information about the effects of stress, smoking, alcohol, lack of exercise, and other health issues. In addition, health psychologists help people cope with chronic problems, such as pain, diabetes, and high blood pressure, as well as unhealthful behaviors, such as anger expression and lack of assertiveness (Davidson, MacGregor, Stuhr, Dixon, & MacLean, 2000; Haerenstam, Theorell, & Kaijser, 2000; Lepore, Ragan, & Jones, 2000).

■ Smoking: Hazardous to Your Health

A custom loathsome to the eye, hateful to the nose, harmful to the brain, dangerous to the lungs, and in the black, stinking fume thereof, nearest resembling the horrible Stygian smoke of the pit that is bottomless.

This is what King James I wrote about smoking in 1604, shortly after Sir Walter Raleigh introduced tobacco to England from the Americas. Today, nearly 400 years later, many people would agree with the king's tirade against the practice.

According to the latest U.S. Public Health Service report, tobacco is the single most preventable cause of death and disease in the United States (Fiore, 2000). Smoking is a major risk factor for coronary heart disease and lung cancer and contributes to cancers of the mouth, larynx, throat, esophagus, bladder, and pancreas (Centers for Disease Control, 2001, 2003). Smoking also contributes to chronic bronchitis, emphysema, and ulcers. Moreover, smoking shortens life (Figure 11.1) (Burns, 2000). This is true for both the smoker and those who breathe secondhand smoke.

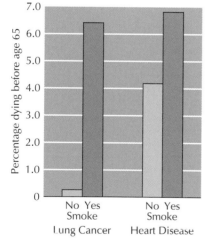

Figure 11.1 *Smoking shortens your life*. This graph shows the chances of a 35-year-old man dying of lung cancer or heart disease before age 65 as a function of smoking heavily or not smoking. Data for women were less complete, but probably would reveal similar risk increases. *Source:* Mattson, Pollack, & Cullen, 1987, p. 427.

What about all the new antismoking laws? Do they help? Ironically, the antismoking laws passed in the 1990s may have made quitting smoking even more difficult for some. First, the fact that smokers have to leave smoke-free environments and group together outdoors on the hottest summer days and the worst winter days to satisfy their habit creates a strong social bond: Together they will suffer the tyranny of nonsmoking laws. Cigarette companies play to this group loyalty (and the individual's "independence" and "perseverance") by showing smokers sitting high up on the ledges of office buildings and on the wings of airplanes in flight "going to any lengths" to have a cigarette. Second, when people cannot smoke in offices, on airplanes, in restaurants, or other public places, the interval between nicotine doses increases, which increases the severity of the withdrawal symptoms (Palfai, Monti, Ostafin, & Hutchinson, 2000). In effect, the smoker gets repeated previews of just how unpleasant quitting is going to be — and who wouldn't rather avoid something unpleasant?

Most people know that smoking is bad for their health and that the more they smoke, the more at risk they are. It is therefore not surprising that most health psychologists and medical professionals are concerned with preventing smoking in the first place and getting those who already smoke to stop.

Smokers unite? Due to increased restrictions, many people are forced to go outside to smoke. Ironically, this may forge stronger bonds between smokers and make them even more resistant to quitting.

Smoking Prevention

The first puff on a cigarette is rarely pleasant. Why, then, do people ever start smoking? The answer is complex. First, smoking usually starts when people are young. The European School Survey Project on Alcohol and Other Drugs (ESPAD) (2001) reported that tobacco smoking was well established by the mid-teens in most European countries and showed few signs of diminishing since the previous ESPAD survey in 1995. A similar survey of U.S. middle schools, grades 6 to 8, found that one in eight students were experimenting with some form of tobacco, such as cigarettes, cigars, and chewing tobacco (Kaufman, 2000). There are many reasons people begin to smoke at such a young age, but peer pressure and imitation of role models (such as celebrities) are particularly strong factors. Young smokers want to look mature and be accepted by their social peers.

Secondly, regardless of the age at which a person begins smoking, once he or she begins to smoke, there is a biological need to continue because of the addictive effects of nicotine. The evidence clearly shows that nicotine is a powerful addictive drug, comparable to heroin, cocaine, and alcohol (Balfour & Ridley, 2000; Pahlavan, Bonnet, & Duda, 2000; Pich et al., 1997). In fact, when we inhale smoke, it takes only seconds for the nicotine to reach the brain, where it increases the release of the neurotransmitters acetylcholine and norepinephrine. Acetylcholine and norepinephrine, in turn, increase alertness, concentration, memory, and feelings of pleasure (McGaughy, Decker, & Sarter, 1999; Picciotto, 1998; Quattrocki, Baird, & Yurgelun-

Part of California's antismoking campaign, this billboard focuses on the dangers of environmental tobacco smoke. Researchers have found that this approach reduces the desire among adolescents to start smoking. Source: California Department of Health Service.

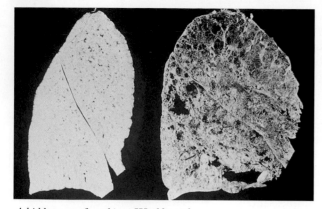

A hidden cost of smoking. Would people continue to smoke if they could see what it does to their lungs? Compare the healthy tissue of the lung of a non-smoker on the left to the blackened, unhealthy lung of the smoker on the right.

Todd, 2000). Several recent research projects have also indicated that nicotine stimulates the release of dopamine, the neurotransmitter most closely related to reward centers in the brain (Noble, 2000; Carboni, Bortone, Giua, & DiChiara, 2000). These neurotransmitters also decrease the symptoms of nicotine withdrawal, anxiety, tension, and pain, which come after a short period without tobacco.

Finally, social pressures and physical addiction combine to create additional benefits (Lazev, Herzog, & Brandon, 1999). For example, smokers learn to associate smoking with pleasant things, such as good food, friends, sex, and, not least, the high that nicotine gives them, so their smoking is rewarded. When smokers are deprived of cigarettes, they go through physical withdrawal with extremely unpleasant symptoms. When they get their next puff, the nicotine relieves the symptoms, so smoking is rewarded. It follows that the best way to reduce the number of smokers is to prevent people from taking their first puff.

If most people begin smoking during adolescence, shouldn't prevention be aimed at this group? Prevention programs for teens face a tough uphill battle. For adolescents, the long-term health disadvantages of heart disease and cancer seem totally irrelevant, whereas smoking itself provides immediate short-term rewards from peers and the addictive, reinforcing properties of nicotine. Many smoking prevention programs therefore focus on immediate short-term problems with smoking, such as bad breath and interference with athletic performance.

Through films and discussion groups, teens also are educated about peer pressure and the media's influence on smoking, given opportunities to role-play refusal skills, taught general social and personal skills needed in decision making, and given strategies for coping with the stresses of adolescence and daily life (Worden, Flynn, Solomon, & Secker-Walker, 1996). Unfortunately, the research shows that the effect of psychosocial prevention programs is small (Baum & Posluszny, 1999). To have even a modest effect, these programs must begin early and continue for many years (Eckhardt, Woodruff, & Elder, 1997).

To reduce the health risk and help fight peer pressure, many schools ban smoking in college buildings and offer more smoke-free dormitories. Another possible deterrent to the college smoking trend results from expensive legal battles and settlements by the tobacco industry and the fact that these expenses are passed on to consumers in the form of higher prices for cigarettes. This increase, added to state and local taxes, brings the cost to over $4 per pack in most states. For a student who smokes a pack of cigarettes a day, the annual cost is nearly $1,500 — more than twice the cost of textbooks for an entire academic year.

Stopping Smoking

To cease smoking is the easiest thing I ever did; I ought to know, for I have done it a thousand times.

MARK TWAIN

Unfortunately, Mark Twain was never able to quit for very long, and many ex-smokers say that stopping smoking was the most difficult thing they ever did. Although some people find the easiest way for them to cope with the physical withdrawal from nicotine is to suddenly and completely stop, the success rate for this "cold turkey" approach is extremely low. Even with medical aids, such as patches, gum, or pills, it is still very difficult to quit (Killen et al., 2000; Patten, 2000). Any program designed to help smokers break their habit must combat the social rewards of smoking as well as the physical addiction to nicotine.

Sometimes the best approach is a combination of cognitive and behavioral techniques and nicotine replacement therapy. Cognitively, smokers can learn to identify stimuli or situations that make them feel like smoking and then change or avoid them (Brandon, Collins, Juliano, & Lazev, 2000). They can also refocus their attention on something other than smoking or remind themselves of the benefits of not smoking (Taylor, Harris, Singleton, Moolchan, & Heishman, 2000). Behaviorally, they might cope with the urge to smoke by chewing gum, exercising, or chewing on a toothpick after a meal instead of lighting a cigarette.

No program to quit smoking will work without a tremendous amount of personal motivation, but the payoffs can be just as tremendous: a more enjoyable and longer life. (See Wetter et al., 1998, for the Agency for Health Care Policy and Research's "Smoking Cessation Clinical Practice Guidelines.")

■ Binge Drinking: A Growing Social Problem

Were you surprised by news reports of two freshmen at Massachusetts Institute of Technology who died from alcohol poisoning after binge drinking at fraternity parties? One of the students had a blood alcohol level of .5888 percent — the equivalent of more than 20 beers in 1 hour and over seven times the legal driving limit in most states. Unlike smoking, alcohol and other drugs can kill directly and immediately when they are taken in large amounts over a short period of time. They also impair the judgment and reaction times of the user, thus contributing to thousands of deaths and injuries from automobile accidents, rapes, and other assaults. (See Module 15 to review the short- and long-term health risks of alcohol.)

Binge drinking occurs when a man consumes five or more drinks in a row or a woman consumes four or more drinks at a time (Weingardt et al., 1998). Approximately 5.1 million Americans between the ages of 12 and 20 years are binge drinkers, and the greatest majority are college students (Wechsler, Lee, Kuo, & Lee, 2000). Binge drinking is a serious health problem for all college-age students, those who drink and those who don't.

What can be done about college binge drinking? Stopping students from binge drinking is very difficult. Students seem to think of it as part of the "college experience." Therefore, any real attack on binge drinking must approach the problem from many different directions. First, it is important to overcome the myths about college drinking and teach the facts. But just learning the facts does not stop people from drinking. The social rewards also must be reduced or removed.

So what are these misconceptions, and how do we reduce the social rewards? Henry Wechsler (1998), the first author of *The Harvard School of Public Health College Alcohol Study*, suggests the following:

* ***Students who binge tend to think that they are just average or moderate drinkers.*** We must make it clear to these students that binge drinking is not the norm. It is not normal or healthy to drink four or five drinks at a sitting, let alone to do that frequently.

* ***Many students believe that binge drinking is harmless to the drinker and to college society.*** But binge drinkers risk AIDS from unprotected sex and can be the victims or perpetrators of assault, rape, and car accident injuries.

* ***Many students think that it's okay to binge drink because the college administration looks the other way.*** College administrations must enforce antidrinking rules and make a greater effort to help students who abuse alcohol. Strict penalties might help repeat offenders.

* ***Members of fraternities and sororities seem to think that drinking is part of the Greek life.*** College communities therefore have a responsibility to work with these organizations so that drinking is not central to social events.

Binge drinking can be fatal. *On many college campuses, it is a tradition to "drink your age" on your 21st birthday. Following this tradition, Bradley McCue, a University of Michigan junior, drank 21 shots of alcohol plus three more to break his friends' record. He died on the morning of his 21st birthday from alcohol poisoning. For more information, contact www.BRAD21.org.*

- ***When students see alumni drinking at tailgate parties and hear their stories of partying until dawn, they think that drinking is what alumni expect them to do at college.*** Any alcohol-control measures directed at students must also apply to visiting alumni. Sporting events should be alcohol free, and colleges should avoid alcohol-related sports promotions.

GENDER & CULTURAL DIVERSITY

Binge Drinking Around the World

After reading the previous section on binge drinking, you may think it is a problem unique to college students in the United States. Unfortunately, binge drinking is a worldwide problem.

- The European School Survey Project (2001) found an overall increase in binge drinking since 1995, especially in Britain, Denmark, Ireland, and Poland. More than 30 percent of school children in those countries reported binge drinking three or more times in the last month.

- In Mexico, a study of drinking patterns at 16 religious fiestas and 13 nonreligious fiestas in the community of Santa María Atzompa found that nearly all the men qualified as binge drinkers at every fiesta. Furthermore, the binge drinking contributed to several outbreaks of violence at the fiestas (Perez, 2000).

- A study in Spain and South America found that young men who reported binge drinking were more likely than others to behave aggressively toward people outside their family (Orpinas, 1999).

- Scientists in Denmark compared the drinking patterns of 56,970 men and women who prefer drinking beer, wine, or spirits (Gronbaek, Tjonneland, Johansen, Stripp, & Overvad, 2000). Results showed that beer drinkers were the least likely of the different types of drinkers to binge, whereas wine drinkers were the most likely to binge.

- Research on alcohol consumption in Russia shows that 44 percent of men are binge drinkers (Bobak, McKee, Rose, & Marmot, 1999).

- The lower rate of binge drinking in Japan has been linked to a genetic mutation that makes it difficult for many Japanese, and other Asians, to metabolize alcohol. Nearly half of the Japanese population is sensitive to alcohol owing to this genetic mutation. Research shows that Japanese who do carry the mutation are much more likely to be binge drinkers than those who do not carry the mutation (Takeshita & Morimoto, 1999; Tu & Israel, 1995).

Binge drinking among young adults is a growing problem, and many teenage and college women are drinking as much as men.

■ Chronic Pain: The Role of Psychologists in Helping Patients Cope

Pain is the most common reason why people seek medical attention. People consult physicians and take medication for pain more than for any other condition or symptom (Price, 2000). Although we try to avoid pain, it is necessary for our survival. Pain alerts us to dangerous or harmful situations, and pain forces us to rest and recover from injury (Watkins & Maier, 2000). But **chronic pain,** pain that continues long past the healing of a wound or pain that is associated with a chronic disease, does not serve a useful function.

Although psychological factors rarely are the source of chronic pain, they can encourage and intensify it, and increase the related anguish and disability (Affleck,

Chronic Pain *Continuous or recurrent pain over a period of 6 months or longer*

Tennen, & Apter, 2001; Fruehwald, Loffler, Eher, Saletu, & Baumhackl, 2001; Snow-Turek, Norris, & Tan, 1996). To treat chronic pain, health psychologists use specific treatment methods, such as behavior modification, biofeedback, and relaxation.

Behavior Modification

Chronic pain is a serious problem with no simple solution. For example, exercise is known to produce an increase in *endorphins*, naturally produced chemicals that attach themselves to nerve cells in the brain and block the perception of pain (Module 5). However, chronic pain patients tend to decrease their activity and exercise. In addition, well-meaning family members often ask chronic pain sufferers, "How are you feeling?" "Is the pain any better today?" Unfortunately, talking about pain focuses attention on it and increases its intensity (Harvey & McGuire, 2000). Furthermore, as the pain increases, anxiety increases, the anxiety itself then increases the pain, which further increases the anxiety, which further increases the pain!

To counteract these hidden personal and family problems and negative cycles, health psychologists may begin a behavior modification program for both the patient with chronic pain and his or her family. The effectiveness of such programs for treating chronic pain was first shown in the late 1970s (Cairns & Pasino, 1977). Researchers established individualized pain management programs, monitored each patient's adherence, and congratulated those who followed through with their pain treatment programs (daily exercise, use of relaxation techniques, and so on). Compared with a control group, patients who used these techniques experienced substantially reduced pain. Today, many pain control programs incorporate similar techniques for rewarding "well behaviors" (Kole-Snijders et al., 1999).

Pain control through biofeedback. Using an electromyograph (EMG), muscular tension is recorded and the patient is taught specific relaxation techniques that reduce tension and help relieve chronic pain.

Biofeedback

In *biofeedback*, information about physiological functions, such as heart rate or blood pressure, is monitored, and the feedback helps the individual learn to control these functions. Such feedback about physiological processes helps reduce some types of chronic pain. Most biofeedback with chronic pain patients is done with the *electromyograph* (EMG). This device measures muscle tension by recording electrical activity in the skin. The EMG is most helpful when the pain involves extreme muscle tension, such as tension headache and lower back pain. Electrodes are attached to the site of the pain, and the patient is instructed to relax. When sufficient relaxation is achieved, the machine signals with a tone or a light. The signal serves as feedback to the patient.

Research shows that biofeedback is sometimes as effective as more expensive and lengthy forms of treatment (Newton-John, Spence, & Schotte, 1995). The reason for its success seems to be that it teaches patients to recognize patterns of emotional arousal and conflict that affect their physiological responses. This self-awareness, in turn, enables them to learn self-regulation skills that help control their pain (McKee, 1991).

Relaxation Techniques

Because the pain always seems to be there, chronic pain sufferers tend to talk and think about their pain whenever they're not thoroughly engrossed in an activity. Watching TV shows or films, attending parties, or any activity that diverts attention from the pain seems to reduce discomfort. Attention might also be diverted with special *relaxation techniques* like those that are taught in so-called "natural childbirth" classes. These techniques focus the birthing mother's attention on breathing and relaxing the muscles, which helps distract her attention from the fear and pain of the birthing process. Similar techniques also can be helpful to chronic pain sufferers. Remember, though, that these techniques do not eliminate the pain; they merely allow the person to ignore it for a time.

Relaxation techniques. Massage is a healthy way to reduce stress and tension related pain.

A Final Note

You are the one who is ultimately responsible for your own health and well-being. Although doctors, nurses, and other health professionals are there for you if you become ill, it is best to do all you can to prevent disease in the first place. By minimizing the harmful effects of stress in our lives, we help our bodies stay well and fight off disease.

Assessment
CHECK & REVIEW

Health Psychology in Action

Because smoking is the single most preventable cause of death and disease in the United States, prevention and cessation of smoking are of primary importance to all health practitioners, including health psychologists. Smoking prevention programs involve educating the public about short- and long-term consequences of smoking, trying to make smoking less socially acceptable, and helping nonsmokers resist social pressures to smoke. Most approaches to help people quit smoking include cognitive and behavioral techniques to aid smokers in their withdrawal from nicotine, along with nicotine replacement therapy (using patches, gum, and pills).

Binge drinking is a serious problem that can lead to rape or assault, to death from alcohol poisoning, or automobile and other accidents. It occurs when a man has five or more drinks in a row and a woman has four or more. To reduce binge drinking, we must overcome the myths about drinking and teach the facts. We also must reduce or remove the social rewards.

Chronic pain is continuous or recurrent pain that persists over a period of six months or more.

Although psychological factors rarely are the source of chronic pain, they can encourage and intensify it. Increased activity, exercise, and dietary changes help to reduce chronic pain. Health psychologists also use behavior modification, biofeedback, and relaxation techniques to treat chronic pain.

Questions

1. Knowing smoking is very dangerous, why is it so difficult for many people to stop?

2. If you are mounting a campaign to prevent young people from taking up smoking, you are likely to get the best results if you emphasize the _____. (a) serious, unhealthy, long-term effects of tobacco use; (b) number of adults who die from smoking; (c) value of having a relatively healthy retirement; (d) short-term detrimental effects of tobacco use.

3. What are the 5 misconceptions about binge drinking, and how can we remove the social reinforcers?

4. An increase in activity and exercise levels benefits patients with pain because exercise increases the release of (a) endorphins; (b) insulin; (c) acetylcholine; (d) norepinephrine.

Answers to Questions can be found in Appendix B.

MODULE 11   ACTIVE LEARNING WORKSHEET

Complete the following, and then check your answers with those in Appendix B.

1. Health psychologists who work as researchers are particularly interested in the relationship between _____ and the _____.
2. When health psychologists work as _____, their goal is to reduce psychological distress or unhealthy behaviors.
3. According to the latest U.S. Public Health Service report, _____ is the single most preventable cause of death and disease in the United States.
4. You read a newspaper article claiming that the rate of birth defects is three times as high for mothers who drink alcohol than for those who do not drink alcohol. Can you conclude that this difference is directly attributable to alcohol consumption, or can you think of other plausible explanations?
5. Your friend avoids visiting his grandmother because "all she ever talks about is her aches and pains." Using information from this module, what advice would you offer your friend regarding his grandmother?

Assessment
KEY TERMS

*To assess your understanding of the **Key Terms*** in this section, write a definition for each (in your own words), and then compare your definitions with those in the text.

Stress and Its Role in Health
approach–approach conflict (p. 101)
approach–avoidance conflict
    (p. 101)
avoidance–avoidance conflict
    (p. 101)
burnout (p. 100)
conflict (p. 101)
distress (p. 98)
eustress (p. 98)
frustration (p. 101)
general adaptation syndrome (GAS)
    (p. 104)

hassles (p. 100)
health psychology (p. 97)
HPA Axis (p. 102)
psychoneuroimmunology [sye-ko-
    NEW-ro-IM-you-NOLL-oh-gee]
    (p. 104)
stress (p. 98)

Stress and Serious Illness
hardiness (p. 111)
posttraumatic stress disorder (PTSD)
    (p. 111)
Type A personality (p. 109)

Type B personality (p. 109)

Coping with Stress
defense mechanisms (p. 114)
emotion-focused forms of coping
    (p. 114)
external locus of control (p. 117)
internal locus of control (p. 117)
problem-focused forms of coping
    (p. 114)

Health Psychology
chronic pain (p. 124)

Achievement
WEB RESOURCES

Huffman Book Companion Site
http://www.wiley.com/college/huffman
    This site is loaded with free Interactive Self-Tests, Internet Exercises, Glossary and Flashcards for key terms, Web links, Handbook for Non-Native Speakers, and other activities designed to improve your mastery of the material in this section.

Stanford University Health Information Library
http://healthlibrary.stanford.edu/
    A general source of scientifically based medical information to help you make informed decisions about your health and health care.

Stress and Its Management
http://stress.about.com/?once=true&
    An excellent site with useful information and tips for handling stress and its management, such as time management, financial problems, night eating, etc.

Free Health Risk Assessment
http://www.youfirst.com/
    This site contains a free personal health assessment useful for identifying your greatest risk factors and links to related information.

Focus on Stress
http://helping.apa.org/work/index.html
    Provides a series of interesting articles about stress.

Burnout Test
http://www.prohealth.com/articles/burnout.htm
    Offers a short self-test on job burnout.

VISUAL SUMMARY

Stress and Health Psychology
(Modules 8, 9, 10, and 11)

Stress and Its Role in Health

Sources of Stress
- *Life changes*: Holmes and Rahe Scale measures stress caused by important life events.
- *Chronic stressors*: Ongoing, long term stress related to political world, family, work, etc.
- **Hassles**: Small, everyday problems that accumulate.
- **Burnout**: Exhaustion resulting from emotionally demanding situations.
- **Frustration**: Negative emotional state from blocked goals.
- **Conflict**: Negative emotional state from 2 or more incompatible goals.
There are 3 types of conflict

Approach-approach conflict:
Two or more desirable goals

Avoidance-avoidance conflict:
Two or more undesirable goals

Approach-avoidance conflict:
Both desirable and undesirable goals

Effects of Stress
- *Sympathetic nervous system activation* increases heart rate, blood pressure, respiration, and muscle tension and releases stress hormones.
- *HPA axis* increases the stress hormone cortisol, which decreases immune system functioning.
  - *Suppressed immune system* leaves body vulnerable to disease.

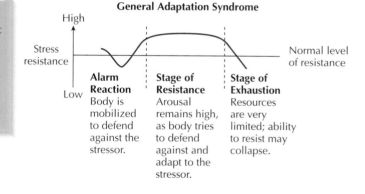

General Adaptation Syndrome

High

Stress resistance

Low

Normal level of resistance

Alarm Reaction
Body is mobilized to defend against the stressor.

Stage of Resistance
Arousal remains high, as body tries to defend against and adapt to the stressor.

Stage of Exhaustion
Resources are very limited; ability to resist may collapse.

Stress and Serious Illness

Cancer
Caused by hereditary dispositions and environmental factors that lead to changes in body chemistry and the immune system

Cardiovascular Disorders
Contributing Factors:
- Stress hormones
- **Type A personality**
- Behaviors such as smoking, obesity, lack of exercise

Postraumatic Stress Disorder (PTSD) and Gastric Ulcers
Exposure to extraordinary stress may lead to PTSD, and chronic stress may increase vulnerability to the *H. pylori* bacterium, which causes gastric ulcers

Coping with Stress

Emotion-Focused Forms of Coping

Emotional and cognitive strategies that change how one appraises a stressful situation.
Defense mechanisms are unconscious strategies that protect the ego and avoid anxiety by distorting reality.

Problem-Focused Forms of Coping

Strategies that deal directly with the stressful situation by applying problem-solving techniques to decrease or eliminate it.

Resources for Effective Coping

Good health, energy, positive beliefs, social skills, social support, material resources, and personal control (e.g., **internal locus of control**) all reduce stress.

Taking Action Against Stress

Exercise and relaxation techniques directly reduce stress.

Health Psychology in Action

Smoking

- *Why do people smoke?* Peer pressure; imitation of role models; addiction (nicotine increases release of neurotransmitters that increase alertness, memory, and well being and decrease anxiety, tension, and pain); learned associations with positive results.
- *Prevention?* Educate about short- and long- term consequences, make smoking less socially acceptable, and help nonsmokers resist social pressures.
- *Stopping?* Use cognitive and behavioral techniques to deal with withdrawal; supplement with nicotine replacement therapy (patches, gum, and pills).

Binge Drinking

Binge drinking: When a man consumes 5 or more drinks in a row, or a woman consumes 4 or more.
How to reduce?
- Overcome the myths and teach facts.
- Reduce or remove social rewards.

Chronic Pain

Chronic pain: Pain lasting over 6 months.
How to reduce?
- Increase activity and exercise.
- Use behavior modification strategies to reinforce changes.
- Employ *biofeedback* with *electromyograph (EMG)* to reduce muscle tension.
- Use relaxation techniques.

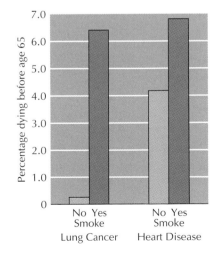

SENSATION AND PERCEPTION

I have just touched my dog. He was rolling on the grass, with pleasure in every muscle and limb. I wanted to catch a picture of him in my fingers, and I touched him as lightly as I would cobwebs. ... He pressed close to me, as if he were fain to crowd himself into my hand. He loved it with his tail, with his paw, with his tongue. If he could speak, I believe he would say with me that paradise is attained by touch. [pp. 3–4]

Thus Helen Keller began her book *The World I Live In*. Her world was totally different from that of most people: She couldn't see it or hear it because she was blind and deaf, but she was as capable and as appreciative of life — if not more so — as any person with all five senses. This was because she made the most of the senses she did have. Excerpts from her book describe how she used these senses:

Through the sense of touch I know the faces of friends, the illimitable variety of straight and curved lines, all surfaces, the exuberance of the soil, the delicate shapes of flowers, the noble forms of trees, and the range of mighty winds. Besides objects, surfaces, and atmospherical changes, I perceive countless vibrations. ... Footsteps, I discover, vary tactually according to the age, the sex, and the manners of the walker. ... When a carpenter works in the house or in the barn near by, I know by the slanting, up-and-down, toothed vibration, and the ringing concussion of blow upon blow, that he is sawing or hammering...

In the evening quiet there are fewer vibrations than in the daytime, and then I rely more largely upon smell. ... Sometimes, when there is no wind, the odors are so

■ Achievement
■ Assessment
■ Application

grouped that I know the character of the country and can place a hayfield, a country store, a garden, a barn, a grove of pines, a farmhouse with the windows open. ... I know by smell the kind of house we enter. I have recognized an old-fashioned country house because it has several layers of odors, left by a succession of families, of plants, perfumes, and draperies. [pp. 43–44, 46, 68–69]

Helen Keller wasn't born deaf and blind. When she was 19 months old, she suffered a fever that left her without sight or hearing and thus virtually isolated from the world. Keller's parents realized they had to find help for their daughter, and after diligently searching, they found Anne Sullivan, a young teacher who was able to break through Keller's barrier of isolation by taking advantage of her sense of touch. One day, Sullivan took Keller to the pumphouse and, as Sullivan (1902) wrote,

I made Helen hold her mug under the spout while I pumped. As the cold water gushed forth, filling the mug, I spelled "w-a-t-e-r" in Helen's free hand. The word coming so close upon the sensation of cold water rushing over her hand seemed to startle her. She dropped the mug and stood as one transfixed. A new light came into her face. [p. 257]

That one moment, brought on by the sensation of cold water on her hand, was the impetus for a lifetime of learning about, understanding, and appreciating the world through her remaining senses. In 1904, Helen Keller graduated cum laude from Radcliffe College and went on to become a famous author and lecturer, inspiring physically limited people throughout the world.

The story of Helen Keller has been told and retold as an example of how people can overcome sensory deficiencies by using their other senses to the optimum. It also provides a wonderful introduction to the two major topics of this section: **sensation,** the process of receiving, converting, and transmitting information from the outside world (outside the brain, not necessarily outside the body), and **perception,** the process of selecting, organizing, and interpreting raw sensory data into useful mental representations of the world.

As you can see in Figure 12.1, the basic function of sensation is *detection* of sensory stimuli, whereas perception generally involves *interpretation* of the same stimuli. Like the central nervous system (CNS) and peripheral nervous system (PNS), the key functions of sensation and perception are somewhat different. But also like the CNS and PNS, the boundary between these two processes is not precise — there is considerable overlap.

We begin this section discussing how we receive sensory information and work our way upward to the top levels of perceptual processing. Psychologists refer to this type of information processing as **bottom-up processing,** taking sensory data in through the sensory receptors, such as the eyes, ears, nose, and tongue, and sending it "upward" to

the brain for analysis. In contrast, **top-down processing** begins with "higher," "top"-level processing involving thoughts, previous experiences, expectations, language, and cultural background and works down to the sensory level. When first learning to read, you used *bottom-up processing.* You initially learned that certain arrangements of lines and "squiggles" represented specific letters. Only later did you realize that these letters joined together to make up words. After years of experience and language training, you quickly perceive the words in this sentence before the individual letters — *top-down processing.* Although top-down processing is far superior for reading, both bottom-up and top-down processing are important to perception.

Sensation *Process of receiving, translating, and transmitting raw sensory data from the external and internal environments to the brain*

Perception *Process of selecting, organizing, and interpreting sensory data into useful mental representations of the world*

Bottom-Up Processing *Information processing that begins "at the bottom" with raw sensory data that feed "up" to the brain*

Top-Down Processing *Information processing that starts "at the top" with the observer's thoughts, expectations, and knowledge and works down*

MODULE 12
SENSATION

Our opening discussion of sensation covers not only what are commonly known as the five senses — vision, hearing, taste, smell, and touch — but also those senses that provide the brain with data from inside the body: the *vestibular sense* (the sense of balance) and *kinesthesis* (the sense of bodily position and movement). After we've covered sensation, we will study perception, where the focus is on how we select, organize, and interpret sensory data. In that module, you discover how we decide what to pay attention to, how we perceive distance, how we see different colors, and whether there is any scientific evidence to support subliminal perception and extrasensory perception (ESP).

Experiencing Sensations: Processing, Thresholds, Adaptation

To experience sensations, we must have both a means of detecting stimuli and a means of converting them into a language the brain can understand. Let's take a closer look at how our sensory organs accomplish both tasks.

Processing

Our eyes, ears, skin, and other sense organs all contain special cells called *receptors,* which receive and process sensory information from the environment. For each sense, these specialized cells respond to a distinct stimulus, such as sound waves or odor molecules.

Through a process called **transduction,** the receptors convert the stimulus into neural impulses, which are sent to the brain. In hearing, for example, tiny receptor cells in the inner ear convert mechanical vibrations (from sound waves) into electrochemical signals. These signals are carried by neurons to the brain. Each type of sensory receptor is designed to detect a wide variety of stimuli and a wide range of stimulation. However, also built into our sensory systems are structures that purposefully reduce the amount of stimuli we receive.

Why would we want to reduce the amount of sensory information we receive? Can you imagine what would happen if you did not have some natural filtering of

How do our sensory organs gather sensory information and convert it into signals the brain can understand?

Transduction *Converting a stimulus to a receptor into neural impulses*

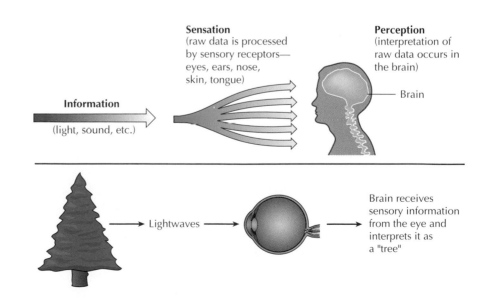

Figure 12.1 *Sensation and perception.* Sensation is the detection and conversion of raw data from the senses. Perception is the interpretation of these raw sensory data by the brain.

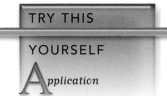

(b)

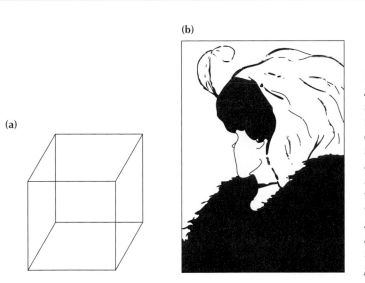

(a)

What is it — sensation or perception? (a) When you stare at this drawing (known as the Necker cube), which area is the top, front, or back of the cube? In the process of sensation, your visual sensory system detects a collection of lines, angles, patterns of color, and so on. But at the perceptual level, you interpret these lines as a geometric shape called a cube. If you stare at it long enough, your perception/interpretation will change. (b) Now look at this drawing of a woman. Do you see a young woman looking back over her right shoulder or an older woman with her chin down on her chest? Although basic sensory input stays the same, your brain's attempt to interpret ambiguous stimuli creates a type of perceptual dance, shifting from one interpretation to another. Source: Gaetz, Weinberg, Rzempoluck, & Jantzen, 1998.

stimuli? You would constantly hear blood rushing through your veins and continually feel your clothes brushing against your skin. Some level of filtering is needed so the brain is not overwhelmed with unnecessary information. It needs to be free to respond to those stimuli that have meaning for survival. Each of our senses is therefore custom designed to respond to only a select range of potential sensory information.

All species have evolved selective receptors that suppress or amplify information to allow survival. For example, hawks have an acute sense of vision but a poor sense of smell. Similarly, we humans cannot sense many stimuli, such as ultraviolet light, microwaves, the ultrasonic sound of a dog whistle, or infrared heat patterns from warm-blooded animals (which rattlesnakes can). However, we can see a candle burning 30 miles away on a dark, clear night, hear the tick of a watch at 20 feet under quiet conditions, smell one drop of perfume in a six-room apartment, and taste 1 teaspoon of sugar dissolved in 2 gallons of water.

In the process of **sensory reduction,** we not only filter incoming sensations, we also analyze the sensations sent through before a neural impulse is finally sent to the cortex of the brain. If cells in the reticular formation within the brainstem (Module 6) decide the information is important, it is passed on to alert the cerebral cortex. This explains why parents of a newborn can sleep through passing sirens and blaring stereos yet awaken to the slightest whimper of their baby.

How does the brain differentiate between various incoming sensations, such as sounds and smells? It depends on the number and type of sensory cells that are activated, on the precise nerve that is stimulated, and ultimately on the part of the brain that the nerve stimulates. Through a process known as **coding,** sounds and smells are interpreted as distinct sensations not because of the environmental stimuli that activate them but because their respective neural impulses travel by different routes and arrive at different parts of the brain. Figure 12.2 illustrates the parts of the brain involved in sensory reception.

Sensory Reduction *Filtering and analyzing incoming sensations before sending a neural message to the cortex*

Coding *Three-part process that converts a particular sensory input into a specific sensation*

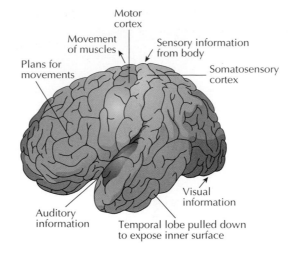

Figure 12.2 *Sensory areas of the brain.* Neural impulses travel from the sensory receptors to various parts of the brain.

Psychophysics *Study of the relation between attributes of the physical world and our psychological experience of them*

Absolute Threshold *The smallest amount of a stimulus needed to detect that the stimulus is present*

Difference Threshold *Minimal difference needed to notice a stimulus change; also called the "just noticeable difference" (JND)*

Sensory Adaptation *Repeated or constant stimulation decreases the number of sensory messages sent to the brain, which causes decreased sensation*

Thresholds

How do we know that humans can hear a watch ticking at 20 feet or smell one drop of perfume in a six-room apartment? The answer comes from research in **psychophysics,** an area of psychology that examines how physical stimuli (such as sound and smell) are related to an individual's psychological reactions to those stimuli. Using knowledge from both physics and psychology, psychophysicists study how the strength or intensity of a stimulus affects an observer.

Suppose you are the parent of a school-age daughter who, like Helen Keller, has just suffered from a serious illness accompanied by high fever. During her period of recovery, you notice that she does not seem to hear as well as before her illness, so you take her to a hearing specialist.

In a test for hearing loss, the specialist uses a tone generator that produces sounds of differing pitches and intensities. Your daughter listens to the sounds over earphones and is asked to indicate the earliest point at which she can hear a tone. She thereby indicates her **absolute threshold,** or the smallest amount of a stimulus (the tone) that she can detect. To test your daughter's **difference threshold,** or *just noticeable difference* (JND), the examiner presents a small change in volume and asks the child to respond when she notices a difference. By noting your daughter's thresholds and comparing them with thresholds of people with normal hearing, the specialist can determine whether your daughter has a hearing loss and, if so, the extent of the loss.

Sensory thresholds exist not only for hearing but also for vision, taste, smell, and the skin senses. In fact, much of the research done in all areas of sensation originally began with the study of various thresholds.

Adaptation

Your friends have invited you to come by to visit their beautiful new baby daughter. As they greet you at their front door, you are overwhelmed by the odor of a nearby diaper pail and even the baby herself. You wonder what's wrong. Why don't they do something about the smell? The answer is **sensory adaptation:** When a constant stimulus is presented for a length of time, sensation often fades or disappears. Receptors higher up in the sensory system get "tired" and actually fire less frequently.

Sensory adaptation makes sense from an evolutionary perspective. Basically, we can't afford to waste attention and time on unchanging, normally unimportant stimuli. "Turning down the volume" on repetitive information helps the brain cope with an overwhelming amount of sensory stimuli and allows time to pay attention to *change.* This helps your friends with their smelly baby, and if you stay long enough, your senses also will adapt — fortunately. Sometimes this adaptation, however, can be dangerous, as when we stop paying attention to that gas leak we noticed in the kitchen.

Although some senses adapt quickly, like smell and touch, we never completely adapt to visual stimuli or extremely intense stimuli, such as the odor of ammonia, the heat of the desert sun, or the pain of a burned hand. Again, from an evolutionary perspective, these limitations on sensory adaptation aid survival. They remind us to avoid strong odors and heat and to do something about the damaged tissue, such as put some ice on that burned hand.

If we don't adapt to pain, how do athletes keep playing despite painful injuries? In certain situations, the body releases natural painkillers called *endorphins* (Module 5). Endorphins act in the same way as morphine to relieve pain by inhibiting pain perception. Both pleasant (the "runner's high," sexual activity) and unpleasant stimuli (injuries, fighting) can release endorphins. Pain relief through endorphins may also be the secret behind *acupuncture*, the ancient Chinese technique of gently twisting thin needles placed in the skin.

In addition to endorphin release, one of the most accepted explanations of pain perception is the **gate-control theory**, first proposed by Ronald Melzack and Patrick Wall (1965). According to this theory, the experience of pain depends partly on whether the neural message gets past a "gatekeeper" in the spinal cord that either blocks pain signals or allows them to pass on to the brain. Normally, the gate is kept shut, either by impulses coming down from the brain itself or by messages coming into the spinal cord from large-diameter fibers that conduct most sensory signals, such as touch and pressure. However, when body tissue is damaged, impulses from smaller pain fibers open the gate.

The gate-control theory helps explain why touch and pressure, such as rubbing your banged elbow, can reduce pain: The large fibers carry competing pressure messages. Messages from the brain itself can also control the pain gate, thus explaining how athletes and soldiers can carry on despite excruciating pain. When we are soothed by endorphins or distracted by competition or fear, our experience of pain can be greatly diminished. On the other hand, when we get anxious or dwell on our pain by talking about it constantly, we can intensify it (Sullivan, Tripp, & Santor, 1998).

Research also suggests that the pain gate may be chemically controlled, that a neurotransmitter called *substance P* opens the pain gate, and that endorphins close it (Cesaro & Ollat, 1997; Liu, Mantyh, & Basbaum, 1997). Other research finds that the brain not only responds to incoming signals from sensory nerves but also is capable of *generating* pain (and other sensations) entirely on its own (Melzack, 1999; Vertosick, 2000). Have you heard of *tinnitus*, the ringing-in-the-ears sensation that sometimes

Gate-Control Theory of Pain *Theory that pain sensations are processed and altered by mechanisms within the spinal cord*

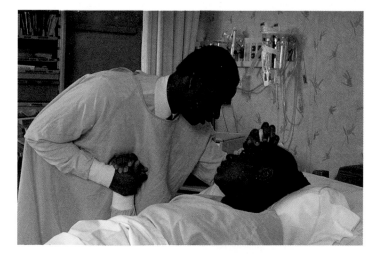

Childbirth and the gate-control theory of pain. Modern childbirth classes teach women to focus their attention away from the pain during childbirth, and the partner (or "labor coach") is encouraged to talk and gently massage the mother's back and neck muscles. Can you see how the gate-control theory helps explain the effectiveness of these techniques?

accompanies hearing loss? In the absence of normal sensory input, nerve cells send conflicting messages ("static") to the brain, and in this case the brain interprets the static as "ringing." A similar process happens with the strange phenomenon of *phantom pain;* wherein people continue to feel pain (and itching or tickling) long after a limb is amputated. The brain interprets the static as pain because it arises in the area of the spinal cord responsible for pain signaling (Vertosick, 2000).

Each of the sensory principles we've discussed thus far — reduction, transduction, coding, thresholds, and adaptation — applies to all the senses. Yet the way in which each sense is processed is uniquely different, as we will see in the remainder of this module.

*A*ssessment
CHECK & REVIEW

Experiencing Sensations

Sensation refers to the process of receiving, converting, and transmitting information from the outside world, whereas **perception** is the process of selecting, organizing, and interpreting raw sensory data into useful mental representations of the world.

Sensory processing includes transduction, reduction, and coding. **Transduction** converts stimuli into neural impulses that are sent to the brain, and we cope with the vast quantities of sensory stimuli through the process of **sensory reduction.** Each sensory system is specialized to **code** its stimuli into unique sets of neural impulses that the brain interprets as light, sound, touch, and so on.

The **absolute threshold** is the smallest magnitude of a stimulus we can detect. The **difference threshold** is the smallest change in a stimulus that we can detect. The process of **sensory adaptation** decreases our sensitivity to constant, unchanging stimuli.

Questions

1. The key functions of sensation and perception are, respectively, (a) stimulation and transduction; (b) transmission and coding; (c) reduction and transduction; (d) detection and interpretation; (e) interpretation and transmission.
2. If a researcher were testing to determine the dimmest light a person could perceive, the researcher would be measuring the _____.
3. Why can't you smell your own perfume or aftershave after a few minutes?
4. The _____ theory of pain helps explain why it sometimes helps to rub or massage an injured thumb. (a) sensory adaptation; (b) gate-control; (c) just noticeable difference; (d) Lamaze.

Answers to Review Questions can be found in Appendix B.

■ How We See and Hear: Our Two Most Important Senses

*A*ssessment

How do our eyes and ears enable us to see and hear?

While on a long train trip, Helen Keller's aunt improvised a doll for 6-year-old Helen out of a few towels. It had no nose, no mouth, no ears, and no eyes — nothing to indicate a face. Helen found this disturbing. Most disturbing, though, was the lack of eyes. In fact, it agitated her so much that she was not content until she found some beads and her aunt attached them for eyes. Uncomprehending as she was of the myriad sensations our eyes bring us, Helen still seemed to know the importance of having eyes.

Vision

Major-league batters can hit a 90-mile-per-hour fastball four-tenths of a second after it leaves the pitcher's hand. How can the human eye receive and process information that quickly? To fully appreciate the marvels of sight, we first need to examine the properties of light, because without it, we wouldn't be able to see. We will then examine the structure and function of the eye, and finally, the way in which visual input is processed.

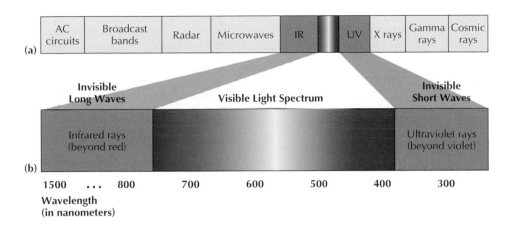

(a)

| AC circuits | Broadcast bands | Radar | Microwaves | IR | | UV | X rays | Gamma rays | Cosmic rays |

Invisible Long Waves   **Visible Light Spectrum**   **Invisible Short Waves**

Infrared rays (beyond red)   Ultraviolet rays (beyond violet)

(b)

1500   ...   800   700   600   500   400   300

Wavelength (in nanometers)

Figure 12.3 *The electromagnetic spectrum.* (a) Gamma radiation and X radiation have short wavelengths, visible light has medium wavelengths, and TV, radio, and AC (alternating current) circuits have long wavelengths. (b) The human eye can see only visible light, a small part of the full spectrum. Visible light with a short wavelength is perceived as blue, visible light with a medium wavelength is green or yellow, and visible light with a long wavelength is red.

Waves of Light   *Light* is a form of electromagnetic energy that moves in waves similar to the movement of waves in the ocean. There are many different types of electromagnetic waves, from short X-rays to long radio waves. Together they form the *electromagnetic spectrum* (Figure 12.3). Most wavelengths are invisible to the human eye; only a small part of the spectrum, known as the *visible spectrum*, can be detected by our visual receptors.

As Table 12.1 shows, light waves vary in length, height, and range — each with a distinct effect on vision. The **wavelength,** the distance between the crest of one wave and the crest of the next, determines its **frequency** (in vision, its **hue** or color). Longer wavelengths produce reddish colors, whereas shorter wavelengths produce bluish colors. The **amplitude,** or height, of a light wave determines its *intensity* (in vision, its *brightness,* in hearing, its *loudness*). Higher waves produce brighter colors, and smaller waves produce dimmer colors. The range of waves — that is, the mixture of length and amplitude — determines its *complexity* (in vision, its *saturation*). The wider range produces more saturated (more varied and complex) color, whereas a narrow range produces less saturated color (less complex and varied; may be a single pure color).

Eye Anatomy and Function   The eye is uniquely designed to capture light and focus it on receptors at the back of the eyeball. The receptors, in turn, convert light energy into neural signals to be interpreted by the brain. Several structures in the eye are involved in the process. We will trace the path of light through these structures — the cornea, pupil, lens, and retina. As we do, please refer to Figure 12.4.

Light waves first enter the eye through a tough, transparent layer called the *cornea,* which is attached to the white, opaque outer wall of the eye. Light passes from the cornea through the *pupil,* an adjustable opening controlled by the *iris* (the colored

Wavelength *Distance between the crests (or peaks) of light or sound waves; the shorter the wavelength, the higher the frequency*

Frequency *How often a light or sound wave cycles — that is, the number of complete wavelengths that pass a point in a given time (e.g., per second)*

Hue *Visual dimension seen as a particular color; determined by the length of a light wave*

Amplitude *Height of a light or sound wave; pertaining to light, it refers to brightness, for sound, it refers to loudness*

What does a butterfly see? The flower on the right was photographed under ultraviolet light. Because butterflies have ultraviolet receptors, this may be what it's like to see like a butterfly.

SUMMARY TABLE 12.1 PROPERTIES OF VISION AND HEARING

Physical properties	**Wavelength:** The distance between successive peaks.	**Wave Amplitude:** The height from peak to trough.	**Range of Wavelengths:** The mixture of waves.
	Long wavelength/low frequency	*Low amplitude/low intensity*	*Low range/low complexity*
	Short wavelength/ high frequency	*High amplitude/ high intensity*	*High range/high complexity*
VISION (Light Waves)	**Hue:** Short wave lengths produce higher frequency and bluish colors; long wavelengths produce lower frequency and reddish colors.	**Brightness:** Great amplitude produces more intensity and bright colors; small amplitude produces less intensity and dim colors.	**Saturation:** Wider range produces more complex color; narrow range produces less complex color.
AUDITION (Sound Waves)	**Pitch:** Shorter wavelengths produce higher frequency and high pitched sounds; long wave-lengths produce lower frequency and low-pitched sounds.	**Loudness:** Great amplitude produces louder (more intense) sounds; small amplitude produces soft sounds.	**Timbre:** Wider range produces more complex sound with a mix of multiple frequencies. Narrower range produces less complex sound with one or a few frequencies.

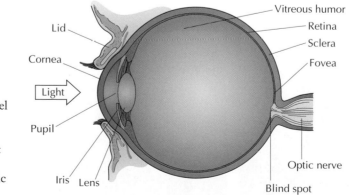

Figure 12.4 *The anatomy of the eye.* Note the path of light waves as they travel from the outside world, enter the eye at the cornea, and pass through the pupil and lens to the retina. In the retina, light waves are transduced (or changed) into neural impulses that move along the optic nerve to the brain.

part of the eye), and then on through the *lens*, a transparent elastic structure. Light waves eventually end up at the back of the eyeball on the *retina*, a group of light receptors, where they are transduced into neural messages and then carried by the *optic nerve* to the brain.

Now that we have the big picture of eye anatomy, and how light information enters and travels to the brain, let's examine how the main structures function.

Cornea, Iris, Pupil, and Lens   The front of the eyeball is covered by the cornea, a protective, transparent tissue that, because of its convex (outward) curvature, helps focus incoming light rays. Directly behind the cornea, is the iris, which provides the color (usually brown or blue) of the eye. Muscles in the iris allow the pupil (or opening) to dilate or constrict in response to light intensity—or even to inner emotions. (Recall from Module 5, that our pupils dilate when we're in sympathetic arousal and constrict when we're in parasympathetic dominance.)

Behind the iris is the lens, which adds to the focusing begun by the cornea. Unlike the cornea, the lens is adjustable. Small muscles change its shape to allow us to focus on objects close to the eye or farther away. This focusing process is known as **accommodation.** When you look at a faraway object, your lens accommodates by thinning and flattening to focus; when your glance shifts to a near object, such as the book you're reading, your lens accommodates by thickening and curving.

Small abnormalities in the eye sometimes interfere with accommodation (Figure 12.5). If you have normal vision, your lens focuses the image of any object — near or far — on the retina at the back of your eye. If you are **nearsighted,** however, your eyeball is deeper than normal in relation to its lens, or your cornea may be too sharply curved. The light rays are focused at a point in front of the retina, and at the retina, the image is blurred. The opposite occurs if you are **farsighted.** Your eyeball is shorter than normal and the light is focused on a point beyond the retina, leading to an inability to focus on objects at close range. Nearsightedness *(myopia)* and farsightedness *(hyperopia)* can occur at any age; however, at about age 40, most people find that they need reading glasses. This is because the lenses start to lose elasticity and the ability to accommodate for near vision *(presbyopia)*. Both nearsightedness and farsightedness are easily remedied with corrective lenses. Advances in laser surgery now make it possible to change the shape of the cornea to correct some visual acuity problems.

Retina   Ultimately, incoming light waves end up on the **retina.** This is an area at the back of the eye that contains blood vessels and a network of neurons that transmit neural information to the occipital lobes of the brain. The retina also contains special light-sensitive cells called **rods** and **cones,** so named for their distinctive shapes (Figure 12.6). There are about 6 million cones and 120 million rods tightly packed together at the back of the retina (Carlson, 1998).

The rods, besides being much more numerous, are also more sensitive to light than the cones. They enable us to see in dim light. This greater sensitivity, however, is achieved at the expense of fine detail and color vision — the job of the cones.

Cones become more numerous toward the center of the retina, and in the center is the **fovea,** a tiny pit filled with cones, responsible for our sharpest vision. Cones function better in bright light and diminish in function as the light dims. Cones enable us not only to see things in fine detail but also to see in color. All cones are sensitive to many wavelengths, but each is maximally sensitive to one color — red, green, or blue. You may have noticed that it is impossible to see the color and fine detail of a flower in near-dark conditions, when only the rods are functioning.

Near the fovea lies an area that has no visual receptors at all and absolutely no vision. This aptly named "blind spot" is where blood vessels and nerve pathways enter and exit the eyeball. Normally, we are unaware of our blind spot because our eyes are

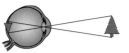

In normal vision, an image is focused on the retina.

In nearsightedness (myopia), the image is focused in front of the retina.

In farsightedness (hyperopia), the image is focused behind the retina.

Figure 12.5 *Normal vision, near-sightedness, and farsightedness.*

Accommodation *Automatic adjustment of the eye, which occurs when muscles change the shape of the lens so that it focuses light on the retina from objects at different distances*

Nearsightedness (Myopia) *Visual acuity problem resulting from cornea and lens focusing an image in front of the retina*

Farsightedness (Hyperopia) *Visual acuity problem resulting from the cornea and lens focusing an image behind the retina*

Retina *Light-sensitive inner surface of the back of the eye, which contains the receptor cells for vision (rods and cones)*

Rods *Receptor cells in the retina that detect shades of gray, are responsible for peripheral vision, and are most sensitive in dim light*

Cones *Receptor cells concentrated near the center of the retina responsible for color vision and fine detail; most sensitive in brightly lit conditions*

Fovea *A tiny pit in the center of the retina filled with cones and responsible for sharp vision*

Figure 12.6 *Structures of the retina.* The retina of the eye is a complicated structure with many different types of cells. The most important are the rods and cones, but light must first pass through the ganglion cells and bipolar neurons.

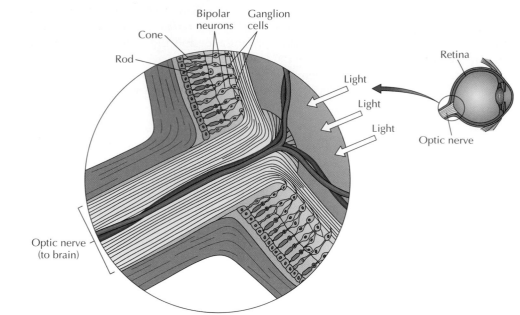

To experience your blind spot, hold the book about 1 foot in front of you, close your right eye, and stare at the X with your left eye. Very slowly, move the book closer to you. You should see the worm disappear and the apple become whole.

always moving. We fill in the information missing from the blind spot with information from adjacent areas on the retina or with images from the other eye.

When the brightness level suddenly changes, how do the rods "take over" from the cones, and vice versa? Think back to the last time you walked into a dark movie theater on a sunny afternoon. You were momentarily blinded. This happens because in bright light, the pigment inside the rods is bleached and they are temporarily nonfunctional. Going from a very light to a very dark setting requires a rapid shift from cones to rods. During the changeover, there is a second or two before the rods are functional enough for you to see. They continue to adjust for 20 to 30 minutes, until your maximum light sensitivity is reached. This process is known as **dark adaptation.** The visual adjustment that takes place when you leave the theater and go back into the sunlight — *light adaptation* — takes about 7 to 10 minutes and is the work of the cones. This adaptation process is particularly important to remember when driving your car from a brightly lit garage into a dark night.

Dark Adaptation *Process whereby rods and cones adjust to allow vision in dim light*

Hearing

In this section, we examine **audition,** the sense of hearing, which we use nearly as much as our sense of vision. In fact, Helen Keller said she "found deafness to be a much greater handicap than blindness. ... Blindness cuts people off from things.

Audition *Sense of hearing*

Deafness cuts people off from people." What is it about hearing that makes it so important? In discussing vision, we talked first about waves of light, then about the anatomy of the eye, and, finally, about problems with vision. We'll follow the same pattern with audition, starting here with waves of sound.

Waves of Sound

Have you heard the philosophical question, "If a tree falls in the forest and there is no one to hear it, does it make a sound?" The answer is based on the fact that *sound* refers to the sensation (which requires a receptor such as a person's ear) and to a physical stimulus. As a physical stimulus, sound is the movement of air molecules in a particular wave pattern. The waves produced are called *sound waves.* They result from rapid changes in air pressure caused by an impact, such as a tree hitting the ground, or by vibrating objects, such as vocal cords or guitar strings.

Like light waves, sound waves vary in three basic ways (see again Table 12.1):

1. **Length** Wavelengths in light correspond to hue or color, whereas wavelengths in sound correspond to **pitch** (the highness or lowness of tones or sounds). Short wavelengths have higher frequency, and the higher the frequency, the higher the pitch. For instance, the faster a person's vocal cords vibrate (the more waves per second), the higher the pitch of the person's voice.

2. **Height** The amplitude (or height) of the sound wave determines **loudness,** intensity of sound, which is measured in units termed *decibels* (the height of light waves determines *brightness*). Figure 12.7 gives decibel ratings for various sounds.

Pitch *Tone or sound determined by the frequency of vibration of the sound waves; the greater the frequency, the higher the pitch*

Loudness *Intensity of sound determined by the amplitude of sound waves; the higher the amplitude, the louder the sound*

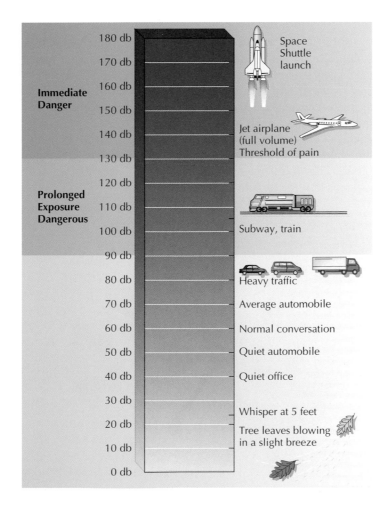

Figure 12.7 *Loudness.* The loudness of a sound is measured in decibels. One decibel is the faintest sound a normal person can hear. This figure lists some familiar sounds and their decibel levels. Normal conversation takes place at about 60 decibels. Constant noise above about 90 decibels can cause permanent nerve damage to the ear.

3. **Range** The range (or mixture) of sound waves determines *timbre*, or complexity of tone. Timbre is the quality of sound that allows us to know whether a note is being played by a violin, trumpet, or oboe.

Ear Anatomy and Function

The ear has three major sections: the *outer ear*, the *middle ear*, and the *inner ear*. The outer ear gathers and delivers sound waves to the middle ear, which amplifies and concentrates the sounds. The inner ear contains the receptor cells that ultimately transduce the mechanical energy created by sounds into neural impulses. As we trace the path of sound waves through the ear, it will help to refer to Figure 12.8.

Sound waves are gathered and funneled into the outer ear by the *pinna*, the external, visible part of the ear that we automatically envision when we think of an ear. The pinna channels the sound waves into the *auditory canal*, a tubelike structure that focuses the sound. At the end of the auditory canal is a thin, tautly stretched membrane known as the *eardrum*, or *tympanic membrane*. As sound waves hit the eardrum, it vibrates. The vibrating eardrum causes the three tiniest bones in the body, the *malleus* (hammer), the *incus* (anvil), and the *stapes* (stirrup), to vibrate. (Together, these three bones are referred to as the *ossicles*.) The stapes presses on a membrane, known as the *oval window*, and causes it to vibrate.

The movement of the oval window creates waves in the fluid that fills the **cochlea**, a snail-shaped structure that contains the *basilar membrane*, on which are located the receptors for hearing. The hearing receptors are known as *hair cells*, and they do in fact resemble hairs. As the waves travel through the cochlear fluid, the hair cells bend from side to side. It is at this point that the mechanical energy of the wave is transduced into electrochemical impulses that are carried by the *auditory nerve* to the brain.

Pitch and Loudness We hear different pitch (low to high) and loudness (soft to loud) by a combination of mechanisms, depending on the frequency (or intensity) of the sound. First, let's discuss how we hear *pitch*. It seems that we hear high-pitched sounds according to the place along the *basilar membrane* that is most stimulated. When we hear a particular sound, it causes the eardrum, the ossicles, and the oval window to vibrate, which in turn produces a "traveling wave" through the fluid in the cochlea. This wave causes some bending of hair cells all along the basilar membrane, but there is a single point where the hair cells are maximally bent for each distinct pitch. This localized maximal bending is described by the **place theory**, which explains how we hear higher-pitched sounds.

www.wiley.com/college/huffman

Cochlea [KOK-lee-uh] *Three-chambered, snail-shaped structure in the inner ear containing the receptors for hearing*

Place Theory *Theory explaining how we hear higher-pitched sounds; different high-pitched sounds bend the basilar membrane hair cells at different locations in the cochlea*

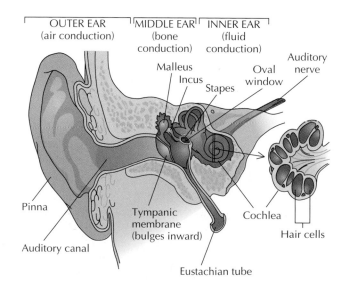

Figure 12.8 *Anatomy of the ear.* Sound waves enter the outer ear, are amplified and concentrated in the middle ear, and then transduced in the inner ear.

OUTER EAR (air conduction)
MIDDLE EAR (bone conduction)
INNER EAR (fluid conduction)
Malleus
Incus
Stapes
Oval window
Auditory nerve
Pinna
Tympanic membrane (bulges inward)
Cochlea
Hair cells
Auditory canal
Eustachian tube

How we hear lower-pitched sounds is explained by the **frequency theory.** According to this theory, we hear a particular low pitch sound because it causes hair cells along the basilar membrane to bend and fire action potentials at the same rate as the frequency of that sound. For example, a sound with a frequency of 90 hertz would produce 90 action potentials per second in the auditory nerve.

How we detect loudness levels also differs according to the frequency and intensity of the sounds. When a sound has a high pitch, we hear it as louder because the neurons fire at a faster rate. Louder sounds produce more intense vibrations, which result in a greater bending of the hair cells, a greater release of neurotransmitters, and consequently a higher firing rate of action potentials. However, there must be an alternate explanation for the perception of the loudness of low sounds, because as just described, rate of firing explains how we hear the pitch of a low sound. Most researchers think that the loudness of lower-pitched sounds is detected by the number of axons that are firing at any one time.

Is it true that loud music can damage your hearing? Yes. There are basically two types of deafness: (1) **conduction deafness,** or middle-ear deafness, which results from problems with the mechanical system that conducts sound waves to the inner ear, and (2) **nerve deafness,** or inner-ear deafness which involves damage to the cochlea, hair cells, or auditory nerve. Disease and biological changes associated with aging can cause nerve deafness. But the most common (and preventable) cause of nerve deafness is continuous exposure to loud sounds that damages the hair cells. If a noise is loud (150 decibels or more), such as a stereo or headphones at full blast, a jackhammer, or a jet airplane engine, even brief exposure can cause permanent deafness. Daily exposure to approximately 85 decibels (such as heavy traffic or motorcycles) can also lead to permanent hearing loss. Obviously, if you cannot avoid such loud noises, earplugs will help reduce the damage. Pay attention to any change in your normal hearing threshold or if you experience *tinnitus,* a whistling or ringing sensation in your ears. These are often the first signs of hearing loss.

Because damage to the nerve or receptor cells is almost always irreversible, the only treatment for nerve deafness is a small electronic device called a *cochlear implant.* If the auditory nerve is intact, the implant bypasses hair cells and directly

Frequency Theory *Theory explaining how we hear lower-pitched sounds; hair cells on the basilar membrane of the cochlea bend and fire action potentials at the same rate as the frequency of the sound*

Conduction Deafness *Middle-ear deafness resulting from problems with transferring sound waves to the inner-ear.*

Nerve Deafness *Inner-ear deafness resulting from damage to the cochlea, hair cells, or auditory nerve.*

Loud noise and nerve deafness. Members of the music group U2 (and their audience) are potential victims of noise-induced nerve deafness, which is irreversible.

A*chievement*

RESEARCH HIGHLIGHT

Tracking Down the Genes for Deafness

Some people suffer hearing loss because of disease (as in Helen Keller's case), accident, or exposure to extremely loud noise. Others are born with a gene that causes deafness. Researchers trying to track down these genes have generally taken one of two approaches. One approach uses animals, such as mice, which have certain known genetic mutations that are naturally occurring or are experimentally induced by the researchers (Self et al., 1998; Wang et al., 1998). The second

approach is to study the genetics of human families that have a large percentage of members who are born deaf or become deaf

later in life (Hahn et al., 2001; Lynch et al., 1997).

Together, the two approaches have located several human deafness genes responsible for producing a type of protein called *myosin,* which is, in turn, instrumental in the development of the auditory hair cells. Mutation of these genes alters the structure of the hair cells, causing the person to be deaf at birth or to go deaf several years after birth. But problems with myosin cannot be the only cause of genetic deafness. It is suspected that many more genetic mutations will be discovered in the next few years.

stimulates the nerve. At present, a cochlear implant produces only a crude approximation of hearing, but the technology is improving. The best bet is to protect your sense of hearing. That means avoiding exceptionally loud noises (rock concerts, jackhammers, stereo headphones at full blast), wearing earplugs when such situations cannot be avoided, and paying attention to bodily warnings. These warnings include a change in your normal hearing threshold and tinnitus.

Assessment
CHECK & REVIEW

How We See and Hear

Light is a form of energy that is part of the electromagnetic spectrum. The **wavelength** of a light determines its **hue**, or color; the **amplitude**, or the height, of a light wave, determines its *intensity*. The range of light waves determines its *complexity*. The function of the eye is to capture light and focus it on visual receptors that convert light energy to neural impulses. Light enters through the pupil and lens to the retina, and then neural impulses travel along the optic nerve to the brain. Cells in the **retina** called **rods** are specialized for night vision, whereas **cones** are specialized for color and fine detail.

The sense of hearing is known as **audition.** We hear sound via sound waves, which result from rapid changes in air pressure caused by vibrating objects. The wavelength of these sound waves is sensed as the **pitch** of the sound, whereas the amplitude of the waves is perceived as *loudness*. The range of sound waves is sensed as *timbre*, the purity or complexity of the tone. The outer ear conducts sound waves to the middle ear, which in turn conducts vibrations to the inner ear, where hair cells in the **cochlea** transduce mechanical energy into neural impulses. The neural message is then carried along the auditory nerve to the brain.

Questions

1. Trace the path of light information as it enters the eye and leaves to go to the brain.
2. The lens of the eye focuses by _____ and _____. The focusing process is known as _____.
3. Trace the path of sound information as it enters the ear and leaves to go to the brain.
4. Explain how place theory differs from frequency theory.

Answers to Questions can be found in Appendix B.

Assessment

How do our other senses enable us to experience the world?

■ Our Other Senses: Smell, Taste, and Other Body Senses

Vision and audition may be the most prominent of our senses, but the others — taste, smell, and the body senses — are also important for gathering information about our environment. The enjoyment of a summer's day comes not only from the visual and auditory beauty of the world but also from the taste of a fresh garden tomato, the smell of honeysuckle, and the feel of a warm, gentle breeze.

Smell and Taste

www.wiley.com/college/huffman

Smell and taste are sometimes referred to as the *chemical senses* because they both involve *chemoreceptors* that are sensitive to certain chemical molecules rather than to electromagnetic or mechanical vibrations. Smell and taste receptors also are located near each other and often interact so closely that we have difficulty separating the sensations. Have you ever noticed how food seems bland when your nose is blocked by a cold and you cannot smell your food?

Olfaction *Sense of smell*

Olfaction   Our sense of smell, or **olfaction,** is remarkably useful and sensitive. We can detect over 10,000 distinct smells (floral, musky, rotten, and so on), and we can smell smoke long before the most sensitive household detector is activated. And blind people can quickly recognize others by their unique odors. (Sighted people can do the same with practice.)

Our sense of smell results from stimulation of receptor cells in the nose (Figure 12.9). These receptors are embedded in a mucus-coated membrane called the *olfactory epithelium*. The olfactory receptors are actually modified neurons, with branched dendrites extending out into the epithelium. When chemical molecules in the air passing through the nose come in contact with the dendrites, they initiate a neural impulse. The impulse travels along the neuron's axon directly to the *olfactory bulb*, a structure just below the frontal lobes where most olfactory information is processed before being sent to other parts of the brain.

Figuring out how we distinguish different odors is complicated for many reasons, not least that we have over 1,000 types of receptors, which allow us to detect the aforementioned 10,000 distinct smells. According to one prominent theory, each odor fits into only one type of olfactory receptor cell, like a key into a lock. This theory is, in fact, called the *lock-and-key theory of olfaction*. Another theory proposes that each olfactory receptor is sensitive to only part of a molecule's structure, and distinct odors activate unique combinations of receptor types (Malnic, Hirono, & Buck, 1999).

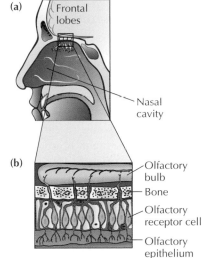

(a) Frontal lobes

Nasal cavity

(b) Olfactory bulb

Bone

Olfactory receptor cell

Olfactory epithelium

Figure 12.9 *Anatomy of the olfactory system.* (a) The nasal cavity contains the olfactory receptors. (b) All olfactory receptors sensitive to the same odor send their axons to the same area of the olfactory bulb.

Achievement
GENDER & CULTURAL DIVERSITY

Do Some People Smell Better Than Others?

No, we are not asking if some people smell like roses and others smell like rotten eggs. The question relates to differences in olfactory sensitivity between people. Research has shown that women and younger adults are better at identifying smells, smokers have a dulled sense of smell, and up to 35 percent of people have some form of *anosmia* (odor blindness) (Dalton, Doolittle, & Breslin, 2002; Frye, Schwartz, & Doty, 1990; Nijjar, 2002; Varney, Pinkston, & Wu, 2001).

Interestingly, some research also finds possible ethnicity differences in smell sensitivity. Using international data from the 1986 National Geographic Smell Survey, C. E. Barber (1997) was able to compare the olfactory sensitivity of several different groups. He compared men to women, young to old, and African to American respondents on one particular odor — androstenone, which is produced by bacteria on the human body and is a component of sweat. Survey respondents included 19,219 Americans and 3,204 Africans of both genders and many different ages.

Barber's research supported earlier findings of increased sensitivity among women and young adults, but African respondents (both men and women) were better than their American counterparts at detecting androstenone. There are many possibilities for the differences in sensitivity, including the environment. Because this was survey research, no one cause can be accurately determined, and the findings of this one study on androstenone cannot be generalized to other odors without further research.

Pheromones [FARE-oh-mones]
Airborne chemicals that affect behavior, including recognition of family members, aggression, territorial marking, and sexual mating

Does smell affect sexual attraction? People have always been interested in increasing their sexual attractiveness. One popular means has been the use of perfumes and, today, aftershave lotions and men's cologne. Is there any scientific basis to such practices? One line of research has focused on **pheromones** — chemical odors we give off that are thought to affect the behavior of others, including their sexual behavior.

Pheromones have been found in a number of animal species and are used to mark trails to food, define territory, and increase sexual arousal and mating behaviors. Although some research supports the idea that pheromones increase sexual behaviors in humans (Cutler, 1999; Jacob, McClintock, Zelano, & Ober, 2002), other findings question the results (Wysocki & Preti, 1998). Despite what the perfume ads might suggest, human sexuality is much more complex than that of other animals.

Nonetheless, human pheromones may explain several interesting phenomena other than sex. For example, researchers have documented an olfactory linkage behind the common belief that women who live together (in an apartment, military barracks, or sorority) eventually develop synchronized menstrual cycles (Stern & McClintock, 1998). Also, mothers and their babies can recognize each other solely on the basis of smell just a few hours after birth. Will other human pheromone phenomena be discovered? Only further study will tell.

Gustation *Sense of taste*

Gustation In modern times, **gustation** (the sense of taste) may be the least critical of our senses. In the past, however, it probably contributed to our survival. The major function of taste is to provide information about substances that are entering our digestive tract so that we can screen out those that may be harmful. This function is aided by the sense of smell. When the sense of smell is eliminated, the enormous variety of tastes can be reduced to five: sweet, sour, salty, bitter, and *umami*. You are undoubtedly familiar with the first four, but umami has been recently added to the list (see the Research Highlight on facing page).

Like smell receptors in the lock-and-key theory, taste receptors respond differentially to the varying shapes of food and liquid molecules. The major taste receptors (or *taste buds*) are clustered within little bumps called *papillae*. You can see these papillae on the surface of your tongue (Figure 12.10).

Why are children so picky about food? In young people, taste buds die and are replaced about every 7 days. As we age, however, the buds are replaced more slowly, so taste diminishes. Thus, children, who have abundant taste buds, often dislike foods

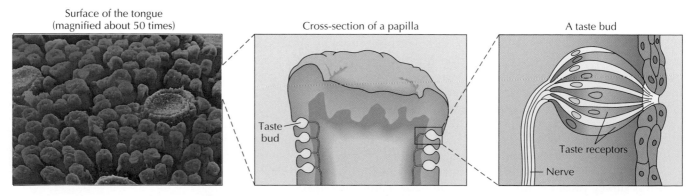

Surface of the tongue
(magnified about 50 times)

Cross-section of a papilla

A taste bud

Taste bud

Taste receptors

Nerve

Figure 12.10 **Taste sensation.** When liquids enter the mouth, or food is chewed and dissolved, the fluid runs over the papillae (the lavender circular areas) and into the pores to the taste buds, which contain the receptors for taste. (The cells shown in blue are support cells.)

Achievement

Discovering a Delicious New Taste

On February 24, 2002, *Nature* magazine provided an early online publication detailing the recent discovery of a fifth taste—*umami* (Nelson et al., 2002). Unlike many scientific discoveries, this one received considerable media attention. Umami is a separate taste and type of taste receptor that is sensitive to glutamate. Glutamate itself is found in meats, meat broths, and monosodium gluta- mate (MSG), and it is a major contributor to the taste of many natural foods, such as meats, fish, and cheese.

Japanese scientists have long acknowl- edged five primary tastes—sweet, sour, salty, bitter, and umami—which means "delicious" or "savory" (Kurihara & Kashiwayanagi, 1998; Lindemann, 2001; Niijima, Togiyama, & Adachi, 1990, Schiffman, 2000). How did Western researchers miss this whole separate taste receptor until 2002? As you recall from Figure 2.2 (p. 11), science requires replica- tion, and it is by nature circular and cumula- tive. The fact that several researchers for many years investigated similar findings before gaining widespread acceptance may demonstrate standard scientific practice. On the other hand, it also might be a good example of Western ethnocentrism. What do you think?

---

with strong or unusual tastes (such as liver and spinach), but as they grow older and lose taste buds, they may come to like these foods.

Some pickiness is related to learning. Many food and taste preferences result from childhood experiences and cultural influences. For example, many Japanese children eat raw fish and some Chinese children eat chicken feet as part of their normal diet, whereas American children might consider these foods "yucky." Likewise, most American children love cheese, which children in some other cultures find repulsive.

Pickiness also relates to the fact that the sense of taste enables humans and ani- mals to discriminate between foods that are safe to eat and foods that are poisonous. Because many plants that taste bitter contain toxic chemicals, an animal is more likely to survive if it avoids bitter-tasting plants (Guinard et al., 1996). On the other hand, humans and animals have a preference for sweet foods that are generally nonpoiso- nous and are good sources of energy.

The Body Senses

Imagine for a moment that you are an Olympic skier and you're anxiously awaiting the starting signal that will begin your once-in-a-lifetime race for the gold medal in the giant slalom. What senses will you need to manage the subtle and ever-changing balance adjustments required for Olympic-level skiing? How will you make your skis carve the cleanest, shortest, fastest line from start to finish? What will enable your arms, legs, and trunk to work in perfect harmony so that you can record the shortest time and win the gold? The senses that will allow you to do all this, and much more, are the body senses. The *body senses* tell the brain how the body is oriented, where and how the body is moving, the things it touches or is touched by, and so on. These senses include the skin senses, the vestibular sense, and the kinesthetic sense.

The Skin Senses   The skin senses are vital. Skin not only protects the internal organs but also provides the brain with basic survival information. With nerve end- ings in the various layers of skin, our skin senses tell us when a pot is dangerously hot, when the weather is freezing cold, and when we have been hurt. Researchers have "mapped" the skin by applying probes to all areas of the body. Mapping shows there are three basic skin sensations: touch (or pressure), temperature, and pain. Receptors for these sensations occur in various concentrations and depths in the skin. For exam- ple, touch (pressure) receptors are maximally concentrated on the face and fingers and

Babies are highly responsive to touch, partly because of the density of their skin receptors.

Figure 12.11 *How do we experience "hot?"*
Researchers use an instrument called a "heat grill" — two pipes twisted together, one containing warm water and the other cold. If you grasp both pipes, you experience intense heat because both warm and cold receptors are activated simultaneously. We do not have separate "hot" receptors.

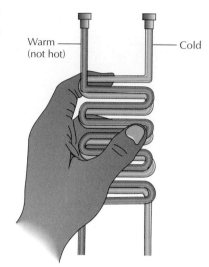

Warm (not hot) — Cold

least in the back and legs. As your hands move over objects, pressure receptors register the indentations created in the skin, allowing perception of texture, and people who are blind learn to read the raised dots that constitute Braille.

The relationship between the types of receptors and the different sensations is not clear. It used to be thought that each receptor responded to only one type of stimulation, but we now know that some receptors respond to more than one. For example, pressure receptors also respond to certain sound waves. And itching, tickling, and vibrating sensations seem to be produced by light stimulation of both pressure and pain receptors.

In conducting studies on temperature receptors, researchers have found that the average square centimeter of skin contains about six cold spots where only cold can be sensed, and one or two warm spots where only warmth can be felt. Interestingly, we don't seem to have separate "hot" receptors. Instead, our cold receptors detect not only coolness but also extreme temperatures — both hot and cold (Craig & Bushnell, 1994). See Figure 12.11.

The Vestibular Sense The *vestibular sense* is the sense of body orientation and position with respect to gravity and three-dimensional space (in other words, it is the sense of balance). Even the most routine activities — riding a bike, walking, or even sitting up — would be impossible without this sense. The vestibular apparatus is located in the inner ear and is composed of the vestibular sacs and the semicircular canals.

The **semicircular canals** provide the brain with balance information, particularly information about rotation of the head. As the head moves, liquid in the canals moves and bends hair cell receptors. At the end of the semicircular canals are the *vestibular sacs*, which contain hair cells sensitive to the specific angle of the head — straight up and down or tilted. Information from the semicircular canals and the vestibular sacs is converted to neural impulses that are then carried to the appropriate section of the brain.

What causes motion sickness? Information from the vestibular sense is used by the eye muscles to maintain visual fixation and sometimes by the body to change body orientation. If the vestibular sense gets overloaded or becomes confused by boat, airplane, or automobile motion, the result is often dizziness and nausea. Random versus expected movements also are more likely to produce motion sickness. Thus, automobile drivers are better prepared than passengers for upcoming movement and are less likely to feel sick (Rolnick & Lubow, 1991). Motion sickness seems to vary with age: Infants are generally immune, children between ages 2 and 12 years have the highest susceptibility, and the incidence declines in adulthood.

Semicircular Canals *Three arching structures in the inner ear containing hair receptors that respond to head movements and provide information on balance*

The Kinesthetic Sense Kinesthesis (from the Greek word for "motion") is the sense that provides the brain with information about bodily posture and orientation, as well as bodily movement. Unlike the receptors for sight, hearing, smell, taste, and balance, which are clumped together in one organ or area, kinesthetic receptors are found throughout the muscles, joints, and tendons of the body. As we sit, walk, bend, lift, turn, and so on, our kinesthetic receptors respond by sending messages to the brain. They tell which muscles are being contracted and which relaxed, how our body weight is distributed, where our arms and legs are in relation to the rest of our body. Without these sensations, we would literally have to watch every step we make.

We rely on kinesthesis constantly yet seldom acknowledge it, because this sense is rarely disturbed in our everyday lives. In one study, an experimenter intentionally disturbed participants' wrist tendon receptors by producing certain vibrations. Participants reported sensations of having multiple forearms and impossible positions of their arms (Craske, 1977). But we don't have to go through experimental procedures to appreciate our kinesthetic sense. All we have to do is observe children learning new skills and remember when we were just learning to ride a bike or catch a football. During the learning process, we consciously move certain body parts and certain muscles, but gradually we learn to operate on "automatic pilot." Our kinesthetic sense needs training in recognizing how various postures and movements should feel.

Kinesthesis *Sensory system for body posture and orientation*

How does she do it? Without her finely tuned vestibular and kinesthetic senses to maintain her balance and coordination, U.S. gymnast Amy Chow would be on her way to the hospital rather than the Olympics.

*A*ssessment

CHECK & REVIEW

Our Other Senses

The sense of smell (**olfaction**) and the sense of taste (**gustation**) are called the chemical senses and are closely interrelated. The receptors for olfaction are at the top of the nasal cavity. According to the lock-and-key theory, we can smell different odors because each three-dimensional odor molecule fits into only one type of receptor. The receptors for gustation are located on the tongue, and are sensitive to five basic tastes: salty, sweet, sour, bitter, and umami.

The body senses are the skin senses, the vestibular sense, and the **kinesthetic** sense.

The skin senses detect pressure, temperature, and pain. They protect the internal organs and provide basic survival information. The vestibular apparatus is located in the inner ear. The kinesthetic sense provides the brain with information about body posture and orientation, as well as body movement. The kinesthetic receptors are spread throughout the body in muscles, joints, and tendons.

Questions

1. The _____ theory of olfaction suggests that we cannot smell carbon monoxide because of the shape of the carbon monoxide molecule. (a) chemoreceptor; (b) lock-and-key; (c) geometric; (d) multi-dimensional.

2. The weightlessness experienced by space travelers as a result of zero gravity has its greatest effect on the _____ senses. (a) visceral; (b) reticular; (c) somasthetic; (d) vestibular.

3. Receptors located in the muscles, joints, and tendons of the body provide _____ information to maintain bodily posture, orientation, and movement.

4. The skin senses include _____. (a) pressure; (b) pain; (c) warmth and cold; (d) all of these

Answers to Questions can be found in Appendix B.

MODULE 12 ACTIVE LEARNING WORKSHEET

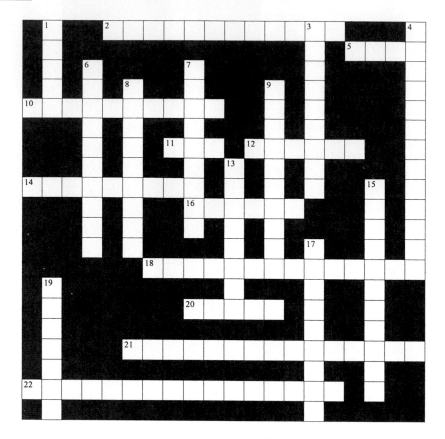

ACROSS

2 The process by which energy stimulating a receptor is converted into neural impulses.

5 Receptor cells in the retina that detect shades of gray, are responsible for peripheral vision, and are most sensitive in dim light.

10 Airborne chemicals that affect behavior, including recognition of family members, aggression, territorial marking, and sexual mating.

11 The visual dimension seen as a particular color; determined by the length of a light wave.

12 The light-sensitive inner surface of the back of the eye, which contains the receptor rods and cones plus other neurons that help in processing visual information.

14 The sense of taste.

16 The three-part process that converts a particular sensory input into a specific sensation.

18 A visual acuity problem that results when the cornea and lens focus an image behind the retina.

20 Visual receptors concentrated near the center of the retina that are responsible for color vision and fine detail. They are most sensitive in daylight or well-lit conditions.

21 Theory that explains how we hear lower-pitched sounds; hair cells on the basilar membrane of the cochlea bend and fire action potentials at the same rate as the frequency of the low sound.

22 The process of filtering and analyzing incoming sensations that occurs before a neural impulse is sent to the cortex.

DOWN

1 Tone or sound determined by the frequency of vibration of the sound waves; the greater the frequency the higher the pitch.

3 The sense of smell.

4 The branch of psychology that studies the relation between attributes of the physical world and our psychological experience of them.

6 The process of selecting, organizing, and interpreting sensory data into usable mental representations of the world.

7 How often a light or sound wave cycles. That is, the number of complete wavelengths that pass a point in a given time (e.g., per second).

8 The height of a light or sound wave; pertaining to light, it refers to brightness.

9 The length of a light or sound wave, measured from the crest of one wave to the crest of the next.

13 The sense of hearing.

15 Theory that explains how we hear higher-pitched sounds; for each distinct higher pitch, hair cells located on the basilar membrane of the cochlea bend maximally at a specific spot.

17 The process of receiving, translating, and transmitting raw sensory data from the external and internal environments to the brain.

19 The three-chambered, snail-shaped structure in the inner that contains the receptors for hearing.

MODULE 13
PERCEPTION

At this point, we are ready to move from sensation and the major senses to perception. Keep in mind, however, that the boundary between the two is ambiguous. Look, for example, at Figure 13.1a. What do you see? Most people see splotches of light and dark, but they perceive no real pattern. If you stare long enough, your brain will try to organize the picture into recognizable shapes or objects, as it does when you lie on your back outdoors and gaze at the clouds on a summer's day. Have you seen the image in the photo yet? If not, try rotating the picture (so that the caption is at the top left). Now do you see it? If you still can't, turn the page and look at Figure 13.1b. Before you *perceived* the cow, you *sensed* only light and dark splotches. Only when you could select relevant splotches and organize them into a meaningful pattern were you able to interpret them as the face of a cow.

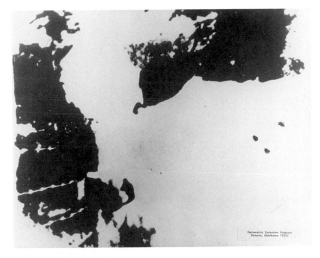

Figure 13.1a *What is it?*

Normally, our perceptions agree with our sensations, but there are times when they do not. This results in an **illusion.** Illusions are false impressions of the physical world that can be produced by actual physical distortions, as in desert mirages, or by errors in the perceptual process, as in the illusions shown in Figures 13.2 and 13.3. Besides being amusing, illusions provide psychologists with a tool for studying the normal process of perception (e.g., Jia et al., 2002; Kramer, Hahn, Irwin, & Theeuwes, 2000). (Be careful not to confuse *illusion* with *hallucination* or *delusion* [Modules 15 and 40]. *Hallucinations* are sensory perceptions that occur without an external stimulus, as in seeing "pulsating flowers" after using LSD [lysergic acid diethylamide] and other hallucinogenic drugs. *Delusions* refer to false beliefs, often of persecution or grandeur, which also may accompany drug or psychotic experiences.)

Illusion *False impression of the environment*

Perception consists of three basic processes: selection, organization, and interpretation of incoming sensations. We will examine how each process contributes to our perception of the world.

◼ Selection: Extracting Important Messages

The first step in perception is *selection:* choosing where to direct our attention. Three major factors are involved in the act of paying attention to some stimuli in our environment and not to others: selective attention, feature detectors, and habituation.

Assessment

How do we decide what to pay attention to in our environment?

Selective Attention

As you sit reading this text, you may be ignoring sounds from another room or the discomfort of the chair you're sitting on. In almost every situation, there is an excess of sensory information, but the brain manages to sort out the important messages and discard the rest (Folk & Remington, 1998; Kramer, Hahn, Irwin, & Theeuwes, 2000). When you are in a group of people, surrounded by various conversations, you can still select and attend to the voices of people you find interesting. This process is known as **selective attention.**

Selective Attention *Filtering out and attending only to important sensory messages*

Feature Detectors

The second major factor in selection is the presence of specialized cells in the brain called **feature detectors** (or *feature analyzers*) that respond only to certain sensory information. In 1959, researchers discovered specialized nerve cells in the optic nerve of a frog, which they called "bug detectors" because they respond only to moving bugs (Lettvin, Maturana, McCulloch, & Pitts, 1959), and in the early 1960s, researchers found feature detectors in cats that respond to specific lines and angles (Hubel, 1963;

Feature Detectors *Specialized cells in the brain that respond only to certain sensory information*

Figure 13.1b *It's a cow!* Now go back to Figure 13.1a and you will easily perceive a cow.

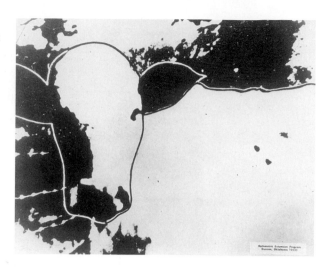

Hubel & Wiesel, 1965, 1979). Similar studies with humans have found feature detectors in the temporal and occipital lobes that respond maximally to faces, and damage to these areas can produce a condition called *prosopagnosia* (*prospon* means "face" and *agnosia* means "failure to know") (Barton, Press, Keenan, & O'Connor, 2002). Interestingly, people with this disorder can recognize that they are looking at a face, but cannot say whose face it is — even if it belongs to a relative or friend or is their own, reflected in a mirror.

Certain basic mechanisms for perceptual selection are thus built into the brain, but a certain amount of interaction with the environment is apparently necessary for feature detector cells to develop normally (Crair, Gillespie, & Stryker, 1998). One well-known study demonstrated that kittens raised in a cylinder with vertically or horizontally striped walls develop severe behavioral and neurological impairments (Blakemore & Cooper, 1970) (Figure 13.4). When "horizontal cats" — those raised with only horizontal lines in their environment — were removed from the cylinder and allowed to roam, they could easily jump onto horizontal surfaces but had great difficulty negotiating objects with vertical lines, such as chair legs. The reverse was true for the "vertical cats": They could easily avoid table and chair legs but never attempted to jump onto horizontal structures. Examination of the visual cortex of these cats revealed that because of their restricted environment, they had failed to develop their potential feature detectors for either vertical or horizontal lines.

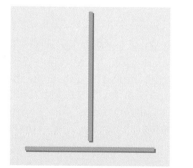

Figure 13.2 *The horizontal-vertical illusion.* Which is longer, the horizontal or the vertical line? People living in areas where they can see long straight lines on the ground, such as roads and shadows of telephone poles, perceive the horizontal line as shorter because of their environmental experiences.

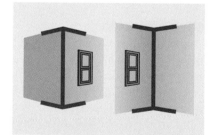

Figure 13.3 *The Müller–Lyer illusion.* Which vertical line is longer? Both are actually the same length, but people who live in urban environments normally see the vertical line on the right as longer than the line on the left. This is because they have learned to make size and distance judgments from perspective cues created by right angles and horizontal and vertical lines of buildings and streets.

Habituation

Another physiological factor important in selecting sensory data is **habituation,** where we quickly *habituate* (or respond less) to predictable and unchanging stimuli. The brain seems "prewired" to pay more attention to changes in the environment than to stimuli that remain constant. For example, when you buy a new CD, you initially listen carefully to all the songs. Over time, your attention declines and you can play the entire CD and not really notice it. This may not matter with CDs — we can always replace them when we become bored. But this same habituation phenomenon also applies to your friends and love life — and people aren't as easily replaced. Attention and compliments from a stranger are almost always more exciting and "valuable" than from long-time friends and lovers. Unfortunately, some people leave good relationships not realizing that they will soon *habituate* to the new person. (This knowledge is another payoff for studying psychology!)

How does habituation differ from sensory adaptation? Good question. Habituation is a perceptual process that occurs in the brain, whereas sensory adaptation occurs when sensory receptors (in the skin, eyes, ears, and so on) actually decrease the number of sensory messages they send to the brain. This is another example of bottom-up versus top-down processing. Sensory adaptation occurs when you first put on your shoes in the morning. Pressure/touch receptors in your feet send multiple messages to your brain, but with time they *adapt* and send fewer messages. You also habituate and your brain "chooses to ignore" the fact that you're wearing shoes. You only notice when something changes — when you break a buckle or shoelace or get a blister from new shoes.

When given a wide variety of stimuli to choose from, we automatically select stimuli that are *intense, novel, moving, contrasting,* and *repetitious.* Parents and teachers often use these same attention-getting principles, but advertisers and politicians have spent millions of dollars developing them to a fine art. The next time you're watching TV, notice the commercial and political ads. Are they louder or brighter than the regular program (intensity)? Do they use talking cows to promote California cheese or computers (novelty)? Is the promoted product or candidate set in *favorable* contrast to the competition? No need to ask about repetition. This is the foundation of all commercial and political ads. Surprisingly, obnoxious advertising does not always deter people from buying the advertised product (or candidate). For sheer volume of sales, the question of whether you like the ad is irrelevant. If it gets your attention, that's all that matters.

A ssessment

VISUAL QUIZ

Figure 13.4 *Nature versus nurture.* Researchers found that kittens reared in a vertical world fail to develop their "innate" ability to detect horizontal lines or objects. On the other hand, kittens restricted to only horizontal lines cannot detect vertical lines. Can you explain why?

Answer: Without appropriate stimulation, brain cells sensitive to vertical or horizontal lines deteriorate during a critical (and irreversible) period in visual development.

Habituation *Tendency of the brain to ignore environmental factors that remain constant*

A ssessment

CHECK & REVIEW

Selection

The selection process allows us to choose which of the billions of separate sensory messages will eventually be processed. **Selective attention** allows us to direct our attention to the most important aspect of the environment at any one time. **Feature detectors** are specialized cells in the brain that distinguish between different sensory inputs. The selection process is very sensitive to changes in the environment. We **habituate** to unchanging stimuli and pay attention when stimuli change in intensity, novelty, location, and so on.

Questions

1. Explain how *illusions* differ from *delusions* and *hallucinations.*
2. Specialized cells in the brain called _____ respond only to certain types of sensory information.
3. Explain why "horizontal cats" could jump onto only horizontal surfaces.
4. You write a reminder on a Post-it and stick it on the door, where you see it every day. A month later, you forget your appointment because of the tendency to ignore constant stimuli, which is known as _____. (a) sensory adaptation; (b) selective perception; (c) habituation; (d) selective attention

Answers to Questions can be found in Appendix B.

How do we organize stimuli in order to perceive form, constancy, depth, and color?

Organization: Form, Constancies, Depth, and Color

Having selected incoming information, we must organize it into patterns and principles that will help us understand the world. In other words, raw sensory data are like the parts of a watch — they must be assembled in a meaningful way before they are useful. We organize sensory data in terms of *form*, *constancy*, *depth*, and *color*.

Form Perception

Look at the first drawing in Figure 13.5. What do you see? Can you draw a similar object on a piece of paper? This is known as an "impossible figure," yet it clearly exists — on this page. The second part of the figure shows a painting by M. C. Escher, a Dutch painter who created striking examples of perceptual distortion. Although drawn to represent three-dimensional objects or situations, the parts don't assemble into logical wholes. Like the illusions studied earlier, impossible figures also help us understand perceptual principles — in this case, the principle of *form organization*.

Gestalt psychologists were among the first to study how the brain organizes sensory impressions. The German word *gestalt* means "whole" or "pattern." Accordingly, Gestaltists emphasized the importance of organization and patterning in enabling us to perceive the whole stimulus rather than perceiving its discrete parts as separate entities. The Gestaltists proposed laws of organization that specify how people perceive form. The most fundamental Gestalt principle or law of organization is that we tend to distinguish between *figure and ground*.

For example, while you are reading this material, your eyes are receiving sensations of black lines and white paper, but your brain is organizing these sensations

VISUAL QUIZ

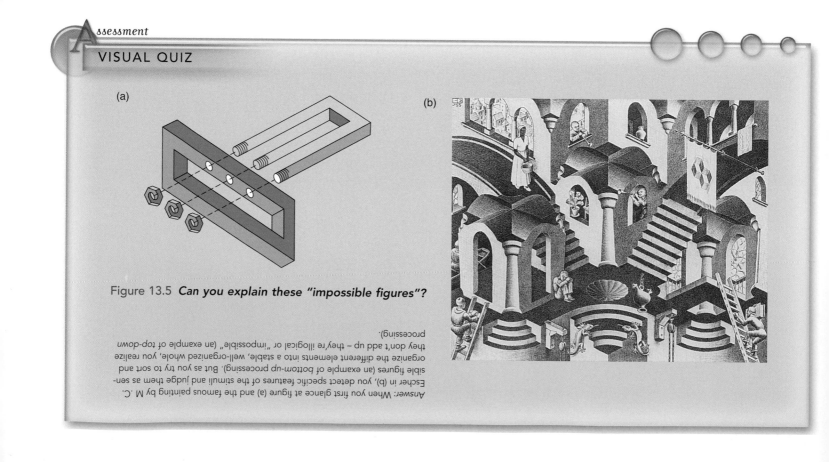

(a)

(b)

Figure 13.5 *Can you explain these "impossible figures"?*

Answer: When you first glance at figure (a) and the famous painting by M. C. Escher in (b), you detect specific features of the stimuli and judge them as sensible figures (an example of *bottom-up* processing). But as you try to sort and organize the different elements into a stable, well-organized whole, you realize they don't add up – they're illogical or "impossible" (an example of *top-down* processing).

into letters and words that are perceived against a backdrop of white pages. The letters constitute the figure and the pages constitute the ground. The discrepancy between figure and ground is sometimes so vague that we have difficulty perceiving which is which, as can be seen in Figure 13.6. This is known as a *reversible figure.* The figure and ground and other basic Gestalt principles are summarized in Figure 13.7. Although these examples are all visual, each law applies to other modes of perception as well.

Figure 13.6 *Figure and ground.* What do you see? A vase or two faces looking at one another? Your answer depends on whether your perceptual expectations lead you to see the vase as figure or as ground.

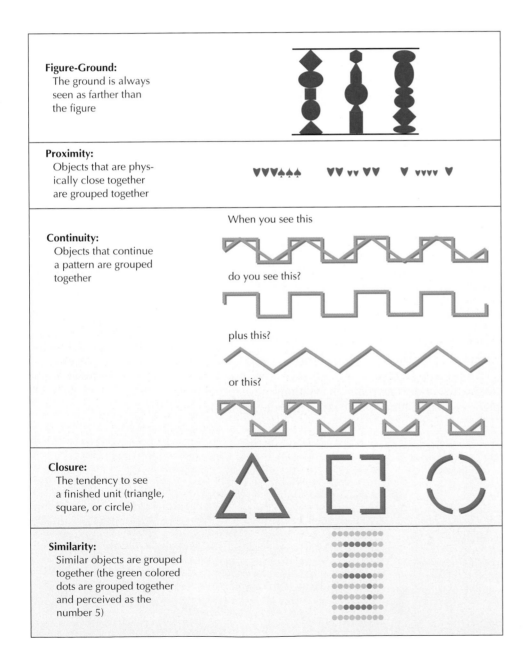

Figure-Ground:
The ground is always seen as farther than the figure

Proximity:
Objects that are physically close together are grouped together

Continuity:
Objects that continue a pattern are grouped together

When you see this

do you see this?

plus this?

or this?

Closure:
The tendency to see a finished unit (triangle, square, or circle)

Similarity:
Similar objects are grouped together (the green colored dots are grouped together and perceived as the number 5)

Summary Figure 13.7 *Basic Gestalt principles of organization.* Figure-ground, proximity, continuity, closure, and similarity are shown here, but the Gestalt principle of contiguity cannot be shown because it involves nearness in time, not visual nearness.

chievement
GENDER & CULTURAL DIVERSITY

Are the Gestalt Laws Universally True?

Are the Gestalt laws of perception universally true for all people? The Gestalt psychologists conducted most of their work with formally educated people from urban European cultures, but A. R. Luria (1976) wondered whether their laws held true for all participants, regardless of their type of education and cultural setting. In what is now a classic study, Luria recruited a wide range of participants living in what was then the USSR, including Ichkeri women from remote villages (with no formal education), collective farm activists (who were semiliterate), and female students in a teachers' school (with years of formal education).

Luria found that when presented with the stimuli shown in Figure 13.8, the formally trained female students were the only ones who identified the shapes by their categorical names. That is, whether circles were made of solid lines, incomplete lines, or solid colors, they called them all circles. However, the other two groups named the shapes according to the objects they resembled. They called a circle a watch, plate, or moon, and referred to the square as a mirror, house, or apricot-drying board. When asked if items 12 and 13 from Figure 13.8 were alike, one woman answered, "No, they're not alike. This one's not like a watch, but that one's a watch because there are dots" (p. 37).

Apparently, the Gestalt laws of perceptual organization are valid only for people who have been schooled in geometrical concepts. But an alternative explanation for Luria's findings has also been suggested. Luria's study, as well as most research on visual perception and optical illusions, relies on two-dimensional presentations — either on a piece of paper or projected on a screen. It may be that experience with pictures and photographs (not formal education in geometrical concepts) is necessary for learning to interpret two-dimensional figures as portraying three-dimensional forms. Westerners who have had years of practice learning to interpret two-dimensional drawings of three-dimensional objects may not remember how much practice it took to learn the cultural conventions about judging the size and shape of objects drawn on paper (Matsumoto, 2000; Price & Crapo, 1999).

Perceptual Constancies

Now that we've seen how form perception contributes to organization, let's examine perceptual constancies. As noted earlier with sensory adaptation and habituation, we are particularly alert to change. However, we also manage to perceive a great deal of consistency in the environment. Without **perceptual constancy** our world would be totally chaotic. Things would seem to grow as we got closer to them, to change shape

Perceptual Constancy *Tendency for the environment to be perceived as remaining the same even with changes in sensory input*

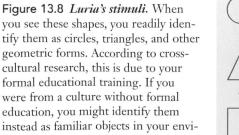

Figure 13.8 *Luria's stimuli*. When you see these shapes, you readily identify them as circles, triangles, and other geometric forms. According to cross-cultural research, this is due to your formal educational training. If you were from a culture without formal education, you might identify them instead as familiar objects in your environment — "the circle is like the moon."

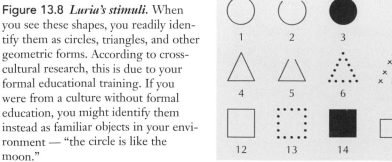

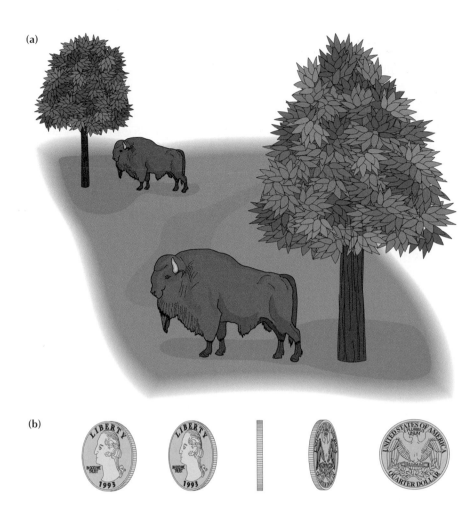

(a)

(b)

(c)

Figure 13.9 *Four types of perceptual constancies.* (a) Although the buffalo in the distance appears much smaller, we perceive it as similar in size to the buffalo in the foreground because of *size constancy*. (b) As the coin is rotated it changes shape, but we perceive it as the same coin because of *shape constancy*. (c) Although this woman's hair and clothing appear different in the shade versus the sun, we know they are the same because of *color* and *brightness constancy*.

as our viewing angle changed, and to change color as light levels changed. The four best-known constancies are visual (Figure 13.9):

1. ***Size constancy.*** Most perceptual constancies are based on prior experience and learning. For example, preschoolers express wonder at the fact that the car parked down the street is only "this high" (as they show about 2 inches between their fingers), whereas the car they are standing next to is taller than they are. Their size judgment is mistaken because they haven't yet had the experiences necessary for learning size constancy. According to this principle, the perceived size of an object remains the same even though the size of its retinal image changes (Figure 13.9a).

   Anthropologist Colin Turnbull (1961) provided a now classic example of an adult who had never developed a sense of size constancy. While studying the Twa people living in the dense rain forest of the Congo River valley in Africa, Turn-bull took a native named Kenge for a Jeep ride to the African plains. Kenge had lived his entire life in an area so dense with foliage that he had never seen distances farther than about 100 yards. Now he was suddenly able to see for almost 70 miles. Lacking perceptual experience with such wide-open spaces, Kenge had great difficulty judging sizes. When he first saw a herd of water buffalo in the distance, he thought they were insects. When Turnbull insisted they were buffalo that were very far away, Kenge was insulted and asked, "Do you think that I am ignorant?" To Kenge's surprise, as they drove toward the "insects," the creatures seemed to grow into buffalo. He concluded that witchcraft was being used to fool him, and after Turnbull showed him a lake so large that its opposite shore couldn't be seen, he asked to be taken back to his rain forest.

2. **Shape constancy.** Other constancies also develop through individual experience. When you look at a chair directly from the front or the back, it has a rectangular shape. When you look at it directly from the side, it has an h shape. Yet you still perceive the chair as having a single shape because your brain remembers past experiences with objects that only seemed to change shape as you moved but actually remained constant. This is known as *shape constancy* (Figure 13.9b).

An ophthalmologist named Adelbert Ames demonstrated the power of shape and size constancies by creating what is now known as the Ames room (see photographs below). On examining this photograph, you might conclude that the person on the left is a midget and the person on the right is a giant. In actuality, both people are normal size. This illusion is based on the unusual construction of the room. As can be seen in the diagram in Figure 13.10, perspective tricks the observer into perceiving the room as square when it is actually shaped like a trapezoid. The illusion is so strong that when a person walks from the left corner to the right, the observer perceives the person to be "growing," even though that is not possible.

If we know the truth of this illusion, why does it still work? Our brain has had a lifetime of interaction with normally constructed rooms, and our desire to perceive the room according to our experience is so powerful that we overrule the truth. This is not a breakdown in perception but rather a result of trying to apply the standard perceptual processes of shape and size constancy to an unusual situation.

3. **Color constancy** and 4. **Brightness constancy.** Other forms of constancy that add stability to our world are *color constancy* and *brightness constancy* (Figure 13.9c). These enable us to perceive things as retaining the same color or brightness levels even though the amount of light may vary. For example, if you place a piece of gray paper in bright sunlight and a piece of white paper in shade, you will still perceive the white as lighter and the gray as darker. This is true regardless of the amount of reflected light actually coming from their surfaces. If you know an object from prior experience, you expect it will be the same color and the same relative brightness in bright light as in low light. That is, you expect it to be its "right" color.

As is the case with shape and size constancy, color constancy and brightness constancy are learned as a result of experience with familiar objects. If an object is unfamiliar, we determine its color and brightness by the actual wavelength of reflected light in combination with the color and brightness of the background.

The Ames room illusion. In the left photo, the woman on the right appears much taller than the boy on the left, but when they reverse positions (the right photo) the boy is taller. For an explanation of how this is possible, see Figure 13.10.

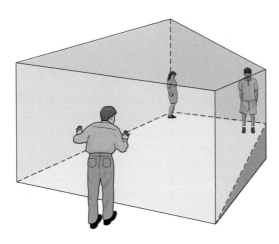

Figure 13.10 *Explanation for the Ames room illusion.* To the viewer peering through the peephole, the room appears perfectly normal. However, in this specially constructed room, the trapezoidal shape and sloping ceilings and floors provide misleading depth cues. Because the brain assumes the two people are the same distance away, it compensates for the differences in retinal size by making the person on the left appear much smaller.

Assessment

CHECK & REVIEW

Organization — Form and Constancies

The Gestalt psychologists set forth laws explaining how people perceive form. The most fundamental principle is the distinction between *figure and ground*. Other principles include proximity, continuity, closure, contiguity, and similarity. Through the **perceptual constancies** of size, shape, color, and brightness, we are able to perceive a stable environment, even though the actual sensory information we receive may be constantly changing. These constancies are based on our prior experiences and learning.

Questions

1. Name the Gestalt principle that is being described: (a) You see a black line on the concrete and realize that it is a single trail of ants. (b) You can read a sentence on a bulletin board even if someone is standing in front of a few words. (c) You see a circle even though part of its curve is erased in three spots.
2. The principle of _____ is at work when, as your brother walks away from you, you don't perceive him to be shrinking.
3. The principle of _____ allows us to see a white blouse as white both in sunlight and in shade.
4. As a flock of Canadian geese files overhead in its familiar V formation, the geese are seen as _____ and the sky as _____. (a) continuity, a closure; (b) a sensation, perception; (c) figure; ground; (d) ground, figure

Answers to Questions can be found in Appendix B.

Depth Perception

The role of experience and learning in organizing perceptions is particularly clear in depth perception. **Depth perception** allows us to accurately estimate the distance of perceived objects and thereby perceive the world in three dimensions. It is possible to judge the distance of objects with nearly all senses. For example, if a person enters a dark room and walks toward you, his or her voice and footsteps get louder, and body smells grow stronger, and you may even be able to feel the slight movement of air from his or her approaching movement. However, in most cases, we rely most heavily on vision to perceive distance. When you add the ability to accurately perceive distance to the ability to judge the height and width of an object, you are able to perceive the world in three dimensions. But no matter which sense you use to perceive the three-dimensional world, perception of depth is primarily learned.

Take the classic example of a patient known as S. B., blind since the age of 10 months, whose sight was restored at age 52. Following the operation that removed cataracts from both eyes, S. B. had great difficulty learning to use his newly acquired vision for judging distance and depth. On one occasion, he was found trying to crawl out of the window of his hospital room. He thought he would be able to lower him-

www.wiley.com/college/huffman

Depth Perception *The ability to perceive three-dimensional space and to accurately judge distance*

self by his hands to the ground below, even though the window was on the fourth floor.

Didn't S. B. have some inborn depth and distance perception? The answer is not clear. As you know, one of the most enduring debates in psychology (and other sciences) is the question of "nature versus nurture," inborn versus learned. In this case, naturists argue that depth perception is inborn, whereas nurturists insist it is learned. Today, most scientists think there is some truth in both viewpoints.

Evidence for the innate position comes from a set of interesting experiments with an apparatus called the *visual cliff* (Figure 13.11). The apparatus consists of a tabletop with a slightly raised platform across the middle. On one side of the platform the tabletop is clear glass, with the red-and-white-checked pattern running down the side of the table and onto the floor several feet below the glass, simulating a steep cliff.

When an infant is placed on the platform and is coaxed by his or her mother to crawl to one side of the table, the infant will readily move to the "shallow" side but will hesitate or refuse to move to the "deep" side (Gibson & Walk, 1960). This reaction is given as evidence of innate depth perception — the infant's hesitation is attributed to fear of the apparent cliff.

Although some have argued that by the time infants are crawling and old enough to be tested they may have *learned* to perceive depth, research with babies at 2 months of age will show a change in heart rate when placed on the deep side of the cliff, but not on the shallow side (Banks & Salapatek, 1983). Similar research with baby chickens, goats, and lambs — animals that walk almost immediately after birth — supports the hypothesis that some depth perception is inborn, as these animals hesitate in stepping onto the steep side.

Once again, the nature–nurture debate continues. However, we all recognize that in our three-dimensional world, the ability to perceive depth and distance is essential. But how do we perceive a three-dimensional world with a two-dimensional receptor system? One mechanism is the interaction of both eyes to produce

Figure 13.11 ***The visual cliff.*** Crawling infants generally refuse to move across this glass surface designed to look like the edge of an elevated platform — even when their mothers stood on the opposite side and coaxed them. This suggests they are able to perceive depth.

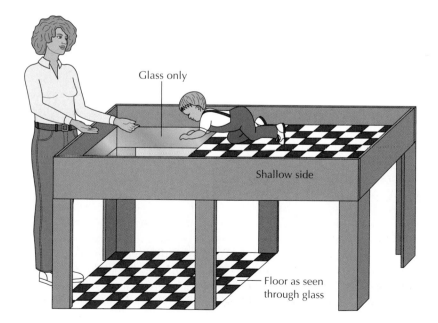

binocular cues; the other involves **monocular cues**, which work with each eye separately. Keep in mind that having two eyes (binocular cues) does help with depth perception. However, we also get similar results with only one eye (monocular cues), as evidenced by the occasional major-league football and baseball players who are blind in one eye.

1. *Binocular cues.* One of the most important cues for depth perception comes from **retinal disparity.** Because our eyes are about $2^1/_2$ inches apart, each retina receives a slightly different view of the world. You can demonstrate this for yourself by pointing at some distant object across the room with your arm extended straight in front of you. Holding your pointing finger steady, close your left eye and then your right. You will notice that your finger seems to jump from one position to another as you change eyes, because of retinal disparity. The brain fuses the different images received by the two eyes into one overall visual image (Figure 13.12). Such *stereoscopic vision* provides important cues to depth.

   As we move closer and closer to an object, a second binocular (and neuromuscular) cue, **convergence,** helps us judge depth. The closer the object, the more our eyes are turned inward, toward our noses (Figure 13.13). Hold your index finger at arm's length in front of you and watch it as you bring it closer and closer until it is right in front of your nose. The amount of strain in your eye muscles created by the convergence, or turning inward of the eyes, is used as a cue by your brain to interpret distance.

   Knowing how convergence operates might help you improve your performance in athletic endeavors. Allen Souchek (1986) found that depth perception is better when looking directly at an object, rather than out of the corner of your eye. Thus, if you turn your body or your head so that you look straight at your tennis opponent or the pitcher, you will more accurately judge the distance of the ball and thereby be more likely swing at the right time.

2. *Monocular cues.* Retinal disparity and convergence are inadequate in judging distances longer than the length of a football field. According to R. L. Gregory (1969), "we are effectively one-eyed for distances greater than perhaps 100 meters." Luckily, we have several monocular cues available separately to each eye. Artists use these same monocular cues to create an illusion of depth on a flat canvas, a three-dimensional world on a two-dimensional surface. Figure 13.14 demonstrates six different monocular cues.

   Two additional monocular cues — ones that cannot be used by artists — are *accommodation* of the lens of the eye and *motion parallax.* As you learned earlier, *accommodation* refers to changes in the shape of the lens of the eye in response to the distance of the object being focused. For near objects, the lens bulges; for far objects, it flattens. Information from the muscles that move the lens is sent to the brain, which interprets the signal and perceives the distance of the object.

   Motion parallax (also known as *relative motion*) refers to the fact that when an observer is moving, objects at various distances move at different speeds across the retinal field. Close objects appear to whiz by, farther objects seem to move slowly, and very distant objects appear to remain stationary. This effect can easily be seen when traveling by car or train. Telephone poles and fences next to the road or track seem to move by very rapidly, houses and trees in the midground seem to move by relatively slowly, and the mountains in the distance seem not to move at all.

Color Perception

We humans may be able to discriminate among 7 million different hues. Is such color perception inborn and culturally universal? Research on many cultures with many different languages suggests that we all seem to see essentially the same colored world (Davies, 1998). Furthermore, studies of infants old enough to focus and move their

Binocular Cues *Visual input from two eyes that allows perception of depth or distance*

Monocular Cues *Visual input from a single eye alone that contributes to perception of depth or distance*

Retinal Disparity *Binocular cue to distance where the separation of the eyes causes different images to fall on each retina*

Convergence *Binocular depth cue in which the closer the object, the more the eyes converge, or turn inward*

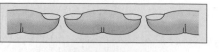

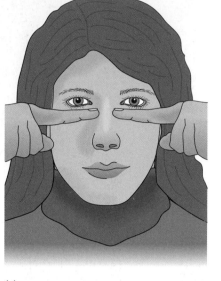

(a)

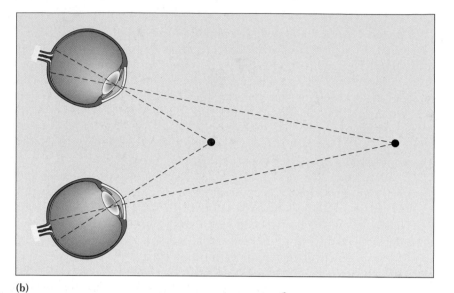

(b)

(c)

Figure 13.12 *Retinal disparity.* (a) Stare at your two index fingers a few inches in front of your eyes with their tips a half inch apart. Do you see the "floating finger?" Move it further away and the "finger" will shrink. Move it closer and it will enlarge. (b) Because of retinal disparity, objects at different distances (such as the "floating finger") project their images on different parts of the retina. Far objects project on the retinal area near the nose, whereas near objects project farther out, closer to the ears. (c) "Magic Eye" images take advantage of retinal disparity. To see the three-dimensional image, stare at this drawing for several minutes, while focusing your eyes beyond it. © Magic Eye 1983 N. E. Thing Enterprises, Inc. Reproduced with permission of Andrews and McMeel. All rights reserved.

Assessment

CHECK & REVIEW

Organization — Depth and Color

Depth perception allows us to accurately estimate the distance of perceived objects and thereby perceive the world in three dimensions. But how do we perceive a three-dimensional world with two-dimensional receptors called eyes? There are two major types of cues: **binocular cues,** which require two eyes, and monocular cues, which require only one eye. The binocular cues are **retinal disparity** and **convergence. Monocular cues** include linear perspective, aerial perspective, texture gradients, interposition, light and shadow, relative size, accommodation, and motion parallax.

Color perception is explained by a combination of two color theories. The **trichro-matic theory** proposes three color systems maximally sensitive to blue, green, and red. The **opponent-process theory** also proposes three color systems but holds that each is sensitive to two opposing colors — blue and yellow, red and green, and black and white — and that they operate in an on-off fashion. The trichromatic system operates at the level of the retina, whereas the opponent-process system occurs in the brain.

Questions

1. The visual cliff is an apparatus designed to study _____ in young children and animals. (a) color discrimination; (b) shape constancy; (c) depth perception; (d) monocular vision.

2. Since Jolly Roger, the pirate, lost one eye in a fight, he can no longer use _____ as a cue for the perception of depth and distance. (a) accommodation; (b) retinal disparity; (c) motion parallax; (d) aerial perspective.

3. After staring at a bright red rectangle for a period of time, a phenomenon known as _____ occurs, which means that if you look away and at a white background, you will see a _____.

4. Explain how the trichromatic theory of color perception differs from the opponent-process theory.

Answers to Questions can be found in Appendix B.

■ Interpretation: Explaining Our Perceptions

After selectively sorting through incoming sensory information and organizing it into patterns, the brain uses this information to explain and make judgments about the external world. This final stage of perception — interpretation — is influenced by several factors, including perceptual adaptation, perceptual set, individual motivation, and frame of reference.

What factors influence how we interpret sensations?

1. *Perceptual adaptation.* What would it be like if your visual field was inverted and reversed? You would certainly have trouble getting around. Things that you expected to be on your right would be on your left, and things you expected to be above your head would be below your head. Do you think you could ever *adapt* to this distorted world?

   To answer such a question, psychologist George Stratton (1897) wore special lenses for 8 days. For the first few days, Stratton had a great deal of difficulty navigating in this environment and coping with everyday tasks. But by the third day, his experience had begun to change and he noted:

   > Walking through the narrow spaces between pieces of furniture required much less care than hitherto. I could watch my hands as they wrote, without hesitating or becoming embarrassed thereby.
   >
   > By the fifth day, Stratton had almost completely adjusted to his strange per-

What if the world were upside down? The student on the right is wearing inverting lenses that literally turn the world upside down — the sky is down, the ground is up. The one on the left is wearing displacement goggles that shift the apparent location of objects 40 degrees to the left. Both have difficulty shaking hands. Interestingly, the human brain adapts to this type of distortion relatively quickly. Within a few days, the upside down world would appear normal.

VISUAL QUIZ

Perceptual set. Do you notice anything unusual in this photo? What happens when you turn the book upside down? Despite the distortion, most people see the first photo as normal. Can you explain why?

Answer: Because of perceptual set, we expect both photos to be the same.

Perceptual Set *Readiness to perceive in a particular manner, based on expectations*

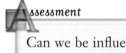

Can we be influenced by subliminal messages, and do some people have ESP?

Figure 13.16 ***Individual motivation and perception.*** Can you see why members of a Jewish organization would be less likely to pay attention (and remember) the other stimuli in this photo when the center item is a swastika?

ceptual environment. His expectations of how the world should be arranged had changed.

2. ***Perceptual set.*** Our previous experiences, assumptions, and expectations also affect how we interpret and perceive the world. If a car backfires, runners at a track meet may jump the gun. People who believe that extraterrestrials occasionally visit the earth may interpret a weather balloon or an odd-shaped cloud as a spaceship. These mental predispositions, or **perceptual sets,** prepare us in a certain way and greatly influence our perception — in other words, we largely see what we expect to see. Studies that used the famous reversible figure of the young/old woman that you saw on page 133 found that when people are led to expect either a young woman or an old woman generally see the one they expect (Leeper, 1935). Perceptual set also explains why labels such as *mental patient, nerd, fag,* or *bitch* can lead to painful and dangerous forms of prejudice and discrimination.

3. ***Individual motivation.*** Our personal needs and interests also influence what we perceive. One experiment recruited participants from a Jewish organization and briefly flashed pictures on a screen (Erdelyi & Applebaum, 1973). When the center symbol was a swastika, the Jewish participants were less likely to recognize and remember the symbols around the edges (Figure 13.16).

4. ***Frame of reference.*** Our perceptions of people, objects, or situations are also affected by their frame of reference, or context. An elephant is perceived as much larger when it is next to a mouse than when it stands next to a giraffe.

■ Subliminal Perception and ESP: Are They for Real?

Several years ago, it was popular to believe that movie theaters were manipulating consumers by subliminally presenting messages like "Eat popcorn" and "Drink Coca-Cola." Similarly, record companies were supposedly embedding subliminal messages in rock music that encouraged violence and sex in listeners. The words on the movie screen and the messages in the music were allegedly presented so quickly that they were below the threshold for awareness. The public was both fascinated and outraged. Politicians rushed to pass laws against the "invisible sell" and the "moral corruption" of our youth. Were they right to be concerned?

Subliminal Perception

There are two major issues surrounding *subliminal perception*. First, is it possible to perceive something without conscious awareness? The answer is clearly yes. Scien-

tific research on **subliminal** (literally, "below the threshold") stimuli demonstrates that information processing does occur even when we are not aware of it (Bouman, 2002; Dimberg, Thunberg, & Elmehed, 2000; Tudorov & Bargh, 2002).

Experimental studies commonly use an instrument called a *tachistoscope* to flash images too quickly for conscious recognition but slowly enough to be registered. For example, in one study the experimenter flashed one of two pictures subliminally (either a happy or angry face) followed by a neutral face. They found this subliminal presentation evoked matching unconscious facial expressions in the participant's own facial muscles (Dimberg, Thunberg, & Elmehed, 2000). The fact that participants were unaware of the subliminal stimuli, as well as their own matching facial response, raises questions regarding our own emotional states. (For example, do we unconsciously become a little more "up" or "down" if we're exposed to good-natured, pleasant people or depressed and angry people?) This study also demonstrates that at least some behaviors can be influenced by subliminal stimuli.

Although subliminal perception *does* occur, the second — and more important — question is "Does it lead to *subliminal persuasion?*" The answer to this question is less clear. Subliminal stimuli are basically *weak* stimuli. At best, they have a modest (if any) effect on consumer behavior and absolutely *no effect* on the minds of youth listening to rock music or citizens' voting behavior (Begg, Needham, & Book-binder, 1993; Trappey, 1996). If you're wondering about buying subliminal tapes promising to help you lose weight or relieve stress, save your money. Blank "placebo" tapes appear to be just as "effective" as subliminal tapes.

In sum, there is evidence that subliminal perception occurs, but the effect on subliminal persuasion is uncertain. When it comes to commercials and self-help tapes, advertisers are better off using *above*-threshold messages — the loudest, clearest, and most attention-getting stimuli possible. And your money and time for weight loss are better spent on the old-fashioned methods of exercise and diet.

Extrasensory Perception

What about a so-called "sixth sense" — beyond our eyes, ears, nose, mouth, and skin? Do some people have the ability to perceive things that cannot be perceived with the usual sensory channels, by using **extrasensory perception (ESP)?** People who claim to have ESP profess to be able to read other people's minds *(telepathy)*, perceive objects or events that are inaccessible to their normal senses *(clairvoyance)*, predict the future *(precognition)*, or move or affect objects without touching them *(psychokinesis)*. Popular tabloids are filled with accounts of psychics claiming to be able to find lost children, talk to the dead, or even predict the stock market (Jaroff, 2001; McDonald, 2001).

Scientific investigations of ESP began in the early 1900s with Joseph B. Rhine. Many of these early experiments, as well as those done by subsequent ESP researchers, involved Zener cards, a deck of 25 cards that bear five different symbols — a plus sign, a square, a star, a circle, and wavy lines. When experimenters want to

Subliminal *Pertaining to any stimulus presented below the threshold of conscious awareness*

Extrasensory Perception *Perceptual, or "psychic," abilities that supposedly go beyond the known senses, including telepathy, clairvoyance, precognition, and psychokinesis*

BIZARRO   By DAN PIRARO

HEY! WE WERE JUST THINKING ABOUT CALLING OUT FOR PIZZA!

I KNOW!

PSYCHIC PIZZA DELIVERED 15 MINUTES *BEFORE* YOU ORDER OR IT'S *FREE!*

Which supposed psychic ability does the Psychic Pizza claim?

ESP and pizza. Can you label the supposed psychic ability of this pizza delivery person?

Answer: Precognition.

study telepathy, for instance, they ask a "sender" to concentrate on a card; then they ask a "receiver" to try to "read the mind" of the sender. By chance alone, the receiver will guess the symbols on about five of the 25 cards correctly. A participant who consistently scores above "chance" is credited with having ESP.

Using Zener cards, Rhine apparently found a few people who scored somewhat better than chance, but his methodology has been severely criticized, particularly in the area of experimental control. In many early experiments, for example, the Zener cards were so cheaply printed that a faint outline of the symbol could be seen from the back. Also, because experimenters knew which cards were correct, they could unknowingly give participants cues through subtle facial gestures.

The most important criticism of both experimental and casual claims of ESP is their lack of stability and replicability — a core requirement for scientific acceptance. Findings in ESP are notoriously "fragile" (Hyman, 1996). A meta-analysis of 30 studies using scientific controls, such as double-blind procedures and maximum security and accuracy in record keeping, reported absolutely no evidence of ESP (Milton & Wiseman, 1999, 2001). As one critic pointed out, positive ESP results usually mean "Error Some Place" (Marks, 1990).

If ESP is so unreliable, why do so many people believe in it? Our fast-paced technological world and rapid scientific progress lead many people to believe that virtually anything is possible, and *possible* is often translated as *probable*. Because ESP is by nature subjective and extraordinary, some people tend to accept it as the best explanation for out-of-the-ordinary experiences. Moreover, as mentioned earlier in this section, our motivations and interests often influence our perceptions. Often, both research participants and researchers are strongly motivated to believe in ESP. They *selectively attend* to things they want to see or hear.

Even the general public seems to want to believe in ESP, as evidenced by the popularity of *the X Files*, children's fairy tales, comic books, and popular movies. It seems that release from natural law is one of the most common and satisfying human fantasies. When it comes to ESP, people eagerly engage in a process known as "the willing suspension of disbelief." We seem to have a hard time accepting our finiteness, and a belief in psychic phenomena offers an increased feeling of power and control.

A Final Note

In this section, we have seen that a number of internal and external factors can affect sensation as well as all three stages of perception — selection, organization, and interpretation. In upcoming modules, we will continue our study of perception by examining how incoming sensory information is processed and retrieved in the different types of memory (Module 20), how perception develops in infants (Module 25), and how we perceive ourselves and others (Module 46).

Helen Keller recognized how crucial sensation and perception are to our lives. She learned to "see" and "hear" with her sense of touch and often recognized visitors by their smell or by vibrations from their walk. Despite the heightened sensitivity of her functioning senses, however, Keller professed a lifelong yearning to experience a normal sensory world. She gave this advice to those whose senses are "normal":

> I who am blind can give one hint to those who see: use your eyes as if tomorrow you would be stricken blind. And the same method can be applied to the other senses. Hear the music of voices, the song of a bird, the mighty strains of an orchestra as if you would be stricken deaf tomorrow. Touch each object as if tomorrow you tactile sense would fail. Smell the perfume of flowers, taste with relish each morsel as if tomorrow you could never smell and taste again. Make the most of every sense; glory in all the facets of pleasure and beauty that the world reveals to you through the several means of contact which nature provides. [1962, p. 23]

CHECK & REVIEW

Interpretation, Subliminal Perception, and ESP

Interpretation, the final stage of perception, can be influenced by perceptual adaptation, **perceptual set,** individual motivation and frame of reference. **Subliminal** (below the threshold) messages can be perceived without our knowing awareness. However, there is little or no evidence of subliminal persuasion. **Extrasensory perception** (ESP) is the supposed ability to perceive things that go beyond the normal senses. ESP research has produced "fragile" results, and critics condemn its lack of experimental control and replicability.

Questions

1. George Stratton's research is important because it demonstrated _____.
   (a) the role of learning in perception;
   (b) innate factors in human perception;
   (c) the difference between sensation and perception;
   (d) the ability of the retina to invert images.
2. Experiments on subliminal perception have _____. (a) supported the existence of the phenomenon but it has little or no effect on persuasion; (b) shown that subliminal perception occurs only among children and some adolescents; (c) shown that subliminal messages affect only people who are highly suggestible; (d) failed to support the phenomenon.
3. The supposed ability to read other people's minds is called _____, perceiving objects or events that are inaccessible to the normal senses is known as _____, predicting the future is called _____, and moving or affecting objects without touching them is known as _____.
4. A major criticism of studies that indicate the existence of ESP is that they _____.

Answers to Questions can be found in Appendix B.

CRITICAL THINKING

Problems with Believing in Extrasensory Perception

The subject of extrasensory perception (ESP) often generates not only great interest but also strong emotional responses. And when individuals feel strongly about an issue, they sometimes fail to recognize the faulty reasoning underlying their beliefs. Belief in ESP is particularly associated with illogical, noncritical thinking. This exercise gives you a chance to practice your critical thinking skills as they apply to ESP. Begin by studying the following types of faulty reasoning:

1. *Fallacy of positive instances:* Noting and remembering events that confirm personal expectations and beliefs (the "hits") and ignoring nonsupportive evidence (the "misses"). Remembering the time the palmist said you would receive a call in the middle of the night (a "hit") but ignoring that she also said that you had three children (a "miss").

2. *Innumeracy:* Failing to recognize chance occurrences for what they are owing to a lack of training in statistics and probabilities. Unusual events are misperceived as statistically impossible (such as predicting a president's illness), and extraordinary explanations, such as ESP, are seen as the logical alternative.

3. *Willingness to suspend disbelief:* Refusing to engage one's normal critical thinking skills because of a personal need for power and control. Although few people would attribute a foreign country's acquisition of top-secret information to ESP, some of these same individuals would willingly believe that a psychic could help them find their lost child.

4. *The "vividness" problem:* Human information processing and memory storage and retrieval are often based on the initial "vividness" of the information. Sincere personal testimonials, theatrical demonstrations, and detailed anecdotes easily capture our attention and tend to be remembered better than rational, scientific descriptions of events. This is the heart of most stories about extraterrestrial visitations.

Now decide which type of faulty reasoning *best* describes each of the following. Although more than one type may be applicable, enter only one number beside each report. Comparing your answers with your classmates' and friends' answers will further sharpen your critical thinking skills.

_____ John hadn't thought of Paula, his old high school sweetheart, for years. Yet one

ACTIVE LEARNING

morning he woke up thinking about her. He was wondering what she looked like and whether she was married now, when suddenly the phone rang. For some strange reason, he felt sure the call was from Paula. He was right. John now cites this call as evidence for his personal experience with extrasensory perception.

_____ A psychic visits a class in introductory psychology. He predicts that out of this class of 23 students, 2 individuals will have birthdays on the same day. When a tally of birthdays is taken, his prediction is supported and many students leave class believing that the existence of ESP has been supported.

_____ A National League baseball player dreams of hitting a bases-loaded triple. Two months later, during the final game of the World Series, he gets this exact triple and wins the game. He informs the media of his earlier dream and the possibility that ESP exists.

_____ A mother sitting alone in her office at work suddenly sees a vivid image of her home on fire. She calls home and awakens the sitter, who then notices smoke coming under the door and quickly extinguishes the fire. The media attributes the mother's visual images to ESP.

MODULE 13   ACTIVE LEARNING WORKSHEET

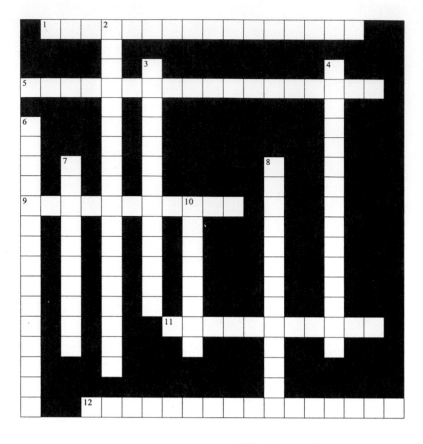

ACROSS

1 Specialized cells in the brain that respond only to certain sensory information.

5 The process whereby the brain sorts out and attends only to the important messages from the senses.

9 The tendency of the brain to ignore environmental factors that remain constant.

11 A binocular depth cue in which the closer the object, the more the eyes converge, or turn inward.

12 A binocular cue to distance in which the separation of the eyes causes different images to fall on each retina.

DOWN

2 The theory first proposed by Thomas Young stating that color perception results from mixing three distinct color systems—-red, green, and blue.

3 Visual input from two eyes that allows perception of depth or distance.

4 A Gestalt law of perceptual organization stating that our perceptions consist of two aspects: the figure, which stands out and has a definite contour or shape, and the ground, which is more distinct.

6 The ability to perceive three-dimensional space and to accurately judge distance.

7 Pertaining to any stimulus presented below the threshold of conscious awareness.

8 Visual input from a single eye alone that contributes to perception of depth or distance.

10 A false impression of the environment.

KEY TERMS

*To assess your understanding of the **Key Terms** in this section, write a definition for each (in your own words), and then compare your definitions with those in the text.*

bottom-up processing (p. 131)
perception (p. 131)
sensation (p. 131)
top-down processing (p. 131)

Experiencing Sensations
absolute threshold (p. 134)
coding (p. 133)
difference threshold (p. 134)
gate-control theory of pain
   (p. 135)
psychophysics (p. 134)
sensory adaptation (p. 134)
sensory reduction (p. 133)
transduction (p. 132)

How We See and Hear
accommodation (p. 139)
amplitude (p. 137)
audition (p. 140)
cochlea (p. 142)

conduction deafness (p. 143)
cones (p. 139)
dark adaptation (p. 140)
farsightedness (hyperopia) (p. 139)
fovea (p. 139)
frequency (p. 137)
frequency theory (p. 143)
hue (p. 137)
loudness (p. 141)
nearsightedness (myopia) (p. 139)
nerve deafness (p. 143)
pitch (p. 141)
place theory (p. 142)
retina (p. 139)
rods (p. 139)
wavelength (p. 137)

Our Other Senses
gustation (p. 146)
kinesthesis (p. 149)
olfaction (p. 144)

pheromones [FARE-oh-mones]
   (p. 146)
semicircular canals (p. 148)

Perception
binocular cues (p. 161)
convergence (p. 161)
depth perception (p. 159)
extrasensory perception (ESP)
   (p. 167)
feature detectors (p. 151)
habituation (p. 153)
illusion (p. 151)
monocular cues (p. 161)
opponent-process theory (p. 163)
perceptual constancy (p. 156)
perceptual set (p. 166)
retinal disparity (p. 161)
selective attention (p. 151)
subliminal (p. 167)
trichromatic theory (p. 163)

WEB RESOURCES

Huffman Book Companion Site
http://www.wiley.com/college/huffman
   This site is loaded with free Interactive Self-Tests, Internet
   Exercises, Glossary and Flashcards for key terms, Web links,
   Handbook for Non-Native Speakers, and other activities
   designed to improve your mastery of the material in this section.

Grand Illusions
http://www.grand-illusions.com/
   Offers an extensive, and exciting, gathering of optical illusions,
   scientific toys, visual effects, and even a little magic.

How We See
http://webvision.med.utah.edu/
   Provides a wealth of information on the organization of the
   retina and visual system, color vision, and related topics.

Interactive Tutorials
http://psych.hanover.edu/Krantz/tutor.html
   Exceptional web site offering numerous demonstrations and
   activities that are both fun and educational.

VISUAL SUMMARY

Sensation and Perception
(Modules 12 and 13)

Experiencing Sensations

Processing

- **Receptors**: Body cells that detect and respond to stimulus energy.
- **Transduction**: A process of converting receptor energy into neural impulses the brain can understand.
- **Sensory reduction**: Filtering and analyzing of sensations before messages are sent to the brain.
- **Coding**: A three-part process that converts sensory input into specific sensations (sight, sound, touch, etc.).

Thresholds

Absolute threshold: Smallest *magnitude* of a stimulus we can detect
Difference threshold: Smallest *change* in a stimulus we can detect

Adaptation

Sensory adaptation: Decreased sensory response to continuous stimulation.

How We See and Hear

Vision

Light is a form of energy and part of the *electromagnetic spectrum*. Light waves vary in:
1) *Length* (the **wavelength** of a light determines **frequency**, which creates **hue**, or color)
2) *Height* (the **amplitude** determines intensity or brightness)
3) *Range* (the mixture of lengths and amplitudes determines complexity or saturation)

Eye anatomy and function

- *Cornea*: Clear bulge at front of eye, where light enters.
- *Pupil*: Hole through which light passes into eye.
- *Iris*: Colored muscles that surround pupil.
- *Lens*: Elastic structure that bulges and flattens to focus an image on retina (a process called **accommodation**).
- **Retina**: Contains visual receptor cells, called **rods** (for night vision) and **cones** (for color vision and fine detail).
- **Fovea:** Pit in the retina responsible for sharp vision.

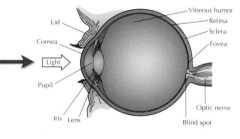

Hearing

Audition (or hearing) occurs via *sound waves*, which result from rapid changes in air pressure caused by vibrating objects. Sound waves vary in:
1) *Length* (the wavelength of a sound determines frequency, which corresponds to **pitch**)
2) *Height* (the amplitude of a sound determines **loudness**)
3) *Range* (the mixture of frequencies and amplitudes in sound wave determines timbre)

How We See and Hear (cont.)

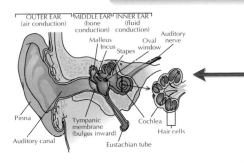

Ear Anatomy and Function

Outer ear conducts sound waves to *eardrum*, which vibrates tiny bones of middle ear that conduct sound vibrations to oval window. Movement of the oval window creates waves in fluid in the **cochlea**, which contains *hair cells* (receptors for hearing) that convert sound energy to neural impulses sent along to the brain.

Our Other Senses

Smell and Taste

Olfaction (sense of smell) *Lock-and-key theory*: Each 3-D odor molecule fits into only one type of receptor.
Gustation (sense of taste) Five basic tastes: salty, sweet, sour, bitter, and umami.

The Body Senses

Skin senses detect touch (pressure), temperature, and pain.
Vestibular sense (or sense of balance) results from receptors in inner ear.
Kinesthesis (body posture, orientation, and body movement) results from receptors in muscles, joints, and tendons.

Perception

Selection

Three major factors:
1) **Selective attention**: The brain sorts out and only attends to most important sensory messages.
2) **Feature detectors**: Specialized brain cells that only respond to specific sensory information.
3) **Habituation**: Tendency of brain to ignore environmental factors that remain constant.

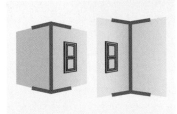

Organization

Four general attributes:
1) **Form**: *Figure and ground, proximity, continuity, closure, contiguity,* and *similarity.*
2) **Constancy**: *Size constancy, shape constancy, color constancy,* and *brightness constancy.*
3) **Depth**: Binocular (2 eyes) **cues** involve **retinal disparity** and **convergence.**
   Monocular (one eye) **cues** include *linear perspective, interposition,* and so on.
4) **Color**: Color perception is a combination of two theories: **trichromatic theory** and **opponent-process theory**.

Interpretation

Four major factors:
1) *Perceptual adaptation*: The brain adapts to changed environment.
2) *Perceptual set*: A readiness to perceive based on expectations.
3) *Individual motivation*: Based on personal interests, needs, and context.
4) *Frame of reference*: Based on context of situation.

Subliminal Perception and ESP

Subliminal stimuli occur below the threshold of our conscious awareness.
Extrasensory perception (ESP) is the supposed ability to perceive things through unknown senses.

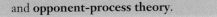

STATES OF CONSCIOUSNESS

On September 4, 1974, an Eastern Airlines flight from Charleston, South Carolina, to Charlotte, North Carolina, crashed, killing the pilot, Captain James Reeves, all of his flight crew, and 68 passengers. The week before, Captain Reeves's hectic work schedule was filled with long flights and work shifts that began anywhere from early morning to late night. Approximately 30 minutes before the crash, Captain Reeves checked in with the Charlotte control tower. Sounding tired and depressed, Reeves complained, "Rest. That's what I need is rest. I don't need all of this [expletive] flying" (cited in Coren, 1996, p. 227).

In October 1996, President Bill Clinton signed into law a bill adding an extra 20 years to a criminal's prison sentence if a certain drug was used to incapacitate the criminal's victim. This was the first time in U.S. history that using a drug was considered a weapon and classified as a crime. What is the drug? Rohypnol — also known as the "date rape drug." Colorless, odorless, and tasteless when dissolved in liquid, Rohypnol can easily be slipped into any drink. Unsuspecting victims have reported waking up naked in fraternity houses, on beaches, or in the homes of their dates, with no recall of the previous several hours (Tattersall, 2000). In addition to the horror of rape and the possibility of sexually transmitted diseases and pregnancy, Rohypnol can also lead to respiratory depression and death.

On May 19, 2002, Cathy Isford, an 18-year-old high school senior, lapsed into a coma after taking Ecstasy on the night of her high school prom. The next day, her doctors determined she could not recover and removed her from all life support. Once used for therapeutic purposes and then by elite club hoppers, Ecstasy, known scientifically as MDMA, is now flooding college dorms, rave parties, and high school campuses (Landry, 2002, Strote, Lee, & Wechsler, 2002). Why? According to users, "it's fun." College students describe melting into "cuddle puddles," groups of writhing individuals massaging and embracing one another on the dance floor. They report that their skin feels "tremblingly alive when caressed." According to 23-year-old, "Katrina," "A guy touching your skin with a cold drink. It's delicious." (Barnes, Graft, Reaves, & Shannon, 2000, p. 67).

What do these three stories have in common? All the situations involve an altered state of consciousness: a fatigued pilot surrendering to much-needed sleep, unsuspecting dates slipping into unconsciousness and amnesia, and party-goers seeking out "cuddle puddles."

What do we mean by "altered consciousness"? And when does a change in consciousness become dangerous? In this section, we begin with a general look at the definition and description of **consciousness,** an organism's awareness of its own self and its surroundings (Damasio, 1999). Next, we examine changes in everyday, waking consciousness, known as *altered* or **alternate states of consciousness** (ASCs). ASCs include sleep and dreaming, chemically induced changes from psychoactive drugs, daydreaming, fantasies, hypnosis, and meditation. The section concludes by exploring why humans throughout history and across cultures have sought alternate states of consciousness.

Consciousness *An organism's awareness of its own self and surroundings (Damasio, 1999)*

Alternate State of Consciousness (ASC) *A mental state other than ordinary waking consciousness, found during sleep, dreaming, psychoactive drug use, hypnosis, and so on*

MODULE 14
CONSCIOUSNESS AND SLEEP AND DREAMS

How can we define and describe consciousness?

■ Understanding Consciousness: What is it?

How Do We Define It?

Our definition of *consciousness* is fairly simple and currently popular: an organism's awareness of its own self and surroundings. We could have chosen another, because psychologists have many definitions of consciousness. The problem is that the concept is difficult to *scientifically* study and define. What, for example, do we mean by "awareness"? What would it be like to be "unaware"? How can we study the contents of our consciousness when the only tool of discovery is the object itself? How can the mind's awareness study itself? Consciousness is a fundamental concept in the field of psychology, yet it eludes simple definition (Damasio, 1999).

In the late nineteenth century, when psychology first became a scientific discipline separate from philosophy, it defined itself as "the study of human consciousness." But such a nebulous area of study eventually led to great dissatisfaction within the field. One group, the behaviorists, led by John Watson, believed that *behavior*, not consciousness, was the proper focus of the new science. In fact, he declared, "the time seems to have come when psychology must discard all references to consciousness; when it need no longer delude itself into thinking that it is making mental states the object of observation" (1913, p. 164).

In recent years, psychology has renewed its original interest in consciousness thanks to research in cognitive and cultural psychology. Also, advances in scientific technology, such as the electroencephalogram (EEG), positron emission tomography (PET), and functional magnetic resonance imaging (fMRI), allow scientific study of brain activity during various states of consciousness. Many neuroscientists believe consciousness will ultimately be linked to patterns of neural activity in the brain, although the precise location or functioning of this "seat of consciousness" has not yet been discovered.

How Do We Describe It?

Consciousness may be easier to *describe* than to define. The first American psychologist, William James, likened consciousness to a stream that's constantly changing yet always the same. It meanders and flows, sometimes where the person wills and sometimes not. However, through the process of *selective attention* (Module 12), we can control our consciousness by deliberate concentration and full attention. For example, at the present moment you are (I hope) fully awake and concentrating on the words on this page. At times, however, your control may weaken, and your stream of consciousness may drift to thoughts of a computer you want to buy, your job, or an attractive classmate.

In addition to meandering and flowing, your "stream of consciousness" also varies in depth. Consciousness is not an all-or-nothing phenomenon — conscious or unconscious. Instead, it exists along a continuum, ranging from high awareness and sharp, focused alertness at one extreme, to middle levels of awareness such as daydreaming, to unconsciousness and coma at the other extreme (Table 14.1).

Controlled Versus Automatic Processes When you're working at a demanding task or learning something new, like how to drive a car, consciousness is at the high end of the continuum. **Controlled processes,** like these, demand focused attention and generally interfere with other ongoing activities. Have you ever been so

Controlled Processes *Mental activities requiring focused attention that generally interfere with other ongoing activities*

SUMMARY TABLE 14.1 LEVELS OF CONSCIOUSNESS

High level of awareness	Controlled processes	High level of awareness, focused attention required	
Middle level of awareness	Automatic processes	Awareness, but minimal attention required	
	Daydreaming	Low level of awareness and conscious effort, somewhere between active consciousness and dreaming while asleep	
Minimal or no awareness	Unconscious mind (a Freudian concept discussed in Module 35)	Reservoir of unacceptable thoughts, feelings, and memories that are too painful or anxiety provoking to be admitted to consciousness	
	Unconscious (biologically based)	Lowest level of awareness due to head injuries, disease, anesthesia during surgery, or coma	

absorbed during an exam that you completely forgot your surroundings until the instructor announced, "Time is up," and asked for your paper? This type of focused attention is the hallmark of controlled processes.

In contrast, **automatic processes** require minimal attention and generally do not interfere with other ongoing activities. Think back to your childhood when you believed it was so difficult to learn to drive a car, yet now you can listen to the radio, think about your classes, and talk to fellow passengers, all while driving. Learning a new task requires complete concentration and *controlled processing*, but once that task is well learned, you can relax and rely on your *automatic processes* (Fanz, Waldie, & Smith, 2000).

Automatic Processes *Mental activities requiring minimal attention and having little impact on other activities*

Automatic processes are generally helpful. However, there are times when we are on "automatic pilot" and don't want to be. Consider the problems of novelist Colin Wilson (1967):

> When I learned to type, I had to do it painfully and with much nervous wear and tear. But at a certain stage a miracle occurred, and this complicated operation was "learned" by a useful robot that I conceal in my subconscious mind. Now I only have to think about what I want to say; my robot secretary does the typing. He is really very useful. He also drives the car for me, speaks French (not very well), and occasionally gives lectures at American universities. [My robot] is most annoying when I am tired, because then he tends to take over most of my functions without even asking me. I have even caught him making love to my wife. [p. 98]

Assessment

CHECK & REVIEW

Understanding Consciousness

Most of our lives are spent in normal, waking **consciousness,** an organism's awareness of its own self and surroundings. However, we also spend considerable time in various **alternate states of consciousness** (ASCs), such as sleep and dreaming, daydreams, sexual fantasies, chemically induced changes from psychoactive drugs, hypnosis, and meditation.

Consciousness has always been difficult to study and define. William James described it as a "flowing stream." Modern researchers emphasize that consciousness exists along a continuum. **Controlled processes,** which require focused attention, are at the highest level of awareness. **Automatic processes,** which require minimal attention, are found in the middle of the continuum. Unconsciousness and coma are at the lowest level of awareness.

Questions

1. _____ is (are) best defined as our awareness of our environments and ourselves. (a) Alternate states of consciousness (ASCs); (b) Consciousness; (c) States of consciousness; (d) Selective attention

2. Why were early psychologists reluctant to study consciousness?

3. Controlled processes require _____ attention, whereas automatic processes need _____ attention.

4. As you read this text, you should _____. (a) be in an alternate state of consciousness; (b) employ automatic processing; (c) let your stream of consciousness take charge; (d) employ controlled processing

Answers to Questions can be found in Appendix B.

Sleep and Dreams: A Third of Our Lives

Having explored the definition and description of everyday, waking consciousness, we now turn to two of our most common alternate states of consciousness (ASCs)—sleep and dreaming. These ASCs are fascinating to both scientists and the general public. Why are we born with a mechanism that forces us to sleep and dream for approximately a third of our lives? How can an ASC that requires reduced awareness and responsiveness to our environment be healthy? What are the functions and causes of sleep and dreams?

The Power of Circadian Rhythms

To understand sleep, you first need to understand that sleep is an integral part of several daily biological rhythms. Each day, our planet cycles from light to dark and back again. Most animals have adapted to this change by developing a 24-hour cycle of activities, or **circadian rhythms** — in Latin, *circa* means "about" and *dies* means "day."

Have you noticed that your energy level, mood, and efficiency change throughout the day? Research shows that alertness, moods, learning efficiency, as well as blood pressure, metabolism, and pulse rate all follow circadian rhythms (Ariznavarreta et al., 2002; Blagrove, 2000; Kunz & Hermann, 2000; Young, 2000). For most people, these activities reach their peak during the day and their low point at night. This corre-

Assessment

What happens to consciousness while we sleep and dream?

Circadian [ser-KAY-dee-an] Rhythms *Biological changes that occur on a 24-hour cycle (circa = about, and dies = day)*

Before reading on, test your personal knowledge of sleep and dreaming by reviewing the common myths below.

- **Myth:** *Everyone needs 8 hours of sleep a night to maintain sound mental and physical health.*

  Although most of us average 7.6 hours of sleep a night, some people get by on an incredible 15 to 30 minutes, whereas others need as much as 11 hours (Doghramji, 2000; Maas, 1999).

- **Myth:** *It is easy to learn complicated things, like a foreign language, while asleep.*

  Although some learning can occur during the lighter stages (1 and 2) of sleep, the processing and retention of this material is minimal (Aarons, 1976; Ogilvie, Wilkinson, & Allison, 1989). Wakeful learning is much more effective and efficient.

- **Myth:** *Some people never dream.*

  In rare cases, adults with certain brain injuries or disorders do not dream (Solms, 1997), but otherwise, adults regularly dream. Even people who firmly believe they never dream report dreams if they are repeatedly awakened during an overnight study in a sleep laboratory. Children also dream regularly. For example, between ages 3 and 8, they dream approximately 20 to 28 percent of their sleep time (Foulkes, 1982, 1993). Apparently, almost everyone dreams, but some people don't remember their dreams.

- **Myth:** *Dreams last only a few seconds.*

  Research shows that some dreams seem to occur in "real time;" that is, a dream that seemed to last 20 minutes probably did last approximately 20 minutes (Dement & Wolpert, 1958).

- **Myth:** *When people experience genital arousal during sleep, it means they are having a sexual dream.*

  When sleepers are awakened during this time, they are no more likely to report sexual dreams than at other times.

- **Myth:** *Dreaming of dying can be fatal.*

  This is a good opportunity to exercise your critical thinking skills. Take time to critically evaluate this common belief. Where did this myth come from? Has anyone ever personally experienced and recounted a fatal dream? How would we scientifically prove or disprove this belief?

sponds to the fact that humans are awake during the light times of the circadian cycle and asleep during the dark periods.

What controls these circadian rhythms? Research shows that the "clock" that regulates these 24-hour rhythms is located in a part of the hypothalamus called the *suprachiasmatic nucleus* (the SCN), which, if damaged, causes animals and humans to fall asleep or wake up at random times (Cohen et al., 1999; Ruby et al., 2002; Vita-terna, Takahashi, & Turek, 2001). Human circadian rhythms are also affected by the *pineal gland*, an endocrine gland in the middle of the brain. The pineal gland helps regulate sleep and arousal by secreting large quantities of the hormone *melatonin* during the night and little or none during the day.

Although research shows that melatonin does seem to bring on sleepiness in humans (e.g., Yang et al., 2001), and many people take over-the-counter versions of it as a "sleeping pill" or dietary supplement, you may want to hesitate before taking it yourself. Melatonin influences not only sleep, but also sexual arousal, the onset of puberty, and possibly the aging process itself. Also, melatonin has not been tested and approved by the FDA, and in the absence of regulation, some supplements are sold that contain 10 times the amount needed to bring on sleepiness (Zhadanova & Wurtman, 1996). Furthermore, there is limited research on the long-term consequences of taking large amounts of melatonin, how it interacts with other medications, or even its overall safety.

Disrupted Circadian Rhythms   Despite the warnings, a growing number of people use melatonin to treat "jet lag" and reset their sleep cycles after working late nights or being on rotating shifts — as in the case of Captain Reeves. The desire to reset the biological clock is understandable because studies clearly show that disruptions in circadian rhythms lead to increased fatigue, decreased concentration, sleep disorders, and other health problems (Garbarino et al., 2002; Katz, Knobler, Laibel, Strauss, & Durst, 2002; Manly, Lewis, Robertson, Watson, & Datta, 2002).

As a student, you may be comforted to know how your late-night study sessions and full or part-time night jobs help explain your fatigue and other complaints. Less comforting is the knowledge that 20 percent of employees in the United States (primarily in the fields of health care, data processing, and transportation) have rotating work schedules that create many of the same problems (Maas, 1999). Although many physicians, nurses, police, and other workers manage to function well despite work schedules that change from day to day or week to week, studies do find that shift work and sleep deprivation lead to decreased concentration and productivity—and increased accidents (Connor et al., 2002; Dement & Vaughan, 1999; Garbarino et al., 2002).

For example, in a major review of Japanese near-collision train incidents, 82 percent took place between midnight and morning (Charland, 1992). Also, some of the worst recent disasters—including the Union Carbide chemical accident in Bhopal, India, the nuclear power plant disaster in Chernobyl, and the Alaskan oil spill from the *Exxon Valdez*—occurred during the night shift. And, as described in the section opener, official investigations of airline crashes often cite pilot shift work and sleep deprivation as possible contributing factors.

Although catastrophic accidents also can be traced to unusual coincidences, we need to recognize that shift workers may be fighting a dangerous battle with their own circadian rhythms. What can be done to help? Some research shows that workers find it easier to adjust when their schedules are shifted from days to evenings to nights (8–4, 4–12, 12–8), probably because it's easier to go to bed later than the reverse. Also, when shifts are rotated every three weeks versus each week, productivity increases and accidents decrease. Finally, some research suggests that brief naps for shift workers (or anyone) can help increase learning potential (Bower, 2002; Tietzel & Lack, 2001).

Not only can rotating work schedules disrupt circadian cycles but so can flying across several time zones. Have you ever taken a long airline flight and felt fatigued, sluggish, and irritable for the first few days after arriving? If so, you experienced symptoms of *jet lag*. Like rotating shift work, jet lag correlates with decreased alertness, decreased mental agility, exacerbation of psychiatric disorders, and overall reduced efficiency (Iyer, 2001; Katz, Knobler, Laibel, Strauss, & Durst, 2002).

Is it true that jet lag is worse when you fly long distances eastward rather than westward? Transcontinental flights in either direction disrupt our circadian cycles, but traveling westward is easier because our bodies adjust more easily to going to sleep later. Why? For some unknown reason, our bodies seem to be on a 25-hour schedule. Research with young adults isolated without daylight or clocks show that participants generally move to a 25-hour day (Moore, 1997).

Sleep Deprivation   Disruptions in circadian cycles due to shift work and jet lag can have serious effects, but what about long-term sleep deprivation? History tells us that during Roman times and in the Middle Ages, sleep deprivation was a form of torture. And today, some armies use loud, blaring music and noise to disrupt their enemy's sleep.

Are you sleep deprived? Take the following two-part test and find out.

Part 1 A typical task used by sleep deprivation researchers is to ask people to trace a star using their nondominant hand while watching their hand in a mirror. Set up a small mirror next to the text and see if you can copy the star below. The task is difficult, and sleep-deprived people typically make many errors.

Part 2 Now give yourself one point each time you answer yes to the following questions:

Do you often fall asleep...

watching TV?

during boring meetings or lectures or in warm rooms?

after heavy meals or after a small amount of alcohol?

while relaxing after dinner?

within five minutes of getting into bed?

In the morning, do you generally...

need an alarm clock to wake up at the right time?

Sleep deprivation. Insufficient sleep can seriously affect your college grades—as well as your physical health, motor skills, and overall mood.

struggle to get out of bed?

hit the snooze bar several times to get more sleep?

During the day, do you...

feel tired, irritable, and stressed out?

have trouble concentrating and remembering?

feel slow when it comes to critical thinking, problem solving, and being creative?

feel drowsy while driving?

need a nap to get through the day?

have dark circles around your eyes?

According to Cornell University psychologist James Maas (1999), if you answered yes to three or more items, you probably are not getting enough sleep.

Source: Quiz adapted and reprinted from Maas, 1999 with permission.

Exploring the scientific effects of severe sleep loss is limited by obvious ethical concerns. Research also is hampered by practical considerations. For example, after about 72 hours without sleep, research participants unwillingly slip into brief, repeated periods of "microsleep," lasting a few seconds at a time. To complicate things further, sleep deprivation increases stress, making it difficult to separate the effects of sleep deprivation from those of stress.

Despite these problems, sleep researchers have documented several hazards related to sleep deprivation that coincide with the previously mentioned effects of disrupted circadian cycles, including mood alterations, reduced concentration and motivation, increased irritability, lapses in attention, reduced motor skills, and increased cortisol levels (a sign of stress) (Carskadon & Dement, 2002; Cho, 2001; Dement & Vaughan, 1999). Experiments with severe sleep deprivation in rats show even more serious side effects and sometimes death (Rechtschaffen, 1997; Rechtschaffen & Bergmann, 1995). But perhaps the greatest danger associated with sleep deprivation comes from pilots, physicians, and other workers whose lapses in attention can cost many lives (McCartt, Rohrbaugh, Hammer, & Fuller, 2000; Paice et al., 2002).

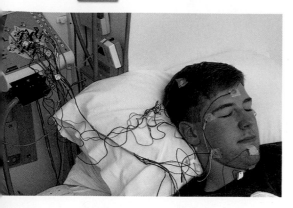

Figure 14.1 *How sleep is studied.* Researchers in a sleep laboratory use sophisticated equipment to record physiological changes during sleep. Electroencephalogram (EEG) electrodes are taped to the scalp to measure brain wave activity. Electromyograph (EMG) electrodes are applied to the chin and mouth to measure muscular activity. Electrooculograph (EOG) electrodes are taped near the eyes to record eye movements. Other devices not shown in this photo record heart rate, respiration rate, and genital arousal.

It is interesting to note, however, that many physiological functions are not significantly disrupted by periods of sleep deprivation (Walsh & Lindblom, 1997). In fact, in 1965, a 17-year-old student named Randy Gardner, who wanted to earn a place in the *Guinness Book of World Records*, stayed awake for 264 consecutive hours. He did become irritable and had to remain active to stay awake, but he did not become incoherent or psychotic (Coren, 1996; Spinweber, 1993). Afterward, Randy slept a mere 14 hours and then returned to his usual 8-hour sleep cycle (Dement, 1992).

Stages of Sleep

Sleep is an important component of our circadian rhythms. Each night, we go through four to five cycles of distinct sleep stages, each with a rhythm of its own and corresponding changes in brain activity and behavior. How do we know this? How can scientists study private mental events like sleep? Surveys and interviews can provide some information about the nature of sleep, but perhaps the most important tool for sleep researchers is a recording of brain activity called the *electroencephalogram* (EEG).

As we move from a waking state to deep sleep, our brains show complex and predictable changes in electrical activity. The EEG records these brain wave changes by means of small disklike electrodes placed on the scalp. The electrodes pick up electrical changes in the nerve cells of the cerebral cortex. The changes are then amplified and recorded on a long roll of paper or computer monitor. These recordings, or electroencephalograms, allow researchers to observe the brain's activity while its owner is asleep. Sleep researchers also use other recording devices, such as those seen in Figure 14.1.

Cycling Through the Stages of Sleep Perhaps the best way to appreciate the methods and findings of sleep researchers is to pretend for a moment that you are a participant in a sleep experiment. When you arrive at the sleep lab, you are assigned one of several "bedrooms." The researcher hooks you up to various physiological recording devices, such as the electroencephalogram (EEG) to measure brain waves, the electromyograph (EMG) to measure muscular activity, and the electrooculogram (EOG) to measure eye movements. If you are like other participants, you will probably need a night or two to adapt to the equipment and return to a normal mode of sleeping.

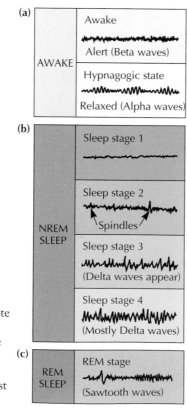

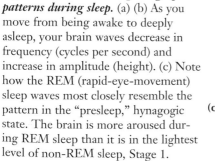

Figure 14.2 *Electroencephalograph patterns during sleep.* (a) (b) As you move from being awake to deeply asleep, your brain waves decrease in frequency (cycles per second) and increase in amplitude (height). (c) Note how the REM (rapid-eye-movement) sleep waves most closely resemble the pattern in the "presleep," hynagogic state. The brain is more aroused during REM sleep than it is in the lightest level of non-REM sleep, Stage 1.

Early Stages of Sleep Once adapted, you are ready for the researchers to monitor your typical night's sleep. As your eyes close and you begin to relax, the researcher in the next room notices that your EEG recordings have moved from the wave pattern associated with normal wakefulness, *beta waves*, to the slower *alpha waves*, which indicate drowsy relaxation (Figure 14.2a). During this relaxed, "presleep" state, you may experience a *hypnagogic state*, which is characterized by feelings of floating, weightlessness, visual images (such as flashing lights or colors), or swift, jerky movements and a corresponding feeling of slipping or falling. Hypnagogic experiences are sometimes incorporated into fragmented dreams and remembered in the morning. They also may explain reported accounts of alien abduction. These alleged encounters typically occur while the victim is falling asleep, and many reports mention "strange flashes of light" and "floating off the bed."

As you continue relaxing, your brain's electrical activity slows even further. You are now in *Stage 1* sleep; your breathing becomes more regular, your heart rate slows, and your blood pressure decreases. At this stage, you could still be readily awakened. No one wakens you, though, so you relax more deeply and slide gently into *Stage 2* sleep. This stage is noted on your electroencephalograph by occasional short bursts of rapid, high-amplitude brain waves known as *sleep spindles*. During Stage 2 sleep, you become progressively more relaxed and less responsive to the external environment. However, even deeper levels of sleep follow Stage 2 — *Stages 3 and 4*. As shown in Figure 14.2b, these stages are marked by the appearance of slow, high-amplitude *delta waves*. It is very hard to awaken you in the deepest stages of sleep, even by shouting and shaking. (Can you see why it is difficult to learn foreign languages or other material from tapes while sound asleep [Wyatt & Bootzin, 1994]?) Stage 4 sleep also is the time when children are most likely to wet the bed and when sleepwalking occurs.

In about an hour, you progress through all four stages of sleep. Then the sequence begins to reverse itself (see Figure 14.3). Although we don't necessarily go through all sleep stages in this sequence, during the course of a night people usually complete four to five cycles of light to deep sleep and back. Each cycle lasts about 90 minutes.

REM Sleep   Figure 14.3 also shows an interesting phenomenon that occurs at the end of the first cycle. You go back through Stage 3, and then to Stage 2, but instead of reentering the calm, relaxed Stage 1, something totally different happens. Quite abruptly, your scalp recordings display a pattern of small-amplitude, fast wave activity similar in many ways to an awake, vigilant person's brain waves. Your breathing and pulse rates become fast and irregular, and your genitals very likely show signs of arousal (an erection or vaginal lubrication). Although your brain and body are giving many signs of active arousal, your musculature is deeply relaxed and unresponsive. This stage is sometimes referred to as "paradoxical sleep" because it is in some ways the deepest sleep and in other ways the lightest. (The term *paradoxical* means "apparently self-contradictory.")

During this stage, rapid eye movements occur under your closed eyelids. Researchers discovered that these eye movements are important because they signal that dreaming is taking place. (Can you see why the muscle "paralysis" of paradoxical sleep is a good thing? Otherwise, we would act out our dreams.) Because of the importance of dreaming, the paradoxical stage is generally known as **rapid eye movement sleep (REM).** And, because REM sleep is so different, Stages 1 to 4 are often collectively called *NREM* (or *non-REM*) sleep.

Although some people believe they do not dream, evidence suggests that we all dream every night even though we may not remember it. Dreaming also occurs during NREM sleep, but less frequently, and the dreams usually contain a simple experience, such as "I dreamed of a house" (Hobson, 2002; Squier & Domhoff, 1998).

What is the purpose of REM and NREM sleep?   In addition to the need for dreaming, which will be discussed in the next section, scientists believe REM sleep may be important for learning and consolidating new memories (Kavanau, 2000; Maquet et al., 2000; Squier & Domhoff, 1998). Further evidence of the importance of REM sleep in complex brain functions comes from the fact that it occurs only in mammals of higher intelligence and is absent in nonmammals such as reptiles (Rechtschaffen & Siegel, 2000). There also is general agreement that it serves an important biological need. When researchers selectively deprive sleepers of REM sleep (by waking them each time they enter the state), most people experience *REM rebound*. That is, they try to "catch up" on REM sleep on subsequent occasions by spending more time than usual in this state (Dement & Vaughan, 1999).

Although REM sleep is important to our biological functioning, the need for NREM sleep may be even greater. When people are deprived of *total* sleep, rather

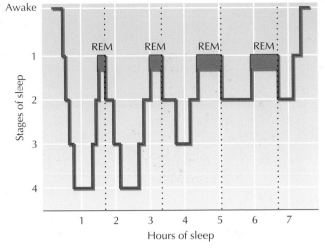

Figure 14.3 *Stages in a typical night's sleep.* During a normal night's sleep, the sleeper moves in and out of various stages of sleep. Starting off alert, the sleeper gradually shifts downward into NREM Stage 1, then NREM Stages 2, 3, and 4. The sleep cycle then reverses. At the peak of the return trip, the sleeper spends some time in REM (rapid-eye-movement) sleep and then the cycle starts downward again. As the night continues, the sleeper repeats the general cycle four to five times. (The dotted lines indicate the boundaries of each cycle.) Note that the periods of Stage 4 and then Stage 3 sleep diminish during the night, whereas REM periods increase in duration. *Source:* Adapted from Julien, 2000, with permission.

Rapid-Eye-Movement (REM) Sleep
A stage of sleep marked by rapid eye movements, high-frequency brain waves, paralysis of large muscles, and dreaming

The sleep cycle in cats. During NREM (non-rapid eye movement) sleep, cats often sleep in an upright position. With the onset of REM sleep, the cat rolls over on its side. *Can you explain why?*

Answer: During REM sleep, large muscles are temporarily paralyzed, which causes the cat to lose motor control and lie down.

than just REM sleep, and then allowed full recovery sleep, their first uninterrupted night has a greater proportion of NREM sleep (Borbely, 1982). In addition, as you may remember from Figure 14.3, when you initially begin to sleep, you spend more time in Stage 1 sleep through Stage 4 sleep (NREM). After this need has been satisfied, the latter parts of the night are devoted to more REM sleep.

The idea that nature first satisfies its need for NREM sleep before going on to REM sleep is also supported by studies showing that adults who are "short sleepers" (5 or fewer hours each night) spend less time in REM sleep than do "long sleepers" (9 or more hours each night). Similarly, infants get more sleep and have a higher percentage of REM sleep than do adults (Figure 14.4). Apparently, the greater the total amount of sleep, the greater the percentage of REM sleep.

Figure 14.4 *Sleep and dreaming over the life span.* Notice that as you get older, the overall amount of sleep, and the proportion of REM (rapid-eye-movement) sleep, both decrease. The most dramatic changes occur during the first 2 to 3 years of life. As an infant, you spent almost 8 hours a day in REM sleep, but at age 70, you spend less than an hour.

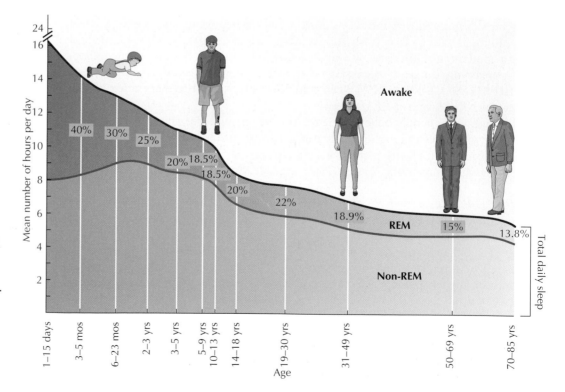

*A*ssessment

CHECK & REVIEW

Circadian Rhythms and Stages of Sleep

Circadian rhythms affect our sleep and waking cycle so that disruptions due to shift work and jet lag can cause serious problems.

A typical night's sleep consists of four to five 90-minute cycles. The cycle begins in Stage 1 and then moves through Stages 2, 3, and 4. After reaching the deepest level of sleep, the cycle reverses up to the **REM** (rapid-eye-movement) state, in which the person often is dreaming.

Questions

1. Biological rhythms that occur on a daily basis are called _____ rhythms. (a) circuitous; (b) chronobiology; (c) calendrical; (d) circadian
2. Jet lag results from _____. (a) sleep deprivation; (b) disruption of the circadian rhythms; (c) the effect of light on the pineal gland; (d) disruption of brain wave patterns that occur at high altitudes.
3. The machine that measures the voltage (or brain waves) that the brain produces is the _____.

4. Just before sleep, brain waves move from _____ waves, indicating normal wakefulness, to _____ waves associated with drowsy relaxation. (a) beta, alpha; (b) theta, delta; (c) alpha, beta; (d) sigma, chi

Answers to Questions can be found in Appendix B.

Theories of Sleep and Dreaming

In addition to the growing body of facts that we now know about sleep and dreaming, scientists also have developed several important, overarching theories, which we'll explore in this section.

Why Do We Sleep? No one knows precisely all the functions sleep serves, but there are two prominent theories. The **repair/restoration theory** suggests that sleep helps us recuperate from depleting, daily activities. Essential factors in our brain or body are apparently repaired or replenished while we sleep. We recover not only from physical fatigue but also from emotional and intellectual demands (Maas, 1999).

In contrast, the **evolutionary/circadian theory** emphasizes the relationship of sleep to basic circadian rhythms. According to this view, sleep evolved so animals could conserve energy when they were not foraging for food or seeking mates. Sleep also serves to keep them still at times when predators are active (Hirshkowitz, Moore, & Minhoto, 1997). The evolutionary/circadian theory helps explain differences in sleep patterns across species (Figure 14.5). Opossums sleep many hours each day because they are relatively safe in their environment and are able to easily find food and shelter. In comparison, sheep and horses sleep very little because their diets require constant foraging for food and because their only defense against predators is vigilance and running away.

Which theory is correct? Both theories have merit. Obviously, we need to repair and restore ourselves after a busy day. But bears don't hibernate all winter simply to recover from a busy summer. Like humans and other animals, they also need to conserve energy when the environment is hostile. It may be that sleep initially served to conserve energy and keep us out of trouble, and over time it has evolved to allow for repair and restoration.

Why Do We Dream? Is there special meaning or information in our dreams? Why do we have bad dreams? Why do we dream at all? These questions have long fascinated writers and poets, as well as psychologists.

Repair/Restoration Theory *Sleep serves a recuperative function, allowing organisms to repair or replenish key factors*

Evolutionary/Circadian Theory *As a part of circadian rhythms, sleep evolved to conserve energy and as protection from predators*

Throughout the ages, humans have wondered about dreams. After dreaming he was a butterfly, Chuang Tzu, a Chinese Taoist (3 B.C.) spoke about the interplay of reality and dreams: "Suddenly I woke up and I was indeed Chuang Tzu. Did Chuang Tzu dream he was a butterfly? Or did the butterfly dream he was Chuang Tzu?"

Figure 14.5 **Average daily hours of sleep for different mammals.** Why does the opossum spend almost 20 hours a day sleeping, while the horse spends only 2 hours?

Answer: According to the evolution-ary circadian theory of sleep, animals that sleep the longest are least threatened by the environment and can easily find food and shelter. Note how the opossum and cat spend longer hours in sleep than the horse and sheep, presumably because of differences in diet and the number of predators.

Manifest Content *According to Freud, the surface content of a dream, which contains dream symbols that distort and disguise the dream's true meaning*

Latent Content *The true, unconscious meaning of a dream, according to Freudian dream theory*

Activation–Synthesis Hypothesis *Hobson's theory that dreams are by-products of random stimulation of brain cells; the brain attempts to combine (or synthesize) this spontaneous activity into coherent patterns, known as dreams*

The Psychoanalytic/Psychodynamic View. One of the oldest and most scientifically controversial explanations for why we dream is Freud's *psychoanalytic view.* In one of his first books, *The Interpretation of Dreams* (1900), Freud proposed that dreams are "the royal road to the unconscious." According to Freud, dreaming is a special state in which forbidden and personally unacceptable desires rise to the surface of consciousness. Therefore, listening to a patient's dreams sometimes offers direct insight into his or her unconscious, as when a lonely person dreams of romance, or an angry child dreams of getting even with the class bully. More often, though, the dream content is so threatening and anxiety producing that it must be couched in symbols. A journey, for example, is often a symbol for death, horseback riding and dancing are symbols for sexual intercourse, and a cigar or a gun might represent a penis. Freud referred to these symbols (the journey, horseback riding, or the gun) as the **manifest content** (or the story line) of the dream and the underlying, true meaning (death, sex, penis) as the **latent content.**

What is the evidence supporting Freud's theory? Modern psychodynamic theorists believe that latent content can be a wish, a fear, or anything that is emotionally important to the dreamer, but traditional Freudian ideas that dreams are generally associated with sexual or aggressive wishes have little or no scientific support (Domhoff, 2003; Fisher & Greenberg, 1996). After being confronted about the symbolic nature of his beloved cigars, Freud himself supposedly remarked, "Sometimes, a cigar is just a cigar."

The Biological View. In contrast to Freud, the **activation–synthesis hypothesis** suggests that dreams are a by-product of random stimulation of brain cells during REM sleep (Hobson, 1988, 2002). On the basis of research conducted on the brain activity of cats during REM sleep, Alan Hobson and Robert McCarley (1977) proposed that specific neurons in the brainstem fire spontaneously during REM sleep and that the cortex struggles to "synthesize" or make sense out of this random stimulation by manufacturing dreams.

Have you ever dreamed that you were trying to run away from a frightening situation but found that you cannot move? The activation–synthesis hypothesis might explain this dream as random stimulation of the amygdala. As you recall from Module 6, the amygdala is a specific brain area linked to strong emotions, especially fear. If your amygdala is randomly stimulated and you feel afraid, you may try to run, but you can't move because your major muscles are temporarily paralyzed during REM sleep. To make sense of this conflict, you might create a dream about a fearful situation in which you were trapped in heavy sand or that someone was holding on to your arms and legs.

This is *not* to say that dreams are totally meaningless. Hobson (1988, 2002) suggests that even if dreams begin with more or less random activity in various brain areas, your interpretation of this activity is not random. The dream that is constructed depends on your individual personality, motivations, memories, and life experiences.

The Cognitive View. According to the cognitive view, dreams are an extension of everyday life — a form of thinking during sleep. Rather than seeing dreams as mysterious messages from the unconscious or the result of random brain stimulation, dreams are simply another type of *information processing:* They help us sift and sort our everyday experiences and thoughts. The brain periodically shuts out sensory input so it can process, assimilate, and update information — a type of *mental housecleaning* similar to disk defragmentation on your computer.

As we discovered earlier, REM sleep increases following stress and intense learning periods, and other research reports strong similarities between dream content and waking thoughts, fears, and concerns (Domhoff, 1996, 1999; Hobson, 2002). For example, college students often report "examination-anxiety" dreams: You can't find your classroom, you're running out of time, your pen or pencil won't work, or you've completely forgotten a scheduled exam and show up totally unprepared (Van de Castle, 1995). (Sound familiar?)

In Sum. The psychoanalytic/psychodynamic, biological, and cognitive views of dreaming offer three perspectives, but numerous questions remain. How would the psychoanalytic/psychodynamic theory explain why human fetuses show REM patterns? Is the fetus working out suppressed wishes and anxieties in the womb? On the other hand, how would the activation-synthesis hypothesis explain complicated,

Dream images. Have you ever had a dream like this? How would you interpret this dream according to the theories discussed in the text?

Application

CRITICAL THINKING

Interpreting Your Dreams

Television, movies, and other popular media often portray dreams as highly significant and easily interpreted. However, scientists are deeply divided about the meaning of dreams and their relative importance. These differences in scientific opinion provide an excellent opportunity for you to practice the critical thinking skill of *tolerance for ambiguity.*

To improve your tolerance for ambiguity (and learn a little more about your own dreams), begin by briefly jotting down a recent and vivid dream. This should be at least three or four paragraphs in length. Now analyze your dream using the following perspectives:

1. According to the psychoanalytic/psychodynamic view, what might be the forbidden, unconscious fears, drives, or desires represented by your dream? Can you identify the manifest content versus the latent content?

2. How would the biological view, the activation–synthesis hypothesis, explain your dream? Can you identify a specific thought that might have been stimulated and then led to this particular dream?

3. Psychologists from the cognitive perspective believe dream analysis provides important information processing, helps us make needed changes in our life, and even suggests solutions to real-life prob-

ACTIVE LEARNING

lems. Do you agree or disagree? Does your dream provide an insight that increases your self-understanding?

Having analyzed your dream from each perspective, can you see how difficult it is to find the one right answer? Higher-level critical thinkers recognize that competing theories are akin to the story of the four blind men who are each exploring separate parts of an elephant. By listening to their description of the trunk, tail, leg, and so on, critical thinkers can synthesize the information and develop a greater understanding. But no one part — or single theory — reveals the whole picture.

storylike dreams or recurrent dreams? What does a fetus have to dream about in response to random brain activity? Finally, according to the information processing approach, how can a fetus sift and sort its "waking" experiences? And how is it that the same dream can often be explained by many theories? To see this for yourself, try the Critical Thinking/Active Learning Exercise on the previous page.

Achievement
GENDER & CULTURAL DIVERSITY

Variations and Similarities in Dreams

Do men and women dream about different things? Are there differences between cultures in dream content? In reference to gender, research shows that men and women tend to share many common dream themes, but women are more likely to dream of children, family and familiar people, household objects, and indoor events. Men, on the other hand, more often dream about strangers, violence, weapons, sexual activity, achievement, and outdoor events (Domhoff, 1996; Hall et al., 1982; Murray, 1995). However, recent evidence suggests that as gender differences and stereotypes lessen, segregation of dream content by gender becomes less distinct (Bursik, 1998; Hobson, 2002).

Likewise, researchers have found both similarities and differences in dream content among cultures. For example, dreams involving basic human needs and fears (like sex, aggression, and death) seem to be found in all cultures. Children around the world often dream about large, threatening, wild animals. People of all ages and cultures dream of falling, being chased, and being unable to do something they need to do. Dreams also typically include more misfortune than good fortune, and the dreamer is more often the victim of aggression than the cause of it (Domhoff, 1996, 1999; Hall & Van De Castle, 1996).

Yet there are also cultural differences. The Yir Yoront, an Australian hunting and gathering group, generally prefer marriage between a man and his mother's brother's daughter (Schneider & Sharp, 1969). Therefore, it is not uncommon (or surprising) that young, single men in the group often report recurrent dreams of aggression from their mother's brother (their future father-in-law) (Price & Crapo, 1999). Similarly, Americans often report embarrassing dreams of being naked in public, but these dreams are rare in cultures where few clothes are worn.

Interestingly, how people interpret dreams and their cultural value also varies across cultures (Matsumoto, 2000; Price & Crapo, 1999). The Iroquois of North America believe that one's spirit uses dreams to communicate unconscious wishes to the conscious mind (Wallace, 1958). They often share their dreams with religious leaders, who help them interpret and cope with their underlying psychic needs to prevent illness and even death. On the other hand, the Maya of Central America shared their dreams and interpretations at communal gatherings as an important means of teaching cultural folk wisdom (Tedlock, 1992). (As a critical thinker, do you notice the close similarity between Freudian theory and the Iroquois concept of dreaming? Some historians believe that Freud borrowed many concepts from the Iroquois — without giving appropriate credit.)

Assessment
CHECK & REVIEW

Theories of Sleep and Dreaming

The exact function of sleep is not known, but according to the **repair/restoration theory,** it is thought to be necessary for its restorative value, both physically and psychologically. According to **evolutionary/circadian theory,** it also has adaptive value.

Three major theories attempt to explain why we dream: The psychoanalytic/psychodynamic view says dreams are disguised symbols of repressed anxieties and desires. The biological (**activation–synthesis hypothesis**) perspective argues that dreams are simple by-products of random stimulation of brain cells. The cognitive view suggests that dreams are an important part of information processing of everyday experiences.

Questions

1. How does the repair/restoration theory of sleep differ from the evolutionary/cir-cadian theory?

2. What are the basic gender and cultural similarities and differences in dreams?

3. Freud believed that dreams were the "royal road to the _____." (a) therapeutic alliance; (b) psyche; (c) latent content; (d) unconscious

4. _____ theory states that dreams are by-products of random stimulation of brain cells, whereas the _____ view suggests dreams serve an information processing function and help us sift and sort our everyday experiences and thoughts. (a) Biological, learning; (b) Cognitive, wish-fulfillment; (c) Activation–synthesis, cognitive; (d) Psychodynamic, infodynamic

Answers to Questions can be found in Appendix B.

Sleep Disorders

Are you one of the lucky people who takes sleep for granted? If so, you may be surprised to discover the following facts (based on, Dement & Vaughan, 1999; Doghramji, 2000; Hobson, 2002; National Sleep Foundation, 2001):

- An estimated two-thirds of American adults suffer from sleep problems, and about 25 percent of children under age 5 have a sleep disturbance. Compared to five years ago, 40 percent of adults say they are spending more time at work, while 38 percent report spending less time sleeping.

- One in five adults is so sleepy during the day that it interferes with their daily activities. And, each year Americans spend more than $98 million on over-the-counter sleep aids and another $50 million on caffeine tablets to keep them awake during the day.

- Twenty percent of all automobile drivers have fallen asleep for a few seconds (microsleep) at the wheel.

The costs of sleep disorders are enormous, not only for the individual but also for the public. Psychologists and other mental health professionals divide sleep disorders into two major diagnostic categories: (1) *dyssomnias*, which involve problems in the amount, timing, and quality of sleep, and (2) *parasomnias*, which include abnormal disturbances occurring during sleep.

Dyssomnias   There are at least three prominent examples of dyssomnias:

1. *Insomnia.* The term *insomnia* literally means "lack of sleep." People with **insomnia** have persistent difficulty falling asleep or staying asleep, or they wake up too early. Many people think they have insomnia if they cannot sleep before an exciting event (this is normal) or because they wrongly assume that everyone must sleep 8 hours a night. Sometimes, too, people think they are not sleeping when they really are. However, a large percentage of the population (as much as 30 percent) genuinely suffers from this disorder, and nearly everybody has insomnia at some time (Doghramji, 2000; Ince, 1995). A telltale complaint of insomnia is that the person feels poorly rested the next day. Most people with serious insomnia have other medical or psychological disorders as well, such as alcohol and other drug abuse, anxiety disorders, and depression (Ohayon, 1997).

Unfortunately, the most popular treatment for insomnia is drugs — either over-the-counter pills, such as Sominex, or prescription tranquilizers and barbiturates. The problem with nonprescription pills is that they generally don't work. Prescrip-

Insomnia *Persistent problems in falling asleep, staying asleep, or awakening too early*

tion pills, on the other hand, do help you sleep, but they decrease Stage 4 and REM sleep, thereby seriously affecting the quality of sleep (Lord, 2000). Frequently prescribed drugs like Ambien, Dalmane, Xanax, and Halcion may be helpful in treating sleeping problems related to anxiety and specific stressful situations, such as losing a loved one. However, chronic users run the risk of psychological and physical drug dependence (Julien, 2001; McKim, 2002). In sum, sleeping pills may be useful for occasional, short-term (two to three nights) use, but they may create more problems than they solve.

Application
APPLYING PSYCHOLOGY TO EVERYDAY LIFE

Self-Help for Insomnia

Are you wondering what is recommended for insomnia other than drugs? A recent large-scale study reported good success from behavior therapy (Smith et al., 2002), and you can use similar techniques in your own life. For example, when you're having a hard time going to sleep, don't keep checking the clock and worrying about your loss of sleep. Instead, remove all TVs, stereos, and books, and limit the use of the bedroom to sleep (and sex). If you need additional help, try some of the following relaxation techniques (Table 14.2).

TABLE 14.2 METHODS FOR ENHANCING SLEEP

You can help yourself to a good night's sleep by preparing during the day and at bedtime. These suggestions come from the Better Sleep Council, a nonprofit education organization in Burtonsville, Maryland.

During the day:
Exercise. Daily physical activity works away tension. But don't exercise vigorously late in the day, or you'll get fired up instead.
Keep regular hours. An erratic schedule can disrupt biological rhythms. Get up at the same time each day.
Avoid stimulants. Coffee, tea, soft drinks, chocolate, and some medications contain caffeine. Nicotine may be an even more potent sleep disrupter.
Avoid late meals and heavy drinking. Overindulgence can shatter your normal sleep pattern.
Stop worrying. Focus on your problems at a set time earlier in the day.
Use presleep rituals. Follow the same routine every evening: listen to music, write in a diary, meditate.

In bed:
Use progressive muscle relaxation. Alternatively tense and relax various muscle groups.
Apply yoga. These gentle exercises help you relax.
Use fantasies. Imagine yourself in a tranquil setting. Feel yourself relax.
Use deep breathing. Take deep breaths, telling yourself you're falling asleep.
Try a warm bath. This can induce drowsiness because it sends blood away from the brain to the skin surface.
* For more information, check these websites:
  • www.sleepfoundation.org
  • www.stanford.edu/~dement

2. **Sleep apnea.** A second major dyssomnia, closely related to insomnia, is sleep apnea. *Apnea* literally means "no breathing." Many people have either irregular breathing or occasional periods of 10 seconds or less without breathing during their sleep. People with **sleep apnea,** however, may fail to breathe for a minute or longer and then wake up gasping for breath. When they do breathe during their sleep, they often snore. Repeated awakenings result in insomnia and leave the person feeling tired and sleepy during the day. However, people are often unaware of these frequent awakenings and may fail to recognize the reason for their daytime fatigue.

Sleep apnea seems to result from blocked upper airway passages or from the brain ceasing to send signals to the diaphragm, thus causing breathing to stop. If you snore loudly or have repeated awakenings followed by gasps for breath, you may be suffering from sleep apnea and should seek medical attention because it can lead to high blood pressure, stroke, and heart attack (Johnson, 2001; Ulfbert, Carter, & Edling, 2000). Treatment depends partly on the severity of the sleep apnea. If the problem occurs only when you're sleeping on your back, sewing tennis balls on the back of your pajama top may help remind you to sleep on your side. Obstruction of the breathing passages also is related to obesity and heavy alcohol use (Christensen, 2000), so dieting and alcohol restriction are often recommended. For others, surgery, dental appliances that reposition the tongue, or ventilating machines may be the answer.

For many years, researchers assumed that snoring (without the accompanying stoppages of breathing in sleep apnea) was a minor problem — except for bed partners. Recent findings, however, suggest that even this "simple snoring" can also lead to heart disease and possible death (Peppard, Young, Palta, & Skatrud, 2000). Although occasional mild snoring remains somewhat normal, it is a possible "warning sign that should prompt people to seek help" (Christensen, 2000 p. 172).

3. **Narcolepsy.** A serious sleep disorder that is somewhat the opposite of insomnia is narcolepsy — sudden and irresistible onsets of sleep during normal waking hours. Narcolepsy afflicts about 1 person in 2,000 and generally runs in families (Johnson, 2001; Kryger, Wald, & Manfrede, 2002; Siegel, 2000). During an attack, REM-like sleep suddenly intrudes into the waking state of consciousness. Victims may experience sudden attacks of muscle weakness or paralysis (known as *cataplexy*). Such people may fall asleep while walking, talking, or driving a car. These attacks are obviously dramatic and can be incapacitating. Can you imagine what it would be like to be driving along the highway or walking across campus and suddenly have a narcoleptic attack?

Although long naps each day and stimulant or antidepressant drugs may help reduce the frequency of attacks, both the causes and cure of narcolepsy are still unknown. Stanford University's Sleep Disorders Center was among the first to selectively breed a group of narcoleptic dogs, which has increased our understanding of the genetics of this disorder (McClintock, 2000). Research on these specially bred dogs has found degenerated neurons in certain areas of the brain (Siegel, 2000). Whether human narcolepsy results from similar degeneration is a question for future research.

Parasomnias The second category of sleep disorders, parasomnias, includes abnormal sleep disturbances such as nightmares and night terrors. **Nightmares,** or bad dreams, occur toward the end of the sleep cycle, during REM sleep. Less common but more frightening are **night terrors,** which occur early in the cycle, during Stage 3 or Stage 4 of NREM sleep. The sleeper may sit bolt upright, screaming and sweating, walk around, talk incoherently, and still be almost impossible to awaken.

Sleep Apnea *Repeated interruption of breathing during sleep because air passages to the lungs are physically blocked*

Narcolepsy [NAR-co-lep-see] *Sudden and irresistible onsets of sleep during normal waking hours. (narco = numbness; lepsy = seizure)*

Nightmares *Anxiety-arousing dreams generally occurring near the end of the sleep cycle, during REM sleep*

Night Terrors *Abrupt awakenings from NREM (non-rapid-eye-movement) sleep accompanied by intense physiological arousal and feelings of panic*

Nightmare or night terror? Can you explain the difference?

Answer: Sitting bolt upright in bed, screaming, and panic are all characteristic of night terrors.

Sleepwalking, which tends to accompany night terrors, usually occurs during NREM sleep (which explains why movement is possible). *Sleep talking*, on the other hand, occurs with about equal probability in REM and NREM sleep. It can include single, indistinct words or long, articulate sentences. It is even possible to engage some sleep talkers in a limited conversation.

Nightmares, night terrors, sleepwalking, and sleep talking are all more common among young children, but they also can occur in adults, usually during times of stress or major life events (Hobson & Silvestri, 1999; Muris, Merckelbach, Gadet, & Moulaert, 2000). Patience and soothing reassurance at the time of the sleep disruption are usually the only treatment recommended for both children and adults.

Sleep Disorders

Many people suffer from numerous sleep problems, which fall into two major diagnostic categories — *dyssomnias* (including insomnia, sleep apnea, and narcolepsy) and *parasomnias* (such as nightmares and night terrors).

People who have repeated difficulty falling or staying asleep or awakening too early experience **insomnia.** A person with **sleep apnea** temporarily stops breathing during sleep, causing loud snoring or poor-quality sleep. **Narcolepsy** is excessive day-time sleepiness characterized by sudden sleep attacks. **Nightmares** are bad dreams that occur during REM (rapid-eye-movement) sleep. **Night terrors** are abrupt awakenings with feelings of panic that occur during NREM sleep.

Questions

Following are four descriptions of people suffering from sleep disorders. Label each type.

1. George awakens many times each night and feels fatigued and poorly rested the next day.
2. While sleeping, Joan often snores loudly and frequently stops breathing temporarily.
3. Tyler is a young child who often wakes up terrified and cannot describe what has happened. These episodes occur primarily during NREM sleep.
4. Xavier complains to his physician about sudden and irresistible onsets of sleep during his normal workday.

Answers to Questions can be found in Appendix B.

ACTIVE LEARNING WORKSHEET   MODULE 14

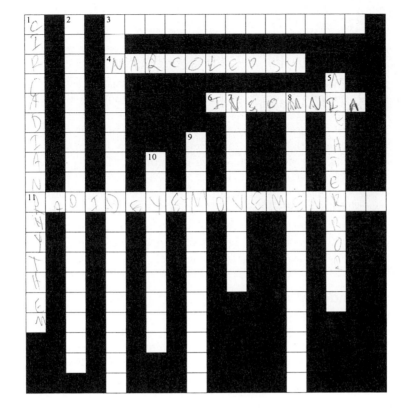

ACROSS

3 An organism's awareness of its own self and surroundings (Damasio, 1999). Consciousness is always about something. It concerns perceptions (of objects and events), thoughts (including verbal thought and mental images, such as dreams and daydreams), feelings, and actions (Farthing, 1992).

4 A disease marked by sudden and irresistible onsets of sleep during normal waking hours. (Narco = numbness, lepsy = seizure)

6 A sleep disorder in which a person has persistent problems in falling asleep or staying asleep or awakens too early.

11 A stage of sleep marked by rapid eye movements, high-frequency brain waves, and dreaming.

DOWN

1 Biological changes that occur on a 24-hour cycle. (Circa = about and dies = day)

2 Mental activities requiring minimal attention; other ongoing activities are generally not affected.

3 Mental activities found at one extreme of the continuum of awareness; they require focused attention and generally interfere with other ongoing activities.

5 Abrupt awakenings from non-REM sleep accompanied by intense physiological arousal and feelings of panic.

7 Anxiety-arousing dreams that generally occur near the end of the sleep cycle, during REM sleep.

8 The surface content of a dream, containing dream symbols that distort and disguise the true meaning of the dream, according to Freudian dream theory.

9 The true, unconscious meaning of a dream, according to Freudian dream theory.

10 A temporary cessation of breathing during sleep.

MODULE 15
DRUGS AND OTHER ROUTES TO ASCs

Assessment

How do psychoactive drugs affect consciousness?

Psychoactive Drugs *Chemicals that change conscious awareness, mood, or perception*

Drug Abuse *Drug taking that causes emotional or physical harm to the drug user or others*

Psychological Dependence *Desire or craving to achieve the effects produced by a drug*

Addiction *Broad term describing a compulsion to use a specific drug or engage in a certain activity*

■ Drugs that Influence Consciousness: A Psychoactive Approach

Since the beginning of civilization, people of all cultures have used — and abused — psychoactive drugs (Abadinsky, 2001; Hanson, Venturelli, & Fleckenstein, 2002). **Psychoactive drugs** are generally defined as chemicals that change conscious awareness or perception. Do you (or someone you know) use caffeine (in coffee, tea, chocolate, or cola) or nicotine (in cigarettes) as a pick-me-up, or alcohol (in beer, wine, and cocktails) to relax and lessen inhibitions? All three — caffeine, nicotine, and alcohol — are psychoactive drugs.

How use differs from abuse and how chemical alterations in consciousness affect a person both psychologically and physically are important topics in psychology. In this section, we begin by clarifying differences in terminology. We then go on to look at the four major categories of psychoactive drugs and "club drugs" like MDMA, the drug that cost Cathy Isford her life.

Understanding Drugs

Have you noticed how difficult it is to have a logical, nonemotional discussion about drugs? In our society, where the most popular drugs are caffeine, tobacco, and ethyl alcohol, people often become defensive when these drugs are grouped with illicit drugs such as marijuana and cocaine. Similarly, users of marijuana are disturbed that their drug of choice is grouped with "hard" drugs like heroin. Most scientists believe there are good and bad uses of *all* drugs. To facilitate our discussion and understanding, we need to clarify several confusing terms and concepts.

Misconceptions and Confusing Terminology   Is drug abuse the same as drug addiction? The term **drug abuse** generally refers to drug taking that causes emotional or physical harm to the individual or others. The drug consumption is also typically compulsive, frequent, and intense. **Addiction** is a broad term referring to a condition in which a person feels compelled to use a specific drug. In recent times, the term *addiction* has been used to describe almost any type of compulsive activity (Doweiko, 1999; Orzack, 1999). People talk about being "addicted" to TV, work, physical exercise, and even the Internet.

Because of problems associated with the terms *addiction* and *drug abuse*, many drug researchers use **psychological dependence** to refer to the mental desire or craving to

William Hogarth's eighteenth century engraving of the social chaos caused by the "gin epidemic." Infant mortality was so high that only one of four babies survived to the age of five. In one section of London, one out of five houses was a gin shop (cited in Levinthal, 2002, p. 188).

History of psychoactive drugs. *Before the Food and Drug Administration (FDA) regulated the sale of drugs, heroin, opium, and cocaine were commonly found in over-the-counter, nonprescription drugs.*

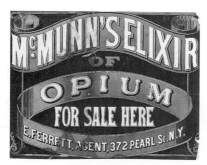

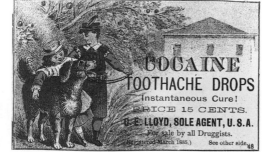

Before we go on, you may want to take the following test to help determine whether you may be physically or psychologically dependent on alcohol or other drugs.

1. Have you gotten into financial difficulties due to drinking or using other drugs?
2. Has drinking alcohol or using other drugs ever been behind your losing a job?
3. Has your efficiency or ambition decreased due to drinking and using other drugs?
4. Is your drinking and drug use jeopardizing your academic performance?
5. Does drinking or using other drugs cause you to have difficulty sleeping?
6. Have you ever felt remorse after drinking and using other drugs?
7. Do you crave a drink or other drug at a definite time daily, or do you want a drink or other drug the next morning?

8. Have you ever had a complete or partial loss of memory because of drinking or using other drugs?
9. Have you ever been to a hospital or institution because of drinking or other drug use?

If you answered yes to these questions, you are more likely to be a substance abuser than someone who answered no.

Source: Bennett et al., "Identifying Young Adult Substance Abusers: The Rutgers Collegiate Substance Abuse Screening Test." *Journal of Studies on Alcohol* 54:522–527. Copyright 1993 Alcohol Research Documentation, Inc., Piscataway, NJ. Reprinted by permission. The RCSAST is to be used only as part of a complete assessment battery because more research needs to be done with this instrument.

achieve the effects produced by a drug. And they use the term **physical dependence** to refer to changes in bodily processes that make a drug necessary for minimum daily functioning. Physical dependence is shown most clearly when the drug is withheld, and the user undergoes painful **withdrawal** reactions, including physical pain and intense cravings. After repeated use of a drug, many of the body's physiological processes adjust to higher and higher levels of the drug, producing a decreased sensitivity, called **tolerance.**

Tolerance leads many users to escalate their drug use and to experiment with other drugs in an attempt to recreate the original pleasurable altered state. In some cases, use of one drug increases tolerance for another. This is known as *cross-tolerance.* Despite the connotations of the words *tolerance* and *cross-tolerance,* it's important to remember that the brain, heart, liver, and other body organs can be seriously damaged.

Although psychological dependence is sometimes considered less dangerous than physical dependence, the effects on the drug user's life can be even more damaging. The craving in psychological dependence can be so strong that the user ingests the drug regularly and maintains a constant drug-induced state. In addition, the psychological aspects of drug taking are often so powerful that an "addict" will return to a drug habit even after all signs of physical dependence are removed.

Physical Dependence *Bodily processes have been so modified by repeated use of a drug that continued use is required to prevent withdrawal symptoms*

Withdrawal *Discomfort and distress, including physical pain and intense cravings, experienced after stopping the use of addictive drugs*

Tolerance *Decreased sensitivity to a drug brought about by its continuous use*

Psychoactive Drugs

For convenience, psychologists divide psychoactive drugs into four broad categories: depressants, stimulants, opiates, and hallucinogens (Table 15.1). In this section, we also explore a modern concern with "club drugs" like Ecstasy, which was mentioned in our section opener.

Depressants   **Depressants** (sometimes called "downers") depress the central nervous system, causing relaxation, sedation, loss of consciousness, and even death. This category includes ethyl alcohol, barbiturates (or sedatives) like Seconal, and antianxiety

Depressants *Psychoactive drugs that act on the central nervous system to suppress or slow bodily processes and reduce overall responsiveness*

SUMMARY TABLE 15.1 EFFECTS OF THE MAJOR PSYCHOACTIVE DRUGS

	Category	Desired Effects	Undersirable Effects
	Depressants (Sedatives) Alcohol, barbiturates, antianxiety drugs (Valium), Rohypnol (roofies), Ketamine (special K), CoHB	Tension reduction, euphoria, disinhibition, drowsiness, muscle relaxation	Anxiety, nausea, disorientation, impaired reflexes and motor functioning, amnesia, loss of consciousness, shallow respiration, convulsions, coma, death
	Stimulants Cocaine, amphetamine, methamphetamine (crystal meth), MDMA (Ecstasy)	Exhilaration, euphoria, high physical and mental energy, reduced appetite, perceptions of power, and sociability	Irritability, anxiety, sleeplessness, paranoia, hallucinations, psychosis, elevated blood pressure and body temperature, convulsions, death
	Caffeine	Increased alertness	Insomnia, restlessness, increased pulse rate, mild delirium, ringing in the ears, rapid heartbeat
	Nicotine	Relaxation, increased alertness, sociability	Irritability, raised blood pressure, stomach pains, vomiting, dizziness, cancer, heart disease, emphysema
	Opiates (Narcotics) Morphine, heroin, codeine	Euphoria, "rush" of pleasure, pain relief, prevention of withdrawal discomfort	Nausea, vomiting, constipation, painful withdrawal, shallow respiration, convulsions, coma, death
	Hallucinogens (Psychedelics) LSD (lysergic acid diethylamide)	Heightened aesthetic responses, cuphoria, mild delusions, hallucinations, distorted perceptions and sensations	Panic, nausea, longer and more extreme delusions, hallucinations, and perceptual distortions ("bad trips"), psychosis
	Marijuana	Relaxation, mild euphoria, increased appetite	Perceptual and sensory distortions, hallucinations, fatigue, lack of motivation, paranoia, possible psychosis

Source: Hanson, Venturelli, & Fleckenstein, 2002; Julien, 2001; National Institute on Drug Abuse, 2002.

TABLE 15.2 ALCOHOL'S EFFECT ON THE BODY AND BEHAVIOR

Blood Alcohol Content (%)	Effect
.05	Relaxed state; increased sociability
.08	Everyday stress lessened
.10[a]	Movements and speech become clumsy
.20	Very drunk; loud and difficult to understand; emotions unstable
.40	Difficult to wake up; incapable of voluntary action
.50	Coma and/or death

[a] Most states use .10 as the threshold level for driving while intoxicated. A few states use .08, whereas some go as high as .12.

Drunk driving. *As in this fatal car accident in Austin, Texas, drunk drivers are responsible for almost half of all highway related deaths in America.*

drugs like Valium. Because tolerance and dependence (both physical and psychological) are rapidly acquired with these drugs, there is strong potential for abuse.

One of the most widely used (and abused) drugs around the world is alcohol. Why? It is primarily a depressant, but at low doses, it has stimulating effects, thus explaining its reputation as a "party drug." The first few drinks seem to relax the inhibitions and thus enliven a person at the same time. But as drinking increases, symptoms of drunkenness appear: Reactions slow, speech slurs, and skilled performance deteriorates (Table 15.2). At the highest doses, the depressant effects can leave the drinker "out of control" and incapable of voluntary action. If blood levels reach 0.5 percent, there is risk of coma and even death from respiratory depression (Doweiko, 1999). One college fraternity pledge, for example, died after a 7-hour drinking binge and approximately 24 drinks. His blood alcohol level was measured at 0.58, which was 6–7 times the legally established limit for driving of a car (Cohen, 1997).

Keep in mind that alcohol's effect is determined primarily by the amount that reaches the brain. Because the liver breaks down alcohol at the rate of about 1 ounce per hour, the number of drinks and the speed of consumption are both very important, and it helps explain why people die after drinking large amounts of alcohol in a short period. In addition, men's bodies are more efficient at breaking down alcohol. Even after accounting for differences in size and muscle-to-fat ratio, women have a higher blood alcohol level than do men following equal doses of alcohol.

Why is mixing alcohol and barbiturates so dangerous? Alcohol should not be combined with *any* other drug, but combining alcohol and barbiturates — two depressants — is particularly dangerous. Together, they can relax the diaphragm muscles to such a degree that the person literally suffocates. Actress Judy Garland is among celebrities known to have died from a barbiturate-and-alcohol mixture.

Alcohol as a Social Concern   In addition to personal health risks, alcohol also plays a major role in our most serious social problems. Did you know, for example, that alcohol is a factor in nearly half of all murders, suicides, spousal abuse, and accidental deaths in the United States (Doweiko, 1999; Murphy & O'Farrell, 1996)? Or did you know that drunk drivers account for about one-half of all highway fatalities, and that medical authorities list alcohol as the third leading cause of birth defects (Butler, Joel, & Jeffries, 2000; Julien, 2001)?

Alcohol does seem to encourage aggressive tendencies (commonly referred to as "beer muscles") and sexual daring and desire (sometimes called "beer goggles") (Allgeier & Allgeier, 2000; Pihl et al., 1997). But it may be that alcohol only releases what's already there. People prone to aggression will become more aggressive, and people prone to being affectionate will become more affectionate. Moral judgments are less thoughtful and attention is focused on the immediate situation rather than future consequences. Even those who believe (when sober) that drinking and driving is wrong often will drive home after drinking at a bar or a friend's house. Although the American Medical Association calls alcohol the most dangerous and physically damaging of all psychoactive drugs, drinking still enjoys wide social acceptance.

Stimulants Whereas depressants are downers, **stimulants** are uppers. They act on the central nervous system to increase its overall activity and responsiveness. Stimulant drugs, such as caffeine, nicotine, amphetamines, and cocaine, produce alertness, excitement, elevated mood, decreased fatigue, and sometimes increased motor activity. They also may lead to serious problems. Let's look more closely at nicotine and cocaine.

Nicotine Like caffeine, nicotine is a widely used legal stimulant, but unlike caffeine it kills many of its users. A sad, ironic example of the dangers of nicotine addiction is Wayne McLaren, the rugged Marlboro Man in cigarette ads, who died of lung cancer at age 51. But McLaren was only one of 400,000 who die from smoking related illnesses each year in the United States. Tobacco kills more than AIDS, legal drugs, illegal drugs, road accidents, murder, and suicide combined (CDC, 2003).

When smoking doesn't kill, it can result in chronic bronchitis, emphysema, and heart disease (CDC, 2001). Countless others are affected by secondhand smoke, by smoke-related fires, and by prenatal exposure to nicotine (Modules 11 and 25). The U.S. Public Health Service considers cigarette smoking the single most preventable cause of death and disease in the United States (Fiore, 2000).

As scientific evidence of the dangers of smoking accumulates and as social pressure from nonsmokers increases, many smokers are trying to kick the habit. But fewer than 1 in 10 actually succeeds (Parker-Pope, 2000). Researchers have found that nicotine activates the same brain areas (nucleus accumbens) as cocaine — a drug well known for its addictive potential (Pich et al., 1997). The reported pleasures of smoking (relaxation, increased alertness, diminished pain and appetite) are so powerfully reinforcing that some smokers continue to smoke — even after having a cancerous lung removed.

Cocaine Sigmund Freud often is cited as a supporter of cocaine use, but few people know that in his later writings Freud called cocaine the "third scourge" of humanity, after alcohol and heroin. Cocaine is a powerful central nervous system stimulant extracted from the leaves of the coca plant. It can be sniffed as a white powder, injected intravenously, or smoked in the form of crack. Cocaine produces feelings of alertness, euphoria, well-being, power, energy, and pleasure.

Although cocaine was once considered a relatively harmless "recreational drug," its potential for physical damage and severe psychological dependence is now recognized (Bonson et al., 2002; Franklin et al., 2002; Hammer, Egilmez, & Emmett-Oglesby, 1997). Even small initial doses of cocaine can be fatal because cocaine interferes with the electrical system of the heart, causing irregular heartbeats and in some cases heart failure. It also can produce heart attacks and strokes by temporarily constricting blood vessels (Kerfoot, Sakoulas, & Hyman, 1996; Kollins & Rush, 2002; Zagnoni & Albano, 2002). The most dangerous form of cocaine is the smokeable, concentrated version known as crack or rock. Its lower price makes it affordable and attractive to a large audience, but its greater potency also makes it more quickly addictive and dangerous.

Opiates **Opiates** (or narcotics), which include morphine and heroin, numb the senses and thus are used medically to relieve pain (Julien, 2001). The classification term *opiates* is used because the drugs are derived from (or are similar to those derived from) the opium poppy. They are attractive to people seeking an alternate state of conscious-

---

Stimulants *Drugs that act on the brain and nervous system to increase their overall activity and general responsiveness*

"There's no shooting—we just make you keep smoking."

Opiates *Drugs derived from opium that function as an analgesic or pain reliever (Opium comes from the Greek word meaning "juice")*

ness because they produce feelings of relaxation and euphoria. They produce their effect by mimicking the brain's own natural chemicals for pain control and mood elevation, called *endorphins*. (Recall from Module 5 that the word *endorphin* literally means "endogenous morphine.")

This mimicking of the body's natural endorphins creates a dangerous pathway to drug abuse. After repeated flooding with artificial opiates, the brain eventually reduces or stops the production of its own opiates. If the user later attempts to stop, the brain lacks both the artificial and normal level of painkilling chemicals and withdrawal can be excruciatingly painful. The euphoria, pain relief, and avoidance of withdrawal all contribute to make opiates like heroin extremely addictive, and, in fact, the recreational use of heroin has doubled since the mid-1980s (Friend, 1997; Leland, 1996). Interestingly, when opiates are used medically to relieve intense pain, they are very seldom habit-forming. However, when taken recreationally, they are strongly addictive (Butler, Joel, & Jeffries, 2000; Doweiko, 1999).

Hallucinogens One of the most intriguing alterations of consciousness comes from **hallucinogens,** drugs that produce sensory or perceptual distortions, including visual, auditory, or kinesthetic hallucinations. According to some reports, colors are brighter and more luminous, patterns seem to pulsate and rotate, and senses may seem to fuse — that is, colors are "heard" or sounds "tasted."

Some cultures have used hallucinogens for religious purposes, as a way to experience "other realities" or to communicate with the supernatural. In Western societies, most people use hallucinogens for their reported "mind-expanding" potential. For example, hallucinogens are highly valued by some artists as a way of increasing creativity. But the experience is not always positive. Terror-filled "bad trips" can occur, and dangerous flashbacks may unpredictably recur long after the initial ingestion. The flashback experience may be brought on by stress, fatigue, marijuana use, illness, emerging from a dark room, and occasionally by intentional effort on the part of the individual (Doweiko, 1999).

Hallucinogens are commonly referred to as *psychedelics* (from the Greek for "mind manifesting"). They include mescaline (derived from the peyote cactus), psilocybin (from mushrooms), phencyclidine (chemically derived), and LSD (lysergic acid diethylamide, derived from ergot, a rye mold). Marijuana (pot, grass, or hashish) is sometimes classified as a hallucinogen because in sufficient dosages, it can produce mental effects similar to the stronger hallucinogens. We will focus on LSD and marijuana in our discussion because they are the most widely used of these drugs.

LSD LSD, an odorless, tasteless, and colorless substance, is one of the most potent drugs known. As little as 10 micrograms of LSD can produce a measurable effect in one individual, and an amount the size of an aspirin is enough to produce effects in 3,000 people. In 1943 Albert Hofman, the Swiss chemist who first synthesized LSD in a laboratory, accidentally licked some of the drug off his finger and later recorded this in his journal:

> Last Friday, April 16, 1943, I was forced to stop my work in the laboratory in the middle of the afternoon and to go home, as I was seized by a peculiar restlessness associated with a feeling of mild dizziness. Having reached home, I lay down and sank in a kind of drunkenness which was not unpleasant and which was characterized by extreme activity of imagination. As I lay in a dazed condition with my eyes closed (I experienced daylight as disagreeably bright) there surged upon me an uninterrupted stream of fantastic images of extraordinary plasticity and vividness and accompanied by an intense, kaleidoscope-like play of colors. This condition gradually passed after about two hours.

HOFMAN (1968), PP. 184–185

Opium field. This farmer in Afghanistan is harvesting raw opium from the field of opium poppies. He starts by making shallow incisions into the seed capsules, allowing the fluid to ooze out. After exposure to air, the fluid oxidizes and hardens into the consistency of heavy syrup, and is then collected plant by plant.

Hallucinogens [hal-LOO-sin-oh-jenz] *Drugs that produce sensory or perceptual distortions called hallucinations*

Vision from an LSD trip?

Perhaps because the LSD experience is so powerful, few people actually "drop acid" on a regular basis, which may account for its relatively low reported abuse rate. However, a recent increase in LSD use by high school and college students has been reported (Connolly, 2000). LSD can be an extremely dangerous drug. Bad LSD trips can be terrifying and may lead to accidents, death, or suicide.

Marijuana Although marijuana is generally classified as a hallucinogen, it has some of the properties of a depressant (including drowsiness and lethargy) and a narcotic (acting as a weak painkiller). In low doses, it also produces mild euphoria, whereas moderate doses lead to an intensification of sensory experiences and the illusion that time is passing very slowly. At the highest doses, marijuana may produce hallucinations, delusions, and distortions of body image (Hanson, Venturelli, & Fleckenstein, 2002). Regardless of its classification, it is one of the most popular of all illegal consciousness-altering drugs today.

The active ingredient in marijuana (cannabis) is THC, or tetrahydracannabinol, which attaches to receptors that are abundant throughout the brain. The presence of these receptors implies that the brain produces some THC-like chemicals of its own. And, in fact, researchers have discovered a brain chemical (called anandamide) that binds to the same receptors that THC was previously found to use. In 1997, a second THC-like chemical (2-AG) was also discovered (Stella, Schweitzer, & Piomelli, 1997). At this point, no one knows the function of anandamide or 2-AG or why the brain has its own marijuana-like receptors.

With the exception of alcohol during the time of Prohibition, there has never been a drug more hotly debated than marijuana. On the positive side, some research has found marijuana therapeutic in the treatment of glaucoma (an eye disease), in alleviating the nausea and vomiting associated with chemotherapy, in increasing appetite, and in treating asthma, seizures, epilepsy, and anxiety (Abadinsky, 2001; Fackelmann, 1997; Julien, 2001; Zagnoni & Albano, 2002).

But marijuana users also report impaired memory, attention, and learning — especially the first few times they use the drug. In addition, chronic marijuana use can lead to throat and respiratory disorders, impaired lung functioning and immune response, declines in testosterone levels, reduced sperm count, and disruption of the menstrual cycle and ovulation (Bourassa & Vaugeois, 2001; Herkenham, 1992;

These young Jamaican girls are members of the Rastafarian Church, which considers marijuana a "wisdom weed." How do you think their experience with the drug might differ from an adult in the United States?

Julien, 2001; O'Leary et al., 2000; Schwartz, 2002). Some studies suggest that mar-ijuana's effects on the brain are disturbingly similar to those produced by highly addictive drugs, such as heroin, cocaine, alcohol, and nicotine (Blum et al., 2000; Goldberg et al., 2000). However, other studies have found little or no lasting nega-tive health effects (e.g., Eisen et al., 2002).

Marijuana also can be habit-forming, but few users experience the intense crav-ings associated with cocaine or opiates. Withdrawal symptoms are rare because the drug dissolves in the body's fats and leaves the body very slowly, which also explains why a marijuana user can test positive for days or weeks after the last use.

Application
APPLYING PSYCHOLOGY TO EVERYDAY LIFE

Club Drug Alert!

As you recall from our section opener, psychoactive drugs like Rohypnol (the date rape drug) and MDMA (Ecstasy) are fast becoming some of our nation's most popu-lar drugs of abuse—especially at "raves," and other all-night dance parties. Other "club drugs," like GHB (gamma-hydroxybutyrate), ketamine (Special K), metham-phetamine (crystal meth), and LSD, also are gaining in popularity (Cowan, 2001; Gal-van et al., 2000; Golub, Johnson, Sifaneck, Chesluk, & Parker, 2002). Although these drugs can produce desirable effects (e.g., Ecstasy's feeling of great empathy and con-nectedness with others), it's important to note that almost all psychoactive drugs may cause serious health problems and, in some cases, even death (National Institute on Drug Abuse, 2002).

High doses of MDMA, for example, can cause dangerous increases in body tem-perature and blood pressure that lead to seizures, heart attacks, and strokes (Kopel-man et al., 2002; Landry, 2002). In addition, research shows that chronic use of MDMA may produce long-lasting, perhaps permanent, damage to the neurons that release the neurotransmitter serotonin (Reneman et al., 2001). As you recall from Module 5, serotonin is critical to emotional regulation, learning, memory, and other cognitive functions.

Club drugs, like all illicit drugs, also are particularly dangerous because there are no truth-in-packaging laws to protect buyers from unscrupulous practices. Sell-ers often substitute unknown, cheaper, and possibly even more dangerous sub-stances for the ones they claim to be selling. Also, club drugs (like most psychoactive drugs) affect motor coordination, perceptual skills, and reaction time necessary for safe driving.

Impaired decision-making is also a serious problem. Just as "drinking and driv-ing don't mix," club drug use may lead to risky sexual behaviors and increased risk of AIDS (acquired immunodeficiency syndrome) and other sexually transmitted dis-eases. When you add in the fact that some drugs, like Rohypnol, are odorless, col-orless, and tasteless, and can easily be added to beverages by individuals who want to intoxicate or sedate others, you can see that the dangers of club drug use go far beyond the drug itself (Kingree, Braithwaite, & Woodring, 2000; National Institute on Drug Abuse, 2002). If you would like more information on the specific dangers and effects of these club drugs, check http://www.drugabuse.gov/ClubAlert/Clubdrugalert.html.

Club drugs developed for Generation X.

Explaining Drug Use

After an exploration of the four major categories of drugs and the problem with club drugs, two basic questions remain: How do psychoactive drugs create alternate states of consciousness? And why do so many people use and abuse them?

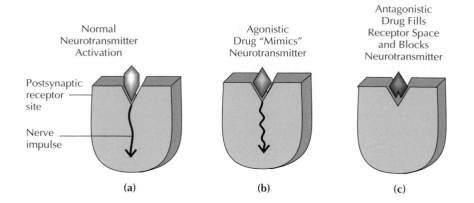

Figure 15.1 *How agonists and antagonists work.* (a) In normal neurotransmitter activation, the neurotransmitter fits easily into the receptor and stimulates the receiving neuron. (b) If an ingested drug has the same molecular shape as a naturally occurring neurotransmitter, it mimics the neurotransmitter's message. This is known as an agonistic drug action. (c) Some psychoactive drugs contain a molecule that is similar enough in shape to a neurotransmitter that it partially fills a receptor site, but dissimilar enough that the receiving neuron does not receive its messages and will not fire. This is known as antagonistic drug action.

How Drugs Work   Psychoactive drugs influence the nervous system in a variety of ways. Alcohol, for example, has a diffuse effect on neural membranes throughout the entire nervous system. Most psychoactive drugs, however, act in a more specific way: by changing the effect of neurotransmitters in two basic ways: They *enhance* the effect or *inhibit* it. Drugs that mimic the action of a particular neurotransmitter, and in so doing enhance the effectiveness of synaptic transmission, are called **agonists.** Drugs that block the action of specific neurotransmitters are called **antagonists** (Figure 15.1).

As you can see in Figure 15.2, most drug action occurs at one of four steps of neural transmission.

Step 1: *Production or synthesis.* Both psychoactive and therapeutic drugs often work by altering the production or synthesis of neurotransmitters. For example, patients with Parkinson's disease have decreased activity in cells that produce dopamine. Usually the treatment is the drug L-dopa (levodopa) because it is converted in the brain to dopamine. Producing what the brain itself cannot, the drug sometimes relieves the tremors, rigidity, and difficulty in movement characteristic of patients with Parkinson's disease. L-dopa can provide added years of nearly normal life, but the disease is progressive and the benefits decrease over time. Finding the early onset of Parkinson-like symptoms in young people, like actor Michael J. Fox, offers important research clues to a major degenerative disease of our aging population.

Step 2: *Storage and release.* Drugs also work by changing the amount of neurotransmitter stored or released by a neuron. As an example, venom from a black widow spider increases the release of the neurotransmitter acetylcholine. More acetylcholine available to the receiving neurons creates an exaggerated stimulant effect: extreme arousal, heightened anxiety, and dangerous increases in blood pressure and heart rate.

Step 3: *Reception.* Drugs also can alter the effect of neurotransmitters on the receiving site of the receptor neuron. Some drugs, called receptor *agonists,* have a

Agonist *Chemical (or drug) that mimics the action of a specific neurotransmitter*

Antagonist *Chemical (or drug) that opposes or blocks the action of a neurotransmitter*

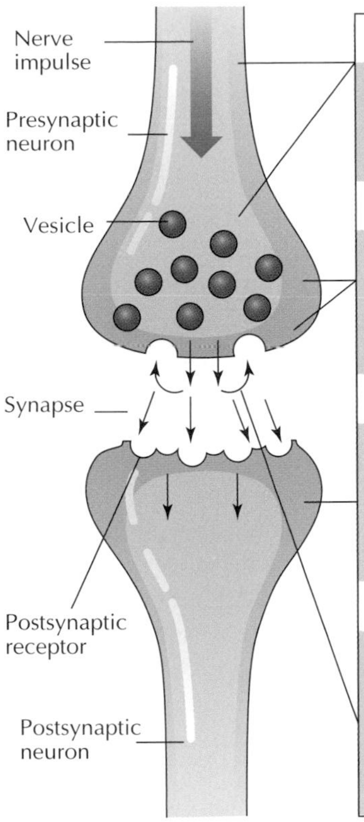

	How neurotransmitters work	Drug increases neural activity	Drug decreases neural activity
Nerve impulse			
Presynaptic neuron	**(Step 1) Production**		
	(1) Neurotransmitter is produced.	Drug serves as a precursor for neurotransmitter synthesis (e.g., L-DOPA is used to make dopamine).	Drug blocks production.
Vesicle	**(Step 2) Storage and release**		
	(2) Neurotransmitter is stored in vesicle. When impulse arrives, neurotransmitter is released.	Drug increases the release of neurotransmitter (e.g., black widow spider venom increases acetylcholine release).	Drug blocks neurotransmitter storage and/or release.
Synapse	**(Step 3) Reception**		
	(3) Neurotransmitter binds to postsynaptic receptors and activates them.	Drug attaches to receptors and activates them (e.g., Nicotine activates acetylcholine receptors and morphine activates endorphin receptors).	Drug blocks neurotransmitter by filling receptor space but doesn't activate the neuron (e.g., drugs for schizophrenia block dopamine).
Postsynaptic receptor	**(Step 4) Inactivation**		
Postsynaptic neuron	(4) Excess neurotransmitter is deactivated by reuptake or enzymatic breakdown.	Drug blocks inactivation of neurotransmitter leaving more in the synapse to stimulate receptors (e.g., cocaine and nicotine block reuptake of dopamine and norepinephrine).	

Figure 15.2 *Psychoactive drugs and neurotransmitters.* Most psychoactive drugs produce their effects by changing the body's supply of neurotransmitters at one of four steps: they can alter production or synthesis (step 1), they can affect storage and release (step 2), they can disrupt the reception by the next neuron (step 3), or they can block the reabsorption (reuptake) of excess neurotransmitters, or the release of enzymes that destroy excess neurotransmitters (step 4). For example, cocaine produces its effects primarily by blocking the reuptake. Because the extra neurotransmitters remain in the synapse, the adjacent neurons continue to fire and the stimulation effects are increased.

molecular structure very similar to that of the body's own neurotransmitters (Figure 15.1). Nicotine is similar to the neurotransmitter acetylcholine, so when it fills the acetylcholine receptors, it produces similar effects (increased stimulation).

Other drugs are similar enough to occupy the same sites as the neurotransmitter but dissimilar enough that they do not cause a response in the receiving neuron. They are called receptor *antagonists*. The problem is that as long as they are attached to the receptors, they prevent the "real" neurotransmitter from getting its message through. As you will see in Module 40, many researchers believe an excess of dopamine causes schizophrenia, so it is often treated with drugs that act as receptor antagonists. These fill the sites and block the action of the excess dopamine, thus relieving the major symptoms of the disorder.

Step 4: Inactivation. After neurotransmitters carry their message across the synapse, the sending neuron normally removes the excess, or leftover neurotransmitter, in two ways: reabsorption (or reuptake) and enzymatic breakdown. If the excess is not removed, the receiving neurons continue to respond as if they were receiving fresh messages. Both nicotine and cocaine work by blocking the reuptake or breakdown of dopamine and other neurotransmitters (Fowler et al., 1996; Koob & Nestler,

1997; Landry, 1997). The normal mood-enhancing effects of these neurotransmitters are thereby increased.

Why People Use and Abuse Drugs In addition to the general desire for altered consciousness, people use and abuse drugs for at least two major reasons: environment and biology.

1. *Environmental factors.* Drug use often is portrayed in movies, TV, and advertisements as an essential accompaniment to all good times — holidays, parties, and celebrations. Movie stars, athletes, and college students are shown drinking alcohol, smoking or chewing tobacco, and occasionally snorting cocaine.

   In addition to seeing such positive portrayals of drug use, often by figures that serve as role models, drug users also learn from personal experience that their drug of choice produces positive emotions. Cocaine induces strong feelings of power and an inflated sense of one's abilities; alcohol and nicotine reduce stress and anxiety; amphetamines increase arousal.

   Some commonly abused drugs (like cocaine and alcohol) also are positively associated with sexual arousal and heightened sexual experiences. But both cocaine and alcohol actually reduce sexual performance (Allgeier & Allgeier, 2000). These drugs maintain their reputation as *aphrodisiacs*, substances that increase sexual desire, because they initially lower inhibition. Furthermore, if users believe cocaine or alcohol will improve their sexual performance and enjoyment, they may act in such a way that they will make this belief come true — at least in the beginning.

   Individual and sociocultural reasons also explain why people use and abuse drugs. Some of these reasons include availability of drugs, economic deprivation, poor school performance (especially in junior high school), low value placed on achievement, inadequate parental warmth and support, lack of religious beliefs, family conflict, poor coping skills, and low social competence (Bryant & Zimmerman, 2002; Dimoff, 2000; Gruber & Machamer, 2000; Hodge, Cardenas, & Montoya, 2001).

2. *Biological forces.* Drug use may begin because of positive associations and other environmental factors, but it is maintained and perpetuated primarily through biological pressures. For example, most natural reinforcers (eating, drinking, and sexual activity) have one thing in common with commonly abused drugs: They stimulate the brain's reward system (see the Research Highlight that follows).

   Genetics also may influence individual differences in drug abuse. For example, certain gene variations may result in a "reward deficiency syndrome," which causes some people to get less pleasure from everyday experiences (Blum, Cull, Braverman, & Comings, 1996). In the past 30 years, a growing body of research also has suggested a biological predisposition toward alcohol/drug dependence (Fehr et al., 2000; Kendler, Gardner, & Prescott, 1997).

   Once drug use is established, it is more likely to continue because removal or withholding of the drug leads to painful withdrawal symptoms. For example, someone who quits opiates after long-term use usually experiences physical symptoms such as rapid breathing, perspiration, tremors, and muscle twitches. The brain produces chemicals closely resembling opiates (endorphins) and contains special receptor sites for them (Module 5). As regular opiate use overloads the endorphin receptor sites, the brain soon stops producing these substances. When the drugs are no longer taken, neither opiates nor endorphins are available for regulating pain and discomfort, and the user experiences excruciating pains of withdrawal. As discussed earlier, problems with withdrawal symptoms are the primary reason people fail in their efforts to stop smoking.

RESEARCH HIGHLIGHT

Addictive Drugs as the Brain's "Evil Tutor"

Why do alcoholics and other addicts continue to take drugs that are clearly destroying their lives? One explanation may be that the brain "learns" to be addicted. Scientists have long known that various neurotransmitters are key to all forms of normal learning. Now evidence suggests that addictive drugs (acting on certain neurotransmitters) teach the brain to want more and more of the destructive substances — whatever the cost. Drugs become the brain's "evil tutor" (Wickelgren, 1998, p. 2045).

How does this happen? The neurotransmitter dopamine has been a primary focus of drug abuse research because of its well-known effect on a part of the brain's reward system known as the *nucleus accumbens* (Blum et al., 2000; DiChiara, 1997; Giros, Jaber, Jones, Wrightman, & Caron, 1996). Nicotine and amphetamines, for example, stimulate the release of dopamine, and cocaine blocks its reuptake. Drugs that increase dopamine activity are most likely to result in physical dependence.

Recently, however, evidence points to the importance of another neurotransmitter, glutamate. Although surges in dopamine caused by drug use appear to activate the brain's reward system, glutamate may explain compulsive drug taking. Even after the initial effects of a drug disappear, gluta-

"That is not one of the seven habits of highly effective people."

©The New Yorker Collection 1998 Leo Cullum from cartoonbank.com. All Rights Reserved.

mate-induced learning encourages the addict to want more and more of the drug and directs the body to get it. Glutamate apparently creates lasting memories of drug use by changing the nature of "conversations" between neurons. Changes in neuronal connections result whenever we learn something and store it in memory. But in this case, glutamate "teaches" the brain to be addicted.

Glutamate's lesson is rarely forgotten. Even when users are highly motivated to end the vicious cycle of drug abuse, glutamate related changes in the brain keep them "hooked." In addition to the well-known intense cravings and pain of withdrawal, the addicted brain also creates cravings at the

mere sight of drug-related items. When 13 cocaine addicts and 5 controls watched films of people using both neutral objects and drug-associated items (such as glass pipes and razor blades), the addicts reported significant cravings. During this same time, positron emission tomography (PET) scans of the addicts' brains showed significant neural activity in brain regions known to release glutamate (Grant et al., 1996). Apparently, activating the glutamate system — through drug use or some reminder of the drug — creates strong cravings, which helps explain the common problem of drug relapse.

As a critical thinker, are you wondering how this new research might help with drug abuse and relapse? Recalling earlier information about agonists and antagonists: What about developing and trying a glutamate antagonist? The good news is that this exact method seems to work. When shown drug-related objects, long-term drug addicts who received a glutamate antagonist reported a significant reduction in cravings and less drug-seeking behavior (Herman & O'Brien, 1997). Drugs that interfere with glutamate transmission are also being tested for the treatment of general drug abuse (Wickelgren, 1998).

CHECK & REVIEW

Drugs and Consciousness

Psychoactive drugs change conscious awareness or perception. **Drug abuse** refers to drug taking that causes emotional or physical harm to the individual or others, whereas **addiction** is a broad term referring to a person's feeling of compulsion to use a specific drug or to engage in certain activities. Psychoactive drug use can lead to psychological dependence or physical dependence or both. **Psychological dependence** is a desire or craving to achieve the effects produced by a drug. **Physical dependence** is a change in bodily processes due to continued drug use that results in **withdrawal** symptoms when the drug is withheld. **Tolerance** is a decreased sensitivity to a drug brought about by its continuous use.

The major categories of psychoactive drugs are **depressants, stimulants, opiates, and hallucinogens.** Depressant drugs slow the central nervous system, whereas stimulants activate it. Opiates numb the senses and relieve pain, whereas hallucinogens produce sensory or perceptual distortions.

Drugs act primarily by changing the effect of neurotransmitters in the brain. Drugs that act as **agonists** mimic neurotransmitters, whereas **antagonists** oppose or block normal neurotransmitter functioning. There are many reasons for drug use and abuse, which fall into the two main categories of environment and biology.

Questions

1. Drugs that change conscious awareness or perception are called _____. (a) addictive; (b) hallucinogenic; (c) psychoactive; (d) mind altering
2. Drug taking that causes emotional or physical harm to the drug user or others is known as _____. (a) addiction; (b) physical dependence; (c) psychological dependence; (d) drug abuse
3. How does physical dependence differ from psychological dependence?
4. Describe four ways psychoactive drugs act on neurotransmitters.

Answers to Questions can be found in Appendix B.

How do alternate states of consciousness, like hypnosis, affect consciousness?

◼ Additional Routes to Alternate States: Daydreams, Fantasies, Hypnosis, and Meditation

As we discovered earlier, ASCs may be reached through everyday activities such as sleep and dreaming or through the chemical means of drugs. In this section, we explore several additional routes for changing consciousness: daydreams and fantasies, hypnosis, and meditation.

Daydreams and Fantasies

In the mildest forms of altered consciousness, *daydreaming* and *fantasies*, attention shifts away from the external world to focus internally on memories, desires, and expectations. Scientists have found that during a typical 24-hour period, we spend as much as one-third of our waking hours daydreaming. And, over 95 percent of both men and women say they have had sexual fantasies while daydreaming. Men's sexual fantasies tend to have more visual images and explicit sexual behaviors, whereas women's fantasies include more touching and romance within a committed and caring relationship (Leitenberg & Henning, 1995; Renaud & Byers, 1999).

Can daydreams and sexual fantasies be dangerous? Daydreaming while sitting in a lecture or driving a car may be counterproductive and potentially dangerous, but under other circumstances, it can be helpful. Most people daydream during quiet, private moments when outside events are boring or automated, such as while waiting at bus stops or washing dishes. It appears that our consciousness responds to an unchanging external world by turning inward and creating more interesting thoughts and images. Daydreaming not only helps us escape and cope with boring tasks and difficult situations but also seems to allow mental and physical relaxation, improve intellectual functioning, and release creative abilities (Klinger, 1987).

Sexual fantasies also serve many purposes. They entertain and excite with no risk of embarrassment, pregnancy, or sexually transmitted diseases (Allgeier & Allgeier, 2000). Many sexual fantasies involve having sex with unavailable or multiple partners — behaviors we would not consider in real life. Such fantasies may lead to feelings of guilt, but thinking about something is not the same as doing it. This lack of distinction between thought and behavior may explain the negativism and uncertainty surrounding both daydreams and fantasies. Just as parents accept that children often think about hitting others but do not accept the actual behavior, we can accept our daydreams about running away to Tahiti with a sexy stranger without the fear of actually doing it.

One cautionary note: Daydreams and fantasies that occupy a great deal of time, or focus on destructive thoughts and behaviors, *can* be harmful. As we will see in Modules 39 and 44, therapists help clients work to "cognitively restructure" these maladaptive or dangerous cognitions.

Hypnosis

"Relax … your body is so tired … your eyelids are so very heavy … your muscles are becoming more and more relaxed … your breathing is becoming deeper and deeper … relax … your eyes are closing and your whole body feels like lead … let go … relax." These are the types of suggestions most hypnotists use to begin hypnosis. Once hypnotized, some people can be convinced they are standing at the edge of the ocean listening to the sound of waves and feeling the ocean mist on their faces. Invited to eat a delicious apple that is actually an onion, the hypnotized person may relish the flavor. Told they are watching a very funny or sad movie, they may begin to laugh or cry at their self-created visions.

What is hypnosis? Scientific research has removed much of the mystery surrounding **hypnosis.** It is defined as a trancelike state of heightened suggestibility, deep relaxation, and intense focus. It is characterized by one or more of the following: (1) narrowed, highly focused attention (the participant is able to "tune out" competing sensory stimuli); (2) increased use of imagination and hallucinations (in the case of visual hallucinations, a person may see things that aren't there or not see things that are); (3) a passive and receptive attitude; (4) decreased responsiveness to pain; and (5) heightened suggestibility (a willingness to respond to proposed changes in perception — "this onion is an apple") (Barber, 2000; David & Brown, 2002; Gay, Philoppot, & Luminet, 2002; Hilgard, 1986, 1992; Spiegel, 1999).

Hypnosis *A trancelike state of heightened suggestibility, deep relaxation, and intense focus*

Five Common Myths and Controversies Hypnotism has been well researched, yet several myths and controversies persist:

1. *Forced hypnosis.* One of the most common misconceptions is that people can be hypnotized against their will. But hypnosis requires the person to make a conscious decision to relinquish control of his or her consciousness to someone else, so it is virtually impossible to hypnotize someone who is unwilling. As a matter of fact, about 8 to 9 percent of people cannot be hypnotized even when they are willing and trying very hard to cooperate. And the notion that people can be hypnotically brainwashed and turned into mindless robots is false. The best potential subjects are those who are able to focus attention, are open to new experiences, and are capable of imaginative involvement or fantasy (Barber, 2000; Ligett, 2000).

2. *Unethical behavior.* A related myth is that hypnosis can make a person behave immorally or take dangerous risks against his or her will. Generally, people will not go against their strongest and most basic values while hypnotized. Participants retain the ability to control their behavior during hypnosis. They are aware of their surroundings and can refuse to comply with the hypnotist's suggestions (Kirsch & Lynn, 1995).

3. *Exceptional memory.* Another myth is that hypnotized people can recall things they otherwise could not. Some research has found that recall memory for some information is occasionally improved under hypnosis because the participant is able to relax and focus intently. However, the number of errors also increases! Furthermore, when pressed to recreate details, hypnotized participants have more difficulty separating fact and fantasy and are more willing to guess (Perry, Orne, London, & Orne, 1996). As you will see in Module 21, all memory is ultimately a *reconstruction* rather than a *reproduction*. Therefore, because memory is normally filled with fabrication and distortion, hypnosis generally increases the potential for error (Baker, 1998; Perry, 1997). Consequently, a growing number of judges and state bar associations ban the use of hypnosis and the testimony of hypnotized individuals from the courtroom (Brown, Scheflin, & Hammond, 1997; McConkey, 1995).

4. *Superhuman strength.* It is also a misconception that under hypnosis, people can perform acts of special, superhuman strength. When nonhypnotized people are

Stage hypnosis. Many people mistakenly believe that people can be hypnotized against their will. Stage hypnotists generally use eager volunteers who want to be hypnotized and willingly cooperate with their suggestions and directions.

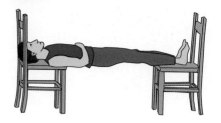

You can recreate a favorite trick that stage hypnotists promote as evidence of superhuman strength under hypnosis. Simply arrange two chairs as shown in the picture. You will see that hypnosis is not necessary — all that is needed is a highly motivated volunteer willing to stiffen his or her body.

simply asked to try their hardest on tests of physical strength, they generally can do anything that a hypnotized person can (Druckman & Bjork, 1994).

5. *Fakery.* Are hypnosis participants faking it and simply playing along with the hypnotist? Or are they actually in a special state of consciousness that changes normal awareness and perception? Although most participants are not consciously faking hypnosis, some researchers believe the effects result from a blend of conformity, relaxation, obedience, suggestion, and role playing (Baker, 1996, 1998; Lynn, Vanderhoff, Shindler, & Stafford, 2002; Stafford & Lynn, 2002). According to this *relaxation/role-playing theory*, hypnosis is a normal mental state in which deeply relaxed, suggestible people allow the hypnotist to direct their fantasies and behavior.

In contrast, the *altered-state theorists* believe that hypnotic effects result from a special altered state of consciousness (Bowers & Woody, 1996; Hilgard, 1978, 1992). They doubt that relaxation, role playing, and suggestion explain instances in which patients endure complex surgeries without drug-induced anesthesia. As in other controversial areas of psychology, there is a group of "unified" theorists here; they suggest that hypnosis is a combination of both relaxation/role playing and a unique alternate state of consciousness.

Therapeutic Uses   From the 1700s to modern times, hypnosis has been used (and abused) by entertainers and quacks, while also being employed as a respected clinical tool by physicians, dentists, and therapists. This curious dual existence began with Franz Anton Mesmer (1734–1815). Mesmer believed that all living bodies were filled with magnetic energy and claimed to use this "knowledge" to cure diseases. After lulling his patients into a deep state of relaxation and making them believe completely in his curative powers, Mesmer passed magnets over their bodies and told them their problems would go away. For some people, it worked — hence the term *mesmerized.*

Mesmer's theories were eventually discredited, but James Braid, a Scottish physician, later put people in this same trancelike state for surgery. Around the same time, however, powerful and reliable anesthetic drugs were discovered, and interest in Braid's technique dwindled. It was Braid who coined the term *hypnosis* in 1843, from the Greek word for sleep.

Today, even with available anesthetics, it is occasionally used in surgery and for the treatment of chronic pain and severe burns (Chaves, 2000; Montgomery, Weltz, Seltz, & Boubjerg, 2002). Hypnosis has found its best use, however, in medical areas in which patients have a high degree of anxiety, fear, and misinformation, such as dentistry and childbirth. Because pain is strongly affected by tension and anxiety, any technique that helps the patient relax is medically useful.

In psychotherapy, hypnosis can help patients relax, remember painful memories, and reduce anxiety. It has had modest success in the treatment of phobias, and in efforts to lose weight, stop smoking, and improve study habits (Ahijevych, Yerardi, & Nedilsky, 2000; Brief hypnosis for needle phobia, 2002; Gemignani et al., 2000).

Many athletes use self-hypnosis techniques (mental imagery and focused attention) to improve performance. Long-distance runner Steve Ortiz, for example, mentally relives all his best races before a big meet. He says that by the time the race actually begins, "I'm almost in a state of self-hypnosis. I'm just floating along" (cited in Kiester, 1984, p. 23).

Meditation

Meditation A group of techniques designed to refocus attention, block out all distractions, and produce an alternate state of consciousness

Meditation refers to a group of techniques designed to refocus attention, block out all distractions, and produce an alternate state of consciousness. Success in meditation requires controlling the mind's natural tendency to wander.

You can enjoy many of the experiences and benefits of meditation with a relaxation technique developed by Herbert Benson (1977):

1. Pick a focus word or short phrase that is calming and rooted in your personal value system (such as *love; peace; one; shalom*).
2. Sit quietly in a comfortable position, close your eyes, and relax your muscles.
3. Focusing on your breathing, breathe through your nose, and as you breathe out, say your focus word or phrase silently to yourself. Continue for 10 to 20 minutes. You may open your eyes to check the time, but do not use an alarm. When you have finished, sit quietly for several minutes, at first with closed eyes and later with opened eyes.
4. Maintain a passive attitude throughout the exercise — permit relaxation to occur at its own pace. When distracting thoughts occur, ignore them and gently return to your repetition.
5. Practice the technique once or twice daily, but not within 2 hours after a meal — the digestive processes seem to interfere with a successful relaxation response.

Some meditation techniques involve body movements and postures, as in t'ai chi and hatha yoga. In other techniques, the meditator remains motionless, attending to a single focal point — gazing at a stimulus (such as a candle flame), observing the breath, or silently repeating a mantra. (A mantra is a special sound, word, or phrase used for mind concentration or spiritual worship.)

Meditation has only recently gained acceptance and popularity in the United States, primarily for its value in promoting relaxation and reducing anxiety. It has, however, been practiced in some parts of the world for centuries. Some believe meditation offers a higher and more enlightened form of consciousness, superior to all other levels, and that it allows meditators to have remarkable control over bodily processes (Bernardi et al., 2001; Flora, 2000).

With sophisticated electronic equipment, researchers have verified that meditation can produce dramatic changes in basic physiological processes such as brain waves, heart rate, oxygen consumption, and sweat gland activity. For the one in four Americans who suffers from high blood pressure, it may be useful to know that meditation has proven somewhat successful in reducing stress and lowering blood pressure (Andreasen, 2000).

What does it feel like when you meditate? In the beginning stages of meditation, people often report a mellow type of relaxation, followed by a mild euphoria. With long practice, some advanced meditators report experiences of profound rapture and joy or strong hallucinations (Smith, 1982). A particularly vivid description is provided by Gopi Khrishna (1999):

> Suddenly, with a roar like that of a waterfall, I felt a stream of liquid light entering my brain through the spinal cord. The illumination grew brighter and brighter, the roaring louder. I experienced a rocking sensation and then felt myself slipping out of my body, entirely enveloped in a halo of light. I felt the point of consciousness that was myself growing wider, surrounded by waves of light. [pp. 4–5]

Achievement
GENDER & CULTURAL DIVERSITY

Consciousness Across Cultures

Throughout recorded history, people have sought ways to alter consciousness. As early as 2500 B.C., the Sumerians recorded their reactions to the drug opium with a symbol that archeologists translate as "joy" or "rejoicing," and the oldest known code of laws, from Hammurabi of Babylonia (ca. 1792–1750 B.C.), regulated the sale of wine.

In a survey of 488 societies in all parts of the world, 90 percent were found to practice institutionally recognized methods of changing consciousness (Bourguignon, 1973). These methods include taking drugs, ritualistic fasting, dancing, chanting, and inducing a trance. Such historical and cultural commonalities have led some researchers to suggest that there is a basic, inborn human need to experience nonordinary reality (Barr, 1999; Jay, 2002; Weil & Rosen, 1993).

Why are people so interested in altering their consciousness? Studies of *kava*, a drink made from the dried roots of a South Pacific Island plant, offer three possible answers to this question ("Hawaii high," 1998; Merlin, Lebot, & Lindstrom, 1992). Though other cultures use different substances or means, most attempts to achieve ASC serve the same functions as kava does for the Pacific Islanders:

1. *Sacred rituals.* Many cultures seek an alternate state of consciousness (ASC) as a pathway to spiritual enlightenment. The earliest use of kava was as a means of communicating with the gods. The islanders believed that the voices of their ancestors could be heard in the nonordinary reality induced by the kava. Similarly, tobacco has always been an integral part of Native American religions (Robicsek, 1992). It serves as a ritual fumigant, a goodwill offering, a sacrifice, and a sacrament. In addition to drug use, individuals in many cultures voluntarily undergo long fasts, isolation, chanting, whirling, and sensory deprivation in search of spiritual enlightenment.

2. *Social interactions.* ASCs also are an integral part of most cultures' social functions. Pacific Islanders often exchange large, elaborately decorated kava plants at festivals and weddings, and political meetings often start with a ritual cup of kava. In small amounts, the drink relaxes the muscles and produces a mild euphoria while leaving the mind alert ("Hawaii high," 1998). Thus, kava is favored both for celebrations and as a means of reducing the frictions of village life (Sahelian, 1998). In comparison, have you noticed how often champagne is used to celebrate weddings, births, and New Year's Eve? In our North American culture, alcohol is a prominent feature of many social interactions.

3. *Individual rewards.* In addition to spiritual and social functions, many ASCs are desirable on an individual level because they provide pleasure and escape from anxiety or stress. In New Guinea and Fiji, people commonly visit kava bars after work for a relaxing cup of kava. The stresses of the day are replaced with a sense of well-being. In Western societies, alcohol serves a similar purpose.

A cautionary note: Due to recent evidence linking kava to liver toxicity and possible death, Canada, the U.K., and other nations have banned its sale (Kava, A supplement to avoid, 2003).

In a wide range of cultures around the world, hallucinogenic drugs, medicinal plants, and trances are used by modern-day shamans to communicate with the spirit world.

A *ssessment*

CHECK & REVIEW

Additional Routes to Alternate States

Daydreaming and sexual fantasies are common forms of mild alternate states of consciousness (ASCs). They serve many functions — primarily positive. **Hypnosis** is an alternate state of heightened suggestibility characterized by relaxation and intense focus. Hypnosis has been used to reduce pain and increase concentration and as an adjunct to psychotherapy. **Meditation** is a group of techniques designed to focus attention, block out all distractions, and produce an alternate state of consciousness. Meditation can produce dramatic changes in physiological processes, including heart rate and respiration.

Although the study of consciousness has waxed and waned among psychologists, the public has historically been very interested — particularly in ASCs. Among peoples of all cultures, ASCs (1) are part of sacred rituals, (2) serve social interaction needs, and (3) provide individual rewards.

Questions

1. Why do some people feel guilty or negative about daydreaming and sexual fantasies?

2. Why is it almost impossible to hypnotize an unwilling participant?

3. _____ is a group of techniques designed to focus attention and produce an alternate state of consciousness. (a) Hypnosis; (b) Scientology; (c) Parapsychology; (d) Meditation

4. List three major functions served by ASCs in all cultures.

Answers to Questions can be found in Appendix B.

MODULE 15 ACTIVE LEARNING WORKSHEET

ACROSS

3 Chemicals that affect the nervous system and cause a change in behavior, mental processes, and conscious experience.

4 Drugs that are derived from opium and function as an analgesic or pain reliever. The word opium derives from the Greek word meaning juice.

9 A chemical (or drug) that opposes or blocks the action of a neurotransmitter.

12 Drug taking that causes emotional or physical harm to the drug user or others.

13 Psychoactive drugs that act on the central nervous system to suppress or slow bodily processes and reduce overall responsiveness.

14 Illicitly manufactured variations on known recreational drugs.

DOWN

1 An alternate state of heightened suggestibility characterized by relaxation and intense focus.

2 A condition in which bodily processes have been so modified by repeated use of a drug that continued use is required to prevent withdrawal symptoms.

5 A decreased sensitivity to a drug brought about by its continuous use.

6 Discomfort and distress, including physical pain and intense cravings, experienced after stopping the use of addictive drugs.

7 Drugs that act on the brain and nervous system, to increase their overall activity and general responsiveness.

8 Drugs that produce sensory distortions or perceptual distortions.

10 A chemical (or drug) that mimics the action of a specific neurotransmitter.

11 A group of techniques designed to focus attention and produce a heightened state of awareness.

ssessment
KEY TERMS

To assess your understanding of the Key Terms in this section, write a definition for each (in your own words), and then compare your definitions with those in the text.

alternate states of consciousness
(ASCs) (p. 175)
consciousness (p. 175)

Understanding Consciousness
automatic processes (p. 177)
controlled processes (p. 176)

Sleep and Dreams
activation–synthesis hypothesis
(p. 186)
circadian [ser-KAY dee-an] rhythms
(p. 178)
evolutionary/circadian theory (p. 185)
insomnia (p. 189)
latent content (p. 186)

manifest content (p. 186)
narcolepsy [NAR co-lep-see] (p. 191)
nightmares (p. 191)
night terrors (p. 191)
rapid-eye-movement (REM) sleep
(p. 183)
repair/restoration theory (p. 185)
sleep apnea (p. 191)

Drugs That Influence Consciousness
addiction (p. 194)
agonist (p. 202)
antagonist (p. 202)
depressants (p. 195)
drug abuse (p. 194)

hallucinogens [hal LU-sin-o-jenz]
(p. 199)
opiates (p. 198)
physical dependence (p. 195)
psychoactive drugs (p. 194)
psychological dependence (p. 194)
stimulants (p. 198)
tolerance (p. 195)
withdrawal (p. 195)

**Additional Routes to Alternate
States**
hypnosis (p. 207)
meditation (p. 208)

chievement
WEB RESOURCES

Huffman Book Companion Site
http://www.wiley.com/college/huffman
This site is loaded with free Interactive Self-Tests, Internet Exercises, Glossary and Flashcards for key terms, Web links, Handbook for Non-Native Speakers, and other activities designed to improve your mastery of the material in this section.

The Association for the Scientific Study of Consciousness
http://assc.caltech.edu/
This site includes transcripts of seminars on various topics in consciousness research, journal articles, bibliographies, and links that cover current and historical issues in consciousness.

Circadian Rhythms
http://stanford.edu/~dement/circadian.html
A rich site offering unlimited information about the biology of circadian rhythms.

Worried about your sleep?
http://www.sleepfoundation.org/
This site provides a self-test for sleep related problems, links to finding sleep services in your community, recent updates in the field, and other vital information.

Everything you wanted to know about sleep but were too tired to ask!
http://www.sleepnet.com/
SleepNet is an educational, noncommercial site developed to improving sleep health worldwide. It contains a sleep test, forum on sleep issues, as well as, many links to sleep lab sites and to sleep disorders.

Worried about your drug use?
http://www.ca.org/ http://www.alcoholics-anonymous.org/
http://www.marijuana-anonymous.org/
Each of these organizations offers basic information and advice on how to deal with problem drug abuse and use. If you want more information, try http://www.nida.nih.gov/ Sponsored by the National Institute on Drug Abuse, this web site contains comprehensive, up-to-date information and national statistics on drug use and related links.

Want more information about MDMA or Ecstasy?
http://dancesafe.org
This web site is dedicated to promoting health and safety within the rave and nightclub community. Click on the link, "Your Brain on Ecstasy," and you will discover an incredible slide show detailing precisely how Ecstasy creates its effects. Also try, http://faculty.washington.edu/chudler/mdma.html This web site provides additional information on Ecstasy, as well as GHB, Rohypnol, and other popular psychoactive drugs.

Interested in Hypnosis?
http://www.hypnosis.org
This commercial site offers extensive information and services related to hypnosis, including free ebooks and free articles.

American Society of Clinical Hypnosis (ASCH)
http://www.asch.net/
The largest U.S. organization for health and mental health care professionals using clinical hypnosis, this site provides information and links for the general public, as well as for members of the organization. A good first stop for researching possible referral services.

VISUAL SUMMARY

States of Consciousness
(Modules 14 and 15)

Sleep and Dreams

- *Sleep as a Biological Rhythm:* 24-hour cycles (**Circadian rhythms**) affect our sleep and waking cycle. Disruptions due to shift work, jet lag and sleep deprivation can cause serious problems.
- *Stages of Sleep:* Typical night's sleep has four to five 90-minute cycles. NREM cycle begins in Stage 1 and then moves through Stages 2, 3, and 4. After reaching deepest level, cycle reverses up to REM state.

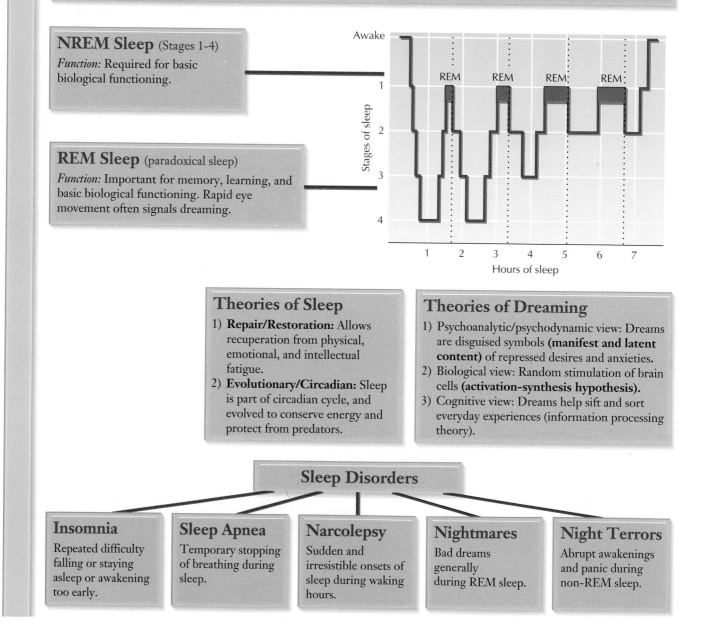

NREM Sleep (Stages 1-4)

Function: Required for basic biological functioning.

REM Sleep (paradoxical sleep)

Function: Important for memory, learning, and basic biological functioning. Rapid eye movement often signals dreaming.

Theories of Sleep

1) **Repair/Restoration:** Allows recuperation from physical, emotional, and intellectual fatigue.
2) **Evolutionary/Circadian:** Sleep is part of circadian cycle, and evolved to conserve energy and protect from predators.

Theories of Dreaming

1) Psychoanalytic/psychodynamic view: Dreams are disguised symbols (**manifest and latent content**) of repressed desires and anxieties.
2) Biological view: Random stimulation of brain cells (**activation-synthesis hypothesis**).
3) Cognitive view: Dreams help sift and sort everyday experiences (information processing theory).

Sleep Disorders

Insomnia
Repeated difficulty falling or staying asleep or awakening too early.

Sleep Apnea
Temporary stopping of breathing during sleep.

Narcolepsy
Sudden and irresistible onsets of sleep during waking hours.

Nightmares
Bad dreams generally during REM sleep.

Night Terrors
Abrupt awakenings and panic during non-REM sleep.

Drugs and Consciousness

Important Terminology

Drug abuse: Drug taking that causes emotional or physical harm to the individual or others.
Addiction: Broad term referring to feelings of compulsion.
Psychological dependence: Desire or craving to achieve effects produced by a drug.
Physical dependence: Change in bodily processes due to continued drug use that results in withdrawal symptoms when the drug is withheld.
Tolerance: Decreased sensitivity to a drug due to its continuous use.

Four Major Categories of Drugs

1) **Depressants** or "downers" (alcohol and barbiturates) slow down central nervous system (CNS).
2) **Stimulants** or "uppers" (caffeine, nicotine, and cocaine) activate CNS.
3) **Opiates** (heroin or morphine) numb senses and relieve pain.
4) **Hallucinogens** or psychedelics (LSD or marijuana) produce sensory or perceptual distortions.

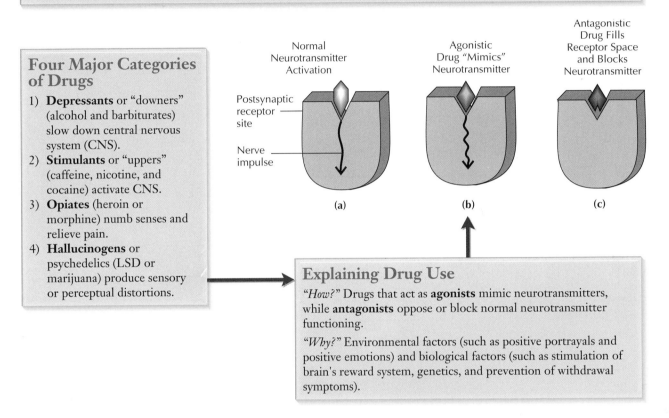

Explaining Drug Use

"*How?*" Drugs that act as **agonists** mimic neurotransmitters, while **antagonists** oppose or block normal neurotransmitter functioning.

"*Why?*" Environmental factors (such as positive portrayals and positive emotions) and biological factors (such as stimulation of brain's reward system, genetics, and prevention of withdrawal symptoms).

Additional Routes to Alternate States

Daydreaming and Sexual Fantasies:

Common forms of mild ASCs that serve mostly positive functions.

Hypnosis:

Trancelike state of heightened suggestibility, deep relaxation, and intense focus.

Meditation:

Group of techniques designed to refocus attention, and block out all distractions.

Consciusness Across Cultures:

ASCs among peoples of all cultures 1) are part of sacred rituals, 2) serve social interaction needs, and 3) provide individual rewards.

LEARNING

O n Sunday morning, June 27, 1998, James Byrd, a disabled 49-year-old African American, was hitchhiking home along Martin Luther King Boulevard in Jasper, Texas, when three young white men pulled up and offered him a ride. But they had no intention of taking him home. Instead, they chained Mr. Byrd by his ankles to the back of their rusted 1982 pickup and dragged him along an old logging road outside of town until his head and right arm ripped from his body.

The three men who committed this grisly murder were quickly captured and brought to justice. Two were sentenced to death and the third was given life imprisonment without

■ Achievement
■ Assessment
■ Application

the possibility of parole. During the trial, jurors recoiled in horror as they viewed photographs of Byrd's dismembered body.

The swift arrest and conviction of James Byrd's murderers brought a measure of comfort to his family, the residents of Jasper, and the nation as a whole. But now as time has passed and the media spotlight has faded, we're left wondering what turns three young men into such callous, hate-filled monsters. Moreover, how do we explain the Imperial Wizard of the Ku Klux Klan who placed a KKK sticker on James Byrd's grave in March 2000?

Despite the nation's collective outrage over this savage murder, hate crimes targeting groups solely on the basis of ethnicity, sexual orientation, gender, or religious preference are as recent as today's newspaper. Why? Where does such hatred come from? Is racism learned?

In the everyday sense, *learning* usually refers to classroom activities, such as math and reading, or motor skills, like riding a bike or playing the piano. But to psychologists, **learning** is much broader. It is formally defined as a relatively permanent change in behavior or mental processes as a result of practice or experience. Most of psychology emphasizes learning. For example, developmental psychologists examine how children learn language and other cognitive and motor skills. Clinical and counseling psychologists explore how previous learning and experiences help explain present-day problems. And social psychologists study how attitudes, social behaviors, and prejudices, such as those evidenced by James Byrd's murderers, are learned through experience.

Tragedies like the murder of James Byrd show us the dark side of human learning, but the very fact that racism and hatred are *learned* offers great hope. What is learned can be unlearned (or at least suppressed). In this section, we will discover how we learn hatred, racism, phobias, and superstitions, as well as love and generosity. Much of this section

focuses on the most basic form of learning called **conditioning,** which is the process of learning associations between environmental stimuli and behavioral responses. We begin with two types of conditioning — classical and operant conditioning. (As you're reading through this section, it may help you organize and learn the material to repeatedly review the summary provided in Table 17.5, p. 238). We also look at cognitive-social learning, and along the way, we discuss how learning theories and concepts can be used to improve your life. We conclude with an exploration of the neurological changes that take place during and after learning and then the evolutionary perspective.

Learning *A relatively permanent change in behavior or mental processes as a result of practice or experience*

Conditioning *Learning associations between environmental stimuli and behavioral responses*

MODULE 16
CLASSICAL CONDITIONING

Assessment

What is classical conditioning, and how can I apply it in everyday life?

Have you noticed that when you're hungry and see a large slice of chocolate cake or a juicy steak, your mouth starts to water? It seems natural that your mouth should water if you put food into it, but why do you salivate at just the sight of the food?

Understanding Classical Conditioning: Pavlov's and Watson's Contributions

The answer to this question was accidentally discovered in the Leningrad laboratory of Ivan Pavlov (1849–1936). Pavlov was a Russian physiologist who was awarded the Nobel Prize for his work on the role of saliva in digestion. One of Pavlov's experiments involved salivary responses in dogs, where he attached a glass funnel to the experimental dogs' salivary glands to collect and measure the output (Figure 16.1). Pavlov wanted to determine whether dry food required more saliva than moist food and if nonfood objects required varying amounts of saliva, depending on how hard it was to spit them out.

Pavlov's (Accidental) Discovery

In the course of Pavlov's research, one of his students noticed that many dogs began to salivate at the sight of the food, the food dish, the smell of the food, or even the person who delivered the food — long *before* food was placed in their mouth. (This is the important, *accidental* part of the discovery, which might have gone unnoticed if the collection tubes had not been in place.) Although this "unscheduled" salivation interfered with Pavlov's research design and irritated him, it also was intriguing. Salivation is a *reflex response*, a largely, involuntary, automatic response to an external stimulus. Why were his dogs reflexively salivating *before* the food was even presented? Why did they salivate to extraneous stimuli other than food?

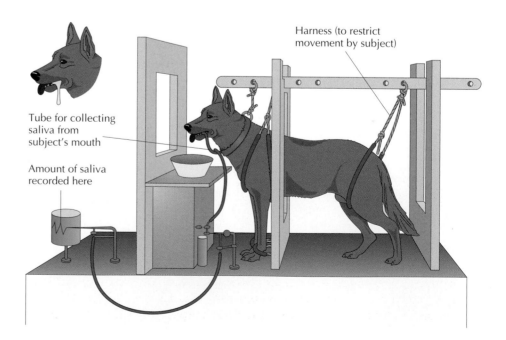

Figure 16.1 *Pavlov's original classical conditioning apparatus.* During Pavlov's initial experiments, a tube was inserted into the dog's salivary gland to collect and measure the saliva produced under different experimental conditions.

Pavlov's scientific training helped him appreciate the significance of what had at first seemed just annoying. A reflex (salivation) that occurred *before* the appropriate stimulus (food) was presented is clearly not inborn and biological. It had to have been acquired through experience — through *learning*. The type of learning that Pavlov described came to be known as **classical conditioning** (as in first [*classical*] learning [*conditioning*]). Classical conditioning is defined as learning that occurs when a neutral stimulus (NS) becomes paired (associated) with an unconditioned stimulus (UCS) to elicit a conditioned response (CR).

To understand this definition, you need to learn five basic terms describing each element of the classical conditioning process: *unconditioned stimulus* (UCS), *unconditioned response* (UCR), *neutral stimulus* (NS), *conditioned stimulus* (CS), and *conditioned response* (CR).

Before Pavlov's dogs *learned* to salivate at something extraneous like the sight of the experimenter, the original salivary reflex was inborn and biological. It consisted of an **unconditioned stimulus** (UCS), food, and an **unconditioned response** (UCR), salivation.

Pavlov's discovery (and great contribution to psychology) was that learning occurs when a **neutral stimulus** (NS) (a stimulus that does not evoke a response) is regularly paired with an unconditioned stimulus. The neutral stimulus then becomes a **conditioned stimulus** (CS), which elicits a **conditioned response** (CR). (*Study tip:* If you're finding this confusing, note that *conditioning* is just another word for *learning*. When you see words like *unconditioned response*, mentally rearrange and think "unlearned response." For additional help, read through the diagram in Figure 16.2, which provides a visual organizer and detailed example from Pavlov's research.)

Does the neutral stimulus always come first? Researchers have investigated four different ways to pair stimuli (Table 16.1) and found that both the timing and the order in which the NS is presented are very important (Chromiak, Barber, & Kyler, 2000; Church & Kirkpatrick, 2001). For example, *delayed conditioning*, where the NS is presented before the UCS and remains until UCR begins, generally yields the fastest learning; whereas *backward conditioning*, where the UCS is presented before the NS, is the least effective.

Watson's Contribution to Classical Conditioning

At this point, you may be wondering what dogs salivating to the sound of a bell has to do with your life — other than explaining why you salivate at the sight of delicious food. In fact, classical conditioning has been shown to be the most basic and fundamental way that all animals, including humans, learn most new responses, emotions, and attitudes. Your love for your parents (or significant other), the hatred and racism that led to the murder of James Byrd, and your drooling at the sight of chocolate cake are largely the result of classical conditioning.

In one of the most famous (and controversial) psychological studies, John Watson and Rosalie Rayner (1920, 2000) experimentally demonstrated how the emotion of fear could be classically conditioned. Albert, a healthy 11-month-old normal child, was brought to Watson's lab at Johns Hopkins University (Figure 16.3). Albert was first allowed to play with a white laboratory rat to find out if he was afraid of rats. Like most infants, "Little Albert" was curious and reached for the rat, showing no fear. Using the fact that infants are naturally frightened (UCR) by loud noises (UCS), Watson stood behind Albert and again put the rat (NS) near him. When the infant reached for the rat, Watson banged a steel bar of Albert's crib with a hammer. As you might imagine, the loud noise frightened Albert and made him cry. The white rat (NS) was paired with the immediate loud noise (UCS) only seven times before the white rat alone produced a **conditioned emotional response** (CER), fear of the rat.

Classical Conditioning *Learning that occurs when a neutral stimulus (NS) becomes paired (associated) with an unconditioned stimulus (UCS) to elicit a conditioned response (CR) (also known as respondent or Pavlovian conditioning)*

Unconditioned Stimulus (UCS) *Stimulus that elicits an unconditioned response (UCR) without previous conditioning*

Unconditioned Response (UCR) *Unlearned reaction to an unconditioned stimulus (UCS) that occurs without previous conditioning*

Neutral Stimulus (NS) *A stimulus that, before conditioning, does not naturally bring about the response of interest*

Conditioned Stimulus (CS) *Previously neutral stimulus that, through repeated pairings with an unconditioned stimulus (UCS), now causes a conditioned response (CR)*

Conditioned Response (CR) *Learned reaction to a conditioned stimulus (CS) that occurs because of previous repeated pairings with an unconditioned stimulus (UCS)*

Conditioned Emotional Response (CER) *A classically conditioned emotional response to a previously neutral stimulus (NS)*

Figure 16.2 *Pavlov's classical conditioning paradigm.* Before conditioning occurs, the neutral stimulus does not elicit a relevant or consistent response. After it is paired several times with an unconditioned stimulus, during conditioning, it becomes a conditioned response and does elicit a response.

 Study Tip

Use this figure to help you visualize and organize the three major phases of classical conditioning and their associated key terms.

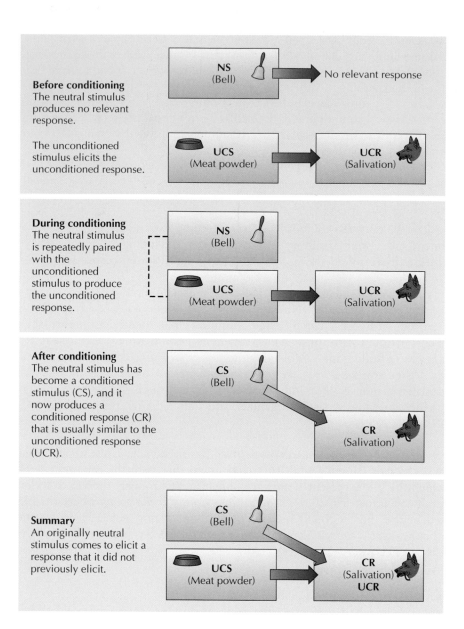

Before conditioning
The neutral stimulus produces no relevant response.

NS (Bell) → No relevant response

The unconditioned stimulus elicits the unconditioned response.

UCS (Meat powder) → UCR (Salivation)

During conditioning
The neutral stimulus is repeatedly paired with the unconditioned stimulus to produce the unconditioned response.

NS (Bell)
UCS (Meat powder) → UCR (Salivation)

After conditioning
The neutral stimulus has become a conditioned stimulus (CS), and it now produces a conditioned response (CR) that is usually similar to the unconditioned response (UCR).

CS (Bell) → CR (Salivation)

Summary
An originally neutral stimulus comes to elicit a response that it did not previously elicit.

CS (Bell)
UCS (Meat powder) → CR (Salivation) UCR

SUMMARY TABLE 16.1 CONDITIONING SEQUENCES

Delayed conditioning (most effective)	NS presented before UCS and remains until UCR begins	Bell presented with food
Simultaneous conditioning	NS presented at the same time as UCS	Bell and food presented simultaneously
Trace conditioning	NS presented and then taken away, or ends before UCS presented	Bell rung, but food presented only once the sound stops
Backward conditioning (least effective)	UCS presented before NS	Food presented before the bell

NS = neutral stimulus; UCR = unconditioned response; UCS = unconditioned stimulus.

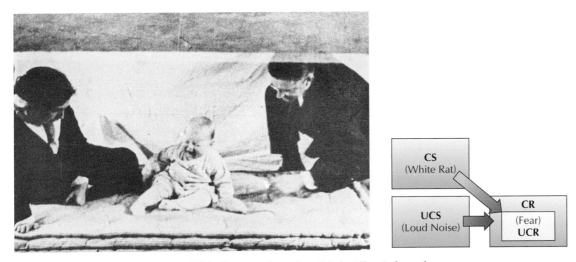

Figure 16.3 *Watson and Rayner.* This diagram shows how Little Albert's fear of rats was conditioned using a loud noise. In the photo, Watson and Rayner are shown with Little Albert who's crying from the loud noise.

Thus, Watson and Rayner's original hypothesis that fears are classically conditioned was confirmed.

Watson and Rayner's experiment could not be performed today because it violates several ethical guidelines for scientific research (Module 2). Moreover, shortly after the experiment, Albert was adopted, and Watson and Rayner ended their experiment without *extinguishing* (removing) Albert's fear, although they knew that such a CER could endure for a long period. This disregard for Albert's well being is a serious criticism of Watson and Rayner's study. Their research methodology also has been criticized. Rather than objectively measuring Albert's fear, Watson and Rayner only subjectively evaluated it, which raises doubt about the degree of fear conditioned (Paul & Blumenthal, 1989).

Despite such criticisms, John B. Watson made important and lasting contributions to psychology. At the time he was conducting research, psychology's early founders were defining the field as the *scientific study of the mind* (Module 1). Watson criticized this focus on individual mental processes, insisting that they were impossible to study objectively. Instead, he emphasized strictly observable behaviors and founded the new school or approach known as *behaviorism*, which explains behavior as a result of observable *stimuli* (in the environment) and observable *responses* (behavioral actions). His study of Little Albert also has had legendary significance for many psychologists. Watson showed us that many of our likes, dislikes, prejudices, and fears are conditioned emotional responses. In Module 38, you also will see how Watson's research in *producing* Little Albert's fears later led to powerful clinical tools for *eliminating* extreme, irrational fears known as *phobias*.

Historical note: Shortly after the Little Albert experiment, Watson was fired from his academic position and no other university would hire him, despite his international fame and scientific reputation. His firing resulted from his scandalous and highly publicized affair with his graduate student Rosalie Rayner and subsequent divorce. Watson later married Rayner and became an influential advertising executive. He is credited with many successful ad campaigns based on classical conditioning, including ones for Johnson & Johnson baby powder, Maxwell House coffee, and Lucky Strike cigarettes (Angelo, 1998; Buckley, 1982, 1989; Hunt, 1993).

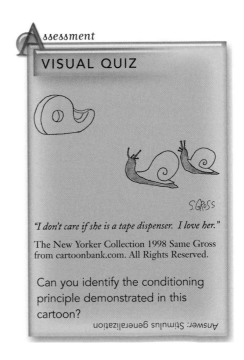

Assessment

VISUAL QUIZ

"I don't care if she is a tape dispenser. I love her."

The New Yorker Collection 1998 Same Gross from cartoonbank.com. All Rights Reserved.

Can you identify the conditioning principle demonstrated in this cartoon?

Answer: Stimulus generalization

Understanding Classical Conditioning

In **classical conditioning,** the type of learning investigated by Pavlov and Watson, an originally **neutral stimulus** (NS) is paired with an **unconditioned stimulus** (UCS) that causes a particular reflex or **unconditioned response** (UCR). After several pairings, the neutral stimulus becomes a **conditioned stimulus** (CS) that alone will produce a **conditioned response** (CR) or **conditioned emotional response** (CER) that is the same as the original reflex response.

There are four conditioning sequences: delayed conditioning, simultaneous conditioning, trace conditioning, and backward conditioning. Delayed conditioning is the most effective, and backward conditioning is the least effective.

Pavlov's work laid a foundation for Watson's insistence that psychology must be an objective science, studying only overt behavior, without considering internal, mental activity. Watson called this position *behaviorism,* and demonstrated in his famous "Little Albert" study that emotional responses can be classically conditioned.

Questions

1. Eli's grandma gives him a Tootsie roll every time she visits. When Eli sees his grandma arriving, his mouth begins to water. In this example the conditioned stimulus (CS) is _____. (a) hunger; (b) Grandma; (c) the Tootsie roll; (d) the watering mouth

2. After conditioning, the _____ elicits the _____.

3. In John Watson's demonstration of classical conditioning with little Albert, the unconditioned STIMULUS was _____. (a) symptoms of fear; (b) a rat; (c) a bath towel; (d) a loud noise

4. A Vietnam War veteran experiences an intense emotional reaction to a clap of thunder. His emotional response is an example of a(n) _____. (a) CS; (b) UCS; (c) CER; (d) UCR

Answers to Questions can be found in Appendix B.

■ Principles of Classical Conditioning: Fine-Tuning the Process

Now that you understand the basics of classical conditioning and how they explain CERs, we can build on this foundation. In this section, we will discuss five important principles of classical conditioning: *stimulus generalization, stimulus discrimination, extinction, spontaneous recovery,* and *higher-order conditioning.*

Generalization and Discrimination

One of Pavlov's early experiments conditioned dogs to salivate at the sound of low-pitched tones. Pavlov and his students later demonstrated that the dogs also would salivate to higher-pitched tones. Though the conditioning at first was to one specific low- and one specific high-pitched tone, the dogs quickly showed conditioning to other high and low tones resembling the conditioned tones.

Stimulus Generalization *Learned response not only to the original stimulus but also to other similar stimuli*

When an event similar to the originally conditioned stimulus (low-pitched tone) triggers the same conditioned response (salivation), it is called **stimulus generalization.** The more the stimulus resembles the conditioned stimulus, the stronger the conditioned response (Hovland, 1937). Have you ever felt afraid when you were driving a car and noticed another car with a rack of spotlights on its roof following close behind? If so, your fear of police cars (which typically have spotlights on their roofs) has *generalized* to all cars with spotlights. Stimulus generalization also occurred in Watson's experiment with Albert. After conditioning, Albert feared rats, as well as a white rabbit, a white glove, cotton balls, and even a white beard on a Santa Claus mask.

Stimulus Discrimination *Learned response to a specific stimulus but not to other, similar stimuli*

Would Little Albert still be afraid of a Santa Claus mask as he grew older? Probably not. Through the process of **stimulus discrimination,** he eventually would learn to recognize differences between rats and other stimuli. Although stimulus generalization seems to naturally follow from initial classical conditioning, organisms only learn to distinguish (or *discriminate*) between an original CS and similar stimuli if they have enough experience with both. Just as you learn to discriminate between the sound of your cellular phone and the ringing of others, when Pavlov repeatedly presented food following a high-pitched tone, but not with a low-pitched tone, the dog gradually learned to distinguish between the two tones. Thus, both Little Albert and Pavlov's dog produced conditioned responses only to specific stimuli — *stimulus discrimination.*

Extinction and Spontaneous Recovery

Classical conditioning, like all learning, is only *relatively* permanent. Most behaviors that are learned through classical conditioning can be weakened or suppressed through **extinction**. Extinction occurs when the UCS is repeatedly withheld whenever the CS is presented, which weakens the previous association. For instance, when Pavlov sounded the tone again and again without presenting food, the dog's salivation gradually declined. Similarly, if you have a classically conditioned fear of the sound of a dentist's drill and later start to work as a dental assistant, your fear would gradually diminish. Can you see the usefulness of this information if you're trying to get over a destructive love relationship? Rather than thinking, "I'll always be in love with this person," remind yourself that over time your feelings will gradually lessen (Figure 16.4).

Does extinction cause us to "unlearn" a classical conditioned response? No, extinction is not *unlearning* (Bouton, 1994). A behavior becomes *extinct* when the response rate decreases and the person or animal no longer responds to the stimulus. It does not mean the person or animal has "erased" the previous learned connection between the stimulus and the response. In fact, if the stimulus is reintroduced, the conditioning is much faster the second time. Furthermore, Pavlov found that if he allowed several hours to pass after the extinction procedure and then presented the tone again, the salivation would spontaneously reappear. This reappearance of a conditioned response after extinction, referred to as **spontaneous recovery,** helps explain why you suddenly feel excited at the sight of your old high school sweetheart even though years have passed (and extinction has occurred). Some people (who haven't read this book and studied this phenomenon) might mislabel this renewed excitement as "lasting love." You, on the other hand, would recognize it as simple *spontaneous recovery*. This phenomenon also explains why couples who've recently broken up sometimes misinterpret and overvalue a similar, sudden "flareup" of feelings, and return to doomed relationships, even knowing they were painful and destructive (Figure 16.5).

Higher-Order Conditioning

Children are not born salivating to the sign of McDonald's golden arches. So why do they beg their parents to stop and eat at one of the restaurants after simply seeing the golden arches on a passing billboard? It is because of **higher-order conditioning,** which occurs when a neutral stimulus (NS) becomes a conditioned stimulus (CS) through repeated pairings with a previously conditioned stimulus (CS).

If you wanted to demonstrate higher-order conditioning in Pavlov's dogs, you would first condition the dogs to salivate to the sound of the bell. Then you would pair a flash of light to the ringing of the bell. Eventually, the dog would salivate to the flash of light alone (Figure 16.6a,b). In a similar fashion, children first learn to pair McDonald's restaurant with food, and later learn that two golden arches are a symbol for McDonald's (Figure 16.6c,d). Their salivation and begging to eat at the restaurant are a classic case of higher-order conditioning (and successful advertising).

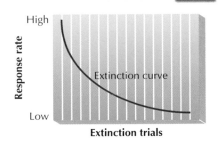

Figure 16.4 *The process of extinction.* In this hypothetical graph from a typical experiment demonstrating extinction, note how the response rate decreases over time and with additional extinction trials.

Extinction *Gradual weakening or suppression of a previously conditioned response (CR)*

Spontaneous Recovery *Reappearance of a previously extinguished conditioned response (CR)*

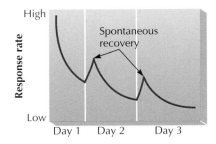

Figure 16.5 *Spontaneous recovery.* A hypothetical graph from a standard extinction experiment, but note that on occasion the extinguished response will "spontaneously reappear."

Higher-Order Conditioning *A neutral stimulus (NS) becomes a conditioned stimulus (CS) through repeated pairings with a previously conditioned stimulus (CS)*

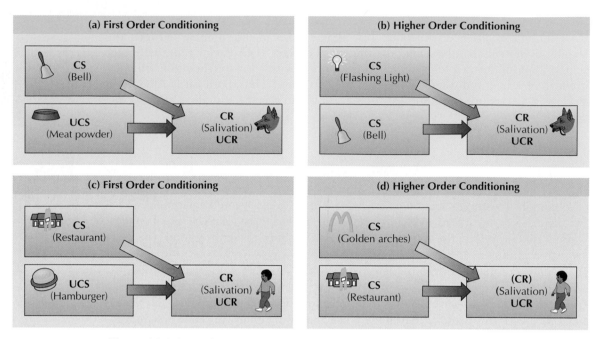

Figure 16.6 *How children learn to salivate for McDonald's.* As you can see in the top two boxes (a and b), *higher-order conditioning* is a two-stage process. In the first stage, a neutral stimulus (such as a bell) is paired with an unconditioned stimulus (such as meat powder) until it becomes a conditioned stimulus that elicits a conditioned response (salivation). During the second stage (higher order conditioning), a different neutral stimulus (such as a flashing light) is paired with the bell until it also becomes a conditioned stimulus. Now examine the bottom two boxes (c and d). Can you see how the same two-stage type of higher-order conditioning helps explain why children become so excited (and salivate) when they see the golden arches?

Application
APPLYING CLASSICAL CONDITIONING TO EVERYDAY LIFE

From Prejudice to Advertisement

As you might expect, advertisers, politicians, film producers, music artists, and others have used classical conditioning to manipulate our purchases, votes, emotions, and motivation. It also helps explain how we sometimes learn prejudices and other problem behaviors. Let's examine several examples, good and bad, from everyday life.

Prejudice

In a classic study in the 1930s, Kenneth Clark and Mamie P. Clark (1939) studied children's reactions to black dolls and to white dolls. They found that given a choice, both black and white children preferred the white dolls. When asked which doll was good and which was bad, both groups of children responded that the white doll was good and nice and that the black doll was bad, dirty, and ugly. The Clarks reasoned that the children, as well as many others in the United States, had *learned* to associate inferior qualities with darker skin and positive qualities with light skin. The Clark study exemplifies the negative effects of classical conditioning, and it played a pivotal role in the famous *Brown v. Board of Education of Topeka* decision in 1954, which ruled that segregation of public facilities was unconstitutional. (This also was the first time social science research was formally cited in a U.S. Supreme Court case to support a legal argument.)

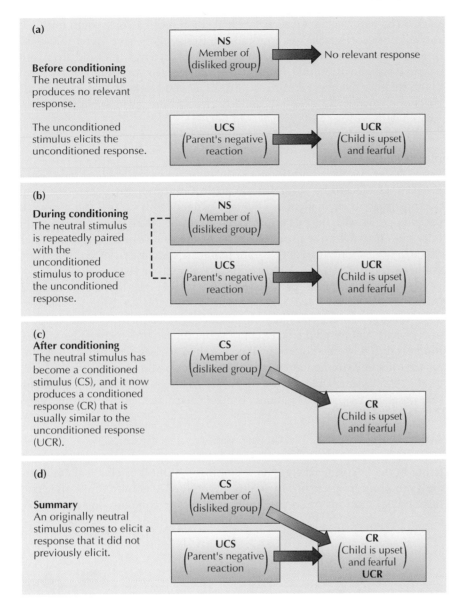

(a)

Before conditioning
The neutral stimulus produces no relevant response.

NS (Member of disliked group) → No relevant response

The unconditioned stimulus elicits the unconditioned response.

UCS (Parent's negative reaction) → UCR (Child is upset and fearful)

(b)

During conditioning
The neutral stimulus is repeatedly paired with the unconditioned stimulus to produce the unconditioned response.

NS (Member of disliked group)

UCS (Parent's negative reaction) → UCR (Child is upset and fearful)

(c)

After conditioning
The neutral stimulus has become a conditioned stimulus (CS), and it now produces a conditioned response (CR) that is usually similar to the unconditioned response (UCR).

CS (Member of disliked group) → CR (Child is upset and fearful)

(d)

Summary
An originally neutral stimulus comes to elicit a response that it did not previously elicit.

CS (Member of disliked group) → CR (Child is upset and fearful) UCR

UCS (Parent's negative reaction) →

As described in the section opener, James Byrd was viciously murdered because of his skin color.

Figure 16.7 *How prejudice may be acquired through classical conditioning.* (a) Before children are conditioned to be prejudiced, they show no response to a member of a different group. (b) Given that children are naturally upset and fearful when they see their parents upset, they can learn to be upset and fearful (UCR) if they see their parents respond negatively (UCS) to a member of a disliked group (NS). (c) After several pairings of the person from this group with their parents' negative reactions, the sight of the other person becomes a conditioned stimulus (CS), and being upset and fearful becomes the conditioned response (CR). (d) A previously unbiased child has now learned to be prejudiced.

If you're thinking this 1930 study no longer applies, follow-up research in the late 1980s found that 65 percent of the African American children and 74 percent of the white children still preferred the white doll (Powell-Hopson & Hopson, 1988). The Clark study provided important insights into the negative effects of prejudice on the victims — African American children. But what about the white children who also strongly preferred the white doll? Was their preference also due to classical conditioning? And did a similar type of classical conditioning contribute to the vicious murder of James Byrd? Although we can't be sure how the hatred and racism that took James Byrd's life originally started, prejudice of many types (racism, ageism, sexism, homophobia, and religious intolerance) can be classically conditioned, as Figure 16.7 shows.

Phobias

Do you know someone who "freaks out" at the sight of a cockroach? At some time during childhood, this person probably learned to associate the NS (cockroach) with a UCS (perhaps seeing a parent flinch at the sight of a cockroach) until a CR (fear at the sight of a cockroach) was conditioned. Researchers have found that classically conditioned emotional responses explain most everyday fears, and even most *phobias*, exaggerated and irrational fears of a specific object or situation (Evans & Rilling, 2000; Rauhut, Thomas, & Ayres, 2002). The good news is that extreme fear of cockroaches, hypodermic needles, spiders, closets, and even snakes can be effectively treated with *behavior modification* (Module 44).

Medical Treatments

Examples of classical conditioning are also found in the medical field. For example, a program conducted by several hospitals in California gives an *emetic* (a nausea-producing drug) to their alcohol-addicted patients. But before the nausea begins, the patient gargles with his or her preferred alcoholic beverage to maximize the taste and odor cues paired with nausea. As a form of classical conditioning, the smell and taste of various alcoholic drinks (NS) are paired with nausea (UCS), making the patient vomit or feel sick (UCR). Afterward, just the smell or taste of alcohol (CS) makes the person sick (CR). Some patients have found this treatment successful, but not all (Module 44).

Although nausea is deliberately produced in this treatment for alcoholism, it is an unfortunate, unintended side effect of some cancer treatment. The nausea and vomiting produced by chemotherapy increase the patient's discomfort, and often generalize to other environmental cues, such as the hospital room color or odor (Stockhorst et al., 2000). Using their knowledge of classical conditioning to change associations, therapists can help cancer patients control their nausea and vomiting response.

Advertising

Beginning with John B. Watson's academic firing and subsequent career in advertising in the 1920s, marketers have employed numerous classical conditioning principles to promote their products. For example, TV commercials, magazine ads, and business promotions often pair their products or company logo (NS) with pleasant

Assessment

VISUAL QUIZ

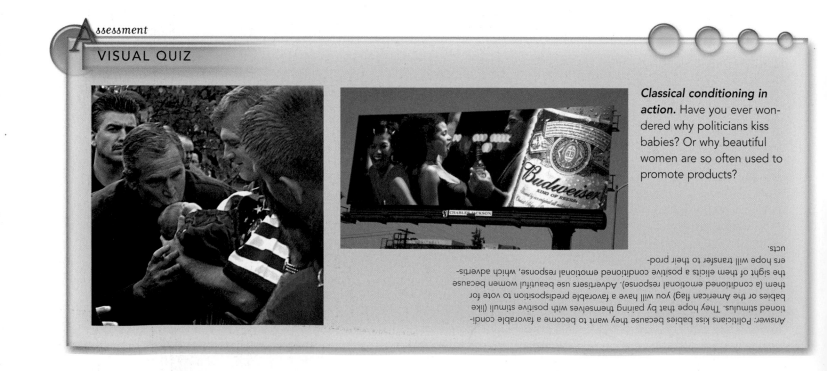

Classical conditioning in action. Have you ever wondered why politicians kiss babies? Or why beautiful women are so often used to promote products?

Answer: Politicians kiss babies because they want to become a favorable conditioned stimulus. They hope that by pairing themselves with positive stimuli (like babies or the American flag) you will have a favorable predisposition to vote for them (a conditioned emotional response). Advertisers use beautiful women because the sight of them elicits a positive conditioned emotional response, which advertisers hope will transfer to their products.

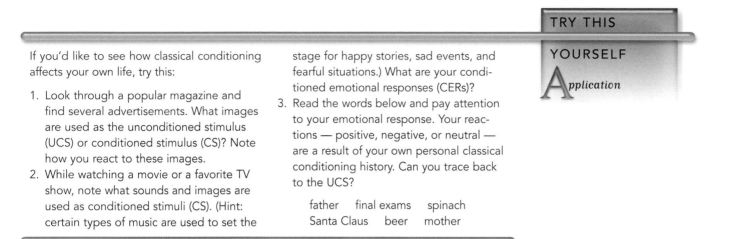

If you'd like to see how classical conditioning affects your own life, try this:

1. Look through a popular magazine and find several advertisements. What images are used as the unconditioned stimulus (UCS) or conditioned stimulus (CS)? Note how you react to these images.
2. While watching a movie or a favorite TV show, note what sounds and images are used as conditioned stimuli (CS). (Hint: certain types of music are used to set the stage for happy stories, sad events, and fearful situations.) What are your conditioned emotional responses (CERs)?
3. Read the words below and pay attention to your emotional response. Your reactions — positive, negative, or neutral — are a result of your own personal classical conditioning history. Can you trace back to the UCS?

    father   final exams   spinach
    Santa Claus   beer   mother

images, such as attractive models and celebrities (CS), which through higher-order conditioning automatically trigger favorable responses (CR). Advertisers hope that after repeated viewings, their products (CS) alone will elicit those same favorable responses (CR) and that we will buy their products or use their services. Researchers caution that these ads also help produce visual stimuli that trigger conditioned responses such as urges to smoke or drink alcohol, which makes addiction recovery more difficult (Dols, Willems, van den Hout, & Bittoun, 2000; Martin et al., 2002; Sargent et al., 2002).

Assessment

CHECK & REVIEW

Principles and Applications of Classical Conditioning

In classical conditioning, **stimulus generalization** occurs when stimuli similar to the original conditioned stimulus (CS) elicit the conditioned response (CR). **Stimulus discrimination** takes place when only the CS elicits the CR. **Extinction** occurs when the unconditioned stimulus (UCS) is repeatedly withheld and the association between the CS and the UCS is weakened. **Spontaneous recovery** happens when a CR that had been extinguished reappears with no prompting. In **higher-order conditioning,** the neutral stimulus (NS) is paired with a CS to which the participant has already been conditioned, rather than with a UCS.

Classical conditioning has many applications in everyday life. It explains how we sometimes learn negative attitudes toward groups of people (prejudice) and phobias. It also is used in some medical treatments and advertising.

Questions

1. Like most college students, your heart rate and blood pressure greatly increase when the fire alarm sounds. If the fire alarm system was malfunctioning and rang every half hour, by the end of the day, your heart rate and blood pressure would no longer increase. Why?
2. A baby is bitten by a dog and then is afraid of all small animals. This is an example of (a) stimulus discrimination; (b) extinction; (c) reinforcement; (d) stimulus generalization.
3. When a conditioned stimulus is used to reinforce the learning of a second conditioned stimulus, _____ has occurred.
4. If you wanted to use higher order conditioning to get Little Albert to fear Barbie dolls, you would present a Barbie doll with _____. (a) the loud noise; (b) the original unconditioned response; (c) the white rat; (d) the original conditioned response

Answers to Questions can be found in Appendix B.

MODULE 16 ACTIVE LEARNING WORKSHEET

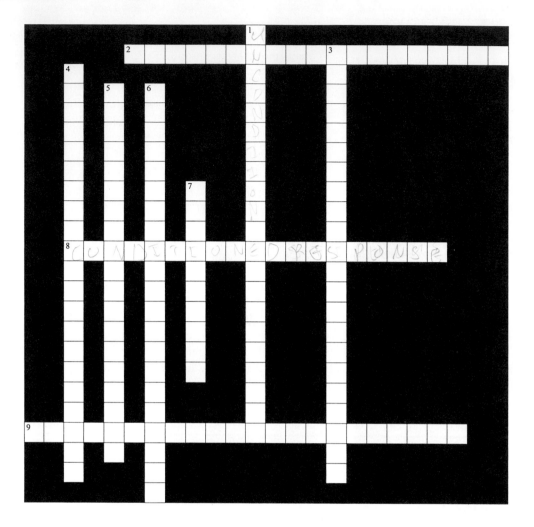

ACROSS

2 Reappearance of a previously extinguished response after a period of time without exposure to the conditioned stimulus.

8 Learned response to a previously neutral stimulus associated with the stimulus

9 Learned response not only to the original stimulus but also to other similar stimuli

DOWN

1 Reflex response evoked by a stimulus without any learning required.

3 Learned response to a specific stimulus but not to other, similar stimuli.

4 A basic form of learning in which an organism involuntarily learns to associate stimuli. (Also known as respondent or Pavlovian conditioning.)

5 A previously neutral stimulus that, through conditioning, now causes a classically conditioned

6 Any stimulus that causes a reflex or emotional response without any learning or conditioning

7 The gradual suppression of a behavior or a response that occurs when a CS is repeatedly

MODULE 17
OPERANT CONDITIONING

Consequences are the heart of **operant conditioning.** In classical conditioning, consequences are irrelevant—Pavlov's dog still got the meat powder whether it salivated or not. But in operant conditioning, the organism performs a behavior (an *operant*) that produces an effect on the environment. These effects, reinforcement or punishment, influence whether the response will occur again in the future. **Reinforcement** strengthens the response and makes it more likely to recur. **Punishment** weakens the response and makes it less likely to recur. If your friends smile and laugh when you tell a joke, your future joke telling is likely to increase. However, if they frown, groan, or ridicule you, your joke telling is likely to decrease.

In addition to differences in their emphasis on consequences, the two types of conditioning differ in another important way. In classical conditioning, the organism's response is *passive* and *involuntary.* It "happens to" the organism's when a UCS follows a NS. In operant conditioning, however, the organism's response is *active* and *voluntary.* The learner "operates" on the environment and produces effects. These effects (or consequences) influence whether the behavior will be repeated.

It's important to mention that these distinctions between classical and operant conditioning are *generally* true — but not *always* true. Technically speaking, classical conditioning does sometimes influence voluntary behavior, and operant conditioning can influence involuntary, reflexive behavior. Furthermore, both forms of conditioning often interact to produce and maintain behavior. But for most purposes, the distinction holds, and it's easier simply to remember that classical conditioning is passive and operant conditioning is active.

In the sections that follow, we will examine the historical contributions of Thorndike and Skinner, the general principles of operant conditioning, and several interesting applications of operant conditioning to real life.

Understanding Operant Conditioning: Thorndike and Skinner

Edward Thorndike (1874–1949), a pioneer of operant conditioning, was among the first to examine how voluntary behaviors are influenced by their consequences. In one of his famous experiments, he put a cat inside a specially built *puzzle box* (Figure 17.1). The only way the cat could get out was by pulling on a rope or stepping on a pedal, whereupon the door would open and the cat could get out to eat. Through trial-and-error, the cat would accidentally pull on the rope or step on the pedal that opened the door. With each additional success, the cat's actions became more purposeful, and it soon learned to open the door immediately.

Thorndike concluded that the frequency of a behavior is modified by its consequences. He is credited with developing the **law of effect**: the probability of an action being repeated is *strengthened* if it is followed by a pleasant or satisfying consequence. In short, rewarded behavior is more likely to reoccur (Thorndike, 1911). Thorndike's law of effect was a first step in understanding how active, *voluntary* behaviors can be modified by their consequences.

B. F. Skinner (1904–1990) extended Thorndike's law of effect to more complex behaviors. As a strict behaviorist, however, Skinner avoided terms like *pleasant, desired,* and *voluntary* because they make assumptions about what an organism feels and wants, and because they imply that behavior is due to conscious choice or intention. He argued that to understand behavior, we should consider only observable, external, or environmental stimuli and responses. We should look outside the learner, not inside.

In keeping with his focus on external, observable behavior, Skinner emphasized that reinforcement (which increases the likelihood of a response) and punishment (which decreases it) are always defined *after the fact.* This emphasis on only reinforc-

Assessment

What is operant conditioning, and how can I apply it in everyday life?

Operant Conditioning *Learning in which voluntary responses are controlled by their consequences (also known as instrumental or Skinnerian conditioning)*

Reinforcement *Strengthens a response and makes it more likely to recur*

Punishment *Weakens a response and makes it less likely to recur*

Law of Effect *Thorndike's rule that the probability of an action being repeated is strengthened when followed by a pleasant or satisfying consequence.*

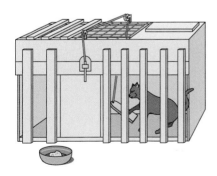

Figure 17.1 *Thorndike box.* Thorndike used a box like this in his trial-and-error experiments with cats. When a cat stepped on a pedal inside the box, the door latch was released and a weight attached to the door pulled it open so the cat could exit. (From Thorndike, 1898).

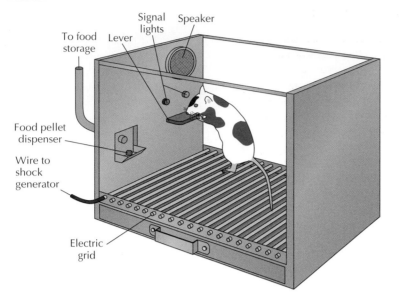

Figure 17.2 *A typical Skinner box.*
Note how food pellets are delivered in the small receiving tray, and how the electric grid on the cage floor can be used to deliver small electric shock.

DENNIS THE MENACE

"I THINK MOM'S USING THE CAN OPENER."

DENNIS THE MENACE® used by permission of Hank Ketcham enterprises and © by North America Syndicate.

Primary Reinforcers *Stimuli that increase the probability of a response because they satisfy a biological need, such as food, water, and sex*

Secondary Reinforcers *Stimuli that increase the probability of a response because of their learned value, such as money and material possessions*

ing or punishing after the behavior is important. Suppose you ask to borrow the family car on Friday night, but your parents say you have to wash the car first. If they let you put off washing the car until the weekend, what is the likelihood that you will do it? From their own "trial-and-error" experiences, most parents have learned to make sure the "payoff" comes *after* the car washing is completed — not before!

In addition to warning that both reinforcement and punishment must come after the response, Skinner also cautions us to check the respondent's behavior to see if it increases or decreases. Sometimes we *think* we're reinforcing or punishing, when we're actually doing the opposite. For example, a professor may think she is encouraging a shy student to talk by repeatedly calling on him or her in class. But the shy student may find this attention very painful, and actually decrease the number of times he or she talks in class. Similarly, men may buy women candy and flowers in an attempt to increase their romantic feelings. However, some women hate candy (imagine that!) or are allergic to flowers, and the man's attempt at reinforcement becomes a punishment instead. Skinner suggests we should watch our target's *actual* responses—not what we *think* the other person should like or do.

To scientifically test his theories, Skinner conducted systematic research. The typical Skinner experiment used an animal, usually a pigeon or a rat, and an apparatus that has come to be called a *Skinner box* (Figure 17.2). Skinner trained a rat to push a lever to receive a food pellet. The rat got a pellet each time it pushed the lever, and the number of responses made by the rat was recorded. Skinner used this basic experimental design to demonstrate a number of operant conditioning principles that are discussed in the next section.

Principles of Operant Conditioning: How It All Works

If you want to learn how to use operant conditioning to improve your everyday life, there are several important principles that you need to understand. We begin with factors involved in *strengthening a response*, including primary and secondary reinforcers, positive and negative reinforcement, schedules of reinforcement, and shaping. Then we discuss principles that *weaken a response*, including positive and negative punishment. We conclude this section with a look at the pros and cons of punishment and with a review of terms that are shared between classical and operant conditioning.

Reinforcement—Strengthening a Response

Earlier, we said that Skinner was a strict behaviorist who insisted that scientific observation be limited to that which can be observed. Therefore, instead of using words like *rewards* (which focus on feelings), Skinner talked about reinforcers and reinforcement in terms of "strengthening the response." As you can see in Table 17.1, reinforcers can be grouped into two major classes:

1. ***Primary and secondary reinforcers.*** One of the chief methods for strengthening a response is with primary and secondary reinforcers. Reinforcers such as food, water, and sex are called **primary reinforcers** because they normally satisfy an unlearned biological need. Reinforcers such as money, praise, attention, and material possessions that have no intrinsic value are called **secondary reinforcers;** the only power they have to reinforce behavior results from their learned value. A baby, for example, would find milk much more reinforcing than a hundred-dollar

SUMMARY TABLE 17.1 HOW REINFORCEMENT STRENGTHENS AND INCREASES BEHAVIORS

	Positive Reinforcement adds to (+) and strengthens behavior	**Negative Reinforcement** takes away (–) and strengthens behavior
Primary Reinforcers	You're hungry and eat a delicious hamburger. Your boyfriend/girlfriend hugs you.	Sunglasses take away the pain of the bright sun. You take an aspirin for your headache, which takes away the pain.
Secondary Reinforcers	You receive $200 as a bonus. You receive a good grade on your psychology exam.	After high sales, your boss says you won't have to work on weekends. Professor says you won't have to take the final exam because you did so well on your unit exam.

bill. Needless to say, by the time this baby has grown to adolescence, he or she will have learned to prefer the money. Among Westerners, money may be the most widely used secondary reinforcer because of its learned association with desirable commodities.

2. ***Positive and negative reinforcement.*** Adding or taking away certain stimuli also strengthens behavior. Suppose you tickle your baby and he smiles at you. His smile increases (or strengthens) the likelihood that you will tickle him again in the future. The smile itself is a *positive reinforcer.* This is called **positive reinforcement.** On the other hand, suppose your baby is upset and crying, so you hug him and he stops crying. In this case, the removal of crying is a *negative reinforcer,* and the *process* is called **negative reinforcement** because the "taking away" of the crying by the hugging increases (or strengthens) the likelihood that you will hug him again in the future when he cries. Both responses reinforce or strengthen your smiling and hugging behavior.

(As a critical thinker, you may be wondering what's happening for the baby in this example. As a parent, you were both *positively* and *negatively reinforced,* whereas in the same two examples your baby was only *positively reinforced.* He learned that his smile caused you to tickle him more, and that his crying caused you to hug him. If you're worried that reinforcing the crying with hugs will create bigger problems, you can relax. Your baby soon will learn to talk and develop "better" ways to communicate.)

Positive Reinforcement *Adding (or presenting) a stimulus, which strengthens a response and makes it more likely to recur*

Negative Reinforcement *Taking away (or removing) a stimulus, which strengthens a response and makes it more likely to recur*

Why Negative Reinforcement is Not Punishment

Most of us hear the term, negative reinforcement, and automatically think of punishment. But it's important to remember that these two terms are actually completely opposite procedures. Reinforcement (either positive or negative) *strengthens a behavior;* whereas punishment *weakens a behavior.*

My students find it easier if they think of positive and negative reinforcement in the mathematical sense (as shown in Table 17.1) rather than as personal values of positive as "good" or negative as "bad." Think of positive reinforcement as something being added (+) that increases the likelihood that the behavior will increase and negative reinforcement as something being taken away (–) that also increases the likelihood that the behavior will continue. For example, if your boss compliments you on a job well done, the compliment is added (+) as a consequence to the good job you did, and your behavior is likely to increase (positive reinforcement). Similarly, if your boss tells you you no longer have to do a boring part of your job because of your excellent work, the taking away (–) of the boring task is a negative reinforcement, and your hard work is likely to increase.

Premack principle *Premack's law that using a naturally occurring high-frequency response will reinforce and increase low-frequency responses*

When I make myself study before I let myself go to the movies, is this negative reinforcement? No, but it is an excellent strategy. You're actually using the **Premack principle,** named after psychologist David Premack, who suggested using any naturally occurring, high-frequency response to reinforce and increase low-frequency responses. Recognizing that you love to go to movies, you intuitively tied your less-desirable, low-frequency activities (studying) to your high-frequency behavior (going to the movies). You also can use the Premack principle in other aspects of your college life, such as making yourself write 4 pages on your term paper or reading 20 pages before you allow yourself to call a friend or have a snack.

Should I use the Premack principle every time I want to go to the movies or just occasionally? The answer is complex and depends on your most desired outcome. To make this decision, you need to understand various *schedules of reinforcement*, or rules that determine when a response will be rewarded and when it will not (Purdy, Markham, Schwartz, & Gordon, 2001).

Schedules of Reinforcement

Continuous Reinforcement *Every correct response is reinforced*

Partial (Intermittent) Reinforcement *Some, but not all, correct responses are reinforced*

The term *schedule of reinforcement* refers to the rate or interval at which responses are reinforced. Although there are numerous schedules of reinforcement, the most important distinction is whether they are *continuous* or *partial*. When Skinner was training his animals, he found that learning was most rapid if the response was reinforced each time it occurred — a procedure called **continuous reinforcement.** However, real life seldom provides continuous reinforcement. You do not get an A each time you write a paper or a date each time you ask, but your behavior persists because your efforts are occasionally rewarded. Most everyday behavior is rewarded on a **partial (or intermittent) schedule of reinforcement,** which involves reinforcing only some responses, not all of them (Sangha et al., 2002).

For effective use of these terms in your own life, remember that continuous reinforcement leads to faster learning than does partial reinforcement. For example, if children (or adults) are rewarded every time they blast an alien starship in a video game *(continuous reinforcement)*, they will learn how to play faster than if they are rewarded for every third or fourth hit *(partial reinforcement)*. On the other hand, imagine having to reward your children every morning for getting up, brushing their teeth, making their beds, dressing, and so on. You simply cannot reward someone constantly for every appropriate response. Although a continuous schedule of reinforcement leads to faster initial learning, it is *not* an efficient system for maintaining long-term behaviors.

It is therefore important to move to a partial schedule of reinforcement once a task is well learned. Why? Because under partial schedules, behavior is more resistant to extinction. Have you noticed that people spend long hours pushing buttons and pulling levers on slot machines in hopes of winning the jackpot? This high response rate and the compulsion to keep gambling in spite of significant losses are evidence of the strong resistance to extinction with partial schedules of reinforcement. This type of partial, intermittent reinforcement also helps parents maintain behaviors like tooth brushing and bed making. After the child has initially learned these behaviors with continuous reinforcement, you should move on to occasional, partial reinforcement.

Four Partial (Intermittent) Schedules of Reinforcement

There are four partial schedules of reinforcement: **fixed ratio (FR)**, **variable ratio (VR)**, **fixed interval (FI)**, and **variable interval (VI)**. Table 17.2 defines these terms and provides examples. (*Study Tip:* Remember that *interval* is *time* based, whereas *ratio* is *response* based.)

How do I know which schedule to choose? The type of partial schedule selected depends on the type of behavior being studied and on the speed of learning desired (Neuringer, Deiss, & Olson, 2000). For example, suppose you want to teach your dog to sit. Initially you reinforce your dog with a cookie every time he sits (continuous reinforcement). To save on your cookie bill and to make his training more resistant to extinction, you eventually switch to one of the partial reinforcement schedules, such as the *fixed ratio* schedule. You would then give your dog a cookie after he sat a certain number of times. The dog must make a fixed number of responses before he receives the reinforcement. As you can see in Figure 17.3, a fixed ratio leads to the

Fixed Ratio (FR) Schedule *Reinforcement occurs after a fixed (predetermined) number of responses*

Variable Ratio (VR) Schedule *Reinforcement occurs unpredictably; the ratio (number or amount) varies*

Fixed Interval (FI) Schedule *Reinforcement occurs after a fixed (predetermined) time has elapsed*

Variable Interval (VI) Schedule *Reinforcement occurs unpredictably; the interval (time) varies*

SUMMARY TABLE 17.2 FOUR SCHEDULES OF REINFORCEMENT

		Definitions	Response Rates	Examples	
Ratio Schedules (response based)	**Fixed ratio (FR)**	Reinforcement occurs after a fixed number of responses	Produces a high rate of response, but a brief dropoff just after reinforcement	Parents pay a child $10 after he washes 2 cars. In a laboratory, a rat receives a food pellet after pressing the bar 7 times.	
	Variable ratio (VR)	Reinforcement occurs unpredictably; the ratio (number and amount) varies	High response rates, no pause after reinforcement, and very resistant to extinction	Slot machines designed to pay out after an average number of responses (maybe every 10 times), but any one machine may pay out on the first response, then seventh, then the twentieth.	
Interval Schedules (time based)	**Fixed interval (FI)**	Reinforcement occurs after a fixed time has elapsed	Responses tend to increase as the time for the next reinforcer is near, but drop off after reinforcement and during interval	You get a monthly paycheck. Rat's behavior is reinforced with a food pellet each time it presses a bar after 20 seconds have elapsed.	
	Variable interval (VI)	Reinforcement occurs unpredictably; the interval (time) varies	Relatively low response rates, but they are steady because the non-human animal or person cannot predict when reward will come	Rat's behavior reinforced with a food pellet after a response and a variable, unpredictable interval of time. In a class with pop quizzes, you study at a slow but steady rate because you can't anticipate the next quiz.	

Shaping *Reinforcement is delivered for successive approximations of the desired response*

Positive Punishment *Adding (or presenting) a stimulus, which weakens a response and makes it less likely to recur*

Negative Punishment *Taking away (or removing) a stimulus, which weakens a response and makes it less likely to recur*

Figure 17.3 *Which is the best schedule of reinforcement?* Each of the different schedules produces its own unique pattern of response, and the best schedule depends on the specific task — see Table 17.2. Note that the "stars" on the lines represent the delivery of a reinforcer. (Adapted from Skinner, 1961.)

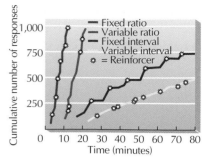

highest overall response rate, but each of the four types of partial schedules has different advantages and disadvantages (Table 17.2).

Shaping

Each of the four schedules of partial reinforcement is important for maintaining behavior. But how do you teach new or complex behaviors like playing the piano or a foreign language? **Shaping** teaches a desired response by reinforcing a series of successive steps leading to the final goal response. It is especially effective for teaching complex or novel behaviors that aren't likely to occur naturally. Skinner believed that shaping explains a wide variety of skills and abilities that each of us possess, from eating with a fork, to playing a musical instrument, to driving a stick-shift car.

Parents, athletic coaches, teachers, and animal trainers all use shaping techniques. For example, if you want to shape a child to make his bed, you could begin by reinforcing when he first gets the sheets and pillows on the bed — even if it's sloppily done. Over time, you would stop reinforcing that level of behavior and only reinforce when he gets the bedspread on the bed and tucked over the pillows. Again, after a little time, you would stop reinforcing until he gets the bedspread on, tucked over the pillows, and straight. Each step in shaping, then, moves slightly beyond the previously learned behavior, allowing the person to link the new step to the behavior previously learned.

Punishment — Weakening a Response

Now that you understand how to *strengthen* a response, we will examine ways to *weaken* undesirable behaviors. Like reinforcement, punishment affects behavior, but it has the opposite effect: it *decreases* the strength of the response — that is, the likelihood that a behavior will be repeated again is weakened. Just as with reinforcement, there are two kinds of punishment, *positive* and *negative* (Skinner, 1953; Gordon, 1989). Also, as with reinforcement, remember to think in mathematical terms of adding and taking away, rather than good and bad (Table 17.3).

Positive punishment is the addition (+) of a stimulus that decreases (or weakens) the likelihood of the response occurring again. If your dog digs a hole every time he sees a gopher mound, and you shout at him to decrease the digging, you are applying positive punishment. **Negative punishment** is the taking away (–) of a stimulus that decreases (or weakens) the likelihood of the response occurring again. Parents use negative punishment when they take the car keys away from a teen who doesn't come home on time. Notice, in *both* positive and negative punishment, the behavior has been punished and the behavioral tendencies have been weakened.

The Tricky Business of Punishment

When we hear the word "punishment," most people think of disciplinary procedures used by parents, teachers, and other authority figures. But punishment is much more than parents giving a child a time-out for misbehaving or teachers giving demerits.

Assessment

VISUAL QUIZ

Operant conditioning in action. Momoko, a five-year-old female monkey, is famous in Japan for her water-skiing, deep-sea diving, and other amazing abilities. Can you imagine how her trainers used shaping to teach this type of behavior?

Answer: The trainers would begin by reinforcing Momoko (with a small food treat) for standing or sitting on the water ski. Then they would reinforce her each time she put her hands on the pole. Next, they would slowly drag the water ski on dry land, and reinforce her for staying upright and holding the pole. Then, they would take Momoko to a shallow and calm part of the ocean and reinforce her for staying upright and holding the pole as the ski moved in the water. Finally, they would take her into the deep part of the ocean.

TABLE 17.3 HOW PUNISHMENT WEAKENS AND DECREASES BEHAVIORS

Positive Punishment (Adds stimulus (+) and weakens the behavior)	Negative Punishment (Takes stimulus away (−) and weakens the behavior)
You have to run 4 extra laps in your gym class because you were late.	You aren't allowed to join the gym class because you were late.
A parent adds chores in response to a child's poor report card.	Your teacher reassigns you to another group because you were talking too much to your friend.
Your boss complains about your performance.	A parent takes away a teenager's driving privileges because he failed to come home on time.

Any process that adds or takes away something that causes the behavior to decrease is *punishment*. By this definition, if parents ignore all the A's on their child's report card and ask repeated questions about the B's and C's, they may unintentionally punish and weaken the likelihood of future A's. Dog owners who yell at or spank their dogs for finally coming to them after being called several times are actually punishing the desired behavior — coming when called. Similarly, college administrators who take away "leftover" money from a department's budget because it wasn't spent by the end of the year are punishing desired behavior — saving money. (Yes, I did add this last example as a subtle message to our college administrators.)

As you can see, punishment is a tricky business. But an advantage of studying psychology is that you now understand how positive and negative punishment (and positive and negative reinforcement) operate, and you can use this knowledge to become a better parent, teacher, and authority figure, as well as a better friend and lover. To help you in these roles, consider the following general discussion and specific suggestions.

First, it's important to acknowledge that punishment plays a significant and unavoidable role in our social world. In his book *Walden Two* (1948), Skinner described a utopian world where reinforcers almost completely replaced punishment. Unfortunately, in our real world, reinforcement is not enough. Dangerous criminals must be stopped and possibly removed from society. Parents must stop their child from running into the street and their teenagers from drinking and driving. And teachers must stop disruptive students in the classroom and bullies on the playground.

There is an obvious need for punishment at times, but it brings problems (MacMillan, 2000; Magee, 2001; Saadeh, Rizzo, & Roberts, 2002). To be effective, punishment should be immediate and consistent. However, in the real world, this is extremely hard to do. Police officers cannot stop every driver every time he or she speeds. To make matters worse, when punishment is not immediate, during the delay the behavior is likely to be reinforced on a partial schedule, which makes it highly resistant to extinction. Think about gambling. For almost everyone, it should be a *punishing* situation — on most occasions, you lose far more money than you win. However, the fact that you occasionally win keeps you "hanging in there."

Perhaps, most important, even if punishment immediately follows the misbehavior, the recipient may learn what *not* to do but doesn't learn what he or she *should* do. Imagine trying to teach a child the word *dog* by only saying "*No!*" each time she said *dog* when it was inappropriate. The child (and you) would soon become very frustrated. It's much more efficient to teach someone by giving him or her clear examples of correct behavior, such as showing a child pictures of dogs and saying "dog" after each photo. Punishment has several other serious side effects, as Table 17.4 shows.

SUMMARY TABLE 17.4 SIDE EFFECTS OF PUNISHMENT

1. Increased aggression. Because punishment often produces a decrease in undesired behavior, at least for the moment, the punisher is in effect rewarded for applying punishment. Thus, a vicious circle may be established in which both the punisher and recipient are reinforced for inappropriate behavior — the punisher for punishing and the recipient for being fearful and submissive. This side effect partially explains the escalation of violence in spousal, child, and elder abuse (Larzelere & Johnson, 1999). In addition to fear and submissiveness, the recipient also might become depressed and/or respond with his or her own form of aggression.

2. Passive aggressiveness. For the recipient, punishment often leads to frustration, anger, and eventually aggression. But most of us have learned from experience that retaliatory aggression toward a punisher (especially one who is bigger and more powerful) is usually followed by more punishment. We therefore tend to control our impulse toward open aggression and instead resort to more subtle techniques, such as showing up late or forgetting to mail a letter for someone. This is known as *passive aggressiveness* (McIlduff & Coghlan, 2000; Stormshak, Bierman, McMahon, & Lengua, 2000).

3. Avoidance behavior. No one likes to be punished, so we naturally try to avoid the punisher. If every time you come home a parent or spouse starts yelling at you, you will delay coming home or find another place to go.

4. Modeling. Have you ever seen a parent spank or hit a child for hitting another child? The punishing parent may unintentionally serve as a "model" for the same behavior he or she is attempting to stop.

5. Temporary suppression. Do you notice that car drivers quickly slow down when they see a police car but quickly resume their previous speed once the police officer is out of sight? Punishment generally suppresses the behavior only temporarily during the presence of the punishing person or circumstances.

6. Learned helplessness. Why do some people stay in abusive homes or marital situations? Research shows that if you repeatedly fail in your attempts to control your environment, you acquire a general sense of powerlessness or *learned helplessness* and you may make no further attempts to escape (Alloy & Clements, 1998; Seligman, 1975; Zhukov & Vinogradova, 2002).

Assessment

VISUAL QUIZ

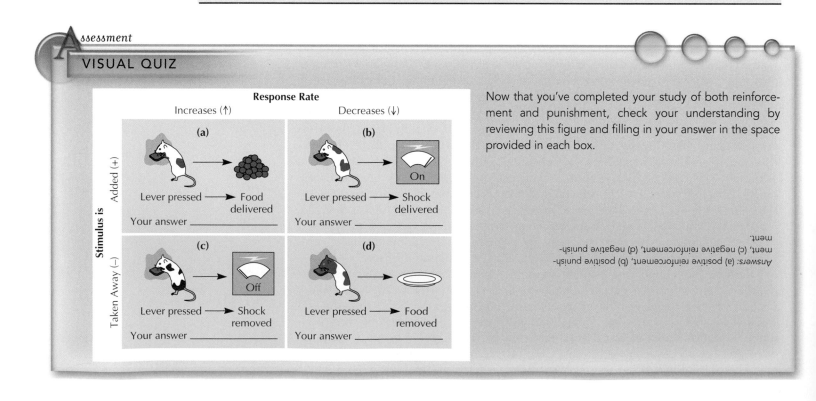

Now that you've completed your study of both reinforcement and punishment, check your understanding by reviewing this figure and filling in your answer in the space provided in each box.

Answers: (a) positive reinforcement, (b) positive punishment, (c) negative reinforcement, (d) negative punishment.

VISUAL QUIZ

Which side effect of punishment is best exemplified by this cartoon?

Answer: The dog's plan to chew up the other shoe while she sleeps is an example of temporary suppression.

Summarizing and Comparing Classical and Operant Conditioning

At this point in the discussion, you may feel overwhelmed by all the terms and concepts for classical and operant conditioning. This is a good time to stop and carefully review Table 17.5, which summarizes and compares the two major types of conditioning.

As you can see, there are several areas of similarity in classical and operant conditioning. For example, in our earlier discussion of the principles of classical conditioning, you learned about *stimulus generalization, stimulus discrimination, extinction,* and *spontaneous recovery.* These same terms also are used in operant conditioning, and your previous learning will help you here. Just as 11-month-old Albert generalized his fear of rats to rabbits and Santa Claus masks, operantly conditioned responses also generalize. After learning the word for *Daddy* (through operant conditioning), children often use this same word for all adult men. This would be a form of *stimulus generalization* (and potential embarrassment to the parents). After parents explain the distinction, the child learns to differentiate (stimulus discrimination) and to only call one man Daddy.

In both classical and operant conditioning, *extinction* occurs when the original source of the learning is removed. In classical conditioning, the CR (Albert's fear of the rat) is extinguished if the CS (the rat) is repeatedly presented without the UCS (the loud noise). In operant conditioning, if the reinforcement (the rat's food pellets) is removed, the response (bar pressing) will gradually decline. Following extinction in either classical or operant conditioning, you also sometimes have *spontaneous recovery.* Just as the classically conditioned fear of rats may spontaneously return, the operantly conditioned bar pressing behaviors may recur.

One final comparison: In classical conditioning, we talked about *higher-order conditioning,* wherein a neutral stimulus (NS) is paired with a conditioned stimulus (CS), which is another stimulus that already produces a learned response. We said that if you wanted to demonstrate higher-order conditioning in Pavlov's dogs, you would first condition the dogs to salivate to the sound of the bell. Then you would pair the flash of light to the ringing of the bell. Eventually, the dog would salivate only to the flash of light.

A similar process, with a different name, also occurs in operant conditioning. If a rat learns that bar pressing produces food *only* when a light is flashing, the rat will soon

SUMMARY TABLE 17.5 AN OVERVIEW OF CLASSICAL AND OPERANT CONDITIONING

	Classical Conditioning	**Operant Conditioning**
Pioneers	Ivan Pavlov John B. Watson	Edward Thorndike B. F. Skinner
Major Terms	Neutral stimulus (NS) Unconditioned stimulus (UCS) Conditioned stimulus (CS) Unconditioned response (UCR) Conditioned response (CR) Conditioned emotional response (CER)	Reinforcers (primary and secondary) Reinforcement (positive and negative) Punishment (positive and negative) Shaping Reinforcement schedules (continuous and partial)
Example	Cringing at the sound of a dentist's drill	A baby cries and you pick it up
Shared Terms	Extinction Spontaneous recovery Generalization Discrimination	Extinction Spontaneous recovery Generalization Discrimination
Major Differences	Involuntary (subject is passive)	Voluntary (subject is active)
Behavior Order	CS must come before the UCS	Reinforcement or punishment come after the behavior

Discriminative Stimulus *A cue that signals when a specific response will lead to the expected reinforcement*

learn to respond only when the light is flashing. The light has become a **discriminative stimulus,** which signals whether a response will pay off or not. We depend on discriminative stimuli many times every day. We pick up the phone only when it rings. We look for the *Women* or *Men* signs on bathroom doors. And children quickly learn to ask Grandma for toys.

Application
APPLYING OPERANT CONDITIONING IN EVERYDAY LIFE

Prejudice, Biofeedback, and Superstition

Operant conditioning has many interesting applications in real life. Here we talk about *prejudice, biofeedback*, and *superstitious behavior.*

Prejudice

Recall the opening story and the three men who murdered James Byrd. What might have reinforced such a behavior? Could it have been attention, notoriety — something else? As you discovered earlier, people can learn prejudice through classical conditioning. We also can learn prejudice through operant conditioning. Because demeaning others gains attention and sometimes approval from others, as well as increases one's self-esteem (at the expense of the victim), prejudice and discrimination are positively

After studying basic operant conditioning principles, can you effectively apply them in your own life? The best method seems to be a combination of the major principles: Reinforce appropriate behavior, extinguish inappropriate behavior, and save punishment for the most extreme cases (such as a 2-year-old running into the street). Here are additional tips:

1. *Feedback.* When using both reinforcement and punishment, be sure to provide immediate and clear feedback to the person or nonhuman animal whose behavior you wish to change. When using punishment, it is particularly important to make clear the desired response, because punishment is merely an indication that the response is undesirable. In other words, give the participant an alternative response to the punished one.

2. *Timing.* Reinforcers and punishers should be presented as close in time to the response as possible. The old policy of "wait till Father gets home" is obviously inappropriate for many reasons. In this case, it is because the delayed punishment is no longer associated with the inappropriate response. The same is true for reinforcement. If you're trying to lose weight, don't say you'll buy yourself a new wardrobe when you lose 30 pounds; reward yourself with a small treat (like a new blouse or shirt) after every few pounds.

3. *Consistency.* To be effective, both reinforcement and punishment must be consistent. Have you ever seen a child screaming for candy in a supermarket? Parents often begin by saying "No." But when the child gets louder or throws a temper tantrum, the parents often give in and buy the candy. Although the parents are momentarily relieved (*negatively rein-forced*) when the screaming stops, can you see how they're creating bigger problems in the long run? First, the child is being *positively reinforced* for the screaming and temper tantrum — and this behavior will increase. To make matters worse, the parents' inconsistency (saying "no" and then occasionally giving in) places begging for candy on a *partial schedule of reinforcement,* which makes it highly resistant to extinction. Like a gambler who continues playing despite the odds, the child will continue the begging, screaming, and temper tantrums in hopes of the occasional payoff.

   Because effective punishment requires constant surveillance and *consistent* responses, it's almost impossible to be a "good punisher." It's best (and easiest) to use consistent reinforcement for good behavior and extinction for bad behavior. Praise the child for happy and cooperative behavior in the supermarket, and extinguish the temper tantrum by consistently refusing the request and ignoring the tantrum.

4. *Order of presentation.* As a teenager, did you ever ask for an extra few dollars as an advance on your allowance, and then forget your promise to mow the grass on Saturday? Did your parents ever make you come home much earlier than your friends because they knew "that all teenagers get into trouble after midnight?" Can you see why the reward of extra money must come *after* the lawn mowing, and why punishment that comes *before* the behavior may create frustration and resentment? Both reinforcement and punishment should come *after* the behavior, never *before.*

reinforced (Fein & Spencer, 1997). People also may have a single punishing experience with a specific member of a group, which they then generalize and apply to all members of the group (Vidmar, 1997) — an example of stimulus generalization.

But the men who killed James Byrd were sentenced to death or life imprisonment. Why would people do anything that they know could bring the death penalty? Punishment does weaken and suppress behavior, but as mentioned before, to be effective it must be consistent and immediate. Unfortunately, this seldom happens. Even worse, as

Figure 17.4 *Biofeedback.* In biofeedback training, internal bodily processes (like blood pressure or muscle tension) are electrically recorded, the information is amplified, and then reported back to the patient through headphones, signal lights, and other means. This information helps the person learn to control bodily processes not normally under voluntary control.

Biofeedback *A bodily function (such as blood pressure or heart rate) is recorded and the information is fed back to an organism to increase voluntary control over that bodily function*

mentioned before, when punishment is inconsistent and the criminal gets away with one or more crimes, that criminal behavior is put on a *partial (intermittent) schedule of reinforcement*, making it more likely to be repeated and to become more resistant to *extinction*.

Biofeedback

In **biofeedback** (short for *biological feedback* and sometimes called *neurofeedback*), information about some biological function, such as heart rate, is conveyed to the individual through some type of signal. Sit quietly for a moment and try to determine your blood pressure. Is it high or low? Is it different from a few minutes ago? You can't tell, can you? For most people, it is impossible to learn to control blood pressure consciously. But if you were hooked up to a monitor that recorded, amplified, and displayed this information to you (biofeedback), you could learn to control it (Figure 17.4).

Researchers have successfully used these biofeedback techniques to treat hypertension and anxiety by lowering blood pressure and muscle tension; epilepsy by changing brain wave patterns; urinary incontinence by gaining better pelvic muscle control; and cognitive functioning, chronic pain, and headache by redirecting blood flow (Jiang, Wang, & Gu, 2002; Lawrence, Wodarski & Wodarski, 2002; Nakao et al., 2000; Penzien, Rains, & Andrasik, 2002; Stetter & Kupper, 2002; Uhlmann & Froescher, 2001).

Biofeedback demonstrates several operant conditioning principles. Something is added (feedback) that increases the likelihood that the behavior will be repeated — *positive reinforcement*. The biofeedback itself is a *secondary reinforcer* because of the learned value of the relief from pain or other aversive stimuli *(primary reinforcer)*. Finally, biofeedback involves *shaping*. The person watches a monitor screen (or other instrument) that provides graphs or numbers indicating their blood pressure (or other bodily states). Like a mirror, the biofeedback reflects back the results of the various strategies the participant uses to gain control. Through trial and error, the participant gets progressively better at lowering heart rate (or making other desired changes). Biofeedback techniques are limited, however, and so far, most successful when used in conjunction with other techniques, such as behavior modification (Module 44).

Application

CRITICAL THINKING

Using Learning Principles to Succeed in College

Psychological theory and research have taught us that an active approach to learning is rewarded by better grades. Active learning means using the SQ4R (Survey, Question, Read, Recite, Review, and Write) study techniques discussed in the Tools for Student Success (pages 41–47). An active learner also rises above old, easy patterns of behavior and applies new knowledge to everyday situations. When you transfer ideas or concepts you learn from class to your personal life, your insight grows.

Now that you have studied the principles of learning, use the following activity to help you apply your new knowledge to achieve your education goals and have an enjoyable college experience:

1. List 3 ways you can positively reinforce yourself for studying, completing assignments, and attending class.

2. Discuss with friends how participating in club and campus activities can reinforce your education commitment.

3. Examine the time and energy you spend studying for an exam in a course you like

ACTIVE LEARNING

with your study effort in a course you don't like. How could you apply the Premack principle to your advantage in this situation?

4. When you take exams, are you anxious? How might this be a classically conditioned response? How could you use the principle of extinction to weaken this response?

Accidental Reinforcement and Superstitious Behavior

B. F. Skinner (1948, 1992) conducted a fascinating experiment to show how accidental reinforcement could lead to *superstitious behaviors*. He set the feeding mechanism in the cages of eight pigeons to release food once every 15 seconds. No matter what the birds did, they were reinforced at 15-second intervals. Six of the pigeons acquired behaviors that they repeated over and over, even though the behaviors were not necessary to receive the food. For example, one pigeon kept turning in counter-clockwise circles, and another kept making jerking movements with its head.

Why did the pigeons engage in such repetitive and unnecessary behavior? Recall that a *reinforcer* increases the probability that a response just performed will be repeated. Although Skinner was not using the food to reinforce any particular behavior, the pigeons associated the food with whatever behavior they were engaged in when the food was originally dropped into the cage. Thus, if the bird was circling counterclockwise when the food was presented, it would repeat that motion to receive more food.

Like Skinner's pigeons, we humans also believe in many superstitions that may have developed from accidental reinforcement. In addition to the superstitions shown in Table 17.6, professional and Olympic-level athletes sometimes carry lucky charms or perform a particular ritual before every competition. Phil Esposito, a hockey player

TABLE 17.6 COMMON WESTERN SUPERSTITIONS

Behavior	Superstition
Wedding plans: *Why do brides wear something old and something borrowed?*	The something old is usually clothing that belongs to an older woman who is happily married. Thus, the bride will supposedly transfer that good fortune to herself. Something borrowed is often a relative's jewelry. This item should be golden, because gold represents the sun, which was once thought to be the source of life.
Spilling salt: *Why do some people throw a pinch of salt over their left shoulder?*	Years ago, people believed good spirits lived on the right side of the body and bad spirits on the left. When a man spilled salt, he believed his guardian spirit had caused the accident to warn him of evil nearby. At the time, salt was scarce and precious. Therefore, to bribe the spirits who were planning to harm him, he would quickly throw a pinch of salt over his left shoulder.
Boasting, making a prediction, or speaking of good fortune: *Why do some people knock on wood?*	Down through the ages, people have believed that trees were homes of gods, who were kind and generous if approached in the right way. A person who wanted to ask a favor of the tree god would touch the bark. After the favor was granted, the person would return to knock on the tree as a sign of thanks.

with the Boston Bruins and the New York Rangers for 18 years, always wore the same black turtleneck and drove through the same tollbooth on his way to a game. In the locker room, he put on all his clothes in the same order and laid out his equipment in exactly the same way he had for every other game. All this because once when he had behaved that way years before, he had been the team's high scorer. Alas, the power of accidental reinforcement.

Assessment

CHECK & REVIEW

Operant Conditioning

In **operant conditioning,** people or animals learn by the *consequences* of their responses. Whether behavior is reinforced or punished (consequences) determines whether the response will occur again. Thorndike and Skinner are the two major contributors to operant conditioning. Thorndike's **law of effect** states rewarded behavior is more likely to recur. Skinner extended Thorndike's work to more complex behaviors but emphasized only external, observable behaviors.

Operant conditioning involves several important terms and principles. **Reinforcement** is any procedure that strengthens or increases a response, whereas **punishment** is any procedure that results in a weakening or decrease. To strengthen a response, we use **primary reinforcers,** which satisfy an unlearned biological need (e.g., hunger, thirst), and **secondary reinforcers,** which have learned value (e.g., money). **Positive reinforcement** (adding something) and **negative reinforcement** (taking something away) increase the likelihood the response will occur again. According to the **Premack principle,** activities or behaviors that are more common or probable in one's life will act as reinforcers for activities that are less probable.

Continuous reinforcement rewards each correct response, whereas a **partial (intermittent) schedule** reinforces for some, not all, designated responses. The four partial reinforcement schedules are **variable ratio (VR), variable interval (VI), fixed ratio (FR),** and **fixed interval (FI).** Complex behaviors can be trained through **shaping,** reinforcing successive approximations of the desired behavior.

Positive punishment (adding something) and **negative punishment** (taking something away) decrease the likelihood the response will occur again. Although some punishment is essential, it has serious side effects.

Operant conditioning has several applications in real life. It helps explain how we learn prejudice through positive reinforcement and stimulus generalization. **Biofeedback,** another application, is the feeding back of biological information, such as heart rate or blood pressure, which a person uses to control normally automatic functions of the body. Operant conditioning also helps explain many superstitions, which involve accidentally reinforced behaviors that are continually repeated because they are believed to cause desired effects.

Questions

1. Define operant conditioning and explain how it differs from classical conditioning.
2. Negative punishment _____ and negative reinforcement _____ the likelihood the response will continue. (a) decreases, decreases; (b) increases, decreases; (c) decreases, increases; (d) increases, increases
3. Partial reinforcement schedules make responses more _____ to extinction.
4. Marshall wears the same necklace to every exam. Explain how his superstitious behavior might have developed.

Answers to Questions can be found in Appendix B.

ACTIVE LEARNING WORKSHEET   MODULE 17

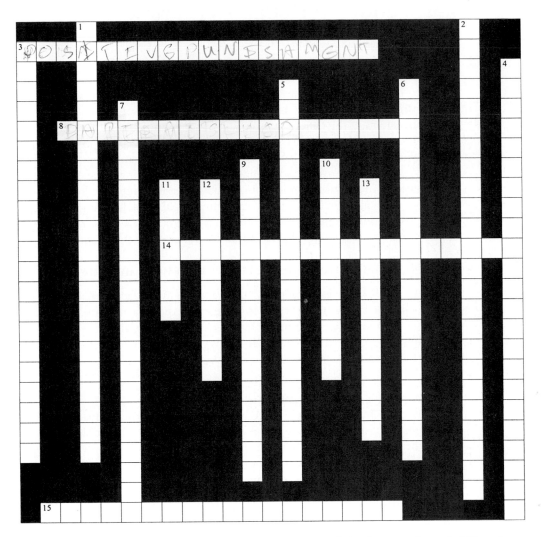

ACROSS

3 The process of adding or presenting a stimulus that decreases the likelihood of that response occurring again.

8 A partial schedule of reinforcement in which a participant must make a certain number of responses before being reinforced.

14 Stimuli that increase the probability of a response because they satisfy a biological need, such as food, water, and sex.

15 The process of taking away or removing a stimulus that decreases the likelihood of that response occurring again.

DOWN

1 A cue that signals when a particular response is likely to be followed by a certain type of consequence.

2 A schedule of reinforcement in which the participant is reinforced for the first response after a specified period of time has elapsed. This period of time varies from one reinforcement to the next.

3 The process of adding or presenting a stimulus that increases the likelihood of that response occurring again.

4 Reinforcement in which every correct response is reinforced.

5 Stimuli that increase the probability of a response because of their learned value, such as money and material possessions.

6 Learning based on consequences. Behavior is strengthened if followed by reinforcement and diminished if followed by punishment

7 The process of taking away or removing a stimulus that increases the likelihood of that response occurring again.

9 Using a response that has a high probability of occurrence to reinforce a response that has a lower probability of occurrence.

10 A procedure for electronically recording, amplifying, and feeding back information about internal bodily changes that would normally be imperceptible (such as blood pressure); aids voluntary regulation of these changes.

11 A procedure in which reinforcement is delivered for successive approximations of the desired response.

12 Any action or event that decreases the likelihood that a response will be repeated.

13 Any action or event that increases the probability that a response will be repeated.

MODULE 18
COGNITIVE-SOCIAL LEARNING

Assessment

How and when do we learn according to cognitive-social theory?

Cognitive-Social Theory *Emphasizes the roles of thinking and social learning in behavior*

Insight *Sudden understanding of a problem that implies the solution*

Is this insight? Grande, one of Wolfgang Köhler's chimps, has just solved the problem of how to get the banana. Is this insight or trial and error? (Also, the chimp in the foreground is engaged in observational learning — our next topic.)

So far, we have examined learning processes that involve associations between a stimulus and an observable behavior. Some behaviorists believe almost all learning can be explained in such stimulus–response terms, but other psychologists feel there is more to learning than can be explained solely by operant and classical conditioning. **Cognitive-social theory** (also called *cognitive-social learning* or *cognitive-behavioral theory*) incorporates the general concepts of conditioning, but rather than a simple S–R (stimulus and response), this theory emphasizes the interpretation or thinking that occurs within the organism—S–O–R (Stimulus–Organism–Response). According to this view, people (as well as, rats, pigeons, and other animals) have attitudes, beliefs, expectations, motivations, and emotions that affect learning. Furthermore, both human and nonhuman animals are social creatures capable of learning new behaviors through observation and imitation of others. We begin with a look at the *cognitive* part of cognitive-social theory, followed by an examination of the *social* aspects of learning.

Insight and Latent Learning: Where are the Reinforcers?

As you'll discover throughout this text, cognitive factors play a large role in human behavior and mental processes. Given that these factors are covered in several other sections (such as Memory, Thinking/Language/Intelligence), our discussion here is limited to the classic research of Wolfgang Köhler and Edward Tolman and their studies of *insight* and *latent learning*.

Köhler's Study of Insight

Early behaviorists likened the mind to a "black box," whose workings could not be observed directly, but German psychologist Wolfgang Köhler wanted to look inside the box. He believed there was more to learning — especially learning to solve a complex problem — than responding to stimuli in a trial-and-error fashion. In several experiments conducted during World War I, Köhler posed different types of problems to chimpanzees and apes to see how they learned to solve them. For example, in one experiment, he placed a banana just outside the reach of a caged chimpanzee. To reach the banana, the chimp would have to use a stick placed near the cage to extend its reach. The chimp did not solve this problem in the random trial-and-error fashion of Thorndike's cats or Skinner's rats and pigeons. Köhler noticed that he seemed to sit and think about the situation for a while. Then, in a flash of **insight** (a sudden understanding), the chimp picked up the stick and maneuvered the banana within its grasp (Kohler, 1925).

Another of Köhler's chimps, an intelligent fellow named Sultan, was put in a similar situation. But this time there were two sticks available to him and the banana was placed even farther away, too far to reach with a single stick. Sultan seemingly lost interest in the banana, but continued to play with the sticks. When he later discovered that the two sticks could be interlocked, he instantly used the now longer stick to pull the banana within grasp. Köhler designated this type of learning *insight learning*, because some internal mental event that we can only describe as "insight" went on between the presentation of the banana and the use of the stick to retrieve it.

Tolman's Study of Latent Learning

Although previous researchers suggested that rats learned mazes through trial-and-error and rewards, Edward C. Tolman (1898–1956) believed they underestimated the rat's cognitive processes and cognitive learning. He noted that rats placed in experimental mazes seemed to pause at certain intersections—almost as if they were *decid-*

ing which route to take. When allowed to roam aimlessly in a maze with no food reward at the end, the rats also seemed to develop a **cognitive map,** or mental representation of the maze.

To test the idea of cognitive learning, Tolman allowed one group of rats to explore a maze in an aimless fashion with no reinforcement. A second group was always reinforced with food whenever they reached the end of the maze. The third group was not rewarded initially (during the first 10 days of the trial), but starting on day 11 they found food at the end of the maze. As expected from simple operant conditioning, the first and third groups were slow to learn the maze; whereas the second group that had reinforcement showed fast, steady improvement. However, when the third group started receiving reinforcement (on the 11th day), their learning of the maze quickly matched the performance of the group that had been reinforced every time (Tolman & Honzik, 1930). For Tolman, this was significant. It proved that the nonreinforced rats had been thinking and building cognitive maps of the area during their aimless wandering, and that their hidden, **latent learning** only showed up when there was a reason to display it (the food reward).

Cognitive learning is not limited to rats. If a new log is placed in its territory, a chipmunk will explore it for a time, but soon move on if no food is found. When a predator comes into the same territory, however, the chipmunk heads directly for and hides beneath the log. Similarly, as a child you may have casually ridden a bike around your neighborhood with no particular reason or destination in mind, and only demonstrated your hidden knowledge of the area when your dad was searching for the closest mailbox. The fact that Tolman's nonreinforced rats quickly caught up to the reinforced ones, that the chipmunk knew about the hiding place under the log, that you knew the location of the mailbox, and recent experimental evidence (Burgdorf, Knutson, & Panksepp, 2000) all provide clear evidence of latent learning and the existence of internal, cognitive maps.

■ Observational Learning: What We See is What We Do

After watching her first presidential debate, my friend's 5-year-old daughter asked, "Do we like him, Mommy?" What form of learning is this? In addition to classical and operant conditioning and cognitive processes (such as insight and latent learning), this child's question shows that we also learn many things through observation and imitation of others—thus the name **observational learning** (or *social learning* or *modeling*). From birth to death, observational learning is very important to our biological, psychological, and social survival (the *biopsychosocial* model). Watching others helps us avoid dangerous stimuli in our environment, it teaches us how to think and feel, and it shows us how to act and interact in social situations.

One of the most compelling examples of observational learning came from the work of Albert Bandura and his colleagues (Bandura, 1997; Bandura, Ross, & Ross, 1961; Bandura & Walters, 1963). Wanting to know whether children learn to be aggressive by watching others be aggressive, Bandura and his colleagues set up several experiments in which children watched a live or televised adult model kick, punch, and shout at a large inflated Bobo doll. Later, the children were allowed to play in the same room with the same toys (see the photo). As Bandura hypothesized, children who had seen the live or televised aggressive model were much more aggressive with the Bobo doll than children who had not seen the aggression. In other words, "Monkey see, monkey do."

We obviously don't copy or model everything we see, however. According to Bandura, learning by observation requires at least four separate processes:

1. *Attention.* Observational learning requires attention. This is why teachers insist on students watching their demonstrations.

2. *Retention.* To learn a complex new dance step, we need to carefully note and remember the instructor's directions and demonstrations.

Cognitive Map *A mental image of a three-dimensional space that an organism has navigated*

Latent Learning *Hidden learning that exists without behavioral signs*

Observational Learning *Learning new behavior or information by watching others (also known as social learning or modeling)*

Bandura's classic Bobo doll study. This child watched while an adult hit the Bobo doll and then imitated the behavior.

Observational learning and modeling. *Note how the bicep circumference of the G.I. Joe action figure has more than doubled since 1964. Can you see how this type of modeling might help explain why men today worry more about their chest and bicep size, and sometimes use steroids to increase their muscle development?* [*Source:* As G.I. Joe bulks up, concern for the 98-pound weakling (1999, May 30), *The New York Times*, p. D2]

3. *Motor reproduction.* Observational learning cannot occur if we lack the motor skills necessary to imitate the model. One of the worst arguments I've ever had with my husband was during his attempts to teach me to downhill ski. Although I paid close attention and remembered his instructions, I repeatedly failed at even the most basic skills—like standing up! Because he was an expert skier of many years, he had forgotten several important steps in the initial learning process, and my motor skills were not up to the task of starting beyond the basics. Our argument was stopped (and our marriage saved) by the arrival of the *professional* ski instructor. (Did you note the way I emphasized "professional"?)

4. *Reinforcement.* We also decide whether we want to repeat the modeled behavior based on whether the model was reinforced. If we see a large number of people making lots of money in the stock market, we're more likely to copy their behavior and less likely to do so when the market collapses.

Application

APPLYING COGNITIVE-SOCIAL LEARNING TO EVERYDAY LIFE

We See, We Do?

Figure 18.1 *John William "Bill" King.* King was sentenced to death for the murder of James Byrd. Note the tattoos on his arm, which include a Satanic image of the Virgin Mary holding a horned baby Jesus, Nazi and racist prison gang insignias, Ku Klux Klan symbols, and the figure of a lynched Black man (Galloway, 1999).

We use cognitive-social learning in many ways in our everyday lives, yet two of the most powerful areas of learning are frequently overlooked—*prejudice* and *media influences.* As you can see in Figure 18.1, one of James Byrd's murderers, Bill King, had numerous tattoos on his body that proudly proclaimed his various prejudices. Did King and his two accomplices learn some of their hatred and prejudice through observation and modeling? King's family and friends insist that he was pleasant and quiet until he began serving an 8-year prison sentence for burglary (Galloway, 1999). What did he learn about prejudice during his prison sentence? Did he model his killing of Byrd after his uncle's well-known killing of a gay traveling salesman a number of years earlier? Or did he learn his prejudices during his numerous years of active membership with the KKK?

Some forms of prejudice also are developed and maintained through the media. Experimental and correlational research clearly show that when children watch television, go to movies, and read books and magazines that portray minorities and women in demeaning and stereotypical roles, they learn to expect these behaviors and to accept them as "natural." Exposure of this kind initiates and reinforces the learning of prejudice (Dovidio, Brigham, Johnson, & Gaertner, 1995).

The media also can teach us what to eat, what toys to buy, what homes and clothes are most fashionable, and what constitutes "the good life." For instance, when a TV commercial shows children enjoying a particular cereal and beaming at their Mom in gratitude (and Mom is smiling back), both children and parents in the audience learn that they too will be rewarded for buying the advertised brand (with happy children) or punished (with unhappy children who won't eat) for buying a competitor's product.

Unfortunately, both children and adults also may be learning more destructive behaviors through observational learning and the media. Correlational evidence from more than 50 studies indicates that observing violent behavior is related to later performing violent behavior (Huesmann & Moise, 1996). As a critical thinker, you may be automatically noting that correlation is not causation. However, over 100 *experimental* studies also have shown a causal link between observing violence and later performing it (Primavera & Herron, 1996).

What about video games? How do they affect behavior? Researchers are just beginning to study these questions. For example, studies have found that students who played more violent video games in junior high and high school also engage in more aggressive behaviors (Anderson & Bushman, 2001; Bartholow & Anderson, 2002). Furthermore, when psychologists Craig Anderson and Karen Dill (2000) experimentally assigned 210 students to first play either a violent or a nonviolent video game and later allowed them to punish their opponent with a loud sound blast, those who played the violent game punished the opponent not only for a longer period of time but also with greater intensity. The researchers hypothesize that video games are more likely to model aggressive behavior because, unlike TV and other media, they are interactive, engrossing, and require the player to identify with the aggressor. Virtual reality games are of particular concern (Unsworth & Ward, 2001).

Video games and aggression. *According to research, playing violent video games increases aggression. These young boys identify with the aggressor and may be more likely to imitate this behavior (Bartholow & Anderson, 2002). What do you think? Do video games affect your behavior or that of your friends?*

Achievement
GENDER & CULTURAL DIVERSITY

Scaffolding as a Teaching Technique in Different Cultures

Learning in the real world is often a combination of classical conditioning, operant conditioning, and cognitive-social learning. This is especially evident in informal situations in which an individual acquires new skills under the supervision of a master teacher. The ideal process used by teachers in these situations is known as *scaffolding* (Wood, Bruner, & Ross, 1976). Like the temporary platform on which construction workers stand, a cognitive *scaffold* provides temporary assistance while a learner acquires new skills. During this type of cognitive scaffolding a more experienced person adjusts the amount of guidance to fit the student's current performance level. In most cases, scaffolding also combines *shaping* and *modeling*, where the teacher selectively reinforces successes of the student and models more difficult parts of the task.

Patricia Marks Greenfield (1984) has described how scaffolding helps young girls learn to weave in Zinacantán, Mexico. Weaving is an important part of the culture of the Zinacantecos, who live in the high-

Scaffolding as a form of learning. *This young Zinacanteco girl is learning to weave through the process of scaffolding.*

lands of southern Mexico. Greenfield videotaped 14 girls at different levels of learning to weave. Each girl was allowed to complete what she was able to do with ease, and then a more experienced weaver created a scaffold by reinforcing correct weaving and modeling more difficult techniques. Interestingly, the teachers appear oblivious of their teaching methods or of the fact that they are teaching at all. Most of the Zinacanteco women believe that girls learn to weave by themselves. Similarly, in our Western culture, many believe that children learn to talk by themselves, and ignore how often children are reinforced (or scaffolded) by others.

Assessment

CHECK & REVIEW

Cognitive-Social Learning

Cognitive-social theory incorporates concepts of conditioning but emphasizes thought processes, or cognitions, and social learning. According to this perspective, people learn through insight, latent learning, observation, and modeling.

Wolfgang Köhler, in working with chimpanzees, demonstrated that learning could occur with a sudden flash of **insight**. Tolman demonstrated that **latent learning** takes place in the absence of reward and remains hidden until some future time when it can be retrieved as needed. A **cognitive map** is a mental image of an area that a person or nonhuman animal has navigated.

According to Albert Bandura, observational learning is the process of learning how to do something by watching others and performing the same behavior in the future. To imitate the behavior of others, we must pay attention, remember, be able to reproduce the behavior, and be motivated by some reinforcement.

Cognitive-social theory helps explain prejudice and media influences. People often learn their prejudices by imitating what they've seen modeled by friends, family, and the media. The media affect our purchasing behaviors as well as our aggressive tendencies. Video games may have a particularly strong influence.

Questions

1. _____ were influential in early studies of cognitive learning. (a) William James and Ivan Pavlov; (b) B. F. Skinner and Edward Thorndike; (c) Wolfgang Köhler and Edward Tolman; (d) Albert Bandura and R. H. Walters.
2. Learning that occurs in the absence of a reward and remains hidden until some future time when it can be retrieved is called _____.
3. Mental images of an area that an organism has navigated are known as _____.
4. Bandura's observational learning studies focused on how _____. (a) rats learn cognitive maps through exploration; (b) children learn aggressive behaviors by observing aggressive models; (c) cats learn problem solving through trial-and-error; (d) chimpanzees learn problem solving through reasoning

Answers to Questions can be found in Appendix B.

MODULE 18   ACTIVE LEARNING WORKSHEET

Enter the correct letter from Column A in the blank space in Column B, and then double-check your answers with those in Appendix B.

Column A	Column B
Albert Bandura	1.____ Mental image of a three-dimensional space.
Anderson and Dill	2.____ Insight learning.
Wolfgang Kohler	3.____ Emphasizes thinking and social learning.
Scaffolding	4.____ Cognitive maps and latent learning.
Insight	5.____ Hidden learning.
Cognitive-social theory	6.____ Combines shaping and modeling.
Edward C. Tolman	7.____ Studied weaving and language learning.
Latent learning	8.____ A sudden flash of understanding.
Cognitive map	9.____ Bobo dolls and observational learning.
Patricia Greenfield	10.____ Violent video games and aggression

MODULE 19
NEUROSCIENCE AND EVOLUTION

As you recall, learning is defined as *a relatively permanent change in behavior and mental processes as a result of practice or experience.* For this change in behavior to persist over time, lasting biological changes must occur within the organism. In this section, we will examine the neurological changes that occur during and after learning. We also will explore the evolutionary advantages of learning.

■ Neuroscience and Learning: Changes in Biochemistry and the Brain

Research conducted on humans and other animals indicates that learning involves at least two important biological changes:

1. ***Biochemistry.*** Neurological research confirms that learning results in alterations in synaptic transmission at specific sites. Because millions of neurons may be activated during an instance of classical conditioning in humans, researchers often use a small sea snail called *Aplysia* to study learning. This particular animal has fewer neurons than any vertebrate, and their neurons are often large (up to 1 mm in diameter) and therefore easier to study.

   When disturbed by a squirt of water, the Aplysia will protectively withdraw its gill. If the squirt continues, the gill withdrawal diminishes (the snail "habituates" – see Module 12). During classical conditioning experiments, the snail repeatedly receives a small electric shock just after being squirted. The Aplysia learns to associate the squirt with the coming shock, and the withdrawal response to the squirt alone becomes stronger. Kandel and his colleagues have shown that this type of learning in the Aplysia coincides with an increase or decrease in the release of specific neurotransmitters by presynaptic and postsynaptic neurons (Bailey & Kandel, 1995; Kandel & Schwartz, 1982; Martinez & Derrick, 1996).

2. ***The Brain's Role in Learning.*** What happens within the brain when something is learned? Every time we learn something new, either consciously or unconsciously, that experience alters the structure of our brain. Experiences that are strong enough to cause learning and memory create new synaptic connections, as well as changes in brain structures.

Evidence that our brains change in structure as a result of experience first began in the 1960s with studies of *enriched* and *deprived environments.* Research on this topic generally involves raising one group of rats in large cages with other rats and many objects to explore. This rat "Disneyland" is colorfully decorated and each cage has ladders, platforms, and cubbyholes to investigate. In contrast, rats in the second group are raised in stimulus-poor, deprived environments. They live alone and have no objects to explore except food and water dispensers. After weeks in these environments, the brains of these two groups of rats are significantly different. The rats in the enriched environment typically develop a thicker cortex, increased nerve growth factor (NGF), more fully developed synapses, more dendritic branching, and improved performance on many tests of learning (Pham, Winblad, Granholm, & Mohammed, 2002; Rosenzweig & Bennett, 1996; Woolf, Zinnerman, & Johnson, 1999).

Admittedly, it is big leap from rats to humans, but research suggests that the human brain also responds to environmental conditions. As we know from Modules 5 and 6, our brains are constantly generating new neurons, and the parts of the brain most involved with learning and memory show the most neuronal growth. In other sections, you will find more information about how the environment, learning, and

Assessment

What neurological changes take place during and after learning? What are the evolutionary advantages to learning?

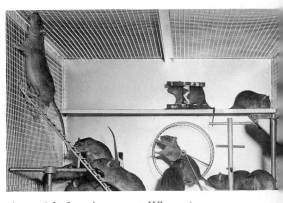

An enriched environment. *When mice and rats live in cages with many objects to explore, their brains develop thicker cerebral cortexes and more efficient synapses.*

Achievement

RESEARCH HIGHLIGHT

Scanning the Brain for Learning

Researchers have long used PET and fMRI brain scans to study various structures in the brain (Module 2). Now they're also using this highly sophisticated technology to scan for learning activity. In Norway, Kenneth Hugdahl (1998) paired a tone (NS) with a shock to the wrist (UCS) and used PET scans to determine which brain areas were activated during the acquisition of a conditioned response. He recorded significant brain acti-

vation in certain right hemisphere frontal lobe areas. In another study, participants were presented with either neutral words (no conditioning) or with threat-related words (higher-order conditioning) (Maddock & Buonocore, 1997). When the fMRI images were compared for the two different conditions, researchers found that the threat words activated a different part of the cerebral cortex than the neutral words.

In addition to these studies, other research has shown that classical condition-

ing activates other areas of the brain, including the thalamus, hippocampus, hypothalamus, amygdala, and cortex (Furmark, Fischer, Wik, Larsson, & Fredrikson, 1997; Schreurs, Shi, Pineda, & Buck, 2000; Steinmetz, 2000). As you can see, learning involves complex processes and numerous brain structures that are not yet well understood (Purdy, Markham, Schwartz, & Gordon, 2001).

memory all affect the brain. How we measure and observe these changes in the living brain is discussed in the following Research Highlight.

■ Evolution and Learning: Biological Preparedness and Instinctive Drift

So far, we have emphasized the learned aspects of behavior, but humans and other animals also are born with certain biological abilities that help ensure their survival. When your fingers touch a hot object, you immediately pull your hand away. When a foreign object approaches your eye, you automatically blink. These simple *reflexes* involve making a specific automatic reaction to a particular stimulus. In addition to reflexes, many species also have a second set of adaptive responses called *instincts*, or species-specific behaviors. For example, the weaverbird is known to tie a particular grass knot to hold its nest together. Even when these birds are raised in total isolation for several generations, they will still tie the same knot.

Although these inborn, innate abilities are important to our evolutionary survival, they are inadequate for coping with a constantly changing environment. Reflexively withdrawing your fingers from a hot object is certainly to your advantage. But what if you saw a sign showing that the hot object was an unusual door handle, which would allow you to escape a burning building? There are numerous important stimuli in our environment that require a flexible approach. Only through learning are we are able to react to spoken words, to written symbols, and other important environmental stimuli. From an evolutionary perspective, *learning* is an adaptation that enables organisms to survive and prosper in a constantly changing world. In this section, we will explore several evolutionary advantages to learning, as well as the limits imposed by an organism's biological heritage.

Classical Conditioning and Biological Preparedness

Years ago, a former student, named Rebecca, was unwrapping her favorite candy bar as she walked to class. After taking the first bite, she stopped eating and looked questioningly at the candy, which was making small movements in her hand. The sight of the small, wiggling maggots filling the candy bar left an immediate and permanent impact. Are you surprised that many years later she still feels nauseated just thinking about this candy bar? Rebecca's response is called a *taste aversion*, and it may have an evolutionary purpose.

Several interesting studies have been done with taste aversion and its link to **biological preparedness,** a built-in (innate) readiness to form associations between certain stimuli and responses. Garcia and his colleagues (1966) produced taste aversion in lab rats by pairing flavored water (NS) and a drug (UCS) that produced gastrointestinal distress (UCR). After being conditioned and recovering from the illness, the rats refused to drink the flavored water (CS) because of the conditioned taste aversion. But, remarkably, Garcia discovered that only certain neutral stimuli could produce the nausea. Pairings of a noise (NS) or a shock (NS) with the nausea-producing drug (UCS) produced no taste aversion. This finding called into question Pavlov's belief that any NS could be conditioned. Garcia suggested that when we are sick to our stomachs, we have a natural, evolutionary tendency to attribute it to food or drink. Being *biologically prepared* to quickly associate nausea with food or drink is adaptive because it helps us avoid that or similar food or drink in the future (Elkins, 1991; Kalat, 1985; Schafe et al., 2000).

Garcia's findings on taste aversion are important for two reasons: First, identifying exceptions to classical conditioning led to a better understanding of biological preparedness. And second, he and his colleagues used their basic research to help solve an economic problem for western ranchers. Coyotes were killing sheep, and the ranchers wanted to kill all coyotes. But this "solution" would have created a larger ecological problem because coyotes eat rabbits and small rodents. In a form of applied research, Garcia and his colleagues used classical conditioning to teach the coyotes not to eat sheep (Gustavson & Garcia, 1974). The researchers began by lacing freshly killed sheep with a chemical that causes extreme nausea and vomiting in coyotes that eat the tainted meat. The conditioning worked so well that the coyotes would run away from the mere sight and smell of sheep. This research has since been applied many times in the wild and in the laboratory with coyotes and with wolves (Gustavson, Kelly, Sweeney, & Garcia, 1976; Ziegler, Gustavson, Holzer, & Gruber, 1983).

Operant Conditioning and Instinctive Drift

Just as later research found that biological preparedness affects classical conditioning, researchers also have found that an animal's natural behavior pattern can interfere with operant conditioning. For example, the Brelands (1961) tried to teach a chicken to play baseball. Through shaping and reinforcement, the chicken first learned to pull a loop that activated a swinging bat, and then learned to actually hit the ball. But instead of running to first base, it would chase the ball as though it were food. Regardless of the lack of reinforcement for chasing the ball, the chicken's natural behavior took precedence. This biological constraint is known as **instinctive drift,** when an animal's conditioned responses tend to shift (or *drift*) toward innate response patterns.

Although animals can be operantly conditioned to perform a variety of novel behaviors (like hitting a baseball), these studies show that reinforcement alone does not determine behavior. Rather, there is a biological tendency in species to favor natural inborn behaviors. Learning theorists initially believed that the fundamental laws of conditioning would apply to almost all species and all behaviors, but recent

Taste aversion. Coyotes find sheep a readily available source of food, but if they are conditioned to develop a taste aversion to sheep, they will avoid them and seek other food.

Biological Preparedness *Built-in (innate) readiness to form associations between certain stimuli and responses*

Instinctive Drift *Conditioned responses shift (or drift) back toward innate response patterns*

Assessment

VISUAL QUIZ

Raccoons can easily learn to play basketball, but they have a very difficult time learning to add coins to a small piggy bank. Can you explain why?

Answer: Because of instinctive drift, the raccoons rub the coins together in an instinctive food-washing response rather than placing them in the piggy bank.

Those who won't forget. *Ross Byrd, left, and Renee Mullins, children of murder victim James Byrd, leaving the Jasper County Courthouse after John "Bill" King was convicted of capital murder.*

findings have identified several limits (such as biological preparedness and instinctive drift) that limit the generality of conditioning principles. As you discovered in Module 2, scientific inquiry is a constantly changing and evolving process.

A Final Note

I began this section with the story of James Byrd because prejudice is a worthy (but unusual) topic for a learning discussion and his story deserved retelling. Although the death of James Byrd shocked many Americans into facing the terrible hatred and racism that still exist in our country, his death (like others) is too quickly forgotten. As you have discovered in this section, however, little (if anything) about prejudice is biologically driven. It is *learned*. Using the *biopsychosocial model*, you can see that the *psychological* component of prejudice (thoughts, values, and beliefs) and *sociocultural* forces (modeling, TV, and other media) are the result of experience and exposure (learning). The good news is that *what we learn we can change* — through retraining, counseling, and self-reflection.

Assessment

CHECK & REVIEW

Neuroscience and Evolution

Learning and conditioning produce relatively permanent changes in biochemistry and various parts of the brain. But not all behaviors are learned. At least some behavior is *innate*, or inborn, in the form of either reflexes or instincts. It appears that all animals are programmed to engage in certain innate behaviors that have evolutionary survival benefits.

Through **biological preparedness** an organism is innately predisposed to form associations between certain stimuli and responses. Taste aversions are classically conditioned associations of food to illness that are rapidly learned, often in a single pairing, and reflect a protective survival mechanism for a species. Findings on **instinctive drift** show there are biological constraints on operant conditioning.

Questions

1. Why do researchers use marine snails (Aplysia) to study learning?
2. How did Garcia condition a taste aversion in coyotes?
3. What is biological preparedness?
4. _____ occurs when an animal's learned responses tend to shift toward innate response patterns.

Answers to Questions can be found in Appendix B.

MODULE 19   ACTIVE LEARNING WORKSHEET

Circle either "T" for true or "F" for false for each of the following statements, and then compare your answers with those in Appendix B.

1. Researchers use small snails (aplysia) to study neuronal activity during learning because they have fewer and larger neurons than most vertebrates. T or F
2. Rats raised in an enriched environment show measurable changes in their brains as a result of their environmental experiences. T or F
3. According to evolutionary psychologists, learning is an adaptation that enables humans to survive and prosper in a constantly changing world.
4. Biological preparedness suggests we would more quickly develop a classically conditioned aversion to spiders and snakes than to spoiled meat. T or F
5. Garcia and his colleagues taught coyotes to avoid sheep by pairing a nausea-inducing drug with freshly killed sheep meat that was later eaten by the coyotes. T or F

KEY TERMS

To assess your understanding of the **Key Terms** in this section, write a definition for each (in your own words), and then compare your definitions with those in the text.

conditioning (p. 217)
learning (p. 217)

Classical Conditioning
classical conditioning (p. 219)
conditioned emotional response
 (CER) (p. 219)
conditioned response (CR) (p. 219)
conditioned stimulus (CS) (p. 219)
extinction (p. 223)
higher-order conditioning (p. 223)
neutral stimulus (NS) (p. 219)
spontaneous recovery (p. 223)
stimulus discrimination (p. 222)
stimulus generalization (p. 222)
unconditioned response (UCR)
 (p. 219)
unconditioned stimulus (UCS) (p. 219)

Operant Conditioning
biofeedback (p. 240)
continuous reinforcement (p. 232)
discriminative stimulus (p. 238)
fixed interval (FI) schedule (p. 233)
fixed ratio (FR) schedule (p. 233)
law of effect (p. 229)
negative punishment (p. 234)
negative reinforcement (p. 231)
operant conditioning (p. 229)
partial (intermittent) reinforcement
 (p. 232)
positive punishment (p. 234)
positive reinforcement (p. 231)
Premack principle (p. 232)
primary reinforcers (p. 230)
punishment (p. 229)
reinforcement (p. 229)

secondary reinforcers (p. 230)
shaping (p. 234)
variable interval (VI) schedule (p. 233)
variable ratio (VR) schedule (p. 233)

Cognitive-Social Learning
cognitive map (p. 245)
cognitive-social theory (p. 244)
insight (p. 244)
latent learning (p. 245)
observational learning (p. 245)

Neuroscience and Evolution
biological preparedness (p. 251)
instinctive drift (p. 251)

WEB RESOURCES

Huffman Book Companion Site
http://www.wiley.com/college/huffman
 This site is loaded with free Interactive Self-Tests, Internet Exercises, Glossary and Flashcards for key terms, Web links, Handbook for Non-Native Speakers, and other activities designed to improve your mastery of the material in this section.

Want to learn more about classical conditioning?
http://www.brembs.net/classical/classical.html
 This site introduces principles of classical conditioning and links to additional sites with important applications of learning techniques.

Interested in Ivan Pavlov?
http://almaz.com/nobel/medicine/1904a.html
 This Nobel Prize Internet Archive provides extensive links and background information on the life and accomplishments of Ivan Petrovich Pavlov.

Want more information about operant conditioning?
http://chiron.valdosta.edu/whuitt/col/behsys/operant.html
 This site provides an overview of operant conditioning, including a brief history, general principles, schedules of reinforcement, examples, and applications.

Interested in biofeedback?
http://www.questia.com/Index.jsp?CRID=behavior_ modification&OFFID=se1
 In addition to background information and related links on the use of biofeedback , this site also offers information and links to other complementary therapies.

Animal training at Sea World
http://www.seaworld.org/infobooks/Training/home.html
 A fascinating look at how operant conditioning, including positive reinforcers, and observational learning are used to train marine animals.

Want more information on cognitive-social learning or observational learning?
http://chiron.valdosta.edu/whuitt/col/soccog/soclrn.html
 This site is an overview of the field, including a brief summary of Bandura's work, research findings, and some general principles.

Interested in the use of taste aversion and wildlife management?
http://www.conditionedtasteaversion.net/
 This site provides a wealth of fascinating information and links related to the use of conditioned taste aversion (CTA) in wildlife.

VISUAL SUMMARY

Learning
(Modules 16, 17, 18, and 19)

Classical Conditioning

Understanding Classical Conditioning

Pioneers: Pavlov and Watson
Process: Involuntary

1) Before **conditioning**, originally **neutral stimulus (NS)** causes no relevant response, while **unconditioned stimulus (UCS)** causes **unconditioned response (UCR)**.
2) During conditioning, NS is paired with UCS that elicits the UCR.
3) After conditioning, previous NS becomes **conditioned stimulus (CS)**, which now causes a **conditioned response (CR)** or **conditioned emotional response (CER)**.

Principles of Classical Conditioning

- **Stimulus generalization**: Stimuli similar to original CS elicit CR.
- **Stimulus discrimination**: Only the CS elicits the CR.
- **Extinction**: Gradual suppression of a learned behavior by repeatedly presenting the CS without the UCS.
- **Spontaneous recovery**: Voluntary reappearance of a previously extinguished CR.
- **Higher order conditioning**: The NS is paired with the CS to which the organism has already been conditioned.

Applying Classical Conditioning to Everyday Life

- *Prejudice*: Negative perceptions of others acquired through classical conditioning processes.
- *Phobias*: Irrational fears developed through association of a feared object with the UCS.
- *Medical treatments*: Using nausea producing drugs, alcoholics learn to pair alcohol (CS) with nausea (CR).
- *Advertising*: Products (NS) are repeatedly paired with pleasant images (UCS) until they become a (CS).

Operant Conditioning

Understanding Operant Conditioning

Pioneers: Thorndike and Skinner
Process: Voluntary

Organisms learn through consequences of their behavior. When responses are reinforced, they are strengthened and likely to increase; when punished, they are weakened and likely to decrease.

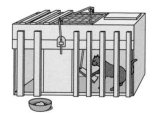

Principles of Operant Conditioning

Strengthening a response occurs through:

1) Primary and secondary reinforcers: **Primary reinforcers**, like food, satisfy a biological need, whereas the value of **secondary reinforcers**, such as money, is learned.
2) Positive and negative reinforcement: **Positive reinforcement** adds something that increases the likelihood of the response, whereas **negative reinforcement** takes away something that increases the likelihood of the response.

Operant Conditioning (cont.)

Principles of Operant Conditioning (cont.)

Additional concepts:

In a **continuous schedule of reinforcement,** every correct response is reinforced, whereas in a **partial (or intermittent) schedule** only some responses are reinforced. Partial schedules include **fixed ratio (FR), variable ratio (VR), fixed interval (FI),** and **variable interval (VI).**

Shaping involves reinforcement for successive approximations of the desired response.

Weakening a response occurs through:
1) **Positive punishment** — adds something that decreases the likelihood of the reponse.
2) **Negative punishment** — takes away something that decreases the likelihood of the response.

Applying Operant Conditioning to Everyday Life

• *Prejudice*: Negative perceptions of others acquired through operant conditioning.

• *Biofeedback*: "Feeding back" biological information (heart rate or blood pressure) for control of normally automatic body functions.

• *Superstitious behavior*: Develops from accidental rewarding of specific behaviors.

Cognitive-Social Learning

Insight and Latent Learning
• *Köhler*: Learning can occur with a sudden flash of understanding (**insight**).
• *Tolman*: Learning can happen without reinforcement and remain hidden until needed (**latent learning**). After navigating their environments people and nonhuman animals create **cognitive maps.**

Observational Learning
• *Bandura*: **Learning** occurs after watching and imitating others.

Applying Cognitive-Social Learning to Everyday Life
• *Prejudice*: Learned by imitating and modeling prejudiced behavior of others.
• *Media influences*: Consumerism, aggression, and other behaviors are partially learned from media models.

Neuroscience and Evolution

Learning and conditioning produce relatively permanent changes in neural connections and various parts of the brain. Evolutionary theorists believe some behavior is unlearned (e.g., reflexes or instincts), and that learning and conditioning are further adaptations that enable organisms to survive and prosper in a constantly changing world.

MEMORY

Core Learning Objectives

As you read Modules 20 and 21, keep the following questions in mind and answer them in your own words:

▶ What are the three major approaches that help explain memory?

▶ What causes forgetting? How can we prevent forgetting of important information?

▶ What are the main memory problems?

When Elizabeth was 14 years old, her mother drowned in their back-yard pool. In her diary she wrote:

Today, July 10, 1959, was the most tragic day of my life. My dearly beloved mother, whom I had just gotten to be really close with, died. We woke up this morning and she was missing, and an hour later we found her in the swimming pool. Only God knows what happened. I know that life must go on and that we all must be brave. I try to tell myself that she is gone only physically and that her soul and her love remain with us. Now that she is gone, I realize how very much I love her and how hard it will be to carry on. I feel so empty inside, like I lost a big part of me. If my mother could hear me I would want her to know that she has all my love and always will (Loftus, 2002, p. 70).

As she grew older, the details surrounding her mother's death became increasingly vague for Elizabeth. At a family reunion some 30 years later, a relative told Elizabeth that she had been the one to find her mother's drowned body. Despite her initial shock and denial, over the next few days the memories slowly started coming back.

I could see myself, a thin, dark-haired girl, looking into the flickering blue-and-white pool. My mother, dressed in her nightgown, is floating face down. I start screaming. I remember the police cars, their lights flashing, and the stretcher with the clean, white

Achievement
Assessment
Application

blanket tucked in around the edges of the body. The memory had been there all along, but I just couldn't reach it (Loftus & Ketcham, 1994, p. 45).

This is the true story of Elizabeth Loftus, who later became a famous experimental psychologist who specializes today in the study of memory.

Now consider the case of a biologically induced memory problem. In 1953, a patient referred to as H.M. had portions of his temporal lobes and underlying parts of the limbic system surgically removed as treatment for his severe epilepsy (which could not be controlled even by high doses of anticonvulsant medication). The surgery was successful in reducing the severity and number of seizures, but his long-term memory was profoundly disrupted (Corkin, 2002). He has no recollection of anything that has happened to him since 1953.

Today, over 50 years after the operation, H.M. cannot rec-

ognize the people who care for him daily, the scientists who have studied him for decades, or even the room where he lives. He spends his days in an always unfamiliar nursing home, often reading the same books and magazines over and over and laughing at the same jokes— each time as though it were the first. He thinks he is still 27 (the age at which he had the operation), and no longer recognizes a photograph of his own face.

Ironically, H.M.'s short-term memory is fine. He can read, solve problems, and converse with ease, but he can only hold and process new information for about 20–30 seconds. As soon as he is distracted, the information is lost—and he cannot recall it later. He is somewhat aware of his memory problems, and he once

described it as, "At this moment everything looks clear to me, but what happened just before? That's what worries me. It's like waking from a dream. I just don't remember" (Milner, 1970, p. 37).

Can you imagine what it would be like to be Elizabeth or H.M.? How could a child forget finding her mother's body? What would it be like to be H.M.—existing only in the present moment, unable to learn and form new memories?

In this section, you will discover several amazing facts related to these two cases, along with numerous concepts and theories that will help improve your everyday life. You also will learn that memory for all of us is not a gigantic library or hard drive, nor is it a video recorder or movie camera that records and stores precise duplicates of our everyday learning and experiences. In fact, it is a highly selective and constructive process subject to serious errors and distortions.

On a more positive note, you will discover that in most cases our memories are highly functional and biologically well adapted for everyday life. Every moment of the day, we rather automatically filter and sort through a barrage of

information and then select, retain, and recover information essential to our survival. In striking contrast to the memory deficits described above, there are also people with exceptional memories. Rajan Mahadevan, for example, earned a place in the *Guinness Book of World Records* by reciting the first 31,811 digits of pi. His exceptional memory is apparently based on elaborate memory devices, which we will discuss near the end of this section (Thompson, Cowan, & Frieman, 1993).

This unit begins with a brief overview of the three most popular theories and models that help explain, "What is memory?" Then we examine several factors and theories that help answer, "Why do we forget?" Next, we explore both common and unusual problems with memory, including amnesia, brain traumas, repressed memories, and eyewitness testimony. We conclude with a summary of the research on specific techniques for memory improvement.

MODULE 20
WHAT IS MEMORY?

Memory *An internal record or representation of some prior event or experience*

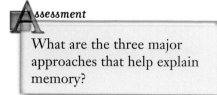

Assessment

What are the three major approaches that help explain memory?

Memory is most often defined as "an internal record or representation of some prior event or experience" (Purdy, Markham, Schwartz, & Gordon, 2001, p. 9). Without memory we have no past because learning is lost. Memory may be our most important and valuable mental process. Realize, however, that this internal record is fallible. It may be composed of less detail (or more) than the actual event or experience. Recognizing the problems and frailties of memory, I have sprinkled memory improvement suggestions throughout this section. Tip number one: *organization*. When you want to learn and remember a large amount of information, you must organize it into meaningful patterns or categories. To provide an example, I have summarized and organized the first section of this unit to create Table 20.1. Like a map that helps you plan your trip, this overview gives you "the big picture," which will help you learn and *organize* upcoming material.

Each of the approaches shown in Table 20.1 and discussed in the upcoming section offers a slightly different but overlapping perspective on the way memory operates and is organized. They also offer you, the reader, a greater understanding of how your memory works — and when it fails. (Specific techniques for improving memory are summarized at the end of this unit.) Let's begin with the first major approach.

Study**T**ip 💡

Studying this table provides a preview of upcoming information and a way to efficiently organize a large amount of information.

SUMMARY TABLE 20.1 AN OVERVIEW OF THREE COMMON MEMORY MODELS

Traditional three-stage memory model Sensory memory → Short-term memory ⇄ Long-term memory	This model suggests humans need to store information for different lengths of time. The first stage, *sensory memory*, holds information just long enough to select items worthy of further processing. The second stage, *short-term memory* (STM), allows time for brief sorting and organizing of information to send on to relatively permanent storage. The third stage, *long-term memory* (LTM), is a relatively permanent storehouse of all our memories.
Encoding, storage, and retrieval approach 	In this model, memory is seen as a *process*, with a variety of control mechanisms operating at each point in the process. At the beginning of the process *(encoding)*, we select certain incoming environmental stimuli and translate (encode) them into neural messages the brain can understand. During storage, we select and organize specific information to save in "files" for permanent storage. At the final point in the process *(retrieval)*, we search these files and bring back the necessary data.
Biological approach 	This approach explains memory by looking at biological changes in the synapses that occur during encoding and storage and at where memories are located when retrieval is required.

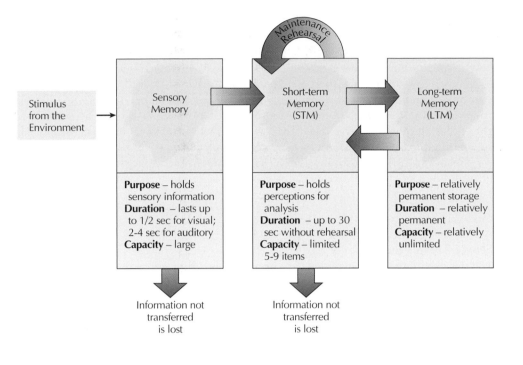

Figure 20.1 *Traditional three-stage memory model.* Each "box" represents a separate memory system that differs in purpose, duration, and capacity. When information is not transferred from sensory memory or short-term memory, it is assumed to be lost. Information stored in long-term memory can be retrieved and sent back to short-term memory for use.

■ Traditional Three-Stage Memory Model: The Need for Differing Storage Times

Since the late 1960s, one of the most widely used models in memory research has been the *traditional three-stage memory model* or the *three-box model* (Atkinson & Shiffrin, 1968; Healy & McNamara, 1996). According to this model, we need different storage "boxes" or stages to house information for various lengths of time. The first stage holds information for exceedingly short intervals, the second retains information for approximately 30 seconds or less (unless renewed), and the third stage provides relatively permanent storage. Because information must pass through each of these stages to get to the next, they are often depicted as three boxes with directional arrows indicating the flow of information (Figure 20.1). Each of these three stages (*sensory*, *short-term*, and *long-term*) has a somewhat different purpose, duration, and capacity.

Sensory Memory

Everything we see, hear, touch, taste, and smell first enters our **sensory memory,** a very brief storage of sensory information. The *purpose* of sensory memory is to retain a relatively exact image of each sensory experience just long enough to locate and focus on relevant bits of information and transfer them on to the next stage of memory. The *duration* of sensory memory varies according to the specific sense. For visual information, known as *iconic memory*, the visual icon (or image) lasts about one-half of a second. Auditory information (what we hear) is held in sensory memory about the same length of time as visual information, one-quarter to one-half of a second, but a weaker "echo," or *echoic memory* of this auditory information, can last up to 2 to 4 seconds (Lu, Williamson, & Kaufman, 1992; Neisser, 1967).

How can such brief sensory messages be measured in a laboratory? One of the earliest researchers, George Sperling (1960), designed a clever experiment that briefly showed people visual arrays of 12 letters arranged in rows (Figure 20.2). Sperling rapidly flashed this three-letter–by–four-letter matrix on a screen. Immediately after the letters flashed off, he asked the participants to recall the letters. Participants generally recalled only 4 or 5 letters but insisted they had seen more letters

Sensory Memory *First memory stage that holds sensory information; relatively large capacity, but duration is only a few seconds*

K	Z	R	A
Q	B	T	P
S	G	N	Y

Figure 20.2 *Experiments with sensory memory.* When George Sperling flashed an arrangement of letters like these for 1/20 of a second, most people could only recall 4 or 5 (of 12). But when instructed to report the top, middle, or bottom row, depending on whether they heard a high, medium, or low tone, they reported almost all the letters correctly. Apparently, all 12 letters are held in sensory memory right after viewing them, but only those that are immediately attended to (with the tone) are noted and processed.

before the memory slipped away. To test this possibility, Sperling devised a "partial report" experiment. Rather than reporting everything from the display, he asked participants to report the first row of letters if they heard a high tone, the second row if they heard a medium tone, and the third row when they heard a low tone. Whatever row or column the participants were asked to recall, they were able to name the letters without any trouble, which indicates that they had memory access to all letters in the matrix for at least a few thousandths of a second. This suggests, then, that all objects in the visual field are available in sensory memory if they can be attended to quickly.

From this and other studies, early researchers assumed that sensory memory had an unlimited capacity. However, later research suggests that sensory memory does have its limits and that the stored images are fuzzier than was once thought (Best, 1999).

Short-Term Memory

Short-Term Memory (STM) *Second memory stage that temporarily stores sensory information and decides whether to send it on to long-term memory (LTM); capacity limited to 5 to 9 items and duration is about 30 seconds*

Just as sensory memory maintains environmental stimuli only long enough to decide whether to send it on, the second stage, **short-term memory** (STM), only temporarily stores and processes the sensory image until it decides whether to send it along to the third stage (long-term memory). Although they share a similar *purpose*, STM does not store exact *duplicates* of sensory information but rather a mixture of perceptual analyses. For example, when your sensory memory registers the sound of your professor's voice, it holds the actual auditory information for a few seconds, and if you decide the voice needs further processing, you send it along to STM. While being transferred from sensory memory, the voice is converted into a larger, more inclusive type of message capable of being analyzed and interpreted during short-term memory. If your STM decides the information is important (or may be on a test), it organizes and sends this information along to relatively permanent storage, called long-term memory (LTM).

The *duration* and *capacity* of STM are relatively limited. STM holds a restricted amount of new information, five to nine items, for up to 30 seconds, by most estimates, although some researchers extend the time to a few minutes (Best, 1999; Kareev, 2000). As with sensory memory, information in STM either is transferred quickly into the next stage (LTM) or it decays and is lost.

www.wiley.com/college/huffman

TRY THIS

YOURSELF

Application

If you'd like a simple demonstration of the duration of visual, *iconic memory*, swing a flashlight in a dark room. Because the image, or *icon*, lingers for a fraction of a second after the flashlight is moved, you see the light as a continuous stream, rather than a succession of individual points.

To appreciate (and remember) auditory, *echoic memory*, think about times when someone interrupted you while you were deeply absorbed in a task. Did you ask them "What?" yet find you could still answer their question without a repeat? Now you know why. If we divert our attention from the absorbing task

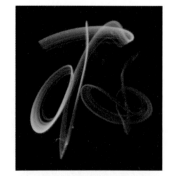

quickly enough, we can "hear again" the echo of what was asked.

How can I increase the duration and capacity of my STM? Look back to the memory model in Figure 20.1 and note the looping arrow at the top labeled "maintenance rehearsal." You can extend the *duration* of your STM almost indefinitely by consciously repeating the information over and over again, a process called **maintenance rehearsal.** You are using maintenance rehearsal when you look up a phone number and repeat it over and over until you dial the number. It is like juggling a set of plates; the plates stay in perfect shape as long as you keep juggling them. Once you stop, however, the plates fall and are destroyed (or the memory is lost).

To extend the *capacity* of STM, you can use **chunking,** grouping separate pieces of information into a single unit (or *chunk*) (Glassman, 1999; Miller, 1956). Have you noticed that numbers on credit cards, your Social Security identification, and telephone number are all grouped into three or four units separated by hyphens? This is because most people find it easier to remember numbers in chunks like *(760) 744–1129* rather than as a string of single digits. Similarly, in reading-improvement courses, students are taught to chunk groups of words into phrases so that fewer eye movements are required and the brain can process the phrases as units rather than as individual words.

Expert chess players also use chunking to organize the information on a game board into meaningful patterns or units. Researchers have found that novice players who look at a standard chessboard with the pieces arranged in a typical play position can remember the positions of only a few pieces. Expert chess players generally remember all the positions (Chase & Simon, 1973; Gobert, 1998). To the expert players, these seemingly randomly arranged pieces form meaningful patterns. Just as you group the letters of this sentence into meaningful words and remember them long enough to understand the meaning, expert chess players group the chess pieces into patterns (or chunks) that can be easily recalled.

If I have room for five to nine units or chunks, why doesn't chunking help me remember even three or four names during introductions? The limited capacity and brief duration of STM both work against you in this situation. Instead of concentrating on the name of someone you meet for the first time, you sometimes use all your short-term memory capacity wondering how you look and thinking about what to say. You might even fill STM space worrying about your memory! People who are good at remembering names repeat the name of each person out loud or silently to keep it entered in STM (maintenance rehearsal). They also make sure that other thoughts don't intrude until they have tested their ability to remember the name. Note that maintenance rehearsal keeps the name available only while you're actively rehearsing. If you want to really learn that name, you will need to transfer it into long-term memory.

Short-Term Memory as a "Working Memory"

So far it sounds as if short-term memory (STM) is just a *passive*, temporary "holding area." Most current researchers (Baddeley, 1992, 2000; Cantor & Engle, 1993) now realize *active* processing of information also occurs in STM — thus the term *working memory.* Today, we think of STM as a three-part *working memory* (Figure 20.3):

1. *Visuospatial sketchpad.* This component is the visual workplace responsible for holding and manipulating visual images and spatial information (Best, 1999; Friedman & Miyake, 2000). Imagine yourself as a food server who's taking multiple orders from three customers at a small table. Using your mind's visuospatial "sketchpad," you can mentally visualize how to fit all the plates of food on their table.

Chess as a type of chunking. World-class chess players such as Garry Kasparov are able to remember groups of pieces by chunking them into meaningful patterns.

Maintenance Rehearsal *Repeating information over and over to maintain it in short-term memory (STM)*

Chunking *Grouping separate pieces of information into a single unit (or chunk)*

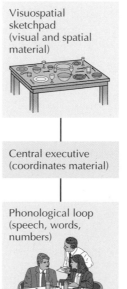

Visuospatial sketchpad (visual and spatial material)

Central executive (coordinates material)

Phonological loop (speech, words, numbers)

Figure 20.3 ***Working memory as a central executive.*** According to this model, working memory serves as a central executive that coordinates the visuospatial sketchpad and the phonological loop.

Problems with short-term memory?
When being introduced to several people at a party, you will be more apt to remember the person's name if you repeat it several times, and focus solely on the person rather than other interfering factors.

2. *Phonological rehearsal loop.* This part involves holding and manipulating verbal information (Best, 1999; Gathercole & Pickering, 2000; Jiang et al., 2000). Picture yourself again as the same food server, and they have given you the following orders: "I want the breakfast special with two scrambled eggs, orange juice, and coffee." "Give me the ham, very well done, with the stack of pancakes, and nothing to drink." "I'll have oatmeal without the raisins, dry toast, coffee, and grapefruit juice." Like a circus performer who keeps a set of plates spinning on the ends of sticks, you can mentally "spin" the food orders by subvocally repeating them. This is why this component is called a phonological (auditory) *rehearsal loop.* You rehearse the order until you reach the kitchen and pass it along to the chef.

3. *Central executive.* This "executive" supervises and coordinates the other two components, as well as material retrieved from LTM. When you mentally combine the verbal food orders (the phonological loop) and their spatial layout on the table (the visuospatial sketchpad), you are using your central executive.

Long-Term Memory

The *purpose* of the third stage, **long-term memory** (LTM), is to serve as a storehouse for information that must be kept for long periods of time. Once information is transferred from STM, it is organized and integrated with other information in LTM. It remains there until we need to retrieve it. Then it is sent back to STM for our use.

Compared to the sensory memory and short-term memory, long-term memory has relatively unlimited *capacity* and *duration* (Klatzky, 1984). Although it may seem that a great deal of information gets lost in your long-term memory storehouse, your problem is more likely a result of poor organization. During the transfer of information from STM to LTM, incoming information is "tagged" or filed, hopefully in the appropriate place. If information is improperly stored, it creates major delays and problems during retrieval. The better you label and arrange things (whether it's your CD collection, your bills, or your memory), the more likely they will be accurately stored and readily available for retrieval.

Long-Term Memory (LTM) *Third stage of memory that stores information for long periods of time; its capacity is virtually limitless and its duration is relatively permanent*

As mentioned at the beginning of this section, good organization is key to a good memory. Admittedly, organization takes time and work. But you'll be happy to know that some memory organization and filing is done automatically while you sleep (Hennevin, Hars, Maho, & Bloch, 1995). Other research shows that sleep itself improves memory (Koulack, 1997; Plihal & Born, 1999).

What about advertising that says you can use tape recordings to learn new skills like foreign languages while you sleep? Do they work? In one early study, participants' brain waves were recorded while they listened to tapes as they slept. Afterward, they were asked questions about the information they heard. Participants who listened to the tapes while in a drowsy state could answer 50 percent of the questions. Listeners in a transition state between drowsiness and light sleep could answer 5 percent of the questions. Listeners who were fully asleep did not remember any information (Simon & Emmons, 1956).

■ Encoding, Storage, and Retrieval: The Processes of Memory

The traditional three-stage memory model remains the leading approach because it offers a convenient way to organize the major findings of memory. However, rather than emphasizing storage time, the second approach, the *encoding, storage, and retrieval model,* focuses on memory *processing*—how information is changed as it moves through the following operations: *encoding, storage,* and *retrieval.* How do you remember the date of your next exam in psychology, the five items you need to buy at the grocery store, or your first romantic kiss? To remember any piece of information, you must first get it into your brain **(encoding),** then you must retain it **(storage),** and later you will need to recover it **(retrieval).**

Each of these three processes represents a different function that is somewhat analogous to the parts and functions of a computer (Figure 20.4). To input data into a computer, you begin by typing letters and numbers on the keyboard, which the computer translates into its own electronic language. In a similar fashion, your brain *encodes* sensory information (sound, visual image, and other senses) into a neural code (language) it can understand and use. Once information is encoded, it must be *stored.* Whereas computer information is stored on a disk or hard drive, your human memories are stored in the brain. Finally, to retrieve information from either the computer or brain, you must search and locate the appropriate "files" and then bring the information up on the computer monitor or to your short-term, working memory where it can be used.

Study **T**ip ◉

As you recall from Module 14, learning a foreign language or anything else requires a highly alert, nonsleepy, attentive level of consciousness, known as controlled processing. To keep this level of attention, you need to actively listen during lectures and actively read while studying your college texts. One of the best ways to stay active is by taking notes while listening and reading. The tools for student success in Module 4, provide additional tips for active learning.

Encoding *Translating information into neural codes (language)*

Storage *Retaining neurally coded information over time*

Retrieval *Recovering information from memory storage*

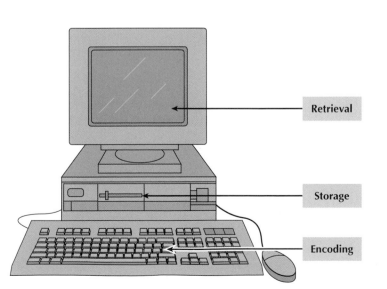

Figure 20.4 ***Memory as a computer.*** The encoding, storage, and retrieval model uses a computer metaphor to explain the three basic functions of our memory system. Similar to a computer, incoming information is first *encoded* (typed on a keyboard and translated into computer language), stored on a disk or the hard drive, and later retrieved and brought to the computer screen to be used.

Parallel Distributed Processing Approach

Like all analogies, this "memory as a computer" model has its limits. Human memories are often fuzzy and fragile compared to the literal, "hard" data stored on a computer disk or hard drive. Critics of both the traditional three-stage model and the encoding, storage, and retrieval approach suggest that the human brain does not operate like a computer. A computer processes instructions and data *sequentially*; units of information follow one after another in a logical, orderly fashion. Human memory, however, occurs *simultaneously*, through the action of multiple networks.

Because of these differences between computers and humans, some cognitive scientists prefer the **parallel distributed processing (PDP)** approach, or *connectionist model* of memory (McClelland, 1995; Sartori & Umilta, 2000). As the name implies, instead of recognizing patterns as a sequence of information bits (like a computer), our brain and memory processes perform multiple, *parallel* operations all at one time. In addition, memory is spread out, or *distributed*, throughout an entire network of processing units. If you're swimming in the ocean and see a large fin nearby, your brain does not conduct a complete search of all fish with fins before urging you to begin a rush to the beach. Instead, you conduct a mental *parallel* search, noting the color of the fish, the fin, and the potential danger all at the same time. Because the processes are parallel, you can quickly process the information — and possibly avoid being eaten by the shark!

The PDP model of how memory works represents the most recent shift in theories of memory. As we just noted, survival in our environment requires instantaneous information processing. The PDP model allows a faster response time, and it also seems consistent with neurological information of brain activity (Module 5) and the parallel processing used when we recognize patterns (Module 13). Therefore, the PDP approach may soon become the standard model for explaining memory.

Parallel Distributed Processing (PDP) *Memory results from connections among interacting processing units, distributed in a vast network, and all operating parallel*

Assessment

CHECK & REVIEW

Three-Stage Memory Model and Encoding, Storage, and Retrieval

The traditional three-stage memory model proposes that information must pass through each of three stages before being stored: *sensory memory, short-term memory,* and *long-term memory.* **Sensory memory** preserves a brief replica of sensory information. It has a large capacity and information lasts between 2 to 4 seconds. Selected information is sent to short-term memory. **Short-term memory** (STM), also called *working memory,* involves memory for current thoughts. Short-term memory can hold five to nine items for about 30 seconds before they are forgotten. Information can be stored longer than 30 seconds through **maintenance rehearsal,** and the capacity of STM can be increased with **chunking. Long-term memory** (LTM) is relatively permanent memory storage with an unlimited capacity.

The encoding, storage, and retrieval approach sees memory as a *process.* It uses similarities between human memory and a computer. Like typing on a keyboard, **encoding** translates information into neural codes that match the brain's language. **Storage** retains neural coded information over time, like saving material on the computer's hard drive or a disk. **Retrieval** gets information out of LTM storage and sends it to STM to be used, whereas the computer retrieves information and displays it on the monitor.

The **parallel distributed processing** (PDP), or *connectionist,* model explains that contents of our memory are represented as a vast number of interconnected units distributed throughout a huge network, all operating in parallel — simultaneously.

Questions

1. According to the three-stage memory model, information must first enter _____, then transfer to _____ and then to _____ to be retained in our memory system.
   (a) sensory memory; short-term memory; permanent memory;
   (b) short-term memory; sensory memory; long-term memory;
   (c) sensory memory; short-term memory; long-term memory;
   (d) working memory; short-term memory; permanent memory

2. Maintenance rehearsal allows us to keep information in _____ memory longer than the typical 30 seconds. (a) short-term; (b) long-term; (c) sensory; (d) permanent

3. Explain how the encoding, storage, and retrieval approach to human memory is analogous to the workings of a computer.

4. How does the PDP approach explain memory?

Answers to Questions can be found in Appendix B.

Integrating the Two Major Approaches: Three-Stage Memory Model Meets Encoding, Storage, and Retrieval

Memory researchers continue to debate the merits and limits of the several models of memory. Given the durability of the *three-stage memory model* and the additional information provided by the *encoding, storage,* and *retrieval* approach, most psychologists currently emphasize an integration of these two models (Figure 20.5). In this section, we will show how an integration of the two major memory models provides a convenient way to organize the major findings on memory, as well as providing a good accounting for those findings. Let's start with encoding.

Integrating Encoding with the Three-Stage Memory Model

When we encode information, we are translating or recording it into a form the brain can recognize and use. As you can see in Figure 20.5, we first encode information when we transfer it from sensory memory to STM. We also perform a second type of encoding during the transfer from STM to LTM. Encoding seems to be related to two major memory strategies: *organization* and *rehearsal*:

1. ***Organization.*** As we discovered earlier, organization is one of the most important elements in memory. It is particularly important during encoding. Two of the most important forms of organization during encoding are *chunking* for STM and *hierarchies* for LTM. To extend the capacity of short-term memory (5 to 9 units), we discussed how to organize the information into chunks. To successfully encode information for LTM, we need to organize these chunks into *hierarchies*, which involves arranging a number of related items into a few broad categories that are further divided and subdivided.

    For example, do you recall how Module 5 organized the large body of information about the nervous system into a hierarchy with smaller and smaller units or chunks? Look at Figure 20.6. Note how the hierarchy for the nervous system is similar to our newly created hierarchy for the current information. Can you see how arranging the information into such hierarchies helps make them more understandable and *memorable?* This is the reason we use so many hierarchies throughout this text (in the form of diagrams, tables, and end-of-section Visual

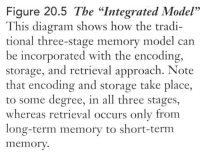

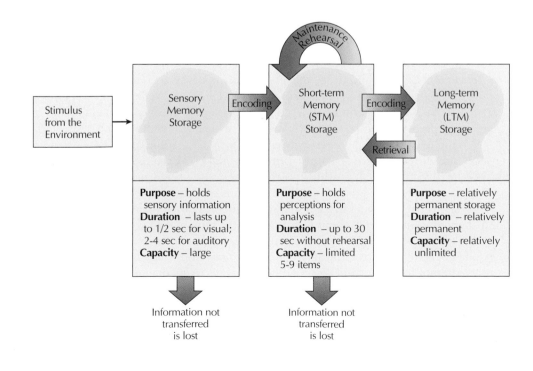

Figure 20.5 *The "Integrated Model"* This diagram shows how the traditional three-stage memory model can be incorporated with the encoding, storage, and retrieval approach. Note that encoding and storage take place, to some degree, in all three stages, whereas retrieval occurs only from long-term memory to short-term memory.

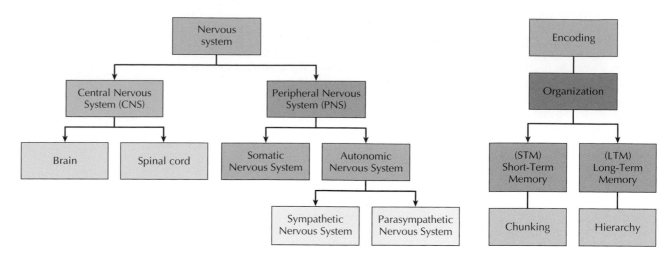

Figure 20.6 *Hierachies are a natural part of LTM.* Just as the diagram of the nervous system helped organize the material in Module 5, a similar diagram of the current information on memory helps you order and arrange the various terms. Encoding, storage, and retrieval in LTM are all improved through the use of hierarchies. This is the reason why this text contains so many tables, figures, and end-of-section Visual Summaries.

Summaries). This also explains why almost all college textbooks are hierarchically arranged. As you can see from the section outlines presented at the beginning of each unit, small subsets of ideas are grouped together as subheadings under a larger, main heading.

If you want to improve your memory in this and other courses, study these hierarchies carefully. Better yet, try making your own hierarchies when studying for exams. Although this may sound difficult, keep in mind that you already possess all the basic skills. Think back to the first day you walked around your college campus. You probably felt overwhelmed by all the buildings, sidewalks, and parking lots, and needed a map just to find your classes. After being on campus for a while, however, the map was discarded because you "naturally" organized all the information into personally meaningful chunks (science building, library, cafeteria) that were further organized into an overall personal hierarchy. Try using these same skills to arrange the large assortment of facts and concepts required for a typical college exam.

2. *Rehearsal.* Like organization, rehearsal also improves encoding for both short-term memory (STM) and long-term memory (LTM). As we learned earlier, if you need to hold information in STM for longer than 30 seconds, you can do a type of juggling act called *maintenance rehearsal,* where you simply keep repeating it over and over. This type of *shallow processing* works for some information that you don't need in long-term memory. But storage in LTM requires *deep processing,* or **elaborative rehearsal,** in which we think *deeply* about new information and tie it into previously stored memories. The previous comparison of the encoding, storage, and retrieval model to a computer is a good example of elaborative rehearsal. When you think deeply about this model and compare it to your previous knowledge of computers, it helps you learn and remember the new model. The immediate goal of elaborative rehearsal is to *understand*—not to memorize. Fortunately, this attempt to understand is one of the best ways to encode new information into long-term memory.

Why? According to Fergus Craik and Robert Lockhart's elaborative rehearsal, or what they call a *levels-of-processing approach* (1972), a deeper analysis of meaning

Elaborative Rehearsal *Linking new information to previously stored material (also known as deeper levels of processing)*

enables us to remember information better because we store it in LTM more effi-ciently. Have you noticed that older students in college classes often receive better grades? Although there are many reasons for this, their longer life and greater num-ber of experiences provide them with more LTM information available for elaborative rehearsal.

If you're a younger student or an older student just returning to college, you may have to work a little harder at *elaborative rehearsal* in your college courses. You can improve this ability and process information at a deeper level by:

- *Making it personal.* If you can't easily tag information to what you already know, create a new, personal example. For example, to encode and store the term *echoic memory*, look for examples of this in other people or yourself. Make a mental note when it happens and store the example with the term *echoic memory*.

- *Expanding (or elaborating on) the information.* To store the term *long-term mem-ory* in your actual LTM, think about what it would be like if you only had STM and could store information for only 30 seconds. Picture the life of H. M. (the man introduced in the opening vignette). The more you elaborate or try to understand something, the more likely you are to remember it.

- *Actively exploring and questioning new information.* Think about the term *iconic memory*. Ask yourself, "Why did they use this term?" Look up the term *icon* in the dictionary and you'll learn that *icon* is from the Greek word for image or likeness.

- *Trying to find meaningfulness.* When you meet people at a party, don't just main-tenance-rehearse their name. Ask about their favorite TV shows, their career plans, political beliefs, or anything else that requires deeper analysis. You'll be much more likely to remember their name.

Integrating Storage with the Three-Stage Memory Model

As we discovered earlier, both sensory memory and STM store a very limited amount of time. Our most important and valuable storehouse is that of LTM. Given that LTM is virtually unlimited in duration and capacity, we obviously collect a vast amount of information over a lifetime. How do we store it? Just as with encoding, organization and hierarchies are key to effective storage in LTM. As you can see in Figure 20.7, LTM appears to be composed of several interacting systems and subsystems — the brain's built-in *hierarchy*. At the top of the hierarchy, you can see that LTM is divided into two major systems — *explicit/declarative memory* and *implicit/nondeclarative memory*.

1. *Explicit/declarative memory.* *Explicit memory* refers to intentional learning or con-scious knowledge. It is *memory with awareness*. If asked to remember your Social Security number, your first kiss, the name of your first-grade teacher, and the name of your current psychology professor, you can report the answers directly (explic-itly). This type of memory also is referred to as *declarative memory*, because, if asked, you consciously know the information and can "declare" it (or state it in words). When people think of memory, they often are referring to this type of declarative memory (Best, 1999; Hayne, Boniface, & Barr, 2000).

   Explicit/declarative memory can be further subdivided into two parts — *semantic memory* and *episodic memory*. **Semantic memory** is memory for general knowledge, rules, events, objective facts, and specific information. It is our inter-nal mental dictionary or encyclopedia of stored knowledge. If you read and remember terms like *semantic*, *episodic*, *explicit/declarative*, and *implicit/nondeclara-tive*, it is because you have stored them in your semantic memory.

   In contrast, **episodic memory** is somewhat like a mental diary (Best, 1999; Tulving, 1985). It records the major events (or *episodes*) that happen to us or take place in our presence. Some of our episodic memories are short-lived (what you ate for breakfast today), whereas others can last a lifetime (your first romantic kiss,

Explicit/Declarative Memory *Sub-system within long-term memory that consciously stores facts, information, and personal life experiences*

Semantic Memory *A part of explicit/declarative memory that stores general knowledge; a mental encyclopedia or dictionary*

Episodic Memory *A part of explicit/declarative memory that stores memories of personally experienced events; a mental diary of a person's life*

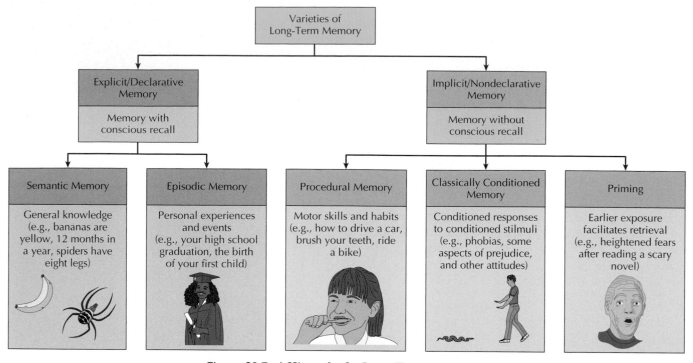

Figure 20.7 *A Hierarchy for Long-Term Memory.* Taking time to study and memorize the separate systems and subsystems for long-term memory can improve your understanding and mastery of this material because it involves *elaborative rehearsal* or a *deeper level of processing.*

your high-school graduation, the birth of your first child). Have you ever wondered why toddlers are quite capable of remembering events they experienced in previous months, yet most of us as adults can recall almost nothing of those years before the age of 3? Why don't we remember our birth, our second birthday, or our family's big move to a new city? These were major events in our life. Research suggests that a concept of "self," sufficient language development, and growth of the frontal lobes of the cortex (along with other structures) may be necessary before these early events (or episodes) can be encoded and retrieved many years later (Harley & Reese, 1999; Simcock & Hayne, 2002; Uehara, 2000).

2. ***Implicit/nondeclarative memory.*** *Implicit memory* refers to unintentional learning or unconscious knowledge. It is *memory without awareness.* For a simple test of implicit memory, try telling someone else how you tie your shoelaces—without demonstrating the actual behavior! Because your memory of this skill is unconscious and hard to describe in words (to "declare"), this type of memory sometimes also is referred to as *nondeclarative.*

Implicit/nondeclarative memory consists of *procedural* motor skills like tying your shoes, riding a bike, and brushing your teeth. It also includes simple, classically conditioned responses, such as fears or taste aversions. As you recall from Module 16, my previous student who ate the candy bar with the crawling maggots has a conditioned emotional response (or *implicit/nondeclarative memory*) that makes her immediately and (unconsciously) nauseated whenever she sees or thinks about this particular candy. (If you're also feeling queasy right now, I apologize. I'm not trying to torture you. I repeat her story because it helps you visualize and remember the term *implicit/nondeclarative memory.*)

In addition to procedural and classically conditioned responses, this type of memory also includes **priming,** where a prior exposure to a stimulus (or *prime*) facilitates

Implicit/Nondeclarative Memory *Subsystem within long-term memory that consists of unconscious procedural skills, simple classically conditioned responses, and priming*

Priming *Prior exposure to a stimulus (or prime) facilitates or inhibits the processing of new information, even when one has no conscious memory of the initial learning and storage*

One way to remember each of these various systems and subsystems is to encode them in your long-term memory (LTM) using *elaborative rehearsal* or a *deeper level of processing*. Our section opening incident included the story of Elizabeth Loftus' unfortunate experiences with her mother's death and the story of H. M. Try your hand at elaborative rehearsal by filling in the following blanks with the name of the correct subdivision of LTM.

1. When Elizabeth Loftus couldn't clearly remember the events and experiences surrounding her mother's death, she was experiencing problems with her _____ memory.
2. The fact that Loftus went on to become a university professor and famous research psychologist suggests that her _____

memory is filled with general knowledge.
3. After his operation, H.M. could not tell the researchers the day of the week, the year, or even about his last meal. His _____ memory was lacking.
4. Because his _____ memory remained intact, H.M. could acquire new manual or problem-solving skills, such as playing tennis.
5. When tested under specialized conditions that do not require conscious remembering, H.M. can approach or even match the performance of normal participants. This suggests that his _____ memory is intact.

Answers: 1. episodic; 2. semantic; 3. declarative; 4. procedural; 5. implicit/nondeclarative.

---

or inhibits the processing of new information (Tulving, 2000). Such priming effects may occur even when we do not consciously remember being exposed to the prime. Have you noticed how your fears are heightened after reading a Stephen King novel, and your romantic feelings increased after watching a romantic movie? This is because your previous experiences *prime* you to more easily notice and recall related instances. (It also suggests a practical way to improve your love life—go to romantic movies.)

In sharp contrast to the loss of explicit/declarative memory, H.M.'s implicit/nondeclarative memory was relatively unaffected. He could remember his previous procedural skills (such as brushing his teeth and dressing himself), and he also can learn some new motor skills, such as writing words upside down (Corkin, 2002; Milner, 1965). Interestingly, each time he was asked to perform the task of upside-down writing, his speed improved, but he had no memory of having performed it before.

Integrating Retrieval with the Three-Stage Memory Model

So far, we've discussed how encoding and storage can be integrated with the three-stage memory model. In this section, we will examine *retrieval*, the process of accessing stored information, and how it also can be integrated with the three-stage model. To do this, we examine two types of retrieval cues — recognition and recall.

Much like *priming*, a **retrieval cue** is a stimulus that can begin a retrieval process from LTM (Klatzky, 1984). There are basically two types of retrieval cues—either specific or general. When you retrieve a memory using a specific cue, it is called **recognition.** You only have to identify (or "recognize") the correct response, as in a multiple-choice exam. When you use a general cue, it is called **recall.** You must retrieve (or recall) previously learned material, as in an essay exam.

If you pick out a particular face you have previously seen from a police lineup, you use *recognition* to check the specific cue (the face) against your LTM contents to see if something matches (Figure 20.8). If, on the other hand, you remember someone's name from a description of that person (a general cue), you are using *recall*, which is a much more difficult task (Bransford, 1979). During recall, you use a general cue to generate a list of material associated with that cue and then search through LTM to

Study**T**ip

To help you remember (and fully appreciate) both explicit/declarative and implicit/nondeclarative memories, think back to the case of H.M. (described in the section opener). What would your life be like if your entire explicit/declarative memory was limited to information stored before a certain moment in your past? After surgery to treat his epilepsy in 1953, H. M. could not encode or store any new factual (semantic) information or personal experiences (episodic memories). As H.M. you wouldn't be in college, which requires lots of storage of new information, and you couldn't fall in love and get married because each time you met your loved one it would (for you) be the first time.

Retrieval Cue *A clue or prompt that helps stimulate recall and retrieval of a stored piece of information from long-term memory*

Recognition *Retrieving a memory using a specific cue*

Recall *Retrieving a memory using a general cue*

Figure 20.8 *Recognition memory.*
Results from a study of recognition memory in which participants were asked to identify pictures of their high school classmates. As you can see, both name recognition and picture recognition remain high, whereas recall memory would be expected to drop significantly over time.

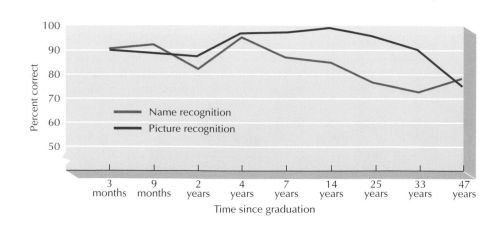

find something that matches the cue (Best, 1999, p. 143). This general cue often isn't enough to locate a single piece of information because the list of possible matches is often quite large. Therefore, the more specific the cue, the more likely you are to retrieve the needed information from your memory. One additional tip: Don't hesitate to ask questions of your professor during exams. Most professors allow this, and their answers often provide valuable retrieval cues.

Application

APPLYING PSYCHOLOGY TO STUDENT LIFE

Using Retrieval Strategies on Exams

Encoding Specificity Principle
Retrieval of information is improved when conditions of recovery are similar to the conditions when information was encoded

As we've just seen, retrieval cues, such as recognition and recall, are frequently used on exams. One lesser known strategy is to recreate the original learning conditions. The ease of retrieval depends on the match between the way information is encoded and later retrieved; this is known as the **encoding specificity principle** (Tulving & Thompson, 1973). Three important research findings are related to this principle that may help improve your exam scores:

TRY THIS

YOURSELF

Application

Close your eyes and try to *recall* the names of Santa's nine reindeer. Most people can only recall 4 to 5 names. Now turn to page 271 for a *recognition* test on the same material.

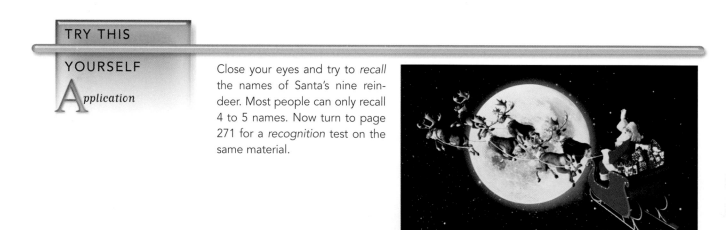

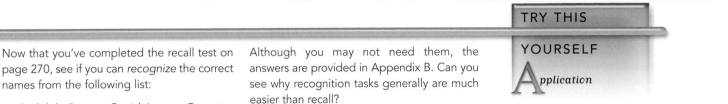

Now that you've completed the recall test on page 270, see if you can *recognize* the correct names from the following list:

Rudolph, Dancer, Cupid, Lancer, Comet, Blitzen, Crasher, Donder, Prancer, Dasher, Vixen

Although you may not need them, the answers are provided in Appendix B. Can you see why recognition tasks generally are much easier than recall?

- *Context and retrieval.* Have you noticed that you do better on a test when you take it in the same seat and classroom where you originally studied the material? This happens because the location is a retrieval cue to the material you studied. Godden and Baddeley (1975) demonstrated how context affects learning and memory in a clever study some years ago. They had underwater divers learn a list of 40 words either on land or underwater. The divers had better recall for lists they had encoded underwater if they also were underwater at retrieval; conversely, lists encoded above water were better recalled above water. This can be one reason why we feel confident about material while studying at home but have trouble recalling it at school later.

- *Mood congruence.* When you're sad or angry, do you tend to remember similar events and circumstances where you were sad or angry in the past? The idea that a given mood tends to evoke memories that are consistent with that mood is called *mood congruence.*

  Research shows that people remember something better if their emotional moods are the same at the time when they learn something and during the time when they try to retrieve it (Kenealy, 1997). If you suffer from test anxiety, you might try recreating the relaxed mood you had while studying by taking deep breaths and reassuring yourself during exams. In addition, you might want to artificially increase your anxiety level while studying by reminding yourself of the importance of good grades or your long-range career plans. By lowering your test anxiety and upping your study anxiety, you create a better balance or match between your exam mood and your study mood. This should improve your retrieval.

- *State-dependent retrieval.* Research also has shown that if you learn something while under the influence of a drug, such as caffeine, you will remember it more easily when you take that drug again than at other times (Baddeley, 1998). Some students have found that drinking a cup of coffee while studying and before an exam does improve their performance. One student jokingly asked if he should drink alcohol as he studied and then again during exams! I reminded him that alcohol and most other drugs impair memory, as well as create serious health and social problems (Module 15).

■ Biological Perspective: Memory's Effect on the Brain and Nervous System

Our two previous models of memory (the traditional three stage and the encoding, storage, and retrieval approach) emphasize how information is processed into memories. In this section, we focus our attention on the biological aspects of memory. It is obvious that something physical must happen in the brain and nervous system when

"I wonder if you'd mind giving me directions. I've never been sober in this part of town before."

How does a sea slug learn and remember? After repeated squirting with water, followed by a mild shock, the sea slug, Aplysia, responds by releasing more neurotransmitters at certain synapses, which allows the circuit to communicate more efficiently. Similar structural changes in human synapses help explain how we also learn and remember.

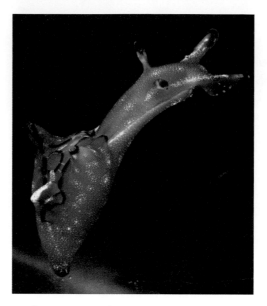

we learn something new. (How else could we later recall and use this information?) In this section, we will first look at neuronal and synaptic changes that occur with memory. Then we will discuss hormonal influences on memory. Finally, in the Research Highlight we explore the anatomy of memory — where memory is located in the brain.

Neuronal and Synaptic Changes in Memory

As you recall from earlier modules learning modifies the brain's neural networks. As a response is learned, specific neural pathways are established that become progressively more excitable and responsive. While you are learning to play tennis, for example, the repeated practice builds neural "pathways" that make it easier and easier to get the ball over the net. This prolonged strengthening of neural firing is called **long-term potentiation (LTP)**. There are at least two ways that LTP can happen:

Long-Term Potentiation (LTP)
Long-lasting increase in neural excitability believed to be a biological mechanism for learning and memory

1. *Repeated stimulation of a synapse can strengthen the synapse by causing the dendrites to grow more spines* (Barinaga, 1999). This would result in more synapses, more receptor sites, and more sensitivity. As seen in Module 19, such structural changes were first demonstrated when rats placed in enriched environments grew more sprouts on their dendrites compared to those of rats raised in deprived environments (Rosenzweig, Benet, & Diamond, 1972).

2. *The ability of a particular neuron to release its neurotransmitters can be increased or decreased.* This is shown from research with *Aplysia*, sea slugs, which can be classically conditioned to reflexively withdraw their gills when squirted with water. After the conditioning occurs, the slugs release more neurotransmitters at certain synapses, and these synapses become more efficient at transmitting signals (see Module 19). Further evidence comes from researchers at Princeton University who have created mice with an added gene, which results in additional receptors for a neurotransmitter named NMDA (*N*-methyl-D-aspartate). These genetic mutant "smart mice" performed significantly better on memory tasks than did normal mice (Tang, Wang, Feng, Kyin, & Tsien, 2001; Tsien, 2000). In fact, they were so far

Improving memory through genetic engineering. Scientists have created mice with an added gene, which so improved their memory they were named "Doogie" after the boy genius on the television show, Doogie Howser, M.D. This "Doogie" mouse stands on an object used in one of their standard learning and memory tests.

superior that the researchers named them Doogie after the boy genius on the TV show *Doogie Howser, M.D.*

Obviously, it is difficult to generalize from sea slugs and mice. However, research on long-term potentiation (LTP) in humans also has been widely supportive (Kikusui, Aoyagi, & Kaneko, 2000; Sutherland & McNaughton, 2000).

Hormonal Changes and Memory

Hormones also have a significant effect on memory. When stressed or excited, we naturally produce hormones that arouse the body, such as epinephrine and cortisol (see Module 8). These hormones in turn affect the amygdala (a subcortical structure involved in emotion), which in turn stimulates the hippocampus and cerebral cortex (other parts of the brain important for memory storage). Research on humans and laboratory animals has shown that direct injections of epinephrine or cortisol, or electrical stimulation of the amygdala, will increase the encoding and storage of new information (Akirav & Richter-Levin, 1999; Buchanan & Lovallo, 2001; McGaugh & Roozendaal, 2002). However, prolonged or excessive stress (and increased levels of cortisol) can interfere with memory (Al'absi, Hugdahl, & Lovallo, 2002; Heffelfinger & Newcomer, 2001; McAllister-Williams & Rugg, 2002).

Can you see why heightened (but not excessive) arousal might enhance memory? To survive, human or nonhuman animals must remember exactly how they got into a dangerous situation and how they got out of it. The naturally produced surge of hormones apparently alerts our brains to "pay attention and remember!"

The power of hormones on memory also can be seen in what are known as *flashbulb memories* — vivid images of circumstances associated with surprising or strongly emotional events (Brown & Kulik, 1977; Davidson & Glisky, 2002). Do you remember the moment you learned about the September 11, 2001, terrorist attacks on the World Trade Center and Pentagon? Is this memory so clear that it seems like a flashbulb went off, capturing every detail of the event in your memory? Assassinations (JFK, Bobby Kennedy, Martin Luther King, Jr.), important personal events (graduation, illnesses, birth of a child), and, of course, horrific terrorist attacks have lasting effects on memory. We secrete fight-or-flight hormones when we initially hear of the event and replay these events in our minds again and again, which makes for stronger memories.

Despite their intensity, flashbulb memories are not as accurate as you might think (Squire, Schmolck, & Buffalo, 2001). For example, in a study of flashbulb memories regarding the verdict in the O.J. Simpson trial, researchers asked participants about their memories 15 months after the verdict and again at 32 months. They found significant alterations in their flashbulb memories (Schmolck, Buffalo, & Squire, 2000). Thus, not even flashbulb memories are immune to alteration. It also is important to note the problems with "hormonally induced memory." If you've ever become so anxious that you "blanked out" during an exam or while giving a speech, you understand that hormones can interfere with both the formation and retrieval of memories.

The terrorist attack on the World Trade Center is a flashbulb memory for most people.

THE FAR SIDE® BY GARY LARSON

I was just getting ready to cross the interstate.

I was down by the edge of the lake at the time.

I was in the glen, just finishing a new burrow when I got the news.

I was looking for crawdads in my favorite creek.

I was under a rock, getting ready to shed.

More facts of nature: All forest animals, to this very day, remember exactly where they were and what they were doing when they heard that Bambi's mother had been shot.

Can you label the memory experience of these forest animals? Can you also recognize the unintended benefit of studying psychology?

Looking for Memory in All the Right Places

So far, our discussion of the biological perspective has focused on the formation of memories as a result of neural changes or hormonal influences. But where is memory stored? What parts of the brain are involved? One of the first scientists to explore this question was Karl Lashley (1890–1958). Believing that memory was *localized,* or stored in a specific brain area, Lashley began with a standard learning maze experiment for rats. Once the maze was learned, he surgically removed tiny portions of the rats' brains and then retested their memory of the maze. After 3 decades of frustrating research, Lashley found that rats were still able to run the maze regardless of the area of cortex he removed (Lashley, 1929, 1950). Lashley joked, "I sometimes feel in reviewing the evidence on localization of the memory trace, the necessary conclusion is that learning is not possible" (1950, p. 477). Failing to locate a single brain site for memory, Lashley ultimately decided memories were not localized. Instead, they were *distributed* throughout the cortex. Later research suggests that Lashley was both right and wrong: Memory tends to be localized *and* distributed throughout the brain — not just the cortex.

Since Lashley's time, the brain structures involved in long-term memory (LTM) have been under investigation for many years. Today, research techniques are so advanced that we can experimentally induce and measure memory-related brain changes as they occur — on-the-spot reporting! For example, James Brewer and his colleagues (1998) used functional magnetic resonance imaging (fMRI) to locate areas of the brain responsible for encoding memories of pictures. They showed 96 pictures of indoor and outdoor scenes to participants while scanning their brains, and then later tested them on their ability to recall those pictures. Brewer and his colleagues identified the right prefrontal cortex and the parahippocampal cortex as the most active during the encoding of the pictures. As you can see in Figure 20.9, these are only two of several brain regions involved in memory storage. Although these multiple storage areas may frustrate you as a student of psychology, keep in mind that this same complexity and ongoing research may someday lead to improved treatment and cures for serious memory disorders such as Alzheimer's disease and senility.

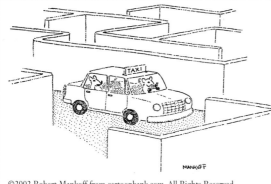

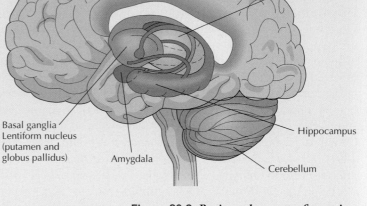

Figure 20.9 *Brain and memory formation.* Damage to any one of these areas can affect encoding, storage, and retrieval of memories.

Brain Area	Known or Suspected Relationship to Memory
Amygdala	Emotional memory (Buchanan & Lovallo, 2001; McGaugh & Roozendaal, 2002)
Basal Ganglia and Cerebellum	Creation and storage of implicit/nondeclarative memories (such as skills, habits, and simple classical conditioned responses) (Baddeley et al., 2000; Jog, Kubota, Connolly, Hillegaart, & Graybiel, 1999; Steinmetz, 1998)
Hippocampal Formation (Hippocampus and Surrounding Area)	Memory recognition; implicit, explicit, spatial, episodic memory; declarative long-term memory; sequences of events (Fernandez et al., 1999; Fortin, Agster, & Eichenbaum, 2002; Heckers et al., 2002)
Thalamus	Formation of new memories and working memory (Bloom & Lazerson, 1988; Johnson & Ojemann, 2001; Manoach et al., 2000)
Cortex	Encoding of explicit/declarative memories; storage of episodic and semantic memories; skill learning; priming; working memory (Abel et al., 2000; Huettel et al., 2002; Romo, Brody, Hernandez, & Lemus, 1999)

Assessment

CHECK & REVIEW

Integration Model and Biological Perspective

Most psychologists currently emphasize an integration of the traditional *three-stage memory model* and the *encoding, storage, and retrieval approach.*

We first encode information when we transfer it from sensory memory to short-term memory, and then again during the transfer from STM to LTM. Organization and rehearsal are important to successful encoding. To improve encoding during STM, we can use the organizational method of *chunking* or the techniques of *maintenance rehearsal.* To improve LTM, we can use the organizational strategy of creating

hierarchies and the technique called *elaborative rehearsal.*

Storage in LTM is divided into two major systems—**explicit/declarative** and **implicit/nondeclarative** memory. Explicit/declarative memory can be further subdivided into two parts—**semantic** and **episodic** memory.

Retrieval from LTM relies on **retrieval cues** (**recognition** and **recall**) and the **encoding specificity principle.**

The biological perspective of memory focuses on changes in neurons (through **long-term potentiation**) and hormones, as well as on searching for the locations of memory in the brain. Memory tends to be localized *and* distributed throughout the brain — not just in the cortex.

Questions

1. What is the difference between semantic and episodic memory?
2. Taking a multiple-choice test requires _____, whereas essay tests involve _____.
3. Describe the two processes involved in LTP.
4. Your vivid memory of what you were doing when you learned about the attack on the World Trade Center is an example of _____. (a) the encoding specificity principle; (b) long-term potentiation; (c) latent learning; (d) a flashbulb memory.

Answers to Questions can be found in Appendix B.

ACTIVE LEARNING WORKSHEET   MODULE 20

Circle the correct answer to the following questions, and then compare your answers with those in Appendix B.

1. _____ is the initial storage of information within the senses; _____ is the working memory where information is briefly stored and processed; and _____ contains information and experiences that have been stored for future use.
    a. maintenance storage; desk top processing; episodic memory
    b. mnemonic memory; semantic memory; episodic memory
    c. sensory; short-term memory; long-term memory
    d. recognition; recall; consolidation

2. A two-year-old wants to remind his parent to take him to the toy store. He keeps saying "Toys-R-Us" over and over, while he's being dressed and eating. Which memory system is he most likely using to retain the name of the toy store while he's being distracted by dressing and eating?
    a. emergency
    b. sensory
    c. short-term
    d. long-term

3. The capacity of your short-term memory can be increased through the use of _____.
    a. elaborative detention
    b. maintenance rehearsal
    c. redintegration
    d. chunking

4. You can improve the likelihood of retrieval of important information if you think deeply about new information and tie it into previously stored memories. This approach is called _____.
   a. recapitulation
   b. redintegration
   c. distributed practice
   d. elaborative rehearsal

5. If you know all the names of your elementary school teachers, their names are stored in your _____ memory, but if you remember that your second grade teacher made you stay after class for chewing gum in class, this information is stored in your _____ memory.
   a. visual; verbal
   b. connotative; denotative
   c. semantic; episodic
   d. lexical; representational

6. If you remember that your Aunt got married on September 18, 2001 because it was exactly a week after the terrorist attack on the World Trade Center, you are using a _____ event to retrieve information from _____ memory.
   a. landmark; long-term
   b. flashbulb; working
   c. landmark; semantic
   d. flashbulb; long-term

7. The subsystem within long-term memory that consciously stores facts, information, and personal life experiences is known as _____.
   a. long-term memory
   b. semantic memory
   c. explicit/declarative memory
   d. sensory memory

8. Your high school graduation and the birth of your first child are memories that are most likely to be stored in your _____ memory.
   a. implict/nondeclarative
   b. episodic
   c. short-term
   d. semantic

9. You just bought a new Subaru car and now you notice that lots of people seem to be driving the same car. This is an example of _____.
   a. egocentrism
   b. priming
   c. the self-serving bias
   d. selective identification

10. When you attend your 20-year high school reunion, you find that you immediately remember most of your classmates, but you worry because you seem to have forgotten most of their names. This is an example of _____.
    a. the superior quality of episodic memories
    b. the decay theory of forgetting
    c. how recognition is easier than recall
    d. state-dependent memory

MODULE 21
MEMORY FAILURES

Assessment

What causes forgetting? How can we prevent forgetting of important information?

■ Why do We Forget? A Number of Causes

Memory is what makes you wonder what you've forgotten.

ANONYMOUS

It may surprise you to learn that forgetting is essential to the proper functioning of memory. Think about what your life would be like if you couldn't forget. Your LTM would be filled with meaningless data, such as what you ate for breakfast every morning of your life. Similarly, think of the incredible pain and sorrow you would continuously endure if you couldn't distance yourself from tragedy through forgetting. Forgetting unnecessary or painful information, then, is essential to our lives. But what about those times when forgetting is an inconvenience or even dangerous? What causes forgetting? How can we prevent forgetting of important information?

Research Findings

These questions have been important issues in psychology ever since Hermann Ebbinghaus, a pioneer memory researcher who often used himself as his only subject, first introduced the experimental study of learning and forgetting in 1885. To measure memory performance, he calculated how long it took him to learn a list of *nonsense syllables*. For his trials, Ebbinghaus chose three-letter nonsense syllables such as *SIB* and *RAL* because they were equally difficult to learn. Furthermore, nonsense syllables don't have the meanings and associations that words do, thus avoiding the complications of previous learning.

After Ebbinghaus memorized lists of nonsense syllables until he knew them perfectly, he retested his memory at regular intervals. He found that 1 hour after he knew a list perfectly, he remembered only 44 percent of the syllables. A day later, he recalled 35 percent, and a week later only 21 percent. Figure 21.1 presents his famous (and somewhat depressing) "forgetting curve."

Do we forget everything this fast? If you were to forget textbook materials and lecture notes this rapidly, you would be able to pass a test only if you took it immediately after studying the material. An hour later, you would fail the test because you would remember less than half of what you had studied. Keep in mind, however, that the forgetting curve in Figure 21.1 applies to meaningless nonsense syllables. Meaningful material is much less likely to be forgotten. The material you study for a test can be retained much longer if you make an effort to make it meaningful through elaborative rehearsal. But meaningful or not, you will still forget some of what you have studied.

On a more cheerful note, after some time passed and he had forgotten the list, Ebbinghaus also calculated the time it took to relearn the same list. He found that relearning a list took less time than the initial learning period; this is known as **relearning** (or the *savings method*). Ebbinghaus's research suggests that we often retain some memory for things we have learned, even when we seem to have forgotten them completely. This finding should be encouraging to you if you studied a foreign language years ago but are no longer proficient in recalling or recognizing the vocabulary. You could expect to relearn the material more rapidly the second time.

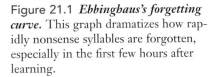

Figure 21.1 *Ebbinghaus's forgetting curve.* This graph dramatizes how rapidly nonsense syllables are forgotten, especially in the first few hours after learning.

Relearning *Learning material a second time, which usually takes less time than original learning (also called the savings method)*

Overcoming Problems with Forgetting

Since Ebbinghaus's original research, scientists have discovered numerous factors that contribute to forgetting — which may have important implications for your life as a student. Two of the most important are the *serial position effect* and *spacing of practice:*

1. *Serial position effect.* When study participants are given lists of words to learn and are allowed to recall them in any order they choose, they remember the words at the beginning *(primacy effect)* and the end of the list *(recency effect)* better than those in the middle, which are quite often forgotten (Jones & Roediger, 1995; Suhr, 2002) (Figure 21.2). The general term, including both the primacy effect and recency effect, is known as the **serial position effect.**

   The reasons for this effect are complex, but they do help explain why material at the beginning and end of a chapter is better remembered than that in the middle, or why you remember the first people you meet at a party and the last. It also has interesting applications for your employment success. If a potential employer calls to set up an interview, you can increase their memory for you and your application by asking to be either the first or last candidate.

2. *Spacing of practice.* Despite their best intentions, students often study in ways that encourage forgetting. In addition to studying in noisy places where attention is easily diverted and interference is maximized, they often try to memorize too much at one time by "cramming" the night before an exam. As the Tools for Student Success section in Module 4 emphasized, the single most important key to improving grades may be *distributed study.* **Distributed practice** refers to spacing your learning periods, with rest periods between sessions. Cramming is called **massed practice** because the time spent learning is massed into long, unbroken intervals. John Donovan and David Radosevich (1999) compared 63 separate studies and found that distributed practice produced superior memory and learning compared with massed practice. Unfortunately, research shows that most students do most of their studying right before the test (Taraban, Maki, & Rynearson, 1999).

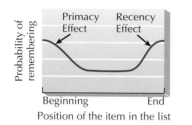

Figure 21.2 *The serial position effect.* If you try to recall a list of similar items, you'll tend to remember the first and last items best.

Serial Position Effect *Remembering information at the beginning and the end of a list better than material in the middle*

Distributed Practice *Practice (or study) sessions are interspersed with rest periods*

Massed Practice *Time spent learning is grouped (or massed) into long, unbroken intervals (also known as cramming)*

Cultural Differences in Memory and Forgetting

How do you remember the dates for all your quizzes, exams, and assignments in college? What memory aids do you use if you need to buy 15 items at the supermarket? Most people from industrialized societies rely on written shopping lists, calendars, books, notepads, or computers to store information and prevent forgetting. Can you imagine living in a culture without these aids? What would it be like if you had to rely solely on your memory to store and retrieve all your past, current, and future information? Would you develop better memory skills if you didn't have the ability to write things down? Do people raised in preliterate societies with rich oral traditions develop better memory skills than do people raised in literate societies?

   Ross and Millson (1970) designed a cross-cultural study to answer these questions. They compared American and Ghanaian college students' abilities to remem-

Culture and memory. *In many societies, tribal leaders pass down vital information through stories related orally. Because of this rich oral tradition, children living in these cultures have better memories for information related through stories than do other children.*

ber stories that were read aloud. Students listened to the stories without taking notes and without being told they would be tested. Two weeks later, all students were asked to write down as much as they could remember. As you might expect, the Ghanaian students had better recall than the Americans. Their superior performance was attributed to their culture's long oral tradition, which requires developing greater skill in encoding oral information (Matsumoto, 2000).

Does this mean that cultures with an oral tradition simply have better memories? Recall from Module 2 that a core requirement for scientific research is *replication* and the generation of related hypotheses and studies. In this case, when other researchers orally presented nonliterate African participants with lists of words instead of stories, they did *not* perform better (Cole, Gray, Glick, & Sharp, 1971). However, when both educated Africans and uneducated Africans were compared for memory of lists of words, the educated Africans performed very well (Scribner, 1979). This suggests that formal schooling helps develop memory strategies for things like lists of words, which preliterate participants may see as unrelated and meaningless.

Wagner (1982) conducted a study with Moroccan and Mexican urban and rural children that helps explain the effect of formal schooling. Participants were presented with seven cards that were then placed facedown in front of them, one at a time. They were then shown a card and asked to point out which of the seven cards was its duplicate. Everyone, regardless of culture or amount of schooling, was able to recall the latest cards presented (the *recency effect*). However, the amount of schooling significantly affected overall recall and the ability to recall the earliest cards presented *(primacy effect)*.

Wagner suggests that the primacy effect depends on *rehearsal* — the silent repetition of things you're trying to remember — and that this strategy is strongly related to schooling. As a child in a typical classroom, you were expected to memorize letters, numbers, multiplication tables, and a host of other basic facts. This type of formal schooling provides years of practice in memorization and in applying these skills in test situations. According to Wagner, memory has two parts: a "hardware" section that does not change across cultures and a "software" part that develops particular strategies for remembering, which are learned.

In summary, research indicates that the "software" (or programming) part of memory is affected by culture. In cultures in which communication relies on oral tradition, people develop good strategies for remembering orally presented stories. In cultures in which formal schooling is the rule, people learn memory strategies that help them remember lists of items. From these studies, we can conclude that across cultures, people tend to remember information that matters to them, and they develop memory skills to match the demands of their environment.

Theories of Forgetting

Five major theories have been offered to explain why forgetting occurs: *decay, interference, motivated forgetting, encoding failure,* and *retrieval failure*. Each theory focuses on a different stage of the memory process or on a particular type of problem in processing information.

Decay Theory   *Decay theory* is based on the commonsense assumption that memory, like all biological processes, degrades with time. Because memory is processed and stored in a physical form — for example, in a network of neurons — the relevant connections between neurons could be expected to decrease over time. It is well documented that skills and memory are degraded if they are not used for a long period of time (Rosenzweig, Barnes, & McNaughton, 2002; Villarreal, Do, Haddad, & Derrick, 2002). In other words, "use it or lose it." But it also is important to point out that conclusive, experimental support for decay theory is difficult to obtain. As we discovered in Module 13's discussion of extrasensory perception (ESP), it is impossible to *prove* ESP (or a previously stored memory) does *not* exist.

Interference Theory   Perhaps the most widely accepted theory, known as *interference theory*, suggests forgetting is caused by one memory competing with or trying to replace another memory (Anderson, Bjork, & Bjork, 1994; Conway & Pleydell-Pearce, 2000; Parkes & White, 2000). Interference is particularly strong among memories for similar events or having similar retrieval cues.

There are two types of interference, *retroactive* and *proactive* (Figure 21.3). When new information leads to forgetting of old material, it is called **retroactive interference** (acting backward in time). Learning your new phone number often causes forgetting of your old phone number (old, "retro" information is forgotten). Conversely, when old information leads to forgetting of new information, it is called **proactive interference** (acting forward in time). Old information (like the Spanish you learned in

Retroactive Interference *New information interferes with remembering old information; backward-acting interference*

Proactive Interference *Old information interferes with remembering new information; forward-acting interference*

Figure 21.3 *Two types of interference.* (a) *Retroactive* (backward acting) *interference* occurs when new information interferes with old information. This example comes from a story about an absent-minded icthyology professor (fish specialist) who refused to learn the name of his college students. Asked why, he said, "Every time I learn a student's name, I forget the name of a fish!" (b) *Proactive* (forward acting) *interference* occurs when old information interferes with new information. Have you ever been in trouble because you used an old partner's name to refer to your new partner? You now have a guilt-free explanation — proactive interference.

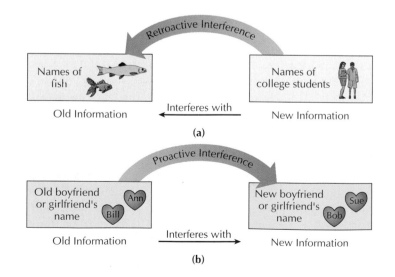

high school) may interfere with your ability to learn and remember your new college course in French.

Motivated Forgetting Theory A third theory of forgetting focuses on our sometimes unconscious wish to forget something unpleasant. According to the *motivated forgetting theory*, we forget for a reason, which leads to inhibition of retrieval. Forgetting the name of a disliked instructor who gave you a low grade, your dental appointment, or that embarrassing speech you made in eighth grade are all examples of motivated forgetting.

People obviously try to inhibit unpleasant or anxiety-producing thoughts or feelings. According to Freudian theory (Module 35), when they do this consciously, telling themselves not to worry about an upcoming final exam, it is called *suppression*. When they do it unconsciously, it is called *repression*. Sigmund Freud claimed that people repressed painful memories to avoid anxiety. If this is the case, appropriate therapy might overcome the repressive mechanisms and cause the repressed memory to be recovered. Memories of child abuse, sexual assault, war atrocities, and so on may create such painful experiences that the individual is highly motivated to forget them. The controversy surrounding *repressed memories* is discussed in Module 21.

Encoding Failure Whose head is on a U.S. penny? What is written at the top of a penny? Despite having seen a real penny thousands of times in your life, most of us have difficulty recognizing the details (Figure 21.4). Although the U.S. penny has eight distinguishing characteristics (Lincoln's head, the date it was minted, which way Lincoln is facing, and so on), the average person can only remember three (Nickerson & Adams, 1979). This is a great example of *encoding failure*. Unless we are coin collectors, we have little motivation to properly encode the details of a penny. Our sensory memory certainly received the information and passed it along (encoded it) to STM. But during STM, we probably decided there was no need to remember the precise details of the penny, so we did not encode it and pass it on for storage in LTM.

Retrieval Failure Theory If you've "blanked out" during an exam or a conversation and remembered the "forgotten" information later, you've had firsthand experience with the *retrieval failure* (or *cue-dependent*) *theory of forgetting*. According to this theory, memories stored in LTM aren't forgotten; they're just momentarily inaccessible as a result of such things as interference, faulty cues, or emotional states.

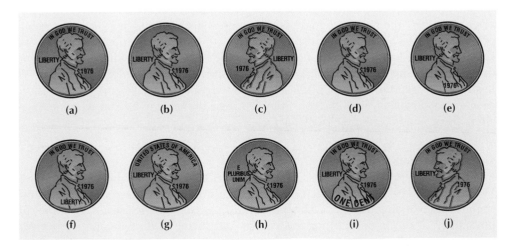

Figure 21.4 *Encoding failure.* Can you identify a drawing of a real penny among fakes?

Tip-of-the-Tongue Phenomenon
A retrieval failure that involves a sensation of knowing that specific information is stored in long-term memory but of being temporarily unable to retrieve it

One of the most common experiences of retrieval *failure* is the **tip-of-the-tongue (TOT) phenomenon** — the feeling that at any second, a word or event you are trying to remember will pop out from the "tip of your tongue" (Brown & McNeill, 1966; Schwartz, 2001; White & Abrams, 2002). Even though you can't say the word, you can often tell how many syllables it has, the beginning and ending letters, or what it rhymes with.

As you might imagine, it is difficult to distinguish retrieval failure from encoding failure. In fact, most memory failures are probably due to poor encoding, rather than retrieval failure (Howe & O'Sullivan, 1997).

Assessment

CHECK & REVIEW

Why do We Forget?

Hermann Ebbinghaus was one of the first researchers to extensively study forgetting. His famous "curve of forgetting" shows that it occurs most rapidly immediately after learning. However, Ebbinghaus also showed that **relearning** usually takes less time than original learning. Two important factors in forgetting are the **serial position effect** (in which material at the beginning and end of the list is remembered better than material in the middle) and spacing of practice (in which **distributed practice** is found to be superior to **massed practice**).

The decay theory of forgetting simply states that memory, like all biological processes, deteriorates as time passes. The interference theory of forgetting suggests

memories are forgotten because of either proactive or retroactive interference. **Proactive interference** occurs when old information interferes with newly learned information. **Retroactive interference** occurs when new information interferes with previously learned information. The motivated forgetting theory states that people forget things that are painful, threatening, or embarrassing. Some material is forgotten because it was never encoded from short-term memory to long-term memory (LTM). Other forgetting occurs because of retrieval failure; information stored in LTM is not forgotten but may at times be inaccessible.

Questions

1. When taking an exam, students often do better with items taken from the first and last of the chapter covered by the exam. This demonstrates the (a) superiority of distributed practice; (b) source amnesia; (c) state-dependent effect; (d) serial position effect.
2. How would you study for a test using distributed practice? Using massed practice?
3. Which theory of forgetting is being described in each of the following examples?
   a. You are very nervous about having to introduce all the people at a party, and you forget a good friend's name.
   b. You meet a friend you haven't seen for 25 years and you cannot remember his name.
   c. You were molested as a child and have completely forgotten the incident.

Answers to Questions can be found in Appendix B.

Assessment

What are the main memory problems?

■ Problems with Memory: Organic and External Causes

What happens when people abruptly lose all memory of their past in cases of amnesia, or slowly lose it with Alzheimer's? Imagine a total loss of memory. With no memories of the past and no way to make new memories, there would be no way to use our previous skills or to learn new ones. We wouldn't know each other, nor would we know ourselves. In fact, our very survival would be in question. In this section, we will discuss the serious personal and social issues associated with memory problems. We begin with organically caused problems (including injury, disease, and amnesia). We then discuss problems with the constructive nature of memory — how we sometimes alter, distort, and create memories.

Organic Causes

Some memory problems are the result of injury and disease (organic pathology). When people are in serious accidents or suffer strokes or other events that cause trauma to the brain, memory loss or deterioration can occur. Disease also can alter the physiology of the brain and nervous system and thereby affect memory processes.

This section focuses on two of the most common causes of organic memory failure: *brain injury* and *Alzheimer's disease.*

The Injured Brain   Have you ever wondered why parents and health professionals are so insistent about wearing a helmet during most sports activities? *Traumatic brain injury* happens when the skull makes a sudden collision with another object. The compression, twisting, and distortion of the brain inside the skull all cause serious and sometimes permanent damage to the brain. The frontal and temporal lobes often take the heaviest hit because they directly impact against the bony ridges inside the skull. In the United States, traumatic brain injury is the leading cause of neurological disorders among Americans ages 15 to 25. These injuries most commonly result from car accidents, falls, blows, and gunshot wounds.

What happens to our memory when we have a serious head injury or trauma? Loss of memory as a result of brain injury or trauma is called *amnesia.* In **retrograde amnesia** (acting backward in time), the patient loses memory for events that occurred *before* the accident yet has no trouble remembering things that happened afterward (old, "retro" memories are lost). Conversely, **anterograde amnesia** (acting forward in time) is a loss of memory for events that occur *after* an accident (Figure 21.5). Anterograde amnesia may result from a surgical injury or from diseases, such as chronic alcoholism. H. M. (the man introduced at the start of this section) suffers from both forms of amnesia. He has trouble remembering events that happened the last several years before the operation *(retrograde amnesia).* Also, for years after the operation, he thought the year was 1953 and that he was only 27 *(anterograde amnesia)* (Corkin, 2002). In most cases, retrograde amnesia is temporary and most patients recover slowly over time. Unfortunately, anterograde amnesia is usually permanent — as is the case with H. M. However, as you recall from the earlier discussion, H.M. (and others with amnesia) show surprising abilities to learn and remember implicit/nondeclarative tasks (such as procedural motor skills). The study of what patients with amnesia can and cannot learn is important for their personal benefit, as well as for our understanding of the basic organization of memory.

Alzheimer's Disease   **Alzheimer's disease** (AD) is a progressive mental deterioration that occurs most commonly in old age (Figure 21.6). The most noticeable early symptoms are disturbances in memory, beginning with typical incidents of forgetful-

Retrograde Amnesia *Loss of memory for events before an injury; backward-acting amnesia*

Anterograde Amnesia *Inability to form new memories after an injury; forward-acting amnesia*

Similar to retroactive and proactive interference, you can remember these two types of amnesia by emphasizing where the amnesia is occurring: In retrograde amnesia, it occurs with old ("retro") information, whereas with anterograde amnesia, it occurs with new information.

Alzheimer's [ALLS-high-merz] Disease *Progressive mental deterioration characterized by severe memory loss*

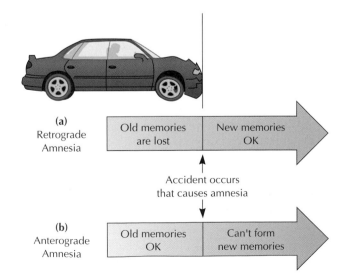

Figure 21.5 *Two types of amnesia.* (a) In *retrograde amnesia*, the individual loses some or all of his or her memories before the injury. This type of amnesia is commonly portrayed in TV soap operas and movies, where the main characters lose almost all memory of their previous jobs, family members, and even their own name. (b) In *anterograde amnesia*, the individual cannot form new memories for events that occur after the injury.

Figure 21.6 ***The effect of Alzheimer's
disease on the brain.*** Note the high
amount of red and yellow color (signs
of brain activity) in the positron emission tomography scans of the normal
brain on the left, and the reduced
activity in the brain of the Alzheimer's
disease patient on the right. The loss is
most significant in the temporal and
parietal lobes, which indicates that
these areas are particularly important
for storing memories.

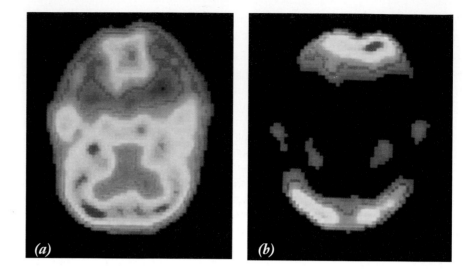

(a)   (b)

ness that everyone experiences from time to time. With AD, however, the forgetfulness
progresses until, in the final stages, the person fails to recognize loved ones, needs total
nursing care, and ultimately dies. Not all types of memory are affected equally. One of
the major differences between normal memory loss and memory loss due to AD is the
latter's extreme decrease in explicit declarative memory (Caltagirone, Perri, Carlesimo,
& Fadda, 2001; Mitchell et al., 2002). They fail to recall facts, information, and personal life experiences, yet they still retain some implicit/nondeclarative memories, such
as simple classically conditioned responses and procedural tasks like tying their
shoelaces.

Autopsies of the brain of people with AD show unusual *tangles* (structures formed
from degenerating cell bodies) and *plaques* (structures formed from degenerating
axons and dendrites). Hereditary AD runs in families and generally strikes its victims
between the ages of 45 and 55. Some experts believe the cause of AD is primarily
genetic, but others think genetic makeup may make some people more susceptible to
environmental triggers (Bernhardt, Seidler, & Froelich, 2002; Ewbank, 2002; Vickers
et al., 2000). In the fall of 2001, a clinical trial began with humans to test a highly
touted vaccine designed to reverse the course of AD. Unfortunately, the tests were
halted after a few months because 15 patients fell ill with brain inflammation. At the
current time, several other variations of the vaccine are being developed and trials are
planned to test them in patients (Martindale, 2002). In addition, a promising new drug
designed to clear away the plaques that clog AD patients' brains is now being tested
on a few human participants (Pepys et al., 2002).

Constructive Processes

Now that we've discussed organic causes of memory problems, you may want to try this
short memory test before we continue discussing additional sources of errors in memory:

Below is a series of words. Take a moment to carefully read through the entire list,
then cover it and write down all the words you can recall in 2 minutes. Now, compare
your recalled words with the original list.

Bed	Awake	Tired	Dream	Wake	Snooze	Snore
Rest	Blanket	Doze	Slumber	Nap	Peace	Yawn
Drowsy	Nurse	Sick	Lawyer	Medicine	Health	Hospital
Dentist	Physician	Patient	Stethoscope	Curse	Clinic	Surgeon

Number of correctly recalled words:

21 to 28 words = excellent memory
16 to 20 words = better than most
12 to 15 words = average
8 to 11 words = below average
7 or fewer = you might need a nap

How did you do? Do you have a good or excellent memory? Did you recall seeing the words *sleep* and *doctor?* If so, you have constructed a false memory. Look back over the list. These words were not there, yet over 65 percent of students will believe they saw these words. Why? The answers are found throughout this section. As we form new memories and sort through the old, we fill in missing pieces, we make "corrections," and rearrange information to make it logically consistent. Thus, the memory that we eventually retrieve is affected not just by the actual direct experiences we have had with the stimulus, but also by our guesses and inferences about its meaning. You falsely remembered *sleep* and *doctor* because they were logically consistent. As mentioned in the section opener, memory is *not* a faithful duplicate of an event; it is a **constructive process** where we actively shape and build on information as it is encoded and retrieved.

When we encode information, we *construct* a mental representation (not an exact recording). Think about a recent, important lecture from your psychology instructor that you (hopefully) encoded for storage in LTM. You obviously did not record a word-for-word copy of the lecture. You summarized, augmented, and tied it in with related memories you have in LTM. Similarly, when we retrieve information, we *reconstruct* the previously *constructed* memories, thus introducing another set of potential errors. If you need to retrieve the stored lecture from your LTM, you repeat the general ideas or facts that were said, while leaving out seemingly unimportant elements or misremembering the details.

Why isn't the original version stored in long-term memory? In addition to problems with general constructive processes that occur during encoding and retrieval, there are two more specific types of construction errors: *source amnesia* and the *sleeper effect*.

1. *Source amnesia.* People sometimes imagine or dream about something and later believe it really happened. Similarly, you might mistakenly recall that you heard specific lecture information from a friend during shared study times or read it in the text, rather than from your psychology professor. This is known as **source amnesia,** which occurs when the true source of the memory is forgotten (Leichtman & Ceci, 1995; Oakes & Hyman, 2001).

2. *Sleeper effect.* With the passage of time, we also tend to confuse reliable information with the unreliable. Research on the **sleeper effect** finds that when we first hear something from an unreliable source we tend to disregard that information in favor of a more reliable source. However, over time, the source of the information is forgotten and the unreliable information is no longer discounted (Underwood & Pezdek, 1998). This sleeper effect can be a significant problem when reliable and unreliable information are intermixed. As a critical thinker, can you see why advertisers of shoddy services or products might benefit from "channel surfing?" What happens to the LTM of the television viewer who skips from news programs to cable talk shows to infomercials? Can you see how a movie star who offers an opinion about a weight-loss diet might later be remembered as a dietary expert?

As a critical thinker, see if you can identify *source amnesia* and the *sleeper effect* in this childhood memory experienced by the famous cognitive and developmental psychologist Jean Piaget (1951):

One of my first memories would date, if it were true, from my second year. I can still see, most clearly, the following scene, in which I believed until I was about fif-

Constructive Process *Organizing and shaping of information during encoding and retrieval that may cause memory errors and distortions*

Source Amnesia *Attributing to a wrong source an event that we have experienced, heard about, read about, or imagined (also called source confusion or source misattribution)*

Sleeper Effect *Tendency to initially discount information from an unreliable source, but later consider it more trustworthy because the source is forgotten*

teen. I was sitting in my pram, which my nurse was pushing in the Champs-Élysées, when a man tried to kidnap me. I was held in by the strap fastened round me while my nurse bravely tried to stand between the thief and me. She received various scratches, and I can still see vaguely those on her face. Then a crowd gathered, a policeman with a short cloak and a white baton came up, and the man took to his heels. I can still see the whole scene, and can even place it near the tube station. When I was about fifteen, my parents received a letter from my former nurse saying that she had been converted to the Salvation Army. She wanted to confess her past faults, and in particular to return the watch she had been given as a reward on this occasion. She had made up the whole story, faking the scratches. I, therefore, must have heard, as a child, the account of this story, which my parents believed, and projected it into the past in the form of a visual memory, which was a memory of a memory, but false. [pp. 187–188]

How did you do? Did you identify *source amnesia* where Piaget falsely attributed his memory to his own experience rather than to his nursemaid's made-up story? Did you note how he incorporated her faked scratches into his own memory of actually seeing the scratches at the time of the "attempted kidnapping?" Because Piaget's parents trusted the nursemaid and considered her information reliable, the *sleeper effect* was not a factor in this false memory. I included it as a small test of your active reading.

Eyewitness Testimony and Repressed Memories

Misremembering the source for a new weight-loss product and Piaget's memory of being saved by a kind nursemaid may be relatively harmless memory problems. But what if the police had mistakenly arrested and convicted an innocent man because of Piaget's nursemaid's false claim? In this section, we will discuss two areas of memory problems that have profound legal and social implications: *eyewitness testimony* and *repressed memories*.

Eyewitness Testimony   You know the old saying "Seeing is believing." But can we really trust what we see — or *think* we see? In the past, one of the best forms

Dangers of eyewitness testimony.
Although 7 eyewitnesses identified the man in the far left photo (Father Pagano) as the "Gentleman Bandit" accused of several armed robberies, the man in the right photo (Robert Clouser) later confessed and was convicted of the crimes.

of trial evidence a lawyer could have was an eyewitness, yet numerous research studies have identified several problems with eyewitness testimony (Dysart, Lindsay, Hammond, & Dupuis, 2002; Loftus, 2000, 2001; Poole & Lindsay, 2002).

In one eyewitness study, participants were shown a film of a car driving through the countryside. Members of one group were asked to estimate how fast the car was going when it passed the barn. Participants in the other group who saw the same film were also asked to estimate the car's speed, but a barn was not mentioned. When all participants were later asked if they saw a barn in the film, six times as many in the group given the misinformation about the barn reported having seen it, even though it never appeared in the film (Loftus, 1982).

It is impossible to determine how often eyewitnesses are mistaken in their recollections of events, but experimental evidence indicates that the error rate might be disturbingly high. For example, in an experiment at the University of Nebraska, participants watched people committing a staged crime. About an hour later, they were asked to pick out suspects from mug shots, and a week later, from a lineup. None of the participants in the staged crime appeared in the mug shots or lineups, yet 20 percent of the eyewitnesses identified innocent people in the mug shots, and 8 percent identified innocent people in the lineup (Brown, Deffenbacher, & Sturgill, 1977).

How could the research participants have been so mistaken? Several properties of memory could combine to create the type of mistaken identity that occurred at the lineup stage. First, we know that seeing a mug shot would lead to familiarity, which might lead to false recognition during the later lineup. Next, we know that memory is constructive, so the participants might have constructed an inaccurate memory of the crime situation using memories instilled by the mug shots.

These problems are so well established and important that judges now allow expert testimony on the unreliability of eyewitness testimony and routinely instruct jurors on its limits (Durham & Dane, 1999; Ramirez, Zemba, & Geiselman, 1996). If you serve as a member of a jury or listen to accounts of crimes in the news, remind yourself of these problems. Also keep in mind that research participants in eyewitness studies generally report their inaccurate memories with great self-assurance and strong conviction (Migueles & Garcia-Bajos, 1999). Eyewitnesses to actual crimes may similarly identify — with equally high confidence — an innocent person.

Repressed Memories   Do you recall the opening story of Elizabeth, who suddenly remembered a childhood scene of finding her mother's drowned body? This is a true story of Elizabeth Loftus, one of the leading experts in modern memory research. The adult recovery of this gruesome childhood memory, although painful, also brought great relief. "I started putting everything into place. Maybe that's why I'm such a workaholic." It also seemed to explain why she had always been fascinated by the topic of memory and had spent so many years on its research.

After all this resolution and relief, however, her brother called to say there had been a mistake! The relative who told Elizabeth that she had been the one to discover her mother's body later remembered it had actually been Aunt Pearl, not Elizabeth Loftus. Other relatives also confirmed that it was Aunt Pearl. Even though Loftus is an expert on memory distortions and false memories, she suffered typical problems of memory construction.

As we've seen throughout this section, our memories are frequently faulty, and researchers have demonstrated that it is relatively easy to create false memories (Braun, Ellis, & Loftus, 2002; Loftus, 1993, 1997, 2001; Mazzoni & Memon, 2003). Seeing the words *sleep* and *doctor* in the previous list, Piaget's kidnapping memory, the eyewitness participants who later recalled a nonexistent barn, and Loftus's memory of finding her mother's body are all examples of false memories.

So what about repressed memories? Can people recover true childhood memories?
Repression, which was mentioned earlier as a part of motivated forgetting, is the supposed unconscious coping mechanism by which anxiety-provoking thoughts are prevented from reaching consciousness. Therefore, thoughts or memories that are extremely frightening to a person, such as memories of childhood sexual abuse, might be repressed. According to some research, these memories are *actively* and *consciously* "forgotten" in an effort to avoid the pain of their retrieval (Anderson, 2001). Others suggest that some memories are so painful they exist only in an *unconscious* corner of the brain, making them inaccessible to the individual (Bertram & Widener, 1999). In these cases, therapy would be necessary to unlock these hidden memories (Davies, 1996).

As you might imagine, this is a complex and controversial topic in psychology. No one doubts that some memories are forgotten and later recovered. When cued by a remark or experience, many people recover memories of long-forgotten events — a childhood trip to Disneyland, the move from one house to another, or details surrounding a painful event. What is questioned is the concept of *repressed memories* of painful experiences (especially childhood sexual abuse), and their storage in the unconscious mind (Goodman et al., 2003; Loftus & Polage, 1999). Critics suggest that most people who have witnessed or experienced a violent crime, or are adult survivors of childhood sexual abuse, have intense, persistent memories. They have trouble forgetting, not remembering.

Some critics also wonder whether therapists retrieve actual memories or inadvertently create false memories. Just as a scientist's *experimenter bias* might unintentionally influence participants' responses (Module 2), clinicians who sincerely believe a client might have been abused as a child may unintentionally influence that client's recall of information. Furthermore, if the clinician mentions possible abuse, the client's own constructive processes may lead him or her to create a false memory.

Remember how Loftus used her relative's suggestion that she found her mother's body to create her own detailed false memory? As a critical thinker, can you see how clients might respond similarly to their therapists' suggestions? Even though the clinician suggests only the possibility of abuse, the client might start to think about movies and books portraying other people's experiences and incorporate this information into his or her own memory and might forget where they originally heard these stories *(source amnesia)*. Over time, they also might forget these originally unreliable sources and see them as reliable (the *sleeper effect*).

Thus, the question "Are recovered memories true or false?" may be impossible to answer. As we've noted before, research clearly demonstrates that *all* our memories are imperfect constructions during encoding and reconstructions during retrieval. Attempting to label some memories as "true" and others as "false" may be misleading and oversimplifying.

The so-called repressed memory debate, however, has grown increasingly bitter, and research on both sides is hotly contested (Lindsay, 1998). This is not just an "academic debate." It has serious implications because civil lawsuits and criminal prosecutions are sometimes based on recovered memories of childhood sexual abuse, and family bonds are sometimes irreparably damaged by false accusations. It is dangerous to trust memory — recovered or repressed — to provide accurate recollections of the past. Researchers are currently seeking more information about the mechanisms underlying delayed remembering. (For more information about this research and the continuing controversy, call or write the American Psychological Association in Washington, D.C. Ask for the pamphlet "Questions and Answers about Memories of Childhood Abuse." Also check the *Psychology in Action* website.)

We will return to this hotly debated issue of repressed memories in Module 41. In the meantime, it is important to remember that child sexual abuse is a fact, not a disputed issue, and we must be careful not to ridicule or condemn people who recover true memories of abuse. In the same spirit, we must protect the innocent from wrongful accusations that come from false memories. We look forward to a time when we can justly balance the interests of the victim with those of the accused.

Elizabeth Loftus

Assessment

CHECK & REVIEW

Problems with Memory

Some memory problems are the result of injury and disease (organic pathology). Forgetting as a result of serious brain injuries or trauma is called *amnesia*. In **retrograde amnesia,** memory for events that occurred *before* the accident is lost. In **anterograde amnesia,** memory for events that occur *after* an accident is lost. **Alzheimer's disease** is a progressive mental deterioration and severe memory loss occurring most commonly in old age.

Memories are not exact duplicates. We actively shape and build on information as it is encoded, stored, and retrieved. There are two major errors that occur during the constructive processes of memory: **source amnesia** and the **sleeper effect.** Two areas of memory problems that have profound legal and social implications are *eyewitness testimony* and *repressed memories*.

Questions

1. Forgetting that results from brain damage or trauma is called _____.

2. Ralph couldn't remember anything that happened to him between the time he fell through the floor of his tree house and found himself in the hospital. His lack of memory for the interval between the events is called _____ amnesia. (a) retroactive; (b) proactive; (c) anterograde; (d) retrograde

3. Explain the difference between source amnesia and the sleeper effect.

4. Why is eyewitness testimony not considered reliable in a court of law?

Answers to Questions can be found in Appendix B.

Application

APPLYING PSYCHOLOGY TO STUDENT LIFE

Improving Memory and Exam Scores

After reading about all the problems and dangers associated with memory, you'll be glad to know that our memories are normally quite accurate and serve us well in most situations. Our memories have evolved to encode, store, and retrieve information vital to our survival. While working to secure our food and shelter, we constantly search and monitor our potentially dangerous environment. Even while sleeping, we process and store important memories. However, when faced with tasks like remembering precise details in a college text, the faces and names of potential clients, or where we left our house keys, our brains are simply not well equipped.

The beauty of the human brain is that we can recognize such limits and develop appropriate coping mechanisms. Just as our ancestors domesticated wild horses and cattle to overcome the physical limits of the human body, we can develop ways to improve our memory for fine detail. The field of psychology provides numerous helpful theories and concepts for improving memory, and concrete suggestions are sprinkled throughout this text. In this section, we will briefly summarize the most effective memory enhancement techniques. Then we close with a discussion of the "seven sins of forgetting," a topic with further tips for improving memory.

Specific Tips   Everyone can improve his or her memory. The harder you work at it, the better your memory will become. Below, we have summarized key points from this section that you can put into practice to improve your memory. (You might also recognize several points that were presented earlier in Tools for Student Success in Module 4.)

- *Pay attention and reduce interference.* If you really want to remember something, you must pay attention to it. So when you're in class, focus on the instructor and sit away from people who might distract you. When you study, choose a place with minimal interferences.

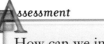

Assessment

How can we improve our memory?

(Left partial column, page behind:)

VISUAL SUMMARY

Memory
(Modules 20 and 21)

What is Memory?

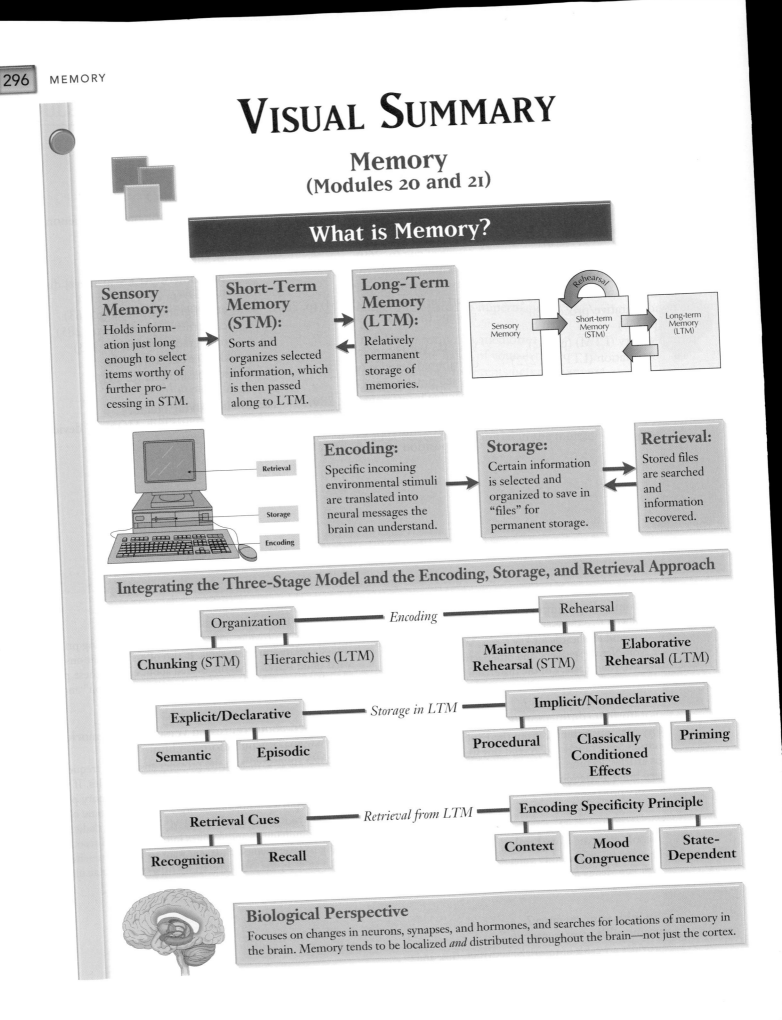

Sensory Memory:
Holds information just long enough to select items worthy of further processing in STM.

Short-Term Memory (STM):
Sorts and organizes selected information, which is then passed along to LTM.

Long-Term Memory (LTM):
Relatively permanent storage of memories.

Encoding:
Specific incoming environmental stimuli are translated into neural messages the brain can understand.

Storage:
Certain information is selected and organized to save in "files" for permanent storage.

Retrieval:
Stored files are searched and information recovered.

Integrating the Three-Stage Model and the Encoding, Storage, and Retrieval Approach

Organization — *Encoding* — Rehearsal

Chunking (STM) | Hierarchies (LTM) | Maintenance Rehearsal (STM) | Elaborative Rehearsal (LTM)

Explicit/Declarative — *Storage in LTM* — Implicit/Nondeclarative

Semantic | Episodic | Procedural | Classically Conditioned Effects | Priming

Retrieval Cues — *Retrieval from LTM* — Encoding Specificity Principle

Recognition | Recall | Context | Mood Congruence | State-Dependent

Biological Perspective
Focuses on changes in neurons, synapses, and hormones, and searches for locations of memory in the brain. Memory tends to be localized *and* distributed throughout the brain—not just the cortex.

Why Do We Forget?

Research Findings

- Ebbinghaus: Forgetting occurs most rapidly immediately after learning, but **relearning** usually takes less time than original learning.
- **Serial position effect**: Material at the beginning and end of the list is remembered better than material in the middle.
- Spacing of practice: **Distributed practice** is better than **massed practice**.

Theories of Forgetting

- *Decay* — Memory deteriorates over time.
- *Interference* — Memories forgotten due to **proactive interference** (old information interferes with new) or **retroactive interference** (new information interferes with old).
- *Motivated Forgetting* — Painful, threatening, or embarassing memories are forgotten.
- *Encoding Failure* — Material from STM to LTM was never successfully encoded.
- *Retrieval Failure* — Information is not forgotten, just temporarily inaccessible.

Problems with Memory

Organic Causes

- *Brain injuries or trauma*: **Retrograde amnesia**, memory is lost for events that occurred before the accident. **Anterograde amnesia** memory is lost for events that occur after an accident.
- *Disease*: **Alzheimer's disease** is a progressive mental deterioration and severe memory loss occurring most commonly in old age.

Constructive Processes

Memory is a **constructive process** with at least 2 major errors:
1) **Source amnesia** where we attribute memories to a wrong source.
2) **Sleeper effect** where we confuse reliable information with unreliable.

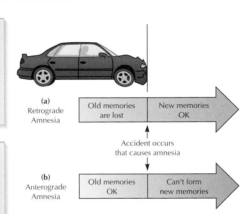

(a) Retrograde Amnesia — Old memories are lost | New memories OK

Accident occurs that causes amnesia

(b) Anterograde Amnesia — Old memories OK | Can't form new memories

Improving Memory

Specific Tips

- Pay attention and reduce interference.
- Use rehearsal techniques (maintenance for STM and elaborative for LTM).
- Improve organization (chunking for STM and hierarchies for LTM).
- Counteract the serial position effect.
- Use time management (distributed versus massed practice).
- Use the encoding specificity principle (including context, mood congruence, and state-dependent retrieval).
- Employ self-monitoring and overlearning.
- Use **mnemonic devices** (method of loci, peg-word, substitute word, and method of word associations).

THINKING, LANGUAGE, AND INTELLIGENCE

H ave you heard about Koko, the gorilla who supposedly "speaks" more than 1,000 words in American Sign Language (ASL)? According to her trainer, Penny Patterson, Koko has used ASL in various ways—to converse with others, talk to herself, rhyme, joke, and even lie (Linden, 1993; Patterson, 2002). Koko also uses signs to communicate her personal preferences, including a strong attraction to cats. After she made repeated requests for a cat as a pet, a litter of three kittens was finally brought to visit Koko. She selected one as her favorite and named him "All Ball" (based on his lack of a tail and her supposed love of rhymes). In their initial encounters, Koko reportedly treated All Ball as she might a baby gorilla—sniffing him, tucking him into her thigh, and trying to get him to nurse. Like a human child with a pet, she also dressed him in linen napkins and hats and played chase games. Assuming these accounts are true, do you think Koko is using true language? Do you consider Koko intelligent?

What about the famous case of the "wild child" known as Genie? From the age of 20 months until authorities rescued her at age 13 years, Genie had been kept locked in a

■ Achievement
■ Assessment
■ Application

tiny, windowless room in solitary confinement. By day, she was kept naked and tied to a chair with nothing to do and no one to talk to. At night, she was put in a kind of straitjacket and "caged" in a covered crib. Genie's abusive father forbade anyone to speak to her for the entire 13 years and refused to have a radio or TV in the home. If Genie made any noise, her father would beat her, while he barked and growled like a dog. After she was discovered at age 13, linguists and psychologists worked with her intensively for many years, but she never progressed much beyond sentences like "Genie, go" (Curtiss, 1977; Rymer, 1993). With her limited language skills, would you say Genie is intelligent?

What about Thomas, a child who attended school for only 3 months? Despite his lack of formal education and progressive deafness throughout his life, Thomas patented over 1,000 inventions — more than any other single individual in history. His insatiable curiosity led him to study fields ranging from metallurgy to plastics, and his long hours of tinkering produced momentous discoveries, including the phonograph, the kinetoscope for motion pictures, and the carbon transmitter for telephones. He has been called the "greatest inventor in American history" (Israel, 1998), yet some have said he was a "technologist rather than a scientist, adding little to original scientific knowledge" (Baldwin, 2001). Did you recognize this as the story of Thomas Edison, the famous inventor of the lightbulb? Would you consider him intelligent?

Being the "greatest inventor in American history" obviously requires a large repertoire of thinking processes and intellectual agility. But don't Genie's survival and Koko's use of sign language also require some form of intelligence? To be intelligent, you must be aware and possess the capacity to learn. But awareness requires thinking, or the mental processing of information. And to express this thinking and intelligence, you need language.

The three topics of this section — thinking, language, and intelligence — are often studied together under the larger umbrella of **cognition,** the mental activities of acquiring, storing, retrieving, and using knowledge. In a real sense, we discuss cognition throughout the text, because psychology is "the scientific study of behavior and *mental processes.*" For example, learning and memory (Modules 16–21) are a core part of cognition. In this section, we focus on three additional aspects — thinking, language, and intelligence.

Cognition *Mental activities involved in acquiring, storing, retrieving, and using knowledge*

MODULE 22
THINKING

Assessment

What is thinking and what are its building blocks? How do we solve problems, and what is creativity?

What is *thinking?* Every time you use information and mentally act on it by forming ideas, reasoning, solving problems, drawing conclusions, expressing thoughts, and comprehending the thoughts of others, you are thinking. We begin this section by exploring how our brains perform this basic (but seemingly magical) act. Next, we examine the building blocks of thought, images, and concepts. Then, we discuss the mental processes involved in problem solving and creativity.

The Thinking Brain: Making Connections

Thought processes are distributed throughout the brain in networks of neurons, much like a tightly interwoven galaxy of shooting stars. Like other psychological functions, however, thought processes also are localized. For example, during problem solving or decision making, our brains are active in a special processing area, the prefrontal cortex, which associates complex ideas, makes plans, forms and initiates attention, and allocates our attention. This area also is involved in multitasking behavior, such as washing the dishes while also talking to your family or friends and simultaneously listening for the doorbell (Koechlin, Basso, Pietrini, Panzer, & Grafman, 1999).

Although many thought processes are localized in the prefrontal cortex, this cortical area also links to other areas of the brain to synthesize information from several senses, as well as to the limbic system, which is the center of our emotions. As you recall from Module 5, Phineas Gage, the railroad foreman whose brain was pierced by an iron rod, suffered damage to his prefrontal cortex. Like Gage, people with damage to this region can solve problems, manipulate information in short-term working memory, and generally have little trouble recalling events from the recent or distant past. However, because the prefrontal cortex is connected to the limbic system, Gage and people with similar injuries have difficulty controlling their emotions and in making connections between their feelings and thoughts (Damasio, 1999). This vital interconnection between thoughts and feelings also helps explain why people who drink too much may make dangerous decisions to drink and drive. Alcohol disrupts communication between the frontal lobes and the limbic system.

Cognitive Building Blocks: The Foundation of Thought

Now that we know the general location of thinking, we need to study its three basic components — *mental images*, *concepts*, and *language*. When you're thinking about your sweetheart, you have a mental *image* of him or her in your mind. You think of him or her in terms of *concepts* or categories, such as woman, man, strong, happy. And you may have in mind *linguistic* statements such as "I wish I could be with him or her right now instead of reading this text." (Study tip: Keep in mind the *Premack principle* from Module 17 — using any naturally occurring, high-frequency responses to reinforce low-frequency responses. If you want to improve your study habits, use "time with your sweetheart" as reinforcement *after* you finish studying.) In this section, we will discuss the role of images and concepts in thinking. Language will be considered in a later section.

Mental Images

Imagine yourself on a warm, sandy ocean beach. Do you see tall palms swaying in the wind? Can you smell the salty ocean water and hear the laughter of the children playing in the surf? What you've just created in your mind's eye is a **mental image,** a mental representation of a previously stored sensory experience, that includes visual, auditory, olfactory, tactile, motor, and gustatory imagery (McKellar, 1972).

Mental Images *A mental representation of a previously stored sensory experience, including visual, auditory, olfactory, tactile, motor, and gustatory imagery (e.g., visualizing a train and hearing its whistle)*

Mental imagery. *Can you imagine what this mountain climber is visualizing in his "mind's eye?" Constant use of mental imagery is critical to his success.*

Where are mental images located? According to research, we all have a fixed-size mental space (similar to the screen of a computer monitor) where we mentally visualize and manipulate our sensory images (Brewer & Pani, 1996; Kosslyn, 1987). In fact, some of our most creative moments come when we're forming mental images and manipulating them. Albert Einstein said that his first insight into relativity theory occurred when he pictured a beam of light and imagined himself chasing after it at its own speed.

Concepts

In addition to mental images, our thinking also involves **concepts** — mental representations of a group or category. We form concepts by grouping together objects, events, activities, or ideas that share similar characteristics (Smith, 1995). Our mental concept of *car* represents a large group of objects that share similar characteristics (vehicles with four wheels, seating space for at least one person, and a generally predictable shape). We also form concepts for abstract ideas, such as *honesty*, *intelligence*, or *pornography*. These abstract ideas, however, are often our own individual constructions that may or may not be shared by others. Therefore, it's generally harder to communicate about honesty than about a car.

Concepts are an essential part of thinking and communication because they simplify and organize information. Imagine being Genie, the "wild child" described at the beginning of this section. If you had been confined to a small, windowless room your entire life, how would you process the world around you without the use of concepts? Normally, when you see a new object or encounter a new situation, you relate it to your existing conceptual structure and categorize it according to where it fits. For example, if you see a rectangular box with moving pictures and sound and people are staring at it, you safely assume it is a TV set. Even though you've never encountered this specific brand before, you understand the concept of a *TV set*. But if you were Genie, how would you process a TV set, a telephone, or even a bathroom, having never seen them and compared them to other TVs, telephones, and rooms?

How do we learn concepts? They develop through the creation and use of three major strategies: *artificial concepts, natural concepts,* and *hierarchies:*

1. ***Artificial concepts.*** We create some of our concepts from logical rules or definitions. Consider the definition of *triangle*, a geometric figure with three sides and three angles. Using this definition, we group together and classify all three-sided

Concept *Mental representation of a group or category that shares similar characteristics (e.g., the concept of a river groups together the Nile, the Amazon, and the Mississippi because they share the common characteristic of being a large stream of water that empties into an ocean or lake)*

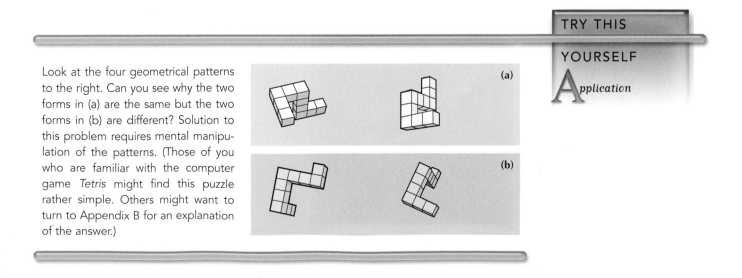

TRY THIS YOURSELF

Application

Look at the four geometrical patterns to the right. Can you see why the two forms in (a) are the same but the two forms in (b) are different? Solution to this problem requires mental manipulation of the patterns. (Those of you who are familiar with the computer game *Tetris* might find this puzzle rather simple. Others might want to turn to Appendix B for an explanation of the answer.)

geometric forms as triangles. If any of the defining features were missing, we would not include the object in the *concept* of triangle. Concepts like "triangle" are called *artificial* (or *formal*) because the rules for inclusion are so sharply defined. Artificial concepts often are found in the sciences and other academic disciplines. As we will see in the upcoming discussion of language, scientists have created specific definitions and rules for the concepts of "language" and "communication."

2. ***Natural concepts.*** In real life, however, we seldom use such precise, artificial definitions. For example, when we see birds in the sky, we don't think "warm-blooded animals that fly, have wings, and lay eggs" — an *artificial concept*. Instead, we use *natural concepts*, called **prototypes,** which are based on a personal "best example" or most typical representative of that concept (Rosch, 1973). When we see flying animals, we can quickly identify them as birds by using our previous prototype or natural concept for a bird. Most of us have a model bird, or prototype, — such as a robin or a sparrow — that captures for us the essence of "birdness."

Prototype *A representation of the "best" or most typical example of a category (e.g., baseball is a prototype of the concept of sports)*

Prototypes provide an efficient mental shortcut, but what happens when we encounter a new item, like *penguin*, where we cannot use our prototype robin? In this case, we need time to review our artificial concept (the definition of *bird*). Because the penguin doesn't fly (but it does lay eggs and is warm-blooded), it takes longer to classify. It's easier to classify a robin because our prototype robin is a "birdier bird" than a penguin.

3. ***Hierarchies.*** Some of our concepts also develop when we create *hierarchies*, in which specific concepts are grouped as subcategories within broader concepts. Note in the hierarchy depicted in Figure 22.1 (a) how the top (superordinate) category of *animals* is very broad and includes lots of members, the midlevel categories of *bird* and *dog*, are more specific but still rather general, and the lowest (subordinate) categories of *parakeet* and *poodle* are the most specific.

Interestingly, research shows that when we first learn something we use the middle categories, which are called *basic-level* concepts (Rosch, 1978). For example, children tend to learn *bird* or *dog* before they learn superordinate concepts like *animals* or subordinate concepts like *parakeet* and *poodle*. Even as adults, when shown a picture of a parakeet, we first classify it as a bird before thinking of the higher concept of *animal* or lower concept of *parakeet*.

Is this your prototype for a sport? Most Americans readily recognize baseball as a prototype for sports. However, if you were from Bermuda where most people watch or play cricket, you would have a different sports prototype.

Study Tip: Recall from Modules 20 and 21 that organization and hierarchies are essential to efficient encoding and storage in LTM. If children did not build a mental hierarchy of *animal*, *bird*, and *parakeet*, they would have a terrible time trying to label or memorize the definition of each. You may have a similar problem if you attempt to simply memorize a long list of a text's Key Terms. It's much easier to master a large amount of material when it's organized into a hierarchy. This is one of the main reasons we include so many tables throughout this text and the visual summaries at the end of each section. It is even better if you develop your own hierarchies.

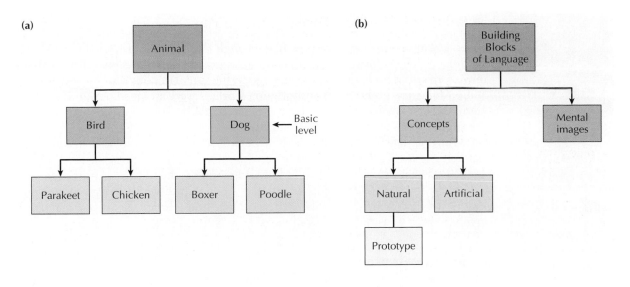

Figure 22.1 *Can hierarchies improve both thinking and exam scores?* (a) When we think, we naturally organize concepts according to superordinate and subordinate classes. We organize concepts, like *animals* or *birds*, with the most general concept at the top and the most specific at the bottom, and research also shows that we use the middle, *basic level* when initially categorizing objects and later add the upper and lower levels. Although they may look complicated, hierarchies significantly reduce the time and effort necessary for learning. For example, when you learn that all animals have mitochondria in their cells, you don't have to relearn that fact each time you learn a new animal species. (b) Hierarchies can be generated from almost any set of interrelated facts and can be used to provide a similar savings in time and effort. For example, instead of focusing on and attempting to memorize the key terms of *concepts*, *mental images*, and *prototype*, you should begin by making a hierarchy of how these terms are interrelated. Once you have this "big picture," it speeds up your mastery of the material, which translates into better exam scores.

Assessment

CHECK & REVIEW

The Thinking Brain and Cognitive Building Blocks

Cognition, or thinking, is defined as mental activities involved in acquiring, storing, retrieving, and using knowledge. Thought processes are distributed throughout the brain in neural networks. However, during problem solving and decision making, our thoughts also are localized for special processing within the frontal lobes.

The prefrontal cortex links to other areas of the brain to synthesize information from several senses. It is also connected to the limbic system. Without connecting thoughts to feelings, solving problems and making decisions would be difficult.

The three basic building blocks of cognition are mental images, concepts, and

language. **Mental images** are mental representations of a sensory experience, including visual, auditory, olfactory, tactile, motor, and gustatory imagery. **Concepts** are mental categories that group objects, events, activities, or ideas that share similar characteristics. (Language is discussed in a later section.)

There are three ways we learn concepts: (1) *Artificial concepts* are formed by logical, specific rules or characteristics. (2) *Natural concepts* are formed by experience in everyday life. When we are confronted with a new item, we compare it with the **prototype** (most typical) of that concept. (3) Concepts are generally organized into *hierarchies*. We most frequently use the middle, basic-level concepts, when first learning material.

Questions

1. All of the following are examples of concepts EXCEPT _____. (a) trees; (b) tools; (c) blue; (d) umbrellas

2. How do we learn concepts?

3. When asked to describe the shape and color of an apple, you probably rely on a _____.

4. For most psychologists, language is a formal _____, whereas the public generally uses fuzzy _____. (a) definition, descriptions; (b) artificial concept, natural concepts; (c) mental image, concepts; (d) superordinate concept, basic-level concepts

Answers to Questions can be found in Appendix B.

A failure of problem solving? On August 12, 2000, the Russian nuclear submarine "Kursk" sank as a result of a torpedo room explosion and all 118 men perished. Would faster or better problem solving have saved them?

▣ Solving Problems: Three Steps to the Goal

Several years ago in Los Angeles, a 12-foot-high tractor-trailer rig tried to pass under a bridge 11 feet 6 inches high. As you might expect, the truck got stuck, unable to move forward or back, thus causing a huge traffic jam. After hours of towing, tugging, and pushing, the police and transportation workers were stumped. About this time, a young boy happened upon the scene and asked, "Why don't you let some air out of the tires?" It was a simple, creative suggestion — and it worked.

Our everyday lives are filled with problems, some easier to solve than others. For example, figuring a way to make coffee without a filter is much easier than rescuing 118 Russian navy seamen trapped inside a submarine at the bottom of the Barents Sea, or finding a lasting relationship. In all cases, though, problem solving requires moving from a *given state* (the problem) to a *goal state* (the solution), a process that usually involves three steps (Bourne, Dominowski, & Loftus, 1979).

Step 1: Preparation

Are you, or someone you know, looking for a long-term love relationship? There are at least three separate components to successful preparation:

- *Identifying given facts.* To find lasting love, it's important to decide what are your most basic, *nonnegotiable* limits and desires. For example, do you want children? Are you willing to move to another city to find love or to be with someone you love? Does your partner have to share your religion?

- *Separating relevant from irrelevant facts.* What are your *negotiable* items? What do you consider irrelevant and easily compromised? Would you consider a relationship with someone who is 10 years older than you? What about 10 years younger? Do you want someone who is college educated? Or is that negotiable?

- *Defining the ultimate goal.* This part of the preparation stage may seem easy, but think again. Are you interested in a long-term relationship with the ultimate goal of marriage and children? If so, dating someone who wants to travel their entire life and never have children is probably not a safe bet. Similarly, if your major enjoyments are camping and outdoor sports, you may not want to date a big-city movie and TV lover.

Step 2: Production

During the *production step*, the problem solver produces possible solutions, called *hypotheses*. There are at least two major approaches to generating hypotheses — *algorithms* and *heuristics*:

Looking for love in all the wrong places. Are singles' bars a good place to find lasting love? Why or why not?

If you're not looking for love, or if you just want a more "hands-on" (excuse the pun) experience with problem solving, try this classic thinking problem (Bartlett, 1958). Your task is to determine the numerals 0 through 9 that are represented by letters, with each letter representing a separate, distinct number. You get one hint before you start: D = 5.

```
    D O N A L D
  + G E R A L D
    R O B E R T
```

Did you try solving this problem with an algorithm? If so, you probably wasted a lot of time. There are 362,880 possible combinations of letters and numbers. At the rate of one combination per minute, 8 hours per day, 5 days a week, 52 weeks a year, it would take nearly 3 years to try all the possible combinations.

A heuristic approach is much easier and quicker. If you successfully solved the problem, you probably used the "creating subgoals" heuristic. You employed previous knowledge of arithmetic to set subgoals, such as determining what number T represents (if D = 5, then D + D = 10, so T = 0, with a carryover of 1 into the tens column). The complete answer is at the end of the next Check & Review section.

- An **algorithm** is a step-by-step procedure that, if followed correctly will always produce the solution. Math problems are ideal for demonstrating algorithms: An algorithm for solving the problem 2×10 is $2 + 2 + 2 + 2 + 2 + 2 + 2 + 2 + 2 + 2$. Algorithms will eventually lead to the correct answer, but for complex problems they may take a long time. Given the limited time you want to spend looking for love, you are unlikely to use algorithms. However, they provide simple ways to balance your checkbook or compute your grade point average. Computers are especially well suited for algorithms because they can quickly perform millions of calculations and logical operations in a step-by-step solution to a problem.

Algorithm *A set of steps that, if followed correctly, will eventually solve the problem*

- A **heuristic** is a simple rule or strategy for problem solving that provides shortcuts, but does not guarantee a solution — it works most of the time, but not always. If you consult married friends or family members regarding your dating problems, they may offer advice (or *heuristics*) such as, "Do what you naturally love to do (dancing, skiing, movies), and you'll find someone with similar interests." Regrettably, this type of general heuristic may not provide the date of your dreams, but there are more specific heuristics for problems like career choices that can be very useful (see Table 22.1).

Heuristic *Strategies, or simple rules, used in problem solving and decision making that do not guarantee a solution, but offer a likely short cut to it*

Step 3: Evaluation

Once the hypotheses are generated, they must be evaluated to see if they meet the criteria defined in step 1. If one or more of the hypotheses meet the criteria, the problem is solved — you know what you want in a partner and the best place to find him or her. If not, then you must return to the production stage and produce more possible solutions. Keep in mind, however, that "action must follow solution." Once the little boy solved the "stuck truck" problem, someone had to follow through and actually let some air out of the tires. Similarly, once you identify your ultimate goal, you must follow through and implement the necessary solution — more and improved dating.

Several heuristics can be particularly helpful in college, including (1) working backward, (2) means–end analysis, and (3) creating subgoals (Table 22.1). Successful college students seem to be particularly good at breaking down a solution into subgoals. When you're faced with a heavy schedule of exams and term papers, try creating subgoals to make the immediate problems more manageable and increase the likelihood of reaching your final goal — a college degree.

Graduating from college requires many skills, including the successful use of several problem solving heuristics.

SUMMARY TABLE 22.1 PROBLEM-SOLVING HEURISTICS

Problem-Solving Heuristics	Description	Example
Working backward	An approach that starts with the solution, a known condition, and works backward through the problem. Once the search has revealed the steps to be taken, the problem is solved.	Deciding you want to be an experimental psychologist, you ask your psychology professor and career counselor to recommend courses, graduate and undergraduate colleges and universities, areas to emphasize, and so on. Then you write the recommended college(s) requesting information on their admission policies and standards. You then plan your current college courses accordingly and work hard to meet (or exceed) the admission standards.
Means–end analysis	The problem solver determines what measure would reduce the difference between the given state and the goal. Once the means to reach the goal are determined, the problem is solved.	Knowing that you need good grades to get into a good graduate school for experimental psychology, you want an A in your psychology course. You ask your professor for suggestions, you interview several A students to compare and contrast their study habits, you assess your own study habits, and then determine the specific means (the number of hours and which study techniques) required to meet your end goal of an A.
Creating subgoals	Large, complex problems are broken down into a series of small subgoals. These subgoals then serve as a series of stepping-stones that can be taken one at a time to reach the original large goal.	Getting a good grade or even passing many college courses requires writing a successful term paper. To do this, you choose a topic, go to the library and Internet to locate information related to the topic, organize the information, write an outline, write the paper, review the paper, rewrite, rewrite again, and submit the final paper on or before the due date.

Application
APPLYING PSYCHOLOGY TO EVERYDAY LIFE

Recognizing Barriers to Problem Solving

Do you find that you can solve some problems easily yet seem to have a mental block when it comes to others? You're not alone; we all encounter barriers that prevent us from effectively solving problems. Five of the most common barriers are *mental sets, functional fixedness, confirmation bias, availability heuristic,* and *representativeness heuristic:*

1. *Mental sets.* Like the police and transportation workers who were trying to pull or shove the truck that was stuck under the bridge, have you ever persisted in attacking problems using the same or similar solutions that have worked in the past? This is known as a **mental set.** Although pulling and shoving obviously works sometimes, in this instance the old solution created a mental barrier to new, and possibly more effective, solutions (such as deflating the tires). The habit (or *mental set*) of working arithmetic problems from the right (ones) column to the left also explains why most people fail to see the solution to the DONALD + GERALD problem. In the same way, looking for love by only going to singles' bars can be a barrier to good dating.

Study tip: Mental sets also block some college students from using the SQ4R (Survey, Question, Read, Recite, Review, and wRite) method or other study techniques described in the Tools for Student Success (Module 4). Their reliance on past study habits blocks them from considering newer and more efficient strategies. If we try to be flexible in our thinking, we can offset the natural tendency toward mental sets. To practice your flexibility, try the nine-dot problem in Figure 22.2, and check your answer with the solution shown in Figure 22.3 on the next page.

2. *Functional fixedness.* The tendency to view objects as functioning only in the usual or customary way is known as **functional fixedness.** Suppose you wanted to make coffee in your automatic coffee maker but were out of filters. Would you dig through the trash looking for an old, dirty filter without thinking of using a paper towel? What if you were given the objects shown in Figure 22.4 and asked to mount the candle on the wall so that it could be easily lit in the normal fashion, with no danger of toppling (Duncker, 1945)? How would you do this? Think about it before you read on.

The solution is to empty the box, use the tacks to attach it to the wall, light the candle, drop some melted wax on the box, then set the candle in the dripped wax (Figure 22.5). In the research test of this problem, participants had a much more difficult time solving the problem when the box was filled with matches than when it was presented with the matches separately. In the former situation, the participants saw the box as only a container for matches and overlooked it as a useful item in itself. When you use a table knife instead of a screwdriver to tighten a screw, you have overcome functional fixedness. (Unfortunately, I cannot find an example of functional fixedness and love relationships. If you have one, please email me <khuffman@palomar.edu>.)

3. *Confirmation bias.* Have you noticed how politicians frequently accept opinion polls that support their political views and ignore those that don't? Have you caught yourself agreeing with friends who support your personal biases regarding relationships (e.g., "opposites attract") and discounting conflicting theories? This inclination to seek out evidence that confirms our preexisting positions or beliefs, while at the same time discounting or overlooking contradictory evidence, is known as **confirmation bias** (Nickerson, 1998). This phenomenon was first demonstrated by British researcher Peter Wason (1968) with the following test:

Can you guess the rule?   2   4   6

Wason asked participants to guess the rule that applied to this same three-numbered set. Before submitting their rule, participants were also asked to generate additional sets of numbers that conformed to their hypothesized rule. The participants generated sets, such as (4, 6, 8) or (1, 3, 5). These sets reflected their

Mental Set *Persisting in using problem-solving strategies that have worked in the past rather than trying new ones*

Functional Fixedness *Tendency to think of an object functioning only in its usual or customary way*

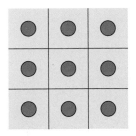

Figure 22.2 *The nine-dot problem.* Draw no more than four lines that run through all nine dots on this page without lifting your pencil from the paper. (See Figure 22.3, page 308, for the solution.)

Figure 22.4 *Overcoming functional fixedness.* Can you use these supplies to mount the candle on a wall so that it can be lit in a normal way — without toppling over?

Confirmation Bias *Tendency to seek out and pay attention only to information that confirms preexisting positions or beliefs, while ignoring or discounting contradictory evidence*

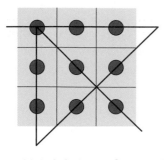

Figure 22.3 *Solution to the nine-dot problem.* People find this puzzle difficult because they see the arrangement of dots as a square. This mental set limits possible solutions because they "naturally" assume they can't go out of the boundaries of the square.

Figure 22.5 *The solution to the candle problem in Figure 22.4.* Use the tacks to mount the matchbox tray to the wall. Light the candle and use some melted wax to mount the candle to the matchbox.

Availability Heuristic *Judging the likelihood or probability of events based on how readily available are other instances in our mind*

Representativeness Heuristic *Estimating the probability of something based on how well the circumstances match our previous prototype*

commonly shared (but unspoken) guess that the rule was "numbers increasing by two." (Is this the same rule you generated?)

Each time the participants presented their list of numbers, Wason assured them their set of numbers conformed to the rule. However, when Wason later informed them that the rule "numbers increasing by 2" was incorrect, they were very frustrated. The actual rule was "numbers in increasing order of magnitude." (Did you guess the correct rule?) The barrier to solving this problem was that participants searched only for confirming information and failed to look for evidence that would disprove their hypothesis. If they had proposed a series, such as 1, 3, 4 instead, they would have discovered that their initial hypothesis was incorrect and they could have easily discovered the correct rule.

4. *Availability heuristic.* Earlier in this module we talked about heuristics as simple rules used in problem solving and decision making that do not guarantee a solution, but offer a likely shortcut to it. Cognitive psychologists Amos Tversky and Daniel Kahneman (1974, 1993) have found these heuristics often provide handy mental shortcuts to problem solving, but they also may lead us to ignore other relevant information.

The **availability heuristic** is a good example of how heuristics may cause even the smartest people to make foolish decisions. When using this heuristic, people judge the likelihood or probability of events based on how easily recalled, or readily *available*, are other instances in their mind. If previous instances are readily recalled, we assume they are common and typical and therefore more likely to occur again in the future (McKelvie & Drumheller, 2001).

Ease of recall often *is* correlated with actual data—but not always. For example, a national study conducted shortly after the horrific attacks on the World Trade Center in 2001 found that the average American participant believed they had a 20.5 percent chance of being hurt in a terrorist attack within the next year (Lerner, Gonzalez, Small, & Fischoff, 2003). Can you see how the vivid media coverage of the attacks created this, thankfully, erroneous availability heuristic and unreasonably high perceptions of risk? Similarly, casinos use loud bells and bright flashing lights to attract attention when someone wins a slot machine jackpot. Although casino owners may not be familiar with Tversky and Kahneman's research on the availability heuristic, their business experience has taught them that calling attention to winners creates a vivid impression. This, in turn, causes nearby gamblers to overestimate the likelihood of winning (and to continue their own gambling).

5. *Representativeness heuristic.* Tversky and Kahneman also identified a second type of heuristic that sometimes leads to erroneous decisions and ineffective problem solving. When using the **representativeness heuristic,** we estimate the probability of something based on how well the event, person, or object matches (or *represents*) our previous prototype. (Remember, a prototype is your most common or representative example.) For instance, if you were looking through questionnaires and noted that John is 6 feet 5 inches with very sloppy handwriting, would you guess that he's a bank president or a NBA basketball player? Because this description matches (or represents) most people's prototype of a basketball player (Beyth-Marom, Shlomith, Gombo, & Lichtenstein, 1985), you might overestimate the probability that this is in fact John's occupation. Statistically, this is not a wise guess. Although the representative heuristic is often adaptive and beneficial, in this case it ignores *base rate information*—the probability of a characteristic occurring in the general population. In the United States, bank presidents outnumber NBA players by about 50 to 1. Therefore, it is much more likely that John is a bank president.

CRITICAL THINKING ACTIVE LEARNING

Solving Problems in College Life

Critical thinking requires adaptive, flexible approaches to thinking and problem solving. Given that your success in college requires overcoming a number of problems in both school and life, the following exercise offers practice in critical thinking, new insights into common college-related problems, and a quick review of terms and concepts discussed in this section.

Before you begin, you may want to review the major problem-solving approaches we discussed — *algorithms* (step-by-step procedures that guarantee solutions) and *heuris-* tics (shortcuts to possible solutions based on previous knowledge and experience). See Table 22.1 for three specific heuristics: *working backward, means–end analysis*, and *creating subgoals*.

Below, you will find two problems.

Problem 1 It is the end of the semester and you have a paper due Friday. Thursday afternoon, after studying for an exam, you turn on your computer to print your paper but can't find the file on your computer. How will you find the file?

Problem 2 The financial aid office has refused to give you your student loan until you verify how much money you made last year. You need to find your pay stubs to verify income.

For each problem, answer the following questions:

1. What was your first step in approaching the problem?
2. Which problem-solving approach did you select and why?
3. Did you consider potential obstacles, such as mental sets, functional fixedness, confirmation bias, availability heuristic, and representativeness heuristic during the problem-solving process?

CHECK & REVIEW

Solving Problems

Problem solving entails three steps: *preparation, production*, and *evaluation*. During the preparation stage, we identify given facts, separate relevant from irrelevant facts, and define the ultimate goal.

During the second production stage, we generate possible solutions, called hypotheses. We typically generate hypotheses by using **algorithms** and **heuristics**. Algorithms, as problem-solving strategies, are guaranteed to lead to a solution eventually, but they are not practical in many situations. Heuristics, or simplified rules based on experience, are much faster but do not guarantee a solution. Three common heuristics are *working backward, means–end analysis*, and *creating subgoals*.

The third evaluation step in problem solving involves judging the hypotheses generated during step two (production stage) against the criteria established in step one (preparation stage).

Five major barriers to successful problem solving are **mental sets, functional fixedness, confirmation bias, availability heuristic,** and **representativeness heuristic.**

Questions

1. List and describe the three stages of problem solving.
2. Rosa is shopping in a new supermarket and wants to find a specific type of mustard. Which problem-solving strategy would be most efficient? (a) algorithm; (b) heuristic; (c) instinct; (d) mental set.
3. Before a new product arrives in the store, a manufacturer goes through several stages, including designing, building, testing a prototype, setting up a production line, and so on. This approach is called (a) working backward; (b) means–end analysis; (c) divergent thinking; (d) creating subgoals.
4. List the five major barriers to problem solving.

Answers to Questions can be found in Appendix B.

Solution to the DONALD + GERALD = ROBERT problem:

$$\begin{array}{r} 526485 \\ +\ 197485 \\ \hline 723970 \end{array}$$

■ Creativity: Finding Unique Solutions

Are you a creative person? Like many students, you may think of only painters, dancers, and composers as creative and may fail to recognize examples of your own creativity. Even when doing ordinary tasks, such as taking notes in class, you are being somewhat creative — unless you're copying the lecture verbatim. Similarly, if you've

www.wiley.com/college/huffman

Thomas Edison with his most famous invention — the light bulb.

ever tightened a screw with a penny or used a magazine to splint a broken arm, you've found creative solutions to problems. All of us, to a greater or lesser degree, exhibit a certain amount of creativity in some aspects of life. Whether a solution or performance is considered creative often depends on its need and usefulness at the time (Weisberg, 1993). Definitions of creativity vary among psychologists and between cultures, but it is generally agreed that **creativity** is the ability to produce valued outcomes in a novel way (Bink & Marsh, 2000; Boden, 2000).

Measuring Creativity

Creative thought is associated with three special characteristics: *originality*, *fluency*, and *flexibility*. As you can see in Table 22.2, Thomas Edison's invention of the lightbulb offers a prime example of each of these characteristics. In addition to the three characteristics of creativity, there is a distinct type of thinking that is related to creativity, called **divergent thinking,** where many possibilities are developed from a single starting point (Baer, 1994). The opposite of divergent thinking is **convergent thinking,** or *conventional thinking*. In this case, lines of thinking *converge* (come together) on the answer, and we select a single correct solution from among several alternatives. You used convergence in the DONALD + GERALD problem to find the one correct number represented by each letter.

Creativity *The ability to produce valued outcomes in a novel way*

Divergent Thinking *Thinking that produces many alternatives or ideas; a major element of creativity (e.g., finding as many uses as possible for a paper clip)*

Convergent Thinking *Narrowing down a list of alternatives to converge on a single correct answer (e.g., standard academic tests generally require convergent thinking)*

TABLE 22.2 THREE ELEMENTS OF CREATIVE THINKING

	Explanations	**Thomas Edison Examples**
Originality	Seeing unique or different solutions to a problem	After noting that electricity passing through a conductor produced a glowing red or white heat, Edison imagined capturing this light for practical uses.
Fluency	Generating a large number of possible solutions	Edison tried literally hundreds of different materials to find one that would heat to the point of glowing white heat without burning up.
Flexibility	Shifting with ease from one type of problem-solving strategy to another	When he couldn't find a long-lasting material, he thought of heating it in a vacuum – thereby creating the first lightbulb.

TRY THIS

YOURSELF

Application

Do you want to test your creativity? Try the following. (See Figure 22.6 for the solution.)

1. In five minutes, see how many words you can make out of the following word.
   HIPPOPOTAMUS

2. In five minutes, list all the things you can do with a paper clip.

3. Find 10 coins and arrange them in the configuration shown here. By moving only two coins, form two rows that each contain 6 coins.

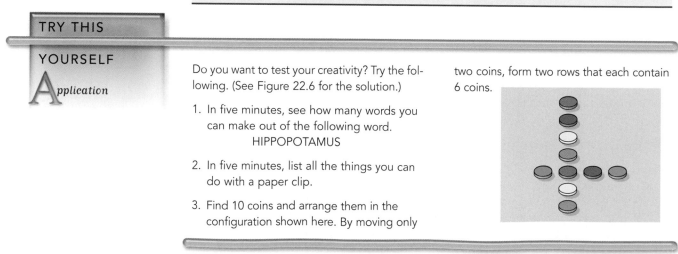

Divergent thinking is the type of thinking most often associated with creativity and is thus the focus of most tests of creativity. In the *Unusual Uses Test*, the person is asked to think of as many uses as possible for an object (such as "How many ways can you use a brick?"). In the *Anagrams Test*, people are asked to reorder the letters in a word to make as many new words as possible. A type of anagram test is found in the following 5 groups of letters. Try rearranging the letters in these words to make new words, and then decide what they share in common. (Answers are listed in the Check & Review for this section.)

1. grevenidt _____   3. ytliibxilef _____   5. yvitcearti _____

2. neleecitlgn _____   4. ptoyropet _____

Researching Creativity

Some researchers view creativity as a special talent or ability and therefore look for common personality traits among people they define as creative (Guilford, 1967; Jausovec & Jausovec, 2000). Other researchers explain the distinction between creative and noncreative people in terms of cognitive processes. That is, creative and noncreative people differ in life experiences, how they encode information, how they store it, and in what information they generate to solve problems (Bink & Marsh, 2000; Cooper, 2000; Jacoby, Levy, & Steinbach, 1992).

According to Sternberg and Lubart's *investment theory* (1992, 1999), creative people are willing to "buy low and sell high" in the realm of ideas. They buy low by championing ideas that they feel have potential but that most people think are worthless or worth very little. Once their creative ideas are supported and highly valued, they "sell high" and move on to another unpopular but promising idea.

Investment theory also suggests that creativity requires the coming together of six different but interrelated resources: intellectual ability, knowledge, thinking style, personality, motivation, and environment (Kaufman, 2002; Sternberg & Lubart, 1999). These resources are summarized in Table 22.3. One way to improve your personal creativity is to study this list and then strengthen yourself in those areas that you think need improvement.

Figure 22.6 *Coin problem solution.* Stack one coin on top of the middle coin so that it shares both the row and the column.

TABLE 22.3 RESOURCES OF CREATIVE PEOPLE

Intellectual Ability	Knowledge	Thinking Style	Personality	Motivation	Environment
Enough intelligence to see problems in a new light	Sufficient basic knowledge of the problem to effectively evaluate possible solutions	Pursue their own novel ideas and can distinguish between the worthy and worthless	Willing to grow and change, take risks, and work to overcome obstacles	Sufficient motivation to accomplish the task; internal rather than external motivation is best	Creative people need to work in an environment that supports creativity

Assessment

CHECK & REVIEW

Creativity

Creativity is the generation of ideas that are original, novel, and useful. Creative thinking involves *originality, fluency,* and *flexibility.* **Divergent thinking,** trying to generate as many solutions as possible, is a special type of thinking involved in creativity. In contrast, **convergent thinking,** or conventional thinking, works toward a single solution to a problem.

The investment theory of creativity proposes that creative people "buy low" by pursuing promising but unpopular ideas, and "sell high" by developing the ideas until they are widely accepted. It also proposes that creativity depends on six specific resources: intellectual ability, knowledge, thinking style, personality, motivation, and environment.

Questions

1. Which of the following items would MOST likely appear on a test measuring creativity? (a) How long is the Ohio River? (b) What are the primary colors? (c) List all the uses of a pot. (d) Who was the first governor of New York?

2. Identify the type of thinking for each of these examples.

   a. You create numerous excuses ("reasons") for not studying.

   b. On a test, you must select one correct answer for each question.

   c. You make a list of ways to save money.

3. According to investment theory, what are the six resources necessary for creativity?

4. As a music teacher, you would like your students to create their own songs. Should you offer a prize as an incentive for the most creative song? Why or why not?

Answers to Questions can be found in Appendix B.

Solutions to the Anagrams Test

1. divergent
2. intelligence
3. flexibility
4. prototype
5. creativity

The answers are key terms found in this section.

MODULE 1

ACTIVE LEARNING WORKSHEET

Enter the correct letter from Column A in the blank space in Column B, and then double-check your answers with those in Appendix B.

Column A	Column B
a. Prototype	1.____ Mental representation of a group or category
b. Functional fixedness	2.____ Best or most typical example of a category
c. Confirmation bias	3.____ Persisting use of old strategies on new problems
d. Divergent thinking	4.____ Producing valued outcomes in a novel way
e. Heuristic	5.____ Thinking that produces many alternatives
f. Algorithm	6.____ Thinking required in most academic tests
g. Convergent thinking	7.____ Agreeing with friends who agree with you
h. Creativity	8.____ Offers a short-cut solution to a problem
i. Mental set	9.____ Set of steps to a problem solution
j. Concept	10.____ Thinking of an object functioning only in its customary way

MODULE 23
LANGUAGE

Any discussion of human thought processes must include a discussion of language. As mentioned earlier, language (along with mental images and concepts) is a foundation or building block of thinking. Language enables us to mentally manipulate symbols, thereby expanding our thinking. Most importantly, whether it's spoken, written, or signed, language allows us to communicate our thoughts, ideas, and feelings.

■ Characteristics of Language: Structure and Production

What is language? Do beavers slapping their tails, birds singing their songs, and ants laying their trails use language? Not according to a strict scientific definition. As we discussed earlier, scientists develop precise definitions and restrictions for certain *artificial concepts*. Psychologists, linguists, and other scientists define *language* as a form of communication whereby we put together sounds and symbols according to specified rules.

Building Blocks of Language

To produce language, we first build words using *phonemes* and *morphemes*. Then we string words into sentences using rules of *grammar* (*syntax* and *semantics*) (Table 23.1):

1. ***Phonemes.*** The smallest basic units of speech or sound are called **phonemes.** These basic speech sounds make up every language. The English language has about 40 or so phonemes. Each one has distinctive features, such as variations in

Assessment

What is language, and how is it related to thinking?

Phoneme [FOE-neem] *Smallest basic unit of speech or sound*

SUMMARY TABLE 23.1 BUILDING BLOCKS OF LANGUAGE

Blocks	Description	Example
Phonemes	The smallest units of sound that make up every language	*p* in pansy; *ng* in sting
Morphemes	The smallest units that carry meaning; they are created by combining phonemes. (*Function morphemes* are prefixes and suffixes. *Content morphemes* are root words.)	*unthinkable* = *un•think•able* (prefix = *un*, root word = *think*, suffix = *able*)
Grammar	A system of rules (syntax and semantics) used to generate acceptable language that enables us to communicate with and understand others	*I enjoy my psychology class.* versus *I my class psychology enjoy.*
Syntax	A system of rules for putting words in order	*I am happy.* versus *Happy I am.*
Semantics	A system of using words to create meaning	*I went out on a limb for you.* versus *Humans have several limbs.*

"If you don't mind my asking, how much does a sentence diagrammer pull down a year?"

© 1981 Thaves. Reprinted with permission.

sound (like the letter *a* in *am* and *ape*) or unvoiced versus voiced components (when we say *s*, we simply hiss; when we say *z*, we do the same but add the voice).

Morpheme [MOR-feem] *Smallest meaningful unit of language, formed from a combination of phonemes*

Grammar *Rules that specify how phonemes, morphemes, words, and phrases should be combined to express thoughts*

Syntax *Grammatical rules that specify how words and phrases should be arranged in a sentence to convey meaning*

2. **Morphemes.** Phonemes are combined to form the second building block of language, morphemes. **Morphemes** are the smallest *meaningful* units of language. Morphemes are divided into two types: (a) *content morphemes*, which hold the basic meaning of a word, such as *cat*, and (b) *function morphemes*, which are prefixes and suffixes, such as *un-*, *dis-*, *-able*, and *-ing*. Function morphemes add additional meaning to the word.

3. **Grammar.** Phonemes, morphemes, words, and phrases are joined together by the third building block of language, the rules of **grammar.** Grammatical rules govern how to combine phonemes into morphemes and words, how to use various classes of words (nouns, verbs, etc.) and their inflections (plurals, verb tenses, etc.), and how to choose and order words to form meaningful sentences. Grammar is made up of two components, syntax and semantics.

- *Syntax.* The grammatical rules for ordering words in sentences are known as rules of **syntax.** By the time we are able to read, our syntactical sense is so highly developed that even a sentence composed of nonsense words sounds as if it makes sense, as long as it follows proper syntax, as in Lewis Carroll's poem, "Jabberwocky":

'Twas brillig, and the slithy toves
Did gyre and gimble in the wabe...

The word arrangement follows the rules of English syntax so well that we feel we know what Carroll is talking about.

Syntax varies from language to language. In English, for example, the verb is usually the second element in a sentence ("He *has driven* to New York"). But in German, the main verb often comes at the very end of a sentence (German word order would be "He *has* to New York *driven*"). English speakers always put the adjective before the noun ("my *precious* love"), but Italian speakers sometimes place the adjective before, and sometimes after, depending on the intended meaning: *Una carrisima amore* means "a very dear, precious love," whereas *un' amore carrisima* means "a very expensive love," one that costs a lot to keep kindled!

Semantics *Meaning, or the study of meaning, derived from words and word combinations*

- *Semantics.* The choosing of words according to the meaning we want to convey is known as **semantics.** When we add *-ed* to the word *walk*, it refers to walking in the past. If we want to refer to a baby sheep, we use the word *lamb*, not the word *limb*, which means something entirely different. Actually, *limb* has several meanings, so we must depend on context to know whether the speaker is referring to an arm or a leg or to one of the larger branches of a tree. Then there is the expression "to go out on a limb," which means not that someone literally climbs a tree but rather that someone takes a risk. Meaning thus depends on many factors, including word choice, context, and whether the intent is literal or figurative, to name just a few.

■ Language and Thought: A Complex Interaction

Our cognitive processes and language are intricately related. Does the fact that you speak English versus Spanish — or Chinese versus Swahili — mean that you reason, think, and perceive the world differently? According to linguist Benjamin Whorf (1956), the language that a person speaks largely determines the nature of that person's thoughts. Whorf's *linguistic relativity* hypothesis suggests that our vocabulary determines how we perceive and categorize the world around us. As proof, Whorf offered a now classic example: Because Eskimos [Inuits] have many words to describe different kinds of snow (*apikak* for "first snow falling," *pukak* for "snow for drinking water," and so on), their richer vocabulary supposedly enables them to perceive and think about snow differently from English speakers, who have only one word — *snow*. People who speak differently languages reportedly have different conceptions of the world around them.

Whorf's hypothesis is certainly intriguing, but most research does not support it. For one thing, he apparently exaggerated the number of Inuit words for snow (Pullum, 1991) and ignored the fact that English speakers have a number of terms like *slush, sleet, hard pack, powder*, and so on. More importantly, Eleanor Rosch (1973) found counterevidence for Whorf's hypothesis when she experimentally tested his ideas with the Dani tribe in New Guinea. Although the Dani language has only two color names, one indicating cool, dark colors and the other warm, bright colors, Rosch found that the Dani could discriminate among color hues just as well as people speaking languages with multiple names for colors. In other words, although it may be easier to express a particular idea in one language than in another, language does not necessarily determine how or what we think.

Whorf apparently went too far with his theory that language *determines* thought, but there is no doubt that language *influences* thought (Lillard, 1998). For example, what happens when people speak two or more languages? Studies have found that people who are bilingual report feeling a different sense of self, depending on the language they are using (Matsumoto, 2000). When using Chinese, they found they tended to behave in ways appropriate to Chinese cultural norms, but when speaking English, they tended to adopt Western norms.

The influence of language on thought also is readily apparent in our word choice. For example, when companies want to alter workers' perceptions, they don't *fire* employees; rather, employees are *outplaced, dehired,* or *nonrenewed*. Similarly, the military uses terms like *preemptive strike* to cover the fact that they attacked first and *tactical redeployment* to refer to a retreat of troops. Our choice of words also has had some embarrassing and financial consequences for North American businesses. When Pepsi-Cola used its "Come alive with Pepsi" slogan in Japan, they later learned that it translated as "Pepsi brings your dead ancestors back from the grave." Words evoke different images and value judgments. Our words, therefore, *influence* not only our thinking but also the thinking of those who hear them.

■ Language Development: From Crying to Talking

From birth, the child has a multitude of ways to communicate. Through such nonverbal means as facial expressions, eye contact, and body gestures, babies only hours old begin to "teach" their parents and caregivers when and how they want to be held, fed, and played with. As early as the late 1800s, Charles Darwin proposed that most emotional expressions, such as smiles, frowns, and looks of disgust, are universal and innate (Figure 23.1). Darwin's contention is supported by the fact that children who are born blind and deaf exhibit the same facial expressions for emotions that sighted and hearing children do.

Stages of Language Development

Eventually, children also communicate verbally. The first, *prelinguistic stage* begins with the newborn baby's reflexive cry. Within a short time, crying becomes more purposeful. At least three distinct patterns have been identified: the basic hunger cry, the anger cry, and the pain cry (Wolff, 1969). Although many child-care texts suggest that each of these cries can be easily identified and responded to by the primary caregivers, most parents find that they must learn through a process of trial and error what actions will satisfy their child.

At about age 2 to 3 months, babies begin **cooing,** producing vowel-like sounds ("ooooh" and "aaaah"). Around age 4 to 5 months they start **babbling,** adding consonants to their vowels ("bahbahbah" and "dahdahdah"). Some parents mark babbling as the beginning of language and consider their child's vocalizations as "words," even though the child typically does not associate a "word" with a specific

Cooing *Vowel-like sounds infants produce beginning around age 2 to 3 months*

Babbling *Vowel/consonant combinations that infants begin to produce at about age 4 to 6 months*

Nature or nurture? *Most children learn to speak in the first few months of life. What does this say about the biological basis for language acquisition?*

Figure 23.1 *Early nonverbal communication.* Can you identify these emotions? Infants as young as 2.5 months can express several basic emotions, including interest, joy, anger, and sadness.

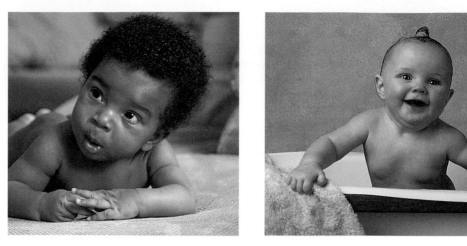

Overextension *Overly broad use of a word to include objects that do not fit the word's meaning (e.g., calling all men "Daddy")*

Telegraphic Speech *Two- or three-word sentences of young children that contain only the most necessary words*

Overgeneralize *Applying the basic rules of grammar even to cases that are exceptions to the rule (e.g., saying "mans" instead of "men")*

Study **T**ip

If you're having difficulty differentiating between overextension and overgeneralization, remember the g in overgeneralize as a cue that this term applies to problems with grammar.

object or person, and despite the fact that all children the world over babble in the same fashion.

The true *linguistic stage* begins toward the end of the first year of life, when babbling begins to sound more like the language of the child's home and when the child seems to understand that sound is related to meaning. At the beginning of this stage, the child is generally limited to a single-utterance vocabulary such as "mama," "go," "juice," or "up." Children manage to get a lot of mileage out of these singular utterances: "Mama" can be used to mean, "I want you to come and get me," "I'm hurt," and "I don't like this stranger." However, their expressive ability more than doubles once they begin to join words into short phrases such as "Go bye-bye," "Daddy milk," and "No night-night!"

At this age, children sometimes overextend the words they use. **Overextension** is using words to include objects that do not fit the word's meaning. For example, having learned the word *doggie*, a child often overextends the word to include all small, furry animals (e.g., kittens, bunnies).

Around age 2 years, most children are creating short but intelligible sentences by linking several words. However, they leave out nonessential, connecting words: "Me want cookie;" "Grandma go bye-bye." This pattern is called **telegraphic speech** because, like telegrams of days gone by, children's speech includes only words directly relevant to meaning, and nothing more.

While increasing their vocabulary at a phenomenal rate during these early years, children also are acquiring a wide variety of rules for grammar, such as adding *-ed* to indicate the past tense and *s* to form plurals. They also make mistakes, however, because they **overgeneralize,** or *overuse* the basic rules of grammar. This results in novel sentences like "I goed to the zoo" and "Two mans."

By age 5 years most children have mastered the basic rules of grammar and typically use about 2,000 words. (Many foreign-language instructors consider this level of mastery adequate for getting by in any given culture.) Past this point, vocabulary and grammar acquisition gradually improve throughout the entire life span.

Theories of Language Development

What motivates children to develop language? Some theorists believe language capability is innate, whereas others claim it is learned through imitation and reinforcement (the nature-versus-nurture controversy again). Although there are staunch supporters of both sides, most psychologists find neither of these extreme positions satisfactory. Most believe that language acquisition is a combination of both nature and nurture — the interactionist position (Casti, 2000; Gottlieb, 2000).

According to the nativist position, language acquisition is primarily a matter of maturation. The most famous advocate of this viewpoint, Noam Chomsky (1968, 1980), suggests that children are born "prewired" to learn language. They possess a type of **language acquisition device** (LAD) that needs only minimal exposure to adult speech to unlock its potential. The LAD enables the child to analyze language and extract the basic rules of grammar.

To support his viewpoint, Chomsky points to the fact that children all over the world go through similar stages in language development at about the same age and in a pattern that parallels motor development. He also cites the fact that babbling is the same in all cultures and that deaf babies babble just like hearing babies.

Although the nativist position enjoys considerable support, it fails to adequately explain individual differences. Why does one child learn rules for English, for example, whereas another learns rules for Spanish? The "nurturists" can explain individual differences and distinct languages. From their perspective, children learn language through a complex system of rewards, punishments, and imitation. Any vocalization attempt ("mah" or "dah") from the young infant is quickly rewarded with smiles and other forms of encouragement. When the infant later babbles "mama" or "dada," proud parents respond even more enthusiastically. (As a critical thinker, can you see how these parents are unknowingly using a type of *shaping* — a concept we discussed in Module 17?)

Language Acquisition Device (LAD) *According to Chomsky, an innate mechanism that enables a child to analyze language and extract the basic rules of grammar*

■ Animals and Language: Can Humans Talk to Nonhuman Animals?

In addition to the nature versus nurture debate on language development, controversy also exists over whether nonhuman animals use language or can be taught to use language. Without question, they communicate. Most species send warnings, signal sexual interest, share location of food sources, and so on. The question is this: Are nonhuman animals capable of mastering the rich complexity of human language?

One of the earliest attempts to answer this question came from psychologists Winthrop and Luella Kellogg (1933), who raised a baby chimpanzee for several years alongside their son of about the same age. Although the chimp learned a few rudimentary, communicative gestures, she never uttered sounds that resembled language. Other early animal language researchers concluded, however, that the Kelloggs probably failed simply because apes do not have the necessary anatomical structure to vocalize the way humans do.

Subsequent studies focused on teaching apes nonvocal languages. One of the most successful was a study by Beatrice and Allen Gardner (1969), who recognized the manual dexterity of chimpanzees and their ability to imitate gestures. The Gardners used American Sign Language (ASL) with a chimp named Washoe. Their success story speaks for itself. By the time Washoe was 4 years old, she had learned 132 signs and was able to combine them into simple sentences such as: "Hurry, gimme toothbrush" and "Please tickle more."

Following the Gardners' success with Washoe, several other language projects have been conducted with apes (Itakura, 1992; Savage-Rumbaugh, 1990). David Premack (1976) taught a chimp named Sarah to "read" and "write" by arranging plastic symbols on a magnetic board. She learned not only to use the plastic symbols but also to follow certain grammatical rules in communicating with her trainers.

Another well-known study was conducted with a chimp named Lana. She learned to push symbols on a computer to get things she wanted, such as food, a drink, a tickle from her trainers, and having her curtains opened (Rumbaugh et al., 1974). And, of course, there is the famous gorilla Koko discussed in the section opener. Penny Patterson (2002) reportedly taught Koko over 1,000 signs in ASL.

A number of language studies also have been done with dolphins. Communication with dolphins is by means of hand signals or audible commands. The commands

Using symbols on a computer, chimps have learned to press specific buttons to get food, drink, or a tickle from the trainers. Does this qualify as true language? Why or why not?

Is Koko using language? *Recall from the section opener, Francine (Penny) Patterson taught a gorilla named Koko to communicate through American Sign Language. At first she rewarded Koko with pieces of fruit if she made any sign that remotely resembled the correct one. Gradually, she reinforced only those gestures that were formed correctly. Today Koko reportedly knows over 1,000 signs and continues to learn new ones.*

may be spoken by trainers or generated by computer and transmitted through an underwater speaker system. In one typical study, dolphins were given commands made up of two- to five-word sentences, such as "Big ball — square — return," which meant they should go get the big ball, put it in the floating square, and return to the trainer (Herman, Richards, & Woltz, 1984).

The interesting part of this experiment was that the commands varied in syntax and content, both of which altered meaning. For example, the next command might be "Square — big ball — return," which meant the dolphin should go to the square first, then get the big ball, then return to the trainer with the ball. Or the command might refer to one of the other objects floating in the pool, thereby changing its content: "Triangle — little ball — square," which required the dolphin to discriminate among various shapes and various sizes of balls to carry out the command. The study demonstrated that dolphins could carry out a great variety of commands that varied in both content and syntax.

Evaluating Animal Language Studies

Although these ape and dolphin studies seem impressive, psychologists nevertheless do not agree on the interpretation of the findings. Most psychologists believe that nonhuman animals communicate at some level, but compared with humans, they express a severely limited repertoire of ideas. The average length of sentences produced and understood by humans also is significantly greater than the two- to five-word sentences used by other animals. Moreover, critics claim that apes and dolphins are unable to learn the rules of grammar and syntax that humans use to convey subtle differences in meaning. They question whether animals can use language in ways that are considered creative or unique and point out that they do not express the concept of time *(tomorrow, last week)*, request information *(How do birds fly?)*, comment on the feelings of others *(Penny is sad)*, express similarities *(That cloud looks like a tree)*, or propose possibilities *(The cat might sit on my lap)* (Jackendoff, 1994).

Other critics raise the issue of operant conditioning (Module 17). They claim that nonhuman animals do not have a conceptual understanding of the complex signs and symbols of language; those who do engage in simple human language are merely imitating symbols to receive rewards. In short, nonhuman animals are not really trying to communicate but are simply performing operantly conditioned responses (Savage-Rumbaugh, 1990; Terrace, 1979). Finally, other critics suggest that much of the data regarding animal language has been anecdotal — and not always well documented. For example, the spectacular claims of Koko's abilities have yet to be published in scientific journals (Lieberman, 1998; Willingham, 2001).

On the other hand, proponents of animal language are quick to point out that chimpanzees and gorillas can use language creatively and have even coined some words of their own. For example, Washoe called a refrigerator "open eat drink" and a swan a "water bird" (Gardner & Gardner, 1971). Koko signed "finger bracelet" to describe a ring and "eye hat" to describe a mask (Patterson & Linden, 1981). Proponents also argue that, as demonstrated by the dolphin studies, animals can be taught to understand basic rules of sentence structure.

Still, the fact remains that the gap between language as spoken and understood by humans and that generated and understood by other animals is considerable. All the evidence seems to suggest that nonhuman animals can learn language at a rudimentary level, but that this language is less complex, creative, and rule-laden than any language used by humans. (As a critical thinker, have you ever thought about an opposite approach to this type of language research? Why don't humans learn nonhuman animal language? Could humans be taught to comprehend and use chimpanzee communication systems, for example?)

"He says he wants a lawyer."

©The New Yorker Collection 1999 Tom Chalkley from cartoonbank.com. All Rights Reserved.

Achievement

RESEARCH HIGHLIGHT

Language and the Brain

In some respects, the brain appears naturally "prewired" to learn language. At birth, the language areas of the temporal cortex are larger in the left than the right hemisphere, and the neurons in the left hemisphere are sensitive to speech sounds. Our neurological understanding of language is just beginning to unfold, but a number of studies provide insight into language and its development.

Functional magnetic resonance imaging (fMRI) studies, for example, indicate that areas of the brain may be organized differently depending on the age at which language is learned. When bilingual individuals learn both languages in childhood, a single region of *Broca's area* is used to produce complex sentences. But when people learn a second language during adolescence, two different regions of *Broca's area* are used (Kim et al., 1997), and the right hemisphere seems to be used more than if the language is learned during childhood (Barinaga, 2000). Finally, recent information suggests that two separate areas of the brain are involved in the processing and production of language.

Broca's area is involved in both speech production and language production, whereas the *supramarginal gyrus* (located in the parietal lobe) combines word meaning with the production of words (Crosson et al., 2001; Grodzinsky, 2000).

Although the brain may seem prepared to learn language, cognitive neuroscientists, linguists, and psychologists debate whether language is inborn and if we have sensitive periods for language acquisition (Plomin & Dale, 2000; Ramus, Hauser, Miller, Morris, & Mehler, 2000). (The *sensitive period hypothesis* suggests that humans most easily learn language between birth and puberty, the time when the brain is becoming increasingly specialized. If learning does not occur during this special time, it may be impossible to later "catch up.")

Genie's case provides an excellent example of the importance of sensitive periods for language development. When first discovered at age 13, she was almost completely silent. Because her father severely punished her for making any vocal sounds, Genie did not sob when she cried nor speak when in a fit of rage. She understood only a few word phrases such as "*stopit*" and "*no more*" (Rymer, 1993). After 8 months of training, Genie had a vocabulary of more than 200 words and was putting together 2-word sentences. However, her language development did not continue in the usual explosive pattern of normal children. According to last reports, Genie's adult language skills are limited to those of a typical 2 or 3 year old (Harris, 1995). This is a conversation between Genie and her foster mother, when Genie was 18:

> GENIE: At school is washing car.
> MOTHER: Whose car did you wash?
> GENIE: People car.
> MOTHER: How many cars did you wash?
> GENIE: Two car. [Curtiss, 1977, p. 28]

Despite years of intensive training, brain scans showed that Genie's left hemisphere remained virtually unresponsive. This suggests that her isolation during critical language-learning years may have failed to trigger innate brain mechanisms, and the cortical tissue normally committed to language may have functionally atrophied.

Assessment

CHECK & REVIEW

Language

Human language is a creative form of communication consisting of symbols put together according to a set of rules. The three building blocks of language are **phonemes, morphemes,** and **grammar.** Phonemes are the basic speech sounds; they are combined to form morphemes, the smallest meaningful units of language. Phonemes, morphemes, words, and phrases are put together by rules of grammar (**syntax** and **semantics**). *Syntax* refers to the grammatical rules for ordering words in sentences; *semantics* refers to meaning in language.

According to Benjamin Whorf's *linguistic relativity hypothesis*, language shapes thought. Generally, Whorf's hypothesis is not supported. However, our choice of vocabulary can influence our mental imagery and social perceptions.

Children go through two stages in their acquisition of language: prelinguistic (crying, **cooing, babbling**) and linguistic (which includes single utterances, **telegraphic speech,** and the acquisition of rules of grammar).

Nativists believe that language is an inborn capacity and develops primarily by maturation. Chomsky suggests that humans possess a **language acquisition device** (LAD) that needs only minimal environmental input. Nurturists emphasize the role of the environment and suggest that language development results from rewards, punishments, and imitating models.

The most successful nonhuman animal language studies have been done with apes using American Sign Language. Dolphins also have been taught to comprehend sentences that vary in syntax and meaning. Some psychologists believe that nonhuman animals can truly learn human language, but others suggest the nonhuman animals are merely responding to rewards.

Questions

1. The basic speech sounds /ch/ and /v/ are known as _____; the smallest meaningful units of language, such as *book*, *pre-*, and *-ing*, are known as _____.

2. Chomsky believes we possess an inborn ability to learn language known as a _____. (a) telegraphic understanding device (TUD); (b) language acquisition device (LAD); (c) language and grammar translator (LGT); (d) overgeneralized neural net (ONN)

3. What is Whorf's *linguistic relativity hypothesis?*

4. Human language differs from the communication of nonhuman animals in that it is (a) used more creatively to express thoughts and ideas; (b) the expression of an innate capability; (c) essential for thought; (d) composed of sounds.

Answers to Questions can be found in Appendix B.

MODULE 23   ACTIVE LEARNING WORKSHEET

PART A

ACROSS

1 Meaning or the study of meaning derived from morphemes, words, and sentences.
4 The most basic unit of speech; an individual speech sound.
5 The rules of a language that specify how phonemes, morphemes, words, and phrases should be combined to meaningfully express thoughts.

DOWN

2 The smallest meaningful unit of language, formed from a combination of phonemes.
3 The grammatical rules that specify in what order the words and phrases should be arranged in a sentence in order to convey meaning.

PART B

Enter the correct letter from Column A in the blank space in Column B, and then double-check your answers with those in Appendix B.

Column A	Column B
a. Telegraphic Speech	1.____ Calling all men "Daddy."
b. Babbling	2.____ 2 or 3 word sentences.
c. Overextension	3.____ Vowel-consonants, such as "ma-ma-ma-ma."
d. Overgeneralization	4.____ Innate capacity to acquire language and grammar.
e. Cooing	5.____ Vowel-like sounds, such as "ee-ee-ee-ee."
f. Language Acquisition Device (LAD)	6.____ Saying "foots" instead of "feet."

MODULE 24
INTELLIGENCE

Are Koko, Genie, and Thomas Edison intelligent? What is intelligence? Are there different types of intelligence?

◾ The Nature of Intelligence: Is it Real?

The term **intelligence** is commonly defined in psychology as the general capacity to profit from experience, acquire knowledge, and adapt to changes in the environment. Although we use the term *intelligence* in our everyday conversation and assume we all share the same definition, we don't. Even among psychologists there is considerable debate over its definition and appropriate methods for measurement. However, there is one area of agreement — it is not a *thing*. It has no mass and it occupies no space. When people talk about intelligence as though it were a concrete, tangible object, they commit an error in reasoning, known as *reification*. Like consciousness, learning, memory, or personality, intelligence is nothing more than a useful *hypothetical, abstract construct*. As you will see later, it is estimated, rather arbitrarily, by scores on intelligence tests. Practically speaking, intelligence is what intelligence tests measure.

Intelligence also is socially constructed, and its definition varies according to the characteristics and skills valued in that culture (Sternberg & Hedlund, 2002; Sternberg & Kaufman, 1998). In fact, many languages have no word that corresponds to our notion of intelligence. The closest Mandarin word is a Chinese character meaning "good brain and talented" (Matsumoto, 2000), which is commonly associated with traits like imitation, effort, and social responsibility (Keats, 1982).

Because of the difficulty in identifying and defining intelligence, it remains a complex and controversial topic. For most Western psychologists, modern research on intelligence has centered on several key questions:

- What is the basis for intelligence? Does it depend more on nature or nurture?

- What are the properties of intelligence? Is it a single general ability or several distinct kinds of mental abilities (intelligences)?

We will discuss several theories that attempt to answer these questions, beginning with Charles Spearman's early theory of *general intelligence*.

Intelligence as a Single Ability

In the early years of intelligence testing, psychologists viewed intelligence as innate, a broad mental ability that included all the cognitive functions. However, Charles Spearman (1923) proposed that intelligence is a single factor, which he termed *general intelligence* (g). He based his theory on his observation that high scores on separate tests of mental abilities, such as spatial and reasoning ability, tend to correlate with each other. Thus, Spearman believed g underlies all intellectual behavior, including reasoning, solving problems, and performing well in all areas of cognition. On the basis of Spearman's work, standardized tests were widely used in the military, schools, and business to measure this general intelligence (Lubinski & Davis, 1992).

Intelligence as Multiple Abilities

About a decade later, L. L. Thurstone (1938) proposed seven primary mental abilities: verbal comprehension, word fluency, numerical fluency, spatial visualization, associative memory, perceptual speed, and reasoning. He felt that Spearman's g had little, if any value. Naturally, at the time, Thurstone's view was rather radical. Many years

Intelligence *General capacity to profit from experience, acquire knowledge, and adapt to changes in the environment*

later, J. P. Guilford (1967) expanded on this number and proposed that as many as 120 factors were involved in the structure of intelligence.

Intelligence Again as a Single Ability

About the same time that Guilford was working, Raymond Cattell (1963, 1971) reanalyzed Thurstone's data and argued against the idea of multiple intelligences. He agreed with Spearman that a single g does exist, but that there are two types of g:

Fluid Intelligence *Aspects of innate intelligence, including reasoning abilities, memory, and speed of information processing, that are relatively independent of education and tend to decline as people age*

Crystallized Intelligence *Knowledge and skills gained through experience and education that tend to increase over the life span*

1. *Fluid intelligence* (gf) refers to reasoning abilities, memory, and speed of information processing. If you were asked to solve analogies or remember a long set of numbers, you would be relying on your fluid intelligence. Being relatively independent of education and experience, it reflects an inherited predisposition, and, like other biological capacities it declines with advancing age (Burns, Nettelbeck, & Cooper, 2000; Schaie, 1993, 1994).

2. *Crystallized intelligence* (gc) refers to knowledge and skills gained through experience and education (Facon & Facon-Bollengier, 1999). You would rely on your crystallized intelligence if you were asked to explain the President's Social Security policy or the difference between a "bear" or "bull" stock market. Crystallized intelligence tends to increase over the life span, which explains why physicians, teachers, musicians, politicians, and people in many other occupations may become more successful with age and can continue working well into old age.

Recent findings show increased frontal lobe activity during very complex tasks, which helps support the idea of g (Duncan & Owen, 2000). Recall from Module 2, however, that correlation does not necessarily imply causation and that other explanations are equally possible. Moreover, other studies find that more intelligent people are likely to show less, not more frontal lobe activation, possibly because tasks are not as challenging to them as to those less intelligent (Haier et al., 1993; Sternberg, 1999).

A Return to Multiple Intelligences

Although there is modern support for the concept of g, many contemporary cognitive theorists see a relationship among diverse mental abilities and point out that most people excel in specific areas of intelligence more than in other areas. So perhaps, as originally suggested by Thurstone and Guilford, mental abilities actually are distinct from one another.

Gardner's theory of multiple intelligences.

One cognitive theorist, Howard Gardner, has proposed a *theory of multiple intelligences* (Figure 24.1). Using his own stringent criteria, Gardner (1983, 1998) has identified the eight (and possibly nine) distinct intelligences shown in Table 24.1. According to Gardner (1999), people come to know their world through these separate intelligences. Also, people have different *profiles of intelligence* because they are stronger in some areas than others, and they use their intelligences differently to learn new material, perform tasks, and solve problems. For example, Richard Hatch, the million-dollar winner on the popular TV program *Survivor*, would undoubtedly score high on *naturalistic* intelligence; whereas Sarah Hughes, the figure skating Gold Medalist of the 2001 Winter Olympics, would score at the top in *bodily/kinesthetic* intelligence.

Gardner's theory has wide-reaching implications for intelligence testing and for education. He believes intelligence testing should consist of assessing a person's strengths rather than coming up with a single "IQ score." He challenges our education system to present material in a variety of learning modes rather than the traditional linguistic and logical–mathematical, and to develop multiple means of assessment rather than the traditional paper-and-pencil tests.

TABLE 24.1 GARDNER'S MULTIPLE INTELLIGENCES AND POSSIBLE CAREERS

Linguistic: language, such as speaking, reading a book, writing a story	**Spatial:** mental maps, such as figuring out how to pack multiple presents in a box or how to draw a floor plan	**Bodily-kinesthetic:** body movement, such as dancing, hitting a baseball, or skiing	**Intra-personal:** understanding oneself, such as setting achievable goals or recognizing self-defeating emotions	**Logical-mathematical:** problem solving or scientific analysis, such as following a logical proof or solving a mathematical problem	**Musical:** musical skills, such as singing a song or playing the piano	**Inter-personal:** social skills, such as talking with other people	**Naturalistic:** Being attuned to nature, such as noticing seasonal patterns or using environmentally safe products	**Spiritual Existential:** (Speculative) Attunement to meaning of life and death and other conditions of life
Career: Novelist, journalist, teacher	**Careers:** Engineer, architect, pilot	**Careers:** Athlete, dancer, ski instructor	**Careers:** Increased success in almost all careers	**Careers:** Mathematician, scientist, engineer	**Careers:** Singer, musician, composer	**Careers:** Salesperson, manager, therapist, teacher	**Careers:** Biologist, naturalist	**Careers:** Philosopher, theologian

Source: Adapted from Gardner, 1983, 1999.

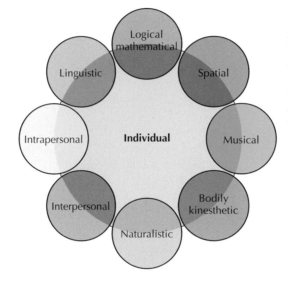

Figure 24.1 *Gardner's theory of multiple intelligences.* Howard Gardner believes there are independent forms of intelligence and that the value of these intelligences may change according to culture. Gardner also proposed a *possible* ninth intelligence, spiritual/existential, shown in Table 24.1.

Sternberg's triarchic (three-part) theory of successful intelligence. On the basis of findings from information processing research, Robert Sternberg (1985, 1999) developed what he called a *triarchic theory of successful intelligence* (Figure 24.1). Sternberg argued that even more important than the outward products of intelligence, such as correct answers on an intelligence test, are the thinking processes we use to arrive at the answers and that theories of intelligence should account for these processes.

The *triarchic theory* proposes three aspects of intelligence: (1) analytic intelligence, (2) creative intelligence, and (3) practical intelligence (Grigorenko, Jarvin, & Sternberg, 2002; Sternberg, 1999). According to Sternberg, people tend to have a stronger aptitude for one or more of these aspects of intelligence. Table 24.2 briefly describes each aspect.

The value of Sternberg's theory of intelligence is that he emphasizes the process underlying thinking rather than just the end product, and he stresses the importance of applying mental abilities to real-world situations rather than testing mental abilities in isolation (e.g., Sternberg et al., 2001; Sternberg & Hedlund, 2002). Sternberg (1998) introduced the term *successful intelligence* to describe the ability to adapt to, shape, and select environments in order to accomplish personal and societal goals.

TABLE 24.2 STERNBERG'S TRIARCHIC THEORY OF SUCCESSFUL INTELLIGENCE

	Analytical Intelligence	**Creative Intelligence**	**Practical Intelligence**
Sample Skills	Good at analysis, evaluation, judgment, and comparison skills	Good at invention, discovery, coping with novelty, and imagination skills	Good at application, implementation, execution, and utilization skills
Methods of Assessment	These skills are assessed by any of the intelligence or scholastic aptitude tests. Questions ask about meanings of words based on context and how to solve number-series problems.	These skills are assessed in many ways, including open-ended tasks, such as designing an invention, writing a short story, drawing a piece of art, creating an advertisement, or solving a scientific problem requiring insight.	Although these skills are more difficult to assess, they can be measured by asking for solutions to practical and personal problems.

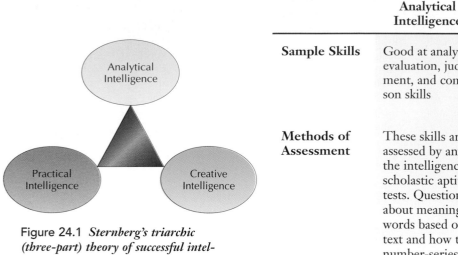

Figure 24.1 *Sternberg's triarchic (three-part) theory of successful intelligence.* According to Robert Sternberg's model, there are three separate and different aspects of intelligence. Each of these components is learned, not the result of genetics. Therefore, each can be strengthened or improved.

Gardner and Sternberg differ on a number of points in their theories, but they agree that intelligence involves multiple abilities. In fact, in modern times, most cognitive scientists believe that, for most people, intelligence is a "very general mental ability" (Arvey et al., 1994).

■ Test Construction: What Makes a Good Test?

Think back to the questions we asked at the very beginning of our discussion of intelligence: Are Genie, Koko, and Thomas Edison intelligent? As you can see, intelligence is difficult to define and measure. But did you know that college admission officers, scholarship committees, and employers might have used scores from your own intelligence tests in their selection of you as a student or employee? How good are these tests? Are they good predictors of student and employee success? To answer these questions, we first need to introduce three general principles of psychological testing: *standardization*, *reliability*, and *validity*.

Standardization *Establishing the norms and uniform procedures for giving and scoring a test*

1. ***Standardization.*** To be useful, intelligence tests (as well as personality, aptitude, and most other tests) must be *standardized*. The term **standardization** has two meanings as it applies to testing (Hogan, 2003). First, every test must have *norms*, or average scores. To develop norms, the test is given to a *representative sample* — a large sample of diverse people who resemble those for whom the test was intended. Norms determine whether an individual's particular score is considered high, low, or average in comparison to the representative sample. Second, *testing procedures* must be standardized. Uniform conditions must exist for taking, giving, and scoring the test. All test takers must get the same instructions, questions, and time limits, and those who administer the test must know exactly how to explain the test and must follow specific, objective standards in their scoring.

2. *Reliability.* Imagine having a stopwatch or oven temperature guide that gave different readings each time you measured. Obviously, every measuring device (including tests) must be consistent. That is, repeated measurements should produce reasonably similar findings. This stability, or **reliability,** of a test is usually determined by retesting to determine whether test scores have changed significantly (Hogan, 2003, p. 142). Retesting can be by the *test-retest method,* comparing participants' scores on two separate administrations of a test, or with the *split-half method,* splitting a test into two equivalent parts and comparing the degree of similarity between the two halves (e.g., whether scores from odd and even questions agree).

Reliability *A measure of the consistency and stability of test scores when the test is readministered*

3. *Validity.* The third important principle of test construction is **validity,** the ability of a test to measure what it is designed to measure. There are several types of validity. The most important is *criterion-related validity,* or the accuracy with which test scores can be used to predict another variable of interest, termed the *criterion.* Criterion-related validity is expressed as the *correlation* between the test score and the criterion. (Recall from Module 2, a correlation is a standard measure of how two variables are related.) A high correlation indicates the two variables are closely related, and low or zero correlation indicates there is little or no relationship between them. If two variables are highly correlated, then one variable can be used to predict the other. Thus, if a test is valid, its scores will be useful in predicting people's behavior in some other specified situation, such as using intelligence test scores to predict grades in college.

Validity *Ability of a test to measure what it was designed to measure*

Can you see why a test that is standardized and reliable, but *not* valid, is worthless? Suppose you are giving someone a test for skin sensitivity. Such a test may be easy to standardize (the instructions specify the exact points on the body to apply the test agent), and it may be reliable (similar results are obtained on each retest), but it would certainly not be valid for predicting college grades.

Although validity is central to a test's success, it is also the core issue in one of the oldest debates in psychology. What are we actually measuring on intelligence tests? If we say we are testing for intelligence but measure only mathematical ability, aren't we by default defining mathematical ability as intelligence? What happens if we only ask questions about acquired knowledge? People with less formal schooling would then be judged as less intelligent. The upcoming section on the origins of intelligence tests will help prepare you for the end-of-section Research Highlight, which explores the current controversy surrounding intelligence tests.

Assessment

CHECK & REVIEW

The Nature of Intelligence and Test Construction

Today, **intelligence** is commonly defined as the general capacity to profit from experience, to acquire knowledge, and adapt to changes in the environment. However, there are several theorists who have defined it differently: Spearman viewed intelligence as "g," a general intelligence; Thurstone saw it as seven distinct mental abilities; Guilford believed it was composed of 120 or more separate abilities; and Cattell viewed it as two types of "g," which he called **fluid intelligence** and **crystallized intelligence.**

In addition to these early theorists, Gardner's theory of multiple intelligences identifies eight (and possibly nine) types of intelligence. He believes that both teaching and assessing should take into account people's learning styles and cognitive strengths. Sternberg's triarchic theory of successful intelligence emphasizes the thinking process rather than the end product (the answer). Sternberg identifies three aspects of intelligence: analytical, creative, and practical intelligences.

For any test to be useful, it must be standardized, reliable, and valid. **Standardization** refers to (a) giving a test to a large number of people in order to determine norms and (b) using identical procedures in administering a test so that everyone takes the test under exactly the same testing conditions. **Reliability** refers to the stability of test scores over time. **Validity** refers to how well the test measures what it is intended to measure.

Questions

1. The g factor originally proposed by Charles Spearman is best defined as (a) skill in the use of language as a tool for thought; (b) general intelligence; (c) the ability to adapt to the environment; (d) the type of intelligence we call common sense.

2. What is the difference between fluid and crystallized intelligences?
3. Explain Sternberg's triarchic theory of successful intelligence.
4. Identify which testing principle — standardization, reliability, or validity — is being described in each of the following statements:

   a. _____ ensures that if the same person takes the same test 2 weeks after taking it the first time, her score will not significantly change.
   b. _____ ensures that a test or other measurement instrument actually

measures what it purports to measure.

   c. _____ ensures that the test has been given to large numbers of people to determine which scores are average, above average, and below average — in short, which scores are representative of the general population.

Answers to Questions can be found in Appendix B.

www.wiley.com/college/huffman

Assessing Intelligence: The Development of the IQ Test

There are many different kinds of IQ tests, and each approaches the measurement of intelligence from a slightly different perspective. Most, however, attempt to measure abilities that allow the test to be a valid predictor of academic performance. In other words, most IQ tests are designed to predict grades in school. To see how that's done, let's take a look at the most commonly used IQ tests.

Individual IQ Tests

The first IQ test to be widely used in the United States was the Stanford–Binet Intelligence Scale (Boake, 2002). It was loosely based on the very first IQ tests developed in France around the turn of the last century by Alfred Binet. In the United States, Lewis Terman (1916) developed the Stanford–Binet (at Stanford University) to test the intellectual ability of U.S.-born children ages 3 to 16. The test is revised periodically — the latest revision was done in 1985. The test items are administered individually (one test-giver and one test-taker) and consist of such tasks as copying geometric designs, identifying similarities, and repeating a sequence of numbers.

In the original version of the Stanford–Binet, results were expressed in terms of a mental age. For example, if a 7-year-old's score equaled that of an average 8-year-old, the child was considered to have a mental age of eight, as measured by the test. To determine the child's **intelligence quotient (IQ),** mental age was divided by the child's chronological age (actual age in years) and multiplied by 100, as follows:

Intelligence Quotient (IQ) *A subject's mental age divided by chronological age and multiplied by 100*

$$IQ = \frac{MA}{CA} \times 100 = \frac{8}{7} \times 100 = 1.14 \times 100 = 114$$

Thus, a 7-year-old with a mental age of 8 would have an IQ of 114. A "normal" child should have a mental age equal to his or her chronological age. (*Normal* in this case refers to the norms or statistics used to standardize the test.)

Today, most intelligence tests, including the Stanford–Binet, no longer compute an IQ. Instead, the test scores are expressed as a comparison of a single person's score to a national sample of similar-aged people. These deviation IQs are computed on the basis of how far the person's score on the test deviates from the national average. On a standardized IQ test such as the Stanford–Binet, the majority of people score within one standard deviation (16 points) above or one standard deviation below the national

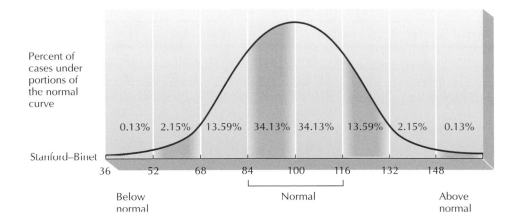

Figure 24.2 *The distribution of scores on the Stanford–Binet Intelligence Test.* Notice that over two-thirds of the people taking the test, 68.26 percent, have an IQ within the normal range.

average, which is 100 points. Figure 24.2 illustrates the typical distribution curve of scores on the Stanford–Binet: The majority (68 percent) of the children taking the test score within the normal range, whereas approximately 16 percent score above 116 and approximately 16 percent score below 84. Even though the actual IQ is no longer calculated, the term *IQ* remains as a shorthand expression for intelligence test scores.

The Wechsler Tests

David Wechsler (pronounced "WEX-ler") developed the most widely used intelligence test, the Wechsler Adult Intelligence Scale (WAIS), in the early 1900s. He later created a similar test for school-age children, the Wechsler Intelligence Scale for Children, third edition (WISC-III; Table 24.3), and one for preschool children, the Wechsler Preschool and Primary Scale (WPPSI).

Like the Stanford–Binet, the Wechsler tests yield an overall intelligence score, but they have separate *verbal* (such as, vocabulary, comprehension, knowledge of general information) and *performance* scores (such as arranging pictures to tell a story, arranging blocks to match a given pattern). Wechsler's approach has three advantages: (1) The WAIS was specifically designed for adults — not children. (2) Different abilities can be evaluated either separately or together. (3) People who are unable to speak or understand English can still be tested. The verbal portion of the test doesn't have to be administered, because each subtest yields its own score.

Have intelligence scores gone up or down over the years? A comparison of intelligence scores over the years indicates that IQ scores increase from one generation to the next, and this increase is found in over 20 different countries (Flynn, 1987, 2000, 2002; Neisser, 1998; Resing & Nijland, 2002). Fluid intelligence scores, typically measured with problem-solving tasks, have increased about 15 points per generation, whereas crystallized intelligence scores, generally assessed by vocabulary and math skills, have increased about 9 points per generation.

The explanation is unclear, but there are at least three possible contributors to this phenomenon, which is termed the *Flynn effect:* (1) the level of public education has increased, (2) people have become more proficient test-takers, and (3) intelligence increases with better nutrition. James Flynn (2000, 2002) believes such increases may reflect the fact that intelligence tests aren't actually measuring intelligence but rather some weak link to intelligence.

Extremes in Intelligence

If you want to judge the validity of any test (academic, intelligence, personality, and so on), one of the best methods is to compare people who score at the extremes. Students who get an A on a major exam should clearly have more information than those

TABLE 24.3 SUBTESTS OF THE WISC-III

Verbal Subtests	Example*
Information	How many senators are elected from each state?
Similarities	How are computers and books alike?
Arithmetic	If one baseball card costs three cents, how much will five baseball cards cost?
Vocabulary	Define *lamp*.
Comprehension	What should you do if you accidentally break a friend's toy?
Performance Subtests	Example below:

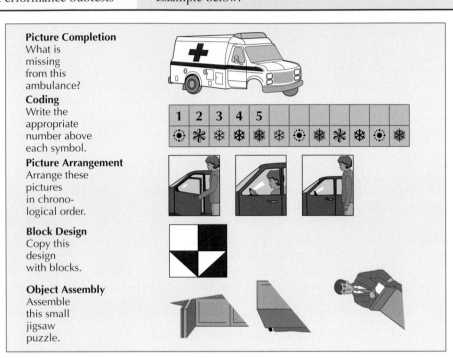

Picture Completion
What is missing from this ambulance?

Coding
Write the appropriate number above each symbol.

Picture Arrangement
Arrange these pictures in chronological order.

Block Design
Copy this design with blocks.

Object Assembly
Assemble this small jigsaw puzzle.

*These examples are similar to those used on the actual test.

who fail. As you will see, the validity of IQ tests is somewhat supported by the fact that individuals who score at the lowest level on standard IQ tests *do* have clear differences in intellectual abilities compared to those who score at the top.

Mental retardation. According to clinical standards, the label *mentally retarded* is applied when someone is significantly below average in general intellectual functioning (IQ less than 70) and has significant deficits in adaptive functioning (such as communicating with others, living independently, social or occupational functioning, and maintaining safety and health) (American Psychiatric Association, 2000). Mental retardation (like most aspects of human behavior) is on a continuum that ranges from mildly to severely retarded. As you can see in Table 24.4, less than 1 to 3 percent of the general population would be classified as mentally retarded, and of this group, 85 percent are only *mildly* retarded.

Children classified as mildly retarded are not easily distinguished from their classmates until they've been in school for several years. Moreover, once they leave academic settings, their mental limits are less noticeable, and many become self-sup-

SUMMARY TABLE 24.4 DEGREES OF MENTAL RETARDATION

Level of Retardation	IQ Scores	Percent of Mentally Retarded Population	Characteristics
Mild	50–70	85	Usually able to become self-sufficient: may marry, have families, and secure full-time jobs in unskilled occupations
Moderate	35–49	10	Able to perform simple unskilled tasks; may contribute to a certain extent to their livelihood
Severe	20–34	3–4	Able to follow daily routines, but with continual supervision; with training, may learn basic communication skills
Profound	below 20	1–2	Able to perform only the most rudimentary behaviors, such as walking, feeding themselves, and saying a few phrases

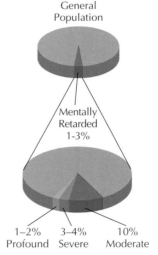

General Population

Mentally Retarded 1-3%

1–2% Profound · 3–4% Severe · 10% Moderate

porting, integrated members of the community. Even those who are part of the moderately retarded group can learn vocational skills that allow them to live in supervised group homes. Furthermore, people can be retarded in most areas yet average or even gifted in others. The most dramatic examples are *savants*, mentally retarded or disturbed people who excel in a specific area, such as rapid calculation, memory, or musical ability. In the movie *Rain Man*, Dustin Hoffman portrayed a savant with exceptional mathematical ability.

What causes mental retardation? Some forms of retardation stem from genetic causes, as is the case with *Down syndrome*, which results from an extra chromosome in the body's cells, *fragile-X syndrome*, an abnormality of the X chromosome caused by a defective gene, and *phenylketonuria* (PKU), a metabolic disorder resulting from an inherited enzyme deficiency. If detected early, PKU is treatable by minimizing phenylalanine in the child's diet. Other causes of retardation are environmental, including alcohol and other drug abuse during pregnancy, extreme deprivation or neglect in early life, and postnatal accidents that damage parts of the brain. However, in many cases, there is no known cause.

Mental Giftedness

At the other end of the intelligence spectrum, we have people with especially high IQs (typically defined as being in the top 1 or 2 percent). Have you ever wondered what happens to people with such superior intellectual abilities?

In 1921, Lewis Terman conducted a long-term study of over 1,500 people, age 3 to 28, who scored 135 or better on IQ tests to see how intelligence relates to occupational and social success. By 1950, when their average age was 40, the number of "Terman Kids [a name bestowed by Terman] who became research scientists, engineers, physicians, lawyers, or college teachers, or who were highly successful in business and

An unusual form of intelligence. *In the movie* Rain Man, *Dustin Hoffman portrayed a savant with exceptional mathematical ability.*

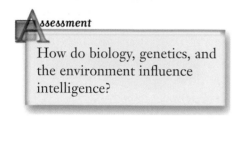

Assessment

How do biology, genetics, and the environment influence intelligence?

(a)

(b)

Figure 24.3 *A test for intelligence?* Which "leg" of the drawing in (a) is longer, the right or the left? Although the answer seems simple, researchers have found that when images like these are flashed for a few milliseconds on a computer screen, the amount of time people need to make correct judgments may reveal something about their intelligence. The second figure (b) appears immediately after figure (a) to block or "mask" the lingering afterimage.

other fields, was many times the number a random group would have provided" (Terman, 1954, p. 41; Leslie, 2000).

On the other hand, not every member of the group was successful, and there were some notable failures. The members who were the most successful tended to have extraordinary motivation and someone at home or school who was especially encouraging (Goleman, 1980). However, many in this gifted group were like others their age of average intelligence. They became alcoholics, got divorced, and committed suicide at close to the national rate (Leslie, 2000). A high IQ is no guarantee for success in every endeavor. It only offers more intellectual opportunities.

■ Explaining Differences in Intelligence: Brain, Genes, and the Environment

Some people are mentally gifted, some are mentally retarded, and most are somewhere in between. To explain these differences, we need to look at the brain, genes, and the environment.

The Brain's Influence on Intelligence

A basic tenet of neuroscience is that all mental activity (including intelligence) results from neural activity in the brain. There are three major questions that have guided neuroscience research on intelligence:

1. ***Does a bigger brain mean greater intelligence?*** It makes logical sense. After all, humans have relatively large brains, and as a species we are more intelligent than dogs, which have smaller brains. Some nonhuman animals, such as whales and dolphins, do have larger brains than humans, but the brains of humans are larger in relation to the size of our bodies. Since the early 1800s, researchers have asked whether "bigger is better" and modern studies using magnetic resonance imaging (MRI) have found a significant correlation between brain size (adjusted for body size) and intelligence (Posthuma et al., 2002; Tisserand, Bosma, Van Boxtel, & Jolles, 2001; Wickett, Vernon, & Lee, 2000). On the other hand, anatomical studies of Einstein's brain found that it was not heavier or larger than normal (Witelson, Kigar, & Harvey, 1999). Some areas were in fact smaller than average, but the area of the brain responsible for processing mathematical and spatial information (the lower region of the parietal lobe) was 15 percent larger. Rather than focusing on brain size, therefore, most of the recent research on the biology of intelligence has focused on the concept of brain functioning.

2. ***Is a faster brain more intelligent?*** The public seems to think so, and neuroscientists have found that a faster response time is indeed related to higher intelligence (Bowling & Mackenzie, 1996; Deary & Stough, 1996, 1997; Posthuma, deGeus, & Boomsma, 2001). A standard experiment flashes simple images like the one in Figure 24.3 and participants must inspect them quickly and make an accurate decision. As simple as it may seem, those participants who respond most quickly also tend to score highest on intelligence tests.

3. ***Does a smart brain work harder?*** As you read in Module 2, PET scans measure brain activity by recording the amount of radioactive glucose used in different parts of the brain. (A more active area of the brain uses more glucose than a less active area). Surprisingly, as can be seen in Figure 24.4, researchers have found that areas of the brain involved in problem solving show *less* activity in people of high intelligence than in people of lower intelligence when they are given the same problem-solving tasks (Haier et al., 1995; Neubauer, 2000; Posthuma, Neale, Boomsma, & de Geus, 2001). Apparently, intelligent brains work smarter, or more efficiently, than less intelligent brains.

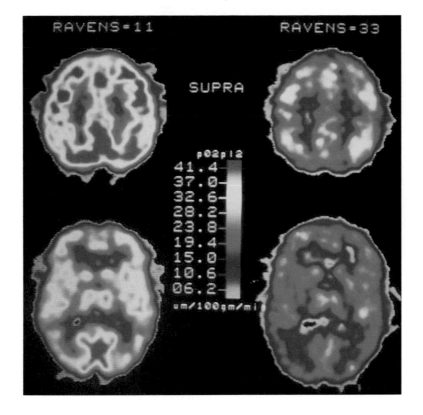

Figure 24.4 *Do intelligent brains work harder?* The PET scans in the left column are from a person with a tested low IQ, whereas the scans on the right are from someone with a high IQ. Note that when solving problems, the brain on the left is more active. (Red and yellow indicate more brain activity.) Contrary to popular opinion, this research suggests that lower IQ brains actually work harder, but less efficiently, than higher IQ brains.

Genetic and Environmental Influences on Intelligence

Like the central tenet of neuroscience (that all behavior is linked to the brain and nervous system), a similar, repeated theme of this text (and most areas of psychology) is that nature and nurture play interacting, *inseparable* roles. In the case of intelligence, any similarities between family members might be due to heredity (family members share similar genetic material) and/or environmental factors (family members share similar living arrangements).

Researchers interested in the role of heredity in intelligence often focus on *twin studies*. Recall from Module 7 that one of the most popular ways to study the relative effects of genetics versus the environment is to use monozygotic (identical, one-egg) twins. Such studies have found significant heredity influences for personality, psychopathology, and intelligence (Lynn, 2002; Phelps, Davis, & Schartz, 1997; Plomin, 2002; Rushton, 2001).

Perhaps the most important and most extensive of all twin studies is the Minnesota Study of Twins, which began in 1979 and continues today. For more than two decades, researchers from the University of Minnesota have been studying identical twins who grew up in different homes (Bouchard, 1994, 1999; Bouchard, McGue, Hur, & Horn, 1998; Markon et al., 2002). Each of these "reared apart" twins was separated from his or her sibling, and adopted by different families early in life and reunited only as adults. Because each twin has identical genetic material but was raised in a different family, researchers have a unique natural experiment that can be used to distinguish the effects of genetics from the effects of the environment. When the IQ data were collected and the statistics computed, researchers found that genetic factors appear to play a surprisingly large role in the IQ score of monozygotic (identical) twins reared apart.

How would you critique these findings? First, adoption agencies tend to look for similar criteria in their choice of adoptive parents. Therefore, the homes of these "reared apart" twins were actually quite similar. In addition, these twins also shared the same nine-month prenatal environment, which also might have influenced their brain development and intelligence (White, Andreasen, & Nopoulos, 2002).

Identical twins reared apart. Jerry Levy and Mark Newman, twins separated at birth, first met each other as adults at a firefighter's annual convention.

What about the famous reunited "Jim twins" that had the same name and almost the same personality? This is one of the most widely publicized cases of the entire Minnesota study. These two children were separated 37 days after their birth and reared with no contact until 38 years later. Despite this lifelong separation, James Lewis and James Springer both had divorced and remarried women named Betty, had undergone police training, loved carpentry, vacationed at the same beach each summer, and had named their firstborn sons James Allan and James Alan (Holden, 1980). This is only a short list of their incredible similarities.

Heredity undoubtedly plays an important role, but can you think of other explanations? One study of *unrelated* pairs of students of the same age and gender also found a striking number of similarities (Wright et al., 1984). People of the same age apparently share a common historical time that influences large aspects of their personality. In addition, do you recall our earlier discussion of the *confirmation bias* (the tendency to seek out and pay attention to information that confirms our existing positions or beliefs, while ignoring contradictory data)? Imagine suddenly finding your long lost identical twin. Wouldn't you be highly excited and thrilled with all your similarities and disinclined to note the differences?

As you can see, the research is inconclusive. Although heredity equips each of us with innate intellectual capacities, the environment significantly influences whether a person will reach his or her full intellectual potential (Dickens & Flynn, 2001; Sangwan, 2001). For example, early malnutrition can cause retarded brain development, which in turn affects the child's curiosity, responsiveness to the environment, and motivation for learning — all of which can lower the child's IQ. We are reminded once again that nature and nurture are inseparable.

Achievement
GENDER & CULTURAL DIVERSITY

The Bell Curve, Stereotype Threat, and IQ Tests

How would you answer the following questions:

1. A symphony is to a composer as a book is to a(n) _____. (a) musician; (b) editor; (c) novel; (d) author

2. If you throw dice and they land with a "7" on top, what is on bottom? (a) snake eyes; (b) box cars; (c) little Joes; (d) eleven

Can you see how the content and answers to these questions might reflect *cultural bias*? People from some backgrounds will find the first question easier, whereas other groups will easily answer the second. Which of these two questions do you think is most likely to appear on standard IQ tests?

As mentioned earlier, one of the most hotly debated and controversial issues in psychology has to do with the accuracy of intelligence tests and what group differences in test scores really mean. In 1969, Arthur Jensen began a heated debate when he argued that intelligence is largely genetic in origin and that, therefore, genetic factors are "strongly implicated" as the cause of ethnic differences in intelligence. A book by Richard J. Herrnstein and Charles Murray titled *The Bell Curve: Intelligence and Class Structure in American Life* reignited this debate in 1994 when the authors claimed that African Americans score below average in IQ because of their "genetic heritage."

Psychologists have responded to these claims with several points:

- **Some ethnic minority children do score differently on IQ tests** (Blanton, 2001; Herrnstein & Murray, 1994; Rushton & Davison, 2000). In the United States,

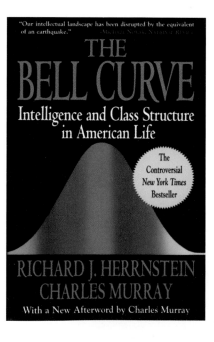

"Our intellectual landscape has been disrupted by the equivalent of an earthquake."

THE BELL CURVE
Intelligence and Class Structure in American Life

The Controversial New York Times Bestseller

RICHARD J. HERRNSTEIN
CHARLES MURRAY

With a New Afterword by Charles Murray

Asian American children score slightly higher on standardized IQ tests than European American children, who in turn score higher than African American, Latino, or Native American children (Brody, 1992; Lynn, 1995; Williams & Ceci, 1997).

- **Members of every ethnic group can be found to have scores at all levels of the IQ scale.** The bell curves of all groups show considerable overlap, and IQ scores and intelligence have their greatest relevance in terms of individuals, not groups (Garcia & Stafford, 2000; Myerson, Rank, Raines, & Schnitzler, 1998; Reifman, 2000). For example, many individual African Americans receive higher IQ scores than many individual white Americans. Most important, even if a trait is primarily genetic (which does not appear to be the case with intelligence), group differences can still be wholly due to the environment (Figure 24.5).

- **Lack of cultural exposure to the concepts required on IQ tests can result in lowered IQ scores.** Therefore, the tests may not be an accurate measure of true capability — they may be culturally biased (Blanton, 2001; Domino, 2000; Greenfield, 1997; Naglieri & Ronning, 2000).

- **Group differences in IQ may have more to do with socioeconomic differences than ethnicity** (McLoyd, 1998; Reifman, 2000). African Americans and most other minorities are far more likely than whites to live in poverty. The environmental effects of poverty, such as poor prenatal care, poorly funded schools, lack of textbooks and other resources, clearly influence intellectual development (Solan & Mozlin, 2001).

- **IQ does have a substantial genetic component, and racial and ethnic differences may reflect underlying hereditary differences** (Plomin & DeFries, 1998; Plomin, 1999; Sternberg & Kaufman, 1998). Note, however, that race and ethnicity, like intelligence itself, are almost impossible to define. For example, depending on the definition that you use, there are between 3 and 300 races, and no race is pure in a biological sense (Beutler et al., 1996; Yee, Fairchild, Weizmann, & Wyatt, 1993).

- **Intelligence is not a fixed characteristic.** As we discovered earlier, research on the so-called *Flynn effect* shows there has been overall increase in IQ since the early 1900s, and this is far too short a time for genetics to have played a role. (Dickens & Flynn, 2001; Flynn, 1987, 1999; Neisser, 1998; Resing & Nijland, 2002). Furthermore, there has been a steady increase in the verbal ability scores of African Americans over time and a slight decline for white Americans (Huang & Hauser, 1998).

- **Differences in IQ scores reflect motivational and language factors.** For example, in some ethnic groups, a child who excels in school is ridiculed for trying to be different from his or her classmates (Pearson, 1995). Moreover, children grow up speaking the language of their culture and the dialect of their neighborhood. If this language or dialect does not match the education system of which they are a part, or the IQ test they take, they are obviously disadvantaged (Tanner-Halverson, Burden, & Sabers, 1993).

- **As we've seen earlier, there are multiple intelligences, and traditional IQ tests do not measure many of them** (Gardner, 1999; Sternberg & Hedlund, 2002).

- **Finally, stereotype threats can significantly reduce test scores of people in stereotyped groups** (Gonzales, Blanton, & Williams, 2002; Josephs, Newman, Brown, & Beer, 2003; Niemann, 2001).

The central thesis of **stereotype threat** is that an individual's performance on an IQ test depends in part on the individual's expectations about how he or she will do. And these expectations are often shaped by cultural stereotypes about the abilities of

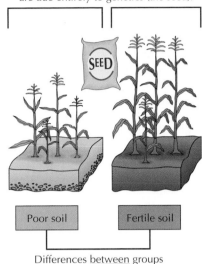

Differences <u>within</u> groups are due entirely to genetics (the seed).

Poor soil   Fertile soil

Differences <u>between</u> groups are due <u>entirely</u> to environment (the soil).

Figure 24.5 *If plants could talk!* Note that even when you begin with the exact same package of seeds (genetic inheritance), the average height of corn plants in the fertile soil will be greater than those in the poor soil (environmental influences). The same is true for intelligence. Therefore, no conclusions can be drawn about possible genetic contributions to the differences between groups.

Stereotype Threat *A person experiences doubt about his or her performance, due to negative stereotypes about his or her group's abilities*

"YOU CAN'T BUILD A HUT, YOU DON'T KNOW HOW TO FIND EDIBLE ROOTS AND YOU KNOW NOTHING ABOUT PREDICTING THE WEATHER. IN OTHER WORDS, YOU DO TERRIBLY ON OUR I.Q. TEST."

an individual's particular age, ethnicity, gender, or socioeconomic class. For example, if the dominant cultural stereotype says, "you can't teach old dogs new tricks" or "women aren't good at math," you can imagine how this might affect many older individuals and women when they take an IQ test.

As you can see, there is no clear answer to this debate. The good news is that Hernstein and Murray's controversial book has provoked considerable discussion and research. For example, Claude Steele and Joshua Aronson (1995) first revealed stereotype threat in an experiment at Stanford University. They recruited African American and white students to take a *performance exam* and informed them that their individual intellectual abilities would be examined. Participants were matched on ability levels prior to the exam, and the exam was composed of questions similar to the Graduate Records Exam (GRE). The results revealed that the African American students performed well below the white students. However, when the researchers repeated the same procedure and told students it was a *laboratory task* instead of a performance exam, there was no difference in African American scores and white scores.

What explains the difference in results?   Subsequent work by Steele and others shows that stereotype threat occurs because members of the stereotyped groups doubt their own abilities. Simply being aware that you are not expected to do well lowers your score — you unintentionally fulfill the negative "self-fulfilling prophecy." Members fear that they will be evaluated in terms of the stereotype, and this worry translates into anxiety, which in turn lowers both the speed and accuracy of their responses to test questions. On the other hand, some individuals cope by "disidentifying," saying to themselves, "The test scores have no influence on how I feel about myself" (Major, Spencer, Schmader, Wolfe, & Crocker, 1998). Unfortunately, this attitude also decreases performance because of the lessened motivation.

Studies show that stereotype threat affects the test performance of many groups, including African Americans, women, Native Americans, Latinos, low-income people, elderly people, and white male athletes (e.g., Aronson, Fried, & Good, 2002; Gonzales, Blanton, & Williams, 2002; Inzlicht & Ben-Zeev, 2000; Niemann, 2001; Steele, James, & Barnett, 2002). This research helps explain some group differences in intelligence and achievement tests. Unfortunately, employers, educators, and clinicians routinely use such tests for many purposes. Yet there is more to intelligence (and achievement) than what is measured by an exam. Relying solely on these tests to make critical decisions affecting individual lives is not warranted and possibly even unethical.

A Final Note

Think back to the questions we asked at the very beginning of our discussion of intelligence: Are Koko, Genie, and Thomas Edison intelligent? How would you answer these questions now? Hopefully, you now understand that all 3 cognitive processes discussed in this section (thinking, language, and intelligence) are complex phenomena, which are greatly affected by numerous, interacting factors. As evidence, let's update our story of Genie. Her life, as you might have guessed, does not have a happy Hollywood ending. Genie's tale is a heartbreaking account of the lasting scars from a disastrous childhood. At the time of her rescue, at age 13, Genie's intellectual performance was at the level of a normal 1 year old. Over the years, she was given thousands of hours of special training and rehabilitation, and by the age of 19 she could use public transportation and was adapting well to her foster home and special classes at school (Rymer, 1993).

Genie was far from normal, however. Her intelligence scores were still close to the cutoff for mental retardation, and, as noted earlier, her language skills were similar to those of a 2 or 3 year old. To make matters worse, she was also subjected to a series of foster home placements — one of which was abusive. At last report, Genie was living in a home for mentally retarded adults (Rymer, 1993).

Assessment

CHECK & REVIEW

Assessing Intelligence/Explaining Differences in Intelligence

Intelligence quotient (IQ) tests do not, and are not intended to, measure overall intelligence. Rather, they are designed to measure verbal and quantitative abilities needed for school success. Several individual IQ tests are in common use. The Stanford–Binet measures primarily the verbal abilities of children ages 3 to 16. The Wechsler tests, consisting of three separate tests for three distinct age levels, measure both verbal and nonverbal abilities. People with IQs of 70 and below are identified as mentally retarded, whereas people with IQs of 135 and above are identified as gifted.

Most neuroscientists believe that all mental activity results from neural activity in the brain. Their research on intelligence has focused on three major questions: 1) Does a bigger brain mean greater intelligence? (Answer: "Not necessarily.") 2) Is a faster brain more intelligent? (Answer: "A qualified yes." And 3) Does a smart brain work harder? (Answer: "No, the smarter brain is more efficient.")

According to the Minnesota Study of Twins Reared Apart, heredity and environment are important, inseparable factors in intellectual development. Heredity equips each of us with innate capacities, but environment significantly influences whether an individual will reach full potential.

Questions

1. Is IQ a true measure of intellectual ability? Why or why not?
2. What are the major differences between the Stanford–Binet and the Wechsler Intelligence Scales?
3. The more efficient brain uses fewer _____ to solve problems than a less efficient brain. (a) parts of the brain; (b) neurotransmitters; (c) synapses, (d) energy resources
4. Which is more important in determining intelligence — heredity or environment?

Answers to Questions can be found in Appendix B.

MODULE 24   ACTIVE LEARNING WORKSHEET

ACROSS

5 The ability of a test to measure what it was designed to measure.

7 Knowledge and learning that we have gained over the course of our lives through an interaction between fluid intelligence and environmental experience.

8 A score on a test that is intended to measure verbal and quantitative abilities.

DOWN

1 A measure of the consistency and stability of test scores when the test is readministered.

2 A psychological predicament in which a person experiences doubt about his or her performance, due to negative stereotypes about his or her group's abilities.

3 The capacity for acquiring new knowledge and solving new problems that is at least partially determined by biological and genetic factors.

4 The process of establishing the norms and uniform procedures for giving and scoring a test.

6 The general capacity to profit from experience, to acquire knowledge, and adapt to changes in the environment.

Assessment
KEY TERMS

To assess your understanding of the **Key Terms** in this section, write a definition for each (in your own words), and then compare your definitions with those in the text.

Thinking
algorithm (p. 305)
availability heuristic (p. 308)
cognition (p. 299)
concept (p. 301)
confirmation bias (p. 307)
convergent thinking (p. 310)
creativity (p. 310)
divergent thinking (p. 310)
functional fixedness (p. 307)
heuristic (p. 305)
mental images (p. 300)
mental set (p. 307)

prototype (p. 302)
representativeness heuristic (p. 308)

Language
babbling (p. 315)
cooing (p. 315)
grammar (p. 314)
language acquisition device (LAD)
   (p. 317)
morpheme [MOR-feem] (p. 314)
overextension (p. 316)
overgeneralize (p. 316)
phoneme [FOE-neem] (p. 313)

semantics (p. 314)
syntax (p. 314)
telegraphic speech (p. 316)

Intelligence
crystallized intelligence (p. 322)
fluid intelligence (p. 322)
intelligence (p. 321)
intelligence quotient (IQ) (p. 326)
reliability (p. 325)
standardization (p. 324)
stereotype threat (p. 333)
validity (p. 325)

Achievement
WEB RESOURCES

Huffman Book Companion Site
http://www.wiley.com/college/huffman
   This site is loaded with free Interactive Self-Tests, Internet Exercises, Glossary and Flashcards for key terms, Web links, Handbook for Non-Native Speakers, and other activities designed to improve your mastery of the material in this section.

Want to test your IQ?
http://www.brain.com/
   This web site (Brain.com) offers a wide range of timed tests of intelligence, mental performance, memory, emotional states, and more.

VISUAL SUMMARY

Thinking, Language, and Intelligence
(Modules 22, 23, and 24)

Thinking

Cognitive Building Blocks

1) **Mental images**: Mind's representation of a sensory experience.
2) **Concepts**: Mental representations of a group or category that share similar characteristics. Concepts arise out of logical rules and definitions (artificial concepts), we then create natural categories or concepts (**prototypes**), and then organize them into successive ranks (hierarchies).
3) **Language:** Method of communication.

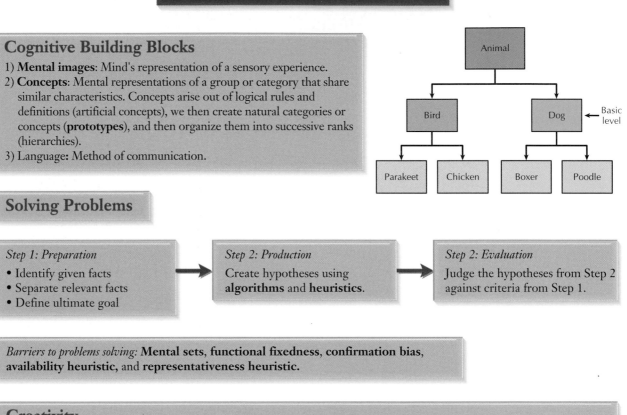

Solving Problems

Step 1: Preparation
• Identify given facts
• Separate relevant facts
• Define ultimate goal

→

Step 2: Production
Create hypotheses using **algorithms** and **heuristics**.

→

Step 2: Evaluation
Judge the hypotheses from Step 2 against criteria from Step 1.

Barriers to problems solving: **Mental sets, functional fixedness, confirmation bias, availability heuristic,** and **representativeness heuristic.**

Creativity

• *Elements of creativity*: Originality, fluency, and flexibility.
• *Measuring creativity*: **Divergent thinking** versus **convergent thinking**.
• *Researching creativity*: Investment theory says creativity is a combination of intellectual ability, knowledge, thinking style, personality, motivation, and environment.

Language

Characteristics of Language

Language is produced from words using **phonemes** (basic speech sounds) and **morphemes** (the smallest meaningful units of a language). The words are strung together into sentences using rules of **grammar**, which includes **syntax** (the grammatical rules for ordering words) and **semantics** (meaning in language).

Language (cont.)

Language Development

Stages

- *Prelinguistic:* Crying → **cooing** (vowel sounds) → **babbling** (vowel/consonant combinations).
- *Linguistic:* One-word utterances → **telegraphic speech** (omits unnecessary, connecting words) → grammatical speech.
- Problems: **Overextension** (e.g., "bunnies" called "dogs") and **overgeneralization** (e.g., "foots," "goed").

Theories

- *Nature:* Language results from maturation. Chomsky´s innate **language acquisition device (LAD)**.
- *Nurture:* Environment and rewards/punishments explain language.

Intelligence

The Nature of Intelligence

Competing theories and definitions:

- Spearman→Intelligence is "g," a general intelligence.
- Thurstone→Intelligence is seven distinct mental abilities.
- Guiliford→Intelligence is composed of 120 or more separate abilities.
- Cattell→Intelligence is two types of "g" (**fluid intelligence** and **crystallized intelligence**).
- Gardner→There are eight or possibly nine types of intelligence.
- Sternberg→Triarchic theory of intelligence (analytical, creative, and practical).

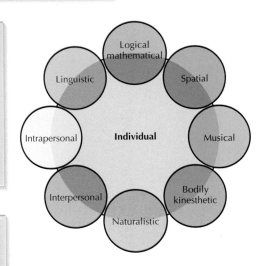

Test Construction

Elements of a useful test:

1) **Standardization:** Test is given to many people to establish norms and identical administrative procedures are used.
2) **Reliability:** The scores are stable over time.
3) **Validity:** The test measures what it is intended to measure.

Assessing Intelligence

Intelligence quotient (IQ) tests do not, and are not intended to, measure overall intelligence. Instead, they are designed to measure verbal and quantitative abilities needed for school success.

- *Stanford–Binet* measures verbal abilities of children ages 3 to 16.
- *Wechsler* measures verbal and nonverbal abilities of three distinct age levels.
- IQs of 70 and below are identified as mentally retarded, whereas IQs of 135 and above are identified as gifted.

Explaining Differences in Intelligence

- Neuroscientists ask: 1) Does a bigger brain mean greater intelligence? Not necessarily. 2) Is a faster brain more intelligent? A qualified yes. 3) Does a smart brain work harder? No, the smarter brain is more efficient.
- The Minnesota Study of Twins Reared Apart found heredity and environment are important, inseparable factors in intellectual development.

LIFE SPAN DEVELOPMENT I

Assessment

Core Learning Objectives

As you read Modules 25 and 26, keep the following questions in mind and answer them in your own words:

▶ How is research in developmental psychology different from research in other areas of psychology?

▶ What are the major physical changes that occur throughout the life span?

▶ How do attachment and parenting styles affect development?

▶ How does cognition, or the way we think about the world, change during the life cycle?

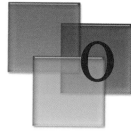

O n December 30, 2001, Tiger Woods was 26 years old. What makes this noteworthy? Consider that during these 26 years, he has won 44 golf tournaments, 32 of those on the PGA tour. With his second Masters victory in 2001, he became the first golfer to ever hold all four major professional championships at the same time. Still not impressed? How about the fact that at the time of his 26th birthday in 2001, Woods had earned almost $26 million from his PGA Tour and over $32 million worldwide from his tournaments, promotional appearances, and endorsements? If money and titles don't excite you, maybe you'll appreciate that at age 3 he shot 48 for nine holes and was featured in Golf Digest. Furthermore, when he competed at the Masters Championship golf tournament in Augusta, Georgia, he was the youngest golfer ever to win that tournament. This win was a first for a minority player of African or Asian heritage at the Masters — a tournament that had its first African American player only two decades earlier (About Tiger, 2002; Lace, 1999; Rosaforte, 2000). A related interesting fact about Tiger Woods is that he calls himself "Cablinasian" because his ethnic heritage is one-quarter white, one-quarter Chinese, one-quarter Thai, an eighth Native American, and an eighth African American (cited in Henslin, 2003). Given these numbers, why do most people consider Tiger Woods to be African American?

In contrast to Tiger Woods' early accomplishments, consider the case of John Glenn. On October 29, 1998, John Glenn spent 9 days in the space shuttle Discovery. What makes this exceptional? Consider that, at age 77, he is the oldest human to travel in space. More remarkable is that 36 years earlier, in 1962, Glenn was the first U.S. astronaut to orbit the

□ Achievement
■ Assessment
■ Application

earth, and in the years between these two historic flights, he served four terms as a senator from Ohio. Why would a distinguished, 77-year-old congressman voluntarily subject himself to months of rigorous training and testing, not to mention the dangers of space travel for a second time? Glenn was interested in the subject of aging, and he knew that the zero gravity condi-

tions of space flights simulate, at advanced speed, what normally happens to our bodies as we age. Glenn's contribution to scientific research demonstrates not only his personal integrity and courage, but also that our lives can be meaningful and productive far longer than common stereotypes would suggest (Cole, 2000).

The accomplishments of Tiger Woods and John Glenn illustrate not only our need to rethink stereotypes about youth, minorities, and older adults, but also the importance of understanding how people grow and develop throughout the entire life span. In this section and the next, we will explore the field of **developmental psychology,** the study of age-related changes in behavior and mental processes throughout the life span, from conception to death (Table 25.1).

To emphasize that development is an ongoing, lifelong *process,* we will take a topical approach (as opposed to a chronological approach, which arbitrarily divides the field

into two periods, childhood–adolescence and adulthood). Thus, in this section, we will trace physical, social–emotional, and cognitive development — one at a time — from conception to death.

Then, in the next set of modules, we will explore moral development, personality development, and special issues related to death and dying, again, one topic at a time. The topical approach allows us to see how any one aspect of development affects an individual over the entire life span.

Developmental Psychology *The study of age-related changes in behavior and mental processes from conception to death*

MODULE 25
TOPICS IN DEVELOPMENT

Assessment

How is research in developmental psychology different from research in other areas of psychology?

■ Studying Development: 3 Major Issues

In all fields of psychology, certain theoretical issues seem to guide the basic direction of research. First, we look at what those issues are in human development, and then we will examine how developmental psychologists conduct their research.

The three most important issues or questions in human development are *nature versus nurture*, *continuity versus stages*, and *stability versus change*.

1. *Nature or nurture.* The issue of "nature versus nurture" has been with us since the beginning of psychology. Even the ancient Greeks had the same debate — Plato arguing for innate knowledge and abilities, and Aristotle, for learning through the five senses. Early philosophers proposed that at birth our minds are a *tabula rasa* (or blank slate) and that the environment determines what messages are written on the slate.

According to the nature position, human behavior and development are governed by automatic, genetically predetermined signals in a process known as **maturation.** Just as a flower unfolds in accord with its genetic blueprint, we humans crawl before we walk and walk before we run. Furthermore, there is an optimal period shortly after birth, one of several **critical periods** during our lifetime, when an organism is especially sensitive to certain experiences that shape the capacity for future development.

Maturation *Development governed by automatic, genetically predetermined signals*

Critical Period *A period of special sensitivity to specific types of learning that shapes the capacity for future development*

TABLE 25.1 LIFE SPAN DEVELOPMENT

Stage	Approximate Age
Prenatal	Conception to birth
Infancy	Birth to 18 months
Early childhood	18 months to 6 years
Middle childhood	6–12 years
Adolescence	12–20 years
Young adulthood	20–45 years
Middle adulthood	45–60 years
Later adulthood	60 years to death

Naturists would therefore say that Tiger Woods's achievements primarily reflect his innate athletic abilities. They would point out that Tiger shot 48 for nine holes at age three, was featured in Golf Digest at age five, and won the Optimist International Junior tournament six times before age 15. On the other side of the debate, those who hold an extreme nurturist position would argue that development occurs by learning through observation and experience. Nurturists would point to the close teaching and strong encouragement from his father and other family members as the major contributors to Tiger's exceptional accomplishments.

2. *Continuity or stages.* Continuity proponents say development is continuous, with new abilities, skills, and knowledge gradually added at a relatively uniform pace. The continuity model, then, suggests that adult thinking and intelligence differ quantitatively from a child's. We simply have more math or verbal skills than children. Stage theorists, on the other hand, believe development occurs at different rates, alternating between periods of little change and periods of abrupt, rapid change. In this section, and the next, we will discuss several stage theories: Piaget's theory of cognitive development, Erikson's psychosocial theory of personality development, and Kohlberg's theory of moral development.

3. *Stability or change.* Have you generally maintained your personal characteristics as you matured from infant to adult (stability)? Or does your current personality bear little resemblance to the personality you displayed during infancy (change)? Psychologists who emphasize stability in development hold that measurements of personality taken during childhood are important predictors of adult personality (McCrae, 2001; McCrae et al., 2000). Of course, psychologists who emphasize change disagree (Ardelt, 2000).

Which of these positions is more correct? Most psychologists do not take a hard line either way. Rather, they prefer an *interactionist perspective.* In the age-old *nature or nurture* debate, for example, psychologists generally believe that development emerges from each individual's unique genetic predisposition *and* from individual experiences in the environment (Carbonneau et al., 2002; Gottlieb, 2000; Maccoby, 2000). More recently, the interactionist position has evolved into the *biopsychosocial model* mentioned throughout this text. In this model, biological factors (genetics, brain functions, biochemistry, and evolution), psychological influences (learning, thinking, emotion, personality, and motivation), and social forces (family, school, culture, ethnicity, social class, and politics) all affect and are affected by one another.

Like the nature versus nurture debate, the continuity versus stage and the stability versus change perspectives also are not a matter of "either-or." Physical development and motor skills, for example, are believed to be primarily continuous in nature, whereas cognitive skills usually develop in discrete stages. Similarly, some traits are stable, whereas others vary greatly across the life span.

We will return to these three questions several times in this section and the next. Now we turn our attention to another aspect of studying development — how developmental psychologists collect their information.

Research Methods

To study development, psychologists use either a *cross-sectional* or *longitudinal* method. The **cross-sectional method** examines individuals of various ages (20, 40, 60, and 80 years) at one point in time — and gives information about age differences. The **longitudinal method** follows a single individual or group of individuals (only 20 year olds) over an extended period of time and gives information about age changes (Figure 25.1).

Imagine you are a developmental psychologist interested in studying intelligence in adults. Which method would you choose — cross-sectional or longitudinal? Before you decide, note the different research results shown in Figure 25.2.

Cross-Sectional Method *Research design that measures individuals of various ages at one point in time and gives information about age differences*

Longitudinal Method *Research design that measures a single individual or group of individuals over an extended period and gives information about age changes*

CROSS-SECTIONAL RESEARCH

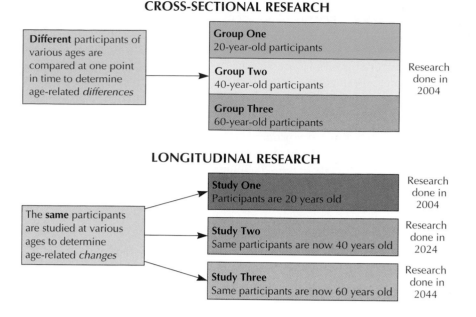

Figure 25.1 *Cross-sectional versus longitudinal research.* Note that cross-sectional research uses different participants and is interested in age-related differences, whereas longitudinal research studies the same participants over time to find age-related changes.

Researchers suggest that the different results may reflect a central problem with cross-sectional studies. They often confuse genuine age differences with *cohort effects*, differences that result from specific histories of the age group studied (Elder, 1998). The decline in intelligence found in cross-sectional research might reflect early educational experiences rather than a true effect of aging. We cannot tell. Age effects and cohort effects are hopelessly tangled.

Longitudinal studies also have their limits. They are expensive in terms of time and money, and their results are restricted in *generalizability*. Because participants often drop out or move away during the extended test period, the experimenter may end up with a self-selected sample that differs from the general population in important ways. As you can see in Table 25.2, each method of research has its own strengths and weaknesses. Keep these differences in mind when you read the findings of developmental research.

Before leaving the topic of research, let's examine the unique contributions cultural psychologists have made to the field of developmental psychology.

Assessment

VISUAL QUIZ

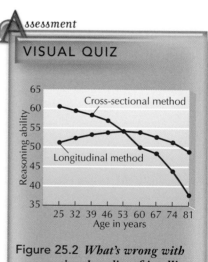

Figure 25.2 *What's wrong with cross-sectional studies of intelligence?*

(·uoissıɯɹəd ɥʇıʍ '⅋661 'əıɐɥɔS ɯoɹɟ pəʇdɐp∀) ·(⅋661 'əıɐɥɔS) 09 əᵷɐ ʇnoqɐ ןıʇun uıᵷəq ʇou səop əɔuəᵷıןןəʇuı uı əuıןɔəp pəꓘɹɐɯ ɐ ʇɐɥʇ punoɟ əʌɐɥ səıpnʇs ןɐuıpnʇıᵷuo˥ ·səuıןɔəp ꓘןןɐnpɐɹᵷ uəɥʇ puɐ pooɥʇןnpɐ ꓘןɹɐə uı ꓘɐəd sʇı səɥɔɐəɹ əɔuəᵷıןןəʇuı ʇɐɥʇ uʍoɥs ꓘןןɐɔıɹoʇsıɥ əʌɐɥ səıpnʇs ןɐuoıʇɔəs-ssoɹƆ :ɹəʍsu∀

TABLE 25.2 ADVANTAGES AND DISADVANTAGES OF CROSS-SECTIONAL AND LONGITUDINAL RESEARCH DESIGNS

	Cross-Sectional	Longitudinal
Advantages	Gives information about age differences Quick Less expensive Typically larger sample	Gives information about age changes Increased reliability More in-depth information per participant
Disadvantages	Cohort effects Restricted generalizability (measures behaviors at only one point in time)	More expensive Time consuming Restricted generalizability (typically smaller sample and dropouts over time)

✳ Achievement
GENDER & CULTURAL DIVERSITY

Cultural Psychology's Guidelines for Developmental Research

How would you answer the following question: "If you wanted to predict how a human child anywhere in the world was going to grow up, what his or her behavior was going to be like as an adult, and you could have only one fact about that child, what fact would you choose to have?"

According to cultural psychologists like Patricia Greenfield (1994, 2000), the answer to this question should be "culture." Yet developmental psychology has traditionally studied people (children, adolescents, and adults) with little attention to the sociocultural context (Brislin, 2000; Valsiner, 2000). In recent times, however, psychologists are paying increasing attention to the following points:

1. ***Culture may be the most important determinant of development.*** If a child grows up in an individualistic/independent culture (such as North America or most of western Europe), we can predict this child will probably be competitive and question authority as an adult. Were this same child reared in a collectivist/interdependent culture (common in Africa, Asia, and Latin America), she or he would most likely grow up to be cooperative and respectful of elders (Delgado-Gaitan, 1994; Segall, Dasen, Berry, & Portinga, 1990).

2. ***Human development, like most areas of psychology, cannot be studied outside its sociocultural context.*** In parts of Korea, most teenagers see a strict, authoritarian style of parenting as a sign of love and concern (Kim & Choi, 1995). Korean American and Korean Canadian teenagers, however, see the same behavior as a sign of rejection. Thus, rather than studying specific behaviors, such as "authoritarian parenting styles," discussed later in this module, researchers in child development suggest that children should be studied only within their *developmental niche* (Harkness & Super, 1996). A developmental niche has three components: the physical and social contexts in which the child lives, the culturally determined rearing and educational practices, and the psychological characteristics of the parents (Bugental & Johnston, 2000).

3. ***Each culture's ethnotheories are important determinants of behavior.*** Within every culture, people have a prevailing set of ideas and beliefs that attempts to explain the world around them (an *ethnotheory*) (Keller, Yovsi, & Voelker, 2002; Rosenthal & Roer-Strier, 2001). In the area of child development, for example, cultures have specific ethnotheories about how children should be trained. As a critical thinker, you can anticipate that differing ethnotheories can lead to problems between cultures. Even the very idea of "critical thinking" is part of our North American ethnotheory regarding education. And it, too, can produce culture clashes.

Concha Delgado-Gaitan (1994) found that Mexican immigrants from a rural background have a difficult time adjusting to North American schools, which teach children to question authority and think for themselves. In their culture of origin, these children are trained to respect their elders, be good listeners, and participate in conversation only when solicited. Children who argue with adults are reminded not to be *malcriados* (naughty or disrespectful).

Cultural influences on development. *How might these two groups differ in their physical, social–emotional, cognitive, and personality development?*

TRY THIS

YOURSELF

Application

If you would like a personal demonstration of the invisibility of culture, try this simple experiment: The next time you walk into an elevator, don't turn around. Remain facing the rear wall. Watch how others respond when you don't turn around, or if you stand right next to them rather than walk to the other side of the elevator. Our North American culture has rules that prescribe the "proper" way to ride in an elevator, and people become very uncomfortable when these rules are violated.

4. *Culture is largely invisible to its participants.* Culture consists of ideals, values, and assumptions that are widely shared among a given group and that guide specific behaviors (Brislin, 2000). Precisely because these ideals and values are widely shared, they are seldom discussed or directly examined. Just as a "fish doesn't know it's in water," we take our culture for granted, operating within it, although being almost unaware of it.

Assessment

CHECK & REVIEW

Studying Development

Developmental psychology is concerned with describing, explaining, predicting, and sometimes modifying age-related behaviors across the entire life span. Three important research issues are *nature or nurture*, *continuity or stages*, and *stability or change*.

Researchers in developmental psychology generally do **cross-sectional** (different participants of various ages at one point in time) or **longitudinal studies** (same participants over an extended period). Each method has advantages and disadvantages.

Cultural psychologists suggest that developmental researchers keep the following points in mind:

- Culture is the most important determinant of development.
- Human development cannot be studied outside its sociocultural context.
- Each culture's ethnotheories are important determinants of behavior.
- Culture is largely invisible to its participants.

Questions

1. Briefly define *developmental psychology*.
2. What three major questions are studied in developmental psychology?
3. Differences in age groups that reflect factors unique to a specific age group are called _____ effects. (a) generational; (b) social–environmental; (c) operational; (d) cohort
4. _____ studies are the most time-efficient method, whereas _____ studies provide the most in-depth information per participant. (a) Correlational, experimental; (b) Fast-track, follow-up; (c) Cross-sectional, longitudinal; (d) Cohort-sequential, cohort-intensive

Answers to Questions can be found in Appendix B.

■ Physical Development: Prenatal to Adulthood

Perhaps the most obvious aspects of development are changes in body proportions and size. In this section, we will look at two separate periods of life: prenatal and early childhood (characterized by rapid change) and adolescence and adulthood (a time of both dramatic and gradual physical change).

Prenatal and Early Childhood

Do you remember being a young child and feeling it would "take forever to grow up?" Contrary to a child's sense of time, the early years of development are a time of rapid

Assessment

What are the major physical changes that occur throughout the life span?

and unparalleled change. In fact, if you continued to develop at the same rapid rate that marks the first 2 years of life, you would weigh several tons and be over 12 feet tall as an adult! Thankfully, physical development slows, yet it is important to note that change continues until the very moment of death.

Prenatal Physical Development Your prenatal development began at *conception*, when your mother's egg, or ovum, united with your father's *sperm* cell (Figure 25.3). At that time, you were a single cell barely $1/175$ of an inch in diameter — smaller than the period at the end of this sentence. This new cell, called a *zygote*, then began a process of rapid cell division that resulted in a multimillion-celled infant (you) some 9 months later.

The vast changes that occur during the 9 months of a full-term pregnancy are usually divided into three stages (Figure 25.4). The **germinal period** begins with fertilization and ends with implantation of the rapidly dividing mass of cells (the zygote) in the wall of the uterus. The outer portion of the zygote forms part of the placenta and umbilical cord, whereas the inner portion becomes the *embryo*. The **embryonic period,** the second stage, begins after implantation and lasts through the eighth week. During this time, the embryo's major organ systems begin to develop. The final stage is the **fetal period,** from the end of the second month until birth. During this period, the *fetus* continues to grow and the organs begin to function. Prenatal growth, as well as growth the first few years after birth, is *proximodistal* (near to far), with the head and upper body developing before the lower body.

Hazards to Prenatal Development During pregnancy, the placenta (the fluid-filled sac in which the fetus develops in-utero) serves as the link for food and excretion of wastes, and it screens out some, but not all, harmful substances. Environmental hazards such as X-rays or toxic waste, drugs, and diseases such as rubella (German measles) can cross the *placental barrier* (Table 25.3, page 349). These influences generally have their most devastating effect during the first 3 months of pregnancy — making this a *critical period* in development.

The pregnant mother obviously plays a primary role in prenatal development, because her health directly influences the child she is carrying. Furthermore, almost everything she ingests can cross the placental barrier (a better term might be *placental sieve*). However, the father also plays a role — other than just fertilization. Environmentally, the father's smoking may pollute the air the mother breathes, and genetically, he may transmit heritable diseases. In addition, research suggests alcohol,

Germinal Period *First stage of prenatal development that begins with conception and ends with implantation in the uterus (the first 2 weeks)*

Embryonic Period *Second stage of prenatal development that begins after uterine implantation and lasts through the eighth week*

Fetal Period *The third, and final, stage of prenatal development (eight weeks to birth), characterized by rapid weight gain in the fetus and the fine detailing of body organs and systems*

Figure 25.3 *The moment of conception.* (a) Note the large number of sperm surrounding the ovum. (b) Although a "joint effort" is required to break through the outer coating, only one sperm will actually fertilize the egg.

(a)

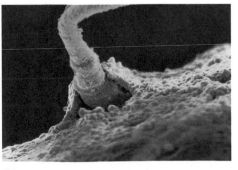

(b)

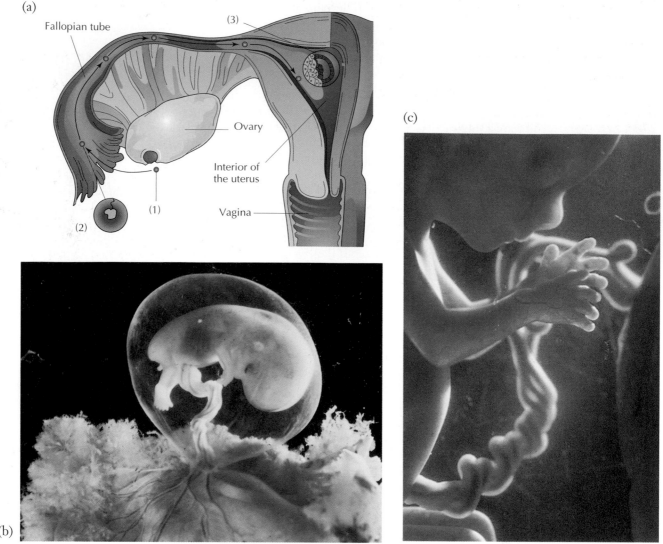

Figure 25.4 *(a) From ovulation to implantation.* After discharge from either the left or right ovary (number 1 on the diagram), the ovum travels to the opening of the fallopian tube. If fertilization occurs (2), it normally takes place in the first third of the fallopian tube. The fertilized ovum is referred to as a *zygote*. When the zygote reaches the uterus, it implants itself in the wall of the uterus (3) and begins to grow tendril-like structures that intertwine with the rich supply of blood vessels located there. After *implantation*, the organism is known as an *embryo. (b) Embryonic period.* This stage occurs from implantation to 8 weeks. At 8 weeks, the major organ systems have become well differentiated. Note that at this stage, the head grows at a faster rate than other parts of the body. *(c) Fetal stage.* This is the period from the end of the second month to birth. At four months all the actual body parts and organs are established. The fetal stage is primarily a time for increased growth and "fine detailing."

Teratogen [TER-ah-toh-jen] *Environmental agent that causes damage during prenatal development; the term comes from the Greek word teras, meaning "malformation"*

opiates, cocaine, various gases, lead, pesticides, and industrial chemicals all can damage sperm (Bandstra et al., 2002; Pollard, 2002; Raloff, 1999; Richardson et al., 2002).

Perhaps the most important, and generally avoidable, danger to the developing fetus comes from drugs — both legal and illegal. Nicotine and alcohol are two major **teratogens,** environmental agents that cause damage during prenatal development. Mothers who smoke tobacco have significantly higher rates of premature births, low-birth-weight infants, and fetal deaths (American Cancer Society, 2002; Day, Richardson, Goldschmidt, & Cornelius, 2000; Windham, Hopkins, Fenster, & Swan, 2000).

SUMMARY TABLE 25.3 SAMPLE ENVIRONMENTAL CONDITIONS THAT ENDANGER THE CHILD

Maternal Factors	Possible Effects on Embryo, Fetus, Newborn, or Young Child	
Malnutrition	Low birth weight, malformations, less-developed brain, greater vulnerability to disease	
Stress exposure	Low birth weight, hyperactivity, irritability, feeding difficulties	
Exposure to X-rays	Malformations, cancer	
Legal and illegal drugs	Inhibition of bone growth, hearing loss, low birth weight, fetal alcohol syndrome, mental retardation, attention deficits in childhood, and death	
Diseases German measles (rubella), herpes, AIDS and toxoplasmosis	Blindness, deafness, mental retardation, heart and other malformations, brain infection, spontaneous abortion, premature birth, low birth weight, and death	*Fetal alcohol syndrome. This child was born with fetal alcohol syndrome (FAS). Note the wide-set eyes and thin upper lip. These subtle facial abnormalities, as well as defective limbs and heart, result from the mother's heavy alcohol consumption during pregnancy. Many children with FAS also are below average in intelligence.*

Sources: Abadinsky, 2001; Butler, Joel, & Jeffries, 2000; Duanel et al., 2002; Rybacki & Long, 1999; Watson, Mednick, Huttunen, & Wang, 1999.

Children of women who smoke during pregnancy also show increased behavioral abnormalities and cognitive problems (Roy, Seidler, & Slotkin, 2002). In addition, researchers have found lower sociability, more negative emotionality, and increased conduct disorders among male children of smokers, as well as increased risk of anti-social behavior and substance abuse in male and female adult children of smokers (Brennan et al., 2002; Piquero et al., 2002; Wakschlag & Hans, 2002).

Alcohol also readily crosses the placenta, affects fetal development, and can result in a neurotoxic syndrome called **fetal alcohol syndrome** (FAS). Prenatal exposure to alcohol can cause facial abnormalities and stunted growth. But the most disabling features of FAS are neurobehavioral problems, ranging from hyperactivity and learning disabilities to mental retardation, depression, and psychoses. Recent research suggests that these problems may be due to widespread neuron death and reduced brain mass caused by alcohol's effect on two important brain neurotransmitters, glutamate and GABA (gamma aminobutyric acid) (Ikonomidou et al., 2000).

Fetal Alcohol Syndrome (FAS) *A combination of birth defects, including organ deformities and mental, motor, and/or growth retardation, that results from maternal alcohol abuse*

Early Childhood Physical Development Although Shakespeare described newborns as capable of only "mewling and puking in the nurse's arms," they are actually capable of much more. Let's explore 3 key areas of change in early childhood: *brain, motor,* and *sensory/perceptual development.*

1. *Brain development.* The brain and other parts of the nervous system grow faster than any other part of the body during both prenatal development and the first 2 years of life. At birth, a healthy newborn's brain is one-fourth its full adult size and will grow to about 75 percent of its adult weight and size by the age of 2 years. At age 5 years, the child's brain is nine-tenths its full adult weight (Figure 25.5, page 350).

It is generally believed that the newborn's brain contains most of the neurons it will ever have. Further brain development and learning occur primarily because neurons grow in size and because the number of axons and dendrites, as well as the extent of their connections, increases (DiPietro, 2000). As children learn and

Figure 25.5 *Body proportions.* Notice how body proportions change as we grow older. At birth, an infant's head is one-fourth its body's size, whereas in adulthood, the head is one-eighth.

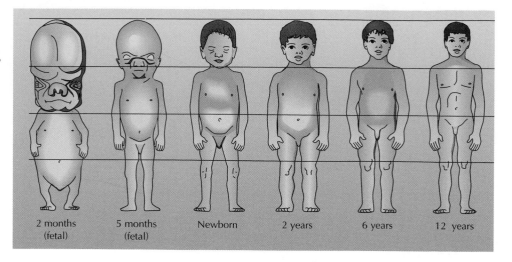

| 2 months (fetal) | 5 months (fetal) | Newborn | 2 years | 6 years | 12 years |

Maturation and motor development.
Some Hopi Indian infants spend a great portion of their first year of life being carried in a cradleboard, rather than crawling and walking freely on the ground. Yet by age one, their motor skills are very similar to those of infants who have not been restrained in this fashion (Dennis & Dennis, 1940).

develop, synaptic connections between active neurons strengthen, and dendritic connections become more elaborate (Figure 25.6). *Synaptic pruning* (reduction of unused synapses) helps support this process. *Myelination*, the accumulation of fatty tissue coating the axons of nerve cells, continues until early adulthood. Myelin increases the speed of neural impulses, and the speed of information processing shows a corresponding increase. In addition, synaptic connections in the frontal lobes and other parts of the brain continue growing and changing throughout the entire life span.

2. *Motor development.* Compared to the hidden, internal changes in brain development, the orderly emergence of active movement skills, known as *motor development*, is easily observed and measured. The newborn's first motor abilities are limited to *reflexes*, involuntary responses to stimulation. For example, the rooting reflex occurs when something touches a baby's cheek: The infant will automatically turn its head, open its mouth, and root for a nipple.

In addition to simple reflexes, the infant soon begins to show voluntary control over movements of various body parts. As you can see in Figure 25.7, page 351, a helpless newborn that cannot even lift her head is soon transformed into an active toddler capable of crawling, walking, and climbing.

3. *Sensory and perceptual development.* At birth, a newborn can smell most odors and distinguish between sweet, salty, and bitter tastes. Breastfed newborns also recognize and show preference for the odor and taste of their mother's milk over another mother's (DiPietro, 2000). The newborn's sense of touch and pain is also highly

Figure 25.6 *Brain growth in the first two years.* As the child learns and acquires new abilities, his or her brain develops increased connections between neurons.

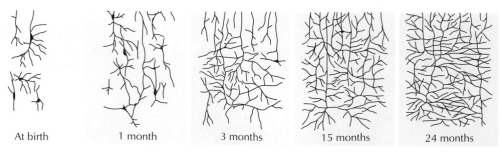

| At birth | 1 month | 3 months | 15 months | 24 months |

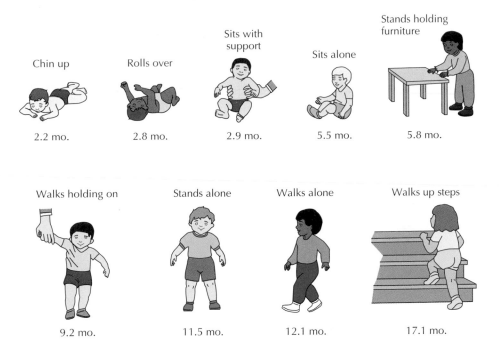

Chin up
2.2 mo.

Rolls over
2.8 mo.

Sits with support
2.9 mo.

Sits alone
5.5 mo.

Stands holding furniture
5.8 mo.

Walks holding on
9.2 mo.

Stands alone
11.5 mo.

Walks alone
12.1 mo.

Walks up steps
17.1 mo.

Figure 25.7 *Milestones in motor development.* In the typical progression of motor abilities, "chin up" occurs at age 2.2 months. However, no two children are exactly alike; all follow their own individual timetable for physical development. (Adapted from Frankenburg et al., 1992, with permission.)

developed, as evidenced by reactions to heel pricks for blood testing and circumcision (Williamson, 1997).

The sense of vision, however, is poorly developed. At birth, a newborn is estimated to have vision between 20/200 and 20/600 (Haith & Benson, 1998). If you have normal 20/20 vision, you can imagine what the infant's visual life is like. The level of detail you see at 200 or 600 feet is what they see at 20 feet. Within the first few months, vision quickly improves, and by six months, it is 20/100 or better. At 2 years, visual acuity reaches a near-adult level of 20/20 (Courage & Adams, 1990).

One of the most interesting findings in infant sensory and perceptual research concerns hearing. Not only can the newborn hear quite well at birth (Matlin & Foley, 1997) but also, during the last few months in the womb, the fetus can apparently hear sounds outside the mother's body (Vaughan, 1996). This raises the interesting possibility of fetal learning, and some have advocated special stimulation for the fetus as a way of increasing intelligence, creativity, and general alertness (e.g., Van de Carr & Lehrer, 1997). Devices such as the "pregaphone" have been specially designed to help eager parents talk to their babies before birth (Figure 25.8).

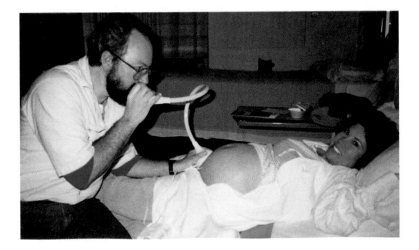

Figure 25.8 *Can a fetus learn before birth?* This father apparently thinks so. He is using a special device called a "pregaphone" to talk to his baby.

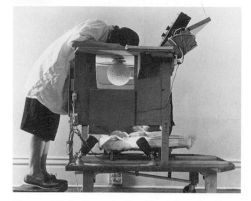

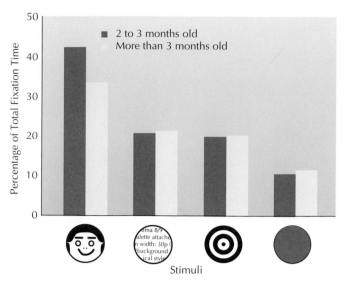

Stimuli

Figure 25.9 *Fantz's "looking chamber."*
Using this specially designed testing apparatus, Fantz and his colleagues measured the length of time infants stared at various stimuli. They found that infants preferred complex rather than simple patterns and pictures of faces rather than nonfaces.

Studies on possible fetal learning have found that newborn infants easily recognize their own mother's voice over that of a stranger. They also show preferences for children's stories (such as *The Cat in the Hat or The King, the Mice, and the Cheese*) that were read to them while they were still in the womb (DeCasper & Fifer, 1980; DeCasper & Spence, 1986; Trotter, 1987). On the other hand, some experts caution that too much or the wrong kind of stimulation before birth can be stressful for both the mother and fetus (Diamond & Hopson, 1998). They suggest that the fetus gets what it needs without any special stimulation.

How can scientists measure perceptual abilities and preferences in such young babies? Newborns and infants obviously cannot talk or follow directions, so researchers have had to create ingenious experiments to evaluate their perceptual skills. One of the earliest experimenters, Robert Fantz (1956, 1963), designed a "looking chamber" in which infants lie on their backs and look at visual stimuli (Figure 25.9).

Researchers also use newborns' heart rate and innate abilities, such as the sucking reflex, to study how they learn and how their perceptual abilities develop. To study the sense of smell, researchers measure changes in the newborns' heart rates when different odors are presented. Presumably, if they can smell one odor but not the other, their heart rate will change in the presence of the first but not the second. From research such as this, we now know that the senses develop very early in life.

Adolescence and Adulthood

Whereas the adolescent years are marked by dramatic changes in appearance and physical capacity, middle age and later adulthood are times of gradual physical changes. We begin with a look at adolescence.

Adolescence   Think back for a moment to your teen years. Were you concerned about the physical changes you were going through? Did you worry about how you differed from your classmates? Changes in height and weight, breast development and menstruation for girls, and a deepening voice and beard growth for boys are important milestones for adolescents. **Puberty,** the period of adolescence when a person becomes capable of reproduction, is a major physical milestone for everyone. It is a clear biological signal of the end of childhood.

Puberty *Biological changes during adolescence that lead to an adult-sized body and sexual maturity*

Although commonly associated with puberty, *adolescence* is the loosely defined psychological period of development between childhood and adulthood. In the United States, it roughly corresponds to the teenage years. It is important to recognize that adolescence is not a universal concept. Some nonindustrialized countries have no need for such a slow transition, and children simply assume adult responsibilities as soon as possible.

The clearest and most dramatic physical sign of puberty is the *growth spurt*, characterized by rapid increases in height, weight, and skeletal growth (Figure 25.10), and significant changes in reproductive structures and sexual characteristics. Maturation and hormone secretion cause rapid development of the ovaries, uterus, and vagina and the onset of menstruation *(menarche)* in the adolescent female. In the adolescent male, the testes, scrotum, and penis develop, and he undergoes *spermarche* (the first ejaculation). The ovaries and testes in turn produce hormones that lead to the development of *secondary sex characteristics*, such as the growth of pubic hair, deepening of the voice, growth of facial hair, growth of breasts, and so on (Figure 25.11).

Once the large and obvious pubertal changes have occurred, further age-related physical changes are less dramatic. Other than some modest increase in height and muscular development during the late teens and early twenties, most individuals experience only minor physical changes until middle age.

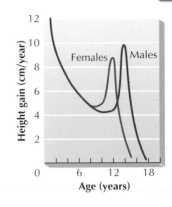

Figure 25.10 *Adolescent growth spurt.* Note the gender differences in height gain during puberty. Most girls are about 2 years ahead of boys in their growth spurt and therefore are taller than most boys between the ages of 10 and 14.

Middle Age

For women, *menopause*, the cessation of the menstrual cycle, which occurs somewhere between ages 45 and 55, is the second most important life milestone in physical development. The decreased production of estrogen (the dominant female hormone) produces certain physical changes. However, the popular belief that menopause (or "the change of life") causes serious psychological mood swings, loss of sexual interest, and depression is *not* supported by current research (Morrison & Tweedy, 2000; Stewart & Ostrove, 1998). In fact, one large-scale study of postmenopausal American women found that almost two-thirds felt relief that their periods had stopped, and over 50 percent did not experience hot flashes (Brim, 1999). When these problems exist, they

Figure 25.11 *Secondary sex characteristics.* Complex physical changes in puberty primarily result from hormones secreted from the ovaries and testes, the pituitary gland in the brain, and adrenal glands near the kidneys.

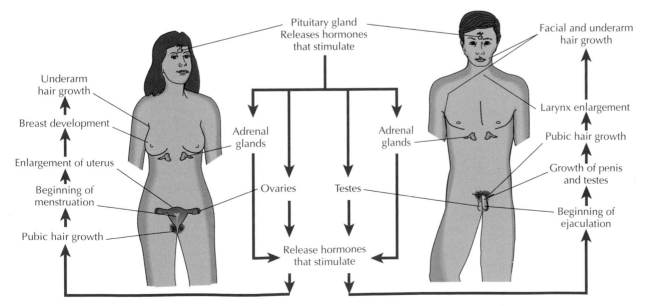

may reflect the social devaluation of aging women, not the physiological process of menopause itself. Given our Western society in which women are highly valued for their youth and beauty, can you understand why such a biological landmark of aging would be difficult for some women, and why women in cultures that derogate aging tend to experience more anxiety and depression during menopause (Mingo, Herman, & Jasperse, 2000; Sampselle, Harris, Harlow, & Sowers, 2002).

For men, youthfulness is less important and the physical changes of middle age are less obvious. Beginning in middle adulthood, men experience a gradual decline in the production of sperm and testosterone (the dominant male hormone), although they may remain capable of reproduction into their eighties or nineties. Physical changes such as unexpected weight gain, decline in sexual responsiveness, loss of muscle strength, and graying or loss of hair may lead some men (and women as well) to feel depressed and to question their life progress. They often see these alterations as a biological signal of aging and mortality (Powell, 1998). Such physical and psychological changes in men are known as the *male climacteric.*

Late Adulthood   After middle age, most physical changes in development are gradual and occur in the heart and arteries and sensory receptors. For example, cardiac output (the volume of blood pumped by the heart each minute) decreases, whereas blood pressure increases due to the thickening and stiffening of arterial walls. Visual acuity and depth perception decline, hearing acuity lessens, especially for high-frequency sounds, and smell sensitivity decreases (Atchley & Kramer, 2000; Medina, 1996).

Ageism *Prejudice or discrimination against an individual based on physical age*

This all sounds depressing. Can anything be done about it? Television, magazines, movies, and advertisements generally portray aging as a time of balding and graying hair, sagging parts, poor vision and hearing, and, of course, no sex life. Such negative portrayals contribute to the widespread **ageism** in our society, and we'll discuss this age-based prejudice in detail in Module 28. For the moment, recognize that aging is not completely bad. Most elderly people are not sick or disabled. In fact, we all know some 50 or 60 year olds who are more physically fit than some 20 year olds.

What about memory problems and inherited genetic tendencies toward Alzheimer's disease and other serious diseases of old age? There's good news on this front, too. The public and most researchers have long thought aging is accompanied by widespread death of neurons in the brain. Although this decline does happen with degenerative disorders like Alzheimer's disease, this is no longer believed to be a part of normal aging. It also is important to remember that age-related memory problems are not on a continuum with Alzheimer's disease (Wilson et al., 2000). That is, normal forgetfulness "does not reflect a predisposition" for serious dementia.

Aging does seem to take its toll on the *speed* of information processing, however. Recall from Module 20 that decreased speed of processing may reflect problems with *encoding* (putting information into long-term storage) and *retrieval* (getting information out of storage). If memory is like a filing system, older people may have more filing cabinets, and it may take them longer to initially file and later retrieve information. Although mental speed declines with age, general information processing and much of memory ability is largely unaffected by the aging process (Baltes, Staudinger, & Lindenberger, 1999; D'Esposito & Weksler, 2000).

In reference to genetic tendencies, scientists Caleb Finch and Rudolf Tanzi (1997) have found that genes have a "relatively minor effect" on our well-being in later years. They discovered that lifestyle and environmental factors (like exercise and good nutrition) "may profoundly influence the outcomes of aging." As illustrated in the section opener's description of John Glenn, many individuals maintain their vigor, interest, and productivity into their later years (Figure 25.12). In fact, recent research shows that cognitive functioning in older adults can be greatly enhanced with simple aerobic training (Calcombe & Kramer, 2003).

Use it or lose it? *Research shows exercise may be the most important factor in maintaining mental and physical abilities throughout the life span.*

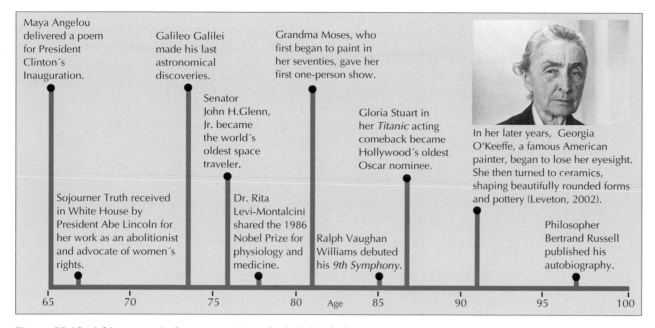

Maya Angelou delivered a poem for President Clinton's Inauguration.

Galileo Galilei made his last astronomical discoveries.

Grandma Moses, who first began to paint in her seventies, gave her first one-person show.

Senator John H.Glenn, Jr. became the world's oldest space traveler.

Gloria Stuart in her *Titanic* acting comeback became Hollywood's oldest Oscar nominee.

In her later years, Georgia O'Keeffe, a famous American painter, began to lose her eyesight. She then turned to ceramics, shaping beautifully rounded forms and pottery (Leveton, 2002).

Sojourner Truth received in White House by President Abe Lincoln for her work as an abolitionist and advocate of women's rights.

Dr. Rita Levi-Montalcini shared the 1986 Nobel Prize for physiology and medicine.

Ralph Vaughan Williams debuted his *9th Symphony*.

Philosopher Bertrand Russell published his autobiography.

65   70   75   80   Age   85   90   95   100

Figure 25.12 *Achievement in later years.* Note the high level of productivity among some of the world's most famous figures. When Georgia O'Keeffe, a famous American painter, began to lose her eyesight, she turned to ceramics, shaping beautifully rounded forms and pottery (Leveton, 2002).

If we set aside contributions from *secondary aging* (changes resulting from disease, disuse, or neglect), we are left to consider *primary aging* (gradual, inevitable age-related changes in physical and mental processes). There are two main theories explaining primary aging and death — programmed theory and damage theory (Cristofalo, 1996; Medina, 1996; Wallace, 1997).

According to the *programmed theory*, aging is genetically controlled. Once the ovum is fertilized, the program for aging and death is set and begins to run. Researcher Leonard Hayflick (1977, 1996) found that human cells seem to have a built-in life span. After about 50 doublings of laboratory-cultured cells, they cease to divide — they have reached the *Hayflick limit.*

The other explanation of primary aging is *damage theory*, which proposes that an accumulation of damage to cells and organs over the years ultimately causes death. Whichever theory is correct, human beings appear to have a maximum life span of about 110 to 120 years. Although we can try to control secondary aging in an attempt to reach that maximum, so far we have no means to postpone primary aging.

"As I get older, I find I rely more and more on these sticky notes to remind me."

Source: Arnic Levin © *The New Yorker* Collection 1996 Arnie Levin from cartoonbank.com

Assessment

CHECK & REVIEW

Physical Development

The prenatal period of development consists of three major stages: the **germinal, embryonic,** and **fetal.** Fetal development can be affected by environmental influences. Poor prenatal nutrition is a leading cause of birth defects, and most prescription and over-the-counter drugs are potentially **teratogenic** (capable of producing birth defects). Doctors advise pregnant women to avoid all unnecessary drugs, especially nicotine and alcohol.

During the prenatal period and the first year of life, the brain and nervous system grow faster than any other part of the body. Early motor development (crawling, standing, and walking) is largely the result of mat-uration. The sensory and perceptual abilities of newborns are relatively well developed.

At **puberty,** the adolescent becomes capable of reproduction and experiences a sharp increase in height, weight, and skeletal growth because of the pubertal growth spurt. Both men and women experience bodily changes in middle age. Many changes in women are related to the hormonal effects of menopause; similar psychological changes in men are called the male climacteric.

Although many of the changes associated with physical aging (such as decreases in cardiac output and visual acuity) are the result of primary aging, others are the result of abuse, disuse, and disease — secondary aging. Physical aging may be genetically built in from the moment of conception (programmed theory), or it may result from the body's inability to repair damage (damage theory).

Questions

1. What are the three stages of prenatal development?
2. Teratogens are _____ that can cause birth defects. (a) DNA fragments; (b) environmental agents; (c) recessive genes; (d) dominant genes
3. The period of life when an individual first becomes capable of reproduction is known as _____. (a) the age of fertility; (b) adolescence; (c) puberty; (d) the adolescent climacteric
4. What is the difference between primary and secondary aging?

Answers to Questions can be found in Appendix B.

■ Social—Emotional Development: Attachment and Parenting Styles

Assessment

How do attachment and parenting styles affect development?

The poet John Donne wrote, "No man is an island, entire of itself." In addition to physical development, developmental psychologists are very interested in social–emotional development. That is, they study how human beings' relations with others grow and change. Two of the most important topics in social–emotional development are those of *attachment* and *parenting styles*.

Attachment

An infant arrives in the world with a multitude of behaviors that encourage a strong bond of attachment with primary caregivers. **Attachment** can be defined as a strong affectional bond with special others that endures over time. Although most research has focused on the attachment between mother and child, fathers, grandparents, and other caretakers may also form attachment bonds with an infant.

In studying attachment behavior, researchers are often divided along the lines of the now-familiar nature-versus-nurture debate. Those who advocate the innate or biological position cite John Bowlby's work (1969, 1989, 2000). He proposed that newborn infants are biologically equipped with verbal and nonverbal behaviors (such as crying, clinging, smiling) and with "following" behaviors (such as crawling and walking after the caregiver) that serve to elicit certain instinctive nurturing responses from the caregiver. The biological argument for attachment is also supported by Konrad Lorenz's (1937) studies of **imprinting.** Lorenz's studies demonstrated how baby geese attach to, and then follow, the first large moving object they see during a certain critical period in their development.

Attachment *A strong affectional bond with special others that endures over time*

Imprinting *An innate form of learning within a critical period that involves attachment to the first large moving object seen*

Is contact comfort biological? When nestled next to a hen, or held in a person's cupped hands, chicks will almost immediately "relax" and close their eyes.

Feeding or Contact Comfort? According to Freud, infants become attached to the caregiver that provides oral pleasure (Module 35). But is there scientific evidence to support Freud's claim? In what is now a classic experiment, Harry Harlow and Robert Zimmerman (1959) set out to experimentally investigate the variables that might affect attachment. They started by creating two types of wire-framed *surrogate* (substitute) "mother" monkeys: one covered by soft terry cloth and one left uncovered. The infant monkeys were fed by either the cloth or the wire mother and had access to both mothers (Figure 25.13).

Harlow and Zimmerman found those monkeys who were "reared" by a cloth mother spent significant amounts of time clinging to the soft material of their surrogate mother. They also developed greater emotional security and curiosity than did monkeys assigned to the wire mother. Monkeys who were given free choice of both mothers also showed strong attachment behaviors toward the cloth mother — even when the wire-framed mother provided all food!

Further evidence of the importance of contact comfort came from later research by Harlow and Harlow (1966), in which monkey babies were exposed to various forms of rejection. Some of the "mothers" contained metal spikes that would suddenly protrude from the cloth covering and push the babies away; others had air jets that would sometimes blow the babies away. Nevertheless, the infant monkeys waited until the rejection was over and then clung to the cloth mother as tightly as before.

On the basis of these and related findings, Harlow concluded that what he called *contact comfort*, the pleasurable tactile sensations provided by a soft and cuddly "parent," is a powerful contributor to attachment. The satisfaction of other physical needs, such as food, is not enough.

Is contact comfort similarly important between human mothers and infants? Several studies suggest that it may be. Touching and massaging premature infants, for example, produce significant physical and emotional benefits (Elliott et al., 2002; Field & Hernandez-Reif, 2001; Gitau et al., 2002). Touch elicits positive emotions and attention from almost all babies. Mothers around the world tend to kiss, nuzzle, nurse, comfort, clean, and respond to their children with lots of physical contact.

For example, Japanese mothers and their children are rarely separated during the first months of life. The mothers touch their infants to communicate with them, breast-feed, carry them around on their backs, and take baths with them. Japanese infants do not even sleep in separate beds (Matsumoto, 2000). Mayan children also sleep alongside their mothers for several years. If a new baby comes along, the older child moves to a bed in the same room or shares a bed with another family member (Morelli, Oppenheim, Rogoff, & Goldsmith, 1992).

As you can see, attachment seems to depend, at least in part, on the hugging, cuddling, and caresses babies naturally receive from their mothers. I use the word *mother* because almost all research in this area has focused on mothers and their infants. However, research also shows the same results apply to fathers and other caregivers (Diener et al., 2002; Grossmann et al., 2002; van Ijzendoorn & De Wolff, 1997).

What happens if a child does not form an attachment? Researchers have investigated this question in two ways: They have looked at children and adults who spent

A**ssessment**

VISUAL QUIZ

Figure 25.13 *Why is this monkey clinging to the cloth figure on the left, rather than to the one on the right that provides milk?*

Answer: Harlow and Zimmerman found that infant monkeys spent more time on the terry-cloth-covered "mother," even when it was the wire "mother" that provided food. They concluded that contact comfort, rather than feeding, was the most important determinant of a monkey's attachment to its caregiver.

A**ssessment**

VISUAL QUIZ

Why are these geese following so closely behind scientist Konrad Lorenz?

Answer: Because they instinctually form a strong attachment and imprint on the first large moving object they see. Usually it is the mother goose, but in this case it was Lorenz.

Friendship and attachment. *These 50-year-old women have remained close friends since kindergarten. Despite heavy schedules, they get together at least once a year for a "summer reunion."*

their early years in institutions without the stimulation and love of a regular caregiver or who lived at home but were physically isolated under abusive conditions.

Infants raised in impersonal or abusive surroundings suffer from a number of problems. They seldom cry, coo, or babble; they become rigid when picked up; and they have few language skills. As for their social–emotional development, they tend to form shallow or anxious relationships. Some appear forlorn, withdrawn, and uninterested in their caretakers, whereas others seem insatiable in their need for affection (Zeanah, 2000). They also tend to show intellectual, physical, and perceptual retardation; increased susceptibility to infection; and neurotic "rocking" and isolation behaviors; in some cases, they die from lack of attachment (Belsky & Cassidy, 1994; Bowlby, 1973, 1982, 2000; Spitz & Wolf, 1946).

Levels of Attachment   Although most children are never exposed to extreme institutional conditions, developmental psychologist Mary Ainsworth and her colleagues (1967, 1978) have found significant differences in the typical level of attachment between infants and their mothers. Moreover, *level of attachment* affects long-term behaviors. Using a method called the *strange situation procedure*, a researcher observes infants in the presence or absence of their mother and a stranger. Ainsworth found that children could be divided into three groups: *securely attached*, *avoidant*, and *anxious/ambivalent*.

1. *Securely attached* (65%). When exposed to the stranger, the infant seeks closeness and contact with the mother, uses the mother as a safe base from which to explore, shows moderate distress on separation, and is happy when the mother returns.

2. *Avoidant* (25%). The infant does not seek closeness or contact with the mother, treats the mother much like a stranger, and rarely cries when the mother leaves the room.

3. *Anxious/Ambivalent* (10%). The infant becomes very upset as the mother leaves the room and when she returns seeks close contact, then squirms angrily to get away.

Ainsworth found that infants with a secure attachment style have caregivers that are sensitive and responsive to their signals of distress, happiness, and fatigue (Ainsworth et al., 1967, 1978; van Ijzendoorn & DeWolff, 1997). On the other hand, avoidant infants had caregivers that were aloof and distant, and anxious/ambivalent infants had inconsistent caregivers that alternated between strong affection and indifference.

Can you see why infants who are securely attached generally develop feelings of emotional security and trust in others? Or why avoidant infants learn to avoid others and suppress their attachment needs, whereas anxious/ambivalent infants tend to be temperamental and anxious that others will not return their affection? It is not surprising that follow-up studies found securely attached children were the most sociable, emotionally aware, enthusiastic, cooperative, persistent, curious, and competent (DeRosnay & Harris, 2002; Goldberg, 2000; Jacobsen & Hofmann, 1997).

Achievement

RESEARCH HIGHLIGHT

Romantic Love and Attachment

If you've been around young children, you've probably noticed how often they share toys and discoveries with a parent and seem much happier when a parent is near. You've probably also thought how cute and

sweet it is when infants and parents coo and share baby talk with each other. But have you noticed that these very same behaviors often occur between you and your adult romantic partner?

Intrigued by these parallels, several researchers have studied the relationship

between an infant's attachment to a parent figure and an adult's love for a romantic partner (Bachman & Zakahi, 2000; Bera, Miralt, Bearor, & Thomas, 2001–2002; Myers & Vetere, 2002). In one study, Cindy Hazan and Phillip Shaver (1987, 1994) discovered that adults who had an avoidant pattern in infancy are uncomfortable with intimacy as adults. They find it hard to trust others, difficult to self-disclose, and rarely report finding "true love" (Cooper, Shaver, & Collins, 1998; Fraley & Shaver, 1997). Anxious/ambivalent adults also have difficulty with intimate relationships, but unlike avoidants, they tend to be obsessed with their romantic partners, fearing their intense love will not be reciprocated. Individuals who are securely attached as infants easily become close to others, expect intimate relationships to endure, and perceive others as generally trustworthy.

Would you like to test your own attachment style? Thinking of your current and past romantic relationships, place a check next to those statements that best describe your feelings.

1. I find it relatively easy to get close to others and am comfortable depending on them and having them depend on me. I don't often worry about being abandoned or about someone getting too close.

2. I am somewhat uncomfortable being close. I find it difficult to trust partners completely or to allow myself to depend on them. I am nervous when anyone gets close, and love partners often want me to be more intimate than is comfortable for me.

3. I find that others are reluctant to get as close as I would like. I often worry that my partner doesn't really love me or won't stay with me. I want to merge completely with another person, and this desire sometimes scares people away.

According to research, 55 percent of adults agree with item I (secure attach-ment), 25 percent choose number 2 (avoidant attachment), and 20 percent choose item 3 (anxious/ambivalent attachment) (adapted from Fraley & Shaver, 1997; Hazan & Shaver, 1987; Shaver & Hazan, 1994). Note that the percentages for these adult attachment styles are roughly equivalent to the percentages for infant–parent attachment.

What your responses to this test may mean is that avoidant and anxious/ambivalent adults have developed intimacy patterns from their early childhood experiences that frustrate, if not destroy, adult love relationships. The avoidant lover may block intimacy by being emotionally aloof and distant, whereas the anxious/ambivalent lover may smother intimacy by being possessive and emotionally demanding.

As you may expect, the securely attached lover has intimacy patterns that foster long-term relationships and is the most desired partner by the majority of adults, regardless of their own attachment styles (Klohnen & Bera, 1998; Pietromonaco & Carnelley, 1994). Studies of adult attachment are significant because they suggest our earliest bonding experiences may have lasting effects. Bowlby (1979), in fact, believed attachment behaviors "characterize human beings from the cradle to the grave" (p. 129).

Evaluating Attachment Theories

Although Hazan and Shaver's research and similar studies are consistent with infant attachment theory, the results are correla-

The importance of attachment. *Researchers have found that the degree and quality of attachments you formed as an infant may carry over to your adult romantic relationships.*

tional rather than experimental. And, as you know from Module 2, it is always risky to infer causation from correlation. Accordingly, the relationship between romantic love style and early infant attachment is subject to several alternative causal explanations. Further research is necessary before we fully understand the link between infant attachment and adult intimate relationships.

Also, be aware that early attachment experiences may predict the future but do not determine it. Despite the significance of the initial infant–parent attachment bond, we are capable of learning new social skills and different attitudes toward relationships in our later interactions with peers, close friends, lovers, and spouses. Unlike diamonds, attachment styles are not necessarily forever.

Parenting Styles

How much of our personality comes from the way our parents treat us as we're growing up? Researchers since the 1920s have studied the effects of different methods of child rearing on children's behavior, development, and mental health. Recent studies done by Diana Baumrind (1980, 1995) found that parenting styles could be reliably divided into three broad patterns: *permissive*, *authoritarian*, and *authoritative*.

1. ***Permissive.*** Permissive parents come in two styles: (a) *permissive-indifferent*, the parent who sets few limits and provides little in the way of attention, interest, or

emotional support, and (b) *permissive-indulgent*, the parent who is highly involved but places few demands or controls on the child. Children of permissive-indifferent parents have poor self-control (becoming demanding and disobedient) and poor social skills. Children of permissive-indulgent parents often fail to learn respect for others and tend to be impulsive, immature, and out of control.

2. ***Authoritarian.*** These parents are rigid and punitive. They value unquestioning obedience and mature responsibility from their children, while remaining aloof and detached. An authoritarian parent might say, "Don't ask questions. Just do it my way or else." Children of authoritarian parents are easily upset, moody, aggressive, and generally have poor communication skills.

3. ***Authoritative.*** These parents are tender, caring, and sensitive toward their children. But they also set firm limits and enforce them, while encouraging increasing responsibility. As you might expect, children do best with authoritative parents. They become self-reliant, self-controlled, and high achieving. They also seem more content, goal oriented, friendly, and socially competent in their dealings with others (Baumrind, 1995; Gonzalez, Holbein, & Quilter, 2002; Parke & Buriel, 1998).

Evaluating Baumrind's Research

Before you conclude that the authoritative pattern is the only way to raise successful children, you should know that many children raised in the other styles also become caring, cooperative adults. Criticism of Baumrind's findings generally falls into three areas: *child temperament*, *child expectations*, and *parental warmth*:

1. ***Child temperament.*** Results may reflect the child's unique temperament and reactions to parental efforts rather than the parenting style per se (Clarke-Stewart, Fitzpatrick, Allhusen, & Goldberg, 2000; McCrae et al., 2000). That is, the parents of mature and competent children may have developed the authoritative style because of the child's behavior rather than vice versa.

2. ***Child expectations.*** Cultural research suggests that a child's expectations of how parents should behave also play an important role in parenting styles (Brislin, 2000; Valsiner, 2000). As we discovered at the beginning of this section, adolescents in Korea expect strong parental control and interpret it as a sign of love and deep concern. Adolescents in North America, however, would interpret the same behavior as a sign of parental hostility and rejection.

3. ***Parental warmth.*** Cross-cultural studies suggest that the most important variable in parenting styles and child development might be the degree of warmth versus rejection parents feel toward their children. On the basis of analyses of over 100 societies, researchers have concluded that, universally, parental rejection adversely affects a child (Rohner, 1986; Rohner & Britner, 2002). The neglect and indifference shown by rejecting parents tend to be correlated with hostile, aggressive children who have a difficult time establishing and maintaining close relationships. These children also are more likely to develop psychological problems that require professional intervention.

Do fathers differ from mothers in their parenting style? Until recently, the father's role in discipline and childcare was largely ignored. But as more fathers have begun to take an active role in childrearing, there has been a corresponding increase in research. From these studies, we now know that fathers are absorbed with, excited about, and responsive to their newborns and that there are few differences in the way children form attachments to either parent (Diener, Mengelsdorf, McHale & Frosch, 2002; Lopez & Hsu, 2002; Rohner & Veneziano, 2001). After infancy, the

Are fathers important? *Although overlooked in the past, the father's role in a child's development is now a topic of active research.*

father becomes increasingly involved with his children, yet he still spends less over-all time in direct childcare than the mother does (Demo, 1992; Hewlett, 1992). But fathers are just as responsive, nurturing, and competent as mothers when they do assume child-care responsibilities.

Assessment

CHECK & REVIEW

Social–Emotional Development

Nativists believe that **attachment** is innate, whereas nurturists believe it is learned. The Harlow and Zimmerman experiments with monkeys raised by cloth or wire surrogate mothers found that contact comfort might be the most important factor in attachment.

Infants who fail to form attachments may suffer serious effects. When attachments are formed, they may differ in level or degree. Research on securely attached, avoidant, and anxious/ambivalent children found significant differences in behaviors that may persist into adulthood.

Parenting styles fall into three major cat-egories: permissive, authoritarian, and auth-oritative. Critics suggest that a child's unique temperament, their expectations of parents, and the degree of warmth versus rejection from parents may be the three most impor-tant variables in parenting styles.

Questions

1. According to Harlow and Zimmerman's research with cloth and wire surrogate mothers, _____ is the most important variable for attachment. (a) availability of food; (b) contact comfort; (c) caregiver and infant bonding; (d) imprinting
2. List the three types of attachment reported by Mary Ainsworth.
3. Using Hazan and Shaver's research on adult attachment styles, match the fol-lowing adults with their probable type of infant attachment:

___1. Mary is nervous around attractive partners and complains that lovers often want her to be more inti-mate than she finds comfortable.
___2. Bob complains that lovers are often reluctant to get as close as he would like.
___3. Rashelle finds it relatively easy to get close to others and seldom worries about being abandoned.

(a) avoidant; (b) secure; (c) anxious/ambiva-lent

4. Briefly summarize Baumrind's three par-enting styles.

Answers to Questions can be found in Appendix B.

MODULE 25   ACTIVE LEARNING WORKSHEET

ACROSS

7 Data collection technique measuring a single individual or group of individuals over an extended period and producing information about age changes.

8 Third stage of prenatal development (eight weeks to birth).

9 External, environmental agent that can cross the placental barrier and cause minor or severe birth defects.

DOWN

1 Branch of psychology that studies age-related behaviors from conception to death.

2 Period of special sensitivity to specific types of learning.

3 Biological growth processes that enable orderly changes in behavior and are relatively uninfluenced by the environment.

4 First stage of pregnancy (conception to two weeks).

5 Period in life when sex organs mature and sexual reproduction becomes possible.

6 Second stage of pregnancy (from uterine implantation through the eighth week).

MODULE 26
COGNITIVE DEVELOPMENT

The following fan letter was written to Shari Lewis (1963), a children's television performer, about her puppet Lamb Chop:

Dear Shari:

All my friends say Lamb Chop isn't really a little girl that talks. She is just a puppet you made out of a sock. I don't care even if it's true. I like the way Lamb Chop talks. If I send you one of my socks will you teach it how to talk and send it back?

RANDI

Assessment

How does cognition, or the way we think about the world, change during the life cycle?

Randi's understanding of fantasy and reality is certainly different from an adult's. Just as a child's body and physical abilities change, his or her way of knowing and perceiving the world also grows and changes. This seems intuitively obvious, but early psychologists — with one exception — focused on physical, emotional, language, and personality development. The one major exception was Jean Piaget (pronounced Pee–ah–ZHAY).

Piaget demonstrated that a child's intellect is fundamentally different from an adult's (Flavell, 1999; Papert, 1999). He showed that an infant begins at a cognitively "primitive" level and that intellectual growth progresses in distinct stages, motivated by an innate need to know. Piaget's theory, developed in the 1920s and 1930s, has proven so comprehensive and insightful that it remains the major force in the cognitive area of developmental psychology today.

To appreciate Piaget's contributions, we need to consider three major concepts: schemas, assimilation, and accommodation. **Schemas** are the most basic units of intellect. They act as patterns that organize our interactions with the environment, like architect's drawings or builder's blueprints.

In the first few weeks of life, for example, the infant apparently has several schemas based on the innate reflexes of sucking, grasping, and so on. These schemas are primarily motor and may be little more than stimulus-and-response mechanisms — the nipple is presented and the baby sucks. Soon, however, other schemas emerge. The infant develops a more detailed schema for eating solid food, a different schema for the concepts of "mother" and "father," and so on. It is important to recognize that schemas, our tools for learning about the world, are enlarged and changed throughout our lives. For example, a computer user previously accustomed to DOS (disk operating system, a text-based format) would need to develop new schemas in order to work with Windows (a graphic user interface).

Assimilation and accommodation are the two major processes by which schemas grow and change over time. **Assimilation** is the process of absorbing new information into existing schemas. For instance, infants use their sucking schema not only in sucking nipples but also in sucking blankets or fingers.

Accommodation occurs when new information or stimuli cannot be assimilated and new schemas are developed or old schemas are changed to better fit with the new information. An infant's first attempt to eat solid food with a spoon is a good example of accommodation. When the spoon first enters her mouth, the child attempts to assimilate it by using the previously successful sucking schema — shaping lips and tongue around the spoon as around a nipple. After repeated trials, she accommodates by adjusting her lips and tongue in a way that moves the food off the spoon and into her mouth.

Schema *Cognitive structures or patterns consisting of a number of organized ideas that grow and differentiate with experience*

Assimilation *In Piaget's theory, absorbing new information into existing schemas*

Accommodation *In Piaget's theory, adjusting old schemas or developing new ones to better fit with new information*

TRY THIS

YOURSELF

Application

Study the "impossible figure" at right. Now take out a piece of paper and try to draw the same figure (without tracing!). Students with artistic training generally find it relatively easy to reproduce, whereas the rest of us find it "impossible." This is because we lack the necessary artistic *schema* and cannot *assimilate* what we see. With practice and training, we could *accommodate* the new information and easily draw the figure.

■ Stages of Cognitive Development: Birth to Adolescence

As a result of assimilation, accommodation, and the corresponding changes in schemas, a child's cognitive abilities undergo an orderly series of increasingly complex changes. When enough changes have occurred, the individual experiences a large developmental shift in his or her point of view. Piaget called these developmental shifts cognitive stages in development (Table 26.1).

SUMMARY TABLE 26.1 PIAGET'S FOUR STAGES OF COGNITIVE DEVELOPMENT

Birth to 2 years	***Sensorimotor*** Abilities: Uses senses and motor skills to explore and develop cognitively. Limits: Beginning of stage lacks *object permanence* (understanding things continue to exist even when not seen, heard, or felt).
Ages 2–7 years	***Preoperational*** Abilities: Has significant language and thinks symbolically. Limits: • Cannot perform "operations." • *Egocentric* thinking (inability to consider another's point of view). • *Animistic* thinking (believing all things are living).
Ages 7–11 years	***Concrete Operational*** Abilities: • Can perform "operations" on concrete objects. • Understands *conservation* (realizing thoughts and changes in shape or appearance can be reversed). Limits: Cannot think abstractly and hypothetically.
Ages 11 years and up	***Formal Operational*** Abilities: Can think abstractly and hypothetically. Limits: *Adolescent egocentrism* at the beginning of this stage, with related problems of the *personal fable* and *imaginary audience*.

According to Piaget, all children go through the same four cognitive stages at approximately the same age, regardless of the culture in which they live. No stage can be skipped, because skills acquired at earlier stages are essential to mastery at later stages. Let's take a closer look at these four stages: sensorimotor, preoperational, concrete operational, and formal operational.

The Sensorimotor Stage

During the **sensorimotor stage,** lasting from birth until "significant" language acquisition (about age 2 years), children explore the world and develop their schemas primarily through their senses and motor activities — hence the term *sensorimotor.*

One important concept acquired during this stage is **object permanence.** At birth and for the next 3 or 4 months, children lack object permanence. They seem to have no schemas for objects they cannot see, hear, or touch — out of sight is truly out of mind (Figure 26.1).

Preoperational Stage

During the **preoperational stage** (roughly ages 2 to 7 years), language advances significantly, and the child begins to think *symbolically* — using symbols, such as words, to represent concepts. Three other qualities characterize this stage:

1. *Concepts are not yet operational.* Piaget labeled this period "preoperational" because the child lacks *operations,* reversible mental processes. For instance, if a preoperational boy who has a brother is asked, "Do you have a brother?" He will easily respond, "Yes." However, when asked, "Does your brother have a brother?" he will answer, "No!" To understand that his brother has a brother, he must be able to *reverse* the concept of "having a brother."

2. *Thinking is egocentric.* Children at this stage have difficulty understanding that there are points of view other than their own. **Egocentrism** refers to the preoperational child's limited ability to distinguish between his or her own perspective and someone else's. (It does not mean "selfishness" in the ordinary sense of the word.) The preschooler who moves in front of you to get a better view of the TV or repeatedly asks questions while you are talking on the telephone is demonstrating egocentrism. They assume that others see, hear, feel, and think exactly as they do. Consider the following telephone conversation between a 3 year old, who is at home, and her mother, who is at work:

Can you see why this stage is called "sensorimotor"?

Sensorimotor Stage *Piaget's first stage (birth to approximately age two years), in which schemas are developed through sensory and motor activities*

Object Permanence *Piagetian term for an infant's understanding that objects (or people) continue to exist even when they cannot be seen, heard, or touched directly*

Preoperational Stage *Piaget's second stage (roughly ages 2 to 7 years), characterized by the ability to employ significant language and to think symbolically, but the child lacks operations (reversible mental processes), and thinking is egocentric and animistic*

Egocentrism *The inability to consider another's point of view, which Piaget considered a hallmark of the preoperational stage*

Assessment

VISUAL QUIZ

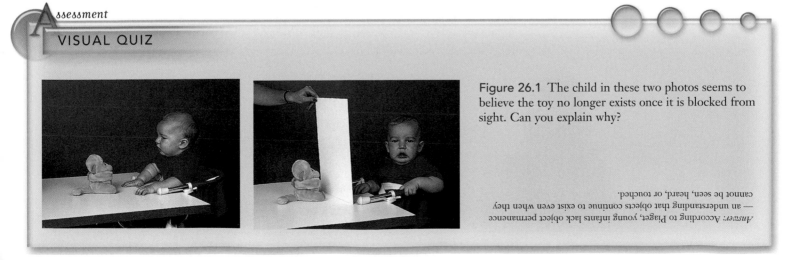

Figure 26.1 The child in these two photos seems to believe the toy no longer exists once it is blocked from sight. Can you explain why?

Answer: According to Piaget, young infants lack object permanence — an understanding that objects continue to exist even when they cannot be seen, heard, or touched.

Concrete Operational Stage
Piaget's third stage (roughly ages 7 to 11 years); the child can perform mental operations on concrete objects and understand reversibility and conservation, but abstract thinking is not yet present

Conservation *Understanding that certain physical characteristics (such as volume) remain unchanged, even when their outward appearance changes*

Mother: Emma is that you?

Emma: (Nods silently.)

Mother: Emma, is Daddy there? Can I speak to him?

Emma: (Twice nods silently.)

Egocentric preoperational children fail to understand that the phone caller cannot see their nodding head.

3. ***Thinking is animistic.*** Children in the preoperational stage believe that objects such as the sun, trees, clouds, and bars of soap have motives, feelings, and intentions (for example, "dark clouds are angry" and "soap sinks to the bottom of the bathtub because it is tired"). *Animism* refers to the belief that all things are living (or animated). Our earlier example of Randi's letter asking puppeteer Shari Lewis to teach her sock to talk like Lamb Chop is also an example of animistic thinking.

   Can preoperational children be taught how to use operations and to avoid egocentric and animistic thinking? Although some researchers have reported success in accelerating the preoperational stage, Piaget did not believe in pushing children ahead of their own developmental schedule. He believed children should be allowed to grow at their own pace, with minimal adult interference (Elkind, 1981, 2000, 2001). In fact, Piaget thought Americans were particularly guilty of pushing children, calling American childhood the "Great American Kid Race."

Concrete Operational Stage

Between the approximate ages of 7 and 11 years, children are in the **concrete operational stage.** During this stage many important thinking skills emerge. Unlike the preoperational stage, concrete operational children are able to perform operations on *concrete* objects. Because they understand the concept of *reversibility*, they recognize that certain physical attributes (such as volume) remain unchanged although the outward appearance is altered, a process known as **conservation** (Figure 26.2).

If you know children in the preoperational or concrete operational stages, you may enjoy testing their grasp of conservation by trying some of the experiments shown in Table 26.2, page 367. The equipment is easily obtained, and you will find their responses fascinating. Keep in mind that this should be done as a game. Do not allow the child to feel that he or she is failing a test or making a mistake.

Figure 26.2 *Test for conservation.* *(a) In the classic conservation of liquids test, the child is first shown two identical glasses with water at the same level. (b) The water is poured from one of the short, wide glasses into the tall, thin one. (c) When asked whether the two glasses have the same amount, or if one has more, the preoperational child replies that the tall, thin glass has more. This is a failure to conserve volume.*

(a)　　　　　(b)　　　　　(c)

This is a sample of experiments used to test Piaget's different types of conservation. Try them with children of various ages. Do the children fit the stages as described by Piaget?

TABLE 26.2

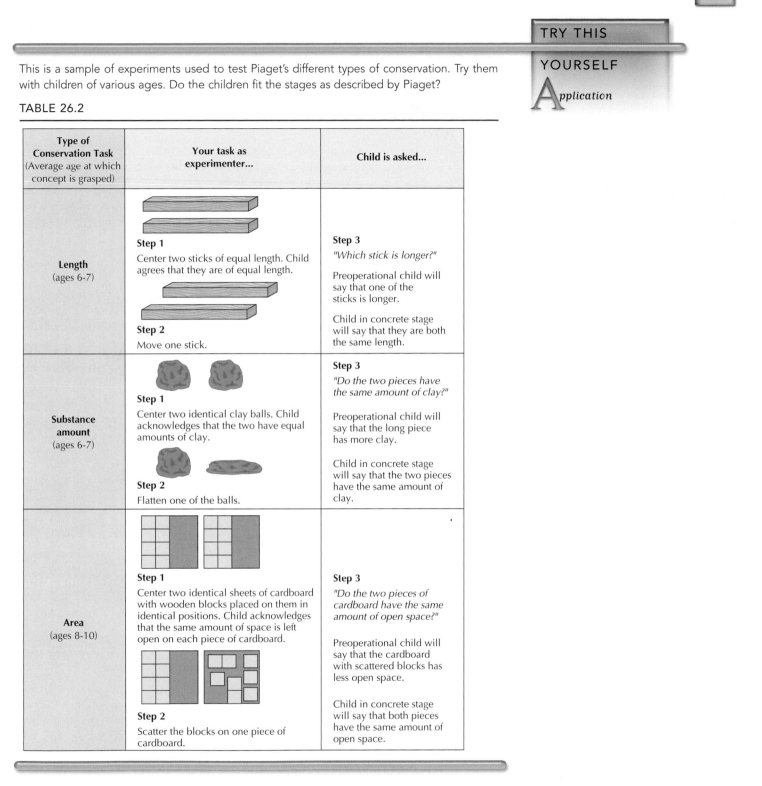

Type of Conservation Task (Average age at which concept is grasped)	Your task as experimenter...	Child is asked...
Length (ages 6-7)	**Step 1** Center two sticks of equal length. Child agrees that they are of equal length. **Step 2** Move one stick.	**Step 3** *"Which stick is longer?"* Preoperational child will say that one of the sticks is longer. Child in concrete stage will say that they are both the same length.
Substance amount (ages 6-7)	**Step 1** Center two identical clay balls. Child acknowledges that the two have equal amounts of clay. **Step 2** Flatten one of the balls.	**Step 3** *"Do the two pieces have the same amount of clay?"* Preoperational child will say that the long piece has more clay. Child in concrete stage will say that the two pieces have the same amount of clay.
Area (ages 8-10)	**Step 1** Center two identical sheets of cardboard with wooden blocks placed on them in identical positions. Child acknowledges that the same amount of space is left open on each piece of cardboard. **Step 2** Scatter the blocks on one piece of cardboard.	**Step 3** *"Do the two pieces of cardboard have the same amount of open space?"* Preoperational child will say that the cardboard with scattered blocks has less open space. Child in concrete stage will say that both pieces have the same amount of open space.

Formal Operational Stage

The final period in Piaget's theory is the **formal operational stage,** which typically begins around age 11 years. In this stage, children begin to apply their operations to abstract concepts, in addition to concrete objects. They also become capable of hypothetical thinking ("What if?"), which allows systematic formulation and testing of concepts.

Formal Operational Stage *Piaget's fourth stage (around age 11 years and beyond), characterized by abstract and hypothetical thinking*

Adolescents considering part-time jobs, for example, may think about possible conflicts with school and friends, the number of hours they want to work, and the kind of work for which they are qualified before they start filling out applications. Formal operational thinking also allows the adolescent to construct a well-reasoned argument based on hypothetical concepts and logical processes. Consider the following argument:

1. If you hit a glass with a feather, the glass will break.

2. You hit the glass with a feather.

What is the logical conclusion? The correct answer, "The glass will break," is contrary to fact and direct experience. Therefore, the child in the concrete operational stage would have difficulty with this task, whereas the formal operational thinker understands that this problem is about abstractions that need not correspond to the real world.

Problems with Early Formal Operational Thinking

Along with the benefits of this cognitive style come several problems. Adolescents in the early stages of the formal operational period demonstrate a type of *egocentrism* different from that of the preoperational child. Although adolescents do recognize that others have unique thoughts and perspectives, they often fail to differentiate between what others are thinking and their own thoughts. This *adolescent egocentrism* has two characteristics that may affect social interactions as well as problem solving:

1. *Personal fable.* As a result of their unique form of egocentrism, adolescents may conclude they alone are having certain insights or difficulties and that no one

---

Application

CRITICAL THINKING

Developing Insight Into Egocentricity: Adult versus Childhood Egocentrism

Piaget asserted that preoperational children (ages two to seven) are egocentric. That is, they are unable to take the perspective of others because of their limited cognitive development. Although Piaget believed that most adults naturally outgrow such egocentric thinking, some research suggests that a tendency toward egocentricity may persist throughout adulthood. Why? It is difficult to outgrow our own egocentricity because we suppress facts that are inconsistent with our conclusions and we fail to notice when our behavior contradicts our self-image.

The best antidote to egocentricity is self-awareness and critical self-analysis. To develop insight into your own egocentricity, use the following rating scale (1 = never behaves in this way, 2 = seldom behaves in this way, 3 = occasionally behaves in this way, 4 = often behaves in this way, 5 = always behaves in this way) to first rate the personality traits of someone you find it hard to get along with. Then using the same scale, rate your best friend and then yourself. Enter your scores in the blank spaces.

ACTIVE LEARNING

	DISLIKED PERSON	BEST FRIEND	SELF
Is aggressive and irritable with others.	___	___	___
Is helpful and courteous to others.	___	___	___
Offers support and encouragement to others.	___	___	___
Takes advantage of others.	___	___	___
Is hard working and reliable.	___	___	___
Is sociable and fun to be with.	___	___	___
Dominates conversations.	___	___	___
Values advice from others.	___	___	___
Is interested in trying new things.	___	___	___
Tries to be fair and just with others.	___	___	___

Compare the values on positive and negative items you assigned for your disliked person versus yourself. Do you think this person would agree with your evaluation? Why or why not? Can you see how your own egocentrism could explain the differences in perception?

Now compare the ratings you assigned for yourself and your best friend. If you are like most people, you will notice a strong similarity. An obvious, and somewhat egocentric, explanation for this is that similarity attracts—we like people who are like us.

Further critical thinking, however, would explain this similarity as the result of *sociocentricity*—the extension of egocentrism to groups. The individual goes from thinking, "I am right!" to "We are right!" When this egocentrism extends to ethnic groups, countries, and religions, it is sometimes referred to as *ethnocentrism*. The best antidote to egocentrism, sociocentrism, and ethnocentrism is to listen carefully and with an open mind to those with whom we disagree and to apply the full force of our critical thinking skills to our own behaviors.

else could understand or sympathize. David Elkind (1967, 2000, 2001) described this as the formation of a *personal fable*, an intense investment in their own thoughts and feelings, and a belief that these thoughts are unique. One student in our class remembered being very upset in junior high when her mother tried to comfort her over the loss of an important relationship. "I felt like she couldn't possibly know how it felt — no one could. I couldn't believe that anyone had ever suffered like this or that things would ever get better."

Several forms of risk taking, such as engaging in sexual intercourse without contraception, driving dangerously, and experimenting with drugs, also seem to arise from the personal fable (Coley & Chase-Lansdale, 1998; Flavell, Miller, & Miller, 2002; Greene et al., 2000). The adolescent has a sense of uniqueness, invulnerability, and immortality. They recognize the dangers of these activities, but think the rules don't apply to them.

2. ***Imaginary audience.*** In early adolescence, people tend to believe they are the center of others' thoughts and attentions, instead of considering that everyone is equally wrapped up in his or her own concerns and plans. In other words, adolescents picture all eyes focused on their behaviors. Elkind referred to this as the *imaginary audience*. This may explain what seems like extreme forms of self-consciousness and concern for physical appearance ("Everyone knows I don't know the answer"; "They're noticing how fat I am and this awful haircut").

If the imaginary audience results from an inability to differentiate the self from others, the personal fable is a product of differentiating too much. Thankfully, these two forms of adolescent egocentrism tend to decrease during later stages of the formal operational period.

Personal fable in action? *Can you see how this type of risk-taking behavior may reflect the personal fable — an adolescent's tendency to believe he or she is unique and special and that dangers don't apply to them?*

■ Assessing Piaget's Theory: Criticisms and Contributions

As influential as Piaget's account of cognitive development has been, it has received significant criticisms. Let's look briefly at two major areas of concern: underestimated abilities and underestimated genetic and cultural influences.

Underestimated Abilities

Research shows that Piaget may have underestimated young children's cognitive development. For example, researchers report that very young infants have a basic concept of how objects move, are aware that objects continue to exist even when screened from view, and can recognize speech sounds, (Baillargeon, 2000; Haith & Benson, 1998).

Research on infant imitation of facial expression also raises questions about Piaget's estimates of early infant abilities. In a series of well-known studies, Meltzoff and Moore (1977, 1985, 1994) found that newborns could imitate such facial movements as tongue protrusion, mouth opening, and lip pursing (Figure 26.3). At age 9 months, infants will imitate facial actions a full day after seeing them (Heimann & Meltzoff, 1996).

Nonegocentric responses also appear in the earliest days of life. For example, newborn babies tend to cry in response to the cry of another baby (Donde, Simion, & Caltran, 1999). And preschoolers will adapt their speech by using shorter, simpler expressions when talking to 2 year olds than to adults (Gelman & Shatz, 1978).

Underestimated Genetic and Cultural Influences

Piaget's model, like other stage theories, has also been criticized for not sufficiently taking into account genetic and cultural differences (Flavell, Miller, & Miller, 2002; Matusov & Hayes, 2000; Matsumoto, 2000; Plomin & Rutter, 1998). During Piaget's time, the genetic influences on cognitive abilities were poorly understood, but as you know from earlier modules and discussions in this text, there has been rapid explosion of information in this field in the last few years. In addition, formal education and specific cultural experiences can also significantly affect cognitive development. Consider the following example from a researcher attempting to test the formal operational skills of a farmer in Liberia (Scribner, 1977):

Contrary to Piaget's belief, children in the preoperational stage are not completely egocentric. They can occasionally take the perspective of another — like the children in this photo.

Figure 26.3 *Infant imitation.* When an adult models a facial expression, even very young infants will respond with a similar expression. Is this true imitation or a simple stimulus–response reflex?

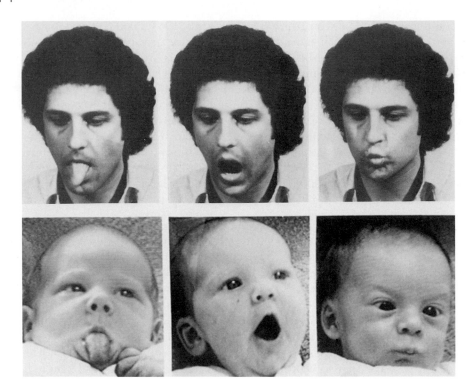

Researcher: All Kpelle men are rice farmers. Mr. Smith is not a rice farmer. Is he a Kpelle man?

Kpelle farmer: I don't know the man. I have not laid eyes on the man myself.

Instead of reasoning in the "logical" way of Piaget's formal operational stage, the Kpelle farmer reasoned according to his specific cultural and educational training, which apparently emphasized personal knowledge. Not knowing Mr. Smith, the Kpelle farmer did not feel qualified to comment on him. Thus, Piaget's theory may have underestimated the effect of culture on a person's cognitive functioning.

Despite criticisms, Piaget's contributions to psychology are enormous. As one scholar put it, "assessing the impact of Piaget on developmental psychology is like assessing the impact of Shakespeare on English literature or Aristotle on philosophy — impossible" (cited in Beilin, 1992, p. 191).

■ Information Processing: A Computer Model of Cognition

An alternative to Piaget's theory of cognitive development is the *information processing model*, which compares the workings of the mind to a computer and studies how information is received, encoded, stored, organized, retrieved, and used by people of different ages. This model offers important insights into two major areas of cognition: attention and memory.

Attention

Attention refers to focusing awareness on a narrowed range of stimuli. Infants pay attention to their environment for only short periods of time. Even toddlers, who can pay attention for longer periods, are easily distracted. When watching television, for example, two-year-olds talk more to other people, play more with toys, and look around the room more than four-year-olds. As they get older, children's attention spans improve and they learn to discriminate between what is and what is not important to concentrate on at any given time (Bjorklund, 1995).

Memory

After children attend to information and take it into their information processing system, they must remember it. Attention determines what information enters the "computer," whereas memory determines what information is saved.

Like attention, memory skills also improve gradually throughout childhood and adolescence (Hayne, Boniface, & Barr, 2000; Richards, 1997). Two-year-olds can repeat back about two digits immediately after hearing them, but 10-year-olds can repeat about six. Improvement comes as children acquire strategies during the school years for storing and retrieving information. For example, they learn to rehearse or repeat information over and over, to use mnemonics (like "i before e except after c"), and to organize their information in ways that facilitate retrieval.

As people grow older, their use of information processing strategies and overall memory continue to change. Recall from Module 24 that fluid *intelligence* (requiring speed or rapid learning) tends to decrease with age, whereas *crystallized intelligence* (knowledge and information gained over the life span) continues to increase until advanced old age.

Despite concerns about "keeping up with 18-year-olds," older returning students often do as well or better than their younger counterparts in college classes. This superior performance in older adult students is due in part to their generally greater academic motivation, but it also reflects the importance of prior knowledge. Cognitive psychologists have demonstrated that the more people know, the easier it is for them to lay down new memories (Chi & Glaser, 1985; Leahy & Harris, 1997). Older students, for instance, generally find this section on development easier to master than younger students. Their interactions with children and greater knowledge about life changes create a framework on which to hang new information.

In summary, the more you know, the more you learn. Thus, having a college degree and stimulating occupation may help you stay mentally sharp in your later years (Mayr & Kliegl, 2000; Powell, 1998).

Haven't studies also shown decreases in older adults' memory capabilities? As mentioned at the beginning of this section, this may reflect problems with cross-sectional versus longitudinal research. In addition, earlier studies often asked participants to memorize simple lists of words or paired association tasks, which older people often find meaningless and uninteresting. When the information is meaningful, an older person's rich web of existing knowledge helps them remember it (Graf, 1990).

Contrary to popular stereotypes of frail and forgetful elderly, growing old, for most of us, will probably be better than expected—and, of course, far better than the alternative!

*A*ssessment

CHECK & REVIEW

Cognitive Development

Jean Piaget's theories of cognitive development are based on the concept of **schemas**, mental patterns or blueprints used to interpret the world. Sometimes existing schemas can be used "as is" and information is **assimilated**; on other occasions, existing schemas must be modified, which calls for **accommodation**.

According to Piaget, cognitive development occurs in an invariant sequence of four stages: **sensorimotor** (birth to 2 years), **preoperational** (between 2 and 7 years), **concrete operational** (between 7 and 11 years), and **formal operational** (age 11 years and up).

In the sensorimotor stage, children acquire **object permanence**. During the preoperational stage, children are better equipped to use symbols, but their thinking is limited by their lack of operations, **egocentrism**, and animism.

In the concrete operational stage, children learn to perform operations (to think about concrete things while not actually doing them). They understand the principles of conservation and reversibility. During the formal operational stage, the adolescent is able to think abstractly and deal with hypothetical situations but again is prone to egotism.

Although Piaget has been criticized for underestimating abilities and genetic and cultural influences, he remains one of the most respected psychologists in modern times.

Psychologists who explain cognitive development in terms of the *information processing model* have found this model especially useful in explaining attention and memory changes across the life span. In contrast to pessimistic early studies, recent research is much more encouraging about age-related changes in information processing.

Questions

1. _____ was one of the first scientists to prove that a child's cognitive processes are fundamentally different from an adult's. (a) Baumrind; (b) Beck; (c) Piaget; (d) Elkind

2. _____ occurs when existing schemas are used to interpret new information, whereas _____ involves changes and adaptations of the schemas. (a) adaptation; accommodation; (b) adaptation; reversibility; (c) egocentrism; postschematization; (d) assimilation; accommodation

3. Match the Piagetian stage with the relevant concept:
   ___1. Egocentrism, animism
   ___2. Object permanence
   ___3. Abstract and hypothetical thinking
   ___4. Conservation, reversibility
   ___5. Personal fable, imaginary audience
   a. Sensorimotor
   b. Preoperational
   c. Concrete operational
   d. Formal operational

Answers to Questions can be found in Appendix B.

MODULE 26   ACTIVE LEARNING WORKSHEET

ACROSS

2 Piagetian term for an infant's understanding that objects (or people) continue to exist even when they cannot directly be seen, heard, or touched.

5 Inability to consider another's point of view.

7 Cognitive structures that grow and differentiate with experience.

8 Reworking schemas to encompass new information, ideas, or objects.

DOWN

1 Piaget's first stage where cognitive development occurs through exploration via sensory perceptions and motor skills.

3 Ability to recognize that a given quantity, weight, or volume remains constant despite changes in shape, length, or position.

4 Piaget's second stage where child gains significant language and thinks symbolically, but lacks operations and thinking is egocentric and animistic.

6 Responding to a new situation in the same manner that is used in a familiar situation.

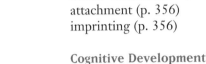

KEY TERMS

To assess your understanding of the **Key Terms** in this section, write a definition for each (in your own words), and then compare your definitions with those in the text.

developmental psychology (p. 341)

Studying Development
critical period (p. 342)
cross-sectional method (p. 343)
longitudinal method (p. 343)
maturation (p. 342)

Physical Development
ageism (p. 354)
embryonic period (p. 347)
fetal alcohol syndrome (FAS) (p. 349)

fetal period (p. 347)
germinal period (p. 347)
puberty (p. 352)
teratogen [TER-ah-toe-jen] (p. 348)

Social—Emotional Development
attachment (p. 356)
imprinting (p. 356)

Cognitive Development
accommodation (p. 363)
assimilation (p. 363)

concrete operational stage (p. 366)
conservation (p. 366)
egocentrism (p. 365)
formal operational stage (p. 367)
object permanence (p. 365)
preoperational stage (p. 365)
schema (p. 363)
sensorimotor stage (p. 365)

WEB RESOURCES

Huffman Book Companion Site
http://www.wiley.com/college/huffman
> This site is loaded with free Interactive Self-Tests, Internet Exercises, Glossary and Flashcards for key terms, Web links, Handbook for Non-Native Speakers, and other activities designed to improve your mastery of the material in this section.

Want to know more about genetics?
http://www.exploratorium.edu/genepool/genepool_home.html
> The "Diving into the gene pool" web site is developed is from the Exploratorium Science Museum in San Francisco, CA. It contains a wealth of information, including "DNA: Your genetic blueprint," "Learning from our relatives," and "Tools for decoding DNA."

Would you like an inside view of prenatal development?
http://www.parentsplace.com/first9months/main.html
> This site contains an extremely detailed, interactive visual of the incredible journey through the first nine months of a baby's development — from conception to birth.

VISUAL SUMMARY

Life Span Development 1
(Modules 25 and 26)

Studying Development

Developmental Psychology:
Studies age related changes in behavior and mental processes from conception to death.

Theoretical Issues
Key Issues:
- Nature vs. Nurture
- Continuity vs. Stages
- Stability vs. Change

Research Methods
Cross–sectional: Different participants, various ages, one point in time. Major problem: cohort effects (a given generation may be affected by specific cultural/historical events).

Longitudinal: Same participants, extended period. Major problem: expensive, time consuming

Physical Development

Prenatal and Newborn
Three major stages: **germinal, embryonic, and fetal.**
- **Teratogens:** Environmental agents capable of producing birth defects.

Newborn and Early Childhood
- Sensory and perceptual abilities are relatively well developed in newborns.
- Motor development comes with **maturation.**

Adolescence
- Adolescence: Psychological period between childhood and adulthood.
- **Puberty:** When sex organs become capable of reproduction.
- Secondary sex characteristics: Hormonally induced changes (pubic hair, breasts, beards).

Adulthood
- Menopause: Cessation of menstruation.
- Male climacteric: Physical and psychological changes in midlife.
- Primary aging: Inevitable, biological changes with age.
- Secondary aging: Accelerated aging due to disease, disuse, or abuse.
- Explanations of primary aging: *Programmed theory* (genetically built-in) and *wear-and-tear theory* (body's inability to repair damage).

Social-Emotional Development

Attachment

- Infant attachment: **Imprinting:** Attaching to first moving object. Harlow's experiments found "contact comfort" very important to **attachment**. Infants who do not attach may suffer serious, lasting effects.
- Adult attachment: Patterns of infant attachment (secure, avoidant, and anxious/ambivalent) may carry over into adult romantic attachments.

Parenting Styles

There are three major categories (permissive, authoritarian, and authoritative), but critics suggest that a child's unique temperament, expectations of parents, and degree of warmth versus rejection from parents may be the most important determinants of parenting styles.

Cognitive Development

Piaget's Major Concepts:

- **Schema:** Cognitive structure for organizing ideas.
- **Assimilation:** Adding new information to an existing schema.
- **Accommodation:** Revising schemas to fit with new information.

Four Stages	**Abilities**	**Limits**
Sensorimotor (Birth to 2 years)	Uses senses and motor skills to explore and develop cognitively.	At beginning of stage, infant lacks **object permanence** (understanding things continue to exist even when not seen, heard, or felt).
Preoperational (Ages 2 to 7)	Has significant language and thinks symbolically.	• Cannot perform "operations." • **Egocentric** thinking (inability to consider another's point of view). • Animistic thinking (believing all things are living).
Concrete Operational (Ages 7 to 11)	• Can perform "operations" on concrete objects. • Understands **conservation** (realizes changes in shape or appearance can be reversed).	Cannot think abstractly and hypothetically.
Formal Operational (11 and up)	Can think abstractly and hypothetically.	Adolescent egocentrism at the beginning of this stage, with related problems of the *personal fable* and *imaginary audience*.

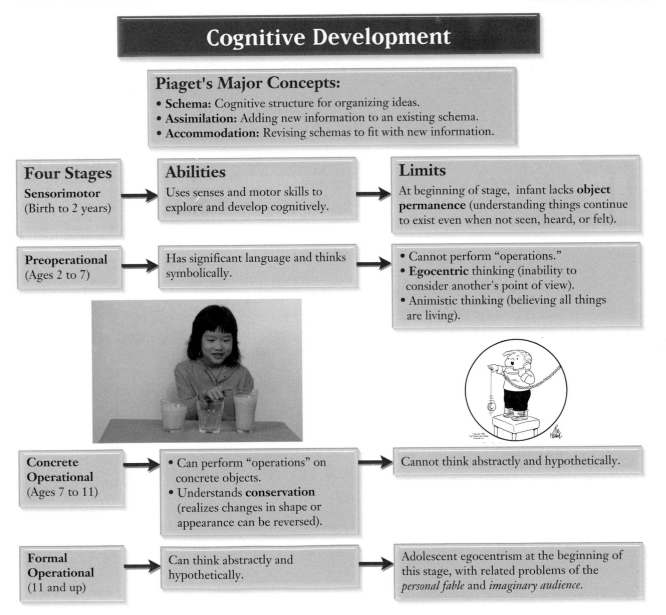

LIFE SPAN DEVELOPMENT II

I n Europe, a woman was near death from a special kind of cancer. There was one drug that doctors thought might save her. It was a form of radium that a druggist in the same town had recently discovered. The drug was expensive to make, but the druggist was charging 10 times what the drug cost him to make. He paid $200 for the radium and charged $2,000 for a small dose of the drug.

The sick woman's husband, Heinz, went to everyone he knew to borrow the money, but he could get together only about $1,000, which is half of what it cost. He told the druggist that his wife was dying and asked him to sell it cheaper or let him pay later. But the druggist said, "No, I discovered the drug, and I'm going to make money from it." So Heinz got desperate and broke into the man's store to steal the drug for his wife. (Kohlberg, 1964, pp. 18–19)

Was Heinz right to steal the drug? What do you consider moral behavior? Is morality "in the eye of the beholder," and everyone simply argues for his or her own self-interest? Or are there universal truths and principles? Whatever your answer, your ability to think, reason, and respond to Heinz's dilemma demonstrates another type of development that is very important to psychology: moral development.

◼ *Achievement*
◼ *Assessment*
◼ *Application*

As we discussed in Module 25, developmental psychology is devoted to the study of age-related changes in behavior and mental processes from conception to death. The previous modules (25 and 26) explored life span changes in physical development, social–emotional development, and cognitive development. In this section, we continue our study with moral development, personality development, and special issues related to grief and death.

I n Module 23, we noted that newborns cry when they hear another baby cry. But did you know that by age 2, most children use words like "good" or "bad" to evaluate actions that are aggressive or that might endanger their own or another's welfare (Kochanska, Casey, & Fukumoto, 1995)? Or that juvenile chimpanzees will soothe a frightened or injured peer, and adult female chimps will "adopt" a motherless baby (Goodall, 1990). How can we explain such early emergence and cross-species evidence of *morality* — the ability to empathize with others and distinguish between right and wrong?

From a biological perspective, some researchers suggest that morality may be prewired and evolutionarily based (e.g., Green et al., 2001; Haidt, 2001; Rossano, 2003). Because behaviors like infant empathic crying and adoption of motherless chimp babies help the species survive, evolution may have provided us with biologically based provisions for moral acts. But like most human behaviors, biology is only one part of the *biopsychosocial model*. In this section, we will focus our attention on the psychological and social factors that explain how moral thoughts, feelings, and actions change over the life span.

MODULE 27
MORAL AND PERSONALITY DEVELOPMENT

Assessment

How does morality change over the life span?

■ Moral Development: Kohlberg's Research

One of the most influential researchers in moral development was Lawrence Kohlberg (1927–1987). He presented what he called "moral stories" like the Heinz dilemma to people of all ages, and on the basis of his findings, he developed a model of moral development (1964, 1984).

What is the right answer to Heinz's dilemma? Kohlberg was interested not in whether participants judged Heinz right or wrong but in the reasons they gave for their decision. On the basis of participants' responses, Kohlberg proposed three broad levels in the evolution of moral reasoning, each composed of two distinct stages (see Table 27.1). Individuals at each stage and level may or may not support Heinz's stealing of the drug, but for different reasons.

Like Piaget's stages of cognitive development (Module 26), Kohlberg believed his stages of moral development were *universal* and *invariant*. That is, they supposedly exist in all cultures, and everyone goes through each of the stages in a predictable fashion. The age trends that are noticed tend to be rather broad:

Preconventional Level *Kohlberg's first level of moral development, in which morality is based on rewards, punishment, and exchange of favors*

Conventional Level *Kohlberg's second level of moral development, where moral judgments are based on compliance with the rules and values of society*

Postconventional Level *Kohlberg's highest level of moral development, in which individuals develop personal standards for right and wrong, and define morality in terms of abstract principles and values that apply to all situations and societies*

1. ***Preconventional level*** (Stages 1 and 2 — birth to adolescence). At this level, moral judgment is *self-centered*. What is right is what one can get away with or what is personally satisfying. Moral understanding is based on rewards, punishments, and exchange of favors. This level is called *preconventional* because children have not accepted society's (*conventional*) rule-making processes.
   • *Stage 1 (punishment and obedience orientation)*. Children at this stage focus on self-interest — obedience to authority and avoidance of punishment. Because they also have difficulty considering another's point of view, they ignore people's intentions in their moral judgments. Thus, a 5-year-old often will say that *accidentally* breaking 15 cups is "badder" and should receive more punishment than *intentionally* breaking 1 cup.
   • *Stage 2 (instrumental-exchange orientation)*. During this stage, children become aware of another's perspective, but their morality is based on reciprocity—an equal exchange of favors. "I'll share my lunch with you because if I ever forget mine you'll share yours with me." "You scratch my back and I'll scratch yours" is the guiding philosophy.

2. ***Conventional level*** (Stages 3 and 4 — adolescence and young adulthood). During this time, moral reasoning advances from being self-centered to *other-centered*. The individual personally accepts *conventional* societal rules because they help ensure social order, and judges morality in terms of compliance with these rules and values.
   • *Stage 3 ("good child" orientation)*. At Stage 3, the primary moral concern is with being nice and gaining approval. People are also judged by their intentions and motives — "His heart was in the right place."
   • *Stage 4 (law-and-order orientation)*. During this stage, the individual takes into account a larger perspective — societal laws. Stage 4 individuals understand that if everyone violated laws, even with good intentions, there would be chaos. Thus, doing one's duty and respecting law and order are highly valued. According to Kohlberg, Stage 4 is the highest level attained by most adolescents and adults.

3. ***Postconventional level*** (Stages 5 and 6 — Adulthood). At this level, individuals develop personal standards for right and wrong. They also define morality in terms of abstract principles and values that apply to all situations and societies. A 20-year-

SUMMARY TABLE 27.1 KOHLBERG'S STAGES OF MORAL DEVELOPMENT

Name of Stage	Moral Reasoning	Heinz's Dilemma Responses	
		Pro	Con
Preconventional level			
Stage 1: punishment–obedience orientation	Morality is what you can get away with	If you let your wife die, you will get in trouble. You'll be blamed for not spending the money to save her and there'll be an investigation of you and the druggist for your wife's death.	You shouldn't steal the drug, because you'll be caught and sent to jail. If you do get away, your conscience would bother you thinking how the police will catch up with you at any minute.
Stage 2: instrumental–exchange orientation	Obey rules to obtain rewards or favors	If you do happen to get caught, you could give the drug back and you wouldn't get much of a sentence. It wouldn't bother you much to serve a little jail term if you had your wife when you got out.	You may not get much of a jail term if you steal the drug, but your wife will probably die before you get out, so it won't do you much good. If your wife dies, you shouldn't blame yourself; it isn't your fault she has cancer.
Conventional level			
Stage 3: good child orientation	Obey rules to get approval	No one will think you're bad if you steal the drug, but your family will think you're an inhuman husband if you don't. If you let your wife die, you'll never be able to look anybody in the face again.	It isn't just the druggist who will think you're a criminal; everyone else will, too. After you steal it, you'll feel bad thinking how you've brought dishonor on your family and yourself, and you won't be able to face anyone again.
Stage 4: law-and-order orientation	Obey laws because they maintain the social order	If you have any sense of honor, you won't let your wife die just because you're afraid to do the only thing that will save her. You'll always feel guilty that you caused her death if you don't do your duty to her.	You're desperate and you may not know you're doing wrong when you steal the drug. But you'll know you did wrong after you're sent to jail. You'll always feel guilty for breaking the law.
Postconventional level			
Stage 5: social-contract orientation	Moral reasoning reflects belief in democratically accepted laws	You'll lose other people's respect, not gain it, if you don't steal. If you let your wife die, it would be out of fear, not out of reasoning it out. So you'd lose self-respect and probably the respect of others, too.	You would lose your standing and respect in the community and violate the law. You'd lose respect for yourself if you're carried away by emotion and forget the long-range point of view.
Stage 6: universal ethics orientation	Moral reasoning reflects individual conscience	If you don't steal the drug and let your wife die, you'll always condemn yourself for it afterward. You wouldn't be blamed and you would have lived up to the outside rule of the law, but you wouldn't have lived up to your own standards of conscience.	If you stole the drug, you wouldn't be blamed by other people, but you'd condemn yourself because you wouldn't have lived up to your own conscience and standards of honesty.

Sources: Kohlberg (1966, 1969); Rest, Turiel, & Kohlberg (1969).

old who judges the "discovery" and settlement of North America by Europeans as immoral because it involved the theft of land from native peoples is thinking in postconventional terms.

- *Stage 5 (social-contract orientation).* Individuals at Stage 5 appreciate the underlying purposes served by laws. When laws are consistent with interests of the majority, they are obeyed because of the "social contract." However, laws can be morally disobeyed if they fail to express the will of the majority or maximize social welfare. For example, during the Vietnam War, some Americans refused to register for the draft because they believed the war was not the will of the majority of Vietnamese or Americans.
- *Stage 6 (universal ethics orientation).* At this stage, "right" is determined by universal ethical principles that *all* religions or moral authorities might view as compelling or fair, such as nonviolence, human dignity, freedom, and equality, whether they conform to existing laws or not. Thus, Mohandas Gandhi, Martin Luther King, and Nelson Mandela intentionally broke laws that violated universal principles, such as human dignity. Few individuals actually achieve Stage 6 (about 1 or 2 percent of those tested worldwide), and Kohlberg found it difficult to separate Stages 5 and 6. Thus, in time, he combined the stages (Kohlberg, 1981).

Moral Behavior

Are the people who achieve higher stages on Kohlberg's scale really more moral than others, or do they just "talk a good game"? Although we might assume that moral reasoning would lead to moral behavior, there is considerable debate over whether Kohlberg's stages accurately predict an individual's actions. Some studies show a positive correlation between higher stages of reasoning and higher levels of moral behavior (Bond, Felter, & Ross, 2000; Borba, 2001; Rest, Narvaez, Bebeau, & Thoma, 1999), but others have found that the pressures of the situation are better predictors of moral behavior (Bandura, 1986, 1991; Bruggeman & Hart, 1996; Nayda, 2002).

In addition to the questionable relationship between moral reasoning and behavior, Kohlberg's model also has been criticized as politically biased (favoring liberals over conservatives), culturally biased (favoring Western ideals of what is morally "advanced"), and gender biased (favoring males over females). The last two points are the focus of our next section.

Achievement
GENDER & CULTURAL DIVERSITY

Insights into Morality

Recall from Module 25 two of the basic questions that guide developmental researchers: "nature or nurture?" and "continuity or stages?" Cross-cultural research on morality confirms that children in different cultures generally do conform to Kohlberg's model and progress sequentially from his first level, the preconventional, to his second, the conventional (Snarey, 1985, 1995; Rest, Narvaez, Bebeau, & Thoma, 1999). Thus, the *nature* and *stage* sides of these two basic questions seem to be supported by cross-cultural studies.

At the same time, cultural *differences* suggest that nurture, or culture, also determines morality. For example, cross-cultural comparisons of responses to Heinz's moral dilemma show that Europeans and Americans tend to consider whether they like or identify with the victim in questions of morality. In contrast, Hindu Indians consider social responsibility and personal concerns two separate issues (Miller & Bersoff, 1998). Researchers suggest that the difference reflects the Indians' broader sense of social responsibility.

In India, Papua New Guinea, China, and Israeli kibbutzim, rather than choosing between the rights of the individual and the rights of society (as the top levels of Kohlberg's model require), most people seek a compromise solution that accommodates both interests (Killen & Hart, 1999; Miller & Bersoff, 1998). Thus, Kohlberg's standard for judging the highest level of morality (the postconventional) may be more applicable to cultures that value individualism over community and interpersonal relationships.

Researcher Carol Gilligan also has criticized Kohlberg's gender bias. Initially, Gilligan believed male and female values reflected two basic approaches to moral reasoning — *justice* versus *caring* (Gilligan, 1977, 1990, 1993; Hoffman, 2000). In the **justice perspective,** morality is based on independence and individual rights. The **care perspective,** on the other hand, defines morality in terms of interdependence and interpersonal responsibility. Gilligan suggested Kohlberg emphasizes the justice perspective and underplays the care perspective in his studies of moral development (Mandel & Midler, 2000).

In the case of Heinz, for example, if you believe Heinz should steal the drug because saving a life is more important than obeying laws, you would be demonstrating justice orientation, according to Gilligan. On the other hand, arguing that Heinz should steal the drug because he has an obligation to help someone he loves would reflect a care orientation.

Recent research supports Gilligan's idea that people have at least two forms of moral reasoning, but most studies have found few if any gender differences in level or type of moral reasoning (Hoffman, 2000; Jaffee & Hyde, 2000; Wark & Krebs, 1996). Both sexes typically use both care and justice orientations. Gilligan now suggests each of us has within ourselves two "voices" of morality — and both voices are valid (Gilligan & Attanucci, 1988).

Gilligan versus Kohlberg. *According to Carol Gilligan, women score "lower" on Lawrence Kohlberg's stages of moral development because they are socialized to assume more responsibility for the care of others.*

Justice Perspective *Gilligan's term for moral reasoning based on independence and individual rights*

Care Perspective *Gilligan's term for moral reasoning that emphasizes interdependence and interpersonal responsibility*

Assessment

CHECK & REVIEW

Moral Development

According to Lawrence Kohlberg, morality progresses through three levels, and each level consists of two stages. At the **preconventional level,** morality is self-centered. What is right is what one can get away with (Stage 1) or what is personally satisfying (Stage 2). **Conventional level** morality is based on a need for approval (Stage 3) and obedience to laws because they maintain the social order (Stage 4). **Postconventional level** morality comes from adhering to the social contract (Stage 5) and the individual's own principles and universal values (Stage 6).

Kohlberg's theory has been criticized for being politically, culturally, and gender biased. Carol Gilligan has suggested that women tend to take a **care perspective** in their moral reasoning, whereas men favor a **justice perspective.** Research shows that in real-life situations, not hypothetical situations, both sexes typically use both the justice and care orientations.

Questions

1. According to Kohlberg's theory of morality, self-interest and avoiding punishment are characteristic of the _____ level, personal standards or universal principles characterize the _____ level, and gaining approval or following the rules describes the _____ level.

2. Calvin would like to wear baggy, torn jeans and a nose ring, but he is concerned that others will disapprove. Calvin is at Kohlberg's _____ level of morality. (a) conformity; (b) approval seeking; (c) conventional; (d) preconventional

3. Five-year-old Tyler believes "bad things are what you get punished for." Tyler is at Kohlberg's _____ level of morality. (a) concrete; (b) preconventional; (c) postconventional; (d) punishment-oriented

4. How is Kohlberg's theory culturally and gender biased?

Answers to Questions can be found in Appendix B.

■ Personality Development: Changes over the Life Span

What were you like as an infant? Do your parents say you were an "easy" baby or a "difficult" one? Are these early differences in personality related to later adult traits? To answer these questions, we explore Stella Thomas and Alexander Chess's temperament theory and Erik Erikson's psychosocial theory.

Assessment

How does personality change from infancy to old age?

Thomas and Chess's Temperament Theory

As an infant, did you lie quietly and seem oblivious to loud noises? Or did you tend to kick and scream and respond immediately to every sound? Did you respond warmly to people, or did you fuss, fret, and withdraw? Your answers to these questions help determine what developmental psychologists call **temperament,** an individual's innate, biological behavioral style and characteristic emotional response.

Temperament *An individual's innate behavioral style and characteristic emotional response*

One of the earliest and most influential theories regarding temperament came from the work of psychiatrists Stella Thomas and Alexander Chess (Thomas & Chess, 1977, 1987, 1991). Thomas and Chess found that approximately 65 percent of the babies they observed could be reliably separated into three categories:

1. *Easy children.* These infants were happy most of the time, relaxed and agreeable, and adjusted easily to new situations (approximately 40 percent).

2. *Difficult children.* Infants in this group were moody, easily frustrated, tense, and over reactive to most situations (approximately 10 percent).

3. *Slow-to-warm-up children.* These infants showed mild responses, were somewhat shy and withdrawn, and needed time to adjust to new experiences or people (approximately 15 percent).

Follow-up studies have found that certain aspects of these temperamental styles tend to be consistent and enduring throughout early childhood and even adulthood (Caspi, 2000; Kagan, 1995, 1998; McCrae et al., 2000; Stams, Juffer, & van Ijzendoorn, 2002). That is not to say every shy, cautious infant ends up a shy adult. Many events take place between infancy and adulthood that shape an individual's development.

One of the most influential factors in early personality development is *goodness of fit* between a child's nature and the social and environmental setting (Eccles et al., 1999; Solomon, 2000; Thompson, 1998). For example, a slow-to-warm-up child does best if allowed time to adjust to new situations, whereas a difficult child thrives in a structured, understanding environment but not in an inconsistent, intolerant home. Alexander Thomas, the pioneer of temperament research, thinks parents should work with their child's temperament, rather than trying to change it. Can you see how this idea of goodness of fit is yet another example of how nature and nurture interact (Gottlieb, 2000; Maccoby, 2000)?

Erikson's Psychosocial Theory

Like Thomas and Chess, Erik Erikson (1902-1994) also emphasized biological forces on development. As a follower of Sigmund Freud, Erikson accepted the importance of inborn factors, but he believed Freud overestimated the importance of sexual drives and the first few years of life, and underestimated the power of social and cultural influences. Therefore, in contrast to Freud's 5 *psychosexual stages* that end in adolescence (Module 35), Erikson identified 8 **psychosocial stages** (Table 27.2) that occur throughout the lifespan. He believed that at each of these 8 stages, we must confront and resolve a specific conflict or crisis, and how we handle these conflicts is a prime determinant of our personality development.

Psychosocial Stages *Erikson's theory that individuals pass through eight developmental stages, each involving a crisis that must be successfully resolved*

SUMMARY TABLE 27.2 ERIKSON'S EIGHT STAGES

Erikson's first stage

Erikson's second stage

Erikson's sixth stage

Erikson's eighth stage

Approximate Age	Psychosocial Crisis	Description
Infancy (0–1)	Trust versus mistrust	Infants learn to trust that their needs will be met by the world, especially by the mother; if not, mistrust develops.
Early childhood (1–3)	Autonomy versus shame and doubt	Toddlers learn to exercise will, to make choices, to control themselves; if not, they become uncertain and doubt that they can do things by themselves.
Play age (3–6)	Initiative versus guilt	Preschool children learn to initiate activities and enjoy their accomplishments; if not, they feel guilty for their attempts at independence.
School age (6–12)	Industry versus inferiority	Elementary school age children develop a sense of industry and learn productive skills their culture requires; if not, they feel inferior.
Adolescence (12–20)	Identity versus role confusion	Adolescents develop a coherent sense of self and their role in society or they face identity and role confusion.
Young adulthood (20–30)	Intimacy versus isolation	Young adults form intimate connections with others; if not they face isolation and consequent self-absorption.
Adulthood (30–65)	Generativity versus stagnation	Middle-aged adults develop concern for establishing, guiding, and influencing the next generation; if not, they experience stagnation (a sense of lifelessness).
Mature (65+)	Ego integrity versus despair	Older people enter a period of reflection and life review. They either achieve a sense of integrity for the lives they've lived and accept death, or yield to despair that their lives cannot be relived.

Source: Adapted from Papalia, Olds, & Feldman (2001). *Human Development* (8 ed.). New York: McGraw-Hill.

Erikson's First Stage In Erikson's first stage (birth to approximately 12 months), the major issue is *trust versus mistrust*. When and how the infant's needs are met determine whether the infant decides the world is a good and satisfying place to live or a source of pain, frustration, and uncertainty.

Stages 2 to 4 According to Erikson, the second stage, *autonomy versus shame and doubt* (ages 1 to 3 years), is a time for developing self-awareness and independence. During the "terrible twos," toddlers continually assert their wills — "no, no" and "me, me." Parents who handle these beginning attempts at independence with patience and good-humored encouragement help their toddlers develop a sense of autonomy. Conversely, if the parents are ridiculing, impatient, or controlling, the child develops feelings of shame and doubt.

During the third stage, *initiative versus guilt* (ages 3 to 6 years), the main issue is the child's desire to initiate activities and the guilt that comes from unwanted or unexpected consequences. When my son was 5 years old, he decided to make himself a grilled cheese sandwich in the toaster. Like all parents, I made mistakes with my children, but in this case I realized that he was "taking initiative" and avoided criticizing him (despite a considerable mess all over the entire kitchen and living room). If caregivers' responses to self-initiated activities are supportive and encouraging (at least most of the time), the child will develop feelings of power and self-confidence versus guilt and doubt.

During Erikson's fourth stage, *industry versus inferiority* (age 6 years through puberty), children develop a sense of industry, or competency, as they begin to practice skills they will use for a lifetime in productive work. Most children in industrialized countries learn to read, write, and count during this stage. How the external world responds to a child's successes and failures determines whether she or he develops feelings of competency and industriousness or feelings of insecurity and inferiority.

Identity Crisis *Erikson's term for an adolescent's search for self, which requires intense self-reflection and questioning*

Stages 5 and 6 Erikson's fifth stage is the period of *identity versus identity confusion*. Erikson believed each individual's personal identity develops from a period of serious questioning and intense soul searching. During this **identity crisis**, adolescents attempt to discover who they are, what their skills are, and what kinds of roles they are best suited to play for the rest of their lives. Failure to resolve the identity crisis may be related to a lack of stable identity, delinquency, or difficulty in maintaining close personal relationships in later life.

Once a firm sense of identity is established, Erikson believed the individual (now in young adulthood) is ready to meet the challenges of *intimacy versus isolation*, stage 6 of development. If close bonds are formed, a basic feeling of intimacy with others will result. If not, the individual may avoid interpersonal commitments and experience feelings of isolation. Erikson's model for stages 5 and 6 suggests that if we are to have close, loving relationships with others, we must first learn who we are and how to be independent.

Erikson's Last Two Stages In the seventh stage, *generativity versus stagnation (middle age)*, the individual expands feelings of love and concern beyond the immediate family group to include all of society. One major drive for this age group is the assistance and guidance of younger generations (Pratt et al., 2001). If this expansion and effort do not occur, an individual stagnates, becoming concerned with only material possessions and personal well-being.

In the final years of life, adults enter the period of *ego integrity versus despair*, Stage 8. Those who have been successful in resolving their earlier psychosocial crises will tend to look back on their lives with feelings of accomplishment and satisfaction. Those who resolved their earlier crises in a negative way or who lived fruitless, self-centered lives may deeply regret lost opportunities or become despondent because they realize it is too late to start over. As the Danish philosopher Søren Kierkegaard said, "Life is lived forward, but understood backward."

Evaluating Erikson's Theory Many psychologists agree with Erikson's general idea that psychosocial crises, which are based on interpersonal and environmental interactions, do contribute to personality development (Brendgen, Vitaro, & Bukowski, 2000; Bugental & Goodnow, 1998; Marcia, 2002). However, Erikson also has his critics. The labels Erikson uses to describe the eight stages may not be entirely appropriate cross-culturally. For example, in individualistic cultures, *autonomy* is highly preferable to *shame and doubt*, but in collectivist cultures, the preferred resolution might be *dependence* or *merging relations* (Matsumoto, 2000). In addition, it is difficult to squeeze an entire lifetime of development into one comprehensive theory.

Despite their limits, Erikson's stages have greatly contributed to the study of North American and European psychosocial development. Moreover, Erikson was among the first theorists to suggest that development continues past adolescence, and his theory encouraged further research.

Myths of Development Having completed our brief overview of lifespan personality development, it's important to clarify a few lingering misconceptions before going on. For example, until recently, most psychologists characterized adolescence as a time of *storm and stress* — great emotional turbulence and psychological strain. Research within the last 20 years, however, has found that storm and stress is largely a myth: Adolescence is no stormier than any other life transition — an observation supported by research in 186 societies (Schlegel & Barry, 1991). And, contrary to Erikson's predicted need for psychological separation from parents in order to establish identity, most teenagers of both sexes remain close to their parents and admire them (Diener & Diener, 1996; Lerner & Galambos, 1998; vanWel, Linssen, & Abma, 2000).

Numerous other beliefs about age-related crises have not been supported by research either. The popular idea of a *midlife crisis* began largely as the result of Gail Sheehy's national best seller *Passages* (1976). Sheehy drew on the theories of Daniel Levinson (1977, 1996) and psychiatrist Roger Gould (1975), as well as her own interviews, and reported a "predictable crisis" at about age 35 for women and 40 for men. Although middle age is typically a time of reexamining one's values and lifetime goals (Smart & Peterson, 1997), Sheehy's book led many people to automatically expect a midlife crisis with drastic changes in personality and behavior. Research suggests that a severe reaction or crisis may actually be quite rare and not typical of what most people experience during middle age (Benazzi, 2000; Brim, 1999; Stewart & Ostrove, 1998).

Many people also believe that when the last child leaves home, most parents experience an *empty nest syndrome* — a painful separation and time of depression for the mother, the father, or both parents. Again, however, research suggests that the empty nest syndrome may be an exaggeration of the pain experienced by a few individuals and an effort to downplay positive reactions (White & Rogers, 1997; Whyte, 1992). For example, one major benefit of the empty nest is an increase in marital satisfaction (Figure 27.1). Furthermore, parent–child relationships do continue once the child leaves home. As one mother said, "The empty nest is surrounded by telephone wires" (Troll, Miller, & Atchley, 1979).

Study Tip

If you're having difficulty remembering Erikson's eight stages, try this mnemonic device based on the peg-word system from Module 21: One is a bun, trust someone. Two is a shoe, or shame on you. Three is a tree for growing initiative. Four is a door to industry. Five is a hive, I'm a busy bee working on my identity. Six are sticks to give someone. Seven is heaven and filled with generativity. Eight is a gate open to integrity. *This study tip was adapted from one developed by Professor Eggleston of McKendree College in Illinois.*

www.wiley.com/college/huffman

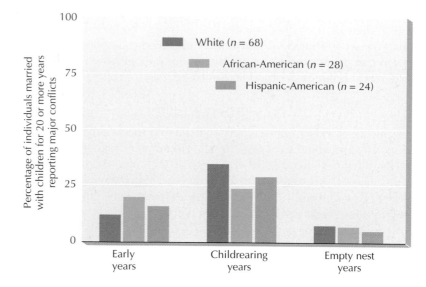

Figure 27.1 *Life span marital satisfaction.* Do you believe children make a marriage happy or that parents experience a depressing empty nest syndrome when they later leave home? Research shows that the highest levels of satisfaction are before children are born and after they leave home (Mackey & O'Brien, 1998, p. 132).

Assessment

CHECK & REVIEW

Personality Development Over The Life Span

Stella Thomas and Alexander Chess emphasize the genetic component of certain traits (such as sociability) and the fact that babies often exhibit differences in **temperament** shortly after birth.

Erik Erikson expanded on Freud's ideas to develop eight **psychosocial stages** of development that cover the entire life span. The four stages that occur during childhood are trust versus mistrust, autonomy versus shame and doubt, initiative versus guilt, and industry versus inferiority.

Erikson believes the major psychosocial **identity crisis of** adolescence is the search for identity versus role confusion. During young adulthood, the individual's task is to establish intimacy over isolation, and during middle adulthood, the person must deal with generativity versus stagnation. At the end of life, the older adult must establish ego integrity or face overwhelming despair at the realization of lost opportunities.

Research shows that adolescent storm and stress, the midlife crisis, and the empty nest syndrome may be exaggerated accounts of a few people's experiences and not typical of most people.

Questions

1. An infant's inborn disposition is known as _____. (a) personality; (b) reflexes; (c) temperament; (d) traits
2. Briefly describe Thomas and Chess's temperament theory.
3. Erikson suggests that problems in adulthood are sometimes related to unsuccessful resolution of one of his eight stages. For each of the following individuals, identify the most likely "problem" stage:
   a. Marcos has trouble keeping friends and jobs because he continually asks for guarantees and reassurance of his worth.
   b. Ann has attended several colleges without picking a major, has taken several vocational training programs, and has had numerous jobs over the last 10 years.
   c. Teresa is reluctant to apply for a promotion even though her coworkers have encouraged her to do so. She worries that she will be taking jobs from others and questions her worth.
   d. George continually obsesses over the value of his life. He regrets that he left his wife and children for a job in another country and failed to maintain contact.
4. Discuss the text's three common myths of development.

Answers to Questions can be found in Appendix B.

ACTIVE LEARNING WORKSHEET   MODULE 27

ACROSS

2 Inborn disposition appearing shortly after birth that characterizes ways of approaching people and situations.

6 Erikson's term for the period of inner conflict when individuals examine their life and values and make decisions about life roles.

7 Kohlberg's second level of moral development where judgments are based on compliance with the rules and values of society.

DOWN

1 Kohlberg's first level of moral development, characterized by moral judgments based on fear of punishment or desire for pleasure.

3 Kohlberg's highest level of moral development where individuals develop personal standards for right and wrong.

4 Gilligan's that emphasizes interpersonal responsibility and interconnectedness with others.

5 Gilligan's term that emphasizes individual rights and views people as differentiated and standing alone.

MODULE 28
ADDITIONAL INFLUENCES ON DEVELOPMENT

Assessment

How do families and career choices influence development?

Theorists like Erikson and Thomas and Chess offer important insights into general personality development. But what about family violence, teen pregnancy, divorce, and occupational choice? How do they influence development? We will explore these questions in the next section.

■ Families: Their Effect on Personality

As we have seen in the discussions of attachment in Module 25 and parenting styles in this one, our families exert an enormous influence on our development. But it is not always for the best. Family violence, teen and single parents, and divorce can have long-lasting effects on individual development.

Family Violence

Families can be warm and loving, but they also can be cruel and abusive. Maltreatment and abuse are more widely recognized than in the past, but it is difficult to measure family violence because it usually occurs in private, and victims are reluctant to report it out of shame, powerlessness, or fear of reprisal. Nevertheless, every year millions of domestic violence, child abuse, and elderly abuse cases are reported to police and service agencies (Anetzberger, 2001; Dube et al., 2002; McCloskey & Bailey, 2000; Safarik, Jarvis, & Nussbaum, 2002).

What causes family violence? Violence occurs more often in families experiencing marital conflict, substance abuse, mental disorders, and economic stress (Melchert, 2000; Fontes, Cruz, & Tabachnick, 2001; Reppucci, Woolard, & Fried, 1999). It is important to remember that abuse and violence occur at all socioeconomic levels. However, abuse and violence occur more frequently in families disrupted by unemployment or other financial distress.

In addition to financial problems, many parents also are socially isolated and lack good communication and parenting skills. Their anxiety and frustration may explode into spouse, child, and elderly abuse. In fact, one of the clearest identifiers of abuse potential is *impulsivity*. People who abuse their children, their spouses, or their elderly parents seem to lack impulse control, especially when stressed. They also respond to stress with more intense emotions and greater arousal (Cicchetti & Toth, 1998). This impulsivity is related not only to psychosocial factors like economic stress and social

Families and personality. Does this remind you of your own family? How did your father, mother, and siblings affect your own personality development?

isolation (with no one to turn to for help or feedback), but also to possible biological influences.

Biologically, three regions of the brain are closely related to the expression and control of aggression: the amygdala, the prefrontal cortex, and the hypothalamus (see Module 6 to review these regions). Interestingly, head injuries, strokes, dementia, schizophrenia, alcoholism, and abuse of stimulant drugs have all been linked to these three areas and to aggressive outbursts (Niehoff, 1999). Research also suggests that low levels of the neurotransmitter serotonin are associated with irritability, hypersensitivity to provocation, and impulsive rage (Oguendo & Mann, 2000; Volavka, 1999).

Is there anything that can be done to reduce this type of aggression? Treatment with antianxiety and serotonin-enhancing drugs like fluoxetine (Prozac) may lower the risk of some forms of impulsive violence. However, given the correlation between spousal, child, sibling, and elder abuse, and because violence affects other family members who are not victims or perpetrators, treatment generally includes the entire family (Briggs & Hawkins, 1999; Emery & Laumann-Billings, 1998).

Most professionals advocate two general approaches in dealing with family violence. *Primary programs* attempt to identify "vulnerable" families and prevent abuse by teaching parenting and marital skills, stress management, and impulse control. These programs also publicize the signs of abuse and encourage people to report suspected cases. *Secondary programs* attempt to rehabilitate families after abuse has occurred. They work to improve social services, establish self-help groups such as Parents Anonymous and AMAC (Adults Molested as Children), and provide individual and group psychotherapy for both victims and abusers.

Teen and Single Parents

Another factor that may affect development is becoming a parent and starting a family at too early an age. Have you heard that the United States has one of the highest rates of teen pregnancy among major industrialized nations (Meschke, Bartholomae, & Zentall, 2000; Miller & Coyl, 2000)? Regrettably, this is a sad fact, but, ironically, today's rate is actually much lower than it has been throughout much of the twentieth century. For example, between 1960 and 1985, the rate of U.S. teen births was 89.1 per 1,000, compared to 52.3 per 1,000 in the mid-1990s (Ventura, Martin, Curtin, & Mathews, 1999).

With this decline, why is everyone so worried about teen pregnancies? Although the total rate has declined substantially, the percentage of *unwed teen births* has soared (Endersbe, 2000; Henshaw, 1998). The higher nonmarital rate is important because single-parent families headed by women are at great risk of poverty. In addition, pregnancy during adolescence also carries with it considerable health risk for both the mother and child (Module 25), decreased chances of marital success, and lower education achievement (Endersbe, 2000; Fullerton, 1997; Roye & Balk, 1997). Pregnancy, in fact, is the most common reason for dropping out of high school. In view of these facts, is it any wonder that teen mothers also report one of the highest levels of depression (Figure 27.2)?

What can be done to reduce the number of teen pregnancies? *Comprehensive health-oriented services* seem to be the most promising avenue for decreasing the rate of pregnancy among high-risk teenagers (Coley & Chase-Lansdale, 1998). The Johns Hopkins Pregnancy Prevention Program, for example, provides complete medical care, contraceptive services, social services (such as counseling), and parenting education. This approach postponed the age of sexual activity onset, increased contraception use, reduced the frequency of sex, and reduced the actual pregnancy rate in the experimental group by 30 percent. During the same period, pregnancy rates in a comparison school rose by 58 percent (Hardy & Zabin, 1991).

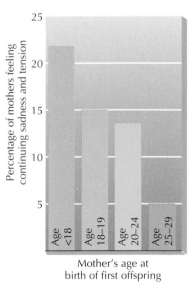

Figure 28.1 *Maternal age and satisfaction.* Note that the age of the mother directly relates to the percentage of reported feelings of sadness and tension.

The Teen Outreach Program is another success story. This program aims to enhance social development among adolescents through structured volunteer community service and classroom discussions of life choices, careers, and relationships (Allen, Philiber, Herrling, & Kupermine, 1997). Research shows that many teen pregnancies are due to poverty and the resulting perception that life options and choices are limited (Brewster, Billy, & Grady, 1993; Luker, 1996).

Most research and social programs (like the two described here) focus on economics: how money (or the lack of it) affects teen pregnancies. But researchers Rebekah Coley & Lindsay Chase-Lansdale (1998) suggest we also should be exploring the *psychological* consequences of early parenting. If adolescence is a time for solidifying identity and developing autonomy from parents, what happens with teen parents? What are the effects on a teen mother if she lives with her mother? What happens to the life span development of the "early" grandparents? What about the teen father? How does early fatherhood affect his course of development? And what about the child who is being raised by a teen mother or teen father or grandparent? How does this affect his or her development? Answers to these questions rest with the next generation of researchers (perhaps some of you who are reading this text).

The Impact of Divorce

> After years of advising other people on their personal problems, I was stunned by my own divorce. I only wish I had someone to write to for advice.
>
> ANN LANDERS

Although there has been a modest decline in the divorce rate since the 1970s, nearly one-half of marriages still end in divorce in the United States. As expected, these breakups have serious implications for both adult and child development (Lengua, Wolchik, Sandler, & West, 2000; Lopez, Melendez, & Rice, 2000). For the adults, both spouses generally experience emotional as well as practical difficulties and are at high risk for depression and physical health problems (Carbone, 2000; Davies & Cummings, 1998). However, many problems assumed to be due to divorce are actually present before marital disruption (Carrere, Buehlman, Gottman, Coan, & Ruckstuhl, 2000; Sigelman, 1999). Thus, for some, divorce can be life enhancing. In a "healthy" divorce, ex-spouses must accomplish three tasks: *let go, develop new social ties*, and, when children are involved, *redefine parental roles* (Everett & Everett, 1994).

In addition to stresses on the divorcing couple, some research shows that children also suffer both short-term and long-lasting effects. Compared with children in continuously intact two-parent families, children of divorce generally exhibit more behavioral problems, poorer self-concepts, more psychological problems, lower academic achievement, and more relationship and social difficulties (Hetherington & Stanley-Hagan, 2002; Melchert, 2000; Tein, Sandler, & Zautra, 2000; van Schaick & Stolberg, 2001). On the other hand, other research finds that children's psychological development is not affected by parental separation per se. Instead, it is related to mother's income, education, ethnicity, childrearing beliefs, depressive symptoms, and behavior (Clarke-Stewart, Vandell, McCartney, Owen, & Booth, 2000). Other researchers have suggested that children may also do better in homes without the constant tension and fighting of an intact, but unhappy, home (Emery, 1999).

Whether children become "winners" or "losers" in a divorce depends on the (1) individual attributes of the child, (2) qualities of the custodial family, (3) continued involvement with noncustodial parents, and (4) resources and support systems available to the child and parents (Carbone, 2000; Gottman, 1998; Hetherington & Stanley-Hagan, 1999). If you or your parents are currently considering or going through divorce, you might want to keep these four factors in mind when making legal and other decisions about children.

Application

CRITICAL THINKING   ACTIVE LEARNING

Are Your Marital Expectations Unrealistic?

When you think about marriage and the roles of husband and wife, what do you imagine? Do you recreate images of television families like those on *The Cosby Show, Everybody Loves Raymond,* or even *The Sopranos?* Research shows that women are more likely than men to report trying to model their family life after what they saw on TV situational comedies, and to expect their significant other to act like the men they've seen on TV (Morrison & Westman, 2001).

When we look at men's expectations, research finds they are more likely to believe certain myths about marriage, such as *Men are from Mars and Women are from Venus* or "affairs are the main cause of divorce." Can you see how these expectations and myths could lead to marital problems (Gottman & Levenson, 2002; Gottman & Notarius, 2000)? For both women and men, marriage therapists and researchers consistently find that *realistic* expectations are a key ingredient in successful marriages (Pasley, Kerpelman, & Guilbert, 2001; Sharp & Ganong, 2000).

Are your expectations realistic? Two important components of critical thinking are *recognizing personal biases* and *valuing truth above self-interest.* Try to use these two skills as you examine your personal marital expectations with the following list of traits and factors based on long-term happy marriages (Gottman & Levenson, 2002; Gottman & Notarius, 2000; Greef & Malherbe, 2001; Harker & Kettner, 2001; Heaton, 2002; Huston et al., 2001; White & Rogers, 2000):

1. **Established "love maps."** In a happy marriage, both partners are willing to share their personal feelings and life goals. This sharing leads to detailed "love maps" of each other's inner emotional life and the creation of shared meaning in the relationship. Is this true for you, or do you have the unrealistic expectation that this type of closeness "naturally" develops, or that the "right partner" will automatically know your innermost thoughts and feelings?

2. **Shared power and mutual support.** Are you willing to fully share power and respect your partner's point of view, even if you disagree? Or have you unconsciously accepted the imbalance of power portrayed by TV sitcoms? Note how the husbands on *The Cosby Show, Everybody Loves Raymond,* and *The Sopranos* are generally portrayed as the "head of the house," but the real power is secretly held by the "little woman." Can you see how this common portrayal might create unrealistic expectations for women, and avoidance of marriage for men?

3. **Conflict management.** Successful couples work hard to solve their solvable conflicts, accept their unsolvable ones, and know the difference. Do you expect your partner to automatically change when you have conflict? Conflict resolution is not about making others change, it involves negotiation and accommodation. Do you idealistically expect to resolve most or all of your problems? Marriage counselors find that most marital conflicts are perpetual—they don't go away. Happy couples recognize these areas and avoid marital "gridlock" with dialogue, patience, and acceptance.

4. **Similarity.** Do you believe "opposites attract"? Although we all know couples who are very different and still happy, research finds that similarity (in values, beliefs, religion, and so on) is one of the best predictors of long lasting relationships (Module 47).

5. **Supportive social environment.** Do you expect that "love conquers all"? Unfortunately, research finds several environmental factors that can overpower or slowly erode even the strongest love, including *age* (younger couples have higher divorce rates), *money* and *employment* (divorce is higher among the poor and unemployed), *parent's marriages* (divorce is higher for children of divorced parents), *length of courtship* (longer is better), and *premarital pregnancy* (no pregnancy is better and waiting a while after marriage is even better).

6. **Positive emphasis.** Do you believe marriage is a place where you can indulge your bad moods and openly criticize one another? Think again. Positive interpretations (how you view your partner's actions), positive affect (cheery emotions, good moods), positive expressions, positive interactions, and a positive rebound to marital conflict are vitally important to lasting, happy marriages. If you'd like a simple test of this finding, pick two or three of your "troublesome" friends, family members, or co-workers, and try giving them four positive comments *before* saying anything even remotely negative. Note how their attitudes and behaviors quickly change. More important, pay attention to the corresponding uplift in your own feelings and responses about this person. Can you see how this type of positivism can dramatically improve marital satisfaction?

Two different kinds of families. The Cosby Show *and* The Sopranos.

Achievement

RESEARCH HIGHLIGHT

Children Who Survive Despite the Odds

Children fortunate enough to grow up with days filled with play and discovery, nights that provide rest and security, and dedicated, loving parents usually turn out fine. But what about those who are raised in violent, impoverished, or neglectful situations? As we saw in the previous discussions of family violence, teen and single parenting, and divorce, a troubled childhood creates significantly higher risk of serious physical, emotional, and behavioral problems. There are exceptions to this rule, however. Some offspring of wonderful, loving parents have serious problems, and some children growing up amid major stressors are remarkably well adjusted.

What is it about children living in harsh circumstances that helps them survive and prosper — despite the odds? The answer holds great interest for both parents and society. Such *resilient* children can teach us better ways to reduce risk, promote competence, and shift the course of development in more positive directions (Masten, 2001). **Resiliency** refers to the ability to adapt effectively in the face of threats.

Resilience has been studied throughout the world in a variety of situations, including poverty, natural disasters, war, and family violence (e.g., Cole & Brown, 2002; Horning & Rouse, 2002; Taylor & Wang, 2000; Wright & Masten, 1997). Two researchers — Ann Masten at the University of Minnesota and Douglas Coatsworth at the University of Miami (1998) — identified several traits of the resilient child and the environmental circumstances that might account for the resilient child's success.

Most children who do well have (1) good intellectual functioning; (2) relationships with caring adults; and, as they grow older, (3) the ability to regulate their attention, emotions, and behavior. These traits obviously overlap. Good intellectual functioning, for example, may help resilient children solve problems or protect themselves from adverse conditions, as well as attract the interest of teachers who serve as nurturing adults. Their greater intellectual skills also may help them learn from their experiences and from the caring adults, so in later life they have better self-regulation skills.

Resiliency and 9-11. *Following the terrorist attack on September 11, 2001, many children and teenagers in New York created moving letters and drawings to express their feelings. Note the red heart in the upper corner of this drawing done by Angelina, a Queens high school student. Is this the sign of a resilient child?*

In times of growing concern about homelessness, poverty, abuse, teen pregnancy, violence, and divorce, studies of successful children can be very important. On the other hand, there is no such thing as an invulnerable child. Masten and Coatsworth remind us, "if we allow the prevalence of known risk factors for development to rise while resources for children fall, we can expect the competence of individual children and the human capital of the nation to suffer" (Masten & Coatsworth, 1998, p. 216).

Resiliency: *The ability to adapt effectively in the face of threats.*

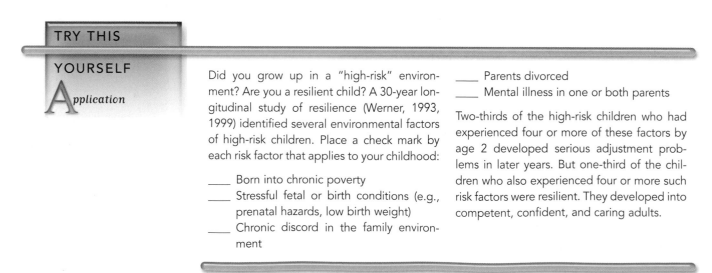

TRY THIS

YOURSELF
Application

Did you grow up in a "high-risk" environment? Are you a resilient child? A 30-year longitudinal study of resilience (Werner, 1993, 1999) identified several environmental factors of high-risk children. Place a check mark by each risk factor that applies to your childhood:

____ Born into chronic poverty
____ Stressful fetal or birth conditions (e.g., prenatal hazards, low birth weight)
____ Chronic discord in the family environment

____ Parents divorced
____ Mental illness in one or both parents

Two-thirds of the high-risk children who had experienced four or more of these factors by age 2 developed serious adjustment problems in later years. But one-third of the children who also experienced four or more such risk factors were resilient. They developed into competent, confident, and caring adults.

■ Occupational Choices: The Effect of Work and Careers

Throughout most of our adult lives, work defines us in fundamental ways. It affects our health, friendships, where we live, and even our leisure activities.

How can I find a rewarding career that suits my personality and interests? Choosing an occupation is one of the most important decisions in our lives, and the task is becoming ever more complex as career options increase as a result of specialization. The *Dictionary of Occupational Titles*, a government publication, currently lists more than 200,000 job categories. One way to learn more about job categories and potential careers is to visit your college career center. Career counselors may suggest that you take vocational interest tests. (You also can try the online version of several vocational interest inventories — http://www.keirsey.com/cgi-bin/newkts.cgi.)

Too often, career choices are made from dreams of high income. Nearly 74 percent of college freshmen surveyed by the Higher Education Research Institute said that being "very well off financially" was "very important" or "essential." Seventy-one percent felt the same way about raising a family ("This year's freshmen," 1995). These young people no doubt expect to combine both family and work roles and "live the good life," but many will have to work long hours just to keep up with the rate of inflation. Given the decline in construction and many high-paying manufacturing jobs (which on the average pay three times the minimum wage), a college education is more important than ever in obtaining higher paying and more satisfying occupations.

Work and careers are a big part of adult lives and self-identity, but the large majority of men and women in the United States choose to retire sometime in their sixties. Like the midlife crisis and empty nest syndrome, the loss of self-esteem and depression that is commonly assumed to accompany retirement may be largely a myth. Life satisfaction after retirement appears to be most strongly related to good health, control over one's life, and participation in community services and social activities (Voltz, 2000; Whitbourne, 2000). This type of active involvement is the key ingredient to a fulfilling old age, according to the **activity theory of aging**. In contrast, other theorists believe successful aging is a natural and graceful withdrawal from life, the **disengagement theory** (Achenbaum & Bengtson, 1994; Cummings & Henry, 1961; McKee & Barlier, 2001; Neugarten, Havighurst, & Tobin, 1968; Rook, 2000).

For obvious reasons, the disengagement theory has been seriously questioned and largely abandoned: Successful aging does *not* require withdrawal from society. I mention this theory because of its historical relevance, and also because of its connection to an influential modern theory, **socioemotional selectivity theory,** which helps explain the predictable decline in social contact that almost everyone experiences as they move into their older years (Carstensen, Pasupathi, Mayr, Nesselroade, & Carstensen, 2000; Lang & Carstensen, 2002). According to this theory, the elderly don't withdraw from society—they're just being more *selective* with their time. They deliberately choose to decrease their total number of social contacts in favor of familiar people that provide emotionally meaningful interactions. As you can see in Figure 27.3, when we begin life, our need for emotional connection is paramount. During childhood, adolescence, and early adulthood, this need declines, and then rises again during late adulthood. The reverse is true for our need for information and knowledge. Can you appreciate the intuitive appeal of this theory? Emotional support is essential to infant survival, information gathering is critical during childhood and early adulthood, and emotional satisfaction is more important in old age—we tend to invest time in those who can be counted on in time of need.

Activity Theory *Successful aging is fostered by a full and active commitment to life*

Disengagement Theory *Successful aging is characterized by mutual withdrawal between the elderly and society*

Socioemotional Selectivity Theory *A natural decline in social contact as older adults become more selective with their time*

Disengagement versus activity. *Although disengagement theory suggests that older people naturally disengage and withdraw from life, activity theory argues that everyone should remain active and involved throughout the entire life span.*

Assessment

VISUAL QUIZ

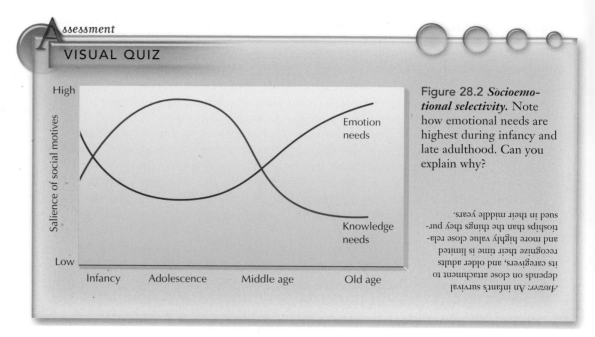

Figure 28.2 *Socioemotional selectivity.* Note how emotional needs are highest during infancy and late adulthood. Can you explain why?

Answer: An infant's survival depends on close attachment to its caregivers, and older adults recognize their time is limited and more highly value close relationships than the things they pursued in their middle years.

Achievement

GENDER & CULTURAL DIVERSITY

Cultural Differences in Ageism

As we've seen in this and the Module 25, there are losses and stress associated with the aging process — although much less than most people think. Perhaps the greatest challenge for the elderly, at least in the United States, is the *ageism* they encounter. In societies that value older people as wise elders or keepers of valued traditions, the stress of aging is much less than in societies that view them as mentally slow and socially useless. In cultures like that in the United States in which youth, speed, and progress are strongly emphasized, a loss or decline in any of these qualities is deeply feared and denied (Powell, 1998).

Aren't there also cultures that honor their elderly? Yes. In Japan, China, and the United States, among African Americans and most tribes of Native Americans, the elderly are more revered. Aging parents are generally respected for their wisdom and experience, are deferred to in family matters, and often are expected to live with their children until they die (Klass, 2000; Martire, Stephens, & Townsend, 2000). However, as these cultures become more urbanized and Westernized, often there is a corresponding decline in respect for the elderly. In Japan, for example, over 80 percent of the elderly lived with their adult children in 1957, as compared to only 55 percent in 1994. Japan has recently made it a legal obligation to care for elderly relatives (Hashizume, 2000; Oshima et al., 1996).

Ageism, gender, and ethnicity in the United States   There also is considerable difference in the status and treatment of different subgroups of the elderly. In the United States, for example, studies show that older men have more social status, income, and sexual partners than do older women. Elderly women, on the other hand, have more friends and are more involved in family relationships but have lower status and income. Contrary to popular stereotype of the "rich old woman," elderly females

Elder respect. Native Americans generally revere and respect the elder members of their tribe. How would aging be different if being old was an honor and blessing versus a dreaded process?

represent one of the lowest income levels in North America (U.S. Bureau of the Census, 2001).

Ethnicity also plays a role in aging in the United States. Ethnic minority elderly, especially African Americans and Latinos, face problems related to both ageism and racism. They are more likely to become ill but less likely to receive treatment, and they are overrepresented among the elderly poor living below the poverty line (Contrada et al., 2000; Harrison & Gardiner, 1999; Markides, 1995).

Other research, however, reports that African Americans are more likely than Anglo-Americans to regard elderly persons with respect (Mui, 1992). Also, compared with whites, other ethnic groups often have a greater sense of community and may have stronger bonds of attachment, owing to their shared traits and experiences with prejudice. Ethnicity itself may therefore provide some benefits. "In addition to shielding them from majority attitudes, ethnicity provides the ethnic elderly with a source of esteem" (Fry, 1985, p. 233).

Assessment

CHECK & REVIEW

Additional Influences on Development

Family violence, teenage pregnancy, and divorce have significant effects on development. However, **resilient** children who survive abusive and stress filled childhoods usually have good intellectual functioning, a relationship with a caring adult, and the ability to regulate their attention, emotions, and behavior.

The kind of work you do and the occupational choices you make can play a critical role in your life. One theory of successful aging, **activity theory**, says people should remain active and involved throughout the entire life span. The other major theory, **disengagement theory**, says the elderly naturally and gracefully withdraw from life because they welcome the relief from roles they can no longer fulfill. Although the disengagement theory is no longer in favor, the **socioemotional selectivity theory** *does* find that the elderly tend to decrease their social contacts as they become more selective with their time.

Questions

1. Efforts to identify and prevent family violence are called _____ programs. (a) directive; (b) redirective; (c) primary; (d) secondary
2. The _____ theory of aging suggests that you should remain active and involved until death, whereas the _____ theory suggests that you should naturally and gracefully withdraw from life.
3. _____ is prejudice against people based on their age. (a) Ethnocentrism; (b) Elder abuse; (c) Ageism; (d) Disengagement
4. Explain how ethnicity may help the elderly overcome some problems of aging.

Answers to Questions can be found in Appendix B.

■ Grief and Death: The Final Stages of Development

www.wiley.com/college/huffman

One unavoidable part of everyone's life is its end. How can we understand and prepare ourselves for death and the grief that comes with the loss of our own life and that of loved others? In this section, we will look at the four stages of grief and then study attitudes toward death and dying. Finally we will then explore death itself as a final developmental crisis.

Assessment

Are these predictable stages for grief and dying?

Grief

What do I do now that you're gone? Well, when there's nothing else going on, which is quite often, I sit in a corner and I cry until I am too numbed to feel. Paralyzed motionless for a while, nothing moving inside or out. Then I think how much I miss you. Then I feel fear, pain, loneliness, desolation. Then I cry until I am too numbed to feel. Interesting pastime.

PETER McWILLIAMS, *HOW TO* SURVIVE *THE* LOSS OF A LOVE

Have you ever felt like this? If so, you are not alone. Loss and grief are an inevitable part of all our lives. Feelings of desolation, loneliness, and heartache, accompanied by painful memories, are common reactions to loss, disaster, or misfortune. Ironically, such painful emotions may serve a useful function. Evolutionary psychologists suggest that bereavement and grief may be adaptive mechanisms for both social animals and humans: The pain may motivate parents and children or mates to search for one another. Obvious signs of distress also may be adaptive because they bring the group to the aid of the bereaved individual.

What does it mean if someone seems emotionless after an important loss?
Grieving is a complicated and personal process. Just as there is no right way to die, there is no right way to grieve (Koppel, 2000). People who restrain their grief may be following the rules for emotional display that prevail in their cultural group. Moreover, outward signs of strong emotion may be the most obvious expression of grief, but this is only one of four stages in the "normal" grieving process (James & Friedman, 1998; Parkes, 1972, 1991).

In the initial phase of grief, *numbness*, bereaved individuals often seem dazed and may feel little emotion other than numbness or emptiness. They also may deny the death, insisting that a mistake has been made.

In the second stage of grief, individuals enter a stage of *yearning*, intense longing for the loved one, and pangs of guilt, anger, and resentment. The bereaved also may experience illusions: They "see" the deceased person in his or her favorite chair or in the face of a stranger, they have vivid dreams in which the deceased is still alive, or they feel the "presence" of the dead person. They also experience strong guilt feelings ("If only I had gotten her to a doctor sooner" "I should have been more loving") and anger or resentment ("Why wasn't he more careful?" "It isn't fair that I'm the one left behind").

Once the powerful feelings of yearning subside, the individual enters the third *disorganization/despair* phase. Life seems to lose its meaning. The mourner feels listless, apathetic, and submissive. As time goes by, however, the survivor gradually begins to accept the loss both intellectually (the loss makes sense) and emotionally (memories are both pleasurable as well as painful). This acceptance, combined with building a new self-identity ("I am a single mother" "We are no longer a couple"), characterizes the fourth and final stage of grief — the *resolution or reorganization* stage.

Grief is obviously not the same for everyone. People vary in the stages of grief that they experience and the length of time for "recovery" (Ellis & Granger, 2002; Satterfield, Folkman, & Acree, 2002; Koppel, 2000). You can help people who are grieving by accepting their individual differences and recognizing that there is no perfect response. Simply say, "I'm sorry," and then let the person talk if he or she wishes. Your quiet presence and caring is generally the best type of support.

When it comes to dealing with your own losses and grief, psychologists offer several techniques that you may find helpful (Ingram, Jones, & Smith, 2001; Kranz & Daniluk, 2002; Napolitane, 1997; Wartik, 1996):

1. ***Recognize the loss and allow yourself to grieve.*** Despite feelings of acute loneliness, remember that loss is a part of everyone's life and accept comfort from others. Take care of yourself by avoiding unnecessary stress, getting plenty of rest, and giving yourself permission to enjoy life whenever possible.

2. ***Set up a daily activity schedule.*** One of the best ways to offset the lethargy and depression of grief is to force yourself to fill your time with useful activities (studying, washing your car, doing the laundry, and so on).

3. ***Seek help.*** Having the support of loving friends and family helps offset the loneliness and stress of grief. Recognize, however, that professional counseling may be necessary in cases of extreme or prolonged numbness, anger, guilt, or depression. (You will learn more about depression and its treatment in Modules 39, 43, 44.)

Attitudes Toward Death and Dying

Cultures around the world interpret and respond to death in widely different ways: "Funerals are the occasion for avoiding people or holding parties, for fighting or having sexual orgies, for weeping or laughing, in a thousand combinations" (Metcalf & Huntington, 1991, p. 62).

Similarly, subcultures within the United States also have different responses to death. Irish Americans are likely to believe the dead deserve a good send-off — a wake with food, drink, and jokes. On the other hand, African Americans traditionally regard funerals as a time for serious grief, demonstrated in some congregations by wailing and singing spirituals (Barley, 1997; Wartik, 1996). Most Japanese Americans, however, try to restrain their grief and smile so as not to burden others with their pain and to avoid the shame associated with losing emotional control (Cook & Dworkin, 1992).

Attitudes toward death and dying also vary with age. As adults, we understand death in terms of three basic concepts: (1) *permanence* — once a living thing dies, it cannot be brought back to life; (2) *universality* — all living things eventually die; and (3) *nonfunctionality* — all living functions, including thought, movement, and vital signs, end at death.

Research shows that permanence, the notion that death cannot be reversed, is the first and most easily understood concept. Preschoolers seem to accept the fact that the dead person cannot get up again, perhaps because of their experiences with dead butterflies and beetles found while playing outside (Furman, 1990).

Understanding of universality comes slightly later, and by the age of 7 years, most children have mastered nonfunctionality and have an adultlike understanding of death. Although adults may fear that discussing death with children and adolescents will make them unduly anxious, those who are offered open, honest discussions of death have an easier time accepting it (Christ, Siegel, & Christ, 2002; Kastenbaum, 1999; Pfeffer et al., 2002).

Grieving. *Individuals vary in their emotional reactions to loss. There is no right or wrong way to grieve.*

The Death Experience

Have you thought about your own death? Would you like to die suddenly and alone, or would you prefer to know ahead of time so you could plan your funeral and spend time saying good-bye to your family and friends? If you find thinking about these questions uncomfortable, it may be because most people in Western societies deny death. Unfortunately, avoiding thoughts and discussion of death and associating aging with death contribute to ageism (Atchley, 1997). Moreover, the better we understand death, and the more wisely we approach it, the more fully we can live until it comes.

During the Middle Ages (from about the fifth century until the 1500s), people were expected to recognize when death was approaching so they could bid their farewells and die with dignity surrounded by loved ones (Aries, 1981). In recent times, Western societies have moved death out of the home and put it into the hospital and funeral parlor. Rather than personally caring for our dying family and friends, we have shifted responsibility to "experts" — physicians and morticians. We have made death a medical failure, rather than a natural part of the life cycle.

This avoidance of death and dying may be changing, though. Since the late 1990s, right-to-die and death-with-dignity advocates have been working to bring death out in the open, and mental health professionals have suggested that understanding the psychological processes of death and dying may play a significant role in good adjustment.

Confronting our own death is the last major crisis we face in life. What is it like? Is there a "best" way to prepare to die? Is there such a thing as a "good death"? After spending hundreds of hours at the bedsides of the terminally ill, Elisabeth Kübler-Ross developed her stage theory of the psychological processes surrounding death (1983, 1997, 1999).

On the basis of extensive interviews with patients, Kübler-Ross proposed that most people go through five sequential stages when facing death: *denial* of the terminal condition ("This can't be true; it's a mistake!"), *anger* ("Why me? It isn't fair!"), *bargaining* ("God, if you let me live, I'll dedicate my life to you!"), *depression* ("I'm losing everyone and everything I hold dear"), and finally *acceptance* ("I know that death is inevitable and my time is near").

Evaluating Kübler-Ross's Theory   Critics of the stage theory of dying stress that each person's death is a unique experience and that emotions and reactions depend on the individual's personality, life situation, age, and so on (Dunn, 2000; Kastenbaum, 1999). Others worry that popularizing such a stage theory will cause further avoidance and stereotyping of the dying ("He's just in the anger stage right now"). In response, Kübler-Ross (1983, 1997, 1999) agrees that not all people go through the same stages in the same way and regrets that anyone would use her theory as a model for a "good death." Dying, like living, is a unique, individual experience.

In spite of the potential abuses, Kübler-Ross's theory has provided valuable insights and spurred research into a long-neglected topic. **Thanatology,** the study of death and dying, has become a major topic in human development. Thanks in part to thanatology research, the dying are being helped to die with dignity by the *hospice* movement, which has created special facilities and trained staff and volunteers to provide loving support for the terminally ill and their families (McGrath, 2002; Parker-Oliver, 2002).

One of the most important contributions by Kübler-Ross (1975) may be her suggestion that:

> It is the denial of death that is partially responsible for [people] living empty, purposeless lives; for when you live as if you'll live forever, it becomes too easy to postpone the things you know you must do. In contrast, when you fully understand that each day you awaken could be the last you have, you take the time that day to grow, to become more of who you really are, to reach out to other human beings (p. 164).

Thanatology [THAN-uh-tall-uh-gee] *The study of death and dying. The term comes from thanatos, the Greek name for a mythical personification of death, and was borrowed by Freud to represent the death instinct*

Application
APPLYING PSYCHOLOGY TO EVERYDAY LIFE

Dealing With Your Own Death Anxiety

Woody Allen once said, "It's not that I'm afraid to die. I just don't want to be there when it happens." Although some people who are very old and in poor health may welcome death, most of us have difficulty facing it. One of the most important elements of critical thinking is self-knowledge, which includes the ability to critically evaluate our deepest and most private fears.

Death Anxiety Questionnaire

To test your own level of death anxiety, indicate your response according to the following scale:

0	1	2
not at all	somewhat	very much

____1. Do you worry about dying?

____2. Does it bother you that you may die before you have done everything you wanted to do?

____3. Do you worry that you may be very ill for a long time before you die?

____4. Does it upset you to think that others may see you suffering before you die?

____5. Do you worry that dying may be very painful?

____6. Do you worry that the persons closest to you won't be with you when you are dying?

____7. Do you worry that you may be alone when you are dying?

____8. Does the thought bother you that you might lose control of your mind before death?

____9. Do you worry that expenses connected with your death will be a burden to other people?

____10. Does it worry you that your will or instructions about your belongings may not be carried out after you die?

____11. Are you afraid that you may be buried before you are really dead?

____12. Does the thought of leaving loved ones behind when you die disturb you?

____13. Do you worry that those you care about may not remember you after your death?

____14. Does the thought worry you that with death you may be gone forever?

____15. Are you worried about not knowing what to expect after death?

Source: Conte, H. R., Weiner, M. B., and Plutchik, R. (1982). Measuring death anxiety: Conceptual, psychometric, and factor-analytic aspects. *Journal of Personality and Social Psychology, 43,* 775–785. Reprinted with permission.

How does your total score compare to the national average of 8.5? When this same test was given to nursing-home residents, senior citizens, and college students, researchers found no significant differences, despite the fact that those tested ranged in age from 30 to 80.

Assessment

CHECK & REVIEW

Grief and Death

Attitudes toward death and dying vary greatly across cultures and among age groups. Although adults understand the *permanence, universality,* and *nonfunctionality* of death, children often don't master these concepts until around age 7 years.

Grief is a natural and painful reaction to a loss. For most people, grief consists of four major stages — *numbness, yearning, disorganization/despair,* and *resolution.*

Elisabeth Kübler-Ross's theory of the five-stage process of dying (*denial, anger, bargaining, depression,* and *acceptance*) offers important insights into the last major crisis we face in life. The study of death and dying, **thanatology,** has become an important topic in human development.

Questions

1. Explain how an adult's understanding of death differs from a preschool child's.
2. Grieving people generally begin with the _____ stage and end with the _____ stage. (a) numbness, bargaining; (b) grief, anger; (c) yearning, acceptance; (d) numbness, resolution

3. Match the following statements with Elisabeth Kübler-Ross's five-stage theory of death and dying:
   ___ a. "I understand that I'm dying, but if I could just have a little more time…"
   ___ b. "I refuse to believe the doctors. I want a fourth opinion."
   ___ c. "I know my time is near. I'd better make plans for my spouse and children."
   ___ d. "Why me? I've been a good person."
   ___ e. "I'm losing everything. I'll never see my children again. Life is so hard."

4. The study of death and dying is known as _____ (a) gerontology; (b) ageism; (c) mortality; (d) thanatology

Answers to Questions can be found in Appendix B.

MODULE 28   ACTIVE LEARNING WORKSHEET

Enter the correct letter from Column A in the blank space in Column B, and then double-check your answers with those in Appendix B.

Column A	Column B
a. Resilience	1.____ Most common reason females drop out of school.
b. Stages of grief	2.____ Prejudice based on age.
c. Disengagement theory	3.____ Study of death and dying.
d. Ageism	4.____ Positive development despite harsh environment.
e. Kubler-Ross	5.____ Natural withdrawal in preparation for death.
f. Teen pregnancy	6.____ Denial, anger, bargaining, depression, acceptance.
g. Thanatology	7.____ Advocates full, active commitment to life.
h. Activity theory	8.____ Has one of the lowest incomes in North America.
i. Elderly females	9.____ Proposed theory of 5 stages of impending death.
j. Stages of death	10.____ Numbness, yearning, disorganization/despair, resolution.

Assessment
KEY TERMS

To assess your understanding of the **Key Terms** in this section, write a definition for each (in your own words), and then compare your definitions with those in the text.

Moral Development
care perspective (p. 381)
conventional level (p. 378)
justice perspective (p. 381)
postconventional level (p. 378)
preconventional level (p. 378)

Personality Development Over the Life Span
identity crisis (p. 384)

psychosocial stages (p. 382)
temperament (p. 382)

Additional Influences on Development
activity theory (p. 393)
disengagement theory (p. 393)
resiliency (p. 392)
socioemotional selectivity theory (p. 393)

Grief and Death
thanatology [THAN-uh-tall-uh-gee] (p. 398)

Achievement
WEB RESOURCES

Huffman Book Companion Site
http://www.wiley.com/college/huffman
 This site is loaded with free Interactive Self-Tests, Internet Exercises, Glossary and Flashcards for key terms, Web links, Handbook for Non-Native Speakers, and other activities designed to improve your mastery of the material in this section.

Want more information about moral development and moral education?
http://tigger.uic.edu/~lnucci/MoralEd/
 The College of Education at the University of Illinois at Chicago developed this comprehensive web site. Their stated mission is to serve "as a link for educators, scholars, and citizens interested in sharing their work and learning about research, practices, and activities in the area of moral development and education."

VISUAL SUMMARY

Life Span Development II
(Modules 27 and 28)

Moral Development

Kohlberg's Three Levels and Six Stages

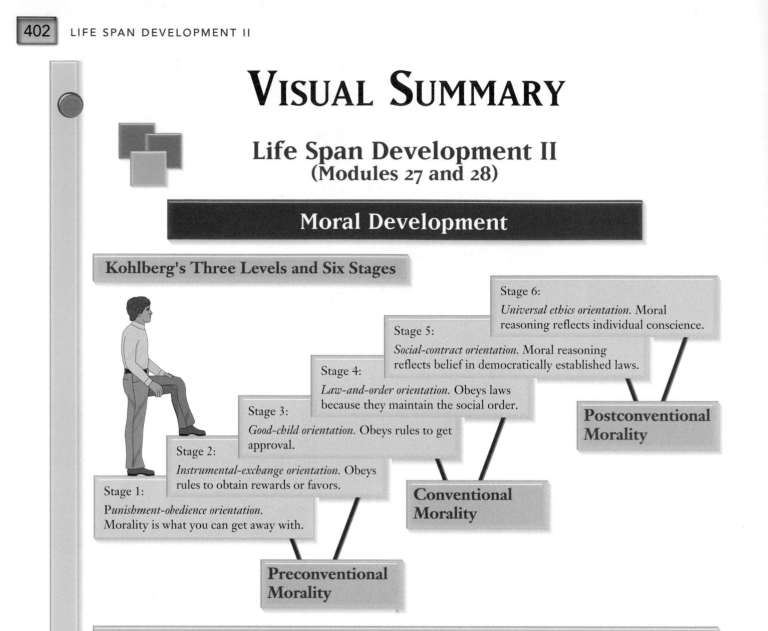

Stage 6:
Universal ethics orientation. Moral reasoning reflects individual conscience.

Stage 5:
Social-contract orientation. Moral reasoning reflects belief in democratically established laws.

Stage 4:
Law-and-order orientation. Obeys laws because they maintain the social order.

Stage 3:
Good-child orientation. Obeys rules to get approval.

Stage 2:
Instrumental-exchange orientation. Obeys rules to obtain rewards or favors.

Stage 1:
Punishment-obedience orientation. Morality is what you can get away with.

Postconventional Morality

Conventional Morality

Preconventional Morality

Criticisms of Kohlberg's theory: Politically, culturally, and gender biased. Gilligan says women take a **care perspective** in their moral reasoning and men a **justice perspective.** In fact, research shows both sexes typically use both perspectives.

Personality Development Over the Life Span

Thomas & Chess's Temperament Theory

Temperament: Basic, inborn disposition.
Three temperament styles: easy, difficult, and slow-to-warm-up. Styles seem consistent and enduring.

Erikson's *Eight* Psychosocial Stages

- Childhood: Trust vs. mistrust, autonomy vs. shame and doubt, initiative vs. guilt, industry vs. inferiority.
- Adolescence: Identity vs. role confusion.
- Young Adulthood: Intimacy vs. isolation.
- Middle Adulthood: Generativity vs. stagnation.
- Older Adult: Ego integrity vs. despair.

Additional Influences on Personality Development

Families
- Family violence, teenage pregnancies, and divorce can damage personality development.
- **Resilience** helps some children survive an abusive or stress-filled childhood.

Occupational Choices
Occupational choice is critically important because most people channel their accomplishment needs into their work.

Aging
Three major theories of aging:

Activity Theory (should remain active)

Disengagement Theory (should gracefully withdraw)

Socioemotional Selectivity: (elderly reduce social contacts because they're more selective)

Grief and Death

Grief
Grief: A natural and painful reaction to a loss, consists of four major stages:

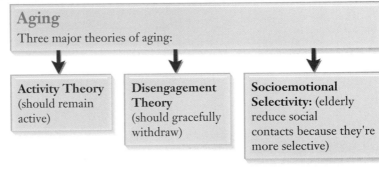

1) numbness → 2) yearning → 3) disorganization and despair → 4) resolution

Attitudes
Attitudes toward death and dying vary greatly across cultures and among age groups. Children generally don't fully understand the permanence, universality, and nonfunctionality of death until around age seven.

Death Experience
- Kübler-Ross proposes a five-stage process of dying (denial, anger, bargaining, depression, and acceptance).
- **Thanatology:** Study of death and dying.

GENDER AND HUMAN SEXUALITY

Assessment

Core Learning Objectives

As you read Modules 29 and 30, keep the following questions in mind and answer them in your own words:

▶ How are sex and gender defined, and how do we develop our gender roles? What are the major sex and gender differences between men and women?

▶ How do scientists study a sensitive topic like sex?

▶ How are men and women alike and different in sexual arousal and response?

▶ What is the latest research on sexual orientation?

▶ What factors contribute to sexual dysfunction and sexually transmitted infections?

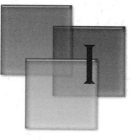

It was an unusual circumcision. The identical twin boys were already 8 months old when their parents took them to the doctor to be circumcised. For many years in the United States, most male babies have had the foreskin of their penis removed during their first week of life, when it is assumed they will experience less pain. The most common procedure is cutting or pinching off the foreskin tissue. In this case, however, the doctor used an electrocautery device, which is used to burn off moles or small skin growths. The electrical current used for the first twin was too high, and the entire penis was accidentally ablated, or removed. (The parents did not let the physician try to circumcise the other twin.)

In anguish over the tragic accident, the parents sought advice from medical experts. Following discussions with John Money and other specialists at John Hopkins University, the parents and doctors made an unusual decision — they would turn the infant with the destroyed penis into a girl.

The first step in the reassignment process occurred at age 17 months, when the child's name was changed — Bruce became "Brenda" (Colapinto, 2000). Brenda was dressed in pink pants and frilly blouses and "her" hair was allowed to grow long. At 21 months, plastic surgery was performed. The child's testes were removed, and external female genitals and an internal, "preliminary" vagina were created. Further plastic surgery to complete the vagina was planned for the beginning of adolescence, when the child's

▢ Achievement

▢ Assessment

▢ Application

physical growth would be nearly complete. At this time she also would begin to take female hormones to complete the boy-to-girl transformation.

According to John Money (Money & Ehrhardt, 1972), the children's mother was surprised and pleased by the striking differences that developed in her two children. By age three, Brenda wore nightgowns and dresses almost exclusively and liked bracelets and hair ribbons. During the preschool years, she reportedly preferred playing with "girl-type" toys and asked for a doll and carriage for Christmas. Her brother asked for a garage with cars, gas pumps, and tools. By age 6, the brother was accustomed to defending his sister if he thought someone was threatening her. The daughter copied the mother in tidying and cleaning up the kitchen, whereas the boy did not. The mother agreed that she encouraged her daughter when she helped with the housework and expected the boy to be uninterested.

During their childhood, both Brenda/Bruce and her brother were brought to Johns Hopkins each year for physical and psychological evaluation. The case was heralded as a complete success, and it became the model for treating infants born with ambiguous genitalia. The story of "John/Joan," (the name used by John Hopkins) was heralded as proof that gender is made — not born.

What first looked like a success was, in fact, a dismal failure. Follow-up studies report that Brenda never really adjusted to her assigned gender (Diamond & Sigmundson, 1997). Despite being raised from infancy as a girl, she did not feel like a girl and avoided most female activities and interests. By age 14, she was so unhappy that she contemplated suicide. The father then tearfully explained what had happened earlier. For the child, "All of a sudden everything clicked. For the first time things made sense, and I understood who and what I was" (Thompson, 1997, p. 83).

AS NATURE MADE HIM
THE BOY WHO WAS RAISED AS A GIRL

JOHN COLAPINTO

What do you think about the parents' and experts' solution to this terrible accident? Is it possible that what makes some children prefer "girl-type" toys and clothes is how parents or others treat them? Or is biology the predictor of our gender-related behaviors? The concepts of gender and sex are not simple. You will learn more about "Brenda" and your own gender development and sexuality in the first section of this module. Then we will discuss four pioneers in sex research and cultural differences in sexual practices and attitudes. The third section describes sexual arousal, response, and orientation. Finally, Module 30 covers sexual dysfunction and sexually transmitted infections, including AIDS (acquired immunodeficiency syndrome).

MODULE 29
SEX AND GENDER

Assessment

How are sex and gender defined, and how do we develop our gender roles? What are the major sex and gender differences between men and women?

Why is it that the first question most people ask after a baby is born is "Is it a girl or a boy?" What would life be like if there were no divisions according to maleness or femaleness? Would your career plans or friendship patterns change? These questions reflect the importance of *sex* and *gender* in our lives. This section begins with a look at the various ways sex and gender can be defined, followed by a discussion of gender role development and sex and gender differences.

◼ Problems with Definition: What Is "Maleness" and "Femaleness"?

When people ask if a newborn is a girl or boy, they're typically thinking of standard biological differences as seen in Figure 29.1. But when they buy gifts for children, they frequently demonstrate their expectations of *femininity* ("She'll like this pretty doll") versus *masculinity* ("This fire truck is perfect for him"). In the case of the male twin who was reassigned as a girl, do you still think of "her" as basically male? Is a man who cross-dresses a woman? The question of what is "male" and "female" can be confusing.

In recent years, researchers have come to use the term **sex** to refer to biological elements (such as having a penis or vagina), or physical activities (such as masturbation and intercourse). **Gender,** on the other hand, encompasses the psychological and sociocultural meanings added to biology (such as "Men should be aggressive" and "Women should be nurturing"). There are at least seven dimensions or elements of *sex* and two of *gender* (Table 29.1).

If you apply the dimensions of sex and gender that are presented in Table 29.1 to the case of the reassigned twin, you can see why it is a classic in the field of human sexuality. Although born a chromosomal male, the child's genital sex was first altered

Sex *Biological maleness and femaleness, including chromosomal sex; also, activities related to sexual behaviors, such as masturbation and intercourse*

Gender *Psychological and sociocultural meanings added to biological maleness or femaleness*

Figure 29.1 *Male and female internal and external sex organs.*

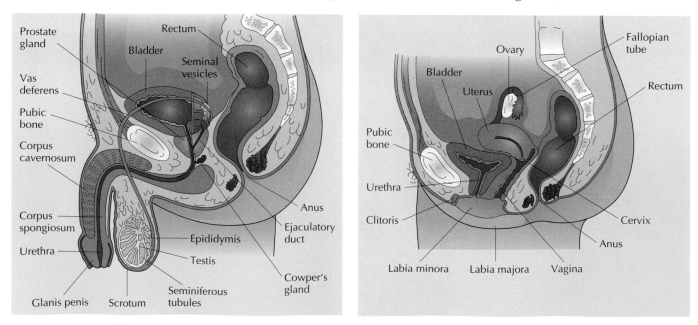

*A*ssessment

This type of "dressing up" is a good example of which dimension of gender?

Answer: Gender role

SUMMARY TABLE 29.1 DIMENSIONS OF SEX AND GENDER

	Male	Female
Sex Dimensions		
1. Chromosomes	XY	XX
2. Gonads	Testes	Ovaries
3. Hormones	Predominantly androgens	Predominantly estrogens
4. External genitals	Penis, scrotum	Labia majora, labia minora, clitoris, vaginal opening
5. Internal accessory organs	Prostate gland, seminal vesicles, vas deferens, ejaculatory duct, Cowper's gland	Vagina, uterus, fallopian tubes, cervix
6. Secondary sex characteristics	Beard, lower voice, wider shoulders, sperm emission	Breasts, wider hips, menstruation
7. Sexual orientation	Heterosexual, gay, bisexual	Heterosexual, lesbian, bisexual
Gender Dimensions		
8. Gender identity (self-definition)	Perceives self as male	Perceives self as female
9. Gender role (societal expectations)	Masculine ("Boys like trucks and sports")	Feminine ("Girls like dolls and clothes")

by the doctor who accidentally removed the penis and later by surgeons who created female genitals. The question was whether surgery, along with female hormones and "appropriate" gender role expectations of the parents, would be enough to create a stable female **gender identity.** Would the child accept the sex reassignment and identify herself as a girl?

At first, it appeared that Brenda's reassignment was successful, and psychology and sociology texts cited this case as evidence of the environment's predominant role in creating gender identity. As she entered adolescence, however, the early "success" began to be questioned. Her appearance and masculine way of walking led classmates to tease her and call her "cave woman." At this age, she also expressed thoughts of becoming a mechanic, and her fantasies reflected discomfort with her female role. She even tried urinating in a standing position. By age 14, she insisted she wanted to live as a boy (Diamond & Sigmundson, 1997).

When the truth finally came out, "Brenda" reclaimed his male gender identity and renamed himself David. After a double mastectomy (removal of both breasts) and construction of an artificial penis, David married a woman and adopted her children. He now says, "I don't blame my parents," but they still feel extremely guilty about their participation in the reassignment. David, his twin brother, and parents all suffered tremendously from the tragic accident and the no less tragic solution. The family members have since reconciled, but David remains angry with the doctors who "interfered with nature" and ruined his childhood.

[A similar botched circumcision occurred in 1985, exactly 20 years after David and his twin brother were born. Although David had announced his decision to live as a male 5 years earlier, "Baby Doe" was also surgically altered and reassigned as a female. The current status of this child is carefully guarded, but limited facts point to

Gender Identity *Self-identification as either a man or a woman*

VISUAL QUIZ

Why do some men cross-dress?

Answer: Men who are transvestites dress like women to release sexual tension and enjoy the other sex's gender role. Contrary to common belief, gay men seldom cross-dress.

Sexual Orientation *Primary erotic attraction toward members of the same sex (homosexual, gay or lesbian), both sexes (bisexual), or other sex (heterosexual)*

Gender Role *Societal expectations for normal and appropriate male and female behavior*

a similarly unhappy outcome (Colapinto, 2000). The consulting specialist was John Money.]

The fact that David ultimately rejected his assigned female gender despite strong pressure from his family and doctors indicates that the most important factor in gender identity may be biological. A recent longitudinal study offers additional evidence of a biological link. Researchers at Johns Hopkins Hospital tracked the development of 27 normal boys, born without a penis, a rare defect known as *cloacal exstrophy*. Twenty-five of these boys were castrated at birth and raised as girls, yet researchers observed many signs of masculine behavior, including lots of "typical" male "rough-and-tumble" play. Fourteen of the children, currently ranging in age from 5 to 16 years, have recently rejected their female reassignment and declared themselves to be boys (Hettena, 2000).

In addition to the gender difficulties involved in David's case and the cases of the boys born without a penis, other gender identity problems may develop when a person feels he or she is trapped in a body of the wrong sex. This is known as *transsexualism* (having a gender identity opposite to biological sex). Although some may see the case of Brenda/Bruce/David as a form of transsexualism, "true" transsexuals are born chromosomally and anatomically one sex, but they have a deep and lasting discomfort with their sexual anatomy. They report feeling as if they are victims of a "birth defect" and they often seek corrective reassignment surgery (Bower, 2001). At one time, the number of men seeking reassignment was much higher than the number of women who wished to be men, but the ratio has narrowed considerably in recent years (Landen, Walinder, & Lundstrom, 1998).

Is a transsexual the same as a transvestite? No, *transvestism* involves individuals (almost exclusively men) who become sexually aroused or gratified by wearing the clothes stereotypical of the other sex (cross-dressing) (Miracle, Miracle, & Baumeister, 2003). In contrast, transsexuals feel that they are really members of the opposite sex imprisoned in the wrong body — their gender identity does not match their gonads, genitals, or internal accessory organs. Transsexuals may also cross-dress, but their motivation is to look like the "right" sex rather than to obtain sexual arousal. Transvestites should also be distinguished from female impersonators (who cross-dress to entertain) and from gay men who occasionally "go in drag" (cross-dress).

Are transvestites and transsexuals also homosexual? When a person is described as *homosexual*, it is because of a **sexual orientation** toward the same sex. (The preferred terms today are *gay* and *lesbian* rather than *homosexual*.) Transvestites are usually heterosexual (Bullough & Bullough, 1997). Transsexuality, on the other hand, has nothing to do with sexual orientation, only with gender identity. In fact, a transsexual can be heterosexual, gay, lesbian, or *bisexual* (being sexually attracted to both males and females).

■ Gender Role Development: Two Major Theories

Sexual orientation and gender identity also should not be confused with **gender roles** — societal expectations for normal and appropriate female and male behavior. Gender roles influence our lives from the moment of birth (when we are wrapped in either a pink or blue blanket) until the moment of death (when we are buried in either a dress or a dark suit). By age two, children are well aware of gender roles. They recognize that boys "should" be strong, independent, aggressive, dominant, and achieving, whereas girls "should" be soft, dependent, passive, emotional, and "naturally" interested in children (Kimmel, 2000; Witt, 1997). The gender role expectations learned in childhood apparently influence us throughout our life.

Early gender role conditioning. *Can you predict the long-term effects of this type of gender role training on young boys and girls? Are these effects primarily good or bad?*

How do we develop our gender roles? The existence of similar gender roles in many cultures suggests that evolution and biology may play a role; however, most research emphasizes two major theories of gender role development: *social learning* and *cognitive developmental.*

Social Learning Theory

Social-learning theorists emphasize the power of the immediate situation and observable behaviors on gender role development. They suggest girls learn how to be "feminine" and boys learn how to be "masculine" in two major ways: (1) They receive rewards or punishments for specific gender role behaviors and (2) they watch and imitate the behavior of others — particularly the same-sex parent (Bandura, 1989, 2000; Bois et al., 2002). A boy who puts on his father's tie or baseball cap wins big, indulgent smiles from his parents. But can you imagine what would happen if he put on his mother's nightgown or lipstick? Parents, teachers, and friends generally reward or punish behaviors according to traditional boy/girl gender role expectations. Thus, a child "socially learns" what it means to be male or female.

Cognitive Developmental Theory

Cognitive-developmental theorists acknowledge that social learning is part of gender development, but, they argue, the social learning model sees gender development as a passive process. Cognitive developmentalists point out that children also actively observe, interpret, and judge the world around them (Bem, 1981, 1993; Liben & Signorella, 1993; Welch-Ross & Schmidt, 1996). As children process this information, they create internal rules governing correct behaviors for boys versus girls. On the basis of these rules, they form *gender schemas* (mental images) of how they should act. (Recall from the discussion of Piaget in Module 26 that a schema is a cognitive structure, a network of associations, which guides perception.)

Thus, a little boy plays with fire trucks and building blocks because his parents smiled approvingly in the past and because he has seen more boys than girls playing with these toys (*social learning theory*). But his internal thought processes (*cognitive developmental theory*) also contribute to his choice of "masculine" toys; he realizes he is a boy, and he has learned that boys "should" prefer fire trucks to dishes and dolls.

Sex and Gender Differences: Nature Versus Nurture

Now that we have looked at the different dimensions of sex and gender and examined gender role development, let's turn our attention to sex and gender differences between males and females.

Sex Differences

Physical anatomy is the most obvious biological difference between men and women (Figure 29.2). The average man is taller, heavier, and stronger than the average woman, but he is also more likely to be bald and color-blind. In addition, men and women differ in their *secondary sex characteristics* (facial hair, breasts, and so on), their signs of reproductive capability (the menarche for girls and the ejaculation of sperm for boys), and their physical reactions to middle age or the end of reproduction (the female menopause and male climacteric).

There also are several functional and structural differences in the brains of men and women. These differences result, at least in part, from the influence of prenatal sex hormones on the developing fetal brain, and they are most apparent in the

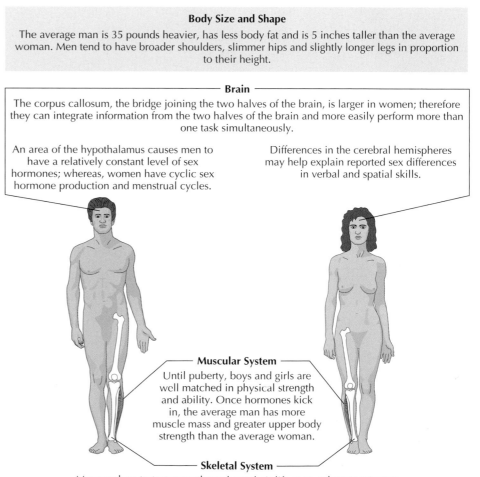

Body Size and Shape
The average man is 35 pounds heavier, has less body fat and is 5 inches taller than the average woman. Men tend to have broader shoulders, slimmer hips and slightly longer legs in proportion to their height.

— **Brain** —
The corpus callosum, the bridge joining the two halves of the brain, is larger in women; therefore they can integrate information from the two halves of the brain and more easily perform more than one task simultaneously.

An area of the hypothalamus causes men to have a relatively constant level of sex hormones; whereas, women have cyclic sex hormone production and menstrual cycles.

Differences in the cerebral hemispheres may help explain reported sex differences in verbal and spatial skills.

Muscular System
Until puberty, boys and girls are well matched in physical strength and ability. Once hormones kick in, the average man has more muscle mass and greater upper body strength than the average woman.

Skeletal System
Men produce testosterone throughout their life span, whereas estrogen production virtually stops when a women goes through menopause. Because estrogen helps rejuvenate bones, women after menopause are more likely to have brittle bones. Women also are more prone to knee damage because a woman's wider hips may place a greater strain on the ligaments joining the thigh to the knee.

Figure 29.2 *Major physical differences between the sexes.*

Source: Adapted from Miracle, Miracle, & Baumeister, 2003, p. 302.

hypothalamus, corpus callosum, and *cerebral hemispheres* (Chipman, Hampson, & Kimura, 2002; Diamond & Sigmundson, 1997; McCarthy, Auger, & Perrot-Sinal, 2002; Swaab et al., 2001). For example, during puberty, the female's hypothalamus directs her pituitary gland to release hormones in a cyclic fashion (the menstrual cycle), whereas the male's hypothalamus directs a relatively steady production of sex hormones. The corpus callosum, the web of nerve fibers connecting the cerebral hemispheres, is larger in adult women and shaped differently in women than in men. Research suggests this difference may explain why men tend to rely on one hemisphere or the other in performing tasks, while women generally use both hemispheres at once. Researchers also have documented differences in the cerebral hemispheres of men and women that may account for reported differences in verbal and spatial skills.

Gender Differences

Do you think there are inborn psychological differences between women and men? Do you believe that women are more emotional and more concerned with aesthetics, whereas men are naturally more aggressive and competitive? Scientists have studied questions such as these; their major findings on gender differences are summarized in Table 29.2. In this section, we will focus on two of their most important findings — regarding cognitive abilities and aggression.

1. *Cognitive abilities.* For many years, researchers have noted that females tend to score higher on tests of verbal skills, whereas males score higher on math and visuospatial tests (Gallagher et al., 2000; Quaiser-Pohl & Lehmann, 2002). As mentioned earlier, some researchers suggest that these differences may reflect biology — that is, structural differences in the cerebral hemispheres, hormones, or in the degree of hemispheric specialization.

   One argument against such a biological model, however, is that male–female differences in verbal ability and math scores have declined in recent years (Brown & Josephs, 1999; Carter, 2000; Halpern, 1997, 2000). This is not true, however, of men in the very highest IQ range. Men in this group still score higher than women on SAT math scores.

2. *Aggression.* One of the clearest and most consistent findings in gender studies is greater physical aggressiveness in males. From an early age, boys are more likely to engage in mock fighting and rough-and-tumble play, and as adolescents and adults, they are more likely to commit aggressive crimes (Camodeca et al., 2002; Hettena, 2000; Moffitt, Caspi, Harrington, & Milne, 2002). But gender differences are clearer for physical aggression (like hitting) than for other forms of aggression (Xie, Cairns, & Cairns, 2002; Zurbriggen, 2000). Early research suggested that females were more likely to engage in more indirect and relational forms of aggression, such as spreading rumors, ignoring, or excluding someone (Bjorkquist, 1994; Crick, 1996). But later studies have not found such clear differences (Feiring et al., 2002; Pakaslahti & Keltikangas-Jaervinen, 2000).

   What causes these gender differences in aggression? Those who take a nature perspective generally cite biological factors. For example, several studies have linked the male gonadal hormone testosterone to aggressive behavior (Book, Starzyk, & Qunisey, 2002; Boyd, 2000; Dabbs & Dabbs, 2000). Other studies have found that aggressive men have disturbances in their levels of serotonin, a neurotransmitter inversely related to aggression (Berman, Tracy, & Coccaro, 1997; Holtzworth-Munroe, 2000; Nelson & Chiavegatto, 2001). In addition, studies on identical twins find that genetic factors account for about 50 percent of aggressive behavior (Cadoret, Leve, & Devor, 1997; Segal & Bouchard, 2000).

Achievement

SUMMARY TABLE 29.2 RESEARCH-SUPPORTED SEX AND GENDER DIFFERENCES

Type of Behavior	More Often Shown by Men	More Often Shown by Women
Sexual	• Begin masturbating sooner in life cycle and have higher overall occurrence rates. • Start sexual life earlier and have first orgasm through masturbation. • Are more likely to recognize their own sexual arousal. • Experience more orgasm consistency in their sexual relations.	• Begin masturbating later in life cycle and have lower overall occurrence rates. • Start sexual life later and have first orgasm from partner stimulation. • Are less likely to recognize their own sexual arousal. • Experience less orgasm consistency in their sexual relations.
Touching	• Are touched, kissed, and cuddled less by parents. • Exchange less physical contact with other men and respond more negatively to being touched. • More likely to initiate both casual and intimate touch.	• Are touched, kissed, and cuddled more by parents. • Exchange more physical contact with other women and respond more positively to being touched. • Less likely to initiate either casual or intimate touch.
Friendship	• Have larger number of friends and express friendship by shared activities.	• Have smaller number of friends and express friendship by shared communication about self.
Personality	• Are more aggressive from a very early age. • Are more self-confident of future success. • Attribute success to internal factors and failures to external factors. • Achievement is task oriented; motives are mastery and competition. • Are more self-validating. • Have higher self-esteem.	• Are less aggressive from a very early age. • Are less self-confident of future success. • Attribute success to external factors and failures to internal factors. • Achievement is socially directed with emphasis on self-improvement; have higher work motives. • Are more dependent on others for self-validation. • Have lower self-esteem.
Cognitive Abilities	• Are slightly superior in mathematics and visuospatial skills.	• Are slightly superior in grammar, spelling, and related verbal skills.

Sources: Crooks & Bauer, 2002; Masters & Johnson, 1961, 1966, 1970; Miracle, Miracle, & Baumeister, 2003.

Nurturists typically point to environmental pressures that encourage "sex-appropriate" behaviors and skills. For example, children's picture books, video games, and TV programs and commercials frequently present women and men in stereotypical gender roles — men as pilots and doctors, women as moms and nurses (Dietz, 1998; Kimmel, 2000).

What if we don't like this part of gender roles? What can we do?

Androgyny

One way to overcome rigid or destructive gender role stereotypes is to encourage **androgyny,** expressing both the "masculine" and "feminine" traits found in each individual. Rather than limiting themselves to rigid gender-appropriate behaviors, androgynous men and women can be assertive and aggressive when necessary, but also gentle and nurturing.

Although some people think *androgyny* is a new term for asexuality or transsexualism, the idea of androgyny has a long history referring to positive combinations of gender roles, like the yin and yang of traditional Chinese religions. Carl Jung (1946, 1959), an early psychoanalyst, described a woman's natural masculine traits and impulses as her "animus" and feminine traits and impulses in a man as his "anima." Jung believed we must draw on both our masculine and feminine natures to become fully functioning adults.

Using personality tests and other similar measures, modern researchers have found that masculine and androgynous individuals generally have higher self-esteem and creativity, are more socially competent and motivated to achieve, and exhibit better overall mental health (Gianakos, 2000; Courtenay, 2000; Hittner & Daniels, 2002; Ward, 2000). It seems that androgyny and masculinity are adaptive for both sexes.

How can you explain this? It seems that traditional masculine characteristics (analytical, independent) are more highly valued than traditional feminine traits (affectionate, cheerful). For example, in business a good manager is still perceived as having predominantly masculine traits (Powell, Butterfield, & Parent, 2002). Also, when college students in 14 different countries were asked to describe their "current self" and their "ideal self," the ideal self-descriptions for both men and women contained more masculine qualities than feminine (Williams & Best, 1990).

This shared preference for male traits helps explain why extensive observations of children on school playgrounds have found that boys who engage in feminine

Androgyny in action. *Combining the traits of both genders helps many couples meet the demands of modern life.*

Androgyny [an-DRAW-juh-nee]
Combining characteristics considered typically male (assertive, athletic) with characteristics considered typically female (yielding, nurturant); from the Greek andro, meaning "male," and gyn, meaning "female"

Would you like to see how androgynous you are? Social psychologist Sandra Bem (1974, 1993) developed a personality measure that has been widely used in research. You can take this version of Bem's test by rating yourself on the following items. Give yourself a number between I (*never or almost never true*) and 7 (*always or almost always true*):

1. _____ Analytical
2. _____ Affectionate
3. _____ Competitive
4. _____ Compassionate
5. _____ Aggressive

6. _____ Cheerful
7. _____ Independent
8. _____ Gentle
9. _____ Athletic
10. _____ Sensitive

Now add up your points for all the odd-numbered items; then add up your points for the even-numbered items. If you have a higher total on the odd-numbered items, you are "masculine." If you scored higher on the even-numbered items, you are "feminine." If your score is fairly even, you may be androgynous.

activities (like skipping rope or playing jacks) lose status. The reverse of this is not true for girls (Leaper, 2000). Even as adults, it is more difficult for males to express so-called female traits like nurturance and sensitivity than for women to adopt traditionally male traits of assertiveness and independence (Kimmel, 2000; Christensen, Hebl, Rothgerber, & Wood, 1997). In short, most societies prefer "tomboys" to "sissies."

Recent studies show that gender roles in our society are becoming less rigidly defined (Kimmel, 2000; Loo & Thorpe, 1998). Asian American and Mexican American groups show some of the largest changes toward androgyny, and African Americans remain among the most androgynous of all ethnic groups (Espin, 1993; Harris, 1996; Huang & Ying, 1989).

Assessment

CHECK & REVIEW

Sex and Gender

The term **sex** is differentiated along seven dimensions: chromosomal sex, gonadal sex, hormonal sex, external genitals, internal accessory organs, secondary sex characteristics, and sexual orientation. **Gender,** on the other hand, is differentiated according to **gender identity** and **gender role.** Transsexualism is a problem with gender identity; transvestism is cross-dressing for sexual arousal. **Sexual orientation** (gay, lesbian, bisexual, or heterosexual) is unrelated to either transsexualism or transvestism. There are two main theories of gender role development: Social-learning theorists focus on rewards, punishments, and imitation, whereas cognitive-developmental theorists emphasize the active, thinking processes of the individual.

Studies of male and female sex differences find several obvious physical differences, such as height, body build, and reproductive organs. There are also important functional and structural sex differences in the brains of human females and males. Looking at gender differences, studies find some differences (such as in aggression and verbal skills), but the cause of these differences (either nature or nurture) is still being debated.

Questions

1. Match the following dimensions of gender with their appropriate meaning:

_____ Chromosomal sex	a. Ovaries and testes
_____ Gender identity	b. XX and XY
_____ Gonadal sex	c. Estrogens and androgens
_____ Gender role	d. One's perception of oneself as male or female
_____ Hormonal sex	e. Breasts, beards, menstruation
_____ Secondary sex characteristics	f. Uterus, vagina, prostate gland, vas deferens
_____ External genitals	g. Labia majora, clitoris, penis, scrotum
_____ Sexual orientation	h. Homosexual, bisexual, heterosexual
_____ Internal accessory organs	i. Differing societal expectations for appropriate male and female behavior

2. Individuals who have the genitals and secondary sex characteristics of one sex but feel as if they belong to the other sex are known as _____. (a) transvestites; (b) heterosexuals; (c) gays or lesbians; (d) transsexuals

3. Briefly summarize the two major theories of gender role development.

4. A combination of both male and female personality traits is called _____. (a) heterosexuality; (b) homosexuality; (c) transsexualism; (d) androgyny

Answers to Questions can be found in Appendix B.

■ The Study of Human Sexuality: A Historical and Cultural Perspective

Assessment

> How do scientists study a sensitive topic like sex?

Sex is used and abused in many ways: as a theme in literature, movies, and music; to satisfy sexual desires; to gain love and acceptance from partners and peer groups; as a way of expressing love or commitment in a relationship; as a way of ending relationships through affairs with others; to dominate or hurt others; and, perhaps most conspicuously, to sell products.

People have probably always been interested in understanding their sexuality, but cultural forces have often suppressed and controlled this interest. During the nineteenth century, for example, polite society avoided mention of all parts of the body covered by

Before we begin our study of human sexuality, try this quiz. The answers are at the bottom, and expanded explanations are found throughout Modules 29 and 30.

Which of the following statements are true and which are false?

1. The breakfast cereal Kellogg's Corn Flakes was originally developed to discourage masturbation.
2. Nocturnal emissions and masturbation are signs of abnormal sexual adjustment.
3. The American Academy of Pediatrics (AAP) no longer recommends routine circumcision for male babies.
4. The American Psychiatric Association and the American Psychological Association (APA) consider homosexuality a type of mental illness.
5. Sexual skill and satisfaction are learned behaviors that can be increased through education and training.
6. If you're HIV positive (have human immunodeficiency virus) you cannot infect someone else; only if you have AIDS (acquired immunodeficiency syndrome) can you spread the disease.
7. Women cannot be raped against their will.

Answers: 1.T 2.F 3.T 4.F 5.T 6.F 7.F

Assessment

clothing. The breast of chickens became known as "white meat," female patients were examined by male doctors in totally dark rooms, and some people even covered piano legs for the sake of propriety (Allen, 2000; Gay, 1983; Money, 1985a).

During this same Victorian period, medical experts warned that masturbation led to blindness, impotence, acne, and insanity (Allen, 2000; Michael, Gagnon, Laumann, & Kolata, 1994). Believing a bland diet helped suppress sexual desire, Dr. John Harvey Kellogg and Sylvester Graham developed the original Kellogg's Corn Flakes and Graham crackers and marketed them as foods that would discourage masturbation (Money, Prakasam, & Joshi, 1991). One of the most serious concerns of many doctors was nocturnal emissions (wet dreams), which were believed to cause brain damage and death. Special devices were even marketed for men to wear at night to prevent sexual arousal (Figure 29.3).

In light of modern knowledge, it seems hard to understand these strange Victorian practices and outrageous myths about masturbation and nocturnal emissions. One of the first physicians to explore and question these beliefs was Havelock Ellis (1858–1939). When he first heard of the dangers of nocturnal emissions, Ellis was frightened — he had personal experience with the problem. His fear led him to frantically search the medical literature, but instead of a cure, he found predictions of gruesome illness and eventual death. He was so upset he contemplated suicide.

Ellis eventually decided he could give meaning to his life by keeping a detailed diary of his deterioration. He planned to dedicate the book to science when he died, but after several months of careful observation, he realized the books were wrong. He wasn't dying. He wasn't even sick. Angry that he had been so misinformed by the "experts," he spent the rest of his life developing reliable and accurate sex information. Today, Havelock Ellis is acknowledged as one of the most important early pioneers in the field of sex research.

Another major contributor to sex research was Alfred Kinsey and his colleagues (1948, 1953). Kinsey and his coworkers personally interviewed over 18,000 participants, asking detailed questions about their sexual activities and preferences. Their results shocked the nation. For example, they reported that 37 percent of

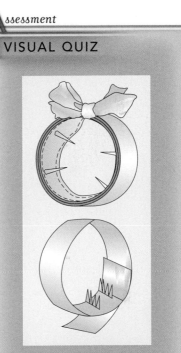

Figure 29.3 *Victorian sexual practice.* During the nineteenth century, men were encouraged to wear spiked rings around their penises at night. Can you explain why?

Answer: The Victorians believed nighttime erections and emissions ("wet dreams") were dangerous. If the man had an erection, the spikes would cause pain and awaken him.

The first sex scientist. Havelock Ellis was one of the first sex researchers to celebrate eroticism and acknowledge female sexuality.

men and 13 percent of women had engaged in adult same-sex behavior to the point of orgasm. However, Kinsey's data were criticized because most research participants were young, single, urban, white, and middle class. Despite the criticism, Kinsey's work is still widely respected, and his data are frequently used as a *baseline* for modern research. In recent years, hundreds of similar sex surveys and interviews have been conducted on such topics as contraception, abortion, premarital sex, and rape (Acierno et al., 2001, 2002; Cloutier, Martin, & Poole, 2002; Laumann, Gagnon, Michael, & Michaels, 1994; Leskin & Sheikh, 2002). By comparing Kinsey's data to the responses found in later surveys, we can see how sexual practices have changed over the years.

In addition to surveys, interviews, and case studies, some researchers have employed direct laboratory experimentation and observational methods. To document the physiological changes involved in sexual arousal and response, William Masters and Virginia Johnson (1961, 1966, 1970) and their research colleagues enlisted several hundred male and female volunteers. Using intricate physiological measuring devices, the researchers carefully monitored participants' bodily responses as they masturbated or engaged in sexual intercourse. Masters and Johnson's research findings are hailed as a major contribution to our knowledge of sexual physiology. Some of their results are discussed in later sections.

Achievement
GENDER & CULTURAL DIVERSITY

A Cross-cultural Look at Sexual Behaviors

Sex researchers interested in both universalities and variations in human sexual behavior conduct cross-cultural studies of sexual practices, techniques, and attitudes (Bhugra, 2000; Beach, 1977; Brislin, 1993, 2000; Ho & Tsang, 2002; Mackay, 2001). Their studies of different societies put sex in a broader perspective and help counteract *ethnocentrism*, the tendency people have to judge their own cultural practices as "normal" and preferable to those of other groups.

For example, do you know that kissing is unpopular in Japan and unknown among some cultures in Africa and South America? Do you find it strange that Apinaye women in Brazil often bite off pieces of their mate's eyebrows as a natural part of sexual foreplay (Goldstein, 1976)? Does it surprise you that members of Tiwi society, off the northern coast of Australia, believe that young girls will not develop breasts or menstruate unless they first experience intercourse (Goodall, 1971)? Or that, the men and women of the Amazonian Yanomamo routinely wear nothing but a thin cord around their waists? But if you were to ask a Yanomamo woman to remove the cord, she would respond in much the same way an American woman would if you asked her to remove her blouse (Miracle, Miracle, & Baumeister, 2003). Furthermore, the Sambia of New Guinea believe that young boys must swallow semen to achieve manhood (Herdt, 1981). Adolescent boys in Mangaia, a small island in the South Pacific, routinely undergo superincision, a painful initiation rite in which the foreskin of the penis is slit and folded back (Marshall, 1971). Figure 29.4 gives other examples of cultural variation in sexuality.

Although other cultures' practices may seem unnatural and strange to us, we forget that our own sexual rituals may appear equally curious to others. If the description of the Mangaian practice of superincision bothered you, how do you feel about our culture's routine circumcision of infant boys? Before you object that infant circumcision in the United States is "entirely different" and "medically safe and necessary," you might want to consider the position now taken by the American Academy of Pediatrics (AAP). In 1999, they decided the previously reported medical benefits of circumcision were so statistically small that the procedure should *not* be routinely

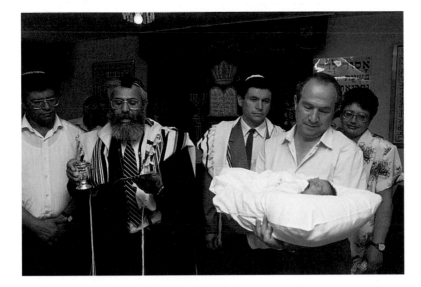

Circumcision and religion. Although circumcision is an important part of some religions, it is relatively rare in most parts of the world.

performed. The AAP does consider it legitimate for parents to take into account cultural, religious, and ethnic traditions in deciding whether to circumcise their sons.

If the controversy over infant male circumcision surprises you, so, too, may information about female genital mutilation. Throughout history and even today, in parts of Africa, the Middle East, and Asia, young girls undergo several types of *female genital mutilation* (FGM), including circumcision (removal of the clitoral hood), *clitoridectomy* (removal of the clitoris), and *genital infibulation* (removal of the clitoris and labia and stitching together the remaining tissue to allow only a small opening for urine and menstrual flow) (Dandash, Refaat, & Eyada, 2001; El-Gibaly et al., 2002; Whitehorn, Ayonrinde, & Maingay, 2002). In most countries, the surgeries are performed on girls between ages 4 and 10 and often without anesthesia or antiseptic conditions (Abusharaf, 1998; McCormack, 2001). The young girls suffer numerous health problems because of these practices — the most serious from genital infibulation. Risks include severe pain, bleeding, chronic infection, and menstrual difficulties. As adults, these women frequently experience serious childbirth complications or infertility.

What is the purpose of these procedures? The main objective is to ensure virginity before marriage (Orubuloge & Caldwell, 1997). Without these procedures, young

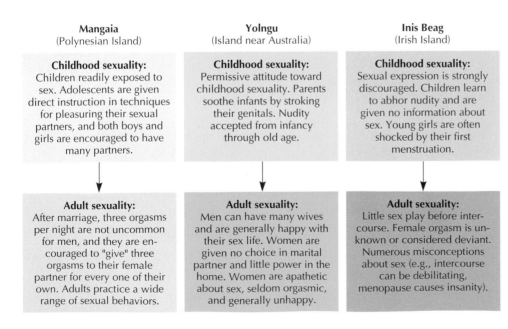

Mangaia (Polynesian Island)	Yolngu (Island near Australia)	Inis Beag (Irish Island)
Childhood sexuality: Children readily exposed to sex. Adolescents are given direct instruction in techniques for pleasuring their sexual partners, and both boys and girls are encouraged to have many partners.	**Childhood sexuality:** Permissive attitude toward childhood sexuality. Parents soothe infants by stroking their genitals. Nudity accepted from infancy through old age.	**Childhood sexuality:** Sexual expression is strongly discouraged. Children learn to abhor nudity and are given no information about sex. Young girls are often shocked by their first menstruation.
Adult sexuality: After marriage, three orgasms per night are not uncommon for men, and they are encouraged to "give" three orgasms to their female partner for every one of their own. Adults practice a wide range of sexual behaviors.	**Adult sexuality:** Men can have many wives and are generally happy with their sex life. Women are given no choice in marital partner and little power in the home. Women are apathetic about sex, seldom orgasmic, and generally unhappy.	**Adult sexuality:** Little sex play before intercourse. Female orgasm is unknown or considered deviant. Numerous misconceptions about sex (e.g., intercourse can be debilitating, menopause causes insanity).

Figure 29.4 *Cross-cultural differences in sexual behavior.* Note: "Inis Beag" is a pseudonym used to protect the privacy of residents of this Irish island. *Sources:* Crooks & Baur, 2002; Ford & Beach, 1951; Marshall, 1971; Messenger, 1971; Miracle, Miracle, & Baumeister, 2003; Money et al., 1991.

girls are considered unmarriageable and without status. As you may imagine, these practices create serious culture clashes. For example, physicians in Western societies are currently being asked by immigrant parents to perform these operations on their daughters. What should the doctor do? Should this practice be forbidden? Or would this be another example of ethnocentrism?

As you can see, it is a complex issue. Canada was the first nation to recognize female genital mutilation as a basis for granting refugee status (Crooks & Baur, 2002), and the United Nations has suspended its regular policy of nonintervention in the cultural practices of nations. The World Health Organization (WHO) and the United Nations International Children's Emergency Fund (UNICEF) have both issued statements opposing female genital mutilation and have developed programs to combat this and other harmful practices affecting the health and well-being of women and children.

*A*ssessment

CHECK & REVIEW

The Study of Human Sexuality

Although sex has always been an important part of human interest, motivation, and behavior, it received little scientific attention before the twentieth century. Havelock Ellis was among the first to study human sexuality despite the repression and secrecy of nineteenth-century Victorian times.

Alfred Kinsey and his colleagues were the first to conduct large-scale, systematic surveys and interviews of the sexual practices and preferences of Americans during the 1940s and 1950s. The research team of William Masters and Virginia Johnson pioneered the use of actual laboratory measurement and observation of human physiological response during sexual activity. Cultural studies are also important sources of scientific information on human sexuality.

Questions

1. During earlier times, it was believed that _____ led to blindness, impotence, acne, and insanity, whereas _____ caused brain damage and death. (a) female orgasms, male orgasms; (b) masturbation, nocturnal emissions; (c) menstruation, menopause; (d) oral sex, sodomy
2. Match the following researchers with their contributions to the study of human sexuality:
   a. Havelock Ellis _____ Based his/their groundbreaking research into human sexuality on personal diaries
   b. William Masters and Virginia Johnson _____ Popularized the use of the survey method in studying human sexuality
   c. Alfred Kinsey _____ Pioneered the use of direct observation and physiological measurement of bodily responses during sexual activities
3. What are the advantages of cultural studies in sex research?
4. Viewing one's own ethnic group (or culture) as central and "correct" and then judging the rest of the world according to this standard is known as _____. (a) standardization; (b) stereotyping; (c) discrimination; (d) ethnocentrism

Answers to Questions can be found in Appendix B.

MODULE 29 ACTIVE LEARNING WORKSHEET

Fill-in the missing blanks, and then compare your answers with those in Appendix B.

1. A transsexual has trouble with his or her _____, whereas a transvestite _____.

2. When asked on a form to identify your "sex," the questioner wants to know _____, whereas "gender" refers to _____.

3. Gender identity refers to _____, whereas gender role encompasses_____.

4. According to research, the two most important gender differences between males and females are in the areas of _____ and _____.

5. Expressing both masculine and feminine traits is known as _____.

MODULE 30
SEXUAL BEHAVIOR AND PROBLEMS

Are women and men fundamentally alike in their sexual responses? Or are they unalterably different? What causes a gay or lesbian sexual orientation? What is sexual prejudice? These are some of the questions we will explore in this section.

■ Sexual Arousal and Response: Gender Differences and Similarities

To understand differences and similarities in male and female sexual behavior, it helps to begin with Masters and Johnson's (1966) four-stage **sexual response cycle** (Figure 30.1):

Stage 1: In the **excitement phase,** which can last from a few minutes to several hours, arousal is initiated through physical factors, such as touching or being touched, or through psychological factors, such as fantasy or erotic stimuli. During this stage, heart rate and respiration increase and blood flows to the pelvic region, causing engorgement of the penis and clitoris. Both men and women may have nipples becoming erect, and both may experience a *sex flush,* or reddening of the upper torso and face.

Stage 2: If stimulation continues, the **plateau phase** begins and heartbeat, respiration rate, and blood pressure continue at a high level. In the man, the penis becomes more engorged and erect while the testes swell and pull up closer to the body. In the woman, the clitoris pulls up under the clitoral hood and the entrance to the vagina contracts while the uterus rises slightly. This movement of the uterus causes the upper two-thirds of the vagina to balloon, or expand. As arousal reaches its peak, both sexes may experience a feeling that orgasm is imminent and inevitable.

Assessment

How are men and women alike and different in sexual arousal and response? What is the latest research on sexual orientation?

Sexual Response Cycle *Masters and Johnson's description of the four-stage bodily response to sexual arousal, which consists of excitement, plateau, orgasm, and resolution*

Excitement Phase *First stage of the sexual response cycle, characterized by increasing levels of arousal and increased engorgement of the genitals*

Plateau Phase *Second stage of the sexual response cycle, characterized by a leveling off in a state of high arousal*

Figure 30.1 *Masters and Johnson's sexual response cycle.* One way to visualize (and remember) the four stages of the sexual response cycle is to compare it to diving off a high diving board. During the *excitement phase* (climbing up the ladder), both men and women become progressively more aroused and excited, resulting in penile and clitoral erection, and vaginal lubrication in women. In the *plateau phase* (walking across the diving board), sexual and physiological arousal continue at a heightened state. The *orgasm phase* (jumping off the diving board) involves rhythmic muscle contractions in both men and women and ejaculation of sperm by men. During the final *resolution phase* (resting and swimming back to the edge), physiological responses return to normal. Note, however, that this is a simplified description that does not account for individual variation. It should *not* be used to judge what's "normal."

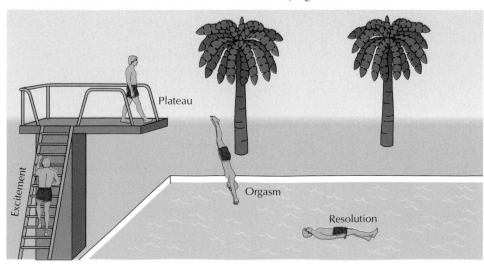

Orgasm Phase *Third stage of the sexual response cycle when pleasurable sensations peak and orgasm occurs*

Resolution Phase *Final stage of the sexual response cycle when the body returns to its unaroused state*

Refractory Period *Phase following orgasm during which further orgasm is considered physiologically impossible*

Stage 3: During the **orgasm phase,** the individual experiences a highly intense and pleasurable release of tension. In the woman, muscles around the vagina squeeze the vaginal walls in and out and the uterus pulsates. Muscles at the base of the penis contract in the man, causing *ejaculation,* the discharge of semen or seminal fluid.

Stage 4: Both male and female bodies gradually return to their preexcitement state during the **resolution phase.** After one orgasm, most men enter a **refractory period,** during which further excitement to orgasm is considered impossible. Many women (and some men), however, are capable of multiple orgasms in fairly rapid succession.

Achievement
GENDER & CULTURAL DIVERSITY

Are There Evolutionary Advantages to Female Nonmonogamy?

In many ways, women and men are similar in their general sexual responses. But it is our differences that attract the most attention. For example, have you heard that men have more sexual drive, interest, and activity than women do? How do scientists investigate such a common belief? There are two major perspectives — evolutionary and social role.

The *evolutionary perspective,* emphasizing the adaptive value of behaviors, suggests that sexual differences (such as men having more sexual partners) evolved from ancient mating patterns that helped the species survive (Buss, 1989, 1999, 2000; Chuang, 2002; Fischman, 2000; Mathes, King, Miller, & Reed, 2002; Schmitt et al., 2001). According to this *sexual strategies theory* (SST), men have a greater interest in sex and multiple partners and are sexually jealous and controlling because these behaviors maximize their chances for reproduction. Women, on the other hand, seek a good protector and provider to increase their chances for survival, as well as that of their offspring. Ultimately, both male and female strategies serve to pass along their genes and ensure the survival of the species.

Although this particular interpretation of the evolutionary perspective suggests that only men have a biological advantage in having multiple sex partners, it is important to note that in at least 18 societies around the world it is *female nonmonogamy* (women having multiple sex partners) that offers survival value to women and children (Beckerman et al., 1999). People in these cultures believe in *partible paternity* (one child having more than one biological father), and pregnant women openly acknowledge their extramarital lovers as "secondary fathers."

This belief that multiple men contribute to the initial impregnation and later "building of the child" seems to benefit both the pregnant woman and her children. Among the Bari of Venezuela and Colombia, Beckerman and his colleagues found that pregnant women with lovers were less likely to miscarry, possibly because of courtship gifts that boosted their nutrition. In addition, 80 percent of children with "extra" fathers lived to age 15, in contrast to 64 percent of children with lone dads.

In contrast to the evolutionary perspective with its biological emphasis, the *social role approach* suggests that gender differences in sexual behavior result from the roles that men and women internalize from their society (Eagly, 1997; Megarry, 2001). For instance, in traditional cultural divisions of labor, women are child bearers and homemakers whereas men are providers and protectors. But as women gain more reproductive freedom and educational opportunities, they also acquire more personal resources and status through means other than mates.

This hypothesis is directly supported by a reanalysis of Buss's original data collected from 37 cultures (Buss et al., 1990). Kasser and Sharma (1999) found that women did indeed prefer resource-rich men, but only when the women lived in cultures with little reproductive freedom and education equality. Therefore, say Kasser and Sharma, the conflict between the evolutionary and social role perspectives may be resolved by examining patriarchal cultural systems that limit women's choices.

If strong patriarchies existed during the Pleistocene epoch, enough time may have passed for psychological mechanisms to evolve in reaction to such environments (Smuts, 1995). If, however, patriarchy emerged only in the past 10,000 years, with the advent of agriculture (Miller & Fishkin, 1997), the time span is too short for evolutionary changes, and the social role explanation may be the best. Kasser and Sharma's theory is intriguing, but further research is necessary.

Sexual Orientation: Contrasting Theories and Myths

What causes homosexuality? What causes heterosexuality? Many have asked the first question, but few have asked the second. As a result, the roots of sexual orientation are poorly understood. However, research has identified several widespread myths and misconceptions about homosexuality (Bell, Weinberg, & Hammersmith, 1981; Fone, 2000; Lamberg, 1998; Mitchell, 2002; Parks, 1998). Every one of the following popular beliefs is false:

- *Seduction theory.* Gays and lesbians were seduced as children by adults of their own sex.

- *"By default" myth.* Gays and lesbians were unable to attract partners of the other sex or had unhappy heterosexual experiences.

- *Poor parenting theory.* Sons become gay because of domineering mothers and weak fathers, whereas daughters become lesbians because their fathers were their primary role model.

- *Modeling theory.* Children raised by gay and lesbian parents usually end up adopting their parents' sexual orientation.

It is important to remember that all of these popular beliefs have been shown to be *false* and that the causes of sexual orientation are still unknown. At this point, however, most studies suggest that genetics and biology play the dominant role in sexual orientation (Bailey, Dunne, Martin, 2000; Cantor, Blanchard, Paterson, & Bogaert, 2002; Hamer & Copeland, 1999; Williams et al., 2000).

For example, a genetic predisposition toward homosexuality is supported by studies on identical male and female twins, fraternal twins, and adopted siblings (Kirk, Bailey, Dunne, & Martin, 2000; Pillard & Bailey, 1995). These studies found that if one identical twin was gay, about 48 to 65 percent of the time so was the second twin. (Note that if the cause were totally genetic, the percentage would be 100.) The rate for fraternal twins was 26 to 30 percent and 6 to 11 percent for adopted brothers or sisters. Estimates of homosexuality in the general population run between 2 and 10 percent.

Some researchers have also hypothesized that prenatal hormone levels affect fetal brain development and sexual orientation. Animal experiments have found that administering male hormones prenatally can cause female sheep and rats to engage in the mounting behavior associated with male sheep and rats (Bagermihl, 1999). Because it is obviously unethical to experiment with human fetuses, we cannot come to any meaningful conclusions about the effect of hormones on fetal development. Furthermore, no well-controlled study has ever found a difference in adult hormone levels between heterosexuals and gays and lesbians (Banks & Gartrell, 1995; Le Vay, 1996).

Hate crimes. The vicious beating and murder of Matthew Shepard in 1998 is a tragic reminder of the costs of sexual prejudice.

Fighting back against sexual prejudice.
These protesters are working to increase
public awareness and acceptance of different
sexual orientations.

Sexual Prejudice *Negative attitudes*
toward an individual because of her or his
sexual orientation

Although the origin of sexual orientation remains a mystery, the fact of being gay or lesbian brings certain difficulties and challenges. Many gays and lesbians endure verbal and physical attacks; disrupted family and peer relationships; and high rates of anxiety, depression, and suicide (Fone, 2000; Fineran, 2002; Herek, 2000; Lock & Steiner, 1999; Tomsen & Mason, 2001).

Some of the hostility supposedly stems from an irrational fear of homosexuality in oneself or others, which Martin Weinberg labeled *homophobia* in the late 1960s. However, this term is too limited and not scientifically acceptable: It implies that antigay attitudes are limited to individual irrationality and pathology. Psychologist Gregory Herek (2000) proposes the term **sexual prejudice** instead, to emphasize multiple causes and to allow researchers to draw on the rich scientific research on prejudice.

Despite the acknowledgment in 1973 by both the American Psychiatric Association and the American Psychological Association that homosexuality is not a mental illness, it continues to be a divisive societal issue in the United States. Seeing *sexual prejudice* as a socially reinforced phenomenon rather than an individual pathology, coupled with political action by gays and lesbians, may help fight discrimination and hate crimes.

Assessment

CHECK & REVIEW

Sexual Behavior

William Masters and Virginia Johnson identified a four-stage **sexual response cycle** during sexual activity — *excitement, plateau, orgasm,* and *resolution.* There are numerous similarities and differences between the sexes, but differences are the focus of most research. According to the *evolutionary perspective,* men engage in more sexual behaviors with more sexual partners because it helps the species survive. The *social role approach* suggests this difference results from traditional cultural divisions of labor.

Although researchers have identified several myths concerning the causes of homosexuality, the origins remain a puzzle. In recent studies, the genetic and biological explanation has gained the strongest support. Despite increased understanding, sexual orientation remains a divisive issue in the United States.

Questions

1. Briefly describe the four stages of Masters and Johnson's sexual response cycle.
2. How do the evolutionary and social role perspectives explain male and female differences in sexual behavior?
3. The genetic influence on sexual orientation has been supported by research reporting that _____.
   a. between identical twins, if one brother is gay, the other brother has a 52 percent chance of also being gay
   b. gay men have fewer chromosomal pairs than straight men, whereas lesbians have larger areas of the hypothalamus than straight women
   c. between adoptive pairs of brothers, if one brother is gay, the other brother has an increased chance of also being gay
   d. parenting style influences adult sexual orientation for men but not for women
4. A homosexual orientation appears to be the result of _____.
   a. seduction during childhood or adolescence by an older homosexual
   b. a family background that includes a dominant mother and a passive, detached father
   c. a hormonal imbalance
   d. unknown factors

Answers to Questions can be found in Appendix B.

■ Sexual Problems: Dysfunction and Disease

When we are functioning well sexually, we tend to take this part of our lives for granted. But what happens when things don't go smoothly? Why does normal sexual functioning stop for some people and never begin for others? What are the major diseases that can be spread through sexual behavior? We will explore these questions in the following section.

Sexual Dysfunction

There are many forms of **sexual dysfunction,** or difficulty in sexual functioning, and their causes are complex (Figure 30.2). In this section, we will discuss how biology, psychology, and social forces (the *biopsychosocial model*) all contribute to sexual difficulties.

Biological Factors   Although many people may consider it unromantic, a large part of sexual arousal and behavior is clearly the result of biological processes (Beauregard, Levesgue, & Bourgouin, 2001; Karama et al., 2002; Meston, 2000). *Erectile dysfunction* (the inability to get or maintain an erection firm enough for intercourse) and *orgasmic dysfunction* (the inability to respond to sexual stimulation to the point of orgasm) often reflect medical conditions such as diabetes, alcoholism, hormonal deficiencies, circulatory problems, and reactions to certain prescription and non-prescription drugs. Hormones also affect sexual drives and behaviors. Testosterone has a clear effect on sex-

Assessment

What factors contribute to sexual dysfunction and sexually transmitted diseases?

Sexual Dysfunction *Impairment of the normal physiological processes of arousal and orgasm*

Figure 30.2 *Sexual problems.* Although sex therapists typically divide sexual dysfunctions into "male," "female," or "both," problems should never be considered "his" or "hers." Couples are almost always encouraged to work together to find solutions. For more information, check www.goaskalice.columbia.edu/Cat6.html. *Sources:* Adapted from Crooks & Baur, 2002; Masters et al., 1995; Miracle, Miracle, & Baumeister, 2003.

Male ♂		Female ♀		Both Male ♂ and Female ♀	
Disorder	**Causes**	**Disorder**	**Causes**	**Disorder**	**Causes**
Erectile dysfunction (impotence) Inability to have (or maintain) an erection firm enough for intercourse *Primary erectile dysfunction* Lifetime erectile problems *Secondary erectile dysfunction* Erection problems occurring in at least 25 percent of sexual encounters	**Physical** — diabetes, circulatory conditions, heart disease, drugs, extreme fatigue, alcohol consumption, hormone deficiencies **Psychological** — performance anxiety, guilt, difficulty in expressing desires to partner, severe antisexual upbringing	**Orgasmic dysfunction** (anorgasmia, frigidity) Inability or difficulty in reaching orgasm *Primary orgasmic dysfunction* Lifetime history of no orgasm *Secondary orgasmic dysfunction* Regularly orgasmic, but no longer is *Situational orgasmic dysfunction* Orgasms occur only under certain circumstances	**Physical** — chronic illness, diabetes, extreme fatigue, drugs, alcohol consumption, hormone deficiencies, pelvic disorders, lack of appropriate or adequate stimulation **Psychological** — fear of evaluation, poor body image, relationship problems, guilt, anxiety, severe antisexual upbringing, difficulty in expressing desires to partner, prior sexual trauma, childhood sexual abuse	**Dyspareunia** Painful intercourse	**Primarily physical** — irritations, infections, or disorders of the internal or external genitals
				Inhibited sexual desire (sexual apathy) Avoids sexual relations due to disinterest	**Physical** — hormone deficiencies, alcoholism, drug use, chronic illness **Psychological** — depression, prior sexual trauma, relationship problems, anxiety
Premature ejaculation Rapid ejaculation beyond the man's control; partner is non-orgasmic in at least 50 percent of their intercourse episodes	**Almost always psychological** — because of guilt, fear of discovery while masturbating, and hurried experiences in cars or motels, man learns to ejaculate as quickly as possible	**Vaginismus** Involuntary spasms of the vagina and penile insertion is impossible or difficult and painful	**Primarily psychological** — learned association of pain or fear with intercourse, due to prior sexual trauma, severe antisexual upbringing, guilt, or lack of lubrication	**Sexual aversion** Avoids sex due to overwhelming fear or anxiety	**Psychological** — severe parental sex attitudes, prior sex trauma, partner pressure, gender identity confusion

ual desire in both men and women, but otherwise, the precise role of hormones in human sexual behavior is not well understood.

In addition to problems resulting from medical conditions and hormones, sexual responsiveness also is affected by the spinal cord and sympathetic nervous system. As discussed in Module 5, some aspects of human behavior are reflexive — that is, unlearned, automatic, and occurring without conscious effort or motivation. Sexual arousal for both men and women is partially reflexive and somewhat analogous to simple reflexes like the eye blink response to a puff of air. Just as the puff of air produces an automatic closing of the eye, certain stimuli, such as stroking of the genitals, can lead to automatic arousal in both men and women. In both situations, nerve impulses from the receptor site travel to the spinal cord, which responds by sending messages to target organs or glands. Normally the blood flow into organs and tissues through the arteries is balanced by an equal outflow through the veins. During sexual arousal, however, the arteries dilate beyond the capacity of the veins to carry the blood away. This results in erection of the penis in men and an engorged clitoris and surrounding tissue in women.

If this is so automatic, why do some people have difficulty getting aroused? Unlike simple reflexes such as the eye blink, negative thoughts or high emotional states may block sexual arousal. Recall from Module 5 that the autonomic nervous system (ANS) is intricately involved in emotional (and sexual) responses. The ANS is composed of two subsystems: the sympathetic, which prepares the body for "fight or flight," and the parasympathetic, which maintains bodily processes at a steady, even balance. The sympathetic branch is dominant during initial excitement; however, sustained arousal (the plateau phase) requires parasympathetic dominance, while the sympathetic branch dominates during ejaculation and orgasm.

Can you see why the parasympathetic branch *must* be in control during arousal? The body needs to be relaxed enough to allow blood to flow to the genital area. This helps explain why young women often have difficulty with sexual arousal and orgasm. The secretive and forbidden conditions of many early sexual experiences create strong anxieties and fear of discovery, fear of loss of respect, and fear of unwanted pregnancy. Many women discover that they need locked doors, committed relationships, and reliable birth control to enjoy sexual relations.

What about men?   Most men also prefer privacy, commitment, and freedom from pregnancy concerns. But as you can see in Table 30.1, relationship status has less of an effect on male orgasms than it does on female orgasms. Apparently, women relax more under these conditions, which allows them to stay in arousal and parasympathetic dominance long enough for orgasm to occur.

Most couples recognize that both sexes have difficulty with arousal if they drink too much alcohol, or when they are stressed, ill, or fatigued. But one of the least recognized blocks of sexual arousal is **performance anxiety,** the fear of being judged in connection with sexual activity. Men commonly experience problems with erections (especially after drinking alcohol) and wonder if their "performance" will satisfy their partner, whereas women frequently worry about their attractiveness and orgasms. Can you see how these performance fears can lead to sexual problems?

Performance Anxiety *Fear of being judged in connection with sexual activity*

TABLE 30.1 SEX AND RELATIONSHIPS

Men ♂	Women ♀	Always or Usually Have an Orgasm with Partner
94%	62%	Dating
95%	68%	Living together
95%	75%	Married

Source: Laumann, Gagnon, Michael, & Michaels, 1994.

"Now, that's product placement!"

Once again, increased anxiety causes the sympathetic nervous system to dominate, which blocks blood flow to the genitals.

Psychological and Social Influences Our bodies may be biologically prepared to become aroused and respond to erotic stimulation, but psychological and social forces also play a role. As we have just seen, fear of evaluation and the consequences of sexual activity are learned, psychological factors that contribute to both male and female sexual dysfunction. *Gender role training*, the *double standard*, and *sexual scripts* are also important social influences.

Gender role socialization begins at birth and continually impacts all aspects of our life, as the story of "Brenda/David" from the beginning of this section shows. Can you imagine how traditional male gender roles — being dominant, aggressive, independent — could lead to different kinds of sexual thoughts and behaviors than traditional female gender roles — being submissive, passive, and dependent? Under this type of gender role training, men are encouraged to explore their sexuality and bring a certain level of sexual knowledge into the relationship, whereas women are expected to stop male advances and refrain from sexual activity until marriage.

Although overt examples of this **double standard** are less evident in modern times, covert or hidden traces of this belief still exist. After examining the gender dif-

Double Standard *Beliefs, values, and norms that subtly encourage male sexuality and discourage female sexuality*

Figure 30.3 *What men and women want.* When asked what they wish they had more of in their sexual relationships, men tended to emphasize activities, whereas women focused more on emotions and the relationship. *Source:* Based on Hatfield & Rapson, 1996, p. 142.

Dating Couples

Men Wish Their Partners Would:
Be more experimental
Initiate sex more often
Try more oral-genital sex
Give more instructions
Be warmer and more involved

Women Wish Their Partners Would:
Talk more lovingly
Be more seductive
Be warmer and more involved
Give more instructions
Be more complimentary

Married Couples

Men Wish Their Partners Would:
Be more seductive
Initiate sex more often
Be more experimental
Be wilder and sexier
Give more instructions

Women Wish Their Partners Would:
Talk more lovingly
Be more seductive
Be more complimentary
Give more instructions
Be warmer and more involved

ferences in Figure 30.3, can you see how items like men wanting women to "initiate sex more often" or women wanting men "to talk more lovingly" might be related to the double standard?

In addition to gender role training and the related double standard, we also learn explicit **sexual scripts** that teach us "what to do, when, where, how, and with whom" (Gagnon, 1990). During the 1950s, societal messages said the "best" sex was at night, in a darkened room, with a man on top and a woman on the bottom. Today, the messages are more bold and varied, partly because of media portrayals. Compare, for example, the sexual scripts portrayed in Figure 30.4.

Sexual scripts, gender roles, and the double standard may all be less rigid today, but a major difficulty remains. Many people and sexual behaviors do not fit society's scripts and expectations. Furthermore, we often "unconsciously" internalize societal messages and then fail to realize how they affect our values and behaviors. For example, modern men and women generally say they want equality, yet both may feel more comfortable if the woman is a virgin and the man has had many partners. Sex therapy

Sexual Scripts *Socially dictated descriptions of "appropriate" behaviors for sexual interactions*

Figure 30.4 *Changing sexual scripts.* (a, b) Television and movies in the 1950s and 1960s allowed only older married couples to be shown in a bedroom setting (and only in long pajamas and separate twin-size beds). Contrast this with today, where very young, unmarried couples are commonly portrayed in one bed, seemingly nude, and engaging in various stages of intercourse. (c, d) Note the change in body postures and clothing in these beach scenes from the 1960s and today.

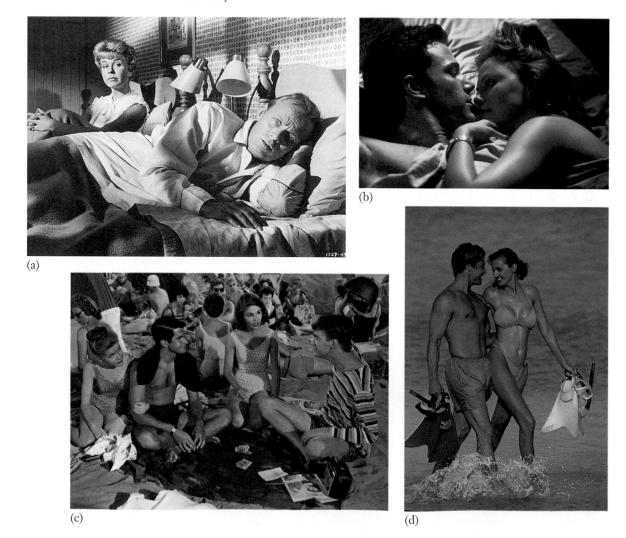

TABLE 30.2 SEXUAL EFFECTS OF COMMONLY ABUSED AND ILLICIT DRUGS

Drugs	Effects
Alcohol	Moderate to high doses inhibit arousal. Chronic abuse causes damage to testes, ovaries, and the circulatory and nervous systems
Tobacco	Decreases blood flow to the genitals, thereby reducing the frequency and duration of erections and vaginal lubrication
Cocaine and Amphetamines	Moderate to high doses and chronic use result in inhibition of orgasm and decrease in erection and lubrication
Barbiturates	Cause decreased desire, erectile disorders, and delayed orgasm

Source: Abadinsky, 2001; Miracle, Miracle, & Baumeister, 2003; Tengs & Osgood, 2001; Wetterling et al., 1999.

encourages partners to examine and sometimes modify inappropriate sexual scripts, gender roles, and beliefs in the double standard.

How do therapists work with sex problems? Clinicians usually begin with interviews and examinations to determine whether the problem is organic, psychological, or, more likely, a combination of both (Donahey & Miller, 2000; Knoll & Abrams, 1998; McCarthy, 2002). Organic causes of sexual dysfunction include medical conditions (such as diabetes mellitus and heart disease) medications (such as antidepressants), and drugs (such as alcohol and tobacco — see Table 30.2). Erectile disorders are the problems most likely to have an organic component. In 1998, a medical treatment for erectile problems, *Viagra*, quickly became the fastest-selling prescription drug in U.S. history. Other medications for both men and women are currently being tested — but they are not the answer to all sexual problems (Bancroft, 2002; Rosen, 2002; O'Sullivan, 2002; Winton, 2001).

Years ago, the major psychological treatment for sexual dysfunction was long-term psychoanalysis, based on the assumption that sexual problems resulted from deep-seated conflicts that originated in childhood. During the 1950s and 1960s, behavior therapy was introduced; it was based on the idea that sexual dysfunction was learned. (See Module 44 for a more complete description of both psychoanalysis and behavior therapy.) It wasn't until the early 1970s and the publication of Masters and Johnson's *Human Sexual Inadequacy* that sex therapy gained national recognition. Because the model that Masters and Johnson developed is still popular and used by many sex therapists, we will use it as our example of how sex therapy is conducted.

Masters and Johnson's Sex Therapy Program Masters and Johnson's approach is founded on four major principles:

1. *A relationship focus.* Unlike forms of therapy that focus on the individual, Masters and Johnson's sex therapy focuses on the relationship between two people. To counteract any blaming tendencies, each partner is considered fully involved and affected by sexual problems. Both partners are taught positive communication and conflict resolution skills.

2. *An integration of physiological and psychosocial factors.* Because medication and many physical disorders can cause or aggravate sexual dysfunctions, Masters and Johnson emphasize the importance of medical histories and exams. They also explore psychosocial factors, such as how the couple first learned about sex and their current attitudes, gender role training, and sexual scripts.

Experiments in sex? *William Masters and Virginia Johnson were the first researchers to use direct laboratory experimentation and observation to study human sexuality.*

TRY THIS

YOURSELF

Application

If you would like to improve your own or your children's current or future sexual functioning, sex therapists would recommend the following:

- *Begin sex education as early as possible.* Children should be given positive feelings about their bodies and an opportunity to discuss sexuality in an open, honest fashion.
- *Avoid goal- or performance-oriented approaches.* Therapists often remind clients that there really is no "right" way to have sex. When couples or individuals attempt to

judge or evaluate their sexual lives or to live up to others' expectations, they risk making sex a *job* rather than pleasure.

- *Communicate openly with your partner.* Mind reading belongs onstage, not in the bedroom. Partners need to tell each other what feels good and what doesn't, and sexual problems should be openly discussed without blame, anger, or defensiveness. If the problem does not improve within a reasonable time, consider professional therapy.

Achievement

RESEARCH HIGHLIGHT

Is Cybersex Harmful?

Lisa, a 42-year-old student, says:

We bought my son a new, powerful computer, and he showed me how to go online to get into chat rooms. I started to log on just to visit and chat, but I soon found my way to chat rooms, where the primary purpose was to discuss sexual fantasies. It was quite a turn-on. I was getting into these intimate discussions with all kinds of men. We talked about our sex lives and what we liked to do in bed. Then it got personal — what we'd like to do to each other. I never wanted to meet these guys face-to-face, but I started to feel like I was still having sex with them.

It all came to a head when my husband saw one of the Internet bills and freaked — it was over $500 for the month. I had to explain the whole thing to him. He felt like I had cheated on him and considered separation, and it took several weeks to restore his trust and convince him I still loved him. I have moved the computer into my son's room, and we've started seeing a family therapist. (Personal communication cited in Blonna & Levitan, 2000, p. 584).

The Internet obviously is a great technological innovation. At school, work, and home, our computers help us work or study

online, gather valuable information, or even to recreationally "surf the Net." But, for some, the Internet can also be harmful (Carnes, 2001; Davis, 2001; Freeman-Longo, 2000; McGrath & Casey, 2002). A survey among 18–64-year-old self-identified cybersex participants found several problems associated with their online sexual activities (Schneider, 2000). For example, two women with no prior history of interest in sadomasochistic sex discovered this type of behavior online and came to prefer it. Others in the survey reported increased problems with depression, social isolation, career loss or decreased job performance, financial consequences, and, in some cases, legal difficulties.

Like Lisa, some Internet users also use cyberspace chat rooms and email to secretly communicate with an intimate other, or as outlets for sexual desires they're unwilling to expose or discuss with their partners. Although these secret liaisons may be exciting, sex therapists are finding that this behavior often leads to a worsening of the participants' relationships with spouses or partners and serious harm to their marriages or primary relationships. "Cybercheating," like traditional infidelity or adultery, erodes trust and connection with the spouse or partner, while the ongoing secrecy, lying, and fan-

tasies increase attraction to the "virtual" relationship (Gwinnell, 2001; Kuriansky, 1998).

What do you think? Does sex require physical contact to count as an "affair"? If you only exchange sexual fantasies with someone on the Internet, are you unfaithful? Is visiting sex sites harmful? When I ask this question in my college classes, some students consider it very harmful and eagerly talk about related relationship problems, whereas others think of it as nothing more than an X-rated movie and seem surprised that anyone would call it "cheating." I encourage them (and you) to openly discuss with their partners what they each consider unacceptable in their relationships — both online and in everyday interactions.

Before going on, I also want to mention that many people have developed healthy, lasting relationships through the Internet, and claim that they are just as intimate (or even more so) than face-to-face relationships. Others suggest that cyber-connecting can be a good rehearsal for the "real" thing. Even some sex therapists see a positive use for the Internet. They find its anonymity allows open, frank, and explicit discussions about sex, which are vital components to successful therapy. As you will see in Module 45, online sex therapy is part of the growing field of mental health therapy, called *telehealth*.

3. *An emphasis on cognitive factors.* Recognizing that many problems result from fears of performance and *spectatoring* (mentally watching and evaluating responses during sexual activities), couples are discouraged from goal setting and judging sex in terms of success or failure.

4. *An emphasis on specific behavioral techniques.* Couples are seen in an intensive 2-week counseling program. They explore their sexual values and misconceptions and practice specific behavioral exercises. "Homework assignments" usually begin with a *sensate focus* exercise in which each partner takes turns gently caressing the other and communicating what is pleasurable. There are no goals or performance demands. Later exercises and assignments are tailored to the couple's particular sex problem.

Sexually Transmitted Infections

Early sex education and open communication between partners are not only important for full sexual functioning; they are also key to avoiding and controlling sexually transmitted infections (STIs), formerly called sexually transmitted diseases (STDs), venereal disease (VD), or social diseases. *STI* is the term used to describe the disorders caused by more than 25 infectious organisms transmitted through sexual activity.

Each year, of the millions of North Americans who contract one or more STIs, a substantial majority are under age 35 (Maguen, Armistead, & Kalichman, 2000; Ross, 2002; Starkman & Rajani, 2002). Also, as Figure 30.4 shows, women are at much greater risk than men of contracting major STIs. It is extremely important for sexually active people to get medical diagnosis and treatment for any suspicious symptoms and to inform their partners. If left untreated, many STIs can cause severe problems, including infertility, ectopic pregnancy, cancer, and even death.

The good news is that most STIs are readily cured in their early stages. See Figure 30.5 for an overview of the signs and symptoms of the most common STIs. As you read through this table, remember that many infected people are *asymptomatic,* meaning lacking obvious symptoms. You can have one or more of the diseases without knowing it, and it is often impossible to tell if a sexual partner is infectious.

Although STIs such as genital warts and chlamydial infections have reached epidemic proportions (Fortenberry, 2002), **AIDS (acquired immunodeficiency syndrome)** has received the largest share of public attention. AIDS results from infection with *human immunodeficiency virus (HIV)*. A standard blood test can determine if someone is **HIV positive,** which means the individual has been infected by one or

AIDS (Acquired Immunodeficiency Syndrome) *Human immunodeficiency viruses (HIVs) destroy the immune system's ability to fight disease, leaving the body vulnerable to a variety of opportunistic infections and cancers*

HIV Positive *Being infected by the human immunodeficiency virus (HIV)*

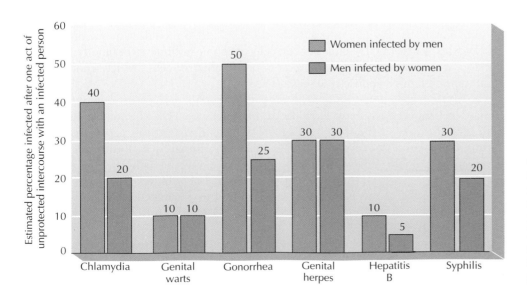

Figure 30.4 *Male-female differences in susceptibility to sexually transmitted infections (STIs).* These percentages represent the chances of infection for men and women after a single act of intercourse with an infected partner. Note that women are at much greater risk than men for four of these six STIs. This is partly because female genitals are more internal.

Figure 30.5 *Common sexually transmitted infections (STIs).* Note that you may have an STI without any of the danger signs but still acquire the complications. Seek medical attention if you suspect that you have come in contact with any of the infections! Follow all medical recommendations. This may include returning for a checkup to make sure that you are no longer infected. Take only medications prescribed by your doctor, and take all of them as directed. Don't share them. If you would like more information, check www.niaid.nih.gov/factsheets/stdinfo.htm. For information on protection from STIs, try www.safesex.org. *Sources:* Adapted from Crooks & Baur, 2002; Miracle, Miracle, & Baumeister, 2003.

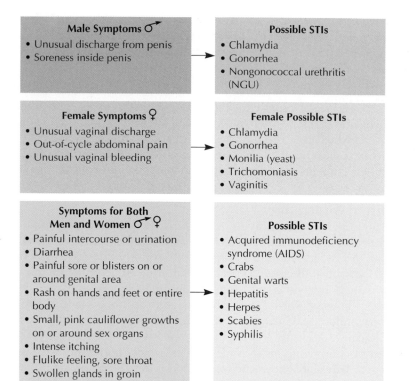

Male Symptoms ♂
- Unusual discharge from penis
- Soreness inside penis

Possible STIs
- Chlamydia
- Gonorrhea
- Nongonococcal urethritis (NGU)

Female Symptoms ♀
- Unusual vaginal discharge
- Out-of-cycle abdominal pain
- Unusual vaginal bleeding

Female Possible STIs
- Chlamydia
- Gonorrhea
- Monilia (yeast)
- Trichomoniasis
- Vaginitis

Symptoms for Both Men and Women ♂♀
- Painful intercourse or urination
- Diarrhea
- Painful sore or blisters on or around genital area
- Rash on hands and feet or entire body
- Small, pink cauliflower growths on or around sex organs
- Intense itching
- Flulike feeling, sore throat
- Swollen glands in groin

Possible STIs
- Acquired immunodeficiency syndrome (AIDS)
- Crabs
- Genital warts
- Hepatitis
- Herpes
- Scabies
- Syphilis

GET IT ON.

NATIONAL CONDOM WEEK ○ FEBRUARY 14-21
1-800-342-2437
National AIDS & STD Hotline

Safe sex is better sex. Use a condom every time.

Courtesy Pharmacist's Planning Service, Inc.

more of the HIV viruses. Being infected with the HIV virus, however, is not the same as having AIDS. AIDS is the final stage of the HIV infection process.

In the beginning of the infection process, the HIV virus replicates rapidly. It is important to know that newly infected individuals are 100 to 1,000 times more infectious than they are throughout the remainder of the disease (Royce, Sena, Cates, & Cohen, 1997). This is especially troubling because most infected people are likely to remain symptom free for months or even years, yet during this time, they can spread the disease to others — primarily through sexual contact.

As the initial HIV infection advances to AIDS, the virus progressively destroys the body's natural defenses against disease and infection. The victim's body becomes increasingly vulnerable to opportunistic infections and cancers that would not be a threat if the immune system were functioning normally. The virus may also attack the brain and spinal cord, creating severe neurological and cognitive deterioration (De Ronchi et al., 2002). The official term *full-blown AIDS* includes anyone infected with HIV who also has a CD4 count of 200 cells per cubic millimeter of blood or less. (The HIV virus destroys CD4 lymphocytes, also called T-cells, which coordinate the immune system's response to disease.)

AIDS is considered one of the most catastrophic diseases of our time. An estimated 34 million people worldwide are infected with HIV (Crooks & Baur, 2002). Recent advances in the treatment of AIDS have increased the survival time of victims, but for almost everyone, AIDS remains an ultimately fatal disorder, and some researchers doubt that a 100 percent effective vaccine will ever be developed. Despite the severity of this disease, there are signs of public complacency due to the false notion that drugs can now cure AIDS and to a reduced emphasis on prevention and education (Boyce, 2001; Vanable, Ostrow, McKirnan, Taywaditep, & Hope, 2000).

Reflecting cutbacks in AIDS education, myths are widespread. For instance, many people still believe AIDS can be transmitted through casual contact, such as a sneeze, handshake, sharing drinking glasses or towels, social kissing, sweat, or tears. Some also think it is dangerous to donate blood, and others are paranoid about gays, because male homosexuals were the first highly visible victims. All of these are false beliefs.

Infection by HIV spreads only by direct contact with bodily fluids — primarily blood, semen, and vaginal secretions. Blood *donors* are at *no* risk whatsoever. Furthermore, AIDS is not limited to the homosexual community. In fact, the AIDS epidemic is now spreading most quickly among heterosexuals, women, African Americans, Hispanics, and children (CDC, 2003).

Application

APPLYING PSYCHOLOGY TO RELATIONSHIPS

Protecting Yourself and Others Against STIs

The best hope for curtailing the HIV/AIDS epidemic is through education and behavioral change. The following "safer sex" suggestions are not intended to be moralistic — but only to help reduce your chances of contracting both HIV/AIDS and other STIs:

1. *Remain abstinent or have sex with one mutually faithful, uninfected partner.* Be selective about sexual partners and postpone physical intimacy until laboratory tests verify that you are both free of STIs.

2. *Do not use intravenous illicit drugs or have sex with someone who does.* If you use intravenous drugs, do not share needles or syringes. If you must share, use bleach to clean and sterilize your needles and syringes.

3. *Avoid contact with blood, vaginal secretions, or semen.* Using latex condoms is the best way to avoid contact. [Until recently, scientists believed condoms and spermicides with nonoxynol-9 would help prevent spread of STIs. Unfortunately, recent research shows it may increase the risk, and the World Health Organization no longer recommends its use (WHO, 2002).]

4. *Avoid anal intercourse, with or without a condom.* This is the riskiest of all sexual behaviors.

5. *Do not have sex if you or your partner are impaired by alcohol or other drugs.* The same is true for your friends. "Friends don't let friends drive [or have sex] drunk."

Application

CRITICAL THINKING | ACTIVE LEARNING

Rape Myths and Rape Prevention

Sexuality can be a source of vitality and tender bonding, but it can also be traumatizing if it becomes a forcible act against the wishes of the other. Rape can be defined as oral, anal, or vaginal penetration forced on an *unwilling, underage,* or *unconscious* victim. As clear-cut as this definition seems, many people misunderstand what constitutes rape. To test your own knowledge, answer true or false to the following:

1. Women cannot be raped against their will.
2. A man cannot be raped by a woman.
3. If you are going to be raped, you might as well relax and enjoy it.
4. All women secretly want to be raped.
5. Male sexuality is biologically overpowering and beyond a man's control.

As you might have expected, all of these statements are false. Tragically, however, these myths are believed by a large number of men and women (Bryant et al., 2001; Morry & Winkler, 2001; Reppucci, Woolard, &

Fried, 1999; Sheldon & Parent, 2002). Using your critical thinking skills, can you explain how each of the following factors might contribute to rape myths?

- Gender role conditioning
- The double standard
- Media portrayals
- Lack of information

If you would like to compare your answers to ours or would like specific information regarding rape prevention, see Appendix B.

Sexual Problems

Many people experience **sexual dysfunction.** They often fail to recognize the role of biology in both sexual arousal and response. Ejaculation and orgasm are partially reflexive. And the parasympathetic nervous system must be dominant for sexual arousal, whereas the sympathetic nervous system must dominate for orgasm to occur. Several aspects of sexual arousal and response are also learned. Early *gender role training*, the **double standard,** and **sexual scripts** teach us what to consider the "best" sex.

Many sexual problems can be helped with sex therapy. William Masters and Virginia Johnson emphasize the couple's relationship, combined physiological and psychosocial factors, cognitions, and specific behavioral techniques. Professional sex therapists offer important guidelines for everyone: Sex education should be early and positive, avoid a goal or performance orientation, and keep communication open.

The most publicized sexually transmitted infection (STI) is **AIDS (acquired immunodeficiency syndrome).** Although AIDS is transmitted only through sexual contact or exposure to infected bodily fluids, many people have irrational fears of contagion. At the same time, an estimated 1 million North Americans are **HIV positive** and therefore carriers.

Questions

1. Briefly explain the roles of the sympathetic and parasympathetic nervous systems in sexual response.
2. Sexual learning that includes "what to do, when, where, how, and with whom" is known as _____. (a) appropriate sexual behavior; (b) sexual norms; (c) sexual scripts; (d) sexual gender roles
3. What are the four principles of Masters and Johnson's sex therapy program?
4. What are five "safer sex" ways to reduce the chances of AIDS and other STIs?

Answers to Questions can be found in Appendix B.

MODULE 30   ACTIVE LEARNING WORKSHEET

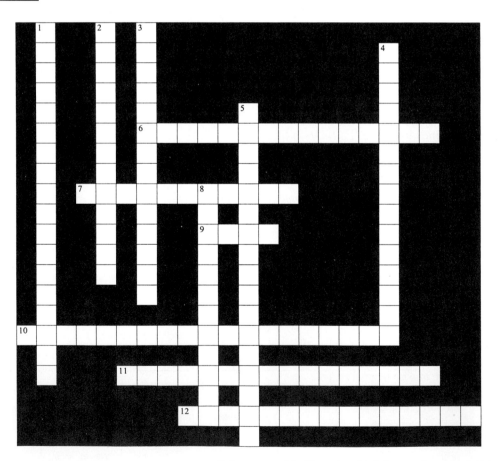

ACROSS

6 First stage of the sexual response cycle, characterized by increasing levels of arousal and increased engorgement of the genitals.

7 Third stage of the sexual response cycle when pleasurable sensations peak and orgasm occurs.

9 A catastrophic illness in which human immunodeficiency viruses (HIV) destroy the immune system's ability to fight disease, leaving the body vulnerable to a variety of opportunistic infections and cancers.

10 Masters and Johnson's description of the bodily response to sexual arousal.

11 Phase following orgasm during which further orgasm is considered physiologically impossible.

12 Final stage of the sexual response cycle when the body returns to its nonaroused state.

DOWN

1 A fear that one will be unable to meet the expectations for sexual "performance" of one's self or one's partner.

2 Socially dictated descriptions of the sequences of behavior that are considered appropriate in sexual interactions.

3 The beliefs, values, and norms that subtly encourage male sexuality and discourage female sexuality.

4 Negative attitudes toward an individual because of her or his sexual orientation.

5 Impairment of the normal physiological processes of arousal and orgasm.

8 Second stage of the sexual response cycle, characterized by a leveling off of high arousal.

Assessment
KEY TERMS

To assess your understanding of the **Key Terms** in this section, write a definition for each (in your own words), and then compare your definitions with those in the text.

Sex and Gender
androgyny
  [an-DRAW-jah nee] (p. 413)
gender (p. 406)
gender identity (p. 407)
gender role (p. 408)
sex (p. 406)
sexual orientation (p. 408)

Sexual Behavior
excitement phase (p. 419)
orgasm phase (p. 420)
plateau phase (p. 419)
refractory period (p. 420)
resolution phase (p. 420)
sexual prejudice (p. 422)
sexual response cycle (p. 419)

Sexual Problems
AIDS (acquired immunodeficiency
  syndrome) (p. 429)
double standard (p. 425)
HIV positive (p. 429)
performance anxiety (p. 424)
sexual dysfunction (p. 423)
sexual scripts (p. 426)

Achievement
WEB RESOURCES

Huffman Book Companion Site
http://www.wiley.com/college/huffman
 This site is loaded with free Interactive Self-Tests, Internet Exercises, Glossary and Flashcards for key terms, Web links, Handbook for Non-Native Speakers, and other activities designed to improve your mastery of the material in this section.

Want more general information about the field of human sexuality?
http://www.sexscience.org/
 The Society for the Scientific Study of Sexuality is an international organization dedicated to the advancement of knowledge about sexuality.

 In addition, http://www.indiana.edu/%7EKinsey/, the Kinsey Institute for research in sex, gender, and reproduction is designed to promote interdisciplinary research and assistance with an array of topics related to gender and sexuality. Another excellent web site, http://www.siecus.org/ The Sexuality Information and Education Council of the U.S. (SIECUS) is a national, nonprofit organization that develops, collects, and disseminates information, promotes comprehensive education about sexuality, and advocates the right of individuals to make responsible sexual choices.

Do you have specific sex questions not answered in these modules?
http://www.goaskalice.columbia.edu/
 Go Ask Alice! is the health question and answer Internet service produced by Columbia University Health Service. "Alice" answers questions about relationships, sexuality, sexual health, nutrition, alcohol, and general health. The stated mission of this site is to increase access to "health information by providing factual, in-depth, straightforward, and nonjudgmental information to assist readers' decision-making about their physical, sexual, emotional, and spiritual health."

Need specific information about STIs?
http://www.cdc.gov/nchstp/dstd/dstp.html
 This site offers frank, accurate details and practical information to prevent and treat STIs.

Would you like more information on gender roles and androgyny?
http://www.utdallas.edu/~waligore/digital/garvey.html
 Loosely based on the Bem Sex Role Inventory discussed in Module 29, this site features a humorous web project, entitled "Genderbender," which offers a self-administered questionnaire with scales to measure masculinity and femininity.

VISUAL SUMMARY

Gender and Human Sexuality
(Modules 29 and 30)

Sex and Gender

Definitions

Sex: Biological dimensions of maleness or femaleness, and physical activities (such as intercourse).
Gender: Psychological and sociocultural meanings of maleness and femaleness.

Gender Role Development

Gender role: Social expectations for appropriate male and female behavior.
Two major theories:

Social learning (reward, punishment, and imitation).

Cognitive Developmental (active thinking processes).

Sex and Gender Differences

Sex differences: Physical differences (like height) and brain differences (function and structure).
Gender differences: Females tend to score somewhat higher in verbal skills. Males score somewhat higher in math and are more physically aggressive.
Androgyny: Combination of masculine and feminine personality traits.

Study of Human Sexuality

Havelock Ellis
Based his research on personal diaries.

Kinsey & Colleagues
Popularized the use of surveys and interviews.

Masters and Johnson
Used direct observation and measurement of human sexual response.

Cultural Studies
Provide insight into universalities and variations in sexual behavior across cultures.

Sexual Behavior

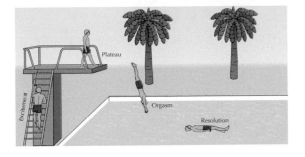

Sexual Arousal and Response

Masters and Johnson's **sexual response cycle: excitement, plateau, orgasm,** and **resolution.** There are numerous similarities of the sexes in this cycle, but differences are the focus of most research. According to the *evolutionary perspective*, males engage in more sexual behaviors with more sexual partners because it helps the species survive. The *social role approach* suggests this difference results from traditional cultural divisions of labor.

Sexual Orientation

Two major theories

Psychosocial ("disturbed family," inability to attract opposite sex, and seduction—all unsupported by research).

Genetic/biological (genetic, prenatal biasing of the brain, and brain differences).

Sexual Problems

Sexual Dysfunctions
Possible causes:

Biological: Anxiety blocks arousal. Parasympathetic nervous system must dominate for sexual arousal to occur, whereas sympathetic nervous system must dominate for orgasm to happen.

Psychological:
- Negative gender role training
- Unrealistic **sexual scripts**
- **Double standard** encourages male sexuality but discourages female's
- **Performance anxiety** created from fear of not meeting partner's sex expectations

Treatment: Masters and Johnson emphasize couple's relationship, combined physiological and psychosocial factors, cognitions, and specific behavioral techniques.

Sexually Transmitted Infections (STIs)

Most publicized STI is **AIDS.** AIDS is transmitted only through sexual contact or exposure to infected bodily fluids, but irrational fears of contagion persist. An estimated one million in the U.S. are **HIV positive** and therefore are carriers.

MOTIVATION AND EMOTION

When Wilt Chamberlain died in October 1999, he left a hole in the heart of his many fans and in the world of professional sports. His list of awards was impressive: 2 NBA championships, scoring the most points in a season (4,029), setting the record for career rebounds (23,924), 7 straight scoring titles, 11 rebound titles, and setting an NBA record by scoring 100 points in a single game against the New York Knicks (Rosenblatt, 1999).

But perhaps his most important accomplishments were leading the league in assists and never fouling out of a game. These feats speak volumes. In a world of professional sports where players attack their opponents, teammates, fans, and referees, Wilt Chamberlain made a graceful difference. He almost never got into a fight. When opposing players tripped and fell, he picked them up. He was over 7 feet tall and dominated the game, but not once did he foul out. Chamberlain appreciated the importance of civility and sportsmanship. This "gentle giant" is missed.

Coach Bobby Knight is another well-known sports figure with an impressive list of accomplishments. Knight was one of the most successful coaches in college basketball, but his success was based on intimidation and boorish behavior. Obscenity-filled shouting

▢ Achievement
▪ Assessment
▪ Application

matches and frequent temper tantrums were used to psychologically terrorize his players as well as college administrators, who continued to give him "just one more chance."

What a contrast. Chamberlain controlled his strength and temper, supported his teammates, and respected his opponents, whereas Knight bullied and abused his players, opponents, coaches, referees, administrators, reporters, and anyone else who just happened to be there (Walton, 2000). Indiana University imposed a "zero tolerance" on Coach Knight's behavior in May 2000. But a few months later, Knight allegedly grabbed and twisted the arm of a student and cursed him for not calling him "Mr. Knight" or "Coach Knight" (Leo, 2000). Apparently, this was the last straw. Indiana University fired Coach Knight on September 10, 2000.

What motivated Chamberlain to be such a joyful and gracious sportsman, despite being a top player in an extremely competitive sport? Why did Coach Knight continue to explode, despite promises to control his temper and the risk to his coaching position? Research in *motivation* and *emotion* attempts to answer such "what" and "why" questions and to explain emotional states such as joy and anger.

Motivation refers to the set of factors that activate, direct, and maintain behavior, usually toward some goal. **Emotion,** on the other hand, refers to a subjective feeling that includes arousal (heart pounding), cognitions (thoughts, values, and expectations), and expressions (smiles, frowns, and running). In other words, motivation energizes and directs behavior, whereas emotion is the "feeling" response. (Both "motivation" and "emotion" come from the Latin *movere*, "to move.")

Motivation and emotion overlap. If you saw your loved one in the arms of another, you might experience a wide variety of emotions (jealously, fear, sadness, and anger), and differing motives may determine how you act in the situation. Your desire for revenge might lead you to look for another partner, whereas your need for love and belonging might motivate you to look for ways to explain the behavior and protect your relationship. There is considerable overlap not only between motivation and emotion but also among motivation, emotion, and most areas of psychology. Moreover, recent advances in neuroscience and cognitive science have made the study of motivation and emotion one of the hot topics in science today. In this section, we will discuss some of the most recent and exciting findings, as well as classic studies in the field.

Motivation *Set of factors that activate, direct, and maintain behavior usually toward a goal*

Emotion *A subjective feeling that includes arousal (heart pounding), cognitions (thoughts, values, and expectations), and expressions (frowns, smiles, and running)*

MODULE 31
MOTIVATION

Assessment

Why do we feel hungry, search for stimulation, and need to achieve?

Research in motivation attempts to answer the "why" questions about human and animal behavior. Why do you spend hours playing a new computer game instead of studying for a major exam? Why do salmon swim upstream to spawn? Behavior results from many motives, some of which have been discussed already. For example, the need for sleep was covered in Module 14, and sexual motivation was discussed in Module 30. Aggression, altruism, and interpersonal attraction will be discussed in Modules 47 and 48. Here, we will focus on three basic motives: hunger and eating, arousal, and achievement. We will also look at the major biological and psychosocial theories that best explain general motivation — or why we do what we do.

■ Hunger and Eating: Multiple Biopsychosocial Factors

What motivates hunger? Is it your growling stomach? Or is it the sight of a juicy hamburger or the smell of a freshly baked cinnamon roll? Although hunger is obviously an internal, biological need, psychological and social forces also heavily influence it. Let's examine some of the major factors.

The Stomach

Walter B. Cannon and A. L. Washburn (1912) conducted one of the earliest experiments exploring the internal factors in hunger. In this study, Washburn swallowed a balloon and then inflated it in his stomach. His stomach contractions and subjective reports of hunger feelings were then simultaneously recorded. Because each time Washburn reported having stomach pangs (or "growling") the balloon also contracted, the researchers concluded that stomach movement caused the sensation of hunger.

What do you think was wrong with this study? As you learned in Module 2, researchers must always control for the possibility of *extraneous variables*, factors that contribute irrelevant data and confuse the results. In this case, it was later found that an empty stomach is relatively inactive and that the stomach contractions experienced by Washburn were an experimental artifact — something resulting from the presence of the balloon. Washburn's stomach had been tricked into thinking it was full and was responding by trying to digest the balloon. Sensory input from the stomach is not essential for feeling hungry, as dieters have learned when they try to "trick" their stomachs into feeling full by eating large quantities of carrots and celery and drinking lots of water. Also, humans and nonhuman animals without stomachs continue to experience hunger.

Does this mean there is no connection between the stomach and feeling hungry? Not necessarily. Receptors in the stomach and intestines detect levels of nutrients, and specialized pressure receptors in the stomach walls signal fullness or a feeling of emptiness (Woods, Schwartz, Baskin, & Seeley, 2000). Furthermore, research has shown that the stomach and other parts of the gastrointestinal tract release chemicals that play a role in hunger. These (and other) chemical signals are the topic of our next section.

Chemical Signals

As we discovered in Module 6, the brain and other parts of the body (including the stomach and other parts of the gastrointestinal tract) produce numerous neurotransmitters, hormones, enzymes, and other chemicals that affect behavior. Research in this area is complex because of the large number of known (and unknown) bodily chemicals and the interactions between them. Hunger and eating are no exception. For example, researchers have shown that glucose, insulin, cholecystokinin (CCK), adiponectin, glucagons, somatostatin, galanin, neuropeptide Y, leptin, serotonin, PPY3-36, and other bodily chemicals have an effect on hunger and *satiety* (a feeling of fullness, or satiation) (e.g., Batterham et al., 2002; Hirosumi et al., 2002; Mulligan et al., 2002; Sawaya et al., 2001; Shimizu-Albergine, Ippolito, & Beavo, 2001; Schwartz & Morton, 2002).

Let's look more closely at two of the most researched of this lengthy (and rapidly growing) list of chemicals — glucose and insulin. Research suggests that the level of *glucose* (a kind of sugar required for energy production) in the blood may be a central factor in hunger. When you've just finished a meal, your glucose level is high and you lose interest in food. Early research suggested low glucose does contribute to hunger, but people with diabetes can have high glucose levels and still be hungry. How could that be explained? Because it is not the *level* of glucose that affects feelings of hunger or satiety, but the *uptake* of glucose that determines hunger.

Thus, in addition to glucose, the body needs *insulin* (a hormone secreted by the pancreas) to uptake or extract glucose from the blood. In nondiabetic people, both glucose and insulin are normally available after food is eaten and hunger feelings are satisfied. In contrast, people with diabetes have low insulin, but when they take their insulin shots, their cells can then use the glucose from food, and they stop feeling hungry.

It's unlikely that any one chemical controls hunger and eating. Other internal factors, such as *thermogenesis* (the heat generated in response to food ingestion), also play a role (Subramanian & Vollmer, 2002). In addition, structures in the brain (our next section) also influence hunger and eating.

The Brain

As explained in Module 6, a part of the brain known as the *hypothalamus* helps regulate eating, drinking, and body temperature. Early research suggested that one area of the hypothalamus, the *lateral hypothalamus* (LH), stimulated eating and another area, the *ventromedial hypothalamus* (VMH), created feelings of satiation and signaled the animal to stop eating. When the VMH area was destroyed in rats, early researchers found that they overate to the point of extreme obesity (Figure 31.1). In contrast, when the LH area was destroyed, the animals starved to death if they were not force-fed.

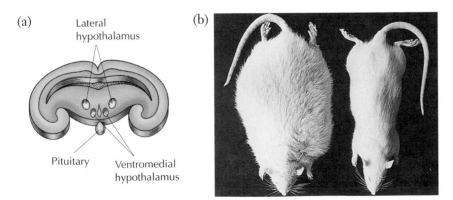

(a) Lateral hypothalamus

Pituitary   Ventromedial hypothalamus

(b)

Figure 31.1 *How the brain affects eating.* (a) This diagram shows a section of a rat's brain viewed from the front with the front half cut away. Note the positions of the ventromedial hypothalamus (VMH) and the lateral hypothalamus (LH). (b) The ventromedial area of the hypothalamus of the rat on the left was destroyed, which led to a tripling of body weight. Compare his size to that of the normal rat on the right.

Later research, however, showed that the LH and VMH areas are not simple on–off switches for eating. For example, lesions to the VMH make animals picky eaters — they reject food that doesn't taste good. Lesions also increase the secretion of insulin, which may in turn cause overeating (Challem, Berkson, Smith, & Berkson, 2000). Today, researchers know that the hypothalamus plays an important role in hunger and eating, but it is not the brain's "eating center." In fact, hunger and eating, like virtually all behavior, are influenced by numerous neural circuits, which run throughout the brain (Berthoud, 2002).

In sum, internal factors such as structures in the brain, numerous chemicals, and messages from the stomach and intestines all seem to play important roles in hunger and eating. But even all these internal factors cannot completely explain what motivates us to reach for that chocolate milkshake.

Psychosocial Factors

As you (and I) know, we often eat for many reasons that are unrelated to internal needs. For example, have you ever ordered dessert after a heavy meal just because you saw a delectable treat on a nearby table? The sight of food and other stimulus cues (such as time of day and food advertisements) act as external triggers on hunger and eating.

In addition to these cues, one of the most important social influences on when, what, where, and why we eat is cultural conditioning. North Americans, for example, tend to eat their evening meal around 6 P.M., whereas people in Spain and South America tend to eat around 10 P.M. When it comes to *what* we eat, have you ever eaten rat, dog, or horsemeat? If you are a typical North American, this might sound repulsive to you, yet most Hindus would feel a similar revulsion at the thought of eating meat from cows.

As you can see, hunger and eating are complex phenomena controlled by numerous biological, psychological, and social factors. These same biopsychosocial forces also play a role in three of our most serious eating disorders — obesity, anorexia nervosa, and bulimia nervosa.

Obesity

Obesity has reached epidemic proportions in the United States and other developed nations (Wadden, Brownell, & Foster, 2002). Well over half of all adults in the United States meet the current criteria for clinical *obesity* (having a body weight 15 percent or more above the ideal for one's height and age). Obesity is a serious and growing problem (no pun intended). It places us at increased risk for a number of medical problems, including heart disease, cancer, arthritis, diabetes, high blood pressure, strokes, and death (American Heart Association, 2003; Dundas et al., 2001; Friedman, 2002; McElroy et al., 2002). Each year billions of dollars are spent treating these health-related problems and consumers spend billions more on largely ineffective weight-loss products and services.

As you're well aware, our culture has a strong preference for thinness and an overt prejudice against being fat. How then can we explain why so many Americans are overweight? The simple answer is overeating and not enough exercise. However, obesity is more than just an imbalance between caloric intake and energy expenditure. We all know some people who can eat anything they want and still not add pounds. As we've seen earlier, this may be a result of their ability to burn calories more effectively (thermogenesis), a higher metabolic rate, and other factors. Adoption and twin studies also suggest that genes may be the culprit. Adoptive children of all weights (ranging from very thin to very obese) tend to resemble their biological parents more than their adoptive parents in body weight (Hewitt, 1997). Heritability for obesity is estimated to range between 30 and 70 percent. Unfortunately, identifying the genes for obesity is difficult. Researchers have isolated over 2,000 genes that contribute to nor-

Portion control? *Can you see why it's difficult to lose pounds or maintain a healthy weight when "I just had a muffin for breakfast" means the one on the right?*

mal and abnormal weight (Ashrafi et al., 2002; Costa, Brennen & Hochgeschwender, 2002; Devlin et al., 2000).

Is there anything that can be done to successfully lose weight? The search for a biological answer to obesity (in the form of drugs or even gene manipulation) is a multimillion-dollar industry. At the current time, however, diet and exercise remain the safest route. For Americans, this is a particularly difficult task. We are among the most sedentary peoples of all nations, and we've become accustomed to large, double (or triple) cheeseburgers, "Big Gulp" drinks, and huge servings of dessert (Lawrence, 2002; Morgan et al., 2002). Europeans are often shocked by the size of food portions in America. We've also learned that meals should be served at least three times a day (whether one is hungry or not); that "tasty" food means adding lots of salt, sugar, and fat; and that food is an essential part of almost all social gatherings and celebrations. To successfully lose (and maintain) weight, we must make permanent lifestyle changes regarding the amount and types of foods we eat and when we eat them.

"Gee, I had no idea you were married to a supermodel."

©The New Yorker Collection 1999 Michael Maslin from cartoonbank.com. All Rights Reserved.

Anorexia Nervosa and Bulimia Nervosa

Interestingly, as obesity has reached epidemic proportions, we've seen a similar rise in two other eating disorders — **anorexia nervosa** (self-starvation and extreme weight loss) and **bulimia nervosa** (intense, recurring episodes of binge eating followed by purging through vomiting or taking laxatives). Contrary to myth, these eating disorders are not restricted to females from upper-middle-class backgrounds. Research shows that more than 50 percent of women in Western industrialized countries show some signs of an eating disorder, and approximately 2 percent meet the DSM-IV-TR criteria for anorexia nervosa or bulimia nervosa (Porzelius et al., 2001). These disorders also are found in all socioeconomic levels. A few men also develop eating disorders, although the incidence is rare compared with that for women (Barry, Grilo, & Masheb, 2002; Hewitt, Coren, & Steel, 2001).

Anorexia Nervosa *Severe loss of weight resulting from an obsessive fear of obesity and self-imposed starvation*

Bulimia Nervosa *Consuming large quantities of food (bingeing), followed by vomiting, extreme exercise, or laxative use (purging)*

Anorexia nervosa is characterized by an overwhelming fear of becoming obese, disturbed body image, need for control, and the use of dangerous measures to lose weight. The fear of fatness does not diminish even with radical and obvious weight loss, and the body image is so distorted that even a skeletal, emaciated body is perceived as fat. Many people with anorexia nervosa not only refuse to eat but also take up extreme exercise regimens — hours of cycling or running or constant walking. The extreme malnutrition often leads to osteoporosis and emaciated bone fractures. Menstruation in women often ceases, and brain computed tomography (CT) scans show enlarged ventricles (cavities) and widened grooves. Such signs generally indicate loss of brain tissue (Wentz, Gillberg, Gillberg, & Rastam, 2000). A significant percentage of individuals with anorexia nervosa ultimately die of the disorder (Gordon, 2000). As you can see, this is a serious and chronic condition that needs immediate and ongoing treatment.

Occasionally the person suffering from anorexia nervosa succumbs to the desire to eat and gorges on food, then vomits or takes laxatives. This type of bingeing and purging is also characteristic of bulimia nervosa, which is much more common than anorexia nervosa (Greeno, Wing, & Shiffman, 2000). Bulimia nervosa is primarily associated with a preoccupation or obsession with weight gain and a deep fear of becoming obese. Individuals suffering from this disorder are not just impulsive eaters; they also show impulsivity in other areas, sometimes by petty shoplifting or alcohol abuse (Bulik, Sullivan, & Kendler, 2002; Corcos et al., 2001; Narduzzi & Jackson, 2000). The vomiting associated with bulimia nervosa causes eroded tooth enamel and tooth loss, severe damage to the throat and stomach, cardiac arrhythmias, metabolic deficiencies, and serious digestive disorders.

What causes anorexia nervosa and bulimia nervosa? There are almost as many suspected causes as there are victims. Some theories focus on physical causes such as hypothalamic disorders, low levels of various neurotransmitters, and genetic or hor-

The extreme thinness of popular television stars and models may contribute to anorexia and bulimia.

monal disorders. Other theories emphasize psychological or social factors, such as a need for perfection, a perceived loss of control, body weight teasing, destructive thought patterns, depression, dysfunctional families, distorted body image, and sexual abuse (e.g., Crowther, Kichler, Shewood, & Kuhnert, 2002; Klump et al., 2002; McCabe & Ricciardelli, 2003; Neumark-Sztainer, Wall, Story, & Perry, 2003).

Culture and Eating Disorders

Cultural factors also play important roles in eating disorders (Dorian & Garfinkel, 2002; Davis, Dionne, & Shuster, 2001). A number of cross-cultural studies have found important differences in perceptions and stereotypes about eating, thinness, and obesity. For instance, Asian and African Americans report fewer eating and dieting disorders and greater body satisfaction than do European Americans (Akan & Grilo, 1995), and Mexican students report less concern about their own weight and more acceptance of fat people than do North American students (Crandall & Martinez, 1996).

Although social pressures for thinness certainly contribute to the development of eating disorders, it is interesting to note that anorexia nervosa also has been found in nonindustrialized areas like the Caribbean island of Curaçao (Riva, Marachi, & Molinari, 2000). On that island, being overweight is socially acceptable and the average woman is considerably heavier than women in North America are, yet some women still have anorexia nervosa. This research suggests that both culture and biology help explain eating disorders. Regardless of the causes, it is important to recognize the symptoms of anorexia and bulimia (Table 31.1) and seek therapy if the symptoms apply to you. There is no question that both disorders are serious and require treatment.

■ Arousal: The Need for Stimulation

Another important motive that influences us is *arousal*, which refers to a general state of alertness and mental and physical activation. Although the hunger motive obviously affects behavior, we are less likely to recognize that all living organisms also need a certain degree of stimulation. According to the *arousal motive* theory, there is an ideal or optimal level of arousal that organisms are motivated to achieve and maintain.

The need for sensory stimulation begins shortly after birth. For example, infants show a marked preference for complex versus simple visual stimuli. Adults also pay more attention, and for a longer period of time, to complex and changing stimuli. Similarly, research with monkeys shows they will perform various tasks for the simple "reward" of a brief look around the laboratory (Butler, 1954). As can be seen in Figure 31.2, they will also learn to open latches for the sheer pleasure of curiosity and manipulation (Harlow, Harlow, & Meyer, 1950).

TABLE 31.1 *DSM-IV-TR*[a] SYMPTOMS OF ANOREXIA NERVOSA AND BULIMIA NERVOSA

Symptoms of Anorexia Nervosa	*Symptoms of Bulimia Nervosa*
• Body weight below 85% of normal for one's height and age • Intense fear of becoming fat or gaining weight, even though underweight • Disturbance in one's body image or perceived weight • Self-evaluation unduly influenced by body weight • Denial of seriousness of abnormally low body weight • Absence of menstrual periods • Purging behavior (vomiting or misuse of laxatives or diuretics)	• Normal or above-normal weight • Recurring binge eating • Eating an amount of food that is much larger than most people would consume • Feeling a lack of control over eating • Purging behavior (vomiting or misuse of laxatives or diuretics) • Excessive exercise to prevent weight gain • Fasting to prevent weight gain • Self-evaluation unduly influenced by body weight

[a] *DSM-IV-TR = Diagnostic and Statistical Manual of Mental Disorders*, fourth edition, revised.

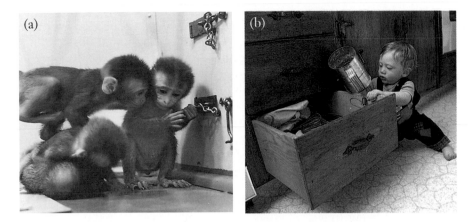

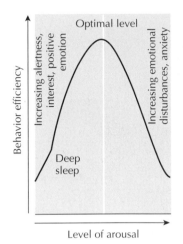

Figure 31.2 *Arousal-seeking behavior.* (a) Monkeys will work very hard at opening latches for the sheer pleasure of satisfying their curiosity. (b) The arousal motive is also seen in young children, who are fascinated by ordinary household objects.

When arousal is too low or too high, performance is diminished, as shown in Figure 31.3. This inverted U-shape curve, so-named because the graph looks like an upside-down letter *U*, also demonstrates that performance is maximized when arousal is at an "optimum" level. Have you noticed this effect while taking exams? When underaroused, your mind wanders, causing you to make careless errors (like filling in the space for option A on a multiple-choice exam when you meant to fill in B). When overaroused, you may become so anxious that you can't remember what you studied. (This kind of forgetting is explained in part by the fact that overarousal seems to interfere with retrieving information from long-term memory [LTM].)

Figure 31.3 *Optimal level of arousal.* Our need for stimulation (the arousal motive) suggests that behavior efficiency increases as we move from deep sleep to increased alertness. However, there is a point at which we become too aroused and performance declines.

Application

APPLYING PSYCHOLOGY TO STUDENT LIFE

Overcoming Test Anxiety

If you do become overly aroused on exam day, you may want to take a class in study skills or test anxiety. You can also try these basic study tips:

Step 1: *Prepare in advance.* Improve your reading, note taking, and study skills by reviewing and practicing the advice in Tools for Student Success in Module 4. The single most important cure for test anxiety is advance preparation and *hard work.* If you are well prepared, you will feel calmer and more in control.

- Read your textbook using the SQ4R (Survey, Question, Read, Recite, Review, and wRite) method.
- Practice good time management and distribute your study time; don't cram the night before.
- Actively listen during lectures and take detailed, and summarizing notes.
- Follow the general strategies for test taking mentioned in Module 4.

Step 2: *Learn to cope with the anxiety.* As you just learned, performance is best at a moderate level of arousal. A few butterflies before and during exams are okay and to be expected, but too much anxiety can interfere with concentration and cripple your performance. To achieve the right amount of arousal, try the following:

- Replace anxiety with relaxed feelings. Practice deep breathing (which activates the parasympathetic nervous system), and the relaxation response (Module 10).
- Desensitize yourself to the test (Module 44).

• Exercise regularly. This is a great stress reliever and promotes deeper and more restful sleep.

Sensation Seeking

Each of us is motivated to achieve an optimal level of arousal, but how do we explain people who seem to have an extreme need for stimulation? What motivates people who hang-glide over deep canyons or go whitewater rafting down dangerous rivers? According to research, these "high sensation seekers" may be biologically "prewired" to need a higher level of stimulation (Zuckerman, 1979, 2000).

Research based on longer versions of Zuckerman's scale suggest four distinct factors that characterize sensation seeking (Franken, 1998; Johnson & Cropsey, 2000): (1) thrill and adventure seeking (skydiving, driving fast, or trying to beat a train), (2) experience seeking (travel, unusual friends, drug experimentation), (3) disinhibition ("letting loose"), and (4) susceptibility to boredom (lower tolerance for repetition and sameness).

TRY THIS YOURSELF *Application*

High sensation-seeking? *Would you be willing to try bungee jumping? If not, are you a low sensation-seeker on Zuckerman's scale?*

Before we continue, circle the choice, A or B, that *best* describes you in each of the following items:

1. A I would like a job that requires a lot of traveling.
   B I would prefer a job in one location.
2. A I am invigorated by a brisk, cold day.
   B I can't wait to get indoors on a cold day.
3. A I get bored seeing the same old faces.
   B I like the comfortable familiarity of everyday friends.
4. A I would prefer living in an ideal society where everyone is safe, secure, and happy.
   B I would have preferred living in the unsettled days of our history.
5. A I sometimes like to do things that are a little frightening.
   B A sensible person avoids activities that are dangerous.
6. A I would not like to be hypnotized.
   B I would like to have the experience of being hypnotized.
7. A The most important goal of life is to live it to the fullest and experience as much as possible.
   B The most important goal of life is to find peace and happiness.
8. A I would like to try parachute jumping.
   B I would never want to try jumping out of a plane, with or without a parachute.
9. A I enter cold water gradually, giving myself time to get used to it.
   B I like to dive or jump right into the ocean or a cold pool.
10. A When I go on a vacation, I prefer the comfort of a good room and bed.
    B. When I go on a vacation, I prefer the change of camping out.
11. A I prefer people who are emotionally expressive even if they are a bit unstable.
    B I prefer people who are calm and even-tempered.
12. A A good painting should shock or jolt the senses.
    B A good painting should convey a feeling of peace and security.
13. A People who ride motorcycles must have some kind of unconscious need to hurt themselves.
    B I would like to drive or ride on a motorcycle.

Scoring

Count 1 point for each of the following items that you have circled: 1A, 2A, 3A, 4B, 5A, 6B, 7A, 8A, 9B, 10B, 11A, 12A, 13B. Add up your total and compare it with the norms below:

0–3: very low need for sensation seeking
4–5: low
6–9: average
10–11: high
12–13: very high

Source: Zuckerman, M. (1978, February). The search for high sensation, *Psychology Today*, pp. 38–46. Copyright © 1978 by the American Psychological Association. Reprinted by permission.

If you scored very high or very low on this test, you might have problems in relationships with individuals who score toward the other extreme. Zuckerman warns that this is true not just between partners or spouses but also between parent and child and therapist and patient. There might also be job difficulties for a high-sensation seeker with a routine clerical or assembly line job or a low-sensation seeker with a highly challenging and variable occupation.

■ Achievement: The Need for Success

Do you wonder what motivated Wilt Chamberlain to achieve such success in basketball or why Coach Bobby Knight drove his players so mercilessly? What about someone like Thomas Edison? Inventing the lightbulb would have been achievement enough for any person, but Edison also received patents for the microphone, the phonograph, and over a thousand other inventions. Even as a child, he spent hours doing experiments and figuring out how things work. What drove Edison?

The key to understanding what motivates Wilt Chamberlain, Bobby Knight, and Thomas Edison lies in what psychologist Henry Murray (1938) identified as a high need for achievement (nAch), or **achievement motivation,** a desire for significant accomplishment. Before you continue reading, complete the Critical Thinking/Active Learning exercise that follows this section. It gives you an opportunity to test your own need for achievement.

Achievement Motivation *Desire to excel, especially in competition with others*

Characteristics of Achievers

How do individuals with a high nAch differ from other people? Researchers have identified several distinguishing traits in these people (McClelland, 1958, 1987, 1993; Mueller & Dweck, 1998; Wigfield & Eccles, 2000).

1. *Preference for moderately difficult tasks.* People high in nAch avoid tasks that are too easy because they offer little challenge or satisfaction. They also avoid extremely difficult tasks because the probability of success is too low. In a ring-toss game, for instance, they often stand at an intermediate distance from the target.

2. *Competitiveness.* High achievement–oriented people are more attracted to careers and tasks that involve competition and an opportunity to excel.

3. *Preference for clear goals with competent feedback.* High achievement–oriented people tend to prefer tasks with a clear outcome and situations in which they can receive feedback on their performance. They also prefer criticism from a harsh but competent evaluator to one who is friendlier but less competent.

4. *Responsibility.* People with high nAch prefer being personally responsible for a project. When they are directly responsible, they can feel satisfied when the task is well done.

5. *Persistence.* High achievement–oriented people are more likely to persist at a task when it becomes difficult. When participants were given an unsolvable task, 47 percent of the high-nAch individuals persisted until time was called. On the other hand, only 2 percent of those who were low on achievement motivation persisted.

6. *More accomplished.* People who have high nAch scores do achieve more than others. They do better on exams, earn better grades in high school and college, and excel in their chosen professions.

What causes some people to be more achievement oriented than others? Achievement orientation appears to be largely learned in early childhood, primarily through interactions with parents. Highly motivated children tend to have parents who encourage independence and frequently reward successes (Maehr & Urdan, 1999). The culture that we are born and raised in also affects achievement needs

Application

CRITICAL THINKING ACTIVE LEARNING

Measuring Your Own Need for Achievement

Are you interested in measuring your own need for achievement? If so, try the following:

Test 1

On the basis of how you feel in *most* situations, answer the following questions honestly with a yes or no:

_____ 1. If offered a choice of tasks, would you pick one that is moderately difficult rather than one that is very difficult or easy?

_____ 2. Do you enjoy tasks more if you compete against others?

_____ 3. Do you prefer tasks that have clear, definable goals and measurable outcomes?

_____ 4. Do you like receiving feedback about how well you are doing when you are working on a project?

_____ 5. Would you rather receive criticism from a harsh but competent evaluator than from one who is friendlier but less competent?

_____ 6. Do you prefer tasks where you are personally responsible for the outcome?

_____ 7. When working on a difficult task, do you persist even when you encounter roadblocks?

_____ 8. Do you typically receive high performance evaluations (e.g., receiving top honors or special recognition in sports, clubs, and other activities)?

Test 2

The Thematic Apperception Test (TAT) consists of a series of ambiguous pictures such as the one shown in Figure 31.4. The TAT is one of the most common methods for measuring achievement motivation. Look closely at the two women in the figure and write a short story answering the following questions:

1. What is happening in this picture, and what led up to it?
2. Who are the people in this picture, and how do they feel?
3. What is going to happen in the next few moments, and in a few weeks?

Scoring

Test 1: Give yourself 1 point for each time you answered yes to the eight questions. On the basis of the characteristics of achievers discussed in the text, people with a higher number of yes answers tend to be high in achievement motivation.

Test 2: Give yourself 1 point each time any of the following is mentioned: (1) defining a problem, (2) solving a problem, (3) obstructions to solving a problem, (4) techniques that

Figure 31.4 *Measuring achievement.*
This card is one of several from the Thematic Apperception Test (TAT). The strength of an individual's need for achievement is measured by stories he or she tells about the TAT photos.

can help overcome the problem, (5) anticipation of success or resolution of the problem. The higher your score on this test, the higher your overall need for achievement.

The higher your score on both tests, the higher your overall need for achievement. Compare your scores with those of your friends and classmates.

(Lubinski & Benbow, 2000). Events and themes in children's literature, for example, often contain subtle messages about what the culture values. In North American and Western European cultures, many children's stories are about persistence and the value of hard work. A study by Richard de Charms and Gerald Moeller (1962) found a significant correlation between the achievement themes in children's literature and the actual industrial accomplishments of various countries. Conversely, can you see how gambling and the lottery — both based on luck of the draw — might appeal to people with a low nAch?

Intrinsic and Extrinsic Motivation and Achievement

Having some understanding of the characteristics of high achievers, let's look at two forms of motivation that affect achievement — *intrinsic* and *extrinsic*. **Intrinsic motivation** comes from within the individual. The person engages in an activity for its own

Intrinsic Motivation *Motivation resulting from personal enjoyment of a task or activity*

sake or for internal satisfaction, with no ulterior purpose or need for an external reward. Some researchers believe this self-motivation comes from an innate need (e.g., Ryan & Deci, 2000). In contrast, **extrinsic motivation** stems from obvious external rewards or avoidance of punishment and is learned through interaction with the environment. Participation in sports and hobbies, like swimming or playing a guitar, is usually intrinsically motivated. Working at a boring job and going to the dentist come from extrinsic motivation. In most people's mind, "play" is intrinsic and "work" is extrinsic.

What do you think would happen if you were suddenly given extrinsic rewards (money, praise, or other incentives) for your current "play" activities? Studies have found that people who are paid or rewarded for something they had previously done for the sheer fun of it often lose enjoyment and interest in the task (Hennessey & Amabile, 1998; Kohn, 2000). One of the earliest experiments to demonstrate this effect involved preschool children who liked to draw (Lepper, Greene, & Nisbett, 1973). The children were all given artist's paper and felt-tipped pens, and one group was promised a "Good Player" certificate with a gold seal and ribbon for their drawings. A second group was asked to draw and then received an unexpected reward when they were done. A third group received no promise of a certificate and no reward was given. A few weeks later, these same children were placed in a situation in which they could draw if they wanted to, and the amount of time they spent drawing was recorded.

What do you think happened? As Figure 31.5 shows, offers of a "Good Player" certificate greatly undermined the children's subsequent interest in drawing.

How can we explain the results of these studies? Apparently, the critical factor in enjoyment of a task is how we interpret our motivation to ourselves. When we perform a task for no apparent reason, we use internal, personal reasons ("I like it"; "It's fun"). But when extrinsic rewards are added, the explanation shifts to external, impersonal reasons ("I did it for the money"; "I did it to please the boss"). This shift generally decreases enjoyment and negatively affects performance.

But doesn't getting a raise or receiving a gold medal increase enjoyment and productivity? Not all extrinsic motivation is bad (Covington & Mueller, 2001; Moneta & Siu, 2002). The problem seems to lie in how extrinsic rewards are used. They are motivating if they are used to inform a person of superior performance or as a special treat. They do not work as motivators if the person experiences them as

Assessment

VISUAL QUIZ

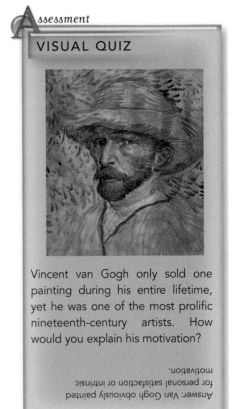

Vincent van Gogh only sold one painting during his entire lifetime, yet he was one of the most prolific nineteenth-century artists. How would you explain his motivation?

Answer: Van Gogh obviously painted for personal satisfaction or intrinsic motivation.

Extrinsic Motivation *Motivation based on obvious external rewards or threats of punishment*

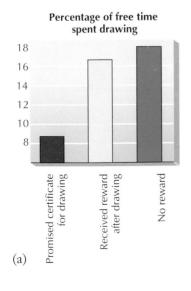

Percentage of free time spent drawing

(a)

(b)

Figure 31.5 *Intrinsic versus extrinsic motivation.* (a) As shown in this graph, children who were given no reward spent more free time drawing. *Source:* Lepper, Greene, & Nisbett, 1973. (b) These children are obviously having fun, yet few adults fingerpaint. Is this because we're too busy or because we were given grades, praise, or other extrinsic rewards that destroyed our early intrinsic motivation?

Reprinted with permission of King Features Syndicate.

pressure or a form of control. First of all, research finds extrinsic rewards do not reduce intrinsic interest if they are based on competency (Deci, 1995). In fact, they may intensify the desire to do well again. Thus, getting a raise or gold medal can inform us and provide valuable feedback about our performance, which may increase enjoyment. On the other hand, if rewards are used to control, like giving children money or privileges for good grades, intrinsic motivation declines.

Second, research with children shows that when extrinsic rewards are perceived as a simple, "no strings attached" treat, their interest in creative tasks increases. As you can see in Figure 31.6 the reverse is true, however, if they see the reward as an external pressure to be creative (Eisenberger & Armeli, 1997; Eisenberger & Rhoades, 2002).

Figure 31.6 *Motivation is in the eye of the beholder.* Do rewards increase motivation or are they seen as coercion or bribery? It depends. Note how a controlling reward and external pressure both lead to extrinsic motivation, whereas an informing reward and "no strings" treat produce intrinsic motivation.

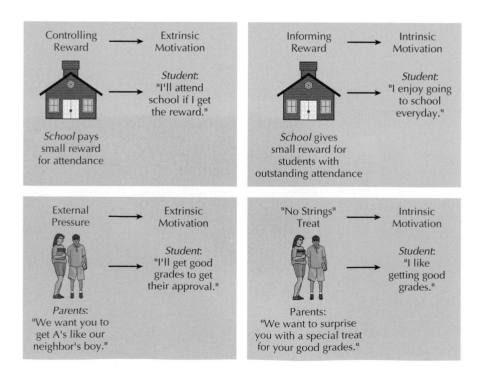

Intrinsic–extrinsic motivation has important implications for raising children, running a business, or even studying this text. Consider the following guidelines for increasing motivation:

1. *Limit concrete extrinsic rewards.* In general, it is almost always better to use the least possible extrinsic reward and for the shortest possible time period. When children are first learning to play a musical instrument, it may help to provide small rewards until they gain a certain level of mastery. But once the child is working happily or practicing for the sheer joy of it, it is best to leave him or her alone. Similarly, if you're trying to increase your study time, begin by rewarding yourself for every significant improvement, but don't interrupt yourself with a reward when you're handling a difficult assignment easily. Save rewards for when you need them. We should emphasize, too, that we're speaking primarily of *concrete* rewards. In contrast, praise and positive feedback generally increase intrinsic motivation (Carton, 1996; Henderlong & Lepper, 2002).
2. *Reward competency.* Use extrinsic rewards to provide feedback for competency or outstanding performance, rather than for simply engaging in the behavior. Schools might enhance intrinsic motivation by giving medals or privileges to students with no absences, rather than giving money for attendance. Similarly, reward yourself with a movie or call to a friend after you've studied *hard* for your scheduled time period or done particularly well on an exam. Don't reward yourself for half-hearted attempts.
3. *Emphasize intrinsic reasons for behaviors.* Rather than thinking about whom you'll impress with good grades or all the great jobs you'll get when you finish college, focus instead on personally satisfying, intrinsic reasons. Think about how exciting it is to learn new things or the value of becoming an educated person and a critical thinker.

Obviously, not all college classes or all aspects of our lives can be intrinsically interesting. Nor should they be. We all have to do many worthwhile things that are obviously extrinsically motivated — going to the dentist, cleaning the house, and studying for exams. It's a good idea, therefore, to save your external reinforcers for the times you're having trouble motivating yourself to do an undesirable task, and avoid "wasting" rewards on well-established intrinsic activities.

CHECK & REVIEW

Understanding Motivation

Motivation is the study of the "whys" of behavior, whereas **emotion** is the study of feelings. Because motivated behaviors are often closely related to emotions, these two topics are frequently studied together. A wide variety of motives are discussed throughout this text. In this section, we focus on hunger, arousal, and **achievement motivation.**

Both biological (stomach, biochemistry, the brain) and psychosocial (visual cues and cultural conditioning) factors affect hunger and eating. A large number of people have eating disorders. Obesity seems to result from biological factors, such as the individual's genetic inheritance, and from numerous psychological factors. **Anorexia nervosa** (extreme weight loss due to self-imposed starvation) and **bulimia nervosa** (excessive consumption of food followed by purging) are both related to an intense fear of obesity.

According to the arousal motive, people seek an optimal level of arousal that maximizes their performance. There are, however, individual differences in this need. According to Zuckerman, high-sensation seekers are biologically "prewired" to need a higher level of stimulation, whereas the reverse is true for low-sensation seekers. Achievement involves the need for success, for doing better than others, and for mastering challenging tasks. Research with **intrinsic** versus **extrinsic motivation** shows that extrinsic rewards can lower interest and achievement motivation.

Questions

1. Compare and contrast motivation and emotion.

2. What are the major biological and psychosocial factors that control hunger and eating behavior?

3. The _____ motive causes us to look for a certain amount of novelty and complexity from our environment for no apparent reason. (a) sensory; (b) social; (c) drive; (d) arousal

4. _____ refers to the desire to perform an act for its own sake, whereas _____

refers to the desire to perform an act because of external rewards or the avoidance of punishment. (a) Personal motivation, external motivation; (b) Internal drive, external drive; (c) Intrinsic motivation, extrinsic motivation; (d) Individual drive, social drive

Answers to Questions can be found in Appendix B.

Assessment

Are we motivated by biological or by psychosocial factors? Or both?

General Theories of Motivation: Biological and Psychosocial

Think back to the introductory stories about Wilt Chamberlain and Bobby Knight while reading the following section. See if you can identify which theory best explains both of their behaviors. We will explore four separate theories that fall into two general categories — biological or psychosocial (Table 12.2).

Biological Theories

Many theories of motivation are biologically based — that is, they look for inborn processes that control and direct behavior. Among these biologically oriented theories are *instinct* and *drive* theories.

Instinct Theories In the earliest days of psychology, researchers like William McDougall (1908) proposed that humans had numerous "instincts," such as repulsion, curiosity, and self-assertiveness. Other researchers later added their favorite

What motivates this behavior? *Which theory best explains this man's love for and collection of banana paraphernalia?*

SUMMARY TABLE 31.2 FIVE THEORIES OF MOTIVATION

Theory	View
Biological Theories	
Instinct	Motivation results from behaviors that are unlearned, uniform in expression, and universal in a species.
Drive-reduction	Motivation begins with a physiological need (a lack or deficiency) that elicits a psychological energy (drive) directed toward behavior that will satisfy the original need.
Psychosocial Theories	
Incentive	Motivation results from environmental stimuli that "pull" the organisms in certain directions.
Cognitive	Motivation reflects thought processes (such as attributions and expectancies) in goal-directed behaviors.
Interactionism	
Maslow's hierarchy of needs	Lower motives (such as physiological and saftey needs) must be satisfied before advancing to higher needs (such as belonging and self-esteem).

"instincts," and by the 1920s, the list became so long it was virtually meaningless. One early researcher found listings for over 10,000 human instincts (Bernard, 1924).

In addition to producing a never-ending list, the label *instinct* led to circular explanations. Have you ever heard someone say that men are just naturally or instinctually aggressive, or that all women have a maternal instinct? When asked for evidence of these instincts, the person (like the researchers did in McDougall's time) most likely points to examples of male aggression or female nurturing. Thus, the explanation of the behavior is the behavior: "They act that way because they naturally act that way." Circular reasoning, however, is not acceptable to science.

In recent years, a branch of biology called *sociobiology* has revived the case for **instincts.** These are rigid and fixed motor response patterns that are not learned, are characteristic of a species, and have an inherited, genetic foundation established in the course of evolution. Instinctual behaviors are obvious in many animals: birds build nests and salmon swim upstream to spawn. But sociobiologists such as Edward O. Wilson (1975, 1978) believe humans also have instincts, like competition or aggression, which are genetically transmitted from one generation to another.

Drive-Reduction Theory

In the 1930s, the concepts of drive and drive reduction began to replace the theory of instincts. According to **drive-reduction theory** (Hull, 1952; Spence, 1951), all living organisms have certain biological *needs* (such as food, water, and oxygen) that must be met if they are to survive. When these needs are unmet, a state of tension (known as a *drive*) is created, and the organism is motivated to reduce it. When we are deprived of food, our biological need creates a state of tension, in this case the hunger *drive*, and we are motivated to find food.

Drive-reduction theory is based largely on the biological concept of **homeostasis** — a state of balance or stability in the body's internal environment. (Homeostasis literally means "standing still.") Body temperature, blood sugar, oxygen level, and water balance are all normally maintained in a state of equilibrium. When this balance is disrupted, a need arises (a drive is created), and we are motivated to restore homeostasis. Drive-reduction theory and homeostasis are summarized in Figure 31.7.

Instincts? *Nurturing of the young is an instinctual behavior for many species.*

Instincts *Behavioral patterns that are (1) unlearned, (2) always expressed in the same way, and (3) universal in a species*

Drive-Reduction Theory *Motivation begins with a physiological need (a lack or deficiency) that elicits a drive toward behavior that will satisfy the original need; once the need is met, a state of balance (homeostasis) is restored and motivation decreases*

Homeostasis *A body's tendency to maintain a relatively stable state, such as a constant internal temperature*

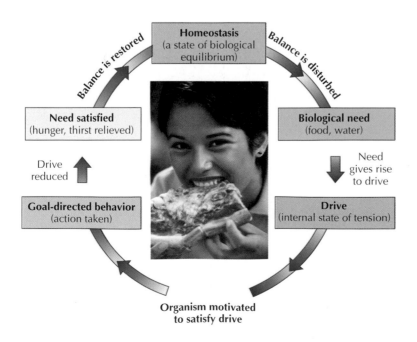

Figure 31.7 *Drive-reduction theory.* Homeostasis, the body's natural tendency to maintain a state of internal balance, is the foundation of drive-reduction theory. When you need food or water, for example, the imbalance creates a drive that motivates you to search for food or water. When the balance is restored, your motivation (to seek food or water) is also decreased.

Psychosocial Theories

Instinct and drive-reduction theories explain some motivations but not all. Why, for example, do we continue to eat after our biological need is completely satisfied? Or why does someone work overtime when his or her salary is sufficient to meet all basic biological needs? These questions are better answered by psychosocial theories that emphasize incentives and cognition.

Incentive Theory — Environmental "Pulls" Although drive theory says internal factors *push* people in certain directions, **incentive theory** says external stimuli *pull* people (Bolles, 1970, 1975; Pfaffmann, 1982). Certain characteristics of external stimuli motivate an individual to act to obtain desirable goals or avoid undesirable events. People initially eat because their hunger "pushes" them, but they continue to eat because the sight of apple pie or ice cream "pulls" them. Many *incentives* drew Wilt Chamberlain to basketball, including fame, status, large financial rewards, and the simple joy of playing the game. But cognitive factors might have provided even more compelling motivation.

Incentive Theory *Motivation results from environmental stimuli, which "pull" the organism in certain directions, rather than internal needs that drive or "push" the organism*

Cognitive Theories — Explaining Things to Ourselves If you receive a high grade in your psychology course, you can interpret that grade in several ways: You earned it because you really studied; you "lucked out"; the textbook was exceptionally interesting and helpful (my preferred interpretation!). According to the cognitive perspective, motivation is directly affected by *attributions*, or how we interpret or think about our own and others' actions. Researchers have found that people who attribute their successes to personal ability and effort tend to work harder toward their goals than people who attribute their successes to luck (Weiner, 1972, 1982).

Expectancies are also important to motivation (Dickhaeuser & Stiensmeier-Pelster, 2002; Higgins, 1997). Your anticipated grade on a test affects your willingness to study — "If I can get an A in the course, then I will study very hard" — just as your expectancies regarding promotions at work affect your willingness to work overtime for no pay.

Interactionism

As we've seen throughout this text, research in psychology generally emphasizes either biological or psychosocial factors (nature or nurture), but in the final analysis, *interactionism* almost always provides the best explanation. Theories of motivation are no exception. One researcher who recognized this interactionism and developed a theory that accounts for both biological and psychosocial needs in motivation was Abraham Maslow (1954, 1970, 1999). Maslow believed that we all have numerous needs that compete for fulfillment but that some needs are more important than others. For example, your need for a good grade in psychology may compete with demands from other classes, but your need for food and shelter is more important than how you do in college.

Hierarchy of Needs *Maslow's theory of motivation that some motives (such as physiological and safety needs) must be met before going on to higher needs (such as belonging and self-actualization)*

As Figure 31.8 shows, Maslow's **hierarchy of needs** *prioritizes* needs, with survival needs at the bottom and social, spiritual needs at the top. Maslow's theory is usually depicted as a pyramid to emphasize that human motivation rests on a foundation of basic biological needs that must be satisfied for survival before higher-level needs can be addressed. As a humanistic psychologist, Maslow also believed that we all have a compelling need to "move up" — to grow, improve ourselves, and ultimately become "self-actualized." (We'll revisit Maslow and other humanistic perspectives in Module 36.7.)

Maslow's hierarchy of needs seems intuitively correct — a starving person would first look for food, then seek love and friendship, and then self-esteem. This prioritizing and the concept of *self-actualization* are important contributions to the study of

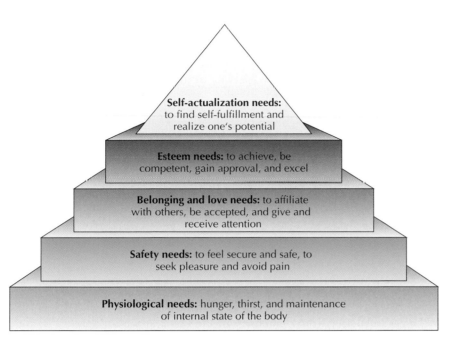

Figure 31.8 *Maslow's hierarchy of needs.* According to Maslow, basic physical necessities must be satisfied before higher-growth needs can be addressed.

Hierarchy of needs. How would Maslow label the needs of these people?

motivation (Frick, 2000; Leclerk, Lefrancois, Dube, Hebert, & Gaulin, 1998; Rowan, 1998). But critics argue that parts of Maslow's theory are poorly researched. People sometimes seek to satisfy higher-level needs even when lower-level needs have not been met (Geller, 1982; Neher, 1991; Williams & Page, 1989).

In some nonindustrialized societies, for example, people may be living in a war zone, subsisting on very little food, and suffering from injury and disease (in other words, not fulfilling Maslow's two most basic needs), yet still seek strong social ties and high self-esteem. During the famine and war in Somalia, many parents sacrificed their own lives to carry starving children hundreds of miles to food distribution centers, and parents at the centers often banded together to share the limited supplies. Because Maslow argued that each individual's own lower needs must be at least partially met before higher needs can influence behavior, these examples "stand Maslow's need hierarchy on its head" (Neher, 1991, p. 97). Although we're normally motivated to fulfill basic needs first, in certain circumstances we can bypass these lower stages and pursue higher-level needs.

Assessment

CHECK & REVIEW

General Theories of Motivation

There are three approaches to explaining motivation: biological (including **instinct** theory and **drive-reduction theory**) psychosocial (including **incentive** and cognitive), and interactionist (Maslow's **hierarchy of needs**).

Instinct theories emphasize inborn, genetic components in motivation. Drive-reduction theory suggests that internal tensions (produced by the body's demand for **homeostasis**) "push" the organism toward satisfying basic needs. According to **incentive** theory, motivation results from the "pull" of external environmental stimuli. Cognitive

theories emphasize the importance of attributions and expectations. Maslow's hierarchy of needs or motives incorporates both biological and psychosocial theories. He believed that basic survival needs must be satisfied before a person can attempt to satisfy higher needs. Critics question the importance of sequentially working upward through these steps.

Questions

1. Define *instinct* and *homeostasis*.
2. Match the following examples with their appropriate theory of motivation: (a) instinct; (b) drive-reduction; (c) incentive; (d) cognitive; (e) Maslow's hierarchy of needs

    _____ i. Joining a club because you want to be accepted by others

    _____ ii. Two animals fighting because of their inherited, evolutionary desire for survival

    _____ iii. Eating to reduce hunger

    _____ iv. Studying hard for an exam because you expect that studying will result in a good grade

    _____ v. Eating because the pie looks so delicious

3. _____ theories emphasize the importance of attributions and expectancies in motivating behaviors. (a) Attribution; (b) Motivational; (c) Achievement; (d) Cognitive

4. According to _____ theory, basic survival and security needs must be satisfied before one can move on to such higher needs as self-actualization. (a) evolutionary; (b) instinct; (c) Maslow's (d) Weiner's

Answers to Questions can be found in Appendix B.

MODULE 31   **ACTIVE LEARNING WORKSHEET**

Enter the correct letter from Column A in the blank space in Column B, and then double-check your answers with those in Appendix B.

Column A

a. Achievement motivation

b. Homeostasis

c. Abraham Maslow

d. Extrinsic motivation

e. Incentive theory

f. Cognitive theory

g. Self-actualization

h. Intrinsic motivation

i. Drive-reduction theory

j. Instincts

Column B

1. ____ Based on external rewards or punishment

2. ____ Innate behavioral patterns

3. ____ Motivation comes from an internal "push"

4. ____ Motivation comes from thought processes

5. ____ Tendency to maintain a relatively stable state

6. ____ Realizing one's potential

7. ____ Motivation comes from an external "pull"

8. ____ Hierarchy of needs

9. ____ Desire to excel, especially in competition

10. ____ Motivation comes from personal enjoyment

MODULE 32
EMOTION

www.wiley.com/college/huffman

We have reviewed the major theoretical explanations for motivation and specific motives like hunger, eating, arousal, and achievement. But as we mentioned at the beginning of this section, motivation is inextricably linked to emotion. In this section, we will explore the three basic components of all emotions and then look at controversies surrounding the polygraph (or "lie detector") test and the concept of emotional intelligence (EQ).

Assessment

What major concepts do I need to know in order to understand emotion?

■ Components of Emotion: Three Basic Ingredients

Emotions play an important role in our lives. They color our dreams, memories, and perceptions, and when they are disturbed they contribute significantly to psychological disorders. But what do we mean by the term *emotion?* In everyday usage, we describe emotions in terms of feeling states — Wilt Chamberlain "felt thrilled" when he set the NBA record against the New York Knicks, Bobby Knight frequently "felt angry" when coaching, and you "feel happy" watching a good basketball game. Psychologists define and study emotions according to their three basic components (cognitive, physiological, and behavioral).

The Cognitive Component

Our thoughts, values, and expectations help determine the type and intensity of our emotional responses. Or, as Shakespeare wrote in *Hamlet*, "There is nothing either good or bad, but thinking makes it so." Consequently, emotional reactions are very individual: What you experience as intensely pleasurable may be boring or aversive for another.

To study the cognitive component of emotions, psychologists typically use self-report techniques such as paper-and-pencil tests, surveys, and interviews. But our cognitions or thoughts about our own and others' emotions are typically difficult to describe and scientifically measure. Individuals differ in their ability to monitor and report on their emotional states. In addition, some people may lie or hide their feelings because of social expectations or as an attempt to please the experimenter. Furthermore, it is often impractical or unethical to artificially create emotions in a laboratory. How can we ethically create strong emotions like anger in a research participant just to study his or her emotional reactions? Finally, memories of emotions are not foolproof. You may remember that trip to Yellowstone as the "best family camping trip ever," whereas your brother or sister may remember it as the "worst." Our individual needs, experiences, and personal interpretations all affect the accuracy of our memories (Module 21).

The Physiological (Arousal) Component

Internal physical changes occur in our bodies whenever we experience an emotion. Imagine walking alone on a dark street in a dangerous part of town. You suddenly see someone jump from behind a stack of boxes and start running toward you. How do you respond? Like most of us, you would undoubtedly interpret the situation as threatening and would run. Your predominant emotion, fear, would involve several physiological reactions, including increased heart rate and blood pressure, dilated pupils, perspiration, dry mouth, rapid or irregular breathing, increased blood sugar, trembling, decreased gastrointestinal motility, and piloerection (goose bumps). Such physiological reactions are controlled by certain brain structures and by the autonomic branch of the nervous system (ANS).

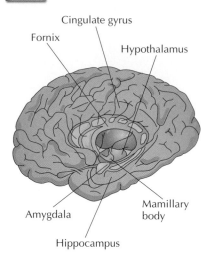

Figure 32.1 *Brain areas involved in emotion.* The limbic system consists of several subcortical structures that form a border (or limbus) around the brainstem. (The red structure in the center is the thalamus.)

The brain. The brain's reticular formation, limbic system, and cerebral cortex play important roles in emotion (Module 6). Each of these structures plays a complex and interwoven role. There is some evidence that emotional reactions, such as Coach Knight's anger at his players, begin with the brainstem's reticular formation, which is responsible for general arousal and motor control (Davidson, 1999; Rosenzweig, Leiman, & Breedlove, 1999).

Situated above the reticular formation, limbic structures (in particular, the *hypothalamus* and *amygdala*) (Figure 32.1) are also involved in recognizing and controlling emotions, particularly during times of attack, defense, and retreat — the fight-or-flight response (Anderson & Phelps, 2000; Dimberg, Thunberg, & Elmehed, 2000; LeDoux, 2002). For example, electrical stimulation of parts of the limbic system can produce a "sham rage" that turns a docile cat into a hissing, slashing animal (Morris et al., 1996). Stimulating adjacent areas can cause the same animal to purr and lick your fingers. (The rage is called sham because it occurs in the absence of provocation and disappears immediately.)

The third part of the brain directly involved in emotions is the cerebral cortex, the outermost layer of the brain that serves as our body's ultimate control and information processing center. Recall from Module 5 that when a 13-pound tamping rod slammed through Phineas Gage's cortex, he could no longer monitor and control his emotions.

Some sensory information travels directly to the limbic system before the cortex can interpret or intervene in the response. Have you ever jumped at a noise on a dark street before you knew whether it was a real threat or just someone's cat? This shortcut from the unexplained noise directly to fear may sometimes embarrass us, but it also protects us from danger. Interestingly, the fact that some neural pathways involved in emotion bypass the cortex also helps explain why people with anxiety disorders often feel afraid without knowing why (Damasio, 1999; LeDoux, 1996).

The autonomic nervous system. As important as the brain is to emotion, it is the ANS that produces the obvious signs of arousal (increased heart rate, fast, shallow breathing, trembling, and so on). These largely automatic responses result from interconnections between the ANS and various glands and muscles (Figure 32.2).

Sympathetic		Parasympathetic
Pupils dilated	**Eyes**	Pupils constricted
Dry	**Mouth**	Salivating
Goose bumps, perspiration	**Skin**	No goose bumps
Respiration increased	**Lungs**	Respiration normal
Increased rate	**Heart**	Decreased rate
Increased epinephrine and norepinephrine	**Adrenal glands**	Decreased epinephrine and norepinephrine
Decreased motility	**Digestion**	Increased motility

Figure 32.2 *Emotion and the autonomic nervous system.* During emotional arousal, the sympathetic branch of the autonomic nervous system (in connection with the brain) prepares the body for fight or flight. Note that digestion and reproductive functions are inhibited during sympathetic dominance — neither is important when you are preparing to attack or run from an enemy. The parasympathetic system is responsible for returning the body to its prearoused state.

The ANS has two major subdivisions: the *sympathetic nervous system* and the *parasympathetic nervous system*. When you are emotionally aroused, the sympathetic branch increases heart rate, respiration, and so on (the fight-or-flight response). When you are relaxed and resting, the parasympathetic branch reverses these effects. The combined action of both systems allows you to respond to emotional arousal and then return to a more relaxed state.

Where does adrenaline fit into this picture? Adrenaline, or, more properly, *epinephrine*, is a hormone secreted from the adrenal glands at the direction of the hypothalamus. Whereas the sympathetic nervous system is almost instantaneously "turned on" along with the limbic system and frontal lobes, epinephrine and norepinephrine, keep the system under sympathetic control until the emergency is over. The damaging effects of prolonged and excessive sympathetic arousal due to stress are discussed in Module 8.

Behavioral (Expressive) Component

Having examined the cognitive and physiological components of emotions, we now turn our attention to how emotions are expressed — the behavioral component. Emotional expression is a powerful form of communication. An infant's smile can create instant bonding, a cry of "fire" can cause crowds to panic, and a sobbing friend can elicit heartbreaking empathy. Though we can talk about our emotions, we more often express them nonverbally through facial expressions, gestures, body position, use of touch, eye gaze, and tone of voice.

Facial expressions may be the most important form of emotional communication, and researchers have developed very sensitive measurement techniques allowing them to detect subtleties of feeling and differentiate honest expressions from fake ones. Perhaps most interesting is the difference between the "social smile" and the "Duchenne smile," the latter is named after French anatomist Duchenne de Boulogne, who first described it in 1862.

In a false, social smile, our voluntary cheek muscles are pulled back, but our eyes are unsmiling. Smiles of real pleasure, on the other hand, use the muscles not only around the cheeks but also around the eyes (Figure 32.3). According to Duchenne de Boulogne, the eye muscle "does not obey the will" and "is put in play only by the sweet emotions of the soul" (cited in Goode, Schrof, & Burke, 1991, p. 127). Studies found that people who show a Duchenne, or real, smile and laughter elicit more positive responses from strangers and enjoyed better interpersonal relationships and personal adjustment (Keltner, Kring, & Bonanno, 1999; Prkachin & Silverman, 2002).

Assessment

VISUAL QUIZ

Figure 32.3 *Duchenne smile.* Which smile looks most sincere? Do you know why?

Answer: (a) A smile of real joy is referred to as a Duchenne smile. Note how the muscles around the eyes also contract. (b) In a social smile, however, only the muscles around the mouth contract.

Achievement
GENDER & CULTURAL DIVERSITY

How Culture and Evolution Affect Emotional Expression

Where do our emotions come from? Do they differ from one culture to the next, or are they the same? Are they a product of our evolutionary past? As you might suspect, researchers have found several answers to these questions.

Cultural Similarities

All people of all cultures have feelings and emotions, and all must learn to deal with them (Matsumoto, 2000). But are these emotions the same across all cultures? Given the seemingly vast array of emotions within our own culture, it may surprise you to learn that some researchers believe all our feelings can be condensed into 7 to 10 *culturally universal* emotions. Table 32.1 presents four theorists's findings; note the strong similarities among the four lists.

How do these theorists explain emotions not on the list, such as love? They would say that love, like many other emotions, is simply a combination of primary emotions with variation in intensity. Robert Plutchik (1984, 1994, 2000) suggested that primary emotions, such as fear, acceptance, and joy, are like colors on a color wheel that combine to form secondary emotions, such as love, submission, awe, and optimism (Figure 32.4).

In addition to all cultures' sharing the same basic emotions, some researchers believe each of these emotions is expressed and recognized in essentially the same way in all cultures. They point to research that finds people from very different cultures display remarkably similar facial expressions when experiencing particular emotions (Biehl et al., 1997; Ekman, 1993; Matsumoto & Kupperbusch, 2001). Moreover, whether respondents are from Western or non-Western societies, they can reliably identify at least six basic emotions: happiness, surprise, anger, sadness, fear, and disgust (Buck, 1984; Matsumoto, 1992, 2000). In other words, across cultures, a frown is recognized as a sign of displeasure, and a smile as a sign of pleasure (Figure 32.5).

Cultural Differences

How do we explain cultural *differences* in emotions? Although we all seem to share reasonably similar facial expressions for some emotions, each culture has its own *display rules* governing how, when, and where to express emotions (Ekman, 1993; Matsumoto

Cultural differences in emotional expression. *Iranian men commonly greet one another with a kiss, whereas men in North America generally shake hands or pat one another's shoulders.*

TABLE 32.1 THE BASIC HUMAN EMOTIONS

Carroll Izard	Paul Ekman and Wallace Friesen	Robert Plutchik	Silvan Tomkins
Fear	Fear	Fear	Fear
Anger	Anger	Anger	Anger
Disgust	Disgust	Disgust	Disgust
Surprise	Surprise	Surprise	Surprise
Joy	Happiness	Joy	Enjoyment
Shame	—	—	Shame
Contempt	Contempt	—	Contempt
Sadness	Sadness	Sadness	—
Interest	—	Anticipation	Interest
Guilt	—	—	—
—	—	Acceptance	—
—	—	—	Distress

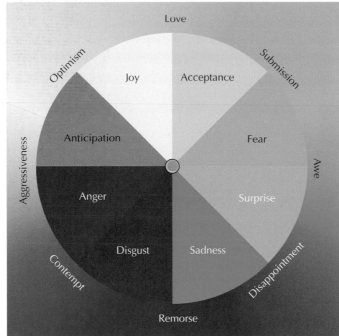

Figure 32.4 *Plutchik's wheel of emotions.* The inner circle represents the eight primary emotions that seem to exist in all cultures. Emotions in the inner circle combine to form secondary emotions located outside the circle. For example, joy and acceptance combine to form love. Robert Plutchik also found that emotions that lie next to each other are more alike than those located farther apart.

& Kupperbusch, 2001; Scherer & Wallbott, 1994). For instance, parents pass along their culture's specific display rules when they respond angrily to some emotions in their children, by being sympathetic to others, and on occasion by simply ignoring them. In this way, children learn which emotions they may express in certain situations and which emotions they are expected to control.

There are almost as many variations in display rules as there are cultures in the world. In Japanese culture, for instance, children learn to conceal negative emotions with a stoic expression or polite smile (Dresser, 1996). Young males in the Masai culture are similarly expected to conceal their emotions in public, but by appearing stern and stony-faced (Keating, 1994).

Figure 32.5 *Can you identify these emotions?* Most people can reliably identify at least six basic emotions — happiness, surprise, anger, sadness, fear, and disgust. On occasion, our facial expressions don't seem to match our presumed emotions, as is the case in the last photo. Oksana Baiul has just won an Olympic medal for figure skating, but she looks sad rather than happy.

Identifying emotions. *Using Plutchik's color wheel, can you identify the primary or secondary emotions of each of these four individuals?*

www.wiley.com/college/huffman

Polygraph *Instrument that measures heart rate, respiration rate, blood pressure, and skin conductivity to detect emotional arousal, which in turn supposedly reflects lying versus truthfulness*

Public physical contact is also governed by display rules. North Americans and Asians are generally not touch-oriented, and only the closest family and friends might hug in greeting or farewell. In contrast, Latin Americans and Middle Easterners often embrace and hold hands as a sign of casual friendship (Axtell, 1998).

The Role of Evolution

Cross-cultural studies of emotional expression tend to support the innate, evolutionary perspective. The idea of universal facial expressions makes adaptive sense because they signal others about our current emotional state (Ekman & Keltner, 1997). Studies with infants also point to an evolutionary basis for emotions. For example, did you know that infants only a few hours old show distinct expressions of emotions that closely match adult facial expressions (Field, Woodson, Greenberg, & Cohen, 1982)? Or that all infants, even those born deaf and blind, show similar facial expressions in similar situations (Eibl-Eibesfeldt, 1980b; Feldman, 1982)? This collective evidence points to a strong biological, evolutionary basis for emotional expression and decoding.

Charles Darwin first advanced the evolutionary theory of emotion in 1872. In his classic book, *The Expression of the Emotions in Man and Animals,* Darwin proposed that expression of emotions evolved in different species as a part of survival and natural selection. For example, fear helps animals avoid danger, whereas expressions of anger and aggression are useful when fighting for mates and necessary resources. Modern evolution theory further suggests that basic emotions (such as fear and anger) originate in the limbic system. Given that higher brain areas (the cortex) developed later than the subcortical limbic system, evolution theory proposes that basic emotions evolved before thought.

The Polygraph: Do "Lie Detector" Tests Really Work?

Having studied the three basic components of all emotions (cognitive, physiological, and behavioral), we can now explore an important controversy related to these components — the *polygraph* (or so-called lie detector) test.

If you suspected your friend of lying or your significant other of having an affair, would you be more or less convinced if they took a polygraph test? Many people believe the polygraph can accurately detect when someone is lying. But can it? The polygraph is based on the theory that when people lie, they feel guilty and anxious. These feelings then supposedly activate their sympathetic nervous system, the activity of which is shown on the polygraph machine.

The polygraph does in fact measure sympathetic nervous system arousal (Figure 32.6). But research shows that lying is only loosely related to anxiety and guilt. Some people become nervous when telling the truth, whereas others remain calm when deliberately lying. Furthermore, a polygraph cannot tell *which* emotion is being felt (nervousness, excitement, sexual arousal, etc.) or whether a response is due to emotional arousal or something else, such as physical exercise.

For all these reasons, most judges, psychologists, and other scientists have serious reservations about using polygraphs as lie detectors (Lykken, 1998). Although proponents contend that polygraph tests are 90 percent or more accurate, actual tests show error rates ranging between 25 and 75 percent. Thus, although people say the innocent have nothing to fear from a polygraph test, the research suggests otherwise (Faigman, Kaye, Saks, & Sanders, 1997; Iacono & Lykken, 1997; Lykken, 1998).

Is there any way to make the polygraph reliable? One suggestion is to use "guilty knowledge" questions — that is, questions based on specific information that only a guilty person would know (such as the time a robbery was committed). The idea is that a guilty person would recognize these specific cues and respond in a different way than an innocent person (Lykken, 1984, 1998; MacLaren, 2001). Expanding on this idea, psychologists have suggested using computers and statistical analyses to improve

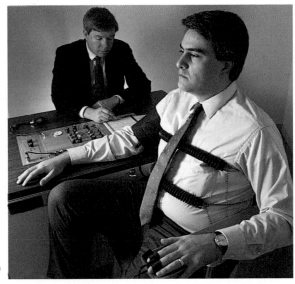

(a)

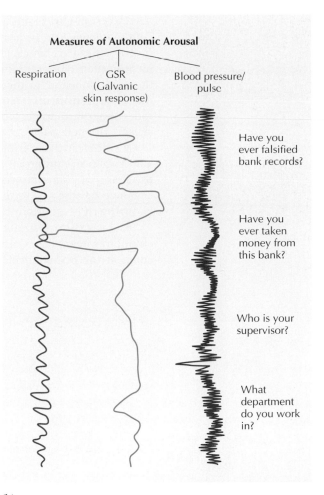

Measures of Autonomic Arousal

Respiration   GSR (Galvanic skin response)   Blood pressure/pulse

Have you ever falsified bank records?

Have you ever taken money from this bank?

Who is your supervisor?

What department do you work in?

(b)

Figure 32.6 *Polygraph tests.* (a) During the administration of a polygraph — or lie detector — test, a band
around the individual's chest measures breathing rate, a
cuff monitors blood pressure, and finger electrodes
measure sweating, or galvanic skin response (GSR). (b)
Polygraph printouts are used to detect lying or dishon-
esty in employees or suspected criminals. Note the
sharp rise in the GSR to the question, "Have you ever
taken money from this bank?" Before concluding that
this response indicates the individual is lying, remember
that research has found error rates ranging between 25
and 75 percent!

polygraph reliability and validity (Saxe & Ben-Shakhar, 1999). Other researchers have
developed a high-definition thermal imaging technique, which reportedly detects
lying by recording the thermal (heat) patterns from people's faces (Paulidis, Eberhardt, & Levine, 2002).

But even with improvements, many psychologists and others still strongly object
to using polygraphs to establish guilt or innocence. In fact, scientific controversy and
public concern led the U.S. Congress to pass a bill that severely restricts the use of
polygraphs in the courts, in government, and in private industry.

■ Emotional Intelligence (EQ): Are You Emotionally Smart?

You've heard of IQ, the intelligence quotient, but what do you know about EQ —
emotional intelligence? According to Daniel Goleman (1995, 2000), **emotional
intelligence (EQ)** involves knowing and managing one's emotions, empathizing with
others, and maintaining satisfying relationships. In other words, an emotionally intelligent person successfully combines the three components of emotions (cognitive,
physiological, and behavioral).

Goleman argued that high EQ explains why people of modest IQ are often more
successful than people with much higher IQ scores. He believes that traditional measures of human intelligence ignore a crucial range of abilities that characterize people
who excel in real life: self-awareness, impulse control, persistence, zeal and self-motivation, empathy, and social deftness.

Emotional Intelligence *Goleman's
term for the ability to know and manage
one's emotions, empathize with others, and
maintain satisfying relationships*

Developing emotional intelligence.
*Adults can help children identify and
understand their own emotions, as well as
how to change them.*

Goleman also suggests that many societal problems, such as domestic abuse and youth violence, can be attributed to a lack of EQ. Therefore, EQ should be fostered in everyone. Parents can help their children develop EQ by encouraging them to identify their emotions and understand how these feelings can be changed and how they are connected to their actions (Bar-On & Parker, 2000; Kuebli, 1999). Schools that have instituted Goleman's ideas say students show not just "more positive attitudes about ways to get along with people, but also improvements in critical thinking skills" (Mitchell, Sachs, & Tu, 1997 p. 62).

Critics fear that a handy term like *EQ* invites misuse, but their strongest reaction is to Goleman's proposals for teaching EQ. For example, Paul McHugh, director of psychiatry at Johns Hopkins University, suggests that Goleman is "presuming that someone has the key to the right emotions to be taught to children. We don't even know the right emotions to be taught to adults" (cited in Gibbs, 1995, p. 68).

EQ is a controversial concept, but most researchers are happy that the subject of emotion is being taken seriously. Further research will increase our understanding of emotion and perhaps even reveal the ultimate value of Goleman's theory.

Assessment

CHECK & REVIEW

Understanding Emotion

All emotions have three basic components: cognitive (thoughts, values, and expectations), physiological arousal (e.g., heart pounding), and behavioral expressions (e.g., smiles, frowns, running). Self-report techniques, such as paper-and-pencil tests, surveys, and interviews, are used to study the cognitive component of emotions.

Studies of the physiological component of emotion find that most emotions involve a general, nonspecific arousal of the nervous system. This arousal involves the reticular formation, limbic system, and cerebral cortex of the brain. The most obvious signs of arousal (trembling, increased heart rate, sweating, and so on) result from activation of the sympathetic nervous system, a subdivision of the autonomic nervous system. The parasympathetic system restores the body to the status quo.

The behavioral component of emotions refers to how we express our emotions, including facial expressions. Most psychologists believe that emotions result from a complex interplay between evolution and culture. Studies have identified 7 to 10 basic emotions that may be universal — experienced and expressed in similar ways across almost all cultures. Display rules for emotional expression differ across cultures.

A **polygraph** measures changes in emotional arousal (increased heart rate, blood pressure, and so on), but research shows it is a poor "lie detector." **Emotional intelligence** (EQ) involves managing one's emotions, empathizing with others, and maintaining satisfying relationships.

Questions

1. Identify the following examples with the appropriate emotional component: (a) cognitive; (b) physiological; (c) behavioral

____ i. Increased heart rate
____ ii. Crying during a sad movie
____ iii. Believing crying is inappropriate for men
____ iv. Shouting during a soccer match

2. When people are emotionally aroused, the _____ branch of the _____ nervous system works to increase heart rate and blood pressure and to activate other crisis responses.

3. The polygraph, or lie detector, measures primarily the _____ component of emotions. (a) physiological; (b) articulatory; (c) cognitive; (d) subjective

4. Knowing and managing one's emotions, empathizing with others, and maintaining satisfying relationships are the key factors in _____. (a) self-actualization; (b) emotional intelligence; (c) emotional metacognition; (d) empathic IQ

Answers to Questions can be found in Appendix B.

Assessment

How are emotional states produced?

■ General Theories of Emotion: Four Major Theories

Researchers generally agree on the three components of emotion (cognition, physiological arousal, and behavioral expression), but there is less agreement on *how* we become emotional. The major theories are the James–Lange theory, Cannon–Bard theory, facial-feedback hypothesis, and Schachter's two-factor theory. Each of these four theories emphasizes different sequences or aspects of the three elements (cognitions, arousal, and expression). As you read about the different theories, you will find it helpful to refer to Figure 32.7.

James—Lange Theory

According to ideas originated by psychologist William James and later expanded by physiologist Carl Lange, emotions depend on feedback from our physiological arousal and behavioral expression. In other words, contrary to popular opinion, which says we cry because we're sad, James wrote: "We feel sorry because we cry, angry because we strike, afraid because we tremble" (James, 1890).

Why would I tremble unless I first felt afraid? According to the **James–Lange theory,** your bodily response of trembling is a reaction to a specific stimulus such as seeing a large snake in the wilderness. In other words, you perceive an event, your body reacts, and then you interpret the bodily changes as a specific emotion (Figure 32.7a). It is your perception of autonomic arousal (palpitating heart, sinking stomach, flushed cheeks), your actions (running, yelling), and changes in your facial expression (crying,

James–Lange Theory *Emotions result from physiological arousal and behavioral expression ("I feel sad because I'm crying"). In this view, each emotion is physiologically distinct*

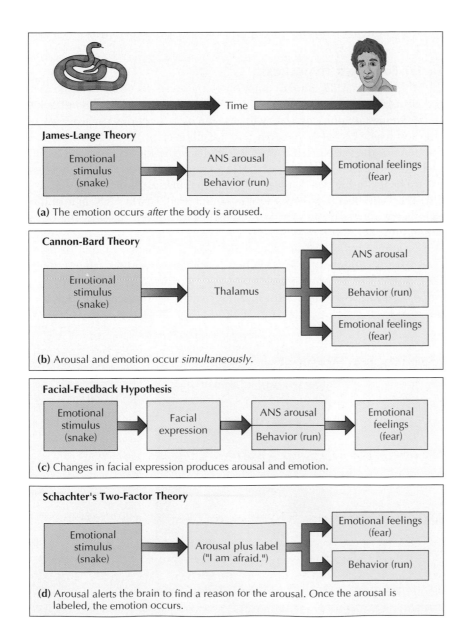

(a) The emotion occurs *after* the body is aroused.

(b) Arousal and emotion occur *simultaneously.*

(c) Changes in facial expression produces arousal and emotion.

(d) Arousal alerts the brain to find a reason for the arousal. Once the arousal is labeled, the emotion occurs.

Figure 32.7 *Four major theories of emotion.* (a) In the James-Lange theory, emotion occurs *after* the body is aroused. (b) In the Cannon-Bard theory, arousal and emotion occur *simultaneously.* (c) The facial-feedback hypothesis proposes that changes in facial expression produce arousal and emotions. (d) In Schachter's two-factor theory, arousal causes us to search for a reason for the arousal; once the arousal is labeled, emotion occurs.

smiling, frowning) that produce what we refer to as emotions. In short, arousal and expression cause emotion. If there is no arousal or expression, there is no emotion.

Cannon—Bard Theory

Whereas the James–Lange theory argues that arousal and expression produce emotion and each emotion has its own distinct physiological reaction, the **Cannon–Bard theory** holds that all emotions are physiologically similar, and arousal, cognitions, and expression occur simultaneously. Walter Cannon (1927) and Philip Bard (1934) proposed that during perception of the emotion-provoking stimuli (seeing the spider) the thalamus sends *simultaneous* messages to both the general body and the cerebral cortex (Figure 32.7b). Messages to the cortex produce the *cognitive experience* of emotion (fear), whereas messages to the autonomic nervous system produce *physiological arousal and behavioral expressions* (heart palpitations, running, widening eyes, and open mouth).

A major point in the Cannon–Bard theory is that all emotions are physiologically similar. In fact, arousal is not a necessary or even major factor in emotion. Cannon supported his position with several experiments in which animals were surgically prevented from experiencing physiological arousal. Yet, these surgically altered animals still showed observable behaviors (like growling and defensive postures) that might be labeled emotional reactions (Cannon, Lewis, & Britton, 1927).

Facial-Feedback Hypothesis

The third major explanation of emotion — the facial–feedback hypothesis — focuses on the *expressive* component of emotions. According to the **facial-feedback hypothesis,** facial changes not only correlate with and intensify emotions but also *cause* or initiate the emotion itself (Ceschi & Scherer, 2001; Keillor et al., 2002; Soussignan, 2002). Contractions of the various facial muscles send specific messages to the brain, identifying each basic emotion. Like James, these researchers suggest that we don't smile because we are happy but rather that we feel happy because we smile (Figure 32.7c).

The facial-feedback hypothesis also supports Darwin's (1872) evolutionary theory that freely expressing an emotion intensifies it, whereas suppressing outward expression diminishes it. Interestingly, recent research suggests that even watching another's facial expressions causes an automatic, *reciprocal* change in our own facial muscles (Dimberg & Thunberg, 1998). When people are exposed to pictures of angry faces, for example, the eyebrow muscles involved in frowning are activated. In contrast, the smile muscles show a significant increase in activity when participants are shown pho-

TRY THIS
YOURSELF
Application

Testing the facial-feedback hypothesis. Hold a pen or pencil between your teeth with your mouth closed, as shown in the left photo. Spend about 15 to 30 seconds in this position. How do you feel? Now hold the pencil between your teeth with your mouth open and your teeth showing, as in the right photo. During the next 15 to 30 seconds, pay attention to your feelings. According to research, pleasant feelings are more likely when teeth are showing. Can you explain why? Source: Adapted from Starck, Martin, & Stepper, 1988.

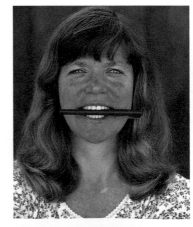
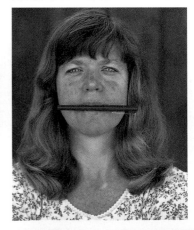

tos of a happy face. In follow-up research using "subliminal perception" techniques discussed in Module 13, scientists have shown that this automatic, matching response occurs even *without* the participant's attention or conscious awareness (Dimberg, Thunberg, & Elmehed, 2000).

This automatic, innate, and sometimes unconscious imitation of facial expressions that match others' expressions has important implications. Have you ever felt depressed after listening to a friend's problems? Your unconscious facial mimicry of the person's sad expression may create similar physiological reactions in your own body. This theory has applications for therapists who constantly work with depressed clients and for actors who simulate emotions for their livelihood. Studies also show that "happy workers are more productive than unhappy workers" (Cote, 1999). Does this mean that unhappy coworkers or a constantly angry boss might affect the happiness (and productivity) of the general workforce? If Darwin was right that expressing an emotion intensifies it and if watching it produces a matching response, maybe we should reconsider traditional advice to "express our anger."

Schachter's Two-Factor Theory

According to psychologist Stanley **Schachter's two-factor theory,** emotions depend on two factors: (1) physical arousal and (2) cognitive labeling of that arousal. Schachter thus agrees with James–Lange that our experience of an emotion comes from a cognitive awareness of our bodily arousal, but he also agrees with Cannon–Bard that emotions are physiologically similar. He reconciles the two theories by proposing that we look to *external* rather than *internal* cues to differentiate and label our emotions. If we cry at a wedding, for example, we interpret our emotion as joy or happiness, but if we cry at a funeral, we label our emotion sadness (Figure 32.7d).

In Schachter and Singer's classic study (1962), participants were given shots of epinephrine and told it was a type of vitamin. Their subsequent arousal and labeling were then investigated (Figure 32.8). One group of participants was *correctly* informed about the expected effects (hand tremors, excitement, and heart palpitations), and a second group was *misinformed* and told to expect itching, numbness, and headache. A third, *uninformed,* group was told nothing about the possible effects.

Following the injection, each participant was placed in a room with a *confederate* (a "stooge" who was part of the experiment but who pretended to be a fellow volunteer). The confederate was told to act happy and cheerful (throwing paper airplanes around the room and shooting wads of paper into the wastebasket) or unhappy and angry (complaining and expressing general dissatisfaction with the entire experiment).

The results of the study confirmed the experimental hypothesis: Participants who did not have an appropriate cognitive label for their emotional arousal (the misinformed group and the uninformed group) tended to look to the situation for an explanation. Thus, those placed with a happy confederate became happy, whereas those with an unhappy confederate became unhappy. Participants in the correctly informed group, on the other hand, knew their physiological arousal was the result of the shot, so their emotions were generally unaffected by the confederate.

Which theory is correct? As you may imagine, each theory has its limitations. For example, the James–Lange theory fails to acknowledge that physical arousal can occur without emotional experience (e.g., when we exercise). This theory also requires a distinctly different pattern of arousal for each emotion. Otherwise, how do we know whether we are sad, happy, or mad? Although research has found subtle differences in positron emission tomography (PET) scan studies of the brain and general physical arousal with basic emotions, such as happiness, fear, and anger (Lane, Reiman, Ahern, & Schwartz, 1997; Levenson, 1992), most people are not aware of these slight variations. Thus, there must be other explanations for why we experience emotion.

Schachter's Two-Factor Theory
Emotions result from physical arousal and cognitive labeling (or interpretation) of that arousal based on external cues

$\mathbb{A}$ssessment

VISUAL QUIZ

"I don't sing because I am happy. I am happy because I sing."

©The New Yorker Collection 1991 Ed Franscino from cartoonbank.com. All Rights Reserved.

Can you identify which of the four major theories of emotion best explains this bird's behavior?

Answer: The James-Lange theory

Figure 32.8 *Schachter's two-factor theory.* A comparison of informed, misinformed, and uninformed participants in Schachter and Singer's classic experiment demonstrates the importance of cognitive labels in emotions.

The Cannon–Bard theory (that the cortex and autonomic nervous system receive simultaneous messages from the thalamus) has received experimental support. For instance, victims of spinal cord damage still experience emotions — often more intensely than before their injuries (Bermond, Fasotti, Nieuwenhuyse, & Schuerman, 1991). Instead of the thalamus, however, other research shows that it is the limbic system, hypothalamus, and prefrontal cortex that are most important in emotional experience (Davidson, 1999; Jansen, Nguyen, Karpitsky, Mettenleiter, & Loewy, 1995).

Research on the facial-feedback hypothesis has found a distinctive physiological response for basic emotions such as fear, sadness, and anger — thus partially confirming James–Lange's initial position (Dimberg, Thunberg, & Elmehed, 2000; Wehrle, Kaiser, Schmidt, & Scherer, 2000). Facial feedback does seem to contribute to the intensity of our subjective emotional experience and our overall moods. Thus, if you want to change a bad mood or intensify a particularly good emotion, adopt the appropriate facial expression. Try smiling when you're sad and extend the smiles when you're happy.

Finally, Schachter's two-factor theory emphasizes the importance of cognitive processes in emotions but his findings have been criticized. For example, research shows that some neural pathways involved in emotion bypass the cortex and go directly to the limbic system. Recall our earlier example of jumping at a strange sound in the dark and then a second later using the cortex to interpret what it was. This and other evidence suggests that emotions can take place without conscious cognitive processes; thus, emotion is not simply the labeling of arousal (Dimberg, Thunberg, & Elmehed, 2000; LeDoux, 1996, 2002; Mineka & Oehman, 2002).

In sum, certain basic emotions are associated with subtle differences in arousal. These differences can be produced by changes in facial expressions or by organs controlling the autonomic nervous system. In addition, "simple" emotions (likes, dislikes, fears, and anger) do not initially require conscious cognitive processes. This allows a quick, automatic emotional response that can later be modified by cortical processes. On the other hand, "complex" emotions (jealously, grief, depression, embarrassment, love) seem to require cognitive elements.

Achievement
RESEARCH HIGHLIGHT

Are Abused Children More Alert to Negative Emotions?

Child abuse has been a tragic part of human history since the beginning of time. Only in modern times have we attempted to scientifically research its causes, treatment, and effects. Seth Pollak at the University of Wisconsin–Madison and his colleagues at the University of Rochester (1997) recently conducted an interesting study of children's responses to parental abuse.

A sample of 23 abused and 21 nonabused children, ranging in age from 7.1 to 11.4 years, were presented with black-and-white slides of the same adult female posing a happy, angry, or neutral expression. All children were asked to press a button when presented with the angry versus neutral face or the happy versus neutral face. Using electrodes attached to the children's

scalp, researchers measured changes in brain electrical activity as the children viewed the happy, angry, and neutral faces.

As expected, both groups of children exhibited the strongest brain activity response to the happy and angry faces, and the weakest response to the neutral face. But the two groups differed in the strength of their response to the happy and angry faces. Although the nonabused children responded equally to the happy and angry faces, the abused children were most alert and responsive to the angry face.

This physiological research supports earlier behavioral observations. For example, in contrast to nonabused children, physically abused infants exhibit negative emotional expressions earlier and more frequently (Gaensbauer & Hiatt, 1984; Sroufe, 1979).

By extending behavioral investigations to include cognitive and physiological

processes, Pollak and his colleagues may help clarify the developmental mechanisms that place maltreated children at risk for maladaptive development. For example, the abused child's heightened reactivity to anger may reflect more efficient and adaptive cognitive organization in a stressful, threatening environment.

However, this greater sensitivity toward negative emotions can create difficulties when abused children interact with others in normal situations (Rogosch, Cicchetti, & Aber, 1995). It may explain why maltreated children often have difficulty in responding to distress and why they react with hostile gestures to other children (Klimes-Dougan & Kistner, 1990; Main & George, 1985). Using earlier studies and the findings of Pollak and his colleagues, future researchers may be able to develop programs to help maltreated children and their parents.

Assessment
CHECK & REVIEW

General Theories of Emotion

There are four major theories to explain what causes emotion. According to the **James–Lange theory,** we interpret the way we feel on the basis of physiological arousal and behavioral expression, such as smiles, increased heart rate and trembling. The **Cannon–Bard theory** suggests arousal, cognitions, and behavioral expression of emotions occur simultaneously.

According to the **facial-feedback hypothesis,** facial movements elicit specific emotions. **Schachter's two-factor theory**

suggests that emotions depend on two factors — physical arousal and a cognitive labeling of the arousal. In other words, people notice what is going on around them, as well as their own bodily responses, and then label the emotion accordingly.

Questions

1. Briefly summarize the four major theories of emotion.
2. We see a bear in the woods, our hearts race as we begin to run, and then we experience fear. This is best explained by the _____ theory. (a) James–Lange; (b)

Cannon–Bard; (c) facial-feedback hypothesis; (d) Schacter's two-factor
3. According to _____, physiological arousal must be labeled or interpreted for an emotional experience to occur. (a) the Cannon–Bard theory; (b) the James–Lange theory; (c) the facial-feedback hypothesis; (d) Schacter's two-factor theory
4. The Cannon–Bard theory of emotion suggests arousal, cognitions, and expression of emotions occur _____.

Answers to Questions can be found in Appendix B.

MODULE 32   ACTIVE LEARNING WORKSHEET

Enter the correct letter from Column A in the blank space in Column B, and then double-check your answers with those in Appendix B.

Column A	Column B
a. Robert Plutchik	1._____ May explain modest IQ and superior success.
b. Polygraph	2._____ Facial expressions, gestures, body posture.
c. Display rules	3._____ Arousal and emotion occur simultaneously.
d. James Lange theory	4._____ Changes in facial expression produce emotion.
e. Daniel Goleman	5._____ Emotion occurs after bodily arousal.
f. Schachter's 2-factor theory	6._____ Emotion results from arousal and labeling.
g. Facial-feedback hypothesis	7._____ Developed theory of emotional intelligence.
h. Cannon-Bard theory	8._____ Measures emotional arousal.
i. Emotional intelligence	9._____ Cultural guidelines for expressing emotion.
j. Emotion's behavioral component	10._____ Suggests primary emotions combine to form secondary emotions.

Assessment
KEY TERMS

To assess your understanding of the **Key Terms** in this section, write a definition for each (in your own words), and then compare your definitions with those in the text.

Understanding Motivation
achievement motivation (p. 445)
anorexia nervosa (p. 441)
bulimia nervosa (p. 441)
emotion (p. 437)
extrinsic motivation (p. 447)
intrinsic motivation (p. 446)
motivation (p. 437)

General Theories of Motivation
drive-reduction theory (p. 451)

hierarchy of needs (p. 452)
homeostasis (p. 451)
incentive theory (p. 452)
instincts (p. 451)

Understanding Emotion
emotional intelligence (EQ) (p. 461)
polygraph (p. 460)

General Theories of Emotion
Cannon–Bard theory (p. 464)

facial-feedback hypothesis (p. 464)
James–Lange theory (p. 463)
Schachter's two-factor theory (p. 465)

Achievement
WEB RESOURCES

Huffman Book Companion Site
http://www.wiley.com/college/huffman
This site is loaded with free Interactive Self-Tests, Internet Exercises, Glossary and Flashcards for key terms, Web links, Handbook for Non-Native Speakers, and other activities designed to improve your mastery of the material in this section.

Want more information on eating disorders?
http://www.mentalhealth.com/p20-grp.html
The Internet Mental Health Eating Disorders provides important information, diagnosis criteria, and treatment for eating disorders.

VISUAL SUMMARY

Motivation and Emotion
(Modules 31 and 32)

Understanding Motivation

Hunger and Eating
- Both *biological* (stomach, biochemistry, brain) and *psychosocial* (emotional needs and cultural conditioning).
- Eating disorders due to combination of biological and psychosocial factors:

1) Obesity: Being significantly above the recommended weight level.

2) Anorexia nervosa: Extreme weight loss due to self-imposed starvation.

3) Bulimia nervosa: Excessive consumption of food followed by purging.

Arousal
Arousal motive: People seek *optimal level* of *arousal* that maximizes their performance. High sensation seekers are biologically "prewired" to need a higher level of stimulation.

Achievement
- **Achievement motivation:** Need for success, doing better than others, and mastering challenging tasks.
- **Intrinsic** vs. **extrinsic motivation:** Research shows extrinsic rewards can lower interest and achievement motivation.

General Theories of Motivation

Biological Theories

- **Instinct theories:** Inborn, genetic component to motivation.

- **Drive-reduction theory:** Internal tensions (produced by body's demand for *homeostasis*) "push" organism to satisfy basic needs.

Psychosocial Theories

- **Incentive theory:** "Pull" of external environmental stimuli.

- *Cognitive theories:* Emphasize thoughts, attributions, and expectations in setting and meeting goals.

Interactionism
Maslow's **hierarchy of needs:** Basic physiological and survival needs must be met before higher needs, such as love and self-actualization.

Understanding Emotion

Three Basic Components

Cognitive
(thoughts, beliefs, and expectations)

Self-report techinques (paper-and-pencil tests, surveys, and interviews) are used to study this component.

Physiological Arousal
(heart rate, respiration rate, etc.)

Emotions are a general, nonspecific arousal of nervous system, involving cerebral cortex, limbic system, and reticular formation.
Obvious signs of arousal: activation of *sympathetic nervous system. Parasympathetic nervous system* restores body to "status quo."

Behavioral Expression
(smiles, frowns, running)

Seven to ten basic, *universal* emotions suggest emotions that may be innate; however, display rules differ across cultures and between men and women.

- **Polygraph**: Measures changes in emotional arousal but is not valid for measuring guilt or innocence.
- **Emotional intelligence (EQ)**: Knowing and managing emotions, empathizing, and maintaining satisfying relationships.

General Theories of Emotion

Four Theories

James–Lange
Feelings are interpreted from physiological arousal and behavioral expressions (smile, racing heart).

Cannon–Bard
Arousal, cognitions, and behavioral expression of emotions occur simultaneously.

Facial–Feedback
Facial muscles elicit specific emotions.

Schachter's Two–Factor
Emotions depend on two factors—physical arousal and cognitive labeling of the arousal.

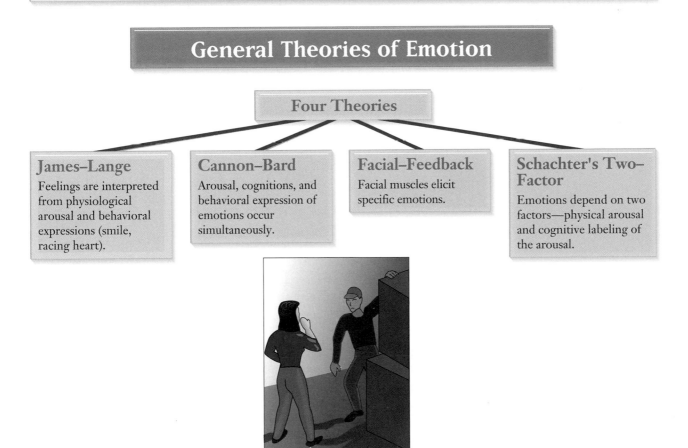

PERSONALITY

C onsider the following personality description. How well does it describe you?

You have a strong need for other people to like you and admire you. You have a tendency to be critical of yourself. You have a great deal of unused capacity that you have not turned to your advantage. Although you have some personality weaknesses, you are generally able to compensate for them. You pride yourself on being an independent thinker and do not accept other opinions without satisfactory proof. Disciplined and self-controlled outside, you tend to be worried and insecure inside. At times, you have serious doubts whether you have made the right decision or done the right thing.

ADAPTED FROM ULRICH, STACHNIK, & STAINTON, 1963

☐ Achievement
■ Assessment
■ Application

What do you think? Does this sound like you? When this same personality description was given to research participants, and they were told that it was written specifically for them on the basis of previous psychological tests, a high percentage reported that the description was "very accurate." Surprisingly, even when participants were informed that this was a made-up assessment based on generalized information, most still believed the description fit them better than a bona fide personality profile developed from scientifically designed tests (Hyman, 1981). Research also shows that about 78 percent of women and 70 percent of men read newspaper horoscopes, and many of them believe these horoscopes are so correct that they were written especially for them (Halpern, 1998). Perhaps most surprising, in a study of nonpsychology and psychology majors and mental health professionals, researchers found widespread acceptance of vague and universal statements as valid descriptors of their individual personalities (Pulido & Marco, 2000).

Why are these pseudo–personality tests so popular? It could be that we think these fortune-tellers and pseudotests have somehow tapped into our unique selves. Actually, however, the traits they supposedly reveal are generalizations shared by almost everyone. Furthermore, the traits are generally positive and flattering — or at least neutral. (Would we like tests revealing that we are "irritable, selfish, and emotionally unstable"?) In this section, rather than these nonscientific methods, we will focus on research–based methods used by psychologists to assess personality.

Before we begin, we need to define *personality*. For most people, "personality" is a relatively simple, everyday concept, as in "He's got a great (or lousy) personality." But for psychologists, personality is an inherently complicated topic, and there are numerous definitions. One of the most widely accepted models defines **personality** as an individual's unique and relatively stable pattern of thoughts, feelings, and actions. Personality describes you as a *person*: how you are different from other people and what patterns of behavior are typical of you. You might qualify as an "extrovert," for example, if you are talkative and outgoing most of the time, or as "conscientious" if you are responsible and self-disciplined most of the time. (Keep in mind that personality is not the same as *character*, which refers to your ethics, morals, values, and integrity.)

Unlike pseudopsychologies presented in supermarket tabloids and newspaper horoscopes, personality theorists focus on empirical studies — the *science* of personality. In line with the basic goals of psychology presented in Module 1, they seek to (1) *describe* individual differences in personality, (2) *explain* how those differences come about, and (3) *predict* individual behavior based on personality findings. Before describing, explaining, or predicting personality, we must *assess* or measure it. Therefore, the first module of this section is personality assessment. We then discuss five major theories: trait, psychoanalytic/psychodynamic, humanistic, social/cognitive, and biological.

Personality *Relatively stable and enduring patterns of thoughts, feelings, and actions*

MODULE 33
PERSONALITY ASSESSMENT

Assessment

How do psychologists
measure personality?

Throughout history, people have sought information about their own and others' personalities. Back in the 1800s, if you wanted to have your personality assessed, you would go to a *phrenologist*. This highly respected person would carefully measure your skull, examine the bumps on your head, and then give you a psychological profile of your unique qualities and characteristics. Phrenologists used a *phrenology* chart to determine which personality traits were associated with bumps on different areas of the skull.

Today, some people consult fortune-tellers, horoscope columns in the newspaper, tarot cards, and even fortune cookies in Chinese restaurants. But modern research has produced various methods for assessing personality, which are used by clinical and counseling psychologists, psychiatrists, and other helping professionals in the diagnosis of patients and to assess progress in therapy. Personality assessment is also used for educational and vocational counseling and by businesses to aid in hiring decisions.

■ How We Measure Personality: Do You See What I See?

Like a detective solving a mystery, modern psychologists typically use numerous methods and a complete *battery* (or series) of tests to fully *assess* personality. This assortment of measures can be grouped in a few broad categories: *interviews*, *observations*, *objective tests*, and *projective tests*.

Interviews

We all use informal "interviews" to get to know other people. When first meeting someone, we ask about their job, college major, family, and hobbies or interests. Psychologists also use interviews — both *structured* and *unstructured*. Unstructured interviews are often used for job and college selection and for diagnosing psychological problems. In an unstructured format, interviewers get impressions and pursue hunches or let a person expand on information that promises to disclose personality characteristics. The interviewee has a chance to explain unique qualifications in his or her own words. Structured interviews, on the other hand, ask specific questions and follow a set of procedures so that the person being evaluated can be evaluated more objectively. The results of a structured interview are often charted on a rating scale to standardize the evaluations and make comparisons easier.

Observation

In addition to structured and unstructured interviews, psychologists also use direct behavioral observation to assess personality. Most of us enjoy "people watching," but observation as a scientific assessment procedure is a methodical process. The psychologist looks for examples of specific behaviors and follows a careful set of evaluation guidelines. For instance, a psychologist might arrange to observe a troubled client's interactions with his or her family. Does the client become agitated by the presence of certain family members and not others? Does he or she become passive and withdrawn when asked a direct question? Through careful observation, the psychologist gains valuable insights into the client's personality, as well as family dynamics.

Objective Tests

Objective personality tests, or *inventories*, are standardized questionnaires that require written responses, typically to multiple-choice or true–false items. Answers to these questions help people to describe themselves — to "self-report." They are considered "objective" tests because they have a limited number of possible responses to items

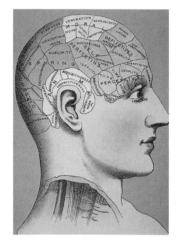

Personality and bumps on the head?
Franz Gall, founder of phrenology, believed that personality could be measured by reading bumps on the skull. Note that terms like sublimity (ability to squelch natural impulses, especially sexual) and ideality (ability to live by high ideals) probably reflect personality traits important in the 1800s. Can you imagine what traits might be measured if we still believed in phrenology? Would we create terms like suppressity (withholding of natural impulses, especially sexual) and computericity (ability to live in the Information Age)?

and empirical standards for constructing test items and scoring. Given that objective tests can be administered to a large number of people in a relatively short period of time and evaluated in a standardized fashion, they are by far the most widely used method for assessing personality.

You have been introduced to several self-report personality tests in this textbook. There was the androgyny scale in Module 29, for example, and the sensation-seeking scale in Module 31. Later in this Module 36, we discuss the locus of control scale. The complete versions of these tests measure one specific personality trait and are used primarily in research. Often, however, psychologists in clinical, counseling, and industrial settings are interested in assessing a range of personality traits all at once. To do this, they generally use *multitrait* (or *multiphasic*) inventories.

Many multitrait tests have been developed, including the Sixteen Personality Factors Questionnaire (16PF) discussed later. The most widely studied and clinically used multitrait test is the **Minnesota Multiphasic Personality Inventory** (MMPI) — or its revision, the MMPI-2 (Butcher, 2000; Butcher & Rouse, 1996). The test consists of over 500 statements that participants respond to with *True, False,* or *Cannot say.* The following are examples of the kinds of statements found on the MMPI:

My stomach frequently bothers me.

I have enemies who really wish to harm me.

I sometimes hear things that other people can't hear.

I would like to be a mechanic.

I have never indulged in any unusual sex practices.

Why are some of these questions about really unusual, abnormal behavior? Although there are many "normal" questions on the full MMPI, the test is designed primarily for clinical and counseling psychologists to diagnose psychological disorders. Table 33.1 shows how MMPI test items are grouped into 10 *clinical scales*, each measuring a different disorder. Depressed people, for example, tend to score higher on one group of questions, whereas people with schizophrenia score higher on a different group. Each group of items is called a *scale*. There are

Minnesota Multiphasic Personality Inventory (MMPI) *The most widely researched and clinically used self-report personality test (MMPI-2 is the revised version)*

TABLE 33.1 SUBSCALES OF THE MMPI-2

Name of Subscale	Typical Interpretations of High Scores
Clinical Scales	
1. Hypochondriasis	Numerous physical complaints
2. Depression	Seriously depressed and pessimistic
3. Hysteria	Suggestible, immature, self-centered, demanding
4. Psychopathic deviancy	Rebellious, nonconformist
5. Masculinity/femininity	Interests like those of other sex
6. Paranoia	Suspicious and resentful of others
7. Psychasthenia	Fearful, agitated, brooding
8. Schizophrenia	Withdrawn, reclusive, bizarre thinking
9. Mania	Distractible, impulsive, dramatic
10. Social introversion	Shy, introverted, self-effacing
Validity Scales	
1. L (lie)	Denies common problems, projects a "saintly" or false picture
2. F (confusion)	Answers are contradictory
3. K (defensiveness)	Minimizes social and emotional complaints
4. ? (cannot say)	Many items left unanswered

also four *validity scales* designed to reflect the extent to which respondents distort their answers, do not understand the items, or are being uncooperative. Research has found that the validity scales effectively detect "pseudopatients" who were asked to fake psychological disturbances or try to appear more psychologically healthy (Bagby, Rogers, & Buis 1994).

Are these tests the same as career inventories? Personality tests, like the MMPI, are often confused with other self-report tests called *vocational interest tests* that help people make career decisions. For example, the *Strong Vocational Interest Inventory* asks whether you would rather write, illustrate, print, or sell a book or whether you'd prefer the work of a salesperson or teacher. This self-report test compares the things you like to do to the responses of people in various occupational groups.

Given your vocational interest test profile, along with your scores on *aptitude tests* (which measure potential abilities) and *achievement tests* (which measure what you have already learned), a counselor can help you identify the types of jobs that best suit you. Most colleges have career counseling centers where you can take vocational interest tests to guide you in your career decisions.

Projective Techniques

Unlike objective tests, **projective tests** use ambiguous, unstructured stimuli, such as inkblots, which can be perceived in many ways. As the name implies, *projective* tests supposedly allow each person to *project* his or her own unconscious conflicts, psychological defenses, motives, and personality traits onto the test materials. Because respondents are unable (or unwilling) to express their true feelings if asked directly, the ambiguous stimuli reportedly provide an indirect, "psychological x-ray" of important unconscious processes. Two of the most widely used projective tests are the *Rorschach Inkblot Test* and the *Thematic Apperception Test* (TAT).

The **Rorschach Inkblot Test,** introduced in 1921 by Swiss psychiatrist Hermann Rorschach, consists of ten inkblots originally developed by spilling ink on paper and folding the paper in half (Figure 33.1). You report what you see in each card and the clinician records your responses verbatim while also observing your gestures and reactions. The clinician later interprets your answers as indications of your unconscious feelings and conflicts. If you report seeing a bear in one of the inkblots, for example, the interpretation might be that you have a strong degree of emotional control (Meloy, Acklin, Gacono, Murray, & Peterson, 1997).

Created by personality researcher Henry Murray in 1938, the **Thematic Apperception Test** (TAT) is another of the most frequently used projective tests. It consists of a series of black-and-white ambiguous pictures, such as Figure 33.2. As mentioned in

"RORSCHACH! WHAT'S TO BECOME OF YOU?"

Projective Tests *Psychological tests using ambiguous stimuli, such as inkblots or drawings, which allow the test taker to project his or her unconscious onto the test material*

Rorschach [ROAR-shock] Inkblot Test *A projective test that presents a set of 10 cards with symmetrical abstract patterns, known as inkblots, and respondents describe what they "see" in the image; their response is thought to be a projection of unconscious processes*

Thematic Apperception Test (TAT) *A projective test that shows a series of ambiguous black-and-white pictures and asks the test taker to create a story related to each; the responses presumably reflect a projection of unconscious processes*

Figure 33.1 *The Rorschach Inkblot Test.* Individuals are shown 10 inkblots like this, one at a time, and asked to report what figures or objects they see in each of them. Their responses are believed to reflect unconscious parts of their personality that *project* onto the ambiguous stimuli. Thus, the Rorschach is known as a *projective* test. (Reproduced with permission.)

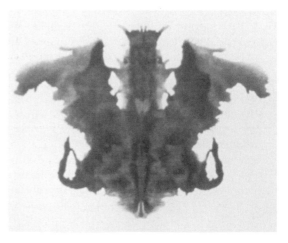

Module 33, the TAT is frequently used to measure achievement motivation, as well as for personality assessment. If you were taking this test, you would be asked to create a story about the picture, including what the characters are feeling and how the story turns out. As with the Rorschach, your responses reportedly reflect your unconscious needs and conflicts. For example, a person who sees a picture of a young girl looking at mannequins in a store window might create a story with angry references to the parents of the girl in the picture. The clinician might infer that the test taker has hidden resentments toward his or her own parents (Davison, Neale, & Kring, 2004).

Are Personality Measurements Accurate? Evaluating the Methods

What do you think of these interpretations of the projective tests? Do they accurately reflect true personality? Let's evaluate each of the various methods of personality assessment, beginning with interviews and observations:

- **Interviews and observations.** Both of these methods can provide valuable insights into personality, but they are time consuming and therefore expensive. Furthermore, just as football fans can disagree over the relative merits of the same quarterback, raters of personality tests frequently disagree in their evaluations of the same individual. Interviews and observations also involve unnatural settings, and as we saw in Module 2, the very presence of an observer can alter the behavior that is being studied.

- **Objective tests.** Tests like the MMPI-2 provide specific, objective information about a broad range of personality traits in a relatively short period of time; however, accuracy largely depends on cooperative and truthful respondents. Thus, objective, self-report inventories are subject to three major criticisms:
  1. **Deliberate deception and social desirability bias.** Some items on self-report inventories are easy to "see through," so respondents may intentionally, or unintentionally, fake particular personality traits. (The validity scales of the MMPI-2 are designed to call attention to this sort of pattern of response.) In addition, some respondents want to look good and will answer questions in ways that they perceive as *socially desirable*.
  2. **Diagnostic difficulties.** When self-report inventories are used for diagnosis, overlapping items sometimes make it difficult to pinpoint a diagnosis (Graham, 1991). In addition, clients with severe disorders sometimes score within the normal range, and normal clients may score within the elevated range (Cronbach, 1990).
  3. **Cultural bias and inappropriate use.** Some critics think that the standards for "normalcy" on objective, self-report tests fail to recognize the impact of culture. For example, respondents from Latino cultures, such as Mexican, Puerto Rican, and Argentinean, on average tend to score differently than respondents from Western cultures on the masculinity–femininity scale on the MMPI-2 (Lucio-Gomez, Ampudia-Rueda, Duran-Patino, Gallegos-Mejia, & Leon-Guzman, 1999). The fact that these groups score higher on traditional gender roles reflects their cultural training more than individual personality traits.

- **Projective tests.** Although projective tests are extremely time consuming to administer and interpret, their proponents suggest that because they have no right or wrong answers, respondents are less able to deliberately fake their responses. In addition, because these tests are unstructured, respondents may be more willing to talk about sensitive, anxiety-laden topics. Critics point out, however, that the reliability and validity of projective tests is among the lowest of all tests of personality (Grove et al., 2002; Wood, Lilienfeld, Nezworski, & Garb, 2001). If you recall from Module 24's discussion of intelligence tests, the two most important measures of a good test are

Figure 33.2 *The Thematic Apperception Test (TAT).* Like the Rorschach, the TAT is a projective test designed to reveal unconscious parts of the personality. Participants are asked to talk about what led up to the pictured situation, what is happening now, and how the story will end. (Reproduced with permission.)

CRITICAL THINKING   ACTIVE LEARNING

Why Are Pseudo Personality Tests So Popular?

Throughout this text, we have emphasized the value of critical thinking, which requires that we recognize *our personal biases and analyze data for value and content.* By carefully evaluating the evidence and credibility of the source, critical thinkers recognize faulty logic and appeals to emotion. When we look at the various problems with pseudo personality evaluations like the one in our introductory incident, we can identify at least three different logical fallacies: the Barnum effect, the fallacy of positive instances, and the self-serving bias.

The Barnum Effect

The first reason we often accept pseudo personality descriptions and horoscope predictions is that we think they are accurate. We tend to believe these tests have somehow tapped into our unique selves, when in fact they are ambiguous, broad statements that fit just about anyone. Being so readily disposed to accept such generalizations is known as the *Barnum effect* — after P.T. Bar-

num, the legendary circus promoter who said, "Always have a little something for everyone" and "There's a sucker born every minute." Reread the bogus personality profile in the introductory incident. Can you see how "You have a strong need for other people to like you and admire you" fits almost everyone? Do you know anyone who doesn't "at times have serious doubts whether [they've] made the right decision or done the right thing"?

The Fallacy of Positive Instances

Now look again at the personality profile and count the number of times both sides of a personality trait are given. ("You have a strong need for other people to like you" and "You pride yourself on being an independent thinker.") According to the *fallacy of positive instances,* we tend to notice and remember events that confirm our expectations and ignore those that are nonconfirming. If we see ourselves as independent thinkers, for example, we ignore the "needing to be liked by others" part. Similarly, horoscope readers easily find "Sagittarius characteristics" in a Sagittarius horoscope but fail to notice when

Sagittarius predictions miss or when the same traits appear for Scorpios or Leos.

The Self-Serving Bias

Now check the overall tone of the personality description. Note how the traits are generally positive and flattering — or at least neutral. According to the *self-serving bias,* we tend to prefer information that maintains a positive self-image (Brown & Rogers, 1991; Gifford & Hine, 1997). In fact, research shows that the more favorable a personality description, the more people believe it, and the more likely they are to believe it is unique to themselves (Guastello, Guastello, & Craft, 1989). (The self-serving bias might also explain why people prefer pseudo personality tests to bona fide tests — they're generally more flattering.)

Taken together, these three logical fallacies help explain the belief in "pop psych" personality tests and newspaper horoscopes. They offer "something for everyone" (the Barnum effect); we pay attention only to what confirms our expectations (the fallacy of positive instances); and we like flattering descriptions (the self-serving bias).

VISUAL QUIZ

Can you name the two logical fallacies found in this cartoon?

Answer: The self-serving bias and Barnum effect.

reliability (Are the results consistent?) and *validity* (Does the test measure what it's designed to measure?). One problem with the Rorschach, in particular, is that interpreting clients' responses depends in large part on the subjective judgment of the examiner, and some examiners are simply more experienced or skilled than others. Also, there are problems with *interrater reliability*. Two examiners may interpret the same response in very different ways.

As you can see, each of these methods has its limits. However, psychologists typically combine results from various methods to create a full picture of individual personality. Having seen how personality is measured and evaluated, we now turn our attention to the major theories that describe, explain, and predict personality.

Assessment

CHECK & REVIEW

Personality Assessment

Personality is defined as an individual's relatively stable and enduring pattern of thoughts, emotions, and actions. Psychologists assess, describe, explain, and predict personality according to different theoretical orientations.

Psychologists use four basic methods to measure or assess personality: interviews, observations, objective tests, and projective techniques. Objective tests, such as the **Minnesota Multiphasic Personality Inventory** (MMPI-2), use paper-and-pencil questionnaires or inventories, which provide objective standardized information about a large number of personality traits. However, they are limited by respondents' deliberate deception and social desirability bias, diagnostic difficulties, and inappropriate use.

Projective tests, such as the **Rorschach Inkblot Test** or the **Thematic Apperception Test** (TAT), ask test takers to respond to ambiguous stimuli. Although these tests reportedly provide insight into unconscious elements of personality, they have low reliability and validity.

Questions

1. Match each personality test with its description:
   (a) a projective test using inkblots;
   (b) an objective, self-report, paper-and-pencil personality test;
   (c) a projective test using drawings of ambiguous human situations
   _____ i. MMPI-2
   _____ ii. Rorschach
   _____ iii. TAT

2. Two important criteria for evaluating the usefulness of tests used to assess personality are _____. (a) concurrence and prediction; (b) reliability and validity; (c) consistency and correlation; (d) diagnosis and prognosis

3. Describe the three logical fallacies that encourage acceptance of pseudo personality tests and horoscopes.

Answers to Questions can be found in Appendix B.

ACTIVE LEARNING WORKSHEET   MODULE 33

Circle either "T" for true or "F" for false, and then compare your answers with those in Appendix B.

1. The Rorschach is the most widely used self-report, objective personality test. T or F

2. The MMPI uses black and whiter photos of ambiguous stimuli to test personality. T or F

3. Noticing and remembering events that confirm our expectations and ignoring nonconfirming events is known as the fallacy of positive instances. T or F

4. Compared to projective tests, objective personality tests generally have higher reliability and validity scores. T or F

5. Projective tests use ambiguous stimuli to allow expression of unconscious feelings and motives. T or F

MODULE 34
TRAIT THEORIES

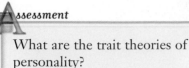

Assessment

What are the trait theories of personality?

Gordon Allport (1897–1967). As a trait theorist, Allport believed personality consisted of a limited number of attributes, which could be arranged into a hierarchy with the most important at the top and the least important at the bottom.

Trait *A relatively stable and consistent characteristic that can be used to describe someone*

Factor Analysis *Statistical procedure for determining the most basic units or factors in a large array of data*

Five-Factor Model (FFM) *Trait theory that explains personality in terms of a Big Five model — openness, conscientiousness, extraversion, agreeableness, and neuroticism*

Study **T**ip

You can easily remember the five factors by noting that together, the first letters of each of the Big Five traits spell the word "ocean."

How would you describe your two or three best friends? Would you say they are funny, loyal, and good-natured? Or adventuresome and trustworthy? The terms you use to describe other people (and yourself) are called **traits**, relatively stable and consistent personal characteristics. Trait theorists are interested in first discovering how people differ (which key traits best describe them) and then in measuring how much they differ (the degree of variation in traits within the individual and among individuals).

■ Early Trait Theorists: Allport, Cattell, and Eysenck

As you may imagine, identifying and measuring essential traits sounds much easier than it actually is. Every individual differs from one another in a great number of ways. An early study of dictionary terms found almost 18,000 words that could be used to describe personality; of these, about 4,500 were considered to fit the researchers' definition of personality *traits* (Allport & Odbert, 1936).

Faced with this enormous list of potential traits, Gordon Allport (1937) believed the best way to understand personality was to study an individual and then arrange his or her unique personality traits into a hierarchy. The most important and pervasive traits were listed at the top and the least important at the bottom.

Later psychologists reduced the wide array of possible personality traits with a statistical technique called **factor analysis.** Raymond Cattell (1950, 1965, 1990) condensed the list of traits to 30 to 35 basic characteristics.

Hans Eysenck (1967, 1982, 1990) reduced the list even further. He described personality as a relationship between three basic types of traits — extroversion–introversion (E), neuroticism (N), and psychoticism (P). These dimensions are assessed with the *Eysenck Personality Questionnaire.*

■ The "Big Five" Model: Five Basic Personality Traits

Factor analysis was also used to develop the most talked about modern trait theory — **five-factor model** (FFM) (McCrae & Costa, 1990, 1997, 1999; McCrae et al., 2000). Combining all the previous research findings and the long list of possible personality traits, researchers discovered that several traits came up repeatedly, even when different tests were used. These five major dimensions of personality, often dubbed the Big Five, are described below.

1. *(O) Openness.* People who rate high in this factor are original, imaginative, curious, open to new ideas, artistic, and interested in cultural pursuits. Low scorers tend to be conventional, down-to-earth, narrower in their interests, and not artistic.

2. *(C) Conscientiousness.* This factor ranges from responsible, self-disciplined, organized, and achieving at the high end to irresponsible, careless, impulsive, lazy, and undependable at the other.

3. *(E) Extroversion.* This factor contrasts people who are sociable, outgoing, talkative, fun loving, and affectionate at the high end with introverted individuals who tend to be withdrawn, quiet, passive, and reserved.

4. *(A) Agreeableness.* Individuals who score high on this factor are good-natured, warm, gentle, cooperative, trusting, and helpful, whereas low scorers are irritable, argumentative, ruthless, suspicious, uncooperative, and vindictive.

5. *(N) Neuroticism (or emotional stability).* People high on neuroticism are emotionally unstable and prone to insecurity, anxiety, guilt, worry, and moodiness.

Study the following figure based on Raymond Cattell's factor analysis findings. Note how Cattell's 16 source traits exist on a continuum with extremes at either end, such as *reserved* and *less intelligent* at the far left and *outgoing* and *more intelligent* at the far right. Average falls somewhere in the middle.

Take a pen and make a dot on the line (from 1 to 10) that represents your own degree of reservation versus outgoingness. Then make a dot for yourself on the other 15 traits. (While making judgments of your traits, try to avoid the self-serving bias described in the previous Critical Thinking/Active Learning exercise.)

Finally, connect the dots. How does your personality profile compare with the profiles of creative artists, airline pilots, and writers?

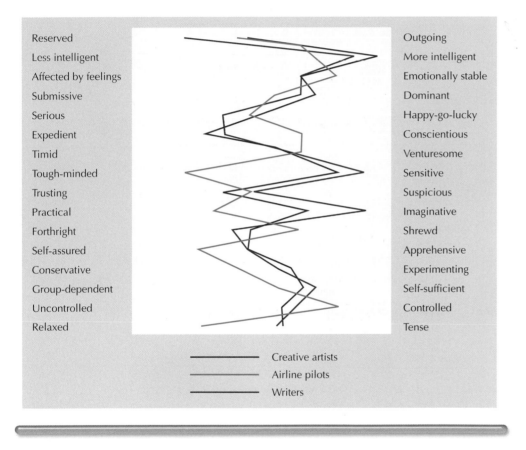

Reserved	Outgoing
Less intelligent	More intelligent
Affected by feelings	Emotionally stable
Submissive	Dominant
Serious	Happy-go-lucky
Expedient	Conscientious
Timid	Venturesome
Tough-minded	Sensitive
Trusting	Suspicious
Practical	Imaginative
Forthright	Shrewd
Self-assured	Apprehensive
Conservative	Experimenting
Group-dependent	Self-sufficient
Uncontrolled	Controlled
Relaxed	Tense

——————— Creative artists
——————— Airline pilots
——————— Writers

People at the other end are emotionally stable, calm, even-tempered, easygoing, and relaxed.

■ Evaluating Trait Theories: The Pros and Cons

As you will see in the Try This Yourself exercise on the next page, David Buss and his colleagues (1991, 1999) found a strong correlation between their survey findings and the Big Five model, which may reflect an evolutionary advantage to people who are more open, conscientious, extroverted, agreeable, and less neurotic. The evolutionary perspective also is confirmed by cross-cultural studies (Chuang, 2002; Mastor, Jin, & Cooper, 2000; McCrae et al., 2000); and comparative studies with chimpanzees and other species (see the accompanying Research Highlight).

Use the following Big Five figure to plot your own profile by placing a dot on each line to indicate your degree of openness, conscientiousness, and so on. Do the same for a current or previous love partner. How do your scores compare? Now look below at Figure 34.1, which reports the characteristics most valued in potential mates. David Buss and his colleagues (1989, 1999) surveyed over 10,000 men and women from 37 different countries and found a surprising level of agreement. Moreover, most elements of the Big Five factors are found at the top of the list. Both men and women prefer dependability (conscientiousness), emotional stability (low neuroticism), pleasing disposition (agreeableness), and sociability (extroversion) to the alternatives.

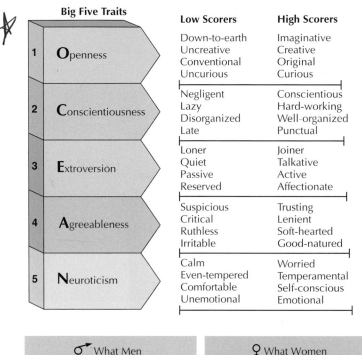

Big Five Traits	Low Scorers	High Scorers
1 **O**penness	Down-to-earth Uncreative Conventional Uncurious	Imaginative Creative Original Curious
2 **C**onscientiousness	Negligent Lazy Disorganized Late	Conscientious Hard-working Well-organized Punctual
3 **E**xtroversion	Loner Quiet Passive Reserved	Joiner Talkative Active Affectionate
4 **A**greeableness	Suspicious Critical Ruthless Irritable	Trusting Lenient Soft-hearted Good-natured
5 **N**euroticism	Calm Even-tempered Comfortable Unemotional	Worried Temperamental Self-conscious Emotional

♂ What Men Want in a Mate

1. Mutual attraction — love
2. Dependable character
3. Emotional stability and maturity
4. Pleasing disposition
5. Good health
6. Education and intelligence
7. Sociability
8. Desire for home and children
9. Refinement, neatness
10. Good looks

♀ What Women Want in a Mate

1. Mutual attraction — love
2. Dependable character
3. Emotional stability and maturity
4. Pleasing disposition
5. Education and intelligence
6. Sociability
7. Good health
8. Desire for home and children
9. Ambition and industriousness
10. Refinement, neatness

Figure 34.1 *The importance of various traits in mate selection around the world.* Note how the top four traits for both men and women are the same, and how closely their desired traits match those of the Big Five. *Source:* Buss et al., 1990, p. 19.

Taken together, these studies suggest that the Big (FFM) model may be a biologically based human universal (MacDonald, 1998). This model is the first to achieve the major goal of trait theory — to describe and organize personality characteristics using the fewest number of traits. Critics argue, however, that the great variation seen in personalities cannot be accounted for by only five traits and that the Big Five model fails to offer *causal* explanations for these traits (Funder, 2001; Matsumoto, 2000; Monte & Sollod, 2003). Trait theories, in general, are subject to three major criticisms:

1. ***Lack of explanation.*** Trait approaches are good at *describing* people but do little to *explain* why they develop certain traits and why traits sometimes change (Digman, 1997).

2. ***Stability versus change.*** Although trait theorists have documented a high level of personality stability after age 30, most theories don't identify which characteristics last a lifetime and which are transient.

3. ***Situational determinants.*** Some personality theorists challenge the entire trait approach on the basis that it cannot be predicted. For example, in a classic study of children's honesty, May, Hartshorne, & Welty (1928) found children might lie at school but not at home, or might cheat on a test but not in an athletic event.

Will this marriage survive? It helps if both parties are over age 30. According to long-term studies of personality (McCrae et al, 2000), most changes in personality occur during childhood, adolescence, and young adulthood. After age 30, most traits are relatively fixed and changes after that point are few and small. Thus, people who marry after age 30 may have a more successful marriage because their personalities are more stable.

Extending the idea that behavior might be *situational*, in 1968, Walter Mischel published a landmark book in the field of personality, *Personality and Assessment*. Rather than seeing personality as the consistent, internal traits of an individual, Mischel thought that people respond to factors and conditions in the external environment. In other words, behavior — and thus personality — is determined almost entirely by the situations in which people find themselves. People are honest or dishonest, for example, not because of their internal personality but because of external rewards or threats of punishment.

Mischel's research findings were persuasive, and many joined his camp. Others, however, held out for the existence of stable traits that cause individuals to behave consistently in a wide range of settings. For years, a heated debate — known as "trait versus situationism" or the "person–situation controversy" — existed in psychology. After two decades of continuing debate and research, the consensus seems to be that situational pressures affect our relatively stable personality traits (Johnson, 1997; Mischel & Shoda, 1999). One prominent personality theorist suggested that the person–situation debate "can at least be declared about 98% over" (Funder, 2000, p. 199). We will return to this *interactionist* position later in Module 36.

Walter Mischel emphasized the power of the situation, or environment, in determining personality. In other words, honesty depends on the threat of detection or potential reward; it is not an internal personality trait.

A chievement

RESEARCH HIGHLIGHT

Do Animals Have Personality?

"It was exactly 33 years ago that I first met one of my oldest and dearest friends. To this day, the most outstanding aspect of her personality remains a quality I noticed the very first time I laid eyes on her: She is one of the most caring and compassionate people I know. She's also a chimpanzee" (Fouts, 2000, p. 68).

These are the words of a famous and highly respected comparative psychologist, Dr. Roger Fouts. What do you think? Do animals have personality? Roger Fouts proposes that "like us, chimps are highly intelligent, cooperative and sometimes violent primates who nurture family bonds, adopt orphans, mourn the death of mothers, practice self-medication, struggle for power and wage war. And that only makes sense, because the

chimp brain and the human brain both evolved from the same brain — that of our common ape ancestor" (Fouts, 2000, p. 68). Other scientists, however, are generally reluctant to ascribe personality traits, emotions, and cognitions to animals, despite the often-cited statistic that humans have 98.4 percent of the same DNA as chimps.

Noting that previous studies on animal personality were scattered across multiple disciplines and various journals, researchers Samuel Gosling and Oliver John attempted to integrate this fragmented literature and summarize what is known about animal personality. They carefully reviewed 19 factor analytic personality studies of 12 different species: guppies, octopi, rats, dogs, cats, pigs, donkeys, hyenas, vervet monkeys, rhesus monkeys, gorillas, and chimpanzees. To integrate the diverse, multispecies information, Gosling and John used the human five-factor model (FFM) discussed earlier. Interestingly, three human FFM dimensions — extraversion, neuroticism, and agreeableness — showed the strongest cross-species generality. How these personality traits are manifested, however, depends on the

Do animals have personality? *Recent research has found that some species of animals demonstrate reliable personality traits similar to the Big Five factors found in human personality.*

species. Although a human who scores low on extroversion "stays at home on Saturday night, or tries to blend into a corner at a large party, the [similarly low scoring] octopus stays in its protective den during feedings and attempts to hide itself by changing color or releasing ink into the water" (Gosling & John, 1999, p. 70).

One nonhuman dimension was also found important for describing animal personality — *dominance*. In adult humans, dominance is part of the extroversion dimension, but it has a wider range of personality implications in animals. Gosling and John explain that unlike most species, humans have multiple dominance hierarchies. The class bully may dominate on the schoolyard, the academically gifted may dominate the classroom, and the artist may win prizes for his or her creations.

Sex differences are another area where cross-species studies provide important information. For example, research on the human FFM consistently shows that women score higher on neuroticism than men (i.e., being more emotional and prone to worry) (Hrebickva, Cermak, & Osecka, 2000; McCrae et al., 1999). However, Gosling and John found a reversal of gender differences among hyenas. It was the males that were most neurotic — being more high-strung, fearful, and nervous (Figure 34.2). They explain that among hyenas, the female is larger and more dominant than the male,

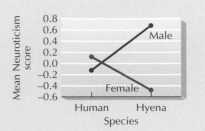

Figure 34.2 *Sex differences in standard (z) scores for neuroticism among humans and hyenas.* The ratings for hyenas are from Gosling (1998); the humans (*n* = 100) were described by peers on the same rating scales used for hyenas.

and the hyena clan is matrilineal, with the mother recognized as the head of the family. Thus, it may be that sex differences in personality are related to the *ecological niches* (the place or function within the ecosystem) occupied by the two sexes in a species.

According to Gosling and John, comparative studies of animals not only provide insight into the existence of animal personality but also offer a fresh perspective on the interplay between social and biological forces in human personality. As Roger Fouts suggested, "In the past few decades, scientific evidence on chimps and other nonhuman primates has poured in to support one basic fact: We have much more in common with apes than most people care to believe" (Fouts, 2000, p. 68).

Assessment

CHECK & REVIEW

Trait Theories

Trait theorists believe personality consists of relatively stable and consistent characteristics. Early theorists like Gordon Allport, Raymond Cattell, and Hans Eysenck used **factor analysis** to identify the smallest possible number of **traits**. More recently, researchers identified a **five-factor model** (FFM), which can be used to describe most

individuals. The Big Five traits are openness, conscientiousness, extroversion, agreeableness, and neuroticism.

General trait theories are subject to three major criticisms: *lack of explanation* (they fail to *explain* why people develop certain traits and why traits sometimes change), *stability versus change* (personality appears stable after age 30, but current theories do not identify which characteris-

tics endure and which are transient), and *situational determinants* (trait theories underestimate the influence of environmental influences).

Questions

1. A relatively stable and consistent characteristic that can be used to describe someone is known as a(n) _____. (a) character; (b) trait; (c) temperament; (d) personality.

2. Match the following personality descriptions with their corresponding Big Five personality factor: (a) openness; (b) conscientiousness; (c) introversion; (d) agreeableness; (e) neuroticism

____ i. Tending toward insecurity, anxiety, guilt, worry, and moodiness

____ ii. Being imaginative, curious, open to new ideas, and interested in cultural pursuits

____ iii. Being responsible, self-disciplined, organized, and high achieving

____ iv. Tending to be withdrawn, quiet, passive, and reserved

____ v. Being good-natured, warm, gentle, cooperative, trusting, and helpful

3. Trait theories of personality have been criticized for all but one of the following reasons. (a) they fail to explain why people develop their traits; (b) they do not include a large number of central traits; (c) they fail to identify which traits last and which are transient; (d) they fail to consider situational determinants of personality.

Answers to Questions can be found in Appendix B.

ACTIVE LEARNING WORKSHEET   MODULE 34

"What's My Trait?"

Using labels from the five-factor model (openness, conscientiousness, extraversion, agreeableness, or neuroticism), identify the major personality trait being expressed in the following sentences:

1. "I enjoy meeting new people and having a fun time."

2. "My employers always like me because they can count on me to show up on time, get my work done properly, and complete whatever task I say I will perform."

3. "New intellectual experiences and ideas are a real treat for me. I like to meet new people and explore new ideas and opinions."

4. "I generally trust others and have a tendency to be compassionate and cooperative."

5. "I am highly anxious, insecure, moody, and often emotionally unstable."

MODULE 35
PSYCHOANALYTIC/PSYCHODYNAMIC THEORIES

Assessment

What is Freud's psychoanalytic theory, and how did his followers build on his theory?

In contrast to trait theories that *describe* personality as it exists, psychoanalytic (or *psychodynamic*) theories of personality attempt to *explain* individual differences by examining how unconscious mental forces interplay with thoughts, feelings, and actions. The founding father of psychoanalytic theory is Sigmund Freud. We will examine Freud's theories in some detail and then briefly discuss three of his most influential followers — Alfred Adler, Carl Jung, and Karen Horney.

Freud's Psychoanalytic Theory: The Power of the Unconscious

Who is the best known figure in all of psychology? Most people immediately name Sigmund Freud. Even before you studied psychology, you probably came across his name in other courses. Freud's theories have been applied in the fields of anthropology, sociology, religion, medicine, art, and literature. Working from about 1890 until he died in 1939, Freud developed a theory of personality that has been one of the most influential and, at the same time, most controversial, in all of science (Gay, 1999; Taylor, 1999).

In discussing Freud's theory, we will focus on four of his most basic and debatable concepts: levels of consciousness, personality structure, defense mechanisms, and psychosexual stages of development.

Levels of Consciousness

What would you think if you heard a flight attendant say, "It's been a real job serving you … I mean joy!"? From a Freudian perspective, this little slip of the tongue (known as a *Freudian slip*) reflects the flight attendant's true, unconscious feelings. Freud believed the unconscious is hidden from our personal awareness but still has an enormous impact on our behavior — and reveals itself despite our intentions.

Freud and his famous couch. *Sigmund Freud (1856–1939) is one of the most influential personality theorists. He developed a major form of therapy (known as psychoanalysis), and treated many patients in the office pictured here.*

"*Good morning, beheaded–uh, I mean beloved.*"

Conscious *In Freudian terms, thoughts or motives that a person is currently aware of or is remembering*

Preconscious *Freud's term for thoughts or motives that one can become aware of easily*

Unconscious *Freud's term for thoughts or motives that lie beyond a person's normal awareness but that can be made available through psychoanalysis*

What exactly is the unconscious? Freud called the mind the *psyche* and believed the unconscious was one of three levels of awareness or consciousness (Figure 35.1). Using the analogy of an iceberg, the first level of awareness, the **conscious,** can be compared to the part of the iceberg above water. This part of the mind consists of all thoughts, feelings, and actions that we are actively aware of at any moment.

Immediately below the conscious realm, and the water's surface, is the somewhat larger **preconscious.** The preconscious includes mental activities not part of our current thoughts but able to be readily brought to mind. For example, the smell of fried chicken at lunch may make you feel inexplicably happy. You are conscious of being happy, but without close examination may not realize the smell reminds you, preconsciously, of your grandmother, whom you adore. The third level, the **unconscious,** lies below the preconscious and forms the bulk of the psyche. According to Freud, the unconscious stores our primitive, instinctual motives, plus anxiety-laden memories and emotions that are prevented from entering the conscious mind.

Just as the enormous mass of iceberg below the surface destroyed the ocean liner *Titanic*, the unconscious may similarly damage our psychological lives. Freud believed most psychological disorders originate from repressed (hidden) memories and instincts (sexual and aggressive) stored in the unconscious.

To treat these disorders, Freud developed *psychoanalysis* — a type of therapy discussed in Module 44. As you can imagine, Freud's concepts of the conscious, preconscious, and unconscious mind, as well as his techniques for uncovering hidden, unconscious motives, are difficult to study scientifically. They have, therefore, been the subjects of great debate in psychology.

Personality Structure

In addition to proposing that the mind functions at three levels of awareness, Freud thought personality was composed of three mental structures: *id, ego,* and *superego.* He believed that each resides, fully or partially, in the unconscious (Figure 35.2) and that each accounts for a different aspect of personality. (Keep in mind that the id, ego, and superego are mental concepts — or hypothetical constructs. They are not physical structures you could see if you dissected a human brain.)

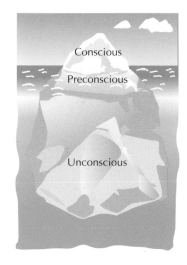

Figure 35.1 *Freud's three levels of consciousness.* The tip of the iceberg is comparable to the conscious mind, open to easy inspection. Directly below the conscious mind lies the preconscious; its contents can be viewed with a little extra effort. The large base of the iceberg is like the unconscious mind, completely hidden from personal inspection. For example, at this moment your conscious mind is focusing on this text, whereas your preconscious may include feelings of hunger and tiredness and thoughts of where you might go for lunch. Your unconscious might contain feelings of hostility toward your parents, repressed sexual desires, aggressive impulses, and irrational thoughts and feelings.

Figure 35.2 *Freud's personality structure.* According to Freud, personality is composed of three structures — the id, ego, and superego. The id operates on the pleasure principle, the ego operates on the reality principle, and the superego is guided by the conscience and ego-ideal. Note how the ego is primarily conscious and preconscious, whereas the id is entirely unconscious.

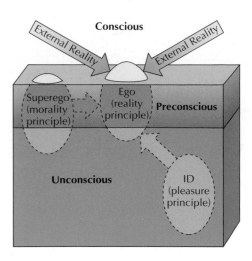

Id *According to Freud, the source of instinctual energy, which works on the pleasure principle and is concerned with immediate gratification*

Pleasure Principle *In Freud's theory, the principle on which the id operates — seeking immediate pleasure*

 Study**T**ip

"Ego" is often confused with pride or boasting. Remember that Freud used this term from the Latin "ego" meaning "I."

Ego *In Freud's theory, the rational part of the psyche that deals with reality by controlling the id, while also satisfying the superego; from the Latin term "ego" meaning "I"*

Reality Principle *According to Freud, the principle on which the conscious ego operates as it tries to meet the demands of the id and superego and the realities of the environment*

Superego *In Freud's theory, the part of the personality that incorporates parental and societal standards for morality*

The Id. The **id** is made up of innate, biological instincts and urges. Like a child, the id is immature, impulsive, and irrational. The id is also totally unconscious and serves as the reservoir of mental energy. When its primitive drives build up, the id seeks immediate gratification to relieve the tension. Thus, the id functions according to what Freud called the **pleasure principle,** the immediate and uninhibited seeking of pleasure and the avoidance of discomfort.

If the id were the only part of the psyche, we might seek pleasure (cheat on our spouses) and avoid pain (lie about our behavior), because this is what the id often urges us to do. However, Freud believed the other two parts of the psyche — the *ego* and the *superego* — control and channel the id's potentially destructive energy.

The Ego The second part of the psyche to develop is the ego, which is capable of planning, problem solving, reasoning, and controlling the id. Unlike the id, which lies entirely in the unconscious, the ego resides primarily in the conscious and preconscious. In Freud's system, the ego corresponds to the self — our conscious identity of ourselves as persons.

One of the ego's tasks is to channel and release the id's energy in ways that are compatible with the external environment. Thus, the ego is responsible for delaying gratification when necessary. Contrary to the id's *pleasure principle*, the ego operates on the **reality principle,** because it has the ability to understand and deal with objects and events in the external environment.

Freud used the example of a rider and his horse to illustrate the relationship of the ego and id:

> In its relation to the id [the ego] is like a man on horseback, who has to hold in check the superior strength of the horse ... Often a rider, if he is not to be parted from his horse, is obliged to guide it where it wants to go; so in the same way the ego is in the habit of transforming the id's will into action as if it were its own.
>
> FREUD 1923/1961; P. 25

The Superego. The final part of the psyche to develop is the **superego,** a set of ethical standards or rules for behavior that resides primarily in the preconscious and unconscious. The superego might be thought of as operating on the *morality principle*, because violating its rules results in feelings of guilt. Have you ever felt the urge to copy someone else's paper during an exam? According to Freud, the desire to cheat and hopefully get a better grade comes from your id. The guilt and conscience that stops you from cheating comes from your superego.

The superego constantly strives for perfection and is therefore as unrealistic as the id. Not only must the ego find objects and events that satisfy the id, but these same objects and events also must not violate the standards of the superego. For this reason, the ego is often referred to as the "harried executive" of the personality — managing, organizing, and directing behavior.

Defense Mechanisms

What happens when the ego fails to satisfy both the id and the superego? Anxiety slips into conscious awareness. Because anxiety is uncomfortable, people avoid it through **defense mechanisms,** which satisfy the id and superego by distorting reality. An alcoholic who uses his paycheck to buy drinks (a message from the id) may feel very guilty (a response from the superego). He may reduce this conflict by telling himself that he deserves a drink for working so hard. This is an example of the defense mechanism of *rationalization.*

Although Freud described many kinds of defense mechanisms, he believed repression was the most important. **Repression** is the mechanism by which the ego prevents the most anxiety-provoking thoughts (in other words, the most unacceptable thoughts) from entering consciousness. It is the first and most basic form of anxiety reduction.

In recent years, repression has become a popular — and controversial — topic because of the number of lawsuits brought by adults who claim *repressed memories* of childhood sexual abuse. As we discussed in Module 21, however, it is difficult to determine the authenticity of such memories. Repression and several other Freudian defense mechanisms (all of which are unconscious) are presented in Table 35.1.

Freudian theory in action? *Can you imagine what the id, ego, and superego of this man and woman might be saying during this flirtation?*

Repression *Freud's first and most basic defense mechanism, which blocks unacceptable impulses from coming into awareness*

SUMMARY TABLE 35.1 SAMPLE PSYCHOLOGICAL DEFENSE MECHANISMS

Defense Mechanism	Description	Example
Repression	Preventing painful or dangerous thoughts from entering consciousness	Forgetting the details of your parent's painful death
Sublimation	Working off unmet desires or unacceptable impulses in activities	Rechanneling sexual desires into school, work, art, sports, hobbies that are constructive
Denial	Protecting oneself from an unpleasant reality by refusing to perceive it	Alcoholics refusing to admit their addiction
Rationalization	Substituting socially acceptable reasons	Justifying cheating on an exam by saying "everyone else does it"
Intellectualization	Ignoring the emotional aspects of a painful experience by focusing on abstract thoughts, words, or ideas	Emotionless discussion of your divorce while ignoring underlying pain
Projection	Transferring unacceptable motives or impulses to others	Becoming unreasonably jealous of your mate while denying your own attraction to others
Reaction formation	Refusing to acknowledge unacceptable urges, thoughts, or feelings by exaggerating the opposite state	Promoting a petition against adult bookstores even though you are secretly fascinated by pornography
Regression	Responding to a threatening situation in a way appropriate to an earlier age or level of development	Throwing a temper tantrum when a friend doesn't want to do what you'd like
Displacement	Substituting a less threatening object for the original object of impulse	Yelling at a coworker after being criticized by your boss

"I'm sorry, I'm not speaking to anyone tonight. My defense mechanisms seem to be out of order."

I see people using defense mechanisms all the time. Is this bad?
Although defense mechanisms do twist the truth and distort reality, research supports Freud's belief that some misrepresentation seems to be necessary for our psychological well-being (Newman Duff, & Baumeister, 1997; Taylor & Armor, 1996). During a gruesome surgery, for example, physicians and nurses may *intellectualize* the procedure as an unconscious way of dealing with their personal anxieties. By focusing on highly objective technical aspects of the situation, they do not become emotionally overwhelmed by the potentially tragic situations they often encounter. Occasional use of defense mechanisms can be healthy as long as it does not become extreme.

Psychosexual Stages of Development

Defense mechanisms have generally withstood the test of time and they are an accepted part of modern psychology (see Module 10). This is not the case for Freud's theory of psychosexual stages of development.

According to Freud, strong biological urges residing within the id supposedly push all children through five universal **psychosexual stages** during the first 12 or so years of life — oral, anal, phallic, latency, and genital (Figure 35.3). The term *psychosexual* reflects Freud's emphasis on *infantile sexuality* — his belief that children experience sexual feelings from birth (although in different forms from those of adolescents or adults).

At each psychosexual stage, the id's impulses and social demands come into conflict. Therefore, if a child's needs are not met or are overindulged at one particular stage, the child may *fixate* and a part of the personality will remain stuck at that stage. Even when individuals successfully pass through one or more of the five stages, they may at times of stress return (or *regress*) to a stage at which earlier needs were badly frustrated or overgratified.

During the first *oral stage* (birth to 12 to 18 months), the erogenous zone is the mouth and the infant receives satisfaction through sucking, eating, biting, and so on. Because the infant is highly dependent on parents and caregivers to provide opportunities for oral gratification, fixation at this stage can easily occur. According to Freud, if the mother overindulges her infant's oral needs, the child may fixate and as an adult become gullible ("swallowing" anything), dependent, and passive. The underindulged child, however, will develop into an aggressive, sadistic person who exploits others. Orally fixated adults may also orient their life around their mouth — overeating, becoming an alcoholic, smoking, talking a great deal, and so on.

During the *anal stage* (between 12 to 18 months and 3 years), the erogenous zone shifts to the anus and the child receives satisfaction by having and retaining bowel movements. Because this is also the time when most parents begin toilet training, the child's desire to control his or her own bowel movements often leads to strong conflict. Adults who are fixated at this stage may display an *anal-retentive* personality and be highly controlled and compulsively neat. Or they may be very messy, disorderly, rebellious, and destructive — the *anal-expulsive* personality.

During the *phallic stage* (between 3 and 6 years), the major center of pleasure is the genitals. Masturbation and "playing doctor" with other children is common during this time. According to Freud, a 3- to 6-year-old boy develops an unconscious sexual longing for his mother and jealousy and hatred for the rival father. This attraction creates a conflict Freud called the **Oedipus complex,** after Oedipus, the legendary Greek king who unwittingly killed his father and married his mother. The young boy eventually experiences guilt and fear of punishment from the rival father, perhaps by castration. This *castration anxiety* and the Oedipus conflict are resolved when the boy represses his sexual feelings for his mother, gives up his rivalry with his father, and begins to *identify* with him instead. If this stage is not resolved completely

Psychosexual Stages *In Freudian theory, five developmental periods (oral, anal, phallic, latency, and genital) during which particular kinds of pleasures must be gratified if personality development is to proceed normally*

Oedipus [ED-uh-puss] Complex *Period of conflict during the phallic stage when children are sexually attracted to the opposite-sex parent and hostile toward the same-sex parent*

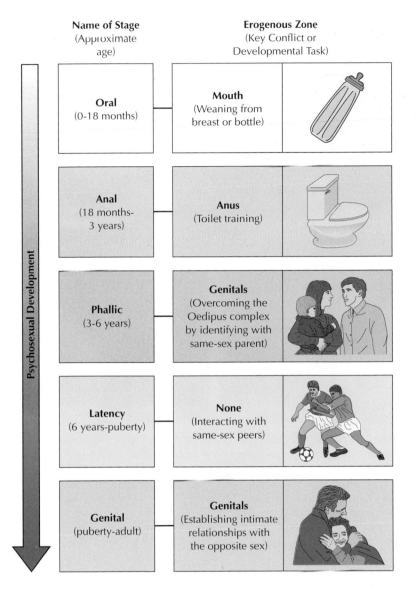

Name of Stage (Approximate age)	Erogenous Zone (Key Conflict or Developmental Task)	
Oral (0-18 months)	**Mouth** (Weaning from breast or bottle)	
Anal (18 months-3 years)	**Anus** (Toilet training)	
Phallic (3-6 years)	**Genitals** (Overcoming the Oedipus complex by identifying with same-sex parent)	
Latency (6 years-puberty)	**None** (Interacting with same-sex peers)	
Genital (puberty-adult)	**Genitals** (Establishing intimate relationships with the opposite sex)	

Psychosexual Development

Figure 35.3 *Freud's five psychosexual stages of development.*

or positively, the boy supposedly grows up resenting his father and generalizes this feeling to all authority figures.

Although Freud admitted that he was unsure about the development of young girls, he believed they did develop a special attachment to their father. Unlike the young boy who develops castration anxiety, however, the young girl discovers that she lacks a penis. This supposedly causes her to develop *penis envy* and hostile feelings toward the mother, who is blamed for the anatomical "deficiency." The conflict is resolved when the little girl suppresses her desire for her father, gives up her rivalry with her mother, and identifies with her instead.

Because Freud believed that most young girls never really overcome penis envy or fully identify with their mothers, he suggested women generally have a lower level of morality than men. (You are undoubtedly surprised or outraged by this statement, but remember that Freud was a product of his times. Most modern psychodynamic theorists reject Freud's notion of penis envy, as we will see below.)

Following the phallic stage is the *latency stage* (from age 6 years to puberty), in which children repress sexual thoughts and engage in nonsexual activities, such as developing social and intellectual skills. The task of this stage is to develop successful interactions with same-sex peers and refinement of appropriate gender roles.

Does art imitate life? Or does art imitate Freud? *According to Freudian interpretation, Shakespeare's* Hamlet *(upper left) portrayed unconscious Oedipal feelings — a young boy's wish to kill his father and marry his mother. The psychiatrist at the end of the movie* Psycho *(top middle) explained the famous murder scene in the shower as a result of "Oedipal problems." Similarly,* Beauty and the Beast *(top right) and* The Little Mermaid *(bottom left) might tap into the young girl's desire for her father and rivalry with her mother. In each of these films, the mother is absent and the young girl has her father all to herself. What about* American Beauty *(bottom right)? How might Freud interpret Kevin Spacey's sexual fantasies about his teenage daughter's best friend?*

With the beginning of adolescence comes the *genital stage*. The genitals are again erogenous zones, and the individual seeks to fulfill his or her sexual desires through emotional attachment to members of the opposite sex. Unsuccessful outcomes at this stage lead to participation in sexual relationships based only on lustful desires, not on respect and commitment.

◼ Neo-Freudian/Psychodynamic Theories: Revising Freud's Ideas

Some initial followers of Freud later rebelled and proposed theories of their own; they became known as *neo-Freudians*. Three of the most influential neo-Freudians were Alfred Adler, Carl Jung, and Karen Horney.

Adler's Individual Psychology

Alfred Adler (1870–1937) was the first to leave Freud's inner circle. He developed a theory he called *individual psychology*. Instead of seeing behavior as motivated by unconscious forces, he believed it is purposeful and goal-directed. He believed that each of us has the capacity to choose and to create. According to Adler, our goals in life provide the source of our motivation — especially those goals that aim to obtain security and

Alfred Adler (1870–1937). *Although initially trained by Freud, Adler developed his own theories (such as the inferiority complex) and later broke away to establish Adlerian psychotherapy and individual psychology.*

overcome feelings of inferiority. Adler believed that almost everyone suffers from an **inferiority complex,** deep feelings of inadequacy that arise from childhood.

Inferiority Complex *Adler's idea that feelings of inferiority develop from early childhood experiences of helplessness and incompetence*

Why are inferiority feelings so common? In Adler's view, we have inferiority feelings because we begin life as completely helpless infants. Every young child feels small, incompetent, and helpless when dealing with skilled adults. These early feelings of inadequacy supposedly result in a *will-to-power* that causes children to strive to develop superiority over others or, more positively, to develop their full potential and gain mastery and control in their lives. Thus, the childhood inferiority complex can lead to negative adult traits of dominance, aggression, and envy, or positive traits such as self-mastery and creativity (Adler, 1964, 1998).

Adler also suggested that the *will-to-power* could be positively expressed through *social interest* — identifying with others and cooperating with them for the social good. In stressing social interest and the positive outcomes of inferiority feelings, Adlerian theory is more optimistic than Freudian theory.

Application
APPLYING PSYCHOLOGY TO EVERYDAY LIFE

Birth Order and Personality

Have you heard that firstborns are more responsible and higher achievers, or that last-borns are more agreeable and accommodating? Adler was one of the first to make a connection between personality and birth order. Do the following descriptions match your adult personality? Check the following Adlerian descriptions to see if your birth order reflects your adult personality.

Firstborns. Adler thought firstborns enjoy a temporary position of privilege and great parental attention. But with the arrival of the second child, the older child is "dethroned." As adults, firstborns tend to be independent and may seek to regain attention through achievements. On the other hand, firstborns can become insecure, cautious, and defensive adults.

Secondborns. Because secondborns live in the shadow of the older sibling, feelings of inferiority are intensified. This supposedly engenders a sense of restlessness and a continual striving to outdo others. The result can be high achievement, or on the negative side, a desire to dominate others. (It's interesting that Adler was a secondborn child.)

The youngest child. Being the baby of the family, the youngest child is the most pampered and most likely to be dependent on others. The youngest child can look to older siblings as models for achievement and superiority, but always being younger, weaker, and less experienced can be discouraging.

The only child. Spending a lot of time around adults without siblings can contribute to a higher level of intellectual ability and academic success. Only children as adults may also become timid, passive, and withdrawn, and need to be pampered.

Adler's descriptions are rather vague and somewhat contradictory. A great deal of research on birth order was conducted during the 1960s and 1970s, but birth order effects turned out to be weaker and less consistent than Adler expected (Parker, 1998). However, recent research has revived the earlier interest and support (Eckstein, 2000; Kitzmann, Cohen, & Lockwood, 2002; Leong et al., 2001; Michalski & Shackelford, 2002; Sulloway, 2000).

Jung's Analytic Psychology

Another early follower turned dissenter, Carl Jung (pronounced "young"), developed *analytical psychology.* Like Freud, Jung (1875–1961) emphasized unconscious processes, but he also believed the unconscious contains positive and spiritual motives as well as sexual and aggressive forces.

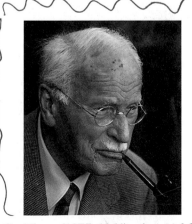

Carl Jung (1875–1961). *An initial follower of Freud, Jung later became a neo-Freudian who is credited with the development of analytical psychology and with identifying the collective unconscious and archetypes.*

Figure 35.4 *The collective unconscious.* According to Jung, humans around the world and throughout history tend to share basic images that are stored in the collective unconscious. Note repeated symbol of the snake in the early Australian aboriginal bark painting, the ancient Egyptian tomb painting, and the fifteenth-century European painting.

Collective Unconscious *Jung's concept of an inherited unconscious that all humans share*

Archetypes *According to Jung, the images or patterns of thoughts, feelings, and behavior that reside in the collective unconscious*

Jung also thought we have two forms of unconscious mind, the *personal unconscious* and the *collective unconscious.* The personal unconscious is created from our individual experiences, whereas the **collective unconscious** is identical in each person and is inherited (Jung, 1936/1969). The collective unconscious consists of primitive images and patterns of thought, feeling, and behavior that Jung called **archetypes.** In other words, the collective unconscious is the ancestral memory of the human race and therefore explains the similarities in religion, art, symbolism, and dream imagery across cultures (Figure 35.4).

Because of archetypal patterns in the collective unconscious, we perceive and react in certain predictable ways. One set of archetypes refers to gender roles. As noted in Module 29, Jung claimed that both males and females have patterns for feminine aspects of personality (*anima*) and masculine aspects (*animus*). The anima and animus within allow each of us to express both masculine and feminine personality traits and to understand and relate to the other sex.

Achievement
GENDER & CULTURAL DIVERSITY

Horney, Freud, and Penis Envy

Karen Horney (pronounced "HORN-eye") was trained as a Freudian psychoanalyst in Germany and came to the United States in 1934. One of her major contributions was a creative blending of Freudian, Adlerian, and Jungian theory, with added concepts of her own (Horney, 1939, 1945).

Horney strongly disagreed with Freud that differences in men and women were biologically based. She thought most of his ideas about female personality reflected male biases and misunderstanding. Instead of "biology is destiny," Horney contended that male–female differences were largely the result of social and cultural factors. Freud's concept of penis envy, for example, reflected women's feelings of cultural inferiority, not biological inferiority, and the appropriate term should be "power envy."

> The wish to be a man … may be the expression of a wish for all those qualities or privileges that in our culture are regarded as masculine, such as strength, courage, independence, success, sexual freedom, and right to choose a partner.
>
> HORNEY, 1926/1967, P. 108

Karen Horney (1885–1952). One of the few women who were trained by Freud, Horney disagreed with his emphasis on biological determinants of personality. She believed penis envy should be called power envy because it resulted from women's lower social status. Horney is also remembered for the concept of basic anxiety.

Horney emphasized that each sex has attributes and powers that are admired by the other and that neither should be seen as inferior or superior. Though Freud's theories have been criticized by a number of recent researchers for their male bias, Horney was one of the first to describe the problem.

Horney is also known for her theories of personality development. Compared to Freud's belief that fixation at any stage of psychosexual development (oral, anal, and so forth) was the strongest influence on adult personality, Horney believed it was the child's relationship to the parents that most influenced adult personality.

If as a child, you felt alone and isolated in a hostile environment and your needs were not met by nurturing parents, Horney believed you would experience extreme feelings of helplessness and insecurity. How people respond to this **basic anxiety** — a major concept in Horney's theory — greatly determines emotional health.

According to Horney, we all search for security in one of three basic and distinct ways. We can move toward people (by seeking affection and acceptance from others); we can move away (by striving for independence, privacy, and self-reliance); or we can move against people (by trying to gain control and power over others). Emotional health requires a balance among these three styles. Exaggerating or overusing one constitutes a neurotic, or emotionally unhealthy, response.

Basic Anxiety *According to Horney, the feelings of helplessness and insecurity that adults experience because as children they felt alone and isolated in a hostile environment*

■ Evaluating Psychoanalytic Theories: Criticisms and Enduring Influence

Freud and his psychoanalytic theories have been enormously influential, but as we said at the onset, his theories have also been the subject of great debate. Five major criticisms are presented here:

1. ***Difficult to test.*** From a scientific point of view, a major problem with psychoanalytic theory is that most of its concepts cannot be empirically tested (Gay, 2000; Lilienfeld, 1999; Macmillan, 2001). How do you conduct an experiment on the id? Or on unconscious conflicts? Scientific standards require testable hypotheses and operational definitions.

2. ***Overemphasis on biology and unconscious forces.*** Like many of the neo-Freudians, modern psychologists believe that Freud overemphasized biological determinants and did not give sufficient attention to learning and culture in shaping behavior. In particular, the psychoanalytic belief that "anatomy is destiny" completely ignores the power of culture to create differences between men and women.

3. ***Inadequate evidence.*** Freud based his theories almost exclusively on the case histories of his patients. His data, therefore, were all subjective, leading critics today to wonder if Freud saw what he expected to see and ignored the rest. (Do you recognize this as the "fallacy of positive instances" described in this section's Critical Thinking/Active Learning exercise?)

   Moreover, Freud's patients were almost exclusively upper-class Viennese women who sought his help because they had serious adjustment problems. Such a small and selective sample may mean that his theory describes only disturbed personality development in upper-class Viennese women in the late 1800s.

4. ***Sexism.*** Many psychologists reject Freud's theories as misogynistic, or derogatory toward women. First, there is the concept of penis envy, which, as you read earlier, Karen Horney, and others since, have rejected. Second, Freud rejected his patients' reports of childhood sexual abuse when colleagues ridiculed him for taking them seriously. His revised position was that the women were expressing unconscious wishes and fantasies. Given our knowledge now of the high rate of rape and incest throughout history, it's entirely possible that Freud was right in initially trusting his patients and wrong to change his position (Masson, 1984, 1992).

Freud and his daughter. *Despite criticisms of sexism, psychoanalysis was one of the few areas where women gained prominent positions in the early twentieth century. Here Freud is walking with his daughter Anna Freud (1895–1982), who also became an influential psychoanalyst.*

5. *Lack of cross-cultural support.* The Freudian concepts that ought to be most easily supported empirically — the biological determinants of personality — are generally not borne out by cross-cultural studies (Crews, 1997).

Today there are few Freudian purists left. Modern psychodynamic theorists and psychoanalysts employ only some of his theories and techniques. Instead, they use empirical methods and research findings to reformulate and refine traditional Freudian theories and methods of assessment (Westen, 1998).

There are many legitimate criticisms of Freud. But even so, many psychologists argue that, wrong as he was on many counts, Freud still ranks as one of the giants of psychology (Breger, 2000; Monte & Sollod, 2003; Weinberger & Westen, 2001). He should be credited and remembered for at least five reasons: (1) the emphasis on the unconscious and its influence on behavior; (2) the conflict among the id, ego, and superego and the resulting defense mechanisms; (3) talking openly about sex in Victorian times; (4) the development of an influential form of therapy, *psychoanalysis*; and (5) the sheer magnitude of his theory.

In reference to this last point, it is hard to overstate Freud's impact on Western intellectual history. He attempted to explain dreams, religion, social groupings, family dynamics, neurosis, psychosis, humor, the arts, and literature. It's easy to criticize Freud if you don't remember that he began his work at the start of the twentieth century and lacked the benefit of modern research findings and technology. To criticize his theory without historical perspective is to criticize the Wright brothers for their crude airplane design. We can only imagine how our current theories will look 100 years from now.

Today, Freud's legacy lives on in our thinking and artistic imagination. Often without realizing the source, we talk about unconscious motives, oral fixations, and repression. We accuse people of being anal or egomaniacs. Right or wrong, Freud has a lasting place among the pioneers in psychology.

Assessment
CHECK & REVIEW

Psychoanalytic/Psychodynamic Theories

Sigmund Freud founded the psychoanalytic approach to personality, which emphasizes the power of the unconscious. The mind (or psyche) reportedly functions on three levels (**conscious, preconscious,** and **unconscious**), and the personality has three distinct structures (**id, ego,** and **superego**). The ego struggles to meet the demands of the id and superego, and when these demands are in conflict, the ego may resort to defense mechanisms to relieve anxiety. According to Freud, all human beings pass through five **psychosexual stages:** oral, anal, phallic, latency, and genital. How specific conflicts at each of these stages are resolved is important to personality development.

Three influential followers of Freud who broke with him were Alfred Adler, Carl Jung, and Karen Horney. Known as neo-Freudians, they emphasized different issues. Adler emphasized the **inferiority complex** and the compensating *will-to-power.* Jung introduced the **collective unconscious** and **archetypes.** Horney stressed the importance of **basic anxiety** and refuted Freud's idea of *penis envy,* replacing it with *power envy.*

Critics of the psychoanalytic approach, especially Freud's theories, argue that it is difficult to test, overemphasizes biology and unconscious forces, has inadequate empirical support, is sexist, and lacks cross-cultural support. Despite these criticisms, Freud remains a notable pioneer in psychology.

Questions

1. Using the analogy of an iceberg, explain Freud's three levels of consciousness.
2. The _____ operates on the pleasure principle, seeking immediate gratification. The _____ operates on the reality principle, and the _____ contains the conscience and ego-ideal, which provide moral guidance for the ego. (a) psyche, ego, id; (b) id, ego, superego; (c) conscious, preconscious, unconscious; (d) oral stage; anal stage; phallic stage
3. Briefly describe Freud's five psychosexual stages.
4. Match the following concepts with the appropriate theorist, Adler, Jung, or Horney:

a. inferiority complex: _____
b. power envy: _____
c. collective unconscious: _____
d. basic anxiety: _____

Answers to Questions can be found in Appendix B.

ACTIVE LEARNING WORKSHEET   MODULE 35

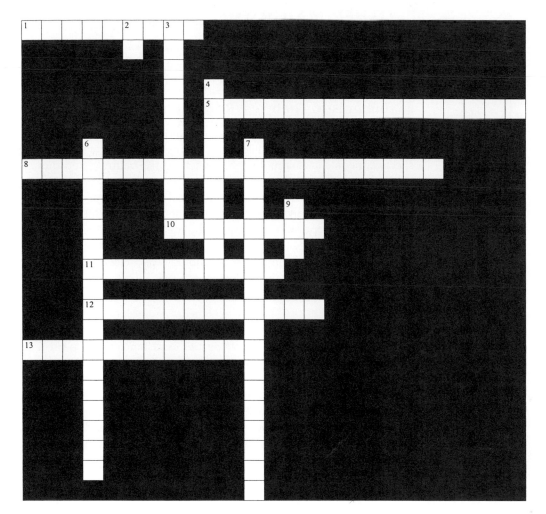

ACROSS

1 In Freudian terms, thoughts or information that a person is currently aware of or is remembering.

5 According to Freud, the principle on which the conscious ego operates as it tries to meet the demands of the unconscious id and the realities of the environment.

8 Jung's concept of an inherited unconscious that all humans share.

10 In psychoanalytic theory, the part of the personality that incorporates parental and societal standards for morality.

11 Freud's first and most basic defense mechanism because it blocks unacceptable impulses from coming into awareness.

12 Freud's term for thoughts or information that one can become aware of easily.

13 According to Horney, the feelings of helplessness and insecurity that adults experience because as children they felt alone and isolated in a hostile environment.

DOWN

2 According to Freud, the source of instinctual energy, which works on the pleasure principle and is concerned with immediate gratification.

3 Freud's term for thoughts, motives, impulses, or desires that lie beyond a person's normal awareness, but that can be made available through psychoanalysis.

4 According to Jung, the images or patterns of thoughts, feelings, and behavior that reside in the collective unconscious.

6 In Freud's theory, the principle on which the id operates—that immediate pleasure is the sole motivation for behavior.

7 Adler's idea that feelings of inferiority develop from early childhood experiences of helplessness and incompetence.

9 In Freud's theory, the rational part of the psyche that deals with reality and attempts to control the impulses of the id while also satisfying the social approval and self-esteem needs of the superego.

MODULE 36
OTHER MAJOR THEORIES

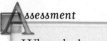

In Module 34, we discovered the trait perspectives, which seeks to describe and classify elements of personality. Module 35 emphasized unconscious processes. In this module, we explore two additional perspectives.

▪ Humanistic Theories: Rogers and Maslou

Humanistic theories of personality emphasize internal experiences — feelings and thoughts — and the individual's own feelings of basic worth. From a humanistic perspective, people are naturally good (or, at worst, neutral), and they possess a positive drive toward self-fulfillment.

According to this view, each individual's personality is created out of his or her unique way of perceiving and interpreting the world. Behavior is controlled by the individual's perception of reality, not by traits, unconscious impulses, or rewards and punishments. To fully understand another human being you must know how he or she perceives the world. Humanistic psychology was developed largely from the writings of Carl Rogers and Abraham Maslow.

Self-Concept *Rogers' term for all the information and beliefs individuals have about their own nature, qualities, and behavior*

Carl Rogers

To humanistic psychologist Carl Rogers (1902–1987), the most important component of personality is the *self*, the part of experience that a person comes to identify early in life as "I" or "me." Today, Rogerians (followers of Rogers) use the term **self-concept** to refer to all the information and beliefs you have as an individual regarding your own nature, unique qualities, and typical behaviors. Rogers was very concerned with the match between a person's self-concept and his or her actual experiences with life. He believed poor mental health and maladjustment developed from an incongruence or disparity between the self-concept and actual life experiences (Figure 36.1).

Mental Health, Congruence, and Self-Esteem   According to Rogers, there is an intimate connection between mental health, congruence, and *self-esteem* — how we feel about ourselves. If our self-concept is congruent (or matches) with our life experiences, we generally have high self-esteem and better mental health. For example, an athletic child living in a family in which athletics are highly valued would have a better chance at higher self-esteem and better mental health than an artistic child in a family in which the arts aren't valued.

These three states (mental health, congruence, and self-esteem) are also part of our innate, biological capacities. Each of us is born into the world with an innate need to survive, grow, and enhance ourselves. We naturally approach and value people and experiences that enhance our growth and fulfillment and avoid those that do not. Therefore, Rogers believed we can — and should — trust our own internal feelings to guide us toward mental health and happiness.

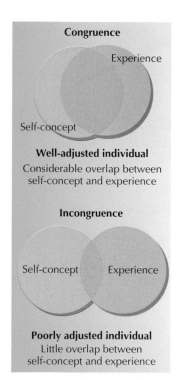

Congruence

Experience

Self-concept

Well-adjusted individual
Considerable overlap between
self-concept and experience

Incongruence

Self-concept   Experience

Poorly adjusted individual
Little overlap between
self-concept and experience

Figure 36.1 *Self-concept and adjustment.* According to Carl Rogers, mental health is related to the degree of congruence (or match) between our self-concept and life experiences. If our self-concept is reasonably consistent with actual life experiences, our "self" is said to be congruent and we are well adjusted. The reverse is true when there is incongruity and little overlap.

If everyone has an inborn, positive drive toward self-fulfillment, why do some people have low self-esteem and poor mental health?   Rogers believed these states generally result from early childhood experiences with parents and other adults who make their love *conditional.* That is, children learn that their acceptance is contingent on behaving in certain ways and expressing only certain feelings. When affection and love seem conditional, children block out the existence of negative impulses and feelings (which others label as "bad"), and their self-concepts and self-esteem become distorted. If a child is angry and hits his younger brother, for example, some parents might punish the child or deny his anger, saying, "Nice children don't hit their brothers; they love them!" To gain parental approval, the child has to deny his true feelings of anger, but inside he secretly suspects he is not a "nice boy" because he *did* hit his brother and didn't love him (at least at that moment).

Can you see how repeated incidents of this type might have a lasting effect on someone's self-esteem? If the child learns that his negative feelings and behaviors (which we all have) are totally unacceptable and unlovable, he may always doubt the love and approval of others because they don't know "the real person hiding inside."

Unconditional Positive Regard   To help a child develop to fullest potential, adults need to create an atmosphere of **unconditional positive regard** — a setting in which children realize that they will be accepted no matter what they say or do. According to child expert Thomas Gordon:

> Acceptance is like the fertile soil that permits a tiny seed to develop into the lovely flower it is capable of becoming. The soil only enables the seed to become the flower. It releases the capacity of the seed to grow, but the capacity is entirely within the seed. As with the seed, a child contains entirely within the organism the capacity to develop. Acceptance is like the soil — it merely enables the child to actualize his potential.
>
> GORDON, 1975, P. 31

To some, unconditional positive regard and acceptance sound like we should allow people to do whatever they please. This is a common misinterpretation. Humanists separate the value of the person from his or her behaviors. They accept the person's positive nature while discouraging destructive or hostile behaviors. Hitting a playmate or grabbing a toy is contrary to the child's positive nature as well as offensive to others. Humanistic psychologists believe in guiding children to control their behavior so they can develop a healthy self-concept and healthy relationships with others.

In the previous example, they would encourage the parent to say, "I know you're angry with your brother, but we don't hit. You won't be allowed to play with him for a while, if you can't control your anger."

Abraham Maslow

Like Rogers, Abraham Maslow believed there is a basic goodness to human nature and a natural tendency toward self-actualization. He saw personality as the expression of the movement from basic physiological needs to the highest level of self-actualization (Figure 36.2).

What exactly is self-actualization?   According to Maslow, **self-actualization** is the inborn drive to develop all one's talents and capacities. It involves understanding one's own potential, accepting oneself and others as unique individuals, and taking a problem-centered approach to life situations (Maslow, 1970). Self-actualization is an ongoing process of growth rather than an end product or accomplishment — such as winning a trophy or graduating from college.

Carl Rogers (1902–1987). As a founder of humanistic psychology, Rogers emphasized the importance of the self-concept. He believed our personality and individual self-esteem are heavily influenced by early childhood experiences, such as whether we receive unconditional positive regard from our adult caregivers.

Unconditional Positive Regard
Rogers' term for positive behavior toward a person with no contingencies attached

Self-Actualization *Maslow's term for the innate tendency toward growth that motivates all human behavior and results in the full realization of a person's highest potential*

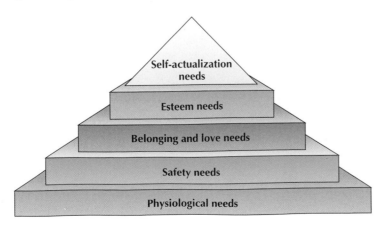

Figure 36.2 *Maslow's hierarchy of needs.* According to Maslow, basic physical necessities must be satisfied before higher-growth needs can be addressed.

Maslow believed that only a few, rare individuals, such as Albert Einstein, Mohandas Gandhi, and Eleanor Roosevelt, become fully self-actualized. However, he saw self-actualization as part of every person's basic hierarchy of needs. (See Module 31 for further discussion of Maslow's theory.)

Evaluating Humanistic Theories

Humanistic psychology was extremely popular during the 1960s and 1970s. It was a refreshing new perspective on personality after the negative determinism of the psychoanalytic approach and the mechanical nature of learning theories. Although this early popularity has declined, many humanistic ideas have been incorporated into approaches for counseling and psychotherapy (Wertz, 1998).

At the same time, humanistic theories have also been criticized (e.g., Funder, 2000). Three of the most important criticisms are:

1. *Naive assumptions.* Critics suggest the humanists are unrealistic, romantic, and even naive about human nature. Are all people as inherently good as they say? Our continuing history of murders, warfare, and other acts of aggression suggests otherwise.

2. *Poor testability and inadequate evidence.* Like many psychoanalytic terms and concepts, humanistic concepts such as unconditional positive regard and self-actualization are difficult to operationally define and scientifically test.

3. *Narrowness.* Like trait theories, humanistic theories have been criticized for merely *describing* personality — rather than *explaining* it. For example, where does the motivation for self-actualization come from? To say that it is an "inborn drive" doesn't satisfy those who favor experimental research and hard data as the way to learn about personalityerimental research and hard data as the way to learn about personality.

CHECK & REVIEW

Humanistic Theories

Humanistic theories emphasize internal experiences, thoughts, and feelings that create the individual's **self-concept.** Carl Rogers emphasized the concepts of *self-esteem* and **unconditional positive regard.** Abraham Maslow emphasized the potential for **self-actualization.** Critics of the humanistic approach argue that these theories are based on naive assumptions and are not scientifically testable or well supported by empirical evidence. In addition, their focus on description, rather than explanation, makes them narrow.

Questions

1. If you took the _____ approach to personality, you would emphasize internal experiences, like feelings and thoughts, and the basic worth of the individual. (a) humanistic; (b) psychodynamic; (c) personalistic; (d) motivational

2. Rogers thought that _____ is necessary for a child's uniqueness and positive self-concept to unfold naturally. (a) permissive parenting; (b) a challenging environment; (c) unconditional positive regard; (d) a friendly neighborhood

3. Abraham Maslow's belief that all people are motivated toward personal growth and development is known as _____.

4. What are three major criticisms of humanistic theories?

Answers to Questions can be found in Appendix B.

What is the social/cognitive perspective on personality?

■ Social/Cognitive Perspective: Bandura and Rotter

According to the social/cognitive perspective, each of us has a unique personality because of our individual history of interactions with the environment, and because we *think* about the world and interpret what happens to us (Cervone & Shoda, 1999). Furthermore, our interpretations are distinctive because of our previous experiences. Two of the most influential social-cognitive theorists are Albert Bandura and Julian Rotter.

Bandura's and Rotter's Approaches

Although Albert Bandura is perhaps best known for his work on observational learning or social learning (Module 18), he has also played a major role in reintroducing thought processes into personality theory. Cognition is central to his concept of **self-efficacy,** which refers to a person's learned expectation of success (Bandura, 1997, 1999, 2000).

How do you generally perceive your ability to select, influence, and control the circumstances of your life? According to Bandura, if you have a strong sense of self-efficacy, you believe you can generally succeed, regardless of past failures and current obstacles. This belief will in turn affect the challenges you accept and the effort you expend in reaching goals.

Doesn't such a belief also affect how others respond to you and thereby affect your chances for success? Precisely! This type of mutual interaction and influence is a core part of another major concept of Bandura's — **reciprocal determinism.** According to Bandura, our cognitions (or thoughts), behaviors, and the environment are interdependent and interactive (Figure 36.3). Thus, a cognition ("I can succeed") will affect behaviors ("I will work hard and ask for a promotion"), which in turn will affect the environment ("My hard work paid off. Now I'm an executive.").

Rotter's Locus of Control Julian Rotter's theory is similar to Bandura's in suggesting that learning creates *cognitive expectancies* that guide behavior and influence the environment (Rotter, 1954, 1990). According to Rotter, your behavior or personality is determined by (1) what you *expect* to happen following a specific action and (2) the *reinforcement value* attached to specific outcomes — that is, the degree to which you prefer one reinforcer to another.

To understand your personality and behavior, for instance, Rotter would want to know your expectancies and what you see as the source of life's rewards and punishments. To secure this information, Rotter would use personality tests that measure your internal versus external *locus of control.* Rotter's tests ask people to respond "true" or "false" to a series of statements, such as "People get ahead in this world primarily by luck and connections rather than by hard work and perseverance," or "When someone doesn't like you, there is little you can do about it."

As you may suspect, *externals* think environment and external forces have primary control over their lives, whereas *internals* think they can control events in their

Self-Efficacy *Bandura's term for learned beliefs that one is capable of producing desired results, such as mastering new skills and achieving personal goals*

Reciprocal Determinism *Bandura's belief that cognitions, behaviors, and the learning environment interact to produce personality*

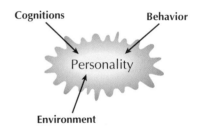

Figure 36.3 *Albert Bandura's theory of reciprocal determinism.* According to Bandura, thoughts (or cognitions), behavior, and the environment all interact to produce personality.

lives through their own efforts. Numerous studies have found that having an internal locus of control is positively associated with higher psychological functioning and better mental health (Hans, 2000; Silvester et al., 2002; Wen, Wang, Zhao, & Sun, 2000).

Evaluating Social/Cognitive Theory

The social/cognitive perspective holds several attractions. First, it emphasizes how the environment affects, and is affected by, individuals. Secondly, it meets most standards for scientific research. It offers testable, objective hypotheses and operationally defined terms and relies on empirical data for its basic principles (Lin, 1998; Stajkovic & Luthans, 1998). Critics, however, believe social/cognitive theory is too narrow. It has been criticized for ignoring unconscious and emotional aspects of personality (Carducci, 1998; Westen, 1998). For example, certain early experiences might have prompted a person to develop an external locus of control.

Both Bandura's and Rotter's theories emphasize cognition and social learning, but they are a long way from a strict behavior theory, which suggests that only environmental forces control behavior. They are also a long way from the biological theories that say inborn, innate qualities determine behavior and personality. Biological theories are the topic of our next section.

Assessment

CHECK & REVIEW

Social/Cognitive Perspective

Social/cognitive theorists emphasize the importance of external events and mental processes: how we interpret and respond to external events. Albert Bandura's social-cognitive approach focuses on **self-efficacy** and **reciprocal determinism,** whereas Julian Rotter emphasizes an internal or external *locus of control.*

Social/cognitive theory is credited for its attention to environmental influences and its scientific standards. However, it has been criticized for its narrow focus and lack of attention to unconscious, emotional, and developmental components of personality.

Questions

1. The social/cognitive approach to personality is most likely to analyze _____.
2. According to _____, thoughts (or cognitions), behavior, and the environment all interact to produce personality. (a) reciprocal determinism; (b) interactionism; (c) confluence theory; (d) reverberating circuits theory
3. According to Bandura, _____ involves a person's belief about whether he or she can successfully engage in behaviors related to personal goals. (a) self-actualization; (b) self-esteem; (c) self-efficacy, (d) self-congruence
4. People with an _____ expect the environment and external forces to control events, whereas those with an _____ believe in personal control.

Answers to Questions can be found in Appendix B.

■ Biological Theories: The "Nature" of Personality

Assessment

How does biology contribute to personality?

As you were growing up, you probably heard comments such as "You're just like your father" or "You're so much like your mother." Does this mean that biological factors you inherited from your parents were the major contributors to your personality? This is the question we first explore in this section. We conclude with a discussion of how all theories of personality ultimately *interact.*

Three Major Contributors

Biological theories of personality focus on the brain, neurochemistry, and genetics. We begin our study with the brain.

The Brain The nineteenth-century phrenologists described at the beginning of Module 33 read bumps on the skull because they believed specific areas of the brain controlled particular personality traits. Today we know that brain structures are not palpable on the skull surface. However, but, dramatic personality changes are common after certain forms of brain damage (Fukutake et al., 2002; Moretti et al., 2001).

Modern biological research also suggests that certain brain areas may contribute to some personality traits. Tellegen (1985), for example, proposes that extroversion and introversion are associated with particular areas of the brain, and research seems to support him. For instance, sociability (or extroversion) is associated with increased electroencephalographic (EEG) activity in the left frontal lobes of the brain, whereas shyness (introversion) shows greater EEG activity in the right frontal lobes (Schmidt, 1999).

A major limitation to research on brain structures and personality is the difficulty identifying which structures are uniquely connected with particular personality traits. Lesioning one structure tends to have wide-ranging effects. Neurochemistry seems to offer more precise data on biological bases of personality. Jerome Kagan (1998), a major personality researcher, believes that most biologically based personality differences rest "on differences in neurochemistry rather than anatomy" (p. 59).

Neurochemistry Do you enjoy skydiving and taking risks in general? Neurochemistry may explain why. Research has found a consistent relationship between sensation seeking and monoamine oxidase (MAO), an enzyme that regulates levels of neurotransmitters such as dopamine (Ibanez, Blanco, & Saiz-Ruiz, 2002; Zuckerman, 1994, 2000). Dopamine also seems to be correlated with novelty seeking and extroversion (Depue & Collins, 1999; Laine, Ahonen, Raesaenen, & Tiihonen, 2001).

How can traits like sensation seeking and extroversion be related to neurochemistry? Studies suggest that high-sensation seekers and extroverts tend to have lower levels of physiological arousal than introverts (Brown & Schmidt, 2000; Dellu, Mayo, Piazza, Le Moal, & Simon, 1993). Their lower arousal apparently motivates them to seek out situations that will elevate their arousal. Moreover, it is believed that a lower threshold is inherited. In other words, personality traits like sensation seeking and extroversion may be inherited. (Also see Module 31 on arousal and sensation seeking.)

Genetics Heredity is what sets the parents of a teenager wondering about each other.

LAURENCE J. PETER

Psychologists have only recently recognized the importance and influence of genetic factors in personality (Borkenau, Riemann, Angleitner, & Spinath, 2001; Murakami & Hayashi, 2002; Plomin & Crabbe, 2000). This relatively new area, called *behavioral genetics*, attempts to determine the extent to which behavioral differences among people are due to genetics as opposed to environment (Module 7).

To measure genetic influence, researchers rely mostly on two kinds of data. First, they compare similarities between identical twins and fraternal twins. For example, studies of the heritability of the Big Five personality traits range from 0.35 to about 0.70 (Bouchard, 1997; Eysenck, 1967, 1991; Lensvelt-Mulders & Hettema, 2001). These correlations suggest that genetic factors contribute about 40 to 50 percent of personality.

Second, researchers compare the personalities of parents, their biological children, and their adopted children. Studies of the Big Five traits of extraversion and neuroticism find that parents' traits correlate moderately with those of their biological children and hardly at all with those of their adopted children (Bouchard, 1997; Jang et al., 1998; Loehlin et al., 1998).

Overall, studies show a strong influence of hereditary factors on personality. At the same time, researchers are careful not to overemphasize the genetic basis (Funder,

Assessment

VISUAL QUIZ

Are people born shy?

Answer: Researchers have found that shyness seems to be innate and that it is one of the most stable, lifelong personality traits.

2001; Maccoby, 2000). Some believe the importance of the unshared environment (aspects of the environment that differ from one individual to another, even within a family) has been overlooked (Saudino, 1997). Others fear that research on "genetic determinism" could be misused to "prove" that an ethnic or racial group is inferior, that male dominance is natural, or that social progress is impossible. There is no doubt that genetics studies have produced exciting and controversial results, but it is also clear that more research is necessary before we have a cohesive biological theory of personality.

The Biopsychosocial Model

When it comes to personality, no one theory is more correct than another. Each provides a different perspective and offers different insights into how a person develops the distinctive set of characteristics we call "personality." As you can see in Figure 36.4, instead of adhering to any one theory, many psychologists believe in the *biopsy-chosocial* approach, the idea that several factors overlap in their contributions to personality (Cervone & Shoda, 1999; Mischel & Shoda, 1999; Robie, Born, & Schmit, 2002). For example, Hans Eysenck (1990), a leading personality theorist, believes certain traits (like introversion and extroversion) may reflect inherited patterns of cortical arousal, as well as social learning, cognitive processes, and the environment. Can you see how someone with an introverted personality, and therefore a higher level of cortical arousal, might try to avoid excessive stimulation by seeking friends and jobs with low stimulation levels?

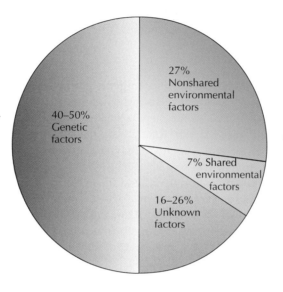

Figure 36.4 *Multiple influences on personality.* Researchers have concluded that personality can be broken down into four major factors: *genetics,* inherited traits (40–50 percent); *nonshared environmental factors,* or how each individual's genetic factors react and adjust to his or her particular environment (27 percent); *shared environmental factors,* involving parental patterns and shared family experiences (7 percent); and *error,* unidentified factors or problems with testing (16–26 percent). *Source:* Bouchard, 1997; Plomin, 1997; Talbot, Duberstein, King, Cox, & Giles, 2000; Wright, 1998.

Eysenck's work exemplifies how trait, biological, and social/cognitive theories can be combined to provide better insight into personality. This trend toward integration and the *biopsychosocial model* is reflected in a growing number of books and articles, and in decreased polarization on certain issues, such as the "either–or" debate between trait theorists and situational determinists discussed earlier.

Achievement
GENDER & CULTURAL DIVERSITY

Cultural Concepts of Self

Up to this point, we have examined only Western theories of personality. The concept of self is central to each of these theories. Personality is seen as a composition of individual parts (traits and motives), and the self is a bounded individual — separate and autonomous from others (Gardner, Gabriel, & Lee, 1999; Matsumoto, 2000). Can you see how the *conscious, preconscious, unconscious, id, ego, superego, inferiority complex, basic anxiety, self-concept, self-esteem,* and *self-actualization* all assume a unique self composed of discrete traits, motives, and abilities? Our Western perspective reflects an *individualistic* perspective.

In *collectivist* cultures, however, the self is inherently linked to others. For example, in Asia, people are described not by a set of enduring traits but in terms of social rela-

The self versus others. *When engaged in exercise or recreation, collectivist cultures are more likely to emphasize group symmetry and connectedness, whereas individualist cultures focus on independent movement and freedom to "do your own thing."*

tionships (Markus & Kitayama, 1998). The person is defined and understood primarily by looking at his or her place in the social unit. Relatedness, connectedness, and interdependence are valued, as opposed to separateness, independence, and individualism.

If you are North American or Western European, you may find the concept of a self, defined in terms of others, almost contradictory. A core selfhood seems intuitively obvious to you. Recognizing that this is not the case in collectivist cultures and among some minorities may prevent misunderstanding. For example, North Americans generally define *sincerity* as behaving in accordance with one's inner feelings, whereas Japanese see it as behavior that conforms to a person's role expectations (carrying out one's duties) (Yamada, 1997). Can you see how Japanese behavior might appear insincere to a North American and vice versa?

Understanding how the individualistic perspective differs from that in collectivist cultures may improve global relations. It also points out limits and biases in our current Western personality theories and the need for continued cross-cultural research.

Assessment

CHECK & REVIEW

Biological Theories

Biological theories emphasize brain structures, neurochemistry, and inherited genetic components of personality. Research on specific traits such as extroversion and sensation seeking support the biological approach. The interactionist approach suggests that the major theories overlap, and each contributes to our understanding of personality. Most theories of personality are biased toward Western, individualistic cultures and their perception of the "self." Recognizing and understanding this bias helps keep our study of personality in perspective.

Questions

1. _____ theories emphasize the importance of genetics in the development of personality. (a) Evolutionary; (b) Phenomenological; (c) Genological; (d) Biological

2. What concerns people about genetic explanations for personality?

3. The _____ approach represents a blending of several theories of personality. (a) unification; (b) association; (c) interactionist; (d) phenomenological

4. Explain how the Western concept of the self reflects an individualistic culture versus a collectivist culture.

Answers to Questions can be found in Appendix B.

MODULE 36   ACTIVE LEARNING WORKSHEET

Enter the correct letter from Column A in the blank space in Column B, and then double-check your answers with those in Appendix B.

Column A

a. Rogers

b. Maslow

c. Bandura

d. Self-Actualization

e. Rotter

f. Tellegen

g. Behavioral Genetics

h. Individualistic Perspective

i. Reciprocal Determinism

j. Unconditional Positive Regard

Column B

1.____ Cognitions, behaviors, and environment interact.

2.____ Positive behavior with no contingencies.

3.____ Self concept.

4.____ Locus of control.

5.____ Studies genetic influences versus environment.

6.____ Emphasizes the self.

7.____ Associates personality with areas of the brain.

8.____ Self-efficacy.

9.____ Realization of highest potential.

10.____ Created hierarchy of needs.

ssessment
KEY TERMS

To assess your understanding of the **Key Terms** in this section, write a definition for each (in your own words), and then compare your definitions with those in the text.

personality (p. 473)

Personality Assessment
Minnesota Multiphasic Personality
Inventory (MMPI-2) (p. 475)
projective tests (p. 476)
Rorschach [ROAR-shock] Inkblot
Test (p. 476)
Thematic Apperception Test (TAT)
(p. 476)

Trait Theories
factor analysis (p. 480)
Five-Factor Model (FFM) (p. 480)
trait (p. 480)

Psychoanalytic/Psychodynamic Theories
archetypes (p. 494)
basic anxiety (p. 495)
collective unconscious (p. 494)
conscious (p. 487)
ego (p. 488)
id (p. 488)
inferiority complex (p. 493)
Oedipus [ED-uh-puss] complex
(p. 490)
pleasure principle (p. 488)
preconscious (p. 487)
psychosexual stages (p. 490)
reality principle (p. 488)

repression (p. 489)
superego (p. 488)
unconscious (p. 487)

Humanistic Theories
self-actualization (p. 499)
self-concept (p. 498)
unconditional positive regard (p. 499)

Social/Cognitive Perspective
reciprocal determinism (p. 501)
self-efficacy (p. 501)

chievement
WEB RESOURCES

Huffman Book Companion Site
http://www.wiley.com/college/huffman
This site is loaded with free Interactive Self-Tests, Internet Exercises, Glossary and Flashcards for key terms, Web links, Handbook for Non-Native Speakers, and other activities designed to improve your mastery of the material in this section.

Would you like to take a free personality test?
http://www.2h.com/personality-tests.html
This commercial site offers a variety of tests, including the Keirsey Temperament Sorter, a Career Values Inventory, and VALS, a measure of your values, attitudes, and life styles. As noted in their stated mission, the sponsors of this site "do not give psychological advice and are not trained in that profession. Tests are only for your entertainment."

Want more information about major personality theorists?
http://www.wynja.com/personality/theorists.html
This web site offers detailed background material on most of the theories and theorists discussed in these modules, includ-

ing Freud, Maslow, and Rogers. It also provides information on lesser-known theorists, such as Kelley, Lewin, and Tart. For even more information about Freudian theory, try http://psychoanalysis.org/. This web site, sponsored by the New York Psychoanalytic Institute and Society, contains a vast array of resources related to psychoanalytic theory and its application. If you want details about Maslow, try http://web.utk.edu/%7Egwynne/maslow.html. This web site offers detailed information about Maslow's hierarchy of needs and its effect on motivation and personality development.

Are you painfully shy?
http://www.shyness.com/encyclopedia.html
Sponsored by the Palo Alto Shyness Clinic in Portola Valley, CA, this web site features a lengthy article written by Lynne Henderson and Philip Zimbardo—two renowned experts in the field. The article details the prevalence and diagnosis of shyness, a research summary, the genetic and environmental influences, as well as suggestions for treatment.

VISUAL SUMMARY
Personality
(Modules 33, 34, 35, and 36)

Personality

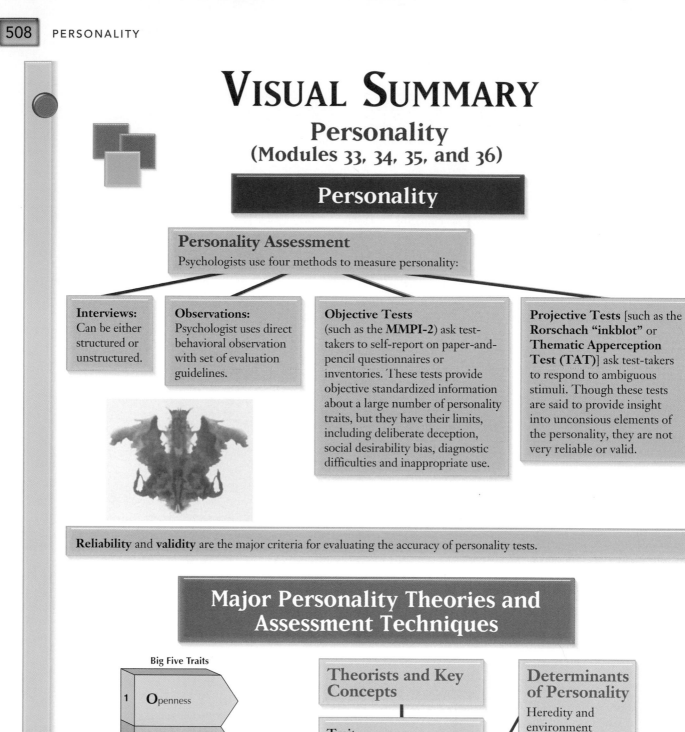

Personality Assessment
Psychologists use four methods to measure personality:

Interviews: Can be either structured or unstructured.

Observations: Psychologist uses direct behavioral observation with set of evaluation guidelines.

Objective Tests (such as the **MMPI-2**) ask test-takers to self-report on paper-and-pencil questionnaires or inventories. These tests provide objective standardized information about a large number of personality traits, but they have their limits, including deliberate deception, social desirability bias, diagnostic difficulties and inappropriate use.

Projective Tests [such as the **Rorschach "inkblot"** or **Thematic Apperception Test (TAT)**] ask test-takers to respond to ambiguous stimuli. Though these tests are said to provide insight into unconsious elements of the personality, they are not very reliable or valid.

Reliability and **validity** are the major criteria for evaluating the accuracy of personality tests.

Major Personality Theories and Assessment Techniques

Big Five Traits

1. **O**penness
2. **C**onscientiousness
3. **E**xtroversion
4. **A**greeableness
5. **N**euroticism

Theorists and Key Concepts

Trait
Early theorists
- Allport: Arranged **traits** in hierarchy.
- Cattell (16PF) and Eysenck (Personality Questionnaire): Used **factor analysis** to reduce number of traits.

Modern theory
- **Five-factor model** (FFM): Openness, conscientious-ness, extroversion, agree-ableness, and neuroticism.

Determinants of Personality
Heredity and environment combine to create personality traits.

Methods of Assessment
Objective (self-report) inventories (e.g., MMPI), observation.

Major Personality Theories and Assessment Techniques (cont.)

Theorists and Key Concepts

Psychoanalytic/Psychodynamic

Freud
- Levels of Consciousness—**conscious, preconscious,** and **unconscious.**
- Personality Structure—**id (pleasure principle), ego (reality principle), superego** (morality principle).
- Defense Mechanisms—**repression** and others.
- **Psychosexual Stages**—oral, anal, phallic, latency, and genital.

NeoFreudians
- Adler—individual psychology, **inferiority complex,** and will-to-power.
- Jung—analytical psychology, **collective unconscious,** and **archetypes.**
- Horney—power envy vs. penis envy and **basic anxiety.**

Determinants of Personality
Unconscious conflicts between id, ego and superego lead to defense mechanisms.

Methods of Assessment
Interviews and projective tests: Rorschach inkblot test, Thematic Apperception Test (TAT).

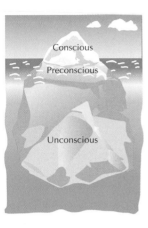

Conscious
Preconscious
Unconscious

Humanistic

Phenomenological perspective
- Rogers—**self-concept,** self-esteem, and **unconditional positive regard.**
- Maslow—**self-actualization.**

Determinants of Personality
Individual's subjective experience of reality.

Methods of Assessment
Interviews, objective (self- report) inventories.

Social/Cognitive
- Bandura—**self-efficacy** and **reciprocal determinism.**
- Rotter—cognitive expectancies and locus of control.

Determinants of Personality
Interaction between cognition and environment.

Methods of Assessment
Observation, objective (self- report) inventories.

Biological
- Brain structures like the frontal lobes may play a role.
- Neurochemistry (dopamine, MAO, and others) may play a role.
- Genetic factors also contribute to personality.

Determinants of Personality
Brain, neurochemistry, genetics.

Methods of Assessment
Animal studies and biological techniques.

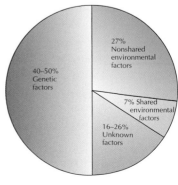

40–50% Genetic factors

27% Nonshared environmental factors

7% Shared environmental factors

16–26% Unknown factors

Interactionism: Major theories overlap and each contributes to our understanding of personality. Cultural comparisons find most theories biased toward Western, individualistic cultures that emphasize the "self."

PSYCHOLOGICAL DISORDERS

Assessment

Core Learning Objectives

As you read Modules 37, 38, 39, 40, and 41, keep the following questions in mind and answer them in your own words:

▶ How do psychologists identify, explain, and classify abnormal behavior?

▶ What are anxiety disorders, and what causes them?

▶ When do disturbances in mood become abnormal?

▶ What are the symptoms and causes of schizophrenia?

▶ How are dissociative disorders and personality disorders identified?

Mary's troubles first began in adolescence. She began to miss curfew, was frequently truant, and her grades declined sharply. During family counseling sessions, it was discovered that Mary also had been promiscuous and had prostituted herself several times to get drug money. She revealed a history of drug abuse, including "everything I can get my hands on." Mary also had ongoing problems with her peers. She quickly fell in love and overly idealized new friends. But when they quickly (and inevitably) disappointed her, she would angrily cast them aside. This pattern of poor grades, cutting classes, and unstable relationships continued throughout high school, two years of college, and a series of clerical jobs. Mary's problems, coupled with a preoccupation with inflicting pain on herself (by cutting and burning) and persistent thoughts of suicide, eventually led to her admittance to a psychiatric hospital at age 26.

DAVISON, NEALE, & KRING, 2004, PP. 408–409

Achievement

Assessment

Application

Jim is a third-year medical student. Over the last few weeks he has been noticing that older men appear to be frightened of him when he passes them on the street. Recently, he has become convinced that he is actually the director of the Central Intelligence Agency and that these men are secret agents of a hostile nation. Jim has found confirmatory evidence for his idea in the fact that a helicopter flies over his house every day at 8:00 a.m. and at 4:30 p.m. Surely, this surveillance is part of the plot to assassinate him.

BERNHEIM & LEWINE, 1979, P. 4

Ken Bianchi, the "Hillside Strangler," terrorized the Los Angeles area for more than a year. Working with his cousin, Angelo Buono, Bianchi used phony police badges to lure victims into his car or home where they were later raped, systematically tortured, and then murdered. Bianchi and Buono killed 10 women aged 12 to 28. Bianchi killed two more after moving to Washington State.

Each of these individuals has a severe psychological problem, and each case raises interesting questions. What caused Mary's unstable relationships and suicidal thoughts, Jim's paranoia, and Ken's cold-blooded murders? Was there something in their early backgrounds to explain their later behaviors? Is there something medically wrong with them? What about less severe forms of abnormal behavior? Is a person who dreams of airplane crashes and refuses to fly mentally ill? Does a compulsively neat student who types all his lecture notes and refuses to write in any textbook need a psychiatric examination? What is the difference between being eccentric and disordered? We address some of these questions in these modules, and the next section focuses on treatment.

The first module begins by exploring the ways psychological disorders are identified, explained, and classified. The heart of this unit is a detailed description of the types of disorders included in the five main categories of psychological disorders (anxiety, schizophrenia, mood disorders, dissociative disorders, and personality disorders).

Unfortunately, there are numerous stereotypes and unwarranted fears about people who suffer from mental disorders. To test your own misconceptions, answer *true* or *false* to the following statements:

_____1. People with psychological disorders act in bizarre ways and are very different from normal people.

_____2. Mental disorders are a sign of personal weakness.

_____3. Mentally ill people are often dangerous and unpredictable.

_____4. A person who has been mentally ill never fully recovers.

_____5. Most mentally ill individuals can work at only low-level jobs.

Each of these five statements is a myth. The facts are provided below and discussed further in these modules.

1. **Fact:** This is true for only a small minority of individuals and during a relatively small portion of their lives. In fact, sometimes even mental health professionals find it difficult to distinguish normal from abnormal individuals without formal screening.

2. **Fact:** Psychological disorders are a function of many factors, such as exposure to stress, genetic disposition, family background, and so on. Mentally disturbed individuals can't be blamed for their problems any more than people who develop Alzheimer's or other physical illnesses.

3. **Fact:** Only a few disorders, such as some psychotic and antisocial personalities, are associated with violence. The stereotype that connects mental illness and violence persists because of prejudice and selective media attention.

4. **Fact:** The vast majority of people who are diagnosed as mentally ill eventually improve and lead normal productive lives. Moreover, mental disorders are generally only temporary. A person may have an episode that lasts for days, weeks, or months and then may go for years — even a lifetime — without further difficulty.

5. **Fact:** Mentally disturbed people are individuals. As such, their career potentials depend on their particular talents, abilities, experience, and motivation, as well as their current state of physical and mental health. Some of the most creative and distinguished people have suffered serious mental disorders, including author Virginia Woolf, composer Robert Schumann, and statesman Winston Churchill.

Sources: Brown & Bradley, 2002; Davison, Neale, & Kring, 2004; Dinan, 2000; Makherjee et al., 2002; O'Flynn, 2001; Volavka, 2002.

MODULE 37
STUDYING PSYCHOLOGICAL DISORDERS

As the introductory cases show, mental disorders vary from person to person and in their severity. Also, like personality, consciousness, and intelligence, *abnormal behavior* is difficult to define. In this section, we will explore how psychologists attempt to identify, explain, and classify abnormal behavior.

Identifying Abnormal Behavior: Four Basic Standards

The behaviors of Mary, Jim, and Ken Bianchi are clearly abnormal. However, most cases of abnormal behavior are not so clear-cut, and people don't fall into one of two extreme categories — "crazy" versus "normal." As we've seen in previous modules, traits like intelligence or creativity lie along a continuum, with most of the population falling somewhere between the two extreme end points. Similarly, on the continuum of normal and abnormal behavior, people can be unusually healthy at one end point, or extremely disturbed at the other — like Mary, Jim, and Ken Bianchi.

Recognizing this continuum, how do we decide when behavior becomes abnormal? Let's begin with one of the most widely accepted definitions of abnormal behavior — patterns of emotion, thought, and action considered pathological (diseased or disordered) for one or more of the following reasons: statistical infrequency, disability or dysfunction, personal distress, or violation of norms (Davison, Neale, & Kring, 2004). As you can see in Figure 37.1, for each of these four criteria abnormal behavior falls along a continuum. Keep in mind that each criterion has its merit and limits and that no single criterion is adequate for identifying all forms of abnormal behavior. Psychologists and other mental health professionals recognize this and seldom label behavior as abnormal unless it meets several of these standards.

1. ***Statistical infrequency. How rare is the behavior?*** A behavior may be judged abnormal if it occurs infrequently in a given population. For example, believing that others are plotting against you is statistically abnormal and it might be a sign of a serious problem called *delusions of persecution*. However, having great intelligence (Albert Einstein), exceptional athletic ability (Kobe Bryant), or an unusual artistic skill (Frida Kahlo) are *not* classified as abnormal by the public (or by psychologists). Therefore, we cannot use statistical infrequency as the sole criterion in determining what is normal versus abnormal.

2. ***Disability or dysfunction. Is there a loss of normal functioning?*** People who suffer from psychological disorders may be unable to get along with others, hold a

ssessment

How do psychologists identify, explain, and classify abnormal behavior?

Abnormal Behavior *Patterns of emotion, thought, and action considered pathological (diseased or disordered) for one or more of these reasons: statistical infrequency, disability or dysfunction, personal distress, or violation of norms*

ssessment

VISUAL QUIZ

Would this behavior be considered abnormal?

Answer: Although it is not statistically "normal" to be such a collector and lover of piercing, the term abnormal behavior is generally restricted to behavior that is considered pathological (diseased or disordered).

Figure 37.1 *The continuum of abnormal behavior.* Rather than in fixed categories, both "abnormal" and "normal" behaviors exist along a continuum.

(Rare) ——————————————— (Common)
Statistical Infrequency
(e.g., believing others are plotting against you)

(Low) ——————————————— (High)
Disability or Dysfunction
(e.g., being unable to go to work due to alcohol abuse)

(Low) ——————————————— (High)
Personal Distress
(e.g., having thoughts of suicide)

(Rare) ——————————————— (Common)
Violation of Norms
(e.g., shouting at strangers)

Normal | Abnormal

job, eat properly, and clean themselves. Their ability to think clearly and make rational decisions also may be impaired. For example, when someone's use of alcohol (or other drugs) is so extreme that it interferes with their normal social or occupational functioning, the person may be diagnosed with a *substance-related disorder.*

3. ***Personal distress. Is the person unhappy?*** The personal distress criterion focuses on the individual's own judgment of his or her level of functioning. For example, someone who drinks heavily every day may realize it is unhealthy and wish to stop. On the other hand, many people with true *alcohol-dependence disorders* deny they have a problem. Also, some serious psychological disorders cause little or no emotional discomfort. A serial killer, for instance, can torture someone without feeling remorse or guilt. The personal distress criterion by itself, then, is not sufficient for identifying all forms of abnormal behavior.

4. ***Violation of norms. Is the behavior culturally abnormal?*** The fourth approach to identifying abnormal behavior is violation of, or nonconforming to, *social norms,* cultural rules that guide behavior in particular situations. Being in such a highly excited state that you forget to pay the rent but pass out $20 bills to strangers is a violation of norms. This type of behavior is common among individuals who are diagnosed with *bipolar disorder.*

   A major problem with this criterion, however, is that cultural diversity can affect what people consider a *violation* of norms (Lopez & Guarnaccia, 2000). Abnormal behavior is often *culturally relative* — understandable only in terms of the culture in which it occurs. In addition, there are also *culture-bound* disorders that are unique and found only in particular cultures, and *culture-general* symptoms that are found in all cultures (Flaskerud, 2000; Green, 1999; Lopez & Guarnaccia, 2000). These terms are discussed in the following Gender and Cultural Diversity Section.

Andrea Yates admitted drowning her five children and was sentenced to life imprisonment despite a vigorous defense and a plea of insanity. What do you think of the verdict?

Insanity *Legal term applied when people cannot be held responsible for their actions or allowed to manage their own affairs because of mental illness*

    What about the term insanity? Where does it fit in? **Insanity** is a legal term indicating that a person cannot be held responsible for his or her actions or cannot manage his or her own affairs because of mental illness. Although *insanity* is often a label for abnormal behavior, mental health professionals generally do not use this term because it confuses legal issues with the general category of abnormal behavior. Think of someone like Andrea Yates, the mother who killed her five small children. The jury did not accept that she was legally insane and found her guilty of murder. Yet her behavior would be considered abnormal by any one or all of our four previous criteria: Her behavior was statistically infrequent, she was clearly dysfunctional and personally distressed, and her behavior was considered abnormal by almost everyone in our culture.

GENDER & CULTURAL DIVERSITY

A Cultural Look at Disorders

Among the Chippewa, Cree, and Montagnais-Naskapi Indians in Canada, there is a disorder called *windigo* — or *wiitiko* — *psychosis,* which is characterized by delusions (irrational beliefs) and cannibalistic impulses. Believing the spirit of a *windigo,* or cannibal giant with heart and entrails of ice, has possessed them, victims become severely depressed (Barnouw, 1985). As the malady begins, the individual typically experiences loss of appetite, diarrhea, vomiting, and insomnia and may see the people around him or her turning into beavers or other edible animals.

    In later stages, the victim becomes obsessed with cannibalistic thoughts. Family members often seek help from a shaman, a folk healer who uses special incantations

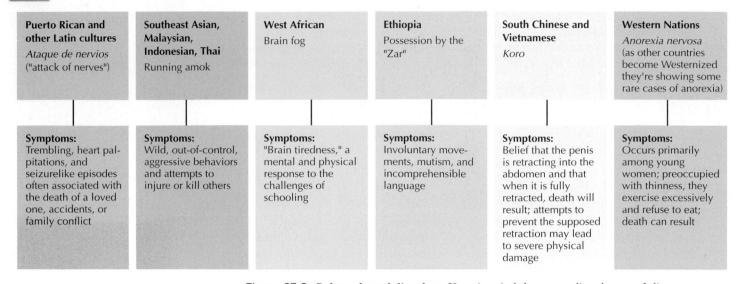

Puerto Rican and other Latin cultures	**Southeast Asian, Malaysian, Indonesian, Thai**	**West African**	**Ethiopia**	**South Chinese and Vietnamese**	**Western Nations**
Ataque de nervios ("attack of nerves")	Running amok	Brain fog	Possession by the "Zar"	*Koro*	*Anorexia nervosa* (as other countries become Westernized they're showing some rare cases of anorexia)
Symptoms: Trembling, heart palpitations, and seizurelike episodes often associated with the death of a loved one, accidents, or family conflict	**Symptoms:** Wild, out-of-control, aggressive behaviors and attempts to injure or kill others	**Symptoms:** "Brain tiredness," a mental and physical response to the challenges of schooling	**Symptoms:** Involuntary movements, mutism, and incomprehensible language	**Symptoms:** Belief that the penis is retracting into the abdomen and that when it is fully retracted, death will result; attempts to prevent the supposed retraction may lead to severe physical damage	**Symptoms:** Occurs primarily among young women; preoccupied with thinness, they exercise excessively and refuse to eat; death can result

Figure 37.2 *Culture-bound disorders.* Keep in mind that some disorders are fading as remote areas become more westernized, and some disorders (such as anorexia nervosa) are spreading as other countries adopt Western values. *Source:* Carmaciu, Anderson, & Markar, 2001; Davison, Neale, & Kring, 2004; Durand & Barlow, 2003; Guarnaccia & Rogler, 1999; Matsumoto, 2000.

and ceremonies to remove the spell of the *windigo* spirit. If they fail to seek help in time, the victim may attack and kill loved ones in order to devour their flesh (Berreman, 1971). As Figure 37.2 shows, *windigo* psychosis is only one of many unique — or culture-bound — mental disorders that have been reported around the world.

Why do cultures develop such unique problems?
In the case of *windigo* psychosis, one explanation is that the disorder developed after fur trade competition depleted game that the Canadian tribes used for food, leading to widespread famine (Bishop, 1974). Facing starvation could have led to cannibalism and the subsequent "creation" of a *windigo* spirit. Belief in spirit possession is a common feature of many cultures, and in this case, people may have used it to explain a socially and psychologically abhorrent behavior, cannibalism (Faddiman, 1997).

Some researchers question the famine explanation for *windigo* psychosis and even the idea of culture-bound disorders (Dana, 1998; Hoek, Van Harten, Van Hoeken, & Susser, 1998). However, there is little doubt that some mental disorders are at least somewhat *culture-bound* (Guarnaccia & Rogler, 1999; Helms & Cook, 1999; Lopez & Guarnaccia, 2000).

Robert Nishimoto (1988) has found several culture-bound and culture-general symptoms that are useful in diagnosing disorders. Using the Langer (1962) index of psychiatric symptoms, Nishimoto gathered data from three diverse groups, Anglo-Americans in Nebraska, Vietnamese Chinese in Hong Kong, and Mexicans living in Texas and Mexico. (The Langer index is a screening instrument widely used to identify psychological disorders that disrupt everyday functioning but do not require institutionalization.) When asked to think about their lives, respondents who needed professional help all named one or more of the same 12 symptoms (Table 37.1).

In addition to the culture-general symptoms (such as "nervousness" or "trouble sleeping"), Nishimoto also found culture-bound symptoms. For example, the Vietnamese Chinese reported "fullness in head," the Mexican respondents had "problems with my memory," and the Anglo-Americans reported "shortness of breath" and "headaches." Apparently people *learn* to express their problems in ways acceptable to others in the same culture (Brislin, 1997, 2000; Widiger & Sankis, 2000). In other

TABLE 37.1 TWELVE CULTURE-GENERAL SYMPTOMS OF MENTAL HEALTH DIFFICULTIES

Nervous	Trouble sleeping	Low spirits
Weak all over	Personal worries	Restless
Feel apart, alone	Can't get along	Hot all over
Worry all the time	Can't do anything worthwhile	Nothing turns out right

Source. Adapted from Brislin, 1993, 2000.

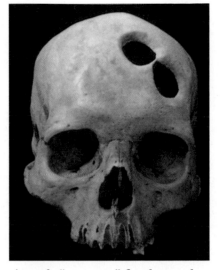

An early "treatment" for abnormal behavior? *During the Stone Age, many believed that demon possession was a primary cause of mental disorders, and one treatment was to bore holes in the skull to allow evil spirits to escape.*

words, most Americans learn that headaches are a common response to stress, whereas Mexicans learn that others will understand their complaints about memory. As you may imagine, it is very important that mental health professionals who work with culturally diverse populations understand that culturally general and culturally bound symptoms exist and what these are for any population.

Culture obviously affects definitions of abnormality, but our concept of what is abnormal also changes over time. Our next section examines historical views of abnormality.

■ Explaining Abnormality: From Superstition to Science

For much of history, abnormal behavior was believed to be caused by evil spirits and witchcraft. During the Stone Age, for example, it was believed that demons could *possess* a person's body and soul and that the only treatment was *trephining*. In this operation, stone instruments were used to bore a hole in the skull to allow the evil spirit to escape. During the Middle Ages (from about the fifth to the fifteenth century A.D.), the troubled person was treated with a religious practice known as *exorcism*, which involved prayer, fasting, noise-making, beating, and drinking terrible-tasting brews. The idea was to make the body so uncomfortable it would be uninhabitable by the Devil. During the fifteenth century, people became even more obsessed with the Devil. Not only could you be possessed, but you also could *choose* to consort with the Devil. These "willing people" (usually women who somehow offended the social

Witchcraft or mental illness? *During the fifteenth century, some people who may have been suffering from mental disorders were accused of witchcraft and tortured or hung.*

An early "Catch 22." *In the Middle Ages, "dunking tests" were used to determine whether people who behaved abnormally were possessed by demons. Individuals who did not drown while being dunked were believed to be guilty of possession and then punished (usually by hanging). Those who did drown were judged to be innocent.*

Medical Model *Perspective that assumes diseases (including mental illness) have physical causes that can be diagnosed, treated, and possibly cured*

Psychiatry *Branch of medicine dealing with the diagnosis, treatment, and prevention of mental disorders*

rules for feminine behavior) were called witches and were tortured, imprisoned for life, or executed (Porta, 2002).

Asylums

As the Middle Ages ended, advances were made in the treatment of mental disorders. By the fifteenth and sixteenth centuries, specialized hospitals, or asylums, began to appear in Europe. Initially designed to provide quiet retreats from the world and to "protect" society (Alexander & Selesnick, 1966), the asylums unfortunately became overcrowded, inhumane "jails."

Improvement came in 1792 when Philippe Pinel, a French physician, was put in charge of a Parisian asylum where the inmates were shackled to the walls of unlighted and unheated cells. Pinel removed inmates from the dungeons and insisted they be treated humanely. Many inmates improved so dramatically they could be released. Pinel's belief that abnormal behavior was caused by "sick" minds soon became the accepted way of viewing people who had previously been feared and punished for their abnormality. Thus, his idea that disturbed individuals had an underlying *physical illness* reflected the **medical model,** which viewed mental illness as having biological causes like other diseases.

Modern Times

Pinel's medical model eventually gave rise to the modern specialty of **psychiatry,** in which disorders are diagnosed as physical illnesses and treatments are prescribed. Unfortunately, when we assume that a mental "disease" exists and label people "mentally ill," we may create new problems. One of the most outspoken critics of the medical model is psychiatrist Thomas Szasz (1960, 1995, 2000). Szasz believes the medical model encourages people to believe they have no responsibility for their actions and that they can find solutions in drugs, hospitalization, or surgery. He contends that mental illness is a "myth" used to label individuals who are peculiar or offensive to others. Furthermore, labels can become self-perpetuating; that is, the person begins behaving according to the diagnosed disorder.

A famous study done by David Rosenhan of Stanford University illustrates problems with diagnostic labels (Rosenhan, 1973). Rosenhan and several colleagues presented themselves to a local mental hospital and complained of hearing voices (a classic symptom of schizophrenia). Although they had no other complaints, they were admitted to the hospital with a diagnosis of schizophrenia. After admission, they stopped their claims of hearing voices and behaved in their normal fashion. The purpose? Rosenhan wanted to see how long it would take the doctors and hospital staff to recognize they were not mentally ill. Surprisingly, none of the pseudopatients was ever recognized as a phony. Once they were inside a mental ward with a label of "schizophrenia," staff members saw only what they expected to see. Interestingly, real patients were not so easily fooled. They were the first to realize that the psychologists were not really mentally ill.

Rosenhan's study offers important insights into problems with labeling mental illness (Hock, 2001). But as you remember from Module 2, the scientific method requires operational definitions, control groups, single- and double-blind procedures, and replication. Unfortunately, none of these standards were met in the Rosenhan study. Despite its limits, the study does increase our awareness of the dangers of diagnostic labels in mental illness.

Today, the medical model remains a founding principle of psychiatry, and diagnosis and treatment of mental disorders continue to be based on the concept of mental *illness.* In contrast, psychology offers a multifaceted approach to explaining abnormal behavior. Each of the seven major perspectives in psychology — psychoanalytic, behavioral, humanistic, cognitive, biological, evolutionary, and sociocultural offers alternative explanations. Figure 37.3 summarizes these perspectives.

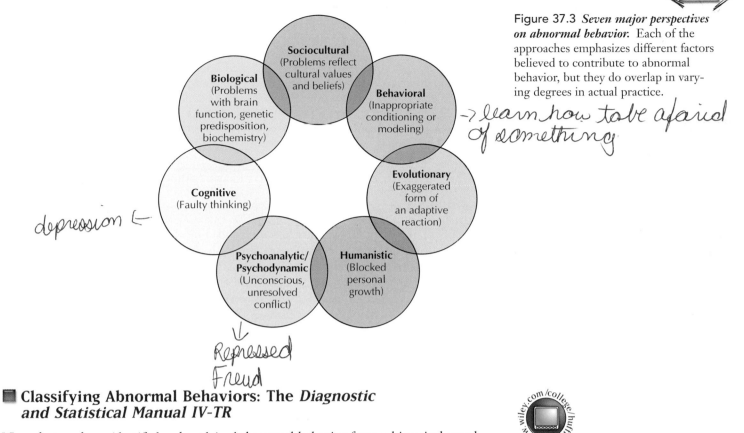

Figure 37.3 *Seven major perspectives on abnormal behavior.* Each of the approaches emphasizes different factors believed to contribute to abnormal behavior, but they do overlap in varying degrees in actual practice.

→ learn how to be afraid of something [handwritten]

depression ← [handwritten]

Repressed Freud [handwritten]

Classifying Abnormal Behaviors: The *Diagnostic and Statistical Manual IV-TR*

Now that we have *identified* and *explained* abnormal behavior from a historical standpoint, we also need a clear and reliable system for *classifying* the wide range of disorders. Just as physicians need agreed-on terms for identifying one set of signs and symptoms as cancer and another as heart disease, psychologists and psychiatrists need agreed-on terms for distinguishing Mary's disruptive behaviors and broken relationships, as described in the opening vignette, from Jim's paranoia. Without a uniform system for classifying and clearly describing psychological disorders, scientific research on them would be almost impossible, and communication among mental health professionals would be seriously impaired. Fortunately, mental health specialists do share a uniform classification system, the ***Diagnostic and Statistical Manual of Mental Disorders,*** fourth edition, text revision (***DSM-IV-TR***) (American Psychiatric Association, 2000). The "IV" simply designates that this is the fourth revision and the "TR" is the text revision of this fourth edition.

Why do they need to keep changing the manual? The major reason for the *DSM* revisions is to incorporate the large volume of new scientific information since the previous edition. Generally, each revision has expanded the list of disorders and changed the descriptions and categories to reflect both the latest in scientific research and changes in the way abnormal behaviors are viewed within our social context (Coolidge & Segal, 1998; Smart & Smart, 1997). For example, the use of the terms **neurosis** and **psychosis** as categories of disorders was significantly revised in *DSM-IV.* In previous editions, *neurosis* was used to describe Freud's idea of the causes of anxiety disorders. He believed anxiety could be felt and expressed directly (through phobias, obsessions, and compulsions) or that the unconscious could convert it into bodily complaints (somatoform disorders). But one way or another, all neurotic conditions were believed to reflect repressed anxiety.

Mental health professionals came to feel that Freud's emphasis on unconscious processes was too limiting and the category too large to be maximally useful. In the *DSM-IV,* conditions previously grouped under neurosis were redistributed as anxiety

Diagnostic and Statistical Manual of Mental Disorders (DSM-IV-TR) *Classification system developed by the American Psychiatric Association used to describe abnormal behaviors; the IV-TR indicates it is the text revision (TR) of the fourth major revision (IV)*

Neurosis *Outmoded term for disorders characterized by unrealistic anxiety and other associated problems*

Psychosis *Serious mental disorders characterized by loss of contact with reality and extreme mental disruption*

disorders, somatoform disorders, and dissociative disorders. Despite these changes, the term *neurosis* continues as a part of everyday language, and clinicians still use it occasionally when discussing disordered behavior presumed to be due to underlying anxiety.

As with neurosis, the conditions grouped under *psychosis* have been redistributed. Individuals with a psychosis suffer extreme mental disruption and loss of contact with reality. They often have trouble meeting ordinary demands of life, making hospitalization necessary. Schizophrenia, some mood disorders, and some disorders due to medical conditions are recognized as psychoses. Though these disorders are now listed as separate categories, the term *psychosis* is still listed in the *DSM-IV-TR* because it is useful in distinguishing between the most severe mental disorders, where the individual loses contact with reality, and the less disruptive disorders.

Understanding the DSM

As a result of continuing scientific research and clinical practice, the current *DSM-IV-TR* is organized according to five major dimensions, called *axes*, which serve as guidelines for making decisions about symptoms (Figure 37.4). Disorders are *diagnosed* along Axis I and II. Axis I describes *state disorders* (the patient's current condition, or "state"), whereas Axis II describes *trait disorders* (enduring problems that seem to be an integral part of the self, rather than something a person acquires). Examples of Axis I disorders are anxiety, substance abuse, and depression. Axis II lists long-running personality disturbances (like antisocial personality disorder) and mental retardation.

The other three axes are used to record important supplemental information. Axis III lists medical conditions that may be important to the person's psychopathology (such as diabetes or hypothyroidism, which can affect mood). Axis IV is reserved for psychosocial and environmental stressors that could be contributing to emotional problems (such as job or housing troubles or the death of a family member). Axis V

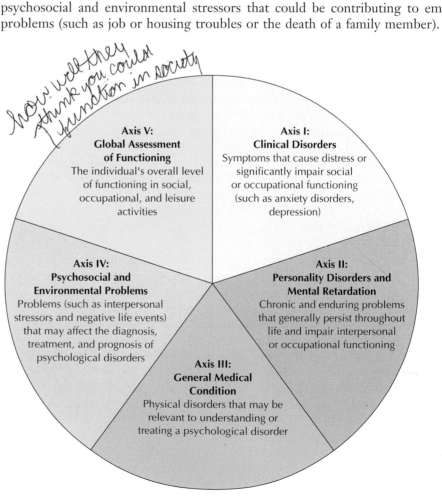

Figure 37.4 *Five axes of DSM-IV-TR.* Each of these five axes serves as a broad category that helps organize the wide variety of mental disorders and acts as a guideline for making decisions. *Source:* Adapted from DSM-IV-TR. American Psychiatric Association, Washington, D.C., 2000.

evaluates a person's overall level of functioning, on a scale from 1 (serious attempt at suicide or complete inability to take care of oneself) to 100 (happy, productive, with many interests).

In sum, the *DSM* offers a comprehensive, well-defined system intended for the diagnosis and classification of psychological disorders. It does not suggest therapies or treatment. The current *DSM-IV-TR* contains over 200 diagnostic categories grouped into 17 major categories (Table 37.2). Owing to space limitations, in Modules 38–41 we focus on only 5 of the 17 categories. We discuss three of the most common categories

TABLE 37.2 SUMMARY OF MAIN CATEGORIES OF MENTAL DISORDERS AND THEIR DESCRIPTIONS IN DSM-IV-TR* (The first five disorders are discussed in Modules 38–41)

1. **Anxiety Disorders:** Problems associated with severe anxiety, such as *phobias*, *obsessive-compulsive disorder*, and *posttraumatic stress disorder*.
2. **Mood Disorders:** Problems associated with severe disturbances of mood, such as *depression*, *mania*, or alternating episodes of both *(bipolar disorder)*.
3. **Schizophrenia and Other Psychotic Disorders:** A group of disorders characterized by major disturbances in perception, language and thought, emotion, and behavior.
4. **Dissociative Disorders:** Disorders in which the normal integration of consciousness, memory, or identity is suddenly and temporarily altered, such as *amnesia* and *dissociative identity disorder*.
5. **Personality Disorders:** Problems related to lifelong maladaptive personality traits, including *antisocial personality disorders* (violation of others' rights with no sense of guilt) or *borderline personality disorders* (impulsivity and instability in mood and relationships).
6. **Substance-related Disorders:** Problems caused by alcohol, cocaine, tobacco, and other drugs.
7. **Somatoform Disorders:** Problems related to unusual preoccupation with physical health or physical symptoms with no physical cause.
8. **Factitious Disorders:** Disorders that the individual adopts to satisfy some economic or psychological need.
9. **Sexual and Gender Identity Disorders:** Problems related to unsatisfactory sexual activity, finding unusual objects or situations arousing, gender identity problems.
10. **Eating Disorders:** Problems related to food, such as *anorexia nervosa* and *bulimia*.
11. **Sleep Disorders:** Serious disturbances of sleep, such as *insomnia* (too little sleep), *sleep terrors*, or *hypersomnia* (too much sleep).
12. **Impulse Control Disorders (not elsewhere classified):** Problems related to *kleptomania* (impulsive stealing), *pyromania* (setting of fires), and *pathological gambling*.
13. **Adjustment Disorders:** Problems involving excessive emotional reaction to specific stressors such as divorce, family discord, or economic concerns.
14. **Disorders usually first diagnosed in infancy, childhood, or early adolescence:** Problems that appear before adulthood, including mental retardation and language development disorders.
15. **Delirium, Dementia, Amnestic, and Other Cognitive Disorders:** Problems caused by known damage to the brain, including Alzheimer's disease, strokes, and physical trauma to the brain.
16. **Mental Disorders due to a general medical condition (not elsewhere classified):** Problems caused by physical deterioration or the brain due to disease, drugs, and so on.
17. **Other conditions that may be a focus of clinical attention:** Problems related to physical or sexual abuse, relational problems, occupational problems, and so forth.

* *Diagnostic Manual of Mental Disorders (DSM-IV-TR).*
Source: American Psychiatric Association, 2000.

Substance-related disorders

Mood disorders

Anxiety disorders

— *anxiety disorders*, *mood disorders*, and *schizophrenia*. We then explore the less common, but fascinating, *dissociative* and *personality disorders*. Before going on, it is important to note that the *DSM-IV-TR* classifies disorders that people have, *not the people themselves*. To reflect this important distinction, this text (like the *DSM-IV-TR*) avoids the use of terms such as *schizophrenic*. Instead, we use the term *a person with schizophrenia*.

Evaluating the DSM-IV-TR

The *DSM-IV* has been praised for carefully and completely describing symptoms, standardizing diagnosis and treatment, facilitating communication among professionals and between professionals and patients, and serving as a valuable educational tool. Critics, on the other hand, suggest it relies too heavily on the medical model and unfairly labels people (Dana, 1998; Roelcke, 1997; Sarbin, 1997). The *DSM-IV* has also been criticized for its possible culture bias. Although it does provide a culture-specific section and a glossary of culture-bound syndromes, the classification of most disorders still reflects a Western European and American perspective (Dana, 1998; Matsumoto, 2000; Smart & Smart, 1997). In addition, some would prefer to see disorders considered not just as *categories* (e.g., mood disorders, anxiety disorders), but also as *dimensions* or degrees of symptoms.

Despite its faults, many consider this fourth revision of the *DSM* the most advanced, scientifically based classification system ever developed (Durand & Barlow, 2003; First, Pincus, & Frances, 1999; Nathan & Langenbucher, 1999). It seems similar to Winston Churchill's description of democracy, it is "the worst system devised by the wit of man, except for all the others."

Assessment

CHECK & REVIEW

Studying Psychological Disorders

Abnormal behavior refers to patterns of emotion, thought, and action considered pathological for one or more of these reasons: statistical infrequency, disability or dysfunction, personal distress, or violation of norms.

In ancient times, people commonly believed that demons were the cause of abnormal behavior. The **medical model,** which emphasizes diseases and illness, later replaced this demonological model. The ***Diagnostic and Statistical Manual of Men-*** ***tal Disorders (DSM-IV-TR)*** classification provides detailed descriptions of symptoms, which in turn allow standardized diagnosis and treatment, and improved communication among professionals and between professionals and patients.

The *DSM* has been criticized for not paying sufficient attention to cultural factors, for relying too heavily on the medical model, and for labeling people.

Questions

1. What are the four major standards for identifying abnormal behavior?

2. In early treatment of abnormal behavior, _____ was used to allow evil spirits to escape, whereas _____ was designed to make the body so uncomfortable it would be uninhabitable by the devil. (a) purging, fasting; (b) trephining, exorcism; (c) demonology, hydrotherapy; (d) the medical model, the dunking test

3. Briefly define *neurosis*, *psychosis*, and *insanity*.

4. What are the chief advantages and disadvantages of the *DSM* system of classifying mental disorders?

Answers to Questions can be found in Appendix B.

ACTIVE LEARNING WORKSHEET   MODULE 37

ACROSS

4 A legal term for people with a mental disorder that implies a lack of responsibility for their behavior and an inability to manage their affairs.

5 Perspective that assumes diseases have physical causes that can be diagnosed, treated, and possibly cured. Using this perspective, abnormal behaviors also have physical causes that can be diagnosed by their symptoms and treated and cured through therapy, including drugs, hospitalization, and so on.

6 Serious mental disorders characterized by loss of contact with reality and extreme mental disruption. Because daily functioning is often impaired, psychotic individuals are more likely to need hospitalization.

DOWN

1 A large group of disorders characterized by unrealistic anxiety and other associated problems.

2 Patterns of emotion, thought, and action considered pathological (diseased or disordered) for one or more of these reasons: statistical infrequency, disability or dysfunction, personal distress, or violation of norms.

3 The specialized branch of medicine dealing with the diagnosis, treatment, and prevention of mental

MODULE 38
ANXIETY DISORDERS

Assessment

What are anxiety disorders and what causes them?

I was 9 years old and sitting alone in the back of a cab as it rumbled over New York City's 59th Street bridge. I noticed the driver was watching me curiously. My feet began tapping and then shaking, and slowly my chest grew tight and I couldn't get enough air in my lungs. I tried to disguise the little screams I made as throat clearings, but the noises began to rattle the driver. I knew a panic attack was coming on, but I had to hold on, get to the studio, and get through the audition. Still, if I kept riding in that car I was certain that I was going to die. The black water was just a few hundred feet below. "Stop!" I screamed at the driver. "Stop right here, please! I have to get out." "Young miss, I can't stop here." "Stop!" I must have looked like I meant it, because we squealed to a halt in the middle of traffic. I got out and began to run. I ran the entire length of the bridge and kept going. Death would never catch me as long as my small legs kept propelling me forward.

(ADAPTED FROM PEARCE AND SCANLON, 2002, P. 69).

These are the words of actress Patty Duke around the time she was starring as Helen Keller, the blind child in *The Miracle Worker*. Patty Duke's flight from the cab and other cases of **anxiety disorder** share one central defining characteristic — unreasonable, often paralyzing, anxiety or fear. The person feels threatened, unable to cope, unhappy, and insecure in a world that seems dangerous and hostile. Anxiety disorders are the most frequently occurring category of mental disorders in the general population, and they are found about twice as often in women as men (Margolis & Swartz, 2003; National Institute of Mental Health, 1999). Fortunately, they also are among the easiest disorders to treat and have one of the best chances for recovery (see Module 44).

◼ Four Major Anxiety Disorders

Symptoms of anxiety, such as rapid breathing, dry mouth, and increased heart rate, plague all of us during final exams, first dates, and visits to the dentist. But some people experience unreasonable anxiety that is so intense and chronic it seriously disrupts their lives. We will consider four major types of anxiety disorders: *generalized anxiety disorder*, *panic disorder*, *phobia*, and *obsessive-compulsive disorder*. (Posttraumatic stress disorder, another major anxiety disorder, was discussed in Module 9.) Although we discuss these disorders separately, it is important to remember that people with one anxiety disorder often have others (Barlow, Esler, & Vitali, 1998).

Generalized Anxiety Disorder

Generalized anxiety disorder is a common chronic problem that affects twice as many women as men and leads to considerable impairment (Brawman-Mintzer & Lydiard, 1996, 1997). As the name implies, **generalized anxiety disorder** is characterized by excessive worrying that lasts for at least six months and that is not focused on any particular object or situation. The anxiety is *unspecific* or *free-floating*. People with this disorder feel afraid of *something* but are unable to articulate the specific fear. They fret constantly and have a hard time controlling their worries. Because of persistent muscle tension and autonomic fear reactions, they may develop headaches, heart palpitations, dizziness, and insomnia. These physical complaints, combined with the intense, long-term anxiety, make it difficult to cope with normal daily activities.

Panic Disorder

Unlike generalized anxiety disorder, which is characterized by chronic, free-floating worry, **panic disorder** is marked by sudden but brief *attacks* of intense apprehension that cause trembling and shaking, dizziness, and difficulty breathing. Patty Duke's

A scene from The Miracle Worker.
As a young girl, Patty Duke won an academy award for her role as Helen Keller, but even at this early age she suffered from a serious anxiety disorder.

Anxiety Disorder *Type of abnormal behavior characterized by unrealistic, irrational fear*

Generalized Anxiety Disorder *Chronic, uncontrollable, and excessive worry not focused on any particular object or situation*

Panic Disorder *Sudden and inexplicable attacks of intense fear; symptoms include difficulty breathing, heart palpitations, dizziness, trembling, terror, and feelings of impending doom*

feeling of suffocation and certainty that she would die if she didn't immediately get out of the cab are characteristic of panic attacks. The American Psychiatric Association (2000) defines a *panic attack* as fear or discomfort that arises abruptly and peaks in 10 minutes or less. Although panic attacks seem to occur from nowhere, they generally happen after frightening experiences, prolonged stress, and even exercise. Many people who have occasional panic attacks interpret them correctly — as a result of a passing crisis or stress. Unfortunately, others begin to worry excessively and some may even quit jobs or refuse to leave home to avoid future attacks. It is labeled *panic disorder* when several apparently spontaneous panic attacks lead to a persistent concern about future attacks. A common complication of panic disorder is *agoraphobia* — anxiety about being trapped in a place or situation where escape is difficult or embarrassing (Craske, 2000; Gorman, 2000). Agoraphobia is one of the phobias discussed in the next section.

Phobia

Phobias involve a strong, irrational fear and avoidance of specific objects or situations. Phobic disorders differ from generalized anxiety disorders and panic disorders because there is a specific stimulus or situation that elicits the strong fear response. Although the objective danger is small or nonexistent and the person recognizes the fear is irrational, they still experience overwhelming anxiety, and a full-blown panic attack may follow. Imagine how it would feel to be so frightened by a spider that you would try to jump out of a speeding car to get away from it. This is how a person suffering from phobia might feel.

The DSM-IV-TR divides phobic disorders into three broad categories:

1. **Agoraphobia.** As discussed earlier, *agoraphobia* often develops following a panic attack. The term agoraphobia comes from the Greek words meaning "fear of the marketplace." People with agoraphobia restrict their normal activities because they fear being in busy, crowded places, or enclosed places like a bus or elevator, or being alone in wide-open places like a deserted beach. Can you see what is common to all these places? The person fears being trapped somewhere they cannot easily escape or would be unable to receive help in an emergency. And the emergency they fear most is having another panic attack. In severe cases, people with agoraphobia become so frightened that they may refuse to leave their home because this is the only place they feel really safe.

2. **Simple Phobias.** A *simple phobia* is a fear of a specific object or situation, such as needles, heights, rats, or spiders. Claustrophobia (fear of closed spaces) and acrophobia (fear of heights) are the simple phobias most often treated by therapists. People with this disorder have especially powerful imaginations, so they vividly anticipate terrifying consequences from encountering the feared object or situation.

    As with all phobias, people with simple phobias generally recognize that their fears are excessive and unreasonable, but they are unable to control their anxiety and will go to great lengths to avoid the feared stimulus. Years ago, a student who had taken my child psychology class wanted to take my general psychology class. However, her anxiety over the *possibility* that our text or the videos might have *pictures* of rats kept her from enrolling. Eventually, she did have therapy and successfully completed the course.

3. **Social Phobias.** Individuals with *social phobias* feel extremely insecure in social situations and have an irrational fear of embarrassing themselves. Fear of public speaking, or of eating in public, are the most common social phobias. Almost everyone experiences "stage fright" when speaking or performing in front of a group. But people with social phobias become so anxious that performance is out of the question. In fact, their fear of public scrutiny and potential humiliation becomes so pervasive that normal life is impossible (den Boer, 2000; Margolis & Swartz, 2003).

Phobia *Intense, irrational fear and avoidance of a specific object or situation*

Phobias reflect an extreme fear of certain objects such as snakes.

As Good as It Gets. *In the film, Jack Nicholson portrays a character struggling with obsessive-compulsive disorder.*

Obsessive-Compulsive Disorder

Intrusive, repetitive thoughts (obsessions), urges to perform repetitive, ritualistic behaviors (compulsions), or both

Obsessive-Compulsive Disorder

Do you remember the movie *As Good As It Gets?* The main character, portrayed by Jack Nicholson, was endlessly counting, checking locks, and repeatedly washing his hands in a seemingly senseless, ritualistic pattern. What's drives this behavior? The answer is **obsessive-compulsive disorder** (OCD), which involves persistent, unwanted thoughts *(obsessions)*, irresistible urges to perform an act or repeated ritual *(compulsions)*, or both. In adults, this disorder is equally common in men and women, however it is more prevalent among boys when the onset is in childhood (American Psychiatric Association, 2000).

Consider the case of billionaire Howard Hughes:

> Due to his unreasonable fear of germs, he made people who worked with him wear white gloves, sometimes several pairs, when handling documents he would later touch. When newspapers were brought to him, they had to be in stacks of three so he could slide the middle one out by grasping it with Kleenex. To escape contamination by dust, he ordered that masking tape be put around the doors and windows of his cars and houses.

FOWLER (1986)

I sometimes find myself worrying about germs and what others might have touched. Would this be considered an obsessive-compulsive disorder? Many people have obsessive thoughts or find they occasionally check stove burners, count steps, or clean their homes and offices past the point of normal standards. People even casually refer to this as "being OC" or "anal." The difference between an OCD and milder forms of obsession and compulsion is that with OCD the repetitive thoughts and ritualistic actions become *uncontrollable* and seriously interfere with a person's life.

For example, a woman with OCD who worries obsessively about germs might compulsively wash her hands hundreds of times a day until they are raw and bleeding. A man might each night check the lights, locks, oven, and furnace 10 times in a ritualistic pattern before he can go to sleep. Most sufferers of OCD do not enjoy these rituals and realize that their actions are senseless. But when they try to stop the behavior, they experience mounting anxiety that is relieved only by giving in to the urges. They simply cannot stop themselves.

Concerned family and friends generally understand that the person cannot stop their obsessions and compulsions, but they also may feel irritated, confused, and

resentful. As with other psychological disorders, therapists may recommend family counseling as well as individual therapies (Module 44).

Causes of Anxiety Disorders: Multiple Roots

The causes of anxiety disorders are a matter of considerable debate, but research has focused primarily on the roles of *psychological, biological,* and *sociocultural* processes (the *biopsychosocial model*).

Psychological

Psychological contributions to anxiety disorders are primarily in the form of faulty cognitive processes and maladaptive learning.

1. People with anxiety disorders have certain cognitive habits that make them vulnerable or prone to fear. They tend to be *hypervigilant* — they constantly scan their environment for signs of danger and seem to ignore signs of safety. They also tend to magnify ordinary threats and failures. For example, most people are anxious in a public speaking situation, but those who suffer from social phobia are excessively concerned about others' evaluation, hypersensitive to any criticism, and obsessively worried about potential mistakes. This intense self-preoccupation not only intensifies the social anxiety, but also leads these people to think they have failed — even when they have been successful. As you will see in Module 44, changing the thinking patterns of anxious people can greatly lessen their fears (Margolis & Swartz, 2003; Wells & Carter, 2001).

2. Phobias and other anxiety disorders can be the result of conditioning (both classical and operant conditioning) and social learning (both modeling and imitation) (Bouton, Mineka, & Barlow, 2001; King, Clowes-Hollins, & Ollendick, 1997). (See Modules 16–18 for a review of these terms.)

   During classical conditioning, for example, a stimulus that is originally neutral (e.g., a harmless spider) becomes paired with a frightening event (the sudden panic attack) so that it becomes a conditioned stimulus that elicits anxiety. After this kind of classical conditioning, the phobia is typically maintained through operant conditioning. The person begins to avoid the anxiety-producing stimulus (in this case, spiders) because avoiding the stimulus reduces the unpleasant feelings of anxiety (a process known as negative reinforcement). However, most people with phobias have no memory of specific instances that led to their fear, and in the face of similar experiences some people develop phobias whereas others do not (Craske, 1999). This suggests that conditioning may not be the only (or best) explanation.

   Social-learning theorists propose that some phobias are the result of modeling and imitation. For example, can you imagine how overprotective, fearful parents may make their children more prone to developing phobias and other anxiety disorders? Howard Hughes's mother, for instance, was extremely protective and worried constantly about his physical health.

   Phobias may also be learned vicariously (in an indirect, secondhand way). One research team showed videotapes to four groups of rhesus monkeys where the tapes were spliced together in a special way to show another monkey apparently experiencing extreme fear of a toy snake, a toy rabbit, a toy crocodile, and flowers (Cook & Mineka, 1989). The "viewing" monkeys were later afraid of the toy snake and crocodile but not of the toy rabbit or flowers, which suggests that phobias have both a learned and biological component.

Vicarious phobias. *Monkeys who watch artificially created videotapes of other monkeys being afraid of either a toy snake, toy rabbit, toy crocodile, or flowers will develop their own set of phobias. The fact that the viewing monkeys only develop fears of snakes and crocodiles demonstrates that phobias are both learned and biological.*

Biological

The fact that the rhesus monkeys selectively learned their phobias may mean that we have an evolutionary predisposition to fear what was dangerous to our ancestors, such as snakes and crocodiles (Mineka & Oehman, 2002; Rossano, 2003). Recent studies show that anxiety disorders also may have a genetic predisposition or may result from disrupted biochemistry or unusual brain activity (Albert, Maina, Ravizza, & Bogetto, 2002; Hettema, Neale, & Kendler, 2001; Jurado et al., 2002; Kendler, Jacobson, Myers, & Prescott, 2002). For example, twin and family studies shows that some individuals with panic disorder seem to be genetically predisposed toward an overreaction of the autonomic nervous system. These people apparently respond more quickly and intensely to stressful stimuli than others. Stress and arousal also seems to play a role in panic attacks. Drugs such as caffeine or nicotine or even hyperventilation (breathing deeper and faster than normal) can trigger an attack, which also suggests a biochemical disturbance.

Sociocultural

Have you heard that we are living in the "age of anxiety?" There has been a sharp rise in anxiety disorders in the past 50 years, particularly in Western industrialized countries. Sociocultural influences on anxiety may include our fast-paced life with decreased job security, increased mobility, and lack of stable family support. As we discovered in Module 8, our evolutionary ancestors were prewired to respond automatically to threatening stimuli. However, today our threats are less identifiable and immediate — but always with us. This may lead some of us to become hypervigilant and predisposed to anxiety disorders.

Further support for sociocultural influences on anxiety disorders is that anxiety disorders can have dramatically different forms in other cultures. For example, the Japanese have a type of social phobia, called *taijin kyofusho* (TKS), which loosely translated means "fear of people." But it is not a fear that people will criticize you, as in the Western version of social phobia. The Japanese disorder is a morbid dread that you will do something to embarrass others. TKS is extremely rare in Western cultures (Dinnel, Kleinknecht, & Tanaka-Matsumi, 2002). In the United States, "we don't think of the fear of embarrassing other people as a psychological syndrome" (cited in Goleman, 1995, p. C-3). But it is so common in Japan that TKS treatment centers, like weight clinics in the United States, are on almost every corner. The difference between Western social phobias and TKS provides another example of a culture-bound disorder and shows us once again how individualist cultures (like ours) emphasize the individual, whereas collectivist cultures (like Japan) focus on others.

Assessment

CHECK & REVIEW

Anxiety Disorders

People with **anxiety disorders** have persistent feelings of threat in facing everyday problems. **Phobias** are exaggerated fears of specific objects or situations, such as agoraphobia, a fear of being in open spaces. In **generalized anxiety disorders,** there is a persistent free-floating anxiety. In **panic disorder,** anxiety is concentrated into brief or lengthy episodes of panic attacks. In **obsessive-compulsive disorder,** persistent anxiety-arousing thoughts (obsessions) are relieved by ritualistic actions (compulsions) such as hand washing. Anxiety disorders are influenced by psychological, biological, and sociocultural factors (the biopsychosocial model). Psychological theories focus on cognitive processes (faulty thinking) and learning (maladaptive reactions). Biological approaches emphasize genetic predisposition, brain abnormalities, and biochemistry. The sociocultural perspective focuses on environmental stressors that increase anxiety and cultural socialization that produces distinct culture-bound disorders like taijin kyofusho (TKS).

Questions

1. Match the descriptions below with the following specific forms of anxiety disorder: (a) generalized anxiety disorder; (b) panic disorder; (c) phobia; (d) obsessive-compulsive disorder (OCD);

___ i. Characterized by severe attacks of extreme anxiety

___ ii. Long-term anxiety that is not focused on any particular object or situation

___ iii. Characterized by irrational fear of an object or situation

___ iv. Characterized by intrusive thoughts and urges to perform repetitive, ritualistic behaviors

2. How do learning theorists and social-learning theorists explain anxiety disorders?

3. Researchers believe that anxiety disorders are probably due to some combination of _____.

Answers to Questions can be found in Appendix B.

ACTIVE LEARNING WORKSHEET

MODULE 38

Complete the following, and then double-check your answers with those in Appendix B.

1. _____ is characterized by chronic, free-floating worry; whereas, _____ is exemplified by sudden and inexplicable attacks of anxiety.

2. _____involve a strong, irrational fear of a specific object or situation, and _____is anxiety about being somewhere where escape is difficult or embarrassing.

3. Irresistible urges to perform an act or ritual are known as _____; whereas _____involve persistent, unwanted thoughts.

4. _____ is a Japanese disorder involving a severe dread of embarrassing others.

5. The fact that rhesus monkeys selectively learn specific phobias suggests an _____ to fear what was dangerous to our ancestors.

MODULE 39
MOOD DISORDERS

Assessment

When do disturbances in mood become abnormal?

Ann had been divorced for eight months when she called a psychologist for an emergency appointment. Although her husband had verbally and physically abused her for years, she had had mixed feelings about staying in the marriage. She had anticipated feeling good after the divorce, but she became increasingly depressed. She had trouble sleeping, had little appetite, felt very fatigued, and showed no interest in her usual activities. She stayed home from work for two days because she "just didn't feel like going in." Late one afternoon she went straight to bed, leaving her two small children to fend for themselves. Then, the night before calling for an emergency therapy appointment, she took five sleeping tablets and a couple of stiff drinks. As she said, "I don't think I wanted to kill myself; I just wanted to forget everything for a while."

MEYER & SALMON, 1988; P. 312

Ann's case is a good example of a *mood disorder* (also known as an *affective disorder*). This category encompasses not only excessive sadness like Ann's but also unreasonable elation and hyperactivity.

■ Understanding Mood Disorders: Major Depressive Disorder and Bipolar Disorder

As the name implies, mood disorders are characterized by extreme disturbances in emotional states. There are two main types of mood disorders — *major depressive disorder* and *bipolar disorder.*

Major Depressive Disorder *Long-lasting depressed mood that interferes with the ability to function, feel pleasure, or maintain interest in life*

Bipolar Disorder *Repeated episodes of mania (unreasonable elation and hyperactivity) and depression*

Major Depressive Disorder

Depression has been recorded as far back as ancient Egypt, when the condition was called melancholia and was treated by priests. We all feel "blue" sometimes, especially following the loss of a job, end of a relationship, or death of a loved one. People suffering from **major depressive disorder,** however, may experience a lasting and continuously depressed mood without a clear trigger or precipitating event. In addition, their sadness is far more intense, interfering with their basic ability to function, feel pleasure, or maintain interest in life (Margolis & Swartz, 2003).

Clinically depressed people are so deeply sad and discouraged that they often have trouble sleeping, are likely to lose (or gain) weight, and may feel so fatigued that they cannot go to work or school or even comb their hair and brush their teeth. They may sleep both day and night, have problems concentrating, and feel so profoundly sad and guilty that they consider suicide. These feelings are without apparent cause and may be so severe that the individual loses contact with reality. As in the case of Ann, depressed individuals have a hard time thinking clearly or recognizing their own problems, but family or friends who recognize the symptoms can encourage them to seek professional help.

Bipolar Disorder

When depression is *unipolar,* the depressive episode eventually ends, and people return to a "normal" emotional level. Some people, however, rebound to the opposite state, known as *mania.* In this type of **bipolar disorder,** the person experiences periods of depression, as well as *mania* (an excessive and unreasonable state of over-excitement and impulsive behavior) (Figure 39.1).

During a manic episode, the person is overly excited, extremely active, and distractible. The person exhibits an unrealistically high self-esteem and an inflated sense of importance or even delusions of grandeur. He or she often makes elaborate plans for becoming rich and famous. The individual is hyperactive and may not sleep for days at a time, yet does not become fatigued. Thinking is speeded up and can change abruptly to new topics, showing "rapid flight of ideas." Speech is also rapid ("pressured speech"), and it is difficult to get a word in edgewise. Poor judgment is common: A person may give away valuable possessions or go on wild spending sprees.

Manic episodes may last a few days to a few months and generally end abruptly. The person's previous manic mood, rapid thinking and speaking style, and hyperactivity are reversed, and the following depressive episode generally lasts three times as long as the manic episode. The lifetime risk for bipolar disorder is low — somewhere between 0.5 and 1.6 percent — but it can be one of the most debilitating and lethal disorders, with a suicide rate between 10 and 20 percent (Goodwin & Ghaemi, 1998; MacKinnon, Jamison, & DePaulo, 1997).

■ Causes of Mood Disorders: Biological versus Psychosocial Factors

Mood disorders differ in their *severity* (how often they occur and how much they disrupt normal functioning), as well as in their *duration* (how long they last). In this section, we will examine the latest research that attempts to explain their causes. These explanations can be categorized as biological and psychosocial.

Biological Factors

Biological factors play a significant role in both major depression and bipolar disorder. Recent research shows the left frontal lobe, which is active during positive emotions, is inactive during depressive episodes (Davidson, 1999). Other research has identified a small area in the prefrontal cortex that may trigger both the sadness of depression and the mania of bipolar disorders (Liotti & Mayberg, 2001; Steffens & Krishnan, 1998).

Several lines of research also suggest that depression and mania may be caused by imbalances of the neurotransmitters norepinephrine and serotonin (Bellivier et al., 1998; Mann et al., 2000). This makes sense because these same neurotransmitters are involved in the capacity to be aroused or energized and in the control of other functions affected by depression such as sleep cycles and hunger. Moreover, drugs that alter the activity of these neurotransmitters also decrease the symptoms of depression (and hence are called *antidepressants*). The drug *lithium* reduces or prevents manic episodes by preventing norepinephrine- and serotonin-sensitive neurons from being overstimulated (Chuang, 1998).

There also is evidence that major depressive disorders, as well as bipolar disorders, may be inherited (Dubovsky & Buzan, 1999; Meltzer, 2000). For example, when one identical twin has a mood disorder, there is about a 50 percent chance that the other twin will also develop the illness (Margolis & Swartz, 2003). It is important to remember, however, that relatives generally have similar environments, as well as similar genes.

Finally, the evolutionary perspective suggests that moderate depression may be an adaptive response to a loss that helps us step back and reassess our goals (Neese, 2000). Consistent with this theory is the observation that primates also show signs of depression when they suffer a significant loss (Suomi, 1991). Clinical, severe depression may just be an extreme version of this generally adaptive response.

Psychosocial Theories

Psychosocial theories of depression focus on disturbances in the person's interpersonal relationships, thought processes, self-concept, and learning history (Agid et al., 1999; Rice & Mirzadeh, 2000). The psychoanalytic explanation sees depression as anger turned inward against oneself when an important relationship or attachment is lost. Anger is assumed to come from feelings of rejection or withdrawal of affection, especially when a loved one dies. The humanistic school says depression results when a person's self-concept is overly demanding or when positive growth is blocked.

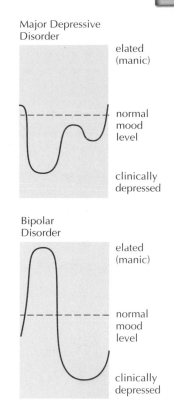

Major Depressive Disorder

elated (manic)

normal mood level

clinically depressed

Bipolar Disorder

elated (manic)

normal mood level

clinically depressed

Figure 39.1 *Mood disorders.* If major depressive disorders and bipolar disorders were depicted on a graph, they might look something like this.

Learned Helplessness *Seligman's term for a state of helplessness or resignation in which people or animals learn that escape from something painful is impossible, and depression results*

The **learned helplessness** theory of depression, developed by Martin Seligman (1975, 1994), is an outgrowth of research on avoidance learning in animals. Seligman has demonstrated that when animals or humans are subjected to pain that they cannot escape; they develop a sense of helplessness or resignation and thereafter do not attempt to escape painful experiences. In other words, the perception that one is unable to change things for the better leads to depression. Seligman also suggests that our general societal emphasis on individualism and diminished involvement with others makes us particularly vulnerable to depression.

The learned helplessness theory may also involve a cognitive element, known as *attribution*, or the explanations people assign to their own and other's behavior. Once someone perceives that his or her behaviors are unrelated to outcomes (learned helplessness), depression is likely to occur. This is particularly true if the person attributes failure to causes that are *internal* ("my own weakness"), *stable* ("this weakness is long-standing and unchanging"), and *global* ("this weakness is a problem in lots of settings") (Gotlieb & Abramson, 1999; Haddad, 2001; Peterson & Vaidya, 2001).

Achievement
GENDER & CULTURAL DIVERSITY

Gender, Culture, and Depression

Research shows certain symptoms of depression seem to exist across cultures: (1) frequent and intense sad affect, (2) decreased enjoyment, (3) anxiety, (4) difficulty in concentrating, and (5) lack of energy (Green, 1999; World Health Organization, 2000). On the other hand, there is evidence of some culture-specific symptoms. For example, feelings of guilt are found more often in North America and Europe. In China, *somatization* (converting depression into bodily complaints) is more frequent than in other parts of the world (Helms & Cook, 1999).

Not only does culture have an impact on depression but so does gender. It is widely accepted that women are more likely than men to suffer depressive symptoms. In North America, the rate of clinical (or severe) depression for women is two to three times the rate for men, and this gender difference holds true in several other countries as well (Angst et al., 2002; Martenyi, Dossenbach, Mraz, & Metcalfe, 2001; Nolen-Hoeksema, Larson, & Grayson, 2000; Ohayon & Schatzberg, 2002).

Why Are Women More Depressed?

Studies regarding the higher rate of female depression can be grouped under *biological* influences (hormones, biochemistry, and genetic predisposition), *psychological* (ruminative thought processes), and *social* factors (greater poverty, work-life conflicts, unhappy marriages, and sexual or physical abuse) (Broderick & Korteland, 2002; Kornstein, 2002; Martenyi, Dossenbach, Mraz, & Metcalfe, 2001; Nolen-Hoeksema, Larson, & Grayson, 2000; Whitney, Kusznir, & Dixie, 2002).

According to the *biopsychosocial model*, some women may inherit a genetic or hormonal predisposition toward depression, and then our society's socialization processes for women may reinforce certain behaviors that increase the chances for depression (Alloy et al., 1999; Nolen-Hoeksema, Larson, & Grayson, 2000). For example, gender roles for women in our culture encourage greater emotional expression, passivity, and dependence, whereas men are socialized toward emotional suppression, activity, and independence.

Can you see how this explanation suggests that we may underestimate male depression? If we socialize men to suppress their emotions and be the "stronger sex," they may be overlooking and underreporting their feelings of sadness and hopelessness, and they may be more reluctant to admit their depressive feelings. Furthermore, the traditionally identified symptoms of depression (sadness, low energy, feelings of helplessness) may cause us to overlook large numbers of depressed men, who show their distress by acting out (aggression), impulsivity (reckless driving and petty crimes), and substance abuse. (Interestingly, in Western society the expression of anger is the one emotion that is more acceptable in men than in women.) It may be that a great number of men are depressed and we just haven't recognized it. In recent years, a separate Gotland Male Depression Scale has been developed to help identify this type of *male depressive syndrome* (Walinder & Rutz, 2002).

Application
APPLYING PSYCHOLOGY TO EVERYDAY LIFE

Suicide and Its Prevention

Whatever the causes of mood disorders, one of the major dangers associated with the condition is the increased risk of suicide. Because of the shame and secrecy associated with suicide, there are many misconceptions and stereotypes. Check your own beliefs with the following exercise.

Decide whether each of the following is true or false:

1. People who talk about suicide are not likely to commit suicide.

2. Suicide usually takes place with little or no warning.

3. Suicidal people are fully intent on dying.

4. Children of parents who attempt suicide are at greater risk of committing suicide.

5. Suicidal people remain so forever.

6. Men are more likely than women to actually kill themselves by suicide.

7. When a suicidal person has been severely depressed and seems to be "snapping out of it," the danger of suicide decreases substantially.

8. Only depressed people commit suicide.

9. Thinking about suicide is rare.

10. Asking a depressed person about suicide will push him or her over the edge and cause a suicidal act that would not otherwise have occurred.

Now let's look at the experts' answers to these questions (Bostwick & Pankratz, 2000; Davison, Neale, & Kring, 2004; Garland & Zigler, 1999; Jamison & Baldessarini, 1999; Oquendo & Mann, 2000):

1. and 2. **False.** About 90 percent of people who are suicidal talk about their intentions. They may say, "If something happens to me, I want you to…" or "Life just isn't worth living." They also leave behavioral clues, such as giving away valued possessions, withdrawing from family and friends, and losing interest in favorite activities.

3. **False.** Only about 3 to 5 percent of suicidal people truly intend to die. Most are just unsure about how to go on living. They cannot see their problems objectively enough to realize that they have alternative courses of action. They often gamble with death, arranging it so that fate or others will save them. Moreover, once the suicidal crisis passes, they are generally grateful to be alive.

4. **True.** Children of parents who attempt or commit suicide are at much greater risk of following in their footsteps. As Schneidman (1969) puts it, "The person

who commits suicide puts his psychological skeleton in the survivor's emotional closet" (p. 22).

5. **False.** People who want to kill themselves are usually suicidal only for a limited period.

6. **True.** Although women are much more likely to attempt suicide, men are more likely to actually commit suicide. Men are more likely to use stronger methods, such as guns versus pills.

7. **False.** When people are first coming out of a depression, they are actually at greater risk because they now have the energy to actually commit suicide.

8. **False.** Although suicide rates are highest for people with major depressive disorders, suicide is also the leading cause of premature death in people who suffer from schizophrenia. Suicide is also a major cause of death in people with anxiety disorders and alcohol and other substance-related disorders. Suicide is not limited to people with depression. Poor physical health, serious illness, substance abuse (particularly alcohol), loneliness, unemployment, and even natural disasters may push many over the edge.

9. **False.** Estimates from various studies are that 40 to 80 percent of the general public has thought about committing suicide at least once in their lives.

10. **False.** Because society often considers suicide a terrible, shameful act, asking directly about it can give the person permission to talk. In fact, *not asking* might lead to further isolation and depression.

How can you tell if someone is suicidal? If you believe someone is contemplating suicide, act on your beliefs. Stay with the person if there is any immediate danger, and encourage him or her to talk to you rather than withdraw. Show the person that you care, but do not give false reassurances that "everything will be okay." This type of response makes the suicidal person feel *more* alienated. Instead, openly ask if the person is feeling hopeless and suicidal. Do not be afraid to discuss suicide with people who feel depressed or hopeless, fearing that you will just put ideas into their heads. The reality is that people who are left alone or who are told they can't be serious about suicide often attempt it.

If you suspect someone is suicidal, it is vitally important that you help the person obtain counseling. Most cities have suicide prevention centers with 24-hour hotlines or walk-in centers that provide emergency counseling. Also, share your suspicions with parents, friends, or others who can help in a suicidal crisis. To save a life, you may have to betray a secret when someone confides in you.

Assessment
CHECK & REVIEW

Mood Disorders

Mood disorders are disturbances of affect (emotion) that may include psychotic distortions of reality. In **major depressive disorder,** individuals experience a long-lasting depressed mood, feelings of worthlessness, and loss of interest in most activities. The feelings are without apparent cause and the individual may lose contact with reality. In **bipolar disorder,** episodes of mania and depression alternate with normal periods. During the manic episode, speech and thinking are rapid, and the person may experience delusions of grandeur and act impulsively.

Biological theories of mood disorders emphasize disruptions in neurotransmitters (especially dopamine and serotonin). There is also evidence of a genetic predisposition for both major depression and bipolar disorder.

Psychosocial theories of mood disorders emphasize disturbed interpersonal relationships, faulty thinking, poor self-concept, and maladaptive learning. **Learned helplessness** theory suggests that depression results from repeatedly failing to escape from a source of stress. Suicide is a serious problem associated with depression, but we can reduce the risk by becoming involved and showing concern.

ACTIVE LEARNING WORKSHEET   MODULE 39

Circle either "T" for true or "F" for false, and then compare your answers with those in Appendix B.

1. Long-lasting depression that interferes with ability to function, feel pleasure, or maintain interest in life is known as major mood dysfunction. T or F

2. In bipolar disorder, the person alternates between depression and mania. T or F

3. Both depression and mania may be caused by imbalances of norepinephrine and serotonin. T or F

4. When one identical twin has a mood disorder, there is about a 20 % chance that the other twin will also develop the illness. T or F

5. People who believe their behavior is unrelated to life outcomes are less likely to become depressed. T or F

MODULE 40
SCHIZOPHRENIA

www.wiley.com/college/huffman

Assessment

What are the symptoms and causes of schizophrenia?

Schizophrenia *Group of psychotic disorders involving major disturbances in perception, language, thought, emotion, and behavior; the individual withdraws from people and reality, often into a fantasy life of delusions and hallucinations*

Imagine for the moment that your daughter has just left for college and you hear voices inside your head shouting, "You'll never see her again! You have been a bad mother! She'll die." Or what if you saw dinosaurs on the street and live animals in your refrigerator? These are actual experiences that have plagued Mrs. T for almost 3 decades (Gershon & Rieder, 1993).

Mrs. T suffers from **schizophrenia,** a disorder characterized by major disturbances in perception, language, thought, emotion, and behavior. All the disorders we have considered so far cause considerable distress, but most sufferers can still function in daily life. Schizophrenia, however, is a form of *psychosis*, a term describing general lack of contact with reality. People with schizophrenia have serious problems caring for themselves, relating to others, and holding a job. In extreme cases, because they lack contact with reality, people with schizophrenia may require institutional or custodial care. To make matters worse, substance abuse rates are very high, perhaps reflecting an attempt to self-medicate (Batel, 2000; Green, 2000).

Schizophrenia is generally considered the most serious and severe form of mental disturbance. According to statistics, 1 of every 100 people develops schizophrenia and approximately half of all people admitted to mental hospitals are diagnosed with schizophrenia (Gottesman, 1991; Kendler, Gallagher, Abelson, & Kessler, 1996: Kessler et al., 1994; Regier et al., 1993). The disorder usually emerges between the late teens and the mid-thirties and only rarely prior to adolescence or after age 45 (American Psychiatric Association, 2000). Although schizophrenia seems to be equally prevalent in men and women, for unknown reasons it typically is more severe and strikes earlier in men than in women (Salyers & Mueser, 2001).

Is schizophrenia the same as "split or multiple personality?" No. Schizophrenia means "split mind," but when Eugen Bleuler coined the term in 1911, he was referring to the fragmenting of thought processes and emotions found in schizophrenic disorders (Neale, Oltmanns, & Winters, 1983). Unfortunately, the public often confuses "split mind" with "split personality." One study of college freshmen found that 64 percent thought having multiple personalities was a common symptom of schizophrenia (Torrey, 1998). But as you will read later, *multiple personality disorder* (now known as *dissociative identity disorder*) is the rare condition of having more than one distinct personality. Schizophrenia is a much more common — and altogether different — type of psychological disorder. What are the symptoms of schizophrenia? What are its causes? And how does it differ cross-culturally?

■ Symptoms of Schizophrenia: Five Areas of Disturbance

Unlike the two previous categories, in which everyone who has an anxiety disorder feels anxiety, and everyone with mood disorders feels depressed or manic, people who suffer from schizophrenia can have significantly different symptoms, yet still be given the same label. This is because schizophrenia is a group or class of disorders, and each case is identified according to some kind of basic disturbance in one or more of the following areas: perception, language, thought, affect (or emotions), and behavior.

Perceptual Symptoms

The senses of people with schizophrenia may be either enhanced (as in the case of Mrs. T) or blunted. The filtering and selection processes that allow most people to concentrate on whatever they choose are impaired, and sensory stimulation is jumbled and distorted. One patient reported:

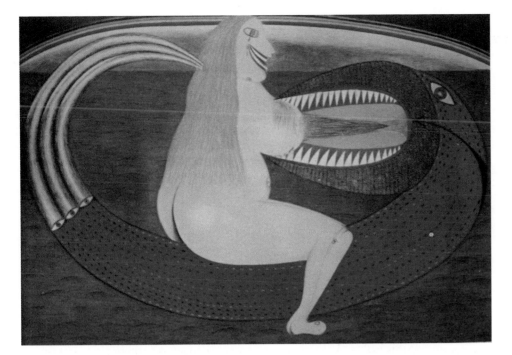

Symptoms of schizophrenia? Disorga-nized thoughts, emotions, and perceptions are sometimes reflected in the artwork of people suffering from schizophrenia.

When people are talking, I just get scraps of it. If it is just one person who is speak-ing, that's not so bad, but if others join in then I can't pick it up at all. I just can't get in tune with the conversation. It makes me feel all open — as if things are closing in on me and I have lost control.

McGhie and Chapman, 1961, p. 106

People with schizophrenia also experience **hallucinations** — they perceive things without external stimuli. Hallucinations can occur in any of the senses (visual, tactile, olfactory), but auditory hallucinations (hearing voices and sounds) are most common in schizophrenia. As with Mrs. T, people with schizophrenia often hear voices speak-ing their thoughts aloud, commenting on their behavior, or telling them what to do. The voices seem to come from inside their own heads or from an external source such as an animal, telephone wires, or a TV set.

On rare occasions, people with schizophrenia will hurt others in response to their distorted internal experiences or the voices they hear. Unfortunately, these cases receive undue media attention and create exaggerated fears of "mental patients." In reality, a person with schizophrenia is most likely self-destructive and at greater risk of suicide than of violence toward others.

Hallucinations *Sensory perceptions that occur without an external stimulus*

Language and Thought Disturbances

For people with schizophrenia, words lose their usual meanings and associations, logic is impaired, and thoughts are disorganized and bizarre. For example, a patient with schizophrenia gave this explanation for the meaning of the proverb "People who live in glass houses shouldn't throw stones":

People who live in glass houses shouldn't forget people who live in stone houses and shouldn't throw glass.

When language and thought disturbances are mild, an individual with schizophrenia jumps from topic to topic. In more severe disturbances, phrases and words are jum-bled together (referred to as *word salad*). Or the person creates artificial words (*neolo-gisms*). For example, the person might say "splisters" for splinters and blisters or "smever" for smart and clever.

Delusions *Mistaken beliefs maintained in spite of strong evidence to the contrary*

The most common thought disturbances experienced by people with schizophrenia are distorted beliefs called **delusions**. In contrast to mistaken beliefs that we all experience from time to time, such as thoughts that a friend is trying to avoid us or that our parents' divorce was our fault, delusions are mistaken beliefs maintained in spite of strong evidence to the contrary.

Mrs. T held the *paranoid delusion* that others were talking about her. In *delusions of grandeur*, people believe they are someone very important, perhaps Jesus Christ or the queen of England. In *delusions of persecution*, individuals believe they are the target of a plot to harm them, as was the case with Jim in our introduction, who believed secret agents were trying to assassinate him. In *delusions of reference*, unrelated events are given special significance, as when a person believes a radio program or newspaper article is giving him or her a special message.

Emotional Disturbances

Changes in emotion, or affect, usually occur in schizophrenia. In some cases, emotions are exaggerated and fluctuate rapidly in inappropriate ways. One person reported:

> It must look queer to people when I laugh about something that has got nothing to do with what I am talking about, but they don't know what's going on inside and how much of it is running around in my head. You see, I might be talking about something quite serious to you and other things come into my head at the same time that are funny and this makes me laugh. If I could only concentrate on one thing at the same time, I wouldn't look half so silly.
>
> (McGhie & Chapman, 1961, p. 104)

In other cases, emotions may become blunted or decreased in intensity. Some people with schizophrenia have *flattened affect* — almost no emotional response of any kind.

Behavioral Disturbances

Disturbances in behavior may take the form of unusual actions that have special meaning. One patient shook his head rhythmically from side to side to try to shake the excess thoughts out of his mind. Another massaged his head repeatedly "to help clear it" of unwanted thoughts. In other cases, the affected person may grimace and display unusual mannerisms. These movements, however, may also be side effects of the medication used to treat the disorder (Module 43).

People with schizophrenia may become *cataleptic* and assume an uncomfortable, nearly immobile stance for an extended period. A few people with schizophrenia also have a symptom called *waxy flexibility*, a tendency to maintain whatever posture is imposed on them.

The abnormal behaviors of individuals with schizophrenia are often related to disturbances in their perceptions, thoughts, and feelings. For example, experiencing a flood of sensory stimuli or overwhelming confusion, a person with schizophrenia will often withdraw from social contacts and refuse to communicate.

■ Types of Schizophrenia: Recent Methods of Classification

For many years, researchers divided the schizophrenias into *paranoid, catatonic, disorganized, undifferentiated*, and *residual* subtypes (Table 40.1). Although these terms are still used in the *DSM-IV-TR* (and sometimes by the public), critics say that they have little value in clinical practice and research. They contend that this classification does not differentiate in terms of prognosis (prediction for recovery), etiology (cause), or response to treatment, and that the undifferentiated type is a catchall for difficult diagnostic cases (American Psychiatric Association, 2000).

For all these reasons, Nancy Andreasen and others (Andreasen, 2000; Andreasen, Flaum, Swayze, Tyrrell, & Arndt, 1990; Toomey, Faraone, Simpson, & Tsuang, 1998) propose an alternative classification system of two groups instead of four:

TABLE 40.1 SUBTYPES OF SCHIZPHRENIA

Paranoid	Dominated by delusions (persecution and grandeur) and hallucinations (hearing voices)
Catatonic	Marked by motor disturbances (immobility or wild activity) and echo speech (repeating the speech of others)
Disorganized	Characterized by incoherent speech, flat or exaggerated emotions, and social withdrawal
Undifferentiated	Meets the criteria for schizophrenia but is not any of the above subtypes
Residual	No longer meets the full criteria for schizophrenia but still shows some symptoms

1. **Positive symptoms** involve *additions* or exaggerations of normal thought processes and behaviors, including bizarre delusions, hallucinations, and disorganized speech.

2. **Negative symptoms** involve the *loss* or absence of normal thought processes and behaviors, including impaired attention, limited or toneless speech, flattened emotions, and social withdrawal.

In addition to these two groups, the latest *DSM-IV-TR* suggests adding another dimension to reflect *disorganization of behavior*. One advantage of either a two- or three-dimension model is that they both acknowledge that the schizophrenias are more than one disorder and that it has multiple causes.

Study**T**ip

If you're having difficulty understanding the distinction between positive and negative symptoms of schizophrenia, think back to what you learned in Module 17 regarding positive and negative reinforcement and punishment. Positive can be seen as "the addition of," whereas negative refers to the "removal or loss of."

▪ Causes of Schizophrenia: Nature and Nurture Theories

There are several theories that attempt to explain the schizophrenias. Biological theories emphasize physical changes in the nervous system based on abnormal brain

"That's the doctor who is treating me for paranoia. I don't trust him."

functioning or inherited predisposition. Psychosocial theories focus on stressful experiences and disturbed family interactions. Keep in mind that because the disorder comes in so many different forms, it may have multiple biological and psychosocial bases.

Biological Theories

An enormous amount of scientific research exists concerning possible biological factors in schizophrenia. Most of this research is in three areas: genetics, neurotransmitters, and brain function:

1. **Genetics.** Genetics undoubtedly plays a primary role in the development of schizophrenia. Although researchers are beginning to identify specific genes related to schizophrenia and have even identified the chromosomal locations of some of them, most genetic studies have focused on twin and adoption research (Bailer et al., 2000; Brustowicz et al., 2000; Gershon et al., 1998; Petronis, 2000). By most estimates, heritability is around 48 percent for identical twins. Figure 40.1 shows the risk of developing schizophrenia in people with differing degrees of relatedness to a person with schizophrenia. As expected, the risk increases with genetic similarity; that is, people who share more genes are more likely to develop the disorder. For example, if one identical twin develops schizophrenia, the other twin has a 48 to 83 percent chance of also developing schizophrenia (Berrettini, 2000; Cannon, Kaprio, Lonnqvist, Huttunen, & Koskenvuo, 1998). But if one sibling develops schizophrenia, the chances of the other sibling developing it are only 9 percent. If you compare these percentages with the risk for the general population (which is around 1 percent), you can appreciate the role of genetics in schizophrenia.

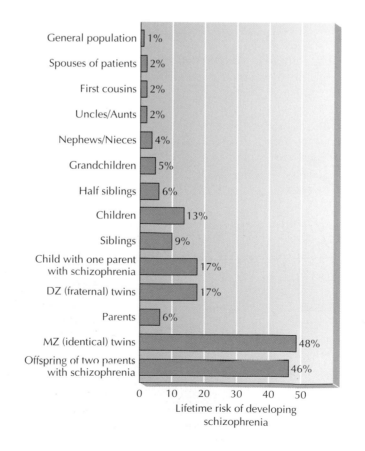

Figure 40.1 *Genetics and schizophrenia.* Your lifetime risk of developing schizophrenia depends, in part, on how closely you are genetically related to someone with schizophrenia. As you evaluate the statistics, bear in mind that the risk in the general population is a little less than 1 percent (the top line on the graph). Risk increases with the degree of genetic relatedness. *Source:* Gottesman, 1991.

2. **Neurotransmitters.** Precisely how genetic inheritance produces schizophrenia is unclear. The most widely held view implicates a dopamine imbalance (Gelman, 1999; Schwartz, Diaz, Pilon, & Sokoloff, 2000). According to the **dopamine hypothesis,** an overactivity of certain dopamine neurons in the brain causes schizophrenia. This hypothesis is based on two important observations:

- Large doses of amphetamines increase the amount of dopamine (Module 15) and can produce the positive symptoms of schizophrenia (such as delusions of persecution) in people with no history of psychological disorders. Low doses of amphetamines worsen symptoms in people who have schizophrenia. Moreover, an amphetamine-induced psychosis is more likely to occur in individuals who have a genetic predisposition but no signs of active schizophrenia.
- Drugs effective in treating the schizophrenias, such as chlorpromazine, block the effects of dopamine in the brain. The result is a reduction or elimination of positive symptoms such as hallucinations.

3. **Brain function.** The third major biological theory for schizophrenia involves possible brain damage. For example, researchers have found larger cerebral ventricles (the normal, fluid-filled spaces in the brain) in some people with schizophrenia (Zipursky, Lambe, Kapur, & Mikulis, 1998). In Figure 40.2a, the enlarged ventricles of one patient with schizophrenia are clearly shown through the technique of magnetic resonance imaging (MRI). (Enlarged cerebral ventricles were found in the brain of John Hinkley Jr., the man who attempted to assassinate President Ronald Reagan.) Keep in mind, however, it could be the case either that the disease itself may result in brain damage or that the damage may cause or worsen the schizophrenia.

Another technique, positron emission tomography (PET) (Figure 40.2c), shows that some people with chronic schizophrenia tend to have a lower level of activity in the frontal and temporal lobes. Because the frontal and temporal lobes are involved in language, attention and memory, damage here might explain the thought and language disturbances that characterize schizophrenia (Buchanan, Vlader, Barta, & Pearlson, 1998; Hazlett et al., 2000).

Dopamine Hypothesis *Theory that overactivity of dopamine neurons may contribute to some forms of schizophrenia*

Figure 40.2 *Two views of schizophrenia.* (a) A three-dimensional magnetic resonance image (MRI) shows structural changes in the shrunken hippocampus (yellow) and enlarged ventricles (gray) of the brain of a patient with schizophrenia. (b) Compare the same regions (the yellow and gray areas) on this person without schizophrenia. (c) These positron emission tomography (PET) scans show variations in the brain activity of normal individuals, people with major depressive disorder, and individuals with schizophrenia. Levels of brain activity correspond to the colors and numbers at the far right of the photo. Higher numbers and warmer colors indicate increased activity.

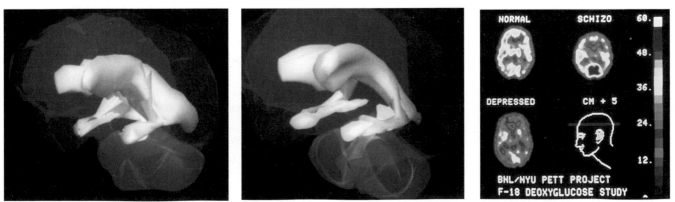

(a)   (b)   (c)

Some research suggests that prenatal viral infections, birth complications, immune responses, and maternal malnutrition also play roles in schizophrenia (Cannon et al., 2002; Koenig, Kirkpatrick, & Lee, 2002; Torrey & Yolken, 2000; Urakubo, 2001).

Psychosocial Theories

We can understand the degree to which psychosocial factors contribute to the development of schizophrenia by looking at genetic statistics for *identical twins*. Remembering that these children share *identical genes*, what would be the percentage chance that both twins would develop schizophrenia if the disorder were completely hereditary? If you guessed 100 percent, you're right. Because the rate is actually only 48 percent, nongenetic factors must contribute the remaining percentage. Other biological factors (such as neurotransmitters and brain structure) may take up part of the "leftover" percentage, but most psychologists believe there are at least two possible nonbiological contributors: stress and family communication.

1. *Stress.* In most theories of schizophrenia, stress plays an essential role in triggering schizophrenic episodes (Jansen, Wied, & Kahn, 2000; Torrey & Yolken, 1998, 2000). According to the *diathesis-stress model* of schizophrenia, a person inherits a predisposition (or *diathesis*) toward schizophrenia and then experiences more stress than he or she can handle, which triggers a schizophrenic episode. Research also suggests that stress may be associated with patient relapse.

2. *Family communication.* Some investigators suggest that communication disorders in parents and family members may be a predisposing factor for schizophrenia. Such disorders include unintelligible speech, fragmented communications, and contradictory messages. In these families, the child might withdraw into a private world and thereby set the stage for later schizophrenia.

Family communication patterns also can negatively affect patients with schizophrenia after hospitalization. In several studies researchers evaluated *expressed emotion* (EE) — levels of criticism and hostility aimed at the family member with schizophrenia and emotional overinvolvement in his or her life. They found greater relapse and worsening of symptoms among hospitalized patients who go home to high-EE families (Hooley & Hiller, 2001; Lefley, 2000).

In sum, there is strong evidence linking schizophrenia to biological factors — genetics, neurotransmitters, and brain function — as well as evidence for psychological, and social factors — the *biopsychosocial model*.

Evaluating the Theories

Critics of the dopamine hypothesis and the brain damage theory argue that they fit only some cases of schizophrenia. Moreover, with both theories, it is difficult to determine cause and effect. That is, does overactivity in dopamine neurons cause schizophrenia, or does schizophrenia cause overactivity of dopamine neurons? Similarly, does brain damage cause schizophrenia, or does schizophrenia cause brain damage? Or is there a third, as yet unknown, factor? Genetic predisposition may be the strongest factor, but as mentioned earlier, the highest correlation, found in identical twins, is only about 50 percent.

The disturbed-communication theories are also hotly debated, and research is equally inconclusive. This uncertainty points to the fact that schizophrenia is probably the result of a combination of known and unknown interacting factors (Figure 40.3).

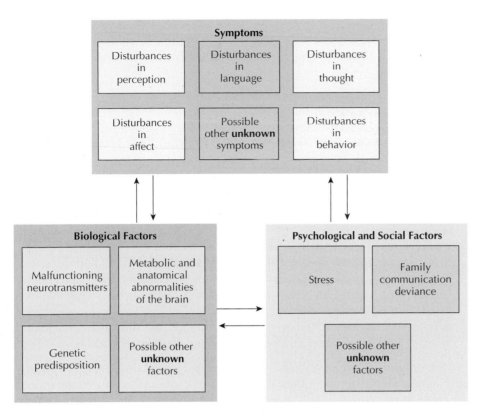

Figure 40.3 **The biopsychosocial model and schizophrenia.** Research shows that schizophrenia may have various causes. Most probably, biological factors interact with psychological and social factors to produce the symptoms. *Source:* Meltzer, 2000.

GENDER & CULTURAL DIVERSITY

Culture and the Schizophrenias

At the beginning of this section, we discussed how some researchers believe that certain mental disorders may be culturally universal; schizophrenia is a prime example. Culturally general symptoms of schizophrenia include delusions, thinking aloud, incoherent speech, difficulty forming emotional ties with others, poor rapport with others, and poor self-insight.

In contrast to these cultural *commonalties*, schizophrenia *differs* across cultures in four important ways:

1. **Prevalence.** Although schizophrenia is one of the more common disorders in the world, the reported incidence within different cultures varies. For example, comparisons of gender differences in Norway found that men tend to develop the disease 3 to 4 years earlier than women, have more and longer hospitalizations, and have poorer social functioning (Raesaenen, Pakaslahti, Syvaelahti, Jones, & Isohanni, 2000). It is unclear whether these differences result from an actual difference in prevalence of the disorder or from differences in definition, diagnosis, or reporting (Kleinman & Cohen, 1997; Lefley, 2000).

2. **Form.** The form or major mode of expression of the schizophrenias also varies across cultures. In Nigeria, for example, the major symptom of schizophrenia is intense suspicion of others, accompanied by bizarre thoughts of personal danger (Katz et al., 1988). However, in Western nations the major symptom is auditory hallucinations. Interestingly, the "sources" of auditory hallucinations have changed

with technological advances. In the 1920s, the voices that people heard came from the radio; in the 1950s, they came from TV; in the 1960s, it was satellites in outer space; and in the 1970s and 1980s, they often came from microwave ovens (Brislin, 2000).

3. **Onset.** As we discussed, some theories suggest that stress may trigger the onset of schizophrenia. Cross-cultural research in sites such as, Algeria, Asia, Europe, South America, and the United States supports the relationship between stress and schizophrenia (Al-Issa, 2000; Benes, 1997; Browne, 2001; Neria et al., 2002; Torrey & Yolken, 1998). Some stressors were shared by many cultures, such as the unexpected death of a spouse or loss of a job, but others were culturally specific, such as feeling possessed by evil forces or being the victim of witchcraft.

4. **Prognosis.** The *prognosis*, or prediction for recovery, from schizophrenia also varies among cultures. Given the advanced treatment facilities and wider availability of trained professionals and drugs in industrialized nations, it may surprise you to learn that the prognosis for people with schizophrenia is better in nonindustrialized societies. This may be because the core symptoms of schizophrenia (poor rapport with others, incoherent speech, etc.) make it more difficult to survive in highly industrialized countries. In addition, individualism is highly encouraged in most industrialized nations, and families and other support groups are less likely to feel responsible for relatives and friends with schizophrenia (Brislin, 2000; Lefley, 2000).

The four culturally specific factors (prevalence, form, onset, and prognosis) support a sociocultural or psychological explanation of schizophrenia. On the other hand, the large number of culturally general symptoms and the fact that schizophrenia is found in almost every society support biological explanations. Can you see how this is just one more example of the importance of the *biopsychosocial model*?

Assessment

CHECK & REVIEW

The Schizophrenias

The schizophrenias are a group of serious psychotic mental disorders that afflict approximately 1 of every 100 people. The five major symptoms are disturbances in perception (impaired filtering and selection, **hallucinations**), language (*word salad, neologisms*), thought (impaired logic, **delusions**), emotion (either exaggerated or blunted emotions), and behavior (social withdrawal, bizarre mannerisms, *catalepsy, waxy flexibility*).

Symptoms of schizophrenia can be divided into a two-dimensioned classification system: *Addition* or exaggeration of normal thought processes and behaviors (e.g., delusions and hallucinations) is classified as *positive symptoms*, whereas loss or absence of normal thought processes and behaviors (e.g., toneless voice and flat emotions) is classified as *negative symptoms*.

Biological theories of the causes of schizophrenia propose genetics (people inherit a predisposition), disruptions in neurotransmitters (the **dopamine hypothesis**), and brain function (such as enlarged ventricles and lower levels of activity in the frontal and temporal lobes). Psychosocial theories of schizophrenia focus on stress and disturbed family communication.

The schizophrenias are the most culturally universal mental disorders in the world. Many symptoms are culturally general (such as delusions), but significant differences also exist across cultures in prevalence, form, onset, and prognosis.

Questions

1. _____ refers to "split mind," whereas _____ refers to "split personality." (a) Psychosis, neurosis; (b) Insanity, multiple personalities; (c) Schizophrenia, dissociative identity disorder; (d) Paranoia, borderline

2. Schizophrenia is also a form of _____, a term describing general lack of contact with reality.

3. Perceptions for which there are no appropriate external stimuli are called _____, and the most common type among people suffering from schizophrenia is _____. (a) hallucinations, auditory; (b) hallucinations, visual; (c) delusions, auditory; (d) delusions, visual

4. List three possible biological and two nonbiological, or psychosocial, causes of schizophrenia.

Answers to Questions can be found in Appendix B.

ACTIVE LEARNING WORKSHEET   MODULE 40

"Name That Symptom"

Schizophrenia is characterized by disturbances in perception, language, thought, affect, and behavior. Identify the type of disturbance in each of the following statements:

1. "I hear voices that tell me what to do."

2. "I become extremely fearful or euphoric for no apparent reason."

3. "My body may assume an uncomfortable, nearly immobile stance for an extended period."

4. "I believe secret agents are trying to assassinate me."

5. "I create new words and sometimes jumble them together."

MODULE 41
OTHER DISORDERS

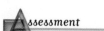

Assessment

How are dissociative disorders and personality disorders identified?

Dissociative Disorder *Amnesia, fugue, or multiple personalities resulting from avoidance of painful memories or situations*

We have now discussed anxiety, schizophrenia, and mood disorders. In this section, we will briefly describe two additional disorders — dissociative and personality disorders.

Dissociative Disorders: When the Personality Splits Apart

Have you seen the movie *The Three Faces of Eve* or *Sybil?* The most dramatic and popularized cases of psychological disorders are **dissociative disorders.** There are several types of dissociative disorders, but all involve a splitting apart (a *dis*-association) of significant aspects of experience from memory or consciousness. Individuals dissociate from the core of their personality by failing to recall or identify past experience (*dissociative amnesia*), leaving home and wandering off (*dissociative fugue*), losing the sense of reality and feeling estranged from the self (*depersonalization disorder*), or by developing completely separate personalities (*dissociative identity disorder*, previously known as *multiple personality disorder*).

Why would someone react this way? We've all had the experience of driving somewhere, arriving at our destination, and then realizing we don't remember a single detail of the drive. This is a very mild form of dissociation. To understand what a dissociative disorder might be like, imagine witnessing a loved one's death in a horrible car accident. Can you see how your mind might cope with the severe emotional pain by blocking out all memory of the event? Putnam (1992) described a heart-wrenching example of a dissociative disorder in a young girl who saw both her parents blown to bits in a minefield, and then tried to carefully piece their bodies back together, bit by bit.

The major problem underlying all dissociative disorders is the need to escape. A history of extreme trauma, usually sexual abuse, is found in nearly all cases (Dickinson, deGruy, Dickinson, & Candib, 1999; Scroppo, Drob, Weinberger, & Eagle, 1998). By developing amnesia, running away, or creating separate personalities, the individual is able to cope with the ongoing trauma or memories of the abuse. Unlike most psychological disorders, environmental variables are reported to be the primary cause, with little or no genetic influence (Waller & Ross, 1997).

Dissociative Identity Disorder

Dissociative Identity Disorder (DID) *Presence of two or more distinct personality systems in the same individual at different times; previously known as multiple personality disorder*

The most severe dissociative disorder is **dissociative identity disorder** (DID), previously known as multiple personality disorder (MPD), in which at least two separate and distinct personalities exist within the same person at the same time. Each personality has unique memories, behaviors, and social relationships. Transition from one personality to another occurs suddenly and is often associated with psychological stress. Usually the original personality has no knowledge or awareness of the existence of the alternate subpersonalities, but all of "them" may be aware of lost periods of time. Often, the alternate personalities are very different from the original personality and may be of the other sex, a different race, another age, or even another species (such as a dog or lion). The disorder is diagnosed more among women than men. Women also tend to have more identities, averaging 15 or more, compared with men, who average 8 (American Psychiatric Association, 2000).

The book and movie *Sybil* portrayed one of the best known cases of DID — that of Sybil Dorsett, a Midwestern schoolteacher with 16 personalities that took turns controlling her body. Instead of thinking of herself as one person who behaved differently at times, Sybil had lapses of memory when she became "another person." When she was "Peggy Lou," she was aggressive and capable of anger; as "Vickie," she was a confident and sophisticated woman who knew of the other personalities.

DID is a controversial diagnosis. As you remember from Module 21, there is considerable debate about whether repressed memories, particularly of childhood sexual abuse, are real or not. Some researchers and mental health professionals even question whether DIDs actually exist. They suggest that many cases are faked or result from false memories and unconscious needs to please the therapist (Lilienfeld et al., 1999; Loftus, 1997; Stafford & Lynn, 2002). These skeptics also believe that therapists may be unintentionally encouraging and thereby over-reporting the incidence of multiple personalities.

Sally Field won an Emmy for her sensitive portrayal of a woman suffering from dissociative identity disorder (DID) in the TV drama Sybil. *Joanne Woodward portrayed the psychiatrist who guided her back to mental health. Although this drama was based on a real-life patient, experts have recently questioned the validity of the case and the diagnosis of DID. Source:* Miller & Kantrowitz, 1999.

Even the authenticity of "Sybil" is now being questioned (Miller & Kantrowitz, 1999). The real-life patient, Shirley Ardell Mason, died in 1998, and some experts are now disputing the original diagnosis of her condition. They suggest that Shirley was highly hypnotizable and suggestible and that her therapist, Cornelia Wilbur, unintentionally "suggested" the existence of multiple personalities.

On the other side of the debate are psychologists who not only accept the validity of multiple personality, but also believe the condition is underdiagnosed (Spiegel & Maldonado, 1999). Consistent with this view, DID cases have been documented in many cultures around the world and there has been a rise in the number of reported cases (American Psychiatric Association, 2000). (However, this also may reflect a growing public awareness of the disorder.)

The stakes in this controversy over childhood memories and dissociation are very high. On the one hand, research has clearly shown that various well-established psychological processes *can* create false memories (Module 21). If careless or overzealous therapists inadvertently create such memories in their patients, the mistaken accusations can irreversibly damage families and even lead to imprisonment of the accused "perpetrators."

On the other hand, evidence also shows that early traumatic experiences *can* cause selective dissociative amnesia (Brown, 2001; Chu et al., 1999; Spiegel, 1995). Moreover, a childhood history of extreme, repeated trauma, usually sexual abuse, is found in almost all cases of DID (Draijer & Langeland, 1999; Lewis et al., 1997). If these people are not believed and do not receive therapy, they are likely to experience lifelong suffering, and their perpetrators will escape legal responsibility.

Obviously, enormous harm can be done to innocent people, either victims or falsely accused perpetrators. Advocates on both sides agree that research must proceed as quickly as possible to clarify and resolve this debate (Kihlstrom, 1997; Pope, 1997).

■ Personality Disorders: Antisocial and Borderline

In Module 33, *personality* was defined as relatively stable and enduring patterns of thoughts, feelings, and actions. What would happen if these stable patterns called personality were so inflexible and maladaptive that they created significant impairment of someone's ability to function socially and occupationally? This is what happens with **personality disorders.** Unlike anxiety or mood disorders, which also involve maladaptive functioning, people with personality disorders generally do not feel upset or anxious about their behavior and may not be motivated to change. There are several types of personality disorders included in this category in *DSM-IV-TR*, but here we will focus on the best-known type, *antisocial personality disorder*, and the most commonly diagnosed, *borderline personality disorder*.

Personality Disorders *Inflexible, maladaptive personality traits that cause significant impairment of social and occupational functioning*

Antisocial Personality *Egocentrism, lack of conscience, impulsive behavior, and manipulation of others*

Antisocial personality? *Between September 14 and October 22, 2002, at least 14 people were allegedly shot by the so-called "Beltway Snipers," 41-year-old John Allen Muhammad (pictured here) and 17-year-old Lee Malvo. Their impulsive behaviors and seeming lack of conscience are two primary characteristics of an antisocial personality disorder.*

Antisocial Personality Disorder

The term **antisocial personality** is used interchangeably with the terms *sociopath* and *psychopath*. These labels describe behavior so far outside the usual ethical and legal standards of society that many consider it the most serious of all mental disorders. Unlike the previous disorders, people with this diagnosis feel little personal distress, but their maladaptive traits generally bring considerable harm and suffering to others (Anderson et al., 1999; Kirkman, 2002). Although it would seem that such people would wind up in jail, many sociopaths avoid problems with the law and harm people in less dramatic ways as con artists, ruthless businesspeople, and "crooked" politicians and CEO's.

Symptoms

Ken Bianchi, who was introduced at the beginning of this section, had the four hallmarks of an antisocial personality disorder: egocentrism, lack of conscience, impulsive behavior, and superficial charm (American Psychiatric Association, 2000). *Egocentrism* refers to a preoccupation with one's own concerns and insensitivity to the needs of others. Dr. Robert Hare described individuals with an antisocial personality disorder as "social predators who charm, manipulate, and ruthlessly plow their way through life, leaving a broad trail of broken hearts, shattered expectations, and empty wallets. Completely lacking in conscience and empathy, they selfishly take what they want and do as they please, violating social norms and expectations without the slightest sense of guilt or regret" (Hare, 1993, p. xi).

Unlike most adults who have learned to sacrifice immediate gratification for the sake of long-range goals, these individuals act on their impulses, without giving thought to the consequences. They are usually serene and poised when confronted with their destructive behavior and feel contempt for anyone they are able to manipulate. They also change jobs and relationships suddenly and often have a history of truancy from school and being expelled for destructive behavior. Even after repeated punishment, they seem to lack insight into the connection between their behavior and its consequences.

Interestingly enough, people with antisocial personalities can be quite charming and persuasive, and they have remarkably good insight into the needs and weaknesses of other people. Even while exploiting someone, they generally inspire feelings of trust. Ken Bianchi (the mass murderer described in our introductory incident) was so good at charming others that he convinced a woman whom he knew only casually to give him an alibi for some of the killings. Bianchi had been charged with several murders and was behind bars when he persuaded her to help him (Magid & McKelvey, 1987).

Causes

Although the causes of antisocial personality disorder are not completely understood, research supports both nature and nurture explanations, and a combination of the two is most likely. Evidence for biological causes comes from twin and adoptive studies that suggest a possible genetic predisposition (Bock & Goode, 1996; Jang, Vernon, & Livesley, 2000). Other studies have found abnormal autonomic activity during stress and reduced gray matter in the frontal lobes (Raine, Lencz, Bihrle, LaCasse, & Colletti, 2000).

Evidence also exists for environmental or psychological causes. Studies have found a high correlation between parenting styles and inappropriate modeling, and antisocial personalities (Farrington 2000; Wootton, Frick, Shelton, & Silverton, 1997). People with antisocial personality often come from homes characterized by emotional deprivation, harsh and inconsistent disciplinary practices, and antisocial behaviors on the part of parents. Still other studies show a strong interaction between both heredity and environment (Paris, 2000; Rutler, 1997).

Borderline Personality Disorder

Of all the personality disorders, **borderline personality disorder** (BPD) is among the most commonly diagnosed (Rutter, 2000). The core features of this disorder are impulsivity and instability in mood, relationships, and self-image. Although "borderline" sounds like it might be a relatively minor disorder, it's not. Originally, the term implied that the person was on the *borderline* between neurosis and schizophrenia (Davison, Neale, & Kring, 2004). The modern conceptualization no longer has this connotation, but the disorder remains as one of the most complex and debilitating of all the personality disorders.

Mary's story of chronic, lifelong dysfunction, described in the section opener, illustrates the serious problems associated with this disorder. People with BPD experience extreme difficulties in relationships and engage in destructive, impulsive behaviors, like Mary's sexual promiscuity and self-mutilation. Others have problems with drinking, gambling, and eating sprees, which also are self-damaging and potentially lethal (Skodol, Oldham, & Gallaher, 1999; Trull, Sher, Minks-Brown, Durbin, & Burr, 2000). Subject to chronic feelings of depression, emptiness, and intense fear of abandonment, they may attempt suicide and sometimes engage in self-mutilating behavior, such as slicing into their forearms or legs with a razor blade (Powell, 2001; Soloff, Lynch, Kelly, Malone, & Mann, 2000).

Have you known someone who fits Mary's description? If so, you know that being a friend, lover, or parent to someone like Mary can be extremely difficult. They can be exciting, friendly, and totally charming one moment, and angry, argumentative, irritable, and sarcastic the next. They also tend to see themselves and everyone else in absolutes — perfect or worthless (Mason & Kreger, 1998). Partly because of their fragile identity, they constantly seek reassurance from others and may quickly erupt in anger at the slightest sign of disapproval or rejection. A simple gesture, missed appointment, or wrong turn of phrase can trigger an angry outburst, even in public situations that would embarrass most people. People with BPD typically have a string of broken friendships, divorces, and lost jobs.

Causes of BPD

People with BPD frequently have a childhood history of neglect; emotional deprivation; and physical, sexual, or emotional abuse (Goodman & Yehuda, 2002; Johnson, Smailes, Cohen, Brown, & Bernstein, 2000). BPD also tends to run in families, and some data suggest impaired functioning of the frontal lobes, an area which controls impulsive behaviors (Bazanis et al., 2002; Nigg & Goldsmith, 1994; Torgersen, 2000; Van Reekum, Conway, Gansler, & White, 1993).

What can be done to help these people?   Prognosis is not favorable. In one study, seven years after treatment, about 50 percent of the original group still had the disorder (Links, Heslegrave, & van Reekum, 1998). Because these people have such an intense emptiness and chronic fear of abandonment, they go from friend to friend, lover to lover, and therapist to therapist looking for someone to "complete" them. Given their troublesome personality traits, however, friends, lovers, and therapists often do "abandon" them — thus deepening their insecurities.

Borderline Personality Disorder (BPD) *Impulsivity and instability in mood, relationships, and self-image*

Alcohol Problems and Comorbidity

Patty Duke's panic attack and flight from the cab ride occurred when she was 9 years old. As she grew older, she also struggled with bipolar disorder and alcohol abuse (Pearce & Scanlon, 2002). This combination of disorders is known as **comorbidity**, or dual diagnosis. Unfortunately, comorbidity is the rule and not the exception in mental disorders. One of the most common comorbid disorders is *alcohol use disorders* (AUDs), which include alcohol abuse and alcohol dependence (see Table 41.1). AUDs overlap with almost all other mental disorders — including anxiety disorders, mood disorders, schizophrenia, and personality disorders (Cassidy, Ahearn, & Carroll, 2001; Green, 2000; Sher, 2000; Verma, Subramaniam, Chong & Kua, 2002).

What Causes This Type of Overlap Between Disorders?

Perhaps the most influential hypothesis is that of self-medication — individuals drink to reduce their symptoms (Batel, 2000; Green, 2000). Research also shows a high genetic correlation between AUDs and other conditions (Heath, 2000). On the other hand, several environmental variables also predict AUDs and comorbid conditions in adolescence, including reduced parental monitoring, distance from teachers, selec-

tive socialization with deviant peers, and disaffiliation with peers (Costello, 2000). Although it may seem contradictory to have both genetic and environmental explanations, we see once again that nature and nurture interact. Researchers suggest that the interaction might result from an alcohol-abusing youth's tendency to seek out deviant peers or that the same genes that contribute to a mother's lax monitoring might also contribute to her child's early experimentation with alcohol (Sher, 2000).

Regardless of the causes or correlates of AUDs and comorbid conditions, it is critical that patients, family members, and clinicians recognize and deal with comorbidity if treatment is to be effective. For example, AUDs often accompany serious depression, and simply stopping drinking is not the only solution (though certainly an important first step). Similarly, people suffering from schizophrenia are far more likely to relapse into psychosis, require hospitalization, neglect their medications, commit acts of violence, and kill themselves when they also suffer from AUDs (Batel, 2000; Green, 2000). Recognizing this pattern and potential danger, many

The high cost of alcohol abuse. *Children of alcoholic parents are at much greater risk of also abusing alcohol and developing related disorders. Is this because of a genetic predisposition, modeling by the parents, or the emotional devastation of growing up with an alcoholic parent?*

individual and group programs that treat schizophrenia now also include methods used in drug abuse treatment.

To sum up, people who suffer from AUDs are at great risk of also experiencing at least one or more other mental disorders. Understanding this *comorbidity* is of great importance to the suffering individual and his or her family. It is also important from a broad social perspective. The pain and destruction experienced by so many people results in enormous costs to society. But as you will see in the next modules, there are many forms of successful therapy that offer hope for everyone.

TABLE 41.1 DSM-IV-TR SUBSTANCE ABUSE AND SUBSTANCE DEPENDENCE

Criteria for substance abuse (alcohol and other drugs)	Criteria for substance dependence (alcohol and other drugs)
Maladaptive use of a substance shown by 1 of the following: • Failure to meet obligations • Repeated use in situations where it is physically dangerous • Continued use despite problems caused by the substance • Repeated substance-related legal problems	*Three or more of the following:* • Tolerance • Withdrawal • Substance taken for a longer time or greater amount than intended • Desire or efforts to reduce or control use • Social, recreational, or occupational activities given up or reduced • Much time spent in activities to obtain the substance • Use continued despite knowing that psychological or physical problems are worsened by it

Comorbidity *Co-occurrence of two or more disorders in the same person at the same time, as when a person suffers from both depression and alcoholism*

Application

CRITICAL THINKING   ACTIVE LEARNING

Testing Your Knowledge of Abnormal Behavior

Applying abstract terminology is an important component of critical thinking. Test your understanding of the six major diagnostic categories of psychological disorders by matching the disorders on the left with the diagnostic categories on the right.

Answers can be found in Appendix B.

Description of Disorder

1. Julie mistakenly believes she has lots of money and is making plans to take all her friends on a trip around the world. She has not slept for days. Last month, she could not get out of bed and talked of suicide.
2. Steve is exceptionally charming and impulsive and apparently feels no remorse or guilt when he causes great harm to others.
3. Chris believes he is president of the United States and hears voices saying the world is ending.
4. Each day, Kelly repeatedly checks and rechecks all stove burners and locks throughout her house and washes her hands hundreds of times.
5. Lee has repeated bouts of uncontrollable drinking, frequently misses his Monday-morning college classes, and was recently fired for drinking on the job.
6. Susan wandered off and was later found living under a new name, with no memory of her previous life.

Possible Diagnosis

a. Anxiety disorder
b. Schizophrenia
c. Mood disorder
d. Dissociative disorder
e. Personality disorder
f. Substance-related disorder

Assessment

CHECK & REVIEW

Other Disorders

In **dissociative disorders,** critical elements of personality split apart. This split is manifested in failing to recall or identify past experiences (*dissociative amnesia*), by leaving home and wandering off (*dissociative fugue*), or by developing completely separate personalities (**dissociative identity disorder** [DID]). Environmental variables are the primary cause of dissociative disorders (e.g., a history of extreme trauma like sexual abuse).

Personality disorders involve inflexible, maladaptive personality traits. The best-known type is the **antisocial personality,** characterized by egocentrism, lack of guilt, impulsivity, and superficial charm. Research suggests this disorder may be related to defects in brain activity, genetic inheritance, or disturbed family relationships. **Borderline personality disorder** (BPD) is the most commonly diagnosed personality disorder. It is characterized by impulsivity and instability in mood, relationships, and self-image.

Questions

1. The major underlying problem for all dissociative disorders is the psychological need to escape from _____.
2. What is DID?
3. A *sociopath* or a *psychopath* would be diagnosed as a(n) _____ personality in the *Diagnostic and Statistical Manual of Mental Disorders*, fourth edition, text revision.
4. One possible biological cause of BPD is _____. (a) childhood history of neglect; (b) emotional deprivation; (c) impaired functioning of the frontal lobes; (d) all of these options.

Answers to Questions can be found in Appendix B.

MODULE 41   ACTIVE LEARNING WORKSHEET

"Name That Disorder"

Given the limited information below, complete each statement with the correct diagnostic label (dissociative identity disorder, antisocial personality, borderline personality disorder, alcohol use disorder).

1. "I am very charming, yet I feel little or no remorse for my dangerous and destructive behaviors."

2. "I suffer from a long list of broken relationships and often engage in impulsive behaviors like drinking, gambling, and sexual promiscuity."

3. "I tend to overuse alcohol and I am at increased risk of one or more other mental disorders."

4. "I have several distinct and separate personalities within my one body."

5. Even when I've suffered repeated punishments, I seem to lack insight into the connection between my behavior and its consequences."

KEY TERMS

To assess your understanding of the **Key Terms** in this section, write a definition for each (in your own words), and then compare your definitions with those in the text.

Studying Psychological Disorders
abnormal behavior (p. 512)
Diagnostic and Statistical Manual of Mental Disorders (DSM-IV-TR) (p. 517)
insanity (p. 513)
medical model (p. 516)
neurosis (p. 517)
psychiatry (p. 516)
psychosis (p. 517)

Anxiety Disorders
anxiety disorder (p. 522)

generalized anxiety disorder (p. 522)
obsessive-compulsive disorder (OCD) (p. 524)
panic disorder (p. 522)
phobia (p. 523)

Mood Disorders
bipolar disorder (p. 528)
learned helplessness (p. 530)
major depressive disorder (p. 528)

Schizophrenia
delusions (p. 536)

dopamine hypothesis (p. 539)
hallucinations (p. 535)
schizophrenia (p. 534)

Other Disorders
antisocial personality (p. 546)
borderline personality disorder (BPD) (p. 547)
comorbidity (p. 548)
dissociative disorder (p. 544)
dissociative identity disorder (DID) (p. 544)
personality disorders (p. 545)

WEB RESOURCES

Huffman Book Companion Site
http://www.wiley.com/college/huffman
  This site is loaded with free Interactive Self-Tests, Internet Exercises, Glossary and Flashcards for key terms, Web links, Handbook for Non-Native Speakers, and other activities designed to improve your mastery of the material in this section.

Want more detailed information about all the disorders discussed in these modules, plus others?
http://www.apa.org/science/lib.html
  Created by the American Psychological Association (APA), this web site offers articles, books, library searches, and links for all the disorders listed in the DSM-IV-TR. If you'd like additional information, try http://www.mentalhealth.com/p20-grp.html. Sponsored by The Internet Mental Health group, this site provides a wealth of resources and information about all the major disorders, including description, diagnosis, treatment, research, and recommended booklets. Also try, http://www.mhsource.com/. Designed primarily for mental health professionals, this web site offers valuable resources and links to specific disorders, their causes, diagnosis, and treatment.

Would you like to see a complete listing of DSM-IV mental disorders?
http://www.behavenet.com/capsules/disorders/dsm4classification.htm
  Although the listing is somewhat obsolete because it is based on the DSM-IV, and not the newer version, DSM-IV-TR, this web site does provide a sample of the exhaustive list of mental disorders and their classification.

Are you depressed?
http://www.medicinenet.com/Depression/article.htm
  Sponsored by MedicineNet.com, this web site offers over 80 articles related to depression. Written by medical authors and editors, these articles discuss the diagnosis, causes, self-help, and professional therapy for depression. If you would like more information, try http://www.blarg.net/~charlatn/Depression.html. This Beyond Madness web site offers numerous resources related to depression and its treatment.

Are you, or someone you know, feeling suicidal?
http://www.spanusa.org/
  Sponsored by the Suicide Prevention Action Network (SPANUSA), this web site is "dedicated to the creation and implementation of effective National Suicide Prevention Strategies." It offers information and tools for suicide prevention. But, as stated on the opening page, "This site is not intended as a crisis or hotline. Local crisis hotline numbers can be found in the front of your local phone book or call 911."

Need additional information about schizophrenia?
http://www.mhsource.com/schizophrenia/index.html
  This is the homepage for the Psychiatric Times, the number one psychiatric publication. Although targeted for the professional, this web site offers valuable, general information and resources for the diagnosis and treatment of schizophrenia.

VISUAL SUMMARY

Psychological Disorders
(Modules 37, 38, 39, 40, and 41)

Studying Psychological Disorders

Identifying Abnormal Behavior

Abnormal behavior: Pattern of emotion, thought, and action considered pathological for one or more of four reasons (statistical infrequency, disability or dysfunction, personal distress, or violation of norms).

Explaining Abnormality

Stone Ages— demon model; treated with *trephining*. ➡ Middle Ages— demon model; treated with exorcism, torture, imprisonment, death. ➡ 18th century— Pinel creates humane asylums to treat the mentally ill. ➡ Modern times— **medical model** dominates (e.g., **psychiatry**).

Classifying Abnormal Behavior

The Diagnostic and Statistical Manual of Mental Disorders (DSM–IV–TR) categorizes disorders according to major similarities and differences and provides detailed descriptions of symptoms.
- *Benefits*: Standardized diagnosis and treatment, improved communication among professionals and between professionals and patients.
- *Problems*: Insufficient attention to cultural factors, supports medical model, and labels may become self-perpetuating.

Major Categories of Psychological Disorders

Anxiety Disorders
Persistent feelings of threat in facing everyday problems

Generalized Anxiety Disorder
Persistent free-floating anxiety

Phobias
Exaggerated fears of specific objects or situations

Panic Disorder
Anxiety concentrated into brief or lengthy episodes of panic attacks

Obsessive-Compulsive Disorder
Persistent anxiety-arousing thoughts (obsessions) are relieved by ritualistic actions (compulsions) such as hand washing

Major Categories of Psychological Disorders (cont.)

Mood Disorders

Mood disorders are disturbances of affect (emotion) that may include psychotic distortions of reality. Two types:

- **Major depressive disorder:** Long-lasting depressed mood, feelings of worthlessness, and loss of interest in most activities. Feelings are without apparent cause and person may lose contact with reality.

- **Bipolar disorder:** Episodes of mania and depression alternate with normal periods. During manic episode, speech and thinking are rapid, and the person may experience delusions of grandeur and act impulsively.

The Schizophrenias

Schizophrenia: serious psychotic mental disorder afflicting approximately one out of every 100 people.

Five major symptoms: Disturbances in
1) Perception (impaired filtering and selection, **hallucinations**).
2) Language (word salad, neologisms).
3) Thought (impaired logic, **delusions**).
4) Emotion (either exaggerated or blunted emotions).
5) Behavior (social withdrawal, bizarre mannerisms, catalepsy, waxy flexibility).

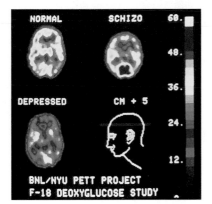

Two-type Classification System:

Positive symptoms—distorted or excessive mental activity (e.g., delusions and hallucinations).

Negative symptoms—behavioral deficits (e.g., toneless voice, flattened emotions).

Other Disorders

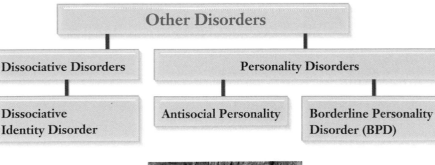

Dissociative Disorders

Personality Disorders

Dissociative Identity Disorder

Antisocial Personality

Borderline Personality Disorder (BPD)

THERAPY

Did you see the latest version of the movie *The House on Haunted Hill?* Do you remember the gruesome "therapy" scenes in the dark asylum? The movie begins with rapid-fire shots of doctors performing surgery without anesthesia, men and women screaming, and mass hysteria as the inmates revolt against the doctors and nurses. A fire starts amid the chaos, and the sadistic director of the asylum pulls a switch, locking down the entire building so that everyone inside, including himself, burns to death. "A sanitarium of horrors, overseen by a surgeon gone mad" is how the fake newsreel coverage of the events describes the scene.

Compare this dimly lit, overcrowded insane asylum with the painfully bright, clinical-looking, mental facility in *One Flew Over the Cuckoo's Nest* or *Terminator 2: Judgment Day.*

Consider, too, how mentally ill people themselves are generally portrayed: They are either cruel, sociopathic criminals (Hannibal Lecter, played by Anthony Hopkins, in *Silence of the Lambs*) or helpless victims who will never be believed again after being labeled insane (Sarah Connor in *Terminator 2*, Bruce Willis in *Twelve Monkeys*, Jack Nicholson in

Achievement
Assessment
Application

One Flew Over the Cuckoo's Nest, *and Winona Ryder in* Girl Interrupted). *And all of them are inescapably trapped in dark, horror-filled asylums or cold, clinical hospitals.*

Since the beginning of the movie age, from The Cabinet of Dr. Caligari *to* Terminator 2, *from* Silence of the Lambs *to* A Beautiful Mind, *mentally ill people and their treatment have been the subject of some of Hollywood's most popular and influential films. The mad or heartless doctors and nurses, "crazy," bizarre patients, and the brutal treatment of mentally ill patients perfectly suit the needs of Hollywood directors hoping to boost ticket sales (adapted from Koenig, 2000).*

In the movie, A Beautiful Mind, *Russell Crowe portrayed Nobel Prize winning mathematician John Nash, who defied therapy and then recovered from his mental disorder. What message does this send to the viewing public?*

What's wrong with these films? Are they only "harmless entertainment," or do they perpetuate harmful stereotypes? According to the Surgeon General's Report on Mental Health, the shame and embarrassment caused by the stigma that surrounds a diagnosis of mental illness is the "most formidable obstacle to future progress in the arena of mental illness and health." Remarking on the film industry's distorted and largely negative portrayal of mental illness and its treatment, the Surgeon General also stated: "We want to help overcome the stereotypes, and help people realize that, just as things go wrong with the heart, the liver and the kidney, things can go wrong with the brain, and there should be no shame in that" (Adams, 2000).

The Surgeon General's report also found that nearly two-thirds of all people who have mental disorders avoid seeking treatment because of financial problems, limited access, lack of awareness, and other situations. At least a part of their resistance to therapy also may be due to Hollywood's negative and one-sided portrayals. This is unfortunate. As you will see in this section, modern therapy can be very effective and prevent much needless suffering (Kopta, Lueger, Saunders, & Howard, 1999). In our coverage of modern forms of therapy, I hope to offset what you might have "learned" from Hollywood films with a balanced, factual presentation of the latest research. To begin, it's important to emphasize that not everyone who seeks professional help is suffering from mental illness. Although psychological disorders are much more prevalent than most people realize, for a large number of people the major goal of therapy is to help with everyday problems in living, such as parent–child conflicts, unhappy marriages, death of a loved one, or adjustment to retirement. In addition, some people enter therapy for greater self-knowledge or personal fulfillment.

Numerous forms of therapy exist to serve varying needs. According to one expert (Kazdin, 1994), there may be over 400 approaches to treatment. To organize our discussion of these treatments, we will focus on two major approaches: (1) **biomedical therapies** that act directly on the patient's brain and nervous system and involve the use of drugs, electroconvulsive therapy (ECT), or psychosurgery, and (2) **psychotherapy,** a collection of various techniques employed to improve psychological functioning and promote adjustment to life. (*Therapy* is a general term including both biomedical therapies and psychotherapies.) Module 45 concludes by exploring several issues in therapy: the ethics of forced institutionalization, effectiveness of therapy, therapy in the electronic age, and women and minorities as clients.

Biomedical Therapy *Using physiological interventions (drugs, electroconvulsive therapy, and psychosurgery) to reduce or alleviate symptoms of psychological disorders*

Psychotherapy *Techniques employed to improve psychological functioning and promote adjustment to life*

MODULE 42
THERAPY ESSENTIALS

What do all therapies have in common?

In the strictest sense, *therapy* refers only to techniques used by professionals (e.g., behavior modification, client-centered therapy, group therapy, and psychoanalysis). The professionals who do therapy include not only psychologists who specialize in mental disorders but also psychiatrists, psychiatric nurses, social workers, counselors, and members of the clergy with special training in pastoral counseling.

This unit focuses on the therapies used primarily by psychologists. The one exception is our discussion of *biomedical therapies* (drug treatments, ECT, and psychosurgery). Although psychiatrists and other medical professionals are generally the only ones who can prescribe biomedical techniques, they often work with psychologists to design the best treatment for their clients. It is also becoming clear that general psychotherapy and biomedical therapies overlap. When successful, they both alter brain functions (Gabbard, 1999). All major forms of therapy are designed to help the client in five specific areas (Figure 42.1). Depending on the individual therapist's training and the client's needs, one or more of these five areas may be emphasized more than the others.

1. *Disturbed thoughts.* Troubled individuals typically suffer some degree of confusion, destructive thought patterns, or blocked understanding of their problems. Therapists work to change these thoughts, provide new ideas or information, and guide individuals toward finding solutions to problems.

2. *Disturbed emotions.* People who seek therapy generally suffer from extreme emotional discomfort. Therapists help clients understand and control their emotions and relieve the discomfort.

3. *Disturbed behaviors.* Therapists help clients eliminate troublesome behaviors and guide them toward more effective lives.

4. *Interpersonal and life situation difficulties.* Therapists help clients improve their relationships with family, friends, and coworkers. They also help them avoid or minimize sources of stress in their lives, such as job demands or family conflicts.

5. *Biomedical disturbances.* Troubled individuals sometimes suffer biological disruptions that directly cause or contribute to psychological difficulties (e.g., chemical imbalances that lead to depression). Therapists help relieve these problems primarily with drugs.

Figure 42.1 *The five most common goals of therapy.* Most therapies focus on one or more of these five goals. As you read about each therapy, see if you can identify which goal(s) would be of most interest to a psychoanalyst, a cognitive therapist, a behaviorist, a psychiatrist, and so on. It will help you differentiate between the approaches to therapy — and it might even help you in an exam on this unit.

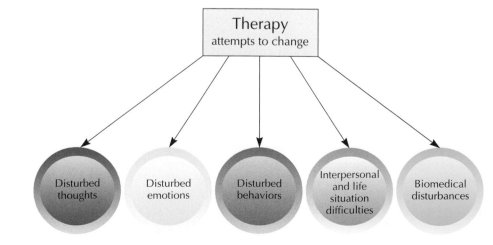

The public often misunderstands therapy. Before we begin our discussion, let's examine some common myths:

- **Myth:** There is one best therapy.
  Fact: Many problems can be treated equally well with all major forms of therapy.
- **Myth:** Therapists can read minds.
  Fact: Good therapists often seem to have an uncanny ability to understand how their clients are feeling and to know when someone is trying to avoid certain topics. This is not due to any special mind-reading ability; rather, it reflects their specialized training and daily experience working with troubled people.

- **Myth:** People who go to therapists are crazy or just weak.
  Fact: Most people seek counseling because of stress in their life or because they realize that therapy can improve their level of functioning. It is difficult to be objective about our own problems, and seeking therapy is a sign not only of wisdom but also of personal strength.
- **Myth:** Only the rich can afford therapy.
  Fact: Although therapy can be expensive, there are many clinics and therapists who charge on a sliding scale based on the client's income. Some insurance plans also cover psychological services.

Although most therapists work with clients in several of these areas, the emphasis varies according to the therapist's training. Psychoanalysts and psychodynamic therapists, for example, generally emphasize unconscious thoughts and emotions. Cognitive therapists focus on their client's faulty thinking and belief patterns, whereas humanistic therapists attempt to alter the client's negative emotional responses. Behaviorists, as the name implies, focus on changing maladaptive behaviors. Therapists who use biomedical techniques attempt to change biological disorders.

Keep in mind that the terms psychoanalyst or cognitive therapist simply refer to the theoretical background and framework that guide a clinician's thinking. Just as Democrats and Republicans approach political matters in different ways, behaviorists and cognitive therapists approach therapy differently. And, just as Democrats and Republicans borrow ideas from one another, clinicians from different perspectives also share ideas and techniques. Clinicians who regularly borrow freely from various theories are said to take an **eclectic approach** (Kopta, Lueger, Saunders, & Howard, 1999).

Eclectic Approach *Combining techniques from various theories to find the most appropriate treatment*

Application
APPLYING PSYCHOLOGY TO WORK

Careers in Mental Health

Do you enjoy helping people and think you would like a career as a therapist? There are dozens of occupational titles related to therapy. Have you wondered how long you will have to go to college or the type of training that is required to be a therapist? Most colleges have counseling or career centers with numerous resources and trained staff who can help you answer these (and other) questions. To get you started, I have included a brief summary in Table 42.1 of the major types of mental health professionals, their degrees, years of required education, and the type of training.

SUMMARY TABLE 42.1 MAJOR TYPES OF MENTAL HEALTH PROFESSIONALS

Occupational Title	Degree	Years of Graduate Education Required and Nature of Training
Clinical Psychologist	Ph.D. (Doctor of Philosophy), Psy.D. (Doctor of Psychology)	(5–7 years) Most often have a doctoral degree and training in research and clinical practice and a supervised one-year internship in a psychiatric hospital or mental health facility. As clinicians, they work with patients suffering from mental disorders, but many also work in colleges and universities as teachers and researchers in addition to having their own private practice.
Counseling Psychologist	M.A. (Master of Arts), Ph.D. (Doctor of Philosophy), Psy.D. (Doctor of Psychology), or Ed.D. (Doctor of Education)	(3–7 years) Similar training to clinical psychologists, but counseling psychologists usually have a master's degree with more emphasis on patient care and less on research. They generally work in schools or other institutions and focus on problems in living rather than mental disorders.
Psychiatrist	M.D. (Doctor of Medicine)	(7–10 years) After four years of medical school, an internship and residency in psychiatry are required, which involves supervised practice in psychotherapy techniques and biomedical therapies. M.D.s are the only mental health specialists who can regularly prescribe drugs.
Psychiatric Social Worker	M.S.W. (Master in Social Work), D.S.W. (Doctorate in Social Work), Ph.D. (Doctor of Philosophy)	(2–5 years) Usually have a master's degree in social work, followed by advanced training and experience in hospitals or outpatient settings working with people who have psychological problems.
Psychiatric Nurse	R.N. (Registered Nurse), M.A. (Master of Arts), Ph.D. (Doctor of Philosophy)	(0–5 years) Usually have a bachelor's or master's degree in nursing, followed by advanced training in the care of mental patients in hospital settings and mental health facilities.
School Psychologist	M.A. (Master of Arts), Ph.D. (Doctor of Philosophy), Psy.D. (Doctor of Psychology), or Ed.D. (Doctor of Education)	(3–7 years) Usually begin with a bachelor's degree in psychology, followed by graduate training in psychological assessment and counseling involving school-related issues and problems.

Assessment

CHECK & REVIEW

Therapy Essentials

Therapy is a general term for both biological and psychological treatments for mental disorders. There are numerous forms of therapy, but they all focus treatment on five basic areas of disturbance — thoughts, emotions, behaviors, interpersonal and life situations, and biomedical problems.

Questions

1. Using therapeutic techniques to improve psychological functioning and promote adjustment to life is known as _____. (a) eclectic therapy; (b) psychoanalysis/psychodynamic therapy; (c) psychotherapy; (d) counseling

2. Match the following therapists with their primary emphasis:

_____ psychoanalysts   (a) faulty thinking and belief patterns
_____ behaviorists   (b) unconscious thoughts and patterns
_____ humanistic therapists   (c) biological disorders
_____ biomedical therapists   (d) negative emotions
_____ cognitive therapists   (e) maladaptive behaviors

Answers to Questions can be found in Appendix B.

ACTIVE LEARNING WORKSHEET   MODULE 42

Completing the following exercise may help provide insight to your own life, as well as, greater understanding of the material in this section.

1. Therapy has five common goals (or areas of attempted change). List them here:

_____

_____

_____

2. Think of the most troublesome area of your life, and identify which of the five goals would be most beneficial for you to change, and why.

_____

_____

_____

3. Considering the 6 major types of therapists discussed in Table 42.1, which therapist would be most appropriate for the problem you described above? Why?

_____

_____

_____

MODULE 43
BIOMEDICAL THERAPIES

What are the major biomedical therapies?

"Before Prozac, she loathed company."

Source: New Yorker Collection 1993. Lee Lorenz from cartoonbank.com

Drug Therapy *Use of chemicals (drugs) to treat physical and psychological disorders*

Biomedical therapies are based on the premise that problem behaviors are caused, at least in part, by chemical imbalances or disturbed nervous system functioning. A physician rather than a psychologist must prescribe biomedical therapies, but psychologists work with patients receiving biomedical therapies and are frequently involved in research programs to evaluate their effectiveness. Despite Hollywood's persistent linking of mental illness with asylums and hospitals, today only people with the most severe and intractable disturbances are institutionalized and abuses like those portrayed in most films are virtually nonexistent. Most people with psychological disorders can be helped with drugs, psychotherapy, or a combination of the two. In this section, we will discuss three types of biomedical therapies: drugs, ECT, and psychosurgery.

Drug Therapy: The Pharmacological Revolution

Since the 1950s, drug companies have developed an amazing variety of chemicals to treat abnormal behaviors. In some cases, **drug therapy** corrects a chemical imbalance. In these instances, using a drug is similar to administering insulin to people with diabetes, whose own bodies fail to manufacture enough. In other cases, drugs are used to relieve or suppress the symptoms of psychological disturbances even if the underlying cause is not thought to be biological. Psychiatric drugs are classified into four major categories: antianxiety, antipsychotic, mood stabilizer, and antidepressant. Table 43.1 gives examples of drugs in each category.

TABLE 43.1 DRUG THERAPY

Type of Drug	Psychological Disorder	Chemical Group	Generic Name	Brand Name
Antidepressant drug	Severe depression (with suicidal tendencies)	Tricyclic antidepressants	Imipramine Amitriptyline	Tofranil Elavil
		Monoamine oxidase inhibitors (MAOIs)	Phenelzine	Nardil
		Second-generation antidepressants	Tranylcypromine Fluoxetine	Parnate Prozac
Antianxiety drugs	Anxiety disorders	Benzodiazepines	Chlordiazepoxide Diazepam	Librium Valium
		Glycerol derivatives	Meprobamate	Miltown Equanil
Antipsychotic drugs	Schizophrenia	Phenothiazines	Chlorpromazine Fluphenazine Thioridazine	Thorazine Prolixin Mellaril
		Butyrophenones	Haloperidol	Haldol
		Dibenzodiazepine	Clozapine	Clozaril
Mood-stabilizer drugs	Bipolar disorder	Antimanic	Lithium carbonate	Lithonate Lithane Eskalith

Antianxiety Drugs

Antianxiety drugs (also known as "minor tranquilizers") create feelings of tranquility and calmness in addition to relieving muscle tension. These drugs have replaced sedatives (which had side effects of drowsiness and sleepiness) in the treatment of anxiety disorders. Antianxiety drugs, such as Valium and Xanax, lower the sympathetic activity of the brain — the crisis mode of operation — so that anxiety responses are diminished or prevented (Margolis & Swartz, 2003; Pollack, 2000).

Antipsychotic Drugs

The medications used to treat schizophrenia and other acute psychotic states are called **antipsychotic drugs,** or *neuroleptics.* They are often referred to as "major tranquilizers," creating the impression they invariably have a strong calming or sedating effect. Some antipsychotic drugs, such as Haldol or Navane, do reduce hallucinations and delusions. But other antipsychotic drugs, such as Clozaril, energize and animate patients. The main effect of antipsychotic drugs is to diminish or eliminate psychotic symptoms, including hallucinations, delusions, withdrawal, and apathy. They are not designed to sedate the patient.

How do these drugs work? The traditional antipsychotics, like Thorazine, appear to decrease activity at the dopamine synapses, which further supports the theory that excessive dopamine contributes to schizophrenia (Module 40). Given the multiple types of dopamine receptors in different parts of the brain, the newer *atypical antipsychotics*, like Clozaril, may be more effective because they target specific dopamine receptors (as well as serotonin receptors) and avoid interfering with others (Roth, Willins, Kristiansen, & Kroeze, 1999).

Mood Stabilizer and Antidepressant Drugs

For people suffering from bipolar disorders, *mood-stabilizer* drugs such as lithium can help manic episodes and depression. Because lithium acts relatively slowly — it can be 3 or 4 weeks before it takes effect — its primary use is in preventing *future* episodes and helping to break the manic–depressive cycle. Lithium also has potentially serious side effects, but recent research also shows that it may increase the volume of gray matter (the so-called thinking part of the brain) (Manji, Husseini, Moore, & Chen, 2000; Webb, Solomon, & Ryan, 2001).

People with depression are usually treated with one of four types of **antidepressant drugs:**

1. *Tricyclics* (named for their chemical structure that contains three rings), such as imipramine, act on multiple neurochemical pathways in the brain, including those of serotonin and catecholamines.

2. *Monoamine oxidase inhibitors* (MAOIs), such as phenelzine, block the enzyme *monoamine oxidase*. Because this enzyme inactivates serotonin and catecholamines, blocking it increases the availability of these helpful neurochemicals.

3. *Selective serotonin reuptake inhibitors* (SSRIs), such as Prozac or Zoloft, work like the tricyclics, but they *selectively* affect only serotonin. They are by far the most commonly prescribed antidepressants.

4. *Atypical antidepressants*, such as Wellbutrin, are a miscellaneous group of drugs used for patients who fail to respond to the other drugs or for people who experience certain side effects (like decreased sexual function) that are common to other antidepressants.

Antianxiety Drugs *Medications used to treat anxiety disorders*

Antipsychotic Drugs *Chemicals administered to diminish or eliminate hallucinations, delusions, withdrawal, and other symptoms of psychosis; also known as neuroleptics or major tranquilizers*

Antidepressant Drugs *Chemicals prescribed to treat depression, some anxiety disorders, and certain eating disorders (such as bulimia)*

■ Electroconvulsive Therapy and Psychosurgery: Promising or Perilous?

Electroconvulsive Therapy (ECT)
Biomedical therapy based on passing electrical current through the brain; used almost exclusively to treat serious depression when drug therapy does not work

In **electroconvulsive therapy** (ECT), also known as *electroshock therapy* (EST), a current of moderate intensity is passed through the brain between two electrodes placed on the outside of the head (Figure 42.2). The electrical current is applied for less than a second, but it triggers widespread firing of neurons, also known as convulsions. The convulsions produce many changes in the central and peripheral nervous systems, including activation of the autonomic nervous system, increased secretion of various hormones and neurotransmitters, and changes in the blood–brain barrier.

During the early years of ECT, some patients received hundreds of treatments (Fink, 1999), but today most receive 12 or fewer treatments. Sometimes the electrical current is applied only to the right hemisphere, which causes less interference with verbal memories and left hemisphere functioning. Modern ECT is used primarily in cases of severe depression that do not respond to antidepressant drugs or psychotherapy. Keep in mind that ECT is almost always used only as a last resort because it produces major brain seizures and may cause varying degrees of memory loss. It is occasionally recommended for suicidal patients because it works faster than antidepressant drugs (Cloud, 2001; Prudic & Sackheim, 1999; Sylvester et al., 2000).

Psychosurgery *Operative procedures on the brain designed to relieve severe mental symptoms that have not responded to other forms of treatment*

The most extreme, and least used, biomedical therapy is **psychosurgery**, brain surgery to reduce psychological symptoms. (It is important to note that psychosurgery is *not* the same as brain surgery used to remove physical problems, such as a tumor or blood clot.) Attempts to change disturbed thinking and behavior by altering the brain have a long history. In Roman times, for example, it was believed that a sword wound to the head could relieve insanity. In 1936, a Portuguese neurologist, Egaz Moniz, treated uncontrollable psychoses by cutting the nerve fibers between the frontal lobes (where association areas for monitoring and planning behavior are found) and the thalamus and hypothalamus. Moniz was awarded the Nobel Prize in medicine in 1949 for developing this technique, called a **lobotomy** (Pressman, 1998; Valenstein, 1998).

Lobotomy *Outmoded medical procedure for mental disorders, which involved cutting nerve pathways between the frontal lobes and the thalamus and hypothalamus*

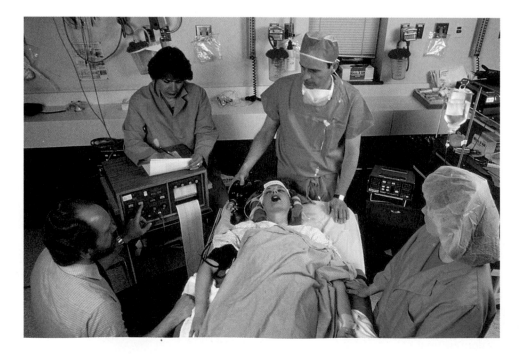

Figure 43.1 *Electroconvulsive therapy (ECT)*. During ECT, electrodes on the forehead apply electric current to the brain, creating a brief cortical seizure. Although ECT is controversial and may seem barbaric to you, for some severely depressed people it is the only hope, and it can be effective in lifting depression.

Although these surgeries did reduce emotional outbursts and aggressiveness, many patients were left with "flat affect" and permanent damage. In the mid-1950s, when antipsychotic drugs came into use, psychosurgery virtually stopped. Recently, however, psychiatrists have been experimenting with a much more limited and precise surgical procedure, called *cingulotomy*, where the cingulum (a small structure in the brain's limbic system known to be involved in emotionality) is partially destroyed. On rare occasions, it is used in the treatment of severely debilitating cases of obsessive-compulsive disorder (OCD), severe depression, and chronic, intractable pain (Cohen et al., 2001; Dougherty et al., 2002; Sotres-Bayon & Pellicer, 2000).

■ Evaluating Biomedical Therapies

Like all forms of therapy, the biomedical therapies have both proponents and critics. We will summarize the research in this area:

1. *Drug therapies.* There are several potential problems with drug therapy. First, although drugs may provide relief of symptoms, they seldom provide "cures" or long-term solutions. Researchers also are still learning about the long-term effects and potential interactions. Furthermore, not all patients are helped by these drugs, and some show only modest improvement. Some patients also develop tolerance to the drugs and become physically dependent. Withdrawal symptoms (such as convulsions and hallucinations) can occur if they suddenly stop taking the drugs. Overdosing with psychotherapeutic drugs intentionally (to get a stronger effect) or unintentionally (by combining them with other drugs, such as alcohol) can be fatal.

Controlling negative side effects is also an important issue with drug therapy. For example, reactions to antipsychotic drugs range from reduced alertness and drowsiness to symptoms similar to Parkinson's disease, including muscle rigidity, tremors, and an unusual shuffling way of walking (Drummond, 2000; Tarsy, Baldessarini, & Tarazi, 2002). Recall from Module 15 that Parkinson's disease is related to a deficit in dopamine, and that the drug L-dopa (levodopa) increases dopamine and reduces the symptoms of Parkinson's. Because antipsychotic drugs work by reducing excess dopamine, you can see how prolonged use could eventually produce Parkinson-like symptoms. Anti-parkinsonian medications can reduce the side effects of antipsychotic drugs, but they have their own side effects, and their use is controversial.

One of the most serious side effects of antipsychotic drugs is a movement disorder called *tardive dyskinesia*, which develop in 15 to 20 percent of the patients. The symptoms generally appear after the drugs have been taken for long periods of time (hence the term *tardive*, from the Latin root for "slow"). They include involuntary movements of the tongue, face, and sometimes other muscles (*dyskinesia*, meaning "disorder of movement") that can be severely disabling. When my students see films about schizophrenia, they often confuse the patient's sucking and smacking of their lips or lateral jaw movements as signs of the disorder rather than signs of the motor disturbances of tardive dyskinesia.

Like antipsychotic medications, mood-stabilizer and antidepressant drugs also have major and minor side effects. Antidepressants may cause dry mouth, fatigue, sexual dysfunction, weight gain, and memory difficulties, whereas mood-stabilizer drugs, such as lithium, can impair memory and cause weight gain. In excessive dosages, lithium can be fatal. Thus, as with other drug therapies, it is important to carefully monitor dosage level and patient reactions (Butler, Joel, & Jeffries, 2000).

What about herbal remedies like St.-John's-Wort to treat depression? Recent controlled studies suggest it may be effective for mild to moderate depression, and that it may have fewer side effects than traditional medications (Jonas, 2002; Lecrubier et al., 2002; Woelk, 2000). However, other studies have found St. John's Wort to be ineffec-

One Flew Over the Cuckoo's Nest. *In this film, the lead character, McMurphy (played by Jack Nicholson), is a persistent problem for the hospital staff. To punish and control him, the staff first used drug therapy, then ECT, and finally psychosurgery — a prefrontal lobotomy. Although this was a popular movie, it also deepened public fear and misconceptions about biomedical therapy.*

tive in the treatment of major depression (Hypericum Depression Trial Study, 2002). Herbal treatments, like kava, valerian, and gingko biloba, also have been used in the treatment of anxiety, insomnia, and memory problems (e.g., Brown & Gerbarg, 2001; Connor & Davidson, 2002). Although these drugs are considered "natural" and therefore "safe," they can produce a number of potentially serious side effects. The quality and amounts of active ingredients vary according to the manufacturer, and the U.S. Food and Drug Administration (US FDA) does not regulate them. For all these reasons, researchers advise a wait-and-see approach (Beaubrun & Gray, 2000; Crone & Gabriel, 2002; Margolis & Swartz, 2003).

Despite the problems associated with psychotherapeutic drugs, they have led to revolutionary changes in mental health. Before the use of drugs, some patients were destined for a lifetime in psychiatric institutions. Today, most improve enough to return to their homes and live successful lives if they continue to take their medication to prevent relapse (Conley, Love, Kelly, & Bartko, 1999).

In sum, medication is an effective and often the most appropriate treatment for many psychological disorders. However, the fact that it is also cost-effective and *generally* fast acting has led to its overuse in some cases. For example, one report found that antidepressants are now prescribed roughly 50 percent of the time a patient walks into a psychiatrist's office (Olfson et al., 1998). Although this reflects in part the increased efficacy of the new medications, it also reflects the economics of health care. Because a psychiatrist can see five or six medication patients in an hour, versus the one person per hour generally seen by a psychotherapist, there is considerable financial incentive to favor drugs over therapy. Yet, most studies that have compared medication alone versus medication plus therapy have found the combination more effective (e.g., Pollack, 2000).

2. *ECT and Psychosurgery.* After nearly half a century of use of ECT, we do not fully understand why an ECT-induced convulsion alleviates depression. Partly because we cannot explain how it works, but also because it seems barbaric, ECT is a controversial treatment (Baldwin & Oxlad, 2000; Cloud, 2001; Pearlman, 2002). Unlike ECT portrayals in movies like *One Flew Over the Cuckoo's Nest* and *The Snake Pit*, patients show few, if any, visible reactions to the treatment, owing to modern muscle-relaxant drugs, which dramatically reduce muscle contractions during the seizure. Although most ECT patients are given an anesthetic such as sodium pentothal to block their memory of the treatment, some patients report that they find the treatment extremely aversive (Johnstone, 1999). However, many others find it life-saving.

Problems with ECT may become obsolete thanks to a recently developed similar treatment known as *repetitive transcranial magnetic stimulation* (rTMS). Unlike ECT, which passes a strong electric current directly through the brain, rTMS delivers a brief but powerful electric current through a coil of wire placed on the head. The coil creates a strong magnetic field that is applied to certain areas in the brain. When used to treat depression, the coil is usually placed over the prefrontal cortex, a region linked to deeper parts of the brain that regulate mood. Treatment with rTMS appears to have a significant effect on major depression, and it has fewer side effects than ECT (Burt, Lisanby, & Sackheim, 2002; Czeh, 2002; DeBattista & Belanoff, 2002).

Because all forms of psychosurgery have potentially serious or fatal side effects and complications, some critics suggest it should be banned altogether. Furthermore, the consequences are irreversible. For these reasons, psychosurgery is considered experimental and remains a highly controversial treatment.

We now turn our attention to those forms of therapy most commonly conducted by psychologists — *psychotherapy.*

Assessment

CHECK & REVIEW

Biomedical Therapies

Biomedical therapies use biological techniques to relieve psychological disorders. **Drug therapy** is the most common form by far. **Antianxiety drugs** (Valium, Xanax) are used to treat anxiety disorders, **antipsychotic drugs** (Haldol, Navane) treat the symptoms of schizophrenia, **antidepressants** (Prozac, Zoloft) treat depression, and mood stabilizers (lithium) can stabilize patients with bipolar disorders. Although drug therapy has been responsible for major improvements in many disorders, there are also problems with dosage levels, side effects, and patient cooperation.

Electroconvulsive therapy (ECT) is used primarily to relieve serious depression when medication has not worked, but it is risky and considered a treatment of last resort. **Psychosurgeries,** such as a **lobotomy,** have been used in the past but are rarely used today.

Questions

1. The dramatic reduction in numbers of hospitalized patients today, as compared with past decades, is primarily attributable to _____. (a) biomedical therapy; (b) psychoanalysis; (c) psychosurgery; (d) drug therapy
2. What are the four major categories of psychiatric drugs?
3. The effectiveness of antipsychotic drugs is thought to result primarily from blockage of _____ receptors. (a) serotonin; (b) dopamine; (c) acetycholine; (d) epinephrine
4. ECT is used primarily to treat _____. (a) phobias; (b) conduct disorders; (c) depression; (d) schizophrenia

Answers to Questions can be found in Appendix B.

ACTIVE LEARNING WORKSHEET   MODULE 43

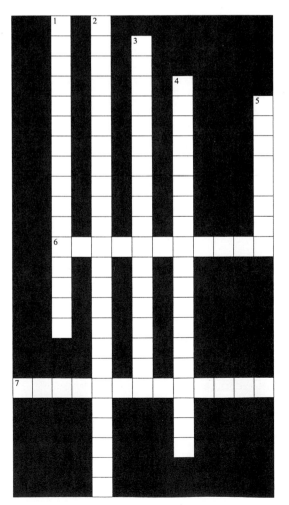

ACROSS

6 Use of chemicals (drugs) to treat physical and psychological disorders.
7 Operative procedures on the brain designed to relieve severe mental symptoms that have not responded to other forms of treatment.

DOWN

1 Medications used to treat anxiety disorders.
2 A biomedical therapy based on passing electrical current through the brain. It is used almost exclusively to treat serious depression when drug therapy does not work.
3 Chemicals administered to diminish or terminate hallucinations, delusions, withdrawal, and other symptoms of psychosis; also known as, neuroleptics or major tranquilizers.
4 Drugs prescribed to treat depression, some anxiety disorders, and certain eating disorders (such as bulimia).
5 Outmoded medical procedure for mental disorders, which involved cutting nerve pathways between the frontal lobes and the thalamus and hypothalamus in hopes of treating psychological disorders.

MODULE 44
PSYCHOTHERAPY

What do you think of when you hear the word *therapy*? When I ask my students this question, they usually describe a small, cluttered office with a sofa where patients recline and tell their secrets to a male therapist with a beard. Does this description match the one in your own mind? If so, it's probably due once again to Hollywood films. In most films, "therapy" is biomedical (drugs, ECT, and psychosurgery). When they do portray "talk therapy," they focus almost exclusively on a Freudian model, with a bearded therapist listening to a patient reclining on a couch. This stereotype has little to do with the realities of modern therapy, however. We begin our discussion of "real" therapy with traditional psychoanalysis (which does use a couch) and its modern counterpart, psychodynamic therapy. Then we explore cognitive, humanistic, and behavior therapies. We conclude with a look at group and family therapies.

Therapist with client.

■ Psychoanalysis/Psychodynamic Therapies: A Focus on the Unconscious

Assessment

What is Freudian psychoanalysis? Are there more modern forms of this therapy?

Why do psychoanalysts use couches in their form of therapy? Freud believed that the unconscious was more accessible when the patient reclined on a couch with only the ceiling to look at. He also felt the therapist should sit out of sight behind the patient. Freud wanted his patients to feel relaxed and nondefensive, almost as if they were talking to themselves rather than revealing information to another person. Traditional psychoanalysts still use a couch, but most modern forms of psychoanalysis do not.

The use of a couch is only one aspect of Freud's original therapy. Why not relax and recline on your own couch for the moment, as you read about the major goals and methods of psychoanalysis.

Goals and Methods

Psychoanalysis *Freudian therapy designed to bring unconscious conflicts, which usually date back to early childhood experiences, into consciousness; also Freud's theoretical school of thought emphasizing the study of unconscious processes*

Psychoanalysis means just what the name implies: A person's psyche (or mind) is analyzed. During psychoanalysis, the therapist (or psychoanalyst) works to bring unconscious conflicts, which are believed to date back to early childhood experiences, into consciousness. This traditional psychoanalysis is based on Sigmund Freud's central belief that abnormal behavior is caused by unconscious conflicts among the three parts of the psyche — the *id, ego,* and *superego.*

Recall from Module 35 that Freud believed primitive urges from the id, or overwhelming feelings of guilt from the superego, caused the ego to develop elaborate defense mechanisms and compulsive or self-defeating behaviors. During psychoanalysis, these unconscious conflicts are brought to consciousness. The patient comes to understand the reasons for his or her behavior and realizes that the childhood conditions under which the conflicts developed no longer exist. Once this realization (or *insight*) occurs, the conflicts can be resolved and the patient is free to develop more adaptive behavior patterns.

How can insight change behavior? Freud explained that becoming aware of a painful conflict permits a release of tension and anxiety. He observed that when his patients relived a traumatic incident, complete with disturbing emotions, the conflict seemed to lose its power to control the person's behavior. This emotional release, known as **catharsis,** frees up psychic energy previously devoted to id, ego, and superego conflicts. Healthier, less anxious living now becomes possible.

Catharsis *In psychoanalytic theory, the release of tension and anxiety through the reliving of a traumatic incident*

Gaining access to unconscious conflicts is not as simple as it sounds. The ego has strong defense mechanisms that block unconscious thoughts from coming to light. To gain insight into the unconscious, the ego must be tricked into relaxing its guard. The five major techniques for making the unconscious "conscious" are free association, dream analysis, analyzing resistance, analyzing transference, and interpretation.

1. *Free association.* Have you ever let your mind wander without attempting to monitor or control the direction of your thinking? If so, you might have noticed that some rather unexpected thoughts pop up. In the process of temporarily removing conscious censorship over thoughts — called **free association** — interesting and even bizarre connections seem to spring into awareness. Freud believed that the first (uncensored) thing to come to a patient's mind was often an important clue to what the person's unconscious wanted to conceal. The analyst's couch and position out of the patient's view are meant to encourage free association.

2. *Dream analysis.* Dream analysis is a classic technique for observing unconscious processes. Freud called dreams "the royal road to the unconscious." Because the ego does not defend itself very well against unconscious conflicts during sleep, these conflicts are supposedly expressed in the form of dreams. Freud felt that dreams could be interpreted on two levels. On a superficial level, there is the *manifest content* of the dream, the immediate and conscious content of dreams. On a deeper level, dreams may be interpreted in terms of their *latent content*, the presumed true meaning hidden behind the manifest content. Thus, according to Freudian dream theory, a therapist might interpret a dream of riding a horse or driving a car (the manifest content) as a desire or concern about sexual intercourse (the latent content).

3. *Analyzing resistance.* When analyzing a patient's behavior and verbalizations, the analyst looks for examples of **resistance,** the defensive tendency of the unconscious to block (or *resist*) from consciousness particularly threatening *repressed* materials. For example, if the patient refuses to talk about certain topics, "forgets," is late, or cancels an appointment, the analyst might think the patient's ego defenses are attempting to keep unconscious conflicts from being revealed. Similarly, if the patient pauses during significant points in conversation or changes topics suddenly, the analyst will try to find out what is causing the resistance by pursuing the topic that preceded the block.

   Although patients generally enter therapy to gain personal insight, they also exhibit resistance because it helps reduce anxiety. The closer the patient and analyst come to the source of the anxiety, the more the patient is motivated to run from it. To help you remember the concept of resistance, think of this classic joke about psychoanalysis: "If patients arrive on time for their appointment, they're compulsive; if they're early, they're dependent; and if late, they're resistant."

4. *Analyzing transference.* During psychoanalysis, the patient may displace (or "transfer") onto his or her relationship with the therapist feelings from an earlier stage in life, generally with the mother, father, or other important figures. This process is known as **transference.** Transference is assumed to have occurred if the patient becomes overly dependent on the analyst or falls in love and seeks to establish an intimate relationship. Rather than taking these reactions and emotions at face value, the analyst interprets them as evidence of unresolved attachments or conflicts in childhood or previous relationships. Transference is considered a valuable part of psychoanalysis because exposing repressed feelings offers the patient a chance to "work through" unconscious conflicts and gain insight into past and current relationships.

5. *Interpretation.* The core of psychoanalytic therapy is **interpretation.** During psychoanalysis, the analyst listens closely and observes patterns and hidden meanings. At the right time, the therapist points out where resistance occurs and what free

Free Association *In psychoanalysis, reporting whatever comes to mind without monitoring its contents*

Resistance *A stage in psychoanalysis when the patient avoids (resists) the analyst's attempts to bring threatening unconscious material to conscious awareness*

Transference *In psychoanalysis, the patient may displace (or transfer) unconscious feelings about a significant person in his or her life onto the therapist*

Interpretation *A psychoanalyst's explanation of a patient's free associations, dreams, resistance, and transference; more generally, any statement by a therapist that presents a patient's problem in a new way*

Application

CRITICAL THINKING

What's Wrong with Movie Portrayals of Therapy?

In the film, *The Prince of Tides*, Barbra Striesand portrays a psychiatrist who falls in love and has sex with her client, Nick Nolte. Before reading on, stop and use your critical thinking skills to explain why this portrayal of sex between a therapist and client might create serious and lasting problems for the therapist, client, and the viewing public.

Therapist: _____

Client: _____

Viewing Public: _____

Now, compare your responses to those listed below.

As we discussed in the section opener, movie portrayals of harmful therapy and unethical therapists create dangerous stereotypes and lasting misconceptions. In this case, the movie treats the sexual relationships

Barbra Streisand in her role as therapist to patient, Nick Nolte, in the movie The Prince of Tides.

between therapist and client as just another romantic encounter, without acknowledging

ACTIVE LEARNING

that the therapist is in serious violation of professional ethics, which may lead to a loss of license and possible criminal charges. Although romance may enliven a movie, therapists must uphold the highest standards of ethical behavior. Sex between patient and therapist is not only unethical, in several states it's also a criminal offense (Dalenberg, 2000; Sloan, Edmond, Rubin, & Doughty, 1998).

In addition to the professional problems for the therapist, the movie overlooks the fact that the client is seeking help and is in a less powerful position during therapy, which increases his or her vulnerability. Intimacy destroys the professional relationship required to help the client. Finally, the public is harmed because these movie portrayals trivialize (and romanticize) a serious breach of professional ethics, and they create a false (and maybe lasting) bad impression that may discourage troubled people from seeking therapy.

---

association, dream analysis, and transference reveal about impulses repressed in the unconscious. For instance, during therapy a man who has trouble with intimacy might look out the window and change the subject whenever anything touches on closeness or feelings. The analyst will attempt to interpret these defensive behaviors and help the patient recognize how he avoids the topic (Davison, Neale, & Kring, 2004, p. 34).

Evaluation

Freud's theories of personality have been enormously influential, yet also the subject of heated debate. The same can be said of his method of therapy. Criticisms of psychoanalysis focus on two major points:

1. ***Limited applicability.*** Freud's methods were developed in the early 1900s for a particular clientele — upper-class Viennese people (primarily women). Although psychoanalysis has been refined over the years, critics say it still seems to suit only a select group of individuals. Success appears to be best with less severe disorders, such as anxiety disorders, and with highly motivated, articulate patients. Critics jokingly proposed the acronym *YAVIS* to describe the perfect psychoanalysis patient: young, attractive, verbal, intelligent, and successful (Schofield, 1964).

Psychoanalysis also is time consuming (often lasting several years with four to five sessions a week) and expensive, and it seldom works well with severe mental disorders, such as schizophrenia. This is logical because psychoanalysis is based on verbalization and rationality — the very abilities most significantly disrupted by

"I dreamt I had a Harem, but they all wanted to talk about the relationship."

Cartoons and couches. *Have you noticed that most cartoons about therapy show a Freudian model with a patient reclining on a couch?*

serious disorders. Critics suggest that spending years on a couch chasing unconscious conflicts from the past allows patients to escape from the responsibilities and problems of adult life — in effect, the patient becomes "couchridden."

2. *Lack of scientific credibility.* The goals of psychoanalysis are explicitly stated — to bring unconscious conflicts to conscious awareness. But how do you know when this goal has been achieved? If patients accept the analyst's interpretations of their conflicts, their "insights" may be nothing more than cooperation with the therapist's belief system. On the other hand, if patients refuse to accept the analyst's interpretations, the analyst may say they're exhibiting resistance. Moreover, the therapist can always explain away a failure. If patients get better, it's because of their insights. If they don't, then the insight was not real — it was only intellectually accepted. Such reasoning does not meet scientific standards. The ability to prove or disprove a theory is the foundation of the scientific approach.

Although psychoanalysts acknowledge that it is impossible to scientifically document certain aspects of their therapy, they insist that most patients benefit (Gabbard, 1999; Ward, 2000). Many analysands (patients) agree. Partially in response to criticism, however, more streamlined forms of psychoanalysis have been developed.

Modern Psychodynamic Therapy

In modern psychoanalytic therapies, known as **psychodynamic,** treatment is briefer (usually only one to two times a week), the patient is seen face to face (rather than

Psychodynamic Therapy *A modern form of psychoanalysis that emphasizes internal conflicts, motives, and unconscious forces*

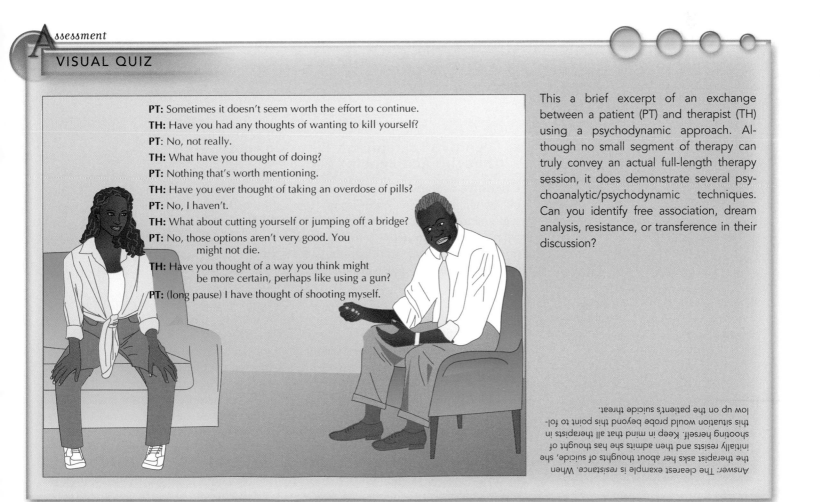

*A*ssessment

VISUAL QUIZ

PT: Sometimes it doesn't seem worth the effort to continue.

TH: Have you had any thoughts of wanting to kill yourself?

PT: No, not really.

TH: What have you thought of doing?

PT: Nothing that's worth mentioning.

TH: Have you ever thought of taking an overdose of pills?

PT: No, I haven't.

TH: What about cutting yourself or jumping off a bridge?

PT: No, those options aren't very good. You might not die.

TH: Have you thought of a way you think might be more certain, perhaps like using a gun?

PT: (long pause) I have thought of shooting myself.

This a brief excerpt of an exchange between a patient (PT) and therapist (TH) using a psychodynamic approach. Although no small segment of therapy can truly convey an actual full-length therapy session, it does demonstrate several psychoanalytic/psychodynamic techniques. Can you identify free association, dream analysis, resistance, or transference in their discussion?

Answer: The clearest example is resistance. When the therapist asks her about thoughts of suicide, she initially resists and then admits she has thought of shooting herself. Keep in mind that all therapists in this situation would probe beyond this point to follow up on the patient's suicide threat.

reclining on a couch), and the therapist takes a more directive approach (rather than waiting for a gradual unveiling of the unconscious). Also, although contemporary psychodynamic therapists try to help clients gain insight into their early childhood experiences and unconscious roots of problems, they focus more attention on conscious processes and current problems. Such refinements have helped make psychoanalysis shorter and more available to an increasing number of people (Leichsenring, 2002; Rutan & Stone, 2000; Sigueland et al., 2002).

Assessment

CHECK & REVIEW

Psychoanalysis/Psychodynamic Therapies

Sigmund Freud developed the psychoanalytic method of therapy to uncover unconscious conflicts and bring them into conscious awareness. The five major techniques of **psychoanalysis** are **free association, dream analysis,** analyzing **resistance,** analyzing **transference,** and **interpretation.** Like psychoanalytic theories of personality, psychoanalysis is the subject of great debate. It is primarily criticized for its limited availability (it is time-consuming, expensive, and suits only a small group of people) and its lack of scientific credibility. Modern **psychodynamic therapies** overcome some of these limitations.

Questions

1. The system of psychotherapy developed by Freud that seeks to bring unconscious conflicts into conscious awareness is known as _____. (a) transference; (b) cognitive restructuring; (c) psychoanalysis; (d) the "hot seat" technique

2. Which psychoanalytic concept best explains the following situations?
   a. Mary is extremely angry with her therapist, who seems unresponsive and uncaring about her personal needs.
   b. Although John is normally very punctual, he is frequently late for his therapy session.
3. What are the two major criticisms of psychoanalysis?
4. How does modern psychodynamic therapy differ from psychoanalysis?

Answers to Questions can be found in Appendix B.

Assessment

What are the major cognitive therapies?

Cognitive Therapy *Therapy that focuses on faulty thought processes and beliefs to treat problem behaviors*

Self-Talk *Internal dialogue; the things people say to themselves when they interpret events*

■ Cognitive Therapies: A Focus on Faulty Thoughts and Beliefs

Cognitive therapy assumes that faulty thought processes and beliefs create problem behaviors and emotions. For example, a cognitive therapist would say that feelings of depression are created by such beliefs as "If I don't do everything perfectly, I am worthless" or "I'm helpless to change my life, so I'll never be happy." When people hold beliefs that are irrational, that are overly demanding, or that fail to match reality, their emotions and behaviors may become disturbed (Beck, 2000, 2001; Ellis, 1996, 2000; Livanou et al., 2002).

Cognitive therapists, like psychoanalysts, analyze a person's thought processes, believing that altering destructive thoughts will enable the person to live more effectively. Also like psychoanalysts, cognitive therapists assume that many of the beliefs that create problem behaviors operate at an unexamined level.

Cognitive therapists also agree with psychoanalysts that exploring an unexamined belief system can produce insight into the reasons for disturbed behaviors. However, instead of believing that a change in behavior occurs because of insight and catharsis, cognitive therapists believe that insight into negative **self-talk,** the unrealistic things a person has been telling himself or herself, is most important. This insight allows the individual to challenge his or her thoughts, to directly change how he or she interprets events, and, ultimately, to change maladaptive behaviors. For example, the irrational statement "If I don't do everything perfectly, I am worthless" can be changed to more adaptive thoughts like "I can accept my limits" or "I can make constructive changes in my behavior." **Cognitive restructuring** is the name for this process of changing destructive thoughts or inappropriate interpretations.

Psychoanalysts focus primarily on childhood relationships within the patient's family, whereas cognitive therapists emphasize the way events and people both inside and outside the family influence beliefs. For example, going to college or boot camp, falling in love, or becoming a parent can change attitudes and beliefs in significant ways, and interactions with teachers, bosses, and friends can create disturbed as well as realistic ways of thinking.

Albert Ellis and Rational-Emotive Therapy

One of the best-known cognitive therapists is Albert Ellis, a former psychoanalytic therapist who developed his own approach, known as **rational-emotive therapy** (RET) (1961, 1997, 2000). Ellis calls RET an A-B-C approach, referring to the three steps involved in creating disturbed responses: (A) an activating event, which is some type of stimulus such as criticism from a boss or a failing grade; (B) the belief system, which is the person's interpretation of the activating experience; and (C) the emotional consequence, which the person experiences (Figure 44.1).

Ellis claims that unless we stop to think about our interpretation of events, we will automatically go from A (the activating event) to C (the emotional consequence). We fail to see that step B (the belief system) actually creates the subsequent emotion. Receiving a failing grade on an exam does not *cause* the emotion of depression. It is step B (the belief that "I'll never get through college") that is the culprit.

When he originally formulated his theory, Ellis emphasized a number of specific irrational beliefs resulting from his A-B-C model, such as "I must have love from everyone" and "I must be thoroughly competent." In recent years, however, he has shifted to a general concept of "demandingness" (Ellis, 1997, 2000; Kottler & Brown, 1999). When people *demand* certain "musts" and "shoulds" from themselves and others, they create emotional distress and behavioral dysfunction that often requires therapeutic intervention. For example, a divorced man whose wife left him for another man might engage in this self-talk: "I *must* be loved by everyone. She *should* not and *must* not reject me. I *demand* that she come back to me, or I'll get even."

Cognitive Restructuring *Process in cognitive therapy to change destructive thinking*

Rational-Emotive Therapy (RET) *Ellis's cognitive therapy to eliminate self-defeating beliefs through rational examination*

Figure 44.1 *The development of irrational misconceptions.* How do our thoughts and beliefs make us unhappy? According to Albert Ellis, our emotional reactions are produced by our interpretation of an event, not by the event itself. For example, if you receive a low exam score, you might explain to yourself and others that your bad mood was a direct result of the low grade. Ellis would argue that the self-talk ("I'll never get through college") between the event and the feeling is what upset you. Furthermore, the bad mood causes you to ruminate on all other bad things in your life, which maintains your negative emotional state. Ellis's theory explains why going jogging or watching television can improve your mood — it breaks the vicious cycle.

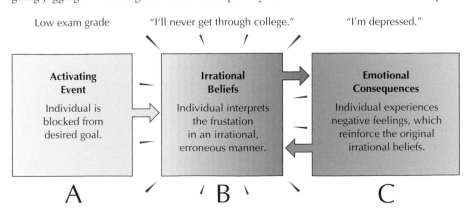

Ellis believes that such unrealistic, unproductive self-talk, "demandingness," and "musturbation" ("He *must* love me." "I *must* get into graduate school.") generally goes unexamined unless the client is confronted directly. In therapy, Ellis often argues with clients, cajoling and teasing them, sometimes in very blunt language. Many clients are shocked by his bluntness — and by their own irrational beliefs. Once clients recognize their self-defeating thoughts, Ellis begins working with them on how to *behave* differently — to test out new beliefs and to learn better coping skills. Reflecting this increased attention to behavioral change, he renamed his therapy *rational-emotive behavior therapy* (REBT).

Aaron Beck and Cognitive-Behavior Therapy

Another well-known cognitive therapist is Aaron Beck (1976, 2000, 2001). Like Ellis, Beck believes that psychological problems result from illogical thinking and from destructive self-talk. But unlike Ellis and psychoanalysts who encourage the client to express thoughts and feelings to gain insight into the origins of maladaptive behaviors, Beck takes a much more active approach. He seeks to provide clients with experiences, both inside and outside the therapy session, which will alter their negative talk in a favorable way. The overall goal is to directly confront and change the behaviors associated with destructive cognitions — hence the term **cognitive-behavior therapy.**

Cognitive-Behavior Therapy *Beck's system for changing destructive thoughts and beliefs as well as associated behaviors*

One of the most successful applications of Beck's theory has been in the treatment of depression. Beck has identified several thinking patterns that he believes are associated with depression. These are among the most important:

1. *Selective perception.* Depression-prone people tend to focus selectively on negative events while ignoring positive events.

2. *Overgeneralization.* On the basis of limited information, depressed people overgeneralize and draw negative conclusions about their self-worth — for example, believing you are worthless because you lost a promotion or failed an exam.

TRY THIS YOURSELF

Application

Although Albert Ellis believes that most people require the help of a therapist to see through their defenses and force them to challenge their self-defeating thoughts, you may be able to change some of your own irrational beliefs and responses with the following suggestions:

1. *Evaluate the consequences.* Emotions such as anger, anxiety, and depression often seem "natural," but they don't have to happen. Rather than perpetuating negative emotions by assuming they must be experienced, focus on whether your reactions make you more effective and enable you to solve your problems.

2. *Identify your belief system.* Find your irrational beliefs by asking yourself why you feel the particular emotions you do. Ellis believes that by confronting your

beliefs, you can discover the irrational assumptions that are creating the problem consequences.

3. *Dispute the self-defeating beliefs.* Once you have identified an overly demanding or irrational belief, argue against it. For example, it is gratifying when people you cherish love you in return, but if they do not, continuing to pursue them or insisting that they must love you will only be self-defeating.

4. *Practice effective ways of thinking.* Continue to examine your emotional reactions to events and situations to create opportunities to dispute irrational beliefs and substitute realistic perceptions. Practice behaviors that are more effective by rehearsing them at home and imagining outcomes that are more successful.

3. *Magnification.* Depressed people tend to exaggerate the importance of undesirable events or personal shortcomings and see them as catastrophic and unchangeable.

4. *All-or-nothing thinking.* Depressed people see things in black-or-white categories. Everything is either totally good or bad, right or wrong, a success or a failure.

Beck's cognitive-behavior therapy works like this: To begin, clients are taught to recognize and keep track of their thoughts. Examples might be: "How come I'm the only one alone at this party" (selective perception) and "If I don't get straight A's, I'll never get a good job" (all-or-nothing thinking). Next, the therapist trains the client to develop ways to test these automatic thoughts against reality. For example, if the client believes that straight A's are necessary for a certain job, the therapist needs to find only one instance of this not being the case to refute the belief. Obviously, the therapist chooses the tests carefully so that they do not confirm the client's negative beliefs but lead instead to positive outcomes.

This approach — identifying dysfunctional thoughts followed by active testing — helps depressed people discover that negative attitudes are largely a product of unrealistic or faulty thought processes. At this point, Beck introduces the second phase of therapy, persuading the client to actively pursue pleasurable activities. Depressed individuals often lose motivation, even for experiences they used to find enjoyable. Simultaneously taking an active rather than passive role and reconnecting with enjoyable experiences help in recovering from depression.

Evaluating Cognitive Therapies

Considerable evidence suggests that Beck's procedures are highly effective with depression, anxiety disorders, bulimia nervosa, anger management, addiction, and even some symptoms of schizophrenia and insomnia (Beck, 2000, 2001; Harvey, Inglis, & Espie, 2002; McMullin, 2000; Tobin, 2000). Ellis's RET has had similar successes with a variety of disorders (Beal & DiGiuseppe, 1998; Ellis, 2000).

Both Beck and Ellis are criticized, however, for ignoring or denying the client's unconscious dynamics and minimizing the importance of the client's past (Butler, 2000). In addition, Ellis is criticized for "preaching an ethical system" (Davison, Neale, & Kring, 2004, p. 579). By labeling his patients' beliefs "irrational" and insisting that they be replaced with "rational" thoughts, Ellis is imposing his own set of standards. Other critics suggest cognitive therapies are successful because they employ behavior techniques, not because they change the underlying cognitive structure (Bandura, 1969, 1997; Wright & Beck, 1999).

■ Humanistic Therapies: Blocked Personal Growth

Humanists believe human potential includes the freedom to become what one wants to be as well as the responsibility to make choices. **Humanistic therapy** therefore assumes that people with problems are suffering from a blockage or disruption of their normal growth potential. This blockage creates a defective self-concept. When obstacles are removed, the individual is free to become the self-accepting and genuine person everyone is capable of being.

Imagine for a minute how you feel when you are with someone who believes you are a good person with unlimited potential, a person whose "real self" is unique and valuable. These are the feelings that are nurtured in humanistic therapy approaches.

Carl Rogers and Client-Centered Therapy

One of the best-known humanistic therapists, Carl Rogers (1961, 1980), developed an approach that encourages people to actualize their potential and relate to others in genuine ways. His approach is referred to as **client-centered therapy.** Using the term *client* instead of *patient* was very significant to Rogers. He believed the label *patient*

Assessment

What is different about humanistic therapies?

Humanistic Therapy *Therapy to maximize personal growth through affective restructuring (emotional readjustment)*

Client-Centered Therapy *Rogers's therapy emphasizing the client's natural tendency to become healthy and productive; techniques include empathy, unconditional positive regard, genuineness, and active listening*

implied being sick or mentally ill, rather than responsible and competent. Treating people as clients emphasizes the fact that *they* are the ones in charge of the therapy and focuses on the equality of the therapist–client relationship.

Client-centered therapy, like psychoanalysis and cognitive therapies, explores thoughts and feelings to obtain insight into the causes for behaviors. For Rogerian therapists, however, the focus is on encouraging healthy emotional experiences. Clients are responsible for discovering their own maladaptive patterns, whereas the therapist provides an accepting atmosphere in which the client can freely explore important thoughts and feelings (Barrett-Lennard, 1999).

How does the therapist create such an atmosphere? Rogerian therapists create a therapeutic relationship by focusing on four important qualities of communication: empathy, unconditional positive regard, genuineness, and active listening.

Empathy *In Rogerian terms, an insightful awareness and ability to share another's inner experience*

1. ***Empathy*** is a sensitive understanding and sharing of another person's inner experience. When we put ourselves in other people's shoes, we enter their inner world. Therapists watch body language and listen for subtle cues to help them understand the emotional experiences of clients. When clients express feelings verbally, they are encouraged to explore them further. The therapist uses open-ended statements such as "You found that upsetting" or "You haven't been able to decide what to do about this" rather than asking questions or offering explanations.

Unconditional Positive Regard *Rogers's term for a nonjudgmental attitude and genuine caring for another*

2. ***Unconditional positive regard*** is genuine caring for people based on their innate value as individuals. Because humanists believe human nature is positive and each person is unique, clients can be respected and cherished without having to prove themselves worthy of the therapist's esteem. Unconditional positive regard allows the therapist to trust that clients have the best answers for their own lives. To maintain a climate of unconditional positive regard, the therapist avoids making evaluative statements such as "That's good" and "You did the right thing," which give the idea that the therapist is judging them and that clients need to receive approval. Humanists believe that when people receive unconditional caring from others, they become better able to value themselves in a similar way.

Genuineness *In Rogerian terms, authenticity or congruence; the awareness of one's true inner thoughts and feelings and being able to share them honestly with others*

3. ***Genuineness,*** or *authenticity*, is being aware of one's true inner thoughts and feelings and being able to share them honestly with others. When people are genuine, they are not artificial, defensive, or playing a role. If a Rogerian therapist were pleased or displeased with a client's progress, for example, he or she would feel free to share those feelings. When therapists are genuine with their clients, they believe their clients will in turn develop self-trust and honest self-expression.

Active Listening *Listening with total attention to what another is saying; it involves reflecting, paraphrasing, and clarifying what the person says and means*

4. ***Active listening*** involves reflecting, paraphrasing, and clarifying what the client says and means. To *reflect* is to hold a mirror in front of the person, enabling that person to see him- or herself. To *paraphrase* is to summarize in different words what the client is saying. To *clarify* is to check that both the speaker and listener are on the same wavelength.

For example, noticing the client's furrowed brow and clenched hands while the client is discussing his marital problems, the clinician might respond, "Sounds like you're angry with your wife and feeling pretty miserable right now." With this one statement, the clinician reflects the client's anger, paraphrases his complaint, and gives feedback to clarify the communication. By being an *active listener*, the clinician communicates that he or she is genuinely interested in what the client is saying.

Evaluation
Supporters say there is empirical evidence for humanistic assumptions (e.g., Bohart, O'Hara, & Leitner, 1998; Hayashi et al., 1998), but critics argue that the basic tenets of humanistic therapy, such as self-actualization and self-awareness, are difficult to test

Would you like to check your understanding of empathy, unconditional positive regard, genuineness, and active listening? Identify the techniques being used in the following excerpt (Shea, 1988, pp. 32–33). Check your responses with those in Appendix B.

THERAPIST (TH): What has it been like coming down to the emergency room today?

CLIENT (CL): Unsettling, to say the least. I feel very awkward here, sort of like I'm vulnerable. To be honest, I've had some horrible experiences with doctors. I don't like them.

TH: I see. Well, they scare the hell out of me, too (smiles, indicating the humor in his comment).

CL: (Chuckles) I thought you were a doctor.

TH: I am (pauses, smiles) — that's what's so scary.

CL: (Smiles and laughs)

TH: Tell me a little more about some of your unpleasant experiences with doctors, because I want to make sure I'm not doing anything that is upsetting to you. I don't want that to happen.

CL: Well, that's very nice to hear. My last doctor didn't give a hoot about what I said, and he only spoke in huge words.

In case you're wondering, this is an excerpt from an actual session — humor and informality can be an important part of the therapeutic process.

scientifically. Most of the research on the outcomes of humanistic therapy relies on client self-reports; however, people undergoing any type of therapy are motivated to justify their time and expense. In addition, research on specific therapeutic techniques, such as Rogerian "empathy" and "active listening" has had mixed results (Gottman, Coan, Carrere, & Swanson, 1998).

Assessment
CHECK & REVIEW

Cognitive and Humanistic Therapies

Cognitive therapy emphasizes the importance of faulty thought processes, beliefs, and negative **self-talk** in the creation of problem behaviors. Albert Ellis's **rational-emotive therapy** (RET) aims to replace a client's irrational beliefs with rational beliefs and accurate perceptions of the world. Aaron Beck's **cognitive-behavior therapy** takes a more active approach with clients by emphasizing changes in both thought processes and behavior.

Evaluations of cognitive therapies find Beck's procedures particularly effective for relieving depression; Ellis has had success with a variety of disorders. Both Beck and Ellis, however, are criticized for ignoring the importance of unconscious processes and the client's history. Some critics also attribute any success with cognitive therapies to the use of behavioral techniques.

Humanistic therapies are based on the premise that problems result when an individual's normal growth potential is blocked. In Carl Rogers's **client-centered therapy**, the therapist offers **empathy, unconditional positive regard, genuineness,** and **active listening** as means of facilitating personal growth. Humanistic therapies are difficult to evaluate scientifically, and research on specific therapeutic techniques has had mixed results.

Questions

1. Cognitive therapists assume that problem behaviors and emotions are caused by _____. (a) faulty thought processes and beliefs; (b) negative self-image; (c) incongruent belief systems; (d) lack of self-discipline

2. What are the three steps (the A-B-C) of Ellis's RET?

3. Beck identified four destructive thought patterns associated with depression (selective perception, overgeneralization, magnification, and all-or-nothing thinking). Using these terms, label the following thoughts:

_____ a. Mary left me, and I'll never fall in love again. I'll always be alone.

_____ b. My ex-spouse is an evil monster and our entire marriage was a sham.

4. Label each of the following Rogerian therapy techniques:

_____ a. A sensitive understanding and sharing of another's inner or phenomenological experience

_____ b. The honest sharing of inner thoughts and feelings

_____ c. A nonjudgmental and caring attitude toward another that does not have to be earned

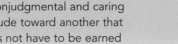

Assessment

How are learning principles used in behavior therapy?

Behavior Therapy *Group of techniques based on learning principles used to change maladaptive behaviors*

▨ Behavior Therapies: Changing Maladaptive Behaviors

Have you ever understood why you were doing something you would rather not do but continued to do it anyway? Sometimes having insight into a problem does not automatically solve it. Take the example of Mrs. D, an agoraphobic woman who had not left her house for $3^1/_2$ years except with her husband. She had undergone $1^1/_2$ years of insight-based therapy and had become well aware of the causes of her problem, but she did not change her behavior. She finally sought the help of a behavior therapist, who, instead of working on her understanding of her problems or attempting to restructure her feelings, systematically trained her to behave differently. After less than 2 months, Mrs. D was able to leave her house and travel alone to appointments (Lazarus, 1971).

Behavior therapy uses learning principles to change behaviors. Behavior therapists do not believe it is necessary to obtain insight or restructure feelings before changes in behavior can occur. The focus in this approach is on the problem behavior itself rather than on any underlying causes. That is not to say the person's feelings and interpretations are disregarded; they are just not emphasized. Behavior therapists believe that abnormal or maladaptive behaviors are learned in the same way that adaptive behaviors are learned. Thus, abnormal behaviors can also be "unlearned."

In behavior therapy, the therapist diagnoses the problem by listing the maladaptive behaviors that occur and the adaptive behaviors that are absent. The therapist

then attempts to decrease the frequency of maladaptive behaviors and increase the frequency of adaptive behaviors. To accomplish this type of change, a behavior therapist draws on principles of classical conditioning, operant conditioning, and modeling (Sarafino, 2000).

Classical Conditioning Techniques

Behavior therapists use the principles of classical conditioning, derived from Pavlov's model for associating two stimulus events, to decrease maladaptive behavior by creating new associations to replace the faulty ones. We will explore two techniques based on these principles: systematic desensitization and aversion therapy.

1. *Systematic desensitization.* Mrs. D's behavior therapist used *systematic desensitization,* a procedure developed by Joseph Wolpe (Wolpe & Plaud, 1997) to extinguish her agoraphobia. **Systematic desensitization** begins with relaxation training, followed by imagining or directly experiencing various versions of a feared object or situation, while remaining deeply relaxed. The goal is to replace an anxiety response with a relaxation response when confronting the feared stimulus (Sturges & Sturges, 1998; Wolpe & Plaud, 1997). It is based on the opposite actions of the sympathetic and parasympathetic branches of the autonomic nervous system. Because the parasympathetic nerves control autonomic functions when we are relaxed and because the sympathetic nerves are dominant when we are anxious, it is physiologically impossible to be both relaxed and anxious at the same time.

Desensitization is a three-step process. First, a client is taught how to maintain a state of deep relaxation that is physiologically incompatible with an anxiety response. Next, the therapist and client construct a *hierarchy*, or ranked listing of 10 or so anxiety-arousing images (Figure 44.2). In the final step, the relaxed client mentally visualizes or physically experiences items at the bottom of the hierarchy and works his or her way to the most anxiety producing images at the top. If any image or situation begins to create anxiety, the client stops momentarily and returns to a state of complete relaxation. Eventually, the fear response is extinguished.

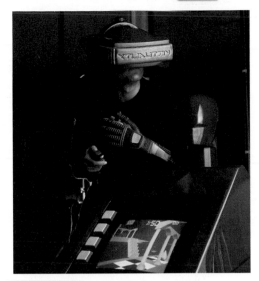

Virtual reality therapy. *Rather than mental imaging or actual physical experiences of a fearful situation, modern therapy can use the latest in computer technology — virtual reality headsets and data gloves. A client with a fear of heights, for example, can have experiences ranging from climbing a stepladder all the way to standing on the edge of a tall building, while never leaving the therapist's office.*

Systematic Desensitization *A gradual process of extinguishing a learned fear (or phobia) by working through a hierarchy of fear-evoking stimuli while staying deeply relaxed*

TRY THIS

YOURSELF

Application

Nearly everyone is somewhat anxious before an important exam. If you find this anxiety helpful and invigorating, skip ahead to the next section. However, if the days and evenings before a major exam are ruined by your anxiety and you sometimes "freeze up" while taking the test, you can benefit from an informal type of systematic desensitization.

Step 1: Review and practice the relaxation technique taught in Module 10.
Step 2: Create a 10-step "test taking" hierarchy — starting with the least anxiety arousing image (perhaps the day your instructor first mentions an upcoming exam) and ending with actually taking the exam.
Step 3: Beginning with the least arousing image — hearing about the exam — picture yourself at each stage, while maintaining a calm, relaxed state. Work your way through all 10 steps. If you become anxious at any stage, stay there, repeating your relaxation technique until the anxiety diminishes.
Step 4: If you start to feel anxious the night before the exam, or even during the exam itself, remind yourself to relax. Take a few moments to shut your eyes and review how you worked through your hierarchy.

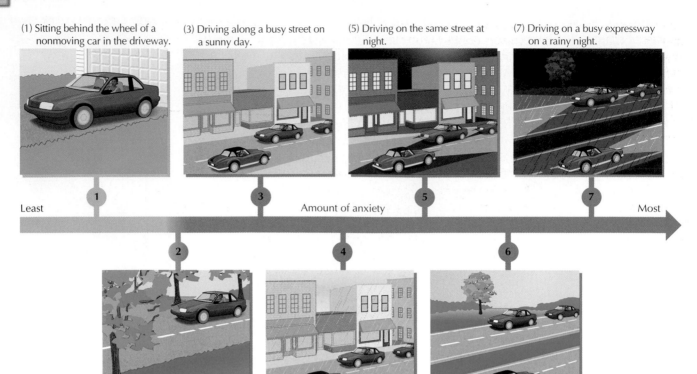

(1) Sitting behind the wheel of a nonmoving car in the driveway.

(3) Driving along a busy street on a sunny day.

(5) Driving on the same street at night.

(7) Driving on a busy expressway on a rainy night.

Least   1   3   Amount of anxiety   5   7   Most

2   4   6

(2) Driving along an empty, quiet street on a sunny day.

(4) Driving on the same street in the rain.

(6) Driving on a busy expressway in the daytime.

Figure 44.2 *desensitization for a driving phobia.* During systematic desensitization, the client begins by constructing a hierarchy, or ranked listing, of anxiety-arousing images or situations starting with one that produces very little anxiety and escalating to those that arouse extreme anxiety. To extinguish a driving phobia, the patient begins with images or actually sitting behind the wheel of a nonmoving car and ends with driving on a busy expressway.

Aversion Therapy *Pairing an aversive (unpleasant) stimulus with a maladaptive behavior*

2. *Aversion therapy.* In sharp contrast to systematic desensitization, **aversion therapy** uses principles of classical conditioning to create anxiety rather than extinguish it. People who engage in excessive drinking, for example, build up a number of pleasurable associations. Because these pleasurable associations cannot always be prevented, aversion therapy provides *negative associations* to compete with the pleasurable ones. Someone who wants to stop drinking, for example, could take a drug called Antabuse that causes vomiting whenever alcohol enters the system. When the new connection between alcohol and nausea has been classically conditioned, engaging in the once desirable habit will cause an immediate negative response (Figure 44.3).

Although this treatment has had some limited success, it has always been controversial. Is it ethical to hurt someone (even when the person has given permission)? It also has been criticized because it does not provide lasting relief (Seligman, 1994). Unlike a similar technique in which sheep meat was tainted with a nausea-producing drug and coyotes quickly learned to avoid sheep (Module 19), humans understand that the nausea is produced by the Antabuse, and do not generalize their learning to the alcohol itself. Once they leave treatment, most alcoholics go back to drinking (and do not continue taking the Antabuse).

Operant Conditioning Techniques

Operant conditioning techniques use shaping and reinforcement to increase adaptive behaviors, and punishment and extinction to decrease maladaptive behaviors.

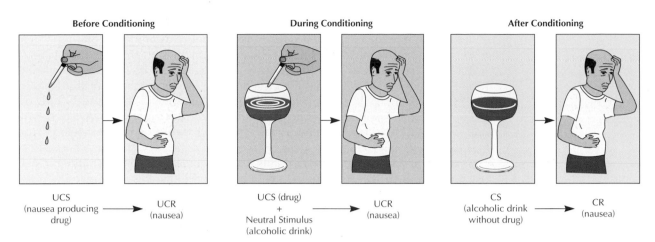

| Before Conditioning | During Conditioning | After Conditioning |

UCS
(nausea producing → UCR
drug) (nausea)

UCS (drug)
+ → UCR
Neutral Stimulus (nausea)
(alcoholic drink)

CS
(alcoholic drink → CR
without drug) (nausea)

Figure 44.3 *Aversion therapy for alcoholism.* Using the principles of classical conditioning, a nausea-producing drug (Antabuse) is paired with alcohol to create an aversion to drinking.

Shaping and reinforcement. In behavior therapy, a behavior to be acquired is called the *target behavior.* Shaping — being rewarded for successive approximations of the target behavior — is one operant technique for eventually performing the target behavior. One of the most successful applications of shaping and reinforcement has been with autistic children. Children with *autism* do not communicate or interact normally with other people. Shaping has been used to develop their language skills. The child is first rewarded for any sounds and then later only for words and sentences.

Shaping is also used to help people acquire social skills. If you are painfully shy, for example, a clinician might first ask you to role-play simply saying hello to someone you find attractive. Then, you might practice behaviors that gradually lead you to suggest a get-together or date. During such *role-playing*, or *behavior rehearsal*, the clinician would give you feedback and reinforcement.

Behavior rehearsal is also the technique behind *assertiveness training*, which teaches people to stand up for themselves. Clients begin with simple situations and progress to practicing effective verbal responses and adaptive behaviors. In treating Mrs. D's agoraphobia, for example, her therapist used role playing to shape assertive behaviors such as standing up to her domineering father.

Adaptive behaviors can also be taught or increased with techniques that provide immediate reinforcement in the form of tokens (Sarafino, 2000). *Tokens* are secondary (conditioned) reinforcers, such as poker chips, "credit" cards, or other tangible objects that can be exchanged for primary rewards such as food, treats, watching TV, a private room, or outings. In an inpatient treatment facility, patients are sometimes rewarded with tokens and gradually shaped toward desirable activities such as taking medication, attending group therapy sessions, or taking part in recreational programs. Patients can also be "fined" for inappropriate behaviors by having tokens taken away.

Doesn't this approach depend too much on the tokens to have any lasting effect? Advocates point out that tokens help people acquire beneficial behaviors that become rewarding in themselves. A full-fledged behavior management program has a series of levels, each requiring increasingly complex behavior. For example, patients might at first be given tokens for merely attending group therapy sessions. Once this behavior is established, they would be rewarded only for actually participating in the sessions. Eventually, the tokens could be discontinued when the patient receives the reinforcement of being helped by participation in the therapy sessions. Tokens have been successfully used in a wide variety of settings, including hospitals, programs for delinquents, classrooms, and individual homes (Bower, 2000; Truchlicka, McLaughlin, & Swain, 1998).

Overcoming agoraphobia. Behavior therapists would use shaping and reinforcement to treat this woman's agoraphobia.

Modeling Therapy *Watching and imitating models that demonstrate desirable behaviors*

Modeling

In addition to using classical and operant conditioning techniques, behavioral therapists also use **modeling therapy,** observing and imitating appropriate behaviors. By watching appropriate people perform desired behaviors, the client learns new behaviors. For example, Bandura and his colleagues (1969) asked clients with snake phobias to watch other (nonphobic) people handle snakes. After only 2 hours of exposure, over 92 percent of the phobic observers allowed a snake to crawl over their hands, arms, and neck. When the client combines live modeling with direct and gradual practice, it is called *participant modeling.*

Modeling is also part of social skills training and assertiveness training. Clients learn how to interview for a job by first watching the therapist role-play the part of the interviewee. The therapist models the appropriate language (assertively asking for a job), body posture, and so forth, and then asks the client to imitate the behavior and play the same role. Over the course of several sessions, the client becomes gradually desensitized to the anxiety of interviews and learns interview skills.

Evaluating Behavior Therapies

Research suggests behavior therapy based on classical and operant conditioning and modeling has been effective with various problems, including phobias, OCD, eating disorders, autism, mental retardation, and delinquency (Agras & Berkowitz, 1999; Sarafino, 2000; Sarkar, Rathee, & Neera, 1999; Wolpe, 1997). Some patients have even returned to their homes and communities after years of institutionalization.

Critics of behavior therapy, however, raise important questions that fall into two major categories:

1. *Generalizability.* What happens after the treatment stops? Can the results be generalized? Critics argue that in the "real world" patients are not consistently reinforced, and their newly acquired behaviors may disappear. To deal with this possibility, behavior therapists work to gradually shape clients toward rewards that are typical of life outside the clinical setting.

2. *Ethics.* Is it ethical for one person to control another's behavior? Are there some situations in which behavior therapy should not be used? In the movie *A Clockwork Orange*, people in positions of power used behavior modification principles to control the general population. Behaviorists reply that rewards and punishments already control our behaviors, and behavior therapy actually increases a person's freedom by making these controls overt. Furthermore, they believe behavior therapy increases self-control by teaching people how to change their own behavior and maintain these changes when they leave the clinical setting.

Assessment

CHECK & REVIEW

Behavior Therapies

Behavior therapies use learning principles to change maladaptive behaviors. Classical conditioning principles are used to change associations. In **systematic desensitization,** the client replaces anxiety with relaxation, and in **aversion therapy,** an aversive stimulus is paired with a maladaptive behavior. *Shaping, reinforcement,* and **modeling** are

behavioral therapy techniques based on operant conditioning principles.

Behavior therapies have been successful with a number of psychological disorders. But they are also criticized for lack of generalizability and the questionable ethics of controlling behavior.

Questions

1. A group of techniques based on learning principles that are used to change mal-

adaptive behaviors is known as _____.
2. In behavior therapy, _____ techniques use shaping, reinforcement, and modeling to increase adaptive behaviors. (a) classical conditioning; (b) modeling; (c) operant conditioning; (d) social learning
3. Describe how shaping can be used to develop desired behaviors.
4. What are the two criticisms of behavior therapy?

Answers to Questions can be found in Appendix B.

Group and Family Therapies: Healing Interpersonal Relationships

The therapies described thus far all consider the individual as the unit of analysis and treatment. In contrast, group and family therapies treat multiple individuals simultaneously. During sessions, therapists often apply psychoanalytic, cognitive, humanistic, and/or behavioral techniques. In this section, we will discuss both group and family therapies.

Assessment

How is psychotherapy done with groups and families?

Group Therapy

Group therapy began as a response to the need for more therapists than were available and for a more economical form of therapy. What began as a practical and economic necessity, however, has become a preferred approach in its own right. In **group therapy,** multiple people meet together to work toward therapeutic goals. Typically, 8 to 10 people meet with a therapist on a regular basis, usually once a week for 2 hours. The therapist can work from any of the psychotherapeutic orientations we've previously discussed, and like individual therapy, members of the group talk about problems in their own lives. Unlike one-on-one therapies, however, the group members also gain from exploring *group process*, or the way members of the group interact with each other.

In addition to being less expensive than one-on-one therapy and providing insights from group processes, group therapy provides other advantages not found in individual therapy (Davison, Neale, & Kring, 2004; Peterson & Halstead, 1998; White & Freeman, 2000).

1. *Group support.* During times of stress and emotional trouble, it is easy to imagine we are alone and that our problems are unique. Knowing that others have similar problems can be very reassuring. In addition, seeing others improve can be a source of hope and motivation.

2. *Feedback and information.* Because group members typically have comparable problems, they can learn from each other's mistakes and share insights. Furthermore, when a group member receives similar comments about his or her behavior from several members of the group, the message may be more convincing than if it comes from a single therapist.

3. *Behavioral rehearsal.* Group members can role-play one another's employer, spouse, parents, children, or prospective dates. By playing and observing different roles in relationships, people gain insight into their problems and practice new social skills.

A variation on group therapy is the **self-help group.** Unlike other group therapy approaches, a professional does not guide these groups. They are simply groups of people who share a common problem and meet to give and receive support. For example, people who are learning to deal with painful life crises find support in organizations like AMAC (Adults Molested as Children), Formerly Employed, and Parents of Murdered Children. Individuals who need help with destructive lifestyles can find it in Alcoholics Anonymous, Debtors Anonymous, and Gamblers Anonymous. Some support groups use their shared pain for public service, like MADD (Mothers Against Drunk Driving). There are even groups for people in happy situations (New Parents, Parents of Twins) where the help may be more instructional than emotional.

Therapists often refer their patients to self-help groups to supplement individual therapy. Someone who has a problem with alcohol, for example, can find comfort and help with others who have "been there." They exchange useful information, share their coping strategies, and gain hope by seeing others overcome or successfully manage their shared problems. Research on self-help groups for alcoholism or obesity find

Group Therapy *A number of people meet together to work toward therapeutic goals*

Self-Help Group *Leaderless or nonprofessionally guided groups in which members assist each other with a specific problem, as in Alcoholics Anonymous*

they can be very effective — either alone or in addition to individual psychotherapy (Davison, Pennebaker, & Dickerson, 2000; Klein, 2000).

Family Therapies

> Mental health problems do not affect three or four out of five persons but one out of one.
>
> DR. WILLIAM MENNINGER

Therapists have long known that dealing with an individual's problem may not be enough. Often, relationships within the family structure must be healed. Because a family is a system of interdependent parts, the problem of any one member unavoidably affects all the others (Barker, 2000; Carr, 2000; Lebow & Gurman, 1995). A teen's delinquency or a parent's drug problem affects each member of the family.

Sometimes the problems parents have with a child arise from conflicts in the marriage; other times a child's behavior creates distress in an otherwise well-functioning couple. The line between *marital* (or *couples*) *therapy* and *family therapy* is often blurred. Given that most married couples have children, our discussion will focus on **family therapy,** in which the primary aim is to change maladaptive family interaction patterns. All members of the family attend therapy sessions, though at times the therapist may also see family members individually or in twos or threes. (The therapist, incidentally, may take any orientation — behavioral, cognitive, etc.)

Many families initially come into therapy believing that one member is *the* cause of all their problems ("Johnny's delinquency" or "Mom's drinking"). However, family therapists generally find that this "identified patient" is the scapegoat (a person blamed for someone else's problems) for deeper disturbances. For example, instead of confronting their own problems with intimacy, the parents may focus all their attention and frustration on the delinquent child (Hanna & Brown, 1999). It is usually necessary to change ways of interacting within the family system to promote the health of individual family members and the family as a whole.

Family therapy is also useful in treating a number of disorders and clinical problems. As we discussed in Module 40, schizophrenic patients are more likely to relapse if their family members express emotions, attitudes, and behaviors that involve criticism, hostility, or emotional overinvolvement (Butzlaff & Hooley, 1998; Linszen, et al., 1997). Family therapy can help family members modify their behavior toward the patient. It also seems to be the most favorable setting for the treatment of adolescent drug abuse (Lebow & Gurman, 1995).

Family Therapy *Treatment to change maladaptive interaction patterns within a family*

Family therapy. *Rather than one-on-one counseling, family therapists generally work with the entire family to improve communication and resolve conflicts.*

Assessment

CHECK & REVIEW

Group and Family Therapies

In addition to being less expensive and more available than individual therapy, **group therapy** has other advantages: It provides group support, feedback, information, and opportunities for behavior rehearsal. A variation on group therapy is the **self-help group** (like Alcoholics Anonymous), which is not guided by a professional.

The aim of **family therapy** is to change maladaptive family interaction patterns.

Because a family is a system of interdependent parts, the problem of any one member unavoidably affects all the others.

Questions

1. In _____, multiple people meet together to work toward therapeutic goals. (a) encounter groups; (b) behavior therapy; (c) group therapy; (d) conjoint therapy
2. What are the major advantages of group therapy?
3. Why do individual therapists often refer their patients to self-help groups?
4. _____ treats the family as a unit, and members work together to solve problems. (a) Aversion therapy; (b) Encounter groups; (c) Self-help groups; (d) Family therapy

Answers to Questions can be found in Appendix B.

Application

CRITICAL THINKING

Synthesizing Multiple Forms of Therapy

When first introduced to the various forms of therapy, many people decide one or two "make sense" and discard the others as worthless. But each approach has its strengths, and the ability to *synthesize* — combine various elements into meaningful patterns — is a valuable critical thinking skill.

Test your own abilities to synthesize, by reviewing each of the six major therapies (psychoanalysis, cognitive, humanistic, behavior, group, and biomedical) and then discussing with your classmates how each therapy might treat the following problems:

Joe is 18 and deeply concerned that he might develop schizophrenia. Both his parents suffered from schizophrenia and close friends have complained about his "crazy thoughts" and depressed moods.

Ann is 35 and very depressed. She has been married for 10 years and always

ACTIVE LEARNING

planned to have a large family. But her husband adamantly refuses to have children. Lately, she finds herself crying at odd times and feels so fatigued she often stays home from work.

Tim is 45 and dissatisfied with his work situation. His coworkers and manager avoid him and complain about his "difficult personality." This is Tim's fifth job in four years. He believes that others secretly envy his intelligence and are plotting against him.

MODULE 44 ACTIVE LEARNING WORKSHEET

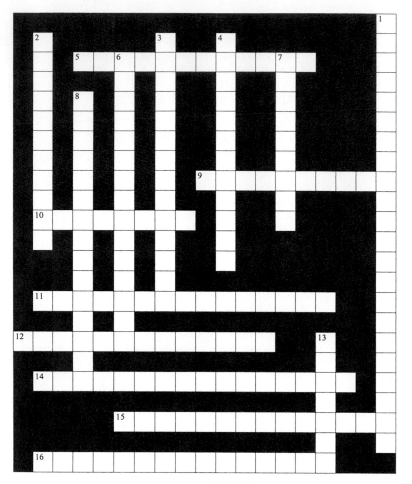

ACROSS

5 In psychoanalysis, the patient may displace (or transfer) thoughts, feelings, fears, wishes and conflicts from past relationships, particularly from childhood, onto new relationships, especially with the therapist.

9 A stage in psychoanalysis when the patient avoids (resists) the analyst's attempts to bring threatening unconscious material to conscious awareness.

10 Internal dialogue; the things people say to themselves when they interpret events.

11 In psychoanalysis, reporting whatever comes to mind without monitoring its contents—regardless of how painful, embarrassing, or irrelevant it may seem. Freud believed that the first thing to come to a patient's mind was often an important clue to what the unconscious mind wants to conceal.

12 A psychological treatment that attempts to change maladaptive interaction patterns among members of a family.

14 Therapy that focuses on faulty thought processes and beliefs to treat problem behaviors.

15 A psychoanalyst's explanation of a patient's free associations, dreams, resistance, and transference; more generally, any statement by a therapist that presents a patient's problem in a new way.

16 A group of techniques based on learning principles that are used to change maladaptive behaviors.

DOWN

1 The process in cognitive therapy by which the therapist and client work to change destructive ways of thinking.

2 In Rogerian terms, authenticity or congruence; the awareness of one's true inner thoughts and feelings and being able to share them honestly with others.

3 A system of therapy developed by Freud that seeks to bring unconscious conflicts, which usually date back to early childhood experiences, into consciousness. Psychoanalysis is also Freud's theoretical school of thought, which emphasizes the study of unconscious processes.

4 Treatment method in which multiple people meet together to work toward therapeutic goals.

6 Behavior therapy technique that pairs an aversive (unpleasant) stimulus with a maladaptive behavior.

7 In psychoanalytic theory, the release of tension and anxiety through the reliving of a traumatic incident.

8 According to Rogers, the ability to listen with total attention to what another is saying. This involves reflecting, paraphrasing, and clarifying what the person says and means.

13 In Rogerian terms, an insightful awareness and ability to share another person's inner experience.

MODULE 45
ISSUES IN THERAPY

Assessment

What are some of the major issues in therapy?

When is it appropriate to institutionalize people against their will? How do you choose a therapist? Is therapy effective? These are all major issues in therapy.

■ Institutionalization: Treating Chronic and Serious Mental Disorders

We all believe in the right to freedom, but when should people be protected from their own mental disorders? What about people who threaten suicide or are potentially violent? Despite Hollywood film portrayals, forced institutionalization of the mentally ill poses serious ethical problems and is generally reserved for only the most serious and life-threatening situations.

Involuntary Commitment

The legal grounds for involuntary commitment vary from state to state. But, generally, people can be sent to psychiatric hospitals if

- They are believed to be dangerous to themselves (usually suicidal) or dangerous to others (potentially violent)

- They are believed to be in serious need of treatment (indicated by bizarre behavior and loss of contact with reality)

- There is no reasonable, less restrictive alternative (Ruzovsky, 1984)

In emergencies, psychologists and other professionals can authorize temporary commitment for 24 to 72 hours. During this observation period, laboratory tests can be performed to rule out medical illnesses that could be causing the symptoms. The patient can also receive psychological testing, medication, and short-term therapy.

Deinstitutionalization

Although the courts have established stringent requirements for involuntary commitment, abuses do occur. In response to the potential for abuse, as well as to problems that come with long-term chronic institutionalization and the expense of properly housing and caring for the mentally ill, many states have a policy of **deinstitutionalization,** discharging as many patients from mental hospitals as soon possible and also discouraging admissions.

Deinstitutionalization *Discharging as many people as possible from state hospitals and discouraging admissions*

Although deinstitutionalization has been a humane and positive step for many (Lariviere et al., 2002; Priebe et al., 2002), some patients are discharged without continuing provision for their protection. Many of these people end up in rundown hotels, understaffed nursing homes, in jail, or living on the street with no shelter or means of support (Bassuk, 2002; Lamb, 2000). [It is important to note that although a sizable percentage of homeless people have mental disorders, the rise in homelessness is also due to such economic factors as increased unemployment, underemployment, and a shortage of low-income housing (Becker, 2001; Seager, 1998; Torrey, 1998).]

What else can be done?   Rather than returning patients to state hospitals, most clinicians suggest expanding and improving community care (Duckworth & Borus, 1999; Lamb, 2000). They recommend that general hospitals be equipped with special psychiatric units where acutely ill patients receive inpatient care. For less disturbed individuals and chronically ill patients, they recommend walk-in clinics, crisis intervention services, improved residential treatment facilities, and psychosocial and vocational rehabilitation. State hospitals would be reserved for the most unmanageable patients.

Deinstitutionalization. *Keeping people locked in large mental institutions creates problems. But deinstitutionalization also creates problems because it forces many former patients onto the streets with no home or medical care.*

Community Mental Health Centers

Community mental health (CMH) centers are a prime example of alternative treatment to institutionalization. CMH centers provide outpatient services such as individual and group therapy and prevention programs. They also coordinate short-term inpatient care and programs for discharged mental patients, such as halfway houses and aftercare services. Psychiatrists, social workers, nurses, and volunteers who live in the neighborhood generally staff CMH centers.

As you can imagine, CMH centers and their support programs are enormously expensive. Investing in primary prevention programs could substantially reduce these costs. Instead of waiting until someone loses his or her job, home, and family, we could develop more intervention programs for high-risk individuals and offer short-term immediate services during crises.

■ Evaluating Therapy: Does It Work? How to Choose?

Have you ever thought about going to a therapist? If you've gone, was it helpful? In this section, we will discuss questions about the effectiveness of therapy and how to find a therapist.

Judging Effectiveness

Scientifically evaluating the effectiveness of therapy can be tricky. How can you trust the perception and self-report of clients or clinicians? Both have biases and a need to justify the time, effort, and expense of therapy.

To avoid these problems, psychologists use controlled research studies. Clients are randomly assigned to different forms of therapy or to control groups who receive no treatment. After therapy, clients are independently evaluated, and reports from friends and family members are collected. Until recently, these studies were simply compared. But with a new statistical technique called *meta-analysis*, which combines and analyzes data from many studies, years of such studies and similar research can be brought together to produce a comprehensive report.

The good news, for both consumers and therapists, is that after years of controlled research and meta-analysis we have fairly clear evidence that therapy does work! Forty to 90 percent of people who receive treatment are better off than people who do not, and short-term treatments, as well as long-term, can be as effective (Kopta, Lueger, Saunders, & Howard, 1999; Kotkin, Daviet, & Gurin, 1996; Sanderson, 1995). Some therapies are more effective than others for specific problems. For example, phobias seem to respond best to systematic desensitization, and OCD can be significantly relieved with cognitive-behavior therapy accompanied by medication (see Seligman, 1994, for a review).

Achievement

RESEARCH HIGHLIGHT

Therapy in the Electronic Age

I never think of the future. It comes soon enough.

ALBERT EINSTEIN

As we've just seen in the previous section, research psychologists and therapists have been hard at work evaluating and improving current forms of traditional therapy, and, like Einstein, they may not have thought much about the future. But like it or not, the electronic age has arrived.

Today millions of people seek advice and "therapy" from radio call-in programs, telephone services with 900 numbers, and, now, websites for online therapy. The newest mental health therapy, called tele-health, has approximately 200 websites and between 350 and 1,000 online counselors offering counseling, group support chats, e-mail correspondence, private instant messages, and videoconferencing therapy (Davison, Pennebaker, & Dickerson, 2000; Kicklighter, 2000; Segal, 2000). These on-line counselors are psychologists, psychiatrists, social workers, licensed counselors, nonlicensed "helpers," and outright "quacks." Together, they treat an estimated 10,000 clients each week (Kicklighter, 2000).

As you might expect, many qualified therapists and academic institutions are concerned about this new form of therapy. They fear, among other things, that without a governing body to regulate this type of

therapy, there are no checks and balances to protect the client from unethical and unsavory practices. However, many of these concerns were recently addressed by the formulation of 10 Interdisciplinary Principles for Professional Practice in Tele-health. According to these principles, psychologists would be required to follow the basic ethical policies of confidentiality, informed consent, and integrity as prescribed by the APA (American Psychological Association) Ethics Code (Reed, McLaughlin, & Milholland, 2000). Questions remain regarding interstate and international licensing conflicts for psychologists and the lack of consumer protection against those practicing without any license at all.

Why Would Anyone Want to Use an Online Counselor?

The Internet and other electronic forms of therapy may sometimes be more effective than traditional therapy. For example, Enid M. Hunkeler and her colleagues (2000) found that depressed patients who received standard care as well as weekly phone calls from health professionals were significantly more likely to show improvement in their depressive symptoms than were patients who did not receive such calls. In another study, Andrew Winzelberg and his colleagues (2000) evaluated an Internet-based program designed for college students with eating disorders and found a significant improvement

in body image and a decrease in drive for thinness.

Studies have long shown that success rates for both physical and mental health are improved with increased contact between patients and their health care providers. Electronic forms of therapy may be the easiest and most cost-effective way of increasing this contact (Schopp, John-stone, & Merrell, 2000). Online clients appreciate having increased access to their therapist, especially during times of crisis. Clients also tend to feel safer discussing sensitive topics in the privacy of their own homes.

On the other hand, critics claim that online therapy is a contradiction in terms — an oxymoron. They say psychotherapy is based on both verbal and nonverbal communication, and it's impossible for online therapists to adequately give therapeutic advice to clients without face-to-face contact. Others are concerned about sending private and confidential thoughts into unsecured cyberspace to a person who may not be a qualified therapist (e.g., Bloom, 1998). David Nickelson, director of technology policy and projects for the American Psychological Association (APA), advises people to first seek face-to-face therapy. "We still need research," Nickelson says, "and it may find that there are just some things therapists and their patients can't do over the Internet" (http://www.apa.org/practice/pf/aug97/tele-heal.html).

Finding a Therapist

If you have time (and the money) to explore options, it is important to "shop around" for a therapist best suited to your specific goals. Consulting your psychology instructor or college counseling system for referrals can be an important first step. However, if you are in a crisis — suicidal thoughts, failing grades, or the victim of abuse — get help fast (Beutler, Shurkin, Bongar, & Gray, 2000; First, Pincus, Frances, 1999). Most communities have telephone hotlines that provide counseling on a 24-hour basis, and most colleges and universities have counseling centers that provide immediate, short-term therapy to students free of charge.

If you are encouraging someone to get therapy, you might offer to help locate a therapist and to go with them for their first visit. If he or she refuses help and the problem affects you, it is often a good idea to seek therapy yourself. You will gain insights and skills that will help you deal with the situation more effectively.

Achievement
GENDER & CULTURAL DIVERSITY

Cultural Variations and the Special Needs of Women in Therapy

All the therapies we have described in this section are based on Western European and American culture. Does this mean they are unique? Or do our psychotherapists do some of the same things that, say, a native healer or shaman does? That is, are there cultural similarities in therapy? Conversely, are there fundamental cultural differences between therapies? Finally, there is the matter of women in therapy: Do women have special needs? Let's take up these issues one at a time.

Cultural Similarities

When we look at therapies in all cultures, we find certain key features in common (Hendrickson, 2002; Jennings & Skovholt, 1999; Matsumoto, 2000; Corey, 2001b). Richard Brislin (1993) has summarized some of these features:

1. *Naming the problem.* One important step toward improving psychological functioning is labeling the problem. People often feel better just by knowing that others experience their problem and that the therapist has had experience with their particular problem.

2. *Qualities of the therapist.* Clients must feel the therapist is caring, competent, approachable, and concerned with finding solutions to their problem.

3. *Establishing credibility.* Word-of-mouth testimonials and status symbols (such as diplomas on the wall) establish the therapist's credibility. Among native healers, in lieu of diplomas, credibility may be established by having served as an apprentice to a revered healer.

4. *Placing the problem in a familiar framework.* If the client believes evil spirits cause psychological disorders, the therapist will direct treatment toward these spirits. Similarly, if the client believes in the importance of early childhood experiences and the unconscious mind, psychoanalysis will be the likely treatment of choice.

5. *Applying techniques to bring relief.* In all cultures, therapy involves action. Either the client or the therapist must do something. Moreover, what they do must fit the client's expectations. For example, the person who believes evil spirits possess him or her expects the shaman to perform a ceremony to expel the demons. In the Western European and American model, clients expect to reveal their thoughts and feelings and provide background information. This "talk therapy" may also have biological or behavioral components, but people who seek therapy generally expect to talk about their problem.

6. *A special time and place.* The fact that therapy occurs outside the client's everyday experiences seems to be an important feature of all therapies. People apparently need to set aside a special time and go to a special place to concentrate on their problems.

Cultural Differences

Although there are basic similarities in therapies across cultures, there are also important differences. In the traditional Western European and American model, clients are encouraged toward self-awareness, self-fulfillment, self-actualization, and modifying self-behavior. The emphasis is on the "self" and on independence and control over one's life — qualities that are highly valued in individualistic cultures. When we look at therapies in collectivist cultures, however, the focus is on interdependence and accepting the realities of one's life (Sue & Sue, 2002).

Japanese *Naikan* therapy is a good example of a collectivist culture's approach to psychological disorders. In *Naikan* therapy, the patient sits quietly from 5:30 A.M. to 9 P.M. for 7 days and is visited by an interviewer every 90 minutes. During this time, the patient is instructed to look at his or her relationships with others from three perspectives: *care received* (recollect and examine the care and kindness you have received from others), *repayment* (recall what you have done to repay the care and kindness of others), and *troubles caused* (think about the troubles and worries you have caused others) (Berry, Poortinga, Segall, & Dasen, 1992).

The goals of *Naikan* therapy are to discover personal guilt for having been ungrateful and troublesome to others and to develop gratitude toward those who have helped the patient. When these goals are attained, the person will have a better self-image and interpersonal attitude.

As you can see, there are pronounced differences between *Naikan* therapy goals and methods and the therapies we have described in this section. Culture affects not only the types of therapy that are developed, it also influences the perceptions of the therapist. For this reason, recognizing cultural differences is very important for building trust between therapists and clients and for effecting behavioral change. Clinicians who work with clients from different cultural backgrounds should learn about their clients' cultures as well as become more aware of their own cultural and ethnic-based values and beliefs (Fuertes & Gelso, 2001; Paniagua, 1998).

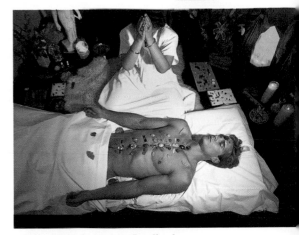

Alternative therapies. In all cultures, therapy involves specific actions or treatments. In this photo, the therapist is using crystal healing, laying on of stones, and meditation.

Women and Therapy

Not only must therapists be sensitive to their clients' cultural backgrounds but they must also be aware of gender differences. Within individualistic Western culture, men and women present different needs and problems to therapists. For example, compared with men, women are more comfortable and familiar with their emotions, have fewer negative attitudes toward therapy, and are more likely to seek psychological help (Komiya, Good, & Sherrod, 2000). Research has identified five major concerns related to women and psychotherapy (Desai & Jann, 2000; Holtzworth-Munroe, 2000; Reppucci, Woolard, & Fried, 1999; Whitney, Kusznir, & Dixie, 2002).

1. *Rates of diagnosis and treatment of mental disorders.* Research has found that women are diagnosed and treated for mental illness at a much higher rate than men are. Is this because women are "sicker" than men as a group, because they are more willing to admit their problems, or because the categories for illness may be biased against women? More research is needed to answer this question.

2. *Stresses of poverty.* Poverty is an important contributor to stress, and stress is directly related to many psychological disorders. Therefore, women bring special challenges to the therapy situation because of their overrepresentation in the lowest economic groups.

3. *Stresses of multiple roles.* Women today are mothers, wives, homemakers, wage earners, students, and so on. The conflicting demands of their multiple roles often create special stresses.

4. *Stresses of aging.* Aging brings special concerns for women. They live longer than men do, but they also tend to be poorer, less educated, and have more serious health problems. Elderly women primarily with age-related dementia also account for over 70 percent of the chronically mentally ill who live in nursing homes in the United States.

5. *Violence against women.* Rape, violent assault, incest, and sexual harassment all take a harsh toll on women's mental health. With the exception of violent assault, these forms of violence are much more likely to happen to women than to men. These violent acts may lead to depression, insomnia, post-traumatic stress disorders, eating disorders, and other problems.

These five areas of concern are important to therapists who treat women. Therapists must be sensitive to possible connections between clients' problems and their gender and/or culture. Rather than prescribing drugs to relieve depression in women, for example, it may be more appropriate for the therapist to explore ways to relieve the stresses of multiple roles or poverty.

Assessment

CHECK & REVIEW

Issues in Therapy

People believed to be mentally ill and dangerous to themselves or others can be involuntarily committed to mental hospitals for diagnosis and treatment. Abuses of involuntary commitments and other problems associated with state mental hospitals have led many states to practice **deinstitutionalization** — discharging as many patients as possible and discouraging admissions. Community services such as community mental health (CMH) centers try to cope with the problems of deinstitutionalization. Research on the effectiveness of psychotherapy has found that 40 to 80 percent of those who receive treatment are better off than those who do not receive treatment.

Therapies in all cultures share six culturally universal features: naming a problem, qualities of the therapist, establishing credibility, placing the problems in a familiar framework, applying techniques to bring relief, and a special time and place. Important cultural differences in therapies also exist. For example, therapies in individualistic cultures emphasize the self and control over one's life, whereas therapies in collectivist cultures emphasize interdependence. Japan's *Naikan* therapy is a good example of a collectivist culture's therapy.

Therapists must take five considerations into account when treating women clients: higher rate of diagnosis and treatment of mental disorders, stresses of poverty, stresses of multiple roles, stresses of aging, and violence against women.

Questions

1. The policy of discharging as many people as possible from state hospitals and discouraging admissions is called _____. (a) disengagement; (b) reinstitutionalization; (c) maladaptive restructuring; (d) deinstitutionalization
2. Name the six features of therapy that are culturally universal.
3. A Japanese therapy designed to help clients develop personal guilt for having been ungrateful and troublesome to others and to develop gratitude toward those who have helped them is known as _____. (a) *Kyoto* therapy; (b) *Okado* therapy; (c) *Naikan* therapy; (d) *Nissan* therapy
4. What are the five major concerns about women in therapy?

Answers to Questions can be found in Appendix B.

MODULE 45   ACTIVE LEARNING WORKSHEET

Completing the following exercise may help provide insight to your own or your friends' lives, as well as, greater understanding of the material in this section.

1. Therapy has six features that are common across all cultures. List them here:

_____
_____
_____

2. Of these six features, which element do you think is most beneficial in helping people change? Why?

_____
_____
_____

3. Which is the least helpful? Why?

_____
_____
_____

4. Considering the 5 major concerns related to women and psychotherapy, which area of concern do you consider most important? Why?

_____
_____
_____

To assess your understanding of the **Key Terms** in this section, write a definition for each (in your own words), and then compare your definitions with those in the text.

biomedical therapy (p. 555)
psychotherapy (p. 555)

Therapy Essentials
eclectic approach (p. 557)

Biomedical Therapies
antianxiety drugs (p. 561)
antidepressant drugs (p. 561)
antipsychotic drugs (p. 561)
drug therapy (p. 560)
electroconvulsive therapy (ECT) (p. 562)
lobotomy (p. 562)
psychosurgery (p. 562)

Psychoanalysis/Psychodynamic Therapies
catharsis (p. 566)

free association (p. 567)
interpretation (p. 567)
psychoanalysis (p. 566)
psychodynamic therapy (p. 569)
resistance (p. 567)
transference (p. 567)

Cognitive and Humanistic Therapies
active listening (p. 574)
client-centered therapy (p. 573)
cognitive-behavior therapy (p. 571)
cognitive restructuring (p. 571)
cognitive therapy (p. 570)
empathy (p. 573)
genuineness (p. 574)
humanistic therapy (p. 573)
rational-emotive therapy (RET) (p. 571)

self-talk (p. 570)
unconditional positive regard (p. 574)

Behavior Therapies
aversion therapy (p. 578)
behavior therapy (p. 576)
modeling therapy (p. 580)
systematic desensitization (p. 577)

Group and Family Therapies
deinstitutionalization (p. 585)
family therapy (p. 582)
group therapy (p. 581)
self-help group (p. 581)

Huffman Book Companion Site
http://www.wiley.com/college/huffman
This site is loaded with free Interactive Self-Tests, Internet Exercises, Glossary and Flashcards for key terms, Web links, Handbook for Non-Native Speakers, and other activities designed to improve your mastery of the material in this section.

Interested in more information on types of therapy?
http://www.grohol.com/therapy.htm
This web site offers a brief overview of four major therapies: psychodynamic/psychoanalytic, cognitive-behavioral/behavioral, humanistic/existential, and eclectic.

Want help finding a therapist?
http://www.helping.apa.org/brochure/index.html
Sponsored by the American Psychological Association (APA), this web site provides general information on psychotherapy, and advice on how to choose a psychotherapist. If you want more information, try www.psychologytoday.com. The home-page of Psychology Today magazine, this web site features the most commonly asked questions in selecting a therapist, help locating a therapist, as well as individual consultations with an expert on-line.

Interested in online therapy?
http://www.counselingnet.com/
Sponsored by Counseling Net, this web site provides free online counseling services for relationship, marital, sexual,

personal, and career problems. Also try, http://netpsych.com/. (Keep in mind the information and warnings regarding electronic therapy discussed in the Research Highlight for this section.)

Want more detailed information about a specific problem and its treatment?
http://www.apa.org/science/lib.html
Created by the American Psychological Association (APA), this Web site offers articles, books, library searches, and links for all the disorders listed in the DSM-IV-TR. If you'd like additional information, try http://www.mentalhealth.com/p20-grp.html. Sponsored by The Internet Mental Health group, this site provides a wealth of resources and information about all the major disorders, including description, diagnosis, treatment, research, and recommended booklets. Also try, http://www.mhsource.com/. Designed primarily for mental health professionals, this web site offers valuable resources and links to specific disorders, their causes, diagnosis, and treatment.

Want help with a substance abuse disorder?
http://www.health.org/
The National Clearinghouse for Alcohol and Drug Information sponsors this site, which provides numerous links to the prevention and treatment of substance abuse. For even more information, try http://www.drugnet.net/metaview.htm. This web site offers a wealth of information and links to resources around the globe.

VISUAL SUMMARY

Therapy
(Modules 42, 43, 44, and 45)

Major Forms of Psychotherapy

- **Psychotherapy:** Various approaches to improving psychological functioning and promoting adjustment to life.
- **Eclectic approach:** Borrows from all forms of therapy.

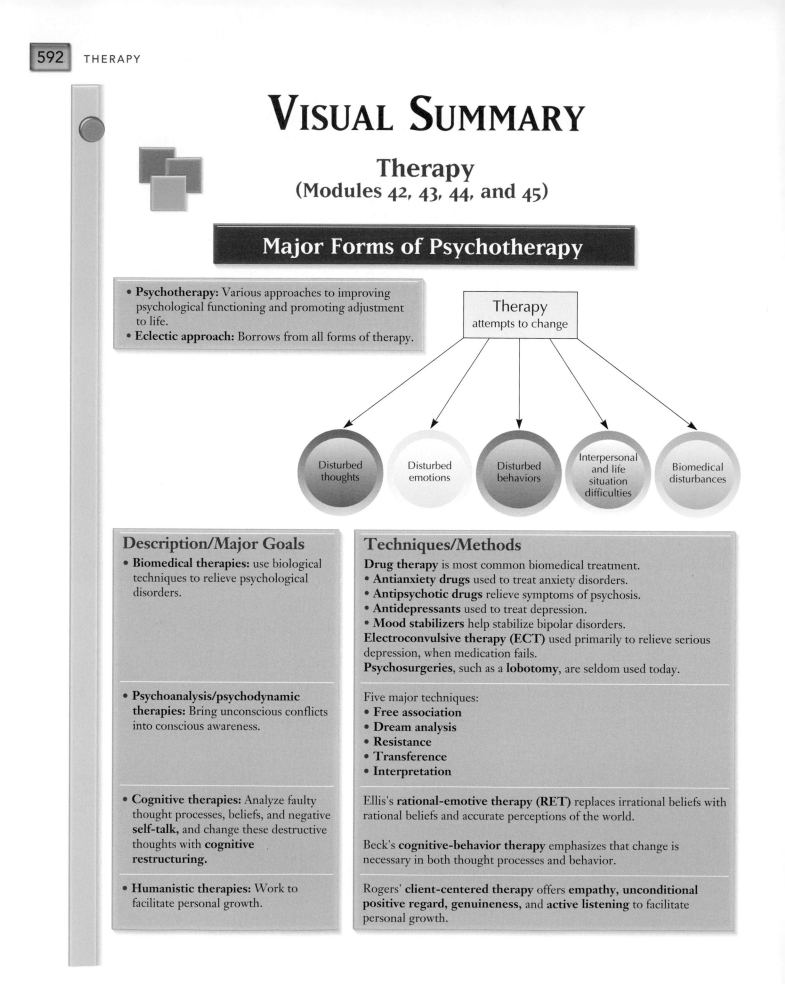

Therapy attempts to change

- Disturbed thoughts
- Disturbed emotions
- Disturbed behaviors
- Interpersonal and life situation difficulties
- Biomedical disturbances

Description/Major Goals

- **Biomedical therapies:** use biological techniques to relieve psychological disorders.

- **Psychoanalysis/psychodynamic therapies:** Bring unconscious conflicts into conscious awareness.

- **Cognitive therapies:** Analyze faulty thought processes, beliefs, and negative **self-talk,** and change these destructive thoughts with **cognitive restructuring.**

- **Humanistic therapies:** Work to facilitate personal growth.

Techniques/Methods

Drug therapy is most common biomedical treatment.
- **Antianxiety drugs** used to treat anxiety disorders.
- **Antipsychotic drugs** relieve symptoms of psychosis.
- **Antidepressants** used to treat depression.
- **Mood stabilizers** help stabilize bipolar disorders.

Electroconvulsive therapy (ECT) used primarily to relieve serious depression, when medication fails.

Psychosurgeries, such as a **lobotomy,** are seldom used today.

Five major techniques:
- **Free association**
- **Dream analysis**
- **Resistance**
- **Transference**
- **Interpretation**

Ellis's **rational-emotive therapy (RET)** replaces irrational beliefs with rational beliefs and accurate perceptions of the world.

Beck's **cognitive-behavior therapy** emphasizes that change is necessary in both thought processes and behavior.

Rogers' **client-centered therapy** offers **empathy, unconditional positive regard, genuineness,** and **active listening** to facilitate personal growth.

Major Forms of Psychotherapy (cont.)

Description/Major Goals

- **Behavior therapies:** Use learning principles to eliminate maladaptive behaviors and substitute healthy ones.

- **Group therapies:** Several clients meet with one or more therapists to resolve personal problems.

- **Family therapies:** Work to change maladaptive family interaction patterns.

Techniques/Methods

Classical conditioning techniques include **systematic desensitization** (client replaces anxiety with relaxation) and **aversion therapy** (an aversive stimulus is paired with a maladaptive behavior).
Operant conditioning techniques include shaping, reinforcement, punishment, extinction, and **modeling therapy** (clients watch and imitate positive role models).

Provide group support, feedback, information, and opportunities for behavior rehearsal.
Self-help groups (like Alcoholics Anonymous) are sometimes considered group therapy, but professional therapists do not conduct them.

Sees family as a system of interdependent parts; therefore treats all members.

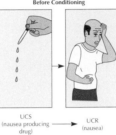  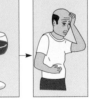

Before Conditioning	During Conditioning	After Conditioning
UCS (nausea producing drug) → UCR (nausea)	UCS (drug) + Neutral Stimulus (alcoholic drink) → UCR (nausea)	CS (alcoholic drink without drug) → CR (nausea)

Issues in Therapy

Institutionalization

- People believed to be mentally ill and dangerous to themselves or others can be involuntarily committed to mental hospitals for diagnosis and treatment.
- Abuses of involuntary commitment and other problems led to **deinstitutionalization** — discharging as many patients as possible and discouraging admissions.
- Community services such as Community Mental Health (CMH) centers offset some problems of deinstitutionalization.

Seeking Therapy

- Forty to 80 percent of those who receive treatment are better off than those who do not.
- Take time to "shop around," but a crisis requires immediate help.
- If others' problems affect you, get help yourself.

Cultural Issues

- Common features of therapy in all cultures: naming a problem, qualities of the therapist, establishing credibility, placing the problems in a familiar framework, applying techniques to bring relief, and a special time and place.
- Differences in therapy between cultures: Individualistic cultures emphasize the "self" and control over one's life. However, therapies in collectivist cultures, like Japan's Naikan therapy, emphasize interdependence.

Women in Therapy

Higher rate of diagnosis and treatment of mental disorders, stresses of poverty, stresses of multiple roles, stresses of aging, and violence against women.

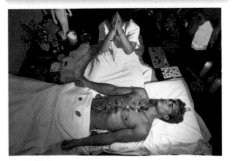

SOCIAL PSYCHOLOGY

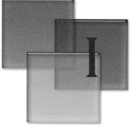

I magine you are one of several people responding to an ad in the local newspaper calling for volunteers for a study on memory. As you arrive at the Yale University laboratory, you are introduced to the experimenter and another participant in the study. The experimenter explains he is studying the effects of punishment on learning and memory. One of you will play the role of the learner and the other will be the teacher. You draw lots, and on your paper is written, "teacher." The experimenter leads you into a room where he straps the other participant — the "learner" — into an "electric chair" apparatus that looks escape-proof. The experimenter then applies electrode paste to the learner's wrist "to avoid blisters and burns" and attaches an electrode that is connected to a shock generator.

You, the "teacher," are shown into an adjacent room and asked to sit in front of this same shock generator, which is wired through the wall to the chair of the learner. As you can see in Figure 46.1, the shock machine consists of 30 switches representing successively higher levels of shock in 15-volt increments. Written labels appear below each group of levers, ranging from Slight Shock to Danger: Severe Shock, all the way to XXX. The experimenter explains it is your job to teach the learner a list of word pairs and to punish any errors by administering a shock. With each wrong answer, you are to give a shock one level

▪ Achievement
▪ Assessment
▪ Application

higher on the shock generator. For example, at the first wrong response, you give a shock of 15 volts; at the second wrong response, 30 volts; and so on.

As the study begins, the learner seems to be having problems with the task. The responses are often wrong. Before long, you are inflicting shocks that must be extremely painful. Indeed, after you administer 150 volts, the learner begins to protest and demands, "Get me out of here. ... I refuse to go on."

You hesitate and wonder what to do. The experimenter asks you to continue. He insists that even if the learner refuses, you must keep increasing the shock levels. But the other person is obviously in pain. What should you do?

Actual participants in this series of studies suffered real conflict and distress when confronted with this problem. The following dialogue took place between the experimenter and one of the "teachers" (Milgram, 1974, pp. 73–74):

TEACHER: I can't stand it. I'm not going to kill that man in there. You hear him hollering?

EXPERIMENTER: As I told you before, the shocks may be painful, but [there is no permanent tissue damage].

LEARNER (screaming): Let me out of here, you have no right to keep me here. Let me out of here, let me out, my heart's starting to bother me, let me out! (Teacher shakes head, pats the table nervously.)

TEACHER: You see, he's hollering. Hear that? Gee, I don't know.

EXPERIMENTER: The experiment requires...

TEACHER (interrupting): I know it does, sir, but I mean — huh! He don't know what he's getting in for. He's up to 195 volts!

(Following this exchange, the teacher continues through 210 volts, 225 volts, 240 volts, 255 volts, and 270 volts, at which point the teacher, with evident relief, runs out of word-pair questions.)

EXPERIMENTER: You'll have to go back to the beginning of that page and go through them again until he's learned them all correctly.

TEACHER: Aw, no, I'm not going to kill that man. You mean I've got to keep going up with the scale? No, sir. He's hollering in there. I'm not going to give him 450 volts.

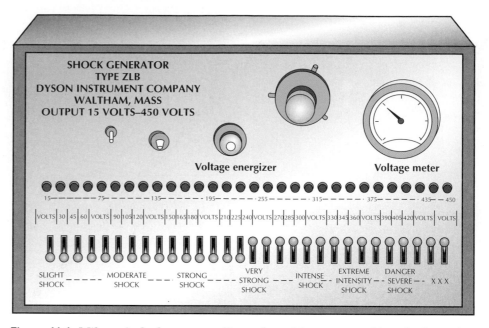

Figure 46.1 *Milgram's shock generator.* Research participants were told to give increasing levels of shocks to someone they had watched being strapped down and connected to this machine. Note how the shock levels are clearly labeled, starting with *Slight Shock*, moving to *Very Strong Shock, Danger, Severe Shock*, and ultimately *XXX*. How would you respond? Would you refuse from the beginning, or would you stop after a few shocks and complaints from the recipient? Would you go all the way to 450 volts?

What do you think happened? Did the man continue? This particular "teacher" continued giving shocks — despite the learner's strong protests. He even continued after the learner refused to give any more answers.

As you might have guessed, this was not a study of punishment and learning. The psychologist who designed the study, Stanley Milgram, was actually investigating *obedience to authority*. Would participants see the experimenter as an authority figure and obey his prompts and commands to shock another human being?

Would you, or others you know, have followed the experimenter's demands in this same situation? In Milgram's public survey, less than 25 percent thought they would go beyond 150 volts. And not one respondent predicted they would go past the 300-volt level. Surprisingly, a full 65 *percent* of the teacher-participants obeyed completely — going all the way to the end of the scale. Even Milgram was surprised.

It is important to recognize that *no* participant-learner ever received an actual shock. The "learner" was an accomplice of the experimenter and simply *pretended* to be shocked. However, the "teachers" were true participants. They believed they were administering real shocks, and they sweated, trembled, stuttered, laughed nervously, and repeatedly protested that they did not want to hurt the learner. They were clearly upset. *But still they obeyed.*

Keep in mind that deception is an important part of some research projects, but Milgram's study would never be undertaken today. The degree of deception and discomfort of the study's participants are now viewed as unethical. Although most par-

Before we begin, test your understanding of social psychology and how it operates in everyday life by answering *true* or *false* to the following statements. Answers are at the end of this activity and expanded explanations are found throughout this section.

1. Groups generally make more conservative decisions than a single individual does.
2. Most people judge others more harshly than they judge themselves.
3. Looks are the primary factor in our initial feelings of attraction, liking, and romantic love.
4. Opposites attract.
5. Romantic love rarely lasts longer than 1 or 2 years.

6. The most effective way to change behavior is to first change the attitude.
7. Prejudice is the same as discrimination.
8. There are positive as well as negative forms of prejudice.
9. Watching a violent sports match or punching a pillow is a good way to release steam and reduce aggression.
10. People are more likely to help another individual when they are alone than when they are in a group.

Answers: 1. False 2. True 3. True 4. False 5. True 6. False 7. False 8. True 9. True 10. True

ticipants *were* visibly upset by the experience, Milgram carefully debriefed everyone after the study and followed up with the participants for several months. Most "teachers" reported the experience as being personally informative and valuable.

Setting aside ethical concerns, one lasting benefit from Milgram's research might be its invaluable insight into human social behavior. For example, many believe only "monsters" would have followed Hitler's commands to torture and kill millions of Jews during World War II, but Milgram's research suggests otherwise. Milgram revealed the conditions that breed obedience, as well as the extent to which "normal" people will obey an authority. As philosopher Hannah Arendt has suggested, the horrifying, thing about the Nazis was not that they were so deviant but that they were so "terrifyingly normal."

Our combination of confusion and fascination over social behaviors like those in Milgram's study is what draws many students and researchers to the field of **social psychology.** Social psychologists study how other people influence our thoughts, feelings, and actions. They explore both the bizarre and the ordinary, from the mindless obedience of religious cults to prejudice, aggression, and attraction. Using the tools of science (experiments, surveys, case studies, self-report, and so on), they seek scientific answers to *social* questions.

Because almost everything we do is social, the subject matter is enormous and varied. We will therefore approach our study by looking at each component of the definition in turn. We begin by exploring topics related to *our thoughts about others* (attribution and attitudes). Next, we examine *our feelings toward others* by looking at prejudice, discrimination, and interpersonal attraction. (Prejudice and discrimination could also be discussed under thoughts or actions. But we consider it under feelings because negative emotions are the central defining characteristic of prejudice.) We conclude with a look at *our actions toward others* (social influence, group processes, aggression, and altruism).

Social Psychology *The study of how other people influence our thoughts, feelings, and actions*

MODULE 46
OUR THOUGHTS ABOUT OTHERS

Assessment

How do our thoughts affect how we explain and judge others?

How could a mother brutalize and torture her child? Why would someone run into a burning building to rescue a stranger? Why did Chris stop going out with me? Trying to understand the world around us often means trying to understand other people's behavior. We look for reasons and explanations for others' behavior (the process of attribution). We also develop thoughts and beliefs (attitudes) about others.

Attribution: Explaining Other's Behavior

How do we explain people's obedience in Milgram's study? When we offer an explanation for behavior, we *attribute* it to something — "the participants were weakwilled," "the experimenter was intimidating," and so on. Psychologists use the term **attribution** to describe statements explaining why people do what they do.

After studying how people explain others' behavior, Fritz Heider (1958) noted that most people begin with a basic question: Does the behavior stem mainly from the person's internal *disposition* or from the external *situation*? If you concluded that participants in Milgram's study acted because of their own personal characteristics, motives, and intentions, you would be making a *dispositional attribution*. On the other hand, if you decided they responded to situational demands and environmental pressures, you would be making a *situational attribution*.

Attribution *Principles used to judge the causes of events, and our own and others' behavior*

Mistaken Attributions

The choice between disposition and situation is central to accurate judgments of why people do what they do. Unfortunately, our attributions are frequently marred by two major errors: the *fundamental attribution error* and the *self-serving bias*.

Fundamental attribution error (FAE) *Misjudging the causes of others' behavior because of overestimating internal personal factors and underestimating external situational influences*

Saliency Bias *Tendency to focus on the most noticeable (salient) factors when explaining the causes of behavior*

1. *The fundamental attribution error — judging the behavior of others.* When we recognize and take into account environmental influences on behavior, we generally make accurate attributions. However, given that people have enduring personality traits (Module 33) and a tendency to take cognitive shortcuts (Module 22), we more often choose dispositional attributions — we blame the person. This bias toward personal, dispositional factors rather than environmental factors is so common in individualistic cultures that it is called the **fundamental attribution error (FAE)** (Fernandez-Dols, 2002; Klein & Licata, 2001; Nisbett, Peng, Choi, & Norenzayan, 2000).

For example, noting that your instructor seems relaxed and talkative in front of the class, you would probably decide that he or she is an extroverted and outgoing person — a *dispositional attribution*. However, outside of class you may be surprised to find him or her shy and awkward on a one-on-one basis or at a party. Similarly, most students think participants in the Milgram study were "weak-willed" and that they would never act like that in the same situation. They blame the person (dispositional attribution) and overlook and underestimate the power of the environment (situational attribution).

Social psychology in action. Can you imagine how Western television programs might affect the thoughts, feelings, and actions of these viewers?

Why do we tend to jump to internal, personal explanations? There are several possible explanations for why we tend to make dispositional rather than situational attributions. The most important reason may be that human personalities and behaviors are more salient (or noticeable) than situational factors. This **saliency bias** helps explain why we focus on participants in Milgram's study versus the situation

VISUAL QUIZ

PEANUTS; drawings by Charles Schulz; 1989 United Features Syndicate, Inc. Reprinted by permission of UFS, Inc.

Can you use terms from this module to explain this cartoon?

Answer: Lucy's criticism of Linus may be the result of the fundamental attribution error, whereas her overlooking of her own faults may be the self-serving bias.

itself. It also explains why people often blame welfare recipients for their joblessness. This type of *blaming the victim* also reflects the fact that large situational factors leading to poverty and joblessness generally are not concrete and conspicuous.

2. ***The self-serving bias — judging our own behavior.*** When we judge others' behavior, we tend to emphasize internal personality factors over external situational causes. But when we explain our own behavior, we favor internal personal attributions for our *successes* and external environmental attributions for our *failures*. This **self-serving bias** is motivated by a desire to maintain our self-esteem, as well as a desire to look good to others (Campbell & Sedikides, 1999; Higgins & Bhatt, 2001; Louie, Curren, & Harich, 2000).

Students who do well on an exam, for instance, often take personal credit ("I really studied" or "I'm smart"). If they fail the test, however, they tend to blame the instructor, the textbook, or the "tricky" questions. Similarly, studies find both partners in divorced couples are more likely to see themselves as the victim, to rate themselves as less responsible for the breakup, and as being more willing to reconcile (Gray & Silver, 1990).

Self-Serving Bias *Taking credit for our successes and externalizing our failures*

Culture and Attributional Biases

Both the FAE and the self-serving bias may depend in part on cultural factors (Matsumoto, 2000). Do you recall the two brutal and widely publicized mass murders in New York City during the 1990s? An intriguing study was conducted that compared all the articles published in the *New York Times* about these murders, with all the same articles in the *World Journal*, a Chinese-language newspaper also published in New York City. Interestingly, they found that the *Times* articles emphasized personality characteristics of the murderers (their traits, attitudes, mental disorders, etc.), whereas the Chinese newspaper focused on situational influences (their living conditions, family and social relationships, etc.).

This and other research shows that Westerners are more likely to make the FAE because of the cultural belief that individuals are responsible for their own actions. However, in most Eastern countries, people are more group oriented and tend to be more aware of situational constraints on behavior (Nisbett, Peng, Choi, & Norenzayan, 2000; Norenzayan & Nisbett, 2000). If you were watching a baseball game in China and the umpire made a bad call, as a Westerner you would probably make a personality attribution ("He's a lousy umpire"), whereas a Chinese spectator would tend to make a situational attribution ("He's under pressure").

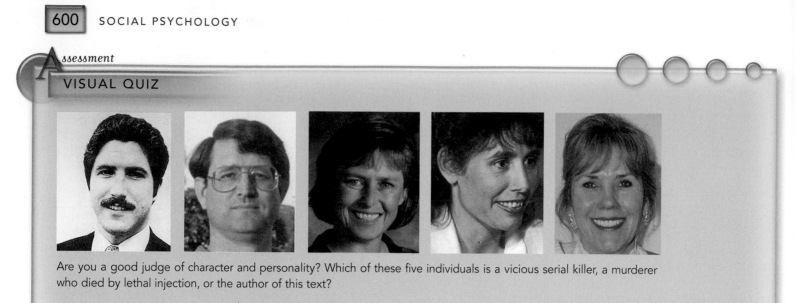

Are you a good judge of character and personality? Which of these five individuals is a vicious serial killer, a murderer who died by lethal injection, or the author of this text?

Answer: Photo 1: Ken Bianchi, rapist and serial killer; photo 4: Karla Faye Tucker, an executed murderer; photo 5: Karen Huffman, author of this text.

Like the FAE, the self-serving bias is also much less common in Eastern nations. In Japan, for instance, the ideal person is someone who is aware of his or her shortcomings and continually works to overcome them — not someone who, thinks highly of himself or herself (Heine & Renshaw, 2002). In the East, where people do not define themselves as much in terms of their individual accomplishments, self-esteem is not related to doing better than others. Rather, fitting in and not standing out from the group is stressed. As the Japanese proverb says, "The nail that sticks up gets pounded down."

This emphasis on group relations in Asian cultures is also true of many Native Americans. For example, when the Wintun Native Americans originally described being with a close relation or intimate friend, they would not say, for example, "Linda and I," but rather, "Linda we" (Lee, 1950). This attachment to community relations instead of individual *selfhood* often seems strange to contemporary Western, individualist societies. But it remains common in collectivist cultures (Markus & Kitayama, 1998).

▌Attitudes: Our Learned Predispositions Toward Others

Attitude *Learned predisposition to respond cognitively, affectively, and behaviorally to a particular object*

An **attitude** is a learned predisposition to respond cognitively, affectively, and behaviorally to a particular object in a particular way. The object can be anything from pizza to people, from diseases to drugs, from abortion to psychology.

Components of Attitudes

Social psychologists generally agree that most attitudes have three components (Figure 46.2): cognitive, affective, and behavioral. The *cognitive component* consists of thoughts and beliefs, such as "Marijuana is a relatively safe drug" or "The dangers of marijuana are greatly underestimated." The *affective*, or *emotional*, *component* involves feelings, such as frustration that our legal system has not legalized marijuana yet or, conversely, that it seems to even consider legalization.

The *behavioral component* consists of a *predisposition* to act in certain ways toward an attitude object. For example, someone who held a positive attitude toward marijuana might write to textbook authors and publishers complaining that we are too critical in our discussion of drugs in Module 15. Someone with a negative attitude, on the other hand, might write to complain that even the use of marijuana as an example could encourage its use.

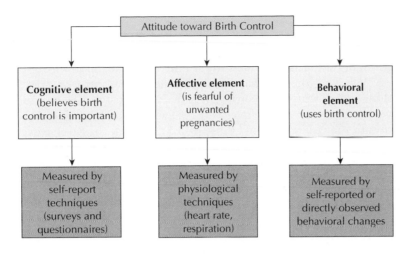

Figure 46.2 *Three components of all attitudes.* When social psychologists study attitudes, they measure each of the three components — cognitive, affective, and behavioral.

Attitude Change Through Cognitive Dissonance

You are not born with your attitudes — they are learned. From earliest childhood, you began forming your attitudes through direct experience (eating pizza) and through indirect observation (listening to your parents discuss social issues). Although attitudes begin in early childhood, they are not permanent. Politicians spend millions of dollars on campaigns because they know attitudes can be shaped and manipulated throughout the entire life span.

Attitude change often results from persuasive appeals (such as TV ads like "Friends Don't Let Friends Drive Drunk"). But an even more efficient method is by creating cognitive dissonance, a perceived discrepancy between an attitude and a behavior or between an attitude and a new piece of information (D'Alessio & Allen, 2002; Stone & Cooper, 2001; Van Overwalle & Jordens, 2002). According to Leon Festinger (1957), who developed **cognitive dissonance theory,** we are highly motivated to change our attitudes when we notice a discrepancy because it creates a state of psychological tension similar to anxiety. Just as the discomfort of being hungry motivates us to find food, the discomfort or tension of cognitive dissonance motivates us to adjust our thinking to eliminate the discrepancy and the accompanying tension (Figure 46.3).

Picture yourself in this situation. You, as an individual who strongly objects to racist and sexist remarks, must give a speech in favor of the Ku Klux Klan (KKK). How do you think this would affect your attitudes? Do you think you would feel more or less favorable toward the KKK afterward?

This is the type of question that led to an original cognitive dissonance experiment conducted by Leon Festinger and J. Merrill Carlsmith (1959). Students selected as participants were given excruciatingly boring tasks for an hour. The experimenters told them that this was a simple performance test, but the actual purpose was to create a negative attitude toward the task. After finishing the task, participants were approached by the experimenter and asked for a favor. The experimenter asked if they would serve as research assistants and tell the next "participant" (who was really a con-

Cognitive Dissonance Theory *Festinger's theory that when we discover inconsistencies between our attitudes, or between our attitudes and behaviors, we experience discomfort and tension, which drives us to make attitudinal changes to restore harmony or consistency*

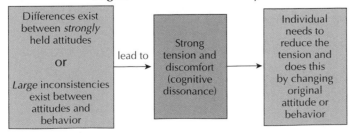

Figure 46.3 *Cognitive dissonance theory.* When differences exist between our strongly held attitudes, or when there are large inconsistencies between our attitudes and behavior, we experience discomfort (*dissonance*) and a need to change either the attitude or the behavior.

federate of the experiment) that the task was "very enjoyable" and "fun." Sometimes the person was offered $1 for helping and sometimes $20. If the person lied to the incoming participant and was paid, he or she was then led to another room and asked about his or her true feelings toward the experimental tasks.

What do you think happened after the participants were coaxed into doing something (lying) that was inconsistent with their actual experiences and attitudes? Would you predict that the people who received $20 for lying would feel more positive toward the task than would those paid $1? In fact, the reverse occurred.

Can you explain this?   Cognitive dissonance theory is essentially a *drive-reduction theory* (Module 31). People have a strong need to feel that their attitudes are in sync with one another and that their attitudes and behavior are consistent. When this harmony is disrupted, people feel distressed; they feel a drive to reduce the dissonance or conflict between their beliefs. Festinger believed that this distress *(dissonance)*, like the feeling of hunger, is unpleasant and that people are strongly motivated to reduce or eliminate it. To relieve the distress and restore balance, we must change either our attitude or behavior.

In the boring task experiment, participants faced a mismatch between their attitude toward the experiment ("That was boring") and their behavior ("I told another participant it was interesting"). To relieve the resulting tension, they changed their original attitude from boredom to "I enjoyed the task."

The reason that the "$1 participants" showed more attitude change was because they experienced a greater amount of cognitive dissonance than did the "$20 participants." Participants who received only $1 either had to change their attitude toward the task or acknowledge they had lied rather cheaply. Because they could not deny they had lied, they changed their attitude.

In contrast, participants who were paid $20 did not need to change their attitude as much because they could readily explain their behavior in terms of the payment ($20 was a considerable amount in the late 1950s). Being paid well for their actions helped relieve the logical inconsistency (the cognitive dissonance) between what they truly believed about the boring task and what they told others. In contrast, the participants who received $1 had *insufficient justification* for lying to another participant and had more motivation to change their attitude to "The task wasn't so boring after all."

Assessment

VISUAL QUIZ

This family has just purchased this new home. Using cognitive dissonance theory, can you predict whether they will like this house more or less after they move in?

Answer: Because moving to a new home involves a great deal of effort and money, the family will need to justify their decision. By focusing only on the positives, they will reduce their cognitive dissonance (and increase their liking of their new home).

Culture and Dissonance

The experience of cognitive dissonance may not be the same in other cultures. It may presume a particular way of thinking about and evaluating the self that is distinctively Western. As noted in earlier modules, North Americans are highly individualistic and independent. For them, making a bad choice or decision has strong, negative effects on self-esteem and a greater motivation for attitude change because we believe this bad choice reflects somehow on our worth as an individual.

Asians, on the other hand, tend to be much more collectivist and interdependent. Consequently, they feel more tension over a potential loss of connection with others than with a threat to their individual self-esteem. Research comparing Japanese and other Asian samples with Canadian and U.S. participants supports this position (Choi & Nisbett, 2000; Markus & Kitayama, 1998).

Assessment

CHECK & REVIEW

Our Thoughts About Others

We explain people's behavior (make **attributions**) by determining whether their actions resulted from internal factors (their own traits and motives) or external factors (the situation). Attribution is subject to several forms of error and bias. **Fundamental attribution error** is the tendency to overestimate internal personality influences when judging the behavior of others. When we explain our own behavior, however, we tend to attribute positive outcomes to internal factors and negative outcomes to external causes **(self-serving bias).**

Attitudes are learned predispositions toward a particular object. Three components of all attitudes are the cognitive responses (thoughts and beliefs), affective responses (feelings), and behavioral tendencies (predispositions to actions). We sometimes change our attitudes because of **cognitive dissonance,** a state of tension or anxiety we feel when two or more attitudes contradict each other or when our attitudes do not match our behaviors. This mismatch and resulting tension motivate us to change our attitude or behavior to restore balance.

Questions

1. The principles people follow in making judgments about the causes of events, others' behavior, and their own behavior are known as _____. (a) impression management; (b) stereotaxic determination; (c) attribution; (d) person perception

2. What is the fundamental attribution error?

3. After hearing about the "shocking" behavior of participants in Stanley Milgram's experiment, most people strongly believe they would have acted differently and easily remember instances in which they have refused to obey others. This may be an example of _____. (a) cognitive dissonance; (b) groupthink; (c) the illusion of invulnerability; (d) the self-serving bias

4. According to _____ theory, people are motivated to change their attitudes because of tension created by a mismatch between two or more competing attitudes or between their attitudes and behavior.

Answers to Questions can be found in Appendix B.

ACTIVE LEARNING WORKSHEET   MODULE 46

Circle either "T" for true or "F" for false, and then compare your answers with those in Appendix B.

1. The tendency to overestimate internal personality factors and underestimate external situational factors is known as the self-serving bias. T or F
2. The tendency to focus on the most noticeable factors when explaining the causes of behavior is known as the saliency bias. T or F
3. The fact that husbands and wives both think they're doing more than their share of household tasks is known as the fundamental attribution error. T or F
4. Both the fundamental attribution error and the self-serving bias are less common in Eastern nations. T or F
5. One of the most efficient ways to change attitudes is through the creation of cognitive dissonance. T or F

MODULE 47
OUR FEELINGS ABOUT OTHERS

Assessment

What feelings are most important in our social interactions?

Prejudice *A learned, generally nega-tive, attitude toward members of a group; it includes thoughts (stereotypes), feelings, and behavioral tendencies (possible dis-crimination)*

Stereotype *A set of beliefs about the characteristics of people in a group that is generalized to all group members; also, the cognitive component of prejudice*

Discrimination *Negative behaviors directed at members of a group*

Figure 47.1 *Prejudice and discrimi-nation.* Note how prejudice can exist without discrimination and vice versa. The only condition in this example without prejudice or discrimination is when someone is given a job simply because he or she is the best candidate.

Having explored our thoughts about others (attribution and attitudes), we now turn our attention to our feelings about others. We begin by examining the negative feel-ings (and thoughts and actions) associated with *prejudice* and *discrimination*. We will then explore the generally positive feelings of *interpersonal attraction*.

■ Prejudice and Discrimination: It's the Feeling That Counts

Prejudice, which literally means *prejudgment*, is a learned, generally *negative* attitude directed toward specific people solely because of their membership in an identified group. Prejudice is not innate. It is learned. It creates enormous problems for its vic-tims, and it also limits the perpetrator's ability to accurately judge others and process information.

Positive forms of prejudice do exist, such as "all women love babies" or "African Americans are natural athletes." However, most research and definitions of prejudice usually focus on the negative forms. (It is also interesting to note that even positive forms of prejudice can be harmful. For example, women might think there must be something wrong with them if they don't like being around babies, or African Ameri-cans might see athletics or entertainment as their major routes to success.)

Like all attitudes, prejudice is composed of three elements: (1) a *cognitive compo-nent* or **stereotype,** thoughts and beliefs held about people strictly because of their membership in a group; (2) an *affective component*, consisting of feelings and emotions associated with objects of prejudice; and (3) a *behavioral component*, consisting of pre-dispositions to act in certain ways toward members of the group (discrimination).

Although the terms *prejudice* and *discrimination* are often used interchangeably, there is an important difference between them. *Prejudice* refers to an *attitude*, whereas **discrimination** refers to *action* (Fiske, 1998). Discrimination often results from prej-udice, but not always (Figure 47.1): People do not always act on their prejudices.

Major Sources of Prejudice and Discrimination

How do prejudice and discrimination originate? Why do they persist? As we explore these questions, you may find your values and beliefs challenged. Use this opportunity to apply your highest critical thinking skills to evaluate your attitudes. We begin with a look at the four most commonly cited sources of prejudice: learning, mental short-cuts, economic and political competition, and displaced aggression.

1. ***Prejudice as a learned response.*** People learn prejudice in the same ways they learn their attitudes toward abortion, divorce, or pizza — through classical and operant conditioning and social learning (Modules 16–18). When chil-dren watch TV and movies and read books and magazines that portray minorities and women in demeaning and stereotypical roles, they learn that such images must be acceptable. When children hear their parents, friends, and teachers expressing prejudice, they imitate them. Exposure of this kind initiates and reinforces the learning of prejudice (Blaine & McElroy, 2002; Durkin & Judge, 2002; Dovidio, Brigham, Johnson, & Gaertner, 1995).

People also learn their prejudices through direct experi-ence. They derogate others and experience a rise in their own self-esteem (Fein & Spencer, 1997). They receive attention and sometimes approval for expressing racist or sexist remarks. Also, they may have a single negative experience with a specific

	Prejudice	
	Yes	**No**
Discrimination — Yes	An African American is *denied* a job because the owner of a business is prejudiced.	An African American is *denied* a job because the owner of a business fears white customers won't buy from an African American salesperson.
Discrimination — No	An African American is *given* a job because the owner of a business hopes to attract African-American customers.	An African American is *given* a job because he or she is the best suited for it.

member of a group that they then generalize and apply to all members of the group (Vidmar, 1997).

2. ***Prejudice as a mental shortcut.*** According to some researchers, prejudice develops as a result of stereotyping, normal thought processes, and everyday attempts to explain a complex social world (Devine & Monteith, 1999; Hehir, 2002; Oliver & Fonash, 2002). Stereotypes (the cognitive component of prejudice) are a by-product of how we cognitively simplify the world through categorization. Stereotyping allows people to make quick judgments about others, thus freeing their mental resources for other activities.

Just as a biologist classifies all living things into categories and mental health professionals classify mental disorders in the *DSM-IV-TR (Diagnostic and Statistical Manual of Mental Disorders*, fourth edition, revised; see Module 37), people use stereotypes to classify others by membership in a specific group ("jocks," "Mexicans," "chicks," and so on). Given that people generally classify themselves as part of the preferred group, they also create ingroups and outgroups.

An *ingroup* is any category that people see themselves belonging to, whereas an *outgroup* consists of all others. People tend to see ingroup members as being more attractive, having better personalities, and engaging in more socially accepted forms of behavior than outgroup members. In other words, cognitively, they practice **ingroup favoritism** (Aboud, 2003; Guimond & Dambrum, 2002; O'Neal, Medlin, Walker, & Jones, 2002).

In addition to ingroup favoritism, people also tend to see more diversity among members of their own ingroup and less among the outgroup (Carpenter & Radhakrisknan, 2002; Hilton & Von Hippel, 1996; Rubin, Hewstone, & Voci, 2001). This "they all look alike to me" tendency is termed the **outgroup homogeneity effect.**

This outgroup homogeneity bias can be particularly dangerous. When members of minority groups are not perceived as varied and complex individuals who have the same needs and feelings as the dominant group, it is easier to perceive them as faceless objects and treat them in discriminatory ways. During the Vietnam War, for example, Asians were labeled "gooks" for whom "life is cheap." Facelessness made it easier to kill large numbers of Vietnamese civilians (Johnson, 1999).

3. ***Prejudice as the result of economic and political competition.*** Still other theorists think prejudice develops out of competition for limited resources and is maintained because it offers significant economic and political advantages to the dominant group (Hughes & Dodge, 1997; Pettigrew, 1998). The competition for resources idea is supported by findings showing lower-class whites in the United States having more racist attitudes than higher-class whites. It may be that the upper class can afford to be less prejudiced because minorities represent less threat to their employment, status, and income. In addition, prejudice is maintained because it serves a function — protecting the interests of the dominant class. The stereotype that blacks are inferior to whites, for example, helps justify a social order in the United States where whites hold disproportionate power.

4. ***Prejudice as a form of displaced aggression.*** Have you ever wondered why lower-class groups tend to blame each other rather than the upper class or the class system itself? As you will see in the section on aggression, frustration often leads people to attack the source of frustration. But when the source is bigger and capable of retaliating, or when the cause of the frustration is ambiguous, people often displace their aggression on an alternative, nonthreatening target. The innocent victim of displaced aggression is known as a *scapegoat*. There is strong historical evidence for the power of scapegoating (Dervin, 2002; Eilenberg & Wyman, 1998; Poppe, 2001). During the Great Depression of the 1930s, Hitler used Jews as scapegoats Germans could blame for their economic troubles. If it is true that a

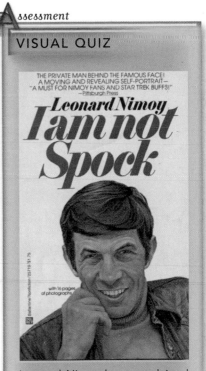

Ingroup Favoritism *Viewing members of the ingroup more positively than members of an outgroup*

Outgroup Homogeneity Effect *Judging members of an outgroup as more alike and less diverse than members of the ingroup*

Figure 47.2 *The price of prejudice.*
Here are two examples of the atrocities associated with prejudice: (a) the Holocaust, when millions of Jews were exterminated by the Nazis and (b) slavery in the United States, where Africans were bought and sold as slaves.

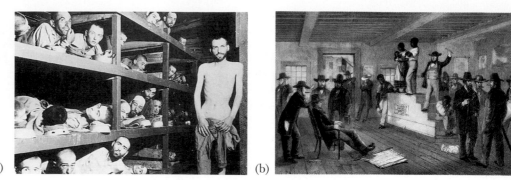

(a)　　　　　　　　　　　　　　(b)

picture is worth a thousand words, then the photos in Figure 47.2 speak volumes about the atrocities resulting from prejudice and discrimination.

Reducing Prejudice and Discrimination

> Let's go hand in hand, not one before another.
>
> WILLIAM SHAKESPEARE

What can be done to combat prejudice? We will look at five approaches: cooperation, superordinate goals, increased contact, cognitive retraining, and cognitive dissonance.

1 and 2. *Cooperation and superordinate goals.* Research shows that one of the best ways to combat prejudice is to encourage *cooperation* rather than *competition* (Brewer, 1996; Walker & Crogan, 1998). Muzafer Sherif and his colleagues (1966, 1998) conducted an ingenious study to show the role of competition in promoting prejudice. The researchers created strong feelings of ingroup and outgroup identification in a group of 11- and 12-year-old boys at a summer camp by physically separating the boys in different cabins and assigning different projects to each group, such as building a diving board or cooking out in the woods.

Once each group developed strong feelings of group identity and allegiance, the researchers set up a series of competitive games, including tug-of-war and touch football, and awarded desirable prizes to the winning teams. Because of this treatment, the groups began to pick fights, call each other names, and raid each other's camps — behaviors the researchers pointed to as evidence of the research-produced prejudice.

After using competition to create prejudice between the two groups, the researchers demonstrated how cooperation could be successfully used to eliminate it. They created "minicrises" and tasks that required expertise, labor, and cooperation from both groups, and prizes were awarded to all. The hostilities and prejudice between groups slowly began to dissipate, and by the end of the camp, the boys voted to return home in the same bus, and the self-chosen seating did not reflect the earlier camp divisions. Sherif's study showed not only the importance of cooperation as opposed to competition but also the importance of *superordinate goals* (the minicrises) in reducing prejudice (Der-Karabetian, Stephenson, & Poggi, 1996).

3. *Increased contact.* A third approach to reducing prejudice is *increasing contact between groups* (Dovidio, Gaertner, & Bachman, 2001; Fiske, 2002; Pettigrew, 1998). But as you just discovered with Sherif's study of the boys at the summer camp, contact can sometimes increase prejudice. It works under only certain conditions: (1) close interaction (if minority students are "tracked" into vocational education courses and white students are primarily in college prep courses, they seldom interact and prejudice is increased), (2) interdependence (both groups must be involved in superordinate goals that require cooperation), and (3) equal status (everyone must be at the same level). Once people have positive experiences with a group, they tend to generalize to other groups (Pettigrew, 1998).

4. **Cognitive retraining.** One of the most recent strategies in prejudice reduction requires taking another's perspective or undoing associations of negative stereotypical traits (Galinsky & Moskowitz, 2000; Kawakami, Dovidio, Moll, Hermsen, & Russin, 2000). For example, in a computer training session, Kawakami and colleagues (2000) instructed participants to *try not to* think of cultural associations when they saw a photograph of an elderly person and to press a *no* button when they saw a photograph of an elderly person with a trait stereotypically associated (e.g., slow, weak) with elderly people. Conversely, they were instructed to press a *yes* button when they saw a photograph of an elderly person with a trait not normally associated with the elderly. After a number of trials, their response times became faster and faster, indicating they were undoing negative associations and learning positive ones. After the training, participants were less likely to activate any negative stereotype of elderly people in another activity, compared with others who did not participate in the training exercise.

   People can also learn to be nonprejudiced if they are taught to selectively pay attention to *similarities* rather than *differences* (Phillips & Ziller, 1997). When we focus on how "black voters feel about affirmative action" or how Jewish people feel about "a Jewish candidate for vice president of the United States," we are indirectly encouraging stereotypes and ingroups versus outgroups. Can you see how this might also apply to gender? By emphasizing gender differences *(Men Are from Mars, Women Are from Venus)*, we may be perpetuating gender stereotypes (Powlishta, 1999).

5. **Cognitive dissonance.** As mentioned earlier, prejudice is a type of attitude that has three basic components — affective (feelings), behavioral tendencies, and cognitive (thoughts). And one of the most efficient methods to change an attitude uses the principle of *cognitive dissonance*, a perceived discrepancy between an attitude and a behavior or between an attitude and a new piece of information (D'Alessio & Allen, 2002; Cook, 2000). Every time you meet a person who does not conform to your prejudiced view, you experience dissonance and an urge to either change your attitude (or your opinion of the person). As a critical thinker, can you see how recent social changes, such as school busing, integrated housing, and increased civil rights legislation, might create cognitive dissonance and a subsequent reduction in prejudice? Moreover, do you recognize how the four methods of reducing prejudice we just described also involve cognitive dissonance? Cooperation and superordinate goals, increased contact, and cognitive retraining all create discrepancy in the prejudiced person, which leads to tension that motivates them to change their attitudes — and reduce their prejudice.

Interpersonal Attraction: Liking and Loving Others

Stop for a moment and think about someone you like very much. Now picture someone you really dislike. Can you explain your feelings? Social psychologists use the term **interpersonal attraction** to refer to the degree of positive feelings toward another. Attraction accounts for a variety of social experiences — admiration, liking, friendship, intimacy, lust, and love. In this section, we will discuss several factors that explain interpersonal attraction.

Interpersonal Attraction *Positive feelings toward another*

Three Key Factors in Attraction: Physical Attractiveness, Proximity, and Similarity

Social psychologists have found three compelling factors in interpersonal attraction — *physical attractiveness*, *proximity*, and *similarity*. Although physical attractiveness and proximity are more influential in the beginning stages of relationships, similarity is the single most important factor in maintaining a long-term relationship.

Physical Attractiveness. Can you remember what first attracted you to your best friend or romantic partner? Was it his or her warm personality, sharp intelligence, or great sense of humor? Or was it looks? Research consistently shows that *physical attractiveness* (size, shape, facial characteristics, and manner of dress) is one of the most important factors in our initial liking or loving of others (Buunk et al., 2002; Herz & Inzlicht, 2002; Li et al., 2002; Sprecher & Regan, 2002; Waynforth, 2001).

Like it or not, attractive individuals are seen by both men and women as more poised, interesting, cooperative, achieving, sociable, independent, intelligent, healthy, and sexually warm (Fink & Penton-Voak, 2002; Langlois et al., 2000; Watkins & Johnston, 2000; Zebrowitz et al., 2002). Perhaps even more distressing, premature infants rated as physically more attractive by nurses caring for them thrive better during their hospital stay. They gain more weight and are released earlier than infants perceived as less attractive, presumably because they receive more nurturing (Badr & Abdallah, 2001). In another study comparing actual court cases, researchers found that judges gave longer prison sentences to unattractive versus attractive defendants — even when they were convicted of comparable crimes (Stewart, 1985).

Achievement
GENDER & CULTURAL DIVERSITY

Physical Attractiveness Across Cultures

If you found the previous list of advantages of physical attractiveness unnerving, you'll be even more surprised to know that some research also shows that judgments of attractiveness appear consistent across cultures, and that in 37 cultures around the world, women are judged more beautiful if they are youthful in appearance (Buss, 1989, 1994, 1999; Cunningham, Roberts, Barbee, Druen, & Wu, 1995; Langlois et al., 2000; Rossano, 2003). For men, on the other hand, maturity and financial resources seem to be more important than appearance in attracting a mate.

How can this be so universally true? Evolutionary psychologists would suggest that this cross-cultural similarity in judgment of attractiveness reflects the fact that good looks generally indicate good health, sound genes, and high fertility. For example, facial and body symmetry appear to be key elements in attractiveness (Fink & Penton-Voak, 2002; Rhodes, Sumich, & Byatt, 1999; Zajonc, 1998) and symmetry seems to be correlated with genetic health. The fact that women prefer men with resources and social status also supports the evolutionary position. Because the responsibility of rearing and nurturing children more often falls on women's shoulders, men with greater resources will have more to invest in children.

Culture and attraction. Which of these women do you find most attractive? Can you see how your cultural background would train you to prefer one look to the others?

In contrast to this seeming universal agreement on standards of attractiveness, there also is evidence that beauty is in "the eye of the beholder." What we judge as beautiful varies somewhat from era to era and culture to culture. For example, the Chinese once practiced foot binding because small feet were considered beautiful in women. All the toes except the big one were bent under a young girl's foot and into the sole. The physical distortion made it almost impossible for her to walk, and she suffered excruciating pain, chronic bleeding, and frequent infections throughout her life (Dworkin, 1974). Even in modern times, cultural demands for attractiveness encourage an increasing number of women (and men) to undergo expensive and often painful surgery to *increase* the size of their eyes, breasts, lips, chest, and penis and *decrease* the size of their nose, ears, chin, stomach, hips, and thighs (Atkins, 2000; Etcoff, 1999).

Given that only a small percentage of people are as attractive as Cameron Diaz or Denzel Washington or have the money (or inclination) for extensive cosmetic surgery, how do the rest of us ever find mates? The good news is that what people judge as "ideally attractive" may be quite different from what they eventually choose for a mate. According to the *matching hypothesis*, men and women of approximately equal physical attractiveness tend to select each other as partners (Reagan, 1998; Sprecher & Regan, 2002). Further good news, as you will see in the following Application section, in that *flirting* offers a "simple" way to increase attractiveness.

Application
APPLYING PSYCHOLOGY TO RELATIONSHIPS

The Art and Science of Flirting

Pretend for the moment that you are watching a man (Tom) and woman (Kaleesha) at a singles bar. As Tom approaches the table, Kaleesha sits up straighter, smiles, and touches her hair. Tom asks her to dance, and Kaleesha quickly nods and stands up while smoothing her skirt. During the dance, she smiles and sometimes glances at him from under her lashes. When the dance finishes, Kaleesha waits for Tom to escort her back to her chair. She motions him to sit in the adjacent chair and they engage in a lively conversation. Kaleesha allows her leg to briefly graze his. When Tom reaches for popcorn from the basket in front of Kaleesha, she playfully pulls it away. This surprises Tom and he frowns at Kaleesha. She quickly turns away and starts talking to her friends. Despite his repeated attempts to talk to her, Kaleesha ignores him.

What happened? Did you recognize Kaleesha's sexual signals? Did you understand why she turned away at the end? If so, you are skilled in the art and science of flirting. If not, you may be very interested in the work of Monica Moore at the University of Missouri (1998). As a scientist interested in describing and understanding flirting and the role it plays in human courtship, Moore has observed and recorded many scenes — in singles bars and shopping malls — like the one with Tom and Kaleesha. Although she prefers the term *nonverbal courtship signaling*, what Moore and her colleagues have spent thousands of hours secretly observing is flirting behavior.

From these naturalistic observations, we know a great deal more about what works and doesn't

work in courtship. First of all, though both men and women flirt, women generally initiate a courtship. The woman signals her interest with glances that may be brief and darting, or direct and sustained. Often she smiles at the same time she gestures with her hands — often with an open or extended palm. Primping (adjusting clothing or patting hair) is also common. A flirting woman will also make herself more noticeable by sitting straighter, with stomach pulled in and breasts pushed out.

Once contact is made and the couple is dancing or sitting at a table, the woman increases the level of flirting. She orients her body toward his, whispers in his ear, and frequently nods and smiles in response to his conversation. Most significant, she touches the man or allows the man to touch her. Like Kaleesha with Tom, allowing her leg to graze his is a powerful indication of her interest.

Women also use play behaviors to flirt. They tease, mock-hit, and tell jokes, not only to inject humor but also to test the man's receptivity to humor. As in the case of Tom's reaction to the popcorn tease, when a man doesn't appreciate the playfulness, a woman often uses rejection signals to cool or end the relationship. Other studies confirm Moore's description of women's nonverbal sexual signaling (Lott, 2000).

Now that you know what to look for, watch for flirting behavior in others — or perhaps in your own life. According to Moore and other researchers, flirting may be the single most important thing a woman can do to increase her attractiveness. Because the burden of making the first approach is usually the man's, men are understandably cautious and welcome a woman clearly signaling her interest.

Two cautions are in order, however. First, signaling interest does not mean that the woman is ready to have sex with the man. She flirts because she wants to get to know the man better; later, she'll decide whether she wants to develop a relationship (Allgeier & Allgeier, 2000). Second, Moore reminds women to "use their enhanced flirting skills only when genuinely interested" (1997, p. 69). Being aware of sexual signals can benefit both men and women, but flirting should be reserved for times when you genuinely want to attract and keep the attention of a particular partner.

Proximity *Attraction based on geographic closeness*

Proximity.   Attraction also depends on people being in the same place at the same time, making **proximity,** or geographic nearness, another major factor in attraction. A study of friendship in college dormitories found that the person next door was more often liked than the person two doors away, the person two doors away was liked more than someone three doors away, and so on (Priest & Sawyer, 1967).

Proximity promotes attraction largely because of *mere exposure*. Just as familiar people become more physically attractive over time, repeated exposure also increases overall liking (Rosano, 2003; Rhodes, Halberstadt, & Brajkouich, 2001; Zajonc, 1998). This makes sense from an evolutionary point of view. Things we have seen before are less likely to pose a threat than novel stimuli. It also explains why modern

Exposure and liking. According to "mere exposure effect," this model would prefer the reversed photo on the left because this is the version she sees in the mirror. However, most people prefer the "normal" photo on the right because this is what is most familiar to them.

Reprinted with special permission of King Features Syndicate.

Opposites attract or similarity?
Research shows that similarity is the single best predictor for long-term relationships. As shown here, however, many people ignore dissimilarities and hope that their chosen partner will change over time.

advertisers tend to run highly redundant ad campaigns, with familiar faces and jingles (Zajonc, 1968, 1998). Repeated exposure increases our liking — and purchases.

We even like *ourselves* better when we see ourselves in a familiar way. When researchers showed college students pictures of themselves or reversed photos (the mirror image), students strongly preferred the reversed photos — that is, the image they were used to seeing in the mirror. Close friends of the same students preferred the true photos of their friend. They were used to seeing this image (Mita, Dermer, & Knight, 1977). (Can you see why people often complain that photos of themselves "never really look like" them?)

One caution. Repeated exposure to a *negative* stimulus can *decrease* attraction, as evidenced by the high number of negative political ads. Politicians have learned that repeatedly running an attack ad associating an opposing candidate with negative cues (like increased taxes) decreases the viewers' liking of the opponent. On the other hand, running ads showing themselves in a positive light (kissing babies, helping flood victims) helps build positive associations and increased liking.

Similarity. Once we've had repeated opportunity to get to know someone through simple physical proximity, and assuming we find him or her attractive, we then need something to hold the relationship together over time. The major cementing factor for long-term relationships, whether liking or loving, is *similarity*. We tend to prefer, and stay with, people (and organizations) who are most like us, those who share our ethnic background, social class, interests, and attitudes (Akers, Jones, & Coyl, 1998; Chen & Kenrick, 2002; Rentsch & McEwen, 2002; Tsui, Porter, & Egan, 2002). In other words, "Birds of a feather flock together."

What about the old saying "Opposites attract"? Although it does seem that these two pieces of common folklore are contradictory, the term *opposites* here probably refers to personality traits rather than to social background or values. An attraction to a seemingly opposite person is more often based on the recognition that in one or two important areas that person offers us something we lack (Dryer & Horowitz, 1997). If you are a talkative and outgoing person, for example, your friendship with a quiet and reserved individual may endure because each of you provides important resources for the other. Psychologists refer to this as **need complementarity,** as compared with the **need compatibility** represented by similarity.

Need Complementarity *Attraction toward those with qualities we admire but personally lack*

Need Compatibility *Attraction based on sharing similar needs*

Loving Others

To complete our discussion of interpersonal attraction, we will explore three perspectives on the mystery of love: liking versus loving, romantic love, and companionate love.

Liking versus loving Because love relationships often develop from friendships and initial feelings of liking for one another, Zick Rubin (1970, 1992) developed

TABLE 47.1 SAMPLE ITEMS FROM RUBIN'S LIKING AND LOVING TEST

Love Scale
1. I feel that I can confide in _____ about virtually everything.
2. I would do almost anything for _____.
3. If I could never be with _____, I would feel miserable.

Liking Scale
1. I think that _____ is unusually well adjusted.
2. I would highly recommend _____ for a responsible job.
3. In my opinion, _____ is an exceptionally mature person.

Source: Rubin, Z. (1970). "Measurement of romantic love," *Journal of Personality and Social Psychology, 16,* 265–273. Copyright © 1970 by the American Psychological Association. Reprinted by permission of the author.

two paper-and-pencil tests to explore the relationship between liking and loving (Table 47.1).

In spite of the apparent simplicity of Rubin's scales, they have proven to be useful indicators of both liking and loving. For example, Rubin hypothesized that "strong love" couples would spend more time gazing into one another's eyes than "weak love" couples. To test his hypothesis, while the couples were waiting for the experiment to begin, Rubin and his assistants secretly recorded the actual amount of eye contact between all couples. As predicted, couples who scored highest on the love scale also spent more time looking into one another's eyes. In addition, Rubin found that although both partners tended to match each other on their love scores, women liked their dating partners significantly more than they were liked in return.

How does love differ from liking on Rubin's scales? Rubin found that liking involves a favorable evaluation of another, as reflected in greater feelings of admiration and respect. He found not only that love is more intense than liking but also that love is composed of three basic elements:

- *Caring*, the desire to help the other person, particularly when help is needed

- *Attachment*, the need to be with the other person

- *Intimacy*, a sense of empathy and trust that comes from close communication and self-disclosure to and from another

Romantic Love When you think of romantic love, do you think of falling in love, a magical experience that puts you on cloud nine? **Romantic love,** also called *passionate love* or *limerence*, has been defined as "any intense attraction that involves the idealization of the other, within an erotic context, with the expectation of enduring for some time in the future" (Jankowiak, 1997, p. 8).

Romantic love has intrigued people throughout history, and its intense joys and sorrows have inspired countless poems, novels, movies, and songs around the world. A cross-cultural study by anthropologists William Jankowiak and Edward Fischer found romantic love in 147 of the 166 societies they studied. The researchers concluded that "romantic love constitutes a human universal, or at the least a near universal" (1992, p. 154).

Problems with Romantic Love Romantic love may be almost universal, but that hardly means it is problem free. First, romantic love is typically short lived. Even

Romantic Love *Intense feeling of attraction to another, within an erotic context and with future expectations*

Symbols of romantic love? *Do you consider this a romantic gesture? How might other cultures signal their attraction and love for one another?*

in the most devoted couples, the intense attraction and excitement generally begin to fade after 6 to 30 months (Hatfield & Rapson, 1996; Livingston, 1999). Although this research finding may disappoint you, as a critical thinker do you really think any emotion of this intensity could last forever? What would happen if other intense emotions, such as anger or joy, were eternal? Moreover, given the time-consuming nature of romantic love, what would happen to other parts of our lives, such as school, career, and family?

Another major problem with romantic love is that it is largely based on mystery and fantasy. People fall in love with others not necessarily as they are but as they want them to be (Fletcher & Simpson, 2000; Levine & Markman, 2001). What happens to these illusions when we are faced with everyday interactions and long-term exposure? Our "beautiful princess" isn't supposed to snore, and our "knight in shining armor" doesn't look very knightly flossing his teeth. And, of course, no princess or knight would ever notice our shortcomings, let alone comment on them.

Is there any way to keep love alive?   If you mean romantic love, one of the best ways to fan the flames is through interference, or some form of frustration that keeps you from fulfilling your desire for the presence of your love. Researchers have found that interference (for example, the parents in Shakespeare's *Romeo and Juliet*) apparently increases the feelings of love (Driscoll, Davis, & Lipetz, 1972).

Because romantic love depends on uncertainty and fantasy, it can also be kept alive by situations in which we never really get to know the other person. This may explain why computer chat room romances or old high school flings have such a tug on our emotions. Because we never really get to test these relationships, we can always fantasize about what might have been.

One of the most constructive ways of keeping romantic love alive is to recognize its fragile nature and nurture it with carefully planned surprises, flirting and flattery, and special dinners and celebrations. In the long run, however, romantic love's most important function might be to keep us attached long enough to move on to companionate love.

Companionate Love.   Companionate love is based on admiration and respect, combined with deep feelings of caring for the person and commitment to the relationship. Studies of close friendships show that satisfaction grows with time as we come to recognize the value of companionship and of having an intimate confidante (Kiraly, 2000; & Hazan, 1991). Companionate love, unlike romantic love, which is very short lived, seems to grow stronger with time and often lasts a lifetime (Figure 47.2).

Companionate love is what we feel for our best friends, and it can be the basis for a strong and lasting marriage. But finding and keeping a long-term relationship is no easy task. Many of our expectations for love are based on romantic fantasies and unconscious programming from fairy tales and TV shows in which everyone lives happily ever after. Therefore, we are often ill equipped to deal with the hassles and boredom that come with any long-term relationship. One tip for maintaining companionate love is to *overlook each other's faults*. Studies of both dating and married couples find that people report greater satisfaction with — and stay longer in — relationships where they have a somewhat idealized or unrealistically positive perception of their partner (Campbell et al., 2001; Fletcher & Simpson, 2000). This makes sense in light of research on cognitive dissonance (discussed earlier). Idealizing our mates allows us to believe we have a good deal — and hence avoids the cognitive dissonance that might naturally arise every time we saw an attractive alternative. As Benjamin Franklin put it, "Keep your eyes wide open before marriage, half shut afterwards."

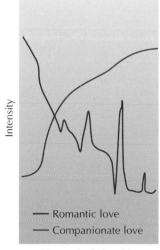

Figure 47.2 *Love over the lifespan.*
Romantic love is high in the beginning of a relationship but tends to diminish over time, with periodic resurgences or "spikes." Companionate love usually increases over time.

Companionate Love *Strong and lasting attraction characterized by trust, caring, tolerance, and friendship*

Companionate versus romantic love.
This couple just celebrated their sixtieth wedding anniversary. Unlike romantic love, which rarely lasts longer than 6 to 30 months, companionate love can last a lifetime.

Assessment

CHECK & REVIEW

Our Feelings About Others

Prejudice is a generally negative attitude directed toward specific people solely because of their membership in a specific group. It contains all three components of attitudes (cognitive, affective, and behavioral). **Discrimination** is not the same as prejudice. It refers to the actual negative behavior directed at members of a group. People do not always act on their prejudices.

The four major sources of prejudice are learning (classical and operant conditioning and social learning), mental shortcuts (categorization), economic and political competition, and displaced aggression (scapegoating). Cooperation, superordinate goals, increased contact, cognitive retraining, and cognitive dissonance reduction are five methods for reducing prejudice and discrimination.

Physical attractiveness is very important to **interpersonal attraction.** Physically attractive people are often perceived as more intelligent, sociable, and interesting than less attractive people. Standards for physical attractiveness vary across cultures and time. Physical **proximity** also increases one's attractiveness. If you live near someone or work alongside someone, you are more likely to like that person. Although people commonly believe that "opposites attract" (**need complementarity**), research shows that similarity (**need compatibility**) is a much more important factor in attraction.

Love can be defined in terms of caring, attachment, and intimacy. **Romantic love** is highly valued in our society, but because it is based on mystery and fantasy, it is hard to sustain. **Companionate love** relies on mutual trust, respect, and friendship and seems to grow stronger with time.

Questions

1. Explain how prejudice differs from discrimination.

2. Saying that members of another ethnic group "all look alike to me" may be an example of _____. (a) ingroup favoritism; (b) the outgroup homogeneity effect; (c) outgroup negativism; (d) ingroup bias

3. Cross-cultural research on physical attractiveness has found all but one of the following. (a) the Chinese once practiced foot binding because small feet were considered attractive in women; (b) in most male dominated societies, physical beauty is the most important attribute in a potential wife; (c) in most Eastern cultures, men prefer women with power and financial status over beauty; (d) for men, maturity and financial resources are more important than appearance in their ability to attract a mate

4. Compare the dangers associated with romantic love with the benefits of companionate love.

Answers to Questions can be found in Appendix B.

ACTIVE LEARNING WORKSHEET   MODULE 47

ACROSS

3 A key factor in attraction involving geographic, residential, and other forms of physical closeness.

6 A generally negative attitude directed toward others because of their membership in a specific group. Like all attitudes, prejudice involves cognitions (thoughts), affect (feelings), and behavioral tendencies.

7 Negative behaviors directed at members of a group.

8 (1) A set of beliefs about the characteristics of people in a group that is generalized to all group members or (2) the cognitive component of prejudice.

DOWN

1 An intense feeling of attraction to another person, within an erotic context and with future expectations.

2 A sharing of similar needs.

4 A cognitive process in prejudice whereby members of an ingroup are viewed in more favorable terms than members of an outgroup.

5 A strong feeling of attraction to another person characterized by trust, caring, tolerance, and friendship. It is believed to provide an enduring basis for long-term relationships.

MODULE 48
OUR ACTIONS TOWARD OTHERS

Having just completed our whirlwind examination of how our thoughts and emotions influence others — and vice versa — we turn to topics associated with actions toward others. We begin with a look at social influence (conformity and obedience) and then continue with group processes (membership and decision making). We conclude by exploring two opposite kinds of behavior — aggression and altruism.

Social Influence: Conformity and Obedience

The society and culture into which we are born influence us from the moment of birth until the moment of death. Our culture teaches us to believe certain things, feel certain ways, and act in accordance with these beliefs and feelings. These influences are so strong and so much a part of who we are that we rarely recognize them. Just as a fish doesn't know it's in water, we are largely unaware of the strong impact cultural and social factors have on all our behaviors. In this section, we will discuss two kinds of *social influence:* conformity and obedience.

Conformity — Going Along with Others

Imagine for a moment that you have volunteered for a psychology experiment on perception. You find yourself seated around a table with six other students. You are all shown a card with three lines labeled A, B, and C, as in Figure 48.1. You are then asked to select the line that is closest in length to a fourth line, X. Each of you is asked to state your choice out loud, in order, around the table. At first, everyone agrees on the correct line, and the experiment seems pretty boring. On the third trial, however, the first participant gives what is obviously a wrong answer. You know that line B is correct, but he says line A. When the second, third, fourth, and fifth participants also say line A, you really start to wonder: "What's going on here? Are they blind? Or am I?"

What do you think you would do at this point in the experiment? Would you stick with your convictions and say line B, regardless of what the others have answered? Or would you go along with the group? In the original version of this experiment, conducted by Solomon Asch (1951), six participants were actually confederates of the experimenter, and seating was arranged so that the one participant who was the real subject was always in the next-to-last position. The six confederates were instructed ahead of time to respond incorrectly on the third trial and selected later trials. This set up was designed to test the participant's degree of **conformity,** or changing one's behavior as a result of real or imagined group pressure.

How did Asch's participants respond? More than one-third conformed and agreed with the group's obviously incorrect choice. This level of conformity is particularly intriguing when it is compared with responses in the control group, which experienced no group pressure and chose correctly virtually 100 percent of the time. Asch's study has been conducted dozens of times, in at least 17 countries, and always with similar results (Bond & Smith, 1996).

Why would so many people conform? To the onlooker, conformity is often difficult to understand, and even the conformer sometimes has a hard time explaining his or her behavior. We can better understand Asch's participants and our own forms of conformity if we look at three factors: (1) *normative social influence,* (2) *informational social influence,* and (3) the role of *reference groups.*

Normative social influence. The first factor, **normative social influence,** refers to conformity to group pressure out of a need for approval and acceptance by

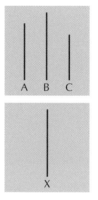

© Sidney Harris

the group. A **norm** is an expected behavior that is adhered to by members of the group. Norms are society's definition of how we "should" behave. They are sometimes explicit, but most often, norms are quite subtle and implicit. Have you ever asked what others are wearing to the party or watched your neighbor's table manners to be sure you pick up the right fork? Such behavior reflects your desire to conform and the power of normative social influence.

An important norm that we conform to in every culture is *personal space* (Axtell, 1998; Hall, 1966, 1983; Sommer, 1969). If someone invades the invisible "personal bubble" that we like to maintain around our bodies, we generally feel very uncomfortable. Imagine yourself as the typical American traveling in several Middle Eastern countries. How would you respond when a local citizen answers your question while standing close enough that you can feel his or her breath? Most Americans, Canadians, and Northern Europeans feel very uncomfortable at this distance (unless talking with a lover), but most Middle Easterners like to be close enough to "read" one another's eyes. If you "naturally" back away during the conversation, the Middle Easterner might think you are cold and standoffish at the same time that you might consider him or her rude and intrusive.

Why do some people like to stand closer than others do?   There are a number of possible explanations. First, culture and socialization have a lot to do with personal space. For reasons unknown, people from Mediterranean, Moslem, and Latin American countries tend to maintain smaller interpersonal distances than do North Americans and Northern Europeans (Axtell, 1998; Steinhart, 1986). Children also tend to

Norm *Cultural rule of behavior prescribing what is acceptable in a given situation*

TRY THIS

YOURSELF

Application

If you want to personally experience the power of social norms, approach a fellow student on campus and ask for directions to the bookstore, library, or some other landmark. As you are talking, move toward the person until you invade his or her personal space. You should be close enough to almost touch toes. How does the person respond? How do you feel?

Now repeat the process with another student, but this time try standing 5 to 6 feet away while asking directions. Which procedure was most difficult for you? Although most people think this will be a fun assignment, they often find it extremely difficult to willingly break our culture's unwritten norms for personal space.

The advantages of conformity. *What would happen to our everyday social functioning if most people did not conform?*

Informational Social Influence
Conforming to group pressure out of a need for direction and information

Reference Groups *People we conform to, or go along with, because we like and admire them and want to be like them*

Obedience *Following direct commands, usually from an authority figure*

stand very close to others until they are socialized to recognize and maintain a greater personal distance. Second, certain relationships, situations, and personalities affect interpersonal distances. Friends stand closer than strangers, women tend to stand closer than men, and violent prisoners prefer approximately three times the personal space of nonviolent prisoners (Axtell, 1998; Gilmour & Walkey, 1981; Roques, Lambin, Jeunier, & Strayer, 1997).

Informational Social Influence.   Have you ever bought a specific brand of ski equipment or automobile simply because of a friend's recommendation? You conform not to gain their approval (normative social influence) but because you assume they have more information than you do. Conforming out of a need for direction and information is considered **informational social influence.** Participants in Asch's experiment might have conformed because they thought the others had more information — especially because they were all unanimous in their judgments. The power of informational influence also was shown when Asch repeated his experiment. When he allowed the participants to privately write down their answers, rather than stating them out loud, their conformity dropped dramatically.

Reference groups.   The third major factor in conformity is the power of **reference groups** — those people we most admire, like, and want to resemble. Attractive actors and popular sports stars are paid millions of dollars to endorse certain products because advertisers know that we want to be as cool as Wesley Snipes or as beautiful as Jennifer Lopez. Of course, we also have more important reference groups in our lives — parents, friends, family, teachers, religious leaders, and so on.

Does this mean that all conformity is bad and even dangerous?   Not at all. In fact, most people conform most of the time because it is in their best interest and everyone else's to do so (Henrich & Boyd, 1998). You stand in line at the bookstore instead of pushing ahead of everyone, and you expect others to wait their turn, too. Conformity allows social life to proceed with order and predictability.

Obedience — Going Along with a Command

A second form of social influence, **obedience,** involves going along with a direct command, usually from someone in a position of authority. Under orders from an experimenter, would you shock a man with a known heart condition who is screaming and asking to be released? Most people assume that few people would do so. But as you recall from Milgram's study described at the opening of this section, approximately two-thirds of the participants administered the full 450 volts. This happened even when the learner had stopped responding (screaming or otherwise) and was apparently either unconscious or dead (Milgram, 1963, 1974).

Even Milgram was surprised by the results of his study. When he polled a group of psychiatrists before the study began, they predicted that most people would refuse to go beyond 150 volts, and that less than 1 percent of those tested would "go all the way." Only someone who was "disturbed and sadistic" would obey to the fullest extent. But as you know, almost two-thirds of the participants, both men and women, of all ages and all walks of life, administered the highest voltage.

Factors in obedience.   As you recall from Module 34, personality researchers are still debating the relative importance of the *person* as opposed to the *situation* in determining behavior. However, Milgram's research suggests when it comes to obedience, *situational factors* are most important. We will examine four of these factors:

1. *Power of authority.* People in positions of authority have an extraordinary — and often underestimated — power to elicit obedience. As Figure 48.2 shows, when an ordinary person instead of the experimenter gave the orders, obedience dropped significantly.

2. *Distance between the teacher and learner.* Look again at Figure 48.2. Note that when the learner was in the same room with the participant (3), only 40 percent obeyed fully. And when the teacher-participant was required to force the learner's hand down on a simulated "shock plate," only 30 percent obeyed (4). Can you see how these results relate to modern warfare? Think how much harder it might be to obey a military command to directly stab and kill one person, compared to the "ease" of dropping a bomb from a high-flying airplane that might kill thousands.

3. *Assignment of responsibility.* Research has also found that when participants are reminded that they will be held responsible for any harm to the victim, obedience is sharply reduced (Hamilton, 1978). Note the sharp contrast in Figure 48.2 between the one condition (5) when participants were asked to just read the list of words while another teacher delivered the shock, compared with the second condition (6) when the teacher was responsible for choosing the level of shock.

4. *Modeling/imitation.* Watching others also can have a tremendous impact on participant obedience. When two confederates (who were acting like "teachers") were instructed to either administer the maximum shock (8) or to openly rebel and refuse to continue (7), actual participants copied either the obedient or the disobedient model (see again Figure 48.2).

One of the most beautiful and historically important examples of the power of modeling and a single act of rebellion occurred in Alabama in 1955. Rosa Parks boarded a bus and as expected in those times she obediently sat in the back section marked "Negroes." When the bus became crowded, the driver told her to give up her seat to a white man. Surprisingly, Parks refused and was eventually forced off the bus by police and arrested. By refusing to obey, she gave impetus to the growing civil

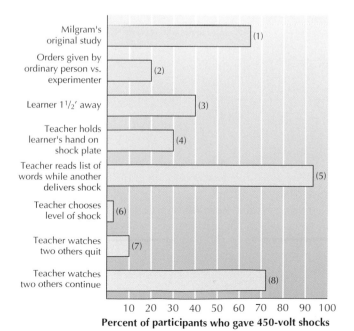

Percent of participants who gave 450-volt shocks

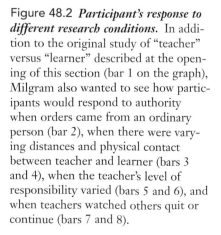

Figure 48.2 *Participant's response to different research conditions.* In addition to the original study of "teacher" versus "learner" described at the opening of this section (bar 1 on the graph), Milgram also wanted to see how participants would respond to authority when orders came from an ordinary person (bar 2), when there were varying distances and physical contact between teacher and learner (bars 3 and 4), when the teacher's level of responsibility varied (bars 5 and 6), and when teachers watched others quit or continue (bars 7 and 8).

Application

CRITICAL THINKING

ACTIVE LEARNING

Would You Have Obeyed Milgram's Directions?

One common intellectual illusion that hinders critical thinking about obedience is the belief that only evil people do evil things or that evil announces itself. For example, the experimenter in Stanley Milgram's study looked and acted like a reasonable person who was simply carrying out a research project. Because he was not seen as personally corrupt and evil, the participants' normal moral guard was down and obedience was maximized.

This relaxed moral guard also might explain obedience to a highly respected military officer or the leader of a religious cult. One of the most infamous cult leaders, Jim Jones, was well known and highly revered for his kindness and "good works" — at least in the beginning. Perhaps because of their relaxed moral guard (combined with the five factors discussed earlier), in 1978 over 900 members of the People's Temple in Guyana committed mass suicide on Jone's order. People who resisted were murdered, but the vast majority took their lives willingly by drinking cyanide-laced Kool-Aid.

In addition, the gradual nature of many obedience situations may explain why so many people were willing to give the maximum shocks in Milgram's study. The initial mild level of shocks may have worked as a

foot-in-the-door technique, in which a first, small request is used as a setup for later, larger requests. Once Milgram's participants complied with the initial request, they might have felt obligated to continue (Chartrand, Pinckert, & Burger, 1999; Sabini & Silver, 1993).

Take this opportunity to think critically about extreme forms of destructive obedience and compare them to everyday examples like the following. Rank each situation by placing a 1 next to the one you believe is the most ethical act of obedience and a 3 next to the least ethical.

_____ Jane is 19 and wants to become a commercial artist. She is offered a scholarship to a good art school, but her parents strongly object to her career choice. After considerable pressure, she gives in and enrolls at the same engineering school her father attended.

_____ Tom is 45 and having serious doubts about his employer's shady business practices, such as double-billing the clients. Although he believes his boss is dishonest and unethical, he cooperates because he really needs the job.

_____ Mary is 20 and a senior in college. She desperately wants to get into a graduate program at a very prestigious school but is fail-

Foot-in-the-door technique. *If this homeowner allows the salesperson to give him a small gift (a "foot-in-the-door" technique), he's more likely to agree to buy something.* **Can you explain why?**

ing an important class. The instructor has suggested she could have an A in his course if she would sexually "cooperate." She agrees.

Although there are no right or wrong answers to your ranking, exploring your thinking about other's responses may help you use what you have learned in this module about conformity and obedience to clarify situations in your past where you were unethically persuaded — and perhaps prevent future problems?

Foot-in-the-Door Technique *Making a small request followed by increasingly larger requests*

rights movement and the repeal of Jim Crow laws in the South. Her act of courage also inspires the rest of us to think about when it is good to obey authorities and when to disobey unethical demands from authorities.

Final Note

Milgram's research provides important insights into situational pressures that can lead normal people to engage in surprising levels of obedience. However, his study remains highly controversial (Berkowitz, 1999; Blass, 1999) and as mentioned earlier it would not be allowed under contemporary standards of research ethics.

Perhaps the most important message is to recognize that obedience, like conformity, can be both good and bad. When police or firefighters order the crowd to step back away from the scene of the crime or the fire, it's important (and adaptive) to quickly obey. However, on some occasions we should not go along with the crowd (conformity) or cooperate with commands from authority (obedience).

Social Influence

The process of social influence teaches important cultural values and behaviors that are essential to successful social living. Two of the most important forms of social influence are conformity and obedience.

Conformity refers to changes in behavior in response to real or imagined pressure from others. People conform for approval and acceptance (**normative social influence**), out of a need for more information (**informational social influence**), and to match the behavior of those they admire and feel similar to (their **reference group**). People also conform because it is often adaptive to do so.

Obedience involves giving in to a command from others. Stanley Milgram's study showed that a surprisingly large number of people would obey orders even when another human being is physically threatened. At least four factors increase or decrease obedience: the power of authority, distance between teacher and learner, assignment of responsibility, and modeling/imitation.

Questions

1. Explain how conformity differs from obedience.

2. A social influence technique in which a first, small request is used as a setup for later requests is known as _____. (a) the lowball technique; (b) the foot-in-the-door technique; (c) infiltration technique; (d) ingratiation

3. Milgram's participants thought they were participating in an experiment designed to study the effect of _____. (a) obedience to authority; (b) arousal on memory; (c) punishment on learning; (d) electric shock on brain-wave activity

4. What are the four factors that increase or decrease obedience?

Answers to Questions can be found in Appendix B.

▨ Group Processes: Membership and Decision Making

Psychologists define a *group* as "two or more persons interacting with one another in such a manner that each person influences and is influenced by each other person" (Shaw, 1981, p. 8). In other words, a group consists of any collection of people who have some mutually recognized relationship with one another. A couple on their first date, a family, a class in psychology, and a basketball team are all considered groups. On the other hand, people riding together in an elevator are not a group.

Group Membership

Have you ever been with friends and found yourself doing something that you might not have done alone? Or have you noticed that you behave differently with your friends than with your parents or with your employer or roommates? In each situation, your behavior is largely the result of your group membership. Although we seldom recognize the power of such membership, social psychologists have identified several important ways that groups affect us. In this section we will explore, first, how the roles we assume influence behavior and, next, how group membership sometimes leads to deindividuation.

Roles in groups.   Every person in a group is expected to play one or more *roles* — a set of behavioral patterns connected with particular social positions. Some roles are very specifically spelled out and regulated (police officer), whereas others are assumed through informal learning and inference (father). Have you ever wondered how these roles affect behavior? This question fascinated social psychologist Philip Zimbardo. In his famous study at Stanford University, 20 carefully screened, well-adjusted young college men were paid $15 a day for participating in a simulation of prison life (Haney, Banks, & Zimbardo, 1978; Zimbardo, 1993).

Deindividuation.   Zimbardo's study shows that the roles we play as members of a group can have a powerful effect on behavior. Perhaps an even more extreme example of group effects occurs during **deindividuation.** To be deindividuated means that

Deindividuation *Increased arousal and reduced self-consciousness, inhibition, and personal responsibility that sometimes occurs in a group, particularly when the members feel anonymous*

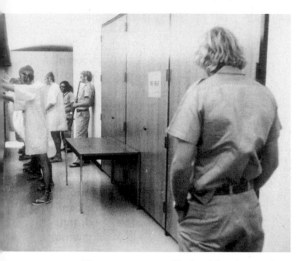

Power corrupts. *Zimbardo's prison study showed how the demands of roles and situations could produce dramatic changes in behavior.*

To appreciate Philip Zimbardo's prison study, pretend you are one of the 20 college students who volunteered to be a participant and that you were randomly assigned to play the role of "prisoner." You're watching TV at home when you unexpectedly hear a loud knock. When you open the door, several uniformed police officers take you outside, spread-eagle you against the police car, frisk you, and inform you that you are being arrested. At the police station, you are photographed, fingerprinted, and booked. You are then blindfolded and driven to your final destination — the "Stanford Prison." Here you are given an ID number (in place of your name) and deloused! You're then issued a shapeless gown to wear, a tight nylon cap to conceal your hair, and no underwear. All prisoners are in similar prisoner clothes; whereas participants who were assigned to be "guards" are outfitted with official-looking uniforms, billy clubs, and whistles. You and the other prisoners are then locked in your cells, and the guards are given complete control. What do you think happens next?

Not even Zimbardo foresaw how the study would turn out. Although some guards were "good guys" who did little favors for the prisoners and others were "tough but fair," they all engaged in some abuse of power. They insisted that prisoners quickly obey all prison rules, as well as their own arbitrary punishments. The slightest disobedience was followed by degrading tasks (such as cleaning the toilet with bare hands) or the loss of "priv-ileges" (such as eating, sleeping, and washing). Most prisoners initially responded to the bossing and punishment with good-humored acceptance. But as demands increased and abuses began, they became passive and depressed. Only one prisoner fought back with a hunger strike, which ended with a forced feeding by the guards.

Four prisoners had to be released within the first 4 days because of severe reactions, including uncontrollable sobbing, fits of rage, severe depression, and, in one case a psychosomatic rash over his entire body. Although the study was planned to last 2 weeks, it was stopped after only 6 days because of the alarming psychological changes in the participants. The guards were seriously abusing their power, and the traumatized prisoners were becoming more and more depressed and dehumanized.

Although this was not a true experiment in that it lacked control groups and clear measurements of the dependent variable, it offers insights into the potential *power of roles* on individual behavior. According to interviews conducted after the study, the students apparently became so absorbed in their roles they forgot they were volunteers in a university study (Zimbardo, Ebbeson, & Maslach, 1977). If this type of personality disintegration and abuse of power could be generated in a mere 6 days in a mock prison with fully informed *volunteers*, can you imagine what happens during life imprisonment, 6-year sentences, or even overnight jail stays?

you feel less self-conscious, less inhibited, and less personally responsible as a member of a group than when you're alone. This is particularly likely under conditions of anonymity. Groups sometimes actively promote deindividuation, such as by requiring uniforms, as a way to increase allegiance and conformity.

Sometimes deindividuation can be positive. We all enjoy being swept along with a crowd's joyous celebration on New Year's Eve and the raucous cheering and shouting during an exciting sports competition. Deindividuation also encourages increased helping behaviors and even heroism, as we will see later in Module 48. Unfortunately, deindividuation also helps explain angry mobs, rioters, and tragic consequences like gang rapes, lynchings, and hate crimes (Akert, 2000; Aronson, Wilson, & Akert, 1999; Green, Glaser, & Rich, 1998).

How does this happen? There are several possible explanations for deindividualization. But one of the most compelling is the fact that the presence of others tends to increase arousal and feelings of anonymity. For example, in one experiment, women who wore KKK-like disguises that completely covered their faces and bodies (see photo) delivered twice as much electric shock to a victim than did women who were not disguised and wore large nametags (Zimbardo, 1970). (As in all such experiments, the "victim" was a confederate who did not receive actual shocks.) It seems that *anonymity* is a powerful disinhibitor, which also helps explain why Halloween masks seem to increase vandalism and why most crimes and riots occur at night — under the cover of darkness. It is important to emphasize, however, that not everyone in a crowd becomes deindividuated. Some people do resist and do maintain their personal values and beliefs.

Deindividuation. *When participants were covered with hoods and white coats, they delivered twice the amount of shock as those who were not covered. Can you see why anonymity, or deindividuation, may increase aggression and other forms of negative social behavior?*

Group Decision Making

Are two heads truly better than one? Does the presence of others improve decision making? Do juries make better decisions than a judge? There are no simple answers to these questions. To formulate some response, we need to look not only at how group discussions affect individual opinions (group polarization) but also at how group membership affects access to accurate information (groupthink).

Group polarization. Most people assume that group decisions are more conservative, cautious, and "middle of the road" than individual decisions. But is this true? Initial investigations indicated that after discussing an issue, groups actually supported *riskier* decisions than decisions they made as individuals before the discussion (Stoner, 1961). Partly because it contradicted the common belief about group caution and moderation, this *risky shift* concept sparked a great deal of research.

Subsequent research shows that the risky shift phenomenon is only part of the picture in group decision making. Although some groups do, in fact, make riskier decisions, others become extremely conservative (Liu & Latane, 1998). Whether the final decision is risky or conservative depends primarily on the dominant preexisting tendencies of the group. That is, as individuals interact and discuss their opinions, their initial positions become more exaggerated. This movement toward one polar extreme or the other is known as **group polarization.**

Why does this happen? The tendency toward group polarization generally results from increased exposure to *persuasive arguments* (Liu & Latane, 1998). When people hear arguments from other people, they are exposed to new information. Because most informal, political, or business groups consist of likeminded individuals, the "new" information generally only reinforces the group's original opinion. Thus, the group's preexisting tendencies are strengthened by the group discussion.

Group Polarization *Group's movement toward either riskier or more conservative behavior, depending on the members' initial dominant tendency*

Groupthink *Faulty decision making that occurs when a highly cohesive group strives for agreement and avoids inconsistent information*

Groupthink. Group decision making may not only be affected by the tendency toward group polarization; another related and equally dangerous tendency is toward **groupthink.** Irving Janis (1972, 1989) defines *groupthink* as "a mode of thinking that people engage in when they are deeply involved in a cohesive ingroup, and when the members' strivings for unanimity override their motivation to realistically appraise alternative courses of action" (p. 9). That is, when groups are strongly cohesive (a family, a panel of military advisers, an athletic team), they generally share a strong desire for agreement (to see themselves as one). This desire

Juries and group polarization. Is group polarization a desirable part of jury deliberation? Yes and no. In an ideal world, attorneys from both sides present the facts of the case. Then, after careful deliberation, the jury moves from its initially neutral position toward the defendant to a more extreme position — either conviction or acquittal. In a not-so-ideal world, the quality of legal arguments from opposing sides may not be equal, the individual members of the jury may not be neutral at the start, and some jurors may unduly influence other jurors.

may lead them to ignore important information or points of view held by outsiders or critics (Vaughn, 1996).

As outlined in Figure 48.3, the process of groupthink begins with group members feeling a strong sense of cohesiveness and relative isolation from the judgments of qualified outsiders. Add a directive leader and little chance for debate, and you have the recipe for a potentially dangerous decision. During the actual discussion process, the members also come to believe they are invulnerable, tend to develop common rationalizations and stereotypes of the outgroup, and exert considerable pressure on anyone who dares to offer a dissenting opinion. Some members actually start to play the role of group "mindguards," working rather like bodyguards to isolate and protect the group from all differences in opinion. The tendency toward groupthink is strongest when members feel threatened and begin to defend their view rather than find the best solution (Turner & Horvitz, 2001).

Presidential embarrassments, such as Franklin Roosevelt's failure to anticipate the attack on Pearl Harbor, John F. Kennedy's disastrous backing of the Bay of Pigs invasion of Cuba, Lyndon Johnson's escalation of the Vietnam War, Richard Nixon's cooperation with the Watergate cover-up, and Ronald Reagan's Iran-Contra scandal have all been blamed on groupthink. It also may have contributed to the 1986 explosion of the space shuttle *Challenger* and the loss in 2003 of *The Columbia* (Esser, 1998; Janis, 1972, 1989; Raven, 1998; Schwartz & Broder, 2003).

Another possible example of groupthink? Two days before the Columbia broke apart in 2003, a NASA engineer warned his supervisors of possible catastrophes on reentry. His message was not forwarded up the chain of command and all seven astronauts died in the explosion (Schwartz & Broder, 2003).

Antecedent Conditions

1 A highly cohesive group of decision makers
2 Insulation of the group from outside influences
3 A directive leader
4 Lack of procedures to ensure careful consideration of the pros and cons of alternative actions
5 High stress from external threats with little hope of finding a better solution than that favored by the leader

⬇

Strong desire for group consensus—The groupthink tendency

⬇

Symptoms of Groupthink

1 Illusion of invulnerability
2 Belief in the morality of the group
3 Collective rationalizations
4 Stereotypes of outgroups
5 Self-censorship of doubts and dissenting opinions
6 Illusion of unanimity
7 Direct pressure on dissenters

⬇

Symptoms of Poor Decision Making

1 An incomplete survey of alternative courses of action
2 An incomplete survey of group objectives
3 Failure to examine risks of the preferred choice
4 Failure to reappraise rejected alternatives
5 Poor search for relevant information
6 Selective bias in processing information
7 Failure to develop contingency plans

⬇

Low probability of successful outcome

Figure 48.3 *Groupthink and marriage.* Few people realize that the decision to marry can be a form of groupthink. (Remember that a "group" can have as few as two members.) While dating, the couple may show several of the antecedent conditions (top box): strong need for cohesiveness ("We agree on almost everything"), insulation from outside influences ("We do almost everything as a couple"), and failure to carefully consider the pros and cons of alternative actions. When planning for marriage, they also sometimes show symptoms of groupthink (middle box). These symptoms include: illusion of invulnerability ("We're different — we won't ever get divorced"), collective rationalizations ("Two can live more cheaply than one"), shared stereotypes of the outgroup ("Couples with problems just don't know how to communicate"), and avoidance of dissenters — anyone who doesn't fully support their decision to marry.

*A*ssessment

CHECK & REVIEW

Group Processes

Groups differ from mere collections of people because group members share a mutually recognized relationship with one another. Group membership affects us through the roles we play. The importance of roles in determining and controlling behavior was dramatically demonstrated in Philip Zimbardo's Stanford Prison Study.

Group membership can also lead to **deindividuation,** in which a person becomes so caught up in the group's identity that individual self-awareness and responsibility are temporarily suspended. **Group polarization** research shows that if most group members initially tend toward an extreme idea, the entire group will polarize in that direction. This is because the other, like-minded, members reinforce the dominant tendency. **Groupthink** is a dangerous type of thinking that occurs when a group's desire for agreement overrules its desire to critically evaluate information.

Questions

1. Zimbardo stopped his prison study before the end of the scheduled 2 weeks because _____.

2. The critical factor in deindividuation is _____. (a) loss of self-esteem; (b) anonymity; (c) identity diffusion; (d) group cohesiveness

3. What are the major symptoms of groupthink?

4. In a groupthink situation, the person who takes responsibility for seeing that dissenting opinions are not expressed is called the _____. (a) censor; (b) mindguard; (c) monitor; (d) whip

Answers to Questions can be found in Appendix B.

Aggression *Any behavior intended to harm someone*

■ Aggression: Explaining and Controlling It

Aggression is any form of behavior intended to harm or injure another living being. Why do people act aggressively? We will explore a number of possible explanations for aggression — both *biological* and *psychosocial*. Then we will look at how aggression can be controlled or reduced.

Biological Factors in Aggression

1. ***Instincts.*** Because aggression has such a long history and is found among all cultures, many theorists believe humans are instinctively aggressive. After personally witnessing the massive death and destruction that occurred during World War I, Sigmund Freud stated that aggressive impulses are inborn. He argued that the drive for violence arises from a basic instinct and that, therefore, human aggression cannot be eliminated (Gay, 1999, 2000; Rohrlich, 1998).

   Evolutionary psychologists and ethologists (scientists who study animal behavior) propose another instinct theory. They believe that aggression evolved because it contributes to Darwin's survival of the fittest. Whereas Freud saw aggression as destructive and disruptive, ethologists believe aggression prevents overcrowding and allows the strongest animals to win mates and reproduce the species (Dabbs & Dabbs, 2000; Lorenz, 1981; Rossano, 2003). Most social psychologists, however, reject both Freud's and the ethologists' view of instinct as the source of aggression.

2. ***Genes.*** Twin studies suggest that some individuals are genetically predisposed to have hostile, irritable temperaments and to engage in aggressive acts (Miles & Carey, 1997; Segal & Bouchard, 2000; Wasserman & Wachbroit, 2000). Remember from Module 2, however, this does *not* mean that these people are doomed to behave aggressively. Aggression develops from a complex interaction of biology, social experience, and each individual's behavior.

3. ***The brain and nervous system.*** Electrical stimulation or severing specific parts of an animal's brain has a direct effect on aggression (Delgado, 1960; Delville, Mansour, & Ferris, 1996; Roberts & Nagel, 1996). Research with brain injuries and organic disorders has also identified possible aggression circuits in the brain — in particular, the hypothalamus, amygdala, and other parts of the brain (Davidson, Putnam, & Larson, 2000; Raine et al., 1998).

4. ***Substance abuse and other mental disorders.*** Substance abuse (particularly alcohol) within the general public is a major factor in most forms of aggression — child abuse, spousal assault, robberies, murders, stabbings, and so on (Casswell & Zhang, 1998; Goodwin, 2000; Shuntich, Loh, & Katz, 1998). Homicide rates are also higher among men with schizophrenia and antisocial disorders, particularly if they also abuse alcohol (Raesaenen et al., 1998; Tiihonen, Isohanni, Rasanen, Koiranen, & Moring, 1997).

5. ***Hormones and neurotransmitters.*** Several studies have linked the male gonadal hormone testosterone to aggressive behavior (Boyd, 2000; O'Connor, Archer, Hair, & Wu, 2002; Sanchez-Martin et al., 2000). However, the relationship between human aggression and testosterone is complex. Testosterone seems to increase aggression and dominance, but dominance itself increases testosterone (Mazur & Booth, 1998). Violent behavior has also been linked with low levels of the neurotransmitters serotonin and GABA (gamma-aminobutyric acid) (Bernhardt, 1997; Brady, Myrick, & McElroy, 1998; LeMarquand et al., 1998; Manuck et al., 1998).

Psychosocial Factors in Aggression

1. ***Aversive stimuli.*** Research shows that aversive stimuli such as noise, heat, pain, insults, and foul odors can increase aggression (Anderson, 2001; Anderson, Ander-

son, Dorr, DeNeve, & Flanagan, 2000; Twenge et al., 2001). Traffic congestion (road rage), cramped airlines (airplane rage), and excessive demands at work (office rage) all reflect another aversive stimuli — *frustration*. Being blocked from achieving a goal increases aggressive tendencies.

John Dollard and his colleagues (1939) noted this relationship between frustration and aggression more than half a century ago. According to the **frustration-aggression hypothesis,** frustration creates anger, which for some may lead to aggression. This does not mean that if you get mad at your boss, you necessarily punch him or her in the nose. You may displace your aggression and take out your anger on your family when you get home. Or you may turn your aggression toward yourself, becoming self-destructive or withdrawing, giving up, and getting depressed.

2. ***Culture and learning.*** As we discovered in Module 18, observational or social learning theory suggests that we learn by watching others. Thus, people raised in a culture with aggressive models will learn aggressive responses (Matsumoto, 2000). In Japan, for example, children are taught very early to value social harmony, and Japan has one of the lowest rates of violence in all industrialized nations (Nisbett, Peng, Choi, & Norenzayan, 2000; Zahn-Waxler, Friedman, Cole, Mizuta, & Himura, 1996). In contrast, the United States is one of the most violent nations, and our children grow up with numerous models for aggression, which they tend to imitate.

3. ***Media and video games.*** Despite protestations that violence in movies, TV, and video games is only entertainment, considerable evidence exists that the media can contribute to aggression in both children and adults (Anderson & Dill, 2000; Bartholow & Anderson, 2002; Gilligan, 2000; Zillman & Weaver, 1999). For example, the latest video games, such as *Doom, Mortal Kombat, Resident Evil,* and *Half-Life,* all feature realistic sound effects and gory depictions of "lifelike" violence, which may teach children that violence is exciting and acceptable. Obviously, most children who play violent video games and watch violent movies and TV shows do not go on to become dangerous killers. However, children do imitate what they see on TV [and, presumably, video games] and seem to internalize as a value that violence is acceptable behavior.

Could it be that aggressive children just tend to prefer violent television and video games? Research suggests it is a two-way street. Laboratory studies, correlational research, and cross-cultural studies among children in five different countries (Australia, Finland, Israel, Poland, and the United States) have all found that exposure to TV violence did increase aggressiveness and that aggressive children tend to seek out violent programs (Aluja-Fabregat & Torrubia-Beltri, 1998; Singer, Slovak, Frierson, & York, 1998).

Culture and learning. *Professional wrestlers, like "Stone Cold" Steven Austin, may serve as models for aggression.*

Frustration-Aggression Hypothesis
Blocking of a desired goal (frustration) creates anger that may lead to aggression

Controlling or Eliminating Aggression

Some therapists advise people to release aggressive impulses by engaging in harmless forms of aggression, such as vigorous exercise, punching a pillow, and watching competitive sports. But studies suggest that this type of *catharsis,* or "draining the aggression reservoir," doesn't really help (Bushman, 2002; Bushman, Baumeister, & Stack, 1999). In fact, as we pointed out in Module 32, expressing an emotion, anger or otherwise, tends to intensify the feeling rather than reduce it.

A second approach, which does seem to effectively reduce or control aggression, is to introduce incompatible responses. Because certain emotional responses, such as empathy and humor, are incompatible with aggression, purposely making a joke or showing some sympathy for the other person's point of view can reduce anger and frustration (Harvey & Miceli, 1999; Kaukianen et al., 1999; Oshima, 2000).

A*chievement*

RESEARCH HIGHLIGHT

America's "Anger Epidemic"

Two supermarket shoppers get in a fist-fight over who should be first in a newly opened checkout lane.

A Continental Airlines flight returns to the Anchorage airport after a passenger allegedly throws a can of beer at a flight attendant and bites a pilot.

A father beats another father to death in an argument over rough play at their sons' hockey practice.

What do you think of these media reports? Although Americans experienced a brief time of closeness and increased civility following the horrific terrorist attacks on September 11, 2001, experts believe the nation is still in the grip of an "anger epidemic," ranging from tantrums in supermarkets and on airplanes to deadly fights over a child's hockey practice (Carson, 2002; Gilligan, 2000; Peterson, 2000). Perhaps most disturbing is the increase in teen violence (Zanigel & Ressner, 2001).

One of the most dramatic examples of teen violence occurred on Tuesday, April 20, 1999, in Littelton, Colorado. On that infamous day, Eric Harris and Dylan Klebold shot and killed 12 fellow Columbine High School students and 1 teacher, wounded many others, and then turned the guns on themselves and committed suicide. Armed with a semiautomatic rifle, two sawed-off shotguns, a semiautomatic handgun, and dozens of homemade bombs, these two young men joined a growing list of recent school shootings in the United States.

Although juvenile massacres are still an aberration, the slaughter at Columbine High "opened a sad national conversation about what turns two boys' souls into poison" (Gibbs, 1999, p. 25). What causes kids to gun down other kids? Can we identify high-risk children at early ages? Is aggressiveness a personality trait that is easily malleable or highly resistant to change?

These are the kinds of questions addressed by researchers Rolf Loeber and

Magda Stouthamer-Loeber (1998) of the University of Pittsburgh. Noting that the numbers of juvenile perpetrators and victims have gradually increased over the past decades, these researchers also cite research demonstrating that highly aggressive children are at risk for adult crime, alcoholism, drug abuse, unemployment, divorce, and mental illness.

Research on juvenile antisocial behavior is voluminous, yet Loeber and Stouthamer-Loeber identify five major misconceptions and controversies that block our understanding of the problem and future research.

1. *Stability of childhood aggression.* Correlation studies give the impression that aggression is highly stable from childhood to adulthood (a review of the literature shows coefficients range from .63 to .92 — very high). In other words, individuals who are aggressive as children are likely to be aggressive as adults. However, Loeber and Stouthamer-Loeber think we are stopping short of the real challenge, researching why some children *don't* go on to become aggressive adults. They cite studies showing that preschool boys commonly show aggressive behaviors and that aggression decreases from preschool to elementary school and from adolescence to adulthood. Knowing why some individuals outgrow aggression could greatly help mental health professionals intervene in high-risk cases.

2. *All serious aggression begins in early childhood.* Loeber and Stouthamer-Loeber suggest we need additional research into violent individuals without a history of early aggression. They go on to suggest three developmental types of aggressive individuals: (a) a life-course type (characterized by aggression in childhood that persists and worsens into adulthood), (b) a limited-duration type (individuals who outgrow aggression), and (c) a late onset type (individuals without a history of aggression). This three-type classification could be more helpful to clinicians, probation officers, and others working with children.

3. *Controversy over single or multiple pathways.* Loeber and Stouthamer-Loeber suggest researchers should spend less time debating whether a single pathway or multiple pathways lead to antisocial behavior and violence. (By "pathways," they mean causes such as genes, culture, learning, or any of the other possible causes discussed at the beginning of this section). Instead, we should research multiple pathways because "casting a wide net" is more likely to produce results than looking at each possibility one at a time.

4. *Simple versus complex causes of aggression.* Loeber and Stouthamer-Loeber looked at three possible causes of aggression in children — family factors, physiology, and genetics. They report that a more complex relationship exists than was previously thought.

Studies of family factors, for example, show a relationship exists between children who live with aggressive parents in a conflict filled home and children who commit personal or violent crimes, but not children who commit property crimes. Similarly, physiological studies link certain hormones (such as testosterone) and neurotransmitters (such as serotonin) to juvenile aggression, but not to property crimes. Genetic studies have produced conflicting results.

5. *Male and female aggression is not the same.* Loeber and Stouthamer-Loeber say the assumption that violence develops in much the same way in women and men is erroneous. Although few gender differences have been recorded in toddlerhood, beginning in preschool and throughout adulthood boys show more personal and physical aggression. Furthermore, several investigators have documented that women tend to use more indirect and verbal aggression and relational aggression (gossip and excluding peers) and are less likely to participate in group fighting, gang fighting, aggravated assault, sexual violence, and homicide. For these reasons, Loeber and Stouthamer-Loeber believe major gender differences exist in aggression, but at the same time, they stress that these variations are pieces of the bigger puzzle that must be addressed by future research.

Following the Columbine massacre, the media offered standard and all-too-familiar answers (violence on TV and in the movies, availability of guns, divorce, and "no-parent" households). But as Loeber and Stouthamer-Loeber document in their analysis of juvenile research studies, the problem is complex and we are a long way from answers.

A third approach to controlling aggression is to improve social and communication skills. Studies show that people with the most deficient communication skills account for a disproportionate share of the violence in society (Trump, 2000; Vance, Fernandez, & Biber, 1998). Unfortunately, little effort is made in our schools or families to teach basic communication skills or techniques for conflict resolution.

Altruism: Why We Help (and Don't Help) Others

After reading about prejudice, discrimination, and aggression, you will no doubt be relieved to discover that human beings also behave in positive ways. People help and support one another by donating blood, giving time and money to charities, helping stranded motorists, and so on. There are also times when people do not help.

Consider the following: In 1964, on Austin Street in Queens, New York, a woman named Kitty Genovese was stabbed to death as she returned to her apartment. Thirty-eight of her neighbors heard her screams and pleas for help: "Oh my God, he stabbed me! Please help me! Please help me!" and watched as she struggled to fight off her assailant. The lights in the windows of the observers' apartments apparently scared off the attacker, who left Kitty lying in the street, wounded but still alive. But when the neighbors turned off their lights and went back to bed, the attacker returned and stabbed her again. Kitty's screams once again awakened her neighbors and again the lights scared off her attacker. But the neighbors went back to bed a second time, and the murderer returned for a third and fatal attack.

Why did the neighbors keep going back to bed, and why didn't the police come? Throughout the entire series of attacks (which lasted for over 35 minutes), only 1 of the 38 neighbors belatedly called the police. Why didn't they respond immediately? More generally, under what conditions do people sometimes help and sometimes ignore others' pleas for help?

Why Do We Help?

Altruism (or prosocial behavior) refers to actions designed to help others with no obvious benefit to oneself. Evolutionary theory suggests that altruism is an instinctual behavior that has evolved because it favors survival of one's genes (Bower, 2000; Roesler, 2002; Ozinga, 2000; Rossano, 2003). As evidence, these theorists cite altruistic acts among lower species (e.g., worker bees living for their mother, the queen) and the fact that altruism in humans is strongest toward one's own children and other relatives. Altruism protects not the individual but the individual's genes. By helping or

Altruism *Actions designed to help others with no obvious benefit to the helper*

Internal Response   **Motivation**   **Behavior**

Person in distress

Egoistic model → Distress (anxiety, annoyance, unpleasantness) → Egoistic motivation (reduces distress) → Helping

Empathy–altruism model → Empathy (concern and compassion for other person) → Altruistic motivation (reduces other's distress) → Helping

Figure 48.4 *Two major explanations for helping.* Do you think the egoistic or the empathy-altruism model is best shown in this photo? Would the young child be motivated to help his pet? Why? According to C. D. Batson and his colleagues, both models motivate helping. Can you explain?

Egoistic Model *Helping that's motivated by anticipated gain — later reciprocation, increased self-esteem, or avoidance of guilt and distress*

Empathy-Altruism Hypothesis *Helping because of empathy for someone in need*

Diffusion of Responsibility *Assuming someone else will take action (or responsibility)*

even dying for your child or sibling, you increase the odds that your genes will be passed on to future generations.

Other research suggests that helping may actually be a form of egoism or disguised self-interest. According to this **egoistic model,** helping is always motivated by some degree of anticipated gain. We help others because we hope for later reciprocation, because it makes us feel good about ourselves, or because it helps us avoid feelings of distress and guilt that loom if we don't help (Cialdini, 2001; Williams, Haber, Weaver, & Freeman, 1998).

Opposing the egoistic model is the **empathy-altruism hypothesis** proposed by C. D. Batson and his colleagues (Batson, 1991, 1998; Batson et al., 1999). As Figure 48.4 shows, Batson thinks some altruism is motivated by simple, selfish concerns (the top part of the diagram), but in other situations, helping is truly selfless and motivated by concern for others (the bottom part of the diagram).

According to the empathy-altruism hypothesis, simply seeing another person's suffering or hearing of his or her need can create *empathy*, a subjective grasp of that person's feelings or experiences. When we feel empathic toward another, we focus on that person's distress, not our own, and are motivated to help the person for his or her own sake (Batson et al., 1999; Kahne, 1999). The ability to empathize may even be innate. Research with infants in the first few hours of life shows that they become distressed and cry at the sound of another infant's cries (Hay, 1994; Hoffman, 1993).

Why Don't We Help?

Many theories have been proposed to explain why people help, but few explain why we do not. How do we explain the Kitty Genovese tragedy? One of the most comprehensive explanations for helping or not helping comes from the research of Bibb Latane and John Darley (1970). They found that whether or not someone helps depends on a series of interconnected events and decisions. The potential helper must first *notice* what is happening, must then *interpret* the event as an emergency, must accept *personal responsibility* for helping, and then must *decide how to help* and actually initiate the helping behavior.

Where did the sequence break down for Kitty Genovese? Kitty's neighbors obviously noticed what was happening and interpreted it as an emergency. The first break in the helping sequence was in their willingness to accept personal responsibility. Newspaper interviews with each of the neighbors described a great deal of anguish, but each of them "naturally" assumed that someone else had already called the police. This is the **diffusion of responsibility** phenomenon — the tendency to assume that someone else will respond and act. It is ironic that if only one neighbor had seen Kitty's attack and known that there were no other witnesses, Kitty might still be alive today.

How Can We Promote Helping?

The most obvious way to increase altruistic behavior is to clarify when help is needed. For example, if you notice a situation in which it seems unclear whether someone needs help, simply ask. On the other hand, if you are the one in need of help, look directly at anyone who may be watching and give specific directions, such as "Call the police."

Helping behaviors could also be encouraged through societal rewards. Some researchers suggest that states need to enact more laws that protect the helper from potential suits and punish people who fail to respond. Certain existing police programs, such as Crime Stoppers, actively recruit public compliance in reporting crime, give monetary rewards, and ensure anonymity. Such programs have apparently been highly effective in reducing crime.

A Final Note

As we close this final module, we sincerely hope that this introduction to psychology has encouraged you to see psychology not only as a science and academic discipline but also as a method for personal and social change. This may sound grandiose. However, if you accept the view that people are rational and behavior can be described, explained, predicted, and changed, then no problem is insurmountable. As you may remember, these are the four goals of psychology discussed in Module 1. I encourage you to share my belief in the transformative nature of psychology and to apply what you have learned from this text and course to your everyday life. I also invite you to continue your exploration of the subject through a career in psychology, or simply as part of your lifelong learning and personal growth.

Assessment

CHECK & REVIEW

Aggression and Altruism

Aggression is any deliberate attempt to harm another living being who is motivated to avoid such treatment. Some researchers believe it is caused by biological factors, such as instincts, genes, the brain and nervous system, substance abuse and other mental disorders, and hormones and neurotransmitters. Other researchers emphasize psychosocial factors, such as aversive stimuli, culture and learning, and media and video games. Releasing aggressive feelings through violent acts or watching violence is not an effective way to reduce aggression. Introducing incompatible responses (such as humor) and teaching social and communication skills is more efficient.

Altruism refers to actions designed to help others with no obvious benefit to one-self. Evolutionary theorists believe altruism is innate and has survival value. Psychological explanations for altruism emphasize the **egoistic model**, which suggests that helping is motivated by anticipated gain, or the **empathy-altruism hypothesis**, which proposes that helping can also be activated when the helper feels empathy for the victim.

Whether or not someone helps depends on a series of interconnected events, starting with noticing the problem and ending with a decision to help. Some people don't help because of the ambiguity of many emergency situations or because of **diffusion of responsibility** (assuming someone else will respond). To increase the chances of altruism, we should reduce ambiguity, increase the rewards for helping, and decrease the costs.

Questions

1. What are the five major biological and three chief psychosocial factors that contribute to aggression?

2. According to research, what are the best ways to reduce aggression?

3. How do evolutionary theorists, the egoistic model, and the empathy-altruism hypothesis explain altruism?

4. Kitty Genovese's neighbors failed to respond to her cries for help because of the _____ phenomenon. (a) empathy-altruism; (b) egoistic model; (c) inhumanity of large cities; (d) diffusion of responsibility

Answers to Questions can be found in Appendix B.

MODULE 48   ACTIVE LEARNING WORKSHEET

ACROSS

3 A type of social influence in which an individual follows direct commands, usually from someone in a position of authority.

6 A type of social influence in which individuals change their behavior as a result of real or imagined group pressure.

7 Cultural rule of behavior that prescribes what is acceptable in a given situation.

8 Any behavior that is intended to harm someone.

9 A condition that results when a highly cohesive group strives for agreement to the point of avoiding inconsistent information; the result is faulty decision-making.

10 Actions designed to help others with no obvious benefit to the helper.

DOWN

1 A group's movement toward either riskier or more conservative behavior, depending upon the members' initial dominant tendency.

2 People to whom we conform (or with whom we go along) because we like and admire them and want to be like them.

4 The increased arousal and reduced self-consciousness, inhibition, and personal responsibility that can occur when a person is part of a group, particularly when the members feel anonymous.

5 The proposal that helping behavior is motivated by anticipated gain—later reciprocation, increased self-esteem, or avoidance of guilt and distress.

Assessment

KEY TERMS

To assess your understanding of the **Key Terms** in this section, write a definition for each (in your own words), and then compare your definitions with those in the text.

social psychology (p. 597)

Our Thoughts About Others
attitude (p. 600)
attribution (p. 598)
cognitive dissonance theory (p. 601)
fundamental attribution error (FAE) (p. 598)
saliency bias (p. 598)
self-serving bias (p. 599)

Our Feelings About Others
companionate love (p. 613)
discrimination (p. 604)

ingroup favoritism (p. 605)
interpersonal attraction (p. 607)
need compatibility (p. 611)
need complementarity (p. 611)
outgroup homogeneity effect (p. 605)
prejudice (p. 604)
proximity (p. 610)
romantic love (p. 612)
stereotype (p. 604)

Our Actions Toward Others
aggression (p. 626)
altruism (p. 629)
conformity (p. 616)

deindividuation (p. 621)
diffusion of responsibility (p. 630)
egoistic model (p. 630)
empathy-altruism hypothesis (p. 630)
foot-in-the-door technique (p. 620)
frustration-aggression hypothesis (p. 627)
group polarization (p. 623)
groupthink (p. 623)
informational social influence (p. 618)
norm (p. 617)
normative social influence (p. 616)
obedience (p. 618)
reference groups (p. 618)

Achievement

WEB RESOURCES

Huffman Book Companion Site
http://www.wiley.com/college/huffman
This site is loaded with free Interactive Self-Tests, Internet Exercises, Glossary and Flashcards for key terms, Web links, Handbook for Non-Native Speakers, and other activities designed to improve your mastery of the material in this section.

Want more general information about social psychology?
http://www.socialpsychology.org/
Sponsored by the Social Psychology Network, this web site is the best starting place for information about the field. As stated on the opening page, this is "the largest social psychology database on the Internet. In these pages, you'll find more than 5,000 links related to psychology."

Interested in love and attraction?
http://www.socialpsychology.org/social.htm
As part of the Social Psychology Network, this link offers tips for online romance, shyness, top 10 rejection lines by women and men, and other interesting topics.

Want to learn more about prejudice and its reduction?
http://www.tolerance.org/
This web site offers self-tests for hidden bias, 101 tools for tolerance, 10 ways to fight hate, and a host of other important topics.

Interested in social influence and persuasion techniques?
http://www.influenceatwork.com/
This is a commercial web site for the Influence at work consulting services group. Robert Cialdini, a renowned expert on

influence, is the president of this organization. You'll find interesting links describing their training and services.

Need information about cults and psychological manipulation?
http://www.csj.org/
AFF, a professional organization, studies psychological manipulation, cult groups, sects, and new religious movements. Through their publications, workshops, programs, and services, they offer practical educational services for families, former group members, professionals, and educators.

Want to learn more about violence and aggression?
http://www.ncovr.heinz.cmu.edu/pls/public/navigation_pkg.
index_page?wh=down&pg=/docs/home.htm
The National Consortium on Violence Research (NCOVR) is a research and training center specializing in violence research. On this web site, they provide important resources and information related to interpersonal violence.

Interested in the Stanford Prison Study?
http://www.prisonexp.org/
As described in Module 48, Philip Zimbardo's prison study is a classic in social psychology. This web site provides an overview of the study, a slide tour, and a discussion of what it tells us about human nature.

VISUAL SUMMARY

Social Psychology
(Modules 46, 47, and 48)

Our Thoughts About Others

Attribution

Attribution: Explaining others' behavior by deciding that their actions resulted from internal factors (their own traits and motives) or external factors (the situation). Problems:

Fundamental attribution error: Tendency to overestimate internal personality influences and underestimate situational factors when judging behavior of others. Why? May be **saliency bias**, focusing on most noticeable (salient) factors.

Self-serving bias: Tendency to explain our own behavior by attributing positive outcomes to internal factors and negative outcomes to external causes.

Attitudes

Attitudes: Learned predispositions toward a particular object. Three components of all attitudes: cognitive, affective, and behavioral tendencies.

Cognitive Dissonance Theory

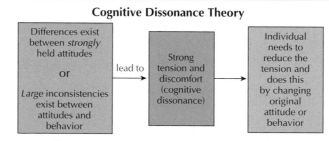

Differences exist between *strongly* held attitudes

or

Large inconsistencies exist between attitudes and behavior

lead to

Strong tension and discomfort (cognitive dissonance)

Individual needs to reduce the tension and does this by changing original attitude or behavior

Our Feelings About Others

Prejudice and Discrimination

Prejudice: Generally negative attitude directed toward people solely because of their membership in a specific group. Contains all three components of attitudes—cognitive (**stereotype**), affective, and behavioral (discrimination).
Discrimination: Refers to the actual negative behavior directed at members of a group. People do not always act on their prejudices. Four major sources of prejudice:

Learning: Classical and operant conditioning and social learning

Cognitive processes: **Ingroup favoritism, outgroup homogeneity effect**

Economic and political competition

Displaced aggression: Scapegoating

Five methods for reducing prejudice and discrimination:
  • Cooperation
  • **Superordinate goals**
  • Increased contact
  • Cognitive retraining
  • Cognitive dissonance

Our Feelings About Others (cont.)

Interpersonal attraction Three key factors:

Physical **proximity** increases attraction largely due to the *mere exposure effect.*

Physical attractiveness is important to initial attraction and more important to men than women, yet standards of beauty vary across cultures and historically.

Although many believe "opposites attract" **(need complementarity)**, research shows **similarity (need compatibility)** is more important.

- *Love:* Rubin defines it in terms of caring, attachment, and intimacy.
- **Romantic love** highly valued in our society, but it's based on mystery and fantasy; thus, hard to sustain.
- **Companionate love** relies on mutual trust, respect, and friendship and grows stronger with time.

Our Actions Toward Others

Social Influence

Conformity: Changes in behavior in response to real or imagined pressure from others.
Four reasons we conform:

For approval and acceptance **(normative social influence).**

Need for more information **(informational social influence).**

To match behavior of those we admire and feel similar to **(reference group).**

We also conform because it is often adaptive to do so.

Obedience: Going along with a direct command. Milgram's experiment showed a high degree of obedience. Why?

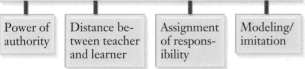

| Power of authority | Distance between teacher and learner | Assignment of responsibility | Modeling/imitation |

Aggression

Aggression: Deliberate attempt to harm another living being who is motivated to avoid such treatment.
- *Biological causes:* Instincts, genes, the brain and nervous system, substance abuse and other mental disorders, hormones, and neurotransmitters.
- *Psychosocial causes:* Aversive stimuli, learning, media, and videogames.
- *Treatment:* Incompatible responses (like humor), social skills, and improved communication help reduce aggression, but expressing it doesn't.

Group Processes

Groups are two or more people interacting and influencing one another's behavior.
- *Group membership* affects us through the roles we play or through **deindividuation**
- *Group decision making* is affected by two key factors:

Group polarization: When most group members initially tend toward an extreme idea, the entire group will move toward that extreme.

Groupthink: Dangerous type of decision making where group's desire for agreement overrules critical evaluation.

Altruism

Altruism: Actions designed to help others with no obvious benefit to oneself.
Why do we help?
- Evolutionary theorists believe altruism is innate and has survival value.
- Psychological explanations suggest helping is motivated by anticipated gain **(egoistic model)** or when helper feels empathy for the victim **(empathy-altruism hypothesis).**
Why don't we help?
- It depends on a series of interconnected events, starting with noticing the problem and ending with a decision to help.
- Many emergency situations are ambiguous.
- We assume others will respond **(diffusion of responsibility).**
How do we increase altruism?
- Reduce ambiguity by giving clear directions to observers.
- Increase rewards, while decreasing costs.

APPENDIX A
Statistics and Psychology

We are constantly bombarded by numbers: "On sale for 30 percent off," "70 percent chance of rain," "9 out of 10 doctors recommend…" The president uses numbers to try to convince us that the economy is healthy. Advertisers use numbers to convince us of the effectiveness of their products. Psychologists use statistics to support or refute psychological theories and demonstrate that certain behaviors are indeed results of specific causal factors.

When people use numbers in these ways, they are using statistics. **Statistics** is a branch of applied mathematics that uses numbers to describe and analyze information on a subject.

Statistics make it possible for psychologists to quantify the information they obtain in their studies. They can then critically analyze and evaluate this information. Statistical analysis is imperative for researchers to describe, predict, or explain behavior. For instance, Albert Bandura (1973) proposed that watching violence on television causes aggressive behavior in children. In carefully controlled experiments, he gathered numerical information and analyzed it according to specific statistical methods. The statistical analysis helped him substantiate that the aggression of his subjects and the aggressive acts they had seen on television were related, and that the relationship was not mere coincidence.

Although statistics is a branch of applied mathematics, you don't have to be a math whiz to use statistics. Simple arithmetic is all you need to do most of the calculations. For more complex statistics involving more complicated mathematics, computer programs are available for virtually every type of computer. What is more important than learning the mathematical computations, however, is developing an understanding of when and why each type of statistic is used. The purpose of this appendix is to help you understand the significance of the statistics most commonly used.

GATHERING AND ORGANIZING DATA

Psychologists design their studies to facilitate gathering information about the factors they want to study. The information they obtain is known as **data (data** is plural; its singular is **datum).** When the data are gathered, they are generally in the form of numbers; if they aren't, they are converted to numbers. After they are gathered, the data must be organized in such a way that statistical analysis is possible. In the following section, we will examine the methods used to gather and organize information.

■ Variables

When studying a behavior, psychologists normally focus on one particular factor to determine whether it has an effect on the behavior. This factor is known as a **variable,** which is in effect anything that can assume more than one value (see Chapter 1). Height, weight, sex, eye color, and scores on an IQ test or a video game are all factors that can assume more than one value and are therefore variables. Some will vary between people, such as sex (you are either male *or* female but not both at the same time). Some may even vary within one person, such as scores on a video game (the same person might get 10,000 points on one try and only 800 on another). Opposed to a variable, anything that remains the same and does not vary is called a **constant.** If researchers use only females in their research, then sex is a constant, not a variable.

In nonexperimental studies, variables can be factors that are merely observed through naturalistic observation or case studies, or they can be factors about which people are questioned in a test or survey. In experimental studies, the two major types of variables are independent and dependent variables.

Drawing by M. Stevens; © 1989 the New Yorker Magazine, Inc.

Independent variables are those that are manipulated by the experimenter. For example, suppose we were to conduct a study to determine whether the sex of the debater influences the outcome of a debate. In this study, one group of subjects watches a videotape of a debate between a male arguing the "pro" side and a female arguing the "con"; another group watches the same debate, but with the pro and con roles reversed. In such a study, the form of the presentation viewed by each group (whether "pro" is argued by a male or a female) is the independent variable because the experimenter manipulates the form of presentation seen by each group. Another example might be a study to determine whether a particular drug has any effect on a manual dexterity task. To study this question, we would administer the drug to one group and no drug to another. The independent variable would be the amount of drug given (some or none). The independent variable is particularly important when using **inferential statistics,** which we will discuss later.

The **dependent variable** is a factor that results from, or depends on, the independent variable. It is a measure of some outcome or, most commonly, a measure of the subjects' behavior. In the debate example, each subject's choice of the winner of the debate would be the dependent variable. In the drug experiment, the dependent variable would be each subject's score on the manual dexterity task.

■ Frequency Distributions

After conducting a study and obtaining measures of the variable(s) being studied, psychologists need to organize the data in a meaningful way. Table A.1 presents test scores from a statistics aptitude test collected from 50 college students. This information is called **raw data** because there is no order to the numbers. They are presented as they were collected and are therefore "raw."

The lack of order in raw data makes them difficult to study. Thus, the first step in understanding the results of an experiment is to impose some order on the raw data. There are several ways to do this. One of the simplest is to create a **frequency distribution,** which shows the number of times a score or event occurs. Although frequency distributions are helpful in several ways, the major advantages are that they

TABLE A.1 STATISTICS APTITUDE TEST SCORES FOR 50 COLLEGE STUDENTS

73	57	63	59	50
72	66	50	67	51
63	59	65	62	65
62	72	64	73	66
61	68	62	68	63
59	61	72	63	52
59	58	57	68	57
64	56	65	59	60
50	62	68	54	63
52	62	70	60	68

TABLE A.2 FREQUENCY DISTRIBUTION OF 50 STUDENTS ON STATISTICS APTITUDE TEST

Score	Frequency
73	2
72	3
71	0
70	1
69	0
68	5
67	1
66	2
65	3
64	2
63	5
62	5
61	2
60	2
59	5
58	1
57	3
56	1
55	0
54	1
53	0
52	2
51	1
50	3
Total	50

allow us to see the data in an organized manner and they make it easier to represent the data on a graph.

The simplest way to make a frequency distribution is to list all the possible test scores, then tally the number of people (N) who received those scores. Table A.2 presents a frequency distribution using the raw data from Table A.1. As you can see, the data are now easier to read. From looking at the frequency distribution, you can see that most of the test scores lie in the middle with only a few at the very high or very low end. This was not at all evident from looking at the raw data.

This type of frequency distribution is practical when the number of possible scores is 20 or fewer. However, when there are more than 20 possible scores it can be even harder to make sense out of the frequency distribution than the raw data. This can be seen in Table A.3, which presents the Scholastic Aptitude Test scores for 50 students. Even though there are only 50 actual scores in this table, the number of possible scores ranges from a high of 1390 to a low of 400. If we included zero frequencies there would be 991 entries in a frequency distribution of this data, making the frequency distribution much more difficult to understand than the raw data. If there are more than 20 possible scores, therefore, a **group** frequency distribution is normally used.

In a **group frequency distribution,** individual scores are represented as members of a group of scores or as a range

TABLE A.3 SCHOLASTIC APTITUDE TEST SCORES FOR 50 COLLEGE STUDENTS

1350	750	530	540	750
1120	410	788	1020	430
720	1080	1110	770	610
1130	620	510	1160	630
640	1220	920	650	870
930	660	480	940	670
1070	950	680	450	990
690	1010	800	660	500
860	520	540	880	1090
580	730	570	560	740

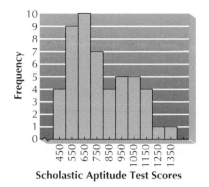

Figure A.1 A histogram illustrating the information found in Table A.4.

of scores (see Table A.4). These groups are called **class intervals.** Grouping these scores makes it much easier to make sense out of the distribution, as you can see from the relative ease in understanding Table A.4 as compared to Table A.3. Group frequency distributions are easier to represent on a graph.

When graphing data from frequency distributions, the class intervals are represented along the **abscissa** (the horizontal or *x* axis), whereas the frequency is represented along the ordinate (the vertical or *y* axis). Information can be graphed in the form of a bar graph, called a **histogram,** or in the form of a point or line graph, called a **polygon.** Figure A.1 shows a histogram presenting the data from Table A.4. Note that the class intervals are represented along the bottom line of the graph (the *x* axis) and the height of the bars indicates the frequency in each class interval. Now look at Figure A.2. The information presented here is exactly the same as that in Figure A.1 but is represented in the form of a polygon rather than a histogram. Can you see how both graphs illustrate the same information? Even though reading information from a graph is simple, we have found that many students have never learned to read graphs. In the next section we will explain how to read a graph.

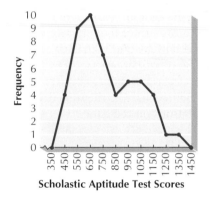

Figure A.2 A polygon illustrating the information found in Table A.4.

How to Read a Graph

Every graph has several major parts. The most important are the labels, the axes (the vertical and horizontal lines), and the points, lines, or bars. Find these parts in Figure A.1.

The first thing you should notice when reading a graph are the labels because they tell what data are portrayed. Usually the data consist of the descriptive statistics, or the numbers used to measure the dependent variables. For example, in Figure A.1 the horizontal axis is labeled "Scholastic Aptitude Test Scores," which is the dependent variable measure; the vertical axis is labeled "Frequency," which means the number of occurrences. If a graph is not labeled, as we sometimes see in TV commercials or magazine ads, it is useless and should be ignored. Even when a graph *is* labeled, the labels can be misleading. For example, if graph designers want to distort the information, they can elongate one of the axes. Thus, it is important to pay careful attention to the numbers as well as the words in graph labels.

Next, you should focus your attention on the bars, points, or lines on the graph. In the case of histograms like the one in Figure A.1, each bar represents the class interval. The width of the bar stands for the width of the class inter-

TABLE A.4 GROUP FREQUENCY DISTRIBUTION OF SCHOLASTIC APTITUDE TEST SCORES FOR 50 COLLEGE STUDENTS

Class Interval	Frequency
1300–1399	1
1200–1299	1
1100–1199	4
1000–1099	5
900–999	5
800–899	4
700–799	7
600–699	10
500–599	9
400–499	4
Total	50

val, whereas the height of the bar stands for the frequency in that interval. Look at the third bar from the left in Figure A.1. This bar represents the interval "600 to 699 SAT Scores," which has a frequency of 10. You can see that this directly corresponds to the same class interval in Table A.4, since graphs and tables are both merely alternate ways of illustrating information.

Reading point or line graphs is the same as reading a histogram. In a point graph, each point represents two numbers, one found along the horizontal axis and the other found along the vertical axis. A polygon is identical to a point graph except that it has lines connecting the points. Figure A.2 is an example of a polygon, where each point represents a class interval and is placed at the center of the interval and at the height corresponding to the frequency of that interval. To make the graph easier to read, the points are connected by straight lines.

Displaying the data in a frequency distribution or in a graph is much more useful than merely presenting raw data and can be especially helpful when researchers are trying to find relations between certain factors. However, as we explained earlier, if psychologists want to make predictions or explanations about behavior, they need to perform mathematical computations on the data.

 ## USES OF THE VARIOUS STATISTICS

The statistics psychologists use in a study depend on whether they are trying to describe and predict behavior or explain it. When they use statistics to describe behavior, as in reporting the average score on the Scholastic Aptitude Test, they are using **descriptive statistics.** When they use them to explain behavior, as Bandura did in his study of children modeling aggressive behavior seen on TV, they are using **inferential statistics.**

■ Descriptive Statistics

Descriptive statistics are the numbers used to describe the dependent variable. They can be used to describe characteristics of a **population** (an entire group, such as all people living in the United States) or a **sample** (a part of a group, such as a randomly selected group of 25 students from Cornell University). The major descriptive statistics include measures of central tendency (mean, median, and mode), measures of variation (variance and standard deviation), and correlation.

Measures of Central Tendency

Statistics indicating the center of the distribution are called **measures of central tendency** and include the mean, median, and mode. They are all scores that are typical of the center of the distribution. The **mean** is what most of us think of when we hear the word "average." The **median** is

TABLE A.5 COMPUTATION OF THE MEAN FOR 10 IQ SCORES

IQ Scores X
143
127
116
98
85
107
106
98
104
116
$\Sigma X = 1{,}100$

$$\text{Mean} = \bar{X} = \frac{\Sigma X}{N} = \frac{1{,}100}{10} = 110$$

the middle score. The **mode** is the score that occurs most often.

Mean   What is your average golf score? What is the average yearly rainfall in your part of the country? What is the average reading test score in your city? When these questions ask for the average, they are really asking for the "mean." The arithmetic **mean** is the weighted average of all the raw scores, which is computed by totaling all the raw scores and then dividing that total by the number of scores added together. In statistical computation, the mean is represented by an "X" with a bar above it ($\bar{X}$, pronounced "X bar"), each individual raw score by an "X," and the total number of scores by an "N." For example, if we wanted to compute the $\bar{X}$ of the raw statistics test scores in Table A.1, we would sum all the X's (ΣX, with Σ meaning sum) and divide by N (number of scores). In Table A.1, the sum of all the scores is equal to 3,100 and there are 50 scores. Therefore, the mean of these scores is

$$\bar{X} = \frac{3{,}100}{50} = 62$$

Table A.5 illustrates how to calculate the mean for 10 IQ scores.

Median   The **median** is the middle score in the distribution once all the scores have been arranged in rank order. If N (the number of scores) is odd, then there actually is a middle score and that middle score is the median. When N is even, there are two middle scores and the median is the mean of those two scores. Table A.6 shows the computation of the median for two different sets of scores, one set with 15 scores and one with 10.

TABLE A.6 COMPUTATION OF MEDIAN FOR ODD AND EVEN NUMBERS OF IQ SCORES

IQ	IQ
139	137
130	135
121	121
116	116
107	108 ← middle score
101	106 ← middle score
98	105
96 ← middle score	101
84	98
83	97
82	N = 10
75	N is even
75	
68	Median = $\dfrac{106 + 108}{2}$ = 107
65	

N = 15
N is odd

Mode Of all the measures of central tendency, the easiest to compute is the **mode,** which is merely the most frequent score. It is computed by finding the score that occurs most often. Whereas there is always only one mean and only one median for each distribution, there can be more than one mode. Table A.7 shows how to find the mode in a distribution with one mode (unimodal) and in a distribution with two modes (bimodal).

There are several advantages to each of these measures of central tendency, but in psychological research the mean is used most often. A book solely covering psychological statistics will provide a more thorough discussion of the relative values of these measures.

TABLE A.7 FINDING THE MODE FOR TWO DIFFERENT DISTRIBUTIONS

IQ	IQ
139	139
138	138
125	125
116 ←	116 ←
116 ←	116 ←
116 ←	116 ←
107	107
100	98 ←
98	98 ←
98	98 ←
Mode = most frequent score	Mode = 116 and 98
Mode = 116	

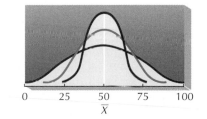

Figure A.3 Three distributions having the same mean but a different variability.

Measures of Variation

When describing a distribution, it is not sufficient merely to give the central tendency; it is also necessary to give a **measure of variation,** which is a measure of the spread of the scores. By examining the spread, we can determine whether the scores are bunched around the middle or tend to extend away from the middle. Figure A.3 shows three different distributions, all with the same mean but with different spreads of scores. You can see from this figure that, in order to describe these different distributions accurately, there must be some measures of the variation in their spread. The most widely used measure of variation is the standard deviation, which is represented by a lowercase s. The standard deviation is a standard measurement of how much the scores in a distribution deviate from the mean. The formula for standard deviation is

$$s = \sqrt{\frac{\Sigma(X - \overline{X})^2}{N}}$$

Table A.8 illustrates how to compute the standard deviation.

TABLE A.8 COMPUTATION OF THE STANDARD DEVIATION FOR 10 IQ SCORES

IQ Scores X	$X - \overline{X}$	$(X - \overline{X})^2$
143	33	1089
127	17	289
116	6	36
98	−12	144
85	−25	625
107	−3	9
106	−4	16
98	−12	144
104	−6	36
116	6	36
ΣX = 1100		$\Sigma(X - \overline{X})^2$ = 2424

Standard Deviation = s

$$= \sqrt{\frac{\Sigma(X - \overline{X})^2}{N}} = \sqrt{\frac{2424}{10}}$$

$$= \sqrt{242.4} = 15.569$$

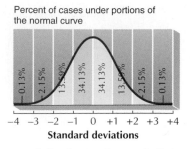

Percent of cases under portions of the normal curve

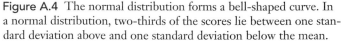

0.13% 2.15% 13.59% 34.13% 34.13% 13.59% 2.15% 0.13%

−4 −3 −2 −1   0 +1 +2 +3 +4
Standard deviations

Figure A.4 The normal distribution forms a bell-shaped curve. In a normal distribution, two-thirds of the scores lie between one standard deviation above and one standard deviation below the mean.

Most distributions of psychological data are bell-shaped. That is, most of the scores are grouped around the mean, and the farther the scores are from the mean in either direction, the fewer the scores. Notice the bell shape of the distribution in Figure A.4. Distributions such as this are called **normal** distributions. In normal distributions, as shown in Figure A.4, approximately two-thirds of the scores fall within a range that is one standard deviation below the mean to one standard deviation above the mean. For example, the Wechsler IQ tests (see Chapter 7) have a mean of 100 and a standard deviation of 15. This means that approximately two-thirds of the people taking these tests will have scores between 85 and 115.

Correlation

Suppose for a moment that you are sitting in the student union with a friend. To pass the time, you and your friend decide to play a game in which you try to guess the height of the next male who enters the union. The winner, the one whose guess is closest to the person's actual height, gets a piece of pie paid for by the loser. When it is your turn, what do you guess? If you are like most people, you will probably try to estimate the mean of all the males in the union and use that as your guess. The mean is always your best guess if you have no other information.

Now let's change the game a little and add a friend who stands outside the union and weighs the next male to enter the union. Before the male enters the union, your friend says "125 pounds." Given this new information, will you still guess the mean height? Probably not — you will probably predict *below* the mean. Why? Because there is a **correlation**, a relationship, between height and weight, with tall people usually weighing more than short people. Since 125 pounds is less than the average weight for males, you will probably guess a less-than-average height. The statistic used to measure this type of relationship between two variables is called a correlation coefficient.

Correlation Coefficient A **correlation coefficient** measures the relationship between two variables, such as height and weight or IQ and SAT scores. Given any two variables, there are three possible relationships between

them: **positive, negative,** and **zero** (no relationship). A positive relationship exists when the two variables vary in the same direction (e.g., as height increases, weight normally also increases). A negative relationship occurs when the two variables vary in opposite directions (e.g., as temperatures go up, hot chocolate sales go down). There is no relationship when the two variables vary totally independently of one another (e.g., there is no relationship between peoples' height and the color of their toothbrushes). Figure A.5 illustrates these three types of correlations.

The computation and the formula for a correlation coefficient (correlation coefficient is delineated by the letter "r") are shown in Table A.9. The correlation coefficient (r) always has a value between +1 and −1 (it is never greater than +1 and it is never smaller than −1). When r is close to +1, it signifies a high positive relationship between the two variables (as one variable goes up, the other variable also goes up). When r is close to −1, it signifies a high negative relationship between the two variables (as one variable goes up, the other variable goes down). When r is 0, there is no linear relationship between the two variables being measured.

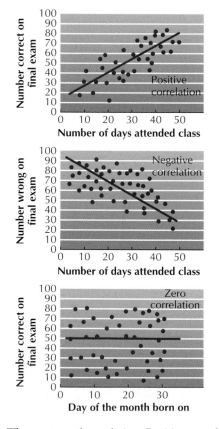

Figure A.5 Three types of correlation. Positive correlation (top): As the number of days of class attendance increases, so does the number of correct exam items. Negative correlation (middle): As the number of days of class attendance increases, the number of incorrect exam items decreases. Zero correlation (bottom): The day of the month on which one is born has no relationship to the number of exam items correct.

TABLE A.9 COMPUTATION OF CORRELATION COEFFICIENT BETWEEN HEIGHT AND WEIGHT FOR 10 MALES

Height (inches) X	X^2	Weight (pounds) Y	Y^2	XY
73	5,329	210	44,100	15,330
64	4,096	133	17,689	8,512
65	4,225	128	16,384	8,320
70	4,900	156	24,336	10,920
74	5,476	189	35,721	13,986
68	4,624	145	21,025	9,860
67	4,489	145	21,025	9,715
72	5,184	166	27,556	11,952
76	5,776	199	37,601	15,124
71	5,041	159	25,281	11,289
700	49,140	1,630	272,718	115,008

$$r = \frac{N \cdot \Sigma XY - \Sigma X \cdot \Sigma Y}{\sqrt{[N \cdot \Sigma X^2 - (\Sigma X)^2]}\sqrt{[N \cdot \Sigma Y^2 - (\Sigma Y)^2]}}$$

$$r = \frac{10 \cdot 115,008 - 700 \cdot 1,630}{\sqrt{[10 \cdot 49,140 - 700^2]}\sqrt{[10 \cdot 272,718 - 1,630^2]}}$$

$$r = 0.92$$

Correlation coefficients can be quite helpful in making predictions. Bear in mind, however, that predictions are just that: *predictions*. They will have some error as long as the correlation coefficients on which they are based are not perfect (+1 or −1). Also, correlations cannot reveal any information regarding causation. Merely because two factors are correlated, it does not mean that one factor causes the other. Consider, for example, ice cream consumption and swimming pool use. These two variables are positively correlated with one another, in that as ice cream consumption increases, so does swimming pool use. But nobody would suggest that eating ice cream *causes* swimming, or vice versa. Similarly, just because Michael Jordan eats Wheaties and can do a slam dunk it does not mean that you will be able to do one if you eat the same breakfast. The only way to determine the cause of behavior is to conduct an experiment and analyze the results by using inferential statistics.

■ Inferential Statistics

Knowing the descriptive statistics associated with different distributions, such as the mean and standard deviation, can enable us to make comparisons between various distributions. By making these comparisons, we may be able to observe whether one variable is related to another or whether one variable has a causal effect on another. When we design an experiment specifically to measure causal effects between two or more variables, we use **inferential statistics** to analyze the data collected. Although there are many inferential statistics, the one we will discuss is the *t* test, since it is the simplest.

t-Test Suppose we believe that drinking alcohol causes a person's reaction time to slow down. To test this hypothesis, we recruit 20 participants and separate them into two groups. We ask the participants in one group to drink a large glass of orange juice with one ounce of alcohol for every 100 pounds of body weight (e.g., a person weighing 150 pounds would get 1.5 ounces of alcohol). We ask the control group to drink an equivalent amount of orange juice with no alcohol added. Fifteen minutes after the drinks, we have each participant perform a reaction time test that consists of pushing a button as soon as a light is flashed. (The reaction time is the time between the onset of the light and the pressing of the button.) Table A.10 shows the data from this hypothetical experiment. It is clear from the data that there is definitely a difference in the reaction times of the two groups: There is an obvious difference between the means. However, it is possible that this difference is due merely to chance. To determine whether the difference is real or due to chance, we can conduct a *t*-test. We have run a sample *t*-test in Table A.10.

TABLE A.10 REACTION TIMES IN MILLISECONDS (MSEC) FOR SUBJECTS IN ALCOHOL AND NO ALCOHOL CONDITIONS AND COMPUTATION OF T

RT (msec) Alcohol X_1	RT (msec) No Alcohol X_2
200	143
210	137
140	179
160	184
180	156
187	132
196	176
198	148
140	125
159	120
$SX_1 = 1,770$	$SX_2 = 1,500$
$N_1 = 10$	$N_2 = 10$
$\bar{X}_1 = 177$	$\bar{X}_2 = 150$
$s_1 = 24.25$	$s_2 = 21.86$

$$S_{\bar{X}_1} = \frac{s}{\sqrt{N_1 - 1}} = 8.08 \qquad S_{\bar{X}_2} = \frac{s}{\sqrt{N_2 - 1}} = 7.29$$

$$S_{\bar{X}_1 - \bar{X}_2} = \sqrt{S_{\bar{X}_1}^2 + S_{\bar{X}_2}^2} = \sqrt{8.08^2 + 7.29^2} = 10.88$$

$$t = \frac{X_1 - X_2}{S_{\bar{X}_1 - \bar{X}_2}} = \frac{177 - 150}{10.88} = 2.48$$

$$t = 2.48, p < .05$$

The logic behind a *t*-test is relatively simple. In our experiment we have two samples. If each of these samples is from the *same* population (e.g., the population of all people, whether drunk or sober), then any difference between the samples will be due to chance. On the other hand, if the two samples are from *different* populations (e.g., the population of drunk people *and* the population of sober people), then the difference is a significant difference and not due to chance.

If there is a significant difference between the two samples, then the independent variable must have caused that difference. In our example, there is a significant difference between the alcohol and the no alcohol groups. We can tell this because *p* (the probability that this *t* value will occur by chance) is less than .05. To obtain the *p*, we need only look up the *t* value in a statistical table, which is found in any statistics book. In our example, because there is a significant difference between the groups, we can reasonably conclude that the alcohol did cause a slower reaction time.

APPENDIX B
Answers to Review Questions, Try This Yourself, and Active Learning Exercises

MODULES 1–4 *Understanding Psychology Page 9* 1. scientific; behavior; mental processes. 2. The process of objectively evaluating, comparing, analyzing, and synthesizing information. Critical thinking has three components: *affective skills* (e.g., empathy and tolerance for ambiguity), *cognitive abilities* (e.g., independent thinking and synthesizing), and *behavioral traits* (e.g., delaying judgment and applying knowledge to new situations). 3. (a). *Description* tells "what" occurred. (b). An *explanation* tells "why" a behavior occurred. (c). *Prediction* specifies the conditions under which a behavior or event is likely to occur. (d). *Change* means applying psychological knowledge to prevent unwanted outcomes or bring about desired goals 4. (a) biopsychology or neuroscience, (b) developmental psychology, (c) cognitive psychology, (d) clinical psychology, (e) industrial/organizational psychology. *Module 1 Active Learning Worksheet Page 9* 1. c. 2. f. 3. a. 4. j. 5. h. 6. g. 7. i. 8. b. 9. e. 10. d. *Scientific Method and Experiments Page 00* 1. (a). literature review (b). developing a testable hypothesis, (c). designing the study and collecting the data, (d). analyzing the data and accepting or rejecting the hypothesis, (e). publishing followed by replication and scientific review, and f). building further theory. 2. In an experiment, the experimenter manipulates and controls the variables, which allows them to isolate a single factor and examine the effect of that factor alone on a particular behavior. 3. c. 4. The two problems for researchers are experimenter bias and ethnocentrism, whereas the two problems for participants are sample bias and participant bias. To guard against **experimenter bias,** researchers employ blind observers, single-blind and **double-blind studies,** and **placebos.** To control for **ethnocentrism,** they use cross-cultural sampling. To offset participant problems with **sample bias,** researchers use random/representative sampling and **random assignment.** To control for participant bias, they rely on many of the same controls in place to prevent experimenter bias, such as double-blind studies. They also attempt to assure anonymity, confidentiality, and sometimes use deception. *Descriptive, Correlational, and Biological Research and Ethical Problems Page 30* 1. d 2. b 3. CT, PET, MRI, fMRI. 4.c. *Module 2 Active Learning Worksheet Page 31*

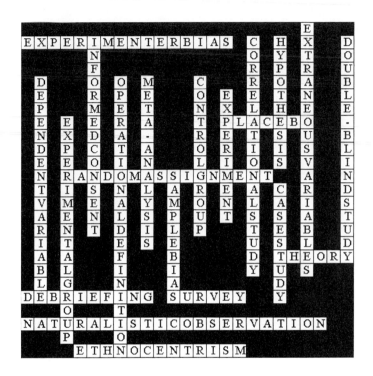

Schools of Psychology Page 38 1. experimental. 2. functionalists. 3. Freud's theories are controversial because of his nonscientific approach, emphasis on sexual and aggressive impulses, and possible sexist bias in his writings and theories. 4. a.
Module 3 Active Learning Worksheet Page 40 1. Gestalt. 2. Behaviorism. 3. Psychoanalytic/Psychodynamic. 4. Cognitive psychology. 5. Evolutionary. 6. Neuroscience/biopsychology. 7. Humanistic. 8. Functionalism. 9. Sociocultural. 10. Eclectic.

MODULES 5–7 *An Overview of the Nervous System Page 58* 1. central; peripheral. 2. d. 3. d. 4. The sympathetic nervous system arouses the body and mobilizes energy stores to deal with emergencies, whereas the parasympathetic nervous system calms the body and conserves the energy stores. *Neurons, Neural Communication, and Chemical Messengers Page 67* 1. Check your diagram with Figure 2.2. 2. c. 3. b. 4. Neurotransmitters are manufactured and released at the synapse, where the messages are picked up and relayed by neighboring neurons. Hormones are released from glands in the endocrine system directly into the bloodstream.

Module 5 Active Learning Worksheet Page 68

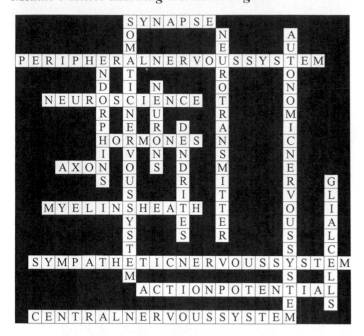

Lower-Level Brain Structures Page 73 1. midbrain, pons, and medulla. 2. cerebellum. 3. b. 4. Because of its role in the production and regulation of emotions, particularly aggression and fear. *The Cerebral Cortex and Hemispheric Specialization Page 83* 1. cerebral cortex. 2. occipital; temporal; frontal; parietal. 3. a. 4. c. *Module 6 Active Learning Worksheet Pages 84*

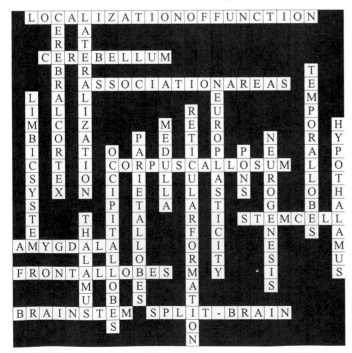

Genetics and Evolutionary Psychology Page 92 1. c. 2. Behavioral geneticists use twin studies, adoption studies, family studies, and genetic abnormalities. 3. Because natural selection favors animals whose concern for kin is proportional to their degree of biological relatedness, most people will devote more resources, protection, love and concern to close relatives, which helps ensure their genetic survival. 4. One possible answer is that in ancient societies men were the "hunters" and women "gatherers." The man's superiority on many spatial relationships and target-directed motor skills, may reflect demands of hunting, whereas activities such as gathering, child-rearing, and domestic tool construction and manipulation may have contributed to the woman's language superiority.

MODULES 8–11 *Sources of Stress Page 102* 1. a. 2. a. 3. a blocked goal; conflict. 4. Choosing between apple pie or pumpkin pie is an example of an approach-approach conflict. Choosing between early morning or evening classes normally is an approach-avoidance conflict. Taking an exam when you're underprepared or not taking the exam and receiving an automatic F is an example of an avoidance-avoidance conflict. *Effects of Stress Page 105* 1. The sympathetic branch of the autonomic nervous system is activated, thereby increasing heart rate, blood pressure, etc. The parasympathetic branch of the autonomic nervous system is activated during low-stress conditions and it lowers heart rate and blood pressure, while increasing activity in the stomach and intestines. 2. The HPA axis increases the level of cortisol, which decreases the immune system. 3. alarm; resistance; exhaustion. 4. c. *Module 8 Active Learning Worksheet Page 106* 1. a. 2. d. 3. c. 4. c. 5. d. 6. b. 7. c. 8. a. 9. d. 10. d. *Stress and Serious Illness Page 112* 1. epinephrine; cortisol. 2. b. 3. A hardy personality is based on three qualities: a commitment to personal goals, control over life, and viewing change as a challenge rather than a threat. 4. Severe anxiety. *Module 9 Active Learning Worksheet Page 113* 1. d. 2. c. 3. a. 4. d. 5. c. 6. b. 7. d. *Coping with Stress Page 118* 1. emotion-focused, problem focused. 2. Rationalization and denial. Defense mechanisms alleviate anxiety but distort reality. 3. internal. 4. The six resources are health and energy, positive beliefs, social skills, social support, material resources, and personal control. Answers will vary depending on personality and individual life style. **Health Psychology in Action Page 126** 1. In addition to social pressures that encourage smoking, nicotine is a powerfully addictive drug and smokers learn to associate positive things with smoking. 2. d. 3. Binge drinkers are just average drinkers — make it clear that binge drinking is not the norm; Binge drinking is harmless — binge drinking causes loss of control that can lead to injury, death, and exposure to sexually transmitted diseases; Okay to binge drink because administration ignores it —

administrators must enforce rules; Binge drinking is just part of fraternity or sorority life   colleges must work within the Greek System to decrease binge drinking; Students see alumni drinking at sports and alumni events — all drinking rules must also apply to alumni. 4. a. ***Module 11 Active Learning Worksheet Page 126*** 1. stress; immune system. 2. practitioners. 3. tobacco. 4. No, you cannot conclude that alcohol is the direct cause of birth defects because this is correlational research. There are other explanations, including; pregnant mothers who drink alcohol might be under additional stress, have less economic and social support, etc. 5. Increased attention to pain increases the perceived level. Therefore, your friend should avoid this topic and divert his grandmother's attention.

MODULES 12–13 *Experiencing Sensations Page 136* 1. c. 2. absolute threshold. 3. The sensory receptors for smell adapt and send fewer messages to the brain. 4. b. ***How We See and Hear Page 144*** 1. Compare your diagram to Figure 4.4. 2. thinning and flattening, thickening and bulging, accommodation. 3. Compare your diagram to figure 4.8. 4. Place theory explains how we hear higher-pitched sounds, whereas frequency theory explains how we hear lower-pitched sounds. ***Our Other Senses Page 149*** 1. b. 2. d. 3. kinesthetic. 4. d. ***Module 12 Active Learning Worksheet Page 150***

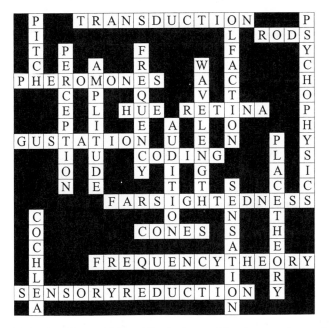

Selection Page 153 1. Illusions are false impressions of the physical world produced by actual physical distortions, hallucinations are sensory perceptions that occur without an external stimulus, and delusions are false beliefs. 2. feature detectors. 3. "Horizontal cats" reared in a horizontal world failed to develop potential feature detectors for vertical

lines or objects. 4. c. ***Organization — Form and Constancies Page 159*** 1. proximity, continuity, closure. 2. size constancy. 3. brightness constancy. 4. c. ***Organization — Depth and Color Page 165*** 1. c. 2. b. 3. color aftereffects, green rectangle. 4. The trichromatic system operates at the level of the retina, whereas the opponent-process system occurs at the level of the brain. ***Interpretation and ESP Page 169*** 1. a. 2. a. 3. telepathy, clairvoyance, precognition, telekinesis. 4. usually cannot be replicated. ***Module 13 Active Learning Worksheet Page 170***

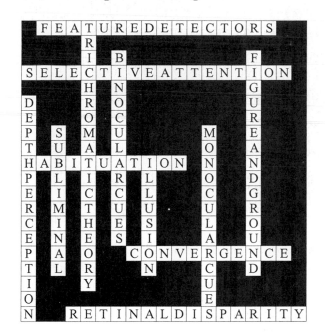

MODULES 14–15 *Understanding Consciousness Page 178* 1. b. 2. They considered it too unscientific and not the proper focus of psychology. 3. focused, minimal. 4. d. ***Circadian Rhythms and Stages of Sleep Page 185*** 1. d. 2. b. 3. electroencephalogram (EEG). 4. a. ***Theories of Sleep and Dreaming Page 189*** 1. Repair/restoration theory suggests we sleep to physically restore our mind and body, whereas evolutionary/circadian theory says that sleep evolved because it helped conserve energy and provided protection from predators. 2. Both men and women have dreams that reflect important life events, but women are more likely to dream of familiar people, household objects, and indoor events, whereas men dream about strangers, violence, sex, achievement, and outdoor events. All cultures dream about basic human needs and fears, but the Yir Yoront men dream of aggression from their mother's brother. Also, Americans dream of being naked in public, whereas cultures wearing few clothes do not dream of being naked. 3. d. 4. c. ***Sleep Disorders Page 192*** 1. insomnia. 2. sleep apnea. 3. night terrors. 4. narcolepsy. ***Module 14 Active Learning Worksheet Pages 193***

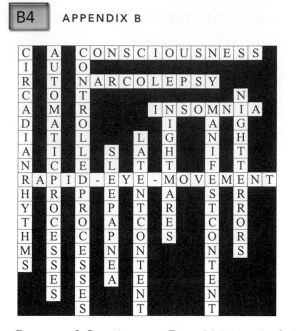

Drugs and Consciousness Page 206 1. c. 2. d. 3. Physical dependence refers to changes in the bodily processes that require continued use of the drug to prevent withdrawal symptoms, whereas psychological dependence refers to the mental desire or craving to achieve the effects produced by the drug. 4. Psychoactive drugs can alter the production, affect storage or release, alter the reception, and block the inactivation of neurotransmitters. **Additional Routes to Alternate States Page 211** 1. They may feel guilty or negative because they do not make a distinction between thought and behavior–thinking is not the same as doing. 2. Hypnosis requires the subject to make a conscious decision to relinquish some personal control of his or her consciousness. 3. d. 4. As a part of sacred rituals, for social interactions, and for individual rewards. **Module 15 Active Learning Worksheet Page 212**

MODULES 16–19 *Understanding Classical Conditioning Page 222* 1. b. 2. conditioned stimulus, conditioned

response. 3. d. 4. c. **Principles and Applications of Classical Conditioning Page 227** 1. You no longer respond to the sound of the fire alarm because your response has been extinquished, which occurs when the UCS is repeatedly withheld, and the association between the CS and the UCS is broken. 2. d. 3. higher-order conditioning. 4. c. **Module 16 Active Learning Worksheet Page 228**

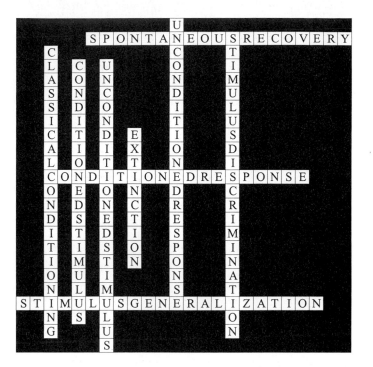

Operant Conditioning Page 242 1. Operant conditioning occurs when organisms learn by the consequences of their responses, whereas in classical conditioning organisms learn by pairing up associations. Operant conditioning is voluntary, whereas classical conditioning is involuntary. 2. c. 3. resistant. 4. Marshall's superstition may be wearing the same necklace to every exam because he believes it is helpful to his performance, although in reality wearing the necklace and previous good luck on exams were only accidentally related. **Module 17 Active Learning Worksheet Page 243**

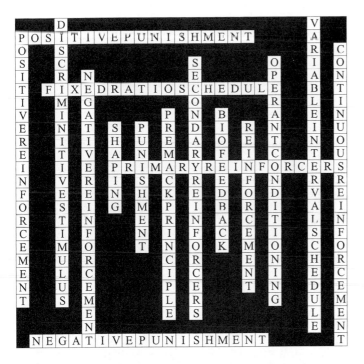

Cognitive-Social Learning Page 248 1. c. 2. latent learning. 3. cognitive maps. 4. b. *Module 18 Active Learning Worksheet Page 248* 1. i. 2. c. 3. f. 4. g. 5. h. 6. d. 7. j. 8. e. 9. a. 10. b. *Neuroscience and Evolution Page 252* 1. Because they have fewer and larger neurons than any vertebrate. 2. Garcia and his colleagues laced freshly killed sheep with a chemical that caused nausea and vomiting in coyotes. After the coyotes ate the tainted meat and became ill, they avoided all sheep. 3. Biological preparedness refers to the fact that organisms are innately predisposed to form associations between certain stimuli and responses. 4. Instinctive drift. *Module 19 Active Learning Worksheet Page 252* 1. T. 2. T. 3. T. 4. F. 5. T.

MODULES 20–21 *Three-Stage Memory Model and Encoding, Storage, and Retrieval Page 264* 1. c. 2. a. 3. Encoding is comparable to typing on a keyboard, storage compares to the hard drive of the computer, and retrieval is analogous to the computer's retrieval of information and its display on the monitor. 4. According to the Parallel Distributed Processing (PDP), or *connectionist*, model, memory resembles a vast number of interconnected units and modules distributed throughout a huge network, all operating in parallel — simultaneously. *Try This Yourself Page 271* Rudolph, Dancer, Cupid, Comet, Blitzen, Donder, Dasher, Prancer, Vixen. *Integration Model and Biological Perspective Page 275* 1. Semantic memory involves remembering facts and how they relate to one another, whereas episodic memory involves remembering where and when an event happened. 2. recognition, recall. 3. Repeated stimulation of a synapse can strengthen the synapse by stimulating the dendrites to grow more spines, and the ability of a particular neuron to release its neurotransmitters can be increased

or decreased. 4. d. *Module 20 Active Learning Worksheet Page 275* 1. c. 2. c. 3. d. 4. d. 5. c. 6. d. 7. c. 8. b. 9. b. 10. c. *Why Do We Forget? Page 282* 1. d. 2. Using distributed practice, you would space your study time into many learning periods with rest periods in between; using massed practice, you would "cram" all your learning into long, unbroken periods. 3. Retrieval failure theory, decay theory, motivated forgetting theory. *Problems with Memory Page 289* 1. amnesia. 2. d. 3. Source amnesia occurs when the true source of the memory is forgotten. The sleeper effect refers to the initial tendency to discount information from an unreliable source, but later consider it more trustworthy because the source is forgotten. 4. Research shows that it is unreliable. *Improving Memory Page 293* 1. Given that the duration of short-term memory is about 30 seconds, to lengthen this time use *maintenance rehearsal*, which involves continuously repeating the material. To effectively encode memory into long-term memory, use *elaborative rehearsal*, which involves thinking about the material and relating it to other information that has already been stored. 2. Because we tend to remember information that falls at the beginning or end of a sequence, be sure to spend extra time with information in the middle of the chapter. 3. organization. 4. Peg-word system, method of loci, method of word associations, substitute word system. *Module 21 Active Learning Worksheet Page 294* 1. c. 2. f. 3. e. 4. g. 5. i. 6. h. 7. j. 8. d. 9. b. 10. a.

MODULES 22–24 *Try This Yourself Page 301* The figures in b are not the same. To solve this problem, mentally rotate one of the objects and then compare the rotated image with the other object to see whether they matched or not. The figures in b were more difficult to solve because they required a greater degree of mental rotation. This is also true of real objects in physical space. It takes more time and energy to turn a cup 20 degrees to the right, than to turn it 150 degrees. *The Thinking Brain and Cognitive Building Blocks Page 303* 1. c. 2. There are at least three methods — artificial concepts, natural concepts, and hierarchies. 3. prototype. 4. b. *Solving Problems Page 309* 1. Preparation, in which we identify the facts, determine which ones are relevant, and define the goal; production, in which we propose possible solutions, or hypotheses; and evaluation, in which we determine whether the solutions meet the goal. 2. b. 3. d. 4. mental sets, functional fixedness, confirmation bias, availability heuristic, and representativeness heuristic. *Creativity Page 312* 1. c. 2. divergent, convergent, divergent. 3. intellectual ability, knowledge, thinking style, personality, motivation, and environment. 4. Probably not because people tend to be less creative when they are working for extrinsic rewards. *Module 22 Active Learning Worksheet Page 312* 1. j. 2. a. 3. i. 4. h. 5. d. 6. g. 7. c. 8. e. 9. f. 10. b *Language Page 320* 1. phonemes, morphemes. 2. b. 3. Language shapes thought. 4. a. *Module 23 Active Learning Worksheet Page 320*

Part A

Part B

1. c. 2. a. e. b. 4. f. 5. e. 6. d.

The Nature of Intelligene and Test Construction Page 326 1. b. 2. Fluid intelligence refers to reasoning abilities, memory, and speed of information processing, whereas crystallized intelligence refers to knowledge and skills gained through experience and education. 3. Sternberg proposed three aspects of intelligence — analytic, creative, and practical. 4.reliability, validity, standardization. ***Assessing Intelligence/Explaining Differences in Intelligence Page 325*** 1. No, an IQ test merely measures verbal and quantitative abilities and predicts school success. 2. The Stanford–Binet is a single test consisting of several sets of various age-level items, whereas the Wechsler consists of three separate tests; also the Stanford–Binet primarily measures verbal abilities, while the Wechsler measures both verbal and performance abilities. 3. d. 4. Both heredity and environment are important, interacting influences. ***Module 24 Active Learning Worksheet Page 326***

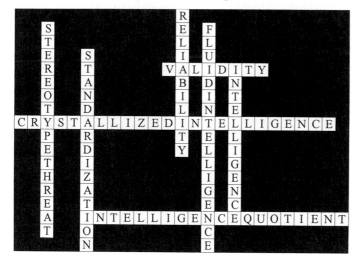

MODULES 25–26 *Studying Development Page 346* 1. Developmental psychology studies age-related changes in behaviors and abilities from conception to death. 2. nature or nurture, continuity or stages, stability or change. 3. d. 4. c. ***Physical Development Page 356*** 1. The three major stages are the germinal period, the embryonic period, and the fetal period. 2. b. 3. c. 4. Primary aging is defined as the inevitable age-related biological changes in physical and mental processes, whereas secondary aging results from abuse, neglect, disuse, or disease. ***Social-Emotional Development Page 361*** 1. b. 2. Securely attached, anxious-avoidant, and anxious-ambivalent; 3. 1a, 2c, 3b. 4. Authoritarian parents value

unquestioning obedience and mature responsibility from their children. Permissive parents either set few limts and provide little attention (the permissive-indifferent), or they're highly involved but few demands (the permissive-indulgent). Authoritative parents are caring and sensitive, but also set firm limits and enforce them. ***Module 25 Active Learning Worksheet Page 362***

Cognitive development Page 372 1. c. 2. d. 3. 1b, 2a, 3d, 4c, 5d. ***Module 26 Active Learning Worksheet Page 372***

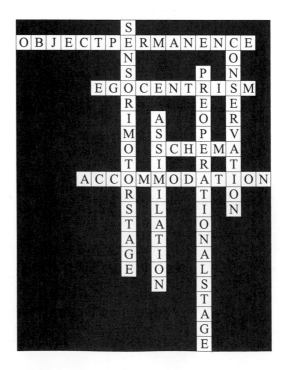

MODULES 27–28 *Moral Development Page 381* 1. Preconventional, postconventional, conventional. 2. c. 3. b. 4. Kohlberg's theory is culturally biased toward individualism versus community and interpersonal relationships. His theory is gender biased because it supposedly favors the male's justice perspective over the female's care perspective. *Personality Development Over the Life Span Page 386.* 1. c. 2. Thomas and Chess describe three categories of temperament — easy, difficult, and slow-to-warm-up — that seem to correlate with stable personality differences. 3. trust versus mistrust, identity versus role confusion, initiative versus guilt, ego integrity versus despair. 4. Research shows that beliefs about adolescent storm and stress, the midlife crisis, and the empty nest syndrome may be exaggerated accounts of a few people's experiences and not those of most people. *Module 27 Active Learning Worksheet Page 387*

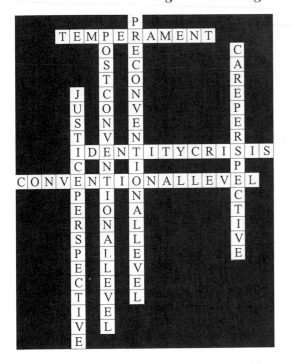

Additional Influences on Development Page 395 1. c. 2. activity; disengagement. 3. c. 4. The social support may help reduce the losses that accompany aging. *Grief and Death Pages 400* 1. Preschool children only understand the permanence of death, they do not yet comprehend the nonfunctionality or universality of death. 2. d. 3. a bargaining, b denial, c resolution, d anger, e despair. 4. d. *Module 28 Active Learning Worksheet Page 400* 1. f. 2. d. 3. g. 4. a. 5. c. 6. j. 7. h. 8. i. 9. e. 10. b.

MODULES 29–30 *Sex and Gender Pages 414* 1. Chromosomal sex b, gender identity d, gonadal sex a, gender role I, hormonal sex c, secondary sex characteristics e, external genitals g, sexual orientation h, internal accessory organs f. 2. d. 3. Social learning theory emphasizes learning through rewards, punishments, and imitation, while cognitive-developmental theory focuses on the active, thinking processes of the individ-

ual. 4. d. *The Study of Human Sexuality Page 418* 1. b. 2. Ellis based his research on personal diaries; Masters and Johnson pioneered the use of direct observation and measurement of bodily responses during sexual activities; Kinsey popularized the use of the survey method. 3. Cultural comparisons put sex in a broader perspective and help counteract ethnocentrism. 4. d. *Module 29 Active Learning Worksheet Page 418* 1. gender identity; cross-dresses for sexual arousal and expression of other gender role. 2. your biological sex; your social role expectations based on masculinity or femininity. 3. self-definition of being male or female; societal expectations of normal and appropriate gender behavior. 4. cognitive abilities; aggression. 5. androgyny. *Sexual Behavior Page 422* 1. Masters and Johnson identified a four-stage sexual response cycle (excitement, plateau, orgasm, and resolution) that acknowledged both similarities and differences between the sexes. However differences are the focus of most research. 2. According to the evolutionary perspective, males engage in more sexual behaviors with more sexual partners because it helps the species survive. The social role perspective suggests this difference reflects a double standard, which subtly encourages male sexuality while discouraging female sexuality. 3. c. 4. d. *Answers to Critical Thinking/Active Learning Exercise Page 431 Gender role conditioning* — A main part of traditional gender conditioning is the belief that women should be the "gatekeepers" for sexuality and men should be the "pursuers." This leads to the myth that male sexuality is overpowering and women are responsible for controlling the situation. *Double standard* — Female gender role also encourages passivity, and women are not taught how to aggressively defend themselves. People who believe the myth that women cannot be raped against their will generally overlook the fact that the female gender role encourages passivity and women are not taught how to aggressively defend themselves. *Media portrayals* — Novels and films typically portray a woman resisting her attacker and then melting into passionate responsiveness. This helps perpetuate the myth that women secretly want to be raped and the myth that she might as well "relax and enjoy it." *Lack of information* — The myth that women cannot be raped against their will overlooks the fact that most men are much stronger and much faster than most women, and a woman's clothing and shoes further hinder her ability to escape. The myth that women cannot rape men ignores the fact that men can have erections despite negative emotions while being raped. Furthermore, an erection is unnecessary, since many rapists (either male or female) often use foreign objects to rape their victims. The myth that all women secretly want to be raped overlooks the fact that if a woman fantasizes about being raped she remains in complete control, whereas in an actual rape she is completely powerless. Also, fantasies contain no threat of physical harm, while rape does.

Tips for Rape Prevention Sex educators and researchers suggest the following techniques for reducing stranger rape (the rape of a person by an unknown assailant) and acquaintance (or date) rape (committed by someone who is known to the victim) (Allgeier & Allgeier, 2003; Crooks &

Baur, 2002). To avoid stranger rape: 1. Follow commonsense advice for avoiding all forms of crime: lock your car, park in lighted areas, install dead-bolt locks on your doors, don't open your door to strangers, don't hitchhike, etc. 2. Make yourself as strong as possible. Take a self-defense course, carry a loud whistle with you, and demonstrate self-confidence with your body language. Research shows that rapists tend to select women who appear passive and weak (Richards et al., 1991). 3. During an attack, run away if you can, talk to the rapist as a way to stall, and/or attempt to alert others by screaming ("Help, rape, call the police") (Shotland & Stebbins, 1980). When all else fails, women should actively resist an attack, according to current research (Fischhoff, 1992; Furby & Fischhoff, 1992). Loud shouting, fighting back, and causing a scene may deter an attack. To prevent acquaintance rape: 1. Be careful on first dates — date in groups and in public places; avoid alcohol and other drugs (Gross & Billingham, 1998). 2. Be assertive and clear in your communication — say what you want and what you don't want. Accept a partner's refusal. If sexual coercion escalates, match the assailant's behavior with your own form of escalation — begin with firm refusals, get louder, threaten to call the police, begin shouting and use strong physical resistance. Don't be afraid to make a scene! *Sexual Problems Page 000* 1. The parasympathetic branch of the autonomic nervous system dominates during sexual arousal, whereas the sympathetic branch dominates during ejaculation and orgasm. 2. c. 3. Relationship focus, integration of physiological and psychosocial factors, emphasis on cognitive factors, emphasis on specific behavioral techniques. 4. Remain abstinent or have sex with one mutually faithful, uninfected partner. Do not use IV drugs or have sex with someone who does. If you do use IV drugs, sterilize or don't share equipment. Avoid contact with blood, vaginal secretions, and semen. Avoid anal intercourse. Don't have sex if you or partner are impaired by drugs. *Module 30 Active Learning Worksheet Page 432*

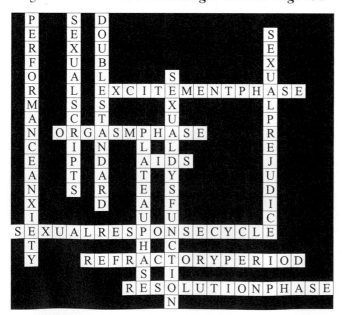

MODULES 31–32 *Understanding Motivation Page 450* 1. Although these two terms often overlap and interact to influence behavior, motivation refers to internal factors that energize and direct behavior, whereas emotion refers to feelings or affective responses. 2. The major biological factors are the stomach, chemical signals, and the brain; while the major psychosocial factors are cultural conditioning and visual stimuli. 3. d. 4. c. *General Theories of Motivation Page 454* 1. An instinct is an unlearned, behavioral pattern that is uniform in expression and universal in a species. Homeostasis is the state of balance or stability in the body's internal environment. 2. a2, b3, c5, d4, e1. 3. d. 4.c. *Module 31 Active Learning Worksheet Page 454* 1.d. 2. j. 3. i. 4. f. 5. b. 6. g. 7. e. 8. c. 9. a. 10. h. *Understanding Emotion Page 462* 1. a3, b1, c2 and c4 2. sympathetic, autonomic. 3. a. 4. b. *General Theories of Emotion Page 467* 1. According to the **James-Lange theory,** emotions are based on physical sensations, such as increased heart rate and trembling, whereas the **Cannon-Bard theory** suggests feelings are created from independent and simultaneous stimulation of both the cortex and the autonomic nervous system. The **facial-feedback hypothesis** suggests facial movements elicit specific emotions, **Schacter's two-factor theory** proposes that emotions depend on physical arousal and a cognitive labeling of the arousal. 2. a. 3. d. 4. simultaneously. *Module 32 Active Learning Worksheet Page 468* 1. i. 2. j. 3. h. 4. g. 5. d. 6. f. 7. e. 8. b. 9. c. 10. a.

MODULES 33–36 *Personality Assessment Page 479* 1. a2, b1, c3. 2. b. 3. 4. People accept pseudopersonality tests because they offer generalized statements that apply to almost everyone (Barnum effect), they notice and remember events that confirm predictions and ignore the misses (fallacy of positive instances), and they prefer information that maintains a positive self-image (self-serving bias). *Module 33 Active Learning Worksheet Page 479* 1. F. 2. F. 3. T. 4. T. 5. T. *Trait Theories Pages 484–485* 1. b. 2. a2, b3, c4, d5, e1. 3. b. *Module 34 Active Learning Worksheet Page 485* 1. extraversion. 2. conscientiousness. 3. openness. 4. agreeableness. 5. neuroticism. *Psychoanalytic/Psychodynamic Page 496* 1. The conscious is the tip of the iceberg and the highest level of awareness; the preconscious is just below the surface but can readily be brought to awareness; the unconscious is the large base of the iceberg and operates below the level of awareness. 2. b. 3. Freud believed an individual's adult personality reflected his or her resolution of the specific crisis presented in each psychosexual stage (oral, anal, phallic, latency, and genital). 4. Adler, Horney, Jung, Horney. *Module 35 Active Learning Worksheet Page 497*

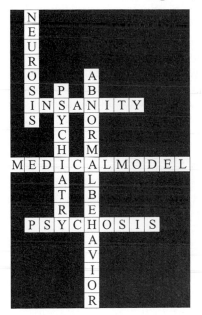

Module 37 Active Learning Worksheet Page 521

Humanistic Theories Page 500 1. a. 2. c. 3. self-actualization. 4. Humanistic theories are criticized for their naive assumptions, poor testability and inadequate evidence, and narrowness in merely describing, not explaining, behavior. *Social/Cognitive Perspective Page 502* 1. How each individual thinks about the world and interprets experiences. 2. a. 3. c. 4. external locus of control, internal locus of control. *Biological Theories Page 505* 1. d. 2. Some researchers emphasize the importance of the unshared environment, while others fear that genetic determinism could be misused to "prove" certain ethnic groups are inferior, male dominance is natural, or that social progress is impossible. 3. c. 4. Western theories emphasize the "self" as separate and autonomous from others, while collectivist cultures see the self as inherently linked to others. *Module 36 Active Learning Worksheet Page 506* 1. i. 2. j. 3. a. 4. e. 5. g. 6. h. 7. f. 8. c. 9. d. 10. b.

MODULES 37–41 *Studying Psychological Disorders Page 520* 1. Statistical infrequency, disability or dysfunction, personal distress, and violation of norms. 2. b. 3. Early versions of the DSM used neurosis to refer to mental disorders related to anxiety, while psychosis is currently used to describe disorders characterized by loss of contact with reality and extreme mental disruption. Insanity is a legal term for people with a mental disorder that implies a lack of responsibility for behavior and an inability to manage their own affairs. 4. The chief advantages of the DSM is that it provides detailed descriptions of symptoms, which in turn allows standardized diagnosis and treatment, and improved communication among professionals and between professionals and patients. The major disadvantage is that the label "mental illness" can lead to social and economic discrimination.

Anxiety Disorders Page 526 1. b I, a II, c III, d IV.   2. Learning theorists most often believe anxiety disorders result from classical and operant conditioning, while social learning theorists argue that imitation and modeling are the cause. 3. Learning, biology, and cognitive processes. *Module 38 Active Learning Worksheet Page 527* 1. Generalized anxiety disorder; panic disorder. 2. Phobias; agoraphobia. 3. compulsions; obsessions. 4. Taijin Kyofusho (TKS). 5. inherited predisposition. *Mood Disorders Page 533* 1. a. 2. c. 3. Seligman believes the individual becomes resigned to pain and sadness and feels unable to change, which leads to depression. 4. It may be due to biological causes (hormones and genes) as well as environmental stressors (poverty, discrimination, unhappy marriages, and sexual or physical abuse). *Module 39 Active Learning Worksheet Page 533* 1. F. 2. T. 3. T. 4. F. 5. F. *Schizophrenia Page 542* 1. c. 2. psychosis, 3. a. 4. Three biological causes might be malfunctioning neurotransmitters, brain abnormalities, and genetic predisposition. Two possible psychosocial causes of schizophrenia may be stress and family communication problems. *Module 40 Active Learning Worksheet Page 543* 1. F. 2. T. 3. T. 4. F. 5. F. *Answers to Active Learning Exercise Page 549* 1. c. 2. e. 3. b. 4. a. 5. f. 6. d. *Other Disorders Pages 549* 1. Stress. 2. Dissociative identity disorder (DID) refers to a dissociative disorder characterized by the presence of two or more distinct personality systems within the same individual. 3. Antisocial personality. 4. d. *Module 41 Active Learning Worksheet Page 550* 1. antisocial personality. 2. borderline personality. 3. alcohol use disorder. 4. dissociative identity disorder. 5. antisocial personality.

MODULES 42–45 *Therapy Essentials Pages 558* 1. c. 2. b psychoanalysts, e behaviorists, d humanistic therapists, c biomedical therapists, a cognitive therapists. 3. clinical or counseling psychologists, psychiatrists, psychoanalysts, social workers, and counselors. *Module 42 Active Learning Worksheet Page 560* 1. disturbed thoughts, disturbed emotions, disturbed behaviors, interpersonal and life situation difficulties, biomedical disturbances. 2. and 3. Answers will vary according to individual life histories. *Biomedical Therapies Page 565* 1. d. 2. antianxiety, antipsychotic, antidepressant, and mood stabilizer. 3. b. 4. c. *Module 43 Active Learning Worksheet Page 565*

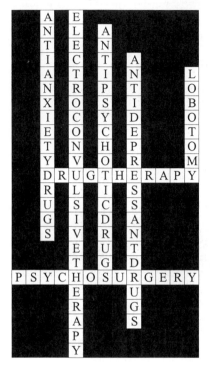

Psychoanalysis/Psychodynamic Therapies Page 570 1. c. 2. Mary is exhibiting transference, reacting to her therapist as she apparently did to someone earlier in her life. John is exhibiting resistance, arriving late because he fears what his unconscious might reveal. 3. Limited applicability, lack of scientific credibility. 4. Psychodynamic therapy is briefer, face-to-face, more directive, and emphasizes current problems and conscious processes. *Try This Yourself Page 575* All four techniques are shown in this example: empathy ("they scare the hell out of me too"), unconditional positive regard (therapist's acceptance and nonjudgmental attitude and caring about not wanting to do "anything that is upsetting" to the client), genuineness (the therapist's ability to laugh and make a joke at his or her own expense); and active listening (therapist demonstrated genuine interest in what the client was saying). *Cognitive and Humanistic Therapies Pages 575–576* 1. a. 2. The activating event, the belief system, the emotional consequence. 3. Magnification, all-or-nothing thinking. 4. Empathy, genuineness, unconditional positive regard. *Behavior Therapies Page 580* 1. behavior therapy. 2. c. 3. By rewarding successive approximations of a

target behavior, the patient is "shaped" toward more adaptive behaviors. 4. Behavior therapy is criticized for lack of generalizability and questionable ethics. *Group and Family Therapies Page 583* 1. c. 2. Group support, feedback and information, behavioral rehearsal. 3. Self-help groups are recommended as a supplement to individual therapy. 4. d. *Module 44 Active Learning Worksheet Page 584*

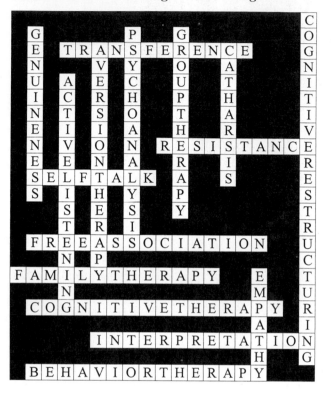

Issues in Therapy Page 590 1. d. 2. Naming the problem, qualities of the therapist, establishment of credibility, placing the problem in a familiar framework, applying techniques to bring relief, a special time and place. 3. c. 4. Rates of diagnosis and treatment of mental disorders, stresses of poverty, stresses of multiple roles, stresses of aging, violence against women.

MODULES 46–48 *Our Thoughts About Others Page 603* 1. c. 2. When judging the causes of others' behaviors, a tendency to overestimate internal personality factors and underestimate external situational factors. 3. d. 4. Cognitive dissonance. *Module 46 Active Learning Worksheet Page 603* 1. F. 2. T. 3. F. 4. T. 5. T. *Our Feelings About Others Page 614* 1. Prejudice is an attitude with behavioral tendencies that may or may not be activated, whereas discrimination is actual negative behavior directed at members of an outgroup. 2. b. 3. c. 4. Romantic love is short lived (6 to 30 months) and largely based on mystery and fantasy, which leads to inevitable disappointment. Companionate love is long lasting and grows stronger with time. *Module 47 Active Learning Worksheet Page 615*

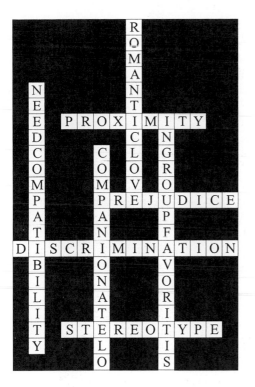

Social Influence Page 621 1. Conformity involves changing behavior in response to real or imagined pressure from others, whereas obedience involves giving in to a command from others. 2. b. 3. c. 4. the power of authority, distance between teacher and learner, assignment of responsibility, and modeling/imitation. *Group Processes Page 625* 1. Guards and prisoners were abusing their roles. 2. b. 3. illusion of invulnerability, belief in the morality of the group, collective rationalizations, stereotypes of the outgroup, self-censorship of doubts and dissenting opinions, illusion of unanimity, and direct pressure on dissenters. 4. b. *Aggression and Altruism Page 631* 1. The five major biological factors are instincts, genes, brain and nervous system, substance use and other mental disorders, hormones and neurotransmitters. The three key psychosocial factors aversive stimuli, culture and learning, and media and video games. 2. Introduce incompatible responses and improve social and communication skills. 3. According to evolutionary theorists, altruism evolved because it favored overall genetic survival. The egoistic model says helping is motivated by anticipated gain for the helper, while the empathy–altruism hypothesis suggests helping is activated when the helper feels empathy for the victim. 4. d. *Module 48 Active Learning Worksheet Page 632*

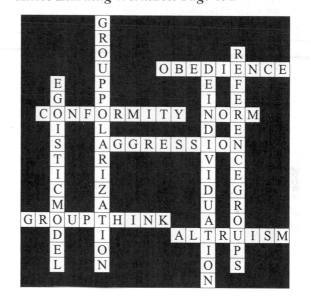

GLOSSARY

Abnormal Behavior Patterns of emotion, thought, and action considered pathological (diseased or disordered) for one or more of these reasons: statistical infrequency, disability or dysfunction, personal distress, or violation of norms *Page 512*

Absolute Threshold The smallest amount of a stimulus needed to detect that the stimulus is present *Page 134*

Accommodation Automatic adjustment of the eye, which occurs when muscles change the shape of the lens so that it focuses light on the retina from objects at different distances *Page 139*

Accommodation In Piaget's theory, adjusting old schemas or developing new ones to better fit with new information *Page 363*

Achievement Motivation Desire to excel, especially in competition with others *Page 445*

Action Potential Neural impulse that carries information along the axon of a neuron. The action potential is generated when positively charged ions move in and out through channels in the axon's membrane *Page 59*

Activation–Synthesis Hypothesis Hobson's theory that dreams are by-products of random stimulation of brain cells; the brain attempts to combine (or synthesize) this spontaneous activity into coherent patterns, known as dreams *Page 186*

Active Listening Listening with total attention to what another is saying; it involves reflecting, paraphrasing, and clarifying what the person says and means *Page 574*

Activity Theory Successful aging is fostered by a full and active commitment to life *Page 393*

Addiction Broad term describing a compulsion to use a specific drug or engage in a certain activity *Page 194*

Ageism Prejudice or discrimination against an individual based on physical age *Page 354*

Aggression Any behavior intended to harm someone *Page 626*

Agonist Chemical (or drug) that mimics the action of a specific neurotransmitter *Page 202*

AIDS (Acquired Immunodeficiency Syndrome) Human immunodeficiency viruses (HIVs) destroy the immune system's ability to fight disease, leaving the body vulnerable to a variety of opportunistic infections and cancers *Page 429*

Algorithm A set of steps that, if followed correctly, will eventually solve the problem *Page 305*

Alternate States of Consciousness (ASCs) A mental state other than ordinary waking consciousness, found during sleep, dreaming, psychoactive drug use, hypnosis, and so on *Page 175*

Altruism Actions designed to help others with no obvious benefit to the helper *Page 629*

Alzheimer's [ALLS-high-merz] Disease Progressive mental deterioration characterized by severe memory loss *Page 283*

Amplitude Height of a light or sound wave; pertaining to light, it refers to brightness, for sound, it refers to loudness *Page 137*

Amygdala [uh-MIG-dull-uh] An almond-shaped lower-level brain structure that is part of the limbic system and is involved in emotion *Page 72*

Androgyny [an-DRAW-juh-nee] Combining characteristics considered typically male (assertive, athletic) with characteristics considered typically female (yielding, nurturant); from the Greek andro, meaning "male," and gyn, meaning "female." *Page 413*

Anorexia Nervosa Severe loss of weight resulting from an obsessive fear of obesity and self-imposed starvation *Page 441*

Antagonist Chemical (or drug) that opposes or blocks the action of a neurotransmitter *Page 202*

Anterograde Amnesia Inability to form new memories after an injury; forward-acting amnesia *Page 283*

Antianxiety Drugs Medications used to treat anxiety disorders *Page 561*

Antidepressant Drugs Chemicals prescribed to treat depression, some anxiety disorders, and certain eating disorders (such as bulimia) *Page 561*

Antipsychotic Drugs Chemicals administered to diminish or eliminate hallucinations, delusions, withdrawal, and other symptoms of psychosis; also known as neuroleptics or major tranquilizers *Page 561*

Antisocial Personality Egocentrism, lack of conscience, impulsive behavior, and manipulation of others *Page 546*

Anxiety Disorder Type of abnormal behavior characterized by unrealistic, irrational fear *Page 522*

Applied Research Research designed to solve practical problems *Page 10*

Approach–Approach Conflict Having to choose between two or more desirable alternatives *Page 101*

Approach–Avoidance Conflict Forced choice between two or more alternatives, which have both desirable and undesirable results *Page 101*

Archetypes According to Jung, the images or patterns of thoughts, feelings, and behavior that reside in the collective unconscious *Page 494*

Assimilation In Piaget's theory, absorbing new information into existing schemas *Page 363*

Association Areas So-called quiet areas in the cerebral cortex involved in interpreting, integrating, and acting on information processed by other parts of the brain *Page 77*

Attachment A strong affectional bond with special others that endures over time *Page 356*

Attitude Learned predisposition to respond cognitively, affectively, and behaviorally to a particular object *Page 600*

Attribution Principles used to judge the causes of events, and our own and others' behavior *Page 598*

Audition Sense of hearing *Page 140*

Automatic Processes Mental activities requiring minimal attention and having little impact on other activities *Page 177*

Autonomic Nervous System (ANS) Subdivision of the peripheral nervous system (PNS) that controls involuntary functions, such as heart rate and digestion. It is further subdivided into the sympathetic nervous system, which arouses, and the parasympathetic nervous system, which calms *Page 55*

Availability Heuristic Judging the likelihood or probability of events based on how readily available are other instances in our mind *Page 308*

Aversion Therapy Pairing an aversive (unpleasant) stimulus with a maladaptive behavior *Page 578*

Avoidance–Avoidance Conflict Forced choice between two or more undesirable alternatives *Page 101*

Axon A long, tubelike structure that conveys impulses away from the neuron's cell body toward other neurons or to muscles or glands *Page 58*

Babbling Vowel/consonant combinations that infants begin to produce at about age 4 to 6 months *Page 315*

Basic Anxiety According to Horney, the feelings of helplessness and insecurity that adults experience because as children they felt alone and isolated in a hostile environment *Page 495*

Basic Research Research conducted to advance scientific knowledge rather than practical application *Page 10*

Behavior Therapy Group of techniques based on learning principles used to change maladaptive behaviors *Page 576*

Behavioral Genetics The study of the effects of heredity on biological, behavioral, and mental processes *Page 86*

Binocular Cues Visual input from two eyes that allows perception of depth or distance *Page 161*

Biofeedback A bodily function (such as blood pressure or heart rate) is recorded and the information is fed back to an organism to increase voluntary control over that bodily function *Page 240*

Biological Preparedness Built-in (innate) readiness to form associations between certain stimuli and responses *Page 251*

Biological Research Scientific studies of the brain and other parts of the nervous system *Page 24*

Biomedical Therapy Using physiological interventions (drugs, electroconvulsive therapy, and psychosurgery) to reduce or alleviate symptoms of psychological disorders *Page 555*

Biopsychosocial Model A unifying theme of modern psychology, which considers biological, psychological, and social processes *Page 36*

Bipolar Disorder Repeated episodes of mania (unreasonable elation and hyperactivity) and depression *Page 528*

Borderline Personality Disorder (BPD) Impulsivity and instability in mood, relationships, and self-image *Page 547*

Bottom-Up Processing Information processing that begins "at the bottom" with raw sensory data that feed "up" to the brain *Page 131*

Brainstem Area at the base of the brain in front of the cerebellum responsible for automatic, survival functions *Page 69*

Bulimia Nervosa Consuming large quantities of food (bingeing), followed by vomiting, extreme exercise, or laxative use (purging) *Page 441*

Burnout Physical, emotional, and mental exhaustion attributable to long-term involvement in emotionally demanding situations *Page 100*

Cannon–Bard Theory Arousal, cognitions, and expression of emotions occur simultaneously; in this view, all emotions are physiologically similar *Page 464*

Care Perspective Gilligan's term for moral reasoning that emphasizes interdependence and interpersonal responsibility *Page 381*

Case Study An in-depth study of a single research participant *Page 21*

Catharsis In psychoanalytic theory, the release of tension and anxiety through the reliving of a traumatic incident *Page 566*

Cell Body The part of the neuron that contains the cell nucleus, as well as other structures that help the neuron carry out its functions *Page 58*

Central Nervous System (CNS) System located centrally in the body that includes the brain and spinal cord *Page 55*

Cerebellum [sehr-uh-BELL-um] Structure at the base of the brain, behind the brainstem, responsible for maintaining smooth movement, balance, and some aspects of perception and cognition *Page 70*

Cerebral Cortex The bumpy, convoluted area on the outside surface of the two cerebral hemispheres that regulates most complex behavior, including receiving sensations, motor control, and higher mental processes *Page 73*

Chromosome Threadlike strands of DNA (deoxyribonucleic acid) molecules that carry genetic information *Page 86*

Chronic Pain Continuous or recurrent pain over a period of 6 months or longer *Page 124*

Chunking Grouping separate pieces of information into a single unit (or chunk) *Page 261*

Circadian [ser-KAY-dee-an] Rhythms Biological changes that occur on a 24-hour cycle (circa = about, and dies = day) *Page 178*

Classical Conditioning Learning that occurs when a neutral stimulus (NS) becomes paired (associated) with an unconditioned stimulus (UCS) to elicit a conditioned response (CR) (also known as respondent or Pavlovian conditioning) *Page 219*

Client-Centered Therapy Rogers's therapy emphasizing the client's natural tendency to become healthy and productive; techniques include empathy, unconditional positive regard, genuineness, and active listening *Page 573*

Cochlea [KOK-lee-uh] Three-chambered, snail-shaped structure in the inner ear containing the receptors for hearing *Page 142*

Coding Three-part process that converts a particular sensory input into a specific sensation *Page 133*

Cognition Mental activities involved in acquiring, storing, retrieving, and using knowledge *Page 299*

Cognitive Dissonance Theory Festinger's theory that when we discover inconsistencies between our attitudes, or between our attitudes and behaviors, we experience discomfort and tension, which drives us to make attitudinal changes to restore harmony or consistency *Page 601*

Cognitive Map A mental image of a three-dimensional space that an organism has navigated *Page 245*

Cognitive Restructuring Process in cognitive therapy to change destructive thinking *Page 571*

Cognitive Therapy Therapy that focuses on faulty thought processes and beliefs to treat problem behaviors *Page 570*

Cognitive-Behavior Therapy Beck's system for changing destructive thoughts and beliefs, as well as associated behaviors *Page 572*

Cognitive-Social Theory Emphasizes the roles of thinking and social learning in behavior *Page 244*

Collective Unconscious Jung's concept of an inherited unconscious that all humans share *Page 494*

Comorbidity Co-occurrence of two or more disorders in the same person at the same time, as when a person suffers from both depression and alcoholism *Page 548*

Companionate Love Strong and lasting attraction characterized by trust, caring, tolerance, and friendship *Page 613*

Concept Mental representation of a group or category that shares similar characteristics (e.g., the concept of a river groups together the Nile, the Amazon, and the Mississippi because they share the common characteristic of being a large stream of water that empties into an ocean or lake) *Page 301*

Concrete Operational Stage Piaget's third stage (roughly ages 7 to 11 years); the child can perform mental operations on concrete objects and understand reversibility and conservation, but abstract thinking is not yet present *Page 366*

Conditioned Emotional Response (CER) A classically conditioned emotional response to a previously neutral stimulus (NS) *Page 219*

Conditioned Response (CR) Learned reaction to a conditioned stimulus (CS) that occurs because of previous repeated pairings with an unconditioned stimulus (UCS) *Page 219*

Conditioned Stimulus (CS) Previously neutral stimulus that, through repeated pairings with an unconditioned stimulus (UCS), now causes a conditioned response (CR) *Page 219*

Conditioning Learning associations between environmental stimuli and behavioral responses *Page 217*

Conduction Deafness Middle-ear deafness resulting from problems with transferring sound waves to the inner-ear. *Page 143*

Cones Receptor cells concentrated near the center of the retina responsible for color vision and fine detail; most sensitive in brightly lit conditions *Page 139*

Confirmation Bias Tendency to seek out and pay attention only to information that confirms preexisting positions or beliefs, while ignoring or discounting contradictory evidence *Page 307*

Conflict Having to choose between two or more incompatible goals or impulses *Page 101*

Conformity Changing behavior as a result of real or imagined group pressure *Page 616*

Conscious In Freudian terms, thoughts or motives that a person is currently aware of or is remembering *Page 487*

Consciousness An organism's awareness of its own self and surroundings (Damasio, 1999) *Page 175*

Conservation Understanding that certain physical characteristics (such as volume) remain unchanged, even when their outward appearance changes *Page 366*

Constructive Process Organizing and shaping of information during encoding and retrieval that may cause memory errors and distortions *Page 285*

Continuous Reinforcement Every correct response is reinforced *Page 232*

Control Group Group that receives no treatment in an experiment *Page 15*

Controlled Processes Mental activities requiring focused attention that generally interfere with other ongoing activities *Page 176*

Conventional Level Kohlberg's second level of moral development, where moral judgments are based on compliance with the rules and values of society *Page 378*

Convergence Binocular depth cue in which the closer the object, the more the eyes converge, or turn inward *Page 161*

Convergent Thinking Narrowing down a list of alternatives to converge on a single correct answer (e.g., standard academic tests generally require convergent thinking) *Page 310*

Cooing Vowel-like sounds infants produce beginning around age 2 to 3 months *Page 315*

Corpus Callosum [CORE-puss] [cah-LOH-suhm] Bundle of nerve fibers connecting the brain's left and right hemispheres *Page 77*

Correlation Coefficient A number that indicates the degree and direction of the relationship between the two variables *Page 22*

Correlational Research Any scientific study in which the researcher observes or measures (without directly manipulating) two or more variables to find relationships between them *Page 22*

Creativity The ability to produce valued outcomes in a novel way *Page 310*

Critical Period A period of special sensitivity to specific types of learning that shapes the capacity for future development *Page 342*

Critical Thinking The process of objectively evaluating, comparing, analyzing, and synthesizing information *Page 4*

Cross-Sectional Method Research design that measures individuals of various ages at one point in time and gives information about age differences *Page 343*

Crystallized Intelligence Knowledge and skills gained through experience and education that tend to increase over the life span *Page 322*

Dark Adaptation Process whereby rods and cones adjust to allow vision in dim light *Page 140*

Debriefing Informing participants after the research about the purpose of the study, the nature of the anticipated results, and any deceptions used *Page 28*

Defense Mechanisms Unconscious strategies used to distort reality and relieve anxiety and guilt *Page 114*

Deindividuation Increased arousal and reduced self-consciousness, inhibition, and personal responsibility that sometimes occurs in a group, particularly when the members feel anonymous *Page 621*

Deinstitutionalization Discharging as many people as possible from state hospitals and discouraging admissions *Page 585*

Delusions Mistaken beliefs maintained in spite of strong evidence to the contrary *Page 536*

Dendrites Branching neuron structures that receive neural impulses from other neurons and convey impulses toward the cell body *Page 58*

Dependent Variable (DV) Variable that is measured; it is affected by (or dependent on) the independent variable *Page 15*

Depressants Psychoactive drugs that act on the central nervous system to suppress or slow bodily processes and reduce overall responsiveness *Page 195*

Depth Perception The ability to perceive three-dimensional space and to accurately judge distance *Page 159*

Descriptive Research Research methods that observe and record behavior without producing causal explanations *Page 19*

Developmental Psychology The study of age-related changes in behavior and mental processes from conception to death *Page 341*

Diagnostic and Statistical Manual of Mental Disorders (DSM-IV-TR) Classification system developed by the American Psychiatric Association used to describe abnormal behaviors; the IV-TR indicates it is the text revision (TR) of the fourth major edition (IV) *Page 517*

Difference Threshold Minimal difference needed to notice a stimulus change; also called the "just noticeable difference" (JND) *Page 134*

Diffusion of Responsibility Assuming someone else will take action (or responsibility) *Page 630*

Discrimination Negative behaviors directed at members of a group *Page 604*

Discriminative Stimulus A cue that signals when a specific response will lead to the expected reinforcement *Page 238*

Disengagement Theory Successful aging is characterized by mutual withdrawal between the elderly and society *Page 393*

Dissociative Disorder Amnesia, fugue, or multiple personalities resulting from avoidance of painful memories or situations *Page 544*

Dissociative Identity Disorder (DID) Presence of two or more distinct personality systems in the same individual at different times; previously known as multiple personality disorder *Page 544*

Distress Unpleasant, objectionable stress *Page 98*

Distributed Practice Practice (or study) sessions are interspersed with rest periods *Page 278*

Divergent Thinking Thinking that produces many alternatives or ideas; a major element of creativity (e.g., finding as many uses as possible for a paper clip) *Page 310*

Dopamine Hypothesis Theory that overactivity of dopamine neurons may contribute to some forms of schizophrenia *Page 539*

Double Standard Beliefs, values, and norms that subtly encourage male sexuality and discourage female sexuality *Page 425*

Double-Blind Study A procedure in which both the researcher and the participants are unaware (blind) of who is in the experimental or control group *Page 17*

Drive-Reduction Theory Motivation begins with a physiological need (a lack or deficiency) that elicits a drive toward behavior that will satisfy the original need; once the need is met, a state of balance (homeostasis) is restored and motivation decreases *Page 451*

Drug Abuse Drug taking that causes emotional or physical harm to the drug user or others *Page 194*

Drug Therapy Use of chemicals (drugs) to treat physical and psychological disorders *Page 560*

Eclectic Approach Combining techniques from various theories to find the most appropriate treatment *Page 557*

Ego In Freud's theory, the rational part of the psyche that deals with reality by controlling the id, while also satisfying the superego; from the Latin term "ego" meaning "I" *Page 488*

Egocentrism The inability to consider another's point of view, which Piaget considered a hallmark of the preoperational stage *Page 365*

Egoistic Model Helping that's motivated by anticipated gain — later reciprocation, increased self-esteem, or avoidance of guilt and distress *Page 630*

Elaborative Rehearsal Linking new information to previously stored material (also known as deeper levels of processing) *Page 266*

Electroconvulsive Therapy (ECT) Biomedical therapy based on passing electrical current through the brain; used almost exclusively to treat serious depression when drug therapy does not work *Page 562*

Embryonic Period Second stage of prenatal development that begins after uterine implantation and lasts through the eighth week *Page 347*

Emotion A subjective feeling that includes arousal (heart pounding), cognitions (thoughts, values, and expectations), and expressions (frowns, smiles, and running) *Page 437*

Emotion-Focused Forms of Coping Coping strategies based on changing one's perceptions of stressful situations *Page 114*

Emotional Intelligence Goleman's term for the ability to know and manage one's emotions, empathize with others, and maintain satisfying relationships *Page 461*

Empathy In Rogerian terms, an insightful awareness and ability to share another's inner experience *Page 574*

Empathy-Altruism Hypothesis Helping because of empathy for someone in need *Page 630*

Encoding Translating information into neural codes (language) *Page 263*

Encoding Specificity Principle Retrieval of information is improved when conditions of recovery are similar to the conditions when information was encoded *Page 270*

Endocrine [EN-doh-krin] System A collection of glands located throughout the body that manufacture and secrete hormones into the bloodstream *Page 66*

Endorphins [en-DOR-fins] Chemical substances in the nervous system that are similar in structure and action to opiates and are involved in pain control, pleasure, and memory *Page 63*

Episodic Memory A part of explicit/declarative memory that stores memories of personally experienced events; a mental diary of a person's life *Page 267*

Ethnocentrism Believing that one's culture is typical of all cultures; also, viewing one's own ethnic group (or culture) as central and "correct" and then judging the rest of the world according to this standard *Page 17*

Eustress Pleasant, desirable stress *Page 98*

Evolutionary Psychology A branch of psychology that studies evolutionary principles, like natural selection and genetic mutations, which affect adaptation to the environment and help explain commonalities in behavior *Page 90*

Evolutionary/Circadian Theory As a part of circadian rhythms, sleep evolved to conserve energy and as protection from predators *Page 185*

Excitement Phase First stage of the sexual response cycle, characterized by increasing levels of arousal and increased engorgement of the genitals *Page 419*

Experiment Carefully controlled scientific procedure that determines whether variables manipulated by the experimenter have a causal effect on other variables *Page 14*

Experimental Group Group that receives a treatment in an experiment *Page 15*

Experimenter Bias Occurs when researcher influences research results in the expected direction *Page 16*

Explicit/Declarative Memory Subsystem within long-term memory that consciously stores facts, information, and personal life experiences *Page 267*

External Locus of Control Believing that chance or outside forces beyond one's control determine one's fate *Page 117*

Extinction Gradual weakening or suppression of a previously conditioned response (CR) *Page 223*

Extrasensory Perception Perceptual, or "psychic," abilities that supposedly go beyond the known senses, including telepathy, clairvoyance, precognition, and psychokinesis *Page 167*

Extrinsic Motivation Motivation based on obvious external rewards or threats of punishment *Page 447*

Facial-Feedback Hypothesis Movements of the facial muscles produce or intensify emotional reactions *Page 464*

Factor Analysis Statistical procedure for determining the most basic units or factors in a large array of data *Page 480*

Family Therapy Treatment to change maladaptive interaction patterns within a family *Page 582*

Farsightedness (Hyperopia) Visual acuity problem resulting from the cornea and lens focusing an image behind the retina *Page 139*

Feature Detectors Specialized cells in the brain that respond only to certain sensory information *Page 151*

Fetal Alcohol Syndrome (FAS) A combination of birth defects, including organ deformities and mental, motor, and/or growth retardation, that results from maternal alcohol abuse *Page 349*

Fetal Period The third, and final, stage of prenatal development (eight weeks to birth), characterized by rapid weight gain in the fetus and the fine detailing of body organs and systems *Page 347*

Five-Factor Model (FFM) Trait theory that explains personality in terms of a Big Five model — openness, conscientiousness, extraversion, agreeableness, and neuroticism *Page 480*

Fixed Interval (FI) Schedule Reinforcement occurs after a fixed (predetermined) time has elapsed *Page 233*

Fixed Ratio (FR) Schedule Reinforcement occurs after a fixed (predetermined) number of responses *Page 233*

Fluid Intelligence Aspects of innate intelligence, including reasoning abilities, memory, and speed of information processing, that are relatively independent of education and tend to decline as people age *Page 322*

Foot-in-the-Door Technique Making a small request followed by increasingly larger requests *Page 620*

Formal Operational Stage Piaget's fourth stage (around age 11 years and beyond), characterized by abstract and hypothetical thinking *Page 367*

Fovea A tiny pit in the center of the retina filled with cones and responsible for sharp vision *Page 139*

Free Association In psychoanalysis, reporting whatever comes to mind without monitoring its contents *Page 567*

Frequency How often a light or sound wave cycles — that is, the number of complete wavelengths that pass a point in a given time (e.g., per second) *Page 137*

Frequency Theory Theory explaining how we hear lower-pitched sounds; hair cells on the basilar membrane of the cochlea bend and fire action potentials at the same rate as the frequency of the sound *Page 143*

Frontal Lobes Cortical lobes at the front of the brain, which govern motor control, speech production, and higher functions, such as thinking, personality, emotion, and memory *Page 73*

Frustration Unpleasant tension, anxiety, and heightened sympathetic activity resulting from a blocked goal *Page 101*

Frustration-Aggression Hypothesis Blocking of a desired goal (frustration) creates anger that may lead to aggression *Page 627*

Functional Fixedness Tendency to think of an object functioning only in its usual or customary way *Page 307*

Fundamental attribution error (FAE) Misjudging the causes of others' behavior because of overestimating internal personal factors and underestimating external situational influences *Page 598*

Gate-Control Theory of Pain Theory that pain sensations are processed and altered by mechanisms within the spinal cord *Page 135*

Gender Psychological and sociocultural meanings added to biological maleness or femaleness *Page 406*

Gender Identity Self-identification as either a man or a woman *Page 407*

Gender Role Societal expectations for normal and appropriate male and female behavior *Page 408*

Gene A segment of DNA (deoxyribonucleic acid) that occupies a specific place on a particular chromosome and carries the code for hereditary transmission *Page 86*

General Adaptation Syndrome Selye's three-phase (alarm, resistance, and exhaustion) reaction to severe stress *Page 104*

Generalized Anxiety Disorder Chronic, uncontrollable, and excessive worry not focused on any particular object or situation *Page 522*

Genuineness In Rogerian terms, authenticity or congruence; the awareness of one's true inner thoughts and feelings and being able to share them honestly with others *Page 574*

Germinal Period First stage of prenatal development that begins with conception and ends with implantation in the uterus (the first 2 weeks) *Page 347*

Glial Cells Cells that provide structural, nutritional, and other support for the neuron, as well as communication within the nervous system; also called glia or neuroglia *Page 58*

Grammar Rules that specify how phonemes, morphemes, words, and phrases should be combined to express thoughts *Page 314*

Group Polarization Group's movement toward either riskier or more conservative behavior, depending on the members' initial dominant tendency *Page 623*

Group Therapy A number of people meet together to work toward therapeutic goals *Page 581*

Groupthink Faulty decision making that occurs when a highly cohesive group strives for agreement and avoids inconsistent information *Page 623*

Gustation Sense of taste *Page 146*

Habituation Tendency of the brain to ignore environmental factors that remain constant *Page 153*

Hallucinations Sensory perceptions that occur without an external stimulus *Page 535*

Hallucinogens [hal-LOO-sin-oh-jenz] Drugs that produce sensory or perceptual distortions called hallucinations *Page 199*

Hardiness Resilient personality that includes a strong commitment to personal goals, control over life, and viewing change as a challenge rather than a threat *Page 111*

Hassles Small problems of daily living that accumulate and sometimes become a major stress *Page 100*

Health Psychology Studies the relationship between psychological behavior and physical health and illness *Page 97*

Heritability A measure of the degree to which a characteristic is related to genetic, inherited factors *Page 87*

Heuristic Strategies, or simple rules, used in problem solving and decision making that do not guarantee a solution, but offer a likely short cut to it *Page 305*

Hierarchy of Needs Maslow's theory of motivation, that some motives (such as physiological and safety needs) must be met before going on to higher needs (such as belonging and self-actualization) *Page 452*

Higher-Order Conditioning A neutral stimulus (NS) becomes a conditioned stimulus (CS) through repeated pairings with a previously conditioned stimulus (CS) *Page 223*

HIV Positive Being infected by the human immunodeficiency virus (HIV) *Page 429*

Homeostasis A body's tendency to maintain a relatively stable state, such as a constant internal temperature *Page 451*

Hormones Chemicals manufactured by endocrine glands and circulated in the bloodstream to produce bodily changes or maintain normal bodily functions *Page 66*

HPA Axis The hypothalamus, pituitary gland, and adrenal cortex, which are activated by stress *Page 102*

Hue Visual dimension seen as a particular color; determined by the length of a light wave *Page 137*

Humanistic Therapy Therapy to maximize personal growth through affective restructuring (emotional readjustment) *Page 573*

Hypnosis A trancelike state of heightened suggestibility, deep relaxation, and intense focus *Page 207*

Hypothalamus [hi-poh-THAL-uh-muss] A small brain structure beneath the thalamus that maintains the body's internal environment and regulates emotions and drives, such as hunger, thirst, sex, and aggression *Page 71*

Hypothesis A specific prediction about how one variable is related to another *Page 12*

Id According to Freud, the source of instinctual energy, which works on the pleasure principle and is concerned with immediate gratification *Page 488*

Identity Crisis Erikson's term for an adolescent's search for self, which requires intense self-reflection and questioning *Page 384*

Illusion False impression of the environment *Page 151*

Implicit/Nondeclarative Memory Subsystem within long-term memory that consists of unconscious procedural skills, simple classically conditioned responses, and priming *Page 268*

Imprinting An innate form of learning within a critical period that involves attachment to the first large moving object seen *Page 356*

Incentive Theory Motivation results from environmental stimuli, which "pull" the organism in certain directions, rather than internal needs that drive or "push" the organism *Page 452*

Independent Variable (IV) Variable that is manipulated to determine its causal effect on the dependent variable *Page 15*

Inferiority Complex Adler's idea that feelings of inferiority develop from early childhood experiences of helplessness and incompetence *Page 493*

Informational Social Influence Conforming to group pressure out of a need for direction and information *Page 618*

Informed Consent Participant's agreement to take part in a study after being told what to expect *Page 27*

Ingroup Favoritism Viewing members of the ingroup more positively than members of an outgroup *Page 605*

Insanity Legal term applied when people cannot be held responsible for their actions or allowed to manage their own affairs because of mental illness *Page 513*

Insight Sudden understanding of a problem that implies the solution *Page 244*

Insomnia Persistent problems in falling asleep, staying asleep, or awakening too early *Page 189*

Instinctive Drift Conditioned responses shift (or drift) back toward innate response patterns *Page 251*

Instincts Behavioral patterns that are (1) unlearned, (2) always expressed in the same way, and (3) universal in a species *Page 451*

Intelligence General capacity to profit from experience, acquire knowledge, and adapt to changes in the environment *Page 321*

Intelligence Quotient (IQ) A subject's mental age divided by chronological age and multiplied by 100 *Page 326*

Interaction A process in which multiple factors mutually influence one another and the outcome—as in the interaction between heredity and environment *Page 6*

Internal Locus of Control Believing that one controls one's own fate *Page 117*

Interpersonal Attraction Positive feelings toward another *Page 607*

Interpretation A psychoanalyst's explanation of a patient's free associations, dreams, resistance, and transference; more generally, any statement by a therapist that presents a patient's problem in a new way *Page 567*

Intrinsic Motivation Motivation resulting from personal enjoyment of a task or activity *Page 446*

James–Lange Theory Emotions result from physiological arousal and behavioral expression ("I feel sad because I'm crying"). In this view, each emotion is physiologically distinct *Page 463*

Justice Perspective Gilligan's term for moral reasoning based on independence and individual rights *Page 381*

Kinesthesis Sensory system for body posture and orientation *Page 149*

Language Acquisition Device (LAD) According to Chomsky, an innate mechanism that enables a child to analyze language and extract the basic rules of grammar *Page 317*

Latent Content The true, unconscious meaning of a dream, according to Freudian dream theory *Page 186*

Latent Learning Hidden learning that exists without behavioral signs *Page 245*

Lateralization Specialization of the left and right hemispheres of the brain for particular operations *Page 77*

Law of Effect Thorndike's rule that the probability of an action being repeated is strengthened when followed by a pleasant or satisfying consequence. *Page 229*

Learned Helplessness Seligman's term for a state of helplessness or resignation in which people or animals learn that escape from something painful is impossible, and depression results *Page 530*

Learning A relatively permanent change in behavior or mental processes as a result of practice or experience *Page 217*

Limbic System An interconnected group of lower-level brain structures involved with the arousal and regulation of emotion, motivation, memory, and many other aspects of behavior and mental processes *Page 71*

Lobotomy Outmoded medical procedure for mental disorders, which involved cutting nerve pathways between the frontal lobes and the thalamus and hypothalamus *Page 562*

Localization of Function Specialization of various parts of the brain for particular functions *Page 69*

Long-Term Memory (LTM) Third stage of memory that stores information for long periods of time; its capacity is virtually limitless and its duration is relatively permanent *Page 262*

Long-Term Potentiation (LTP) Long lasting increase in neural excitability believed to be a biological mechanism for learning and memory *Page 272*

Longitudinal Method Research design that measures a single individual or group of individuals over an extended period and gives information about age changes *Page 343*

Loudness Intensity of sound determined by the amplitude of sound waves; the higher the amplitude, the louder the sound *Page 141*

Maintenance Rehearsal Repeating information over and over to maintain it in short-term memory (STM) *Page 261*

Major Depressive Disorder Long-lasting depressed mood that interferes with the ability to function, feel pleasure, or maintain interest in life *Page 528*

Manifest Content According to Freud, the surface content of a dream, which contains dream symbols that distort and disguise the dream's true meaning *Page 186*

Massed Practice Time spent learning is grouped (or massed) into long, unbroken intervals (also known as cramming) *Page 278*

Maturation Development governed by automatic, genetically predetermined signals *Page 342*

Medical Model Perspective that assumes diseases (including mental illness) have

physical causes that can be diagnosed, treated, and possibly cured *Page 516*

Meditation A group of techniques designed to refocus attention, block out all distractions, and produce an alternate state of consciousness *Page 208*

Medulla [muh-DUL-uh] Structure at the base of the brainstem responsible for automatic body functions such as breathing and heart rate *Page 69*

Memory An internal record or representation of some prior event or experience *Page 258*

Mental Images A mental representation of a previously stored sensory experience, including visual, auditory, olfactory, tactile, motor, and gustatory imagery (e.g., visualizing a train and hearing its whistle) *Page 300*

Mental Set Persisting in using problem solving strategies that have worked in the past rather than trying new ones *Page 307*

Meta-analysis Statistical procedure for combining and analyzing data from many studies *Page 13*

Midbrain Neural centers located near the top of the brainstem involved in coordinating movement patterns, sleep, and arousal *Page 69*

Minnesota Multiphasic Personality Inventory (MMPI) The most widely researched and clinically used self-report personality test (MMPI-2 is the revised version) *Page 475*

Mnemonic [nih-MON-ik] Device Memory-improvement technique based on encoding items in a special way *Page 291*

Modeling Therapy Watching and imitating models that demonstrate desirable behaviors *Page 580*

Monocular Cues Visual input from a single eye alone that contributes to perception of depth or distance *Page 161*

Morpheme [MOR-feem] Smallest meaningful unit of language, formed from a combination of phonemes *Page 314*

Motivation Set of factors that activate, direct, and maintain behavior usually toward a goal *Page 437*

Myelin [MY-uh-lin] Sheath A layer of fatty insulation wrapped around the axon of some neurons, which increases the rate at which nerve impulses travel along the axon *Page 59*

Narcolepsy [NAR-co-lep-see] Sudden and irresistible onsets of sleep during normal waking hours. (narco = numbness; lepsy = seizure) *Page 191*

Natural Selection The driving mechanism behind evolution that allows individuals with genetically influenced traits that are adaptive in a particular environment to stay alive and produce offspring *Page 90*

Naturalistic Observation Observing and recording behavior in the participant's natural state or habitat *Page 19*

Nature–Nurture Controversy Ongoing dispute over the relative contributions of nature (heredity) and nurture (environment) to the development of behavior and mental processes *Page 6*

Nearsightedness (Myopia) Visual acuity problem resulting from cornea and lens focusing an image in front of the retina *Page 139*

Need Compatibility Attraction based on sharing similar needs *Page 611*

Need Complementarity Attraction toward those with qualities we admire but personally lack *Page 611*

Negative Punishment Taking away (or removing) a stimulus, which weakens a response and makes it less likely to recur *Page 234*

Negative Reinforcement Taking away (or removing) a stimulus, which strengthens a response and makes it more likely to recur *Page 231*

Nerve Deafness Inner-ear deafness resulting from damage to the cochlea, hair cells, or auditory nerve *Page 143*

Neurogenesis [nue-roh-JEN-uh-sis] The division and differentiation of nonneuronal cells to produce neurons *Page 82*

Neuron Individual nerve cell responsible for processing, storing, and transmitting information throughout the body *Page 58*

Neuroplasticity The brain's ability to reorganize and change its structure and function throughout the life span *Page 82*

Neuroscience An interdisciplinary field studying how biological processes relate to behavioral and mental processes *Page 53*

Neurosis Outmoded term for disorders characterized by unrealistic anxiety and other associated problems *Page 517*

Neurotransmitter Chemicals manufactured and released by neurons that alter activity in other neurons *Page 61*

Neutral Stimulus (NS) A stimulus that, before conditioning, does not naturally bring about the response of interest *Page 219*

Night Terrors Abrupt awakenings from NREM (non-rapid-eye-movement) sleep accompanied by intense physiological arousal and feelings of panic *Page 191*

Nightmares Anxiety-arousing dreams generally occurring near the end of the sleep cycle, during REM sleep *Page 191*

Norm Cultural rule of behavior prescribing what is acceptable in a given situation *Page 617*

Normative Social Influence Conforming to group pressure out of a need for acceptance and approval *Page 616*

Obedience Following direct commands, usually from an authority figure *Page 618*

Object Permanence Piagetian term for an infant's understanding that objects (or people) continue to exist even when they cannot be seen, heard, or touched directly *Page 365*

Observational Learning Learning new behavior or information by watching others (also known as social learning or modeling) *Page 245*

Obsessive-Compulsive Disorder Intrusive, repetitive thoughts (obsessions), urges to perform repetitive, ritualistic behaviors (compulsions), or both *Page 624*

Occipital [ahk-SIP-uh-tuhl] **Lobes** Cortical lobes at the back of the brain responsible for vision and visual perception *Page 77*

Oedipus [ED-uh-puss] **Complex** Period of conflict during the phallic stage when children are sexually attracted to the opposite-sex parent and hostile toward the same-sex parent *Page 490*

Olfaction Sense of smell *Page 144*

Operant Conditioning Learning in which voluntary responses are controlled by their consequences (also known as instrumental or Skinnerian conditioning) *Page 229*

Operational Definition A precise description of how the variables in a study will be observed and measured (For example, drug abuse might be operationally defined as "the number of missed work days due to excessive use of an addictive substance.") *Page 12*

Opiates Drugs derived from opium that function as an analgesic or pain reliever (Opium comes from the Greek word meaning "juice") *Page 198*

Opponent-Process Theory Hering's theory that color perception is based on three systems of color opposites — blue–yellow, red–green, and black–white *Page 163*

Orgasm Phase Third stage of the sexual response cycle when pleasurable sensations peak and orgasm occurs *Page 420*

Outgroup Homogeneity Effect Judging members of an outgroup as more alike and less diverse than members of the ingroup *Page 605*

Overextension Overly broad use of a word to include objects that do not fit the word's meaning (e.g., calling all men "Daddy") *Page 316*

Overgeneralize Applying the basic rules of grammar even to cases that are exceptions to the rule (e.g., saying "mans" instead of "men") *Page 316*

Panic Disorder Sudden and inexplicable attacks of intense fear; symptoms include difficulty breathing, heart palpitations, dizziness, trembling, terror, and feelings of impending doom *Page 522*

Parallel Distributed Processing (PDP) Memory results from connections among interacting processing units, distributed in a vast network, and all operating parallel *Page 264*

Parasympathetic Nervous System Subdivision of the autonomic nervous system (ANS) responsible for calming the body and conserving energy *Page 56*

Parietal [puh-RYE-uh-tuhl] **Lobes** Cortical lobes at the top of the brain where bodily sensations are interpreted *Page 75*

Partial (Intermittent) Reinforcement Some, but not all, correct responses are reinforced *Page 232*

Perception Process of selecting, organizing, and interpreting sensory data into useful mental representations of the world *Page 131*

Perceptual Constancy Tendency for the environment to be perceived as remaining the same even with changes in sensory input *Page 156*

Perceptual Set Readiness to perceive in a particular manner, based on expectations *Page 137*

Performance Anxiety Fear of being judged in connection with sexual activity *Page 424*

Peripheral Nervous System (PNS) All nerves and neurons outside the brain and spinal cord. Its major function is to connect the CNS to the rest of the body *Page 55*

Personality Relatively stable and enduring patterns of thoughts, feelings, and actions *Page 473*

Personality Disorders Inflexible, maladaptive personality traits that cause significant impairment of social and occupational functioning *Page 545*

Pheromones [FARE-oh-mones] Airborne chemicals that affect behavior, including recognition of family members, aggression, territorial marking, and sexual mating *Page 146*

Phobia Intense, irrational fear and avoidance of a specific object or situation *Page 523*

Phoneme [FOE-neem] Smallest basic unit of speech or sound *Page 313*

Physical Dependence Bodily processes have been so modified by repeated use of a drug that continued use is required to prevent withdrawal symptoms *Page 195*

Pitch Tone or sound determined by the frequency of vibration of the sound waves; the greater the frequency, the higher the pitch *Page 141*

Place Theory Theory explaining how we hear higher-pitched sounds; different high-pitched sounds bend the basilar membrane hair cells at different locations in the cochlea *Page 142*

Placebo [pluh-SEE-bo] An inactive substance or fake treatment used as a control technique, usually in drug research, or given by a medical practitioner to a patient *Page 17*

Plateau Phase Second stage of the sexual response cycle, characterized by a leveling off in a state of high arousal *Page 419*

Pleasure Principle In Freud's theory, the principle on which the id operates — seeking immediate pleasure *Page 488*

Polygraph Instrument that measures heart rate, respiration rate, blood pressure, and skin conductivity to detect emotional arousal, which in turn supposedly reflects lying versus truthfulness *Page 460*

Pons Structure at the top of the brainstem involved in respiration, movement, waking, sleep, and dreaming *Page 69*

Positive Punishment Adding (or presenting) a stimulus, which weakens a response and makes it less likely to recur *Page 234*

Positive Reinforcement Adding (or presenting, a stimulus, which strengthens a response and makes it more likely to recur *Page 231*

Postconventional Level Kohlberg's highest level of moral development, in which individuals develop personal standards for right and wrong, and define morality in terms of abstract principles and values that apply to all situations and societies *Page 378*

Posttraumatic Stress Disorder (PTSD) Anxiety disorder following exposure to a life-threatening or other extreme event that evoked great horror or helplessness; characterized by flashbacks, nightmares, and impaired functioning *Page 111*

Preconscious Freud's term for thoughts or motives that one can become aware of easily *Page 487*

Preconventional Level Kohlberg's first level of moral development, in which morality is based on rewards, punishment, and exchange of favors *Page 378*

Prejudice A learned, generally negative, attitude toward members of a group; it includes thoughts (stereotypes), feelings, and behavioral tendencies (possible discrimination) *Page 604*

Premack principle Premack's law that using a naturally occurring high-frequency response will reinforce and increase low-frequency responses *Page 232*

Preoperational Stage Piaget's second stage (roughly ages 2 to 7 years), characterized by the ability to employ significant language and to think symbolically, but the child lacks operations (reversible mental processes), and thinking is egocentric and animistic *Page 365*

Primary Reinforcers Stimuli that increase the probability of a response because they satisfy a biological need, such as food, water, and sex *Page 230*

Priming Prior exposure to a stimulus (or prime) facilitates or inhibits the processing of new information, even when one has no conscious memory of the initial learning and storage *Page 268*

Proactive Interference Old information interferes with remembering new information; forward-acting interference *Page 280*

Problem-Focused Forms of Coping Coping strategies that use problem-solving strategies to decrease or eliminate the source of stress *Page 114*

Projective Tests Psychological tests using ambiguous stimuli, such as inkblots or drawings, which allow the test taker to project his or her unconscious onto the test material *Page 476*

Prototype A representation of the "best" or most typical example of a category (e.g., baseball is a prototype of the concept of sports) *Page 302*

Proximity Attraction based on geographic closeness *Page 610*

Psychiatry Branch of medicine dealing with the diagnosis, treatment, and prevention of mental disorders *Page 516*

Psychoactive Drugs Chemicals that change conscious awareness, mood, or perception *Page 194*

Psychoanalysis Freudian therapy designed to bring unconscious conflicts, which usually date back to early childhood experiences, into consciousness; also Freud's theoretical school of thought emphasizing the study of unconscious processes *Page 566*

Psychodynamic Therapy A modern form of psychoanalysis that emphasizes internal conflicts, motives, and unconscious forces *Page 569*

Psychological Dependence Desire or craving to achieve the effects produced by a drug *Page 194*

Psychology The scientific study of behavior and mental processes *Page 4*

Psychoneuroimmunology [sye-koh-NEW-roh-IM-you-NOLL-oh-gee] Interdisciplinary field that studies the effects of psychological factors on the immune system *Page 104*

Psychophysics Study of the relation between attributes of the physical world and our psychological experience of them *Page 134*

Psychosexual Stages In Freudian theory, five developmental periods (oral, anal, phallic, latency, and genital) during which particular kinds of pleasures must be gratified if personality development is to proceed normally *Page 490*

Psychosis Serious mental disorders characterized by loss of contact with reality and extreme mental disruption *Page 517*

Psychosocial Stages Erikson's theory that individuals pass through eight developmental stages, each involving a crisis that must be successfully resolved *Page 382*

Psychosurgery Operative procedures on the brain designed to relieve severe mental symptoms that have not responded to other forms of treatment *Page 562*

Psychotherapy Techniques employed to improve psychological functioning and promote adjustment to life *Page 555*

Puberty Biological changes during adolescence that lead to an adult-sized body and sexual maturity *Page 352*

Punishment Weakens a response and makes it less likely to recur *Page 229*

Random Assignment Participants are assigned to experimental conditions on the basis of chance, thus minimizing the possibility of biases or preexisting differences in the groups *Page 18*

Rapid-Eye-Movement (REM) Sleep A stage of sleep marked by rapid eye movements, high-frequency brain waves, paralysis of large muscles, and dreaming *Page 183*

Rational-Emotive Therapy (RET) Ellis's cognitive therapy to eliminate self-defeating beliefs through rational examination *Page 571*

Reality Principle According to Freud, the principle on which the conscious ego operates as it tries to meet the demands of the id and superego and the realities of the environment *Page 488*

Recall Retrieving a memory using a general cue *Page 269*

Reciprocal Determinism Bandura's belief that cognitions, behaviors, and the learning environment interact to produce personality *Page 501*

Recognition Retrieving a memory using a specific cue *Page 269*

Reference Groups People we conform to, or go along with, because we like and admire them and want to be like them *Page 618*

Refractory Period Phase following orgasm during which further orgasm is considered physiologically impossible *Page 420*

Reinforcement Strengthens a response and makes it more likely to recur *Page 229*

Relearning Learning material a second time, which usually takes less time than original learning (also called the savings method) *Page 277*

Reliability A measure of the consistency and stability of test scores when the test is readministered *Page 325*

Repair/Restoration Theory Sleep serves a recuperative function, allowing organisms to repair or replenish key factors *Page 185*

Representativeness Heuristic Estimating the probability of something based on how well the circumstances match our previous prototype *Page 308*

Repression Freud's first and most basic defense mechanism, which blocks unacceptable impulses from coming into awareness *Page 489*

Resiliency The ability to adapt effectively in the face of threats. *Page 392*

Resistance A stage in psychoanalysis when the patient avoids (resists) the analyst's attempts to bring threatening unconscious material to conscious awareness *Page 567*

Resolution Phase Final stage of the sexual response cycle when the body returns to its unaroused state *Page 420*

Reticular Formation (RF) Diffuse set of neurons in the core of the brainstem that screens incoming information and arouses the cortex *Page 69*

Retina Light-sensitive inner surface of the back of the eye, which contains the receptor cells for vision (rods and cones) *Page 139*

Retinal Disparity Binocular cue to distance where the separation of the eyes causes different images to fall on each retina *Page 161*

Retrieval Recovering information from memory storage *Page 363*

Retrieval Cue A clue or prompt that helps stimulate recall and retrieval of a stored piece of information from long-term memory *Page 269*

Retroactive Interference New information interferes with remembering old information; backward-acting interference *Page 280*

Retrograde Amnesia Loss of memory for events before an injury; backward-acting amnesia *Page 283*

Rods Receptor cells in the retina that detect shades of gray, are responsible for peripheral vision, and are most sensitive in dim light *Page 139*

Romantic Love Intense feeling of attraction to another, within an erotic context and with future expectations *Page 612*

Rorschach [ROAR-shock] Inkblot Test A projective test that presents a set of 10 cards with symmetrical abstract patterns, known as inkblots, and respondents describe what they "see" in the image; their response is thought to be a projection of unconscious processes *Page 476*

Saliency Bias Tendency to focus on the most noticeable (salient) factors when explaining the causes of behavior *Page 598*

Sample Bias Occurs when research participants are not representative of the larger population *Page 17*

Schachter's Two-Factor Theory Emotions result from physical arousal and cognitive labeling (or interpretation) of that arousal based on external cue *Page 465*

Schema Cognitive structures or patterns consisting of a number of organized ideas that grow and differentiate with experience *Page 363*

Schizophrenia Group of psychotic disorders involving major disturbances in perception, language, thought, emotion, and behavior; the individual withdraws from people and reality, often into a fantasy life of delusions and hallucinations *Page 534*

Secondary Reinforcers Stimuli that increase the probability of a response because of their learned value, such as money and material possessions *Page 230*

Selective Attention Filtering out and attending only to important sensory messages *Page 151*

Self-Actualization Maslow's term for the innate tendency toward growth that motivates all human behavior and results in the full realization of a person's highest potential *Page 499*

Self-Concept Rogers' term for all the information and beliefs individuals have about their own nature, qualities, and behavior *Page 498*

Self-Efficacy Bandura's term for learned beliefs that one is capable of producing desired results, such as mastering new skills and achieving personal goals *Page 501*

Self-Help Group Leaderless or nonprofessionally guided groups in which members assist each other with a specific problem, as in Alcoholics Anonymous *Page 581*

Self-Serving Bias Taking credit for our successes and externalizing our failures *Page 599*

Self-Talk Internal dialogue; the things people say to themselves when they interpret events *Page 570*

Semantic Memory A part of explicit/declarative memory that stores general knowledge; a mental encyclopedia or dictionary *Page 267*

Semantics Meaning, or the study of meaning, derived from words and word combinations *Page 314*

Semicircular Canals Three arching structures in the inner ear containing hair receptors that respond to head movements and provide information on balance *Page 148*

Sensation Process of receiving, translating, and transmitting raw sensory data from the external and internal environments to the brain *Page 131*

Sensorimotor Stage Piaget's first stage (birth to approximately age two years), in which schemas are developed through sensory and motor activities *Page 365*

Sensory Adaptation Repeated or constant stimulation decreases the number of sensory messages sent to the brain, which causes decreased sensation *Page 134*

Sensory Memory First memory stage that holds sensory information for a few seconds with relatively large capacity *Page 259*

Sensory Reduction Filtering and analyzing incoming sensations before sending a neural message to the cortex *Page 133*

Serial Position Effect Remembering information at the beginning and the end of a list better than material in the middle *Page 278*

Sex Biological maleness and femaleness, including chromosomal sex; also, activities related to sexual behaviors, such as masturbation and intercourse *Page 406*

Sexual Dysfunction Impairment of the normal physiological processes of arousal and orgasm *Page 423*

Sexual Orientation Primary erotic attraction toward members of the same sex (homosexual, gay or lesbian), both sexes (bisexual), or other sex (heterosexual) *Page 408*

Sexual Prejudice Negative attitudes toward an individual because of her or his sexual orientation *Page 422*

Sexual Response Cycle Masters and Johnson's description of the four-stage bodily response to sexual arousal, which consists of excitement, plateau, orgasm, and resolution *Page 419*

Sexual Scripts Socially dictated descriptions of "appropriate" behaviors for sexual interactions *Page 426*

Shaping Reinforcement is delivered for successive approximations of the desired response *Page 234*

Short-Term Memory (STM) Second memory stage that temporarily stores sensory information and decides whether to send it on to long-term memory (LTM); capacity limited to 5 to 9 items and duration is about 30 seconds *Page 260*

Sleep Apnea Repeated interruption of breathing during sleep because air passages to the lungs are physically blocked *Page 191*

Sleeper Effect Tendency to initially discount information from an unreliable source, but later consider it more trustworthy because the source is forgotten *Page 285*

Social Psychology The study of how other people influence our thoughts, feelings, and actions *Page 597*

Socioemotional Selectivity Theory A natural decline in social contact as older adults become more selective in their friendships. *Page 393*

Somatic Nervous System (SNS) A subdivision of the peripheral nervous system (PNS) that connects to sensory receptors and controls skeletal muscles *Page 55*

Source Amnesia Attributing to a wrong source an event that we have experienced, heard about, read about, or imagined (also called source confusion or source misattribution) *Page 285*

Split-Brain A surgical separation of the brain's two hemispheres used medically to treat severe epilepsy; split-brain patients provide data on the functions of the two hemispheres *Page 77*

Spontaneous Recovery Reappearance of a previously extinguished conditioned response (CR) *Page 223*

Standardization Establishing the norms and uniform procedures for giving and scoring a test *Page 324*

Stem Cell Precursor (immature) cells that give birth to new specialized cells; a stem cell holds all the information it needs to make bone, blood, brain — any part of a human body — and can also copy itself to maintain a stock of stem cells *Page 82*

Stereotype A set of beliefs about the characteristics of people in a group that is generalized to all group members; also, the cognitive component of prejudice *Page 604*

Stereotype Threat A person experiences doubt about his or her performance, due to negative stereotypes about his or her group's abilities *Page 333*

Stimulants Drugs that act on the brain and nervous system to increase their overall activity and general responsiveness *Page 198*

Stimulus Discrimination Learned response to a specific stimulus but not to other, similar stimuli *Page 222*

Stimulus Generalization Learned response not only to the original stimulus but also to other similar stimuli *Page 222*

Storage Retaining neurally coded information over time *Page 263*

Stress A nonspecific response of the body to any demand made of it; the arousal, both physical and mental, to situations or events that we perceive as threatening or challenging *Page 98*

Subliminal Pertaining to any stimulus presented below the threshold of conscious awareness *Page 167*

Superego In Freud's theory, the part of the personality that incorporates parental and societal standards for morality *Page 488*

Survey Research technique that assesses behaviors and attitudes of a sample or population *Page 20*

Sympathetic Nervous System Subdivision of the autonomic nervous system (ANS) responsible for arousing the body and mobilizing its energy during times of stress; also called the "fight or flight" system *Page 56*

Synapse [SIN-aps] Junction between the axon tip of the sending neuron and the dendrite or cell body of the receiving neuron; during an action potential, chemicals called neurotransmitters are released and flow across the synaptic gap *Page 61*

Syntax Grammatical rules that specify how words and phrases should be arranged in a sentence to convey meaning *Page 314*

Systematic Desensitization A gradual process of extinguishing a learned fear (or phobia) by working through a hierarchy of fear-evoking stimuli while staying deeply relaxed *Page 577*

Telegraphic Speech Two- or three-word sentences of young children that contain only the most necessary words *Page 316*

Temperament An individual's innate behavioral style and characteristic emotional response *Page 382*

Temporal Lobes Cortical lobes above the ears involved in audition (hearing), language comprehension, memory, and some emotional control *Page 75*

Teratogen [TER-ah-toh-jen] Environmental agent that causes damage during prenatal development; the term comes from the Greek word teras, meaning "malformation" *Page 348*

Thalamus [THAL-uh-muss] A brain structure at the top of the brainstem that relays sensory messages to the cerebral cortex *Page 71*

Thanatology [THAN-uh-tall-uh-gee] The study of death and dying. The term comes from thanatos, the Greek name for a mythical personification of death, and was borrowed by Freud to represent the death instinct *Page 398*

Thematic Apperception Test (TAT) A projective test that shows a series of ambiguous black-and-white pictures and asks the test taker to create a story related to each; the responses presumably reflect a projection of unconscious processes *Page 476*

Theory An interrelated set of concepts, which explains a body of data *Page 12*

Tip-of-the-Tongue Phenomenon A retrieval failure that involves a sensation of knowing that specific information is stored in long-term memory but of being temporarily unable to retrieve it *Page 282*

Tolerance Decreased sensitivity to a drug brought about by its continuous use *Page 195*

Top-Down Processing Information processing that starts "at the top" with the observer's thoughts, expectations, and knowledge and works down *Page 131*

Trait A relatively stable and consistent characteristic that can be used to describe someone *Page 480*

Transduction Converting a stimulus to a receptor into neural impulses *Page 132*

Transference In psychoanalysis, the patient may displace (or transfer) unconscious feelings about a significant person in his or her life onto the therapist *Page 567*

Trichromatic Theory Young's theory that color perception results from mixing three distinct color systems — red, green, and blue *Page 163*

Type A Personality Behavior characteristics including intense ambition, competition, exaggerated time urgency, and a cynical, hostile outlook *Page 109*

Type B Personality Behavior characteristics consistent with a calm, patient, relaxed attitude toward life *Page 109*

Unconditional Positive Regard Rogers' term for positive behavior toward a person with no contingencies attached *Page 499, 574*

Unconditioned Response (UCR) Unlearned reaction to an unconditioned stimulus (UCS) that occurs without previous conditioning *Page 219*

Unconditioned Stimulus (UCS) Stimulus that elicits an unconditioned response (UCR) without previous conditioning *Page 219*

Unconscious Freud's term for thoughts or motives that lie beyond a person's normal awareness but that can be made available through psychoanalysis *Page 487*

Validity Ability of a test to measure what it was designed to measure *Page 325*

Variable Interval (VI) Schedule Reinforcement occurs unpredictably; the interval (time) varies *Page 233*

Variable Ratio (VR) Schedule Reinforcement occurs unpredictably; the ratio (number or amount) varies *Page 233*

Wavelength Distance between the crests (or peaks) of light or sound waves; the shorter the wavelength, the higher the frequency *Page 137*

Withdrawal Discomfort and distress, including physical pain and intense cravings, experienced after stopping the use of addictive drugs *Page 195*

REFERENCES

Aarons, L. (1976). Evoked sleep-talking. *Perceptual and Motor Skills, 31,* 27–40.

Abadinsky, H. (2001). *Drugs: An introduction* (4th ed.). Stamford, CT: Thomson Learning.

Abi-Dargham, A. (1998). Increased striatal dopamine transmission in schizophrenia. *American Journal of Psychiatry, 155,* 761–767.

Aboud, F. E. (2003). The formation of ingroup favoritism and out-group prejudice in young children: Are they distinct attitudes? *Developmental Psychology, 39(1),* 48–60.

About James Randi. (2002). Detail biography. www.randi.org/jr/bio.html.

Abusharaf, R. (1998, March/April). Unmasking tradition. *The Sciences,* 22–27.

Achenbaum, W. A., & Bengtson, V. L. (1994). Re-engaging the disengagement theory of aging: On the history and assessment of theory development in gerontology. *Gerontologist, 34,* 756–763.

Acierno, R., Brady, K., Gray, M., Kilpatrick, D. G., Resnick, H., & Best, C. L. (2002). Psychopathology following interpersonal violence: A comparison of risk factors in older and younger adults. *Journal of Clinical Geropsychology, 8(1),* 13–23.

Acierno, R., Gray, M., Best, C., Resnick, H., Kilpatrick, D., Saunders, B., & Brady, K. (2001). Rape and physical violence: Comparison of assault characteristics in older and younger adults in the National Women's Study. *Journal of Traumatic Stress, 14(4),* 685–695.

Acklin, M. W. (1999). Behavioral science foundations of the Rorschach Test: Research and clinical applications. *Assessment, 6(4),* 319–326.

Adamopoulos, J., & Kashima, Y. (1999). *Social psychology and cultural context.* Thousand Oaks, CA: Sage.

Adelman, P. K., & Zajonc, R. B. (1989). Facial efference and the experience of emotion. In M. R. Rosenzweig & L. W. Porter (Eds.), *Annual review of psychology* (pp. 249–280). Palo Alto, CA: Annual Reviews Inc.

Adler, A. (1964). The individual psychology of Alfred Adler. In H. L. Ansbacher & R. R. Ansbacher (Eds.), *The individual psychology of Alfred Adler.* New York: Harper & Row.

Adler, A. (1998). *Understanding human nature.* Center City: MN: Hazelden Information Education.

Adler, N. E., Boyce, T., Chesney, M. A., Cohen, S., Folkman, S., Kahn, R. L., & Syme, L. (1994). Socioeconomic status and health: The challenge of the gradient. *American Psychologist, 49,* 15–24.

Adolphs, R., Tranel, D., & Damasio, A. R. (1998). The human amygdala in social judgment. *Nature, 393,* 470–474.

Adrianson, L. (2001). Gender and computer-mediated communication: Group processes in problem solving. *Computers in Human Behavior, 17(1),* 71–94.

Affleck, G., Tennen, H., & Apter, A. (2001). Optimism, pessimism, and daily life with chronic illness. In E. C. Chang (Ed), *Optimism & pessimism: Implications for theory, research, and practice* (pp. 147–168). Washington, DC: American Psychological Association.

Agid, O., Shapira, B., Zislin, J., Ritsner, M., Hanin, B., Murad, H., Troudart, T., Bloch, M., Heresco-Levy, U., & Lerer, B. (1999). Environment and vulnerability to major psychiatric illness: A case control study of early parental loss in major depression, bipolar disorder, and schizophrenia. *Molecular Psychiatry, 4,* 163–172.

Agras, W. S., & Berkowitz, R. I. (1999). Behavior therapies. In R. E. Hales, S. C. Yudofsky, & J. A. Talbott (Eds.), *American Psychiatric Press textbook of psychiatry.* Washington, DC: American Psychiatric Press.

Ahijevych, K., Yerardi, R., & Nedilsky, N. (2000). Descriptive outcomes of the American Lung Association of Ohio hypnotherapy smoking cessation program. *International Journal of Clinical & Experimental Hypnosis, 48(4),* 374–387.

Ainsworth, M. D. S. (1967). *Infancy in Uganda: Infant care and the growth of love.* Baltimore: Johns Hopkins University Press.

Ainsworth, M. D. S., Blehar, M., Waters, E., & Wall, S. (1978). *Patterns of attachment: Observations in the strange situation and at home.* Hillsdale, NJ: Erlbaum.

Akan, G. E., & Grilo, C. M. (1995). Sociocultural influences on eating attitudes and behaviors, body image, and psychological functioning: A comparison of African American, Asian American, and Caucasian college women. *International Journal of Eating Disorders, 18,* 181–187.

Akers, J. F., Jones, R. M., & Coyl, D. D. (1998). Adolescent friendship pairs: Similarities in identity status development, behaviors, attitudes, and intentions. *Journal of Adolescent Research, 13,* 178–201.

Akirav, I., & Richter-Levin, G. (1999). Biphasic modulation of hippocampal plasticity by behavioral stress and basolateral amygdala stimulation in the rat. *Journal of Neuroscience, 19,* 10530–10535.

Al'absi, M., Hugdahl, K., & Lovallo, W. R. (2002). Adrenocortical stress responses and altered working memory performance. *Psychophysiology, 39(1),* 95–99.

Albarracin, D., & Wyer, R. S., Jr. (2000). The cognitive impact of past behavior: Influences on beliefs, attitudes, and future behavioral decisions. *Journal of Personality & Social Psychology, 79(1),* 5–22.

Albert, U., Maina, G., Ravizza, L., & Bogetto, F. (2002). An exploratory study on obsessive-compulsive disorder with and without a familial component: Are there any phenomenological differences? *Psychopathology, 35(1),* 8–16.

Alden, L. E., & Wallace, S. T. (1995). Social phobia and social appraisal in successful and unsuccessful social interactions. *Behaviour Research and Therapy, 33(5),* 497–505.

Alexander, F. G., & Selesnick, S. T. (1966). *The history of psychiatry.* New York: Harper & Row.

Alexander, M., & Hegarty, J. R. (2000). Measuring staff burnout in a community home. *British Journal of Developmental Disabilities, 46,* 51–62.

Al-Issa, I. (2000). Culture and mental illness in Algeria. In I. Al-Issa (Ed.), *Al-Junun: Mental illness in the Islamic world* (pp. 101–119). Madison, CT: International Universities Press, Inc.

Allen, J. P., Philiber, S., Herrling, S., & Kupermine, G. P. (1997). Preventing teen pregnancy and academic failure: Experimental evaluation of a developmentally based approach. *Child Development, 64,* 729–742.

Allen, P. L. (2000). *The wages of sin: Sex and disease, past and present.* Chicago: University of Chicago Press.

Allen, R. P., & Mirabile, J. (1997, June 18). Cited in E. Woo, How to get A's, not Zzz's. *Los Angeles Times,* p. 34.

Alloy, L. B., & Clements, C. M. (1998). Hopelessness theory of depression. *Cognitive Therapy and Research, 22,* 303–335.

Alloy, L. B., Abramson, L. Y., Whitehouse, W. G., Hogan, M. E., Tashman, N. A.,

Steinberg, D. L., Rose, D. T., & Donovan, P. (1999). Depressogenic cognitive styles: Predictive validity, information processing and personality characteristics, and developmental origins. *Behaviour Research and Therapy, 37,* 503–531.

Allport, G. W., & Odbert, H. S. (1936). Trait-names: A psycho-lexical study. *Psychological Monographs: General and Applied, 47,* 1–21.

Allport, G. (1937). *Personality: A psychological interpretation.* New York: Holt, Rinehart and Winston.

Almeida, D. M., & Kessler, R. C. (1998). Everyday stressors and gender differences in daily distress. *Journal of Personality and Social Psychology, 75,* 670–680.

Aluja-Fabregat, A., & Torrubia-Beltri, R. (1998). Viewing of mass media violence, perception of violence, personality and academic achievement. *Personality and Individual Differences, 25,* 973–989.

Amabile, T. (2000). *Creativity in context.* Boulder, CO: Westview.

Ambrose, M. L., & Kulik, C. T. (1999). Old friends, new faces: Motivation research in the 1990s. *Journal of Management, 25(3),* 231–292.

American Cancer Society. (2000). Pregnant women may have ample motivation to quit smoking, but few have access to smoking cessation programs tailored to their maternal condition. Available: http://www2. cancer.org/zine/index.cfm?fn=001_11031998_0

American Heart Association (2003). Obesity and overweight. Available: http://www.networkforgood.org/offsiteframe/?siteURL=http://www.americanheart.org/

American Heart Association. (2000). Heart Patient Information. Available: http://americanheart.org/Patient_Information/hindex.html

American Psychiatric Association Work Group on Alzheimer's Disease & Related Dementias. (1997). Practice guideline for the treatment of patients with Alzheimer's disease and other dementias of late life. *American Journal of Psychiatry, 154(5,* Suppl), 1–39.

American Psychiatric Association. (2000). *Diagnostic and statistical manual of mental disorders* (4th ed. TR). Washington, DC: American Psychiatric Press.

Ammerman, A. S., Lindquist, C. H., Lohr, K. N., & Hersey, J. (2002). The efficacy of behavioral interventions to modify dietary fat and fruit and vegetable intake: A review of the evidence. *Preventive Medicine: An International Journal Devoted to Practice & Theory, 35(1),* 25–41.

Andersen, B. L. (1998). Psychology's science in responding to the challenge of cancer. *Psychological Science Agenda, 11(1),* 14–15.

Anderson, A. K., & Phelps, E. A. (2000). Expression without recognition: Contributions of the human amygdala to emotional communication. *Psychological Science, 11(2),* 106–111.

Anderson, C. A. (2001). Heat and violence. *Current Directions in Psychological Science, 10(1),* 33–38.

Anderson, C. A., & Bushman, B. J. (2001). Effects of violent video games on aggressive behavior, aggressive cognition, aggressive affect, physiological arousal, and prosocial behavior: A meta-analytic review of the scientific literature. *Psychological Science, 12(5),* 353–359.

Anderson, C. A., Anderson, K. B., Dorr, N., DeNeve, K. M., & Flanagan, M. (2000). Temperature and aggression. *Advances in Experimental Social Psychology, 32,* 63–133.

Anderson, M. C. (2001). Active forgetting: Evidence for functional inhibition as a source of memory failure. *Journal of Aggression, Maltreatment & Trauma, 4(2),* 185–210.

Anderson, M. C., Bjork, R. A. & Bjork, E. L. (1994). Remembering can cause forgetting: Retrieval dynamics in long-term memory. *Journal of Experimental Psychology: Learning, Memory, and Cognition, 20,* 1063–1087.

Anderson, S. W., Bechara, A., Damasio, H., Tranel, D., & Damasio, A. R. (1999). Impairment of social and moral behavior related to early damage in human prefrontal cortex. *Nature Neuroscience, 2,* 1032–1037.

Andrade, T. G. C. S., & Graeff, F. G. (2001). Effect of electrolytic and neurotoxic lesions of the median raphe nucleus on anxiety and stress. *Pharmacology, Biochemistry & Behavior, 70(1),* 1–14.

Andreasen, J. (2000). Meditation meets behavioural medicine: The story of experimental research on meditation. *Journal of Consciousness Studies, 7(11–12),* 17–73.

Andreasen, N. C. (1997). The role of the thalamus in schizophrenia. *Canadian Journal of Psychiatry, 155,* 1784–1786.

Andreasen, N. C. (1999). Understanding the causes of schizophrenia. *New England Journal of Medicine, 340(8),* 645–647.

Andreasen, N. C. (2000). Schizophrenia: The fundamental questions. *Brain Research Reviews, 31,* 106–112.

Andreasen, N. C., Flaum, M., Swayze, V. W., Tyrrell, G., & Arndt, S. (1990). Positive and negative symptoms in schizophrenia. *Archives of General Psychiatry, 47,* 615–621.

Anetzberger, G. J. (2001). Elder abuse identification and referral: The importance of screening tools and referral protocols. *Journal of Elder Abuse & Neglect, 13(2),* 3–22.

Angst, J., Gamma, A., Gastpar, M., Lepine, J. P., Mendlewicz, J., & Tylee, A. (2002). Gender differences in depression: Epidemiological findings from the European DEPRES I and II studies. *European Archives of Psychiatry & Clinical Neuroscience, 252(5),* 201–209.

Anooshian, L. J. (1997). Distinctions between implicit and explicit memory: Significance for understanding cognitive development. *International Journal of Behavioral Development, 21,* 453–478.

Apkarian, A. V., Darbar, A., Kraus, B. R., Gelnar, P. A., & Szeverenyi, N. M. (1999). Differentiating cortical areas related to pain perception from stimulus identification: Temporal analysis of fMRI activity. *Journal of Neurophysiology, 81,* 2956–2963.

Ardelt, M. (2000). Still stable after all these years? Personality stability theory revisited. *Social Psychology Quarterly, 63(4),* 392–405.

Aries, P. (1981). *The hour of our death.* (H. Weaver, Trans.). New York: Knopf.

Ariznavarreta, C., Cardinali, D. P., Villanua, M. A., Granados, B., Martin, M., Chiesa, J. J., Golombek, D. A., Tresguerres, J. A. F. Circadian rhythms in airline pilots submitted to long-haul transmeridian flights. (2002). *Aviation, Space, & Environmental Medicine, 73(5),* 445–455.

Arnett, J. J. (2000). High hopes in a grim world: Emerging adults' view of their futures and "Generation X.' *Youth & Society, 31(3),* 267–286.

Arnsten, A. F. (1998). The biology of being frazzled. *Science, 280,* 1711–1712.

Aronson, E., Wilson, T. D., & Akert, R. A. (1999). *Social psychology: The heart and the mind* (3rd ed.). New York: Freeman.

Aronson, J., Fried, C. B., & Good, C. (2002). Reducing the effects of stereotype threat on African American college students shaping theories of intelligence. *Journal of Experimental Social Psychology, 38(2),* 113–125.

Arvey, R. D., et al. (1994, December 13). Mainstream science on intelligence. *The Wall Street Journal,* p. A18.

Asch, S. E. (1951). Effects of group pressure upon the modification and distortion of judgment. In H. Guetzkow (Ed.), *Groups, leadership, and men.* Pittsburgh: Carnegie Press.

Ashrafi, K., Chang, F. Y., Watts, J. L., Fraser, A. G., Kamath, R. S., Ahringer, J., & Ruvjun, G. (2002). Genome-wide RNAi analysis of Caenorhabditis elegans fat regulatory genes. *Nature, 421,* 268–272.

Aspinall, S. Y. (1996). Educating children to cope with death: A preventive model. *Psychology in the Schools, 33,* 341–349.

Atchley, P., & Kramer, A. F. (2000). Age related changes in the control of attention in depth. *Psychology & Aging, 15*(1), 78–87.

Atchley, R. C. (1997). *Social forces and aging* (8th ed.). Belmont, CA: Wadsworth.

Atkinson, R. C., & Shiffrin, R. M. (1968). Human memory: A proposed system and its control processes. In K. W. Spence & J. T. Spence (Eds.), *The psychology of learning and motivation* (Vol. 2). New York: Academic Press.

Avis, N. E. (1999). Women's health at midlife. In S. L. Willis & J. D. Reid (Eds.), *Life in the middle: Psychological and social development in middle age.* San Diego: Academic Press.

Axtell, R. E. (1998). *Gestures: The do's and taboos of body language around the world,* revised and expanded ed. New York: Wiley.

Bacciagaluppi, M. (1998). Recent advances in evolutionary psychology and psychiatry. *Journal of the American Academy of Psychoanalysis, 26,* 5–13.

Bachman, G., & Zakahi, W. R. (2000). Adult attachment and strategic relational communcation: Love schemas and affinity-seeking. *Communication Reports, 13*(1), 11–19.

Backstrom, J. R., Chang, M. S., Chu, H., Niswender, C. M., & Sanders–Bush, E. (1999). Agonist-directed signaling of serotonin 5-HT-sub(2C) receptors: Differences between serotonin and lysergic acid diethylamide (LSD). *Neuropsychopharmacology, 21*(Supl, 2), 77S–81S.

Baddeley, A. D. (1992). Working Memory. *Science, 255,* 556–559.

Baddeley, A. D. (2000). Short-term and working memory. In E. Tulving, F. I. M. Craik, et al. (Eds.), *The Oxford handbook of memory.* New York: Oxford University Press.

Baddeley, A. (1998). Recent developments in working memory. *Current Opinion in Neurobiology, 8,* 234–238.

Badr, L. K., & Abdallah, B. (2001). Physical attractiveness of premature infants affects outcome at discharge from the NICU. *Infant Behavior & Development, 24(1),* 129–133.

Baer, J. (1994). Divergent thinking is not a general trait: A multi-domain training experiment. *Creativity Research Journal, 7,* 35–36.

Bagby, R. M., Rogers, R., & Buis, T. (1994). Detecting malingered and defensive responding on the MMPI–2 in a forensic inpatient sample. *Journal of Personality Assessment, 62,* 191–203.

Bagemihl, B. (1999). *Biological exuberance: Animal homosexuality and natural diversity.* New York: St Martins Press.

Bailer, U., Leisch, F., Meszaros, K., Lenzinger, E., Willinger, U., Strobl, R., Gebhardt, C., Gerhard, E., Fuchs, K., Sieghart, W., Kasper, S., Hornik, K., & Aschauer, H. N. (2000). Genomes scan for susceptibility loci for schizophrenia. *Neuropsychobiology, 42*(4), 175–182.

Bailey, C. H., & Kandel, E. R. (1995). Molecular and structural mechanisms underlying long-term memory. In M. S. Gazzanig, et al. (Eds.), *The cognitive neurosciences.* Cambridge, MA: MIT Press.

Bailey, J. M., Dunne, M. P., & Martin, N. G. (2000). Genetic and cnvironmental influences on sexual orientation and its correlates in an Australian twin sample. *Journal of Personality & Social Psychology,78*(3), 524–536.

Baillargeon, R. (2000). Reply to Bogartz, Shinskey, and Schilling; Schilling; and Cashon and Cohen. *Infancy, 1,* 447–462.

Baker, D., Telfer, M., Richardson, C. E., & Clark, G. R. (1970). Chromosome errors in men with antisocial behavior: Comparison of selected men with Klinefelter's syndrome and XYY chromosome pattern. *Journal of the American Medical Association, 214,* 869–878.

Baker, R. A. (1996). *Hidden memories.* New York: Prometheus Books.

Baker, R. A. (1998). A view of hypnosis. *Harvard Mental Health Letter, 14,* 5–6.

Baldwin, N. (2001). *Edison: Inventing the century.* Chicago: University of Chicago Press.

Baldwin, S., & Oxlad, M. (2000). *Electroshock and minors: A fifty year review.* New York: Greenwood Publishing Group.

Balfour, D. J. K., & Ridley, D. L. (2000). The effects of nicotine on neural pathways implicated in depression: A factor in nicotine addiction? *Pharmacology, Biochemistry & Behavior, 66*(1), 79–85.

Baltes, B. B., & Parker, C. P. (2000). Reducing the effects of performance expectations on behavioral ratings. *Organizational Behavior & Human Decision Processes, 82*(2), 237–267.

Baltes, P. B., Staudinger, U. M., & Lindenberger, U. (1999). Lifespan psychology: Theory and application to intellectual functioning. *Annual Reviews of Psychology, 50,* 471–507.

Bancroft, J. (2002). The medicalization of female sexual dysfunction: The need for caution. *Archives of Sexual Behavior, 31(5),* 451–455.

Bandstra, E. S., Morrow, C. E., Vogel, A. L., Fifer, R. C., Ofir, A. Y., Dausa, A. T., Xue, L., & Anthony, J. C. (2002). Longitudinal influence of prenatal cocaine exposure on child language functioning. *Neurotoxicology & Teratology, 24*(3), 297–308.

Bandura, A. (1969). *Principles of behavior modification.* New York: Holt, Rinehart and Winston.

Bandura, A. (1986). *Social foundations of thought and action: A social cognitive theory.* Englewood Cliffs, NJ: Prentice Hall.

Bandura, A. (1989). Social cognitive theory. In R. Vasta (Ed.), *Annals of child development* (Vol. 6). Greenwich, CT: JAI Press.

Bandura, A. (1991). Social cognitive theory of moral thought and action. In W. M. Kurtines & J. L. Gewirtz (Eds.), *Handbook of moral behavior and development: Vol. 1. Theory.* Hillsdale, NJ: Erlbaum.

Bandura, A. (1997). *Self-efficacy: The exercise of control.* New York: Freeman.

Bandura, A. (1999). Social cognitive theory of personality. In L. A Pervin, & O. P. John (Eds.), *Handbook of personality: Theory and Research.* New York: Guilford Press.

Bandura, A. (2000). Exercise of human agency through collective efficacy. *Current Directions in Psychological Science, 9*(3), 75–83.

Bandura, A., & Walters, R. H. (1963). *Social learning and personality development.* New York: Holt, Rinehart and Winston.

Bandura, A., Blanchard, E. B., & Ritter, B. J. (1969). The relative efficacy of desensitization and modeling therapeutic approaches for inducing behavioral, affective, and attitudinal changes. *Journal of Personality and Social Psychology, 13,* 173–199.

Bandura, A., Ross, D., & Ross, S. (1961). Transmission of aggression through imitation of aggressive models. *Journal of Abnormal & Social Psychology, 63,* 575–582.

Bandura, A., Ross, D., & Ross, S. (1963). Imitation of film-mediated aggressive models. *Journal of Abnormal & Social Psychology, 66,* 3–11.

Banks, A., & Gartrell, N. K. (1995). Hormones and sexual orientation: A questionable link. *Journal of Homosexuality, 28*(3–4), 247–268.

Banks, M. S., & Salapatek, P. (1983). Infant visual perception. In M. M. Haith & J. J. Campos (Eds.), *Handbook of child psychology.* New York: Wiley.

Bannon, A. W., Decker, M. W., Kim, D. J. B., Campbell, J. E., & Arneric, S. P. (1998). ABT-594, a novel cholinergic channel modulator, is efficacious in nerve ligation and diabetic neuropathy models of neuropathic pain. *Brain Research, 801,* 158–163.

Barber, C. E. (1997). Olfactory acuity as a function of age and gender: A comparison of African and American samples. *International Journal of Aging and Human Development, 44,* 317–334.

Barber, N. (2000). On the relationship between country sex ratios and teen pregnancy rates: A replication. *Cross-Cultural*

Research: The Journal of Comparative Social Science, 34, 26–37.

Barber, T. X. (2000). A deeper understanding of hypnosis: Its secrets, its nature, its essence. *American Journal of Clinical Hypnosis, 42*(3–4), 208–272.

Bard, C. (1934). On emotional expression after decortication with some remarks on certain theoretical views. *Psychological Review, 41*, 309–329.

Barinaga, M. (1999). Learning visualized, on the double. *Science, 286*, 1661.

Barker, P. (2000). *Basic family therapy.* Malden, MA: Blackwell Science, Inc.

Barker, R. A., & Dunnett, S. B. (1999). *Neural repair, transplantation, and rehabilitation.* Hove, England: Psychology Press/Taylor & Francis.

Barley, N. (1997). *Grave matters: A lively history of death around the world.* Austin, TX: Henry Holt & Company.

Barlow, D. H. (1999). *Anxiety and its disorders: The nature and treatment of anxiety and panic* (2nd ed.). New York: Guilford.

Barlow, D. H., & Durand, V. M. (2001). *Abnormal psychology* (2nd ed.). Belmont, CA: Wadsworth.

Barlow, D. H., Esler, J. L., & Vitali, A. E. (1998). Psychosocial treatments for panic disorders, phobias, and generalized anxiety disorder. In P. E. Nathan, J. M. Gorman, et al. (Eds.), *A guide to treatments that work* (pp. 288–318). New York: Oxford University Press.

Barnes, E., Graft, B., Reaves, J. A., & Shannon, E. (2000, March 13). It's all the rave. *Time*, pp. 64–66.

Barnouw, V. (1985). *Culture and personality* (4th ed.). Homewood, IL: Dorsey Press.

Baron, J., Roediger, H. L. III, & Anderson, M.C. (2000). Human factors and the Palm Beach ballot. *APS Observer, 13*(10), 5–7.

Baron, R. (2000). *Social psychology* (7th ed.). Boston: Allyn & Bacon.

Bar-On, R. (2000). *The handbook of emotional intelligence.* New York: Jossey-Bass.

Barr, A. (1999). *Drink: A social history of America.* New York: Carroll & Graf.

Barrett–Lennard, G. T. (1999). *Carl Rogers' helping system: Journey and substance.* Thousand Oaks, CA: Corwin Press.

Barry, D. T.,Grilo, C. M., & Masheb, R. M. (2002). Gender differences in patients with binge eating disorder. *International Journal of Eating Disorders, 31*(1), 63–70.

Barstow, D. G. (1999). Female genital mutilation: The penultimate gender abuse. *Child Abuse and Neglect, 23*(5), 501–510.

Bartholow, B. D., & Anderson, C. A. (2002). Effects of violent video games on aggressive behavior: Potential sex differ-

ences. *Journal of Experimental Social Psychology, 38*(3), 283–290.

Bartholow, B. D., & Anderson, C. A. (2002). Effects of violent video games on aggressive behavior: Potential sex differences. *Journal of Experimental Social Psychology,2 May Vol 38(3) 283–290*

Bartlett, F. C. (1958). *Thinking.* London: Allen & Unwin.

Barton, J. J. S., Press, D. Z., Keenan, J. P., & O'Connor, M. (2002). Lesions of the fusiform face area impair perception of facial configuration in prosopagnosia. *Neurology, 58*(1), 71–78.

Bartsch, R. A., Judd, C. M., Louw, D. A., Park, B., & Ryan, C. S. (1997). Cross-national outgroup homogeneity: United States and South African stereotypes. *South African Journal of Psychology, 27*(3), 166–170.

Bassett, H., & Lloyd, C. (2001). Occupational therapy in mental health: Managing stress and burnout. *British Journal of Occupational Therapy, 64*(8), 406–411.

Batel, P. (2000). Addiction and schizophrenia. *European Psychiatry, 15*, 115–122.

Batson, C. D. (1991). *The altruism question: Toward a social-psychological answer.* Hillsdale, NJ: Erlbaum.

Batson, C. D. (1998). Altruism and prosocial behavior. In D. T. Gilbert, S. T. Fiske, and G. Lindzey (Eds.), *The handbook of social psychology, Vol. 2* (4th ed.) (pp. 282–316). Boston, MA: McGraw-Hill.

Batson, C. D., et al. (1999). Two threats to the common good: Self-interested egoism and empathy and empathy-induced altruism. *Personality and Social Psychology Bulletin, 25*, 3–16.

Batterham, R. L., Cowley, M. A., Small, C. J., Herzog, H., Cohen, M. A., et al. (2002). Gut hormone PYY 3–36 physiologically inhibits food intake. *Nature, 418*, 650–654.

Baum, A., & Posluszny, D. M. (1999). Health psychology: Mapping biobehavioral contributions to health and illness. *Annual Review of Psychology, 50*, 137–163.

Baumeister, R. J. (1998). The self. In D. T. Gilbert, S. T. Fiske, and G. Lindzey (Eds.), *The handbook of social psychology, Vol. 2* (4th ed.) (pp. 680–740). Boston, MA: McGraw-Hill.

Baumrind, D. (1980). New directions in socialization research. *American Psychologist, 35*, 639–652.

Baumrind, D. (1995). *Child maltreatment and optimal caregiving in social contexts.* New York: Garland.

Bazanis, E., Rogers, R. D., Dowson, J. H., Taylor, P., Meux, C., Staley, C., Nevinson-Andrews, D., Taylor, C., Robbins, T. W., & Sahakian, B. J. (2002). Neurocognitive deficits in decision-making and planning of patients with DSM-III-R borderline per-

sonality disorder. *Psychological Medicine, 32*(8), 1395–1405.

Beach, F. A. (1977). *Human sexuality in four perspectives.* Baltimore: The Johns Hopkins University Press.

Beal, D., & DiGiuseppe, R. (1998). Training supervisors in rational emotive behavior therapy. *Journal of Cognitive Psychotherapy, 12*, 127–137.

Beaubrun, G., & Gray, G. E. (2000). A review of herbal medicines for psychiatric disorders. *Psychiatric Services, 51*(9), 1130–1134.

Beaumont, G. (2000). Antipsychotics-The future of schizophrenia treatment. *Current Medical Research and Opinion, 16*, 37–42.

Beauregard, M., Levesque, J., & Bourgouin, P. (2001). Neural correlates of conscious self-regulation of emotion. *Journal of Neuroscience, 21*(18), 6993–7000.

Bechara, A., Damasio, H., Damasio, A. R., & Lee, G. P. (1999). Different contributions of the human amygdala and ventromedial prefrontal cortex to decision-making. *Journal of Neuroscience, 19*, 5473–5481.

Bechara, A., Tranel, D., Damasio, H., & Damasio, A. R. (1996). Failure to respond automatically to anticipated future outcomes following damage to prefrontal cortex. *Cerebral Cortex, 6*, 215–225.

Beck, A. T. (1976). *Cognitive therapy and the emotional disorders.* New York: International Universities Press.

Beck, A. T. (2000). *Prisoners of hate.* New York: Harperperennial.

Beck, A. T., Brown, G. K., Steer, R. A., Kuyken, W., & Grisham, J. (2001). Psychometric properties of the Beck Self-Esteem Scales. *Behaviour Research & Therapy, 39*(1), 115–124.

Beck, J. S. (1995). *Cognitive therapy: Basics and beyond.* New York: Guilford.

Becker, H., & Kunstmann, W. (2001). The homeless mentally ill in Germany. *International Journal of Mental Health, 30*(3), 57–73.

Beckerman, S., Hardy, S. B., Baker, R. R., Crocker, W. H., Valentine, P., & Hawkes, K. (1999). Partible paternity: Matings with multi-ple men leading to multiple fathers per child. *Meeting of the American Association for the Advancement of Science.* January, Anaheim, CA.

Beckett-Camarata, E. J., Camarata, M. R., & Barker, R. T. (1998). Integrating internal and external customer relationships through relationship management: A strategic response to a changing global environment. *Journal of Business Research, 41*(1), 71–81.

Beeckmans, K., Michiels, K. (1996). Personality, emotions and the temporolimbic system: A neuropsychological approach. *Acta Neurologica Belgica, 96*, 35–42.

Begg, I. M., Needham, D. R., & Bookbinder, M. (1993). Do backward messages unconsciously affect listeners? No. *Canadian Journal of Experimental Psychology, 47,* 1–14.

Begley, S. (2000, January 1). Rewiring your gray matter. *Newsweek,* pp. 63, 65.

Beilin, H. (1992). Piaget's enduring contribution to developmental psychology. *Developmental Psychology, 28,* 191–204.

Bekaroglu, M., Soylu, C., Soylu, N., & Bilici, M. (1997). Bipolar affective disorder associated with Klinefleter's syndrome: A case report. *Israel Journal of Psychiatry & Related Sciences, 34,* 308–310.

Bell, A. P., Weinberg, M. S., & Hammersmith, S. K. (1981). *Sexual preference: Its development in men and women.* Bloomington: Indiana University Press.

Bellivier, F., Leboyer, M., Courtet, P., Buresi, C., Beufils, B., Samolyk, D., et al. (1998). Association between the tryptophan hydroxylase gene and manic-depressive illness. *Archives of General Psychiatry, 55,* 33–37.

Belsky, J., & Cassidy, J. (1994). Attachment: Theory and evidence. In M. Rutter & D. Hay (Eds.), *Development through life: A handbook for clinicians* (pp. 373–402). Oxford, England: Blackwell.

Bem, S. L. (1974). The measurement of psychological androgyny. *Journal of Consulting and Clinical Psychology, 42*(2), 155–162.

Bem, S. L. (1981). Gender schema theory: A cognitive account of sex typing. *Psychological Review, 88,* 354–364.

Bem, S. L. (1993). *The lenses of gender: Transforming the debate on sexual inequality.* New Haven, CT: Yale University Press.

Benes, F. M. (1997). The role of stress and dopamine-GABA interactions in the vulnerability for schizophrenia. *Journal of Psychiatric Research, 31*(2), 257–275.

Benson, H. (1977). Systematic hypertension and the relaxation response. *New England Journal of Medicine, 296,* 1152–1156.

Berger, T. W., & Thompson, R. F. (1982). Hippocampal cellular plasticity during extinction of classically conditioned nictitating membrane behavior. *Behavioural Brain Research, 4*(1), 63–76.

Berkowitz, L. (1990). On the formation and regulation of anger and aggression. *American Psychologist, 45,* 494–503.

Berkowitz, L. (1999). Evil is more than banal: Situationism and the concept of evil. *Personality and Social Psychology Review, 3*(3), 246–253.

Berman, M. E., Tracy, J. I., & Coccaro, E. F. (1997). The serotonin hypothesis of aggression revisited. *Clinical Psychology Review, 17*(6), 651–665.

Bermond, B., Fasotti, L., Nieuwenhuyse, B., & Schuerman, J. (1991). Spinal cord lesions, peripheral feedback, and intensities of emotional feelings. *Cognition and Emotion, 5,* 201–220.

Bernard, L. L. (1924). *Instinct.* New York: Holt.

Bernardi, L., Sleight, P., Bandinelli, G., Cencetti, S., Fattorini, L., Wdowczyc-Szulc, J., & Lagi, A. (2001). Effect of rosary prayer and yoga mantras on autonomic cardiovascular rhythms: Comparative study. *BMJ: British Medical Journal, 323*(7327), 1446–1449.

Bernhardt, P. C. (1997). Influences of serotonin and testosterone in aggression and dominance: Convergence with social psychology. *Current Directions in Psychological Science, 6,* 44–48.

Bernhardt, T., Seidler, A., & Froelich, L. (2002). Der Einfluss von psychosozialen Faktoren auf das Demenzerkrankungsrisiko. Psychosocial risk factors and dementia—A review. *Fortschritte der Neurologie, Psychiatrie, 70*(6), 283–288.

Bernheim, K. F., & Lewine, R. R. J. (1979). *Schizophrenia: Symptoms, causes, and treatments.* New York: Norton.

Berreman, G. (1971). *Anthropology today.* Del Mar, CA: CRM Books.

Berrettini, W. H. (2000). Genetics of psychiatric disease. *Annual Review of Medicine, 51,* 465–479.

Berrettini, W. H. (2000). Susceptibility loci for bipolar disorder: Overlap with inherited vulnerability to schizophrenia. *Biological Psychiatry, 47*(3), 245–251.

Berry, J. W., Poortinga, Y. A., Segall, M. H., & Dasen, P. R. (1992). *Cross-cultural psychology: Research and applications.* New York: Cambridge University Press.

Berthoud, H. (2002). Multiple neural systems controlling food intake and body weight. *Neuroscience & Biobehavioral Reviews, 26*(4), 393–428.

Bertram, K., & Widener, A. (1998). Repressed memories: The real story. *Professional Psychology: Research & Practice, 29,* 482–487.

Bertram, K., & Widener, A. (1999). Repressed memories: Just the facts. *Professional Psychology: Research & Practice, 30,* 625–626.

Best, D. L., & Williams, J. E. (1994). Masculinity/femininity in the self and ideal self-descriptions of university students in fourteen countries. In A. M. Bouvy, F. J. R. van de Vijver, P. Boski, & P. Schmitz (Eds.), *Journeys into cross-cultural psychology* (pp. 297–306). Amsterdam: Swets & Zeitlinger.

Best, J. B. (1999). *Cognitive psychology,* (5th ed.) Belmont, CA: Wadsworth.

Beutler, L. E., Brown, M. T., Crothers, L., Booker, K., et al. (1996). The dilemma of factitious demographic distinctions in psychological research. *Journal of Consulting and Clinical Psychology, 64,* 892–902.

Beutler, L. E., Shurkin, J. N., Bongar, B. M., & Gray, J. (2000). *A consumers guide to psychotherapy.* Oxford: Oxford University Press.

Beyth-Marom, Shlomith, D., Gombo, R., & Shaked, M. (1985). *An elementary approach to thinking under uncertainty.* Hillsdale, NJ: Erlbaum.

Bhugra, D. (2000). Disturbances in objects of desire: Cross-cultural issues. *Sexual & Relationship Therapy, 15*(1), 67–78.

Biehl, M., Matsumoto, D., Ekman, P., Hearn, V., Heider, K., Kudoh, T., & Ton, V. (1997). Matsumoto and Ekman's Japanese and Caucasian facial expressions of emotion (JACFEE): Reliability data and cross–national differences. *Journal of Nonverbal Behavior, 21,* 3–21.

Binder, J. R., et al. (1997). Human brain language areas identified by functional magnetic resonance imaging. *Journal of Neuroscience, 17,* 353–362.

Bink, M. L., & Marsh, R. L. (2000). Cognitive regularities in creative activity. *Review of General Psychology, 4*(1), 59–78.

Bishop, C. A. (1974). *The northern Objibwa and the fur trade.* Toronto: Holt, Rinehart, and Winston.

Bishop, K. M., & Wahlsten, D. (1997), Sex differences in the human corpus callosum: Myth or reality? *Neuroscience and Biobehavioral Reviews, 21,* 581–601.

Bjorkqvist, K. (1994). Sex differences in physical, verbal, and indirect aggression: A review of recent research. *Sex Roles, 30,* 177–188.

Blagrove, M. (2000). Sleep, sleep deprivation, sleepiness, circadian rhythms, sleep neurophysiology, sleep disorders, and dreaming. In D. S.Gupta, & R. M. Gupta (Eds.),*Psychology for psychiatrists* (pp. 198–214). London, England: Whurr Publishers, Ltd.

Blaine, B., & McElroy, J. (2002). Selling stereotypes: Weight loss infomercials, sexism, and weightism. *Sex Roles, 46*(9–10), 351–357.

Blakemore, C., & Cooper, G. F. (1970). Development of the brain depends on the visual environment. *Nature, 228,* 477–478.

Blanchard, J. J., Squires, D., Henry, T., Horan, W. P. Bogenschutz, M., et al., (1999). Examining an affect regulation model of substance abuse in schizophrenia: The role of traits and coping. *Journal of Nervous and Mental Disease, 187,* 72–79.

Blanton, C. K. (2000). "They cannot master abstractions, but they can often be made efficient workers": Race and class in the intelligence testing of Mexican Americans and African Americans in Texas during the

1920s. *Social Science Quarterly, 81*(4), 1014–1026.

Blass, T. (1999). The Milgram Paradigm after 35 years: Some things we now know about obedience to authority. *Journal of Applied Social Psychology, 29*(5), 955–978.

Bliwise, D. L. (1997). Sleep and aging. In M. R. Pressman & W. C. Orr (Eds.), *Understanding sleep: The evaluation and treatment of sleep disorders.* Washington, DC: American Psychological Association.

Blonna, R., & Levitan, J. (2000). *Healthy sexuality.* Englewood, CO: Morton.

Bloom, F. E., & Lazerson, A. (1988). Brain, mind, and behavior (2nd ed.). New York: W. H. Freeman.

Bloom, J. W. (1998). The ethical practice of Web-Counseling. *British Journal of Guidance & Counseling, 26*(1), 53–59.

Blum, K., Braverman, E. R., Holder, J. M., Lubar, J. F., Monastra, V. J., Miller, D., Lubar, J. O., Chen, T. J. H., & Comings, D. E. (2000). Reward deficiency syndrome: A biogenetic model for the diagnosis and treatment of impulsive, addictive, and compulsive behaviors. *Journal of Psychoactive Drugs, 32*(Suppl), 1–68.

Blum, K., Cull, J. G., Braverman, E. R., & Comings, D. E. (1996). Reward deficiency syndrome. *American Scientist, 84,* 132–145.

Boake, C. (2002). From the Binet-Simon to the Wechsler-Bellevue: Tracing the history of intelligence testing. *Journal of Clinical & Experimental Neuropsychology, 24*(3), 383–405.

Bobak, M., McKee, M., Rose, R., & Marmot, M. (1999). Alcohol consumption in a national sample of the Russian population. *Addiction, 94*(6), 857–866.

Bock, G. R., & Goode, J. A. (Eds.) (1996). *Genetics of criminal and antisocial behavior.* Chichester, England: Wiley.

Boden, M. A. (2000). State of the art: Computer models of creativity. *Psychologist, 13*(2), 72–76.

Bohart, A. C., O'Hara, M., & Leitner, L. M. (1998). Empirically violated treatments: Disenfranchisement of humanistic and other psychotherapies. *Psychotherapy Research, 8,* 141–157.

Bois, J. E., Sarrazin, P. G., Brustad, R. J., Trouilloud, D. O., & Cury, F. (2002). Mothers' expectancies and young adolescents' perceived physical competence: A yearlong study. *Journal of Early Adolescence, 22*(4), 384–406.

Boivin, D. B., Czeisler, C. A., & Waterhouse, J. W. (1997). Complex interaction of the sleep-wake cycle and circadian phase modulates mood in healthy subjects. *Archives of General Psychiatry, 54,* 145.

Bolles, R. C. (1970). Species–specific defense reactions and avoidance learning. *Psychological Review, 77,* 32–48.

Bolles, R. C. (1975). Theory of motivation (2nd ed.). New York: Harper & Row.

Bonavia, M. T., & Pardo, I. Q. (1999). Par-Creencias directivas y participacion de los empleados. Management culture and employee involvement. *Revista de Psicologia del Trabajo y de las Organizaciones, 15*(3), 367–383.

Bond, F. W., & Bunce, D. (2000). Mediators of change in emotion-focused and problem-focused worksite stress management intervention. *Journal of Occupational Health Psychology, 5,* 153–163.

Bond, M. H., & Smith, P. B. (1996). Cross-cultural social and organizational psychology. *Annual Review of Psychology, 47,* 205–235.

Bonder, B. R., Zadorzny, C., & Martin, R. J. (1998). Dressing in Alzheimer's disease: Executive function and procedural memory. *Clinical Gerontologist, 19,* 88–92.

Bonson, K. R., Grant, S. J., Contoreggi, C. S., Links, J. M., Metcalfe, J., Weyl, H. L., Kurian, V., Ernst, M., & London, E. D. (2002). Neural systems and cue-induced cocaine craving. *Neuropsychopharmacology, 26*(3), 376–386.

Book, A. S., Starzyk, K. B., & Qunisey, V. L. (2001). The relationship between testosterone and aggression: A meta-analysis. *Aggression & Violent Behavior, 6*(6), 579–599.

Book, H. E., & Luborsky, L. (1998). *Brief psychodynamic psychotherapy.* Washington, DC: American Psychological Association.

Borba, M. (2001). *Building moral intelligence: The seven essential virtues that teach kids to do the right thing.* New York: Jossey-Bass.

Borbely, A. A. (1982). Circadian and sleep-dependent processes in sleep regulation. In J. Aschoff, S. Daan, & G. A. Groos (Eds.), *Vertebrate circadian rhythms* (pp. 237–242). Berlin: Springer/Verlag.

Borkenau, P., Riemann, R., Angleitner, A., & Spinath, F. M. (2001). Genetic and environmental influences on observed personality: Evidence from the German Observational Study of Adult Twins. *Journal of Personality & Social Psychology, 80*(4), 655–668.

Born, J. Lange, T., Hansen, K., Molle, M., & Fehm, H. L. (1997). Effects of sleep and circadian rhythm on human circulating immune cells. *Journal of Immunology, 158,* 4454–4464.

Bostwick, J. M., & Pankratz, V. S. (2000). Affective disorders and suicide risk: A reexamination. *American Journal of Psychiatry, 157*(12), 1925–1932.

Bouchard, T. J. Jr. (1997). The genetics of personality. In K. Blum & E. P. Noble (Eds.), *Handbook of psychiatric genetics.* Boca Raton, FL: CRC Press.

Bouchard, T. J., Jr. (1994). Genes, environment, and personality. *Science, 264,* 1700–1701.

Bouchard, T. J., Jr. (1999). The search for intelligence. *Science, 284,* 922–923.

Bouchard, T. J., Jr., & Hur, Y. (1998). Genetic and environmental influences on the continuous scales of the Myers-Briggs Type Indicator: An analysis based on twins reared apart. *Journal of Personality, 66,* 135–149.

Bouchard, T. J., Jr., Mcgue, M., Hur, Y., & Horn, J. M. (1998). A genetic and environmental analysis of the California Psychological Inventory using adult twins reared apart and together. *European Journal of Personality, 12,* 307–320.

Bouman, M. A. (2002). De Vries-Weber gain control and dark adaptation in human vision. Journal of the Optical Society of America A: *Optics, Image Science & Vision, 19*(2), 254–265.

Bourassa, M., & Vaugeois, P. (2001). Effects of marijuana use on divergent thinking. *Creativity Research Journal, 13*(3–4), 411–416.

Bourguignon, E. (1973). Introduction: A framework for the comparative study of altered states of consciousness. In E. Bourguignon (Ed.), *Religion, altered states of consciousness and social change.* Columbus: Ohio State University Press.

Bourne, L. E., Dominowski, R. L., & Loftus, E. F. (1979). *Cognitive processes.* Englewood Cliffs, NJ: Prentice Hall.

Bouton, M. E. (1994). Context, ambiguity, and classical conditioning. *Current Directions in Psychological Science, 2,* 49–53.

Bouton, M. E., Mineka, S., & Barlow, D. H. (2001). A modern learning theory perspective on the etiology of panic disorder. *Psychological Review, 108*(1), 4–32.

Bower, B. (2002, June 1). Snooze power: Midday nap may awaken learning potential. *Science News, 161,* 341–342.

Bower, B. (1999). Criminal links to prenatal smoking. *Science News, 155,* 203.

Bower, B. (2000). Cooperative strangers turn a mutual profit. *Science News, 157,* 231.

Bower, G. H., Thompson-Schill, S. & Tulving, E. (1994). Reducing retroactive interference: An interference analysis. *Journal of Experimental Psychology: Learning, Memory, and Cognition, 20,* 51–66.

Bower, H. (2001). The gender identity disorder in the DSM-IV classification: A critical evaluation. *Australian & New Zealand Journal of Psychiatry, 35*(1), 1–8.

Bowers, K. S., & Woody, E. Z. (1996). Hypnotic amnesia and the paradox of intentional forgetting. *Journal of Abnormal Psychology, 105,* 381–390.

Bowlby, J. (1969). *Attachment and loss, Vol. I: Attachment.* New York: Basic Books.

Bowlby, J. (1973). *Attachment and loss, Vol. II: Separation and anxiety.* New York: Basic Books.

Bowlby, J. (1979). *The making and breaking of affectional bonds.* London, England: Tavistock.

Bowlby, J. (1982). Attachment and loss: Retrospect and prospect. *American Journal of Orthopsychiatry, 52,* 664–678.

Bowlby, J. (1989). *Secure attachment.* New York: Basic Books.

Bowlby, J. (2000). *Attachment.* New York: Basic Books.

Bowler, D. F. (2001). "It's all in your mind": The final common pathway. *Work: Journal of Prevention, Assessment & Rehabilitation, 17(3),* 167–174.

Bowling, A. C., & Mackenzie, B. D. (1996). The relationship between speed of information processing and cognitive ability. *Personality & Individual Differences, 20(6),* 775–800.

Boyce, N. (2001, February 19). Aids is far from over. *U.S. News & World Report,* p. 56.

Boyd, N. (2000). *The beast within: Why men are violent.* London: Greystone Books, Ltd.

Brady, K. T., Myrick, H., & McElroy, S. (1998). The relationship between substance use disorders, impulse control disorders, and pathological aggression. *American Journal on Addictions, 7(3),* 221–230.

Bragdon, A. D., & Gamon, D. (1999). *Building left-brain power: Left-brain conditioning exercises and tips to strengthen language, math, and uniquely human skills.* Thousand Oaks, CA: Brainwaves Books.

Brandon, T. H., Collins, B. N., Juliano, L. M., & Lazev, A. B. (2000). Preventing relapse among former smokers: A comparison of minimal interventions through telephone and mail. *Journal of Consulting and Clinical Psychology, 68(1),* 103–113.

Brannigan, A. (1997). Self control, social control and evolutionary psychology: Towards an integrated perspective on crime. *Canadian Journal of Criminology, 39,* 403–431.

Bransford, J. D. (1979). *Human cognition.* Belmont, CA: Wadsworth.

Braun, K. A., Ellis, R., & Loftus, E. F. (2002). Make my memory: How advertising can change our memories of the past. *Psychology & Marketing, 19(1),* 1–23.

Brawman-Mintzer, O., & Lydiard, R. B. (1996). Generalized anxiety disorder: Issues in epidemiology. *Journal of Clinical Psychiatry, 57,* 3–8.

Brawman-Mintzer, O., & Lydiard, R. B. (1997). Biological basis of generalized anxiety disorder. *Journal of Clinical Psychiatry, 58,* 16–25.

Bredeson, C. (2000). *John Glenn returns to orbit: Life on the space shuttle.* New York: Enslow Publishers.

Breedlove, S. M. (1997). Sex on the brain. *Nature, 389,* 801–804.

Breger, L. (2000). *Freud: Darkness in the midst of vision.* New York: Wiley.

Breland, K., & Breland, M. (1961). The misbehavior of organisms. *American Psychologist, 16,* 681–684.

Brennan, P. A., Grekin, E. R., Mortensen, E. L., & Mednick, S. A. (2002). Relationship of maternal smoking during pregnancy with criminal arrest and hospitalization for substance abuse in male and female adult offspring. *American Journal of Psychiatry, 159(1),* 48–54.

Breslau, N., & Klein, D. F. (1999). Smoking and panic attacks: An epidemiologic investigation. *Archives of General Psychiatry, 56,* 1141–1147.

Brewer, J. B., Zhao, Z., Desmond, J. E., Glover, G. H., & Gabrieli, J. D. (1998). Making memories: Brain activity that predicts how well visual experience will be remembered. *Science, 281,* 1185–1187.

Brewer, M. B. (1996). When contact is not enough: Social identity and intergroup cooperation. *International Journal of Intercultural Relations, 20(3–4),* 291–303.

Brewer, W. F., & Pani, J. R. (1996). Reports of mental imagery in retrieval from long-term memory. *Consciousness & Cognition: An International Journal, 5,* 265–287.

Brewin, C. R., Andrews, B., Rose, S., & Kirk, M. (1999). Acute stress disorder and posttraumatic stress disorder in victims of violent crime. *American Journal of Psychiatry, 156,* 360–366.

Brewster, K. L., Billy, J. O. G., & Grady, W. R. (1993). Social context and adolescent behavior: The impact of community on the transition to sexual activity. *Social Forces, 71,* 713–740.

Briggs, F., & Hawkins, R. M. F. (1999). The importance of parent participation in child protection curricula. In L. E. Berk, *Landscapes of development* (pp. 323–338). Belmont, CA: Wadsworth.

Brim, O. (1999). The MacArthur Foundation study of midlife development. Vero Beach, FL: *MacArthur Foundation.*

Brislin, R. B. (2000). *Understanding culture's influence on behavior.* Ft. Worth, TX: Harcourt.

Brislin, R. W. (1993). *Understanding culture's influence on behavior.* Orlando, FL: Harcourt Brace Jovanovich.

Brislin, R. W. (1997). *Understanding culture's influence on behavior.* San Diego: Harcourt Brace.

Brkich, M., Jeffs, D., & Carless, S. A. (2002). A global self-report measure of person-job fit. *European Journal of Psychological Assessment, 18(1),* 43–51.

Broderick, P. C., & Korteland, C. (2002). Coping style and depression in early adolescence: Relationships to gender, gender role, and implicit beliefs. *Sex Roles, 46(7–8),* 201–213.

Brody, N. (1992). *Intelligence* (2nd ed.). San Diego, CA: Academic Press.

Brook, J. S., Richter, L., & Whiteman, M. (2000). Effects of parent personality, upbringing, and marijuana use on the parent–child attachment relationship. *Journal of the American Academy of Child & Adolescent Psychiatry, 39(2),* 240–248.

Brown, D. (2001). (Mis)representations of the long-term effects of childhood sexual abuse in the courts. *Journal of Child Sexual Abuse, 9(3–4),* 79–108.

Brown, D., Scheflin, A. W., & Hammond, D. C. (1997). *Memory, trauma treatment and the law.* New York: Norton.

Brown, E, Deffenbacher, K., & Sturgill, K. (1977). Memory for faces and the circumstances of encounter. *Journal of Applied Psychology, 62,* 311–318.

Brown, J. D. (1991). Accuracy and bias in self-knowledge. In C. R. Snyder & D. F. Forsyth (Eds.), *Handbook of social and clinical psychology: The health perspective.* New York: Pergamon Press.

Brown, J. D., & Rogers, R. J. (1991). Self-serving attributions: The role of physiological arousal. *Personality and Social Psychology Bulletin, 17,* 501–506.

Brown, K., & Bradley, L. J. (2002). Reducing the stigma of mental illness. *Journal of Mental Health Counseling, 24(1),* 81–87.

Brown, L. S., & Burman, E. (1997). Editor's introduction: The delayed memory debate: Why feminist voices matters. *Feminism and Psychology, 7,* 7–16.

Brown, R. P., & Gerbarg, P. L. (2001). Herbs and nutrients in the treatment of depression, anxiety, insomnia, migraine, and obesity. *Journal of Psychiatric Practice, 7(2),* 75–91.

Brown, R., & Kulik, J. (1977). Flashbulb memories. *Cognition, 5,* 73–99.

Brown, R., & McNeill, D. (1966). The "tip of the tongue" phenomenon. *Journal of Verbal Learning and Verbal Behavior, 5,* 325–337.

Browne, K. O. (2001). Cultural formulation of psychiatric diagnoses. *Culture, Medicine & Psychiatry, 25(4),* 411–425.

Bruggeman, E. L., & Hart, K. J. (1996). Cheating, lying, and moral reasoning by religious and secular high school students. *Journal of Educational Research, 89,* 340–344.

Brundin, P., Pogarell, O., Hagell, P., Piccini, P., Widner, H., Schrag, A., Kupsch, A., Crabb, L., Odin, P., Gustavii, B., Bjoerklund, A., Brooks, D. J., Marsden, C. D.,

Oertel, W. H., Quinn, N. P., Rehncrona, S., & Lindvall, O. (2000). Bilateral caudate and putamen grafts of embryonic mesencephalic tissue treated with lazaroids in Parkinson's disease. *Brain, 123*(7), 1380–1390.

Brustowicz, L. M., Hodgkinson, K. A., Chow, E. W. C., Honer, W. G., & Bassett, A. S. (2000). Location of a major susceptibility locus for familial schizophrenia on chromosome 1q21–q22. *Science, 288,* 678–682.

Bryant, A. L., & Zimmerman, M. A. (2002). Examining the effects of academic beliefs and behaviors on changes in substance use among urban adolescents. *Journal of Educational Psychology, 94*(3), 621–637.

Bryant, J. A., Mealey, L., Herzog, E. A., & Rychwalski, W. L. (2001). Paradoxical effect of surveyor's conservative versus provocative clothing on rape myth acceptance of males and females. *Journal of Psychology & Human Sexuality, 13*(1), 55–66.

Buchanan, R. W., Vlader, K., Barta, P. E., & Pearlson, G. D. (1998). Structural evaluation of the prefrontal cortex in schizophrenia. *American Journal of Psychiatry, 155,* 1049–1055.

Buchanan, T. W., & Lovallo, W. R. (2001). Enhanced memory for emotional material following stress-level cortisol treatment in humans. *Psychoneuroendocrinology, 26*(3), 307–317.

Buchsbaum, M. S., & Hazlett, E. A. (1998). Positron emission tomography studies of abnormal glucose metabolism in schizophrenia. *Schizophrenia Bulletin, 24,* 343–364.

Buck, R. (1984). *The communication of emotion.* New York: Guilford Press.

Buckley, K. W. (1982). The selling of a psychologist: John Broadus Watson and the application of behavioral techniques to advertising. *Journal of the History of the Behavioral Sciences, 18,* 207–221.

Buckley, K. W. (1989). *Mechanical man: John Broadhus Watson and the beginnings of behaviorism.* New York: Guilford Press.

Bugental, B. B., & Goodnow, J. J. (1998). Socialization process. In W. Damon & N. Eisenberg (Eds.), *Handbook of child psychology* (5th ed.). New York: John Wiley & Sons.

Bugental, D. B., & Johnston, C. (2000). Parental and child cognitions in the context of the family. *Annual Review of Psychology, 51,* 315–344.

Buka, S. L., Goldstein, J. M., Seidman, L. J., Zornberg, G., Donatelli, J. A., Denny, L. R., & Tsuang, M. T. (1999). Prenatal complications, genetic vulnerability, and schizophrenia: The New England longitudinal studies of schizophrenia. *Psychiatric Annals, 29,* 151–156.

Bulik, C. M., Sullivan, P. F., & Kendler, K. S. (2002). Medical and psychiatric morbidity in obese women with and without binge eating. *International Journal of Eating Disorders, 32*(1), 72–78.

Bullough, B., & Bullough, V. (1997). Are transvestites necessarily heterosexual? *Archives of Sexual Behavior, 26,* 1–12.

Burg, M. W. (1995). Anger, hostility, and coronary heart disease: A review. *Mind/Body Medicine, 1,* 159–172.

Burgdorf, J., Knutson, B., & Panksepp, J. (2000). Anticipation of rewarding electrical brain stimulation evokes ultrasonic vocalization in rats. *Behavioural Neuroscience, 114*(2), 320–327.

Burgess, C., O'Donohoe, A., & Gill, M. (2000). Agony and ecstasy: A review of MDMA effects and toxicity. *European Psychiatry, 15*(5), 287–294.

Burke, R. J., & Greenglass, E. R. (2000). Hospital restructuring and nursing staff well-being: The role of coping. *International Journal of Stress Management, 7,* 49–59.

Burns, D. M. (2000). Cigarette smoking among the elderly: Disease consequences and the benefits of cessation. *American Journal of Health Promotion, 14*(6), 357–361.

Burns, N. R., Nettelbeck, T., & Cooper, C. J. (2000). Event-related potential correlates of some human cognitive ability constructs. *Personality & Individual Differences, 29*(1), 157–168.

Bursik, K. (1998). Moving beyond gender differences: Gender role comparisons of manifest dream content. *Sex Roles, 38,* 203–214.

Bushman, B. J. (2002). Does venting anger feed or extinguish the flame? Catharsis, rumination, distraction, anger and aggressive responding. *Personality & Social Psychology Bulletin, 28*(6), 724–731.

Bushman, B. J., Baumeister, R. F., & Stack, A. D. (1999). Catharsis, aggression, and persuasive influence: Self-fulfilling or self-defeating prophecies? *Journal of Personality and Social Psychology, 76,* 367–376.

Buss, D. H. (1999). *Evolutionary Psychology: The new science of the mind.* Boston: Allyn & Bacon.

Buss, D. M. and 40 colleagues. (1990). International preferences in selecting mates: A study of 37 cultures. *Journal of Cross-Cultural Psychology, 21,* 5–47.

Buss, D. M. (1989). Sex differences in human mate preferences: Evolutionary hypotheses tested in 37 cultures. *Behavioral and Brain Sciences, 12,* 1–49.

Buss, D. M. (1991). Evolutionary personality psychology. *Annual Review of Psychology, 42,* 459–491.

Buss, D. M. (1994). The strategies of human mating. *American Scientist, 82,* 238–249.

Buss, D. M. (2000). *The dangerous passion: Why jealousy is as necessary as love and sex.* New York: Free Press.

Buss, D. M., Shackelford, T. K., Choe, J., Buunk, B. P., Dijkstra, P. (2000). Distress about mating rivals. *Personal Relationships, 7*(3), 235–243.

Butcher, J. N. (2000). Revising psychological tests: Lessons learned from the revision of the MMPI. *Psychological Assessment, 12*(3), 263–271.

Butcher, J. N., & Rouse, S. V. (1996). Personality: Individual differences and clinical assessment. *Annual Review of Psychology, 47,* 87–111.

Butler, K. Joel, J. C., & Jeffries, M. (2000). *Clinical handbook of psychotropic drugs.* New York: Wiley.

Butler, R. A. (1954, February). Curiosity in monkeys. *Scientific American, 190,* 70–75.

Butterworth, B. (1999). A head for figures. *Science, 284,* 928–929.

Butzlaff, R. L., & Hooley, J. M. (1998). Expressed emotion and psychiatric relapse. *Archives of General Psychiatry, 55,* 547–552.

Buunk, B. P., Dijkstra, P., Fetchenhauer, D., & Kenrick, D. (2002). Age and gender differences in mate selection criteria for various involvement levels. *Personal Relationships, 9*(3), 271–278.

Byrne, R. S., & Fone, B. (2000). *Homophobia: A history.* New York: Metropolitan Books.

Cacioppo, J. T., & Gardner, W. L. (1999). Emotion. *Annual Review of Psychology, 50,* 191–214.

Cacioppo, J. T., Petty, R. E., Feinstein, J. A., Jarvis, W. B. G. (1996). Dispositional differences in cognitive motivation: The life and times of individuals varying in need for cognition. *Psychological Bulletin, 119*(2), 197–253.

Cadoret, R. J., Leve, L. D., & Devor, E. (1997). Genetics of aggressive and violent behavior. *Psychiatric Clinics of North America, 20,* 301–322.

Cagnacci, A., Kraeuchi, K., Wirz-Justice, A., & Volpe, A. (1997). Homeostatic versus circadian effects of melatonin on core body temperature in humans. *Journal of Biological Rhythms, 12,* 509–617.

Cahill, L., Vazdarjanova, A., & Setlow, B. (2000). The basolateral amygdala complex is involved with, but is not necessary for, rapid acquisition of Pavlovian "fear conditioning." *European Journal of Neuroscience, 12*(8), 3044–3050.

Cairns, D., & Pasino, J. A. (1977). Comparison of verbal reinforcement and feedback in the operant treatment of disability due to chronic back pain. *Behavior Therapy, 8*(4), 621–630.

Caltagirone, C., Perri, R., Carlesimo, G. A., & Fadda, L. (2001). Early detection and diagnosis of dementia. *Archives of Gerontology & Geriatrics, Suppl 7,* 67–75.

Campbell, L., Simpson, J. A., Kashy, D. A., & Fletcher, G. J. O. (2001). Ideal standards, the self, and flexibility of ideals in close relationships. *Personality & Social Psychology Bulletin, 27(4),* 447–462.

Campbell, W. K., & Sedikides, C. (1999). Self-threat magnifies the self-serving bias: A meta-analytic integration. *Review of General Psychology, 3,* 23–43.

Campfield, L. A., Smith, F. J., Rosenbaum, M., & Hirsch, J. (1996). Human eating: Evidence for a physiological basis using a modified paradigm. *Neuroscience and Biobehavioral Reviews, 20,* 133–137.

Cannon, A. (2002, January 14). One life, in ashes. *U.S.News & World Report,* p. 23.

Cannon, T. D., Kaprio, J., Lonnqvist, J., Huttunen, M., & Koskenvuo, M. (1998). The genetic epidemiology of schizophrenia in a Finnish twin cohort. *Archives of General Psychiatry, 55,* 67–74.

Cannon, T. D., Rosso, I. M., Hollister, J., Megginson, B., Carrie, E., Sanchez, L. E., & Hadley, T. (2000). A prospective cohort study of genetic and perinatal influences in the etiology of schizophrenia. *Schizophrenia Bulletin, 26,* 351–366.

Cannon, T. D., van Erp, T. G. M., Rosso, I. M., Huttunen, M., Loenqvist, J., Pirkola, T., Salonen, O., Valanne, L., Poutanen, V., & Standertskjoeld-Nordenstam, C. (2002). Fetal hypoxia and structural brain abnormalities in schizophrenic patients, their siblings, and controls. *Archives of General Psychiatry, 59(1),* 35–41.

Cannon, W. B. (1927). The James-Lange theory of emotions: A critical examination and an alternative theory. *American Journal of Psychology, 39,* 106–124.

Cannon, W. B., & Washburn, A. (1912). An explanation of hunger. *American Journal of Physiology, 29,* 441–454.

Cannon, W. B., Lewis, J. T., & Britton, S. W. (1927). The dispensability of the sympathetic division of the autonomic nervous system. *Boston Medical Surgery Journal, 197,* 514.

Cantor, J. M., Blanchard, R., Paterson, A. D., & Bogaert, A. F. (2002). How many gay men owe their sexual orientation to fraternal birth order? *Archives of Sexual Behavior, 31(1),* 63–71.

Cantor, J., & Engle, R. (1993). Working-memory capacity as long-term memory activation: An individual differences approach. *Journal of Experimental Psychology: Learning, memory, and Cognition, 19(5),* 1101–1114.

Carbone, J. (2000). *From partners to parents: 2nd revolution in family law.* New York: Columbia University Press.

Carboni, E., Borone, L., Giua, C. & Di Chiara, G. (2000). Dissociation of physical abstinence signs from changes in extracellular dopamine in the nucleus accumbens and in the prefrontal cortex of nicotine dependent rats. *Drug and Alcohol Dependence, 58(1–2),* 93–102.

Carbonneau, R., Rutter, M., Silberg, J. L., Simonoff, E., & Eaves, L. J. (2002). Assessment of genetic and environmental influences on differential ratings of within-family experiences and relationships in twins. *Psychological Medicine, 32(4),* 729–741.

Carducci, B. J. (1998). *The psychology of personality: Viewpoints, research, and applications.* Pacific Grove, CA: Brooks/Cole.

Carducci, B. J. (2000). *Shyness: A bold new approach.* New York: Harperperennial.

Carlson, N. R. (1998). *Physiology of behavior* (6th ed.). Boston: Allyn and Bacon.

Carmaciu, C. D., Anderson, C. S., & Markar, H. R. (2001). Secondary koro with unusual features in a Briton. *Transcultural Psychiatry, 38(4),* 528–533.

Carnes, P. J. (2001). Cybersex, courtship, and escalating arousal: Factors in addictive sexual desire. *Sexual Addiction & Compulsivity, 8(1),* 45–78.

Caron, S. L. (1998). *Cross-cultural perspectives on human sexuality.* Boston: Allyn and Bacon.

Carpenter, S., & Radhakrishnan, P. (2002). The relation between allocentrism and perceptions of ingroups. *Personality & Social Psychology Bulletin, 28(11),* 1528–1537.

Carr, A. (2000). *Family therapy: Concepts, process, and practice.* New York: Wiley.

Carrere, S., Buehlman, K. T., Gottman, J. M., Coan, J. A., & Ruckstuhl, L. (2000). Predicting marital stability and divorce in newlywed couples. *Journal of Family Psychology, 14(1),* 42–58.

Carskadon, M. A., & Dement, W. C. (2002). *Adolescent sleep patterns.* New York: Cambridge University Press.

Carstensen, L. L. (1995). Evidence for a life-span theory of socioemotional selectivity. *Current Directions in Psychological Science, 4(5),* 151–156.

Carstensen, L. L., Pasupathi, M., Mayr, U., & Nesselroade, J. R. (2000). Emotional experience in everyday life across the adult life span. *Journal of Personality & Social Psychology, 79(4),* 644–655.

Carter, S. (2000). Math skill, confidence multiplying for girls. *The Oregonian,* March 4, A1 & A11.

Carton, J. S. (1996). The differential effects of tangible rewards and praise on intrinsic motivation: A comparison of cognitive evaluation theory and operant theory. *Behavior Analyst, 19,* 237–255.

Cartwright, J. (2000). *Evolution and human behavior.* Harvard, MA: MIT Press.

Caspi, A. (2000). The child is father of the man: Personality continuities from childhood to adulthood. *Journal of Personality and Social Psychology, 78(1),* 158–172.

Cassidy, F., Ahearn, E. P., & Carroll, B. J. (2001). Substance abuse in bipolar disorder. *Bipolar Disorders, 3(4),* 181–188.

Casswell, S. & Zhang, J. F. (1998). Impact of liking for advertising and brand allegiance on drinking and alcohol-related aggression: A longitudinal study. *Addiction, 93(8),* 1209–1217.

Casti, J. L. (2000). *Paradigms regained: A further exploration of the mysteries of modern science.* New York:Morrow.

Castillo, R. J. (1997). *Culture and mental illness: A client-centered approach.* Pacific Grove, CA: Brooks/Cole.

Cattell, R. B. (1950). *Personality: A systematic, theoretical, and factual study.* New York: McGraw-Hill.

Cattell, R. B. (1963). Theory of fluid and crystallized intelligence: A critical experiment. *Journal of Educational Psychology, 54,* 1–22.

Cattell, R. B. (1965). *The scientific analysis of personality.* Baltimore: Penguin.

Cattell, R. B. (1971). *Abilities: Their structure, growth, and action.* Boston, MA: Houghton Mifflin.

Cattell, R. B. (1990). Advances in Cattellian personality theory. In L. A. Pervin (Ed.), *Handbook of personality: Theory and research.* New York: Guilford Press.

Ceci, S. J., & Bjork, R. A. (2000). Psychological science in the public interest: The case for juried analyses. *Psychological Science, 11(3),* 177–178.

Ceci, S. J., Rosenblum, T., deBruyn, & Lee, D. Y. (1997). A bio-ecological model of intellectual development: Moving beyond h2. In R. J. Sternberg & E. L. Grigorenko (Eds.), *Intelligence, heredity, & environment.* New York: Cambridge University Press.

Centers for Disease Control (CDC). (2002). The burden of chronic diseases as causes of death. Available: http://www.cdc.gov/nccd-php/statbook/pdf/section1.pdf

Centers for Disease Control (CDC). (2003). The Tobacco Atlas: Deaths. Available: Http://www.5.who.int/tobacco/repository/stp84/36%209%20Deaths.pdf

Centers for Disease Control. (1999). Trends in the HIV & AIDS Epidemic. Available: http://www.cdc.gov/hiv/stats/trends98. pdf

Centers for Disease Control. (2000). Tracking the Hidden Epidemics: Trends in STDs in the United States, 2000. Available: http://www.cdc.gov/nchstp/dstd/Stats_Trends/Trends2000.pdf

Centers for Disease Control. (2001). Heart disease still main cause of death in US. *Morbidity and Mortality Weekly Report, 50,* 90–93.

Centers for Disease Control. (2001). *Women and Smoking: A Report of the Surgeon General – 2001.* Available: http://www.cdc.gov/tobacco/sgr/sgr_forwomen/at aglance.htm#Health_Consequences *Cerebral Cortex, 12(9),* 900–907.

Cervone, D., & Shoda, Y. (1999). Beyond traits in the study of personality coherence. *Current Directions in Psychological Science, 8(1),* 27–32.

Cesaro, P., & Ollat, H. (1997). Pain and its treatments. *European Neurology, 38,* 209–215.

Ceschi, G., & Scherer, K. R. (2001). Controler l'expression faciale et changer l'emotion : Une approche developpementale. The role of facial expression in emotion: A developmental perspective. *Enfance, 53(3),* 257–269.

Chaban, M. (2000). *The life work of Dr. Elisabeth Kubler-Ross and its impact on the death awareness movement.* Baltimore: Edwin Mellen Press.

Challem, J., Berkson, B., Smith, M. D., & Berkson, B. (2000). *Syndrome X: The complete program to prevent and reverse insulin resistance.* New York: Wiley.

Charland, W. A. (1992, January). Nightshift narcosis. *The Rotarion, 160,* 16–19.

Chartrand, T., Pinckert, S., & Burger, J. M. (1999). When manipulation backfires: The effects of time delay and requester on the foot-in-the-door technique. *Journal of Applied Social Psychology, 29,* 211–221.

Chase, W. G., & Simon, H. A. (1973). The mind's eye in chess. In W. Chase (Ed.), *Visual information processing.* New York: Academic Press.

Chaves, J. F. (2000). Hypnosis in the management of anxiety associated with medical conditions and their treatment. In D. I. Mostofsky & D. H. Barlow (Eds.), *The management of stress and anxiety in medical disorders* (pp. 119–142). Needham Heights, MA: Allyn & Bacon.

Chen, F., & Kenrick, D. T. (2002). Repulsion or attraction?: Group membership and assumed attitude similarity. *Journal of Personality & Social Psychology, 83(1),* 111–125.

Cheng, H., & Furnham, A. (2001). Attributional style and personality as predictors of happiness and mental health. *Journal of Happiness Studies, 2(3),* 307–327.

Chi, I., & Chou, K. (1999). Financial strain and depressive symptoms among Hong Kong Chinese elderly: A longitudinal study. *Journal of Gerontological Social Work, 32,* 41–60.

Chin, G. (2000). Memory maps in the brain. *Science, 287,* 13.

Chipman, K., Hampson, E., & Kimura, D. (2002). A sex difference in reliance on vision during manual sequencing tasks. *Neuropsychologia, 40(7),* 910–916.

Cho, K. (2001). Chronic 'jet lag' produces temporal lobe atrophy and spatial cognitive deficits. *Nature Neuroscience, 4(6),* 567–568.

Choi, I., & Nisbett, R. E. (2000). Cultural psychology of surprise: Holistic theories and recognition of contradiction. *Journal of Personality & Social Psychology, 79(6),* 890–905.

Chomsky, N. (1957). Syntactical structures. The Hague: Mouton.

Chomsky, N. (1965). *Aspects of the theory of syntax.* Cambridge, MA: MIT Press.

Chomsky, N. (1968). *Language and mind.* New York: Harcourt, Brace, World.

Chomsky, N. (1980). *Rules and representations.* New York: Columbia University Press.

Christ, G. H., Siegel, K., & Christ, A. E. (2002). Adolescent grief: "It never really hit me...until it actually happened." JAMA: *Journal of the American Medical Association, 288(10),* 1269–1278.

Christensen, D. (2000). Is snoring a dizzease? Nighttime snoring may serve as a wake-up call for future illness. *Science News, 157,* 172–173.

Christensen, D. (2001). Making sense of centenarians. *Science News, 159,* 156–157.

Chromiak, W., Barber, T. A., & Kyler, K. J. (2000). Selective associations in day-old chicks: When do CS traces become available for sickness-conditioned learning? *Behavioral Neuroscience, 114(1),* 117–124.

Chu, J.A., Frey, L.M., Ganzel, B.L., & Matthews, J.A. (1999). Memories of childhood abuse: Dissociation, amnesia, and corroboration. *American Journal of Psychiatry, 156,* 749–755.

Chuang, D. (1998). Cited in J. Travis, Stimulating clue hints how lithium works. *Science News, 153,* 165.

Chuang, Y. (2002). Sex differences in mate selection preference and sexual strategy: Tests for evolutionary hypotheses. *Chinese Journal of Psychology, 44(1),* 75–93.

Church, R. M., & Kirkpatrick, K. (2001). Theories of conditioning and timing. In R. R. Mowere, S. B. Klein (Eds.), *Handbook of contemporary learning theories.* Mahwah, NJ: Lawrence Erlbaum.

Cialdini, R. B. (2001). The science of persuasion. *Scientific American, 284(2),* 76–81.

Cialdini, R. (1993). *Influence: Science and practice* (3rd ed.). New York: HarperCollins.

Cicchetti, D., & Toth, S. L. (1998). Perspectives on research and practice in developmental psychopathology. In W. Damon, I. E. Siegel, & K. A. Renninger (Eds.), *Handbook of child psychology* (5th ed.) (pp. 479–584). New York: Wiley.

Clark, K. B., & Clark, M. P. (1939). The development of consciousness of self and the emergence of racial identification in Negro preschool children. *Journal of Social Psychology, 10,* 591–599.

Clarke-Stewart, K. A., Fitzpatrick, M. J., Allhusen, V. D., & Goldberg, W. A. (2000). Measuring difficult temperament the easy way. *Journal of Developmental and Behavioral Pediatrics, 21(3),* 207–220.

Clarke-Stewart, K. A., Vandell, D. L., McCartney, K., Owen, M. T., & Booth, C. (2000). Effects of parental separation and divorce on very young children. *Journal of Family Psychology, 14(2),* 304–326.

Classen, C., Koopman, C., Hales, R., & Spiegel, D. (1998). Acute stress disorder as a predictor of posttraumatic stress symptoms. *American Journal of Psychiatry, 155,* 620–624.

Cloud, J. (2001, February 26). New sparks over electroshock. Time, 60–62.

Cloutier, S., Martin, S. L., & Poole, C. (2002). Sexual assault among North Carolina women: Prevalence and health risk factors. *Journal of Epidemiology & Community Health, 56(4),* 265–271.

Cockerill, I. M., & Riddington, M. E. (1996). Exercise dependence and associated disorders: A review. *Counseling Psychology Quarterly, 9,* 119–129.

Cohen, A. (1997, September 8). Battle of the binge. *Time,* pp. 54–56.

Cohen, B., Novick, D., & Rubinstein, M. (1996). Modulation of insulin activities by leptin. *Science, 274,* 1185–1188.

Cohen, D. B. (1999). *Stranger in the nest: Do parents really shape their child's personality, intelligence, or character?* New York: Wiley.

Cohen, R. A., & Albers, H. E. (1991). Disruption of human circadian and cognitive regulation following a discrete hypothalamic lesion: A case study. *Neurology, 41,* 726–729.

Cohen, R. A., Barnes, J., Jenkins, M., & Albers, H. E. (1997). Disruption of short-duration timing associated with damage to the suprachiasmatic region of the hypothalamus. *Neurology, 48(6),* 1533–1539.

Cohen, R. A., Paul, R., Zawacki, T. M., Moser, D. J., Sweet, L., & Wilkinson, H. (2001). Emotional and personality changes following cingulotomy. *Emotion, 1(1),* 38–50.

Cohen, S., & Herbert, T. B. (1996). Health psychology: Psychological factors and physical disease from the prespective of human psychoneuroimmunology. *Annual Review of Psychology, 47,* 113–142.

Cohen, S., & Williamson, G. M. (1991). Stress and infectious disease in humans. *Psychological Bulletin, 109,* 5–24.

Cohen, S., Doyle, W. J., & Skoner, D. P. (1999). Psychological stress, cytokine production, and severity of upper respiratory illness. *Psychosomatic Medicine, 61,* 175–180.

Cohen, S., Frank, E., Doyle, W. J., et al. (1998). Types of stressors that increase susceptibility to the common cold in healthy adults. *Health Psychology, 17,* 214–223.

Cohen, S., Hamrick, N., Rodriguez, M. S., Feldman, P. J., Rabin, B. S., & Manuck, S. B. (2002). Reactivity and vulnerability to stress-associated risk for upper respiratory illness. *Psychosomatic Medicine, 64(2),* 302–310.

Colapinto, J. (2000). *As nature made him: The boy that was raised as a girl.* New York: HarperCollins.

Colcombe, S., & Kramer, A. F. (2003). Fitness effects on the cognitive function of older adults: A meta-analytic study. *Psychological Science, 14,* in press.

Cole, D. L. (1982). Psychology as a liberating art. *Teaching of Psychology, 9,* 23–26.

Cole, E., & Brown, R. S. (2002). Psychological needs of post-war children in Kosovo: A preliminary analysis. *School Psychology International, 23(2),* 131–147.

Cole, M. D. (2000). *John Glenn: Astronaut and senator.* New York: Enslow Publishers.

Cole, M., Gray, J., Glick, J. A., & Sharp, D. W. (1971). *The cultural context of learning and thinking.* New York: Basic Books.

Coley, R. L., & Chase-Lansdale, P. L. (1998). Adolescent pregnancy and parenthood: Recent evidence and future directions. *American Psychologist, 53(2),* 152–166.

Conley, R. R., Love, R. C., Kelly, D. L., & Bartko, J. J. (1999). Rehospitalization rates of patients recently discharged on a regimen of risperidone or clozapine. *American Journal of Psychiatry, 156,* 863–868.

Connolly, S. (2000). *LSD (just the facts).* Baltimore: Heinemann Library.

Connor, J., Norton, R., Ameratunga, S., Robinson, E., Civil, I., Dunn, R., Bailey, J., & Jackson, R. (2002). Driver sleepiness and risk of serious injury to car occupants: Population based case control study. BMJ: *British Medical Journal, 324(7346),* 1125–1128.

Connor, K. M., & Davidson, J. R. T. (2002). A placebo-controlled study of Kava kava in generalized anxiety disorder. *International Clinical Psychopharmacology, 17(4),* 185–188.

Contrada, R. J., Ashmore, R. D., Gary, M. L., Coups, E., Egeth, J. D., Sewell, A., Ewell, K., Goyal, T. M., & Chasse, V. (2000). Ethnicity-related sources of stress and their effects on well-being. *Current Directions in Psychological Science, 9(4),* 136–139.

Converging PET findings in depression and normal sadness. *American Journal of Psychiatry, 156,* 675–682.

Conway, M. A., & Pleydell-Pearce, C. W. (2000). The construction of autobio-graphical memories in the self-memory system. *Psychological Review, 107,* 261–288.

Conyne, R. K. (1999). *Failures in group work.* Thousand Oaks, CA: Sage.

Cook M., & Mineka, S. (1989). Observational conditioning of fear to fear-relevant versus fear-irrelevant stimuli in rhesus monkeys. *Journal of Abnormal Psychology, 98,* 448–459.

Cook, A. S., & Dworkin, D. S. (1992). *Helping the bereaved: Therapeutic interventions for children, adolescents, and adults.* New York: Basic Books.

Cook, E. W., Hodes, R. L., & Lang, P. J. (1986). Preparedness and phobia: Effects of stimulus content on human visceral conditioning. *Journal of Abnormal Psychology, 95,* 195–207.

Cook, P. F. (2000). Effects of counselors' etiology attributions on college students' procrastination. *Journal of Counseling Psychology, 47(3),* 352–361.

Coolidge, F., & Segal, D. (1998). Evolution of personality disorder diagnosis in the Diagnostic and Statistical Manual of Mental Disorders. *Clinical Psychology Review, 18,* 585–599.

Cooper, E. E. (2000). Spatial-temporal intelligence: Original thinking processes of gifted inventors. *Journal for the Education of the Gifted, 24(2),* 170–193.

Cooper, M. L., Shaver, P. R., & Collins, N. L. (1998). Attachment styles, emotion regulation, and adjustment in adolescence. *Journal of Personality and Social Psychology, 74(5),* 1380–1397.

Coplan, R. J., Hastings, P. D., Lagace-Seguin, D. G., & Moulton, C. E. (2002). Authoritative and authoritarian mothers' parenting goals, attributions, and emotions across different childrearing contexts. *Parenting: Science & Practice, 2(1),* 1–26.

Corballis, M. C. (1998). Sperry and the Age of Aquarius: Science, values and the split brain. *Neuropsychologia, 36,* 1083–1087.

Corcos, M., Nezelof, S., Speranza, M., Topa, S., Girardon, N., Guilbaud, O., Taieeb, O., Bizouard, P., Halfon, O., Venisse, J. L., Perez-Diaz, F., Flament, M., & Jeammet, Ph. (2001). Psychoactive substance consumption in eating disorders. *Eating Behaviors, 2(1),* 27–38.

Coren, S. (1996). *Sleep thieves: An eye-opening exploration into the science and mysteries of sleep.* New York: Freeman.

Corey, G. (2001a). *Case approach to counseling and psychotherapy.* Belmont, CA: Wadsworth.

Corey, G. (2001b). *The art of integrative counseling.* Belmont, CA: Wadsworth.

Costa, J. L., Brennen, M. B., & Hochgeschwender, U. (2002). The human genetics of eating disorders: Lessons from the leptin/melanocortin system. Child &
Adolescent *Psychiatric Clinics of North America, 11(2),* 387–397.

Costa, L., Bauer, L., Kuperman, S., Porjesz, B., O'Connor, S., Hesselbrock, V., Rohrbaugh, J., & Begleiter, H. (2000). Frontal P300 decrements: Alcohol dependence, and antisocial personality disorder. *Biological Psychiatry, 47(12),* 1064–1071.

Cote, S. (1999). Affect and performance in organizational settings. *Current Directions in Psychological Science, 8(2),* 65–68.

Cotman, C. W. & Berchtold, N. C. (2002). Exercise: A behavioral intervention to enhance brain health and plasticity. *Trends in Neurosciences, 25(6),* 295–301.

Courage, M. L., & Adams, R. J. (1990). Visual acuity assessment from birth to three years using the acuity card procedures: Cross-sectional and longitudinal samples. *Optometry and Vision Science, 67,* 713–718.

Courtenay, W. H. (2000). Engendering health: A social constructionist examination of men's health beliefs and behaviors. *Psychology of Men and Masculinity, 1(1),* 4–15.

Courtney, S. M., Ungerleider, L. G., Keil, K., & Hazby, J. V. (1998). Object and spatial visual working memory activate separate neural systems in human cortex. *Cerebral Cortex, 6,* 39–49.

Couzin, J. (1999, September 13). A good trend spoiled. *U. S. News & World Report,* p. 55.

Covington, M. V. (1999). Caring about learning: The nature and nurturing of subject matter appreciation. *Educational Researcher, 34,* 127–136.

Covington, M. V. (2000). Intrinsic versus extrinsic motivation in schools: A reconciliation. *Current Directions in Psychological Science, 9(1),* 22–25.

Covington, M. V., & Mueeller, K. J. (2001). Intrinsic versus extrinsic motivation: An approach/avoidance reformulation. *Educational Psychology Review, 13(2),* 157–176.

Cowan, R. L. (2001). Patient's page: Ecstasy. *Journal of the Gay & Lesbian Medical Assn, 5(1),* 25–26.

Cowen, P. J. (2002). Cortisol, serotonin and depression: All stressed out? *British Journal of Psychiatry, 180(2),* 99–100.

Craig, A. D., & Bushnell, M. C. (1994). The thermal grill illusion: Unmasking the burn of cold pain. *Science, 265,* 252–255.

Craik, F. I. M., & Lockhart, R. S. (1972). Levels of processing: A framework for memory research. *Journal of Verbal Learning and Verbal Behavior, 11,* 671–684.

Craik, F. I. M., Moroz, T. M., Moscovitch, M., Stuss, D. T., Winocur, G., Tulving, E., & Kapur, S. (1999). In search of the self: A positron emission tomography study. *Psychological Science, 10,* 26–34.

Crair, M. C., Gillespie, D. C., & Stryker, M. P. (1998). The role of visual experience in the development of columns in cat visual cortex. *Science, 279*, 566–570.

Crandall, C. S., & Martinez, R. (1996). Culture, ideology, and antifat attitudes. *Personality and Social Psychology Bulletin, 22*, 1165–1176.

Craske, B. (1977). Perception of impossible limb positions induced by tendon vibration. *Science, 196*(4285), 71–73.

Craske, M. (2000). *Mastery of your anxiety and panic: Therapist guide* (3rd ed.). New York: Academic Press.

Craske, M.G. (1999). *Anxiety disorders: Psychological approaches to theory and treatment.* Boulder, CO: Westview.

Crews, F. (1997). The verdict on Freud. *Psychological Science, 7*(2), 63–68.

Crick, N. R. (1996). The role of overt aggression, relational aggression, and prosocial behavior in the prediction of children's future social adjustment. *Child Development, 67*, 2317–2327.

Cristofalo, V. J. (1996). Ten years later: What have we learned about human aging from studies of cell cultures? *Gerontologist, 36*, 737–741.

Croizet, J., & Claire, T. (1998). Extending the concept of stereotype threat to social class: The intellectual underperformance of students from low socioeconomic backgrounds. *Personality and Social Psychology Bulletin, 24*, 588–594.

Cronbach, L. (1990). *Essentials of psychological testing.* New York: Harper & Row.

Crone, C. C., & Gabriel, G. (2002). Herbal and nonherbal supplements in medical-psychiatric patient populations. *Psychiatric Clinics of North America, 25*(1), 211–230.

Crooks, R., & Baur, K. (2002). Our sexuality (8th ed.). Pacific Grove: Brooks/Cole.

Crosson, B. (1999). Subcortical mechanisms in language: Lexical-semantic mechanisms and the Thalamus. *Brain & Cognition, 40*, 414–438.

Crosson, B., Sadek, J. R., Maron, L., Goekcay, D., Mohr, C. M., Auerbach, E. J., Freeman, A. J., Leonard, C. M., & Briggs, R. W. (2001). Relative shift in activity from medial to lateral frontal cortex during internally versus externally guided word generation. *Journal of Cognitive Neuroscience,13*(2), 272–283.

Crowder, R. G. (1976). *Principles of learning and memory.* Hillsdale, NJ: Erlbaum.

Crowther, J. H., Kichler, J. C., Shewood, N. E., & Kuhnert, M. E. (2002). The role of familial factors in bulimia nervosa. Eating Disorders: The *Journal of Treatment & Prevention, 10*(2), 141–151.

Cunningham, M. R., Roberts, A. R., Barbee, A. P. Druen, P. B., & Wu, C. (1995).

"Their ideas of beauty are on the whole, the same as ours": Consistency and variability in the cross-cultural perception of female physical attractiveness. *Journal of Personality and Social Psychology, 68*, 261–279.

Curtiss, S. (1977). *Genie: A psycholinguistic study of a modern-day "wild child."* New York: Academic Press.

Cutler, W. B., (1999). Human sex-attractant hormones: Discovery, research, development, and application in sex therapy. *Psychiatric Annals, 29*, 54–59.

Czeh, B., Welt, T., Fischer, A. K., Erhardt, A., Schmitt, W., Mueller, M. B., Toschi, N., Fuchs, E., & Keck, M. E. (2002). Chronic psychosocial stress and concomitant repetitive transcranial magnetic stimulation: Effects on stress hormone levels and adult hippocampal neurogensis. *Biological Psychiatry, 52*(11), 1057–1065.

D'Alessio, D., & Allen, M. (2002). Selective exposure and dissonance after decisions. *Psychological Reports, 91*(2), 527–532.

D'Imperio, R. L., Dubow, E. F., & Ippolito, M. F. (2000). Resilent and stress-affected adolescents in an urban setting. *Journal of Clinical and Child Psychology, 29*, 129–142.

D'Sa, C., & Duman, R. S. (2002). Antidepressants and neuroplasticity. *Bipolar Disorders, 4*(3), 183–194.

Dabbs, J. M., & Dabbs, M. G. (2000). *Heroes, rogues, and lovers: Testosterone and behavior.* New York: McGraw-Hill.

Dackis, C. A., & O'Brien, C. P. (2001). Cocaine dependence: A disease of the brain's reward centers. *Journal of Substance Abuse Treatment, 21*(3), 111–117.

Dadds, M. R., Bovbjerg, D. H., Redd, W. H., & Cutmore, T. R. H. (1997). Imagery in human classical conditioning. *Psychological Bulletin, 122*, 89–103.

Dade, L. A., Zatorre, R. J., & Jones-Gotman, M. (2002). Olfactory learning: Convergent findings from lesion and brain imaging studies in humans. *Brain, 125*, 86–101.

Dager, S. R., et al. (1999). Human brain metabolic response to caffeine and the effects of tolerance. *American Journal of Psychiatry, 156*, 229–237.

Dalenberg, C. J. (2000). *Countertransference and the treatment of trauma.* Washington, DC: American Psychological Association.

Daley, S. E., Burge, D., & Hammen, C. (2000). Borderline personality disorder symptoms as predictors of 4-year romantic relationship dysfunction in young women: Addresing issues of specificity. *Journal of Abnormal Psychology, 109*(3), 451–460.

Dalton, M. A., Tickle, J. J., Sargent, J. D., Beach, M. L., Ahrens, M. B., & Heatherton, T. F. (2002). The incidence and context of tobacco use in popular movies from 1988

to 1997. *Preventive Medicine: An International Journal Devoted to Practice & Theory, 34*(5), 516–523.

Dalton, P., Doolittle, N., & Breslin, P. A. S. (2002). Gender-specific induction of enhanced sensitivity to odors. *Nature Neuroscience,* DOI: 10.1038/nn803.

Daly, M. P. (1999). Diagnosis and management of Alzheimer disease. *Journal of the American Board of Family Practice, 5*, 375–385.

Damasio, A. R. (1994). *Descartes' error.* New York: Putnam's Sons.

Damasio, A. R. (1999). *The feeling of what happens: Body and emotion in the making of consciousness.* New York: Harcourt Brace.

Damasio, H., Grabowski, T., Frank, R., Galaburda, A. M., & Damasio, A. R. (1994). The return of Phineas Gage: Clues about the brain from the skull of a famous patient. *Science, 264*, 1102–1105.

Dana, R. H. (1998). Cultural identity assessment of culturally diverse groups: 1997. *Journal of Personality Assessment, 70*, 1–16.

Dandash, K. F., Refaat, A. H., & Eyada, M. (2001). Female genital mutilation: A prospective view. *Journal of Sex & Marital Therapy, 27*(5), 459–464.

Darwin, C. R. (1872). *The expression of the emotions in man and animals.* London: John Murray.

Darwin, C. (1859). *On the origin of species.* London: Murray.

Davidson, K., MacGregor, M. W., Stuhr, J., Dixon, K., & MacLean, D. (2000). Constructive anger verbal behavior predicts blood pressure in a population-based sample. *Health Psychology, 19*, 55–64.

Davidson, P. S. R., & Glisky, E. L. (2002). Is flashbulb memory a special instance of source memory? Evidence from older adults. *Memory, 10*(2), 99–111.

Davidson, R. J. (1992). Emotion and affective style: Hemispheric substrates. *Psychological Science, 3*, 39–43.

Davidson, R. J. (2000). Affective style, psychopathology, and resilience: Brain mechanisms and plasticity. *American Psychologist, 55*(11), 1196–1214.

Davidson, R. J., Putnam, K. M., Larson, C. L. (2000). Dysfunction in the neural circuitry of emotion regulation—a possible prelude to violence. *Science, 289*(5479), 591–594.

Davidson, R. (1999, April). Cited in Ruksnis, E. (1999). The emotional brain and the emergence of affective neuroscience. *APS Observer,* 13.

Davies, I. (1998). A study of colour grouping in three languages: A test of the linguistic relativity hypothesis. *British Journal of Psychology, 89*, 433–452.

Davies, J. M. (1996). Dissociation, repression and reality testing in the countertransference: the controversy over memory and false memory in the psychoanalytic treatment of adult survivors of childhood sexual abuse. *Psychoanalytic Dialogues, 6,* 189–218.

Davies, P. T., & Cummings, E. M. (1998). Exploring children's emotional security as a mediator of the link between marital relations and child adjustment. *Child Development, 69,* 124–139.

Davila, J., Burge, D., & Hammen, C. (1997). Why does attachment style change? *Journal of Personality and Social Psychology, 73,* 826–838.

Davis, C. G., Nolen-Hoeksema, S., & Larson, J. (1998). Making sense of loss and benefiting from the experience: Two construals of meaning. *Journal of Personality and Social Psychology, 75*(2), 561–574.

Davis, C., Dionne, M., & Shuster, B. (2001). Physical and psychological correlates of appearance orientation. *Personality & Individual Differences, 30*(1), 21–30.

Davis, K. D., Kiss, Z. H., Luo, L. et al. (1998). Phantom sensations generated by thalamic microstimulation. *Nature, 391,* 385–387.

Davis, M. (1999). Oral contraceptive use and hemodynamic, lipid, and fibrinogen Responses to smoking and stress in women. *Health Psychology, 18,* 122–130.

Davis, R. A. (2001). A cognitive-behavioral model of pathological Internet use. *Computers in Human Behavior, 17*(2), 187–195.

Davison, G. C., & Neale, J. M. (2001). Abnormal psychology (8th ed.). New York: Wiley.

Davison, G.C., Neale, J.M., & Kring, A.M. (2004). *Abnormal psychology (9th. ed.).* New Jersey: Wiley.

Davison, K. P., Pennebaker, J. W., & Dickerson, S. S. (2000). Who talks? The social psychology of illness support groups. *American Psychologist, 55*(2), 205–217.

Day, N. L., Richardson, G. A., Goldschmidt, L., & Cornelius, M. D. (2000). Effects of prenatal tobacco exposure on preschoolers' behavior. *Journal of Developmental & Behavioral Pediatrics, 21*(3), 180–188.

Day, N. L., Zuo, Y., Richardson, G. A., Goldschmidt, L., Larkby, C. A., & Cornelius, M. D. (1999). Prenatal alcohol use and offspring size at 10 years of age. *Alcoholism: Clinical & Experimental Research, 23*(5), 863–869.

De Brabander, B., Hellemans, J., boon, C., & Gerits, P. (1996). Locus of control, sensation seeking, and stress. *Psychological Reports, 79,* 1307–1312.

de Charms, R., & Moeller, G. H. (1962). Values expressed in American children's readers: 1800–1950. *Journal of Abnormal and Social Psychology, 64*(2), 136–142.

De Ronchi, D., Faranca, I., Berardi, D., Scudellari, P., Borderi, M., Manfredi, R., & Fratiglioni, L. (2002). Risk factors for cognitive impairment in HIV-1–infected persons with different risk behaviors. *Archives of Neurology, 59* (5), 812–818.

De Rosnay, M., & Harris, P. L. (2002). Individual differences in children's understanding of emotion: The roles of attachment and language. *Attachment & Human Development, 4*(1), 39–54.

Deary, I. J., & Stough, C. (1996). Intelligence and inspection time: Achievements, prospects, and problems. *American Psychologist, 51,* 599–608.

Deary, I. J., & Stough, C. (1997). Looking down on human intelligence. *American Psychologist, 52,* 1148–1149.

DeBattista, C., & Belanoff, J. (2002). Novel strategies in the treatment of psychotic major depression. *Psychiatric Annals, 32*(11), 695–698.

DeCasper, A. J., & Fifer, W. D. (1980). Of human bonding: Newborns prefer their mother's voices. *Science, 208,* 1174–1176.

DeCasper, A. J., & Spence, M. J. (1986). Prenatal maternal speech influences newborn's perception of speech sounds. *Infant Behavior and Development, 9,* 133–150.

Deci, E. L. (1995). Why we do what we do: The dynamics of personal autonomy. New York: Putnam's Sons.

Deffenbacher, K. A. (1980). Eyewitness accuracy and confidence: Can we infer anything about their relationship? *Law and Human Behavior, 4,* 243–260.

Dehaene, S., Spelke, E., Pinel, P., Stanescu, R., & Tsivkin, S. (1999). Sources of mathematical thinking: Behavioral and brain-imaging evidence. *Science, 284,* 970–974.

Debue, T. (2000). From deception trials to control reagents: The introduction of the control group about a century ago. *American Psychologist, 55,* 264–268.

Delahanty, D. L., Liegey Dougall, A., Hayward, M., Forlenza, M., Hawk, L. W. & Baum, A. (2000). Gender differences in cardiovascular and natural killer cell reactivity to acute stress following a hassling task. *International Journal of Behavioral Medicine, 7,* 19–27.

Delgado, J. M. R. (1960). Emotional behavior in animals and humans. *Psychiatric Research Report, 12,* 259–271.

Delgado-Gaitan, C. (1994). Socializing young children in Mexican-American families: An intergenerational perspective. In P. M. Greenfield & R. R. Cocking (Eds.), *Cross-cultural roots of minority child development* (pp. 55–86). Hillsdale, NJ: Erlbaum.

Dellu, F., Mayo, W., Piazza, P. V., LeMoal, M., & Simon, H. (1993). Individual differences in behavioral responses to novelty in rats: Possible relationship with the sensation-seeking trait in man. *Personality and Individual Differences, 14,* 411–418.

Delville, Y., Mansour, K. M., & Ferris. C. F. (1996). Testosterone facilitates aggression by modulating vasopressin receptors in the hypothalamus. *Physiology and Behavior, 60,* 25–29.

Dement, W. C. (1992, March). The sleepwatchers. *Stanford,* pp. 55–59.

Dement, W. C., & Vaughan, C. (1999). *The promise of sleep.* New York: Delacorte Press.

Dement, W. C., & Wolpert, F. (1958). The relation of eye movements, bodily motility, and external stimuli to dream content. *Journal of Experimental Psychology, 53,* 543–553.

Demo, D. H. (1992). Parent–child relations: Assessing recent changes. *Journal of Marriage and the Family, 54,* 104–117.

DeMoranville, B.M., Jackson, I., Ader, R., Madden, K. S., Felten, D. L., Bellinger, D. L., & Schiffer, R.B. (2000). Endocrine and immune systems. In B. S. Schiffer, & R. B. Schiffer, et al. (Eds), *Synopsis of neuropsychiatry* (pp. 133–153). Philadelphia: Lippincott Williams & Wilkins Publishers.

den Boer, J. A. (2000). Social anxiety disorder/social phobia: Epidemiology, diagnosis, neurobiology, and treatment. *Comprehensive Psychiatry, 41*(6), 405–415.

Dennis, W., & Dennis, M. G. (1940). Cradles and cradling customs of the Pueblo Indians. *American Anthropologist, 42,* 107–115.

Depue, R. A., & Collins, P. F. (1999). Neurobiology of the structure of personality: Dopamine, facilitation of incentive motivation, and extraversion. *Behavioral & Brain Sciences, 22*(3), 491–569.

Der-Karabetian, A., Stephenson, K., & Poggi, T. (1996). Environmental risk perception, activism and world-mindedness among samples of British and U. S. College students. *Perceptual and Motor Skills, 83*(2), 451–462.

Dervin, D. (2002). From American Taliban to Taliban America: The role of the delegate, the rule of group-fantasy post-9/11. *Journal of Psychohistory, 30*(2), 155–163.

Desai, H. D., & Jann, M. W. (2000). Major depression in women: A review of the literature. *Journal of the American Pharmaceutical Association, 40,* 525–537.

DeValois, R. L. (1965). Behavioral and electrophysiological studies of primate vision. In W. D. Neff (Ed.), *Contributions to sensory physiology* (Vol. 1). New York: Academic Press.

Devine, P. G., & Monteith, M. J. (1999). Automaticity and control in stereotyping. In

S. Chaiken, Y. Trope, et al. (Eds.), *Dual-process theories in social psychology*, pp. 339–360. New York: Guilford Press.

Devlin, M. J., Yanovski, S. Z., & Wilson, G. T. (2000). Obesity: What mental health professionals need to know. *American Journal of Psychiatry, 157(6)*, 854–866.

Diamond, M. (2000). Sex and gender: Same or different? *Feminism & Psychology, 10*, 46–54.

Diamond, M., & Hopson, J. (1998). *Magic trees of the mind: How to nurture your child's intelligence, creativity, and healthy emotions from birth through adolescence.* New York: Dutton.

Diamond, M., & Sigmundson, H. K. (1997). Sex reassignment at birth: Long-term review and clinical implications. *Archives of Pediatrics and Adolescent Medicine, 151*, 298–304.

Diana, E. M., & Webb, J. M. (1997). Using geographic maps in classrooms: The conjoint influence of individual differences and dual coding on learning facts. *Learning & Individual Differences, 9*, 195–214.

DiChiara, G. (1997). Alcohol and dopamine. *Alcohol Health & Research World, 21*, 108–114.

Dickens, W. T., & Flynn, J. R. (2001). Heritability estimates versus large environmental effects: The IQ paradox resolved. *Psychological Review, 108(2)*, 346–369.

Dickhaeuser, O., & Stiensmeier-Pelster, J. (2002). Gender differences in computer work: Evidence for the model of achievement-related choices. *Contemporary Educational Psychology, 27(3)*, 486–496.

Dickinson, L. M., deGruy, F. V., Dickinson, W. P., & Candib, L. M. (1999). Health related quality of life and symptom profiles of female survivors of sexual abuse. *Archives of Family Medicine, 8*, 35–43.

Diederich, N. J., & Goetz, C. G. (2000). Neuropsychological and behavioral aspects of transplants in Parkinson's disease and Huntington's disease. *Brain & Cognition, 42(2)*, 294–306.

Diener, E., & Biswas-Diener, R. (2002). Will money increase subjective well-being? *Social Indicators Research, 57(2)*, 119–169.

Diener, E., & Diener, C. (1996). Most people are happy. *Psychological Science, 7*, 181–185.

Diener, E., & Lucas, R. E. (2000). Explaining differences in societal levels of happiness: Relative standards, need fulfillment, culture and evaluation theory. *Journal of Happiness Studies, 1(3)*, 41–78.

Diener, E., & Seligman, M. E. P. (2002). Very happy people. *Psychological Science, 13(1)*, 81–84.

Diener, E., Lucas, R. E., Oishi, S., & Suh, E. M. (2002). Looking up and down:

Weighting good and bad information in life satisfaction judgments. *Personality & Social Psychology Bulletin, 28(4)*, 437–445.

Diener, E., Napa, S., C., Oishi, S., Dzokoto, V., & Suh, E. M. (2000). Positivity and the construction of life satisfaction judgments: Global happiness is not the sum of its parts. *Journal of Happiness Studies, 1(2)*, 159–176.

Diener, M. L., Mengelsdorf, S. C., McHale, J. L., & Frosch, C. A. (2002). Infants' behavioral strategies for emotion regulation with fathers and mothers: Associations with emotional expressions and attachment quality. *Infancy, 3(2)*, 153–174.

Diener, M. L., Mengelsdorf, S. C., McHale, J. L., & Frosch, C. A. (2002).Infants' behavioral strategies for emotion regulation with fathers and mothers: Associations with emotional expressions and attachment quality. *Infancy, 3(2)*, 153–174.

Dietz, T. L. (1998). An examination of violence and gender role portrayals in video games. *Sex Roles, 38*, 425–442.

Digman, J. M. (1997). Higher-order factors of the Big Five. *Journal of Personality and Social Psychology, 73*, 1246–1256.

DiLalla, D. L., Carey, G., Gottesman, I. I., & Bouchard, T. J., Jr. (1996). Heritability of MMPI personality indicators of psychopathology in twins reared apart. *Journal of Abnormal Psychology, 105*, 491–499.

Dimberg, U., & Thunberg, M. (1998). Rapid facial reactions to emotion facial expressions. *Scandinavian Journal of Psychology, 39(1)*, 39–46.

Dimberg, U., Thunberg, M., & Elmehed, K. (2000). Unconscious facial reactions to emotional facial expressions. *Psychological Science, 11(1)*, 86–89.

Dimoff, T. A. (2000). *How to recognize substance abuse.* New York: CSS Publishing.

Dinan, T. G. (2000). Antidepressants and violence: Cause for concern or media hype? *Human Psychopharmacology Clinical & Experimental, 15(6)*, iii-iv.

Dinnel, D. L., Kleinknecht, R. A., & Tanaka-Matsumi, J. (2002). A cross-cultural comparison of social phobia symptoms. *Journal of Psychopathology & Behavioral Assessment, 24(2)*, 75–84.

Doby, V., & Caplan, R. D. (1995). Organizational stress as threat to reputation: Effects on anxiety at work and at home. *Academy of Management Journal, 38*, 1105–1123.

Doghramji, K. (2000, December). Sleepless in America: Diagnosing and treating insomnia. [On-line serial]. Available: http://psychiatry. medscape. com/Medscape/psychiatry/ClinicalMgmt/CM. v02/public/index-CM. v02. html

Dollard, J., Doob, L., Miller, N., Mowrer, O. H., & Sears, R. R. (1939). *Frustration and aggression.* New Haven, CT: Yale University Press.

Dols, M., Willems, B., van den Hout, M., & Bittoun, R. (2000). Smokers can learn to influence their urge to smoke. *Addictive Behaviors, 25(1)*, 103–108.

Domhoff, G. W. (1999). New directions in the study of dream content using the Hall and Van de Castle coding system. *Dreaming, 9*, 115–137.

Domhoff, G. W. (2001). A new neurocognitive theory of dreams. *Dreaming, 11(1)*, 13–33.

Domhoff, G. W. (2003). *The scientific study of dreams: Neural networks, cognitive development, and content analysis.* Washington, DC: American Psychological Association.

Domhoff, G. (1996). *Finding meaning in dreams: A quantitative approach.* New York: Plenum.

Domino, G., & Morales, A. (2000). Reliability and validity of the D-48 with Mexican American college students. *Hispanic Journal of Behavioral Sciences, 22(3)*, 382–389.

Donahey, K. & Miller, S. (2001). Applying a common factors perspective to sex therapy. *Journal of Sex Education and Therapy, 25*, 221–230.

Dondi, M., Simion, F., & Caltran, G. (1999). Can newborns discriminate between their own cry and the cry of another newborn infant? *Developmental Psychology, 35*, 418–426.

Donovan, J. J., & Radosevich, D. J. (1999). A meta-analytic review of the distribution of practice effect: Now you see it, now you don't. *Journal of Applied Psychology, 84*, 795–805.

Dorfman, A. (2002, May). Send in the roborats. *Time*, p. 61.

Dorian, L., & Garfinkel, P. E. (2002). Culture and body image in Western culture. *Eating & Weight Disorders, 7(1)*, 1–19.

Dorion, A. A., Chantome, M., Hasboun, D., Zouaoui, A., Marsault, C., Capron, C., & Duyme, M. (2000). Hemispheric asymmetry and corpus callosum morphometry: A magnetic resonance imaging study. *Neuroscience Research, 36(1)*, 9–13.

Dougherty, D. D., Baer, L., Cosgrove, G. R., Cassem, E. H., Price, B. H., Nierenberg, A. A., Jenike, M. A., & Rauch, S. L. (2002). Prospective long-term follow-up of 44 patients who received cingulotomy for treatment-refractory obsessive-compulsive disorder. *American Journal of Psychiatry, 159(2)*, 269–275.

Dovidio, J. F., Brigham, J. C., Johnson, B. T., & Gaertner, S. L. (1995). Stereotyping, prejudice, and discrimination: Another look. In N. Macrae, M. Hewstone, & C. Stangor

(Eds.), *Foundations of stereotypes and stereotyping*. New York: Guilford.

Dovidio, J. F., Gaertner, S. L., Bachman, B. A. (2001). Racial bias in organizations: The role of group processes in its causes and cures. In M. E. Turner (Ed.), *Groups at work: Theory and research* (pp. 415–444). Mahwah, NJ: Erlbaum.

Doweiko, H. E. (1999). *Concepts of chemical dependency*. Pacific Grove, CA: Brooks/Cole.

Draijer, N., & Langeland, W. (1999). Childhood trauma and perceived parental dysfunction in the etiology of dissociative symptoms in psychiatric inpatients. *American Journal of Psychiatry, 156*, 379–385.

Dresser, N. (1996). *Multicultural manners: New rules of etiquette for a changing society*. New York: Wiley.

Driscoll, R., Davis, K. E., & Lipetz, M. E. (1972). Parental interference and romantic love: The Romeo and Juliet effect. *Journal of Personality and Social Psychology, 24*, 1–10.

Druckman, D., & Bjork, R. A. (Eds.) (1994). *Learning, remembering, believing: Enhancing human performance*. Washington, DC: National Academy Press.

Druckman, D., & Swets, J. A. (1988). *Enhancing human performance: Issues, theories, and techniques*. Washington, DC: National Academy Press.

Drummond, E. (2000). *The complete guide to psychiatric drugs*. New York: Wiley.

Dryer, D. C., & Horowitz, L. M. (1997). When do opposites attract? Interpersonal complementarity versus similarity. *Journal of Personality and Social Psychology, 72*, 592–603.

Dube, S. R., Anda, R, F., Felitti, V. J., Edwards, V. J., & Williamson, D. F. (2002). Exposure to abuse, neglect and household dysfunction among adults who witnessed intimate partner violence as children: Implications for health and social services. *Violence & Victims, 17(1)*, 3–18.

Dubovsky, S. L., & Buzan, R. (1999). Mood disorders. In R. E. Hales, S. C. Yudofsky, & J. A. Talbott (Eds.), *American psychiatric press textbook of psychiatry*. Washington, DC: American Psychiatric Press.

Duckworth, K., & Borus, J. F. (1999). Population-based psychiatry in the public sector and managed care. In A. M. Nicholi (Ed.), *The Harvard guide to psychiatry*. Cambridge, MA: Harvard University Press.

Dukes Conrad, S., & Stevens Morrow, R. (2000). Borderline personality organization, dissociation, and willingness to use force in intimate relationships. *Psychology of Men & Masculinity, 1(1)*, 37–48.

Duncan, J., & Owen, A. M. (2000). Common regions of the human frontal lobe recruited by diverse cognitive demands. *Trends in Neurosciences, 23(10)*, 475–483.

Duncan, W. J. (2001). Stock ownership and work. *Organizational Dynamics, 30(1)*, 1–11.

Duncker, K. (1945). On problem-solving. *Psychological Monographs, 58*, 361–362.

Dundas, R., Morgan, M., Redfern, J., Lemic-Stojcevic, N., & Wolfe, C. (2001). Ethnic differences in behavioural risk factors for stroke: Implications for health promotion. *Ethnicity & Health, 6(2)*, 95–103.

Dunlap, J. (1998). Circadian rhythms: An end in the beginning. *Science, 280*, 1548–1549.

Dunn, M. (2000). *Good death guide: Everything you wanted to know but were afraid to ask*. New York: How to Books.

Durand, M. V., & Barlow, D. H. (2003). *Essentials of abnormal psychology (3rd ed.)*. Belmont Park, CA: Thompson Learning.

Durham, M. D., & Dane, F. C. (1999). Juror knowledge of eyewitness behavior: Evidence for the necessity of expert testimony. *Journal of Social Behavior & Personality, 14*, 299–308.

Durkin, K., & Judge, J. (2001). Effects of language and social behaviour on children's reactions to foreign people in television. *British Journal of Developmental Psychology, 19(4)*, 597–612.

Dworkin, A. (1974). *Woman hating*. New York: E. P. Dutton.

Dworkin, B. R., & Miller, N. E. (1986). Failure to replicate visceral learning in the acute curarized rat preparation. *Behavioral Neuroscience, 100*, 299–314.

Dysart, J. E., Lindsay, R. C. L., Hammond, R., & Dupuis, P. (2001). Mug shot exposure prior to lineup identification: Interference, transference, and commitment effects. *Journal of Applied Psychology, 86(6)*, 1280–1284.

Eagly, A. H. (1997). Sex differences in social behavior: Comparing social role theory and evolutionary psychology. *American Psychologist, 52*, 1303–1382.

Eagly, A. H., & Wood, W. (1999). The origins of sex differences in human behavior: Evolved dispositions versus social roles. *American Psychologist, 54*, 408–423.

Easterlin, R. A. (2001). Life cycle welfare: Trends and differences. *Journal of Happiness Studies, 2(1)*, 1–12.

Eccles, J. S., Buchanan, C. M., Flanagan, C., Fuligni, A., Midgley, C., & Yee, D. (1999). Control versus autonomy during early adolescence. In L. E. Berk, *Landscapes of development* (pp. 393–406). Belmont, CA: Wadsworth.

Eckhardt, L., Woodruff, S. I., & Elder, J. P. (1997). Relative effectiveness of continued, lapsed, and delayed smoking prevention intervention in senior high school students. *American Journal of Health Promotion, 11(6)*, 418–421.

Eckstein, D. (2000). Empirical studies indicating significant birth-order-related personality differences. *Journal of Individual Psychology, 56(4)*, 481–494.

Eckstein, D., & Goldman, A. (2001). The Couples' Gender-Based Communication Questionnaire (CGCQ). *Family Journal-Counseling & Therapy for Couples & Families, 9(1)*, 62–74.

Edwards, B. (1999). The new drawing on the right side of the brain. Baltimore: J P Tarcher.

Edwards, K. J., Hershberger, P. J., Russell, R. K., & Markert, R. J. (2001). Stress, negative social exchange, and health symptoms in university students. *Journal of American College Health, 50(2)*, 75–79.

Ehlers, A. & Steil, R. (1995). Maintenance of intrusive memories in posttraumatic stress disorder: A cognitive approach. *Behavioral & Cognitive Psychotherapy, 23*, 217–249.

Eibl-Eibesfeldt, I. (1980b). Strategies of social interaction. In R. Plutchik & H. Kelerman (Eds.), Emotion: Theory, research, and experience. New York: Academic Press.

Eichenbaum, H. (1999a). Conscious awareness, memory and the hippocampus. *Nature Neuroscience, 2*, 775–776.

Eilenberg, M. E., & Wyman, S. E. (1998). Scapegoating in an early adolescent girls group. *Journal of Child and Adolescent Group Therapy, 8(1)*, 3–11.

Eisen, S. A., Chantarujikapong, Sta, Xian, H., Lyons, M. J., Toomey, R., True, W. R., Scherrer, J. F., Goldberg, J., & Tsuang, M. T. (2002). Does marijuana use have residual adverse effects on self-reported health measures, sociodemographics and quality of life? A monozygotic co-twin control study in men. *Addiction, 97(9)*, 1137–1144.

Eisenberg, N. (2000). Emotion, regulation, and moral development. *Annual Review of Psychology, 51*, 665–697.

Eisenberger, R., & Armeli, S. (1997). Can salient reward increase creative performance without reducing intrinsic creative interest? *Journal of Personality and Social Psychology, 72*, 652–663.

Eisenberger, R., & Cameron, J. (1996). Detrimental effects of reward: Reality or myth? *American Psychologist, 51*, 1153–1166.

Eisenberger, R., & Rhoades, L. (2002). Incremental effects of reward on creativity. *Journal of Personality & Social Psychology, 81(4)*, 728–741.

Ekman, P. (1993). Facial expression and emotion. *American Psychologist, 48*, 384–392.

Ekman, P., & Friesen, W. V. (1971). Constants across cultures in the face and emotion. *Journal of Personality and Social Psychology, 17*, 124–129.

Ekman, P., & Keltner, D. (1997). Universal facial expressions of emotion: An old controversy and new findings. In U. C. Segerstrale & P. Molnar (Eds.), *Nonverbal communication: Where nature meets culture.* Mahwah, NJ: Erlbaum.

Elder, G. (1998). The life course as developmental theory. *Current Directions in Psychological Science, 69,* 1–12.

El-Gibaly, O., Ibrahim, B., Mensch, B.S., Clark, W.H. (2002). The decline of female circumcision in Egypt: Evidence and interpretation. *Social Science & Medicine, 54(2),* 205–220.

Elkind, D. (1999). Authority of the brain. *Journal of Developmental & Behavioral Pediatrics, 20(6),* 432–433.

Elkind, D. (1967). Egocentrism in adolescence. *Child Development, 38,* 1025–1034.

Elkind, D. (1981). *The hurried child.* Reading, MA: Addison-Wesley.

Elkind, D. (1998). *Reinventing childhood: Raising and educating children in a changing world.* New York: Modern Learning.

Elkind, D. (1999). Authority of the brain. *Journal of Developmental & Behavioral Pediatrics, 20(6),* 432–433.

Elkind, D. (2000). A quixotic approach to issues in early childhood education. *Human Development, 43(4–5),* 279–283.

Elkins, R. L. (1991). An appraisal of chemical aversion (emetic therapy) approaches to alcoholism treatment. *Behaviour Research & Therapy, 29(5),* 387–413.

Elliott, M. R., Reilly, S. M., Drummond, J., & Letourneau, N. (2002). The effect of different soothing interventions on infant crying and on parent-infant interaction. *Infant Mental Health Journal, 23(3),* 310–328.

Ellis, A. (1961). *A guide to rational living.* Englewood Cliffs, NJ: Prentice-Hall.

Ellis, A. (1996). Better, deeper, and more enduring brief therapy. New York: Institute for Rational Emotive Therapy.

Ellis, A. (1997). Using Rational Emotive Behavior Therapy techniques to cope with disability. *Professional Psychology: Research and Practice, 28,* 17–22.

Ellis, A. (2000). *How to control your anxiety before it controls you.* Charleston, SC: Citadel Press.

Ellis, J. L., et al. (1999). Development of muscarine analgesics derived from epibatidine: Role of the M-sub-4 receptor subtype. *Journal of Pharmacology & Experimental Therapeutics, 288,* 1143–1150.

Ellis, R. T., & Granger, J. M. (2002). African American adults' perceptions of the effects of parental loss during adolescence. *Child & Adolescent Social Work Journal, 19(4),* 271–284.

Ellman, S. J., Spielman, A. J., Luck, D., Steiner, S. S., & Halperin, R. (1991). REM deprivation: A review. In S. A. Ellman & J. S. Antrobus (Eds.), *The mind in sleep: Psychology and psychophysiology* (2nd ed., pp. 329–368). New York: Wiley.

Emery, R. E. (1999). *Marriage, divorce, and children's adjustment* (2nd ed). Thousand Oaks, CA: Sage.

Emery, R. E., & Laumann-Billings, L. (1998). An overview of the nature, causes, and consequences of abusive family relationships: Toward differentiating maltreatment and violence. *American Psychologist, 53(2),* 121–135.

Endersbe, J. (2000). *Teen pregnancy: Tough choices.* New York: Life Matters.

Engle, V. G. & Graney, M. J. (2000). Biobehavioral effects of therapeutic touch. *Journal of Nursing Scholarship, 32(3),* 287–293.

Ennis, N. E., Hobfoll, S. E., Schroeder, K. E. E. (2000). Money doesn't talk, it swears: How economic stress and resistance resources impact inner-city women's depressive mood. *American Journal of Community Psychology, 28,* 149–173.

Erdelyi, M. H., & Applebaum, A. G. (1973). Cognitive masking: The disruptive effect of an emotional stimulus upon the perception of contiguous neutral items. *Bulletin of the Psychonomic Society, 1,* 59–61.

Eriksson, P. S., Perfilieva, E., Bjork-Eriksson, T., Alborn, A. M., Nordborg, C., Peterson, D. A., & Gage, F. H. (1998). Neurogenesis in the adult human hippocampus. *Nature Medicine, 4(11),* 1313–1317.

Espin, O. M. (1993). Feminist theory: Not for or by white women only. *Counseling Psychologist, 21,* 103–108.

Esposito, S., Prange, A. J., & Golden, R. N. (1998). The thyroid axis and mood disorders: Overview and future prospects. *Psychopharmacology Bulletin, 33,* 205–217.

Esser, J. K. (1998). Alive and well after 25 years: A review of groupthink research. *Organizational Behavior and Human Decision Processes, 73,* 116–141.

Etcoff, N. (1999). *Survival of the prettiest: The science of beauty.* New York: Doubleday.

Ethical Principles of Psychologists and Code of Conduct. (1992). *American Psychologist, 47,* 1597–1611.

European School Survey Project on Alcohol and Other Drugs (ESPAD) (2001). Substance abuse increasing among European adolescents. *Reuters Medical News for the Professional* [On-line]. Available: psychiatry.medscape.com/reuters/prof/2001/02/02.21

Evans, G. W., Hygge, S., & Bullinger, M. (1995). Chronic noise and psychological stress. *Psychological Science, 6(6),* 333–338.

Evans, M. J., & Kaufman, M. H. (1981). Establishment in culture of pluripotential cells from mouse embryos. *Nature, 292,* 153–156.

Evans, R. B. E., & Rilling, M. (2000). How the challenge of explaining learning influenced the origins and development of John B. Watson's behaviorism. *American Journal of Psychology, 113(2),* 275–301.

Everett, C., & Everett, S. V. (1994). *Healthy divorce.* San Francisco: Jossey-Bass.

Ewart, C. K., & Fitzgerald, S. T. (1994). Changing behaviour and promoting well-being after heart attack: A social action theory approach. *Irish Journal of Psychology, 15(1),* 219–241.

Ewart, C. K., & Kolodner, K. B. (1994). Negative affect, gender, and expressive style predict elevated ambulatory blood pressure in adolescents. *Journal of Personality and Social Psychology, 66,* 596–605.

Ewbank, D. C. (2002). A multistate model of the genetic risk of Alzheimer's disease. *Experimental Aging Research, 28(4),* 477–499.

Exner, J. E., Jr. (1997). The future of Rorschach in personality assessment. *Journal of Personality Assessment, 68(1),* 37–46.

Eyler, F., Behnke, M., Conlon, M., Woods, N., & Wobie, K. (1998). Birth outcome from a prospective, matched study of prenatal crack cocaine use: I. Interactive and dose effects on health and growth. *Pediatrics, 101,* 229–237.

Eysenck, H. J. (1967). *The biological basis of personality.* Springfield, IL: Charles C Thomas.

Eysenck, H. J. (1982). *Personality, genetics, and behavior: Selected papers.* New York: Prager.

Eysenck, H. J. (1990). Biological dimensions of personality. In L. A. Pervin (Ed.), *Handbook of personality: Theory and research.* New York: Guilford Press.

Eysenck, H. J. (1991). *Smoking, personality, and stress: Psychosocial factors in the prevention of cancer and coronary heart disease.* New York: Springer-Verlag.

Fackelmann, K. (1997). Marijuana on trial: Is marijuana a dangerous drug or a valu-able medicine? *Science News, 151,* 178–179, 183.

Facon, B., & Facon-Bollengier, T. (1999). Chronological age and crystallized intelligence of people with intellectual disability. *Journal of Intellectual Disability Research, 43(6),* 489–496.

Faddiman, A. (1997). *The spirit catches you and you fall down.* New York: Straus & Giroux.

Faigman, D. L., Kaye, D., Saks, M. J., & Sanders, J. (1997). *Modern scientific evidence: The law and science of expert testimony.* St. Paul, MN: West.

Fantz, R. L. (1956). A method for studying early visual development. *Perceptual and Motor Skills, 6,* 13–15.

Fantz, R. L. (1963). Pattern vision in newborn infants. *Science, 140,* 296–297.

Fanz, E. A., Waldie, K. E., & Smith, M. J. (2000). The effect of callostomy on novel versus familiar bimanual actions: A neural dissociation between controlled and automatic processes. *Psychological Science, 11*(1), 82–85.

Farber, P. L. (2000). *Finding order in nature: The naturalist tradition from Linnaeus to E. O. Wilson.* Baltimore: Johns Hopkins Univ. Press.

Farrington, D. P. (2000). Psychosocial predictors of adult antisocial personality and adult convictions. *Behavioral Sciences & the Law, 18*(5), 605–622.

Farthing, W. G. (1992). The psychology of consciousness. Englewood Cliffs, NJ: Prentice Hall.

Fava, G. A., et al. (1998). Prevention of recurrent depression with cognitive behavioral therapy. *Archives of General Psychiatry, 55*(9), 816–820.

Febr, C., Grintschuk, N., Szegedi, A., Angbelescu, I., Klawe, C., Singer, P., Hiemke, C., & Dahmen, N. (2000). The HTR1B 861G > C receptor polymorphism among patients suffering from alcoholism, major depression, anxiety disorders and narcolepsy. *Psychiatry Research, 97*(1), 1–10.

Fein, S., & Spencer, S. J. (1997). Prejudice as self-image maintenance: Affirming the self through derogating others. *Journal of Personality and Social Psychology, 73*(1), 31–44.

Feiring, C., Deblinger, E., Hoch-Espada, A., & Haworbt T. (2002). Romantic relationship aggression and attitudes in high school students: The role of gender, grade, and attachment and emotional styles. *Journal of Youth & Adolescence, 31*(5), 373–385.

Feldman, R. S. (1982). *Development of nonverbal behavior in children.* Seacaucus, NJ: Springer-Verlag.

Fenton, G. W. (1998). Neurosurgery for mental disorder. *Irish Journal of Psychological Medicine, 15,* 45–48.

Fernandez, G., et al. (1999). Real-time tracking of memory formation in the human rhinal cortex and hippocampus. *Science, 285,* 1582–1585.

Fernandez, G., Hufnagel, A., Helmstaedter, C., Zetner, J., Elger, C. E. (1996). Memory function during low intensity hippocampal electrical stimulation in patients with temporal lobe epilepsy. *European Journal of Neurology, 3,* 335–344.

Fernandez, G., Weyerts, H., Schrader-Boelsche, M., Tendolkar, I., Smid, H. G. O. M., Tempelmann, C., Hinrichs, H., Scheich, H., Elger, C. E., Mangun, G. R., &

Heinze, H- J. (1998). Successful verbal encoding into episodic memory engages the posterior hippocampus: A parametrically analyzed functional magnetic resonance imaging study. *Journal of Neuroscience, 18*(5), 1841–1847.

Fernandez-Dols, J., Carrera, P., & Russell, J. A. (2002). Are facial displays social? Situational influences in the attribution of emotion to facial expressions. *Spanish Journal of Psychology, 5*(2), 119–124.

Ferry, B., Roozendaal, B., & McGaugh, J. L. (1999). Involvement of alpha 1-adrenoceptors in the basolateral amygdala in modulation of memory storage. *European Journal of Pharmacology, 372,* 9–16.

Festinger, L. A. (1957). *A theory of cognitive dissonance.* Evanston, IL: Row, Peterson.

Festinger, L. A., & Carlsmith, L. M. (1959). Cognitive consequences of forced compliance. *Journal of Abnormal and Social Psychology, 58,* 203–210.

Field, K. M., Woodson, R., Greenberg, R., & Cohen, D. (1982). Discrimination and imitation of facial expressions by neonates. *Science, 218,* 179–181.

Field, T., & Hernandez-Reif, M. (2001). Sleep problems in infants decrease following massage therapy. *Early Child Development & Care, 168,* 95–104.

Finch, C. E., & Tanzi, R. E. (1997). Genetics of aging. *Science, 278,* 407–411.

Fineran, S. (2002). Sexual harassment between same-sex peers: Intersection of mental health, homophobia, and sexual violence in schools. *Social Work, 47*(1), 65–74.

Fink, B., & Penton-Voak, I. (2002). Evolutionary psychology of facial attractiveness. *Current Directions in Psychological Science, 11*(5), 154–158.

Fink, M. (1999). *Electroshock: Restoring the mind.* London: Oxford University Press.

Finkel, D., & Pedersen, N. L. (2000). Contribution of age, genes, and environment to the relationship between perceptual speed and cognitive ability. *Psychology & Aging, 15*(1), 56–64.

Finley, W. H., McDanal, C. E., Finley, S. C., & Rosecrans, C. J. (1973). Prison survey for the XYY karyotype in tall inmates. *Behavior Genetics, 3,* 97–100.

Finnoy, O. J. (2000). Job satisfaction and stress symptoms among personnel in child psychiatry in Norway. *Nordic Journal of Psychiatry, 54*(6), 397–403.

Fiore, M. C. (2000). A clinical practice guideline for treating tobacco use and dependence: A US Public Health Service Report. *Journal of the American Medical Association, 283*(24), 3244–3254.

First, M. B., Pincus, H. A., & Frances, A. (1999). Another perspective on "Putting

DSM-IV in perspective." *American Journal of Psychiatry, 156*(3), 499–500.

Firth, C. D., & Firth, U. (1999). Interacting minds—A biological basis. *Science, 286,* 1692–1695.

Fischman, J. (2000, February 7). Why we fall in love. *U. S. News & World Report,* pp. 42–48.

Fisher, S. E., Vargha-Khadem, F., Watkins, K. E., et al. (1998). Localisation of a gene implicated in a severe speech and language disorder. *Nature Genetics, 18,* 168–170.

Fisher, S., & Greenberg, R. P. (1996). *Freud scientifically reappraised: Testing the theories and therapy.* New York: Wiley.

Fiske, S. T. (2002). What we know about bias and intergroup conflict, the problem of the century. *Current Directions in Psychological Science, 11*(4), 123–128.

Fiske, S. T. (1998). Stereotyping, prejudice, and discrimination. In D. T. Gilbert, S. T. Fiske, and G. Lindzey (Eds.), *The handbook of social psychology,* Vol. 2 (4th ed.) (pp. 357–411). Boston, MA: McGraw-Hill.

Flaskerud, J. H. (2000). Ethnicity, culture, and neuropsychiatry. *Issues in Mental Health Nursing, 21*(1), 5–29.

Flavell, J. H. (1999). Cognitive development: Children's knowledge about the mind. *Annual Reviews of Psychology, 50,* 21–45.

Flavell, J. H., Miller, P. H., & Miller, S. A. (2002). *Cognitive development* (4th ed.). Upper Saddle River, NJ: Prentice-Hall.

Fletcher, G. J. O., & Simpson, J. A. (2000). Ideal standards in close relationships: Their structure and functions. *Current Directions in Psychological Science, 9*(3), 102–105.

Flexser, A. J., & Tulving, E. (1978). Retrieval independence in recognition and recall. *Psychological Review, 85,* 153–171.

Flexser, A. J., & Tulving, E. (1982). Priming and recognition failure. *Journal of Verbal Learning and Verbal Behavior, 21,* 237–248.

Flora, M. E. (2000). *Meditation: Key to spiritual awakening.* New York: CDM Publications.

Flynn, J. R. (1987). Massive IQ gains in 14 nations: What IQ tests really measure. *Psychological Bulletin, 101,* 171–191.

Flynn, J. R. (1998). IQ gains over time: Toward finding the causes. In U. Neisser (Ed.), *The rising curve: Long-term gains in IQ and related measures.* Washington, DC: American Psychological Association.

Flynn, J. R. (2000). IQ gains and fluid g. *American Psychologist, 55*(5), 543.

Foa, E. B., Franklin, M. E., Perry, K. J., & Herbert, J. D. (1996). Cognitive biases in generalized social phobia. *Journal of Abnormal Psychology, 105*(3), 433–439.

Fold, M. A., & Friedman, S. (2000). Cadet basic training: an ethnographic study of stress and coping. *Military Medicine, 165,* 147–152.

Folk, C. I., & Remington, R. W. (1998). Selectivity in distraction by irrelevant featural singletons: Evidence for two forms of attentional capture. *Journal of Experimental Psychology: Human Perception and Performance, 24,* 1–12.

Folkman, S., Lazarus, R. S., Gruen, R. J., & DeLongis, A. (1986). Appraisal, coping, health-status, and psychological symptoms. *Journal of Personality and Social Psychology, 50,* 571–579.

Fone, B. R. S. (2000). *Homophobia: A history.* New York: Metropolitan Books.

Fontes, L. A., Cruz, M., & Tabachnick, J. (2001). Views of child sexual abuse in two cultural communities: An exploratory study among African Americans and Latinos. Child Maltreatment: *Journal of the American Professional Society on the Abuse of Children, 6(2),* 103–117.

Fortenberry, J. D. (2002). Unveiling the hidden epidemic of sexually transmitted diseases. *JAMA: Journal of the American Medical Association, 287(6),* 768–769.

Fortin, N. J., Agster, K. L.. & Eichenbaum, H. B. (2002). Critical role of the hippocampus in memory for sequences of events. *Nature Neuroscience, 5(5),* 458–462.

Foster, T. C., & Dumas, T. C. (2001). Mechanism for increased hippocampal synaptic strength following differential experience. *Journal of Neurophysiology, 85(4),* 1377–1383.

Foulkes, D. (1982). *Children's Dreams.* New York: Wiley.

Foulkes, D. (1993). Children's dreaming. In D. Foulkes & C. Cavallero (Eds.), *Dreaming as cognition,* pp. 114–132. New York: Harvester Wheatsheaf.

Fowler, I. L., Carr, V. J., Carter, N. T., & Lewin, T. J. (1998). Patterns of current and lifetime substance use in schizophrenia. *Schizophrenia Bulletin, 24,* 443–455.

Fowler, J. S., Volkow, N. D., Wang, G. J., Pappas, N., Logan, J., MacGregor, R., Alexoff, D., Shea, C., Shyler, D., Wolf, A. P., Warner, D., Zazulkova, I., & Cilento, R. (1996). Inhibition of monoamine oxidase B in the brains of smokers. *Nature, 379,* 733–736.

Fowler, R. D. (1986, May). Howard Hughes: A psychological autopsy. *Psychology Today,* pp. 22–33.

Fowles, D. C. (1992). Schizophrenia: Diathesis-stress revisited. *Annual Review of Psychology, 43,* 303–336.

Fraley, R. C., & Shaver, P. R. (1997). Adult attachment and the suppression of unwanted thoughts. *Journal of Personality and Social Psychology, 73,* 1080–1091.

Frances, A., & First, M. B. (1998). Your mental health: A layman's guide to the psychiatrist's bible. New York: Scribners.

Franken, R. E. (1998). *Human motivation* (4th ed.). Pacific Grove, CA: Brooks/Cole.

Franklin, T. R., Acton, P. D., Maldjian, J. A., Gray, J. D., Croft, J. R., Dackis, C. A., O'Brien, C. P., & Childress, A. R. (2002). Decreased gray matter concentration in the insular, orbitofrontal, cingulate, and temporal cortices of cocaine patients. *Biological Psychiatry, 51(2),* 134–142.

Franz, E. A., Waldie, K. E., & Smith, M. J. (2000). The effect of callostomy on novel versus familiar bimanual actions: A neural dissociation between controlled and automatic processes? *Psychological Science, 11 (1),* 82–85.

Frazier, L. (2000). Coping with disease-related stressors in Parkinson's disease. *Gerontologist, 2000, 40,* 53–63.

Frederick, C. M., & Morrison, C. S. (1999). Date selection choices in college students: Making a potential love connection. *North American Journal of Psychology, 1(1),* 41–50.

Fredrickson, M., Wik, G., Fischer, H., & Andersson, J. (1995). Affective and attentive neural networks in humans: A PET study of Pavlovian conditioning. *Neuroreport: An International Journal for the Rapid Communication of Research in Neuroscience, 7(1),* 97–101.

Fredrikson, M., Wik, G., & Fischer, H. (1999). Higher hypothalamic and hippocampal neural activity in type A than type B women. *Personality & Individual Differences, 26,* 265–270.

Freeman-Longo, R. E. (2000). Children, teens, and sex on the Internet. *Sexual Addiction & Compulsivity, 7(1–2),* 75–90.

Freud, S. (1900/1953). The interpretation of dreams. In J. Stratchey (Ed. and Trans.), *The standard edition of the complete psychological works of Sigmund Freud* (Vols. 4 and 5). London: Hogarth Press. (Original work published 1900).

Freud, S. (1961). The ego and the id. In J. Stratchey (Ed. and Trans.), *The standard edition of the complete psychological works of Sigmund Freud* (Vol. 19). London: Hogarth Press. (Original work published 1923).

Frick, Willard B. (2000). Remembering Maslow: Reflections on a 1968 interview. *Journal of Humanistic Psychology, 40(2),* 128–147.

Friedman, H. S., Hawley, P. H., & Tucker, J. S. (1994). Personality, health, and longevity. *Current Directions in Psychological Science, 4(2),* 37–41.

Friedman, J. (2002). Diabetes: Fat in all the wrong places. *Nature, 415,* 268–269.

Friedman, M., & Rosenman, R. H. (1959). Association of specific overt behavior patterns with blood and cardiovascular findings: Blood cholesterol level, blood clotting time, incidence of arcus senilis and clinical coronary artery disease. *Journal of the American Medical Association, 169,* 1286–1296.

Friedman, M., Thoresen, C. E., Gill, J. J., Ulmer, D., Powell, L. H., Price, V. A., Brown, B., Thompson, L., Rabin, D. D., Breall, W. S., Bourg, E., Levy, R., & Dixon, T. (1986). Alteration of Type A behavior and its effect on cardiac recurrences in past myocardial infarction patients: Summary results of the Recurrent Coronary Prevention Project. *American Heart Journal, 112,* 653–665.

Friedman, N. P., & Miyake, A. (2000). Differential roles for visuospatial and verbal working memory in situation model construction. *Journal of Experimental Psychology, 129,* 61–83.

Friend, T. (1997, February 5). Heroin spreads across the USA. *USA Today,* p. 2, 4.

Fritz, G. K., & McQuaid, E. L. (2000). Chronic medical conditions: Impact on development. In A. J. Sameroff, & M. Lewis, et al., (Eds.), *Handbook of developmental psychopathology* (2nd ed.) (pp. 277–289). New York: Kluwer Academic/Plenum Publishers.

Fruehwald, S., Loffler, H., Eher, R., Saletu, B., & Baumhackl, U. (2001). Relationship between depression, anxiety, and quality of life: A study of stroke patients compared to chronic low back pain and myocardial ischemia patients. *Psychopathology, 34(1),* 50–56.

Fry, C. L. (1985). Culture, behavior, and aging in the comparative perspective. In J. E. Birren, K. W. Schaie, et al. (Eds.), *Handbook of the psychology of aging* (2nd ed.), pp, 216–244. New York: Van Nostrand Reinhold Co.

Frye, R. E., Schwartz, B. S., & Doty, R. L. (1990). Dose-related effects of cigarette smoking on olfactory function. *Journal of the American Medical Association, 263,* 1233–1236.

Fu, S., Sun, J., Chen, S., & Luo, H. (2002). Mental health of the elderly in the community. Chinese Mental Health *Journal, 16(3),* 169–171.

Fuchs, E., & Segre, J. A. (2000). Stem Cells: A New Lease on Life. *Cell, 100(1),* 143–155.

Fukutake, T., Akada, K., Ito, S., Okuda, T., Ueki, Y. (2002). Severe personality changes after unilateral left paramedian thalamic infarct. *European Neurology, 47(3),* 156–160.

Fullerton, D. (1997). A review of approaches to teenage pregnancy. *Nursing Times, 93,* 48–49.

Fulton, S., Woodside, B., & Shizgal, P. (2000). Modulation of brain reward circuitry by leptin. *Science, 287,* 125–128.

Funder, D. C. (2000). Personality. *Annual Review of Psychology, 52,* 197–221.

Funder, D. C. (2001). The really, really fundamental attribution error. *Psychological Inquiry, 12(1),* 21–23.

Fung, H. H., Lai, P., & Ng, R. (2001). Age differences in social preferences among Taiwanese and mainland Chinese: The role of perceived time. *Psychology & Aging, 16(2),* 351–356.

Furnham, A. (2001). Vocational preference and P-O fit: Reflections on Holland's theory of vocational choice. *Applied Psychology: An International Review, 50(1),* 5–29.

Furman, E. (1990, November). Plant a potato learn about life (and death). *Young Children, 46(1),* 15–20.

Furmark, T., Fischer, H., Wik, G., Larsson, M., & Fredrikson, M. (1997). The amygdala and individual differences in human fear conditioning. *Neuroreport: An International Journal for the Rapid Communication of Research in Neuroscience, 8(18),* 3957–3960.

Gabbard, G. O. (1999). Psychodynamic therapy in an age of neuroscience. *Harvard Mental Health Letter, 15(7),* 4–5.

Gable, S. L., Reis, H. T., & Downey, G. (2003). He said, she said: A quasi-signal detection analysis of daily interactions between close relationship partners. *Psychological Science, 14,* in press.

Gabrieli, J. D., Brewer, J. B., & Poldrack, R. A. (1998). Images of medial temporal lobe functions in human learning and memory. *Neurobiology of Learning & Memory, 70,* 275–283.

Gaensbauer, T. J., & Hiatt, S. (1984). Facial communication of emotion in early infancy. In N. Fox & R. Davidson (Eds.), *The psychobiology of affective development* (pp. 207–230). Hillsdale, NJ: Erlbaum.

Gaertner, S. L., Dovidio, J. F., Rust, M. C., Nier, J. A., Banker, B. S., Ward, C. M., Mottola, G. R., & Houlette, M. (1999). Reducing intergroup bias: Elements of intergroup cooperation. *Journal of Personality and Social Psychology, 76(3),* 388–402.

Gaetz, M., Weinberg, H. Rzempoluck, E., & Jantzen, K. J. (1998). Neural network classifications and correlational analysis of EEG and MEG activity accompanying spontaneous reversals of the Necker Cube. *Cognitive Brain Research, 6,* 335–346.

Gage, F. H. (2000). Mammalian neural stem cells. *Science, 287,* 1433–1438.

Gagnon, J. H. (1990). The explicit and implicit use of the scripting perspective in sex research. *Annual Review of Sex Research, 1,* 1–43.

Galinsky, A. D., & Moskowitz, G. B. (2000). Perspective-taking: Decreasing stereotype expression, stereotype accessibility, and in-group favoritism. *Journal of Personality & Social Psychology, 78(4),* 708–724.

Gallagher, A. M., De Lisi, R., Holst, P. C., McGillicuddy-De Lisi, A. V., Morely, M., Cahalan, C. (2000). Gender differences in advanced mathematical problem solving. *Journal of Experimental Child Psychology, 75(3),* 165–190.

Gallistel, C. R., & Gibbon, J. (2000). Time, rate, and conditioning. *Psychological Review, 107(2),* 289–344.

Galloway, J. L. (1999, March 8). Into the heart of darkness. *U. S. News and World Report,* pp. 25–32.

Galvan, J., Unikel, C., Rodriguez, E., Ortiz, A., Soriano, A., & Flores, J. C. (2000). General perspective of flunitracepam (Rohypnol) abuse in a sample of drug users of Mexico City. *Salud Mental, 23(1),* 1–7.

Garbarino, S., Beelke, M., Costa, G., Violani, C., Lucidi, F., & Ferrillo, F. (2002). Brain function and effects of shift work: Implications for clinical neuropharmacology. *Neuropsychobiology, 45(1),* 50–56.

Garcia, G. M., & Stafford, M. E. (2000). Prediction of reading by Ga and Gc specific cognitive abilities for low-SES White and Hispanic English-speaking children. *Psychology in the Schools, 37(3),* 227–235.

Garcia, J., Ervin, F. R., & Koelling, R. A. (1966). Learning with prolonged delay of reinforcement. *Psychonomic Science, 5(3),* 121–122.

Garcia, S. D., & Khersonsky, D. (1997). 'They are a lovely couple': Further examination of perceptions of couple attractiveness. *Journal of Social Behavior and Personality, 12,* 367–380.

Gardner, B. T., & Gardner, R. A. (1971). Two-way communication with an infant chimpanzee. In A. M. Schrier & F. Stollnitz (Eds.), *Behavior of nonhuman primates* (Vol. 4). New York: Academic Press.

Gardner, H. (1983). *Frames of mind.* New York: Basic Books.

Gardner, H. (1986). From testing intelligence to assessing competencies. A pluralistic view of intellect. *Roeper Review, 8(3),* 147–150.

Gardner, H. (1988). Creativity: An interdisciplinary perspective. *Creativity Research Journal, 1,* 8–26.

Gardner, H. (1991). *The unschooled mind: How children think & how schools should teach.* New York: Basic Books.

Gardner, H. (1998). A multipliciaty of intelligences. *Scientific American Presents Exploring Intelligence, 9,* 18–23.

Gardner, H. (1999, February). Who owns intelligence? *Atlantic Monthly,* pp. 67–76.

Gardner, R. A., & Gardner, B. T. (1969). Teaching sign language to a chimpanzee. *Science, 165,* 664–672.

Gardner, W. L., Gabriel, S., & Lee, A. Y. (1999). "I" value freedom, but "we" value relationships: Self-construal priming mirrors cultural differences in judgment. *Psychological Science, 10(4),* 321–326.

Garland, A. F., & Zigler, E. (1999). Adolescent suicide prevention: Current research and social policy implications. In L. E. Berk, *Landscapes of development* (pp. 407–426). Belmont, CA: Wadsworth.

Garnefski, N. (2000). *Journal of the American Academy of Child and Adolescent Psychiatry, 39,* 1175–1181.

Gasper, K. & Clore, G. L. (2002). Attending to the big picture: Mood and global versus local processing of visual information. *Psychological Science, 13(1),* 34–40.

Gathercole, S. E., & Pickering, S. J. (2000). Working memory deficits in children with low achievements in the national curriculum at 7 years of age. *British Journal of Educational Psychology, 70,* 177–194.

Gaudine, A. P., & Saks, A. M. (2001). Effects of an absenteeism feedback intervention on employee absence behavior. *Journal of Organizational Behavior, 22(1),* 15–29.

Gay, M-C., Philippot, P., & Luminet, O. (2002). Differential effectiveness of psychological interventions for reducing osteoarthritis pain: A comparison of Erickson hypnosis and Jacobson relaxation. *European Journal of Pain, 6,* 1–16.

Gay, P. (1983). *The bourgeois experience: Victoria to Freud. Vol. 1: Education of the senses.* New York: Oxford University Press.

Gay, P. (1999, March 29). Psychoanalyst Sigmund Freud. *Time,* 65–69.

Gay, P. (2000). *Freud for historians.* Replica Books.

Gazzaniga, M. S. (1970). *The bisected brain.* New York: Appleton-Century-Crofts.

Gazzaniga, M. S. (1995). Consciousness and the cerebral hemispheres. In M. S.

Gazzaniga, M. S. (2000). *The mind's past.* University California Press.

Geller, L. (1982). The failure of self-actualization theory: A critique of Carl Rogers and Abraham Maslow. *Journal of Humanistic Psychology, 22,* 56–73.

Gelman, R., & Shatz, M. (1978). Appropriate speech adjustments: The operation of conversational constraints on talk to two-year-olds. In M. Lewis & L. A. Rosenblum (Eds.), *Interaction, conversation, and the development of language* (pp. 27–61). New York: Wiley.

Gelman, S. (1999). *Schizophrenia and medication: A history.* New York: Rutgers University Press.

Gemignani, A., Santarcangelo, E., Sebastiani, L., Marchese, C., Mammoliti, R., Simoni, A., & Ghelarducci, B. (2000). Changes in autonomic and EEG patterns induced by hypnotic imagination of aversive stimuli in man. *Brain Research Bulletin, 53(1),* 105–111.

George, M. S., Sackeim, H. A., Rush, A. J., Marangell, L. B., Nahas, Z., Husain, M. M., Lisanby, S., Burt, T., Goldman, J., & Ballenger, J. C. (2000). Vagus nerve stimulation: A new tool for brain research and therapy. *Biological Psychiatry, 47(4),* 287–295.

Gershon, E. S. et al., (1998). Closing in on genes for manic-depressive illness and schizophrenia. *Neuropsychopharmacology, 18,* 233–242.

Gershon, E. S., & Rieder, R. O. (1993). Major disorders of mind and brain. Mind and brain: *Readings from Scientific American magazine* (pp. 91–100). New York, NY: Freeman.

Geschwind, N. (1979). Specialization of the human brain. *Scientific American, 241,* 180–199.

Gianakos, I. (2000). Gender roles and coping with work stress. *Sex Roles, 42,* 1059–1079.

Giancola, P. R. (2000). Temperament and antisocial behavior in preadolescent boys with or without a family history of a substance use disorder. *Psychology of Addictive Behaviors, 14(1),* 56–68.

Gibbs, N. (1995, October 2). The EQ factor. *Time,* pp. 60–68.

Gibbs, N. (1999, May 3). Crime: The Littleton massacre. *Time,* 20–36.

Gibbs, W. W. (1995). Seeking the criminal element. *Scientific American,* pp. 100–107.

Gibson, E. J., & Walk, R. D. (1960). The visual cliff. *Scientific American, 202(2),* 67–71.

Gifford, R., & Hine, D. W. (1997). "I'm cooperative, but you're greedy": Some cognitive tendencies in a commons dilemma. *Canadian Journal of Behavioural Science, 29(4),* 257–265.

Gilbert, D.T., & Ebert, J. E. J. (2002). Decisions and revisions: The affective forecasting of changeable outcomes. *Journal of Personality & Social Psychology, 82(4),* 503–514.

Gilligan, C. (1977). In a different voice: Women's conception of morality. *Harvard Educational Review, 47(4),* 481–517.

Gilligan, C. (1990). Teaching Shakespeare's sister. In C. Gilligan, N. Lyons, & T. Hanmer (Eds.), *Mapping the moral domain* (pp. 73–86). Cambridge, MA: Harvard University Press.

Gilligan, C. (1993). Adolescent development reconsidered. In A. Garrod (Ed.), *Approaches to moral development: New research and emerging themes.* New York: Teachers College Press.

Gilligan, C., & Attanucci, J. (1988). Two moral orientations. In C. Gilligan, J. V. Ward, et al. (Eds.), *Mapping the moral domain: A contribution of women's thinking to psychological theory and education,* (pp. 73–86). Cambridge, MA: Harvard University Press.

Gilligan, J. (2000). *Violence: Reflections on a Western epidemic.* London: Jessica Kingsley.

Gilmour, D. R., & Walkey, F. H. (1981). Identifying violent offenders using a video measure of interpersonal distance. *Journal of Consulting and Clinical Psychology, 49,* 287–291.

Ginty, D. D., Kornhauser, J. M., Thompson, M. A., Bading, H., Mayo, K. E., Takahashi, J. S., & Greenberg, M. E. (1993). Regulation of CREB phosphorylation in the suprachiasmatic nucleus by light and a circadian clock. *Science, 260,* 238–241.

Giovagnoli, A. R. (2001). Relation of sorting impairment to hippocampal damage in temporal lobe epilepsy. *Neuropsychologia, 39(2),* 140–150.

Giros, B., Jaber, M., Jones, S. R., Wightman, R. M., & Caron, M. G. (1996). Hyperlocomotion and indifference to cocaine and amphetamine in mice lacking the dopamine transporter. *Nature, 379,* 606–612.

Gitau, R., Modi, N., Gianakoulopoulos, X., Bond, C., Glover, V., & Stevenson, J. (2002). Acute effects of maternal skin-to-skin contact and massage on saliva cortisol in preterm babies. *Journal of Reproductive & Infant Psychology, 20(2),* 83–88.

Glassman, A. H., & Shapiro, P. A. (1998). Depression and the course of coronary artery disease. *American Journal of Psychiatry, 155,* 4–11.

Glassman, R. B. (1999). A working memory "theory or relativity": Elasticity in temporal, spatial, and modality dimensions conserves item capacity in radial maze, verbal tasks and other cognition. *Brain Research Bulletin, 48,* 475–489.

Gleaves, D. H. (1996). The sociocognitive model of dissociative identity disorder: A reexamination of the evidence. *Psychological Bulletin, 120,* 42–59.

Gluck, M. A., & Myers, C. E. (1997). Psychobiological models of hippocampal function in learning and memory. *Annual Review of Psychology, 48,* 481–514.

Gobert, F. (1998). Expert memory: A comparison of four theories. *Cognition, 66,* 115–152.

God, M. A., & Friedman, B., (2000). Cadet basic training: An ethnographic study of stress and coping. *Military Science, 165,* 147–152.

Goddard, A. W., et al. (1996). Plasma levels of gamma-aminobutyric acid and panic disorder. *Psychiatry Research, 63,* 223–225.

Godden, D. R., & Baddeley, A. D. (1975). Context-dependent memory in two natural environments: On land and underwater. *British Journal of Psychology, 66,* 325–331.

Goebel, M. U., & Mills, P. J. (2000). Acute psychological stress and exercise and changes in peripheral leukocyte adhesion molecule expression and density. *Psychosomatic Medicine, 62(5),* 664–670.

Gold, M. A., & Friedman, S. B. (2000). Cadet basic training: An ethnographic study of stress and coping. *Military Medicine, 165(2),* 147–152.

Gold, P. E., Cahill, L., & Wenk, G. L. (2002). Ginkgo Biloba: A cognitive enhancer? *Psychological Science in the Public Interest, 3(1),* 2–11.

Goldberg, S. (2000). *Attachment and development.* New York: Edward Arnold.

Goldberger, L., & Breznitz, S. (1993). *Handbook of stress.* New York: Free Press.

Golden, G., & Lemonick, M. D. (2000, July 3). The race is over. *Time,* pp. 18–23.

Goldman, J., Nahas, Z., & George, M. S. (2000). What is transcranial magnetic stimulation? *Harvard Mental Health Letter, 17(5),* 8.

Goldstein, B. (1976). *Introduction to human sexuality.* New York: McGraw-Hill.

Goleman, D. P. (2000). *Working with emotional intelligence.* New York: Bantam Doubleday.

Goleman, D. (1980, February). 1,528 little geniuses and how they grew. *Psychology Today,* pp. 28–53.

Goleman, D. (1995). *Emotional intelligence: Why it can matter more than IQ.* New York: Bantam.

Goleman, D. (1995, December 5). Making room on the couch for culture. *New York Times,* C1–C3, C4.

Golombok, S., & Tasker, F. (1996). Do parents influence the sexual orientation of their children? Findings from a longitudinal study of lesbian families. *Developmental Psychology, 32,* 3–11.

Golub, A., Johnson, B. D., Sifaneck, S. J., Chesluk, B., & Parker, H. (2001). Is the U.S. experiencing an incipient epidemic of hallucinogen use? *Substance Use & Misuse, 36(12),* 1699–1729.

Gong, J., Chen, F., Jiang, Z., Chen, M., & Guo, X. (2000). 1 /Investigation of goiter incidence and intelligence level in children in light-iodine-deficient areas. *Chinese Journal of Clinical Psychology, 8(2),* 107–108, 110.

Gonzales, P. M., Blanton, H., & Williams, K. J. (2002). The effects of stereotype threat and double-minority status on the test performance of Latino women. *Personality & Social Psychology Bulletin, 28*(5), 659–670.

Gonzalez, A. R., Holbein, M. F. D., & Quilter, S. (2002). High school students' goal orientations and their relationship to perceived parenting styles. *Contemporary Educational Psychology, 27*(3), 450–470.

Goodall, J. (1990). *Through a window: My thirty years with the chimpanzees of Gombe.* Boston: Houghton-Mifflin.

Goodall, J. (1971). *Tiwi wives.* Seattle, WA: University of Washington Press.

Goode, E. E., Schrof, J. M., & Burke, S. (1991, June 24). Where emotions come from. *U. S. News and World Report,* pp. 54–60.

Goodman, G. S., Ghetti, S., Quas, J. A., Edelstein, R. S., Alexander, K. W., Redlich, A. D., Cordon, I. M., & Jones, D. P. H. (2003). A prospective study of memory for child sexual abuse: New findings relevant to the repressed-memory controversy. *Psychological Science, 14,* in press.

Goodwin, D. W. (2000). *Alcoholism: The facts.* London: Oxford University Press.

Goodwin, F. K., & Ghaemi, S. N. (1998). Understanding manic-depressive illness. *Archives of General Psychiatry, 55,* 23–25.

Gordon, T. (1975). *Parent effectiveness training.* New York: Plume.

Gordon, W. C. (1989). *Learning and memory.* Pacific Grove, CA: Brooks/Cole.

Gorman, C. (2001, February 5). Repairing the damage. *Time,* 53–58.

Gorman, J. (2000). Neuroanatomical hypothesis of panic disorder revised. *American Journal of Psychiatry, 57,* 493–505.

Gosling, S. D. (1998). Personality dimensions in spotted hyenas (Crocuta crocuta). *Journal of Comparative Psychology, 112,* 107–118.

Gosling, S. D., & John, O. P. (1999). Personality dimensions in nonhuman animals: A cross-species review. *Current Directions in Psychological Science, 8*(3), 69–75.

Gotlieb, I. H., & Abramson, L. Y. (1999). Attributional theories of emotion. In T. Dalgleish & M. Power (Eds.), *Handbook of cognition and emotion.* New York: Wiley.

Gottesman, I. I. (1991). *Schizophrenia genesis: The origins of madness.* New York: Freeman.

Gottlieb, G. (2000). Environmental and behavioral influences on gene activity. *Current Directions in Psychological Science, 9*(3), 93–97.

Gottman, J. M. (1998). Psychology and the study of marital processes. *Annual Review of Psychology, 49,* 169–197.

Gottman, J. M., & Levenson, R. W. (1999). What predicts change in marital interaction over time? A study of alternative models. *Family Process, 38,* 143–158.

Gottman, J. M., & Levenson, R. W. (2002). A two-factor model for predicting when a couple will divorce: Exploratory analyses using 14–year longitudinal data. *Family Process, 41*(1), 83–96.

Gottman, J. M., & Notarius, C. I. (2000). Decade review: Observing marital interaction. *Journal of Marriage & the Family, 62*(4), 927–947.

Gottman, J. M., Coan, J., Carrere, S., & Swanson, C. (1998). Predicting happiness and stability from newlywed interactions. *Journal of Marriage and the Family, 60,* 42–48.

Gould, E., Reeves, A. J., Graziano, M. S., & Gross, C. G. (1999). Neurogenesis in the neocortex of adult primates. *Science, 286,* 548–552.

Gould, E., Tanapat, P., Hastings, N. B., & Shors, T. J. (1999). Neurogenesis in adulthood: a possible role in learning. *Trends in Cognitive Science, 3*(5), 186–1992.

Gould, R. L. (1975, August). Adult life stages: Growth toward self-tolerance. *Psychology Today,* pp. 74–78.

Graham, J. R. (1991). Comments on Duckworth's review of the Minnesota Multiphasic Personality Inventory-2. *Journal of Counseling and Development, 69,* 570–571.

Grant, S., et al. (1996). Activation of memory circuits during the cue-elicited cocaine craving. *Proceedings of the National Academy of Sciences, 93,* 12040.

Gray, J. D., & Silver, R. C. (1990). Opposite sides of the same coin: Former spouses' divergent perspectives in coping with their divorce. *Journal of Personality & Social Psychology, 59*(6), 1180–1191.

Greeff, A. P., & Malherbe, H. L. (2001). Intimacy and marital satisfaction in spouses. *Journal of Sex & Marital Therapy, 27*(3), 247–257.

Green, A. I. (2000). What is the relationship between schizophrenia and substance abuse? *Harvard Mental Health Letter, 17*(4), 8.

Green, D. P., Glaser, J., Rich, A. (1998). From lynching to gay bashing: The elusive connection between economic conditions and hate crime. *Journal of Personality and Social Psychology, 75,* 82–92.

Green, J. T., & Woodruff-Pak, D. S. (2000). Eyeblink classical conditioning: Hippocampal formation is for neutral stimulus associations as cerebellum is for association-response. *Psychological Bulletin, 126*(1), 138–158.

Green, J. W. (1999). *Cultural awareness in the human services: A multi-ethnic approach.* Needham Heights, MA: Allyn & Bacon.

Green, J.D., Sommerville, R.B., Nystrom, L.E., Darley, J.M., & Cohen, J.D. (2001). An fMRI investigation of emotional engagement in moral judgment. *Science, 293,* 2105–2108.

Greenberg, J., Pyszcynski, T., Solomon, S., Pinel, E., et al., (1993). Effects of self-esteem on vulnerability-denying defensive distortions: Further evidence of an anxiety-buffering function of self-esteem. *Journal of Experimental Social Psychology, 29*(3), 229–251.

Greene, K., Kremar, M., Walters, L. H., Rubin, D. L., Hale, J., & Hale, L. (2000). Targeting adolescent risk-taking behaviors: The contributions of egocentrism and sensation-seeking. *Journal of Adolescence, 23,* 439–461.

Greenfield, P. M. (1984). A theory of the teacher in the learning activities of everyday life. In B. Rogoff & J. Lave (Eds.), *Everyday Cognition* (pp. 117–138). Cambridge, MA: Harvard University Press.

Greenfield, P. M. (1994). *Cross-cultural roots of minority child development.* Hillsdale, NJ: Erlbaum.

Greenfield, P. M. (1997). You can't take it with you: Why ability assessments don't cross cultures. *American Psychologist, 52,* 1115–1124.

Greenfield, P. M. (2000). Three approaches to the psychology of culture: Where do they come from? Where can they go? *Asian Journal of Social Psychology, 3*(33), 223–240.

Greenfield, P. M., Maynard, A., E., & Childs, C. P. (2000). History, culture, learning, and development. Cross-Cultural Research: *The Journal of Comparative Social Science, 34*(4), 351–374.

Greeno, C. G., Wing, R. R., & Shiffman, S. (2000). Binge antecedents in obese women with and without binge eating disorder. *Journal of Consulting & Clinical Psychology, 68*(1), 95–102.

Greenwald, A. G., & Banaji, M. R. (1995). Implicit social cognition: Attitudes, self-esteem, and stereotypes. *Psychological Review, 102,* 4–27.

Gregory, R. L. (1969). Apparatus for investigating visual perception. *American Psychologist, 24*(3), 219–225.

Griffeth, R. W., & Gaertner, S. (2001). A role for equity theory in the turnover process: An empirical test. *Journal of Applied Social Psychology, 31*(5), 1017–1037.

Griffith, M. A., & Dubow, E. F., & Ippolito, M. F. (2000). Developmental and cross-situational differences in adolescents' coping strategies. *Journal of Youth and Adolescence, 29,* 183–204.

Griffiths, A. W. (1971). Prisoners of XYY constitution: Psychological aspects. *British Journal of Psychiatry, 119,* 193–194.

Grigorenko (Eds.), Intelligence, heredity, and environment. New York: Cambridge University Press.

Grigorenko, E. L., Jarvin, L., & Sternberg, R. J. (2002). School-based tests of the triarchic theory of intelligence: Three settings, three samples, three syllabi. *Contemporary Educational Psychology, 27(2),* 167–208.

Grisaru, N., Bruno, R., & Pridmore, S. (2001). Effect on the emotions of healthy individuals of slow repetitive transcranial magnetic stimulation applied to the prefrontal cortex. *Journal of ECT, 17(3),* 184–189.

Grodzinsky, Y. (2000). The neurology of syntax: Language use without Broca's area. *Behavioral & Brain Sciences, 23*(1), 1–71.

Grossi, G., Perski, A., Lundberg, U., & Soares, J. (2001). Associations between financial strain and the diurnal salivary cortisol secretion of long-term unemployed individuals. *Integrative Physiological & Behavioral Science, 36(3),* 205–219.

Grossmann, K., Grossmann, K. E., Fremmer-Bombik, E., Kindler, H., Scheuerer-Englisch, H., & Zimmermann, P. (2002). The uniqueness of the child-father attachment relationship: Fathers' sensitive and challenging play as a pivotal variable in a 16–year longitudinal study. *Social Development, 11(3),* 307–331.

Groth-Marnat, G. (1990). *Handbook of psychological assessment* (2nd ed.). New York: Wiley.

Grove, W. M., Barden, R. C., Garb, H. N., & Lilienfeld, S. O. (2002). Failure of Rorschach-Comprehensive-System-based testimony to be admissible under the Daubert-Joiner-Kumho standard. *Psychology, Public Policy, & Law, 8(2),* 216–234.

Growe, R., Schmersahl, K., Perry, R., & Henry, R. (2002). A knowledge base for cultural diversity in administrator teaching. *Journal of Instructional Psychology, 29(3),* 205–212.

Gruber, E., & Machamer, A. M. (2000). Risk of school failure as an early indicator of other health risk behaviour in American high school students. *Health, Risk & Society, 2*(1), 59–68.

Grunberg, L., Moore, S., Anderson-Connolly, R., & Greenberg, E. (1999). Work stress and self-reported alcohol use: The moderating role of escapist reasons for drinking. *Journal of Occupational Health Psychology, 4,* 29–36.

Guadagno, R. E., & Cialdini, R. B. (2002). Online persuasion: An examination of gender differences in computer-mediated interpersonal influence. *Group Dynamics, 6(1),* 38–51.

Guarnaccia, P. J., & Rogler, L. H. (1999). Research on culture-bound syndromes:

New directions. *American Journal of Psychiatry, 156*(9), 1322–1327.

Guastello, S. J., Guastello, D. D., & Craft, L. L. (1989). Assessment of the Barnum effect in computer-based test interpretations. *Journal of Psychology, 123,* 477–484.

Guidelines for the treatment of animals in behavioural research and teaching. (2000). *Animal Behaviour, 59* (1), 253–257.

Guidelines for the treatment of animals in behavioural research and teaching (2002). *Animal Behaviour, 63(1),* 195–199.

Guilford, J. P. (1967). *The nature of human intelligence.* New York: McGraw-Hill.

Guimond, S., & Dambrum, M. (2002). When prosperity breeds intergroup hostility: The effects of relative deprivation and relative gratification on prejudice. *Personality & Social Psychology Bulletin, 28(7),* 900–912.

Guinard, J., et al. (1996). Does consumption of beer, alcohol, and bitter substances affect bitterness perception? *Physiology & Behavior, 49,* 625–631.

Gump, L. S., Baker, R. C., & Roll, S. (2000). Cultural and gender differences in moral judgment: A study of Mexican Americans and Anglo-Americans. *Hispanic Journal of Behavioral Sciences, 22(1),* 78–93.

Gunnar, M. R., & Donzella, B. (2002). Social regulation of the cortisol levels in early human development. *Psychoneuroendocrinology, 27(1–2),* 199–220.

Gur, R., Mozley, L., Mozley, P., Resnick, S., Karp, J., Alavi, A., Arnold, S., & Gur, R. (1995). Sex differences in regional cerebral glucose metabolism during a resting state. *Science, 267,* 528–531.

Gurevich, E. V., Bordelon, Y., Shapiro, R. M., Arnold, S. E., Gur, R. E., & Joyce, J. N. (1997). Mesolimbic dopamine D3 receptors and use of antipsychotics in patients with schizophrenia. *Archives of General Psychiatry, 54,* 225–232.

Gustavson, C. R., & Garcia, J. (1974, August). Pulling a gag on the wily coyote. *Psychology Today,* pp. 68–72.

Gustavson, C. R., Kelly, D. J., Sweeney, M., & Garcia, J. (1976). Prey-lithium aversions: I. Coyotes and wolves. *Behavioral Biology, 17,* 61–72.

Guthrie, R. V. (1998). *Even the rat was white.* Boston: Allyn & Bacon.

Gutkin, J. (1989). A study of "flashbulb" memories for the moment of the explosion of the space shuttle Challenger. *Unpublished manuscript,* Emory University, Atlanta.

Gwinnell, E. (2001). Risk factors for the development of Internet adultery. *Journal of Sex Education & Therapy, 26,* 45–49.

Haddad, Y. (2001). The role of negative attributional style and depression in predicting academic performance of males and

females after receiving unacceptable grades. *Dirasat: Educational Sciences, 28(1),* 209–228.

Haerenstam, A., Theorell, T., & Kaijser, L. (2000). Coping with anger-provoking situations, psychosocial working conditions, and ECG-detected signs of coronary heart disease. *Journal of Occupational Health Psychology, 5*(1), 191–203.

Hagarty, P. (1997). Materializing the hypothalamus: A performative account of the "gay brain." *Feminism & Psychology, 7,* 355–372.

Hagerty, M. R. (2000). Social comparisons of income in one's community: Evidence from national surveys of income and happiness. *Journal of Personality & Social Psychology, 78(4),* 764–771.

Hagerty, M. R. (2000). Social comparisons of income in one's community: Evidence from national surveys of income and happiness. *Journal of Personality & Social Psychology, 78(4),* 764–771.

Hahn, H., Trant, M. R., Brownstein, M. J., Harper, R. A., Milstien, S., & Butler, I. J. (2001). Neurologic and psychiatric manifestations in a family with a mutation in exon 2 of the guanosine triphosphate-cyclohydrolase gene. *Archives of Neurology, (5),* 749–755.

Haidt, J. (2001). The emotional dog and its rational tail: A social intuitionist approach to moral judgment. *Psychological Review, 108,* 814–834.

Haier, R. J. (1993). Cerebral glucose metabolism and intelligence. In P. A. Vernon (Ed.), *Biological approaches to the study of human intelligence.* Norwood, NJ: Ablex.

Haier, R. J., Chueh, D., Touchette, P., Lott, I., Buchsbaum, M. S., MacMillan, D., Sandman, C., LaCasse, L., & Sosa, E. (1995). Brain size and cerebral glucose metabolic rate in non-specific mental retardation and Down Syndrome. *Intelligence, 20,* 191–210.

Haith, M. M., & Benson, J. B. (1998). Infant cognition. In W. Damon & R. M. Lerner (Eds.), Handbook of child psychology (Vol. 1). New York: John Wiley & Sons.

Halford, J. C. G., & Blundell, J. E. (2000). Separate systems for serotonin and leptin in appetite control. *Annals of Medicine, 32(3),* 222–232.

Hall, C. S., & Van de Castle, R. L. (1966). *The content analysis of dreams.* New York: Appleton-Century-Crofts.

Hall, C., Domhoff, G. W., Blick, K. A., & Weesner, K. E. (1982). The dreams of college men and women in the 1950 and 1980: A comparison of dream contents and sex differences. *Sleep, 5,* 188–194.

Hall, E. T. (1966). *The hidden dimension.* New York: Doubleday.

Hall, E. T. (1983, June). A conversation with Erik Erikson. *Psychology Today*, pp. 22–30.

Hall, W. G., Arnold, H. M., & Myers, K. P. (2000). The acquisition of an appetite. *Psychological Science, 11*(2), 101–105.

Hall, W. G., Moore, A., & Myers, K. P. (2000). The acquisition of an appetite. *Psychological Science, 11*(2), 101–105.

Halpern, D. F. (1997). Sex differences in intelligence: Implications for education. *American Psychologist, 52*, 1091–1102.

Halpern, D. F. (1998). Teaching critical thinking for transfer across domains. *American Psychologist, 53*, 449–455.

Halpern, D. F. (2000). *Sex differences in cognitive abilities.* Hillsdale, NJ: Erlbaum.

Hamer, D. H., & Copeland, P. (1999). *Living with our genes: Why they matter more than you think.*

Hamid, P. N., & Chan, W. T. (1998). Locus of control and occupational stress in Chinese professionals. *Psychological Reports, 82*, 75–79.

Hamilton, V. L. (1978). Obedience and responsibility: A jury simulation. *Journal of Personality and Social Psychology, 36*, 126–146.

Hammer, R. P., Egilmez, Y., & Emmett-Oglesby, M. W. (1997). Neural mechanisms of tolerance to the effects of cocaine. *Behavioural Brain Research, 84*, 225–239.

Haney, C., Banks, C., & Zimbardo, P. (1978). Interpersonal dynamics in a stimulated prison. *International Journal of Criminology and Penology, 1*, 69–97.

Hanna, S. M., & Brown, J. H. (1999). *The practice of family therapy: Key elements across models* (2nd ed.). Belmont, CA: Brooks/Cole.

Hans, T. A. (2000). A meta-analysis of the effects of adventure programming on locus of control. *Journal of Contemporary Psychotherapy, 30*(1), 33–60.

Hanson, G., Venturelli, P. J., & Fleckenstein, A. E. (2002). *Drugs and society* (7th ed.). New York: Jones & Bartlett.

Hardy, J. B., & Zabin, L. S. (1991). *Adolescent pregnancy in an urban environment: Issues, programs, and evaluation.* Baltimore: Urban and Schwarzenberg.

Hare, R. D. (1993). *Without conscience: The disturbing world of the psychopaths among us.* New York: Pocket Books.

Harker, L., & Keltner, D. (2001). Expressions of positive emotion in women's college yearbook pictures and their relationship to personality and life outcomes across adulthood. *Journal of Personality & Social Psychology. Jan80*(1), 112–124.

Harkness, S., & Super, C. M. (1996). *Parents' cultural belief systems: Their origins, expressions, and consequences.* New York: Guilford Press.

Harley, K., & Reese, E. (1999). Origins of autobiographical memory. *Developmental Psychology, 35*, 1338–1348.

Harlow, H. F., & Harlow, M. K. (1966). Learning to love. *American Scientist, 54*, 244–272.

Harlow, H. F., & Zimmerman, R. R. (1959). Affectional responses in the infant monkey. *Science, 130*, 421–432.

Harlow, H. F., Harlow, M. K., & Meyer, D. R. (1950). Learning motivated by a manipulation drive. *Journal of Experimental Psychology, 40*, 228–234.

Harlow, J. M. (1848). Passage of an iron rod through the head. *Boston Medical and Surgical Journal, 39*, 389–393.

Harlow, J. (1868). Recovery from the passage of an iron bar through the head. *Publications of the Massachusetts Medical Society, 2*, 237–246.

Harmon, R. J., Bender, B. G., Linden, M. G., & Robinson, A. (1998). Transition from adolescence to early adulthood: Adaptation and psychiatric status of women with 47, XXX. *Journal of the American Academy of Child & Adolescent Psychiatry, 37*, 286–291.

Harmon-Jones, E. (2000). Cognitive dissonance and experienced negative affect: Evidence that dissonance increases experienced negative affect even in the absence of aversive consequences. *Personality & Social Psychology Bulletin, 26*(12), 1490–1501.

Harris, A. C. (1996). African American and Anglo American gender identities: An empirical study. *Journal of Black Psychology, 22*, 182–194.

Harris, J. C. (1995). *Developmental neuropsychiatry Vol. 1.* New York: Oxford University Press.

Harris, R., & Harris, C. (2000). *20–minute retreats.* Thousand Oaks, CA: Owl books.

Harrison, L., & Gardiner, E. (1999). Do the rich really die young? Alcohol-related mortality and social class in Great Britain, 1988–94. *Addiction, 94*(12), 1871–1880.

Hartup, W. W., & van Lieshout, C. F. M. (1995). Personality development in social context. In J. T. Spence, J. M. Darley, & D. J. Foss (Eds.), *Annual review of psychology, 46*, 655–687.

Harvey, A. G., & McGuire, B.E. (2000). Suppressing and attending to pain-related thoughts in chronic pain patients. *Behaviour Research & Therapy, 38*(11), 1117–1124.

Harvey, L., Inglis, S. J., & Espie, C. A. (2002). Insomniacs' reported use of CBT components and relationship to long-term clinical outcome. *Behaviour Research & Therapy, 40*(1), 75–83.

Harvey, M. G., & Miceli, N. (1999). Antisocial behavior and the continuing itragedy of the commons. *Journal of Applied Social Psychology, 29*, 109–138.

Haselton, M. G., & Buss, D. M. (2001). The affective shift hypothesis: The functions of emotional changes following sexual intercourse. *Personal Relationships, 8*(4), 357–369.

Hashizume, Y. (2000). Gender issues and Japanese family-centered caregiving for frail elderly parents or parents-in-law in modern Japan: From the sociocultural and historical perspectives. *Public Health Nursing, 17*(1), 25–31.

Hatfield, E., & Rapson, R. L. (1996). *Love and Sex: Cross-cultural perspectives.* Needham Heights, MA: Allyn & Bacon.

Hay, D. F. (1994). Prosocial development. *Journal of Child Psychology and Psychiatry, 35*, 29–71.

Hayashi, S., Kuno, T., Morotomi, Y., Osawa, M., Shimizu, M., & Suetake, Y. (1998). Client-centered therapy in Japan: Fujio Tomoda and taoism. *Journal of Humanistic Psychology, 38*, 103–124.

Hayflick, L. (1977). The cellular basis for biological aging. In C. E. Finch & L. Hayflick (Eds.), *Handbook of the biology of aging* (pp. 159–186). New York: Van Nostrand Reinhold.

Hayflick, L. (1996). *How and why we age.* New York: Ballantine Books.

Hayne, H., Boniface, J., & Barr, R. (2000). The development of declarative memory in human infants: Age-related changes in deferred imitation. *Behavioral Neuroscience, 114*(1), 77–83.

Hayward, M. D., Friedman, S., & Chen, H. (1998). Career trajectories and older men's retirement. *Journal of Gerontology: Social Sciences, 53*, S91–S103.

Hazan, C., & Shaver, P. R. (1994). Attachment as an organizational framework for research on close relationships. *Psychological Inquiry, 5*, 1–22.

Hazan, C., & Shaver, P. (1987). Romantic love conceptualized as an attachment process. *Journal of Personality and Social Psychology, 52*, 511–524.

Hazan, C., & Zeifman, D. (1994). Sex and the psychological tether. In K. Bartholomew & D. Perlman (Eds.), *Attachment processes in adulthood. Advances in personal relationships* (Vol. 5) (pp. 151–178). London: Jessica Kingsley.

Hazlett, E. A., Buchbaum, M. S., Byne, W., Wei, T-C., Spiegel-Cohen, J., Geneve, C., Kinderlehrer, R., Haznedar, M. M., Shihabuddin, L., & Siever, L. J. (1999). Three-dimensional analysis with MRI and PET of the size, shape, and function of the thalamus in the schizophrenia spectrum. *American Journal of Psychiatry, 156*(8), 1190–1199.

Healy, A. F., & McNamara, D. S. (1996). Verbal learning and memory: Does the modal model still work? *Annual Review of Psychology, 47,* 143–172.

Heaton, T. B. (2002). Factors contributing to increasing marital stability in the US. *Journal of Family Issues, 23(3),* 392–409.

Hebb, D. O. (1949). *The organization of behavior.* New York: Wiley.

Hebb, D. O. (1955). Drive and the CNS (central nervous system). *Psychological Review, 62,* 243–254.

Hebb, D. O. (1966). *A textbook of psychology* (2nd ed.) Philadelphia: Saunders.

Heckers, S., Weiss, A. P., Alpert, N. M., & Schacter, D. L. (2002). Hippocampal and brain stem activation during word retrieval after repeated and semantic encoding.

Heffelfinger, A. K., & Newcomer, J. W. (2001). Glucocorticoid effects on memory function over the human life span. *Development & Psychopathology, 13(3),* 491–513.

Hehir, T. (2002). Eliminating ableism in education. *Harvard Educational Review, 72(1),* 1–32.

Heider, F. (1958). *The psychology of interpersonal relations.* New York: Wiley.

Heimann, M., & Meltzoff, A. N. (1996). Deferred imitation in 9- and 14-month-old infants. *British Journal of Developmental Psychology, 14,* 55–64.

Heine, S. J., & Lehman, D. R. (1997). Culture, dissonance, and self-affirmation. *Personality and Social Psychology Bulletin, 23,* 389–400.

Heine, S. J., & Renshaw, K. (2002).Interjudge agreement, self-enhancement, and liking: Cross-cultural divergences. *Personality & Social Psychology Bulletin, 28(5),* 578–587.

Hejmadi, S., Davidson, R. J., & Rozin, P. (2000). Exploring Hindu Indian emotion expressions: Evidence for accurate recognition by Americans and Indians. *Psychological Science, 11,* 183–187.

Helms, J. E. (1992). Why is there no study of cultural equivalence in standardized cognitive ability testing? *American Psychologist, 47,* 1083–1101.

Helms, J. E., & Cook, D. A. (1999). *Using race and culture in counseling and psychotherapy: Theory and process.* Boston: Allyn & Bacon.

Henderlong, J., & Lepper, M. R. (2002). The effects of praise on children's intrinsic motivation: A review and synthesis. *Psychological Bulletin, 128(5),* 774–795.

Henke, P. G. (1992). Stomach pathology and the amygdala. In J. P. Aggleton (Ed), *The amygdala: Neurobiological aspects of emotion, memory, and mental dysfunction* (pp. 323–338). New York: Wiley.

Hennessey, B. A., & Amabile, T. M. (1998). Reward, intrinsic motivation, and creativity. *American Psychologist, 53,* 674–675.

Hennevin, E., Hars, B., Maho, C., & Bloch, V. (1995). Processing of learned information in paradoxical sleep: Relevance for memory. *Behavioral Brain Research, 69,* 125–135.

Henrich, J., & Boyd, R. (1998). The evolution of conformist transmission and the emergence of between group differences. *Evolution and Human Behavior, 19,* 215–241.

Hensch, T. K., & Stryker, M. P. (1996). Ocular dominance plasticity under metabotropic glutamate receptor blockade. *Science, 272,* 554–557.

Henshaw, S. K. (1998). Unintended pregnancy in the United States. *Family Planning Perspectives, 30,* 24–29, 46.

Henslin, J. M. (2003). *Sociology: A down-to-earth approach.* Boston: Allyn & Bacon.

Herbst, J. H., Zonderman, A. B., McCrae, R. R., & Costa, P. T., Jr. (2000). Do the dimensions of the Temperament and Character Inventory map a simple genetic architecture? Evidence from molecular genetics and factor analysis. *American Journal of Psychiatry, 157(8),* 1285–1290.

Herdt, G. H. (1981). *Guardians of the flutes: Idioms of masculinity.* New York: McGraw-Hill.

Herek, G. (2000). The psychology of prejudice. *Current Directions in Psychological Science, 9(1),* 19–22.

Herkenham, M. (1992). Cannabinoid receptor localization in brain: Relationship to motor and reward systems. *Annals of the New York Academy of Sciences, 654,* 19–32.

Herman, B. H., & O'Brien, C. P. (1997). Clinical medications development for opiate addiction: Focus on nonopiods and opiod antagonists for the amelioration of opiate withdrawal symptoms and relapse prevention. *Seminars in Neuroscience, 9,* 158.

Herman, L. M., Richards, D. G., & Woltz, J. P. (1984). Comprehension of sentences by bottlenosed dolphins. *Cognition, 16,* 129–139.

Herman, S. M. (1998). The relationship between therapist-client modality similarity and psychotherapy outcome. *Journal of Psychotherapy Practice and Research, 7,* 56–64.

Hermelin, E., & Robertson, I. T. (2001). A critique and standardization of meta-analytic validity coefficients in personnel selection. *Journal of Occupational & Organizational Psychology, 74(3),* 253–277.

Herrnstein, R. J., & Murray, C. (1994). *The bell curve: Intelligence and class structure in American life.* New York: Free Press.

Herz, R. S., & Inzlicht, M. (2002). Sex differences in response to physical and social factors involved in human mate selection: The importance of smell for women. *Evolution & Human Behavior, 23(5),* 359–364.

Hetherington, E. M., & Stanley-Hagan, M. (2000). Diversity among stepfamilies. In D. H. Demo, K. R. Allen, et al. (Eds.), *Handbook of family diversity.* (pp. 173–196).New York: Oxford University Press.

Hetherington, E. M., & Stanley-Hagan, M. (1999). The adjustment of children with divorced parents: A risk and resiliency perspective. *Journal of Child Psychology & Psychiatry & Allied Disciplines, 40(1),* 129–140.

Hetherington, E. M., Bridges, M., & Insabella, G. M. (1998). What matters? What does not?: Five perspectives on the association between marital transitions and children's adjustment. *American Psychologist, 53(2),* 167–184.

Hettema, J. M., Neale, M. C., & Kendler, K. S. (2001). A review and meta-analysis of the genetic epidemiology of anxiety disorders. *American Journal of Psychiatry, 158(10),* 1568–1578.

Hewitt, P. L., Coren, S., & Steel, G. D. (2001). Death from anorexia nervosa: Age span and sex differences. *Aging & Mental Health, 5(1),* 41–46.

Hewlett, B. S. (1992). Introduction. In B. S. Hewlett (Ed.), *Father-child relations: Cultural and biosocial contexts.* New York: Aldine de Gruyter.

Higgins, E. T. (1997). Beyond pleasure and pain. *American Psychologist, 52,* 1280–1300.

Higgins, N. C., & Bhatt, G. (2001). Culture moderates the self-serving bias: Etic and emic features of casual attributions in India and in Canada. *Social Behavior & Personality, 29(1),* 49–61.

Hikosaka, O., Miyashita, K., Miyachi, S., Sakai, K., & Lu, X. (1998). Differential roles of the forntal cortex, basal ganglia, and cerebellum in visuomotor sequence learning. *Neurobiology of Learning & Memory, 70,* 137–149.

Hilgard, E. R. (1978). Hypnosis and consciousness. *Human Nature, 1,* 42–51.

Hilgard, E. R. (1986). *Divided consciousness: Multiple controls in human thought and action* (expanded ed.). New York: Wiley-Interscience.

Hilgard, E. R. (1992). Divided consciousness and dissociation. *Consciousness and Cognition, 1,* 16–31.

Hilton, J. L., & von Hippel, W. (1996). Stereotypes. In J. T. Spence, J. M. Darley, & D. J. Foss (Eds.), *Annual Review of Psychology, 47* (pp. 237–271). Palo Alto, CA: Annual Review.

Hinshaw, S. P., Zupan, B. A., Simmel, C., Nigg, J. T., & Melnick, S. (1997). Peer status in boys with and without attention-deficit hyperactivity disorder: Predictions from overt and covert antisocial behavior, social isolation, and authoritative parenting beliefs. *Child Development, 68,* 880–896.

Hirono, N., et al. (1997). Procedural memory in patients with mild Alzheimer's disease. *Dementia & Geriatric Cognitive Disorders, 8,* 210–216.

Hirosumi, J., Tuncman, G., Chang, L., Gorgun, C. Z., Uysal, K. T., Maeda, K., Karin, M., & Hotamisligil, G. S. (2002). Obesity is closely associated with insulin resistance and establishes the leading risk factor for type 2 diabetes mellitus, yet the molecular mechanisms. *Nature, 420,* 333–336.

Hirshkowitz, M., Moore, C. A., & Minhoto, G. (1997). The basics of sleep. In M. R. Pressman & W. C. Orr (Eds.), *Understanding sleep: The evaluation and treatment of sleep disorders.* Washington, DC: American Psychological Association.

Hittner, J. B., & Daniels, J.R. (2002). Gender-role orientation, creative accomplishments and cognitive styles. *Journal of Creative Behavior, 36(1),* 62–75.

Ho, P. S. Y., & Tsang, A. K. T. (2002). The things girls shouldn't see: Relocating the penis in sex education in Hong Kong. *Sex Education, 2(1),* 61–73.

Hobson, J. A. (2002). *Dreaming: An introduction to the science of sleep.* New York: Oxford University Press.

Hobson, J. A. (1988). *The dreaming brain.* New York: Basic Books.

Hobson, J. A. (1999). *Dreaming as delirium: How the brain goes out of its mind.* Cambridge, MA: MIT Press.

Hobson, J. A., & McCarley, R. W. (1977). The brain as a dream state generator: An activation-synthesis hypothesis of the dream process. *American Journal of Psychiatry, 134,* 1335–1348.

Hobson, J. A., & Silvestri, L. (1999). Parasomnias. *The Harvard Mental Health Letter, 15(8),* 3–5.

Hock, R. (2001). *Forty studies that changed psychology: Explorations into the history of psychological research* (4th ed). Englewood Cliffs, NJ: Prentice Hall.

Hock, R. (1998). *Forty studies that changed psychology: Explorations into the history of psychological research.* Englewood Cliffs, NJ: Prentice Hall.

Hodge, D.R., Cardenas, P., & Montoya, H. (2001). Substance use: Spirituality and religious participation as protective factors among rural youths. *Social Work Research, 25(3),* 153–162.

Hoek, H. W., Van Harten, P. N., Van Hoeken, D., & Susser, E. (1998). Lack of relation between culture and anorexia nervosa: Results of an incidence study on Curacao. *New England Journal of Medicine, 338,* 1231–1232.

Hoffman, A. M., & Summers, R. W. (2000). *Teen violence: A global view.* New York: Greenwood Publishing Group.

Hoffman, M. L. (1993). Empathy, social cognition, and moral education. In A. Garrod (Ed.), *Approaches to moral development: New research and emerging themes.* New York: Teachers College Press.

Hoffman, M. L. (2000). Empathy and moral development: Implications for caring and justice. New York: Cambridge University Press.

Hoffman, P. (1997). The endorphin hypothesis. In W. P. Morgan, et al., (Eds.), *Physical activity and mental health. Series in health psychology and behavioral medicine* (pp. 163–177). Washington, DC: Taylor & Francis.

Hofman, A. (1968). Psychotomimetic agents. In A. Burger (Ed.), *Drugs affecting the central nervous system* (Vol. 2). New York: Dekker.

Hogan, T.P. (2003). *Psychological testing: A practical introduction.* New York: Wiley.

Hogben, M. (1998). Factors moderating the effect of televised aggression on viewer behavior. *Communication Research, 25,* 220–247.

Holden, C. (1980). Identical twins reared apart. *Science, 207,* 1323–1325.

Holmes, T. H., & Rahe, R. H. (1967). The social readjustment rating scale. *Journal of Psychosomatic Research, 11,* 213–218.

Holtzworth-Munroe, A. (2000). A typology of men who are violent toward their female partners: Making sense of the heterogeneity in husband violence. *Current Directions in Psychological Science, 9(4),* 140–143.

Hong, S. (2000). Exercise and psychoneuroimmunology. *International Journal of Sport Psychology, 31(2),* 204–227.

Hooley, J. M., & Gotlib, I. H. (2000). A diathesis-stress conceptualization of expressed emotion and clinical outcome. *Applied & Preventive Psychology, 9(3),* 135–151.

Hooley, J. M., & Hiller, J. B. (2001). Family relationships and major mental disorder: Risk factors and preventive strategies. In B. R. Sarason & S. Duck (Eds.), *Personal relationships: implications for clinical and community psychology.* New York: Wiley.

Hooley, J. M., & Hiller, J. B. (2000). Personality and expressed emotion. *Journal of Abnormal Psychology, 109,* 40–44.

Horenczyk, G., & Tatar, M. (2002). Teachers' attitudes toward multiculturalism and their perceptions of the school organizational culture. *Teaching & Teacher Education, 18(4),* 435–445.

Horney, K. (1939). *New ways in psychoanalysis.* New York: International Universities Press.

Horney, K. (1945). *Our inner conflicts: A constructive theory of neurosis.* New York: Norton.

Horning, L. F., & Rouse, K. A. G. (2002). Resilience in preschoolers and toddlers from low-income families. *Early Childhood Education Journal, 29(3),* 155–159.

Horowitz, J. M. (1999, March 29). Good news. *Time,* p. 19.

Hovland, C. I. (1937). The generalization of conditioned responses: II. The sensory generalization of conditioned responses with varying intensities of tone. *Journal of Genetic Psychology, 51,* 279–291.

Howe, M. L., & O'Sullivan, J. T. (1997). What children's memories tell us about recalling our childhoods: A review of storage and retrieval processes in the development of long-term retention. *Developmental Review, 17,* 148–204.

Hoyert, D. L., & Rosenberg, H. M. (1999). Mortality from Alzheimer's disease: an update. *National Vital Statistics Report, 47(20),* 1–8.

Hrebickva, M., Cermak, I., & Osecka, L. (2000). Development of personality structure from adolescence to old age: Preliminary findings. *Studia Psychologica, 42(3),* 163–166.

Huang, L. N., & Ying, Y. (1989). Japanese children and adolescents. In J. T. Gibbs & Ln N. Huang (Eds.), *Children of color.* San Francisco: Jossey-Bass.

Huang, M., & Hauser, R. M. (1998). Trends in Black–White test-score differentials: II. The WORDSUM Vocabulary Test. In U. Neisser (Ed.), *The rising curve: Long-term gains in IQ and related measures* (pp. 303–334). Washington, DC: American Psychological Association.

Hubel, D. H. (1963). The visual cortex of the brain. *Scientific American, 209,* 54–62.

Hubel, D. H., & Wiesel, T. N. (1965). Receptive fields and the functional architecture in two nonstriate visual areas (18 and 19) of the cat. *Journal of Neurophysiology, 28,* 229–289.

Hubel, D. H., & Wiesel, T. N. (1979). Brain mechanisms of vision. *Scientific American, 241,* 150–162.

Hudley, C., & Graham, S. (2001). Stereotypes of achievement striving among early adolescents. *Social Psychology of Education, 5(2),* 201–224.

Huesmann, L. R., & Moise, J. (1996, June). Media violence: A demonstrated public health threat to children. *Harvard Mental Health Letter,* pp. 5–7.

Huettel, S. A., Mack, P. B., & McCarthy, G. (2002). Perceiving patterns in random series: Dynamic processing of sequence in prefrontal cortex. *Nature Neuroscience, 5(5),* 485–490.

Huffcutt, A. I., Conway, J. M., Roth, P. L., & Stone, N. J. (2001). Identification and meta-analytic assessment of psychological constructs measured in employment interviews. *Journal of Applied Psychology, 86(5),* 897–913.

Hugdahl, K. (1998). Cortical control of human classical conditioning: Autonomic and positron emission tomography data. *Psychophysiology, 35,* 170–178.

Hughes, D., & Dodge, M. A. (1997). African American women in the workplace: Relation-ships between job conditions, racial bias at work, and perceived job quality. *American Journal of Community Psychology, 25(5),* 581–599.

Hull, C. (1952). *A behavior system.* New Haven, CT: Yale University Press.

Hulme, C., et al. (1997). Word-frequency effects on short-term memory tasks: Evidence for a redintegration process in immediate serial recall. *Journal of Experimental Psychology: Learning, Memory, & Cognition, 23,* 1217–1232.

Hulme, C., Newton, P., Cowan, N., Stuart, G., & Brown, G. (1999). Think before you speak: Pauses, memory search, and trace redintegration processes in verbal memory span. *Journal of Experimental Psychology: Learning, Memory, & Cognition, 25,* 447–463.

Humphreys, G. W., & Muller, H (2000). A search asymmetry reversed by figure-ground assignment. *Psychological Science, 11,* 196–200.

Hunkeler, N. et al. (2000). Efficacy of nurse telehealth care and peer support in augmenting treatment of depression in primary care. *Archives of Family Medicine, 9,* 700–708.

Hunsley, J., & Bailey, J. M. (1999). The clinical utility of the Rorschach: Unfulfilled promises and an uncertain future. *Psychological Assessment, 11(3),* 266–277.

Hunt, M. (1993). *The story of psychology.* New York: Doubleday.

Hur, Y., Bouchard, T. J., Jr., & Eckert, E. (1998). Genetic and environmental influences on self-reported diet: A reared-apart twin study. *Physiology & Behavior, 64,* 629–636.

Huston, T. L., Caughlin, J. P., Houts, R. M., Smith, S. E., & George, L. J. (2001). The connubial crucible: Newlywed years as predictors of marital delight, distress, and divorce. *Journal of Personality & Social Psychology, 80(2,)* 237–252.

Hyde, J. S., & Linn, M. C. (1988). *The psychology of gender: Advances through meta-analysis.* Baltimore: The Johns Hopkins University Press.

Hyde, J., Fenneman, E., & Lamon, S. (1990). Gender differences in mathematics performance: A meta-analysis. *Psychological Bulletin, 107,* 139–155.

Hyman, I. E., & Kleinknecht, E. E. (1999). False childhood memories: Research, theory, and applications. In L. M. Williams, & V. L. Banyard (Eds.), *Trauma and memory.* Thousand Oaks, CA: Sage.

Hyman, I. E., & Loftus, E. F. (1998). Errors in autobiographical memory. *Clinical Psychology Review, 18,* 933–947.

Hyman, R. (1981). Cold reading: How to convince strangers that you know all about them. In K. Fraizer (Ed.), *Paranormal borderlands of science* (pp. 232–244). Buffalo, NY: Prometheus.

Hyman, R. (1996). The evidence for psychic functioning: Claims vs. reality. *Skeptical Inquirer, 20,* 24–26.

Hypericum Depression Trial Study Group (2002). Effect of Hypericum performatum (St John's wort) in major depressive disorder: A randomized controlled trial. *JAMA: Journal of the American Medical Association, 287(14),* 1807–1814.

Iacono, W. G., & Lykken, D. T. (1997). The validity of the lie detector: Two surveys of scientific opinion. *Journal of Applied Psychology, 82(3),* 426–433.

Ibanez, A., Blanco C., & Saiz-Ruiz, J. (2002). Neurobiology *and genetics of pathological gambling.* Psychiatric Annals, 32(3), 181–185.

Ikonomidou, C., Bittigau, P., Ishimaru, M. J., Wozniak, D. F., Koch, C., Genz, K., Price, M. T., Stefovska, V., Horster, F., Tenkova, T., Dikranian, K., & Olney, J. W. (2000). Ethanol-induced apoptotic neurodegeneration and fetal alcohol syndrome. *Science, 287,* 1056–1060.

Ince, S. (1995). *Sleep disturbance.* Boston, MA: Harvard Medical School.

Ingram, K. M., Jones, D. A., & Smith, N. (2001). Grant Adjustment among people who have experienced AIDS-related multiple loss: The role of unsupportive social interactions, social support, and coping. *Omega: Journal of Death & Dying, 43(4),* 287–309.

International Human Genome Sequencing Consortium (IHGSC). (2001). Initial sequencing and analysis of the human genome. *Nature, 409,* 860–921.

Inzlicht, M., & Ben-Zeev, T. (2000). A threatening intellectual environment: Why females are susceptible to experiencing problem-solving deficits in the presence of males. *Psychological Science, 11(5),* 365–371.

Irwin, M., Mascovich, A., Gillin, J. C., Willoughby, R., et al. (1994). Partial sleep deprivation reduced natural killer cell activity in humans. *Psychosomatic Medicine, 56(6),* 493–498.

Israel, P. (1998). *Edison: A Life of Invention.* New York: Wiley.

Itakura, S. (1992). Symbolic association between individuals and objects by a chimpanzee as an initiation of ownership. *Psychological Reports, 70,* 539–544.

Iyer, P. (2001). *The global soul: Jet lag, shopping malls, and the search for home.* London: Vintage Books.

Jablensky, A. (1999). Schizophrenia: Epidemiology. *Current Opinion in Psychiatry, 12,* 19–28.

Jackson, C. J., Furnham, A., Forder, L., & Cotter, T. (2000). The structure of the Eysenck Personality Profiler. *British Journal of Psychology, 91,* 233–239.

Jacob, S., McClintock, M. K., Zelano, B., & Ober, C. (2002). Peternally inherited HLA alleles are associated with women's choice of male odor. *Nature Genetics,* DOI: 10.1038/ng830.

Jacobsen, T., & Hofmann, V. (1997). Children's attachment representations: Longitudinal relations to school behavior and aca-demic competency in middle childhood and adolescence. *Developmental Psychology, 33,* 703–710.

Jacoby, L. L., Levy, B. A., & Steinbach, K. (1992). Episodic transfer and automaticity: Integration of data-driven and conceptually-driven processing in rereading. *Journal of Experimental Psychology: Learning, Memory, & Cognition, 18(1),* 15–24.

Jaffee, S., & Hyde, J. S. (2000). Gender differences in moral orientation: A meta-analysis. *Psychological Bulletin, 126(5),* 703–726.

James, J. W., & Friedman, R. (1998). *The grief recovery handbook: The action program for moving beyond death, divorce, and other losses.* New York: Harpercollins.

James, W. (1890). *The principles of psychology* (Vol. 2). New York: Holt.

Jamison, K. R., & Baldessarini, R. J. (1999). Effects of medical interventions on suicidal behavior. *Journal of Clinical Psychiatry, 69,* 4–6.

Jang, K. L., McCrae, R. R., Angleitner, A., Riemann, R., & Livesley, W. J. (1998). Heritability of facet-level traits in a cross-culture twin sample: Support for a hierarchical model of personality. *Journal of Personality and Social Psychology, 74(6),* 1556–1565.

Jang, K. L., Vernon, P. A., & Livesley, W. J. (2000). Personality disorder traits, family environment, and alcohol misuse: A multivaritate behavioural genetic analysis. *Addiction, 95,* 873–888.

Janis, I. L. (1972). *Victims of groupthink: A psychological study of foreign-policy decisions and fiascoes.* Boston: Houghton Mifflin.

Janis, I. L. (1989). *Crucial decisions: Leadership in policymaking and crisis management.* New York: Free Press.

Jankowiak, W. (1997). *Romantic passion: A universal experience.* New York: Columbia University Press.

Jankowiak, W., & Fischer, E. (1992). Cross-cultural perspective on romantic love. *Ethnology, 31,* 149–155.

Jansen, A. S. P., Nguyen, X. V., Karpitskiy, V., Mettenleiter, T. C., & Loewy, A. D. (1995). Central command neurons of the sympathetic nervous system: Basis of the fight-or-flight response. *Science, 270,* 644–646.

Jansen, L. M. C., Wied, C. C. G., & Kahn, R. S. (2000). Selective impairment in the stress response in schizophrenic patients. *Psychopharmacology, 149,* 319–325.

Jaroff, L. (2001, March 5). Talking to the dead. *Time,* 52.

Jausovec, N., & Jausovec, K. (2000). Correlations between ERP parameters and intelligence: A reconsideration. *Biological Psychology, 55(2),* 137–154.

Jay, M. (2002). *Emperors of dreams: Drugs in the Nineteeth Century.* New York: Dedalus Ltd.

Jegalian, K., & Lahn, B. T. (2001, February). Why the Y is so weird. *Scientific American,* 56–61.

Jenkins, S. R., & Baird, S. (2002). Secondary traumatic stress and vicarious trauma: A validational study. *Journal of Traumatic Stress, 15(5),* 423–432.

Jennings, L., & Skovholt, T. M. (1999). The cognitive, emotional, and relational characteristics of master therapists. *Journal of Counseling Psychology, 46(1),* 3–11.

Jerome, L. W., DeLeon, P. H., James, L. C., Folen, R., Earles, J., & Gedney, J. J. (2000). The coming of age of telecommunications in psychological research and practice. *American Psychologist, 55(4),* 407–421.

Jia, H., Yu, L., Bi, H., Wang, K., Liu, Z., & Zie, S. (2002). Perception of the cabin attitude change in hypergravity. *Aviation, Space, & Environmental Medicine, 73(3),* 191–193.

Jiang, R., Wang, Y., & Gu, B. (2002). EEG biofeedback on cognitive function of children with ADHD. *Chinese Mental Health Journal, 16(6),* 407–410.

Jiang, Y., Olson, I. R., & Chun, M. M. (2000). Organization of visual short-term memory. *Journal of Experimental Psychology: Learning, memory, and cognition, 26,* 683–702.

Jog, M. S., Kubota, Y., Connolly, C. I., Hillegaart, V., & Graybiel, A. M. (1999). Building neural representations of habits. *Science, 286,* 1745–1749.

Johnson, D. (1991). Animal rights and human lives: Time for scientists to right the balance. *Psychological Science, 1,* 213–214.

Johnson, J. A. (1997). Units of analysis for the description and explanation of personality. In R. Hogan, J. Johnson, & S. Briggs (Eds.), *Handbook of personality psychology.* New York: Academic Press.

Johnson, J. G., Cohen, P., Brown, J., Smailes, E. M., & Bernstein, D. P. (1999). Childhood maltreatment increases risks for personality disorders during early adulthood. *Archives of General Psychiatry, 56,* 600–606.

Johnson, J., Smailes, E., Cohen, P., Brown, J., & Bernstein, D. (2000). Associations between four types of childhood neglect and personality disorder symptoms during adolescence and early adulthood: Findings of a community-based longitudinal study. *Journal of Personality Disorders, 14,* 171–187.

Johnson, K. P. (2002). The sleepy teenager. *Harvard Mental Health Letter, 18(5),* 6–8.

Johnson, M. D., & Ojemann, G. A. (2000). The role of the human thalamus in language and memory: Evidence from electrophysiological studies. *Brain & Cognition, 42,* 218–230.

Johnson, M. H. (1997). *Developmental cognitive neuroscience: An introduction.* Cambridge, MA: Blackwell.

Johnson, M., & Helgeson, V. S. (2002). Sex differences in response to evaluative feedback: A field study. *Psychology of Women Quarterly, 26(3),* 242–251.

Johnson, T. J., & Cropsey, K. L. (2000). Sensation seeking and drinking game participation in heavy-drinking college students. *Addictive Behaviors, 25(1),* 109–116.

Johnston, J. J. (1978). Answer-changing behavior and grades. *Teaching of Psychology, 5*(1), 44–45.

Johnstone, L. (1999). Adverse psychological effects of ECT. *Journal of Mental Health (UK), 8(1),* 69–85.

Jonas, W. (2002). St John's wort and depression. *JAMA: Journal of the American Medical Association, 288(4),* 446.

Jones, P. B., Rantakallio, P., Hartikainen, A., Isohanni, M., & Sipila, P. (1998). Schizophrenia as a long-term outcome of pregnancy, delivery, and perinatal complications: A 28-year follow-up of the 1966 North Finland General Population Birth Cohort. *American Journal of Psychiatry, 155,* 355–364.

Jones, R. (2002). In the news: From stem cells to neurons? *Nature Reviews Neuroscience, 3,* 84.

Jones, T., & Roediger, H. L. (1995). The experiential basis of serial position effects. *European Journal of Cognitive Psychology, 7,* 65–80.

Joseph, R. (2000). The evolution of sex differences in language, sexuality, and visual-spatial skills. *Archives of Sexual Behavior, 29(1),* 35–66.

Josephs, R. A., Newman, M. L., Brown, R. P., & Beer, J. M. (2003). Status, testosterone, and human intellectual performance: Stereotype threat as status concern. *Psychological Science, 14,* in press.

Jouvet, M. (1999). Sleep and Serotonin: An unfinished story. *Neuropsychopharmacology, 21*(Suppl, 2), 24S–27S.

Joyce, C. A., Paller, K. A., McIsaac, H. K., & Kutas, M. (1998). Memory changes with normal aging: Behavioral and electrophysiological measures. *Psychophysiology, 35,* 669–678.

Judge, T. A., & Ilies, R. (2002). Relationship of personality to performance motivation: A meta-analytic review. *Journal of Applied Psychology, 87(4),* 797–807.

Judge, T. A., & Watanabe, S. (1993). Another look at the job satisfaction-life satisfaction relationship. *Journal of Applied Psychology, 78(6),* 939–948.

Julien, R. M. (2001). *A primer of drug action: A concise, nontechnical guide to the actions, uses, and side effects of psychoactive drugs.* New York: Freeman.

Jung, C. G. (1946). *Psychological types.* New York: Harcourt Brace.

Jung, C. G. (1959). The archetypes and the collective unconscious. In H. Read, M. Fordham, & G. Adler (Eds.), *The collected works of C. G. Jung,* Vol. 9. New York: Pantheon.

Jung, C. (1969). The concept of the collective unconscious. In *Collected works* (Vol. 9, Part 1). Princeton, NJ: Princeton University Press. (Original work published 1936).

Jurado, M. A., Junque, C., Vallejo, J., Salgado, P., & Grafman, J. (2002). Obsessive-compulsive disorder (OCD) patients are impaired in remembering temporal order and in judging their own performance. *Journal of Clinical & Experimental Neuropsychology, 24(3),* 261–269.

Kagan, J. (1998). Biology and the child. In W. Damon & R. M. Lerner (Eds.), *Handbook of child psychology* (Vol. 1). New York: John Wiley & Sons.

Kahne, J. (1999). Personalized philanthropy: Can it support youth and build civic commitments? *Youth and Society, 30,* 367–387.

Kalat, J. W. (1985). Taste-aversion learning in ecological perspective. In T. D. Johnston & A. T. Pietrewicz (Eds.), *Issues in the ecological study of learning.* Hillsdale, NJ: Erlbaum.

Kamii, C., & Housman, L. B. (1999). *Young children reinvent arithmetic: Implications of Piaget's theory.* New York: Teachers College Press.

Kandel, E. R., & Schwartz, J. H. (1982). Molecular biology of learning: Modification of transmitter release. *Science, 218,* 433–442.

Kandel, E., Abel, T. (1995). Neuropeptides, adenylyl cyclase, and memory storage. *Science, 268,* 825–826.

Kanner, A. D., Coyne, J. C., Schaefer, C., & Lazarus, R. S. (1981). Comparison of two modes of stress management: Daily hassles and uplifts versus major life events. *Journal of Behavioral Medicine, 4,* 1–39.

Karama, S., Lecours, A. R., Leroux, J., Bourgouin, P., Beaudoin, G., Joubert, S., & Beauregard, M. (2002). Areas of brain activation in males and females during viewing of erotic film excerpts. *Human Brain Mapping, 16(1),* 1–13.

Karni, A., Tanne, D., Rubenstein, B. S., Askenasy, J. J. M., & Sagi, D. (1994, July 29). Dependence on REM sleep of overnight improvement in perceptual skill. *Science, 265,* 679–682.

Kasser, T., & Sharma, Y. S. (1999). Reproductive freedom, educational equality, and females' preference for resource-acquisition characteristics in mates. *Psychological Science, 10(4),* 374 377.

Kastenbaum, R. (1999). Dying and bereavement. In J. C. Cavanaugh & S. K. Whitbourne (Eds.), *Gerontology: An interdisciplinary perspective.* New York: Oxford University Press.

Katula, J. A., Blissmer, B. J., McAuley, E. (1999). Exercise and self-efficacy effects on anxiety reduction in healthy, older adults. *Journal of Behavioral Medicine, 22(3),* 233–247.

Katz, G., Knobler, H. Y., Laibel, Z., Strauss, Z., & Durst, R. (2002). Time zone change and major psychiatric morbidity: The results of a 6–year study in Jerusalem. *Comprehensive Psychiatry, 43(1),* 37–40.

Katz, M., Marsella, A., Dube, K., Olatawura, M., et al. (1988). On the expression of psychosis in different cultures: Schizophrenia in an Indian and in a Nigerian community. *Culture, Medicine, and Psychiatry, 12,* 331–355.

Kaufman, J. C. (2002). Dissecting the golden goose: Components of studying creative writers. *Creativity Research Journal, 14(1),* 27–40.

Kaukiainen, A., Bjoerkqvist, K., Lagerspetz, K., Oesterman, K., Salmivalli, C. et al. (1999). The relationship between social intelligence, empathy, and three types of aggression. *Aggressive Behavior, 25,* 81–89.

Kaul, R. E. (2002). A social worker's account of 31 days responding to the Pentagon disaster: Crisis intervention training and self-care practices. *Brief Treatment & Crisis Intervention, 2(1),* 33–37.

Kava: A supplement to avoid. (2003, March). *Consumer Reports, 68(3),* 8.

Kavanau, J. L. (2000). Sleep, memory maintenance, and mental disorders. *Journal of Neuropsychiatry & Clinical Neurosciences, 12(2),* 199–208.

Kawakami, K., Dovidio, J. F., Moll, J., Hermsen, S., & Russin, A. (2000). Just say no (to stereotyping): Effects of training in the negation of stereotypic associations on stereotype activation. *Journal of Personality & Social Psychology, 78(5),* 871–888.

Kazdin, A. E. (1994). Methodology, design, and evaluation in psychotherapy research. In A. E. Bergin & S. L. Garfield (Eds.), *Handbook of psychotherapy and behavior change* (4th ed.). New York: Wiley.

Keane, T. M., Taylor, K. L., & Penk, W. E. (1997). Differentiating posttraumatic stress disorder (PTSD) from major depression (MDD) and generalized anxiety disorder (GAD). *Journal of Anxiety Disorders, 11,* 317–328.

Keating, C. R. (1994). World without words: Messages from face and body. In W. J. Lonner & R. Malpass (Eds.), *Psychology and culture* (pp. 175–182). Boston: Allyn & Bacon.

Keats, D. M. (1982). Cultural bases of concepts of intelligence: A Chinese versus Australian comparison. In P. Sukontasarp, N. Yongsiri, P. Intasuwan, N. Jotiban, & C. Suvannathat (Eds.), *Proceedings of the Second Asian Workshop on Child and Adolescent Development* (pp. 67–75). Bangkok: Burapasilpa Press.

Keenan, J. P., Nelson, A., O'Connor, M., & Pascual-Leone, A. (2001). Self-recognition and the right hemisphere. *Nature, 409(6818),* 305.

Keillor, J. M., Barrett, A. M., Crucian, G. P., Kortenkamp, S., & Heilman, K. M. (2002). Emotional experience and perception in the absence of facial feedback. *Journal of the International Neuropsychological Society, 8,* 130–135.

Keller, H. (1962). Quoted in R. Harrity & R. G. Martin, *The three lives of Helen Keller* (p. 23). Garden City, NY: Doubleday.

Keller, H., & Greenfield, P. M. (2000). History and future of development in cross-cultural psychology. *Journal of Cross-Cultural Psychology, 31(1),* 52–62.

Keller, H., Yovsi, R. D., & Voelker, S. (2002). The role of motor stimulation in parental ethnotheories: The case of Cameroonian Nso and German women. *Journal of Cross-Cultural Psychology, 33(4),* 398–414.

Kellogg, W. N., & Kellogg, L. A. (1933). *The ape and the child.* New York: McGraw-Hill.

Kelly, I. W. (1998). Why astrology doesn't work. *Psychological Reports, 82,* 527–546.

Kelly, I. W. (1999, November/December). Debunking the debunkers: A response to an astrologer's debunking of skeptics. *Skeptical Inquirer,* 37–43.

Keltner, D., Capps, L., Kring, A. M., Young, R. C., & Heerey, E. A. (2001). Just teasing: A conceptual analysis and empirical review. *Psychological Bulletin, 127(2),* 229–248

Keltner, D., Kring, A. M., & Bonanno, G. A. (1999). Fleeting signs of the course of life: Facial expression and personal adjustment. *Current Directions in Psychological Science, 8(1),* 18–22.

Kempermann, G. (2002). Why new neurons? Possible functions for adult hippocampal neurogenesis. *Journal of Neuroscience, 22,* 635–638.

Kendler, K. S. (1996). Parenting: A genetic-epidemiologic perspective. *The American Journal of Psychiatry, 153,* 11–20.

Kendler, K. S., Gallagher, T. J., Abelson, J. M., & Kessler, R. C. (1996). Lifetime prevalence, demographic risk factors, and diagnostic validity of nonaffective psychosis as assessed in a U. S. community sample. *Archives of General Psychiatry, 53,* 1022–1031.

Kendler, K. S., Gardner, C. O., & Prescott, C. A. (1997). Religion, psychopathology, and substance use and abuse: A multimeasure, genetic-epidemiologic study. *American Journal of Psychiatry, 154,* 322–329.

Kendler, K. S., Jacobson, K. C., Myers, J., & Prescott, C. A. (2002). Sex differences in genetic and environmental risk factors for irrational fears and phobias. *Psychological Medicine, 32(2),* 209–217.

Kendler, K. S., Karkowski, L. M., & Prescott, C. A. (1999). Fears and phobias: Reliability and heritability. *Psychological Medicine, 29,* 539–553.

Kendler, K. S., Neale, M., Kessler, R. C., Heath, A., & Eaves, L. (1992). The genetic epidemiology of phobias in women: The interrelationship of agoraphobia, social phobia, situational phobia, and simple pho-bia. *Archives of General Psychiatry, 49,* 273–281.

Kenealy, P. M. (1997). Mood-state-dependent retrieval: The effects of induced mood on memory reconsidered. *Quarterly Journal of Experimental Psychology: Human Experimental Psychology, 50A,* 290–317.

Kerfoot, P., Sakoulas, G., & Hyman, S. E. (1996). Cocaine. In L. S. Friedman, N. F. Fleming, D. H. Roberts, & S. E. Hyman (Eds.), *Source book of substance abuse and addiction.* Baltimore: Williams & Wilkins.

Kessler, R. C., McGonagle, K. A., Zhao, S., Nelson, C. B., Hughes, M., Eshleman, S., Wittchen, H., & Kendler, K. S. (1994). Lifetime and 12–month prevalence of DSM-III-R psychiatric disorders in the United States. *Archives of General Psychiatry, 51,* 8–19.

Kessler, R. C., Zhao, S., Katz, S. J., Kouzis, A. C., Frank, R. G., Edlund, M., & Leaf, P. (1999). Past year use of outpatient services for psychiatric problems in the National Comorbidity Survey. *American Journal of Psychiatry, 156,* 115–123.

Kiecolt-Glaser, J. K., & Glaser, R. (2001). Stress and immunity: Age enhances the risk. *Current Directions in Psychological Science, 10*(1), 18–21.

Kiecolt-Glaser, J. K., McGuire, L., & Robles, T. F., & Glaser R. (2002). Psychoneuroimmunology: Psychological influences on immune function and health. *Journal of Consulting & Clinical Psychology, 70*(3), 537–547.

Kiernan, J. (2002). The experience of therapeutic touch in the lives of five postpartum women. *American Journal of Maternal/Child Nursing, 27*(1), 47–53.

Kihlstrom, J. F. (1997). Memory, abuse, and science. *American Psychologist, 52,* 994–995.

Kikusui, T., Aoyagi, A., & Kaneko, T. (2000). Spatial working memory is independent of hippocampal CA1 long-term potentiation in rats. *Behavioral Neuroscience, 114,* 700–706.

Killen, J. D., Fortmann, S. P., Schatzberg, A. F., Hayward, C. S., Sussman, L., Rothman, M., Strausberg, L. & Varady, A. *Nicotine patch and paroxetine for smoking cessation.* (2000). *Journal of Consulting & Clinical Psychology, 68*(5), 883–889.

Killen, M., & Hart, D. (1999). *Morality in everyday life: Developmental perspectives.* New York: Cambridge University Press.

Kilpatrick, D. G., Best, C. L., Vernonen, L. J., Amick, A. E., Villeponteaux, L. A., Ruff, G. A. (1985). Mental health correlates of criminal victimization: A random community survey. *Journal of Consulting and Clinical Psychology, 53,* 866–873.

Kim, J-H., Auerbach, J. M., Rodriquez-Gomez, J. A., Velasco, I., Gavin, D., Lumelsky, N., Lee, S-H., Nguyen, J., Sanchez-Pernaute, R., Bankiewicz, K., & McKay, R. (2002). Dopamine neurons derived from embryonic stem cells function in an animal model of Parkinson's disease. *Nature, 418,* 50–56.

Kim, K. H. S., Relkin, N. R., Lee, K-M., & Hirsch, J. (1997). Distinct cortical areas associated with native and second languages. *Nature, 388,* 171–174.

Kimmel, M. S. (2000). *The gendered society.* London: Oxford University Press.

King, A. C., Baumann, K., O'Sullivan, P., Wilcox, S., & Castro, C. (2002). Effects of moderate-intensity exercise on physiological, behavioral, and emotional responses to family caregiving: A randomized controlled trial. *Journals of Gerontology: Series A: Biological Sciences & Medical Sciences, 57A*(1), M26–M36.

King, N. J., Clowes-Hollins, V., & Ollendick, T. H. (1997). The etiology of childhood dog phobia. *Behaviour Research and Therapy, 35,* 77.

Kingree, J. B., Braithwaite, R., & Woodring, T. (2000). Unprotected sex as a function of alcohol and marijuana use among adolescent detainees. *Journal of Adolescent Health, 27*(3), 179–185.

Kingree, J. B., Braithwaite, R., & Woodring, T. (2000). Unprotected sex as a function of alcohol and marijuana use among adolescent detainees. *Journal of Adolescent Health, 27*(3), 179–185.

Kinney, H. C., Korein, J., Panigrahy, A., Dikkes, P., & Goode, R. (1994). Neuropatho-logical findings in the brain of Karen Ann Quinlan: The role of the thalamus in the persistent vegetative state. *New England Journal of Medicine, 330,* 1469–1475.

Kinsbourne, M. (1972). Eye and head turning indicates cerebral lateralization. *Science, 176,* 539–541.

Kinsey, A. C., Pomeroy, W. B., & Martin, C. E. (1948). *Sexual behavior in the human male.* Philadelphia: Saunders.

Kinsey, A. C., Pomeroy, W. B., Martin, C. E., & Gebbard, P. H. (1953). *Sexual behavior in the human female.* Philadelphia: Saunders.

Kinzel, A., & Nanson, J. (2000). Education and debriefing: Strategies for preventing crises in crisis-line volunteers. *Crisis, 21*(3), 26–134.

Kiraly, Z. (2000). The relationship between emotional self-disclosure of male and female adolescents' friendship. (gender differences, ninth-grade). *Dissertation Abstracts International: Section B: The Sciences & Engineering, 60*(7–B), 3619.

Kirchner, J. E., Owen, R. R., Nordquist, C., & Fischer, E. P. (1998). Diagnosis and management of substance use disorders among inpatients with schizophrenia. *Psychiatric Services, 49,* 82–85.

Kirk, K. M., Bailey, J. M., Dunne, M. P., & Martin, N. G. (2000). Measurement models for sexual orientation in a community twin sample. *Behavior Genetics, 30*(4), 345–356.

Kirkman, C. A. (2002). Non-incarcerated psychopaths: Why we need to know more about the psychopaths who live amongst us. *Journal of Psychiatric & Mental Health Nursing, 9*(2), 155–160.

Kitamura, T., Nakamura, M., Miura, I., & Fujinawa, A. (1997). Symptoms of neuroses: Profile patterns and factor structure of clinic attenders with non-psychotic functional psychiatric disorders. *Psychopathology, 30,* 191–199.

Kitayama, S. (2000). Collective construction of the self and social relationships: A rejoinder and some extensions. *Child Development, 71*(5), 1143–1146.

Kitayama, S., Markus, H. R., & Kurokawa, M. (2000). Culture, emotion, and well-being: Good feelings in Japan and the United States. *Cognition & Emotion, 14*(1), 93–124.

Kitzmann, K. M., Cohen, R., & Lockwood, R. L. (2002). Are only children missing out? Comparison of the peer-related social competence of only children and siblings. *Journal of Social & Personal Relationships, 19*(3), 299–316.

Klass, D. (2000). Response to Colin Murray Parkes' comments on my article "Developing a cross-cultural model of grief." *Omega: Journal of Death & Dying, 41*(1), 327–330.

Klatzky, R. L. (1984). *Memory and awareness.* New York: Freeman.

Klein, E., Kreinin, I., Chistyakov, A., Koren, D., Mecz, L. Marmur, S., Sen-Shachar, D., & Feinsod, M. (1999). Therapeutic efficacy of right prefrontal slow repetitive transcranial magnetic stimulation in major depression. *Archives of General Psychiatry, 56*(4), 315–320.

Klein, L. L. (2000). *The support group sourcebook: What they are, how you can find one, and how they can help you.* New York: Wiley.

Klein, O. & Licata, L. (2001). Explaining differences between social groups: The impact of group identification on attribution. *Swiss Journal of Psychology - Schweizerische Zeitschrift fuer Psychologie - Revue Suisse de Psychologie, 60*(4), 244–252.

Kleinknecht, R. A., Dinnel, D., & Kleinknecht, E. E. (1997). Cultural factors in social anxiety: A comparison of social phobia symptoms and taijin kyofusho. *Journal of Anxiety Disorders, 11,* 157–177.

Kleinman, A., & Cohen, A. (1997, March). Psychiatry's global challenge. *Scientific American,* 86–89.

Klimes-Dougan, B., & Kistner, J. (1990). Physically abused preschoolers' responses to peers' distress. *Developmental Psychology, 26,* 599–602.

Klinger, E. (1987, October). The power of daydreams. *Psychology Today,* pp. 37–44.

Klohnen, E. C., & Bera, S. (1998). Behavioral and experiential patterns of avoidantly and securely attached women across adulthood: A 31-year longitudinal perspective. *Journal of Personality and Social Psychology, 74*(1), 211–223.

Klump, K. L., Wonderlich, S., Lehoux, P., Lilenfeld, L.R. R., & Bulik, C. M. (2002). Does environment matter? A review of nonshared environment and eating disorders. *International Journal of Eating Disorders, 31*(2), 118–135.

Knecht, S., Floeel, A., Draeger, B., Breitenstein, C., Sommer, J., Henningsen, H.,

Ringelstein, E. B., & Pascual-Leone, A. (2002). Degree of language lateralization determines susceptibility to unilateral brain lesions. *Nature Neuroscience, 5(7),* 695–699.

Knight, B. G., Silverstein, M., McCallum, t. J., & Fox, L. S. (2000). A Socioculturals. Stress and coping model for mental health outcomes among African American caregivers in Southern California. *Journals of Gerontology: Series B: Psychological Sciences & Social Sciences, 55B,* 142–150.

Knoblauch, K., Vital-Durand, F., & Barbur, J. L. (2000). Variation of chromatic sensitivity across the life span. *Vision Research, 41(1),* 23–36.

Knoll, L., & Abrams, J. (1998). Evaluation of penile ultrasonic velocitometry versus penile duplex ultrasonography to assess penile arte-rial hemodynamics. *Urology, 51,* 89–93.

Kobak, R. R., & Hazan, C. (1991). Attachment in marriage: Effects of security and accuracy of working models. *Journal of Personality & Social Psychology, 60(6),* 861–869.

Kobasa, S. (1979). Stressful life events, personality, and health: An inquiry into hardiness. *Journal of Personality and Social Psychology, 37,* 1–11.

Kobasa, S. (1990). Stress-resistant personality. In R. E. Ornstein, C. Swencionis, et al. (Eds.), *The healing brain: A scientific reader.* New York: Guilford Press.

Kobasa, S., Maddi, S., & Kahn, S. (1982). Hardiness and health: A prospective study. *Journal of Personality and Social Psychology, 42,* 168–177.

Kobun, K., & Reyes, O. (2000). A descriptive study of urban Mexican American adolescents' perceived stress and coping. *Hispanic Journal of Behavioral Sciences, 22,* 163–178.

Kochanska, G., Casey, R. J., & Fukumoto, A. (1995). Toddlers' sensitivity to standard violations. *Child Development, 66,* 643–656.

Koechlin, E., Basso, G., Pietrini, P., Panzer, S., & Grafman, J. (1999). The roll of the anterior prefrontal cortex in human cognition. *Nature, 399,* 148–151.

Koenig, J. I., Kirkpatrick, B., & Lee, P. (2002). Glucocorticoid hormones and early brain development in schizophrenia. *Neuropsychopharmacology, 27(2),* 309–318.

Koenig, S. (2000). The inmates and the asylum: How Hollywood depicts mental hospitals.

Koerner, A. F., & Fitzpatrick, M. A. (2002). Nonverbal communication and marital adjustment and satisfaction: The role of decoding relationship relevant and relationship irrelevant affect. *Communication Monographs, 69(1),* 33–51.

Kohlberg, L. (1964). Development of moral character and moral behavior. In L. W. Hoffman & M. L. Hoffman (Eds.), *Review of child development research* (Vol. 1). New York: Sage.

Kohlberg, L. (1966). A cognitive-developmental analysis of children's sex-role concepts and attitudes. In E. E. Maccoby (Ed.), *The development of sex differences.* Stanford, CA: Stanford University Press.

Kohlberg, L. (1969). Stage and sequence: The cognitive-developmental approach to socialization. In D. A. Goslin (Ed.), *Handbook of socialization theory and research.* Chicago: Rand McNally.

Kohlberg, L. (1981). *The meaning and measurement of moral development.* Worcester, MA: Clark University Press.

Kohlberg, L. (1984). *The psychology of moral development: Essays on moral development* (Vol. II). San Francisco: Harper & Row.

Kohler, W. (1925). *The mentality of apes.* New York: Harcourt, Brace.

Kohn, A. (2000). *Punished by rewards: The trouble with gold stars, incentive plans, A's, and other bribes.* New York: Houghton Mifflin.

Kole-Snijders, A. M., Vlaeyen, J. W., Goossens, M. E., Rutten-van Moelken, M. P., & Breukelen, G., & von Eek, H. (1999). Chronic low-back pain: What does cognitive coping skills training add to operant behavioral treatment? Results of a randomized clinical trial. *Journal of Consulting & Clinical Psychology, 67,* 931–944.

Kollins, S. H., & Rush, C. R. (2002). Sensitization to the cardiovascular but not subject-rated effects of oral cocaine in humans. *Biological Psychiatry, 51(2),* 143–150.

Komiya, N., Good, G. E., & Sherrod, N. B. (2000). Emotional openness as a predictor of college students' attitudes toward seeking psychological help. *Journal of Counseling Psychology, 47(1),* 138–143.

Koob, G. F., & Nestler, E. J. (1997). Neurobiology of drug addiction. *Journal of Neuropsychiatry and Clinical Neuroscience, 9(3),* 482–497.

Kopelman, M. D., Reed, L. J., Marsden, P., Mayes, A. R., Jaldow, E., Laing, H., & Isaac, C. (2002). Amnesic syndrome and severe ataxia following the recreational use of 3,4–methylene-dioxymethamphetamine (MDMA, 'ecstasy') and other substances. *Neurocase, 7(5),* 423–432.

Koppel, J. (2000). *Good/Grief.* New York: Harperperennial.

Kopta, S. M., Lueger, R. J., Saunders, S. M., & Howard, K. I. (1999). Individual psychotherapy outcome and process research: Challenges leading to a greater turmoil or a positive transition? *Annual Review of Psychology, 50,* 441–469.

Kornstein, S. G. (2002). Chronic depression in women. *Journal of Clinical Psychiatry, 63(7),* 602–609.

Koslowsky, M., Sagie, A., & Stashevsky, S. (2002). Introduction: Cultural relativism and universalism in organizational behaviors. *International Journal of Cross Cultural Management, 2(2),* 131–135.

Kosslyn, S. M. (1987). Seeing and imagining in the cerebral hemispheres: A computational approach. *Psychological Review, 94,* 148–175.

Kotkin, M., Daviet, C., & Gurin, J. (1996). The Consumer Reports mental health survey. *American Psychologist, 51(10),* 1080–1082.

Kottler, J. A., & Brown, R. W. (1999). *Introduction to therapeutic counseling.* Monterey, CA: Brooks/Cole.

Koulack, D. (1997). Recognition memory, circadian rhythms, and sleep. *Perceptual & Motor Skills, 85,* 99–104.

Kouri, E. M., Lukas, S. E., Pope, H. G. Jr., & Olivia, P. S. (1998). ?Increased aggressive responding in male volunteers following administration of gradually increased doses of testosterone cypionate?: Erratum. *Drug and Alcohol Dependence, 50,* 255.

Kraaij, V., Arensman, E., & Spinhoven, P. (2002). Negative life events and depression in elderly persons: A meta-analysis. *Journals of Gerontology: Series B: Psychological Sciences & Social Sciences, 57B(1),* 87–94.

Kramen-Kahn, B., & Hansen, N. D. (1998). Rafting the rapids: Occupational hazards, rewards, and coping strategies of psychotherapists. *Professional Psychology: Research & Practice, 29(2),* 130–134.

Kramer, A. F., Hahn, S., Irwin, D. E., & Theeuwes, J. (2000). Age differences in the control of looking behavior. *Psychological Science, 11(3),* 210–217.

Krantz, D. S., & McCeney, M. K. (2002). Effects of psychological and social factors on organic disease: A critical assessment of research on coronary heart disease. *Annual Review of Psychology, (1),* 341–369.

Krantz, D. S., Gruenberg, N. E., & Baum, A. (1985). Health psychology. *Annual Review of Psychology, 36,* 349–383.

Kranz, K., & Daniluk, J. C. (2002). Gone but not forgotten: The meaning and experience of mother-loss for midlife daughters. *Women & Therapy, 25(1),* 1–18.

Krishna, G. (1999). *The dawn of a new science.* Los Angeles: Institute for Consciousness Research.

Krug, E. G., Kresnow, M., Peddicord, J., Dahlberg, L. Powell, K. E., Crosby, A. E., & Annest, J. L. (1998). Suicide after natural disasters. *New England Journal of Medicine, 338,* 373–378.

Kryger, M. H., Roth, T., & Dement, W. C. (2000). *Principles and practice of sleep medicine* (3rd ed.). New York: W. B. Saunders.

Kryger, M. H., Walld, R., & Manfreda, J. (2002). Diagnoses received narcolepsy patients in the year prior to diagnosis a sleep specialist. *Sleep: Journal of Sleep & Sleep Disorders Research, 25(1),* 36–41.

Kübler-Ross, E. (1983). *On children and death.* New York: Macmillan.

Kübler-Ross, E. (1997). *Death: The final stage of growth.* New York: Simon & Schuster.

Kübler-Ross, E. (1999). *On death and dying.* New York: Simon & Schuster.

Kuebli, J. (1999). Young children's understanding of everyday emotions. In L. E. Berk, *Landscapes of development* (pp. 123–136). Belmont, CA: Wadsworth.

Kunz, D., & Hermann, W. M. (2000). Sleep-wake cycle, sleep-related disturbances, and sleep disorders: A chronobiological approach. *Comparative Psychology, 41,* 104–105.

Kuriansky, J. (1998). *The complete idiot's guide to a healthy relationship.* New York: Alpha Books.

Kurihara, K., & Kashiwayanagi, M. (1998). Introductory remarks on umami taste. *Annals of the New York Academy of Sciences, 855,* 393–397.

Kushner, S. A., Dewey, S. L., & Kornetsky, C. (1999). The irreversible gamma-aminobutyric acid (GABA) transminase inhibitor gamma-vinyl-GABA blocks cocaine self-administration in rats. *Journal of Pharmacology & Experimental Therapeutics, 290,* 797–802.

Lace, W. W. (1999). *Tiger Woods: Star golfer.* New York: Enslow.

Laine, T., Pekka, J., Ahonen, A., Raesaenen, P., & Tiihonen, J. (2001). Dopamine transporter density and novelty seeking among alcoholics. *Journal of Addictive Diseases, 20(4),* 91–96.

Laird, J. D., & Bressler, C. (1992). The process of emotional experience: A self-perception theory. In M. S. Clark (Ed.), *Review of personality and social psychology* (pp. 213–234). Newbury Park, CA: Sage.

Lakein, A. (1998). *Give me a moment and I'll change your life: Tools for moment management.* New York: Andrews McMeel Publishing.

Lal, S. K. L., et al. (1998). Effect of feedback signal and psychological characteristics on blood pressure self-manipulation capability. *Psychophysiology, 35(4),* 405–412.

Lamb, H. R. (2000). Deinstitutionalization and public policy. In R. W. Menninger & J.C. Nemiah (Eds.), *American psychiatry after World War II.* Washington, DC: American Psychiatric Press.

Lamb, H. R., & Weinberger, L. E. (2000). Commentary: A major advance in the laws pertaining to community treatment for persons with severe mental illness. *Journal of the American Academy of Psychiatry & the Law, 28(2),* 149–153.

Lamb, M. E. (1996). *The role of the father in child development* (3rd ed.). New York: Wiley.

Lamberg, L. (1998). Gay is okay with APA-Forum honors landmark 1973 events. *Journal of the American Medical Association, 280,* 497–499.

Landen, M., Walinder, J., & Lundstrom, B. (1998). Clinical characteristics of a total cohort of female and male applicants for sex reassignment: A descriptive study. *Acta Psychiatrica Scandinavia, 97,* 189–194.

Landry, D. W. (1997). Immunotherapy for cocaine addiction. *Scientific American, 276,* 42–45.

Landry, M.J. (2002). MDMA: A review of epidemiologic data. *Journal of Psychoactive Drugs, 34(2),* 163–169.

Lane, R. D., Reiman, E. M., Ahern, G. L., & Schwartz, G. E. (1997). Neuroanatomical correlates of happiness, sadness, and disgust. *American Journal of Psychiatry, 154,* 926–933.

Lang, F. R., & Carstensen, L. L. (2002). Time counts: Future time perspective, goals, and social relationships. *Psychology & Aging, 17(1),* 125–139.

Langella, M., Colarieti, L., Ambrosini, M. V., & Giuditta, A. (1992). The sequential hypothesis of sleep function: A correlative analysis of sleep variables in learning and nonlearning rats. *Physiology and Behavior, 51(2),* 227–238.

Langer, T. (1962). A twenty-two item screening score of psychiatric symptoms indicating impairment. *Journal of Health and Human Behavior, 3,* 269–276.

Langlois, J. H., Kalakanis, L., Rubenstein, A. J., Larson, A., Hallam, M., & Smoot, M. (2000). Maxims or myths of beauty? A meta-analytic and theoretical review. *Psychological Bulletin, 126(3),* 390–423.

Lannon, C. M., Bailey, A. G. D., Fleischman, A. R., Kaplan, G. W., Shoemaker, C. T., Swanson, G. T., & Couston, A. (1999). Circumcision policy statement. *Pediatrics, 103,* 686–693.

Lanyon, R. I., & Goodstein, L. D. (1997). *Personality assessment.* New York: Wiley.

Lapsley, D. K. (1996). *Moral psychology.* Boulder, CO: Westview.

Lariviere, N., Gelinas, I., Mazer, B., Tallant, B., & Paquette, I. (2002). Discharging older adults with a severe and chronic mental illness in the community. *Canadian Journal of Occupational Therapy, 69(2),* 71–83.

Laruelle, M., Abi-Dargham, A., Gil, R., Kegeles, L., & Inis, R. (1999). Increased dopamine transmission in schizophrenia: Relationship to illness phases. *Biological Psychiatry, 46 (1),* 56–72.

Larzelere, R. E., & Johnson, B. (1999). Evaluations of the effects of Sweden's spanking ban on physical child abuse rates: A literature review. *Psychological Reports, 85(2),* 381–392.

Lashley, K. (1929). *Brain mechanisms and intelligence.* Chicago: University of Chicago Press.

Lashley, K. (1950). In search of the engram. *Symposia of the Society of Experimental Biology, 4,* 454–482.

Latane, B., & Darley, J. M. (1970). *The unresponsive bystander: Why doesn't he help?* New York: Appleton-Century-Crofts.

Latham, G. P. (2001). The reciprocal effects of science on practice: Insights from the practice and science of goal setting. *Canadian Psychology, 42(1),* 1–11.

Laumann, E., Gagnon, J., Michael, R., & Michaels, S. (1994). *The social organization of sexuality: Sexual practices in the United States.* Chicago: University of Chicago Press.

Laurelle, M., Abi-dargham, A., Gil, R., Kegeles, L., & Innis, R. (1999). Increased dopamine transmission in schizophrenia: Relationship to illness phases. *Biological Psychiatry, 46,* 56–72.

Lawrence, S. A. (2002). Behavioral interventions to increase physical activity. *Journal of Human Behavior in the Social Environment, 6(1),* 25–44.

Lawrence, S. A., Wodarski, L. A., & Wodarski, J. (2002). Behavioral medicine paradigm: Behavioral interventions for chronic pain and headache. *Journal of Human Behavior in the Social Environment, 5(2),* 1–14.

Lazarus, A. A. (1971). *Behavior therapy and beyond.* New York: McGraw-Hill.

Lazarus, R. S. (1999). Stress and emotion: A new synthesis. New York: Springer.

Lazarus, R. S., & Folkman, S. (1984). *Stress appraisal and coping.* New York: Springer.

Lazev, A. B., Herzog, T. A., & Brandon, T. H. (1999). Classical conditioning of environmental cues to cigarette smoking. *Experimental & Clinical Psychopharmacology, 7(1),* 56–63.

Leaper, C. (2000). Gender, affiliation, assertion, and the interactive context of parent–child play. *Developmental Psychology, 36(3),* 381–393.

Leaper, C., Anderson, K., & Sanders, P. (1998). Moderators of gender effects on parents' talk to their children: A meta-analysis. *Developmental Psychology, 34,* 3–27.

Lebow, J. L., & Gurman, A. S. (1995). Research assessing couple and family therapy. In J. T. Spence, J. M. Darley, & D. F. Foss (Eds.), *Annual Review of Psychology, 46* (pp. 27–57). Palo Alto, CA: Annual Review.

Leclerk, G., Lefrancois, R., Dube, M., Hebert, R., & Gaulin, P. (1998). The self-actualization concept: A content validation.

Journal of Social Behavior & Personality, 11, 69–84.

Lecrubier, Y., Clerc, G., Didi, R., & Kieser, M. (2002). Efficacy of St. John's wort extract WS 5570 in major depression: A double-blind, placebo-controlled trial. *American Journal of Psychiatry, 159(8),* 1361–1366.

LeDoux, J. (2002). *Synaptic self: How our brains become who we are.* New York: Viking.

LeDoux, J. E. (1992). Systems and synapses of emotional memory. In L. R. Squire, N. M. Weinberger, G. Lynch, & J. L. McGuagh (Eds.), *Memory: Organization and locus of change.* New York: Oxford University Press.

LeDoux, J. E. (1996). Sensory systems and emotion: A model of affective processing. *Integrative Psychiatry, 4,* 237–243.

LeDoux, J. (1996). *The emotional brain: The mysterious underpinnings of emotional life.* New York: Simon & Schuster.

Lee, D. (1950). The conception of the self among the Wintu Indians. In D. Lee (Ed.), *Freedom and culture.* Englewood Cliffs, NJ: Prentice-Hall.

Lee, L., et al. (1999). Are reporting errors due to encoding limitations or retrieval failure? Surveys of child vaccination as a case study. *Applied Cognitive Psychology, 13,* 43–63.

Leeper, R. W. (1935). A study of a neglected portion of the field of learning: The development of sensory organization. *Journal of Genetic Psychology, 46,* 41–75.

Lefley, H. P. (2000). Cultural perspectives on families, mental illness, and the law. *International Journal of Law and Psychiatry, 23,* 229–243.

Lehrman, S. (1995). U. S. stalls over tests of marijuana to treat AIDS patients. *Nature, 374,* 7–8.

Leibowitz, S. F., & Alexandr, J. T. (1998). Hypothalamic serotonin in control of eating behavior, meal size, and body weight. *Biological Psychiatry, 44,* 851–864.

Leichsenring, F. (2002). Zur Wirksamkeit tiefenpsychologisch fundierter und psychodynamischer Therapie. Eine Uebersicht unter Beruecksichtigung von Kriterien der Evidence-Based Medicine./The effectiveness of psychodynamic therapy. A review using criteria of evidence-based medicine. *Zeitschrift fuer Psychosomatische Medizin und Psychotherapie, 48(2),* 139–162.

Leichtman, M. D., & Ceci, S. J. (1995). The effects of stereotypes and suggestions on preschoolers' reports. *Developmental Psychology, 31,* 568–578.

Leitenberg, H., & Henning, K. (1995). Sexual fantasy. *Psychological Bulletin, 117,* 469–496.

Leland, J. (1996, August 26). The fear of heroin is shooting up. *Newsweek,* pp. 55–56.

LeMarquand, D. G., Pihl, R. O., Young, S. N., Tremblay, R. E., Seguin, J. R., Palmour, R. M., & Benkelfat, C. (1998). Tryptophan depletion, executive functions, and disinhibition in aggressive, adolescent males. *Neuropsychopharmacology, 19(4),* 333–341.

Lembke, A., & Ketter, T. A. (2002). Impaired recognition of facial emotion in mania. *American Journal of Psychiatry, 159(2),* 302–304.

Lemery, K. S., Goldsmith, H. H., Klinnert, M. D., & Mrazek, D. A. (1999). Developmental models of infant and childhood temperament. *Developmental Psychology, 35,* 189–204.

Lemonick, M. D. (1998, April 13). Emily's little experiment. *Time,* p. 67.

Lemonick, M. D. (2000, July 3). The genome is mapped. Now what? *Time,* pp. 24–29.

Lengua, L. J., Wolchik, S. A., Sandler, I. N., & West, S. G. (2000). The additive and interactive effects of parenting and temperament in predicting problems of children of divorce. *Journal of Clinical Child Psychology, 29(2),* 232–244.

Lenhart, R. S., & Ashby, J. S. (1996). Cognitive coping strategies and coping modes in relation to chronic pain disability. *Journal of Applied Rehabilitation Counseling, 27,* 15–18.

Lensvelt-Mulders, G., & Hettema, J. (2001). Analysis of genetic influences on the consistency and variability of the Big Five across different stressful situations. *European Journal of Personality, 15(5),* 355–371.

Leo, S. (2000, December 6). Verbal judo for beginners. *Time,* p. 6.

Leonard, B. E. (1996). Serotonin receptors and their function in sleep, anxiety disorders and depression. *Psychotherapy & Psychosomatics, 65,* 66–75.

Leonard, B. E. (2000). Stress, depression, and the immune system. *Stress Medicine, 16(3),* 133–137.

Leong, F. T. L., Hartung, P. J., Goh, D., & Gaylor, M. (2001). Appraising birth order in career assessment: Linkages to Holland's and Super's models. *Journal of Career Assessment, 9(1),* 25–39.

Lepore, S. J., Ragan, J. D., & Jones, S. (2000). Talking facilitates cognitive-emotional processes of adaptation to an acute stressor. *Journal of Personality and Social Psychology, 78(3),* 499–508.

Lepper, M. R., Greene, D., & Nisbett, R. E. (1973). Undermining children's intrinsic interest with extrinsic rewards: A test of the overjustification hypothesis. *Journal of Personality and Social Psychology, 28,* 129–137.

Lerner, J. S., Gonzalez, R. M., Small, D. A., & Fischhoff, B. (2003). Effects of fear and anger on perceived risks of terrorism: A national field experiment. *Psychological Science, 14,* in press.

Lerner, R. M., & Galambos, N. L. (1998). Adolescent development: Challenges and opportunities for research, programs, and policies. *Annual Review of Psychology, 49,* 413–446.

Leserman, J., Petitto, J. M., Golden, R. N., Gaynes, B. N., Gu, H., Perkins, D. O., Silva, S. G., Folds, J. D., & Evans, D. L. (2000). Impact of stressful life events, depression, social support, coping, and cortisol on progression to AIDS. *American Journal of Psychiatry, 157(8),* 1221–1228.

Leslie, M. (2000). The Vexing Legacy of Lewis Terman. Stanford Magazine, Available: http://www.stanfordalumni.org/jg/mig/news_magazine/magazine/julaug00/index.html

Lettvin, J. Y., Maturana, H. R., McCulloch, W. S., & Pitts, W. H. (1959). What the frog's eye tells the frog's brain. *Proceedings of the Institute of Radio Engineers, 47,* 1940–1951.

Levenson, R. W. (1992). Autonomic nervous system differences among emotions. *Psychological Science, 3,* 23–27.

Leveton, D. (2002, August 23). "O'Keeffe, Georgia," World Book Online Americas Edition, http://www.worldbookonline.com/ar?/na/ar/co/ar400900.htm.

Levin, E. D., Torry, D., Christopher, N. C., Yu, X., Einstein, G, & Schartz-Bloom, R. D. (1997). Is binding to nicotinic acetylcholine and dopamine receptors related to working memory in rats? *Brain Research Bulletin, 43,* 295–304.

Levine, D. (2000). Virtual attraction: What rocks your boat. *CyberPsychology & Behavior, Aug3(4),* 565–573.

Levine, J. R. (2001). *Why do fools fall in love: Experiencing the magic, mystery, and meaning of succesful relationships.* New York: Jossey-Bass.

Levinson, D. J. (1977). The mid-life transition, *Psychiatry, 40,* 99–112.

Levinson, D. J. (1996). *The seasons of a woman's life.* New York: Knopf.

Lewis, D. O., Yeager, C. A., Swica, Y., Pincus, J. H., & Lewis, M. (1997). Objective documentation of child abuse and dissociation in 12 murderers with dissociative identity disorder. *American Journal of Psychiatry, 154,* 1703–1710.

Lewis, S. (1963). *Dear Shari.* New York: Stein & Day.

Li, F., Wang, E., & Zhang, F. (2002). The multitrait-multirater approach to analyzing rating biases. *Acta Psychologica Sinica, 34(1),* 89–96.

Li, N. P., Bailey, J. M., Kenrick, D. T., & Linsenmeier, J. A. W. (2002). The necessities and luxuries of mate preferences: Testing the tradeoffs. *Journal of Personality & Social Psychology, 82(6)*, 947–955.

Li, N. P., Bailey, J. M., Kenrick, D., & Linsenmeier, J. A. W. (2002). The necessities and luxuries of mate preferences: Testing the tradeoffs. *Journal of Personality & Social Psychology, 82(6)*, 947–955.

Liben, L. S., & Signorella, M. L. (1993). Gender-schematic processing in children: The role of initial interpretations of stimuli. *Developmental Psychology, 29*, 141–149.

Libkuman, T. M., Nichols-whitehead, P., Griffith, J., & Thomas, R. (1999). Source of arousal and memory for detail. *Memory & Cognition, 27*, 166–190.

Lieberman, P. (1998). *Eve spoke: Human language and human evolution.* New York: W.W. Norton and Company.

Liggett, D. R. (2000). Enhancing imagery through hypnosis: A performance aid for athletes. *American Journal of Clinical Hypnosis, 43(2)*, 149–157.

Lilienfeld, L. R., Kaye, W. H., Greeno, C. G., Merikangas, K. R., Plotnicov, K., et al. (1999). Psychiatric disorders in women with bulimia nervosa and their first-degree relatives: Effects of comorbid substance dependence. *International Journal of Eating Disorders, 22*, 253–264.

Lilienfeld, S. O., Wood, J. M., & Howard, N. G. (2000). The scientific status of projective techniques. *Psychological Science in the Public Interest, 1(2)*, 27–66.

Lilienfeld. S. O. (1999). Projective measures of personality and psychopathology: How well do they work? *Skeptical Inquirer, 23*, 32–39.

Lillard, A. (1998). Ethnopsychologies: Cultural variations in theories of mind. *Psychological Bulletin, 123*, 3–32.

Lin, C. (1998). Comparison of the effects of perceived self-efficacy on coping with chronic cancer pain and coping with chronic low back pain. *Clinical Journal of Pain, 14*, 303–310.

Lindemann, B. (2001). Receptors and transduction in taste. *Nature, 413(6852)*, 219–225.

Linden, E. (1993), March 22). Can animals think? *Time*, pp. 54–61.

Lindsay, D. S. (1998). Depolarizing views on recovered memory experiences. In S. J. Lynn & K. M. McConkey (Eds.), *Truth in memory.* New York: Guilford Press.

Links, P. S., Heslegrave, R., & van Reekum, R. (1998). Prospective follow-up of borderline personality disorder: Prognosis, prediction outcome, and Axis II comorbidity. *Canadian Journal of Psychiatry, 43*, 265–270.

Linszen, D. H., et al. (1997). Patient attributes and expressed emotion as risk factors for psychotic relapse. *Schizophrenia Bulletin, 23*, 119–130.

Linzer, M., Gerrity, M., Douglas, J. A., McMurray, J. E., Williams, E. S., Konrad, T. R., & Society of General Medicine Career Satisfaction Study Group (2002). Physician stress: Results from the physician worklife study. *Stress & Health: Journal of the International Society for the Investigation of Stress, 18(1)*, 37–42.

Liotti, M., & Mayberg, H. S. (2001). The role of functional neuroimaging in the neuropsychology of depression. *Journal of Clinical & Experimental Neuropsychology, 23(1)*, 121–136.

Liptak, A. (2003, January 23). Circumcision opponents use the legal system and legislatures. Available: http://www.nytimes.com/2003/01/23/national/23CIRC.html?todaysheadlines

Liu, H., Mantyh, P, & Basbaum, A. I. (1997). NMDA-receptor regulation of substance P release from promary afferent nociceptors. *Nature, 386*, 721–724.

Liu, J. H., & Latane, B. (1998). Extremitiza-tion of attitudes: Does thought-and-discussion-induced polarization cumulate? *Basic and Applied Social Psychology, 20*, 103–110.

Livanou, M., Basoglu, M., Marks, I. M., De Silva, P., Noshirvani, H., Lovell, K., & Thrasher, S. (2002). Beliefs, sense of control and treatment outcome in post-traumatic stress disorder. *Psychological Medicine, 32(1)*, 157–165.

Livingston, J. A. (1999). Something old and something new: Love, creativity, and the enduring relationship. *Bulletin of the Menninger Clinic, 63*, 40–52.

Loay, D., & Loay, M. D. (2000). *Sexually-Transmitted diseases.* Baltimore: Merit Publishing International.

Lobel, T. E. (1994). Sex typing and the social perception of gender stereotypic and non-stereotypic behavior: The uniqueness of feminine males. *Journal of Personality and Social Psychology, 66*, 379–385.

Lock, J., & Steiner, H. (1999). Gay, lesbian, and bisexual youth risks for emotional, physical, and social problems: Results from a community-based survey. *Journal of the American Academy of Child & Adolescent Psychiatry, 38(3)*, 297–304.

Lock, M. (1998). Menopause: Lessons from anthropology. *Psychosomatic Medicine, 60*, 410–419.

Locke, E. A., & Latham, G. P. (2002). Building a practically useful theory of goal setting and task motivation: A 35–year odyssey. *American Psychologist, 57(9)*, 705–717.

Loeber, R., & Stouthamer-Loeber, M. (1998). Development of juvenile aggres-

sion and violence: Some common misconceptions and controversies. *American Psychologist, 53*, 242–259.

Loehlin, J. C., McCrae, R. R., Costa, P. T., & John, O. (1998). Heritabilities of common and measure-specific components of the Big Five personality factors. *Journal of Research in Personality, 32*, 431–453.

Loftus, E. (2002, May/June). My story: Dear Mother. *Psychology Today*, pp. 67–70.

Loftus, E. E., & Ketcham, K. (1994). *The myth of repressed memories: False memories and allegations of sexual abuse.* New York: St. Martin's Press.

Loftus, E. F. (2001). Imagining the past. *Psychologist, 14(11)*, 584–587.

Loftus, E. F. (1982). Memory and its distortions. In A. G. Kraut (Ed.), *The G. Stanley Hall Lecture Series* (Vol. 2, pp. 123–154). Washington, DC: American Psychological Association.

Loftus, E. F. (1993). The reality of repressed memories. *American Psychologist, 48*, 518–537.

Loftus, E. F. (1997). Memory for a past that never was. *Current Directions in Psychological Science, 6(3)*, 60–65.

Loftus, E. F. (2000). Remembering what never happened. In E. Tulving, et al. (Eds.), *Memory, consciousness, and the brain: The Tallinn Conference*, pp. 106–118. Philadelphia, PA: Psychology Press/Taylor & Francis.

Loftus, E. F., & Polage, D. C. (1999). Repressed memories: When are they real? When are they false? *Psychiatric Clinics of North America, 22*, 61–70.

Loftus, E. (1993). Psychologists in the eyewitness world. *American Psychologist, 48*, 550–552.

Lohman, J., & Jarvis, P. A. (2000). Adolescent stressors, coping strategies, and psychological health studied in the family context. *Journal of Youth & Adolescence, 29*, 15–43.

Loo, R., & Thorpe, K. (1998). Attitudes toward women's roles in society. *Sex Roles, 39*, 903–912.

Lopez, F. G., Melendez, M. C., & Rice, K. G. (2000). Parental divorce, parent–child bonds, and adult attachment orientations among college students: A comparison of three racial/ethnic groups. *Journal of Counseling Psychology, 47(2)*, 177–186.

Lopez, F., & Hsu, P-C. (2002). Further validation of a measure of parent-adult attachment style. *Measurement & Evaluation in Counseling & Development, 34(4)*, 223–237.

Lopez, J. C. (2002). Brain repair: A spinal scaffold. *Nature Reviews Neuroscience, 3*, 256.

Lopez, S. R., & Guarnaccia, P. J. J. (2000). Cultural psychopathology: Uncovering the social world of mental illness. *Annual Review of Psychology, 51,* 571–598.

Lorenz, K. Z. (1981). *The foundations of ethology.* New York: Springer-Verlag.

Lorenz, K. (1937). The companion in the bird's world. *Auk, 54,* 245–273.

Lott, D. A. (2000). *The new flirting game.* London: Sage.

Louie, T. A., Curren, M. T., & Harich, K. R. (2000). "I knew we would win": Hindsight bias for favorable and unfavorable team decision outcomes. *Journal of Applied Psychology, 85*(2), 264–272.

Lu, L., Kao, S-F., Cooper, C. L., & Spector, P. E. (2000). Managerial stress, locus of control, and job strain in Taiwan and UK: A comparative study. *International Journal of Stress Management, 7*(3), 209–226.

Lu, Z. L., Williamson, S. J., & Kaufman, L. (1992). Behavioral lifetime of human auditory sensory memory predicted by physiological measures. *Science, 258,* 1668–1670.

Lubinski, D., & Benbow, C. P. (2000). States of excellence. *American Psychologist, 55*(1), 137–150.

Lubinski, D., & Dawis, R. V. (1992). Aptitudes, skills, and proficiencies. In M. D. Dunnette & L. M. Hough (Eds.), *The handbook of industrial/organizational psychology* (pp. 1–59). Palo Alto, CA: Consulting Psychologists Press.

Lucio-Gomez, E., Ampudia-Rueda, A., Duran-Patino, C., Gallegos-Mejia, L., & Leon-Guzman, I. (1999). La nueva version del Inventario Multifasico de la Personalidad de Minnesota para adolescentes Mexicanos. /The new version of the Minnesota Multiphasic Personality Inventory for Mexican adolescents. *Revista Mexicana de Psicologia, 16*(2), 217–226.

Luft, A., Skalej, M., Stefanou, A., Klose, U., & Voight, K. (1998). Comparing motion-and imagery-related activation in the human cerebellum: A functional MRI study. *Human Brain Mapping, 6*(2), 105–113.

Luker, K. (1996). *Dubious conceptions: The politics of teenage pregnancy.* Cambridge, MA: Harvard University Press.

Luria, A. R. (1976). *Cognitive development: Its cultural and social foundations.* Cambridge, MA: Harvard University Press.

Luthar, S. S. (1999). *Poverty and children's adjustment.* Thousand Oaks, CA: Sage.

Lykken, D. T. (1984). Polygraphic interrogation. *Nature, 307,* 681–684.

Lykken, D. T. (1988). The case against polygraph testing. In A. Gale (Ed.), *The polygraph test: Lies, truth, and science.* London: Sage.

Lykken, D. T. (1998). *A tremor in the blood: Uses and abuses of the lie detector.* New York: Plenum Press.

Lynch, E. D., Lee, M. K., Morrow, J. E., Welcsh, P. L., LeÛn, P. E., & King, M. (1997). Nonsyndromic deafness DFNA1 associated with mutation of a human homolog of the Drosophila gene diaphanous. *Science, 278,* 1315–1318.

Lynn, R. (2002). Racial and ethnic differences in psychopathic personality. *Personality & Individual Differences, 32*(2), 273–316.

Lynn, R. (1995). Cross-cultural differences in intelligence and personality. In D. H. Saklofske & M. Zeidner (Eds.), *International handbook of personality and intelligence.* New York: Plenum.

Lynn, S. J., Vanderhoff, H., Shindler, K., & Stafford, J. (2002). Defining hypnosis as a trance vs. cooperation: Hypnotic inductions, suggestibility, and performance standards. *American Journal of Clinical Hypnosis, 44*(3–4), 231–240.

Lyons, M. J., et al. (1998). A registry-based twin study of depression in men. *Archives of General Psychiatry, 55,* 468–472.

Maas, J. B. (1999). *Power sleep.* New York: HarperPerennial.

Maccoby, E. E. (2000). Parenting and its effects on children: On reading and misreading behavior genetics. *Annual Review of Psychology, 51,* 1–27.

MacDonald, K. (1998). Evolution, culture, and the five-factor model. *Journal of Cross-Cultural Psychology, 29*(1), 119–149.

Mackay, D. G., Stewart, R., & Burke, D. M. (1998a). H. M. 's language production deficits: Implications fro relations between memory, semantic binding, and the hippocampal system. *Journal of Memory & Language, 38,* 28–69.

Mackay, D. G., Stewart, R., & Burke, D. M. (1998b). H. M. revisited: Relations between language comprehension, memory, and the hippocampal system. *Journal of Cognitive Neuroscience, 10,* 377–394.

Mackay, J. (2001). Global sex: Sexuality and sexual practices around the world. *Sexual & Relationship Therapy, 16*(1), 71–82.

Mackey, R. A., & O'Brien, B. A. (1998). Marital conflict management: Gender and ethnic differences. *Social Work, 43*(2), 128–141.

Mackey, R. A., O'Brien, B. A.(1998) Marital conflict management: Gender and ethnic differences. *Social Work, 43*(2), 128–141.

Mackey, W. C. (2001). Support for the existence of an independent man-to-child affiliative bond: Fatherhood as a biocultural invention. *Psychology of Men & Masculinity, 2*(1), 51–66.

MacKinnon, D. F., Jamison, K. R., & DePaulo, J. R. (1997). Genetics of manic-depressive illness. *Annual Review of Neuroscience, 10,* 355–373.

MacLaren, V.V. (2001). A qualitative review of the Guilty Knowledge Test. *Journal of Applied Psychology, 86*(4), 674–683.

MacMillan, H. L. (2000). Child maltreatment: What we know in the year 2000. *Canadian Journal of Psychiatry, 45*(8), 702–709.

Macmillan, M. (2001). The reliability and validity of Freud's methods of free association and interpretation. *Psychological Inquiry, 12*(3), 167–175.

Macmillan, M. B. (1986). A wonderful journey through skull and brains: The travels of Mr. Gage's tamping iron. *Brain and Cognition, 5,* 67–107.

Macmillan, M. B. (2000). *An odd kind of fame: Stories of Phineas Gage.* Cambridge, MA: MIT Press.

Macmillan, M. (1997). *Freud evaluated.* Cambridge, MA: MIT Press.

Maddi, S. R., Khoshaba, D. M., Persico, M., Lu, J., Harvey, R., & Bleecker, F. (2002). The personality construct of hardiness: II. Relationships with comprehensive test of personality and psychopathology. *Journal of Research in Personality, 36*(1), 72–85.

Maddock, R. J., & Buonocore, M. H. (1997). Activation of left posterior cingulate gyrus by the auditory presentation of threat-related words: An fMRI study. *Psychiatry Research: Neuroimaging, 75,* 1–14.

Maeda, H. (1977). Septum and aggression: A review. *Kyushu Neuropsychiatry, 23*(1), 7–16.

Maehr, M. L., & Urdan, T. C. (2000). *Advances in motivation and achievement: The role of context.* Greewich, CT: JAI Press.

Magee, S. K., & Ellis, J. (2001). The detrimental effects of physical restraint as a consequence for inappropriate classroom behavior. *Journal of Applied Behavior Analysis, 34*(4), 501–504.

Magid, K., & McKelvey, C. A. (1987). *High risk: Children without a conscience.* New York: Bantam.

Maguen, S., Armistead, L., & Kalichman, S. (2000). Predictors of HIV antibody testing among gay, lesbian, and bisexual youth. *Journal of Adolescent Health, 26,* 252–257.

Main, M., & George, C. (1985). Responses of abused and disadvantaged toddlers todistress in agemates: A study in the day care setting. *Developmental Psychology, 21,* 407–412.

Malnic, B., Hirono, J., & Buck, L. B. (1999). Combinatorial receptor codes for odors. *Cell, 96,* 713–715.

Manji, H. K., & Lenox, R. H. (1998). Lithium: A molecular transducer of mood-stabilization in the treatment of bipolar disorders. *Neuropsychopharmacology, 19,* 161–166.

Manji, H. K., Moore, G. J., & Chen, G. (2000). Clinical and preclinical evidence for the neurotrophic effects of mood stabilizers: Implications for the pathophysiology and treatment of manic-depressive illness. *Biological Psychiatry, 48*(8),740–754.

Manly, T., Lewis, G. H., Robertson, I. H., Watson, P. C., & Datta, A. K. (2002). Coffee in the cornflakes: Time-of-day as a modulator of executive response control. *Neuropsychologia, 40*(1), 1–6.

Mann, J. J., Huang, Y., Underwood, M. D., Kassir, S. A., Oppenheim, S., Kelly, T. M., Dwork, A. J., & Arango, V. (2000). A serotonin transporter gene promoter polymorphism (5-HTTLPR) and prefrontal cortical binding in major depression and suicide. *Archives of General Psychiatry, 57*(8), 729–738.

Manoach, D. S., Gollub, R. L., Benson, E. S., Searl, M., Goff, D. C., Halpern, E., Saper, C., & Rauch, S. L. (2000). Schizophenia subjects show aberrant fMRI activation of dorsolateral prefrontal cortex and basal ganglia during working memory performance. *Biological Psychiatry, 48*, 99–109.

Manuck, S. B., Flory, J. D., McCaffery, J. M., Matthews, K. A., Mann, J. J., & Muldoon, M. F. (1998). Aggression, impulsivity, and central nervous system serotonergic responsivity in a nonpatient sample. *Neuropsychopharmacology, 19*(4), 287–299.

Maquet, P., et al. (1997). Functional neuroanatomy of human slow wave sleep. *Journal of Neuroscience, 17,* 2807–2812.

Maquet, P., Laureys, S., Peigneux, P., Fuchs, S., Petiau, C., Phillips, C., Aerts, J., Del Fiore, G., Degueldre, C., Meulemans, T., Luxen, A., Franck, G., Van Der Linden, M., Smith, C., & Cleeremans, A. (2000). Experience-dependent changes in cerebral activation during REM sleep. *Nature Neuroscience, 3,* 831–836.

Marcia, J. E. (2002). Identity and psychosocial development in adulthood. *Identity, 2*(1), 7–28.

Maren, S. (1999). Long-term potentiation in the amygdala: A mechanism for emotional learning and memory. *Trends in Neurosciences, 22,* 561–567.

Margolis, S., & Swartz, K. L. (2003). *Depression and anxiety. Johns Hopkins White Papers.* Baltimore: Johns Hopkins Medical Institutions.

Markides, K. S. (1995). Aging and ethnicity. *The Gerontologist, 35,* 276–277.

Markon, K. E., Krueger, R. F., Bouchard, T. J., & Gottesman, I. I. (2002). Normal and abnormal personality traits: Evidence for genetic and environmental relationships in the Minnesota Study of Twins Reared Apart. *Journal of Personality, 70*(5), 661–693.

Marks, D. F. (1990). Comprehensive commentary, insightful criticism. *Skeptical Inquirer, 14,* 413–418.

Markus, H. R., & Kitayama, S. (1998). The cultural psychology of personality. *Journal of Cross-Cultural Psychology, 29,* 63–87.

Marmot, M. G., & Wilkinson, R. G. (1999). *Social determinants of health.* Oxford: Oxford University Press.

Marshall, D. S. (1971). Sexual behavior in Mangaia. In D. S. Marshall & R. C. Suggs (Eds.), *Human sexual behavior* (pp. 103–162). Englewood Cliffs, NJ: Prentice Hall.

Martenyi, F., Dossenbach, M., Mraz, K., & Metcalfe, S. (2001). Gender differences in the efficacy of fluoxetine and maprotiline in depressed patients: A double-blind trial of antidepressants with serotonergic or norepinephrinergic reuptake inhibition profile. *European Neuropsychopharmacology, 11*(3), 227–232.

Martin, S. E., Snyder, L. B., Hamilton, M., Fleming-Milici, F., Slater, M. D., Stacy, A., Chen, M., & Grube, J. W. (2002). Alcohol advertising and youth. Alcoholism: *Clinical & Experimental Research, 26*(6), 900–906.

Martinez, J. L., & Derrick, B. E. (1996). Long-term potentiation and learning. *Annual Review of Psychology, 47,* 173–203.

Martire, L. M., Stephens, M. A. P., & Townsend, A. L. (2000). Centrality of women's multiple roles: Beneficial and detrimental consequences for psychological well-being. *Psychology & Aging, 15*(1), 148–156.

Maslach, C. (1982). *Burnout: The cost of caring.* Englewood Cliffs, NJ: Prentice Hall.

Maslow, A. H. (1954). *Motivation and personality.* New York: Harper & Row.

Maslow, A. H. (1970). Motivation and personality (2nd ed.). New York: Harper & Row.

Maslow, A. H. (1999). *Toward a psychology of being* (3rd ed.). New York: Wiley.

Mason, P. T., & Kreger, R. (1998). Stop walking on eggshells: Taking your life back when someone you care about has borderline personality disorder. New York: New Harbinger Publishers.

Masson, J. M. (1992). The assault on truth: Freud's suppression of the seduction theory. New York: Harper Perennial.

Mast, M. (2002). Dominance as expresses and inferred through speaking time: A meta-analysis. *Human Communication Research, 28*(3), 420–450.

Masten A. S., & Coatsworth, J. D. (1998). The development of competence in favorable and unfavorable environments. *American Psychologist, 53*(2), 205–220.

Masten, A. S. (2001). Ordinary magic: Resilience processes in development. *American Psychologist, 56,* 227–238.

Masten, A. S. (1998). Resilience comes of age: Reflections on the past and outlook for the next generation of research. In M. D. Glantz, J. Johnson, & L. Huffman (Eds.), *Resilience and development: Positive life adaptations.* New York: Plenum.

Masters, W. H., & Johnson, V. E. (1966). *Human sexual response.* Boston: Little, Brown.

Masters, W. H., & Johnson, V. E. (1970). Human sexual inadequacy. Boston: Little, Brown.

Masters, W., & Johnson, V. (1961). Orgasm, anatomy of the female. In A. Ellis & A. Abarbonel (Eds.). *Encyclopedia of Sexual Behavior,* Vol. 2. New York: Hawthorn.

Mastor, K. A., Jin, P., & Cooper, M. (2000). Malay culture and personality: A Big Five perspective. *American Behavioral Scientist, 44*(1), 95–111.

Mathes, E.W., King, C. A., Miller, J. K., & Reed, R.M. (2002). An evolutionary perspective on the interaction of age and sex differences in short term sexual strategies.

Matlin, M. W., & Foley, H. J. (1997). *Sensation and perception* (4th ed.). Boston: Allyn and Bacon.

Matsumoto, D. (1992). More evidence for the universality of a contempt expression. *Motivation and Emotion, 16,* 363–368.

Matsumoto, D. (2000). *Culture and psychology: People around the world.* Belmont, CA: Wadsworth.

Matsumoto, D., & Kupperbusch, C. (2001). Idiocentric and allocentric differences in emotional expression, experience, and the coherence between expression and experience. *Asian Journal of Social Psychology, 4*(2), 113–131.

Mattson, M.E., Pollack, E. S., & Cullen, J. W. (1987). What are the odds that smoking will kill you? *American Journal of Public Health, 77,* 425–431.

Matusov, E., & Hayes, R. (2000). Sociocultural critique of Piaget and Vygotsky. *New Ideas in Psychology, 18*(2–3), 215–239.

Matuszek, P. A. C. (2000). A biofeedback-enhanced stress management program for the fire service. *Dissertation Abstracts International: Section B: The Sciences & Engineering, 60*(7–B), 3212.

May, M. A., Hartshorne, H., & Welty, R. E. (1928). Personality and character tests. *Psychological Bulletin, 25,* 422–443.

Mayberg, H. S., Liotti, M., Brannan, S. K., McGinnis, S., Mahurin, R. K., Jerabek, P. A., Silva, J. A., Tekell, J. L., Martin, C. C., Lancaster, J. L., & Fox, P. T. (1999). Reciprocal limbic-cortical function and negative mood. *American Journal of Psychiatry, 156,* 675–682.

Mayer, J. D., & Salovey, P. (1997). What is emotional intelligence? In P. Salovey & D.

Sluyter (Eds.), *Emotional development, emotional literacy, and emotional intelligence.* New York: Basic Books.

Mayford, M., Barzilai, A., Keller, F., Schachter, S., & Kandel, E. R. (1992). Modulation of an NCAM-related adhesion molecule with long-term synaptic plasticity in aplysia. *Science, 256,* 638–644.

Mazur, A., & Booth, A. (1998). Testosterone and dominance in men. *Behavioral and Brain Sciences, 21,* 353–363.

Mazzoni, G., & Memon, A. (2003). Imagination can create false autobiographical memories. *Psychological Science, 14,* in press.

McAllister-Williams, R. H., & Rugg, M. D. (2002). Effects of repeated cortisol administration on brain potential correlates of episodic memory retrieval. *Psychopharmacology, 160(1),* 74–83.

McAndrew, F. T., Akande, A., Turner, S., & Sharma, Y. (1998). A cross-cultural ranking of stressful life events in Germany, India, South Africa, and the United States. *Journal of Cross-Cultural Psychology, 29,* 717–727.

McArthur, L. Z., & Berry, D. S. (1987). Cross-cultural agreement in perceptions of baby-faced adults. *Journal of Cross-Cultural Psychology, 18,* 165–192.

McCabe, M. P., & Ricciardelli, L. A. (2003). Body image and strategies to lose weight and increase muscle among boys and girls. *Health Psychology, 22(1),* 39–46.

McCall, M. (1997). The effects of physical attractiveness on gaining access to alcohol: When social policy meets social decision making. *Addiction, 92,* 597–600.

McCall, R. B. (1994). Academic underachievers. *Current Directions in Psychological Science, 3,* 15–19.

McCarthy, B. W. (2002). Sexual secrets, trauma, and dysfunction. *Journal of Sex & Marital Therapy, 28(4),* 352–360.

McCarthy, M. M., Auger, A. P., & Perrot-Sinal, T. S. (2002). Getting excited about GABA and sex differences in the brain. *Trends in Neurosciences, 25(6),* 307–312.

McCartt, A. T., Rohrbaugh, J. W., Hammer, M. C., & Fuller, S. Z. (2000). Factors associated with falling asleep at the wheel among long-distance truck drivers. *Accident Analysis and Prevention, 32(4),* 493–504.

McClelland, D. C. (1958). Risk-taking in children with high and low need for achievement. In J. W. Atkinson (Ed.), *Motives in fantasy, action, and society.* Princeton, NJ: Van Nostrand.

McClelland, D. C. (1987). Characteristics of successful entrepreneurs. *Journal of Creative Behavior, 3,* 219–233.

McClelland, D. C. (1993). Intelligence is not the best predictor of job performance. *Current Directions in Psychological Science, 2,* 5–6.

McClelland, J. L. (1995). Constructive memory and memory distortions: A parallel-distributed processing approach. In D. L. Schachter (Ed.), *Memory distortions: How minds, brains, and societies reconstruct the past* (pp. 69–90). Cambridge: Harvard University Press.

McCloskey, L. A., & Bailey, J. A. (2000). The intergenerational transmission of risk for child sexual abuse. *Journal of Interpersonal Violence, 15(10),* 1019–1035.

McConkey, K. M. (1995). Hypnosis, memory, and the ethics of uncertainty. *Australian Psychologist, 30,* 1–10.

McCormack, F. (2001). SiaAmma. *Ms.,* February/March, 13.

McCrae, R. E., & Costa, P. T. Jr. (1990). *Personality in adulthood.* New York: Guilford Press.

McCrae, R. R. (2001). Facts and interpretations of personality trait stability: A reply to Quackenbush. *Theory & Psychology, 11(6),* 837–844.

McCrae, R. R., & Costa, P. T. Jr. (1999). A five-factor theory of personality. In L. A. Pervin, & O. P. John (Eds.), *Handbook of personality: Theory and research.* New York: Guilford Press.

McCrae, R. R., & Costa, P. T. Jr., de Lirna, M. P., Simoes, A., Ostendorf, F., Angleitner, A., Marusic, I., Bratko, D., Caprara, G. V., Barbaranelli, C., Chae, J. H., & Piedmont, R. L. (1999). Age differences in personality across the adult life span: Parallels in five cultures. *Developmental Psychology, 35,* 466–477.

McCrae, R. R., & Costa, P. T. (1997). Personality trait structure as a human universal. *American Psychologist, 52,* 509–516.

McCrae, R. R., Costa, P. T., Jr., Ostendorf, F., Angleitner, A., Hrebickova, M., Avia, M. D., Sanz, J., Sanchez-Bernardos, M. L., Kusdil, M. E., Woodfield, R., Saunders, P. R., & Smith, P. B. (2000). Nature over nurture: Temperament, personality, and life span development. *Journal of Personality & Social Psychology, 78(1),* 173–186.

McDonald, C., & Murray, R. M. (2000). Early and late environmental risk factors for schizophrenia. *Brain Research Reviews, 31,* 130–137.

McDonald, J. W., Liu, X. Z., Qu, Y., Liu, S., Mickey, S. K., Turetsky, D., Gottlieb, D. I., & Choi, D. W. (1999). Transplanted embryonic stem cells survive, differentiate, and promote recovery in injured rat spinal cord. *Nature & Medicine, 5,* 1410–1412.

McDonald, M. (2001, January 8). Psst! Want a hot tip? Try a crystal ball. *U.S. News & World Report,* 34.

McDougall, W. (1908). *Social psychology.* New York: Putnam's Sons.

McElroy, S. L., Frye, M. A., Suppes, T., Dhavale, D., Keck, P. E., Jr., Leverich, G. S., Altshuler, L., Denicoff, K. D., Nolen, W. A., Kupka, R., Grunze, H., Walden, J., & Post, R. M. (2002). Correlates of overweight and obesity in 644 patients with bipolar disorder. *Journal of Clinical Psychiatry, 63(3),* 207–213.

McEntee, D. J., & Halgin, R. P. (1999). Cognitive group therapy and aerobic exercise in the treatment of anxiety. *Journal of College Student Psychotherapy, 13(3),* 37–55.

McGaugh, J. L. (1989). Modulation of memory storage processes. In P. R. Soloman, G. R. Goethals, C. M. Kelley, & B. R. Stephens (Eds.), *Memory: Interdisciplinary approaches.* New York: Springer-Verlag.

McGaugh, J. L. (1990). Significance and remembrance: The role of neuromodulatory systems. *Psychological Science, 1,* 15–25.

McGaugh, J. L., & Roozendaal, B. (2002). Role of adrenal stress hormones in forming lasting memories in the brain. *Current Opinion in Neurobiology, 12(2),* 205–210.

McGaughy, J., Decker, M. W., Sarter, M. (1999). Enhancement of sustained attention performance by the nicotine acetylcholine receptor agonist ABT-418 in intact but not basal forebrain-lesioned rats. *Psychopharmacology, 144(2),* 175–182.

McGaughy, J., et al. (1997). Lack of effects of lesins of the dorsal norandrenergic bundle on behavioral vigilance. *Behavioral Neuroscience, 111,* 646–652.

McGeoch, J. A. (1942). *The psychology of human learning.* New York: Longmans, Green.

McGhie, A., & Chapman, H. (1961). Disorders of attention and perception in early schizophrenia. *British Journal of Medical Psychology, 34,* 103–116.

McGhie, A., & Chapman, I. S. (1961). Disorders of attention and perception in early schizophrenia. *British Journal of Medical Psychology, 34,* 103–116.

McGrath, M.G., & Casey, E. (2002). Forensic psychiatry and the Internet: Practical perspectives on sexual predators and obsessional harassers in cyberspace. *Journal of the American Academy of Psychiatry & the Law, 30(1),* 81–94.

McGrath, P. (2002). Qualitative findings on the experience of end-of-life care for hematological malignancies. *American Journal of Hospice & Palliative Care, 19(2),* 103–111.

McGraw, D. (1999, March 1). Justice delayed. U. S. *News and World Report,* pp. 76–79.

McIlduff, E., & Coghlan, D. (2000). Reflections: Understanding and contending with passive-aggressive behaviour in teams and organizations. *Journal of Managerial Psychology, 15(7–8),* 716–732.

McKay, R. et al. (2002). Dopamine neurons derived from embryonic stem cells function in an animal model of Parkinson's disease. *Nature, 417*, 302–307.

McKee, M. G. (1991). Contributions of psychophysiologic monitoring to diagnosis and treatment of headache pain: A case study. *Headache Quarterly, 2*, 327–330.

McKee, P., & Barber, C. E. (2001). Plato's theory of aging. *Journal of Aging & Identity, 6(2)*, 93–104.

McKellar, P. (1972). Imagery from the standpoint of introspection. In P. W. Sheehan (Ed.), *The function and nature of imagery.* New York: Academic Press.

McKim, W. A. (2002). Drugs and behavior: An introduction to behavioral pharmacology (5th ed). Englewood Cliffs, NJ: Prentice Hall.

McKnight, J. D., & Glass, D. C. (1995). Perceptions of control, burnout, and depressive symptomatology. *Journal of Consulting and Clinical Psychology, 63*, 490–494.

McLoyd, V. C. (1998). Socio-economic disadvantage and child development. *American Psychologist, 53*, 185–204.

McMillan, T. M., Robertson, I, H., & Wilson, B. A. (1999). Neurogesesis after brain injury: Implications for neurorehabilitation. *Neuropsychological Rehabilitation, 9*, 129–133.

McMullin, R. E. (2000). *The new handbook of cognitive therapy techniques.* New York: W. W. Norton & Company.

Medina, J. J. (1996). *The clock of ages: Why we age.* Cambridge, MA: Cambridge University Press.

Medora, N. P., Larson, J. H., Hortacsu, N., & Dave, P. (2002). Perceived attitudes towards romanticism: A cross-cultural study of American, Asian-Indian, and Turkish young adults. *Journal of Comparative Family Studies, 33(2)*, 155–178.

Megarry, T. (2001). What made us human? Reflections on sex and gender in human evolution. *Psychology, Evolution & Gender, 3(2)*, 167–188.

Meisenzahl, E. M., Dresel, S., F. T., Schmitt, G. J. E., Preuss, U. W., Rossmueller, B., Tatsch, K., Mager, T., Hahn, K., & Moeller, H. J. (2000). D-sub-2 receptor occupancy under recommended and high doses of olanzapine: An iodine-123–iodobenzamide SPECT study. *Journal of Psychopharmacology, 14(4)*, 364–370.

Melamed, S., Ugarten, U., Shirom, A., Kahana, L., Lerman, Y., & Froom, P. (1999). Chronic burnout, somatic arousal, and elevated salivary cortisol levels. *Journal of Psychosomatic Research, 46*, 591–598.

Melchert, T. P. (2000). Clarifying the effects of parental substance abuse, child sexual abuse, and parental caregiving on adult adjustment. *Professional Psychology: Research & Practice, 31(1)*, 64–69.

Meloy, J. R., Acklin, M. W., Gacono, C. B., Murray, J. F., & Peterson, C. A. (Eds.) (1997). Contemporary Rorschach interpretation. Mahwah, NJ: Erlbaum.

Meltzer, H. Y. (2000). Genetics and etiology of schizophrenia and bipolar disorder. *Biological Psychiatry, 47*, 171–173.

Meltzoff, A. N., & Moore, M. K. (1977). Imitation of facial and manual gestures by human neonates. *Science, 198*, 75–78.

Meltzoff, A. N., & Moore, M. K. (1985). Cognitive foundations and social functions of imitation and intermodal representation in infancy. In J. Mehler & R. Fox (Eds.), *Neonate cognition: Beyond the blooming buzzing confusion.* Hillsdale, NJ: Erlbaum.

Meltzoff, A. N., & Moore, M. K. (1994). Imitation, memory, and the representation of persons. *Infant Behavior and Development, 17*, 83–99.

Melzack, R. (1999). Pain and stress: A new perspective. In R. J. Gatchel & D. C. Turk (Eds.), *Psychosocial factors in pain: Critical perspectives.* New York: Guilford Press.

Melzack, R., & Wall, P. D. (1965). Pain mechanisms: A new theory. *Science, 150*, 971–979.

Melzack, R., Israel, R., Lacroix, R., & Schultz, G. (1997). Phantom limbs in people with congenital limb deficiency or amputation in early childhood. *Brain, 120*, 1603–1620.

Mennin, D. S., Heimberg, R. G., & Holt, C. S. (2000). Panic, agoraphobia, phobias, and generalized anxiety disorder. In M. Hersen & A. S. Bellack (Eds.), *Psychopathology in adulthood (2nd ed.).* Needham Heights, MA: Allyn & Bacon.

Merckelbach, H., Arntz, A., Arrindell, W. A., & DeJong, P. J. (1992). Pathways to spider phobia. *Behaviour Research and Therapy, 30*, 543–546.

Merckelbach, H., de Jong, P. J., Muris, P., & van den Hout, M. A. (1996). The etiology of specific phobias: A review. *Clinical Psychology Review, 16*, 337–361.

Merikle, P. M., & Skanes, H. E. (1992). Subliminal self-help audiotapes: A search for placebo effects. *Journal of Applied Psychology, 77*, 772–776.

Merlin, M., Lebot, V., & Lindstrom, L. (1992). *Kava: The Pacific drug.* New Haven, CT: Yale University Press.

Meschke, L. L., Bartholomae, S., & Zentall, S. R. (2000). Adolescent sexuality and parent-adolescent processes: Promoting healthy teen choices. Family Relations: *Interdisciplinary Journal of Applied Family Studies, 49(2)*, 143–154.

Messenger, J. (1971). Sex and repression in an Irish folk community. In D. Marshall & R. Suggs (Eds.), *Human sexual behavior: Variations in the ethnographic spectrum.* Englewood Cliffs, NJ: Prentice Hall.

Meston, C. M., & Frohlich, P. F. (2000). The neurobiology of sexual function. *Archives of General Psychiatry, 57(11)*, 1012–1030.

Metcalf, P., & Huntington, R. (1991). *Celebrations of death: The anthropology of mortuary ritual* (2nd ed.). Cambridge, England: Cambridge University Press.

Meyer, R. G., & Salmon, P. (1988). *Abnormal psychology* (2nd ed.). Boston: Allyn & Bacon.

Michael, R., Gagnon, J., Laumann, E., & Kolata, G. (1994). *Sex in America.* Boston: Little, Brown.

Michalski, R. L., & Shackelford, T. K. (2002). An attempted replication of the relationships between birth order and personality. *Journal of Research in Personality, 36(2)*, 182–188.

Migueles, M, & Garcia-Bajos, E. (1999). Recall, recognition, and confidence patterns in eyewitness testimony. *Applied Cognitive Psychology, 13*, 257–268.

Miles, C., & Hardman, E. (1998). State-dependent memory produced by aerobic exercise. *Ergonomics, 41*, 20–28.

Miles, D. R., & Carey, G. (1997). Genetic and environmental architecture on human aggression. *Journal of Personality and Social Psychology, 72*, 207–217.

Milgram, S. (1963). Behavioral study of obedience. *Journal of Abnormal and Social Psychology, 67*, 371–378.

Milgram, S. (1974). *Obedience to authority: An experimental view.* New York: Harper & Row.

Miller, B., & Coyl, D. D. (2000). Adolescent pregnancy and childbearing in relation to infant adoption in the United States. *Adoption Quarterly, 1 4(1)*, 3–25.

Miller, F. A. (1998). Strategic culture change: The door to achieving high performance and inclusion. *Public Personnel Management, 27(2)*, 151–160.

Miller, G. A. (1956). The magical number seven, plus or minus two: Some limits on our capacity for processing information. *Psychological Review, 63*, 81–97.

Miller, G. E., & Cohen, S. (2001). Psychological interventions and the immune system: A meta-analytic review and critique. *Health Psychology, 20(1)*, 47–63.

Miller, J. G., & Bersoff, D. M. (1998). The role of liking in perceptions of the moral responsibility to help: A cultural perspective. *Journal of Experimental Social Psychology, 34*, 443–469.

Miller, J. (1998). The enemy inside: An exploration of the defensive processes of introjecting and identifying with the aggressor. *Psychodynamic Counseling, 4*(1), 55–70.

Miller, L. C., & Fishkin, S. A. (1997). On the dynamics of human bonding and reproductive success: Seeking windows on the adapted-for-human-environmental interface. In J. A. Simpson & D. T. Kenrick (Eds.). *Evolutionary social psychology* (pp. 197–236). Mahwah, NJ: Erlbaum.

Miller, L. C., Putcha-Bhagavatula, A., & Pedersen, W. C. (2002). Men's and women's mating preferences: Distinct evolutionary mechanisms? *Current Directions in Psychological Science, 11*(3), 88–93.

Miller, M. A., & Rahe, R. H. (1997). Life changes scaling for the 1990s. *Journal of Psychosomatic Research, 43,* 279–292.

Miller, M., & Kantrowitz, B. (1999, January 25). Unmasking Sybil: A reexamination of the most famous psychiatric patient in history. *Newsweek,* pp. 11–16.

Miller, N. E. (1991). Commentary on Ulrich: Need to check truthfulness of statements by opponents of animal research. *Psychological Science, 2,* 422–424.

Miller, N. E., & DiCara, L. (1967). Instrumental learning of heart rate changes in curarized rats: Shaping and specificity to discriminative stimulus. *Journal of Comparative and Physiological Psychology, 63,* 12–19.

Miller, T. O., Smith, T. W., Turner, C. W., Guijarro, M. L., & Hallet, A. J. (1996). A meta-analytic review of research on hostility and physical health. *Psychological Bulletin, 119,* 322–348.

Milner, B. (1965). Memory disturbance after bilateral hippocampal lesions. In P. Milner & S. Glickman (Eds.), *Cognitive processes and the brain.* Princeton, NJ: Van Nostrand.

Milner, B. (1970). Memory and the medial temporal regions of the brain. In K. H. Pribram & D. E. Broadbent (Eds.), *Cognitive processes and the brain.* Princeton, NJ: Van Nostrand.

Milner, B. (1970). Memory and the temporal regions of the brain. In K. H. Pribram & D.E. Broadbent (Eds.), *Biology of memory.* New York: Academic Press.

Milton, J., & Wiseman, R. (2001). Does psi exist? Reply to Storm and Ertel 2000. *Psychological Bulletin, 127*(3), 434–438.

Milton, J., & Wiseman, R. (2001). Does psi exist? Reply to Storm and Ertel. *Psychological Bulletin, 127,* 434–438.

Milton, J., & Wiseman, R. (1999). Does psi exist? Lack of replication of an anomalous process of information transfer. *Psychological Bulletin, 125,* 387–391.

Min, P. G. (2001). Changes in Korean immigrants' gender role and social status, and their marital conflicts. *Sociological Forum, 16*(2), 301–320.

Mineka, S., & Oehman, A. (2002). Phobias and preparedness: The selective, automatic, and encapsulated nature of fear. *Biological Psychiatry, 51*(9), 927–937.

Mingo, C., Herman, C. J., & Jasperse, M. (2000). Women's stories: Ethnic variations in women's attitudes and experiences of menopause, hysterectomy, and hormone replacement therapy. *Journal of Women's Health and Gender Based Medicine, 9,* S27–S38.

Miracle, T. S., Miracle, A. W., & Baumeister, R. F. (2003). *Human sexuality: Meeting your basic needs.* Upper Saddle River, NJ: Pearson Education, Inc.

Miralt, G., Bearor, K., & Thomas, T. (2001).-(2002). Adult romantic attachment among women who experienced childhood maternal loss. *Omega: Journal of Death & Dying, 44*(1), 97–104.

Mischel, W., & Shoda, Y. (1999). Integrating dispositions and processing dynamics within a unified theory of personality: The cognitive-affective personality system. In L. A. Pervin, & O. P. John (Eds.), *Handbook of personality: Theory and research.* New York: Guilford Press.

Mita, T. H., Dermer, M., & Knight, J. (1977). Reversed facial images and the mere-exposure hypothesis. *Journal of Personality & Social Psychology, 35*(8), 597–601.

Mitchell, E., Sachs, A., Tu, J. I-Chin (1997, September 29). Teaching feelings 101. *Time,* p. 62.

Mitchell, S. A. (2002). Psychodynamics, homosexuality, and the question of pathology. *Studies in Gender & Sexuality, 3*(1), 3–21.

Mitchell, T. W., Mufson, E. J., Schneider, J. A., Cochran, E. J., Nissanov, J., Han, L., Bienias, J. L., Lee, V. M., Trojanowski, J. Q., Bennett, D. A., & Arnold, S. E. (2002). Parahippocampal tau pathology in healthy aging, mild cognitive impairment, and early Alzheimer's disease. *Annals of Neurology, 51*(2), 182–189

Moffitt, T. E., Caspi, A., Harrington, H., & Milne, B. J. (2002). Males on the life-course-persistent and adolescence-limited antisocial pathways: Follow-up at age 26 years. *Development & Psychopathology, 14*(1), 179–207.

Mohr, P. B., & Larsen, K. (1998). Ingroup favoritism in umpiring decisions in Australian football. *Journal of Social Psychology, 138*(4), 495–504.

Moneta, G. B., & Siu, C. M. Y. (2002). Trait intrinsic and extrinsic motivations, academic performance, and creativity in Hong Kong college students. *Journal of College Student Development, 43*(5), 664–683.

Money, J. (1985a). Sexual reformation and counter-reformation in law and medicine. *Medicine and Law, 4,* 479–488.

Money, J., & Ehrhardt, A. A. (1972). *Man and woman, boy and girl.* Baltimore: The Johns Hopkins University Press.

Money, J., Prakasam, K. S., & Joshi, V. N. (1991). Semen-conservation doctrine from ancient Ayurvedic to modern sexological theory. *American Journal of Psychotherapy, 45,* 9–13.

Monk, T. H. (1997). Shift work. In M. R. Pressman and W. C. Orr (Eds.), *Understanding sleep: The evaluation and treatment of sleep disorders. Application and practice in health psychology* (pp. 249–266). Washington, DC: American Psychological Association.

Monte, C. F., & Sollod, R.N., (2003). *Beneath the mask: An introduction to theories of personality.* Hoboken, NJ: Wiley.

Montgomery, G. H., Weltz, C. R., Seltz, M., & Bovbjerg, D. H. (2002). Brief presurgery hypnosis reduces distress and pain in excisional breast biopsy patients. *International Journal of Clinical & Experimental Hypnosis, 50*(1), 17–32.

Moore, M. M. (1998). The science of sexual signaling. In G. C. Brannigan, E. R. Allgeier, & A. R. Allgeier (Eds.), *The sex scientists* (pp. 61–75). New York: Longman.

Moore, R. Y. (1997). Circadian rhythms: Basic neurobiology and clinical applications. *Annual Review of Medicine, 48,* 253–266.

Moore, T. E. (1995). Subliminal self-help auditory tapes: An empirical test of perceptual consequences. *Canadian Journal of Behavioral Science, 27,* 9–20.

Mor Barak, M., & Levin, A. (2002). Outside of the corporate mainstream and excluded from the work community: A study of diversity, job satisfaction and well-being. *Community, Work & Family, 5*(2), 133–157.

Moran, C. C., & Massam, M. M. (1999). Differential influences of coping humor and humor bias on mood. *Behavioral Medicine, 25*(1), 36–42.

Morelli, G. A., Oppenheim, D., Rogoff, B., & Goldsmith, D. (1992). Cultural variations in infant sleeping arrangements: Questions of independence. *Developmental Psychology, 28,* 604–613.

Morelli, G. A., Rogoff, B., Oppenheim, D., & Goldsmith, D. (1999). Cultural variations in infants' sleeping arrangements: Questions of independence. In L. E. Berk, *Landscapes of development* (pp. 65–80). Belmont, CA: Wadsworth.

Moretti, R., Torre, P.,Antonello, R. M., & Cazzato, G. (2001). Fronto-temporal dementia versus Alzheimer disease. *Archives of Gerontology & Geriatrics, 7,* 273–278.

Morgan, C. M., Tanofsky-Kraff, M., Wilfley, D. E., & Yanovski, J. A. (2002). Childhood obesity. *Child & Adolescent Psychiatric Clinics of North America, 11(2),* 257–278.

Morgan, M. J., McFie, L., Fleetwood, L. H., & Robinson, J. A. (2002). Ecstasy (MDMA): Are the psychological problems associated with its use reversed by prolonged abstinence? *Psychopharmacology, 159(3),* 294–303.

Morgan, S. (2001). Brief hypnosis for needle phobia. *Australian Journal of Clinical & Experimental Hypnosis, 29(2),* 107–115.

Morgenstern, J., Labouvie, E., McCrady, S., Kahler, C. W., & Frey, R. M. (1997). Affiliation with Alcoholics Anonymous after treatment: A study of the therapeutic effects and mechanisms of action. *Journal of Consulting and Clinical Psychology, 65,* 768–777.

Morgenstern, J., Langenbucher, J., Labouvie, E., & Miller, K. J. (1997). The comorbidity of alcoholism and personality disorders in a clinical population: Prevalence rates and relation to alcohol typology variables. *Journal of Abnormal Psychology, 106,* 74–84.

Mori, E., Ikeda, M., Hirono, N., Kitagaki, H., Imamura, T., & Shimomura, T. (1999). Amygdalar volume and emotional memory in Alzheimer's disease. *American Journal of Psychiatry, 156,* 216–222.

Morris, J. S., Frith, C. D., Perrett, D. L., Rowland, D., Young, A. W., Calder, A. J., & Dolan, R. J. (1996). A differential neural response in the human amygdala to fearful and happy expressions. *Nature, 383,* 812–815.

Morris, N., & Raabe, B. (2002). Some legal implications of CBT stress counseling in the workplace. *British Journal of Guidance & Counseling, 30(1),* 55–62.

Morrison, C., & Westman, A. S. (2001). Women report being more likely than men to model their relationships after what they have seen on TV. *Psychological Reports, 89(2),* 252–254.

Morrison, M. F., & Tweedy, K. (2000). Effects of estrogen on mood and cognition in aging women. *Psychiatric Annals, 30(2),* 113–119.

Morry, M. M., & Winkler, E. (2001). Student acceptance and expectation of sexual assault. *Canadian Journal of Behavioural Science, 33(3),* 188–192.

Moscoso, S. (2000). A review of validity evidence, adverse impact and applicant reactions. *International Journal of Selection & Assessment, 8(4),* 237–247.

Moss, A. J., Allen, K. f., Gioviano, G. A., & Mills, S. L. (1992). *Recent trends in adolescent smoking, smoking-update correlates, and expectations about the future. Advance Data No. 221* (from Vital and Health Statistics of the Centers for Disease Control and Prevention p. 537).

Mueller, C. M., & Dweck, C. S. (1998). Praise for intelligence can undermine children's motivation and performance. *Journal of Personality & Social Psychology, 75,* 33–52.

Muente, T. F. (1997). Event-related brain potentials to unfamiliar faces in explicit and implicit memory tasks. *Neuroscience Research, 28,* 223–233.

Mui, A. C. (1992). Caregiver strain among black and white daughter caregivers: A role theory perspective. *The Gerontologist, 32,* 203–212.

Muir, G. D., & Steeves, J. D. (1997). Sensorimotor stimulation to improve locomotor recovery after spinal cord injury. *Trends in Neurosciences, 20,* 72–77.

Mukherjee, R., Fialho, A., Wijetunge, A., Checinski, K., & Surgenor, T. (2002). The stigmatisation of psychiatric illness: The attitudes of medical students and doctors in a London teaching hospital. *Psychiatric Bulletin, 26(5),* 178–181.

Mulac, A., Bradac, J. J., & Gibbons, P. (2001). Empirical support for the gender-asculture hypothesis: An intercultural analysis of male/female language differences. *Human Communication Research, 27(1),* 121–152.

Mulford, M., Orbell, J., Shatto, C., & Stockard, J. (1998). Physical attractiveness, opportunity, and success in everyday exchange. *American Journal of Sociology, 103,* 1565–1592.

Mulligan, C., Moreau, K., Brandolini, M., Livingstone, B., Beaufrere, B., & Boirie, Y. (2002). Alterations of sensory perceptions in healthy elderly subjects during fasting and refeeding. A Pilot Study. *Gerontology, 48(1),* 39–43.

Murakami, K., & Hayashi, T. (2002). Interaction between mind-heart and gene. *Journal of International Society of Life Information Science, 20(1),* 122–126.

Muris, P., Merckelbach, H., Gadet, B., & Moulaert, V. (2000). Fears, worries, and scary dreams in 4– to 12–year-old children: Their content, developmental pattern, and origins. *Journal of Clinical Child Psychology, 29(1),* 43–52.

Murphy, C. M., & O'Farrell, T. J. (1996). Marital violence among alcoholics. *Current Directions in Psychological Science, 5(6),* 183–186.

Murphy, G., Athanasou, J., & King, N. (2002). Job satisfaction and organizational citizenship behaviour: A study of Australian human-service professionals. *Journal of Managerial Psychology, 17(4),* 287–297.

Murphy, S. T., & Zajonc, R. (1993). Affect, cognition, and awareness: Affective priming with optimal and suboptimal stimulus exposures. *Journal of Personality and Social Psychology, 64,* 723–739.

Murray, B. (1995, October). Americans dream about food, Brazilians dream about sex. *APA Monitor,* p. 30.

Murray, H. A. (1938). *Explorations in personality.* New York: Oxford University Press.

Murray, S. l., & Holmes, J. G. (1993). Seeing virtues in faults: Negativity and the transformation of interpersonal narratives in close relationships. *Journal of Personality and Social Psychology, 65,* 707–722.

Murray, S. L., & Holmes, J. G. (1997). A leap of faith? Positive illusions in romantic relationships. *Personality and Social Psychology Bulletin, 23,* 586–604.

Myers, D. G. (2000). The funds, friends, and faith of happy people. *American Psychologist, 55(1),* 56–67.

Myers, L. B., & Vetere, A. (2002). Adult romantic attachment styles and health-related measures. *Psychology, Health & Medicine, 7(2),* 175–180.

Myerson, J., Rank, M. R., Raines, F. Q., & Schnitzler, M. A. (1998). Race and general cognitive ability: The myth of diminishing returns to education. *Psychological Science, 9,* 139–142.

Nadon, R., Hoyt, I. P., Register, P. A., & Kihlstrom, J. F. (1991). Absorption and hypnotizability: Context effects reexamined. *Journal of Personality and Social Psychology, 60,* 144–153.

Naglieri, J. A., & Ronning, M. E. (2000). Comparison of White, African American, Hispanic, and Asian children on the Naglieri Nonverbal Ability Test. *Psychological Assessment, 12(3),* 328–334.

Nakao, M., Nomura, S., Shimosawa, T., Fujita, T., & Kuboki, T. (2000). Blood pressure biofeedback treatment of white-coat hypertension. *Journal of Psychosomatic Research, 48(2),* 161–169.

Nakao, M., Nomura, S., Shimosawa, T., Yoshiuchi, K., Kuboki, T., et al. (1997). Clinical effects of blood pressure biofeedback treatment on hypertension by autoshaping. *Psychosomatic Medicine, 59,* 331–338.

Napolitane, C. (1997). *Living and loving after divorce.* New York: Signet.

Narduzzi, K. J., & Jackson, T. (2000). Personality differences between eating-disordered women and a nonclinical comparison sample: A discriminant classification analysis. *Journal of Clinical Psychology, 56(6)* 699–710.

Nathan, P. E., & Langenbucher, J. W. (1999). Psychopathology. *Annual Review of Psychology, 50,* 79–107.

National Center for Health Statistics. (2001). Trends in Causes of Death Among the Elderly. *Centers for Disese Control,* Available: http://navigation.helper.realnames.com/framer/1/112/default.asp?realna

me=National+Center+for+Health+Statistics&url=http%3A%2F%2Fwww%2Ecdc%2Egov%2Fnchswww%2F&frameid=1&providerid=112&uid=30011018

National Institute of Mental Health. (1999). *Facts about anxiety disorders.* Available: http://www.nimh.nih.gov/anxiety/adfacts.cfm

National Institute on Drug Abuse (2002). Club drugs: Community drug alert bulletin. http://www.drugabuse.gov/ClubAlert/Clubdrugalert.html.

National Sleep Foundation (2001). Less fun, less sleep, more work: An American portrait. http://www.sleepfoundation.org/PressArchivs/lessfun_lesssleep.html.

Nayda, R. (2002). Influences on registered nurses' decision-making in cases of suspected child abuse. *Child Abuse Review, 11(3),* 168–178.

Neale, J. M., Oltmanns, T. F., & Winters, K. C. (1983). Recent developments in the assessment and conceptualization of schizophrenia. *Behavioral Assessment, 5,* 33–54.

Neese, R. M. (2000). Is depression an adaptation? *Archives of General Psychiatry, 57,* 14–20.

Neher, A. (1991). Maslow's theory of motivation: A critique. *Journal of Humanistic Psychology, 31,* 89–112.

Neisser, U. (1967). *Cognitive psychology.* New York: Appleton-Century-Crofts.

Neisser, U. (1998). Introduction: Rising test scores and what they mean. In U. Neisser (Ed.), *The rising curve: Long-term gains in IQ and related measures.* Washington, DC: American Psychological Association.

Neisser, U., & Harsch, N. (1992). Phantom flashbulbs: False recollections of hearing the news about Challenger. In E. Winograd, & U. Neisser (Eds.), *Affect and accuracy in recall: Studies of "flashbulb" memories.* New York: Cambridge University Press.

Neisser, U., Boodoo, G., Bouchard, T. J., Jr., Boykin, A. W., Brody, N., Ceci, S. J., Halpern, D. F., Loehlin, J. C., Perloff, R., Sternberg, R. J., & Urbina, S. (1996). Intelligence: Knowns and unknowns. *American Psychologist, 51,* 77–101.

Nelson, C. (1997). The neurobiological basis of early memory development. In N. Cowan (Ed.), *The development of memory in childhood. Studies in developmental psychology* (pp. 41–82). Hove, HK: Erlbaum.

Nelson, G., Chandrashekar, J., Hoon, M. A., Feng, L., Zhao, G., Ryba, N. J. P., & Zuker, C. S. (2002). An amino-acid taste receptor. *Nature, 416,* 199–202.

Nelson, R. J., & Chiavegatto, S. (2001). Molecular basis of aggression. *Trends in Neurosciences, 24(12),* 713–719.

Neria, Y., Bromet, E. J., Sievers, S., Lavelle, J., & Fochtmann, L. J. (2002).

Trauma exposure and posttraumatic stress disorder in psychosis: Findings from a first-admission cohort. *Journal of Consulting & Clinical Psychology, 70(1),* 246–251.

Nesbitt, M. N., & Penn, N. E. (2000). Gender stereotypes after thirty years: A replication of Rosenkrantz, et al. (1968). *Psychological Reports, 87,* 493–511.

Nestler, E. J., & Landsman, D. (2001). Learning about addiction from the genome. *Nature, 409,* 834–835.

Nestler, E. J., & Landsman, D. (2001).Learning about addiction from the genome. *Nature, 409(6822),* 834–835.

Neubauer, A. C. (2000). Physiological approaches to human intelligence: A review. *Psychologische Beitrage, 42(2),* 161–173.

Neumark-Sztainer, D., Wall, M. M., Story, M., & Perry, C. L. (2003). Correlates of unhealthy weight-control behaviors among adolescents: *Implications for prevention programs.* Health Psychology, 22(1), 88–98.

Neuringer, A., Deiss, C., & Olson, G. (2000). Reinforced variability and operant learning. *Journal of Experimental Psychology: Animal Behavior Processes, 26(1),* 98–111.

New, M., & Berliner, L. (2000). Mental health service utilization by victims of crime. *Journal of Traumatic Stress, 13(4),* 693–707.

Newman, J. (1997). Putting the puzzle together: II. Towards a general theory of the neural correlates of consciousness. *Journal of Consciousness Studies, 4,* 100–121.

Newman, L. S., Duff, K., & Baumeister, R. (1997). A new look at defensive projection: Thought suppression, accessibility, and biased person perception. *Journal of Personality and Social Psychology, 72,* 980–1001.

Newton-John, T. O., Spence, S. H., & Schotte, D. (1995). Cognitive-behavioral therapy versus EMG biofeedback in the treatment of chronic low back pain. *Behaviour Research & Therapy, 33,* 691–697.

NIAAA. (2000). Research on Relationships Between Alcohol and Violence. *National Institute on Alcohol Abuse and Alcoholism,* Available: http://www.niaaa. nih.gov/extramural/relation.htm

Nicholson, N. (1997). Evolutionary psychology: Toward a new view of human nature and organizational society. *Human Relations, 50,* 1053–1078.

Nickell, J. (1996, May/June). A study of fantasy proneness in the thirteen cases of alleged encounters in John Mack's Abduction. *Skeptical Inquirer, 54,* 18–20.

Nickerson, R. S., & Adams, M. J. (1979). Long-term memory for a common object. *Cognitive Psychology, 11,* 287–307.

Nickerson, R. (1998). Confirmation bias: A ubiquitous phenomenon in many guises. *Review of General Psychology, 2,* 175–220.

Nicolson, R., Bhalerao, S., & Solman, L. (1998). 47, XYY karyotypes and pervasive developmental disorders. *Canadian Journal of Psychiatry, 43,* 619–622.

Niedenthal, P. M., Brauer, M., Robin, L., & Innes-Ker, A. H. (2002). Adult attachment and the perception of facial expression of emotion. *Journal of Personality & Social Psychology, 82(3),* 419–433.

Niehoff, D. (1999). *The biology of violence: How understanding the brain, behavior, and environment can break the vicious cycle of aggression.* New York: Free Press.

Niemann, Y. F. (2001). Stereotypes about Chicanas and Chicanos: Implications for counseling. *Counseling Psychologist, 29(1),* 55–90.

Nigg, J. T., & Goldsmith, H. H. (1994). Genetics of personality disorders: Perspectives from personality and psychopathology research. *Psychological Bulletin, 115,* 346–380.

Niijima, A., Togiyama, T., & Adachi, A. (1990). Cephalic-phase insulin release induced taste stimulus of monosodium glutamate (umami taste). *Physiology & Behavior, 48(6),* 905–908.

Nijjar, R. K. (2002). Olfactory impairment increases as a function of age in persons with Down syndrome. *Neurobiology of Aging, 23(1),* 65–73.

Nisbett, R. E., Peng, K., Choi, L., & Norenzayan, A. (2000). Culture and systems of thought: Holistic vs. analytic cognition. *Psychological Review, 21,* 34–45.

Nishimoto, R. (1988). A cross-cultural analysis of psychiatric symptom expression using Langer's twenty-two item index. *Journal of Sociology and Social Welfare, 15,* 45–62.

Nishimura, H., et al. (1999). Sign language "heard" in the auditory cortex. *Nature, 397,* 116.

Noble, E. P. (2000). Addiction and its reward process through polymorphisms of the D-sub-2 dopamine receptor gene: A review. *European Psychiatry, 15(2),* 79–89.

Nolen-Hoeksema, S., Larson, J., & Grayson, C. (2000). Explaining the gender difference in depressive symptoms. *Journal of Personality and Social Psychology, 77,* 1061–1072.

Norenzayan, A., & Nisbett, R. E. (2000). Culture and causal cognition. *Current Directions in Psychological Science, 9(4),* 132–135.

O'Connor, D. B., Archer, J., Hair, W. M., Wu, F. C. W. (2002). Exogenous testosterone, aggression, and mood in eugonadal and hypogonadal men. *Physiology & Behavior, 75(4),* 557–566.

O'Connor, D. B., Archer, J., Hair, W. M.. * Frederick, C. W. Exogenous testosterone, aggression, and mood in eugonadal and hypogonadal men. *Physiology & Behavior, 75(4),* 557–566.

O'Connor, F. L. (1998). The role of serotinin and dopamine in schizophrenia. *Journal of the American Psychiatric Nurses Association, 4*, S30–S34.

O'Flynn, D. (2001). Approaching employment. Mental health, work projects and the Care Programme Approach. *Psychiatric Bulletin, 25(5)*, 169–171.

O'Leary, D. S., Block, R. I., Flaum, M., Schultz, S. K., Ponto, L. L. Boles, Watkins, G. L., Hurtig, R. R., Andreasen, N. C., Hichwa, R. D. (2000). Acute marijuana effects on rCBF and cognition: A PET study. *Neuroreport: For Rapid Communication of Neuroscience Research, 11(17)*, 3835–3841.

O'Neal, M. F., Medlin, J., Walker, K. L., & Jones, L. R. (2002). Effects of participant ethnicity, target physiognomy, and target gender on college students' judgments of cheating. *Journal of Black Psychology, 28(3)*, 276–289.

O'Sullivan, J. D. (2002). Apomorphine as an alternative to sildenafil in Parkinson's disease. *Journal of Neurology, Neurosurgery & Psychiatry, 72(5)*, 681.

Oakes, M. A., & Hyman, I. E., Jr. (2001). The role of the self in false memory creation. *Journal of Aggression, Maltreatment & Trauma, 4(2)*, 87–103.

Ogilvie, R. D., Wilkinson, R. T., & Allison, S. (1989). The detection of sleep onset: Behavioral, physiological, and subjective convergence. *Sleep, 12(5)*, 458–474.

Ohayon, M. M. (1997). Prevalence of DSM-IV diagnostic criteria of insomnia: Distinguishing insomnia related to mental disorders from sleep disorders. *Journal of Psychiatric Research, 31*, 333–346.

Okazaki, S., & Sue, S. (2000). Implications of test revisions for assessment with Asian Americans. *Psychological Assessment, 12(3)*, 272–280.

Olds, J., & Milner, P. M. (1954). Positive reinforcement produced by electrical stimulation of septal area and other regions of rat brains. *Journal of Comparative and Physiological Psychology, 47*, 419–427.

Olfson, M., Marcus, S., Pincus, H. A., Zito, J. M., Thompson, J. W., & Zarin, D. A. (1998). Antidepressant prescribing practices of outpatient psychiatrists. *Archives of General Psychiatry, 55*, 310, 316.

Oliver, M. B., & Fonash, D. (2002). Race and crime in the news: Whites' identification and misidentification of violent and nonviolent criminal suspects. *Media Psychology, 4(2)*, 137–156.

Omori, M., Murata, T., Kimura, H., Koshimoto, Y., Kado, H., Ishimori, Y., Ito, H., & Wada, Y. (2000). Thalamic abnormalities in patients with schizophrenia revealed by proton magnetic resonance spectroscopy. *Psychiatry Research: Neuroimaging, 98 (3)*, 155–162.

Oquendo, M. A., & Mann, J. J. (2000). The biology of impulsivity and suicidality. *Psychiatric Clinics of North America, 23(1)*, 11–25.

Orth-Gomer, K., et al. (1994). Lipid lowering through work stress reduction. *International Journal of Behavioral Medicine, 1*, 204–214.

Orubuloye, I., Caldwell, J., & Caldwell, P. (1997). Perceived male sexual needs and male sexual behavior in southwest Nigeria. *Social Science and Medicine, 44*, 1195–1207.

Orzack, M. H. (1999). Computer addiction: Is it real or virtual. *The Harvard Mental Health Letter, 15(7)*, 8.

Oshima, I., Inazawa, K., Okagami, K., Yoshizumi, A., & Inomata, Y. (1996). Attitudes towards community living and determining factors among chronic institutionalized patients in Japan: The analysis of a nationwide self-rating survey. *Seishin Igaku (Clinical Psychiatry), 38(12)*, 1248–1256.

Oshima, K. (2000). Ethnic jokes and social function in Hawaii. *Humor: International Journal of Humor Research, 13(1)*, 41–57.

Oshiro, Y. Fuijita, N., Tanaka, H., Hirabuki, N., Nakamura, H., Yoshiya, I. (1998). Functional mapping of pain-related activation with echo-planar MRI: Significance of the SII-insular region. *Neuroreport: An International Journal for the Rapid Communication of Research in Neuroscience, 9*, 2285–2289.

Otero, G. A., Aguirre, D. M., Porcayo, R., & Fernandez, T. (1999). Psychological and electroencephalographic study in school children with iron deficiency. *International Journal of Neuroscience, 99(1–4)*, 113–121.

Overmier, J. B., & Murison, R. (2000). Anxiety and helplessness in the face of stress predisposes, precipitates, and sustains gastric ulceration. *Behavioural Brain Research, 110(1–2)*, 161–174.

Ozinga, J. A. (2000). *Altruism.* New York: Praeger Pub.

Page, T. L. (1994). Time is the essence: Molecular analysis of the biological clock. *Science, 263*, 1570–1572.

Pahlavan, F., Bonnet, P., & Duda, D. (2000). Human motor responses to simultaneous aversive stimulation and failure on a valued task. *Psychological Reports, 86*, 232–242.

Paice, E., Rutter, H., Wetherell, M., Winder, B., & McManus, I. C. (2002). Stressful incidents, stress and coping strategies in the pre-registration house officer year. *Medical Education, 36(1)*, 56–65.

Pajer, K., Gardner, W., Kirillova, G. P., & Vanyukov, M. M. (2001). Sex differences in cortisol level and neurobehavioral disinhibition in children of substance abusers. *Journal of Child & Adolescent Substance Abuse,10(4)*, 65–76.

Pakaslahti, L., & Keltikangas-Jaervinen, L. (2000). Comparison of peer, teacher and self-assessments on adolescent direct and indirect aggression. *Educational Psychology, 20(2)*, 177–190.

Palfai, T. P., Monti, P. M., Ostafin, B., & Hutchinson, K. (2000). Effects of nicotine deprivation on alcohol-related information processing and drinking behavior. *Journal of Abnormal Psychology, 109*, 96–105.

Pandey, R. N. (2002). The use of induced abortion as a contraceptive: *The case of Mongolia. Journal of Biosocial Science, 34(1)*, 91–108.

Paniagua, F. A. (1998). *Assessing and treating culturally diverse clients: A practical guide* (2nd ed.). London: Sage.

Papert, S. (1999, March 29). *Child psychologist Jean Piaget. Time*, 105–107.

Parasuraman, S., & Purohit, Y. S. (2000). Distress and boredom among orchestra musicians: The two faces of stress. *Journal of Occupation Health Psychology, 5(1)*, 74–83.

Paris, J. (1998). Does childhood trauma cause personality disorders in adults? *Canadian Journal of Psychiatry, 43*, 148–153.

Paris, J. (2000). Childhood precursors of personality disorder. *Psychiatric Clinics of North America, 23*, 77–88.

Park, R. (2000). *Voodoo science: The road from foolishness to fraud.*Oxford University Press.

Parke, R. D., & Buriel, R. (1998). Socialization in the family: Ethnic and ecological perspectives. In W. Damon (Ed.), *Handbook of child psychology* (Vol. 3). New York: Wiley.

Parker, W. D., (1998). Birth order effects in the academically talented. *Gifted Child Quarterly, 42*, 29–36.

Parker-Oliver, D. (2002). Redefining hope for the terminally ill. *American Journal of Hospice & Palliative Care, 19(2)*, 115–120.

Parkes, C. M. (1972). *Bereavement: Studies of grief in adult life.* New York: International Universities Press.

Parkes, C. M. (1991). Attachment, bonding, and psychiatric problems after bereavement in adult life. In C. M. Parkes, J. Stevenson-Hinde, & P. Marris (Eds.), *Attachment across the life cycle.* London: Tavistock/Routledge.

Parkes, M., & White, K. (2000). Glucose attenuation of memory impairments. *Behavioral Neuroscience, 114*, 307–319.

Parkinson, J. A., Willoughby, P. J., Robbins, T. W., & Everitt, B. J. (2000). Disconnection of the anterior cingulated cortex and nucleus accumbens core impairs Pavlovian approach behavior: Further evidence for limbic cortical-ventral striatopallidal systems. *Behavioral Neuroscience, 114(1)*, 42–63.

Parks, C. A. (1998). Lesbian parenthood: A review of the literature. *American Journal of Orthopsychiatry, 68,* 376–389.

Pasley, K., Kerpelman, J., & Guilbert, D. E. (2001). Gendered conflict, identity disruption, and marital instability: Expanding Gottman's model. *Journal of Social & Personal Relationships, 18(1),* 5–27.

Patten, C. A. (2000). A critical evaluation of nicotine replacement therapy for teenage smokers. *Journal of Child & Adolescent Substance Abuse, 9(4),* 51–75.

Patterson, D. R., & Ptacek, J. T. (1997). Baseline pain as a moderator of hypnoticanalgesia for burn injury treatment. *Journal of Consulting and Clinical Psychology, 65,* 60–67.

Patterson, F., & Linden, E. (1981). *The education of Koko.* New York: Holt, Rinehart and Winston.

Patterson, P. (2002). Penny's journal: Koko wants to have a baby. Available: http://www.koko.org/world/journal.phtml?offset=5

Paul, D. B., & Blumenthal, A. L. (1989). On the trail of little Albert. *The Psychological Record, 39,* 547–553.

Pavlidis, I., Eberhardt, N. L., & Levine, J. A. (2002). Seeing through the face of deception. *Nature, 415(6867),* 35.

Payne, J. D., Nadel, L., Allen, J. J. B., Thomas, K. G. F., & Jacobs, W. J. (2002). The effects of experimentally induced stress on false recognition. *Memory, 10(1),* 1–6.

Pearlman, C. (2002). Electroconvulsive therapy in clinical psychopharmacology. *Journal of Clinical Psychopharmacology, 22(4),* 345–346.

Penev, P. D., Zee, P. C., & Turek, F. W. (1997). Serotonin in the spotlight. *Nature, 385,* 123.

Penfield, W. (1958). Functional localization in temporal and deep Sylvian area. *Research Publications of the Association for Research in Nervous & Mental Disease, 36,* 210–226.

Penfield, W. (1975). *The mystery of the mind.* Princeton, NJ: Princeton University Press.

Pengilly, J. W., & Dowd, E. T. (2000). Hardiness and social support as moderators of stress. *Journal of Clinical Psychology, 56,* 813–820.

Pennisi, E. (1997). The architecture of hearing. *Science,* 1223–1224.

Penzien, D. B., Rains, J., C., & Andrasik, F. (2002). Behavioral management of recurrent headache: Three decades of experience and empiricism. *Applied Psychophysiology & Biofeedback, 27(2),* 163–181.

Peppard, P. E., Young, T., Palta, M., & Skatrud, J. (2000). Prospective study of the association between sleep-disordered breathing and hypertension. *New England Journal of Medicine, 342(19),* 1378–1384.

Perez, L. A., Peynircioglu, Z. F., & Blaxton, T. A. (1998). Developmental differences in implicit and explicit memory performance. *Journal of Experimental Psychology: Learning, Memory, & Cognition, 25,* 644–663.

Perez, R. L. (2000). Fiesta as tradition, fiesta as change: Ritual, alcohol, and violence in a Mexican community. *Addiction, 95(3),* 365–373.

Perkins, K. A., Levine, M., Marcus, M., Shiffman, S., D'Amico, Miller, A., Keina, A., Ashcom, J., & Broge, M. (2000). Tobacco withdrawl in women and menstrual cycle phase. *Journal of Counseling and Clinical Psychology, 68,* 176–180.

Perreault, S., & Bourhis, R. Y. (1999). Ethnocentrism, social identification, and discrimination. *Personality & Social Psychology Bulletin, 25(1),* 92–103.

Perry, C. (1997). Admissability and per se ex-clusion of hypnotically elicited recall in American courts of law. *International Journal of Clinical and Experimental Hypnosis, 45,* 266–279.

Perry, R. J., & Hodges, J. R. (1999). Attention and executive deficits in Alzheimer's disease: A critical review. *Brain, 122,* 383–404. *Personality & Social Psychology Review, 6(3),* 204–231.

Persons, J. B., Davidson, J., & Tompkins, M. A. (2000). *Essential components of cognitive-behavior therapy for depression.* Washington, DC: American Psychological Association.

Pert, C. B., & Snyder, S. H. (1973). The opiate receptor: Demonstration in nervous tissue. *Science, 179,* 1011–1014.

Pert, C. B., Snowman, A. M., & Snyder, S. H. (1974). Localization of opiate receptor binding in presynaptic membranes of rat brain. *Brain Research, 70,* 184–188.

Peskind, E. R. (1998). Pharmacologic approaches to cognitive deficits in Alzheimer's disease. *Journal of Clinical Psychiatry, 59,* 22–27.

Peterson, A. L. & Halstead, T. S. (1998). Group cognitive behavior therapy for depression in a community setting: A clinical replication series. *Behavior Therapy, 29,* 3–18.

Peterson, C., & Vaidya, R. S. (2001). Explanatory style, expectations, and depressive symptoms. *Personality & Individual Differences, 31(7),* 1217–1223.

Peto, R., Lopez, A. D., Boreham, J., Thun, M., & Hath, C., Jr. (1992). Mortality from tobacco in developed countries: Indirect estimates from national vital statistics. *Lancet, 339,* 1268–1278 (p. 536).

Petrinovich, L. F. (1999). *Darwinian dominion: Animal welfare and human interests.* Cambridge, MA: MIT Press.

Petronis, A. (2000). The genes for major psychosis: Aberrant sequence or regulation? *Neuropsychopharmacology, 23,* 1–12.

Pettigrew, T. F. (1998). Reactions towards the new minorities of Western Europe. *Annual Review of Sociology, 24,* 77–103.

Pettit, J.W., Kline, J. P., Gencoz, T., Gencoz, F., & Joiner, T. E., (2001). Are happy people healthier? The specific role of positive affect in predicting self-reported health symptoms. *Journal of Research in Personality, 35(4),* 521–536.

Pfaffmann, C. (1982). Taste: A model of incentive motivation. In D. W. Pfaff (Ed.), *The physiological mechanisms of motivation.* New York: Springer-Verlag.

Pfeffer, C. R., Jiang, H., Kakuma, T., Hwang, J., & Metsch, M. (2002). Group intervention for children bereaved the suicide of a relative. *Journal of the American Academy of Child & Adolescent Psychiatry, 41(5),* 505–513.

Pham, T.M., Winblad, B., Granholm, A-C., & Mohammed, A. H. (2002). Environmental influences on brain neurotrophins in rats. *Pharmacology, Biochemistry & Behavior, 73(1),* 167–175.

Phelps, J. A., Davis, J. O., & Schartz, K. M. (1997). Nature, nurture, and twin research strategies. *Current Directions in Psychological Science, 6,* 117–120.

Phillips, S. T., & Ziller, R. C. (1997). Toward a theory and measure of the nature of nonprejudice. *Journal of Personality and Social Psychology, 72,* 420–434.

Piaget, J. (1951). *Play, dreams, and imitation in childhood.* New York: Norton.

Picciotto, M. R. (1998). Common aspects of the action of nicotine and other drugs of abuse. *Drug and Alcohol Dependence, 51,* 165–172.

Pich, E. M., Chiamulera, C., & Caarboni, L. (1999). Molecular mechanisms of the positive reinforcing effect of nicotine. *Behavioural Pharmacology, 10(6–7),* 587–596.

Pich, E. M., Pagliusi, S. R., Tessari, M., Talabot-Ayer, D., Van Huijsduijnen, R. H., & Chiamulera, C. (1997). Common neural substrates for the addictive properties of nicotine and cocaine. *Science, 275,* 83–86.

Pietromonaco, P. R., & Carnelley, K. B. (1994). Gender and working models of attachment: Consequences for perception of self and romantic relationships. *Personal Relationships, 1,* 3–26.

Pihl, R. O., Lau, M. L., & Assaad, J-M. (1997). Aggressive disposition, alcohol, and aggression. *Aggressive Behavior, 23,* 11–18.

Pilcher, J. J., & Huffcutt, A. I. (1996). Effects of sleep deprivation on performance: A meta-analysis. *Sleep, 19,* 318–326.

Pillard, R. C., & Bailey, M. J. (1995). A biological perspective on sexual orientation. *The Psychiatric Clinics of North America, 18,* 71–84.

Pines, A. M. (1993). Burnout. In L. Goldberger & S. Breznitz (Eds.), *Handbook of stress: Theoretical and clinical aspects.* New York: Free Press.

Pinto, C., Dhavale, H., Nair, S., Patil, B., & Dewan, M. (2000). Borderline personality disorder exists in India. *Journal of Nervous & Mental Disease, 188,* 386–388.

Piquero, A. R., Gibson, C. L., Tibbetts, S. G., Turner, M. G., & Katz, S. H. (2002). Maternal cigarette smoking during pregnancy and life-course-persistent offending. *International Journal of Offender Therapy & Comparative Criminology, 46(2),* 231–248.

Plihal, W., & Born, J. (1999). Effects of early and late nocturnal sleep on priming and spatial memory. *Psychophysiology, 36,* 571–582.

Plomin, R. (1990). The role of inheritance in behavior. *Science, 248,* 183–188.

Plomin, R. (1997, May). Cited in B. Azar, Nature, nurture: Not mutually exclusive. *APA Monitor,* p. 32.

Plomin, R. (1999). Genetics and general cognitive ability. *Nature, 402,* C25–C29.

Plomin, R., & Caspi, A. (1999). Behavioral genetics and personality. In L. A. Pervin, & O. P. John (Eds.), *Handbook of personality: Theory and research.* New York: Guilford Press.

Plomin, R., & Crabbe, J. (2000). DNA. *Psychological Bulletin, 126,* 806–828..

Plomin, R., & Craig, I. (2002). "Genetic research on cognitive ability": Author's reply. *British Journal of Psychiatry, 180(2),* 185–186.

Plomin, R., & Dale, P. S. (2000). Genetics and early language development: A UK study of twins. In D. V. M. Bishop & L. B. Leonard (Eds.), *Speech and language impairments in children: Causes, characteristics, intervention, and outcome.* Oxford: Oxford University Press.

Plomin, R., & Petrill, S. A. (1997). Genetics and Intelligence: What's new? *Intelligence, 24,* 53–77.

Plomin, R., & Rutter, M. (1998). Child development, molecular genetics and what to do with genes once they are found. *Child Development, 69,* 68–71.

Plomin, R., DeFries, J. C., McClearn, G. E., & Rutter, M. (1997). *Behavioral genetics* (3rd ed.). New York: Freeman.

Plous, S. (1991). An attitude survey of animal rights activists. *Psychological Science, 2,* 194–196.

Plous, S. (1998). Signs of change within the animal rights movement: Results from a follow-up survey of activists. *Journal of Comparative Psychology, 112,* 48–54.

Plutchik, R. (1984). Emotions: A general psychoevolutionary theory. In K. R. Scherer, & P. Ekman (Eds), *Approaches to emotion.* Hillsdale, NJ: Erlbaum.

Plutchik, R. (1994). *The psychology and biology of emotion.* New York: HarperCollins.

Plutchik, R. (2000). *Emotions in the practice of psychotherapy: Clinical implications of affect theories.* Washington, DC: American Psychological Association.

Podsakoff, P. M., MacKenzie, S. B., Paine, J. B., & Bachrach, D. G. (2000). Organizational citizenship behaviors: A critical review of the theroetical and empirical literature and suggestions for future research. *Journal of Management, 26(3),* 513–563.

Pollack, M. H. (2000). What are the current treatments for panic disorder. *Harvard Mental Health Letter, 16(11),* 8.

Pollak, S. D., Cicchetti, D., Klorman R., & Brumaghim, J. T. (1997). Cognitive brain event-related potentials and emotion processing in maltreated children. *Child Development, 68,* 773–787.

Pollard, I. (2000). Substance abuse and parenthood: Biological mechanisms-bioethical challenges. *Women & Health, 30(3),* 1–24.

Pomponio, A. T. (2001). *Psychological consequences of terror.* New York: Wiley.

Pontieri, F. E., Tanda, G., Orzi, F., & DiChiara, G. (1996). Effects of nicotine on the nucleus accumbens and similarity to those of addictive drugs. *Nature, 382,* 255–257.

Poole, D. A. & Lindsay, D. S. (1995). Interviewing preschoolers: Effects of nonsuggestive techniques, parental coaching and leading questions on reports of nonexperienced events. *Journal of Experimental Child Psychology, 60,* 129–154.

Poole, D. A., & Lindsay, D. S. (2002). Reducing child witnesses' false reports of misinformation from parents. *Journal of Experimental Child Psychology, 81(2)* 117–140.

Pope, K. S. (1997). Science as careful questioning: Are claims of a false memory syndrome epidemic based on empirical evidence? *American Psychologist, 52,* 997–1006.

Poppe, E. (2001). Effects of changes in GNP and perceived group characteristics on national and ethnic stereotypes in central and Eastern Europe. *Journal of Applied Social Psychology, 31(8),* 1689–1708.

Porter, R. (2002). *Madness: A brief history.* New York: Oxford University Press.

Porzelius, L. K., Dinsmore, B. D., & Staffelbach, D. (2001). Eating disorders. In M. Hersen & V. B. Van Hasselt (Eds.), *Advanced abnormal psychology* (2nd ed.). Netherlands: Klewer Academic Publishers.

Posthuma, D., de Geus, E. J. C., & Boomsma, D. I. (2001). Perceptual speed and IQ are associated through common genetic factors. *Behavior Genetics, 31(6),* 593–602.

Posthuma, D., de Geus, E. J. C., Baare, W. E. C., Hulshoff Pol, H. E., Kahn, R. S., Boomsma, D. I. (2002). The association between brain volume and intelligence is of genetic origin. *Nature Neuroscience, 5(2),* 83–84.

Posthuma, D., Neale, M. C., Boomsma, D. I., & de Geus, E. J. C. (2001). Are smarter brains running faster? Heritability of alpha peak frequency, IQ, and their interrelation. *Behavior Genetics, 31(6),* 567–579.

Powell, D. H. (1998). *The nine myths of aging: Maximizing the quality of later life.* San Francisco: Freeman.

Powell, G. N., Butterfield, D. A., & Parent, J. D. (2002). Gender and managerial stereotypes: Have the times changed? *Journal of Management, 28(2),* 177–193.

Powell, K. F. (2001). An investigation of self-injurious behaviors and the relationship between traumatic experiences and self-injurious behavior in prison. *Dissertation Abstracts International: Section B: The Sciences & Engineering, 61(7–B),* 3856.

Powell, R. A., & Gee, T. L. (1999). The effects of hypnosis on dissociative identity disorder: A reexamination of the evidence. *Canadian Journal of Psychiatry, 44,* 914–916.

Powell-Hopson, D., & Hopson, D. S. (1988). Implications of doll color preferences among Black preschool children and White preschool children. *Journal of Black Psychology, 14,* 57–63.

Powlishta, K. K. (1999). Gender segregation among children: Understanding the "cootie phenomenon." In L. E. Berk, (Ed.), *Landscapes of development* (pp. 281–294). Belmont, CA: Wadsworth.

Prall, R. C. (2000). *The rights of children in separation and divorce: The essential handbook for parents.* Austin, TX: Landmark Editions.

Pratt, L. A., Ford, D. E., Crum, R. M., Armenian, H. K., Gallo, J. J., & Eaton, W. W. (1996). Depression, psychotropic medication, and risk of myocardial infarction: Prospective data from Baltimore ECA follow-up. *Archives of Internal Medicine, 94,* 3123–3129.

Premack, D. (1976). Language and intelligence in ape and man. *American Scientist, 64(6),* 674–683.

Pressman, J. D. (1998). *Last resort psychosurgery and the limits of medicine.* Cambridge, MA: Cambridge University Press.

Pressman, M. R., & Orr, W. C. (Eds.) 1997). *Understanding sleep: The evaluation and treatment of sleep disorders.* Washington, DC: American Psychological Association.

Price, D. D. (2000). Psychological and neural mechanisms of the affective dimension of pain. *Science, 288,* 1769–1772.

Price, R. H., & Crapo, R. H. (1999). *Cross-cultural perspectives in introductory psychology.* Belmont, CA: Wadsworth.

Priebe, S., Hoffmann, K., Isermann, M., & Kaiser, W. (2002). Do long-term hospitalised patients benefit from discharge into the community? *Social Psychiatry & Psychiatric Epidemiology, 37(8),* 387–392.

Priest, R. F., & Sawyer, J. (1967). Proximity and peership: Bases of balance in interpersonal attraction. *American Journal of Sociology, 72,* 633–649.

Primavera, L. H., & Herron, W. G. (1996). The effect of viewing television violence on aggression. *International Journal of Instructional Media, 23,* 91–104.

Prkachin, K. M., & Silverman, B. E. (2002). Hostility and facial expression in young men and women: Is social regulation more important than negative affect? *Health Psychology, 21(1),* 33–39.

Provencio, I., Rollag, M. D., & Castrucci, A. M. (2002). Photoreceptive net in the mammalian retina. *Nature, 415(6871),* 493.

Prudic, J., & Sackheim, H. A. (1999). Electroconvulsive therapy and suicide risk. *Journal of Clinical Psychiatry, 60,* 104–110.

Pryor, J. P. (2002). Pharmacotherapy of erectile dysfunction. *Sexual & Relationship Therapy, 17(4),* 389–400.

Psychological Reports, 90, 949–956.

Pulido, R., & Marco, A. (2000). El efecto Barnum en estudiantes universitarios y profesionales de la psicologia en Mexico. /The Barnum effect in university students and psychology professionals in Mexico. *Revista Intercontinental de Psicoanalisis Contemporaneo, 2(2),* 59–66.

Pullum, G. K. (1991). *The great Eskimo vocabulary hoax and other irreverent essays on the study of language.* Chicago: University of Chicago Press.

Purdy, J. E., Markham, M. R., Schwartz, B. L., & Gordon, W. C. (2001). *Learning and memory* (2nd ed.). Belmont, CA: Wadsworth.

Putnam, F. W. (1992). Altered states: Peeling away the layers of multiple personality. *Science, 32(6),* 30–36.

Qu, T., Brannen, C. L., Kim, H. M., & Sugaya, K. (2001). Human neural stem cells improve cognitive function of aged brain. *Neuroreport: For Rapid Communication of Neuroscience Research, 12,* 1127–1132.

Quaiser-Pohl, C., & Lehmann, W. (2002). Girls' spatial abilities: Charting the contributions of experiences and attitudes in different academic groups. *British Journal of Educational Psychology, 72(2),* 245–260.

Quattrocki, E., Baird, A., & Yurgelun-Todd, D. (2000). Biological aspects of the link between smoking and depression. *Harvard Review of Psychiatry, 8(3),* 99–110.

Quinn, J. F., & Strelkauskas, A. J. (1993). Psycho immunologic effects of Therapeutic Touch on practitioners and recently bereaved recipients: A pilot study. *ANS Advanced Nursing Science, 15(4),* 13–26.

Rabin, B. S. (2002). Can stress participate in the pathogenesis of autoimmune disease? *Journal of Adolescent Health, 30(4, Suppl.),* 71–75.

Rae-Dupree, J. (May, 2002). Know your genes, know yourself. *U.S. News & World Report,* 62–63.

Raesaenen, P. M., Tiihonen, J., Isohanni, M., Rantakallio, P., Lehtonen, J., & Moring, J. (1998). Schizophrenia, alcohol abuse, and violent behavior: A 26-year follow up study of an unselected birth cohort. *Schizophrenia Bulletin, 24,* 437–441.

Raesaenen, S., Pakaslahti, A., Syvaelahti, E., Jones, P. B., & Isohanni, M. (2000). Sex differences in schizophrenia: A review. *Nordic Journal of Psychiatry, 54,* 37–45.

Rafferty, F. T. (1999). Evolutionary psychology. *Journal of the American Academy of Child & Adolescent Psychiatry, 38,* 641–642.

Ragavan, C. (2001, February 5). Cracking down on ecstasy. *U.S. News & World Report,* pp. 14–17.

Raine, A., Lencz, T, Bihrle, S., LaCasse, L., & Colletti, P. (2000). Reduced prefrontal gray matter volume and reduced autonomic activity in antisocial personality disorder. *Archives of General Psychiatry, 57,* 119–127.

Raine, A., Meloy, J. R., Bihrle, S., Stoddard, J., LaCasse, L., & Buchsbaum, M. S. (1998). Reduced prefrontal and increased subcortical brain functioning assessed using positron emission tomography in predatory and affective murderers. *Behavioral Sciences & the Law, 16(3),* 319–332.

Raine, A., Reynolds, C., Venables, P. H., & Mednick, S. A. (2002). Stimulation seeking and intelligence: A prospective longitudinal study. *Journal of Personality & Social Psychology, 82(4),* 663–674.

Raloff, J. (1999). Common pollutants undermine masculinity. *Science News, 155,* 213.

Ramachandran, V. S., & Blakeslee, S. (1998). *Phantoms in the brain.* New York: William Morrow.

Ramirez, G., Zemba, D., & Geiselman, R. E. (1996). Judges' cautionary instructions on eyewitness testimony. *American Journal of Forensic Psychology, 14,* 31–66.

Ramus, F., Hauser, M. D., Miller, C., Morris, D., & Mehler, J. (2000). Language discrimination by human newborns and by cotton-top tamarin monkeys. *Science, 288(5464),* 349–351.

Randi, J. (1997). *An encyclopedia of claims, frauds, and hoaxes of the occult and supernatural: James Randi's decidedly skeptical definitions of alternate realities.* New York: St Martin's Press.

Rathus, S. A., & Nevid, J. S. (2002). *Psychology and the challenges of life: Adjustment in the new millennium (8th ed.).* New York: Wiley.

Rauhut, A. S., Thomas, B. L., & Ayres, J. J. B. (2002). Treatments that weaken Pavlovian conditioned fear and thwart its renewal in rats: Implications for treating human phobias. *Journal of Experimental Psychology: Animal Behavior Processes, 27(2),* 99–114.

Raven, B. H. (1998). Groupthink: Bay of Pigs and Watergate reconsidered. *Organizational Behavior and Human Decision Processes, 73,* 352–361.

Ray, W. J. (2003). *Methods: Toward a science of behavior and experience.* (7ed). Wadsworth: Belmont, CA.

Rechtschaffen, A. (1997, August). Cited in T. Geier, What is sleep for? *U. S. News and World Report,* pp. 17–21.

Rechtschaffen, A., & Bergmann, B. M. (1995). Sleep deprivation in the rat by the disk-over-water method. *Behavioural Brain Research, 69,* 55–63.

Reed, G. M., McLaughlin, C. J., & Milholland, K. (2000). Ten interdisciplinary principles for professional practice in telehealth: Implications for psychology. *Professional Psychology: Research and Practice, 31(2),* 170–178.

Refaat, A., Dandash, K. F., El Defrawi, M. H., & Eyada, M. (2001). Female genital mutilation and domestic violence among Egyptian women. *Journal of Sex & Marital Therapy, 27(5),* 593–598.

Regan, P. C. (1998). What if you can't get what you want? Willingness to compromise ideal mate selection standards as a function of sex, mate value, and relationship context. *Personality & Social Psychology Bulletin, 24(12),* 1294–1303.

Regan, P. C. (2000). The role of sexual desire and sexual activity in dating relationships. *Social Behavior & Personality, 28(1),* 51–60.

Regier, D. A., Narrow, W. E., Rae, D. S., Mander-scheid, R. W., Locke, B. Z., & Goodwin, F. K. (1993). The de facto US mental and addictive disorders service system. *Archives of General Psychiatry, 50,* 85–93.

Reh, T. A. (2002). Neural stem cells: Form and function. *Nature Neuroscience, 5,* 392–394.

Reid, I. C., & Stewart, C. A. (2001). How antidepressants work: New perspectives on the pathophysiology of depressive disorder. *British Journal of Psychiatry, 178,* 299–303.

Reifman, A. (2000). Revisiting the Bell Curve. *Psychology, 11,* 21–29.

Reiner, W. (1997). To be male or female-that is the question. *Archives of Pediatric and Adolescent Medicine, 151,* 224–225.

Renaud, C. A., & Byers, E. S. (1999). Exploring the frequency, diversity and content of university students' positive and negative sexual cognitions. *Canadian Journal of Human Sexuality, 8(1),* 17–30.

Reneman, L., Booij, J., de Bruin, K., Reitsma, J. R., de Wolff, F. A., Gunning, W. B., den Heeten, G. J., & van den Brink, W. (2001). Effects of dose, sex, and long-term abstention from use on toxic effects of MDMA (Ecstasy) on brain serotonin neurons. *Lancet, 358(9296),* 1864–1869.

Renner, M. J., & Mackin, R. S. (1998). A life stress instrument for classroom use. *Teaching of Psychology, 25,* 46–48.

Rentsch, J. R., & McEwen, A. H. (2002). Comparing personality characteristics, values, and goals as antecedents of organizational attractiveness. *International Journal of Selection & Assessment, 10(3),* 225–234.

Repetti, R. L. (1993). Short-term effects of occupational stressors on daily mood and health complaints. *Health Psychology, 12,* 125–131.

Reppucci, N. D., Woolard, J. L., & Fried, C. S. (1999). Social, community, and preventive interventions. *Annual Review of Psychology, 50,* 387–418.

Resing, W. C., & Nijland, M. I. (2002). Worden kinderen intelligenter? Een kwart eeuw onderzoek met de Leidse Diagnostische Test. /Are children becoming more intelligent? Twenty-five years' research using the Leiden Diagnostic Test. *Kind en Adolescent, 23(1),* 42–49.

Rest, J. R., Turiel, E., & Kohlberg, L. (1969). Relations between level of moral judgment and preference and comprehension of the moral judgments of others. *Journal of Personality, 37,* 225–252.

Rest, J., Narvaez, D., Bebeau, M., & Thoma, S. (1999). A neo-Kohlbergian approach: The DIT and schema theory. *Educational Psychology Review, 11(4),* 291–324.

Rest, J., Thoma, S., & Edwards, L. (1997). Designing and validating a measure of moral judgment: Stage preference and stage consistency approaches. *Journal of Educational Psychology, 89,* 5–28.

Reutens, D. C., Savard, G., Andermann, F., Dubeau, F., & Olivier, A. (1997). Results of surgical treatment in temporal lobe epilepsy with chronic psychosis. *Brain, 120,* 1929–1936.

Reynolds, G. P. (1999). Dopamine receptors, antipsychotic action and schizophrenia. *Journal of Psychopharmacology, 13,* 202–203.

Rhodenizer, L., Bowers, C. A., & Bergondy, M. (1998). Team practice schedules: What do we know? *Perceptual & Motor Skills, 87,* 31–34.

Rhodes, G., Halberstadt, J., & Brajkovich, G. (2001). Generalization of mere exposure effects to averaged composite faces. *Social Cognition,19(1),* 57–70.

Rhodes, G., Sumich, A., & Byatt, G. (1999). Are average facial configurations attractive only because of their symmetry? *Psychological Science, 10(1),* 52–58.

Rice, K. G., & Mirzadeh, S. A. (2000). Perfectionism, attachment, and adjustment. *Journal of Counseling Psychology, 47(2),* 238–250.

Rice, M. E. (1997). Violent offender research and implications for the criminal justice system. *American Psychologist, 52,* 414–423.

Richardson, D. R., & Green, L. R. (1999). Social sanction and threat explanations of gender effects on direct and indirect aggression. *Aggressive Behavior, 25(6),* 425–434.

Richardson, G. A., Ryan, C., Willford, J., Day, N. L., & Goldschmidt, L. (2002). Prenatal alcohol and marijuana exposure: Effects on neuropsychological outcomes at 10 years. *Neurotoxicology & Teratology, 24(3),* 311–320.

Richter, J. S. (2001). Eating disorders and sexuality. In J. J. Robert-McComb (Ed), *Eating disorders in women and children: Prevention, stress management, and treatment* (pp. 201–208). Boca Raton, FL: CRC Press.

Robbins, S. P. (1996). *Organizational behavior: Concepts, controversies, and applications.* Englewood Cliffs, NJ: Prentice Hall.

Robbins, T. W. (1997). Arousal systems and attentional processes. *Biological Psychology, 45,* 57–71.

Robert-McComb, J. J. (2001). Eating disorders. In J. J. Robert-McComb (Ed), *Eating disorders in women and children: Prevention, stress management, and treatment* (pp. 3–37). Boca Raton, FL: CRC Press.

Roberts, W. W., & Nagel, J. (1996). First-order projections activated by stimulation of hypothalamic sites eliciting attack and flight in rats. *Behavioral Neuroscience, 110,* 509–527.

Robertson, D. A., Gernsbacher, M. A., Guidotti, S. J., Robertson, R. R. W., Irwin, W., Mock, B. J., & Campana, M. E. (2000). Functional neuroanatomy of the cognitive process of mapping during discourse comprehension. *Psychological Science, 11(3),* 255–260.

Robicsek, F. (1992, Sept./Oct.). Sacred smoke. *Utne Reader,* pp. 90–91.

Robie, C., Born, M., & Schmit, M. J. (2001). Personal and situational determinants of personality responses: A partial reanalysis and reinterpretation of the Schmit et al. (1995) data. *Journal of Business & Psychology, 16(1),* 101–117.

Robins, L. N., & Regier, D. A. (1991). *Psychiatric disorders in America: The epidemiological catchment area.* New York: The Free Press.

Rodgers, J. L., Cleveland, H. H., van den Oord, E., & Rowe, D. C. (2000). Resolving the debate over birth order, family size, and intelligence. *American Psychologist, 55(6),* 599–612.

Roelcke, V. (1997). Biologizing social facts: An early 20th century debate on Kraepelin's concepts of culture, neurasthenia, and degeneration. *Culture, Medicine, and Psychiatry, 21,* 383–403.

Rogers, C. R. (1961). *On becoming a person.* Boston: Houghton Mifflin.

Rogers, C. R. (1980). A way of being. Boston: Houghton Mifflin.

Rogosch, F. A., Cicchetti, D., & Aber, J. L. (1995). The role of child maltreatment in early deviations in cognitive and affective processing abilities and later peer relationship problems. *Development and Psychopathology, 7,* 591–609.

Rohner, R. P., & Britner, P. A. (2002).Worldwide mental health correlates of parental acceptance-rejection: Review of cross-cultural and intracultural evidence. *Cross-Cultural Research: The Journal of Comparative Social Science, 36(1),* 15–47.

Rohner, R. P., Veneziano, R. A. (2001). The importance of father love: History and contemporary evidence. *Review of General Psychology, 5(4),* 382–405.

Rohner, R. (1986). *The warmth dimension.* Newbury Par, CA: Sage.

Rohrlich, J. B. (1998). The meanings of aggression. *Psychiatric Annals, 28,* 246–249.

Rolnick, A., & Lubow, R. E. (1991). Why is the driver rarely motion sick? The role of controllability in motion sickness. *Ergonomics, 34(7),* 867–879.

Romo, R., Brody, C. D., Hernandez, A., & Lemus, L. (1999). Neuronal correlates of parametric working memory in the prefrontal cortex. *Nature, 399,* 470–473.

Rook, K. S. (2000). The evolution of social relationships in later adulthood. In S. H. Qualls & N. Abeles (Eds.), *Psychology and the aging revolution.* Washington, DC: American Psychological Association.

Roozendaal, B., & McGaugh, J. L. (1999). Role of norepinephrine in mediating stress hormone regulation of long-term memory storage: a critical involvement of the amygdala. *Biological Psychiatry, 46,* 1140–1152.

Roques, P. Lambin, M., Jeunier, B., Strayer, F. (1997). Multivariate analysis of personal space in a primary school classroom. *Enfance, 4,* 451–468.

Rosa, L., Rosa, E., Sarner, L., Barrett, S. (1998). A close look at therapeutic touch. *Journal of the American Medical Association, 279,* 1005–1010.

Rosaforte, T. (2000). *Raising the bar: The championship years of Tiger Woods.* New York: St. Martin's Press.

Rosch, E. H. (1973). Natural categories. *Cognitive Psychology, 4,* 328–350.

Rosch, E. (1978). Principles of organization. In E. Rosch & H. L. Lloyd (Eds.), *Cognition and categorization.* Hillsdale, NJ: Erlbaum.

Rose, C. R., & Konnerth, A. (2002). Exciting glial oscillations. *Nature Neuroscience, 4,* 773–774.

Rose, S. A., & Feldman, J. F. (1997). Memory and speed: Their role in the relation of infant information processing to later IQ. *Child Development, 68,* 630–641.

Rosen, R. C. (2002). Sexual function assessment and the role of vasoactive drugs in female sexual dysfunction. *Archives of Sexual Behavior, 31(5),* 439–443.

Rosenblatt, R. (1999, October 25). The way we look at giants. *Time,* p. 142.

Rosenhan, D. (1973). On being sane in insane places. *Science, 197,* 250–258.

Rosenheck, R., Cramer, J., Allan, E., Erdos, J., Frisman, J. et al. (1999). Cost-effectiveness of clozapine in patients with high and low levels of hospital use. *Archives of General Psychiatry, 56,* 565–572.

Rosenthal, M. K., & Roer-Strier, D. (2001). Cultural differences in mothers' developmental goals and ethnotheories. *International Journal of Psychology, 36(1),* 20–31.

Rosenthal, N. E. (1998). *Winter blues: Seasonal affective disorder.* New York: Guilford.

Rosenzweig, E. S., Barnes, C. A., & McNaughton, B. L. (2002). Making room for new memories. *Nature Neuroscience, 5(1),* 6–8.

Rosenzweig, M. R. (1966). Environmental complexity, cerebral change, and behavior. *American Psychologist, 21,* 321–332.

Rosenzweig, M. R., & Bennett, E. L. (1996). Psychobiology of plasticity: Effects of training and experience on brain and behavior. *Behavioural Brain Research, 78(1),* 57–65.

Rosenzweig, M. R., Bennet, E. L., & Diamond, M. C. (1972). Brain changes in response to experience. *Scientific American, 226,* 22–29.

Rosenzweig, M. R., Leiman, A. L., & Breedlove, S. M. (1999). *Biological psychology: An introduction to behavioral, cognitive, and clinical neuroscience.* Sunderland, MA: Sinauer Associates.

Ross, B. M., & Millson, C. (1970). Repeated memory of oral prose in Ghana and New York. *International Journal of Psychology, 5,* 173–181.

Ross, M. W. (2002). Sexuality and health challenges: Responding to a public health imperative. *Journal of Sex Research, 39(1),* 7–9.

Rossano, M. J. (2003). *Evolutionary psychology: The science of human behavior and evolution.* Hoboken, NJ: Wiley.

Roth, B. L., Willins, D. L., Kristiansen, K., & Kroeze, W. K. (1999). Activation is hallucinogenic and antagonism is therapeutic: Role of 5-HT 2A receptors in atypical antipsychotic drug actions. *Neuroscientist, 5,* 254–262.

Rotter, J. B. (1954). *Social learning and clinical psychology.* Englewood Cliffs, NJ: Prentice Hall.

Rotter, J. B. (1990). Internal versus external control of reinforcement: A case history of a variable. *American Psychologist, 45,* 489–493.

Rottnek, M. (2000). *Sissies and tomboys: Gender nonconformity and homosexual childhood.* New York: New York University Press.

Rovee-Collier, C. (1999). The development of infant memory. *Current Directions in Psychological Science, 8,* 80–85.

Rowan, J. (1998). Maslow amended. *Journal of Humanistic Psychology, 38,* 81–92.

Roy, T. S., Seidler, F. J., & Slotkin, T. A. (2002). Prenatal nicotine exposure evokes alterations of cell structure in hippocampus and somatosensory cortex. *Journal of Pharmacology & Experimental Therapeutics, 300(1),* 124–133.

Royce, R., Sena, A., Cates, W., & Cohen, M. (1997). Sexual transmission of HIV. *New England Journal of Medicine, 336,* 1072–1078.

Roye, C., & Balk, S. (1997). Evaluation of an intergenerational program for pregnant and parenting adolescents. *Maternal-Child Nursing Journal, 24,* 32–36.

Rozee, P. D., & Koss, M. P. (2001). Rape: A century of resistance. *Psychology of Women Quarterly, 25(4),* 295–311.

Rozin, P. (1996). Towards a psychology of food and eating: From motivation to module to model to marker, morality, meaning, and metaphor. *Current Directions in Psychological Science, 5,* 18–24.

Rubin, L. B. (1992). The empty nest. In J. M. Henslin (Ed.), *Marriage and family in a changing society* (4th ed., pp. 261–270). New York: Free Press.

Rubin, M., Hewstone, M., & Voci, A. (2001). Stretching the boundaries: Strategic perceptions of intragroup variability. *European Journal of Social Psychology, 31(4),* 413–429.

Rubin, Z. (1970). Measurement of romantic love. *Journal of Personality and Social Psychology, 16,* 265–273.

Ruble, D. N., & Martin, C. L. (1998). Gender development. In W. Damon & R. M. Lerner (Eds.), *Handbook of child psychology* (Vol. 1). New York: Wiley.

Ruby, N. F., Dark, J., Burns, D. E., Heller, H. C., & Zucker, I. (2002). The suprachiasmatic nucleus is essential for circadian body temperature rhythms in hibernating ground squirrels. *Journal of Neuroscience, 22(1),* 357–364.

Rudd, M. D., Ellis, T. E., Rajab, M. H., & Wehrly, T. (2000). Personality types and suicidal behavior: An exploratory study. *Suicide & Life-Threatening Behavior, 30(3),* 199–212.

Ruffin, C. L. (1993). Stress and health-little hassles vs. major life events. *Australian Psychologist, 28,* 201–208.

Rug, M. D., et al. (1998). Dissociation of the neural correlates of implicit and explicit memory. *Nature, 392,* 595–598.

Rumbaugh, D. M., et al. (1974). Lana (chimpanzee) learning language: A progress report. *Brain & Language, 1(2),* 205–212.

Rushton, J. P. (2001). Black-White differences on the g-factor in South Africa: A "Jensen Effect" on the Wechsler Intelligence Scale for Children—Revised. *Personality & Individual Differences, 31(8),* 1227–1232.

Russell, J., Baur, L. A., Beumont, P. J. V., Byrnes, S., Gross, G., Touyz, S., Abraham, S., & Zipfel, S. (2001). Altered energy metabolism in anorexia nervosa. *Psychoneuroendocrinology, 26(1),* 51–63.

Rust, J. (1999). Discriminant validity of the "big five" personality traits in employment settings. *Social Behavior & Personality, 27(1),* 99–108.

Rutan, J. S., & Stone, W. N. (2000). *Psychodynamic group psychotherapy* (3rd ed.). New York: Guilford Press.

Rutler, M. L. (1997). Nature–nurture integration: The example of antisocial behavior. *American Psychologist, 52,* 390–398.

Ruxton, G. D. (1998). Experimental design: Minimizing suffering may not always mean minimizing number of subjects. *Animal Behaviour, 56(2),* 511–512.

Ruzovsky, F. A. (1984). *Consent to treatment: A practical guide.* Boston: Little, Brown.

Ryan, R. M., & Deci, E. L. (2000). Self-determination theory and the facilitation of intrinsic motivation, social development, and well-being. *American Psychologist, 55(1),* 68–78.

Rybacki, J. J., & Long, J. W. (1999). The essential guide to prescription drugs 1999. New York: Harper/Perennial.

Rybash, J. M. (2000). Adult development and aging. Columbus, OH: Brown and Benchmark.

Rye, D. B. (1997). Contributions of the pedunculopontine region to normal and altered REM sleep. Sleep, 20, 757–788.

Rymer, R. (1993). Genie: An abused child's first flight from silence. New York: HarperCollins.

Saadeh, W., Rizzo, C. P., & Roberts, D. G. (2002). Spanking. Clinical Pediatrics, 41(2), 87–88.

Saarinen, T. F. (1987). Centering of mental maps of the world. Discussion paper. Tucson, AZ: University of Arizona, Department of Geography and Regional Development.

Sabini, J., & Silver, M. (1993). Critical thinking and obedience to authority. In J. Chaffee (Ed.), Critical thinking (2nd ed.) (pp. 367–376). Palo Alto, CA: Houghton Mifflin.

Saenger, P. (1996). Current concepts: Turner's syndrome. New England Journal of Medicine, 335, 1749–1754.

Safarik, M. E., Jarvis, J. P., & Nussbaum, K. E. (2002). Sexual homicide of elderly females: Linking offender characteristics to victim and crime scene attributes. Journal of Interpersonal Violence, 17(5), 500–525.

Sahelian, R. (1998). Kava: The miracle antianxiety herb. New York: St Martins.

Salisbury, D. F., et al. (1998). First-episode schizophrenic psychosis differs from first-episode affective psychosis and controls in P300 amplitude over left temporal lobe. Archives of General Psychiatry, 55, 173–180.

Saltus, R. (2000, June 22). Brain cells are coaxed into repair duty. Boston Globe, A18.

Salyers, M.P., & Mueser, K.T. (2001). Schizophrenia. In M. Hersen & V.B. Van Hasselt (Eds.), Advanced abnormal psychology (2nd ed.). New York: Klewer Academic/Plenum.

Sampselle, C. M., Harris, V. Harlow, S. D., Sowers, M. F. (2002). Midlife development and menopause in African American and Caucasian women. Health Care for Women International, 23(4), 351–363.

Sanchez-Martin, J. R., Fano, E., Ahedo, L., Cardas, J., Brain, P. F., & Azpiroz, A. (2000). Relating testosterone levels and free play social behavior in male and female preschool children. Psychoneuroendocrinology, 25(8), 773–783.

Sanders, M. A. (2001). Minimizing stress in the workplace: Whose responsibility is it? Work: Journal of Prevention, Assessment & Rehabilitation, 17(3), 263–165.

Sanderson, W. C. (1995, March). Which therapies are proven effective? APA Monitor, p. 4.

Sangha, S., McComb, C., Scheibenstock, A., Johannes, C., & Lukowiak, K. (2002). The effects of continuous versus partial reinforcement schedules on associative learning, memory, and extinction in Lymnaea stagnalis. Journal of Experimental Biology, 205, 1171–1178.

Sangwan, S. (2001). Ecological factors as related to I.Q. of children. Psycho-Lingua, 31(2), 89–92.

Sano, M., Stern, Y., Cote, L., Williams, J. B., & Mayeux, R. (1990). Depression in Parkinson's disease: A biochemical model. Archives of Neurology, 48, 1052–154.

Sapolsky, R. M. (1994). Why zebras don't get ulcers: A guide to stress, stress related diseases, and coping. New York: Freeman.

Sapolsky, R. M. (1996a). Stress, glucocorticoids, and damage to the nervous system: The current state of confusion. Stress: The International Journal on the Biology of Stress, 1, 1–19.

Sapolsky, R. M. (1996b). Why stress is bad for your brain. Science, 273, 749–750.

Sapolsky, R. (1999, March). Stress and your shrinking brain. Discover, pp. 116–120.

Sarafino, E. P. (2000). Behavior modification: Understanding principles of behavior change. Mayfield.

Sarafino, E. P. (2002). Health psychology: Biopsychosocial interactions (4th ed.). New York: Wiley.

Sarbin, T. R. (1997). On the futility of psychiatric diagnostic manuals (DSMs) and the return of personal agency. Applied and Preventive Psychology, 6, 233–243.

Sargent, J. D., Dalton, M. A., Beach, M. L., Mott, L. A., Tickle, J. J., Ahrens, M. B., & Heatherton, T. F. (2002). Viewing tobacco use in movies: Does it shape attitudes that mediate adolescent smoking? American Journal of Preventive Medicine, 22(3), 137–145.

Sarkar, P., Rathee, S. P., & Neera, N. (1999). Comparative efficacy of pharmacotherapy and biofeedback among cases of generalized anxiety disorder. Journal of Projective Psychology & Mental Health, 6, 69–77.

Sartori, G., & Umilta, C. (2000). The additive factor method in brain imaging. Brain & Cognition, 42, 68–71.

Satterfield, J. M., Folkman, S., & Acree, M. (2002). Explanatory style predicts depressive symptoms following AIDS-related bereavement. Cognitive Therapy & Research, 26(3), 393–403.

Saudino, K. J. (1997). Moving beyond the heritability question: New directions in behavioral genetic studies of personality. Current Directions in Psychological Science, 6, 86–90.

Savage-Rumbaugh, E. S. (1990). Language acquisition in a nonhuman species: Implications for the innateness debate. Developmental Psychobiology, 23, 599–620.

Savitsky, K., Medvec, V. H., & Gilovich, T. (1997). Remembering and regretting: The Zeigarnik effect and the cognitive availability of regrettable actions and inactions. Personality & Social Psychology Bulletin, 23, 248–257.

Sawaya, A. L., Fuss, P. J., Dallal, G. E., Tsay, R., McCrory, M. A., Young, V., & Roberts, S. B. (2001). Meal palatability, substrate oxidation and blood glucose in young and older men. Physiology & Behavior, 72(1–2), 5–12.

Saxe, L., & Ben-Shakhar, G. (1999). Admissibility of polygraph tests: The application of scientific standards post- Daubert. Psychology, Public Policy, & Law, 5(1), 203–223.

Scanlan, J. M., Vitaliano, P. P., Ochs, H., Savage, M. V., & Borson, S. (1998). CD4 and CD8 counts are associated with interactions of gender and psychosocial stress. Psychosomatic Medicine, 60, 644–653.

Schachter, S., & Singer, J. E. (1962). Cognitive, social, and physiological determinants of emotional state. Psychological Review, 69, 379–399.

Schacter, D. L. (1999). The seven sins of memory: Insights from psychology and cognitive neuroscience. American Psychologist, 54, 182–203.

Schafe, G. E., Fitts, D. A., Thiele, T. E., LeDoux, J. E., & Bernstein, I. L. (2000). The induction of c-Fos in the NTS after taste aversion learning is not correlated with measures of conditioned fear. Behavioral Neuroscience, 114(1), 99–106.

Schaie, K. W. (1993). The Seattle longitudinal studies of intelligence. Current Directions in Psychological Science, 2, 171 175.

Schaie, K. W. (1994). The life course of adult intellectual development. American Psychologist, 49, 304–313.

Schapira, A. H. V. (1999). Clinical review: Parkinson's disease. British Medical Journal, 318(3), 311–314.

Scheiber, B., & Selby, C. (2000). Therapeutic touch. Buffalo, NY: Prometheus Books.

Scherer, K. R., & Wallbott, H. G. (1994). Evidence for universal and cultural variation of differential emotion response patterning. Journal of Personality and Social Psychology, 66(2), 310–328.

Schiffer, F, Zaidel, E, Bogen, J, & Chasan-Taber, S. (1998). Different psychological status in the two hemispheres of two split-brain patients. Neuropsychiatry, Neuropsychology, & Behavioral Neurology, 11, 151–156.

Schiffman, S. S. (2000). Taste quality and neural coding: Implications from psychophysics and neurophysiology. Physiology & Behavio, 69(1/2), 147–159.

Schmajuk, N. A., & DiCarlo, J J. (1991). A neural network approach to hippocampal function in classical conditioning. *Behavioral Neuroscience, 105*(1), 82–110.

Schmidt, L. A. (1999). Frontal brain electrical activity in shyness and sociability. *Psychological Science, 10*(4), 316–320.

Schmidt, M. E., Fava, M., Robinson, J. M., & Judge, R. (2000). The efficacy and safety of a new enteric-coated formulation of fluoxetine given once weekly during the continuation treatment of major depressive disorder. *Journal of Clinical Psychiatry, 61*(11), 851–857.

Schmidt, N. B., Lerew, D. R., & Jackson, R. J. (1999). Prospective evaluation of anxiety sensitivity in the pathogenesis of panic: Replication and extension. *Journal of Abnormal Psychology, 108*, 532–537.

Schmitt, D. P., Shackelford, T. K., Duntley, J., Tooke, W., & Buss, D. M. (2001). The desire for sexual variety as a key to understanding basic human mating strategies. *Personal Relationships, 8*(4), 425–455.

Schmolck, H., & Squire, L. R. (2001). Impaired perception of facial emotions following bilateral damage to the anterior temporal lobe. *Neuropsychology, 15*(1), 30–38.

Schmolck, H., Buffalo, E. A., & Squire, L. R. (2000). Memory distortions develop over time: Recollections of the O.J. Simpson trial verdict after 15 and 32 months. *Psychological Science, 11*(1), 39–45.

Schmolck, H., Buffalo, E. A., & Squire, L. R. (2000). Memory distortions develop over time: Recollections of the O. J. Simpson trial verdict after 15 and 32 months. *Psychological Science, 11*, 39–45.

Schneider, D. M., & Sharp, L. (1969). *The dream life of a primitive people: The dreams of the Yir Yoront of Australia.* Ann Arbor, MI: University of Michigan.

Schneider, J. P. (2000). A qualitative study of cybersex participants: Gender differences, recovery issues, and implications for therapists. *Sexual Addiction & Compulsivity, 7*(4), 249–278.

Schneidman, E. S. (1981). Suicide. *Suicide and Life-Threatening Behavior, 11*(4), 198–220.

Schofield, W. (1964). *Psychotherapy: The purchase of friendship.* Englewood Cliffs, NJ: Prentice Hall.

Scholnick, E. K. et al. (1999). *Conceptual development: Piaget's legacy.* Mahwah, NJ: Erlbaum.

Schooler, N. R. et al. (1997). Relapse and rehospitalization during maintenance treatment of schizophrenia: The effects of dose reduction and family treatment. *Archives of General Psychiatry, 54*, 453–463.

Schopp, L., Johnstone, B., & Merrell, D. (2000). Telehealth and neuropsychological assessment: New opportunities for psychologists. *Professional Psychology: Research & Practice, 31*(2), 179–183.

Schreurs, B. G., Shi, T., Pineda, S. III, & Buck, D. L. (2000). Conditioning the unconditioned response: Modification of the rabbit's (Oryctolagus cuniculus) unconditioned nictitating membrane response. *Journal of Experimental Psychology: Animal Behavior Processes, 26*(2), 144–156.

Schuh, K. J., & Griffiths, R. R. (1997). Caffeine reinforcement: The role of withdrawal. *Psychopharmacology, 130*, 320–326.

Schulz, R. & Heckhausen, J. (1996). A lifespan model of successful aging. *American Psychologist, 51*, 702–714.

Schwartz, B. L. (2001). The relation of tip-of-the-tongue states and retrieval time. *Memory & Cognition, 29*(1), 117–126.

Schwartz, J., & Broder, J. M. (2003, February 13). Engineer warned of dire effects of liftoff damage. Available: http://www.nytimes.com/2003/02/13/national/nationalspecial/13SHUT.html?th

Schwartz, J-C., Diaz, J., Pilon, C., & Sokoloff, P. (2000). Possible implications of the dopamine D-sub-3 receptor in schizophrenia and in antipsychotic drug actions. *Brain Research Reviews, 31*, 277–287.

Schwartz, M. W., & Morton, G. J. (2002). Obesity: Keeping hunger at bay. *Nature, 418*, 595–597.

Schwartz, R.H. (2002). Marijuana: A decade and a half later, still a crude drug with underappreciated toxicity. *Journal of the American Academy of Child & Adolescent Psychiatry, 41*(10), 1215.

Scribner, S. (1977). Modes of thinking and ways of speaking: Culture and logic reconsidered. In P. N. Johnson-Laird & P. C. Wason (Eds.), *Thinking: Readings in cognitive science* (pp. 324–339). New York: Cambridge University Press.

Scribner, S. (1979). Modes of thinking and ways of speaking: Culture and logic reconsidered. In I. O. Freedle (Ed.), *New directions in discourse processing* (pp. 223–243). Norwood, NJ: Able.

Scroppo, J. C., Drob, S. L., Weinberger, J., & Eagle, P. (1998). Identifying dissociative identity disorder: A self-report and projective study. *Journal of Psychology, 107*, 272–284.

Scully, J. A., Tosi, H., & Banning, K. (2000). Life event checklists: Revisiting the Social Readjustment Rating Scale after 30 years. *Educational & Psychological Measurement, 60*(6), 864–876.

Seager, S. B. (1998). *Street crazy: The tragedy of the homeless mentally ill.* New York: Westcom Press.

Seamon, J. G., McKenna, P. A., & Binder, N. (1998). The mere exposure effect is differentially sensitive to different judgment tasks. *Consciousness and Cognition: An International Journal, 7*, 85–102.

Sears, S., & Urizar, G. G., & Evans, G. D. (2000). Examining a stress-coping model of burnout and depression in extension agents. *International Journal of Stress Management, 7*, 49–59.

Seedat, S., & Stein, D. J. (2000). Trauma and post-traumatic stress disorder in women: A review. *International Clinical Psychopharmacology, 15*(Supp3), S25–S33.

Segal, N. L. (2000). Virtual twins: New findings on within-family environmental influences on intelligence. *Journal of Educational Psychology, 92*(3), 442–448.

Segal, N. L., & Bouchard, T. J. (2000). *Entwined lives: Twins and what they tell us about human behavior.* New York: Plumsock.

Segal, N. L., Topolski, T. D., Wilson, S. M., Brown, K. W., et al. (1995). Twin analysis of odor identification and perception. *Physiology and Behavior, 57*, 605–609.

Segall, M. H., Dasen, P. R., Berry, J. W., & Portinga, Y. H. (1990). *Human behavior in global perspective: An introduction to cross-cultural psychology.* Elmsford, NY: Pergamon Press.

Segerstrale, U. (2000). *Defenders of the truth: The battle for science in the sociobiology debate and beyond.* London: Oxford University Press.

Self, T., Aahony, M., Fleming, J., Walsh, J., Brown, S. D., & Steel, K. P. (1998). Shaker-1 mutations reveal roles for myosin VIIA in both development and function of cochlear hair cells. *Development, 125*, 557–566.

Seligman, M. E. P. (1975) *Helplessness: On depression, development, and death.* San Francisco: Freeman.

Seligman, M. E. P. (1994). *What you can change and what you can't.* New York: Alfred A. Knopf.

Seligman, M. E. P. (1995). The effectiveness of psychotherapy: The Consumer Reports study. *American Psychologist, 50*, 965–974.

Selye, H. (1936). A syndrome produced by diverse nocuous agents. *Nature, 138*, 32.

Selye, H. (1974). *Stress without distress.* New York: Harper & Row.

Senior, C., Ward, J., & David, A. S. (2002). Representational momentum and the brain: An investigation into the functional necessity of V5/MT. *Visual Cognition, 9*, 81–92.

Seppa, N. (2000). Silencing a gene slows breast-tumor fighter. *Science News, 157*, 407.

Seppa, N. (2001). Sedentary off-hours link to Alzheimer's. *Science News, 159*, 148.

Shafer, A. B. (2000). Relation of the Big Five to Biodata and aspects of the self. *Per-*

sonality & Individual Differences, 28, 1017–1035.

Shapiro, K. J. (1997). The separate world of animal research. *American Psychologist, 52(11),* 1250.

Sharp, E. A., & Ganong, L. H. (2000). Raising awareness about marital expectations: Are unrealistic beliefs changed by integrative teaching? Family Relations: Interdisciplinary *Journal of Applied Family Studies, 49(1),* 71–76.

Shaver, P., R., & Hazan, C. (1994). Attachment. In A. L. Weber & J. H. Harvey (Eds.), *Perspectives on close relationships* (pp. 110–130). Boston: Allyn & Bacon.

Shaw, M. E. (1981). *Group dynamics: The psychology of small group behavior* (3rd ed.). New York: McGraw-Hill.

Shaywitz, B. A., Bennett, A., Shaywitz, S. E., Pugh, K. R., Constable, R. T., et al. (1995). Sex differences in the functional organization of the brain for language. *Nature, 373,* 607–609.

Shaywitz, S. E., Shaywitz, B. A., Pugh, K. R., Fulbright, R. K., Skudlarski, P., Mencl, W. E., Constable, R. T., Naftolin, F., Palter, S. F., Marchione, K. E., Katz, L., Shankweiler, D. P., Fletcher, J. M., Lacadie, C., Keltz, M., & Gore, J. C. (1999). Effect of estrogen on brain activation patterns in postmenopausal women during working memory tasks. *Journal of the American Medical Association, 28,* 1197–1202.

Sheehy, G. (1976). *Passages: Predictable crises of adult life.* New York: Dutton.

Sheldon, J. P., & Parent, S. L. (2002). Clergy's attitudes and attributions of blame toward female rape victims. *Violence Against Women, 8(2),* 233–256.

Sher, L. (2000). Psychological factors, immunity, and heart disease. *Psychosomatics, 41,* 372–373.

Sherif, M. (1966). *In common predicament: Social psychology of intergroup conflict and cooperation.* Boston: Houghton Mifflin.

Sherif, M. (1998). Experiments in group conflict. In J. M. Jenkins, K. Oatley et al.(Eds.), *Human emotions: A reader* (pp. 245–252). Malden, MA: Blackwell Publishers Inc.

Sherman, J. W., & Bessenoff, G. R. (1999). Stereotypes as source-monitoring cues: On the interaction between episodic and semantic memory. *Psychological Science, 10(2),* 106–110.

Sherrid, P. (2001, February 26). After the breakthrough. *U.S. News & World Report,* p. 48.

Shimizu-Albergine, M., Ippolito, D. L., & Beavo, J. A. (2001). Downregulation of fasting-induced cAMP response element-mediated gene induction by leptin in neuropeptide Y neurons of the arcuate nucleus. *Journal of Neuroscience, 21(4),* 1238–1246.

Shiraev, E., & Levy, D. (2000). *Introduction to cross-cultural psychology: Critical thinking and contemporary applications.* Boston: Allyn & Bacon.

Shukla, P. V. (2001). Management people for higher performance in under-developed region. *Psycho-Lingua, 31(1),* 25–32.

Shultz, T. R., Leveille, E., & Lepper, M. R. (1999). Free choice and cognitive dissonance revisited: Choosing 'lesser evils' versus 'greater goods.' *Personality and Social Psychology Bulletin, 25,* 40–48.

Shum, M. S. (1998). The role of temporal landmarks in autobiographical memory processes. *Psychological Bulletin, 124,* 423–442.

Shuntich, R. J., Loh, D., & Katz, D. (1998). Some relationships among affection, aggression and alcohol abuse in the family setting. *Perceptual and Motor Skills, 86,* 1051–1060.

Siegel, A., & Brutus, M. (1990). Neural substrates of aggression and range in the cat. *Progress in Psychobiology and Physiological Psychology, 14,* 135–143.

Siegel, J. M. (2000, January). Narcolepsy. *Scientific American,* pp. 76–81.

Sigelman, C. K. (1999). *Life-span human development* (3rd ed.). Pacific Grove, CA: Brooks/Cole.

Silver, E. (1995). Punishment or treatment? Comparing the lengths of confinement of successful and unsuccessful insanity defendants. *Law & Human Behavior, 19(4),* 375–388.

Silverman, I., & Phillips, K. (1998). The evolutionary psychology of spatial sex differences. In C. Crawford, & D. L. Krebs (Eds.), *Handbook of evolutionary psychology: Ideas, issues, and applications.* Mahwah, NJ: Erlbaum.

Silvester, J., Anderson-Gough, F. M., Anderson, N. R., & Mohamed, A. R. (2002). Locus of control, attributions and impression management in the selection interview. *Journal of Occupational & Organizational Psychology, 75(1),* 59–76.

Simcock, G., & Hayne, H. (2002). Breaking the barrier? Children fail to translate their preverbal memories into language. *Psychological Science, 13(3),* 225–231.

Simon, C. W., & Emmons, W. H. (1956). Responses to material presented during various stages of sleep. *Journal of Experimental Psychology, 51,* 89–97.

Simon, G. E. (1998). Management of somatoform and factitious disorders. In P. E. Nathan & J. M. Gorman (Eds.), *A guide to treatments that work* (pp. 408–422). New York: Oxford University Press.

Singer, M. I., Slovak, K., Frierson, T., & York, P. (1998). Viewing preferences, symptoms of psychological trauma, and violent behaviors among children who watch television. *Journal of the American Academy of Child and Adolescent Psychiatry, 37,* 1041–1048.

Siqueland, L., Crits-Christoph, P., Gallop, R., Barber, J. P., Griffin, M. L., Thase, M. E., Daley, D., Frank, A., Gastfriend, D. R., Blaine, J., Connolly, M. B., & Gladis, M. (2002). Retention in psychosocial treatment of cocaine dependence: Predictors and impact on outcome. *American Journal on Addictions, 11(1),* 24–40.

Skinner, B. F. (1948). Superstition in the pigeon. *Journal of Experimental Psychology, 38,* 168–172.

Skinner, B. F. (1953). *Science and human behavior.* New York: Macmillan.

Skinner, B. F. (1992). "Superstition" in the pigeon. *Journal of Experimental Psychology: General, 121(3),* 273–274.

Skodol, A. E., Oldham, J. M., & Gallaher, P. E. (1999). Axis II comorbidity of substance use disorders among patients referred for treatment of personality disorders. *American Journal of Psychiatry, 156,* 733–738.

Skuse, et al. (1997). Evidence from Turner's syndrome of an imprinted X-linked locus affecting cognitive function. *Nature, 387,* 705–708.

Slade, J. (1999). Nicotine. In B. S. McCrady, & E. E. Epstein (Eds). *Addictions: A comprehensive guidebook* (pp. 162–170). New York: Oxford University Press.

Sloan, L., Edmond, T., Rubin, A., & Doughty, M. (1998). Social workers' knowledge of and experience with sexual exploitation by psychotherapists. *Journal of the National Association of Social Workers, 43,* 43–53.

Slovenko, R. (1995). *Psychiatry and criminal culpability.* New York: Wiley.

Smart, D. W., & Smart, J. F. (1997). DSM-IV and culturally sensitive diagnosis: Some observations for counselors. *Journal of Counseling and Development, 75,* 392–398.

Smart, R., & Peterson, C. (1997). Super's career stages and the decision to change careers. *Journal of Vocational Behavior, 51,* 358–374.

Smith, A. (1982). *Powers of mind.* New York: Summit.

Smith, C. A., & Kirby, L. D. (2001). Affect and cognitive appraisal processes. In J. P. Forgas (Ed.), *Handbook of affect and social cognition,* pp. 75–92. Mahwah, NJ: Lawrence Erlbaum.

Smith, E. E. (1995). Concepts and categorization. In E. E. Smith, D. N. Osherson, et al. (Eds.), *Thinking: An invitation to cognitive science,* Vol. 3 (2nd ed.), (pp. 3–33). Cambridge: MIT Press.

Smith, P. B., Dugan, S., & Trompenaars, F. (1997). Locus of control and affectivity by gender and occupational status: A 14-nation study. *Sex Roles, 36,* 51–77.

Smuts, B. (1995). The evolutionary origins of patriarchy. *Human Nature, 6,* 1–32.

Snarey, J. R. (1985). Cross-cultural universality of social-moral development: A critical review of Kohlbergian research. *Psychological Bulletin, 97,* 202–233.

Snarey, J. R. (1995). In communitarian voice: The sociological expansion of Kohlbergian theory, research, and practice. In W. M. Kurtines & J. L. Gerwirtz (Eds.), *Moral development: An introduction* (pp. 109–134). Boston: Allyn & Bacon.

Snow-Turek, A. L., Norris, M. P., & Tan, G. (1996). Active and passive coping strategies in chronic pain patients. *Pain, 64,* 445–462.

Sobel, D. S., & Ornstein, R. (1996). Rx: Healthy Thinking. *Mental Medicine Update, 4,* 3–6.

Sobieski, D. J. (2000, July 24). Letters. *Time,* p. 3.

Solan, H. A., & Mozlin, R. (2001). Children in poverty: Impact on health, visual development, and school failure. *Issues in Interdisciplinary Care, 3(4),* 271–288.

Solms, M. (1997). *The neuropsychology of dreams.* Mahwah, NJ: Lawrence Erlbaum.

Soloff, P. H., Lynch, K. G., Kelly, T. M., Malone, K. M., & Mann, J. (2000). Characteristics of suicide attempts of patients with major depressive episode and borderline personality disorder: A comparative study. *American Journal of Psychiatry, 157,* 601–608.

Solomon, M. (2000). The fruits of their labor: A longitudinal exploration of parent personality and adjustment in their adult children. *Journal of Personality, 68(2),* 281–308.

Solomon, M., & Englis, B. G. (1994). Observations: The big picture: Product complementarity and integrated communications. *Journal of Advertising Research, 34(1),* 57–63.

Sommer, R. (1969). *Personal space.* Englewood Cliffs, NJ: Prentice Hall.

Son, L. K., & Metcalfe, J. (2000). Metacognitive and control strategies in study-time allocation. *Journal of Experimental Psychology: Learning, Memory, & Cognition, 26(1),* 204–221.

Song, H-J, Stevens, C. F., & Gage, F. H. (2002). Neural stem cells from adult hippocampus develop essential properties of functional CNS neurons. *Nature Neuroscience, 5,* 438–445.

Sotres-Bayon, F., & Pellicer, F. (2000). The role of the dopaminergic mesolimbic system in the affective component of chronic pain. *Salud Mental, 23(1),* 23–29.

Soussignan, R. (2002). Duchenne smile, emotional experience, and autonomic reactivity: A test of the facial feedback hypothesis. *Emotion, 2(1),* 52–74.

Spearman, C. (1923). *The nature of "intelligence" and the principles of cognition.* London: Macmillan.

Spencer, P., & Vanden-Boom, E. (1999). Year after the death of Michigan State U. Student, family advocates sensible drinking. Lansing, MI: University Wire.

Sperling, G. (1960). The information available in brief visual presentations. *Psychological Monographs, 74* (Whole No. 498).

Spiegel, D. (1995). Hypnosis and suggestion. In D. L. Schachter (Ed.), *Memory distortion: How minds, brains, and societies reconstruct the past.* Cambridge, MA: Harvard University Press.

Spiegel, D. (1999). An altered state. *Mind/Body Health Newsletter, 8(1),* 3–5.

Spiegel, D., & Maldonado, J. R. (1999). Dissociative disorders. In R. E. Hales, S. C. Yudofsky, & J. C. Talbott (Eds.), *American psychiatric press textbook of psychiatry.* Washington, DC: American Psychiatric Press.

Spinweber, C. L. (1993). Randy Gardner. In M. A. Carskadon (Ed.), *Encyclopedia of sleep and dreaming.* New York: Macmillan.

Spitz, R. A., & Wolf, K. M. (1946). The smiling response: A contribution to the ontogenesis of social relations. *Genetic Psychology Monographs, 34,* 57–123.

Spokane, A. R., Meir, E. I., & Catalano, M. (2000). Person-environment congruence and Holland's theory: A review and reconsideration. *Journal of Vocational Behavior, 57(2),* 137–187.

Sprecher, S., & Regan, P. C. (2002). Liking some things (in some people) more than others: Partner preferences in romantic relationships and friendships. *Journal of Social & Personal Relationships, 19(4),* 463–481.

Sprecher, S., & Regan, P. C. (2002). Liking some things (in some people) more than others: Partner preferences in romantic relationships and friendships. *Journal of Social & Personal Relationships, 19(4),* 463–481.

Springer, S. P., & Deutsch, G. (1998). *Left brain, right brain.* New York: Freeman.

Squier, L. H., & Domhoff, G. W. (1998). The presentation of dreaming and dreams in introductory psychology textbooks: A critical examination. *Dreaming, 10,* 21–26.

Squire, L. R., & Zola, S. M. (1998). Episodic memory, semantic memory, and amnesia. *Hippocampus, 8,* 205–211.

Squire, L. R., Schmolck, H., & Buffalo, E. A. (2001). Memory distortions develop over time: A reply to Horn. *Psychological Science, 121(2),* 182.

Sroufe, L. A. (1979). Socioemotional development. In J. Osofsky (Ed.), *Handbook of infant development* (pp. 462–516). New York: Wiley.

Stafford, J., & Lynn, S. J. (2002). Cultural scripts, memories of childhood abuse, and multiple identities: A study of role-played enactments. *International Journal of Clinical & Experimental Hypnosis, 50(1),* 67–85.

Stahl, S. M. (1997). Mental illness may be damaging to your brain. *Journal of Clinical Psychiatry, 58,* 289–290.

Stajkovic, A. D., & Luthans, F. (1998). Self-efficacy and work-related performance: A meta-analysis. *Psychological Bulletin, 124,* 240–261.

Stake, J. E. (1997). Integrating expressiveness and instrumentality in real-life settings: A new perspective on the benefits of androgyny. *Sex Roles, 37,* 541–564.

Stams, Geert-Jan J. M., Juffer, F., & van IJzendoorn, M. H. (2002). Maternal sensitivity, infant attachment, and temperament in early childhood predict adjustment in middle childhood: The case of adopted children and their biologically unrelated parents. *Developmental Psychology, 38(5),* 806–821.

Starkman, N. & Rajani, N. (2002). The case for comprehensive sex education. *AIDS Patient Care & STD's, 16(7),* 313–318.

Steele, C. M., & Aronson, J. (1995). Stereotype threat and the intellectual test performance of African Americans. *Journal of Personality and Social Psychology, 69,* 797–811.

Steele, J., James, J. B., & Barnett, R. C. (2002). Learning in a man's world: Examining the perceptions of undergraduate women in male-dominated academic areas. *Psychology of Women Quarterly, 26(1),* 46–50.

Steffens, D. C., & Krishnan, K. R. R. (1998). Strutural neuroimaging and mood disorders: Recent findings, implications for classification, and future directions. *Biological Psychiatry, 43,* 705–712.

Stein, F. (2001). Occupational stress, relaxation therapies, exercise and biofeedback. *Work: Journal of Prevention, Assessment & Rehabilitation, 17(3),* 235–246.

Steinhart, P. (1986, March). Personal boundaries. *Audubon,* pp. 8–11.

Stella, N., Schweitzer, P., & Piomelli, D. (1997). A second endogenous cannabinoid that modulates long-term potentiation. *Na-ture, 382,* 677–678.

Stephan, W., Berscheid, E., & Walster, E. (1971). Sexual arousal and heterosexual perception. *Journal of Personality and Social Psychology, 20(1),* 93–101.

Stepkoe, A., Cropley, M. & Joekes, K. (2000). Task demands and the pressures of everyday life: Associations between cardiovascular reactivity and work blood pressure and hearth rate. *Health Psychology, 19,* 46–54.

Sterman, M. B. (1996). Physiological origins and functional correlates of EEG rhythmic activities: Implications for self-regulation. *Biofeedback and Self Regulation, 21,* 3–33.

Stern, K., & McClintock, M. K. (1998). Regulation of ovulation by human pheromones. *Nature, 392,* 177–179.

Sternberg, R. J. (1985). *Beyond IQ: A triarchic theory of human intelligence.* New York: Cambridge University Press.

Sternberg, R. J. (1998). Principles of teaching for successful intelligence. *Educational Psychologist, 33,* 65–72.

Sternberg, R. J. (1999). The theory of successful intelligence. *Review of General Psychology, 3,* 292–316.

Sternberg, R. J., & Hedlund, J. (2002). Practical intelligence, g, and work psychology. *Human Performance, 15(1–2),* 143–160.

Sternberg, R. J., & Kaufman, J. C. (1998). Human abilities. *Annual Review of Psychology, 49,* 479–502.

Sternberg, R. J., & Lubart, T. I. (1992). Buy low and sell high: An investment approach to creativity. *Current Directions in Psychological Science, 1(1),* 1–5.

Sternberg, R. J., Nokes, C., Geissler, P. W., Prince, R., Okatcha, F., Bundy, D. A., & Grigorenko, E. L. (2001). The relationship between academic and practical intelligence: A case study in Kenya. *Intelligence, 29(5),* 401–418.

Stetter, F., & Kupper, S. (2002). Autogenic training: A meta-analysis of clinical outcome studies. *Applied Psychophysiology & Biofeedback, 27(1),* 45–98.

Stevenson, H. L., & Stigler, J. (1992). *The learning gap: Why our schools are failing and what we can learn from Japanese and Chinese education.* New York: Summit Books.

Stewart, A. J., & Ostrove, J. M. (1998). Women's personality in middle age: Gender, history, and midcourse corrections. *American Psychologist, 53(11),* 1185–1194.

Stewart, T., Doan, K. A., Gingrich, B. E., & Smith, E. (1998). The actor as context for social judgments: Effects of prior impressions and stereotypes. *Journal of Personality and Social Psychology, 75,* 1132–1154.

Stip, E. (2000). Novel antipsychotics: Issues and controversies. Typicality of atypical antipsychotics. *Journal of Psychiatry & Neuroscience, 25,* 137–153.

Stockhorst, U., Spennes-Saleh, S., Koerholz, D., Goebel, U., Schneider, M. E., Steingrueber, H-J., & Klosterhalfen, S. (2000).

Anticipatory symptoms and anticipatory immune responses in pediatric cancer patients receiving chemotherapy: Features of a classically conditioned response? *Brain, Behavior & Immunity, 14(3),* 198–218.

Stolerman, I. P., & Jarvis, M. J. (1995). The scientific case that nicotine is addictive. *Psychopharmacology, 117,* 2–10.

Stone, J., & Cooper, J. (2001). A self-standards model of cognitive dissonance. *Journal of Experimental Social Psychology, 37(3),* 228–243.

Stoner, J. A. (1961). A comparison of individual and group decisions involving risk. *Unpublished master's thesis,* School of Industrial Management, MIT, Cambridge, MA.

Stormshak, E. A., Bierman, K. L., McMahon, R. J., & Lengua, L. J., Conduct Problems Prevention Research Group. (2000). Parenting practices and child disruptive behavior problems in early elementary school. *Journal of Clinical Child Psychology, 29(1),* 17–29.

Strack, F., Martin, L. L., & Stepper, S. (1988). Inhibiting and facilitating conditions of the human smile: A nonobstrusive test of the facial feedback hypothesis. *Journal of Personality and Social Psychology, 54,* 768–777.

Stratton, G. M. (1897). Vision without inversion of the retinal image. *Psychological Review, 4(4),* 341–360.

Strote, J., Lee, J.E., & Wechsler, H. (2002). Increasing MDMA use among college students: Results of a national survey. *Journal of Adolescent Health, 30(1),* 64–72.

Strubbe, J. H., & van Dijk, G. (2002). The temporal organization of ingestive behaviour and its interaction with regulation of energy balance. *Neuroscience & Biobehavioral Reviews, 26(4),* 485–498.

Sturges, J. W., & Sturges, L. V. (1998). In vivo systematic desensitization in a single-session treatment of an 11-year-old girl's elevator phobia. *Child & Family Behavior Therapy, 20(4),* 55–62.

Subramanian, S., & Vollmer, R. R. (2002). Sympathetic activation fenfluramine depletes brown adipose tissue norepinephrine content in rats. *Pharmacology, Biochemistry & Behavior, 73(3),* 639–646.

Sue, D. W., & Sue, D. (1999). *Counseling the culturally different.* New York: Wiley.

Sue, D.W., & Sue, D. (2002). *Counseling the culturally diverse: Theory and practice.* New York: Wiley.

Suhr, J. A. (2002). Malingering, coaching, and the serial position effect. *Archives of Clinical Neuropsychology, 17(1),* 69–77.

Sullivan, M. J. L., Tripp, D. A., & Santor, D. (1998). Gender differences in pain and pain behavior: The role of catastrophizing. Paper presented at the annual meeting of

the American Psychological Association, San Francisco.

Sulloway, F. J. (2000). Birth order, sibling competition, and human behavior. In P. C. Davies & H. R. Holcombs (Eds.), The evolution of minds: Psychological and philosophical perspectives. Boston: Kluwer Academic.

Suomi, S. J. (1991). Adolescent depression and depressive symptoms: Insights from longitudinal studies with rhesus monkeys. *Journal of Youth & Adolescence, 20,* 273–287.

Surgenor, L. J., Horn, J., Plumridge, E. W., & Hudson, S. M. (2002). Anorexia nervosa and psychological control: A reexamination of selected theoretical accounts. *European Eating Disorders Review, 10(2),* 85–101.

Sutherland, G. R., & McNaughton, B. (2000). Memory trace reactivation in hippocampal and neocortical neuronal ensembles. *Current Opinion in Neurobiology, 10,* 180–186.

Suzuki, L. A., & Valencia, R. R. (1997). Race-ethnicity and measured intelligence: Educational implications. *American Psychologist, 52,* 11–3–1114.

Svendsen, C. N. (2002). Neurobiology: The amazing astrocyte. *Nature, 417,* 29–32.

Swaab, D. F., Chung, W. C. J., Kruijver, F. P. M., Hofman, M. A., & Ishunina, T. A. (2001). Structural and functional sex differences in the human hypothalamus. *Hormones & Behavior, 40(2),* 93–98.

Swets, J. A., Dawes, R. M., & Monahan, J. (2000). Psychological science can improve diagnostic decisions. *Psychological Science in the Public Interest, 1,* 1–26.

Sylvester, A. P., Mulsant, B. H., Chengappa, K. N. R., Sandman, A. R., & Haskett, R. F. (2000). Use of electroconvulsive therapy in a state hospital: A 10–year review. *Journal of Clinical Psychiatry, 61,* 534–544.

Szasz, T. (2000). Second commentary on "Aristotle's function argument." *Philosophy, Psychiatry, & Psychology, 7,* 3–16.

Szasz, T. S. (1960). The myth of mental illness. *American Psychologist, 15,* 113–118.

Szasz, T. S. (1987). *Insanity: The idea and its consequences.* New York: Wiley.

Szasz, T. (1995, May/June). Idleness and lawlessness in the therapeutic state. *Society,* pp. 30–35.

Takeshita, T., & Morimoto, K. (1999). Self-reported alcohol-associated symptoms and drinking behavior in three ALDH2 genotypes among Japanese University students. *Alcoholism: Clinical & Experimental Research, 23(6),* 1065–1069.

Talbot, N. L., Duberstein, P. R., King, D. A., Cox, C., & Giles, D. E. (2000). Personality traits of women with a history of childhood sexual abuse. *Comprehensive Psychiatry, 41*, 130–136.

Tanaka, T., Yoshida, M., Yokoo, H., Tomita, M., & Tanaka, M. (1998). Expression of aggression attenuates both stress-induced gastric ulcer formation and increases in noradrenaline release in the rat amygdala assessed intracerebral microdialysis. *Pharmacology, Biochemistry & Behavior, 59(1)*, 27–31.

Tanda, G., Pontieri, F. E., & Di Chiara, G. (1997). Cannabinoid and heroin activation of mesolimbic dopamine transmission by a common 1 opioid receptor mechanism. *Science, 276*, 2048–2050.

Tang, Y.-P., Wang, H., Feng, R., Kyin, M., & Tsien, J. Z. (2001). Differential effects of enrichment on learning and memory function in NR2B transgenic mice. *Neuropharmacology, 41(6)*, 779–790.

Tang, Y.-P., Shimizu, E., Dube, G. R., Rampon, C., Kerchner, G. A., Zhuo, M., Liu, G., & Tsien, J. Z. (1999). Genetic enhancement of learning and memory in mice. *Nature, 401*, 63–69.

Tanner, B. L. (1992). Mental disorders, psychiatric patients and suicide. In R. W. Marls, A. L. Berman, J. T. Maltsberger, & R. I. Yufit (Eds.), *Assessment and prediction of suicide* (pp. 227–320).

Tanner-Halverson, P., Burden, T., & Sabers, D. (1993). WISC-III normative data for Tohono O'odham Native-American children. In B. A. Bracken & R. S. McCallum (Eds.), *Journal of Psychoeducational Assessment Monograph Series, Advances in Psychoeducational Assessment: Wechsler Intelligence Scale for Children–Third Edition* (pp. 125–133). Germantown, TN: Psychoeducational Corporation.

Taraban, R., Maki, W. S., & Rynearson, K. (1999). Measuring study time distributions: Implications for designing computer-based courses. *Behavior Research Methods, Instruments & Computers, 31*, 263–269.

Tarsy, D., Baldessarini, R. J., & Tarazi, F. I. (2002). Effects of newer antipsychotics on extrapyramidal function. *CNS Drugs, 16(1)*, 23–45.

Tart, C. T. (1986). Consciousness, altered states, and worlds of experience. *Journal of Transpersonal Psychology, 18*, 159–170.

Tattersall, C. (2000). *Date rape drugs.* Thousand Oaks, CA: Rosen Publishers.

Taub, E., Gitendra, U., & Thomas, E. (2002). New treatments in neurorehabilitation founded on basic research. *Nature Reviews Neuroscience, 3*, 228–236.

Tauscher, J., Pirker, W., de Zwann, M., Asenbaum, S., Bruecke, T., & Kasper, S. (1999). In vivo visualization of serotonin transporters in the human brain during fluoxetine treatment. *European Neuropsychopharmacology, 9*, 117–179.

Taylor, E. (1999). William James and Sigmund Freud: "The future of psychology belongs to your work." *Psychological Science, 10(6)*, 465–469.

Taylor, M. J. (2000). The influence of self-efficacy on alcohol use among American Indians. *Cultural Diversity and Ethnic Minority Psychology, 6*, 152–167.

Taylor, R. C., Harris, N. A., Singleton, E. G., Moolchan, E. T., & Heishman, S. J. (2000). Tobacco craving: Intensity-relate effects of imagery scripts in drug abusers. *Experimental and Clinical Psychopharmacology, 8(1)*, 75–87.

Taylor, R. D., & Wang, M. C. (2000). *Resilience across contexts: Family, work, culture, and community.*

Taylor, S. E., & Armor, D. A. (1996). Positive illusions and coping with adversity. *Journal of Personality, 64*, 873–898.

Tedlock, B. (1992). Zuni and Quiche dream sharing and interpreting. In B. Tedlock (Ed.), *Dreaming: Anthropological and psychological interpretations.* Santa Fe, NM: School of American Research Press.

Tein, J-Y, Sandler, I. N., Zautra, A. J. (2000). Stressful life events, psychological distress, coping, and parenting of divorced mothers longitudinal study. *Journal of Family Psychology, 14(1)*, 27–42.

Tellegen, A. (1985). Structures of mood and personality and their relevance to assessing anxiety with an emphasis on self-report. In A. H. Tuma & J. D. Maser (Eds.), *Anxiety and the anxiety disorders* (pp. 681–706). Hillsdale, NJ: Erlbaum.

Temple, C. M., & Marriott, A. J. (1998). Arithmetical ability and disability in Turner's syndrome: A cognitive neuropsychological analysis. *Developmental Neuropsychology, 14*, 47–67.

Tengs, T., & Osgood, N. D. (2001). The link between smoking and impotence: Two decades of evidence. *Preventive Medicine: An International Journal Devoted to Practice & Theory, 32(6)*, 447–452.

Tennant, C. (1999). Life stress, social support, and coronary heart disease. *Australian & New Zealand Journal of Psychiatry, 33*, 636–641.

Terman, L. M. (1916). The measurement of intelligence. Boston: Houghton Mifflin.

Terman, L. M. (1954). Scientists and nonscientists in a group of 800 gifted men. *Psychological Monographs, 68(7)*, 1–44.

Terrace, H. S. (1979, November). How Nim Chimpsky changed my mind. *Psychology Today*, pp. 65–76.

Tett, R. P., & Murphy, P. J. (2002). Personality and situations in co-worker preference: Similarity and complementarity in worker compatibility. *Journal of Business & Psychology, 17(2)*, 223–243.

Thomas, A., & Chess, S. (1977). *Temperament and development.* New York: Brunner/Mazel.

Thomas, A., & Chess, S. (1987). Roundtable: What is temperament: Four approaches. *Child Development, 58*, 505–529.

Thomas, A., & Chess, S. (1991). Temperament in adolescence and its functional significance. In R. M. Lerner, A. C. Petersen, & J. Brooks-Gunn (Eds.), *Encyclopedia of adolescence* (Vol. 2). New York: Garland.

Thompson, C. P., Cowan, T. M., & Frieman, J. (1993). *Memory search by a mnemonist.* Hillsdale, NJ: Erlbaum.

Thompson, D. (1997, March 24). A boy without a penis. *Time*, 83.

Thompson, M., & Kaslow, N. J. (2000). Childhood maltreatment, PTSD, and suicidal behavior among African American females. *Journal of Interpersonal Violence, 15*, 3–16.

Thompson, R. A. (1998). Early sociopersonality development. In W. Damon & R. M. Lerner (Eds.), *Handbook of child psychology* (Vol. 1). New York: John Wiley & Sons.

Thompson, V. A., & Paivio, A. (1994). Memory for pictures and sounds: Independence of auditory and visual codes. *Canadian Journal of Experimental Psychology, 48*, 380–398.

Thorndike, E. L. (1898). Animal intelligence. *Psychological Review Monograph, 2(8)*.

Thorndike, E. L. (1911). *Animal intelligence.* New York: Macmilan.

Thunberg, M., & Dimberg, U. (2000). Gender differences in facial reactions to fear-relevant stimuli. *Journal of Nonverbal Behavior, 24(1)*, 45–51.

Thurstone, L. L. (1938). *Primary mental abilities.* Chicago: University of Chicago Press.

Tice, D. M., & Baumeister, R. F. (1997). Longitudinal study of procrastination, performance, stress, and health: The costs and benefits of dawdling. *Psychological Science, 8*, 454–458.

Tien, J. Y., Sandler, I. N., & Zautra, A. J. (2000). Stressful life events, psychological distress, coping, and parenting of divorced mothers longitudinal study. *Journal of Family Psychology, 14(1)*, 27–41.

Tierney, M. C., Varga, M., Hosey, L., Grafman, J., & Braun, A. (2001). PET evaluation of bilingual language compensation following early childhood brain damage. *Neuropsychologia, 39(2)*, 114–121.

Tietzel, A. J., & Lack, L. C. (2001). The short-term benefits of brief and long naps following nocturnal sleep restriction. *Sleep: Journal of Sleep Research & Sleep Medicine, 24(3)*, 293–300.

Tiffany, S. T., Sanderson, L., & Flash, C. A. (2000). Effects of transdermal nicotine patches on abstinence-induced and cue-induced craving in cigarette smokers. *Journal of Consulting and Clinical Psychology, 68,* 233–240.

Tiihonen, J., Isohanni, M., Rasanen, P., Koiranen, M., & Moring, J. (1997). Specific major mental disorders and criminality: A 26-year prospective study of the 1966 northern Finland birth cohort. *American Journal of Psychiatry, 154,* 840–845.

Tisserand, D. J., Bosma, H., Van Boxtel, M. P. J., & Jolles, J. (2001). Head size and cognitive ability in nondemented older adults are related. *Neurology, 56(7),* 969–971.

Tobin, D. L. (2000). *Coping strategies therapy for bulimia nervosa.* Washington, DC: American Psychological Association.

Todorov, A., & Bargh, J. A. (2002). Automatic sources of aggression. *Aggression & Violent Behavior, 7(1),* 53–68.

Tolman, E. C., & Honzik, C. H. (1930). Introduction and removal of reward and maze performance in rats. *University of California Publications in Psychology, 4,* 257–275.

Tolman, E. C., Ritchie, B. F., & Kalish, D. (1946). Studies in spatial learning: II. Place learning versus response learning. *Journal of Experimental Psychology, 36,* 221–229.

Tolosa, E., Marti, M. J., Valldeoriola, F., & Molinuevo, J. L. (1998). History of levodopa and dopamine agonists in Parkinson's disease treatment. *Neurology, 50(6, Suppl 6),* S2–S10.

Tomsen, S., & Mason, G. (2001). Engendering homophobia: Violence, sexuality and gender conformity. *Journal of Sociology, 37(3),* 257–273.

Toomey, R., Faraone, S. V., Simpson, J. C., & Tsuang, M. T. (1998). Negative, positive, and disorganized symptom dimensions in schizophrenia, major depression, and bipolar disorder. *Journal of Nervous and Mental Disease, 186,* 470–476.

Torgersen, S. (2000). Genetics of patients with borderline personality disorder. *Psychiatric Clinics of North America, 23,* 1–9.

Torrey, E. F. (1998). *Out of the shadows: Confronting America's mental illness crisis.* New York: Wiley.

Torrey, E. F., & Yolken, R. H. (1998). Is household crowding a risk factor for schizophrenia and bipolar disorder? *Schizophrenia Bulletin, 24,* 321–324.

Torrey, E. F., & Yolken, R. H. (2000). Familial and genetic mechanisms in schizophrenia. *Brain Research Reviews, 31,* 113–117.

Toth, J. P., & Reingold, E. M. (1996). *Beyond perception: Conceptual contributions to* unconscious influences of memory. Oxford, England: Oxford University Press.

Tracy, J. A., Thompson, J. K., Krupa, D. J., & Thompson, R. F. (1998). Evidence of plasticity in the pontocerebellar condition stimulus pathway during classical conditioning of the eyeblink response in the rabbit. *Behavioral Neuroscience, 112,* 267–285.

Trappey, C. (1996). A meta-analysis of consumer choice and subliminal advertising. *Psychology and Marketing, 13,* 517–530.

Travis, J. (2000). Human genome work reaches milestone. *Science News, 158,* 4.

Travis, J. (2000). Nerve connections come ready to assemble. *Science News, 157,* 262.

Troll, S. J., Miller, J., & Atchley, R. C. (1979). *Families in later life.* Belmont, CA: Wadsworth.

Trotter, R. J. (1987, January). The play's the thing. *Psychology Today,* pp. 27–34.

Truchlicka, M., McLaughlin, T. F., & Swain, J. C. (1998). Effects of token reinforcement and response cost on the accuracy of spelling performance with middle-school special education students with behavior disorders. *Behavioral Interventions, 13(1),* 1–10.

Trudeau, L. S., Russell, D. W., de la Mora, A., Schmitz, M.F. (2001). Comparisons of marriage and family therapists, psychologists, psychiatrists, and social workers in job-related measures and reactions to managed care in Iowa. *Journal of Marital & Family Therapy, 27(4),* 501–507.

Trull, T., Sher, K. J., Minks-Brown, C., Durbin, J., & Burr, R. (2000). Borderline personality disorder and substance use disorders: A review and integration. *Clinical Psychology Review, 20,* 235–253.

Trump, K. S. (2000). *Classroom killers? Hallway hostages? How schools can prevent and manage school crises.* Thousand Oaks, CA: Sage.

Tsien, J. Z. (2000, April). Building a brainier mouse. *Scientific American,* pp. 62–68.

Tsui, A. S., Porter, L. W., & Egan, T. D. (2002). When both similarities and dissimilarities matter: Extending the concept of relational demography. *Human Relations, 55(8),* 899–929.

Tu, G-C., & Israel, Y. (1995). Alcohol consumption by Orient in North America is predicted largely by a single gene. *Behavior Genetics, 25(1),* 59–65.

Tulving, E, & Markowitsch, H. J. (1998). Episodic and declarative memory: Role of hippocampus. *Hippocampus, 8,* 198–204.

Tulving, E. (2000). Concepts of memory. In E. Tulving & F. I. M. Craik (Eds.), *The Oxford handbook of memory.* New York: Oxford University Press.

Tulving, E. (1985). How many memory systems are there? *American Psychologist, 40(4),* 385–398.

Tulving, E., & Thompson, D. M. (1973). Encoding specificity and retrieval processes in episodic memory. *Psychological Review, 80,* 352–373.

Turk, D. C. (1994). Perspectives on chronic pain: The role of psychological factors. *Current Directions in Psychological Science, 3,* 45–48.

Turnbull, C. M. (1961). Some observations regarding the experiences and behavior of the Bamputi pygmies. *American Journal of Psychology, 74,* 304–308.

Tversky, A., & Kahneman, D. (1974). Judgment under uncertainty: Heuristics and biases. *Science, 185,* 1124–1131.

Tversky, A., Kahneman, D. (1993). Probabilistic reasoning. In A. I. Goldman (Ed.), *Readings in philosophy and cognitive science.* Cambridge, MA: The MIT Press.

Twenge, J. M., Baumeister, R. F., Tice, D. M., & Stucke, T. S. (2001). If you can't join them, beat them: Effects of social exclusion on aggressive behavior. *Journal of Personality & Social Psychology, 81(6),* 1058–1069.

U.S. Bureau of the Census. (1999). *Historical Poverty Tables.* Available: http://www. census.gov/hhes/poverty/histpov/hstpov3.html

Udry, J. R. (1998). Doing sex research on adolescents. In G. G. Brannigan, E. R. Allgeier, & A. R. Allgeier (Eds.), *The sex scientists* (pp. 49–60). New York: Longman.

Uecker, A. (1997). Neuroanatomical correlates of implicit and explicit memory for structurally possible and impossible visual objects. *Learning & Memory, 4,* 337–355.

Uehara, I. (2000). Differences in episodic memory between four- and five-year-olds: False information versus real experiences. *Psychological Reports, 86(3,Pt1),* 745–755.

Uhlmann, C., & Froescher, W. (2001). Biofeedback treatment in patients with refractory epilepsy: Changes in depression and control orientation. *Seizure, 10(1),* 34–38.

Ulfberg, J., Carter, N., & Edling, C. (2000). Sleep-disorder breathing and occupational accidents. *Scandinavian Journal of Work, Environment, & Health, 26(3),* 237–242.

Ulrich, R. E., Stachnik, T. J., & Stainton, N. R. (1963). Student acceptance of generalized personality interpretations. *Psychological Reports, 13,* 831–834.

Underwood, J., & Pezdek, K. (1998). Memory suggestibility as an example of the sleeper effect. *Psychonomic Bulletin & Review, 5,* 449–453.

Unni, L. K. (1998). Beyond Tarcine: Recently developed cholinesterase inhibitors for the treatment of Alzheimer's disease. *CNS Drugs, 10,* 447–460.

Unsworth, G., & Ward, T. (2001). Video games and aggressive behaviour. *Australian Psychologist, 36(3),* 184–192.

Urakubo, A., Jarskog, L. F., Lieberman, J. A., & Gilmore, J. H. (2001). Prenatal exposure to maternal infection alters cytokine expression in the placenta, amniotic fluid and fetal brain. *Schizophrenia Research, 47(1),* 27–36.

Vagg, P. R., Spielberger, C. D., & Wasala, C. F. (2002). Effects of organizational level and gender on stress in the workplace. *International Journal of Stress Management, 9(4),* 243–261.

Vaillant, G. E. (2000). Adaptive mental mechanisms: Their role in a positive psychology. *American Psychologist, 55(1),* 89–98.

Valenstein, E. S. (1998). *Blaming the brain: The truth about drugs and mental health.* New York: Free Press.

Valsiner, J. (2000). *Culture and human development.* Thousand Oaks, CA: Sage.

Van de Carr, F. R., & Lehrer, M. (1997). *While you are expecting: Your own prenatal classroom.* New York: Humanics Publishing.

Van de Castle, R. L. (1995). *Our dreaming mind.* New York: Ballantine Books.

van der Aalsvoort, G. M., & Harinck, F. J. H. (2001–2002). Scaffolding: Classroom teaching behavior for use with young students with learning disabilities. *Journal of Classroom Interaction, 36(2)-37(1),* 29–39.

Van Dierendonck, D., Schaufeli, W. B., & Buunk, B. P. (2001). Burnout and inequity among human service professionals: A longitudinal study. *Journal of Occupational Health Psychology, 6(1),* 43–52.

van IJzendoorn, M. H., & De Wolff, M. S. (1997). In search of the absent father: Meta-analyses of infant-father attachment: A rejoinder to our discussants. *Child Development, 68,* 604–609.

Van Overwalle, F., & Jordens, K. (2002). An adaptive connectionist model of cognitive dissonance.

Van Reekum, R., Conway, C. A., Gansler, D., & White, R. (1993). Neurobehavioral study of borderline personality disorder. *Journal of Psychiatry and Neuroscience, 18,* 121–129.

van Schaick, K., & Stolberg, A. L. (2001). The impact of paternal involvement and parental divorce on young adults' intimate relationships. *Journal of Divorce & Remarriage, 36(1–2),* 99–122.

Van Wel, F., Linssen, & Abma, R. (2000). The parental bond and the well-being of adolescents and young adults. *Journal of Youth & Adolescence, 29,* 307–318.

Vanable, P. A., Ostrow, D. G., McKirnan, D. J., Taywaditep, K. J., & Hope, B. A. (2000). Impact of combination therapies on HIV risk perceptions and sexual risk among HIV-Positive and HIV-Negative gay and bisexual men. *Health Psychology, 19(2),* 134–145.

Vance, J. E., Fernandez, G., & Biber, M. (1998). Educational progress in a population of youth with aggression and emotional disturbance: The role of risk and protective factors. *Journal of Emotional and Behavioral Disorders, 6,* 214–221.

VanLaningham, J., Johnson, D. R., & Amato, P. (2001). Marital happiness, marital duration, and the U-shaped curve: Evidence from a five-wave panel study. *Social Forces, 79(4),* 1313–1341.

Varney, N. R., Pinkston, J. B., & Wu, J. C. (2001). Quantitative PET findings in patients with posttraumatic anosmia. *Journal of Head Trauma Rehabilitation, 3,* 253–259.

Vaughan, C. (1996). *How life begins: The science of life in the womb.* New York: Times Books.

Vaughn, D. (1996). *The Challenger launch decision: Risky technology, culture, and deviance at NASA.* Chicago: University of Chicago Press.

Veatch, T. C. (1998). A theory of humor. *Humor: International Journal of Humor Research, 11,* 161–215.

Venter, C. et al., (2001). The sequence of the human genome. *Science,* 291, 1304–1323.

Ventura, S. J., Martin, J. A., Curtin, S. C., & Mathews, T. J. (1997). Report of final natality statistics, 1995. *Monthly Vital Statistics Report, 45*(11, Suppl. 2). Hyattsville, MD: National Center for Health.

Verma, S. K., Subramaniam, M., Chong, S., & Kua, E. H. (2002). Substance abuse in schizophrenia: A Singapore perspective. *Social Psychiatry & Psychiatric Epidemiology, 37(7),* 326–328.

Vermeulen, R. J., Drukarch, B, Wolters, E. C., & Stoof, J. C. (1999). Dopamine D-sub(1) receptor agonists: The way forward for the treatment of Parkinson's disease. *CNS Drugs, 11,* 83–91.

Vertosick, F. T. (2000). *Why we hurt: The natural history of pain.* New York: Harcourt, Inc.

Vickers, J. C., et al. (2000). The cause of neuronal degeneration in Alzheimer's disease. *Progress in Neurobiology, 60,* 139–165.

Vidmar, N. (1997). Generic prejudice and the presumption of guilt in sex abuse trials. *Law and Human Behavior, 21(1),* 5–25.

Villarreal, D. M., Do, V., Haddad, E., & Derrick, B. E. (2002). MDA receptor antagonists sustain LTP and spatial memory: Active processes mediate LTP decay. *Nature Neuroscience, 5(1),* 48–52.

Villarreal, D. M., Do, V., Haddad, E., & Derrick, B. E. (2002). NMDA receptor antagonists sustain LTP and spatial memory: Active processes mediate LTP decay. *Nature Neuroscience, 5(1),* 48–52.

Vitaterna, M. H., Takahashi, J. S., & Turek, F. W. (2001). Overview of circadian rhythms. *Alcohol Research & Health, 25(2),* 85–93.

Volavka, J. (2002). Risk for individuals with schizophrenia who are living in the community. *Psychiatric Services, 53(4),* 484–485.

Volavka, J. (1990). Aggression, electroencephalography, and evoked potentials: A critical review. *Neuropsychiatry, Neuropsychology, and Behavioral Neurology, 3,* 249–259.

Volavka, J. (1999). The neurobiology of violence: An update. *Journal of Neuropsychiatry & Clinical Neurosciences, 11,*(3) 307–314.

Von Bergen, C. W., Soper, B., Foster, T. (2002). Unintended negative effects of diversity management. *Public Personnel Management, 31(2),* 239–251.

Voyer, D., Voyer, S., & Bryden, M. (1995). Magnitude of sex differences in spatial abilities: A meta-analysis and consideration of critical variables. *Psychological Bulletin, 117,* 250–270.

Vuilleumier, P., Reverdin, A., & Landis, T. (1997). Four legs: Illusory reduplication of the lower limbs after bilateral parietal lobe damage. *Archives of Neurology, 54,* 1534–1547.

Wadden, T. A., Brownell, K. D., & Foster, G. D. (2002). Obesity: Responding to the global epidemic. *Journal of Consulting & Clinical Psychology, 70(3),* 510–525.

Wadden, T. S., Vogt, R. A., Anderson, R. E., Bartlett, S. J., Foster, G. D., Kuehnel, R. H., Wilk, J., Weinstock, R., Buckenmeyer, P., Berkowitz, R. I., & Steen, S. N. (1997). Exer-cise in the treatment of obesity: Effects of four interventions on body composition, resting energy expenditure, appetite, and mood. *Journal of Consulting and Clinical Psychology, 65,* 269–277.

Wade, T. J., & Abez, H. (1997). Social cognition and evolutionary psychology: Physical attractiveness and contrast effects on women's self-perceived body image. *International Journal of Psychology, 32,* 35–42.

Wagner, D. A. (1982). Ontogeny in the study of culture and cognition. In D. A. Wagner & H. W. Stevenson (Eds.), *Cultural perspectives on child development* (pp. 105–123). San Francisco: Freeman.

Wakschlag, L. S., & Hans, S. L. (2002). Maternal smoking during pregnancy and conduct problems in high-risk youth: A developmental framework. *Development & Psychopathology, 14(2),* 351–369.

Walinder, J., & Rutz, W. (2001). Male depression and suicide. *International Clinical Psychopharmacology, 16(Suppl2),* S21–S24.

Walker, E. F., & Diforio, D. (1997). Schizophrenia: A neural diathesis-stress model. *Psychological Review, 104,* 667–685.

Walker, I., & Crogan, M. (1998). Academic performance, prejudice, and the Jigsaw classroom: New pieces to the puzzle. *Journal of Community and Applied Social Psychology, 8,* 381–393.

Wallace, A. F. C. (1958). Dreams and wishes of the soul: A type of psychoanalytic theory among the seventeenth century Iroquois. *American Anthropologist, 60,* 234–248.

Wallace, D. C. (1997, August). Mitochondrial DNA in aging and disease. *Scientific American,* 40–47.

Waller, N. G., & Ross, C. A. (1997). The prevalence and biometric structure of pathological dissociation in the general population: Taxometric and behavior genetics findings. *Journal of Abnormal Psychology, 106,* 499–510.

Wallerstein, J. S., & Corbin, S. B. (1999). The child and the vicissitudes of divorce. In R. M. Galatzer-Levy, & L. Kraus (Eds), *The scientific basis of child custody decisions* (pp. 73–95). New York: Wiley.

Wallerstein, J. S., & Lewis, J. (1998). The long-term impact of divorce on children: A first report from a 25-year study. *Family & Conciliation Courts Review, 36*(3), 368–383.

Walsh, J. K., & Lindblom, S. S. (1997). Psychophysiology of sleep deprivation and disruption. In M. R. Pressman, W. C. Orr, et al. (Eds.), *Understanding sleep: The evaluation and treatment of sleep disorders. Application and practice in health psychology* (pp. 73–110). Washington, DC: American Psychological Association.

Walton, B. (2000, May 29). Basketball's tarnished knight. *Time,* p. 96.

Wang, A., Laing, Y., Fridell, R. A., Probst, F. J., Wilcox, E. R., Touchman, J. W., Morton, C. C., Morell, R. J., Noben-Trauth, K., Camper, S. A., & Friedman, T. B. (1998). Association of unconventional myosin MY015 mutations with human nonsyndromic deafness DFNB3. *Science, 280,* 1447–1451.

Wang, D. L. (1999). Object selection based on oscillatory correlation. *Neural Networks, 12,* 579–592.

Wang, D. L., & Terman, D. (1997). Image segmentation based on oscillatory correlation. *Neural Computation, 9,* 805–836.

Wang, M., Irwin, R., & Hautus, M. J. (1998). Discriminability in length of lines in the Müller-Lyer figure. *Perception & Psycho-physics, 60,* 511–517.

Wang, S., Mason, J., Charney, D., & Yehuda, R. (1997). Relationships between hormonal profile and novelty seeking in combat-related posttraumatic stress disorder. *Biological Psychiatry, 41,* 145–151.

Ward, C.A. (2000). Models and measurements of psychological androgyny: A cross-cultural extension of theory and research. *Sex Roles, 43*(7–8), 529–552.

Ward, I. (2000). *Introducing psychoanalysis.* Thousand Oaks, CA: Totem Books.

Wark, G. R., & Krebs, D. L. (1996). Gender and dilemma differences in real-life moral judgment. *Developmental Psychology, 32,* 220–230.

Wartik, N. (1996). Learning to mourn. *American Health, 15*(4), 76–79, 96.

Wason, P. C. (1968). Reasoning about a rule. *Quarterly Journal of Experimental Psychology, 20*(3), 273–281.

Wasserman, D., & Wachbroit, R. S. (2000). *Genetics and criminal behavior.* Cambridge, MA: Cambridge University Press.

Watkins, L. M., & Johnston, L. (2000). Screening job applicants: The impact of physical attractiveness and application quality. *International Journal of Selection & Assessment, 8*(2), 76–84.

Watkins, L. R., & Maier, S. F. (2000). The pain of being sick: Implications of immune-to-brain communication for understanding pain. *Annual Review of Psychology, 51,* 29–57.

Watson, J. B., & Rayner, R. (1920). Conditioned emotional reactions. *Journal of Experimental Psychology, 3,* 1–14.

Watson, J. B., & Rayner, R. (2000). Conditioned emotional reactions. *American Psychologist, 55*(3), 313–317.

Watson, J. B., Mednick, S. A.; Huttunen, M., Wang, X. (1999). Prenatal teratogens and the development of adult mental illness. *Development & Psychopathology, 11*(3), 457–466.

Watson, J. (1913). Psychology as the behaviorist views it. *Psychological Review, 20,* 158–177.

Watson, J. (2000, July 3). The double helix revisited. *Time,* p. 30.

Waye, K. P., Bengtsson, J., Rylander, R., Hucklebridge, F., Evans, P., & Clow, A. (2002). Low frequency noise enhances cortisol among noise sensitive subjects during work performance. *Life Sciences, 70(7),* 745–758.

Waynforth, D. (2001). Mate choice trade-offs and women's preference for physically attractive men. *Human Nature, 12(3),* 207–219.

Weaver, C. A., & Kelemen, W. L. (1997). Judgments of learning at delays: Shifts in response patterns or increased metamemory accuracy? *Psychological Science, 8,* 318–321.

Webb, A. L., Solomon, D. A., & Ryan, C. A. (2001). Lithium levels and toxicity among hospitalized patients. *Psychiatric Services, 52*(2), 229–231.

Webb, W. B. (1992). *Sleep the gentle tyrant* (2nd ed.). Bolton, MA: Anker.

Wechsler, H., Dowdall, G. W., Maenner, G., Gledhill-Hoyt, J., & Lee, H. (1998). Changes in binge drinking and related problems among American college students between 1993 and 1997: Results of the Harvard School of Public Health College Alcohol Study. *Journal of American College Health, 47,* 57–68.

Wechsler, H., Lee, J. E., Kuo, M., & Lee, H. (2000). College binge drinking in the 1990's: A continuing problem: Results of the Harvard School of Public Health 1999 College Alcohol Study. *Journal of American College Health, 48,* 199–210.

Wechsler, H., Rigotti, N. A., Gledhill-Hoyt, J., & Lee, H. (1998). Increased levels of cigarette use among college students: A cause for national concern. *Journal of the American Medical Association, 280*(19), 1673–1678.

Wegerer, V., Moll, H., Bagli, M., Rothenberger, A., Ruether, E., & Huether, G. (1999). Persistently increased density of serotonin transporters in the frontal cortex of rats treated with fluoxetine during early juvenile life. *Journal of Child & Adolescent Psychopharmacology, 9*(1), 13–24.

Wehrle, T., Kaiser, S., Schmidt, S., & Scherer, K. R. (2000). Studying the dynamics of emotional expression using synthesized facial muscle movements. *Journal of Personality and Social Psychology, 78*(1), 105–119.

Weil, A., & Rosen, W. (1993). *From chocolate to morphine: Everyday mind-altering drugs.* Boston: Houghton Mifflin.

Weil, M. M., & Rosen, L. D. (1997). *Coping with technology @work @home @play.* New York: Wiley.

Weinberger, J., & Westen, D. (2001). Science and psychodynamics: From arguments about Freud to data. *Psychological Inquiry, 12(3),* 129–132.

Weiner, B. (1972). *Theories of motivation.* Chicago: Rand-McNally.

Weiner, B. (1982). The emotional consequences of causal attributions. In M. S. Clark & S. T. Fiske (Eds.), *Affect and cognition.* Hillsdale, NJ: Erlbaum.

Weingardt, K. R., Baer, J. S., Kivlahan, D. R., Roberts, L. J., Miller, E. T., & Marlatt, G. A. (1998). Episodic heavy drinking among college students: Methodological issues and longitudinal perspectives. *Psychology of Addictive Behaviors, 12*(3), 155–161.

Weisberg, R. W. (1993). *Creativity: Beyond the myth of genius.* New York: W. H. Freeman.

Welchman, K. (2000). *Erik Erikson: His life, work, and significance.* London: Oxford University Press.

Welch-Ross, M. K., & Schmidt, C. R. (1996). Gender-schema development and children's constructive story memory: Evidence for a developmental model. *Child Development, 67*, 820–835.

Wells, A., & Carter, K. (2001). Further tests of a cognitive model of generalized anxiety disorder: Metacognitions and worry in GAD, panic disorder, social phobia, depression, and nonpatients. *Behavior Therapy, 32(1)*, 85–102.

Wen, W., Wang, Y., Zhao, G., & Sun, J. (2000). 1/Research on the relationship between social support and psychological control and mental health. *Chinese Mental Health Journal, 14(4)*, 258–260.

Werner, E. E. (1993). Risk resiliency and recovery: Perspectives from the Kauai Longitudinal Study. *Development and Psychopathology, 5*, 503–515.

Werner, E. E. (1995). Resilience in development. *Current Directions in Psychological Science, 5*, 112–116.

Werner, E. E. (1999). Risk, resilience, and recovery: Perspectives from the Kauai Longi-tudinal Study. In L. E. Berk, *Landscapes of development* (pp. 445–460). Belmont, CA: Wadsworth.

Werner, J. S., & Wooten, B. R. (1979). Human infant color vision and color perception. *Infant Behavior and Development, 2(3)*, 241–273.

Wertz, F. J. (1998). The role of the humanistic movement in the history of psychology. *Journal of Humanistic Psychology, 38*, 42–70.

Westen, D. (1998). Unconscious thought, feeling, and motivation: The end of a century-long debate. In R. F. Bornstein & J. M. Masling (Eds.), *Empirical perspectives on the psychoanalytic unconscious.* Washington, DC: American Psychological Association.

Wetter, D. W., Fiore, M. C., Gritz, E. R., Lando, H. A., Stitzer, M. L., Hasselblad, V., & Baker, T. B. (1998). The Agency for Health Care Policy and Research Smoking Cessation Clinical Practice Guideline: Findings and implications for psychologists. *American Psychologist, 53(6)*, 657–669.

Wetterling, T., Veltrup, C., Driessen, M., & John, U. (1999). Drinking pattern and alcohol-related medical disorders. *Alcohol & Alcoholism, 34(3)*, 330–336.

Whelan, T. A., & Kirkby, R. J. (2000). Parent adjustment to a child's hospitalization. *Journal of Family Studies, 6*, 46–64.

Whitbourne, S. (2000). *Adult development and aging: Biopsychosocial perspectives.* New York: Wiley.

White, J. R., & Freeman, A. S. (2000). *Cognitive-behavioral group therapy for specific problems and populations.* Washington, DC: American Psychological Association.

White, K. K., & Abrams, L. (2002). Does priming specific syllables during tip-of-the-tongue states facilitate word retrieval in older adults? *Psychology & Aging, 17(2)*, 226–235.

White, L. K., & Rogers, S. J. (1997). Strong support but uneasy relationships: Coresidence and adult children's relationships with their parents. *Journal of Marriage and the Family, 59*, 62–76.

White, L., & Rogers, S. J. (2000). Economic circumstances and family outcomes: A review of the 1990s. *Journal of Marriage & the Family, 62(4)*, 1035–1051.

White, N. M., & Milner, P. M. (1992). The psychobiology of reinforcers. *Annual Review of Psychology, 43*, 443–471.

White, T., Andreasen, N. C., & Nopoulos, P. (2002). Brain volumes and surface morphology in monozygotic twins. *Cerebral Cortex, 12(5)*, 486–493.

White, W. F. (1997). Why students can't remember: The problem of forgetting. *Journal of Instructional Psychology, 24*, 140–143.

Whitehorn, J., Ayonrinde, O., & Maingay, S. (2002). Female genital mutilation: Cultural and psychological implications. *Sexual & Relationship Therapy, 17(2)*, 161–170.

Whiteside, M. F., & Becker, B. J. (2000). Parental factors and the young child's post-divorce adjustment: A meta-analysis with implications for parenting arrangements. *Journal of Family Psychology, 14(1)*, 5–26.

Whitney, D. K., Kusznir, A., & Dixie, A. (2002). Women with depression: The importance of social, psychological and occupational factors in illness and recovery. *Journal of Occupational Science, 9(1)*, 20–27.

Whorf, B. L. (1956). Science and linguistics. In J. B. Carroll (Ed.), *Language, thought and reality.* Cambridge, MA: MIT Press.

Whyte, M. K., (1992, March-April). Choosing mates – the American way. *Society*, pp. 71–77.

Wickelgren, I. (2002). Animal studies raise hopes for spinal cord repair. Available: Http://www.sciencemag.org/cgi/content/full/297/5579/178

Wickelgren, I. (1998). Teaching the brain to take drugs. *Science, 280*, 2045–2047.

Wickelgren, I. (1999). Rat spinal cord function partially restored. *Science, 286*, 1826–1827.

Wickett, J. C., Vernon, P. A., & Lee, D. H. (2000). Relationships between factors of intelligence and brain volume. *Personality & Individual Differences, 29(6)*, 1095–1122.

Widiger, T. A., & Sankis, L. M. (2000). Adult psychopathology. *Annual Review of Psychology, 51*, 377–404.

Wigfield, A., & Eccles, J. S. (2000). Expectancy-value of achievement motiva-tion. *Contemporary Educational Psychology, 25(1)*, 68–81.

Williams, A. L., Haber, D., Weaver, G. D., & Freeman, J. L. (1998). Altruistic activity: Does it make a difference in the senior center? *Activities, Adaptation and Aging, 22(4)*, 31–39.

Williams, D. E., & Page, M. M. (1989). A multi-dimensional measure of Maslow's hierarchy of needs. *Journal of Research in Person-ality, 23*, 192–213.

Williams, J. E., & Best, D. L. (1990). *Sex and psyche: Gender and self viewed cross-cultur-ally.* Newbury Park, CA: Sage.

Williams, T. J., Pepitone, M. E., Christensen, S.E., Cooke, B. M., Huberman, S. D., Breedlove, N. J., Breedlove, T. J., Jordan, C. I., & Breedlove, M. (2000). Finger length patterns and human sexual orientation. *Nature, 404(6777)*, 455–456.

Williams, W. M., & Ceci, S. J. (1997). Are Americans becoming more or less alike? Trends in race, class, and ability differences in intelligence. *American Psychologist, 52*, 1126–1235.

Williamson, M. (1997). Circumcision anesthesia: A study of nursing implication for dorsal penile nerve block. *Pediatric Nursing, 23*, 59–63.

Willingham, D.B. (2001). *Cognition: The thinking animal.* Upper Saddle River, NJ: Prentice Hall.

Willner, P. (1997). The dopamine hypothesis of schizophrenia: current status, future prospects. *International Clinical Psychopharmacology, 12*, 297–308.

Wilson, C. (1967). Existential psychology: A novelist's approach. In J. F. T. Bugental (Ed.), *Challenges of humanistic psychology.* New York: McGraw-Hill.

Wilson, E. O. (1975). *Sociobiology: The new synthesis.* Cambridge, MA: Harvard University Press.

Wilson, E. O. (1978). *On human nature.* Cambridge, MA: Harvard University Press.

Wilson, R. S., Gilley, D. W., Bennett, D. A., Beckett, L. A., & Evans, D. A. (2000). Person-specific paths of cognitive decline in Alzheimer's disease and their relation to age. *Psychology & Aging, 15(1)*, 18–28.

Windle, M. (1999). *Alcohol use among adolescents.* Thousand Oaks, CA: Sage.

Winnubst, J. A. M., Buunk, B. P., & Marcelissen, F. H. G. (1988). Social support and stress: Perspectives and processes. In S. Fisher & J. Reason (Eds.), *Handbook of life stress, cognition and health.* New York: Wiley.

Winton, M. (2001). The medicalization of male sexual dysfunctions: An analysis of sex therapy journals. *Journal of Sex Education and Therapy, 26*, 231–239.

Winzelberg, A., Eppstein, D., Eldredge, K. L., Wilfley, D., Dasmahpatra, R., Taylor,

C. B., & Dev, P. E. (2000). Effectiveness of an Internet-based program for reducing risk factors for eating disorders. *Journal of consulting and Clinical Psychology*, *68(2)*, 346–350.

Wirshing, D. A., Marshall, B. D., Green, M. F., Mintz, J. et al. (1999). Risperidone in treatment-refractory schizophrenia. *American Journal of Psychiatry*, *156*, 1374–1379.

Wisniewski, A. B. (1998). Sexually-dimorphic patterns of cortical asymmetry, and the role for sex steroid hormones in determining cortical patterns of lateralization. *Psychoneuroendocrinology*, *23*, 519–547.

Witelson, S. F., Glazer, I. I., & Kigar, D. I. (1994). Sex differences in numerical density of neurons in human auditory association cortex. *Society for Neuroscience Abstracts*, *30*, (Abstract No. 582. 12).

Witelson, S. F., Kigar, D. L., & Harvey, T. (1999). The exceptional brain of Albert Einstein. *The Lancet*, *353*, 2149–2153.

Witt, S. D. (1997). Parental influences on children's socialization to gender roles. *Adolescence*, *32*, 253–259.

Woelk, H. (2000). Comparison of St. John's wort and imipramine for treating depression: Randomised controlled trial. BMJ: *British Medical Journal*, *321(7260)*, 536–539.

Wolff, P. (1969). The natural history of crying and vocalization in early infancy. In B. M. Foss (Ed.), *Determinants of infant behavior* (Vol. IV). London: Methuen.

Wolpe, J. (1997). Thirty years of behavior therapy. *Behavior Therapy*, *28*, 633–635.

Wolpe, J., & Plaud, J. J. (1997). Pavlov's contributions to behavior therapy. *American Psychologist*, *52(9)*, 966–972.

Wong, J., & Checkland, D. (2000). *Teen pregnancy and parenting: Social and ethical issues*. Toronto: University of Toronto Press.

Wood, D., Bruner, J. S., & Ross, G. (1976). The role of tutoring in problem solving. *Journal of Child Psychology & Psychiatry & Allied Disciplines*, *17(2)*, 89–100.

Wood, J. M., Lilienfeld, S. O., Nezworski, M. T., & Garb, H. N. (2001). Coming to grips with negative evidence for the comprehensive system for the Rorschach: A comment on Gacono, Loving, and Bodholdt, Ganellen, and Bornstein. *Journal of Personality Assessment*, *77(1)*, 48–70.

Wood, W., Christensen, P. N., Hebl, M. R., & Rothgerber, H. (1997). Conformity to sex-typed norms, affect, and the self-concept. *Journal of Personality and Social Psychology*, *73*, 523–535.

Woods, E. R., Lin, Y. G., Middleman, A., Beckford, P., Chase, L., & DuRant, R. H. (1997). The associations of suicide attempts in adolescents. *Pediatrics*, *99*, 791–796.

Woods, S. C., & Ramsay, D. S. (2000). Pavlovian influences over food and drug intake. *Behavioural Brain Research*, *110(1–2)*, 175–182.

Woods, S. C., & Ramsay, D. S. (2000). Pavlovian influences over food and drug intake. *Behavioural Brain Research*, *110(1–2)*, 175–182.

Woods, S. C., Schwartz, M. W., Baskin, D. G., & Seeley, R. J. (2000). Food intake and the regulation of body weight. *Annual Review of Psychology*, *51*, 255–277.

Woolf, N. J., Zinnerman, M. D., & Johnson, G.V.W. (1999). Hippocampal microtubule-associated protein-2 alterations with contextual memory. *Brain Research*, *821(1)*, 241–249.

Wootton, J. M., Frick, P. J., Shelton, K. K., & Silverthorn, P. (1997). Ineffective parenting and childhood conduct problems: The moderating role of callous-unemotional traits. *Journal of Consulting and Clinical Psychology*, *65*, 301–308.

Worden, J. K., Flynn, B. S., Solomon, L. J., & Secker-Walker, R. H. (1996). Using mass media to prevent cigarette smoking among adolescent girls. *Health Education Quarterly*, *23(4)*, 453–468.

World Health Organization (WHO). (2002). Nonoxynol-9 ineffective in preventing HIV infection. Available: http://www.who.int/inf/en/pr-2002-55.html.

World Health Organization. (2000). *Epidemiology of Mental Disorders and Psychosocial Problems.* Available: http://www. who.int/dsa/cat98/men8.htm

Wright, D. B., Self, G., & Justice, C. (2000). Memory conformity: Exploring misinformation effects when presented by another person. *British Journal of Psychology*, *91*, 189–202.

Wright, J. H., & Beck, A. T. (1999). Cognitive therapies. In R. E. Hales, S. C. Yudofsky, & J. A. Talbott (Eds.), *American Psychiatric Press textbook of psychiatry*. Washington, DC: American Psychiatric Press.

Wright, M. O., & Masten, A. S. (1997). Vulnerability and resilience in young children. In J. D. Noshpita (Series Ed.) & S. Greenspan, S. Weider, & J. Osofsky (Vol. Eds.), *Handbook of child and adolescent psychiatry: Vol. 1. Infants and preschoolers: Development and syndromes* (pp. 202–224). New York: Wiley.

Wright, W. (1998). *Born that way: Genes, behavior, personality.* New York: Knopf.

Wu, W., Yamaura, T., Murakami, K., Murata, J., Matsumoto, K., Watanabe, H., & Saiki, I. (2000). Social isolation stress enhanced liver metastasis of murine colon 26–L5 carcinoma cells by suppressing immune responses in mice. *Life Sciences*, *66(19)*,1827–1838.

Wyatt, J. K., & Bootzin, R. R. (1994). Cognitive processing and sleep: Implications for enhancing job performance. *Human Performance*, *7*, 119–139.

Wysocki, C. J., & Preti, G. (1998). Pheromonal influences. *Archives of Sexual Behavior*, *27*, 627–629.

Xie, H., Cairns, R. B., & Cairns, B. D. (2002). The development of social aggression and physical aggression: A narrative analysis of interpersonal conflicts. *Aggressive Behavior*, *28(5)*, 341–355.

Yamada, H. (1997). *Different games, different rules: Why Americans and Japanese misunderstand each other.* London: Oxford University Press.

Yang, C., Spielman, A. J., D'Ambrosio, P., Serizawa, S., Nunes, J., & Birnbaum, J. (2001). A single dose of melatonin prevents the phase delay associated with a delayed weekend sleep pattern. Sleep: *Journal of Sleep Research & Sleep Medicine*, *24(3)*, 272–281.

Yee, A. H., Fairchild, H. H., Weizmann, F., & Wyatt, G. E. (1993). Addressing psychology's problem with race. *American Psychologist*, *48*, 1132–1140.

Yehuda, R., Halligan, S. L., & Bierer, L. M. (2002). Cortisol levels in adult offspring of Holocaust survivors: Relation to PTSD symptom severity in the parent and child. *Psychoneuroendocrinology*, *27(1–2)*, 171–180.

Yehuda, R., Schmeidler, J., Wainberg, M., Binder-Brynes, K, & Duvdevani, T. (1998). Vulnerability to posttraumatic stress disorder in adult offspring of Holocaust survivors. *American Journal of Psychiatry*, *155*, 1163–1171.

Yeung, R. R. (1996). The acute effects of exercise on mood state. *Journal of Psychosomatic Research*, *40*, 123–141.

Yoo, S. H., & Sung, K. (1997). Elderly Koreans' tendency to live independently from their adult children: Adaptation to cultural differences in America. *Journal of Cross-Cultural Gerontology*, *12(3)*, 225–244.

Yoshihama, M., & Horrocks, J. (2002). Posttraumatic stress symptoms and victimization among Japanese American women. *Journal of Consulting & Clinical Psychology*, *70(1)*, 205–215.

Young, M. W. (2000, March). The tick-tock of the biological clock. *Scientific American*, 64–71.

Young, T. (1802). Color vision. *Philosophical Transactions of the Royal Society*, p. 12.

Yudolfsky, S., & Silver, J. (1987). Treating performance anxiety. *The Harvard Mental Health Letter*, *4(6)*, 8.

Zagnoni, P. G., & Albano, C. (2002). Psychostimulants and epilepsy. *Epilepsia*, *43*, 28–31.

Zahn-Waxler, C., Friedman, R. J., Cole, P. M., Mizuta, I., & Himura, N. (1996). Japanese and United States preschool children's responses to conflict and distress. *Child Development, 67*, 2462–2477.

Zaichenko, M. I., Mikhailova, N. G., & Raigorodskii, Y.V. (2001). Neuron activity in the prefrontal cortex of the brain in rats with different typological characteristics in conditions of emotional stimulation. *Neuroscience & Behavioral Physiology, 31(3),* 299–304.

Zaidel, D. W. (1985). Hemifield tachistoscopic presentations and hemispheric specialization in normal subjects. In D. F. Benson, E. Zaidel, et al. (Eds.), *The dual brain: Hemispheric specialization in humans* (Vol. 18). New York: Guilford Press.

Zaidel, E. (1998). Stereognosis in the chronic split brain: Hemispheric differences, ipsilateral control and sensory integration across the midline. *Neuropsychologia, 36* (10), 1033–1047.

Zajonc, R. B. (1968). The attitudinal effects of mere exposure. *Journal of Personality and Social Psychology, 9,* 1–27.

Zajonc, R. B. (1998). Emotions. In D. T. Gilbert, S. T. Fiske, & G. Lindzey (Eds.), *The handbook of social psychology,* Vol. 2 (4th ed.) (pp. 591–632). Boston, MA: McGraw-Hill.

Zanarini, M. C., Williams, A. A., Lewis, R. E., Reich, R. B., Vera, S. C., et al. (1997). Reported pathological childhood experiences associated with the development of borderline personality disorder. *American Journal of Psychiatry, 154,* 1101–1106.

Zanigel, R., & Ressner, J. (2001). The copycat? Did Columbine inspire a new plot—or a fantasy? *Time,* p. 73.

Zboril-Benson, L. R. (2002). Why nurses are calling in sick: The impact of health-care restructuring. *Canadian Journal of Nursing Research/Revue canadienne de recherche en sciences infirmieres, 33(4),* 89–107.

Zeanah, C. H. (2000). Disturbances of attachment in young children adopted from institutions. *Journal of Developmental & Behavioral Pediatrics, 21(3),* 230–236.

Zebrowitz, L. A., Hall, J. A., Murphy, N. A., & Rhodes, G. (2002). Looking smart and looking good: Facial cues to intelligence and their origins. *Personality & Social Psychology Bulletin, 28(2),* 238–249.

Zelinski, E. M., & Stewart, S. T. (1998). Individual differences in 16-year memory changes. *Psychology & Aging, 13,* 622–630.

Zetik, D. C., & Stuhlmacher, A. F. (2002). Goal setting and negotiation performance: A meta-analysis. *Group Processes & Intergroup Relations, 5(1),* 35–52.

Zhadanova, I., & Wurtman, R. (1996, June). How does melatonin affect sleep? *The Harvard Mental Health Letter, 12(12),* 8.

Zhou, J., Hofman, M., Gooren, L., & Swaab, D. (1995). A sex difference in the human brain and its relation to transsexuality. *Nature, 378,* 68–70.

Zhukov, D. A., & Vinogradova, K. P. (2002). Learned helplessness or learned inactivity after inescapable stress? Interpretation depends on coping styles. *Integrative Physiological & Behavioral Science, 37(1),* 35–43.

Ziegler, J. M., Gustavson, C. R., Holzer, G. A., & Gruber, D. (1983). Anthelmintic-based taste aversions in wolves (Canis lupus). *Applied Animal Ethology, 3-sup-4,* 373–377.

Zillman, D., & Weaver, J. B. (1999). Effects of prolonged exposure to gratuitous media violence on provoked and unprovoked hostile behavior. *Journal of Applied Social Psychology, 29,* 145–165.

Zimbardo, P. G. (1970). The human choice: Individuation, reason, and order versus deindividuation, impulse, and chaoe. In W. J. Arnold & D. Levine (Eds.), *Nebraska symposium on motivation.* Lincoln: University of Nebraska Press.

Zimbardo, P. G., Ebbeson, E. B., & Maslach, C. (1977). *Influencing attitudes and changing behavior.* Reading, MA: Addison-Wesley.

Zimbardo, P. (1993). Stanford prison experiment: A 20-year retrospective. *Invited presentation at the meeting of the Western Psycho-logical Association,* Phoenix, AZ.

Zipursky, R. B., Lambe, E. K., Kapur, S., & Mikulis, D. J. (1998). Cerebral gray matter volume deficits in first episode psychosis. *Archives of General Psychiatry, 55,* 540–546.

Zuckerman, M. (1979). *Sensation seeking: Beyond the optimal level of arousal.* Hillsdale, NJ: Erlbaum.

Zuckerman, M. (1994). *Behavioral expressions and biosocial bases of sensation seeking.* New York: Cambridge University Press.

Zuckerman, M. (1995). Good and bad humors: Biochemical bases of personality and its disorders. *Psychological Science, 5,* 325–332.

Zuckerman, M. (1996). Item revisions in the Sensation Seeking Scale Form V (SS-V). *EDRA: Environmental Design Research Association, 20(4),* 515.

Zuckerman, M., & Kuhlman, D. M. (2000). Personality and risk-taking: Common biosocial factors. *Journal of Personality, 68(6),* 999–1029.

Zurbriggen, E. L. (2000). Social motives and cognitive power-sex associations: Predictors of aggressive sexual behavior. *Journal of Personality & Social Psychology, 78(3),* 559–581.

Zweigenhaft, R. L. (2002). Birth order effects and rebelliousness: Political activism and involvement with marijuana. *Political Psychology, 23(2),* 219–233.

PHOTO CREDITS

Modules 1–4 Opener (left): ©Brian Payne. Opener (right): Photo by Christian Steiner. Courtesy Antonio Damasio. Page 5: Bruce Ayres/Stone/Getty Images. Page 6: Courtesy James Randi Educational Foundation. Page 8 (top): Photo ©Chris Casaburi. Courtesy Candace Pert. Page 8 (center top): Courtesy Dan Belleck. Page 8 (center bottom): Mark Richards/PhotoEdit. Page 8 (bottom): Ed Kashi/Liaison Agency, Inc./Getty Images. Page 16: ©Peter S. Mueller. Page 19: Anna Clopet-Saola/Liaison Agency, Inc./Getty Images. Page 25 (top): Robert Burke/Liaison Agency, Inc./Getty Images. Page 25 (bottom): Alexander Tsiaras/Stock Boston. Page 26 (top): Mehau Kulyk/Photo Researchers. Page 26 (center): N.I.H/Photo Researchers. Page 26 (bottom): Scott Camazine/Photo Researchers. Page 27: ©John Chase. Page 29: Jonathan Selig/Stone/Getty Images. Page 33: ©The New Yorker Collection 1994 Sam Gross from cartoonbank.com. All Rights Reserved. Page 34 (top): Corbis Images. Page 34 (bottom): Keystone/The Image Works. Page 35 (top): Corbis Images. Page 35 (center): Bruce Hoertel/Liaison Agency, Inc./Getty Images. Page 35 (bottom): Psychology Archives, The University of Akron. Page 36 (top): Deborah Feingold/Archive Photos/Getty Images. Page 36 (bottom): Time Inc. Picture Collection. Page 39 (left): Tamara Reynolds/Stone/Getty Images. Page 39 (center left): Tim Davis/Stone/Getty Images. Page 39 (center right): Visuals Unlimited. Page 39 (right): Ken Lucas/Visuals Unlimited.

Modules 5–7 Opener: From Damasio H, Grabowski T, Frank R, Galaburda AM, AR, "The Return of Phineas Gage: Clues about the brain from a famous patient." SCIENCE, 53, 1994. Department of Neurology and Image Analysis Facility, University of Iowa. Page 56: Tony Freeman/PhotoEdit. Page 62: Courtesy E.R. Lewis, Berkeley. Page 64: Alex Wong/Liaison Agency, Inc./Getty Images. Page 65 (left): Jack Fields/Corbis Images. Page 65 (right): Reuters New Media Inc./Corbis Images. Page 70: Science Pictures Limited/Photo Researchers. Page 71 & 74: ©AP/Wide World Photos. Page 75: The Natural History Museum. Page 82 (top): Courtesy Dr. Fred Gage, The Salk Institute. Page 82 (bottom): From P. Piccini et al., "Nature Neuroscience 2." 1137, (1999). Page 83 (top): A. Tannenbaum/Corbis Sygma. Page 87: Courtesy of Dr. Nancy L. Segal, author, "Entwined Lives: Twins and What They Tell Us About Human Behavior," 2000, NY: Plume. Page 88: Courtesy Karen Huffman. Page 89: ©AP/Wide World Photos. Page 90: Non Sequitur by Wiley ©2000. Distributed by Universal Press Syndicate. All Rights Reserved.

Modules 8–11 Opener (left): Stan Honda/Agence France Presse. Opener (right): Mitch Jacobson/U.S. News & World Report. Page 100: Will & Deni McIntyre/Photo Researchers. Page 103 (top left): Damon Kiesow/Liaison Agency, Inc./Getty Images. Page 103 (top right): Alex Wong/Liaison Agency, Inc./Getty Images. Page 103 (bottom): A. Operti/American Museum of Natural History Library. Page 104: Bonnier Alba. Page 109 (top right): Howard Sochurek/Corbis Stock Market. Page 108 (top left): Biophoto Associates/Photo Researchers. Page 109 (bottom): ©1997 by Randy Glasbergen. Page 116: ©AP/Wide World Photos. Page 117: Arthur Tilley/Stone/Getty Images. Page 121: Spencer Grant/PhotoEdit. Page 121: Courtesy California Department of Health Services. Funded by Tobacco Tax Initiative. Page 122: Auerbach/Visuals Unlimited. Page 123: Courtesy B.R.A.D., Photo provided by Cindy McCue. Page 124: Bob Daemmrich/The Image Works. Page 125 (top): James Schnepf/Liaison Agency, Inc./Getty Images. Page 125 (bottom): Damien Lovegrove/Photo Researchers.

Modules 12–13 Opener: Corbis-Bettman. Page 135: Doug Martin/Photo Researchers. Page 137: Leonard Lessin/Photo Researchers. Page 143: Jed Jacobson/Liaison Agency, Inc./Getty Images. Page 143: W & D McIntyre/Photo Researchers. Page 146: Omikron/Photo Researchers. Page 147: Jeff Greenberg/PhotoEdit. Page 149: ©AP/Wide World Photos. Page 151 & 152: Courtesy Optometric Extension Program Foundation, Santa Ana, CA. Page 153: Courtesy Colin Blakemore from Schmitt & Worden, "The Neurosciences Third Study Program," MIT Press. Page 154 (bottom): Cordon Art B.V. Page 155 (top): Courtesy Kasier Porcelain, Ltd. Page 157: Werner Bokelberg/The Image Bank/Getty Images. Page 158 (top): Bizarro ©1991 by Dan Piraro. Reprinted with permission of Universal Press Syndicate. All Rights Reserved. Page 158 (bottom): Baron Wolman/Woodfin Camp & Associates. Page 160: ©Enrico Ferorelli. Page 162: ©1999 Magic Eye, Inc., http://magiceye.com. Page 162: Hilarie Kavanagh/Stone/Getty Images. Page 163: Courtesy Graham-Field Surgical Company. Page 166 (top left): Kelly Jordan/Corbis Sygma. Page 165 (top right): Courtesy Karen Huffman. Page 166 (bottom): Erdely: M.H., Appelbaum, A.G. (19973). "Cognitive Masking: The disruptive effect of an emotional stimulus upon the perception of contiguous neutral items." Bulletin of the Psychonomic Society, 1, 59–61. Page 167: ©1998 ZITS Partnership. Reprinted with special permission of King Features Syndicate. Page 168: ©Dan Piraro, Chronicle Features.

Modules 14–15 Opener (top): Jeffery Zaruba/Stone/Getty Images. Opener (bottom): Corbis Images. Page 177 (top): Patrick Ramsey/International Stock Photo. Page 177 (center top): Ariel Skelley/Corbis Stock Market. Page 177 (center): Richard Hutchings/Photo Researchers. Page 177 (center bottom): Paul Merideth/Stone/Getty Images. Page 177 (bottom): David Madison/Duomo Photography, Inc. Page 181: Topham Picturepoint/The Image Works. Page 182: Hank Morgan/Rainbow. Page 184 (left): Michael & Barbara Reed/Animals Animals NYC. Page 184 (right): J. P. Thomas/Jacana/Photo Researchers. Page 185: Richard Cummins/Corbis Images. Page 187: A. Rousseau/The Image Works. Page 192: Zigy Kaluzny/Stone/Getty Images. Page 194 (left & center): Courtesy The New York Historical Society. Page 194 (right): Archivo Iconografico/Corbis Images. Page 196 (top): Philip Habib/Stone/Getty Images. Page 196 (top center): Deborah Gilbert/The Image Bank/Getty Images. Page 196 (center): Adam Hart-Davis/Photo Researchers. Page 196 (bottom center): Uwe Schmid/OKAPIA/Photo Researchers. Page 196 (bottom): Fredrik Skold/The Image Bank/Getty Images. Page 197: L. Kolvoord/The Image Works. Page 198: ©The New Yorker Collection 2001 Michael Shaw from cartoonbank.com. All Rights Reserved. Page 199 (top): ©AP/Wide World Photos. Page 199 (bottom): Tom & DeeAnn McCarthy/Corbis Stock Market. Page 200: ©2002 Daniel Laine/Matrix International, Inc. Page 201: ©AP/Wide World Photos. Page 205: ©The New Yorker Collection 1998 Leo Cullum from cartoonbank.com. All Rights Reserved. Page 207: Bob Daemmrich/Stock Boston. Page 210: Lindsay Hebberd/Corbis Images.

Modules 16–19 Opener: Greg Smith/Corbis SABA. Page 218: Drawing by John Chase. Page 221 (top): Courtesy Benjamin Harris. Page 221 (bottom): ©The New Yorker Collection 1998 Sam Gross from the cartoonbank.com. All Rights Reserved. Page 225: ©AP/Wide World Photos. Page 226 (left): Tannen Maury/The Image Works. Page 226 (right): Bill Aaron/PhotoEdit. Page 230: DENNIS THE MENACE® used by permission of Hank Ketcham Enterprises, Inc. and © by North America Syndicate. Page 234: Kaku Kurita/Liaison Agency, Inc./Getty Images. Page 237: ©The New Yorker Collection 1991

TEXT AND ILLUSTRATION CREDITS

Modules 1–4 Figure 1.1: From Caccioppo, Petty, and Jarvis; *Dispositional Differences in Cognitive Motivation*, Psychological Bulletin, 119(2), pg. 197–253, © 1996 American Psychological Association. Table 1.4: From Plous, S., *An attitude survey of animal rights activists*, American Psychological Society (1991). Copyright © 1991 American Psychological Society. Reprinted by permission of the American Psychological Society and S. Plous.

Modules 5–7 Figures 7.3 and 7.4: From Kimura, D.; *Sex Differences in the Brain*, Scientific American, Sept. 1992, pg. 120 © 1992 Jared Schneidman Designs.

Modules 8–11 Figure 8.2: From Selye; *Stress Without Distress*, © 1974 Harper & Row Publishers. Critical Thinking/Active Learning Exercise (pg. 104): Robbins, S. P., *Organizational behavior: Concepts, controversies, and applications* ©1996 Prentice-Hall, Englewood Cliffs, NJ reprinted with permission. Table 8.1: From Holmes & Rahe, *The social readjustment rating scale*, © 1967 Journal of Psychosomatic Research, 11 pg. 213–218. Figure 11.1: From Mattson, Pollack & Cullen; "*What are the Odds that Smoking Will Kill You?*," American Journal of Public Health, 77, pgs. 425–431 , © 1987 American Journal of Public Health. Table 9.1: From Pomponio, © 2002 John Wiley & Sons.

Modules 12–13 Figure 13.6: From Luria, A. R., *Cognitive development: Its cultural and social foundations*, Harvard University Press (1976). Reprinted by permission of Harvard University Press. Copyright © 1976 by the President and Fellows of Harvard College. Figure 13.16: From Erdelyi, M.H. & Applebaum, A.G., *Cognitive Masking*, © 1973 Bulletin of the Psychonomic Society I, pg. 59–61.

Modules 14–15 Figure 14.3: From Julien; *A Primer of Drug Action*, © 2000 W.H. Freeman. Figure 14.4: From William, Karacan, and Hursch; *Electroencephalography of Human Sleep*, © 1974 John Wiley & Sons. Prose: From Benson, Herbert, "Systematic hypertension and the relaxation response". *New England Journal of Medicine*, 296, 1977. Reprinted with permission.

Modules 20–21 Figure 20.8: From Bahrick, Bahrick, and Wittlinger; *Those Unforgettable High School Days*, Reprinted with permission from Psychology Today Magazine, © 1978 Sussex Publishers, Inc. Figure 21.2: From Murdock, Jr.; *The Serial Effect of Free Recall*, the Journal of Experimental Psychology, 64(5) pg. 482–488, Figure 1 pg. 483, © 1962 American Psychological Association.

Modules 22–24 Try This Yourself pg. 281: From Shepard and Metzler; *Mental Rotation of Three-Dimensional Objects*, © 1971 American Association for the Advancement of Science. Figure 24.1: From Gardner; The Atlantic Monthly, Feb. 1999 pp. 67–76, © 1999 Howard Gardner. Table 8.6: From Sternberg; *Beyond IQ*, © 1985 Cambridge University Press. Figure 24.1: From Sternberg; *The Theory of Successful Intelligence*, Review of General Psychology, 3, pg. 292–316, © 1999 American Psychological Association.

Modules 25–26 Figure 25.2: From Schaie; *The life course of Adult Intellectual Abilities*, American Psychologist, 49, pg. 304–313, © 1994 The American Psychological Association. Reprinted with permission. Table 26.2: From Clarke-Stewart and Friedman; *Child Development*, © 1985 John Wiley & Sons. Reprinted with permission. Figure 25.7: From Frankenburg & Dodds, *Denver II Training Manual* © 1991 Denver Developmental Materials. Figure 25.10: From Tanner, J. M., Whitehouse, R. N., and Takaislu, M., "Male/female growth spurt." *Archives of Diseases in Childhood*, 41, 454–471, 1966. Reprinted with permission. Application: From Schaie, K. W. The life course of adult intellectual abilities. *American Psychologist*, 49, 304–313, 1994. Copyright © 1994 by the American Psychological Association. Reprinted with permission. Figure 25.12: From Chart of elderly achievers. In *The brain: A user's manual*. Copyright © 1982 by Diagram Visual Information.

Modules 27–28 Achievement 10.1: Adapted from *Handbook of socialization theory and research* (1969) D. A. Goslin (ed.). Reprinted by permission of Houghton Mifflin. Table 27.2: From Papalia, Olds & Feldman; *Human Development* 8e, © 2001 McGraw-Hill. Reprinted with permission. Figure 27.2: From Brown, Adams, and Kellam, *Research in community and mental health* (1981). Reprinted with permission. Figure 27.3: From Cartensen et al.; *The Social Context of Emotion*, Annual Review of Geriatrics & Gerontology, 17, pg. 331, © 1997 Springer Publishing Company, Inc., New York 10012. Used by permission.

Modules 29–30 Figure 29.2: From Miracle, Miracle, & Baumeister; *Human Sexuality: Meeting Your Basic Needs*, Study Guide Figure 10.4, pg. 302, Reprinted by Permission of Pearson Education, Inc. © 2003 Pearson Education. Figure 30.1: From Hebb, D. O., *Organization of behavior*, John Wiley and Sons, Inc. Copyright © 1949. Reprinted by permission of D. O. Hebb and J. Nichols Hebb Paul, sole executor and daughter. Figure 30.2: From Hat- field, Elaine and Rapson, Richard L, *Love, sex, and intimacy*. Copyright © 1993 by Elaine Hat- field and Richard L. Rapson. Reprinted by permission of Addison-Wesley Educational Publishers Inc. Figure 30.4: From Strong, DeVault, and Sayad, *Core concepts in human sexuality*. Mountain View, California: Mayfield. Reprinted by permission. Try This Yourself: From Hyde, Janis S., *Half the human experience: The psychology of women (fifth edition)*. Copyright © 1995 by D. C. Heath & Company, Lexington, Mass. Reprinted by permission of Houghton-Mifflin Co. Table 30.2: From Laumann et al.; *The Social Organization of Sexuality*, © 1994 University of Chicago Press.

Modules 31–32 Table 31.1: From Diagnostic and Statistical Manual of Mental Disorders; fourth edition text revision, Washington DC, © 2000 American Psychiatric Association. Figure 31.4: From Murray, H. H. *Thematic Apperception Test (TAT) card*. Harvard University Press. Printed with permission. Figure 31.5: From Lepper, Greene, and Nisbett; *Undermining Children's Intrinsic Interest In Extrinsic Rewards*, Journal of Personality and Social Psychology, 8e, pg. 129–137, © 1973 American Psychological Association. Figure 31.8: From Maslow; "*A Theory of Motivation*," in Motivation and Personality, 3e © 1997. Reprinted by permission of Pearson Education, Inc., Upper Saddle River, NJ. Figure 32.4: From Plutchik; *Emotion: A Psychoevolutionary Synthesis*, © 1980 Published by Allyn and Bacon, Boston, MA. Copyright © 1980 by Pearson Education. Adapted by permission of the publisher. Try This Yourself, pg. 416–417: From Zuckerman; "*The Search for High Sensation*", Psychology Today, pp. 38–46, Reprinted with permission from Psychology Today Magazine, © 1978 Sussex Publishers, Inc.

Modules 33–36 Figure 34.1: From Buss et al., "*International Preferences in Selecting Mates*," Journal of Cross-Cultural Psychology, 21, pp. 5–47, © 1990 Sage Publications, Inc. Try This Yourself, pg. 451: From Cattell; "*Personality Pinned Down*," Psychology Today, pg. 44, Reprinted With Permission From Psychology Today Magazine, © 1974 Sussex Publishers, Inc. Figure 34.2: From Gosling, "*Personality Dimensions in Spotted Hyenas*," Journal of Comparative Psychology, 112, pp. 107–118, © 1974 American Psychological Association.

Name Index

SUBJECT INDEX

Abnormal behavior. *See also*
  Psychological disorders
  culture and, 513–515
  explanations for, 515–516
  standards for identifying, 512–513
Abscissa, A3
Absentmindedness, 292
Absolute threshold, 134
Accommodation, 161, 363
  visual, 139
Acetylcholine (ACh), 63, 65, 202
Achievement feature, xiii
Achievement motivation, 445–449
  characteristics of achievers and,
    445–449
  intrinsic and extrinsic motivation
    and, 446–449
Achievement tests, 476
Acquired immunodeficiency
    syndrome (AIDS), 429–431
Action potentials, 59–61
Activation-synthesis hypothesis,
    186–187
Active learning, xi–xiv. *See also*
    Critical Thinking/Active
    Learning issues
  Achievement feature for, xiii
  Application feature for, xii–xiii
  Assessment feature for, xiii–xiv
Active listening, 45
  in client-centered therapy, 574
Active reading, process for, 41–43
Activity theory of aging, 393
AD (Alzheimer's disease), 87,
    283–284
Adaptation
  general adaptation syndrome and,
    104
  to light and dark, 140
  perceptual, 165–166
  sensory, 134–136
Addiction, 205
  definition of, 194
Adolescence, 342
  parenthood during, 389–390
  physical development during,
    352–353
  psychosocial development during,
    383, 384, 385
Adolescent egocentrism, 368–369
Adoption studies, 87
Adrenaline, 63
  emotion and, 457
Adulthood, 342
  physical development during,
    353–355
  psychosocial development during,
    384, 385
Adults Molested as Children
    (AMAC), 389, 581
Advertising, classical conditioning
    and, 226–227
Aerial perspective, 163
Affect, flattened, 536

Affective component
  of attitudes, 600
  of prejudice, 604
Aftereffects, color, 163
Age differences. *See also* Aging
  in attitudes toward death and
    dying, 397
  in smell sense, 145
Ageism, 354
  cultural differences in, 394–395
Aggression, 626–628
  biological factors in, 626
  brain and, 72
  controlling or eliminating,
    627–628
  in families, 388–389
  psychosocial factors in, 626–627
  sex differences in, 411, 412
  as side effect of punishment, 236
Aging
  activity theory of, 393
  disengagement theory of, 393
  memory decline associated with,
    371
  primary, 355
  secondary, 355
  socioemotional selectivity theory
    of, 393
Agonist drugs, 65, 202
Agoraphobia, 523
AIDS (acquired immunodeficiency
    syndrome), 429–431
Alarm reaction, 104
Alcoholics Anonymous, 581
Alcohol use/abuse, 548
  alcohol-dependence disorders
    and, 513
  aversion therapy for, 578, 579
  binge drinking and, 123–124
  effects of, 197
  mixing with barbiturates, 197
  during pregnancy, 349
  as social concern, 196–197
  treatment of, 226
Alcohol use disorders (AUDs), 548
Algorithms, 305
All-or-none law, 60
All-or-nothing thinking in
    depression, 573
Alpha waves, 182
Alternate states of consciousness
    (ASCs), 175, 178–210
  daydreaming as, 177, 206
  dreaming as. *See* Dreaming
  drugs and. *See* Psychoactive drugs
  fantasies as, 206
  hypnosis and, 207–208
  meditation and, 208–209
  motivation for seeking, 210
  sleep as. *See* Dreaming; Sleep
Altruism, 628–631
  lack of, reasons for, 630–631
  promoting, 631
  reasons for, 629–630

Alzheimer's disease (AD), 87,
    283–284
AMAC (Adults Molested as
    Children), 389, 581
American Psychological Association
    (APA), 27
  ethical principles of, 27–30
American Psychological Society
    (APS), 27
Ames room illusion, 158, 159
Amnesia, 283
  dissociative, 544
  source, 285, 286, 288
Amphetamines, dopamine and, 539
Amplitude
  of light waves, 137, 138
  of sound waves, 141
Amygdala, 72
  emotion and, 456
  memory and, 274
Anal-expulsive personality, 490
Anal-retentive personality, 490
Anal stage of development, 490, 491
Analytic intelligence, 324
Analytic psychology, 493–494
Androgyny, 413–414
Angina, 108–111
Animals
  language in, 317–318
  personality in, 483–484
  as research subjects, ethical
    principles guiding research
    with, 29
Animism in preoperational stage,
    366
Anonymity, 623
Anorexia nervosa, 441–442
Anosmia, 145
ANS (autonomic nervous system),
    55–57
  emotion and, 455–457
Antagonist drugs, 65, 202, 203
Anterograde amnesia, 283
Antianxiety drugs, 560, 561
Antidepressant drugs, 529, 560, 561,
    563
Antipsychotic drugs, 560, 561, 563
Antisocial personality disorder,
    545–547
Anvil (bone), 142
Anxiety
  basic, 495
  castration, 490
  posttraumatic stress disorder and,
    111–112
  test, overcoming, 443–444
Anxiety disorders, 522–527
  causes of, 525–526
  generalized, 522
  obsessive-compulsive disorder,
    524–525
  panic disorder, 522–523
  phobias, 523
  treatment of, 560, 561

Anxious/ambivalent infants, 358
APA (American Psychological
    Association), 27
  ethical principles of, 27–30
Apes, language in, 317–318
Aphasia, 74, 76
Aphrodisiacs, 204
Apnea, sleep, 191
Application feature, xi
Applied research, 10
Approach-approach conflict, 101
Approach-avoidance conflict, 101
APS (American Psychological
    Society), 27
Aptitude tests, 476
Archetypes, 494
Arousal, 442–445
  emotion and, 455–457, 463
  sensation seeking and, 444–445
Artificial concepts, 301–302
ASCs. *See* Alternate states of
    consciousness (ASCs)
Assertiveness training, 579
Assessment feature, xiii–xiv
Assimilation, 363
Association areas, 77
Asylums, 516
Atherosclerosis, 108–111
Athoritative parenting style, 360
Attachment
  failure to form, 357–358
  feeding and contact comfort and,
    356–358
  levels of, 358
  romantic love and, 358–359
Attention
  cognitive development and, 370
  memory improvement and,
    289–290
  selective, 151, 168, 176
Attitudes, 600–603
  cognitive dissonance and,
    601–602
  components of, 600
  coping with stress and, 116
  toward death and dying, 397
  prejudice as. *See* Prejudice
  success and, 47
Attraction, interpersonal. *See*
    Interpersonal attraction
Attractiveness, physical. *See* Physical
    attractiveness
Attribution, 452, 598–600
  biases in, culture and, 599–600
  dispositional and situational, 598
  learned helplessness and, 530
  mistaken, 598–599
Atypical antidepressants, 561
Atypical antipsychotics, 561
Audiences, imaginary, 369
Audition. *See* Hearing
Auditory canal, 142
Auditory cortex, 75
Auditory nerve, 142